Edexcel AS/A level
ECONOMICS

Alain Anderton

Edited by Dave Gray

6th EDITION

ALWAYS LEARNING

PEARSON

Published by Pearson Education Limited, 80 Strand, London, WC2R 0RL.

www.pearsonschoolsandfecolleges.co.uk

Copies of official specifications for all Edexcel qualifications may be found on the website: www.edexcel.com

Text © Alain Anderton 2015

Edited by Dave Gray

Designed by Pearson Education

Typeset by Waring-Collins

Original illustrations © Pearson Education 2015

Illustrated by Tech-Art

Cover design by Elizabeth Amoux for Pearson Education

Indexed by Sophia Clapham, Index-Now

Picture research by Rebecca Sodergren

Cover photo/illustration © nelsonsiregar / Getty Images

The right of Alain Anderton to be identified as author of this work has been asserted by him in accordance with the Copyright, Designs and

Patents Act 1988.

First published 2015

20

10 9 8

British Library Cataloguing in Publication Data

A catalogue record for this book is available from the British Library

ISBN (Student Book bundle) 978 1 447 99055 0

ISBN (ActiveBook) 978 1 447 98356 9

ISBN (Kindle edition) 978 1 447 98357 6

Printed and bound in Great Britain by Bell and Bain Ltd, Glasgow

Websites

Pearson Education Limited is not responsible for the content of any external internet sites. It is essential for tutors to preview each website before using it in class so as to ensure that the URL is still accurate, relevant and appropriate. We suggest that tutors bookmark useful websites and consider enabling students to access them through the school/college intranet.

A note from the publisher

In order to ensure that this resource offers high-quality support for the associated Pearson qualification, it has been through a review process by the awarding body. This process confirms that this resource fully covers the teaching and learning content of the specification or part of a specification at which it is aimed. It also confirms that it demonstrates an appropriate balance between the development of subject skills, knowledge and understanding, in addition to preparation for assessment.

Endorsement does not cover any guidance on assessment activities or processes (e.g. practice questions or advice on how to answer assessment questions), included in the resource nor does it prescribe any particular approach to the teaching or delivery of a related course.

While the publishers have made every attempt to ensure that advice on the qualification and its assessment is accurate, the official specification and associated assessment guidance materials are the only authoritative source of information and should always be referred to for definitive guidance.

Pearson examiners have not contributed to any sections in this resource relevant to examination papers for which they have responsibility.

Examiners will not use endorsed resources as a source of material for any assessment set by Pearson.

Endorsement of a resource does not mean that the resource is required to achieve this Pearson qualification, nor does it mean that it is the only suitable material available to support the qualification, and any resource lists produced by the awarding body shall include this and other appropriate resources.

Contents

How to use this book

This Student Book contains a wealth of features that will help you to access the course content, prepare for your exams, and take your knowledge and understanding further. The pages below show some of the key features and explain how they will support you in developing the skills needed to succeed on your A level Economics course.

FEATURES

'**Key points**' These provide a clear overview of the content covered in the topic.

Key points

1. Indirect taxes can be either ad valorem taxes or specific taxes.
2. The imposition of an indirect tax is likely to lead to a rise in the unit price of a good which is less than the unit value of the tax.
3. The incidence of indirect taxation is likely to fall on both consumer and producer.
4. The more elastic the demand curve or the more inelastic the supply curve, the greater will be the incidence of tax on producers and the less will be the incidence of tax on consumers.
5. Tax revenues from an indirect tax will be greater the more inelastic the demand for the product.
6. Subsidies will lower the price of a good for consumers, but not all of the subsidy will be received by consumers because some will be received by producers.

'**Starter activity**' These activities are designed to help you start thinking about the topics and issues you will be covering in the unit.

Starter activity

The government announces a new sugar and fat tax that will increase the standard rate of Value Added Tax (VAT) on selected products from its current 20 per cent to 30 per cent. These products include fizzy drinks and chocolate bars. What is Value Added Tax and how is it calculated? By how many per cent do you think the price of these products will increase in shops? Will it have any impact on consumption of these items?

'**Key terms**' These are highlighted in the text and complex terminology or jargon clearly defined in a handy box at the end of each unit.

Key Terms

Ad valorem tax - tax levied as a percentage of the value of the good.
Incidence of tax - the tax burden on the taxpayer.
Specific or unit tax - tax levied on volume.
Subsidy - a grant given which lowers the price of a good, usually designed to encourage production or consumption of a good.

'**Questions**' Throughout each unit you will find questions that test your understanding of topics and help you to build your analytical and critical thinking skills.

Question 1

Figure 1

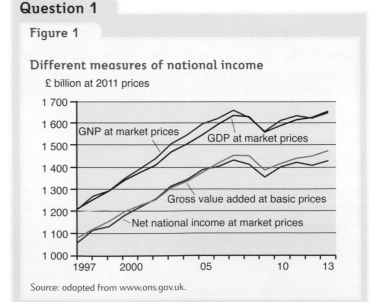

Different measures of national income
£ billion at 2011 prices

Source: adapted from www.ons.gov.uk.

(a) Briefly explain the difference between each measure of national income shown on the graph.
(b) 'Changes in GDP at market prices broadly reflect changes in other measures of national income over time.' To what extent do the data support this?

'Thinking like an economist' These features provide opportunities for you to explore an aspect of economics in more detail. The information in these features goes beyond the specification and will help you to deepen your understanding and to view issues like an economist.

'Data response question' These exam-style, case study questions contain an authentic piece of writing that provides you with an opportunity to practise your own extended writing and to develop your ability to combine your knowledge, skills and understanding with the breadth and depth of the subject of economics.

'Maths tips' These will help you to simplify complex calculations and will provide practical worked examples to help you apply new methods or formulae to your own work.

'Preparing for your exams' At the end of this book you'll find a detailed exam preparation section to help consolidate your learning. Exam-style questions, mark schemes and answers, together with useful tips for how to approach the exams, will give you extra confidence in your performance.

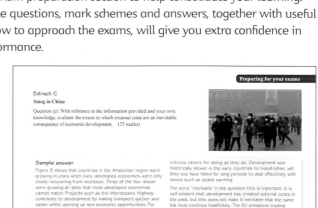

Question 2

Table 1 GDP (£billion), population (millions) and prices (Year 1 = 100)

Year	GDP (£bn)	Population (millions)	Price index Year 1 = 100
1	100	1.00	100
2	120	1.20	100
3	150	1.25	200
4	200	1.25	250

The table gives data for GDP (at nominal prices), population and prices for 4 years. Calculate: (a) GDP per capita at nominal prices; (b) total GDP at real Year 1 prices; (c) GDP per head at Year 1 prices.

Maths tip

How to calculate real GDP from nominal GDP is covered in Unit 2. To calculate numbers at Year 1 prices, divide nominal GDP by the ratio of the change in prices over the period. For example, prices increased 2.5 times (250 ÷ 100) between Year 1 and Year 4. So real GDP in Year 4 at Year 1 prices was £200 billion ÷ 2.5.

Getting the most from your online ActiveBook

This book comes with 3 years' access to ActiveBook* – an online, digital version of your textbook. Follow the instructions printed on the inside front cover to start using your ActiveBook.

Your ActiveBook is the perfect way to personalise your learning as you progress through your A level Economics course. You can:

● access your content online, anytime, anywhere.
● use the inbuilt highlighting and annotation tools to personalise the content and make it really relevant to you.

Highlight tool
Use this to pick out key terms or topics so you are ready and prepared for revision.

Annotations tool
Use this to add your own notes; for example, links to your wider reading, such as websites or other files. Or make a note to remind yourself about work that you need to do.

*for new purchases only. If this access code has already been revealed, it may no longer be valid. If you have bought this textbook secondhand, the code may already have been used by the first owner of the book.

Introduction

Teachers and students of economics are critical groups of people. Constantly dissatisfied with the materials that they use, they face the problems of limited resources, a wide variety of needs and a constantly changing world. The 6th edition of AS/A level Edexcel Economics is intended to go some way to resolving this example of the basic economic problem. A number of features are included in the book which we believe will help this task – these can be read about in the 'How to use this book' section on page iv.

The study of economics relies upon the understanding of both applied economics and economic theory. Many books cover this separately but Economics contains a systematic approach to applied economics, alongside the discussion of economic theory.

Economics students must understand the real-world application of their study. This book has endeavoured to include a variety of different realistic data that cover a broad period of time. An understanding of the relevance of economics to history will be invaluable to the student; from throughout the post-war era, with particular emphasis on the turbulent times of the 1970s and 1980s to the more recent financial crisis of 2007-08.

Comprehensive course coverage
This book covers the material found in all four themes of the Edexcel A level Economics specification:

● **Theme 1** Introduction to markets and market failure
● **Theme 2** The UK economy – performance and policies
● **Theme 3** Business behaviour and the labour market
● **Theme 4** A global perspective

By covering all four themes of the specification in detail Economics takes students through the course, ensuring they gain all the skills and understanding they need to be able to be successful in their exams. Units in Theme 1 and Theme 2 allow students to gain an in-depth understanding of microeconomic and macroeconomic concepts, with content in Theme 3 and Theme 4 developing a breadth and depth of knowledge and understanding, and applications to more complex concepts and models.

Acknowledgements

The publisher would like to thank the following for their kind permission to reproduce their photographs:

(Key: b-bottom; c-centre; l-left; r-right; t-top)

123RF.com: 134, 137, 269, 271, 281, 311, 333, 334, 349tc, 392, 405t, 422, 431, 433, 490, Alicephoto 118, Baloncici 123, Markos Dolopikos 24t, Dotshock 78, Alina Isakovich 237, kzenon 332, Kampee Patisena 68, sean pavone 198tr, Nadiya Vlashchenko 5; **Alamy Images:** Amana Images inc 88, Clive Sawyer 504, Kathy deWitt 34b, Dex Image. Yoshio Sawargai 405b, Directphoto Collection 77, Keith Douglas 527, dpa picture alliance archive 226b, Mark Dyball 259t, Richard Ellis 83b, Jeff Gilbert 446, David J. Green 89, 146, Greg Balfour Evans 300, 498, Sue Heaton 170t, Horizons WWP 13b, imageBROKER 209, Lou Linwei 557, Purple Marbles 137b, Stefano Paterna 541, Prisma Bildagentur AG 113, Purepix 288, RosaIreneBetancourt 3 437, T.M.O.Buildings 275, Westend61 GmbH 258tr; **Corbis:** Fancy. Veer 20t; **Fotolia.com:** 29, diego cervo 369, chalabala 308, delkoo 105, emde71 251, Fotolyse 151, HappyAlex 385, Nataliya Hora 412, industrieblick 400, Michael Jung 115, 349b, Kadmy 55, Kara 195, KB3 282, Kletr 270, ktasimar 522, Oleksiy Mark 319, MasterLu 198tl, Monkey Business 13t, 16, Monkey Business 13t, 16, project1photography 87, Route66 439, terex 413, Anastasiia Usoltceva 71, Robert Wilson 295; **Getty Images:** American Stock Archive 206, Anadolu Agency 139, Tony Anderson 317t, Bloomberg 104, 168, 390, 444, Peter Macdiarmid 167, Jonathan Maddock 289t, Spencer Platt 463, Dougal Waters 20b; **Imagestate Media:** Michael Duerinckx 296; **Pearson Education Ltd:** Studio 8 112, 344, Rob Judges 34t, Naki Kouyioumtzis 198bl, Debbie Rowe 66; **Photolibrary.com:** Malcolm Fife 259c, Image Source 258tl, Monty Rakusen. Cultura 359; **Reproduced with kind permission of Unilever PLC and group companies:** 37; **Rex Features:** 119, 199, Quilai Shen 22; **Shutterstock.com:** 21, 38, 264, Adisa 263, Andrey Arkusha 349t, bikeriderlondon 15, Diego Cervo. 293t, Chungking 82, Deklofenak 11, Dziewul 14, eldirector77. 274, fiphoto 293b, Foodpics 49, Michael G. Mill 90, Martin Good 406, Holbox 258br, Alex Hubenov 258bl, Image Point Fr. 259b, Jim Parkin 416, Jurand 126, Dmitry Kalinovsky 377, Kletr 81, Levent Konuk 257, l i g h t p o e t 307, Lapass77 226t, Lucky Business 317b, Paul Maguire 40, Merzzie 170b, michaeljung 339, Monkey Business Images 91, 262, Luciano Mortula 198br, Nightman1965 250, PHOTOCREO Michal Bednarek 376, Pics-xl 24b, Marco Prati 33, r.nagy 225, Sozaijiten 478, Pete Spiro 10, ssuaphotos 101, Rikard Stadler 69, STILLFX 95, Tumarkin Igor - ITPS 144, Vankad 349bc, wavebreakmedia. 228, Zurbagan 24c

Cover images: Front: **Getty Images:** nelsonsiregar

All other images © Pearson Education

The publisher would like to thank the following individuals and organisations for their approval and permission to reproduce their materials:

p.41 AHDB Dairy; **p.410** American Iron and Steel Institute; **p.556** *Markets, Consumers and Firms*, B. Ellis and N. Wall, Anforme; **p.95** Action on Smoking and Health (ASH); **p. 393** Association of South East Asian Nations (ASEAN); **pages 37, 118, 173, 225, 402, 421, 139, 142, 503, 504, 510, 531, 549** Bank of England; **p.301** Barclays; **p.103** Beeton's Book of Household Management; **pages 47, 68, 132, 389** BP; **p.508** Brian Deer; **p.286** BT; **pages 209 and 210** Captial Economics; **p.31** Central Intelligence Agency; **p.553** Cornwall Energy; **p.61** Department for Communities and Local Government (DCLG); **p.48** Department of Energy & Climate Change (DECC); **p.511** Department for Work and Pensions; **p.150** DIW Berlin; **p.552** Economics Today; **p.431** Eesti Pank; **p.446** Eurostat; **p.225** Fathom Consulting; **pages 3, 4, 5, 6, 16, 20, 21, 26, 27, 28, 33, 41, 49, 52, 62, 65, 66, 69, 72, 75, 77, 78, 80, 82, 86, 87, 88, 94, 97, 98, 101, 104, 105, 113, 115, 123, 126, 131, 151, 154, 182, 183, 187, 188, 201, 205, 209, 212, 214, 216, 218, 219, 220, 224, 225, 228, 230, 231, 232, 233, 247, 248, 250, 251, 256, 257, 260, 261, 263, 264, 265, 269, 270, 271, 274, 276, 280, 281, 282, 292, 297, 298, 301, 302, 308, 311, 315, 317, 318, 319, 321, 322, 324, 325, 326, 328, 329, 334, 337, 339, 358, 359, 361, 362, 364, 365, 367, 369, 371, 373, 374, 377, 383, 386, 396, 399, 401, 402, 405, 406, 409, 410, 412, 413, 416, 418, 422, 428, 429, 432, 433, 436, 437, 445, 446, 451, 454, 455, 457, 467, 470, 471, 475, 477, 482, 484, 485, 488, 491, 495, 496, 497, 498, 501, 503, 505, 506, 514, 517, 518, 532, 536, 537, 540, 543** © the Financial Times, All Rights Reserved; **p.241** Food and Agriculture Organization (FAO); **470** Freedom House; **p.62** Globefish; **p.296** Go-ahead; **pages 12, 72, 78, 174, 296, 324, 402, 553** gov.uk; **p.445** Haver Analytics; **p.174** Higher Education Statistics Agency; **p.78** HM Customs and Excise; **pages 522 and 523** HM Revenue and Customs; **pages 224, 225, 511, 519, 547** HM Treasury; **p.99** Health and Safety Executive; **pages 327, 328, 524, 530, 531** House of Commons Library; **pages 131** IFS Green budget; **224, 511; p.256** IHS Global; **pages 6, 418** IMF; **p.355** Incomes Data Services; **p.269** Jefferies; **p.368** Living Wage Foundation; **pages 367 and 368** Low Pay Commission Report; **p.508** Margaret Thatcher Foundation; **p.241** Marine Management Organisation; **p.491** McKinsey; **p.216** Migration Watch; **p.225** National archives; **p.40, 174** Nationwide; **p.393** North America Free Trade Agreement (NAFTA); **pages 163, 224, 512, 521** Office for Budget Responsibility; **pages 279 and 328** Office for Fair Trading; **pages 6, 7, 8, 9, 10, 11, 40, 54, 55, 57, 59, 61, 71, 72, 88, 112, 115, 117, 121, 122, 133, 134, 144, 146, 152, 154, 155, 161, 165, 167, 168, 173, 174, 176, 178, 180, 181, 183, 189, 190, 193, 194, 195, 199, 202, 206, 207, 224, 225, 301, 340, 341, 342, 343, 344, 345, 346, 353, 354, 356, 357, 358, 376, 384, 385, 395, 414, 421, 440, 443, 448, 450, 452, 453, 454, 457, 461, 462, 507, 512, 513, 527, 533, 548, 549** Office for National Statistics; **p.553** Ofgem; **pages 30, 107, 108, 113, 125, 169, 197, 198, 206, 207, 209, 210, 220, 389, 390, 402, 420, 422, 426, 438, 442, 443, 445, 463, 464, 477, 514, 522, 525, 528, 534, 542, 548** Organisation for Economic Co-operation and Development (OECD); **p.337** Resolution Foundation; **p.500** Scotland's Referendum; **pages 71, 72, 281** Society of Motor Manufacturers and Traders (SMMT); **p.199** The Budget Speech; **p.393** The European Free Trade Association; **p.453** The Smith Institute; **p.241** The State of World Fisheries and Aquaculture (SOFIA); **p.327** The UK Competition Regime; **pages 62, 69, 72, 182, 214, 224, 263, 265, 269, 270, 271, 328, 358, 367, 386, 429, 433, 438, 467, 475, 491, 532, 536, 537, 542, 543** Thomson Reuters Datastream; **p.95** Tobaccofreekids.org; **p.11** UK Cinema Association; **p.499** UK Parliament; **p.240** UKpia.com; **p.393** Union of South American Nations; **21, pages 31, 445, 479, 514** United Nations; **pages 413** United Nations Conference on Trade and Development; **page 468** United Nations Development Programme; **p.31** United States Census Bureau; **455** US Department of Health and Human Services (HHS); **p.288** Virgin trains; **p.61** Valuation Office Agency; **pages 80, 156, 158, 159, 175, 182, 445, 465, 466, 469, 472, 489, 490, 556** World Bank, **pages 370, 393, 413** World Trade Organization.

Every effort has been made to trace the copyright holders and we apologise in advance for any unintentional omissions. We would be pleased to insert the appropriate acknowledgement in any subsequent edition of this publication.

1 Economics as a social science

1. Economics is generally classified as a social science and uses the scientific method as the basis for its investigation.
2. Economics is the study of how groups of individuals make decisions about the allocation of scarce resources.
3. Economists build models and theories to explain economic interactions.
4. The ceteris paribus assumption is used in building models.
5. Positive economics deals with statements of 'fact' that can either be refuted or supported. Normative economics deals with value judgements, often in the context of policy recommendations.

Starter activity

'The UK should leave the European Union.' Is this a fact or is it a value judgement? If you wanted to argue for or against the UK leaving the European Union, what factual arguments could you use? And what emotional arguments could you put forward?

Which of these arguments are economic and which are non-economic?

The scientific method

There are many sciences covering a wide field of knowledge. What links them all is a particular method of work or enquiry called the **scientific method**. The scientific method at its most basic is relatively easy to understand. A scientist:

● postulates (puts forward) a **theory** - the scientist puts forward a hypothesis which is capable of refutation (e.g. the Earth travels round the Sun, the Earth is flat, a light body will fall at the same speed as a heavy body);

● gathers evidence to either support the theory or refute it - astronomical observation gives evidence to support the theory that the earth travels round the sun; on the other hand, data refute the idea that the Earth is flat; gathering evidence may be done through controlled experiments;

● accepts, modifies or refutes the theory - the Earth does travel round the Sun; a light body will fall at the same speed as a heavy body although it will only do so under certain conditions; the Earth is not flat.

Theories which gain universal acceptance are often called **laws**. Hence we have the law of gravity, Boyle's law, and in economics the laws of demand and supply.

Economics - the science

In natural sciences, such as physics or chemistry, it is relatively easy to use the scientific method. In physics, much of the work can take place in laboratories. Observations can be made with some degree of certainty. Control groups can be established. It then becomes relatively easy to accept or refute a particular hypothesis.

This is much more difficult in **social sciences** such as economics, sociology, politics and anthropology. In economics, it is often not possible to set up experiments to test hypotheses. It is often not possible to establish control groups or to conduct experiments in environments which enable one factor to be

varied whilst other factors are kept constant. The economist has to gather data in the ordinary everyday world where many variables are changing over any given time period. It then becomes difficult to decide whether the evidence supports or refutes particular hypotheses.

Economists sometimes come to very different conclusions when considering a particular set of data as their interpretations may vary. For example, an unemployment rate of six per cent in Scotland compared to a national average of three per cent may indicate a failure of government policy to help this area. Others may conclude that policy had been a success as unemployment may have been far greater without the use of policy.

It is sometimes argued that economics cannot be a science because it studies human behaviour and human behaviour cannot be reduced to scientific laws. There is an element of truth in this. It is very difficult to understand and predict the behaviour of individuals. However, nearly all economics is based on the study of the behaviour of groups of individuals. The behaviour of groups is often far more predictable than that of individuals. Moreover, we tend to judge a science on its ability to establish laws which are certain and unequivocal. But even in a hard science such as physics, it has become established that some laws can only be stated in terms of probabilities. In economics, much analysis is couched in terms of 'it is likely that' or 'this may possibly happen'. Economists use this type of language because they know they have insufficient data to make firm predictions. In part it is because other variables may change at the same time, altering the course of events. However, it is also used because economists know that human behaviour, whilst broadly predictable, is not predictable to the last £1 spent or to the nearest one penny of income.

Theories and models

The terms 'theory' and '**model**' are often used interchangeably. There is no exact distinction to be made between the two. However, an economic theory is generally expressed in looser terms than a model. For instance, 'consumption is dependent upon income' might be an economic theory.
'$C_t = 567 + 0.852Y_t$' where 567 is a constant, C_t is current consumption and Y_t current income would be an economic model. Theories can often be expressed in words. But economic models, because they require greater precision in their specification, are often expressed in mathematical terms.

The purpose of modelling

Why are theories and models so useful in a science? The universe is a complex place. There is an infinite number of interactions happening at any moment in time. Somehow we all have to make sense of what is going on. For instance, we assume that if we put our hand into a flame, we will get burnt. If we see a large hole in the ground in front of us we assume that we will fall into it if we carry on going in that direction.

One of the reasons why we construct theories or models is because we want to know why something is as it is. Some people are fascinated by questions such as 'Why do we fall downwards and not upwards?' or 'Why can birds fly?'. More importantly we use theories and models all the time in deciding how to act. We keep away from fires to prevent getting burnt. We avoid holes in the ground because we don't want to take a tumble.

Simplification

One criticism made of economics is that economic theories and models are 'unrealistic'. This is true, but it is equally true of Newton's law of gravity, Einstein's Theory of Relativity or any theory or model. This is because any theory or model has to be a simplification of reality if it is to be useful. Imagine, for instance, using a map which described an area perfectly. To do this it would need to be a full scale reproduction of the entire area which would give no practical advantage. Alternatively, drop a feather and a cannonball from the top of the Leaning Tower of Pisa. You will find that they don't descend at the same speed, as one law in physics would predict, because that law assumes that factors such as air resistance and friction don't exist.

If a model is to be useful it has to be simple. The extent of simplification depends upon its use. If you wanted to go from London to Tokyo by air, it wouldn't be very helpful to have maps which were on the scale of your local A to Z. On the other hand, if you wanted to visit a friend in a nearby town it wouldn't be very helpful to have a map of the world with you. The local A to Z is very much more detailed (i.e. closer to reality) than a world map but this does not necessarily make it more useful or make it a 'better' model.

Simplification implies that some factors have been included in the model and some have been omitted. It could even be the case that some factors have been distorted to emphasise particular points in a model. For instance, on a road map of the UK, cartographers will almost certainly not have attempted to name every small village or show the geological formation of the area. On the other hand, they will have marked in roads and motorways which will appear several miles wide according to the scale of the map.

Assumptions and ceteris paribus

All sciences make assumptions when developing models and theories. In the case of the feather and the cannonball being dropped from the Leaning Tower of Pisa, both would fall at equal speed if it were assumed that there was no air resistance. Making assumptions allows the scientist to simplify a problem to make it manageable to solve.

An important way in which economists simplify reality is to adopt the **ceteris paribus** condition. Ceteris paribus is Latin for 'all other things being equal' or 'all other things remaining the same'. For example, in demand theory, economists consider how price affects the amount demanded by buyers of a good. To isolate the price factor, they assume that all other factors that affect demand, such as income or the price of other goods, remain unchanged. Then economists see what happens to quantity demanded as the price of the good changes.

Positive and normative economics

Economics is concerned with two types of investigation. **Positive economics** is the scientific or objective study of the subject. It is concerned with finding out how economies and markets actually work. **Positive statements** are statements about economics which can be proven to be true or false. They can be supported or refuted by evidence. For example, the statement 'The UK economy is currently operating on its production possibility frontier' is a positive statement. Economists can search for evidence as to whether there are unemployed resources or not. If there are large numbers of unemployed workers, then the statement is refuted. If unemployment is very low, and we know that all market economies need some unemployment for the efficient workings of labour markets as people move between jobs, then the statement would be supported. Statements about the future can be positive statements too. For example, 'The service sector will grow by 30 per cent in size over the next five years' is a positive statement. Economists will have to wait five years for the proof to support or refute the statement to be available. However, it is still a statement which is capable of being proved or disproved.

Question 1

In 2014 it was reported that Britain's Minister of State for Crime Prevention had questioned whether police should respond to calls from petrol retailers whose customers drive off without paying. Norman Baker suggested that petrol stations encouraged crime by refusing to insist on prepayment at the pumps. They did this because they wanted more business in their shops. One of the fastest-growing offences is motorists filling their cars with petrol and driving off without paying. In London, the practice increased nearly sevenfold between 2010 and 2012, according to official statistics.

However, Brian Madderson, Chair of the Petrol Retailers' Association, disagreed. 'The police have no right whatsoever to interfere with our business model. We only live as forecourt retailers these days by dint of our shop sales. The (profit) margin on fuel has almost disappeared and the reason is the supermarkets selling at or below cost.' Neil Saunders, Managing Director at research group Conlumino, dismissed the minister's comments as 'wholly ignorant'. 'Retailers spend millions each year to try and combat shoplifting. Short of turning their stores into prison camps, retailers cannot prevent this.'

Source: adapted from © the *Financial Times* 2.8.2014, All Rights Reserved.

Explain which are the positive statements and which are the normative statements in this passage.

Normative economics is concerned with value judgements. It deals with the study of and presentation of policy prescriptions about economics. **Normative statements** are statements which cannot be supported or refuted. Ultimately, they are opinions about how economies and markets should work. For example, 'The government should increase the state pension', or 'Manufacturing companies should invest more' are normative statements.

Economists tend to be interested in both positive and normative economics. They want to find out how economies work. But they also want to influence policy debates. Normative economics also typically contains positive economics within it. Take the normative statement 'The government should increase the state pension'. Economists putting forward this value judgement are likely to back up their opinion with positive evidence. They might state that 'The average pensioner has a disposable income of 40 per cent of the average worker'; and 'The average pensioner only goes on holiday once every four years'. These are positive statements because they are capable of proof or disproof. They are used to build up an argument which supports the final opinion that state pensions should be raised.

Normative statements tend to contain words like 'should' and 'ought'. However, sometimes positive statements also contain these words. 'Inflation should be brought down' is a normative statement because it is not capable of refutation. 'Inflation should reach 5 per cent by the end of the year' is a positive statement. At the end of the year, if inflation has reached five per cent, then the statement will have been proven to be correct.

Key Terms

Ceteris paribus - all things being equal; the assumption that, whilst the effects of a change in one variable are being investigated, all other variables are kept constant.

Law - a theory or model which has been verified by empirical evidence.

Normative economics - the study and presentation of policy prescriptions involving value judgements about the way in which scarce resources are allocated.

Normative statement - a statement which cannot be supported or refuted because it is a value judgement.

Positive economics - the scientific or objective study of the allocation of resources.

Positive statement - a statement which can be supported or refuted by evidence.

Scientific method - a method which subjects theories or hypotheses to falsification by empirical evidence.

Social science - the study of societies and human behaviour using a variety of methods, including the scientific method.

Theory or model - a hypothesis which is capable of refutation by empirical evidence.

Thinking like an economist

The Scottish Independence vote

In September 2014, Scotland voted against becoming an independent country by a majority of 55 per cent to 45 per cent. In a letter to the *Financial Times*, John Barstow, from the Executive Council of the trade union Usdaw, a trade union representing shop workers, said that the no verdict was 'excellent news for all our livelihoods'. This is a value judgement with which those leading the campaign for Scottish independence would have disagreed.

In the letter, he stated that 'Usdaw has been in total unison with household names such as Marks and Spencer, J Sainsbury and Tesco in supporting the integrity of the UK'. This is a positive statement which can be supported or refuted by looking at evidence. In this case, John Barstow was arguably correct in so far as the three companies mentioned had come out in support of the 'No' campaign.

John Barstow went on to say that 'retail is a complex activity involving not just outlets, but also distribution depots, manufacturing chains, administration offices and even some banking'. Again this is mainly a positive statement, capable of being supported or refuted by evidence. It could be argued that the word 'complex' is a value judgement. Complex implies that there is an opposite, which is simple. However, most economists probably would argue that distribution is a complex activity.

He then stated: 'Hence the simplicity of a strong UK single market is an essential base for expanding this sector and the livelihoods within it'. Those in favour of independence for Scotland would have disagreed with this statement. They might have argued that a single market is not 'simple' and that the increase in complexity arising out of independence would have been so minimal as to be unimportant. They would possibly also have taken issue with saying that a single market is an 'essential base for expanding this sector'. Whether or not there is a single market, there are consumers wanting to buy from shops.

Much of this debate would involve positive statements, supporting or refuting the argument put forward by John Barstow. Ultimately, though, the way in which the letter is written, comparing a 'complex' system in retail with a 'simple' system in a single market suggests that he is putting forward his own value judgement: that a vote for independence would have been bad both for Scotland and the UK it left behind.

Source: adapted from © the *Financial Times* 19.9.2014, All Rights Reserved.

Net migration

2014 figures showed that net migration in the UK (the total number of people entering the country to live minus the number of people leaving to live abroad) soared by more than a third to 212 000 in the year to September. This dealt a blow to David Cameron's hope that he would reach his target of 'tens of thousands' by May 2015.

The 58 000 rise in immigrants was largely due to a surge in arrivals from within the European Union, with 60 000 more arriving from countries such as Spain, Portugal, Italy and Poland than in the previous 12 months. Non-EU immigration was down by 25 000.

The latest data give evidence to support fears that the UK's education exports are suffering as a result of government controls.

Statisticians estimated that there were 25 000 fewer immigrants from New Commonwealth countries, particularly India and Pakistan, coming to study in the UK. Foreign students are important for universities because they pay higher than average fees, subsidising UK students who pay lower fees.

Responding to the data, it was reported that James Brokenshire, Minister for Security and Immigration, said he and his team were building an immigration system that was 'fair to British citizens and legitimate migrants', whilst being 'tough on those who abuse the system or flout the law'. But Yvette Cooper, Shadow Home Secretary, said the figures showed that the net migration target was 'in tatters'. Nigel Farage, UKIP leader, said the figures showed 'just what a failure the government has been' on controlled immigration.

Source: adapted from © the *Financial Times* 28.2.2014, All Rights Reserved.

Q

1. Explain the difference between positive and normative statements. Illustrate your answer with at least two examples of positive statements from the data and two examples of normative statements.

2. Discuss the possible impact on the UK economy of '25 000 fewer immigrants … coming to study in the UK' per year.

Evaluation

Think of the main points about which you could write a paragraph. These could include the impact on housing and health care, lost export income for the UK and the impact on the balance of payments, lost income for universities and its consequences, lost income for businesses that rely on university and student spending, as well as long-term loss of business contacts when foreign students return home and run their own businesses. Then weigh up which of these is most important or less important.

2 Economic data

Theme 1
Theme 2
Theme 3
Theme 4

Key points

1. Economic data are collected not only to verify or refute economic models but to provide a basis for economic decision making.
2. Data may be expressed at nominal (or current) prices or at real (or constant) prices. Data expressed in real terms take into account the effects of inflation.
3. Indices are used to simplify statistics and to express averages.
4. Data can be presented in a variety of forms such as tables or graphs.
5. All data should be interpreted with care given that data can be selected and presented in a wide variety of ways.

Starter activity

When your great grandparents started work, what did they earn? In 1950, average UK earnings were £350 per year. Is that £350 the same as £350 a year today? In 2013, average earnings were £26 500. What could you have bought with £26 500 in 1950?

In 2013, the average earnings of bar staff were £7 317, secretaries £16 384, teachers £32 547 and doctors £70 646. How many times more did a teacher earn than a secretary or a doctor more than bar staff? Is there an easy way to display the relative earnings of different workers?

Source: with information from www.ons.gov.uk.

The collection and reliability of data

Economists collect data for two main reasons.

- The scientific method requires that theories be tested. Data may be used to refute or support a theory. For instance, an economist might gather data to support or refute the hypothesis that 'Cuts in the marginal rate of income tax will increase the incentive to work', or that 'An increase in the real value of unemployment benefit will lead to an increase in the number of people unemployed'.
- Economists are often required to provide support for particular policies. Without economic data it is often difficult, if not impossible, to make policy recommendations. For instance, in his Budget each year the Chancellor of the Exchequer has to make a statement to the House of Commons outlining the state of the economy and the economic outlook for the next 12 months. Without a clear knowledge of where the economy is at the moment, it is impossible to forecast how it might change in the future and to recommend policy changes to steer the economy in a more desirable direction.

Collecting economic data is usually very difficult and sometimes impossible. Some macroeconomic data - such as the balance of payments figures or the value of national income - are collected from a wide variety of sources. The figures for the balance of payments on current account are compiled from returns made by every exporter and importer on every item exported and imported. Not surprisingly, the information is inaccurate. Some exporters and importers will conceal transactions to avoid tax. Others will not want to be bothered with the paperwork.

Other macroeconomic data such as the Consumer Prices Index (used to measure inflation) or the Labour Force Survey (used to measure employment and unemployment) are based

Question 1

How do you double the size of your economy overnight to become the largest economy in Africa? The answer is to revise your estimate of the output of the economy, called GDP (Gross Domestic Product). This is what Nigeria has done. Yesterday, it was reported that it announced its GDP for 2013 was $509 billion, 89 per cent larger than previously stated. Previous estimates were based on a way of calculating GDP set in 1990 that failed to capture many of Nigeria's growth industries. For example, under the old method, telecoms including mobiles accounted for 0.8 per cent of GDP. Under the new method, it is 8.6 per cent of GDP. Under the old method, the film industry was not even measured. Under the new method, it accounts for 1.4 per cent of GDP.

Source: adapted from © the *Financial Times* 7.4.2014, All Rights Reserved.

Figure 1

Top African countries by GDP, 2013

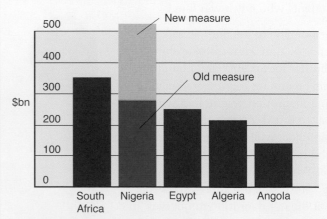

Source: adapted from IMF estimates.

(a) Explain why the estimates of GDP in 2013 using the 1990 method of calculation were unreliable.

(b) Suggest why a European company might be more prepared to invest in new facilities in Nigeria rather than South Africa in 2014 compared to 2012.

on surveys. Surveys are only reliable if there is accurate sampling and measuring and are rarely as accurate as a complete count.

Some macroeconomic data are very reliable statistically but do not necessarily provide a good measure of the relevant economic variable. In the UK, the unemployment Claimant Count is calculated each month at benefit offices throughout the country. It is extremely accurate but no economist would argue that the figure produced is an accurate measure of unemployment. There is general agreement that some people who claim benefit for being unemployed are not unemployed and conversely there are many unemployed people who are not claiming benefit.

In microeconomics use is again made of survey data, with the limitations that this implies. Economists also make use of more experimental data, gathering evidence for case studies. For instance, economists might want to look at the impact of different pricing policies on entry to sports centres. They might study a small number of sports centres in a local area. The evidence gathered would be unlikely decisively to refute or support a general hypothesis such as 'Cheap entry increases sports centre use'. But it would be possible to conclude that the evidence tended to support or refute the hypothesis.

In economics it is difficult to gather accurate data and, for that reason, academic economists mostly qualify their conclusions.

Real and nominal values

There are many different measures in use today such as tonnes, litres, kilograms and kilometres. Often, we want to be able to compare these different measures. For instance, an industrialist might wish to compare oil measured in litres, and coal measured in kilograms. One way of doing this is to convert oil and coal into therms using gross calorific values. In economics, by far the most important measure used is the value of an item measured in monetary terms, such as pounds sterling, US dollars or euros. One problem in using money as a measure is that inflation (the general change in prices in an economy) erodes the purchasing power of money.

For instance, in 1948 the value of output of the UK economy (measured by gross domestic product at market prices) was £11.6 billion. In 2013, 65 years later, it was £1 713.3 billion. It would seem that output had increased about 148 times (£1 713.3 billion ÷ £11.6 billion) - an enormous increase. In fact, output increased by only a fraction of that amount. This is because most of the measured increase was an increase not in output but in prices. Prices over the period rose about 29 fold. Stripping the inflation element out of the increase leaves us with an increase in output of 5.2 times.

Values unadjusted for inflation are called **nominal values**. These values are expressed at **current prices** (i.e. at the level of prices existing during the time period being measured).

If data are adjusted for inflation, then they are said to be at **real values** or at **constant prices**. To do this in practice involves taking one period of time as the **base period**. Data are then adjusted assuming that prices were the same throughout as in the base period.

For instance, a basket of goods costs £100 in year 1 and £200 in year 10. Prices have therefore doubled. If you had £1 000 to spend in year 10, then that would have been equivalent to £500 at year 1 prices because both amounts would have bought five baskets of goods. On the other hand, if you had £1 000 to spend in year 1, that would be equivalent to £2 000 in year 10 prices because both would have bought you 10 baskets of goods.

Taking another example, the real value of UK output in 1948 at 1948 prices was the same as its nominal value (i.e. £11.6 billion). The real value of output in 2013 at 1948 prices was £57.8 billion. It is much lower than the nominal 2013 value because prices were much higher in 2013.

On the other hand, at 2013 prices, the real value of output in 1948 was £320.2 billion, much higher than the nominal value because prices in 2013 were much higher than in 1948. Further examples are given in Table 2.

UK government statistics expressed in real terms are adjusted to prices three or four years previously. In 2014, figures were expressed at 2011 prices.

Question 2

Table 1 Components of final demand at current prices

	Index of prices 2010=100	£ billion at current prices		
		Households' expenditure	Government expenditure	Fixed investment
2010	100.0	953.3	336.6	250.2
2011	104.5	985.8	337.3	260.8
2012	107.4	1022.1	343.9	268.8
2013	110.1	1059.1	346.8	281.5

Source: adapted from www.ons.gov.uk.

Using a calculator or a spreadsheet, work out for the period 2010-2013 (a) at constant 2010 prices and (b) at constant 2013 prices the values of:

(i) households' expenditure;
(ii) government expenditure;
(iii) fixed investment.

Present your calculations in the form of two tables, one for 2010 prices and the other for 2013 prices.

Table 2 Nominal and real values

Nominal value	Inflation between year 1 and 2	Real values	
		Value at year 1 prices	Value at year 2 prices
Example 1 £100 in year 1	10%	£100	£110
Example 2 £500 in year 1	50%	£500	£750
Example 3 £200 in year 2	20%	£166.66	£200
Example 4 £400 in year 2	5%	£380.95	£400

Note: £100 at year 1 prices is worth £100 x 1.1 (i.e. 1+10%) in year 2 prices £200 at year 2 prices is worth £200 ÷ 1.2 in year 1 prices.

Indices

It is often more important in economics to compare values than to know absolute values. For instance, we might want to compare the real value of output in the economy in 2003 and 2013. Knowing that the real value of output (GDP at market prices at 2013 prices) in 2003 was £1 471.1 billion and in 2013 was £1 656.5 billion is helpful, but the very large numbers make it difficult to see at a glance what, for instance, was the approximate percentage increase. Equally, many series of statistics are averages. The Retail Prices Index (the measure of the cost of living) is calculated by working out what it would cost to buy a typical cross-section or 'basket' of goods. Comparing say £458.92 in one month with £475.13 the next is not easy.

So, many series are converted into **index number** form. One time period is chosen as the base period and the rest of the statistics in the series are compared to the value in that base period. The value in the base period is usually 100. The figure 100 is chosen because it is easy to work with mathematically. Taking the example of output again, if 1948 were taken as the base year, then the value of real output in 1948 would be 100, and the value of real output in 2013 would be 517.3. Alternatively if 2013 were taken as the base year, the value of output would be 100 in 2013 and 19.3 in 1948. Or with 2003 as the base year, the value of output in 1948 would be 21.8 whilst in 2013 it would be 112.6. Further examples are given in Table 3.

Table 3 Converting a series into index number form

		Consumption		
		Index number if base year is:		
Year	£ millions	year 1	year 2	year 3
1	500	100.0	83.3	62.5
2	600	120.0	100.0	75.0
3	800	160.0	133.3	100.0

Note: The index number for consumption in year 2, if year 1 is the base year, is (600 ÷ 500) x 100.

Question 3

Table 4 Consumers' expenditure at current prices

	£ billion		
	Food & Drink	Clothing & Footwear	Restaurants & Hotels
2010	82.8	51.0	87.3
2011	86.4	54.6	93.6
2012	90.9	56.1	97.4
2013	95.2	59.7	101.5

Source: adapted from www.ons.gov.uk.

Using a calculator or a spreadsheet, convert each category of expenditure into index number form using as the base year: (a) 2010 and (b) 2013.

Present your calculations in the form of two tables, one for each base year.

The interpretation of data

Data can be presented in many forms and be used both to inform and mislead the reader. To illustrate these points, consider inflation figures for the UK economy. Inflation is the general rise in prices in an economy. If there has been two per cent inflation over the past year, it means that prices on average have increased by 2 per cent. One way in which inflation figures can be presented is in tabular form as in Table 5. The data could also be presented in graphical form as in Figure 2(a).

Figure 2

UK Inflation (CPI)

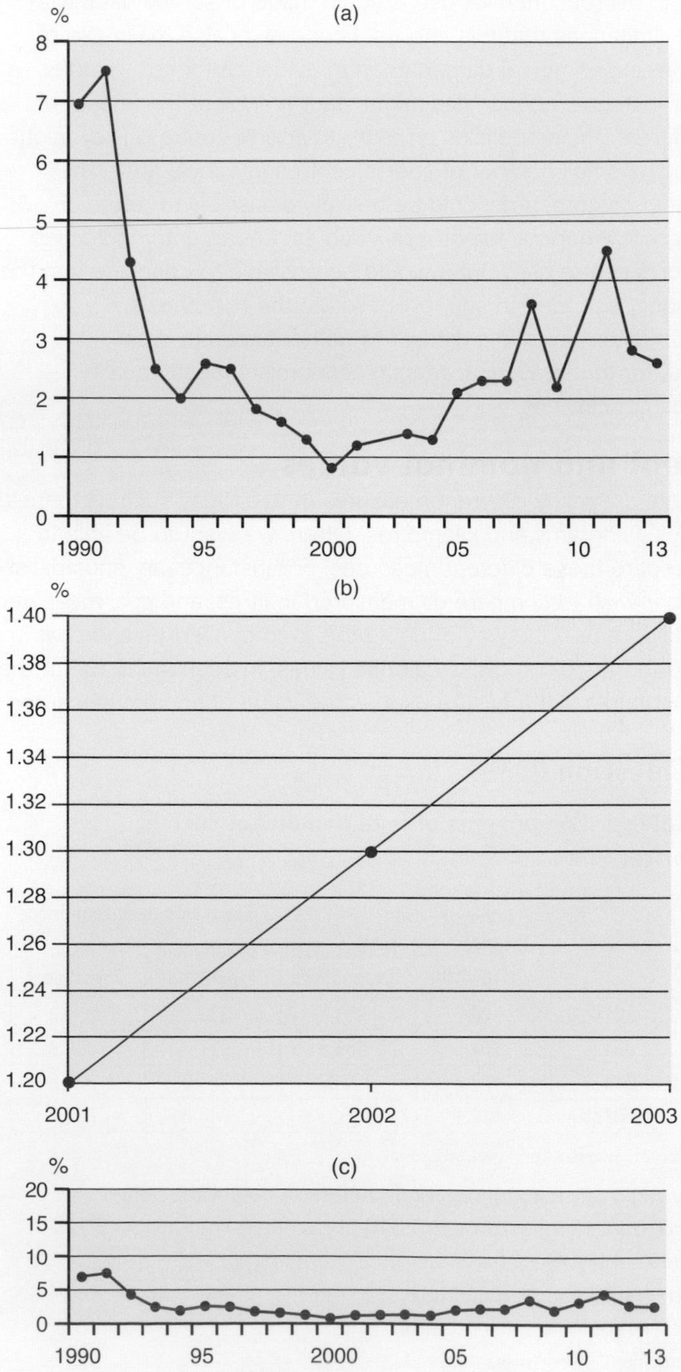

Source: adapted from www.ons.gov.uk.

Table 5 UK inflation (CPI)

Year	Inflation %	Year	Inflation %
1990	7.0	2002	1.3
1991	7.5	2003	1.4
1992	4.3	2004	1.3
1993	2.5	2005	2.1
1994	2.0	2006	2.3
1995	2.6	2007	2.3
1996	2.5	2008	3.6
1997	1.8	2009	2.2
1998	1.6	2010	3.3
1999	1.3	2011	4.5
2000	0.8	2012	2.8
2001	1.2	2013	2.6

Source: with information from www.ons.gov.uk.

Graphs must be interpreted with some care. Figure 2(b) gives a distorted view of inflation between 2001 and 2003. Figure 2(a) shows that there was almost no change in inflation over these three years. But looking at Figure 2(b), it would seem that there has been a massive change in inflation. This is because in Figure 2(b) the vertical scale starts at 1.20 per cent and ends at 1.40 per cent and on the horizontal scale, only three years are covered. Figure 2(c) distorts the data in a different way. By compressing the scale on the vertical axis in relation to the horizontal axis, it looks as though there has been hardly any change in inflation between 1990 and 2013.

Graphs are sometimes constructed using log scales for the vertical axis. This has the effect of gradually compressing values on the vertical axis as they increase. The vertical distance between 0 and 1, for instance, is larger per unit than between 999 and 1 000.

Data can also be expressed in verbal form. For example, Figure 2(a) shows that inflation was lower at 2.6 per cent at the end of the period in 2013 than at the start in 1990 when it was seven per cent. Over the period 1990-2013, inflation ranged from a high of 7.5 per cent in 1991 to a low of 0.8 per cent in 2000. When expressing data in verbal form, it can become very tedious to describe each individual change. For instance, it would be inappropriate to say 'Inflation in 1990 was seven per cent. Then it rose to 7.5 per cent in 1991 before falling to 4.2 per cent in 1992. Then in 1993 it fell again to 2.5 per cent and again in 1994 to 2.0 per cent'. When expressing data in verbal form, it is important to pick out the main trends and perhaps give a few key figures to illustrate these trends.

Key Terms

Base period - the period, such as a year or a month, with which all other values in a series are compared.
Index number - an indicator showing the relative value of one number to another from a base of 100. It is often used to present an average of a number of statistics.
Nominal values - values unadjusted for the effects of inflation (i.e. values at current prices).
Real values - values adjusted for inflation (i.e. values at constant prices).

Question 4

Figure 3

Unemployment rate, %

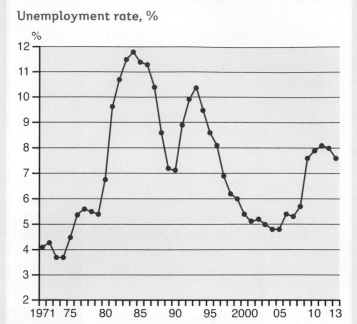

Figure 4

Unemployment rate, %

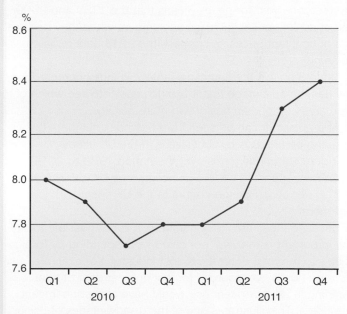

Consider each graph in turn.

(a) What does each show?

(b) Explain why each seems to give a different picture of unemployment in the UK for the period 2010-2011.

9

Thinking like an economist

Spending on tourism

Tourism is a major industry in the UK. Is it a growing industry? There is a number of ways in which growth can be measured but one is total spending by holidaymakers, defined as tourists, who spent at least one night away on holiday.

Table 6 shows how total spending on tourism has grown between 1989 and 2013. It divides tourists into three categories - UK tourists who take a holiday within the country, foreign tourists who come to the UK and UK tourists who take holidays abroad. The figures in Table 6 are expressed at current prices.

This means that inflation is not taken into account. If there had been very high inflation over the period 1989-2013, the volume of tourism could have declined given the data in Table 6. In fact, consumer (RPI) prices over the 24-year period rose 117 per cent. So real growth in spending is anything that is above that 117 per cent rise.

Table 7 shows the figures in Table 6 expressed at constant 2013 prices, i.e. after the inflation element has been stripped out and adjusted to the level of prices in 2013. Taking 2013 as the reference year for prices means that the 1989 and 2000 data at current prices increase as numbers when they become data at constant prices. In contrast, the 2013 data remain the same.

Table 8 shows the figures in Table 7 in index number form. This has the advantage that it is much easier to see which of the three areas of tourism has grown more quickly.

At a glance, it can be seen from the index numbers that spending on holidays by UK citizens in the UK fell by 32.9 per cent in real terms over the period 1989 to 2013. In contrast, spending on foreign holidays by UK citizens grew by 71.8 per cent. Foreign visitors to the UK spent 39.4 per cent more.

Because these are index numbers, it is not possible to say how important is the 24.7 per cent rise in spending by foreign visitors to the total domestic tourist industry. For example, if foreign holidays accounted for just one per cent of total spending, a 24.7 per cent rise would have almost no impact on tourism. This illustrates one of the disadvantages of using index numbers.

To assess the relative impact of the increase in foreign tourists, we have to look back to Table 7. Total spending on tourism in the UK by UK citizens and by foreigners at constant 2013 prices fell from £52.1 billion to £45.9 billion, a 11.9 per cent fall over the period 1989 to 2013. The data show that a very large fall in spending by UK residents on holidays in the UK has outweighed a smaller increase in spending by foreigners on UK holidays. UK citizens are spending more on holidays in 2013 than in 1989, but they have substituted foreign holidays for domestic holidays.

Table 6 Spending on tourism at current prices, £ million

	£ millions at current prices		
	Spending on holidays by UK citizens in the UK	Spending in the UK by foreign visitors	Spending on foreign holidays by UK residents
1989	17 071	6 945	9 357
2000	26 133	12 805	24 251
2013	24 861	21 011	34 900

Source: adapted from www.ons.gov.uk.

Table 7 Spending on tourism at constant 2013 prices, £ million

	£ millions at constant 2013 prices		
	Spending on holidays by UK citizens in the UK	Spending in the UK by foreign visitors	Spending on foreign holidays by UK residents
1989	37 060	15 077	20 314
2000	38 383	18 807	35 618
2013	24 861	21 011	34 900

Source: adapted from www.ons.gov.uk.

Table 8 Spending on tourism at constant 2013 prices, 1989=100

	1989 = 100		
	Spending on holidays by UK citizens in the UK	Spending in the UK by foreign visitors	Spending on foreign holidays by UK residents
1989	100.0	100.0	100.0
2000	103.6	124.7	175.3
2013	67.1	139.4	171.8

Source: adapted from www.ons.gov.uk.

Data Response Question

Cinema data

Q

1. Describe the main trends in cinema admissions shown in the data.

2. Explain the advantages and disadvantages of using index numbers to present data. Illustrate your answer from the data.

3. 'Revenues per screen and the number of screens cannot carry on rising.'
   (a) To what extent do the data support this statement for the period 1987-2013?
   (b) Discuss whether it is likely to be true in the future.

Table 9 Cinema exhibitor statistics, UK₁

	Number of sites	Number of screens	Number of admissions	at current prices			at constant 2013 prices		
				Gross box office takings	Revenue per admission	Revenue per screen	Gross box office takings	Revenue per admission	Revenue per screen
			millions	£millions	£	£000	£millions	£	£000
1987	492	1 035	66.8	123.8	1.85	119.6	303.9	4.54	293.6
1995	728	2 003	114.6	354.2	3.09	176.8	594.2	5.18	396.6
2006	783	3 440	156.6	762.1	4.87	221.5	962.2	6.15	279.7
2013	747	3 897	165.5	1082.1	5.84	277.7	1082.1	5.84	277.7

Source: adapted from www.ons.gov.uk; www.cinemauk.org.uk.

Table 10 Cinema exhibitor statistics, UK₁

	Number of sites	Number of screens	Number of admissions	at current prices			at constant 2013 prices		
				Gross box office takings	Revenue per admission	Revenue per screen	Gross box office takings	Revenue per admission	Revenue per screen
1987	100.0	100.0	100.0	100.0	100.0	100.0	100.0	100.0	100.0
1995	148.0	193.5	171.6	286.1	167.0	148.9	195.5	114.0	101.8
2006	159.1	332.4	234.4	615.6	263.2	185.2	316.6	135.5	95.3
2013	151.8	376.5	247.8	874.1	315.7	232.2	356.1	128.6	94.6

Source: adapted from www.ons.gov.uk; www.cinemauk.org.uk.

1. 1987 data are Great Britain; 1995, 2006 and 2013 data are UK.

Evaluation

For question 3(a), look carefully at the data. What has happened to the number of screens? Then, for revenues per screen, are the data telling the same story at current prices and at constant prices? Do the data support or refute the statement at the start of the question? For 3(b), is there a limit on the number of screens there is likely to be in the future and what might set that limit? What impact could changes in technology have on cinema? What about inflation? Come to a conclusion by weighing up your arguments.

3 The economic problem

Key points

1. Nearly all resources are scarce.
2. Human wants are infinite.
3. Scarce resources and infinite wants give rise to the basic economic problem - resources have to be allocated between competing uses.
4. Allocation involves choices and each choice has an opportunity cost.
5. An economy is a social organisation through which decisions about what, how and for whom to produce are made.
6. The factors of production - land, labour capital and enterprise - are combined together to create goods and services for consumption.
7. The rewards to the owners of the factors of production include rents, royalties, wages, interest and profit.

Starter activity

What are you going to do tomorrow? What alternatives do you have? What could you do with your time? If it turns out you can't do what you have planned, what is the next best alternative?

Just as your time tomorrow is a scarce resource, so is the money you have. How do you plan to spend it? What is the next best alternative purchase?

Scarcity

It is often said that we live in a global village. The world's resources are finite; there are only limited amounts of land, water, oil, food and other resources on this planet. Economists therefore say that resources are **scarce**.

Scarcity means that economic agents, such as individuals, firms, governments and international agencies, can only obtain a limited amount of resources at any moment in time. For instance, a family has to live on a fixed budget; it cannot have everything it wants. A firm might want to build a new factory but not have the resources to be able to do so. A government might wish to build new hospitals or devote more resources to its foreign aid programme but not have the finance to make this possible. Resources which are scarce are called **economic goods**.

Not all resources are scarce. There is more than enough air on this planet for everyone to be able to breathe as much as they want. Resources which are not scarce are called **free goods**. In the past many goods such as food, water and shelter have been free, but as the population of the planet has expanded and as production has increased, so the number of free goods has diminished. Recently, for instance, clean beaches in many parts of the UK have ceased to be a free good to society. Pollution has forced water companies and seaside local authorities to spend resources cleaning up their local environment. With the destruction of the world's rain forests and increasing atmospheric pollution, the air we breathe may no longer remain a free good. Factories may have to purify the air they take from the atmosphere, for instance. This air would then become an economic good.

Infinite wants

People have a limited number of **needs** which must be satisfied if they are to survive as human beings. Some are material needs, such as food, water, heat, shelter and clothing. Others are psychological and emotional needs such as self-esteem and being loved. People's needs are finite. However, no one would choose to live at the level of basic human needs if they could enjoy a higher standard of living.

This is because human **wants** are unlimited. It doesn't matter whether the person is a doctor in Africa, a manager in India, a farmer in the UK or the richest individual in the world, there is always something which that person wants more of. This can include more food, a bigger house, a longer holiday, a cleaner environment, more love, more friendship, better relationships, more self-esteem, greater fairness or justice, peace, or more time to listen to music, meditate or cultivate the arts.

Question 1

Time was when people used to take their car out for a Sunday afternoon 'spin'. The novelty of owning a car and the freedom of the road made driving a pleasant leisure pursuit. Today, with 35.8 million vehicles registered in the UK, a Sunday afternoon tour could easily turn into a nightmare traffic jam.

Of course, many journeys are trouble free. Traffic is so light that cars do not slow each other down. But most rush hour journeys today occur along congested roads where each extra car on the road adds to the journey time of every other car. When London introduced a £5 a day 'congestion charge', a fee for cars to use roads in central London, the amount of traffic dropped by 17 per cent. This was enough to reduce journey times considerably.

Traffic congestion also greatly increases the amount of pollution created by cars. Our ecosystem can cope with low levels of emissions, but, as cities like Paris and Athens have discovered, high levels of traffic combined with the wrong weather conditions can lead to sharp increases in pollution levels. The car pollutes the environment anyway because cars emit greenhouse gases. Nearly one fifth of CO_2 emissions in the UK come from road transport.

Source: adapted from www.gov.uk.

Explain whether roads are, in any sense, a 'free good' from an economic viewpoint.

Question 2

Draw up a list of minimum human needs for a teenager living in the UK today. How might this list differ from the needs of a teenager living in Ethiopia?

The basic economic problem

Resources are scarce but wants are infinite. It is this which gives rise to the **basic economic problem** and which forces economic agents to make choices. They have to allocate their scarce resources between competing uses.

Economics is the study of this **allocation of resources** - the choices that are made by economic agents. Every **choice**

Question 3

Over the past 20 years, university students have come under increasing financial pressure. Previously, the government had paid all student tuition fees. It had also given a grant to students to cover their living expenses, although this grant was means tested according to the incomes of parents.

In 1999, grants for living expenses were replaced completely by student loans. By 2012, university tuition fees had risen to a maximum of £9 000 per year. Together with living expenses, the cost of a university education to a student living away from home on a three year course could easily reach £50 000 in total.

What might be the opportunity cost of the £50 000 in fees and living expenses:

(a) to parents if they pay them on behalf of their children;

(b) to students if they have to borrow the money to pay them?

involves a range of alternatives. For instance, should the government spend £10 billion in tax revenues on nuclear weapons, better schools or greater care for the elderly? Will you choose to become an accountant, an engineer or a vicar?

These choices can be graded in terms of the benefits to be gained from each alternative. One choice will be the 'best' one and a rational economic agent will take that alternative. But all the other choices will then have to be given up. The benefit lost from the next best alternative is called the **opportunity cost of the choice**. For instance, economics may have been your third choice at A level. Your fourth choice, one which you didn't take up, might have been history. Then the opportunity cost of studying economics at A level is studying history at A level.

For **consumers**, opportunity cost is what has to be given up when spending on an item. For instance, the opportunity cost of a chocolate bar might be two packets of crisps. For **producers**, the opportunity cost of buying a machine might be the wages of four workers for three years. For **government**, the opportunity cost of a fighter plane might be building two new primary schools.

Free goods have no opportunity cost. No resources need be sacrificed when someone, say, breathes air or swims in the sea.

What is an economy?

Economic resources are scarce whilst human wants are infinite. An economy is a system which attempts to solve this basic economic problem. There are many different levels and types of economy. There is the household economy, the local economy, the national economy and the international economy. There are free market economies which attempt to solve the economic problem with the minimum intervention of government and command economies where the state makes most resource allocation decisions. Although these economies are different, they all face the same problem.

Economists distinguish three parts to the economic problem.

- **What** is to be produced? An economy can choose the mix of goods to produce. For instance, what proportion of total output should be spent on defence? What proportion should be spent on protecting the environment? What proportion should be invested for the future? What proportion should be manufactured goods and what proportion services?
- **How** is production to be organised? For instance, are smartphones to be made in the UK, Japan or Taiwan? Should car bodies be made out of steel or fibreglass? Would it be better to automate a production line or carry on using unskilled workers?
- **For whom** is production to take place? What proportion of output should go to workers? How much should pensioners get? What should be the balance between incomes in the UK and those in Bangladesh?

An economic system needs to provide answers to all these questions.

Economic resources

Economists commonly distinguish four types of resources available for use in the production process. They call these resources the **factors of production**.

Land is not only land itself but all natural resources below the earth, on the ground, in the atmosphere and in the sea. Everything from gold deposits to rainwater and natural forests are examples of land. **Non-renewable resources**, such as coal, oil, gold and copper, are land resources which once used will never be replaced. If we use them today, they are not available for use by our children or our children's children. **Renewable resources**, on the other hand, can be used and replaced. Examples are fish stocks, forests, or water. **Sustainable resources** are a particular type of renewable resource. Sustainable resources are ones which can be exploited economically and which will not diminish or run out. A forest is a renewable resource. However, it is only a sustainable resource if it survives over time despite economic activities such as commercial logging or farming. It ceases to be a sustainable resource if it is cleared to make way for a motorway. **Non-sustainable resources** are resources which are diminishing over time due to economic exploitation. Oil is a non-sustainable resource because it cannot be replaced.

Labour is the workforce of an economy - everybody from housepersons to doctors, vicars and cabinet ministers. Not all workers are the same. Each worker has a unique set of inherent characteristics including intelligence, manual dexterity and emotional stability. But workers are also the products of education and training. The value of a worker is called their **human capital**. Education and training will increase the value of that human capital, enabling the worker to be more productive.

Question 4

Consider your household economy.

(a) What is produced by your household (e.g. cooking services, cleaning services, accommodation, products outside the home)?

(b) How is production organised (e.g. who does the cooking, what equipment is used, when is the cooking done)?

(c) For whom does production take place (e.g. for mother, for father)?

(d) Do you think your household economy should be organised in a different way? Justify your answer.

Key Terms

Basic economic problem - resources have to be allocated between competing uses because wants are infinite whilst resources are scarce.

Capital - as a factor of production is the stock of manufactured resources used in the production of goods and services.

Choice - economic choices involve the alternative uses of scarce resources.

Economic goods - goods that are scarce because their use has an opportunity cost.

Entrepreneurs - individuals who seek out profitable opportunities for production and take risks in attempting to exploit these.

Enterprise or entrepreneurship - as a factor of production is the seeking out of profitable opportunities for production and taking risks in attempting to exploit these.

Factors of production - the inputs to the production process: land, labour, capital and enterprise or entrepreneurship.

Fixed capital - economic resources such as factories and hospitals which are used to transform working capital into goods and services.

Free goods - goods that are unlimited in supply and which therefore have no opportunity cost.

Human capital - the value of the productive potential of an individual or group or workers; it is made up of the skills, talents, education and training of an individual or group and represents the value of future earnings and production.

Labour - as a factor of production is the workforce.

Land - as a factor of production, is all natural resources.

Needs - the minimum that is necessary for a person to survive as a human being.

Non-renewable resources - resources, such as coal or oil, which once exploited cannot be replaced.

Non-sustainable resource - a resource which can be economically exploited in such as a way that its stock is being reduced over time.

Opportunity cost - the benefits forgone of the next best alternative.

Renewable resources - resources, such as fish stocks or forests, that can be exploited over and over again because they have the potential to renew themselves.

Scarce resources - resources that are limited in supply so that choices have to be made about their use.

Sustainable resource - renewable resource that is being economically exploited in such a way that it will not diminish or run out.

Wants - desires for the consumption of goods and services.

Working or circulating capital - resources that are in the production system waiting to be transformed into goods or other materials before being finally sold to the consumer.

Capital is the manufactured stock of tools, machines, factories, offices, roads and other resources which is used in the production of goods and services. Capital is of two types. **Working** or **circulating capital** is stocks of raw materials, semi-manufactured and finished goods which are waiting to be sold. These stocks circulate through the production process till they are finally sold to a consumer. **Fixed capital** is the stock of factories, offices, plant and machinery. Fixed capital is fixed in the sense that it will not be transformed into a final product as working capital will. It is used to transform working capital into finished products.

Enterprise or **entrepreneurship** is the fourth factor of production. It is the seeking out of profitable opportunities for production and taking risks in attempting to exploit these. **Entrepreneurs** are individuals who:

- organise production - organise land, labour and capital in the production of goods and services;
- take risks - with their own money and the financial capital of others; they buy factors of production to produce goods and services in the hope that they will be able to make a profit but in the knowledge that at worst they could lose all their money and go bankrupt.

Entrepreneurs are typically the owners of small and medium sized businesses who run those businesses on a day to day basis. However, managers in companies can also be entrepreneurial if they both organise resources and take risks on behalf of their company.

The rewards to the factors of production

Owners of the factors of production receive payments when they allow other economic agents to use them for a period of time. Owners of land may receive rent or lease payments. If 'land' is a resource like oil, copper or gold, owners may receive a royalty, a share of the money raised in sales of the resource.

In a modern economy, individuals may offer themselves for hire as workers. The reward to labour is the wage or earnings they receive.

Owners of capital such as machinery, factories or hospitals, can earn a variety of types of income from renting or leasing these physical assets. They might receive rent or lease income. They might also receive a share of any profits made from their use.

Entrepreneurs earn profit from their activities, risking their financial capital and organising the factors of production to produce goods and services.

Thinking like an economist

The opportunity costs of going to university

Most students of A level economics are 17-18-year-olds. Before they have completed their A level courses, they have some serious choices to make. One is whether to stay on in education, typically by doing a university degree, or whether to try to find a job, aged 18.

The opportunity costs of going to university are the benefits foregone from the next best alternative. Getting a job at 18 is not guaranteed, but if students do get employment after school or college, they will be able to earn a wage and spend that money. Getting a job at 18 will almost certainly lead students to being better off financially for three years than those heading off to university. However, for many, working is a less pleasant experience than being a student.

Once students have gained a degree, on average they are likely to earn more over a lifetime than those who don't have a degree. This is true even after any student debt has been deducted from total earnings over a lifetime and the three years of potential earnings have been discounted. A study published in 2010, for example, by the Centre for Market and Public Organisation at Bristol University, found that female graduates getting an upper second class degree would earn approximately 20 per cent more over their lifetimes than if they had not obtained a degree. Graduates are also less likely to be unemployed.

When student fees were raised to £9 000 per year by many universities, some predicted that there would be a sharp fall in student numbers. This has not happened. Despite the increased cost, the return to the average student of getting a degree is still positive. The opportunity costs of going to university - the

benefits foregone - are lower than the lifetime rewards of being a graduate.

This is the reason why the majority of those studying A levels choose to go to university.

Data Response Question

The National Health Service faces tough choices

Politicians and health officials must be more honest with the public about the tough choices facing the National Health Service (NHS), according to Sir Andrew Dillon, the head of NICE (the National Institute for Health and Care Excellence). It is the responsibility of NICE to decide which drugs are value for money and can be prescribed by the NHS and which drugs will not be available to NHS patients.

Andrew said: 'The NHS has to exercise choices, sometimes, in order to ensure its resources are allocated as fairly as possible'. The NHS spends £13 billion a year on pharmaceuticals, about 12 per cent of its total budget.

It was reported this month that NICE ruled that two cancer drugs - Zytiga® for prostate cancer and Kadcyla® for breast cancer - were not cost-effective for the NHS, the latest expensive cancer medicines to be rejected by the agency. Roche, the Swiss pharmaceuticals company, said the refusal to back its Kadcyla drug, which typically extends life by about six months at a cost of £90 000, showed that the UK's drug evaluation system was 'no longer fit for purpose'.

It has been suggested that the price of new medicines will continue rising - particularly for cancer - because drug companies expect to make a profit on their heavy investment in research and development. Sir Andrew pointed out that, whatever the funding for the NHS, there will always be an 'opportunity cost'. Choosing to expand treatment in one area meant that 'something else cannot be done'.

Source: adapted from © the *Financial Times* 23.8.2014, All Rights Reserved.

Q

1. Define the term 'opportunity cost'.

2. Explain why the NHS has to make 'tough choices' about what it offers patients.

3. Discuss, from an economic viewpoint, whether it should be a committee of cancer experts that decides which drugs should be offered on the NHS or an independent committee like NICE.

Evaluation

It is very important in a question like this to use economic terms like scarcity, choice, opportunity cost and positive and normative statements. What value judgements do you think the two types of committee would make? Would they come to different conclusions about a drug like Kadcyla? Would it be in the best interests of all NHS patients if choices about which drugs to buy were made by cancer experts?

4 Production possibility frontiers

Key points

1. The production possibility frontier (PPF) shows the maximum potential output of an economy.
2. Growth in the economy will shift the PPF outwards whilst a shift inwards of the PPF shows that the productive potential of an economy has declined.
3. Consuming more in the present at the expense of producing capital goods can lead to lower growth of the potential output of an economy in the future.
4. Production at a point inside the PPF indicates an underuse or an inefficient use of resources.
5. The PPF shows only what could be produced but not what should be produced.

Starter activity

Your Economics A level group decided to raise money for charity. It took each person a day to take part and you raised £500. You can give the money to two charities. Which two charities would you chose? How much would you give to each? If you give £100 more to one charity, how much less to do you give to the other? What would have been the likely outcome if half the group had given excuses and not taken part in the fund-raising activity? Answers to these questions illustrate opportunity cost, choice and production possibility frontiers.

The problem of scarcity

Over a period of time, resources are scarce and therefore only a finite amount can be produced. For example, an economy might have enough resources at its disposal to be able to produce 30 units of manufactured goods and 30 units of non-manufactured goods. If it were now to produce more manufactured goods, it would have to give up some of its production of non-manufactured items. This is because the production of a manufactured item has an opportunity cost - in this case the production of non-manufactured items. The more manufactured goods that are produced, the less non-manufactured goods can be produced.

This can be shown in Figure 1. The curved line is called the **production possibility frontier (PPF)** - other names for it include **production possibility curve** or **boundary**, and **transformation curve**. The PPF shows the different combinations of economic goods which an economy is able to produce if all resources in the economy are fully and efficiently employed. The economy therefore could be:

- at the point C on its PPF, producing 30 units of manufactured goods and 30 units of non-manufactured goods;
- at the point D, producing 35 units of manufactured goods and 20 units of non-manufactured goods;
- at the point A, devoting all of its resources to the production of non-manufactured goods;
- at the points B or E or anywhere else along the line.
  Production cannot take place to the right of the PPF, such as at the point G. This is because the PPF shows the maximum output of the economy. It can operate within the boundary,

Figure 1

The production possibility frontier

ABCDE is a production possibility frontier. It shows the different combinations of goods which can be produced if all resources are fully and efficiently utilised. The economy can produce at any point on the line. It cannot produce at G because the PPF shows the maximum that can be produced. It can produce within the PPF, such as at F, but less will be produced than the maximum possible.

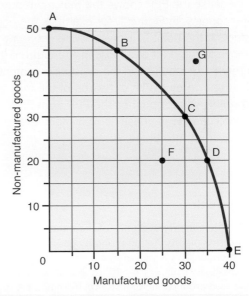

for example at F, but the economy is producing less than its maximum.

Opportunity cost

The production possibility frontier illustrates clearly the principle of opportunity cost. Assume that the economy is producing at the point C in Figure 1 and it is desired to move to the point D. This means that the output of manufactured goods will increase from 30 to 35 units. However, the opportunity cost of that (i.e. what has to be given up because of that choice) is the lost output of non-manufactured goods, falling from 30 to 20 units. The opportunity cost at C of increasing manufacturing production by five units is 10 units of non-manufactured goods.

Another way of expressing this is to use the concept of the **margin**. In economics, the margin is a point of possible

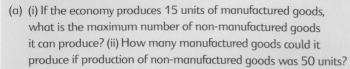

Question 1

The production possibility frontier of an economy is as shown in Figure 1.

(a) (i) If the economy produces 15 units of manufactured goods, what is the maximum number of non-manufactured goods it can produce? (ii) How many manufactured goods could it produce if production of non-manufactured goods was 50 units?

(b) The economy is currently operating at point C. What is the opportunity cost of increasing production of non-manufactured goods by (i) 15 units; (ii) 20 units?

(c) The economy is at D. What is the marginal cost of increasing production of non-manufactured goods to the point (i) C; (ii) B?

change. At the point C in Figure 1, the economy could produce more manufactured goods, but at the cost of giving up non-manufactured goods. For example, the marginal cost of five more units of manufactured goods would be 10 fewer units of non-manufactured goods. This is shown by the movement from C to D along the boundary.

Economic growth or decline

The economy cannot produce at any point outside its existing PPF. This is because the PPF shows the maximum potential output of an economy. In Figure 1, for example, the economy cannot produce at the point G. However, the economy might be able to move to the right of its PPF in the future if there is economic growth. An increase in the productive potential of an economy is shown by a shift outwards of the PPF. In Figure 2 economic growth pushes the PPF from PP to QQ, allowing the economy to increase its maximum level of production, say, from A to B.

Growth in the economy can happen if:

- the quantity of resources available for production increases; for instance there might be an increase in the number of workers in the economy, or new factories and offices might be built;
- there is an increase in the quality of resources; education will make workers more productive whilst technical progress will allow machines and production processes to produce more with the same amount of resources.

Production possibility frontiers can shift inwards as well as outwards. The productive potential of an economy can fall. For example, war can destroy economic infrastructure. A rapid fall in the number of workers in a population can reduce potential output. Some environmentalists predict that global warming will devastate world agriculture and this will have a knock-on effect on all production. Global warming could therefore lead to a shift inwards of the world's PPF.

Many economies experience high levels of unemployment of workers. Factories and machines may lie idle when this occurs. Production then occurs **within** the boundary and **not on** the boundary such as at the point F in Figure 1. If resources became fully employed, the economy could move from inside the boundary to a point on the boundary. In Figure 1, this would mean a move from the point F to, say, D or E.

Consumption vs investment

There is a potential conflict between consuming now and economic growth fuelled by investment. If an economy produces an extra £10 billion worth of restaurant meals for consumers, then they are better off today. If, however, that £10 billion had been spent on new factories, offices or new machinery, the productive potential of the economy is likely to increase. As a result, consumers may then be better off in the future.

Figure 2

Economic growth

An increase in the quantity or quality of the inputs to the production process means that an economy has increased its productive potential. This is shown by a shift to the right of the production possibility frontier from PP to QQ. It would enable the economy to move production, for instance, from point A to point B.

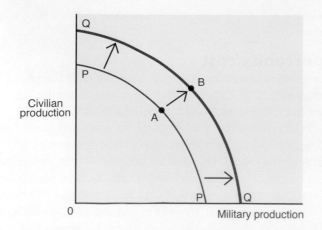

Figure 3

Consumption vs investment

Country B, which initially devotes more resources to investment (the production of capital goods) has a higher growth rate than Country A which initially produces more consumer goods. Eventually, Country B produces more capital and consumer goods than Country A because of higher growth.

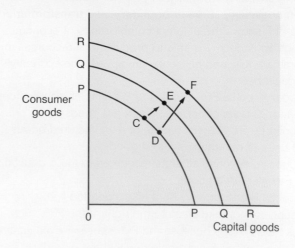

This conflict can be shown in Figure 3. **Consumer goods**, such as food, holidays or DVDs, are shown on the vertical axis. **Capital goods**, such as factories, offices, roads, machines and equipment, are shown on the horizontal axis. Two economies, A and B, at the start are the same size in terms of overall production and population. However, country A produces more consumer goods and fewer capital goods than country B. So initially country A produces at the point C whilst country B produces at the point D.

Over time, both economies grow. However, because country B has invested more, devoting more of its finite resources to capital goods, it grows faster. Ten years later, growth in country A has shifted its PPF to QQ and is producing at the point E. However, the PPF of country B has shifted to RR and country B is producing at the point F. At the start of the period, consumers in country A were better off than in country B because consumption of consumer goods was higher. But at the end, consumers in country B are better off. At the point F, country B is producing more of both consumer and capital goods than country A which produces at E.

The production possibility frontiers in Figures 1 and 2 have been drawn concave to the origin (bowing outwards) rather than as straight lines or as convex lines. This is because it has been assumed that not all resources in the economy are as productive in one use compared to another.

Efficiency

The production possibility frontier shows the maximum amount that can be produced from a given number of resources. Therefore, for an economy, the boundary shows the level of output where all resources are fully and efficiently employed. In Figure 1, there is full and efficient utilisation of resources at all points along the boundary AE.

Efficiency on the boundary is of two types. There is **productive efficiency**, which means that production takes place at lowest cost. Productive efficiency occurs when a given set of resources produces the maximum number of goods. All points on the boundary are productively efficient because they show a combination of goods produced at the lowest cost for that combination.

However, not all points on the boundary are **allocatively efficient**. Allocative efficiency occurs when social welfare is maximised. Not every combination of goods produced will maximise welfare and there could be just one point which does this.

Choice

The PPF by itself gives no indication of which combination of goods will be produced in an economy. All it shows is the combination of goods which an economy could produce if output were maximised from a given fixed amount of resources. It shows a range of possibilities and much of economics is concerned with explaining why an economy, ranging from a household economy to the international economy, chooses to produce at one point either on or within its PPF rather than another.

Question 2

Draw a production possibility frontier. The vertical axis shows the production of public sector goods and the horizontal axis shows production of private sector goods. The economy is currently producing at point A on the frontier where 50 per cent of all production is devoted to public sector goods and 50 per cent to private sector goods.

(a) Mark the following points on your drawing.
   (i) Point A.
   (ii) Point B which shows production following the election of a government which increases government spending on both education and the National Health Service.
   (iii) Point C where unemployment is present in the economy.
   (iv) Point D where the government takes over production of all goods and services in the economy.

(b) Draw another diagram putting on it the original production possibility frontier you drew for (a), labelling it AA.
   (i) Draw a new production possibility frontier on the diagram, labelling it PP, which shows the position after a devastating war has hit the economy.
   (ii) Draw another PPF labelling it QQ which shows an increase in productivity in the economy such that output from the same amount of resources increases by 50 per cent in the public sector but twice that amount in the private sector.

Key Terms

Capital goods - goods that are used in the production of other goods such as factories, offices, roads, machines and equipment.
Consumer goods - goods and services that are used by people to satisfy their needs and wants.
Margin - a point of possible change.
Production possibility frontier (also known as the production possibility curve or the production possibility boundary or the transformation curve) - a curve which shows the maximum potential level of output of one good given a level of output for all others goods in the economy.

Thinking like an economist

Water shortages

In many circumstances, water is a free good. It falls from the sky or can be collected from rivers with no opportunity cost. However, with the world's population predicted to rise to over 11 billion, water is becoming an ever scarcer resource in many countries.

Scarcity is being felt not just by consumers but also by producers. For example, the world's oil and gas supplies could be transformed by the relatively new process of fracking – forcing liquid through rocks to release oil and gas trapped in the rocks. But each US well requires on average two million gallons of water to extract all the oil or gas in the well. Many wells are in areas of relative water shortage. Hence, Antero Resources, a US shale gas company, is planning to spend $525 million on a pipeline to carry water to its operations to increase reliability of supplies.

Countries and industries where water is scarce therefore face a trade-off between investing in water facilities or using the money for other purposes. If there is not enough water, there is an immediate conflict between household consumption for drinking and cleaning, and its use by industry including farming and manufacturing. If industry faces water restrictions, in the short term there will be less production forcing the production possibility frontier inwards. In the long term, if there is too little investment in water infrastructure, production will be lower than if more had been invested today. In other words, the production possibility frontier will be to the left of where it might otherwise have been.

Source: adapted from © the *Financial Times* 15.7.2014, All Rights Reserved.

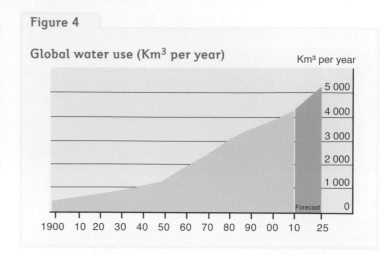

Figure 4

Global water use (Km³ per year)

Data Response Question

Civil war in Syria

In 2011, protests against the government broke out in Syria. The country has been governed by the Baath party since 1963. For nearly 40 years the party had ruthlessly suppressed opponents through torture and killing to maintain power. Since 2011, the country has descended into civil war with Western governments imposing bans on exports to the country. Not surprisingly, output measured by gross domestic product has fallen sharply. Millions of people have been forced to flee their homes. Most have been internally displaced but several million have become refugees in neighbouring countries. Thousands of schools have been destroyed or are being used as shelter for displaced persons. A lack of access to health care and scarcity of medications have led to catastrophic health situations in several regions in Syria. In the meantime, spending on armaments has soared.

Source: with information from © the *Financial Times* 21.2.2015, All Rights Reserved.

China

Since the mid-1970s, many indicators have suggested that China's economy has been growing dramatically. In 2014 it was growing by nearly 10 per cent per annum. This meant that output would be doubling roughly every seven years. It is not difficult to understand why the Chinese economy has been so successful. By the mid-1970s, it already had a relatively well educated workforce compared to other poor developing countries. However, some sources suggested its economy was otherwise inefficient and backward. From the mid-1970s, there was a gradual easing of Communist control of the economy that allowed ordinary Chinese people to set up their own businesses in a more free market style economy. Exports began to be encouraged. This linked China to the global economy. Finally, there was a considerable flow of investment money and technological know-how into China. Foreign investors were keen to take advantage of cheap labour and found the lure of what would soon become the world's largest economy irresistible.

Table 1 China, average annual growth in output (%), 1971-2014

	1971-80	1981-1990	1991-2000	2001-2011	Percentage 2012-2014
Yearly average growth in output (%)	6.3	9.4	10.5	10.3	7.7

Source: adapted from unstats.un.org, United Nations Statistics Division, © 2015 United Nations. Reprinted with the permission of the United Nations.

Replacing Trident

The UK currently has four nuclear-powered submarines able to fire nuclear missiles, but they are coming to the end of their service life. It is estimated that replacing the four submarines and their nuclear missiles will cost at least £25 billion.

Source: adapted from © the *Financial Times* 17.7.2013, All Rights Reserved.

1. What is a production possibility frontier for an economy?

2. Explain why a production possibility frontier might shift inwards or outwards. Illustrate you answer with examples from the data.

3 A peace group has put forward a proposal that the UK should not replace its fleet of Trident submarines. Using production possibility frontiers, evaluate the possible economic implications of this proposal.

Evaluation

Identify the alternative ways in which the resources used to build a new fleet of replacement Trident submarines could be used, including spending on alternative defence goods. Mention opportunity cost and choice. Which would be consumer goods and which would be capital goods? Which might be the best alternative uses and why?

5 Specialisation and the division of labour

Starter activity

Take any piece of clothing that you are wearing right now. Where was it sold? Where was it manufactured? Where did the raw materials for it come from? How many firms do you think might have been involved in getting it to you? Why do you think so many firms were involved in the chain of supply?

Specialisation

When he was alone on his desert island, Robinson Crusoe found that he had to perform all economic tasks by himself. When Man Friday came along he quickly abandoned this mode of production and specialised. **Specialisation** is the production of a limited range of goods by an individual or firm or country in co-operation with others so that together a complete range of goods is produced.

Specialisation can occur between nations. For instance, a country like Honduras produces bananas and trades those for cars produced in the United States. **Globalisation** is currently intensifying this process of specialisation between nations. Specialisation can also occur within economies. Regional economies specialise. In the UK, Cornwall specialises in tourism whilst London specialises in financial services.

Specialisation by individuals is called the **division of labour**. Adam Smith, in a passage in his famous book *An Enquiry into the Nature and Causes of the Wealth of Nations* (1776), described the division of labour amongst pin workers. He wrote:

A workman not educated to this business ... could scarce ... make one pin in a day, and certainly could not make twenty. But in the way in which this business is now carried on, ... it is divided into a number of branches ... One man draws out the wire, another straightens it, a third cuts it, a fourth points, a fifth grinds it at the top for receiving the head; to make the head requires two or three distinct operations; to put it on is a peculiar business, to whiten the pins is another; it is even a trade by itself to put them into the paper.

He pointed out that one worker might be able to make 20 pins a day if he were to complete all the processes himself. But ten workers together specialising in a variety of tasks could, he estimated, make 48 000 pins.

This enormous increase in **productivity** (output per unit of input employed) arises from both increases in **labour productivity** (output per worker) and **capital productivity** (output per unit of capital employed).

- Specialisation enables workers to gain skills in a narrow range of tasks. These skills enable individual workers to be far more productive than if they were jacks-of-all-trades. In a modern economy a person could not possibly hope to be able to take on every job which society requires.
- The division of labour makes it cost-effective to provide workers with specialist tools. For instance, it would not be profitable to provide every farm worker with a tractor. But it is possible to provide a group of workers with a tractor which they can then share.
- Time is saved because a worker is not constantly changing tasks, moving around from place to place and using different machinery and tools.

Question 1

(a) Explain, with the help of the photograph, what is meant by 'specialisation'.

(b) What might be some of the (i) advantages to firms and (ii) disadvantages to workers of the division of labour shown in the photograph?

- Workers can specialise in those tasks to which they are best suited.

The division of labour has its limits. If jobs are divided up too much, the work can become tedious and monotonous. Workers feel alienated from their work. This will result in poorer quality of work and less output per person. Workers will do everything possible to avoid work - going to the toilet, lingering over breaks and reporting sick for instance. The size of the market too will limit the division of labour. A shop owner in a village might want to specialise in selling health foods but finds that in order to survive she has to sell other products as well.

Over-specialisation also has its disadvantages. For example, the north of England, Wales, Scotland and Northern Ireland have suffered high unemployment since the 1950s as their traditional heavy industry, such as coal mining and shipbuilding, declined and was not replaced by enough new service sector jobs. Another problem with specialisation is that a breakdown in part of the chain of production can cause chaos within the system. Honda's Japanese car production plant in Swindon halved its production in April and May 2011 because of a shortage of parts from Japan after a tsunami disrupted production in Japan. Similarly, London businesses can be crippled by an Underground strike or a bus strike.

Sectors of the economy

Economies are structured into three main sectors. In the **primary sector** of the economy, raw materials are extracted and food is grown. Examples of primary sector industries are agriculture, forestry, fishing, oil extraction and mining. In the **secondary** or **manufacturing sector**, raw materials are transformed into goods. Examples of secondary sector industries are motor manufacturing, food processing, furniture making and steel production. The **tertiary** or **service sector** produces services such as transport, sport and leisure, distribution, financial services, education and health.

Most firms tend to operate in just one of these sectors, specialising in producing raw materials, manufactured goods or services. Some very large firms, such as BP, operate across all three sectors, from the extraction of oil to its refining and sale to the public through petrol stations.

Question 2

Table 1 Shops selling grocery items in Burscough

Type	Number
Small independent grocers	1
Convenience store grocers	1
Supermarket grocers	2

Burscough is a town in Lancashire which has shops selling grocery items such as fresh vegetables, dairy products or tinned food.

(a) Who might be the buyers and sellers in the local Burscough market for grocery products?

(b) What is the relationship between this market and the market for (i) meat and (ii) petrol?

Economies can also be split into two sectors: the public sector and the private sector. The **public sector** is the state or government sector of the economy. Production of goods and services is achieved by organisations such as government departments, local authorities or state owned businesses. The **private sector** is that part of the economy owned by private individuals, companies and charities. For example, in the UK, the public sector organises schooling for most children. So a state primary school is part of the public sector. However, some parents choose to pay for their children to go to schools that are in the private sector. Most health care is provided by the public sector through the National Health Service. However, there is also a smaller private health care sector where companies such as Nuffield Health and individual doctors provide patient services.

Markets

Markets play a fundamental role in almost all economies today. Markets are where buyers and sellers meet. For economists, markets are not just street markets. Buying and selling can take place online, in newspapers and magazines, through mail order or over the telephone in financial deals in the City of London, or on industrial estates as well as in high street shopping centres. A **market** is any convenient set of arrangements by which buyers and sellers communicate to exchange goods and services.

Economists group buyers and sellers together. For instance, there is an international market for oil where large companies and governments buy and sell oil. There are also national markets for oil. Not every company or government involved in the buying and selling of oil in the UK, say, will be involved in the US or the Malaysian oil markets. There are also regional and local markets for oil. In your area there will be a small number of petrol filling stations (sellers of petrol) where you (the buyers) are able to buy petrol. All these markets are interlinked but they are also separate. A worldwide increase in the price of oil may or may not filter down to an increase in the price of petrol at the pumps in your local area. Equally, petrol prices in your area may increase when prices at a national and international level remain constant. Sometimes, economists refer to **sub-markets**. This is a term used to describe a market within a larger market. For example, the market for diesel fuel in the UK is a sub-market of the market for all oil-based fuels in the UK. Equally the market for all oil-based fuels in the UK is a sub-market of the international market for fuels.

How buyers and sellers are grouped together and therefore how markets are defined depends upon what is being studied. We could study the tyre industry or we could consider the market for cars and car components which includes part but not all of the tyre industry. Alternatively, we might want to analyse the market for rubber, which would necessitate a study of rubber purchased by tyre producers.

Many Western economists argue that specialisation, exchange and the market lie at the heart of today's economic prosperity in the industrial world. Whilst it is likely that the market system is a powerful engine of prosperity, we shall see that it does not always lead to the most efficient allocation of resources.

Money and exchange

Specialisation has enabled people to enjoy a standard of living which would be impossible to achieve through self-sufficiency. Specialisation, however, necessitates exchange. Workers can only specialise in refuse collecting, for instance, if they know that they will be able to exchange their services for other goods and services such as food, housing and transport.

Exchange for most of history has meant barter - swapping one good for another. However, barter has many disadvantages and it would be impossible to run a modern sophisticated economy using barter as a means or medium of exchange. It was the development of money that enabled trade and specialisation to transform economies into what we know today. Money is anything which is widely accepted as payment for goods received, services performed, or repayment of past debt. In a modern economy, it ranges from notes and coins to money in bank accounts and deposits in building society accounts.

The functions of money

Most people today in Britain, if asked 'what is money?', would reply 'notes and coins'. What is it about notes and coins that make them money, and is there anything else which possesses these same properties? If something is to be money, it must fulfil four functions (i.e. it must do four things).

A medium of exchange This is the most important function of **money**. Money is used to buy and sell goods and services. A worker accepts payment in money because she knows that she will be able to use that money to buy products in the shops.

There is no money in a **barter** economy. Exchange is conducted directly by swapping one good with another. For instance, a farmer might pay a dozen eggs to have his horse shod or a woman might trade a carpet for a cow. This requires a **double coincidence of wants**. If the blacksmith didn't want eggs, then he might refuse to shoe the farmer's horse. If the woman with a carpet was offered a horse instead of a cow, again she might refuse to trade. Barter requires that each party to the transaction wants what the other has to trade. This is costly and difficult, if not impossible, and therefore trade is discouraged. Without trade there can be no specialisation. Without specialisation, there can be little or no increase in living standards. So barter is associated with types of economy where individuals or small groups are self-reliant, and the need for trade is small.

Money separates the two sides of a barter transaction. The farmer can sell his eggs for money. The blacksmith will accept money for shoeing the farmer's horse because he knows that he will be able buy the goods that he wants with the money.

A measure of value Money acts as a unit of account. If a dress costs £30 and a skirt costs £15, we know that the value of one dress equals the value of two skirts. At times of very high inflation, such as in Germany in 1923, money ceases to act as a unit of account. Prices may change by the hour. A dress costing £30 in the morning might only buy one skirt in the evening. High inflation therefore destroys the ability of money to perform this function. It is very difficult under a barter system to establish an agreed unit of account as people's opinions of the value of certain items differ greatly.

A store of value A worker who receives wages is unlikely to spend the money immediately. She may defer spending because it is more convenient to spend the money later. She will do this only if what she can buy in the future is approximately equal to what she can buy today. So money links the present and the future. It acts as a store of value. High inflation destroys this link because money in the future is worth far less than money today. In the German hyperinflation of 1923, people started to refuse payment in German money because it would lose so much value by the time they had spent it.

Question 3

Explain which of these items might be considered 'money' and which would not.

A method of deferred payment If people lend money today, they will only do so if they think that they will be able to buy roughly the same amount of goods when it is paid back. In trade, a company which accepts an order at a fixed price today for delivery and payment in a year's time will only do so if it is confident that the money it receives will have a value which can be assessed today. So again money must link different time periods when it comes to borrowed as well as saved money.

When money ceases to have this function, credit and borrowing collapse and this is very damaging to investment and economic growth in an economy.

Forms of money in a modern economy

In a modern economy there is a number of assets which can be classified as money.

Cash Cash means notes and coins. Cash is a token money. It has little or no intrinsic value (unlike gold which would be classified along with items such as pigs and cigarettes as commodity money). It is issued either by government or with the permission of government. Government reinforces the acceptability of cash by making it legal tender. This means that it must be accepted by law as a means of payment.

Cash is not perfect money. In the UK it is an almost perfect medium of exchange. But inflation affects three of the functions of money - those of a measure of value, a store of value and a method of deferred payment. In 1975 for instance, UK inflation was nearly 25 per cent. Anyone holding £1 at the beginning of the year could only buy 75 pence worth of goods with it at the end of the year. The higher the rate of inflation, the less it can be said that cash is a 'good' money.

Money in current accounts Banks and building societies in the UK offer customers current account facilities. Current accounts have two distinguishing features. First, cash can be withdrawn on demand from the account if it is in credit. So deposits can be immediately converted into money if the account holder so wishes. Second, account holders are provided with a cheque book and debit card. Cheques and debit cards can be used to purchase goods and services. Cheque book money therefore is a medium of exchange. It is not perfect because people and firms can refuse to accept cheques and debit cards in a transaction. Moreover, little or no interest is offered on accounts and so current account deposits lose value over time with inflation, damaging their store of value function. But deposits in current accounts are nearly as good a form of money as cash.

Near monies Near Monies are assets which fulfil some but not all of the functions of money. In particular, they act as measures of value and stores of value but cannot be used as mediums of exchange. However, they are convertible into a medium of exchange quickly and at little cost. (The ease with which an asset can be converted into money without loss of value is termed **liquidity**. The more liquid an asset, the more easily it is convertible into money.) In the UK, the most obvious type of near monies is **time deposits** with banks and building societies. They pay higher rates of interest than current accounts. They are therefore used more for saving and less for making transactions than current accounts. Depositors need to give notice if they wish to withdraw from the account (hence the term 'time' deposit). Alternatively, many accounts offer instant access if an interest rate penalty is paid (i.e. the saver loses money for the privilege of instant withdrawal).

Question 4

Emma Higgins has £250 in a building society share account. She owns a £100 000 house but owes £50 000 in the form of a mortgage loan. Her current account at her bank is in credit by £200 and she has an overdraft facility of £300. In her purse she has £20 in cash. She has recently purchased £50 worth of goods using her credit card. Her credit card limit is £1 000.

Explain how much money Emma Higgins possesses.

Key Terms

Barter - swapping one good for another without the use of money.
Capital productivity - output per unit of capital employed.
Division of labour - specialisation by workers, who perform different tasks at different stages of production to make a good or service, in co-operation with other workers.
Labour productivity - output per worker.
Market - any convenient set of arrangements by which buyers and sellers communicate to exchange goods and services.
Money - any item, such as a coin or a bank balance, which fulfils four functions: a medium of exchange, a measure of value, a store of value and a method of deferred payment.
Money substitutes - anything which can be used as a medium of exchange but which are not stores of value. Examples are charge cards or credit cards.
Primary sector - extractive and agricultural industries.

Private sector - the part of the economy owned by individuals, companies and charities.
Productivity - output per unit of input employed.
Public sector - the part of the economy where production is organised by the state or the government.
Secondary or manufacturing sector - industries involved in the production of goods, mainly manufactured goods.
Specialisation - a system of organisation where economic units such as households or nations are not self-sufficient but concentrate on producing certain goods and services and trading the surplus with others.
Sub-market - a market which is a distinct and identifiable part of a larger market.
Tertiary or service sector - industries involved in the production of services.

Non-money financial assets All financial assets can be converted into money. However, for most assets the potential penalties for doing this are great. There can be a long waiting time for withdrawal and there can be considerable loss of money from conversion. This impairs their functions as measures of value and stores of value. Economists do not classify these assets as money. Shares, for instance, are easily sold, but it can take up to a month to receive the money from the sale. Shares can also change value rapidly and are therefore not a good store of value (when share prices fall) or a method of deferred payment (when share prices rise).

Money substitutes Money is not the only means of payment for goods and services. Charge cards and credit cards have become increasingly important over the past 40 years as a medium of exchange. But they are not stores of value. This is because possession of a card does not show that the cardholder has money in the card account. The card only represents an ability to borrow money instantly. So credit cards, for example, are not money but they are **money substitutes** (i.e. they are used instead of money).

Thinking like an economist

Slave labour and the supply chain

Specialisation can have a dark side. According to the International Labour Organisation, about 21 million men, women and children are in slavery, including bonded labour and forced child labour. You might have bought something which was in part produced by what some people call 'slave labour'.

No UK sellers will admit that their products have a slave labour component. However, according to a 2014 survey by the Chartered Institute of Purchasing and Supply, nearly three quarters of managers responsible for buying products for their businesses admitted that they had 'zero visibility' on the early parts of their supply chain. The problem arises because of specialisation. Many goods and services sold in the UK have very long supply chains. There may be hundreds of businesses involved in the production of a single item. A mobile phone seller, for example, might have a component of the phone made in China or India. That relatively unimportant component may

have been made using slave labour in a manufacturing plant. Slave or bonded labour might have also been used in small-scale mining of the metal used in the component. Even in transport, there might be a trace of slave labour in the supply chain of the transport company. So at every stage, in primary, secondary and tertiary industries there is a risk.

Large companies selling directly to consumers are particularly vulnerable to bad publicity about slave labour. They tend to be the companies that attempt to investigate their supply chain and inspect production facilities across the world. But with so many separate businesses involved, it is usually impossible for them to guarantee that no slave labour has been used. Specialisation allows slavery to be a hidden problem to the consumer at the end of the production chain.

Source: adapted from © the *Financial Times* 21.7.2014, All Rights Reserved.

Data Response Question

Antler

Antler, the luggage company, is bringing suitcase production back to Britain for the first time in 20 years, according to the *Financial Times*. The Atom suitcase, part of Antler's range, will be manufactured and assembled by Linecross, a plastics company which is based in Rutland in the East Midlands. It will use a fabric made by Scotland's Don & Low, which is used in protective helmets and armour for military vehicles. The material is moulded and then coated in plastic.

Many British companies, like Antler, use Chinese suppliers to make their

products. Julie Reynolds, chief executive of Antler, admitted that it was more expensive to manufacture in Britain because labour costs were higher. However, it allowed the use of more advanced materials. It also cut shipping costs. 'You are shipping a lot of empty air when you ship suitcases' she said. Manufacturing in Britain also had the advantage that it was quicker to get supplies to customers when needed because of the time it took to ship supplies from half way across the world.

Source: adapted from © the *Financial Times* 13.5.2014, All Rights Reserved.

Q

1. Getting an Antler suitcase to a customer usually involves firms operating in the primary, secondary and tertiary sectors. Explain why this is the case.

2. Suggest reasons why making suitcases involves specialisation.

6 Types of economy

Key points

1. The function of an economic system is to resolve the basic economic problem.
2. Markets allocate resources determining what is to be produced, how it is to be produced and for whom production is to take place.
3. Resources can be allocated by planning rather than markets, as for example happens within firms and by governments.
4. Free market economies, mixed economies and planned economies are three different types of economic system.
5. There are various ways in which economic systems can be evaluated including choice, quality and innovation, efficiency, economic growth, income distribution and risk.

Starter activity

To what extent is your household a planned economy? Is all the spending controlled by one person or perhaps two people? Does anyone in the family get paid for doing jobs for the family like washing up, tidying their rooms or gardening? Would it be better if anyone who did a job within the house got paid? Would it be better if you had to pay rent for your room and money for the food you ate?

Economic systems

The function of an economy is to resolve the basic economic problem - resources are scarce, but wants are infinite. Resources therefore need to be allocated. This allocation has three dimensions.

What is to be produced? Should it be pizzas, tanks or holidays for example?

How is it to be produced? For example, is it going to be produced in London or in Manchester? Is it going to be made using the latest technology or by hand? Is production going to be automated or is it going to labour intensive?

For whom it is to be produced? Should products be equally distributed amongst the population? Should a small number of people be able to secure 100 times the amount that the majority gain? Should people living in the UK enjoy 200 times the number of products available to people in Bangladesh?

An **economic system** is a complex network of individuals, organisation and institutions which allocates resources. This is done within social systems, such as the family or the local neighbourhood, and legal systems such as the British or EU legal systems.

Within an economic system, there are various 'actors'.

Individuals They are consumers and workers. They may own factors of production which they supply for production purposes.

Groups Firms, trade unions, political parties, families and charities are just some of the groups which might exist in an economic system.

Government Government might range from a local parish council, to a local police authority, to a national parliament or supranational body like the European Commission. One key role of government is to exercise power. It establishes or influences the relationships between individuals and groups, for instance through the passing of laws or the enforcement of laws.

The allocation of resources

In rich industrialised economies, over the past 100 years, there have been two main ways in which resources have been allocated.

The market mechanism The market mechanism allocates resources through bringing together buyers and sellers who agree on a price for the product or resource being sold. In the market for crisps, for example, crisp manufacturers sell their products via shops and supermarkets to buyers like you. In the market for teachers, schools hire (i.e. buy the services of) teachers and teachers sell their labour. In the market for copper, copper mining companies sell to buyers which include manufacturing companies.

Planning Planning allocates resources through administrative decisions. Planning occurs within families when individuals make decisions about who in the family is to get what. For example, adults will make decisions about children's Christmas presents or how much the household spends on heating. Firms are also planned economies where managers decide how to allocate resources. At a national level, governments and government bodies such as the National Health Service, allocate resources through planning. For example, in a budget, the Chancellor will announce plans for how the government will spend money.

Question 1

Black Friday is an American import. In America, on the last Friday of November, shops offer large discounts to encourage customers to spend and for the past two years, UK retailers have copied the idea. This year, some supermarkets got more than they bargained for. The *Financial Times* reported that police were called to at least seven Tesco stores in the Manchester area after brawls took place between customers competing for the bargains on offer. Online, websites for Tesco, Currys and Argos all struggled. Currys, the electrical retailer, left shoppers on its website waiting up to an hour in a virtual queue.

Source: adapted from © the *Financial Times* 29.11.2014, All Rights Reserved.

Explain, using the data as an example, how consumers, firms and government interact in a market economy like the UK.

Types of economy

In rich, industrialised economies, three main types of economy can be distinguished.

Free market economies In **free market economies** (also called **free enterprise economies** or **capitalist economies** or **market economies**), the majority of resources are allocated through markets rather than through government and planning. There are no examples of pure free market economies in the world today. However, Hong Kong and the United States have a great proportion of their resources allocated by the market than economies such as Sweden or Germany. In the United States, public (i.e. government) spending accounts for around 37.5 per cent of total output. The government, through the planning mechanism, allocates resources, for example for education, defence, roads, policing and the justice system. Hong Kong and the United States therefore tend to be called 'free market economies'.

Mixed economies In **mixed economies**, more resources are allocated through government planning than in free market economies. Typically between 40 per cent and 60 per cent of resources are allocated by government and the free market. Two key areas which distinguish free market and mixed economies are welfare benefits and healthcare. In mixed economies, there tends to be a greater redistribution of income through welfare benefits such as state pensions, unemployment and sickness benefits and child benefits. Mixed economies also tend to be ones where the healthcare system is administered and financed by the state, as in the UK. In pure free market economies, healthcare would be entirely financed by the private sector and, in theory, there would be no welfare benefit system.

Command economies In **command** (or **planned** or **centrally planned**) **economies**, most resources are allocated by the state and the market mechanism only plays a small part. The largest

planned economy today is China although it is moving towards a mixed economy. Cuba and North Korea are two other examples. Before 1990, the Soviet Union and Eastern European countries such as Poland and Romania were also planned economies.

An evaluation of different types of economy

The different types of economy have advantages and disadvantages.

Choice Comparing the United States with the former Soviet Union in 1985, or North Korea or Cuba today, it is clear that individual citizens on average have more choice in free market economies. Planning tends to produce uniform products. So in the Soviet Union, everything from cars to shoes to food was mass-produced in large quantities but with little variety. In a market economy, consumers can choose between thousands of different variants of hundreds of different cars. As workers, in a market economy, people have choices about which jobs to apply for. In planned economies, there tends to be much more direction with workers being allocated jobs. Citizens also have far less income after tax in planned economies than in free market economies. The amount they are free to spend on products of their choice is therefore much smaller. However, choice has its limitations. In free market economies, those with high incomes or high levels of education have far more choice than those with low incomes or low levels of education. Choice for an unemployed worker in a high-unemployment area might very limited indeed.

Quality and innovation One advantage claimed of a free market economy is that there are strong incentives built into the system to innovate and produce high-quality goods. Companies which fail to do both are likely to be driven out of business by more efficient firms. However, this assumes that consumers or buyers have the power to make free choices. In practice, many markets are dominated by a few large producers which manipulate the market through advertising and other forms of marketing in order to exploit the consumer. So whilst choice and innovation are greater than under planned systems, the advantages of free market economies may not be as great as it might at first seem.

Efficiency The planned economies of the Soviet Union and Eastern Europe proved to be inefficient. One major problem was that workers and managers had little incentive to work efficiently. Usually guaranteed their jobs, they only had to meet their minimum work targets to stay out of trouble. Markets tend to lead to greater efficiency because of competition. Firms in a competitive market have to be efficient to survive and make a profit. However, competition in many markets in mixed and free market economies is limited because a few large firms dominate those markets. Also, large firms are mini-planned economies in themselves and often struggle to maintain efficient production through planning in exactly the same way that planned economies such as the Soviet Union struggled to be efficient.

Economic growth One frequently made claim is that the more market orientated an economy, the higher will be the rate of

Question 2

North Korea is one of the last planned economies in the world. But it is slowly moving in a more market-orientated direction. In the 1990s, the break up of another planned economy, the Soviet Union, brought mass famine to North Korea with an estimated 1 million deaths. The Soviet Union had been North Korea's main trading partner and had subsidised its economy. When that trade and subsidy disappeared, North Korea's income fell significantly. It was during this time that informal markets, particularly for food, sprang up. Today, these informal markets provide an estimated two-thirds of the population with their main source of income. However, officially, agriculture is all collectivised, with the state owning all farms and directing production. So too with industry. On the other hand, the government has established a small number of Special Economic Zones where foreign companies can set up and employ North Korean workers to produce goods for export. It wants to expand their number.

Source: adapted from © the *Financial Times* 12.3.2014, 2.9.2014, All Rights Reserved.

Explain what it might mean for North Korea as a planned economy to move 'in a more market orientated direction'.

growth of its overall economy. Markets are assumed to be dynamic whilst government control is assumed to dampen innovation and best practice. The planned economies of the Soviet Union and Eastern Europe certainly fell behind in terms of growth. Planning the whole economy produced large inefficiencies. However, both mixed and free market economies at the same level of development seem to grow at very similar rates over the long term. Free market economies do not seem to have higher rates of growth than mixed economies over time.

Distribution of income and wealth Free market economies tend to have higher levels of inequality than mixed or planned economies. This is because resources produced by government through the planning process tend to be distributed more equally than would be the case in a free market. Higher income earners and wealth owners also tend to pay a larger proportion of tax in mixed compared to free market economies.

Risk Free market economies tend to expose their citizens to far more risk than mixed or planned economies. For example, there tends to be far less provision for risks associated with ill health, unemployment and old age in free market economies. The well off can afford to spend their way out of problems. However, the poor can be left with no healthcare, no job, no house and no food. In mixed and planned economies, there tend to be a 'cradle to the grave' bundle of services and benefits provided by government for citizens.

Political freedom All planned economies in the 20th and 21st century have curbed political freedoms to enforce control. Almost all have been totalitarian police states. In contrast, both free market and mixed economies in the rich industrialised world have been associated with political freedom.

Over the past fifty years, most planned economies have disappeared. Apart from North Korea, the few that remain, such as China, are moving towards a more market economy. Equally, there has been a tendency for the size of government in free market economies to grow. Amongst mixed economies, those such as Sweden and Norway, which at one point saw their government spending rise to over 60 per cent of GDP, have tended to move back towards a more market-orientated allocation of resources.

Smith, Hayek and Marx

Three writers who have profoundly influenced thinking about economic systems are Adam Smith, Friedrich Hayek and Karl Marx.

Adam Smith Adam Smith published his famous book, *An Enquiry into the Nature and Causes of the Wealth of Nations*, in 1776. In the book he explained how the **invisible hand** of the market would allocate resources to everyone's advantage. He argued that the selfish pursuit of profit by every individual could lead to a whole economy where benefit was maximised. He attacked the economic system of his day which restricted free trade through protectionism, economic restrictions and legal barriers. Adam Smith is often seen as an advocate of free market economies and laissez-faire government. Laissez-faire means that the government should leave markets as much as possible to regulate themselves. However, there are many points in his writings where he recognises that the state has an important

role to play in providing a framework within which free markets can operate. He saw that individuals and firms would attempt to distort markets to gain more for themselves. He also saw that the poor needed to be defended from those who owned property. For example, he argued that businesses would attempt to combine together to raise prices at the expense of the consumer. He wrote that employers would drive wages down as low as possible whether or not workers could survive on these incomes. He also argued that the state had to provide those goods and services which free markets would otherwise not provide. The whole legal and judicial framework for enforcing property law, for example, needed to be provided by the state. So too did goods such as roads and bridges.

Friedrich Hayek Friedrich Hayek was a 20th-century Austrian economist who moved to the UK in 1931. His most famous book is *The Road to Serfdom* published in 1944. It was enormously influential in the development of Margaret Thatcher's economic thinking in the 1970s and 1980s. In it, he argued that ever-greater control of the economy by the state leads to totalitarianism and the loss of freedom by the individual. He was reacting to the loss of individual freedom in the Soviet Union under Joseph Stalin and Germany under Adolf Hitler. He correctly saw that individuals were forced to comply with state wishes through the threat of imprisonment and death. However, he then said that greater state control over the economy in both the UK and the USA also led to a loss of freedom for the individual. For Hayek, the poor in the UK and the USA were better off than in Germany or the Soviet Union because at least they had their personal freedom. Proponents of free markets have used Hayek's thoughts to argue that free unregulated markets are better than regulated markets or direct state provision and control because the liberties of the individual are maintained in free markets. He also said that central planning by governments led to the will of a small minority of individuals being imposed on the whole of society. Critics would argue, however, that this occurs in free market economies too. Those who own property are able to impose their will on everyone else. In a free market economy, the poor have very few 'spending votes' compared to the rich. In free market economies, the rich are also able to buy influence over political processes, influencing political decision making. The poor then become politically disenfranchised as well as being economically marginalised.

Karl Marx Karl Marx was a 19th-century German thinker and writer and is often credited with founding modern sociology. His most famous book is *Das Capital*, the first part of which was published in 1867. He correctly saw that there was a great gulf between the economic fortunes of the owners of property and workers in 19th-century Europe. He wanted to see that gulf eliminated. He developed a theory which said that it was historically inevitable that workers, the proletariat, would rise up in revolution against property owners and violently seize control of the means of production. A new democratic society would arise which would lead to equality and where property would be owned by everyone collectively. Karl Marx, although he advocated violent revolution, would probably not have approved of the Marxist state created by Joseph Stalin in the Soviet Union in the 1920s, 1930s and 1940s. The problem for Marxists was how to go from a capitalist free market economy to a utopian economy where somehow everyone owned everything to the benefit of all. Joseph Stalin solved this problem by creating a command economy where the state owned most resources. Command economies ultimately have not been anywhere near as successful as free market and mixed economies at delivering economic benefit to their citizens. Also, as Hayek pointed out, they came to rely on the abuse of political power to enforce their decisions.

> **Key Terms**
>
> **Command or planned or centrally planned economy** - an economic system where government, through a planning process, allocates resources in society.
> **Economic system** - a complex network of individuals, organisations and institutions and their social and legal interrelationships which allocates resources.
> **Free market economy, or free enterprise economy or capitalist economy or market economy** - an economic system that resolves the basic economic problems mainly through the market mechanism.
> **Mixed economy** - an economy where both the free market mechanism and the government planning process allocate significant proportions of total resources.

Thinking like an economist

Mixed economies

The fundamental shape of today's UK economy was formed between 1945 and 1951 in the years following the Second World War. A Labour government created the Welfare State, including a free National Health Service and a system of cradle to the grave benefits that eliminated the worst of the poverty seen before 1945.

In common with most industrialised economies the UK saw the rate of growth government spending rise faster than national income in the 1950s, 1960s and 1970s. The result was that government spending as a percentage of GDP rose.

1980s saw an attempt by a Conservative government under Margaret Thatcher to reduce the role of the state significantly and shift the economy back to being more market orientated. The 'Thatcher revolution' was influential throughout the industrialised world. It led to a debate that is still ongoing today about what should be left for market forces to provide and what should be done by the state.

Sweden was one country which was influenced by this debate. Along with Norway and Denmark, it had created a large welfare state which helped create much greater equality in society than in, for example, the USA. However, in the early 1990s, it experienced a banking crisis and a major recession. This led to government spending soaring to 71 per cent of GDP as can be seen in Figure 1. In the years that followed, Sweden recognised that its government spending was too high. By 2014, it had fallen to a little over 50 per cent, not much more than the average for the Euro area.

When the world experienced a banking crisis and major recession in 2008, like Sweden before, government spending as a proportion of GDP tended to rise in most countries. This was because government spending itself rose at a time when GDP

Figure 1

Government spending as a percentage of GDP[1]

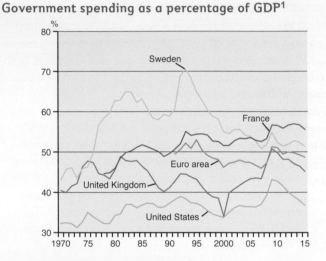

1. Data for 2014 and 2015 are estimates.
Source: adapted from OECD, Economic Outlook.

was falling. In the UK, government spending as a proportion of GDP rose to 51 per cent in 2009. In 2010, a new coalition government with a Conservative party Chancellor, George Osborne, vowed to cut public spending. This was to reduce government borrowing.

However, it was also designed to reduce the size of the state and shift the UK away from Scandinavian and other European mixed economies towards a more free market US-style mix of private and public sectors. The debate about whether the UK should be a mixed economy rather than a free market economy is therefore still very much alive.

Data Response Question

The US economy

Money goes a long way in the United States for the ordinary foreign tourist. Prices are cheap and service is good. The free market means the tourist has the choice of everything from the most luxurious five-star hotel to a tent or caravan, a Michelin-star restaurant to a burger joint, or a walk in the wilderness to a place at a gaming table in Las Vegas.

However, the US economy is a divided economy. Tourists tend to be served by the half of Americans who are on low wages. According to the 2013 US census, half of all households earn $52 000 or less per year whilst one fifth of households earn $22 000 or less. The bottom half of Americans can't expect to see much increase in their incomes over the coming decades. After all, as Figure 2 shows, since 1980, the bottom fifth of income earners have seen almost no change in their before-tax income. Contrast that with the top five per cent who have seen their incomes grow 72 per cent. The top one cent have seen their incomes rise by nearly 300 per cent. The USA is truly a winner-takes-all society.

Free market rhetoric is strong in the USA. The free market is supposed to deliver superior growth to the 'socialist' countries of Europe. But the evidence is out for that position. At least some of the difference in growth rates is accounted for by the high immigration rates to the USA. More workers means more output and so higher GDP. But it doesn't mean higher output per person.

Free market rhetoric also condemns the government financed health care systems of Europe as 'communist'. In America, it has been a hotly defended freedom to have so little money that you can't afford to visit the doctor, let alone have a life-saving operation. This is changing with the introduction of 'Obamacare', an insurance scheme designed to give medical access to all.

However, the free market medical care system, to date, has left life expectancy in 2014 in the richest country in the world at only 79.6 years - ranked 42nd by the CIA *World Factbook*. For 'socialist' Sweden, it is 81.9 years and for Japan it is 84.5 years.

Social mobility is also a real problem in the United States. Barack Obama was exceptional. He was the first person in living memory to be elected President who wasn't already a millionaire. Even then, he and his wife were in the top one per cent of income earners when he began to run for president in 2007. Just as in the UK or in Sweden, individuals in the USA can make it from poverty to riches. But most wealthy people are the sons and daughters of rich parents. The chances of a child from a poor background today making it to the top of the income pile are very low.

Source: with information from www.cia.gov.

Figure 2

Growth in real household income before tax and non-cash benefits by income quintile, USA, (%), 1980-2013

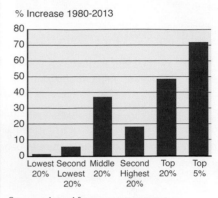

% Increase 1980-2013

Source: adapted from www.census.gov.

1. Using the USA as an example, explain how resources are allocated in a free market economy.

2. To what extent does the free market economy of the USA perform better than mixed economies such as Sweden when judged by (a) economic growth; (b) distribution of income and wealth; (c) risk for individuals?

Evaluation

Look carefully at the data in the table and in the figure, as well as reading the text. Take each part and argue whether the USA or Sweden does better, supporting your argument with data. Then come to an overall conclusion on the three factors in the question.

Table 1 Annual average real growth in GDP per head and GDP (%)

	GDP per head at constant purchasing power parities % increase at 2005 prices					GDP at constant purchasing power parity increase at 2005 prices
	1971-80	1981-1990	1991-2000	2001-2013	1971-2013	1971-2013
Canada	2.8	1.4	1.8	0.8	1.7	2.8
France	3.0	1.9	1.6	0.5	1.7	2.2
Germany	2.8	2.2	1.6	0.9	1.8	2.0
Italy	3.3	2.3	1.6	-0.5	1.5	1.8
Japan	3.2	4.1	0.9	0.7	2.1	2.6
Sweden	1.6	1.9	1.8	1.2	1.6	2.0
United Kingdom	1.8	2.6	2.8	0.8	1.9	2.2
United States	2.1	2.4	2.2	0.8	1.8	2.8

Source: adapted from stats.oecd.org.

Key points

1. Neoclassical economic theory assumes that economic actors are rational.
2. Consumers are assumed to maximise their utility, workers their rewards from working, firms their profit and government the welfare of citizens.
3. In neoclassical economic theory, economic actors make decisions at the margin.

Starter activity

In front of you is a bag of crisps, a chocolate bar, a can of fizzy lemonade and a doughnut. If you could choose just one of these to eat or drink right now, which would you choose? What would be your second choice if that product was not available? Which would be your least favourite item? In real life, do you always act in a rational manner, maximising your net benefits from the money you spend?

Rational economic decision making

Much of the economics that is taught at A level and on university degree courses is based on **neo-classical theory**. It is a body of economics that was developed from the 1870s onwards. In this book, almost all the **microeconomics** - the study of individual markets - is based on neo-classical theory. Equally, **macroeconomics** taught at A level is mainly a fusion of neoclassical theory with the ideas of John Maynard Keynes, a very famous economist of the 1920s and 1930s.

One of the key assumptions of neo-classical theory is that economic agents, such as individuals or firms, make decisions in a rational way. The word 'rational' has a precise meaning in neoclassical theory. It is that economic agents are able to rank the order of different outcomes from an action in terms of their net benefits to them. They then act in a way that will maximise these net benefits. For example, you might prefer cheese and onion crisps to salt and vinegar crisps. All other things being equal, you are a rational economic decision maker if you choose a pack of cheese and onion crisps when given a choice with salt and vinegar crisps.

When making a decision, there is often a number of factors which will influence an economic agent. For example, you might want to buy a packet of crisps now. You could buy them now from your nearest corner shop two minutes walk away at a cost of 30p or you could go to a local supermarket ten minutes walk away at a cost of 20p. Alternatively, you could simply go without the packet of crisps.

There are two costs here. One is the cost of the packet - 20p or 30p. The other is the value of your time and effort to get the packet. If you value eight minutes of your time at more than 10p, you will buy at the local corner shop. If you value two minutes of your time at, say, £20, you probably won't buy a packet at all because the benefit from consuming them is probably not worth the £20.30 it will cost at the local corner shop.

Maximisation

Another key assumption of neo-classical theory is that economic agents act in a way that will maximise their net benefits.

Consumers Consumers are assumed to maximise their **economic welfare**, sometimes referred to, or measured by **utility** or satisfaction from consuming goods. In a world where their resources are scarce, they have to make choices. So they have to compare the utility to be gained from consuming an extra unit of a product with its opportunity cost. If there is £2 to be spent, would it be best spent on chocolate, a magazine or a gift to charity, for example.

Workers Workers are assumed in neo-classical theory to want to maximise their own welfare at work. Workers take a number of different considerations into account when deciding where to work and how long to work. Pay is usually a key consideration. But other factors, such as job security, how long it takes to commute to work, the satisfaction derived from doing a particular job with a particular group of other workers and the cost of looking for alternative employment, are all important too.

Firms Neo-classical theory assumes that the owners of firms want to maximise their reward from ownership. This means that firms will aim to maximise their profits.

Governments Governments are assumed to want to maximise the welfare of citizens. They take decisions that will lead to increased welfare for the country as a whole.

Neo-classical theory recognises that these assumptions about the goals of economic actors can be simplistic. For example, large firms tend to be run not by their owners, the shareholders, but by managers. Not surprisingly, managers can often take decisions that will benefit themselves rather than the shareholders who have employed them. Governments tend to maximise the welfare of all citizens. However, governments around the world may be corrupt. They then take decisions that will tend to benefit the members of the government rather than citizens. Equally, governments tend to reward their own supporters at the expense of other citizens. In a democracy, there is little point in taking decisions that will reward the core voters of other parties. Rather, decisions are taken which will benefit your own core voters and those who might vote for you in an election.

Neo-classical theory also recognises that not every decision will be made in a rational way. However, neo-classical economists would argue that their theories will be correct so long as most economic agents act in a rational way most of the time.

The margin

Some economic theories assume that economic agents will act rationally in a way that maximises their total net benefit. For example, consumers will act to maximise their total utility. However, there are problems with this approach. One of the key elements of neo-classical economic theory is that it is much simpler to assume that decisions are taken at the margin. For example, when you decide whether or not you want to buy a packet of crisps now, you don't review all your spending decisions. What you do, according to neo-classical economists, is that you look at the one decision in isolation. What will give the greatest utility: to buy a packet of crisps now, or not to buy? For a firm, it may investigate whether to take on an extra worker. The firm doesn't review all its spending decisions when making this one decision. Instead, it considers whether or not profit will be increased by taking on the extra worker.

Marginal analysis is fundamental to the study of economics today both at A level and at university level. A quick look at the index of a standard economics textbook will show how many different marginal variables there are, for example, marginal utility, marginal cost, marginal benefit, marginal product, marginal rate of tax and the marginal propensity to consume.

Key Terms

Economic welfare - the level of well-being or prosperity or living standards of an individual or group of individuals such as a country.

Macroeconomics - the study of the economy as a whole, including inflation, growth and unemployment.

Microeconomics - the study of the behaviour of individuals or groups such as consumers, firms or workers, typically within a market context.

Neo-classical theory - a theory of economics which typically starts with the assumption that economic agents will maximise their benefits and act rationally, and which develops how resources will be allocated in markets and at what price through the forces of demand and supply; the margin is a key concept in neo-classical theory.

Utility or economic welfare - the satisfaction or benefit derived from consuming a good or a set of goods.

Thinking like an economist

Ryanair

In 2014, the *Financial Times* reported that the no-frills airline company, Ryanair, had seen a fall in its net profits over the past 12 months. The company was quoted as saying that the results were 'disappointing' and announced a number of measures to improve future profitability.

Neo-classical economic theory assumes that shareholders expect their companies to maximise profits. In the case of Ryanair, the company has grown fast since it was founded in 1985. Its success is based on low prices and low costs. By having lower costs than most of its rivals, it can afford to offer lower priced air tickets to its customers and make a profit. Low airfares have been so attractive to customers that the company has grown to be one of the largest airlines in Europe.

Ryanair's customers are arguably maximising their utility when they buy a Ryanair flight. Typically they shop around for the cheapest flight to their chosen destination. The *Financial Times* reported that Ryanair had been voted the worst of 100 big brands in the UK market for customer relations by the readers of the consumer magazine, *Which?* In calculating their utility in a rational manner, customers who buy tickets are offsetting any negative utility they may suffer from customer service with the savings in price on the airfare.

Following the announcement of lower profits, Ryanair announced that it would make improvements to its customer service in an attempt to increase sales and profits. This could be seen to be a recognition on the part of Ryanair that some potential customers were not flying Ryanair because they valued better service more than saving, say, £40 on a flight.

Source: adapted from © the *Financial Times* 19.5.2014, All Rights Reserved.

Data Response Question

Private vs state schools

Is it rational for parents to send their children to private schools? The cost of sending a child to a day school now averages £12 000 per year. This can double for boarding school education and for a top public school it is £35 000 a year. For the cost of sending a child to a top public school for five years, parents could afford to buy themselves a holiday house in Spain or France. They couldn't, however, buy a flat in central London or a private jet.

Some parents prefer to use the postcode system to get their children into the 'right' school. Buying a house in the catchment area of a high-achieving state school is now very common, particularly in London. Unlike with private school fees, the cost of buying a more expensive house can be recouped once the children have got into their school simply by selling up and moving somewhere cheaper. Moving north can also be a solution. It is much cheaper in most other areas of the UK to buy into a property which is in the catchment area of a good school than in London and the south east. However, average earnings are also much lower outside of the London and the south east, limiting the buying power of parents shopping around for the best education.

A more fundamental question to ask is why one person would spend so much money benefitting another person. Parents get little direct benefit from the schooling of their children. It is the children themselves who get the main benefit, partly in terms of better qualifications and motivation which lead to higher paid jobs as adults. Clearly, there is utility to be gained by parents when they spend money on their own children's education which they don't gain when other children are educated.

Q

1. Explain what 'rationality' means in economics, using the purchase of private education as an example.

2. Assume that the government wants to maximise the economic welfare of its citizens whilst consumers want to maximise their utility. Evaluate whether the government, in order to maximise economic welfare, should abolish all private schools in the UK and make the education system entirely state funded and run.

Evaluation

In your answer, focus on economic arguments. Would parents who currently send their children to private schools be better off or worse off? What about parents who send their children to state schools? How might some parents bend any pure state-run system to their benefit? What would be likely to happen to taxes if private schools were abolished? Explain two other ways in which society might benefit or lose out if private schools were abolished. In your conclusion, weigh up the advantages and disadvantages.

8 Demand

Key points

1. Demand is the quantity of goods or services that will be bought over a period of time at any given price.
2. Demand for a good will rise or fall if there are changes in the conditions of demand such as incomes, the price of other goods, tastes, and the size of the population.
3. A change in price is shown by a movement along the demand curve.
4. A change in any other variable affecting demand, such as income, is shown by a shift in the demand curve.

Starter activity

'Demand for instant coffee fell by five per cent in the UK last year.' What do you think is meant by 'demand'? What might have caused a drop in demand of five per cent?

Demand

A market exists wherever there are buyers and sellers of a particular good. Buyers demand goods from the market whilst sellers supply goods to the market.

Demand has a particular meaning in economics. Demand is the quantity of goods or services that will be bought at any given price over a period of time. For instance, approximately two million new cars are bought each year in the UK today at an average price of, say, £8 000. Economists would say that the annual demand for cars at £8 000 would be two million units.

Demand and price

If everything else were to remain the same (this is known as the ceteris paribus condition), what would happen to the quantity demanded of a product as its price changed? If the average price of a car were to fall from £8 000 to £4 000, then it is not difficult to guess that the quantity demanded of cars would rise. On the other hand, if the average price rose to £40 000, very few cars would now be sold.

This is shown in Table 1. As the price of cars rises then, ceteris paribus, the quantity of cars demanded will fall. Another way of expressing this is shown in Figure 1. Price is on the vertical axis and quantity demanded over time is on the horizontal axis. The curve is downward sloping showing that as price falls, quantity demanded rises. This **demand curve** shows the quantity that is demanded at any given price. When price changes there is said to be a movement along the curve. For instance, there is a **movement along** the curve from the point A to the point B, a fall of 1 million cars a year, when the price of cars rises from £8 000 to £16 000. There is an

Figure 1

The demand curve

The demand curve is downward sloping, showing that the lower the price, the higher will be the quantity demanded of a good. In this example, only 0.4 million cars per year are demanded at a price of £40 000 each, but a reduction in price to £4 000 increases quantity demanded to 4 million units per year.

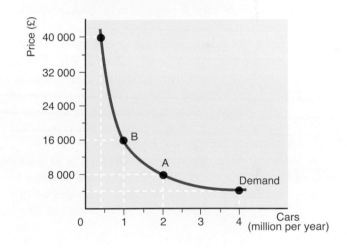

extension of demand when the quantity demanded rises. There is a **contraction of demand** when the quantity demanded falls.

It is important to remember that the demand curve shows **effective demand**. It shows how much would be bought (i.e. how much consumers can afford to buy and would buy) at any given price and not how much buyers would like to buy if they had unlimited resources.

Economists have found that in almost all cases, rises in price lead to falls in quantity demanded. The demand curve is therefore almost always downward sloping. Mathematically, it means that there is an inverse relationship between price and quantity demanded.

Conditions of demand

Changes in price will lead to a change in quantity demanded. These changes are shown by movements along the demand curve. However, there are many other factors apart from price which can cause demand for a product to change. These other factors are collectively called the **conditions of demand**. Changes in the conditions of demand cause a **shift in the demand curve** either to the right or to the left.

Table 1 The demand schedule for cars	
Price (£)	Demand (million per year)
4 000	4.0
8 000	2.0
16 000	1.0
40 000	0.4

35

Question 1

Stagecoach operates both bus and train services. It charges different prices to different passengers for the same journeys depending, for instance, on when they travel, their age, whether they are making a single or return journey or whether they have a season ticket. Using a demand curve diagram, explain what happens when:

(a) children are charged half price for a bus journey instead of being charged full price;

(b) senior citizens are given a free bus pass paid for by the local authority rather than having to pay the full fare;

(c) Stagecoach increases its prices on a route by 5 per cent;

(d) passengers can get a 60 per cent reduction by buying a day return if they travel after 9.30 compared to having to pay the full fare.

Demand and income

One condition of demand is income. Demand for a normal good rises when income rises. For instance, a rise in income leads consumers to buy more cars. A few goods, known as inferior goods, fall in demand when incomes rise.

The effect of a rise in income on demand is shown in Figure 2. Buyers are purchasing OA of clothes at a price of OE. Incomes rise and buyers react by purchasing more clothes at the same price. At the higher level of income they buy, say, OB of clothes. A new demand curve now exists, D_2. It will be to the right of the original demand curve because at any given price more will be demanded at the new higher level of income.

Economists say that a rise in income will lead to an **increase in demand** for a normal good such as clothes. An increase in demand is shown by a shift in the demand curve. (Note that

an increase in quantity demanded would refer to a change in quantity demanded resulting from a change in price and would be shown by a movement along the curve.) In Figure 2, the original demand curve D_1 shifts to the right to its new position D_2. Similarly, a fall in income will lead to a **fall in demand** for a normal good. This is shown by a **shift** to the left of the demand curve from D_1 to D_3. For instance, at a price of OE, demand will fall from OA to OC.

Two points need to be made. First, the demand curves in Figure 2 have been drawn as straight lines. These demand curves drawn show a hypothetical (or imaginary) position. They are drawn straight purely for convenience and do not imply that actual demand curves for real products are straight. Second, the shifts in the demand curves are drawn as parallel shifts. Again this is done for convenience and neatness but it is most unlikely that a rise or fall in income for an actual product would produce a precisely parallel shift in its demand curve.

Question 2

Table 2 Demand curve for tyre manufacturer

Quantity demanded (million tyres)	Price (£)
10	20
20	16
30	12
40	8
50	4

Table 2 shows the demand curve facing a tyre manufacturer.

(a) Draw a demand curve for tyres from the above data.

(b) An increase in income results in an increase in quantity demanded of tyres of: (i) 5 million; (ii) 10 million; (iii) 15 million; (iv) 25 million. For each of these, draw a new demand curve on your diagram.

(c) Draw a demand curve for tyres which would show the effect of a fall in income on the original demand for tyres.

(d) Draw a demand curve for tyres which would show that no products were demanded when their price was £8.

> **Maths Tip**
> Remember that price always goes on the vertical axis and quantity on the horizontal axis on a demand diagram.

The price of other goods

Another important factor which influences the demand for a good is the price of other goods. For instance, in the great drought of 1976 in the UK, the price of potatoes soared. Consumers reacted by buying fewer potatoes and replacing them in their diet by eating more bread, pasta and rice.

This can be shown on a demand diagram. The demand curve for pasta in Figure 3 is D_1. A rise in the price of potatoes leads to a rise in the demand for pasta. This means that at any given price a greater quantity of pasta will be demanded. The new demand curve D_2 will therefore be to the right of the original demand curve.

Figure 2

A change in income

An increase in income will raise demand for a normal good. At a price of OE, for instance, demand will rise from OA to OB. Similarly, at all other prices, an increase in income will result in a level of demand to the right of the existing demand curve. So the demand curve will shift to the right from D_1 to D_2. A fall in income will result in less being demanded at any given price. Hence the demand curve will shift to the left, from D_1 to D_3.

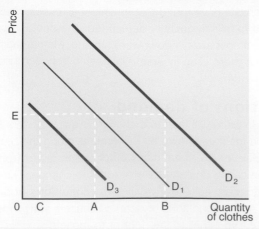

Figure 3

A rise in the price of other goods

A rise in the price of potatoes will lead to a rise in the demand for substitute goods. So the demand for pasta will increase, shown by a shift to the right in the demand curve for pasta from D_1 to D_2.

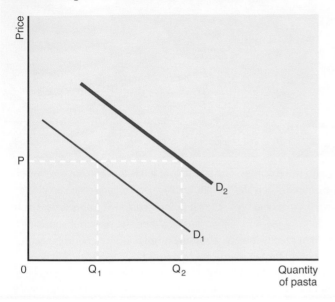

Question 3

Figure 4

Brent crude oil price, £ per barrel, 2007-15

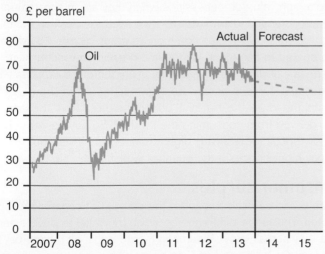

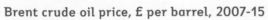

Source: adapted from *Bank of England Inflation Report*, February 2014.

Between 2009 and 2011, the price of Brent crude oil rose from around £20 a barrel to around £80 a barrel. In early 2014, the price of oil was predicted to remain high for the foreseeable future because of growing demand for oil from emerging countries such as China. Explain, using diagrams, what effect you would expect very high prices for crude oil to have on the demand in the UK for:

(a) oil-fired central heating systems; (b) luxury cars with high petrol consumption; (c) rail travel; (d) ice-cream; (e) air travel.

Question 4

Figure 5

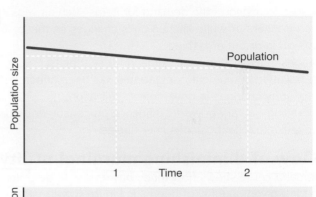

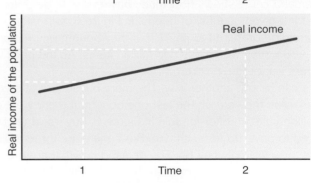

Studies show that products which lower your cholesterol are good for your health

Explain the likely effect on demand for Flora pro.activ of each of the four factors shown in the data - advertising, medical reports, population and income. Use a separate demand diagram for each factor to illustrate your answer.

Not all changes in prices will affect the demand for a particular good. A rise in the price of tennis balls is unlikely to have much impact on the demand for carrots, for instance. Changes in the price of other goods as well may have either a positive or negative impact on demand for a good. A rise in the price of tennis rackets is likely to reduce the demand for tennis balls as some buyers decide that tennis is too expensive a sport. On the other hand, the demand for cinema places, alcoholic drink or whatever other form of entertainment consumers choose to buy instead of tennis equipment, will increase.

Other factors

There is a wide variety of other factors which affect the demand for a good apart from price, income and the prices of other goods. These include:

- changes in population - an increase in population is likely to increase demand for goods;
- changes in fashion - the demand for items such as wigs or flared trousers or white kitchen units changes as these items go in or out of fashion;
- changes in legislation - the demand for seat belts, anti-pollution equipment or cigarettes has been affected in the past by changes in government legislation;
- advertising - a very powerful influence on consumer demand that seeks to influence consumer choice.

The law of diminishing marginal utility

The demand curve shows how much buyers would be prepared to pay for a given quantity of goods. In Figure 6, for instance, they would be prepared to pay 10p if they bought one million items. At 8p, they would buy two million items. As the price falls, so buyers want to buy more.

This can be put another way. The more buyers are offered, the less value they put on the last one bought. If there were only one million units on offer for sale in Figure 6, buyers would be prepared to pay 10p for each one. But if there are three million for sale, they will only pay 6p. The demand curve, therefore, shows the value to the buyer of each item bought. The first unit bought is worth almost 12p to a buyer. The one millionth unit is worth 10p. The four millionth unit would be worth 4p.

This illustrates the **law of diminishing marginal utility**. The value, or utility, attached to consuming the last product bought falls as more units are consumed over a given period of time. A student might be prepared to pay £5 to watch a film on a Saturday. The student might be prepared to watch a second film that day, but values the second film less than the first. Eventually, the student would begin to experience negative marginal utility and would pay not to have watch yet another film.

Adam Smith, writing in the 18th century, was puzzled why consumers paid a high price for goods such as diamonds, which were unnecessary to human existence, whilst the price of necessities such as water was very low. This problem is known as the **paradox of value**. The law of diminishing marginal utility can, however, explain this paradox. If there are few goods available to buy, as with diamonds, then consumers are prepared to pay a high price for them because their marginal utility is high. If goods are plentiful, then consumers are only prepared to pay a low price because the last one consumed

Question 5

Samira loves clothes. The first pair of jeans that she bought herself, she adored. Then she bought another pair of jeans but she didn't wear them as much as her first pair of jeans. Two years later, she had five pairs of jeans in her wardrobe. When she went out shopping, she didn't really look at jeans any more and spent her money on other items for her wardrobe. Samira's brother, Intzar, had one pair of jeans, which he wore frequently. When his mum suggested that he might like to buy another pair, he said he had better things to spend his money on. He would only buy another pair when his existing pair had fallen apart.

How does this illustrate the law of diminishing marginal utility?

has low marginal utility. This doesn't mean to say that they don't place a high value on necessities when they are in short supply. In times of famine, diamonds can be traded for small amounts of food. If diamonds were as common as water, buyers would not be prepared to pay much for the last diamond bought.

The law of diminishing marginal utility therefore explains why the demand curve is downward sloping. The higher the quantity bought, the lower the marginal utility (the utility from the last one) derived from consuming the product. So buyers will only pay low prices for relatively high amounts purchased, but they will pay higher prices if the quantity available for sale is lower.

Consumer surplus

Figure 6 can be used to explain the concept of **consumer surplus**. This is the difference between the value to buyers and what they actually pay. Assume in Figure 6 that all buyers pay a price of 6p for a product. The buyer who bought the millionth unit would have been prepared to pay 10p for that unit. So that buyer has gained a consumer surplus of 4p (10p - 6p) on that unit. The buyer who bought the two millionth unit would have been prepared to pay 8p for the unit. So the consumer surplus on the two millionth unit is 2p (8p - 6p). The buyer who bought the three millionth unit gained no consumer surplus. The price paid was exactly equal to the value or utility of 6p placed by the buyer on the unit.

The total consumer surplus at a price of 6p is shown by the shaded area in Figure 6. It is the sum of all the vertical lines between the price of 6p and the demand curve, which shows the value that buyers are placing on marginal units purchased.

Figure 6

Consumer surplus

The demand curve shows the price that the buyer would be prepared to pay for each unit. Except on the last unit purchased, the price that the buyer is prepared to pay is above the market price that is paid. The difference between these two values is the consumer surplus. It is represented by the shaded area under the demand curve.

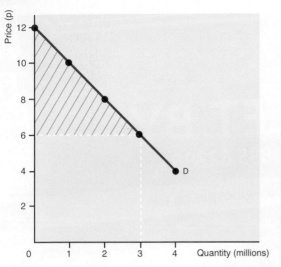

Key Terms

Conditions of demand - factors other than price, such as income or the price of other goods, which lead to changes in demand and are associated with shifts in the demand curve.

Consumer surplus - the difference between how much buyers are prepared to pay for a good and what they actually pay.

Contraction of demand - when quantity demanded for a good falls because its price rises; it is shown by a movement up the demand curve.

Demand curve - the line on a price/quantity diagram which shows the level of effective demand at any given price.

Demand or effective demand - the quantity purchased of a good at any given price, given that other determinants of demand remain unchanged.

Extension of demand - when quantity demanded for a good increases because its price falls; it is shown by a movement down the demand curve.

Law of diminishing marginal utility - the value or utility that individual consumers gain from the last product consumed falls the greater the number consumed. So the marginal utility of consuming the sixth product is lower than the second product consumed.

Shift in the demand curve - a movement of the whole demand curve to the right or left of the original caused by a change in any variable affecting demand except price.

Question 6

Demand for a good is zero at £200. It then rises to 50 million units at £100 and 75 million at £50.

(a) Draw the demand curve for prices between 0 and £200.

(b) Shade the area of consumer surplus at a price of £60.

(c) Is consumer surplus larger or smaller at a price of £40 compared to £60? Explain your answer.

Thinking like an economist

The demand for housing

There are two main housing markets in the UK. In the rental market, tenants rent properties from landlords. In the owner-occupied market, people buy a property to live in it. The demand for houses in these two markets is driven by a number of factors.

Price The higher the price of a property, either its purchase price or its rent, the lower will be the quantity demanded. Historically, the long-term trend for house prices and rents has been upwards. However, there have been periods of sharp falls in house prices such as in the late 1980s and 2008-11. Higher prices and rents tend to disadvantage house buyers and those looking for rented accommodation. They limit what they can afford.

Interest rates Most houses are bought partly with mortgages (money borrowed to purchase property). The higher the rate of interest, the higher will be the monthly repayments on a mortgage. For those using a mortgage, higher interest rates therefore effectively raise the price of the house. Higher interest rates therefore tend to reduce quantity demanded.

Incomes Over the long term, rising incomes have significantly increased demand for houses, shifting the demand curve to the right. Figure 7 shows how real GDP (the income of the country after inflation has been taken into account) has increased approximately two and a half times between 1975 and 2014, whilst real house prices have increased by almost as much.

Population As Table 3 shows, the population of the UK has been growing. Much of it in recent years has been due to immigration of workers from the EU. The number of households (a group of people living together in one dwelling) is growing even faster. With an ageing population, the long-term trend has been for more single pensioner households and fewer households with parents and children.

Other factors Other factors have affected the demand for housing in the UK. One very damaging factor has been speculation. Some house buyers purchase property mainly because they hope they will be able to be able to sell it later at a profit. Speculation has caused a number of housing bubbles in the last forty years. Prices have risen fast only to crash later

as in the first decade of the twenty-first century. This can leave some of those who bought at the height of the bubble with negative equity. This means they owe more money on the mortgage they used to buy a property than its current sale value.

Table 3 Population and number of households, UK

	Population millions	Number of households millions
1961	52.8	16.7
1971	55.9	19.0
1981	56.4	20.7
1991	57.8	22.9
2001	59.1	24.6
2011	62.3	26.3
2013	64.1	26.4

Source: adapted from www.ons.gov.uk.

Figure 7

Average UK house prices, at current and constant prices, £, index of real GDP at market prices 1975 Q1=100

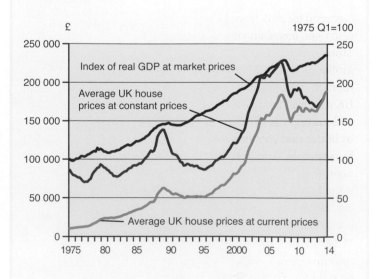

Source: adapted from www.nationwide.co.uk.

Data Response Question

Booming demand leads to higher milk prices

In March 2014, it was reported that UK dairy farmers were doing well. Costs of production had been falling, whilst the prices they received for their milk had been rising significantly. This was despite the fact that UK consumers have seen a cut in their spending power over the past four years due to the recession, which has in itself cut demand for dairy products. Rising food prices in general and rising prices for dairy products in UK supermarkets have also dampened demand.

However, demand for dairy products has been rising globally. Low and middle-income countries, such as China, have been growing fast. Their populations have used their growing incomes in part to finance a more varied diet. This includes substantially increasing their consumption of products such as milk and cheese. China might be a long way away from a dairy farm in Devon, but the dairy market is a global market. Products such as dried milk powder and cheese are traded globally. To meet this demand, Dairy Crest has recently invested £45 million in its cheese plant in Cornwall to increase production of whey powder for export to Asia.

Demand for milk from UK farms has also been increasing domestically. Dairy processors have been investing in new facilities in the UK. The aim is to produce more in the UK of what is bought in UK supermarkets by customers. This will cut imports of dairy products such as butter and yoghurts into the UK. For example, Arla, the Danish co-operative that makes Lurpak butter and is the UK's largest dairy operation, has created the world's biggest fresh milk processing plant in Aylesbury. Müller Wiseman, another of Britain's major milk processors, has spent £17 million on a butter plant in Shropshire.

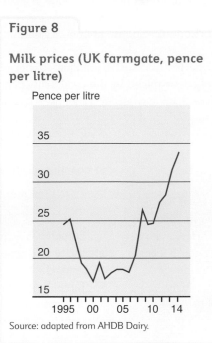

Figure 8

Milk prices (UK farmgate, pence per litre)

Pence per litre

Source: adapted from AHDB Dairy.

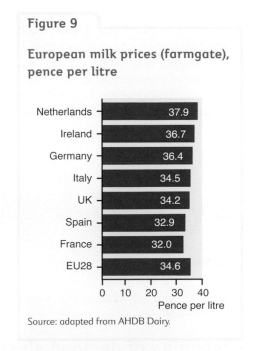

Figure 9

European milk prices (farmgate), pence per litre

	Pence per litre
Netherlands	37.9
Ireland	36.7
Germany	36.4
Italy	34.5
UK	34.2
Spain	32.9
France	32.0
EU28	34.6

Source: adapted from AHDB Dairy.

Source: adapted from © the *Financial Times* 15.3.2014, All Rights Reserved.

Part of the reason for wanting to produce more in the UK has been recent food safety scares. In 2013, demand for minced beef products fell dramatically when it was found that some products had horse meat in them rather than beef. Being able to trace a dairy product back to a UK farm reassures British customers.

If the UK became self-sufficient in dairy products and cut out all imports, British dairy farmers would have to increase yearly production from the current 14 billion litres to between 17 billion and 19 billion litres. On top of that, the National Farmers' Union forecasts that global demand for dairy production will grow by 2.3 per cent per year for the next decade.

Evaluation

In your answer to question 3, explain the advantages and the disadvantages to farmers of increasing their herds. Which of these advantages and disadvantages are likely to be more important? Come to an overall conclusion about whether the advantages outweigh the disadvantages.

1. The data describe a number of factors that might have influenced demand for farm milk in the UK in recent years. Using a demand curve diagram for each example, explain the effect on demand of the changes in:
   (a) the price of dairy products in UK supermarkets;
   (b) incomes of UK consumers;
   (c) world demand for dairy products;
   (d) scares about the quality of food purchased in the UK.

2. Explain, using a demand curve diagram, the impact of 'rising prices for dairy products in UK supermarkets' on the consumer surplus enjoyed by UK consumers on dairy products.

3. Briefly evaluate whether British dairy farmers should have increased the size of their herds of dairy cattle in 2014.

9 Price elasticity of demand

1. Elasticity is a measure of the extent to which quantity responds to a change in a variable which affects it, such as price or income.
2. Price elasticity of demand measures the proportionate response of quantity demanded to a proportionate change in price.
3. Price elasticity of demand varies from zero, or perfectly inelastic, to infinity or perfectly elastic.
4. The value of price elasticity of demand is mainly determined by the availability of substitutes and by time.
5. The price elasticity of demand for a good will determine whether a change in the price of the good results in a change in its total expenditure/revenue.

Starter activity

How much is the price of your favourite chocolate bar, like a Twix or Mars Bar? If it goes up in price by 10 per cent, what do you think will be the change in quantity bought by all its buyers? How much is the price of a cinema ticket for a 17 or 18-year old student? If it goes up in price by 10 per cent, what do you think will be the change in the number of tickets bought? In thinking about this, you are thinking about what economists call 'price elasticity of demand'.

The meaning of demand elasticity

The quantity demanded of a good is affected by changes in the price of the good, changes in price of other goods, changes in income and changes in other relevant factors. Elasticity is a measure of just how much the quantity demanded will be affected by a change in price or income or other factor.

Assume that the price of gas increases by one per cent. If quantity demanded consequently falls by 20 per cent, then there is a very large drop in quantity demanded in comparison to the change in price. The price elasticity of gas would be said to be very high. If quantity demanded falls by 0.01 per cent, then the change in quantity demanded is relatively insignificant compared to the large change in price and the price elasticity of gas would be said to be low.

Different elasticities of demand measure the proportionate response of quantity demanded to a proportionate change in the variables which affect demand. So price elasticity of demand measures the responsiveness of quantity demanded to changes in the price of the good. Income elasticity measures the responsiveness of quantity demanded to changes in consumer incomes. Cross elasticity measures the responsiveness of quantity demanded to changes in the price of another good. Economists could also measure population elasticity, tastes elasticity or elasticity for any other variable which might affect quantity demanded, although these measures are rarely calculated.

Price elasticity of demand

Economists choose to measure responsiveness in terms of proportionate or percentage changes. So **price elasticity of demand** - the responsiveness of changes in quantity demanded to changes in price - is calculated by using the formula:

$$\frac{\text{percentage change in quantity demanded}}{\text{percentage change in price}}$$

Sometimes, price elasticity of demand is called **own price elasticity of demand** to distinguish it from cross price elasticity of demand.

Table 1 shows a number of calculations of price elasticity. For instance, if an increase in price of 10 per cent leads to a fall in quantity demanded of 20 per cent, then the price elasticity of demand is 2. If an increase in price of 50 per cent leads to a fall in quantity demanded of 25 per cent then price elasticity of demand is ½.

Table 1 Price elasticity

Percentage change in quantity demanded	Percentage change in price	Elasticity
20	10	2
25	50	0.5
28	7	4
3	9	0.333

Elasticity is sometimes difficult to understand at first. It is essential to memorise the formulae for elasticity. Only then can they be used with ease and an appreciation gained of their significance.

Alternative formulae

Data to calculate price elasticities are often not presented in the form of percentage changes. These have to be worked

Question 1

Table 2 Price elasticity of demand

	Percentage change in quantity demanded	Percentage change in price
(a)	10	5
(b)	60	20
(c)	4	8
(d)	1	9
(e)	5	7
(f)	8	11

Calculate the price elasticity of demand from the data in Table 2.

out. Calculating the percentage change is relatively easy. For instance, if consumers have 10 apples and buy another five, the percentage change in the total number of apples is of 50 per cent. This answer is worked out by dividing the change in the number of apples they have (i.e. 5) by the original number of apples they possessed (i.e. 10) and multiplying by 100 to get a percentage figure. So the formula is:

$$\text{percentage change} = \frac{\text{new value - original value}}{\text{original value}}$$

$$= \frac{\text{change}}{\text{original value}} \times 100\%$$

Price elasticity of demand is measured by dividing the percentage change in quantity demanded by the percentage change in price. Therefore an alternative way of expressing this is $\Delta Q_D/Q_D \times 100$ (the percentage change in quantity demanded Q_D) divided by $\Delta P/P \times 100$ (the percentage change in price P). The 100s cancel each other out, leaving a formula of:

$$\frac{\Delta Q_D}{Q_D} \div \frac{\Delta P}{P} \quad \text{or} \quad \frac{\Delta Q_D}{Q_D} \times \frac{P}{\Delta P}$$

This is mathematically equivalent to:

$$\frac{P}{Q_D} \times \frac{\Delta Q_D}{\Delta P}$$

Examples of calculations of elasticity using the above two formulae are given in Figure 1.

Figure 1

Calculations of elasticity of demand

Example 1
Quantity demanded originally is 100 at a price of £2. There is a rise in price to £3 resulting in a fall in demand to 75.
Therefore the change in quantity demanded is 25 and the change in price is £1.
The price elasticity of demand is:

$$\frac{\Delta Q_D}{Q_D} \div \frac{\Delta P}{P} = \frac{-25}{100} \div \frac{1}{2} = -\tfrac{1}{2}$$

Example 2
Quantity demanded originally is 20 units at a price of £5 000. There is a fall in price to £4 000 resulting in a rise in demand to 32 units.
Therefore the change in quantity demanded is 12 units resulting from the change in price of £1 000.
The price elasticity of demand is:

$$\frac{P}{Q_D} \times \frac{\Delta Q_D}{\Delta P} = \frac{5\,000}{20} \times \frac{12}{-1\,000} = -3$$

Elastic and inelastic demand

Different values of price elasticity of demand are given special names. These values ignore minus signs and just refer to the number itself.

- Demand is price **elastic** if the value of elasticity is greater than one. If demand for a good is price elastic, then a percentage change in price will bring about an even larger percentage change in quantity demanded. For instance,

Question 2

Table 3 Price elasticity of demand

	Original values		New values	
	Quantity demanded	Price (£)	Quantity demanded	Price (£)
(a)	100	5	120	3
(b)	20	8	25	7
(c)	12	3	16	0
(d)	150	12	200	10
(e)	45	6	45	8
(f)	32	24	40	2

Calculate the price elasticity of demand for the data in Table 3.

Maths Tip
Price elasticity of demand is a concept where it is essential to memorise the formula. If you don't, you can't put the numbers in the right place to calculate an answer.

if a 10 per cent rise in the price of tomatoes leads to a 20 per cent fall in the quantity demanded of tomatoes, then price elasticity is 20 ÷ 10 or 2. Therefore the demand for tomatoes is elastic. Demand is said to be **perfectly elastic** if the value of elasticity is infinity (i.e. a fall in price would lead to an infinite increase in quantity demanded whilst a rise in price would lead to the quantity demanded becoming zero).

- Demand is price **inelastic** if the value of elasticity is less than one. If demand for a good is price inelastic then a percentage change in price will bring about a smaller percentage change in quantity demanded. For instance, if a 10 per cent rise in the price of tube fares on London Underground resulted in a one per cent fall in journeys made, then price elasticity is 1 ÷ 10 or 0.1. Therefore, the demand for tube travel is inelastic. Demand is said to be **perfectly inelastic** if the value of elasticity is zero (i.e. a change in price would have no effect on quantity demanded).

- Demand is of **unitary elasticity** if the value of elasticity is exactly 1. This means that a percentage change in price will lead to an exact and opposite change in quantity demanded. For instance, a good would have unitary elasticity if a 10 per cent rise in price led to a 10 per cent fall in quantity demanded.

This terminology is summarised in Table 4.

Question 3

Explain whether you think that the following goods would be elastic or inelastic in demand if their price increased by 10 per cent whilst all other factors remained constant:

(a) petrol;

(b) fresh tomatoes;

(c) holidays offered by a major tour operator;

(d) a Ford car;

(e) a Mars Bar;

(f) *GQ* magazine.

Table 4 Elasticity: summary of key terms

	Verbal description of response to a change in price	Numerical measure of elasticity (ignoring the minus sign)	Changes in total expenditure/ revenue as price rises
Perfectly inelastic	Quantity demanded does not change at all as price changes	Zero	Increases
Inelastic	Quantity demanded changes by a smaller percentage than does price	Between 0 and 1	Increases
Unitary elasticity	Quantity demanded changes by exactly the same percentage as does price	1	Constant
Elastic	Quantity demanded changes by a larger percentage than does price	Between 1 and infinity	Decreases
Perfectly elastic	Buyers are prepared to purchase all they can obtain at some given price but none at all at a higher price	Infinity	Decreases to zero

Figure 2

Price elasticity along a straight demand curve

Price elasticity varies along the length of a straight demand curve, moving from infinity, where it cuts the price axis, to (-)1 half way along the line, to zero where it cuts the quantity axis.

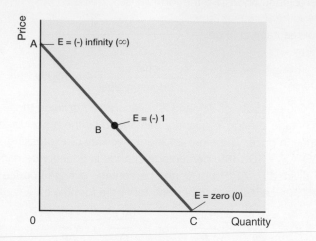

Graphical representations

Figure 2 shows a straight line graph. It is a common mistake to conclude that elasticity of a straight line demand curve is constant all along its length. In fact nearly all straight line demand curves vary in elasticity along the line.

- At the point A, price elasticity of demand is infinity. Here quantity demanded is zero. Putting Q = 0 into the formula for elasticity:

$$\frac{\Delta Q_D}{Q_D} \div \frac{\Delta P}{P}$$

  we see that zero is divided into ΔQ_D. Mathematically there is an infinite number of zeros in any number.
- At the point C, price elasticity of demand is zero. Here price is zero. Putting P = 0 into the formula for elasticity, we see

that P is divided into ΔP giving an answer of infinity. Infinity is then divided into the fraction $\Delta Q_D \div Q_D$. Infinity is so large that the answer will approximate to zero.
- At the point B exactly half way along the line, price elasticity of demand is 1.

  It is worth noting that the elasticity of demand at a point can be measured by dividing the distance from the point to the quantity axis by the distance from the point to the price axis, BC ÷ AB. In Figure 2, B is half way along the line AC and so BC = AB and the elasticity at the point B is -1.

  Two straight line demand curves discussed earlier do not have the same elasticity all along their length.

  Figure 3(a) shows a demand curve which is perfectly inelastic. Whatever the price, the same quantity will be demanded.

Figure 3

Perfectly elastic and inelastic demand curves and unitary elasticity

A vertical demand curve (a) is perfectly inelastic, whilst a horizontal demand curve (b) is perfectly elastic. A curve with unitary elasticity (c) is a rectangular hyperbola with the formula PQ = k where P is price, Q is quantity demanded and k is a constant value.

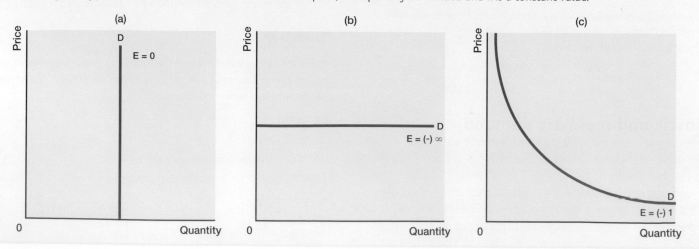

Figure 3(b) shows a perfectly elastic demand curve. Any amount can be demanded at one price or below it whilst nothing will be demanded at a higher price.

Figure 3(c) shows a demand curve with unitary elasticity. Mathematically it is a rectangular hyperbola. This means that any percentage change in price is offset by an equal and opposite change in quantity demanded.

Another common mistake is to assume that steep demand curves are always inelastic and demand curves which have a shallow slope are always elastic. In Figure 4, two demand curves are drawn. In Figure 4(a), the demand curve has a very shallow slope. The part that is drawn is indeed elastic but this is only because it is just the top half of the line which is drawn. If the whole line were drawn, the bottom half would be inelastic even though the gradient of the line is shallow. Similarly, in Figure 4(b), the demand curve has a very steep slope. The part that is shown is indeed price inelastic but this is only because it is the bottom half of the line. The top half of the steep line would be elastic.

Two technical points

In general, price elasticity of demand is written as if it were a positive number. In fact any downward sloping demand curve always has a negative elasticity. This is because a rise in one variable (price or quantity) is always matched by a fall in the other variable. A rise is positive but a fall is negative and a positive number divided by a negative one (or vice versa) is always negative. However, economists often find it convenient to omit the minus sign in price elasticity of demand because it is easier to deal in positive numbers whilst accepting that the value is really negative.

A second point relates to the fact that elasticities over the same price range can differ. For example, at a price of £2, demand for a good is 20 units. At a price of £3, demand is 18 units. Price elasticity of demand for a rise in price from £2 to £3 is:

$$\frac{P}{Q_D} \times \frac{\Delta Q_D}{\Delta P} = \frac{2}{20} \times \frac{-2}{1} = -\frac{1}{5}$$

However, price elasticity of demand for a fall in price from £3 to £2 is:

$$\frac{P}{Q_D} \times \frac{\Delta Q_D}{\Delta P} = \frac{3}{18} \times \frac{-2}{1} = -\frac{1}{3}$$

The price elasticity for a rise in price is therefore less than for a fall in price over the same range.

The determinants of price elasticity of demand

The exact value of price elasticity of demand for a good is determined by a wide variety of factors. Economists, however, argue that two factors in particular can be singled out: the availability of substitutes and time.

The availability of substitutes The better the substitutes for a product, the higher the price elasticity of demand will tend to be. For instance, salt has few good substitutes. When the

Figure 4

Slopes of straight line demand curves

Figure 4(a) shows an elastic demand curve but it is only elastic because it is the top half of the line, not because it has a shallow gradient. Similarly, Figure 4(b) shows an inelastic demand curve but it is only inelastic because it is the bottom half of the line, not because it has a steep gradient.

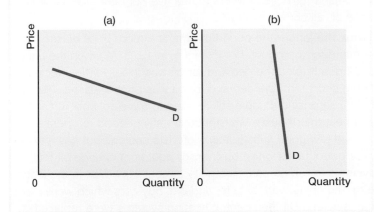

price of salt increases, the demand for salt will change little and therefore the price elasticity of salt is low. On the other hand, spaghetti has many good substitutes, from other types of pasta, to rice, potatoes, bread, and other foods. A rise in the price of spaghetti, all other food prices remaining constant, is likely to have a significant effect on the demand for spaghetti. Hence the elasticity of demand for spaghetti is likely to be higher than that for salt.

Question 4

Figure 5

Demand

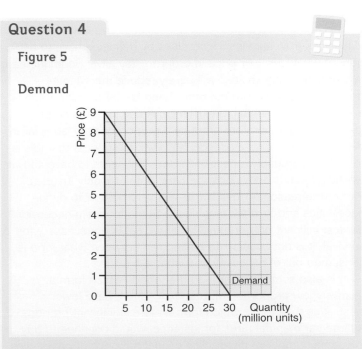

Consider Figure 5.

(a) Between what prices is demand (i) elastic and (ii) inelastic?

(b) At what price is demand (i) perfectly inelastic, (ii) perfectly elastic and (iii) equal to 1?

45

Width of market definition The more widely the product is defined, the fewer substitutes it is likely to have. Spaghetti has many substitutes, but food in general has none. Therefore the elasticity of demand for spaghetti is likely to be higher than that for food. Similarly the elasticity of demand for boiled sweets is likely to be higher than for confectionery in general. A five per cent increase in the price of boiled sweets, all other prices remaining constant, is likely to lead to a much larger fall in demand for boiled sweets than a five per cent increase in the price of all confectionery.

Time The longer the period of time, the more price elastic is the demand for a product. For instance, in 1973-74 when the price of oil quadrupled the demand for oil was initially little affected. In the short term the demand for oil was price inelastic. This is hardly surprising. People still needed to travel to work in cars and heat their houses whilst industry still needed to operate. Oil had few good substitutes. Motorists couldn't put gas into their petrol tanks whilst businesses could not change oil-fired systems to run on gas, electricity or coal. However, in the longer term motorists were able to, and did, buy cars which were more fuel efficient. Oil-fired central heating systems were replaced by gas and electric systems. Businesses converted or did not replace oil-fired equipment. The demand for oil fell from what it would otherwise have been. Taking the 10 year period to 1985, and given the changes in other variables which affected demand for oil, estimates suggest that the demand for oil was slightly elastic. It is argued that in the short term, buyers are often locked into spending patterns through habit, lack of information or because of durable goods that have already been purchased. In the longer term, they have the time and opportunity to change those patterns.

It is sometimes argued that necessities have lower price elasticities than luxuries. Necessities by definition have to be bought whatever their price in order to stay alive. So an increase in the price of necessities will barely reduce the quantity demanded. Luxuries on the other hand are by definition goods which are not essential to existence. A rise in the price of luxuries should therefore produce a proportionately large fall in demand. There is no evidence, however, to suggest that this is true. Food, arguably a necessity, does not seem to have a lower elasticity than holidays or large cars, both arguably luxuries. Part of the reason for this is that it is very difficult to define necessities and luxuries empirically. Some food is a necessity but a significant proportion of what we eat is unnecessary for survival. It is not possible to distinguish between what food is consumed out of necessity and what is a luxury.

It is also sometimes argued that goods which form a relatively low proportion of total expenditure have lower elasticities than those which form a more significant proportion. A large car manufacturer, for instance, would continue to buy the same number of paper clips even if the price of paper clips doubled because it is not worth its while to bother changing to an alternative. On the other hand, its demand for steel would be far more price elastic. There is no evidence to suggest that this is true. Examples given in textbooks, such as salt and matches, have low price elasticities because they have few good substitutes. In the case of paper clips, manufacturers of paper

Question 5

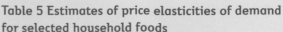

Table 5 Estimates of price elasticities of demand for selected household foods

	Price elasticity of demand
Nuts	-0.7
Fresh vegetables	-1.0
Blue fish	-0.5
Milk	-0.7
Beef	-0.6
Poultry	-0.9
Pork	-0.8
Fresh Fruit	-1.0
Eggs	-0.6

Source: adapted from *Family Food* 2011, Defra.

(a) Using the data in the table, calculate the percentage change in quantity demanded if the price of (i) nuts goes up by 10 per cent; (ii) fresh vegetables falls by 7.6 per cent; (iii) pork goes up by two per cent.

(b) Calculate the change in total revenue for sellers if the price of (a) a unit of fresh fruit goes up by 4p from an average price of £1 when one million units were being sold before the price change; (b) a dozen eggs goes up 10p from an average price of £2 when two million units were being sold before the price change.

(c) An increase in the price of which foods shown in the data would be most likely to lead (i) the greatest and (ii) the least change in household expenditure? Explain your answer.

(d) Suggest reasons why the demand for some foods in Table 5 is more price inelastic than the demand for others.

clips would long ago have raised prices substantially if they believed that price had little impact on the demand for their product.

Price elasticity of demand and total revenue/expenditure

Price elasticity of demand and changes in **total revenue** or **total expenditure** of a product are linked. Total expenditure is the amount that buyers spend on the product. Total revenue is the amount that sellers receive from selling the product. It will be assumed here that the two are the same amounts, although in practice they may be different if, for example, there are taxes on the sale of the product. Total expenditure or total revenue can be calculated by multiplying price and quantity:

Total expenditure = quantity purchased x price

or

Total revenue = quantity sold x price

For instance, if you bought five apples at 10 pence each, your total expenditure would be 50 pence and the total revenue of the seller would be 50p. If the price of apples went up, you might spend more, less, or the same on apples depending upon your price elasticity of demand for apples. Assume that the price of apples went up 40 per cent to 14p each. You might react by buying fewer apples. If you now buy four apples (i.e. a fall in demand of 20 per cent), the price elasticity of demand is 20 ÷ 40 or 0.5. Your expenditure on apples will also rise (from 50 pence to 56 pence). If you buy two apples (i.e. a fall in quantity demanded of 60 per cent), your elasticity of demand is 60 ÷ 40 or 1.5 and your expenditure on apples will fall (from 50 pence to 28 pence).

These relationships are what should be expected. If the percentage change in price is larger than the percentage change in quantity demanded (i.e. elasticity is less than 1, or inelastic), then expenditure will rise when prices rise. If the percentage change in price is smaller than the percentage change in quantity demanded (i.e. elasticity is greater than 1 or elastic), then spending will fall as prices rise. If the percentage change in price is the same as the change in quantity demanded (i.e. elasticity is unity), expenditure will remain unchanged because the percentage rise in price will be equal and opposite to the percentage fall in demand. These relationships are summarised in Table 4 on page 44.

Key Terms

Elastic demand - where the price elasticity of demand is greater than 1. The responsiveness of demand is proportionally greater than the change in price. Demand is perfectly elastic if price elasticity of demand is infinity.
Inelastic demand - where the price elasticity of demand is less than 1. The responsiveness of demand is proportionally less than the change in price. Demand is perfectly inelastic if price elasticity of demand is zero.
Price elasticity of demand or own price elasticity of demand - the proportionate response of changes in quantity demanded to a proportionate change in price, measured by the formula:

$$\frac{P}{Q_D} \times \frac{\Delta Q_D}{\Delta P}$$

Unitary elasticity - where the value of price elasticity of demand is 1. The responsiveness of demand is proportionally equal to the change in price.
Total expenditure - quantity bought times the average price of a product.
Total revenue - quantity sold times the average price of a product.

Thinking like an economist

The price of oil

Oil is a key world commodity. In the 1950s and 1960s, the price of oil was relatively stable at around $2 a barrel. Since 1970, however, the price of oil has proved volatile. Both the actual price of oil (i.e. at current prices) and the real price of oil adjusted for inflation (i.e. at constant prices) have fluctuated but overall have increased dramatically, as can be seen in Figure 6. There has been a number of price spikes in that period.

- Between 1972 and 1974, there was a surge in world demand for oil as economies boomed. At the same time, a 1973 war between Israel and its neighbours led Arab countries to restrict the supply of oil. Following the war, Arab countries realised that, through OPEC, the oil cartel, they could keep the price of oil high by agreeing to restrict output.
- Between 1978 and 1980, the sharp increase in price was caused by a revolution in Iran, a major world oil producer, which saw a sharp fall in Iranian oil output.
- In the 1980s, OPEC found it difficult to maintain discipline in terms of restricting output of oil. The sharp rises in the price of oil had substantially reduced world demand for oil. The fall in UK demand can be seen in Figure 7. In 1990, however, yet another war, the first Gulf War against Iraq, led to fears that oil output would fall and produce another spike in the oil price.
- In the 2000s, growing demand for oil from China, combined with tight supply, led to a price surge. The world recession of 2008-2010, led to a fall in world demand

and prices. However, in 2011, oil prices regained their pre-recession levels as demand increased again and supply remained tight.

Figure 6

Spot crude oil price[1], US$ per barrel at current and constant (2012 US$) prices

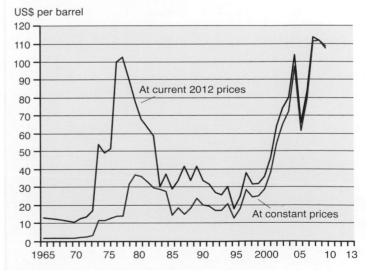

1. 1965-1983 Arabian Light, 1984-2013 Brent.
Source: adapted from *BP Statistical Review of World Energy*.

Price elasticity of demand for oil

Economic theory would suggest that a rise in the price of oil would lead to a fall in quantity demanded. Looking at Figure 7, it can be seen that the sharp rise in the price of oil from $2.48 a barrel to $36.83 a barrel between 1972 and 1980 was associated with a sharp decline in the UK consumption of oil from 101.5 million tonnes in 1973 to a low of 67.2 million tonnes in 1983. A 1385 per cent rise in the price of oil was associated with a 34 per cent fall in demand. Other factors affecting the UK demand for oil were changing over this ten year period. Incomes rose, for example, and more fuel efficient technology was developed. However, these figures would suggest that the demand for oil at the time was price inelastic.

Figure 7 shows that the UK demand for oil over most of the period since 1990 has remained fairly stable at between 75 and 79 million tonnes per year. However, the recession that started in 2008 pushed down incomes and was arguably the main factor driving annual UK demand for oil below 70 million tonnes. Overall, though, the large rises in oil prices since 2000 seem to have had little impact on quantity demanded, again suggesting a very low price elasticity of demand for oil.

Table 6 shows estimates of the price elasticity of demand for oil for high income countries (OECD economies such as the UK or the USA) and middle and low income countries (non-OECD countries such as Brazil or Tanzania). Demand is highly inelastic for both groups of countries.

Figure 7

Oil consumption, million tonnes oil equivalent, UK

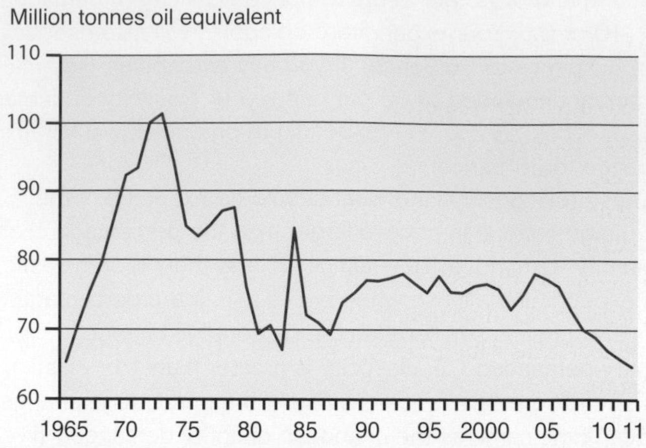

Source: adapted from www.decc.gov.uk.

Table 6 Estimated price elasticities of demand for oil

	Short term	Long term
OECD	-0.025	-0.093
Non-OECD	-0.007	-0.035

Source: adapted from *World Economic Outlook, April 2011*, IMF.

Short-term and long-term price elasticities

In the short term, demand for oil is likely to be highly price inelastic. This is supported by the estimates shown in Table 6.

Consumers of oil have little choice but to buy oil to run their cars, trains or heating systems. In the longer term, demand for oil is likely to be less inelastic. This is what Table 6 would suggest. This is partly because consumers can substitute oil for other forms of energy such as gas and coal. It is also because of energy-saving measures which make it economical, for example, to install insulation in lofts or develop more fuel-efficient cars.

OPEC and some of its member countries like Saudi Arabia are aware that too high a price for oil could result in a long-term decline in demand for oil despite rising world incomes. A large-scale switch from petrol-driven vehicles to ones powered by hydrogen, for example, could bring the price of oil down to below $10 a barrel. This would have a significant impact on economies such as Saudi Arabia, which are highly dependent on oil revenues for their prosperity. It is in the interests of these countries to have an oil price which is as high as possible but is not so high that it encourages the long-term development of technologies which considerably reduce the demand for oil.

Data Response Question

Fatty food clampdown

Food and drink manufacturers are fighting fiercely against measures that would restrict sales of their foods. The mayor of New York, Michael Bloomberg, announced a ban ten days ago on the sale of 'supersized' sugary drinks in restaurants, cinemas and stadiums. Hungary, France and Denmark have imposed higher taxes on unhealthy foods in order to discourage demand. In Denmark, for example, its 'fat tax' of DKr16 (£4.62) per kilogram of saturated fat in a product will increase the price of a burger by about 24p and that of a small pack of butter by about 64p.

Industry representatives say that measures such as these simply raise prices for consumers but have little effect on their eating habits. They also hit poor consumers hardest. Health experts say that restricting availability of unhealthy foods and raising their prices sharply will lead to healthier diets and fewer health problems.

Source: adapted from © The *Financial Times*, 4.10.2011 and 9.6.2012.

Campaigners for health food eating have suffered setbacks as well as triumphs. In November 2012, the Danish government announced it was repealing its 'fat tax'. Apart from being unpopular with consumers, it said that retailers had found it difficult to administer the tax. It also said that too many Danish consumers were now shopping across the border in Sweden and Germany for products subject to the fat tax. In 2013, Michael Bloomberg's ban on supersized sugary drinks was declared illegal in court. This was not before the ban was subject to protests and late-night comedy ridicule.

Source: adapted from © the *Financial Times*, 20.11.2013 All Rights Reserved.

Table 7 Estimates of price elasticities of demand for selected foods

	Price elasticity
Cheeses	-0.6
Fats (e.g. butter)	-0.5
Beef	-0.6
Sweets	-0.5
Sausage	-0.6
Drink	-0.8
Fresh fruit	-1.0
Fresh vegetables	-1.0

Source: adapted from *Family Food 2011*, Defra.

Evaluation

In your answer to question 3, you need to explain **both** the costs and benefits of a fat tax to those on low incomes. Which costs and which benefits are the most important? Then in your conclusion, explain whether the benefits outweigh the costs or vice versa. Overall, will they be net beneficiaries of a 'fat tax'? Include information both from the data and your own knowledge. Make sure you use Table 7 to assess the statement by food and drink manufacturers that raising prices will have 'little effect' on eating habits.

Q

1. Given the information in Table 7, assume that the price elasticity of demand for butter is -0.5 and that for a beef burger is -0.6. There is a rise in taxes on butter and beef burgers. By how much would quantities demanded fall if there were a rise in price of (a) butter of 20 per cent and (b) beef burgers of 50 per cent?

2. Define inelastic demand and suggest why cheeses and beef have such low price elasticities of demand.

3. Discuss whether 'fat taxes' are likely to benefit those on low incomes.

Income and cross elasticities

Key points

1. Income elasticity of demand measures the proportionate response of quantity demanded to a proportionate change in income.
2. An increase in income will lead to an increase in demand for normal goods but a fall in demand for inferior goods.
3. Normal goods have a positive income elasticity of demand but inferior goods have a negative income elasticity of demand.
4. Cross elasticity of demand measures the proportionate response of quantity demanded of one good to a proportionate change in price of another good.
5. Substitutes have a positive cross elasticity of demand whilst complements have a negative cross elasticity of demand.

Starter activity

What is the good or service on which you spend the most? It might be chocolate, downloads or clothes for example. If your income went up by 50 per cent, what do you think would happen to the number and percentage of these items you would buy? If the price of these items went up by a quarter (25 per cent), what would happen to your spending on the item on which you spend the next highest amount?

Income elasticity of demand

The demand for a good will change if there is a change in consumers' incomes. **Income elasticity of demand** is a measure of that change. If the demand for housing increased by 20 per cent when incomes increased by five per cent, then the income elasticity of demand would be said to be positive and relatively high. If the demand for food were unchanged when income rose, then income elasticity would be zero. A fall in demand for a good when income rises gives a negative value to income elasticity of demand.

The formula for measuring income elasticity of demand is:

$$\frac{\text{percentage change in quantity demanded}}{\text{percentage change in income}}$$

So the numerical value of income elasticity of a 20 per cent rise in demand for housing when incomes rise by five per cent is +20/+5 or +4. The number is positive because both the 20 per cent and the five per cent are positive. On the other hand, a rise in income of 10 per cent which led to a fall in quantity demanded of a product of five per cent would have an income elasticity of -5/+10 or -½. The minus sign in -5 shows the fall in quantity demanded of the product. Examples of items with a high income elasticity of demand are holidays and recreational activities, whereas washing up liquid tends to have a low income elasticity of demand.

Just as with price elasticity, it is sometimes easier to use alternative formulae to calculate income elasticity of demand.

The above formula is equivalent to:

$$\frac{\Delta Q}{Q} \div \frac{\Delta Y}{Y}$$

where Δ is change, Q is quantity demanded and Y is income. Rearranging the formula gives another two alternatives:

$$\frac{Y}{Q} \times \frac{\Delta Q}{\Delta Y} \quad \text{or} \quad \frac{\Delta Q}{Q} \times \frac{Y}{\Delta Y}$$

Examples of the calculation of income elasticity of demand are given in Table 1. Some economists use the terms 'elastic' and 'inelastic' with reference to income elasticity. Demand is

Table 1 Calculation of income elasticity of demand

Original quantity demanded	New quantity demanded	Original income (£)	New income (£)	$\frac{\Delta Q}{Q}$	÷	$\frac{\Delta Y}{Y}$	Numerical value
20	25	16	18	5/20	÷	2/16	+2
100	200	20	25	100/100	÷	5/20	+4
50	40	25	30	-10/50	÷	5/25	-1
60	60	80	75	0/60	÷	5/80	0
60	40	27	30	-20/60	÷	3/27	-3

Question 1

Table 2 Income elasticity of demand

| | Original | | New | |
	Quantity demanded	Income £	Quantity demanded	Income £
(a)	100	10	120	14
(b)	15	6	20	7
(c)	50	25	40	35
(d)	12	100	15	125
(e)	200	10	250	11
(f)	25	20	30	18

Calculate the income elasticity of demand from the data in Table 2.

income inelastic if it lies between +1 and -1. If income elasticity of demand is greater than +1 or less than -1, then it is elastic.

Normal and inferior goods

The pattern of demand is likely to change when income changes. It would be reasonable to assume that consumers will increase their demand for most goods when their income increases. Goods for which this is the case are called **normal goods**.

However, an increase in income will result in a fall in demand for other goods. These goods are called **inferior goods**. There will be a fall in demand because consumers will react to an increase in their income by purchasing products which are perceived to be of better quality. Commonly quoted examples of inferior goods are:

- bread - consumers switch from this cheap, filling food to more expensive meat or convenience foods as their incomes increase;
- margarine - consumers switch from margarine to butter, although this has become less true recently with greater health awareness;
- bus transport - consumers switch from buses to their own cars when they can afford to buy their own car.

A good can be both a normal and an inferior good depending on the level of income. Bread may be a normal good for people on low incomes (i.e. they buy more bread when their income increases). But it may be an inferior good for higher income earners.

Normal and inferior goods are shown on Figure 1. D_1 is the demand curve for a normal good. It is upward sloping because demand increases as income increases. D_2 is the demand curve for an inferior good. It is downward sloping, showing that demand falls as income increases. D_3 is the demand curve for a good which is normal at low levels of income, but is inferior at higher levels of income.

Figure 1

Normal and inferior goods

On the quantity-income diagram, a normal good such as D_1 has an upward sloping curve, whilst an inferior good such as D_2 has a downward sloping curve. D_3 shows a good which is normal at low levels of income but is inferior at higher levels of income.

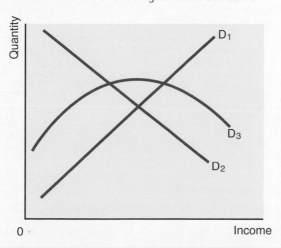

Question 2

Table 3 Quantity of food purchased by UK households: average per person per week, grams

	Grams per person per week			
	1980	1990	2000	2012
Sugar	392	211	132	91
Chicken and other poultry	141	164	170	192
Bananas	91	130	214	214
White bread	668	451	461	266
Fresh potatoes	1 176	1 008	727	478
Butter	106	42	37	41

Source: adapted from *Family Food Statistics*, Defra.

Household incomes per person rose between each of the years shown in the table. Assuming that all other factors remained constant, which of the goods shown in Table 3 are normal goods and which are inferior goods?

Inferior goods and income elasticity

Inferior goods can be distinguished from normal goods by their income elasticity of demand. The formula for measuring income elasticity is:

$$\frac{\text{percentage change in quantity demanded}}{\text{percentage change in income}}$$

A normal good will always have a positive income elasticity because quantity demanded and income either both increase (giving a plus divided by a plus) or both decrease (giving a minus divided by a minus). An inferior good, however, will always have a negative elasticity because the signs on the top and bottom of the formula will always be opposite (a plus divided by a minus or a minus divided by a plus giving a minus answer in both cases).

For instance, if the demand for bread falls by two per cent when incomes rise by 10 per cent then it is an inferior good. Its income elasticity is -2/+10 or -0.2.

Necessities and luxuries

Some economists distinguish between **necessities** (or basic goods) and **luxuries** (or superior goods). They state that necessities have an income elasticity of less than +1 whilst luxury goods have an income elasticity of greater than +1. The problem with this distinction is that many products which have an income elasticity of less than +1 would hardly be classified as 'necessities' by most consumers. For example, most foods have an income elasticity of less than +1 and would therefore all be classified as necessities. Yet should a fruit juice be just as much a necessity as tea, milk or meat? Whilst it can be useful to discuss necessities and luxuries in theory, putting a precise value on these in terms of income elasticity of demand may not be particularly helpful.

Question 3

Greggs, the bakery chain, did well out of the recession starting in 2008 with growing sales and profit. Its 1 500 outlets found a ready market with cash-strapped customers, many of whom were seeing their incomes decline. Budget breakfasts and low-cost pastries, value sandwiches and a national network of stores helped it grow its sales at the expense of more upmarket competitors.

As the economy began to climb out of recession in 2013, its sales actually fell. Greggs responded with a turnround plan. It concentrated on refurbishing outlets rather than opening new ones to make them more attractive. Menus were changed to include better coffee and more breakfast options to attract more upmarket customers who might otherwise buy from chains like Pret or even the supermarkets. It also added 'Balanced Choice', a range of low-calorie sandwiches designed to appeal to better off customers.

Source: adapted from © the *Financial Times* 15.3.2012, 1.7.2014, 30.7.2014, All Rights Reserved.

(a) Why might the data suggest that many of Greggs' products are inferior goods?

(b) Explain why these products would have negative income elasticities.

(c) Suggest why Greggs changed its sales strategy when incomes began to rise as the economy came out of recession in 2013. In your answer, explain the difference between inferior and normal goods.

Cross elasticity of demand

Cross elasticity of demand or **cross-price elasticity of demand** measures the proportionate response of the quantity demanded of one good to the proportionate change in the price of another. For example, it is a measure of the extent to which demand for pork increases when the price of beef goes up.

The formula for measuring cross elasticity of demand for good X with respect to the price of good Y is:

$$\frac{\text{percentage change in quantity demanded of good X}}{\text{percentage change in price of good Y}}$$

For example, if the quantity demanded of good X falls by 20 per cent as a result of a 10 per cent rise in the price of good Y, then the cross elasticity for good X with respect to the price of good Y is -2.0 (-20 % ÷ 10 %). More examples of the calculation of cross elasticity of demand are given in Table 4.

Some economists use the terms 'elastic' and 'inelastic' with reference to cross elasticity. If cross elasticity of demand is greater than +1 or less than -1, then it is elastic. If it lies between +1 and -1, then it is inelastic.

Substitutes and complements

The quantity demanded for some goods can be significantly affected by changes in the price of some other goods.

Table 4 Calculation of cross elasticity of demand

Original quantity demanded of Good X	New quantity demanded of Good X	Original price of Good Y	New price of Good Y	$\frac{\Delta Q_X}{Q_X}$	÷	$\frac{\Delta P_Y}{P_Y}$	Numerical value
16	20	8	10	4/16	÷	2/8	+1
50	30	10	11	-20/50	÷	1/10	-4
36	26	9	8	-10/36	÷	-1/9	+2.5
24	36	12	14	12/24	÷	2/12	+3
57	57	9	11	0/57	÷	2/9	0

Substitutes A rise in the price of a good such as beef would increase the quantity demanded of pork or chicken. This is because pork or chicken are **substitutes** for beef. A substitute is a good which can be replaced by another good. Examples of substitutes for British consumers are:

• Coca-Cola and Pepsi-Cola;
• a holiday in Spain and a holiday in Turkey;
• an Indian takeaway and a Chinese takeaway.

Two goods which are substitutes will have a positive cross elasticity. An increase (positive) in the price of one good such as a holiday in Spain, leads to an increase (positive) in the quantity demanded of a substitute such as a holiday in Turkey.

Complements A rise in price of a good such as cheese would lead to a fall in the quantity demanded of a good such as macaroni. This is because macaroni and cheese are **complements**. A complement is a good which is demanded because it is used with another good. Examples of complements are:

• tennis rackets and tennis balls;
• washing machines and soap powder;
• foreign holidays and sun cream;
• tablets and apps.

Two goods which are complements will have a negative cross elasticity. An increase (positive) in the price of one good such as foreign holidays leads to a fall (negative) in demand for a complement such as sun cream.

Question 4

Table 5 Cross elasticity of demand

	Original		New	
	Quantity demanded of good X	Price of good Y £	Quantity demanded of good X	Price of good Y £
(a)	100	5	180	6
(b)	40	40	13	17
(c)	200	10	170	13
(d)	90	6	30	4
(e)	72	12	54	13
(f)	126	18	140	16

For (a) to (f), calculate the cross elasticity of demand of good X with respect to the price of good Y from the data in Table 5.

However, for many products, the quantity demanded is little affected by the price of some other goods. For example, a rise in the price of soap powder is likely to have little impact on the demand for foreign holidays.

Goods which are not related The demand for some products is unlikely to be affected by the price of other products. For example, a rise in the price of cement is unlikely to have any impact on the demand for chocolate bars. The cross elasticity of two goods which have little relationship to each other would be zero. So a rise in the price of cement of 10 per cent is likely to have no effect (i.e. 0 per cent change) on the demand for chocolate bars. The cross elasticity of demand for cement to the price of chocolate bars is 0% ÷ 10% which is zero.

Key Terms

Complement - a good that is purchased with other goods to satisfy a want. Complements have a negative cross elasticity of demand with each other.
Cross elasticity or cross-price elasticity of demand - a measure of the responsiveness of quantity demanded of one good to a change in price of another good. It is measured by dividing the percentage change in quantity demanded of one good by the percentage change in price of the other good.
Income elasticity of demand - a measure of the responsiveness of quantity demanded to a change in income. It is measured by dividing the percentage change in quantity demanded by the percentage change in income.
Inferior good - a good where demand falls when income increases (i.e. it has a negative income elasticity of demand).
Normal good - a good where demand increases when income increases (i.e. has a positive income elasticity of demand).
Substitute - a good which can be replaced by another to satisfy a want. Substitutes have a positive cross elasticity of demand with each other.

Thinking like an economist

Food substitutes

Many foods are substitutes for each other. Eggs are a substitute for fish; fish is a substitute for meat. Economic theory would suggest that these goods would therefore have a positive cross elasticity of demand. An increase in the price of one would lead to an increase in demand for the substitute good, whilst a fall in price of one good would lead to a fall in demand for another. Equally, some foods are complements. They are consumed together and so a rise in the price of one would lead to a fall in demand for the other. Complements have negative cross elasticities.

Family Food 2011, a report on the 2011 Family Food Module of the Living Costs and Food Survey, gives some evidence for this. Table 6 shows estimates of the cross elasticity of demand for three foods: cheeses, cream and milk. In red, going across diagonally, are the own-price elasticities of demand for each good. For example, the price elasticity of demand for cheese is -0.650 (i.e. it is price inelastic). In black, reading across the rows are the figures for cross elasticity of demand for a product with respect to the price of another. For example, the cross elasticity of demand for cheese with respect to the price of cream is +0.082. The cross elasticity of demand for cream with respect to the price of milk is +1.131.

The data in Table 6 would suggest that milk and cream are substitutes because their cross elasticities are positive. A 10 per cent rise in the price of milk leads to an 11.31 per cent rise in quantity demanded of cream. Interestingly, though, the cross elasticity of demand for milk with respect to the price of cream is almost zero at +0.046.

Table 6 Estimates of price and cross elasticity of demand for cheeses, cream and milk, 2009

	Elasticity with respect to the price of		
	Cheeses	Cream	Milk
Cheeses	-0.650	+0.082	-0.090
Cream	-0.667	-0.582	+1.131
Milk	-0.096	-0.046	-0.827

Source: adapted from Defra, *Family Food 2011*.

When cross elasticities are negative, it shows that goods might be complements to each other. Table 7 shows cross elasticities of demand for different pork products. All but one of the cross elasticities are negative. For example, a 10 per cent rise in the price of pork fillet and steak leads to a 0.039 fall in quantity demanded for pork joints. However, the cross elasticity values are very small, suggesting that different types of pork are only very weak substitutes for each other.

Table 7 Estimates of price and cross elasticity of demand for pork products, 2009

	Elasticity with respect to the price of		
	Joints	Chops	Fillet and steak
Joints	-0.958	-0.013	-0.039
Chops	+0.007	-0.920	-0.023
Fillet and steak	-0.031	-0.031	-1.006

Source: adapted from Defra, *Family Food 2011*.

Where changes in the price of one good have no effect on the quantity demanded of another good, the cross elasticity of demand is zero. Table 8 shows cross elasticities for six food and drinks products. Seven of the nine cross elasticities are zero. For example, a rise in the price of beef, sausages or salmon had no effect on the quantity demanded of fresh vegetables in 2009. The two cross elasticities which were not zero were very close to zero, again suggesting little or no link between price changes in one product and quantity demanded of another.

Table 8 Estimates of price and cross elasticity of demand for six food products, 2009

	Elasticity with respect to the price of		
	Beef	Sausages	Salmon
Cheese	-0.000	-0.000	0.000
Alcohol	-0.003	-0.001	0.000
Fresh vegetables	0.000	-0.000	0.000

Source: adapted from Defra, *Family Food 2011.*

Data Response Question

Clothing, footwear and transport

Decile groups

A population can be split into 10 equal groups. These are called decile groups. In Table 10, on the next page, the groups are households, which are split according to their gross income. So the first decile group is the tenth of households which have the lowest income. The fifth decile group is the tenth of households between 40 and 50 per cent of the total, whilst the tenth decile group is made up of the highest 10 per cent of households by gross income. In Table 10 data for the other seven decile groups are available, but are not printed here in order to simplify the data.

Measuring income elasticity of demand

Income elasticity of demand is measured by dividing the percentage change in quantity demanded of a good or a basket of goods by the percentage change in income of consumers. Quantity demanded is a physical number, like 100 washing machines or 1 000 shirts. However, when data for quantity are not available, a good proxy variable is expenditure. This is quantity times price. If prices remain the same as expenditure changes, then the percentage change in quantity will be the same as the percentage change in expenditure.

Figure 2

Expenditure on clothing and footwear as a percentage of total expenditure by gross income decile group, 2012

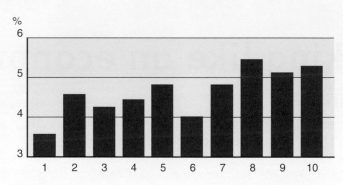

Source: adapted from ONS, *Family Spending* 2013

Figure 3

Expenditure on transport as a percentage of total expenditure by gross income decile group, 2012

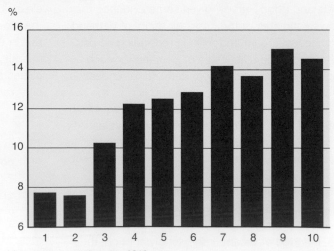

Source: adapted from ONS, *Family Spending* 2013

Gross and disposable income

Gross income is income before income tax, National Insurance contributions and welfare benefits have been taken into account.

Disposable income is equal to gross income minus income tax and employees' National Insurance contributions plus welfare benefits.

Table 9 Clothing and footwear and transport as a percentage of total household expenditure, real disposable income per household, 1980 to 2012

	Clothing and footwear %	Transport %	Real disposable income per household 1980=100
1980	8.1	14.6	100
1995-96	5.9	14.9	129
2012	4.8	13.1	177

Source: adapted from ONS, *Family Spending* 2013.

Table 10 Average weekly expenditure per household on clothing and footwear and transport (£) by gross income decile group, 2012

	First decile	Fifth decile	Tenth decile
Men's outer garments	1.60	3.40	14.20
Men's under garments	0.10	0.40	0.80
Women's outer garments	2.50	7.30	18.50
Women's under garments	0.50	1.10	2.20
Boys' outer garments (5-15)	0.20	0.50	1.60
Girls' outer garments (5-15)	0.30	1.20	1.90
Infants' outer garments (under 5)	0.20	0.70	1.10
Children's under garments (under 16)	0.10	0.50	0.70
Accessories	0.20	0.70	1.90
Haberdashery and clothing hire	0.00	0.10	0.40
Dry cleaners, laundry and dyeing	0.10	0.20	1.10
Footwear	1.30	3.80	11.80
Total clothing and footwear	**7.10**	**19.90**	**56.20**
Purchase of vehicles	2.40	14.10	48.30
Petrol, diesel and other motor oils	5.10	22.10	47.30
Other motoring costs	3.60	10.80	29.00
Rail and tube fares	0.90	1.90	11.70
Bus and coach fares	0.80	1.40	1.60
Combined fares	0.40	0.20	2.30
Other travel and transport	1.30	2.00	13.90
Total transport	**14.50**	**52.50**	**154.10**
Total expenditure per household on all goods and services £	189.30	422.60	1 065.60
Range of total gross income per household £	0-169	438-541	1397+

Source: adapted from ONS, *Family Spending* 2013.

1. Describe how spending on clothing and footwear and on transport (a) varies with income and (b) has changed over time.

2. Using the data, explain whether 'clothing and footwear' is likely to have a higher income elasticity of demand than transport.

3. Using Table 10, explain which components of clothing and footwear and transport are likely to have the highest income elasticities.

4. Using the data in Table 10 and the concept of income elasticity of demand, discuss whether bus and coach transport has a future in the UK.

Evaluation

Look at Table 10 to see what happens to spending on bus and coach fares as different income groups are compared. Does this suggest that bus and coach travel is an inferior good? In the future, average incomes are likely to rise (they have doubled over the past 30 years). Is demand for bus and coach travel likely to rise with this rise in incomes? Looking at Table 10, is car and rail transport likely to replace bus and coach travel?

11 Supply

Key points

1. A rise in price leads to a rise in quantity supplied, shown by a movement along the supply curve.
2. A change in supply can be caused by factors such as a change in costs of production, technology and the price of other goods. This results in a shift in the supply curve.
3. The market supply curve in a perfectly competitive market is the sum of each firm's individual supply curves.

Starter activity

A large mining company is deciding whether to develop a new gold mine in West Africa on land that has been found to contain gold ore deposits. What factors do you think will determine whether it goes ahead with the project and starts to produce gold?

Supply

In any market there are buyers and sellers. Buyers demand goods whilst sellers supply goods. **Supply** in economics is defined as the quantity of goods that sellers are prepared to sell at any given price over a period of time. For instance, in September 2014, UK farmers sold 1.1 billion litres of milk at an average price of 30.81 pence per litre. So economists would say that the supply of milk at 30.81 pence per litre over the one month period was 1.1 billion litres.

Supply and price

If the price of a good increases, how will producers react? Assuming that no other factors have changed, they are likely to expand production to take advantage of the higher prices and the higher profits that they can now make. In general, quantity supplied will rise (there will be an **extension of supply**) if the price of the good also rises, all other things being equal.

This can be shown on a diagram using a supply curve. A supply curve shows the quantity that will be supplied over a period of time at any given price. Consider Figure 1 which shows the supply curve for wheat. Wheat is priced at £110 per tonne. At this price only the most efficient farmers grow wheat. They supply 110 million tonnes per year. However, if the price of wheat rose to £140 per tonne, farmers already growing wheat might increase their acreage of wheat, whilst other non-wheat growing farmers might start to grow wheat. Farmers would do this because at a price of £140 per tonne it is possible to make a profit on production even if costs are higher than at a production level of 110 million units.

A fall in price will lead to a **fall in quantity supplied, or contraction of supply**. This is shown by a **movement along** the supply curve. At a lower price, some firms will cut back on relatively unprofitable production whilst others will stop producing altogether. Some of the latter firms may even go out of business, unable to cover their costs of production from the price received.

An upward sloping supply curve assumes that:
- firms are motivated to produce by profit - so this model does not apply, for instance, to much of what is produced by government;

Figure 1

The supply curve

The supply curve is upward sloping, showing that firms increase production of a good as its price increases. This is because a higher price enables firms to make profit on the increased output whereas at the lower price they would have made a loss on it. Here, an increase in the price of wheat from £110 to £140 per tonne increases quantity supplied from 110 million tonnes to 150 million tonnes per year.

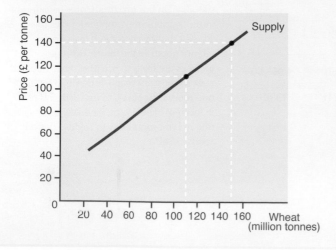

Question 1

Table 1 Price and quantity supplied

Price (£)	Quantity supplied (million units per year)
5	5
10	8
15	11
20	14
25	17

(a) Draw a supply curve from the above data.

(b) Draw new supply curves assuming that quantity supplied at any given price:
   (i) increased by 10 units; (ii) increased by 50 per cent;
   (iii) fell by 5 units; (iv) halved.

• the cost of producing a unit increases as output increases (a situation known as rising marginal cost) - this is not always true but it is likely that the prices of factors of production to the firm will increase as firms bid for more land, labour and capital to increase their output, thus pushing up costs.

Conditions of supply

Changes in price will lead to a change in quantity supplied. These changes are shown by movements along the supply curve. However, there are many other factors apart from price which can cause supply of a product to change. These other factors are collectively called the **conditions of supply**. Changes in the conditions of supply cause a shift in the supply curve either to the right or to the left. The conditions of supply include the costs of production, technology and the prices of other goods.

Costs of production

The supply curve is drawn on the assumption that the general costs of production in the economy remain constant (part of the **ceteris paribus** condition). If other things change, then the supply curve will shift. If the costs of production increase at any given level of output, firms will attempt to pass on these increases in the form of higher prices. If they cannot charge higher prices then profits will fall and firms will produce less of the good or might even stop producing it altogether. A rise in the costs of production will therefore lead to a decrease in supply.

Question 2

Figure 2

Average annual percentage change in earnings

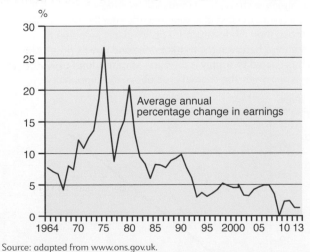

Source: adapted from www.ons.gov.uk.

(a) Explain how a change in earnings can shift the supply curve of a product to the left.

(b) Discuss in which years the supply curves for goods made in the UK are likely to have shifted (i) furthest and (ii) least far to the left according to the data.

Figure 3

A rise in the costs of production

A rise in the costs of production for a firm will push its supply curve upwards and to the left, from S_1 to S_2. For any given quantity supplied, firms will now want a higher price to compensate them for the increase in their costs.

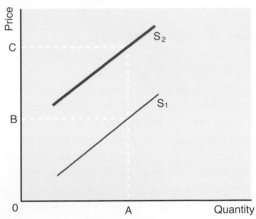

This can be seen in Figure 3. The original supply curve is S_1. A rise in the costs of production means that at any given level of output firms will charge higher prices. At an output level of OA, firms will increase their prices from OB to OC. This increase in prices will be true for all points on the supply curve. So the supply curve will **shift** upwards and to the left to S_2 in Figure 3. There will have been a **fall in supply**. (Note that a fall in quantity supplied refers to a change in **quantity supplied** due to a change in price and would be shown by a movement along the supply curve.) Conversely a fall in the costs of production will lead to an increase in supply of a good. This is shown by a shift to the right in the supply curve.

Technology

Another factor which affects supply of a particular good is the state of technology. The supply curve is drawn on the assumption that the state of technology remains unchanged. If new technology is introduced to the production process it should lead to a fall in the costs of production. This greater **productive efficiency** will encourage firms to produce more at the same price or produce the same amount at a lower price

Question 3

Explain, using supply curves, why it cost £10 000 in 1970 for a machine that could do the same as a calculator which cost £100 in 1975 and £5 today.

or some combination of the two. The supply curve will shift downwards and to the right. It would be unusual for firms to replace more efficient technology with less efficient technology. However, this can occur at times of war or natural disasters. If new technical equipment is destroyed, firms may have to fall back on less efficient means of production, reducing supply at any given price, resulting in a shift in the supply curve to the left.

The prices of other goods

Changes in the prices of some goods can affect the supply of a particular good. For instance, if the price of beef increases substantially there will be an increase in the quantity of beef supplied. More cows will be reared and slaughtered. As a result there will be an increase in the supply of hides for leather. At the same price, the quantity of leather supplied to the market will increase. An increase in the price of beef therefore leads to an increase in the supply of leather. On the other hand, an increase in cattle rearing is likely to be at the expense of production of wheat or sheep farming. So an increase in beef production is likely to lead to a fall in the supply of other agricultural products as farmers switch production to take advantage of higher profits in beef.

Other factors

A number of other factors affect supply. These include:
- the goals of sellers - if for some reason there is a change in the profit levels which a seller expects to receive as a reward for production, then there will be a change in supply; for instance, if an industry such as the book retailing industry went from one made up of many small sellers more interested in selling books than making a profit to one where the industry was dominated by a few large profit-seeking companies, then supply would fall;
- government legislation - anti-pollution controls which raise the costs of production, the abolition of legal barriers to setting up business in an industry, or tax changes, are some examples of how government can change the level of supply in an industry;
- expectations of future events - if firms expect future prices to be much higher, they may restrict supplies and stockpile goods; if they expect disruptions to their future production because of a strike they may stockpile raw materials, paying for them with borrowed money, thus increasing their costs and reducing supply;
- the weather - in agricultural markets, the weather plays a crucial role in determining supply, bad weather reducing supply, good weather producing bumper yields;
- producer cartels - in some markets, producing firms or producing countries band together, usually to restrict supply; this allows them to raise prices and increase their profits or revenues; the best known cartel today is OPEC, which restricts the supply of oil onto world markets.

Producer surplus

The supply curve shows how much will be supplied at any given price. In Figure 4, firms will supply 10 million units at 10p whereas they will supply 25 million units at 20p. Assume that

Question 4

Explain, using diagrams, how you would expect supply of the following goods in 2014 to be affected by the events stated, all other things being equal.

(a) Rubber. Rubber plantations in Laos, first planted in 2007, begin to yield natural rubber in 2014.

(b) Office space in London. The government introduced new regulations in 2013 allowing office space to be converted into dwellings.

(c) Corn. US farmers respond in 2014 to rising prices for soyabeans by increasing their planting soyabeans on land which in 2013 was used to grow corn.

the price that firms receive is actually 20p. Some firms will then receive more than the lowest price at which they are prepared to supply. For instance, one firm was prepared to supply the 10 millionth unit at 10p. The firm receives 20p, which is 10p more. This 10p is producer surplus. It is the difference between the market price which the firm receives and the price at which it is prepared to supply. The total amount of producer surplus earned by firms is shown by the area between the supply curve and horizontal line at the market price. It is the sum of the producer surplus earned at each level of output.

Price elasticity of supply

Price elasticity of demand measures the responsiveness of changes in quantity demanded to changes in price. Equally, the responsiveness of quantity supplied to changes in price

Figure 4

Producer surplus

The supply curve shows how much will be supplied at any given price. Except on the last unit supplied, the supplier receives more for the good than the lowest price at which it is prepared to supply. This difference between the market price and lowest price at which a firm is prepared to supply is producer surplus. Total producer surplus is shown by the shaded area above the supply curve.

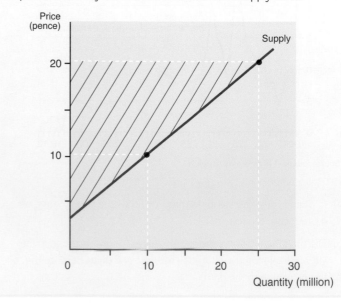

Figure 5

Elasticity of supply

The elasticity of supply of a straight line supply curve varies depending upon the gradient of the line and whether it passes through the origin.

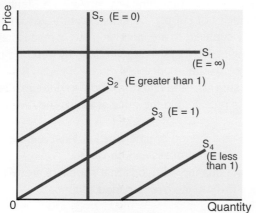

can also be measured - this is called **price elasticity of supply**. The formula for measuring the price elasticity of supply is:

$$\frac{\text{percentage change in quantity supplied}}{\text{percentage change in price}}$$

This is equivalent to:

$$\frac{\Delta Q_s}{Q_s} \div \frac{\Delta P}{P}$$

or

$$\frac{P}{Q_s} \times \frac{\Delta Q_s}{\Delta P}$$

where Q_s is quantity supplied, P is price and Δ is change.

The supply curve is upward sloping (i.e. an increase in price leads to an increase in quantity supplied and vice versa). Therefore price elasticity of supply will be positive because the top and bottom of the formula will be either both positive or both negative.

As with price elasticity of demand, different ranges of elasticity are given different names. Price elasticity of supply is:
- perfectly inelastic (zero) if there is no response in quantity supplied to a change in price;
- inelastic (between zero and one) if there is a less than proportionate response in quantity supplied to a change in price;
- unitary (one) if the percentage change in quantity supplied equals the percentage change in price;
- elastic (between one and infinity) if there is a more than proportionate response in quantity supplied to a change in price;
- perfectly elastic (infinite) if producers are prepared to supply any amount at a given price.

These various elasticities are shown in Figure 5. It should be noted that any straight line supply curve passing through the origin has an elasticity of supply equal to 1. This is best understood if we take the formula:

$$\frac{P}{Q_s} \times \frac{\Delta Q_s}{\Delta P}$$

Question 5

Figure 6

Supply

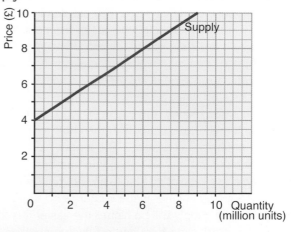

Source: adapted from www.ons.gov.uk.

Calculate from Figure 6 the elasticity of supply of a change in price from: (a) £4 to £6; (b) £6 to £8; (c) £8 to £10; (d) £9 to £7; (e) £7 to £5.

$\Delta Q_s/\Delta P$ is the inverse of (i.e. 1 divided by) the slope of the line, whilst P/Q_s, assuming that the line passes through the origin, is the slope of the line. The two multiplied together must always equal 1.

Determinants of elasticity of supply

As with price elasticity of demand, there are four factors which determine supply elasticity across a wide range of products.

Availability of substitutes Substitutes here are not consumer substitutes but producer substitutes. These are goods which a producer can easily produce as alternatives. For instance, one model of a car is a good producer substitute for another model in the same range because the car manufacturer can easily switch resources on its production line. On the other hand, carrots are not substitutes for cars. The farmer cannot easily switch from the production of carrots to the production of cars. If a product has many substitutes then producers can quickly and easily alter the pattern of production if its price rises or falls. Hence its elasticity of supply will be relatively high. However, if a product has few or no substitutes, then producers will find it difficult to respond flexibly to variations in price. If there is a fall in price, a producer may have no alternative but either to carry on producing much the same quantity as before or withdraw from the market. Price elasticity of supply is therefore low.

Time The shorter the time period, the more difficult producers find it to switch from making one product to another. So in the short term, supply is likely to be more price inelastic than in the long term. There is a number of reasons why this is the case.
- Some items take a long time to make. For example, if there is a crop failure of a product like hazelnuts, it will take until the next growing season to increase supply again whatever price the market sets for hazelnuts in the short term.

- If there is no spare capacity to make more of a product, it will be difficult to increase supply very much even if prices rise sharply. The more spare capacity, the less constraint this places on increasing supply in response to price rises.
- With some products, it is easy and relatively cheap to hold stocks to supply the market when they are demanded. With others, it is impossible to hold stocks. For example, large stocks of wheat are kept around the world which can be released if prices rise, so keeping price elasticity of supply relatively high. However, it is impossible in most cases to store electricity. So when there is a sharp rise in price of electricity in a free market, there is unlikely to be much response in terms of extra supply in the short term if the system is working at full capacity. The longer the time period, the easier it is for the market to build up appropriate stocks or to build excess capacity if stocks are not possible. So price elasticity of supply is higher in the longer term.
- Price elasticity of supply will be higher the easier it is for a firm to switch production from one product to another or for firms to enter the market to make the product.

The short run and the long run

The phrases 'short term' and 'long term' have no precise meaning in economics. For example, 'short term' might be until the next harvest, or the next delivery from China. The long term might be three months or it could be 30 years.

However, **short run** and **long run** have precise meanings in microeconomics. The long run is when all factors of production involved in making a good are variable. This means they can all be changed. The short run is defined as being a period of time

Key Terms

Conditions of supply - factors other than price, such as income or the price of other goods, which lead to changes in supply and are associated with shifts in the supply curve.
Long run - the period of time when all factor inputs can be varied but the state of technology remains constant.
Price elasticity of supply - a measure of the responsiveness of quantity supplied to a change in price. It is measured by dividing the percentage change in quantity supplied by the percentage change in price.
Producer surplus - the difference between the market price which firms receive and the price at which they are prepared to supply.
Short run - the period of time when at least one factor input to the production process can be varied.
Supply - the quantity of goods that suppliers are willing to sell at any given price over a period of time.

when at least one factor of production is fixed. This means it cannot be changed.

For producers, price elasticity of supply is likely to be higher in the long run than in the short run. In the long run, producers can change their methods of production to increase or decrease quantity supplied in response to price changes. In the short run, there could be capacity problems. For example, a producer might not be able to increase production this week or this month because all its machines are in constant use. A coffee grower might not be able to increase supply of coffee beans because it only has a fixed number of coffee bushes.

Thinking like an economist

The supply of new housing

There is a number of different markets within the housing market, each of which has its own supply. One way of subdividing the housing market is into the market for new dwellings and the market for second hand dwellings. Approximately 90 per cent of house sales in the UK are of existing dwellings. The remaining 10 per cent is of new dwellings.

Figure 7 shows that new dwellings are of two types. Most new dwellings are sold privately, either to owner-occupier buyers or as buy-to-let properties. In 2012-13, 109 330 new properties were sold in this way. The other source of new dwellings is 'social landlords'. In practice, this means housing associations. They mainly rent out properties to those for whom owner occupation might be unsuitable. This includes those on below average incomes or the elderly. Social landlords receive most of their funding for new houses from the government. So the supply of new social housing is dependent on the political priorities of governments rather than market forces. Note that local authorities which supply council housing effectively no longer build new houses. Although they own and rent out a large stock of houses, they play little part in the new housing market.

Factors affecting the supply of new private housing

Economic theory would suggest that the supply of new private housing would be affected by a variety of factors including price, costs and government legislation.

Price A rise in the price of new housing should lead to a rise in quantity supplied. Figure 8 shows a peak in the price of new houses in 2007. Rising house prices since 1990 had seen a growth in the supply of new housing to the market as Figure 7 shows. The fall in new property prices in 2008 and 2009 was associated with a slump in new house builds. Despite a rise in house prices from 2010, the number of private sector houses built remained subdued. This would suggest that other factors apart from price were causing the depression in the number of new house builds.

Costs Costs of new housing have risen over time. Figure 9 shows that the price of land for building rose between 1994 and 2008 when there was a sharp drop. The drop in the cost of land for building following 2008 will have contributed to the drop in the price of new dwellings shown in Figure 8. There is a similar pattern shown in Figure 10. Wages of workers in the construction industry rose to 2008, pushing up costs of

Figure 7

Annual completions of new houses: UK

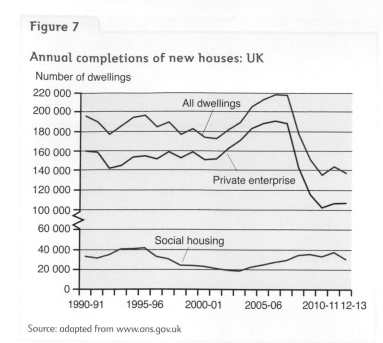

Source: adapted from www.ons.gov.uk

Figure 8

Average prices of new dwellings: UK

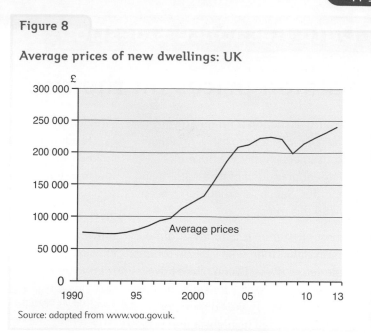

Source: adapted from www.voa.gov.uk.

Figure 9

Average price of building land, £m per hectare[1], UK

Source: adapted from www.communities.gov.uk.
1. 1994-2003 annual figures, 2004-2010 January figures.

Figure 10

Construction: average weekly earnings £, UK

Source: adapted from www.ons.gov.uk.

construction. After 2008, wages stagnated, helping to keep the cost of building new houses constant.

Government regulation House building companies often argue that they would build more houses if only government regulations were relaxed. All new houses need planning permission. The vast majority of the land in the UK which is not already built on is not available for building. A whole variety of restrictions such as Green Belt regulations and limited access to National Parks prevent any sort of development outside urban areas. Even within built-up areas, there is a very limited amount of land available for new house building. Getting planning permission for this land takes years. Initial applications are usually refused because planners feel that the development is inappropriate. The planning regime therefore ensures that house builders cannot respond quickly to large changes in house prices. If the planning regime were relaxed, this would push the supply curve for new housing to the right, allowing more houses to be built at the same price.

Technology Some argue that the supply of housing could increase if UK house builders adopted new technology in their construction techniques. In the UK, the typical dwelling is still built using bricks and mortar. On the Continent and in the USA, many houses are built using pre-fabricated techniques where much of the dwelling is built off site and then assembled on-site. These techniques, it is argued, would produce lower cost houses, pushing the supply curve to the right.

The supply of new housing is a major political issue in the UK. The environmental and rural lobbies argue that almost all new housing must be built within existing urban areas to prevent the 'concreting over' of the UK. Planning regulations effectively ensure that this is what actually occurs. The result is that the lack of supply forces building land prices up and increases the cost of new homes. The only way to increase supply substantially would be to ease planning restrictions, building in what is now countryside. This is unlikely to occur in the immediate future given the strength of the environmental and rural lobbies.

Data Response Question

Salmon prices on the rise

The price of salmon is on an upward trend. Demand for the fish is growing as consumers worldwide have a greater appreciation of its health-giving properties. Supply is struggling to keep up with this trend.

Almost all salmon sold today is farmed salmon rather than wild salmon caught in the sea or rivers. Rising prices have led to increased profits for salmon farmers. Norway Royal Salmon, for example, reported its highest profits in its 21-year history in 2013.

However, despite the incentive of rising profits, there are factors which are holding back the expansion of the industry. In Norway, the largest producer of farmed salmon, production by private firms is restricted by the government, which issues licences.

There is also a limit on the number of salmon which can be farmed in one place because of the risk of disease.

Worldwide, the price of fish feed is rising as a result of more fish farming and limited catches of anchovies, an important source of fish feed.

The weather too can impact on supply. In 2013, Norway suffered colder than usual seawater which inhibited the growth of salmon and so the total tonnage of salmon produced fell.

Source: adapted from © the *Financial Times* 15.3.2014, All Rights Reserved.

Evaluation

Question 3 asks how easily the quantity supplied of salmon can be changed in response to changes in its price. In your answer, write about the short term - if the price of salmon doubled today, for example, could the quantity supplied of salmon double in the next year? What are the constraints on increasing supply? Then consider the long term. What are the constraints on increasing supply and how important are they? Come to an overall conclusion about the short term and long term.

1. Using Figure 11, identify two significant features of the data shown. In your answer, back up your comments with data.

2. Using supply curve diagrams, explain the effects on the supply of salmon of the following described in the article:
   (a) a change in profits by fish farmers;
   (b) licences issued by governments to salmon farmers;
   (c) a change in fish feed prices;
   (d) changes in the weather.

3. Discuss whether the price elasticity of supply of salmon is likely to be high or low.

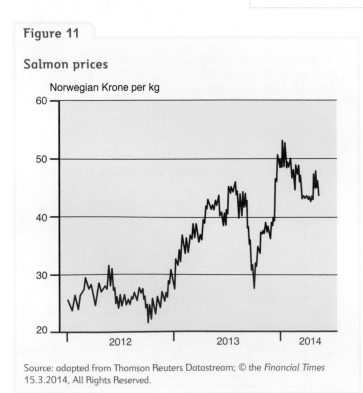

Figure 11

Salmon prices

Source: adapted from Thomson Reuters Datastream; © the *Financial Times* 15.3.2014, All Rights Reserved.

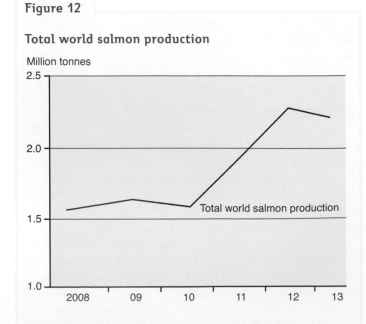

Figure 12

Total world salmon production

Source: adapted from Food and Agriculture Organization of the United Nations, *GLOBEFISH HIGHLIGHTS, January-Sept 2014*, 31.1.2015, Rome, Italy. Reproduced with permission.

12 Price determination

Key points

1. The equilibrium or market clearing price is set where demand equals supply.
2. Changes in demand and supply will lead to new equilibrium prices being set.
3. A change in demand will lead to a shift in the demand curve, a movement along the supply curve and a new equilibrium price.
4. A change in supply will lead to a shift in the supply curve, a movement along the demand curve and a new equilibrium price.
5. Markets do not necessarily tend towards the equilibrium price.
6. Changes in supply and demand will affect consumer and producer surplus.
7. The equilibrium price is not necessarily the price which will lead to the greatest economic efficiency or the greatest equity.

Starter activity

Do you eat your 'five a day' - five portions of fruit and vegetables? What is your favourite fruit? What is its price? How is this price determined? To answer that, you need to think about demand for and supply of the fruit.

Equilibrium price

Buyers and sellers come together in a market. A price (sometimes called the **market price**) is struck and goods or services are exchanged. Consider Table 1. It shows the demand and supply schedule for a good at prices between £2 and £10.

- If the price is £2, demand will be 12 million units but only two million units will be supplied. Demand is greater than supply and there is therefore **excess demand** (i.e. too much demand in relation to supply) in the market. There will be a **shortage** of products on the market. Some buyers will be lucky and they will snap up the two million units being sold. But there will be a 10 million unit shortfall in supply for the rest of the unlucky buyers in the market. For instance, it is not possible to buy some luxury cars without being on a waiting list for several years because current demand is too great.
- If the price is £10, buyers will not buy any goods. Sellers on the other hand will wish to supply 10 million units. Supply is greater than demand and therefore there will be **excess supply**. There will be a glut or surplus of products on the market. 10 million units will remain unsold. A sale in a shop is often evidence of excess supply in the past. Firms tried to sell the goods at a higher price and failed.
- There is only one price where demand equals supply. This is at a price of £6 where demand and supply are both six million units. This price is known as the **equilibrium price**. This is the only price where the demand of buyers equals the supply of sellers in the market. It is also known as the **market-clearing price** because all the products supplied to the market are bought or cleared from the market, but no buyers are left frustrated in their wishes to buy goods.

An alternative way of expressing the data in Table 1 is shown in Figure 1. The equilibrium price is where demand equals supply. This happens where the two curves cross, at a price of

Table 1 A demand and supply schedule

Price (£)	Quantity demanded (million units per month)	Quantity supplied (million units per month)
2	12	2
4	9	4
6	6	6
8	3	8
10	0	10

£6 and a quantity of six million units. If the price is above £6, supply will be greater than demand and therefore excess supply will exist. If the price is below £6, demand is greater than supply and therefore there will be excess demand.

Changes in demand and supply

It is explained in Unit 8 and Unit 11 that a change in price would lead to a change in quantity demanded or supplied, shown by a movement along the demand or supply curve. A change in any other variable, such as income or the costs of production,

Figure 1

Equilibrium

At £6, the quantity demanded is equal to the quantity supplied. The market is said to be in equilibrium at this price.

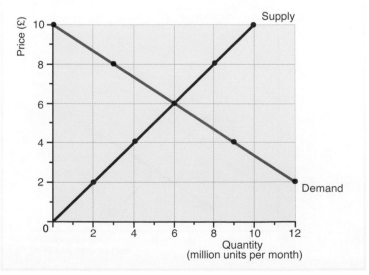

would lead to an **increase** or **decrease** in demand or supply and therefore a **shift** in the demand or supply curve.

Demand and supply diagrams provide a powerful and simple tool for analysing the effects of changes in demand and supply on equilibrium price and quantity.

Consider the effect of a rise in consumer incomes. This will lead to an increase in the demand for a normal good. In Figure 2(a) this will push the demand curve from D_1 to D_2. As can be seen from the diagram, the equilibrium price rises from P_1 to P_2. The quantity bought and sold in equilibrium rises from Q_1 to Q_2. The model of demand and supply predicts that an increase in incomes, all other things being equal (the **ceteris paribus** condition), will lead to an increase both in the price of the product and in the quantity sold. Note that the increase in income **shifts** the demand curve and this then leads to a **movement along** the supply curve.

Figure 2(b) shows the market for televisions in the early 2000s. In the early 2000s, many manufacturers introduced flat screen, slimline televisions. As a result, there was a boom in sales of these televisions and a slump in sales of older, more bulky sets. In economic terms the demand for older, bulky sets fell. This is shown by a shift to the left in the demand curve.

Question 1

Table 2 Demand and supply

Price (£)	Quantity demanded (million units)	Quantity supplied (million units)
30	20	70
20	50	50
10	80	30

(a) Plot the demand and supply curves shown in Table 2 on a diagram.

(b) What is the equilibrium price?

(c) In what price range is there
   (i) excess demand and
   (ii) excess supply?

(d) Will there be a glut or a shortage in the market if the price is:
   (i) £10; (ii) £40; (iii) £22; (iv) £18; (v) £20?

The equilibrium level of sales in Figure 2(b) falls from OB to OA whilst equilibrium price falls from OF to OE. Note again that a shift in the demand curve leads to a movement along the supply curve.

Figure 2

Shifts in the demand and supply curves

Shifts in the demand or supply curves for a product will change the equilibrium price and the equilibrium quantity bought and sold.

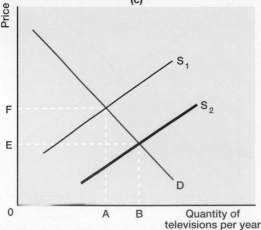

(a)

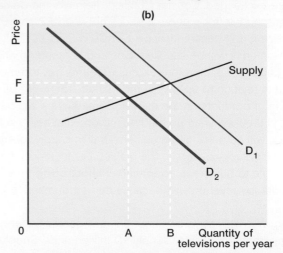

(b)

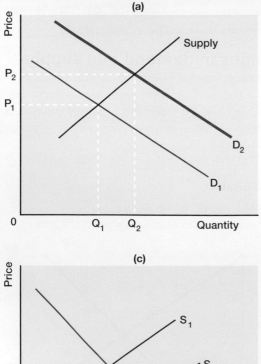

(c)

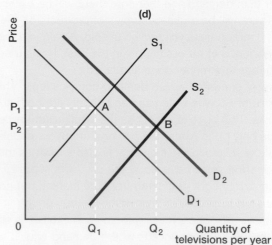

(d)

Prices of television sets have fallen since the 1970s. The main reason for this was an increase in productive efficiency due to the introduction of new technology, enabling costs of production to fall. A fall in costs of production is shown by the shift to the right in the supply curve in Figure 2(c). At any given quantity of output, firms will be prepared to supply more television sets to the market. The result is an increase in quantity bought and sold from 0A to 0B and a fall in price from 0F to 0E. Note that there is a shift in the supply curve which leads to a movement along the demand curve.

So far we have assumed that only one variable changes and that all other variables remain constant. However, in the real world, it is likely that several factors affecting demand and supply will change at the same time. Demand and supply diagrams can be used to some extent to analyse several changes. For instance, in the 2000s the demand for flat screen and high definition (HD) television sets increased due to rising real incomes. At the same time, supply increased too because of an increase in productive efficiency. Overall, the price of television sets fell slightly. This is shown in Figure 2(d). Both the demand and supply curves shift to the right. This will lead to an increase in quantity bought and sold. In theory, depending upon the extent of the shifts in the two curves, there could be an increase in price, a fall in price or no change in the price. Figure 2(d) shows the middle of these three possibilities.

Do markets clear?

It is very easy to assume that the equilibrium price is either the current market price or the price towards which the market moves. Neither is correct. The market price could be at any level. There could be excess demand or excess supply at any point in time.

Question 2

The Olympic Torch was carried by around 8 000 people up and down the UK in the run-up to the 2012 London Olympic Games. Torch bearers were given the opportunity to buy their torch for £215. Almost immediately after the first torches were carried, a 2012 Olympic torch appeared on eBay, the electronic auction site, with a price tag of £150 000. More appeared for auction and prices of around £10 000 were being paid. In the long term, these sorts of prices are unlikely to be maintained. By 2014, torches were being offered for sale on eBay for £2 300 and the price is likely to fall further. Torches from the 2008 Beijing Olympics are selling for around £2 000 on eBay, for example. A rarer torch from the 1948 London Olympics recently sold for £6 250 at a Christie's auction. Only 1 720 torches were made for the 1948 Olympics.

Source: adapted from © the *Financial Times* 26.5.2012, All Rights Reserved.

(a) Explain, using a demand and supply diagram, how the second hand price of a 2012 Olympic torch is set.

(b) Why were the first few 2012 Olympic torches sold likely to have a higher price than 2012 Olympic torches sold in 2014?

(c) Explain, using a demand and supply diagram, why it is likely that, in ten years time, a 1948 Olympic torch is likely to fetch a higher price at auction than a 2012 Olympic torch.

Nor will market prices necessarily tend to change to their equilibrium prices over time. One of the most important controversies in economics today is the extent to which markets tend towards market-clearing prices.

The argument put forward by neo-classical free market economists is that markets do tend to clear. Let us take the example of the coffee market. In this market, there are many producers (farmers, manufacturers, wholesalers and retailers) that are motivated by the desire to make as large a profit as possible. When there is excess demand for coffee (demand is greater than supply), coffee producers will be able to increase their prices and therefore their profits and still sell all they produce. If there is excess supply (supply is greater than demand), some coffee will remain unsold. Producers then have a choice. Either they can offer coffee for sale at the existing price and risk not selling it or they can lower their price to the level where they will sell everything offered. If all producers choose not to lower their prices, there is likely to be even greater pressure to reduce prices in the future because there will be unsold stocks of coffee overhanging the market. Therefore when there is excess demand, prices will be driven upwards whilst prices will fall if there is excess supply.

This can be shown diagrammatically. In Figure 3, there is excess demand at a price of OE. Buyers want to purchase AC more of coffee than is being supplied. Shops, manufacturers and coffee growers will be able to increase their prices and their production and still sell everything they produce. If they wish to sell all their output, they can increase their prices to a maximum of OF and their output to a maximum OB, the market-clearing price and production levels. This they will do because at higher prices and production levels they will be able to make more profit. If there is excess supply, coffee producers will be left with unsold stocks. At a price of OG, output left unsold will be AC. Producers in a free market cannot afford to build up stocks forever. Some producers will lower prices and the rest will be forced to follow. Production and prices will go on falling until

Figure 3

The operation of market forces in the coffee market

Market pressure will tend to force down coffee prices when there is excess supply, such as at price OG, but force up coffee prices when there is excess demand, such as at price OE.

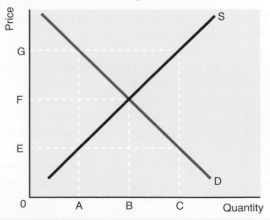

Question 3

The rent on office buildings in London has been increasing fast as the economy has recovered from recession according to newspaper sources. In 2013, for example, rents in the West End of London were up nine per cent, with prime office space at £120 per square foot. However, rents in the City of London, the financial heart of the capital, have fallen behind. Rents were up less than five per cent, with prime office space at £59.50 per square foot.

In the West End of London, with fairly inelastic supply of prime office space, the increase in rents has been driven by increased demand from a variety of industries such as technology, media and creative businesses. The City of London, in contrast, is dominated by financial companies many of which are still suffering from the after-effects of the financial crash of 2008. Demand for office space in the City is still increasing but not as much as in the rest of London. Also, a number of large office developments, such as the Shard, have recently been completed in the City. This has increased supply of office space. Rather than letting out these new developments at knock-down rents, developers have preferred to allow office space to remain empty. By March 2014, less than one third of the Shard which opened in February 2013, had been let. Until this excess supply of office space has been rented out, City of London rent increases are likely to lag behind those in the rest of London.

Source: adapted from © the *Financial Times* 3.3.2014, All Rights Reserved.

(a) Using demand and supply diagrams, explain why rents were increasing more slowly in the City of London than in the rest of the capital.

(b) Using another demand and supply diagram, explain why there is excess supply of office space in the City.

equilibrium output and price is reached. This is usually referred to as a **stable equilibrium** position.

These pressures which force the market towards an equilibrium point are often called **free market forces**. However, critics of the market mechanism argue that free market forces can lead away from the equilibrium point in many cases. In other markets, it is argued that market forces are too weak to restore equilibrium. Some economists give the labour market as an example of this. In other markets, there are many forces such as government legislation, trade unions and multinational monopolies which more than negate the power of the market.

Consumer and producer surplus

Consumer and producer surplus can be shown on a demand and supply diagram. In Figure 4, the equilibrium price is OJ. Consumer surplus, the difference between how much buyers are prepared to pay for a good and what they actually pay, is the area JHG. Producer surplus, the difference between the market price which firms receive and the price at which they are prepared to supply, is shown by the area JGF.

The amounts of consumer and producer surplus will change if either demand or supply change. For example, in Figure 5, demand increases, shown by a shift to the right in the demand curve. For suppliers, an increase in demand results in higher equilibrium output and higher prices. Suppliers will experience an increase in producer surplus from FGJ to FKM shown in Figure 5(a). For consumers, the increase in demand shows that they are prepared to pay a higher price for the same quantity bought. They place a greater value on the good. So their consumer surplus also increases, from JGH to MKL shown in Figure 5(b). Conversely, if there is a fall in demand, shown by a shift to the left in the demand curve, consumer and producer surplus will both fall.

Figure 6 shows what happens if the supply increases, shown by a shift to the right in the supply curve. For suppliers, an increase in supply results in higher equilibrium output but lower prices. Suppliers will experience an increase in producer surplus from JKH to FGM shown in Figure 6(a). For consumers, the increase in supply will lead to an increase in quantity bought. So their consumer surplus also increases from HKL to MGL shown in Figure 6(b). Conversely, if there is a fall in supply, shown by a shift to the left in the supply curve, consumer and producer surplus will both fall.

Figure 4

Consumer and producer surplus

Consumer surplus is the shaded area JGH, showing how much more consumers are prepared to pay for buying a total of 0A goods. Producer surplus is FGJ, showing how much less they would have been prepared to accept in revenue for supplying 0A than they actually received.

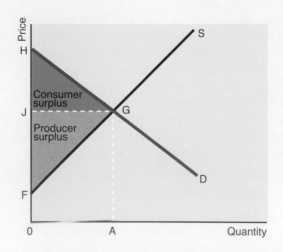

Figure 5

Changing consumer and producer surplus with a rise in demand

A rise in demand from D_1 to D_2 increases producer surplus from FGJ to FKM and consumer surplus from JGH to MKL.

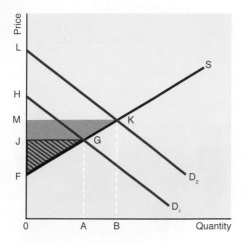

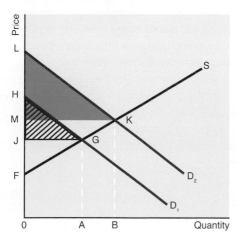

Figure 6

Changing consumer and producer surplus with a rise in supply

A rise in supply from S_1 to S_2 increases producer surplus from JKH to FGM and consumer surplus from HKL to MGL.

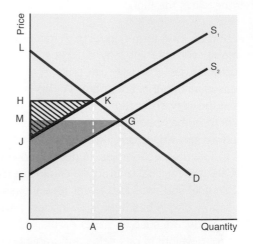

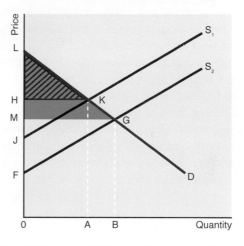

Points to note

Equilibrium is a very powerful concept in economics but it is essential to remember that the equilibrium price is unlikely to be the most desirable price or 'right' price in the market. The most desirable price in the market will depend upon how one defines 'desirable'. It may be, for instance, the one which leads to the greatest economic efficiency, or it may be the one which leads to greatest equity. Alternatively it may be the one which best supports the defence of the country.

Demand can also equal supply without there being equilibrium. At any point in time, what is actually bought must equal what is actually sold. There can be no sellers without buyers. So actual demand (more often referred to as realised or ex post demand in economics) must always equal actual (or **realised** or **ex-post**) supply. Equilibrium occurs at a price where there is no tendency to change. Price will not change if, at the current price, the quantity that consumers wish to buy (called **planned** or **desired** or **ex-ante** demand) is equal to the quantity that suppliers wish to sell (called planned or desired or ex-ante supply).

Therefore only in equilibrium will planned demand equal planned supply.

Key Terms

Equilibrium price - the price at which there is no tendency to change because planned (or desired or ex ante) purchases (i.e. demand) are equal to planned sales (i.e. supply).
Excess demand - where demand is greater than supply.
Excess supply - where supply is greater than demand.
Free market forces - forces in free markets which act to reduce prices when there is excess supply and raise prices when there is excess demand.
Market-clearing price - the price at which there is neither excess demand nor excess supply but where everything offered for sale is purchased.

Thinking like an economist

The price of gas

The world price of gas has a direct impact on households in the UK. The higher the price, the higher the gas bills for households tend to be.

Most gas is sold on long-term contracts. A gas producer, like Shell or ExxonMobil, will enter into, say, a 10 year or 20 year deal to sell a customer gas at a particular price. A relatively small percentage of gas is sold in the 'spot market'. This is the market for sales of gas in the very short term.

The long-term trend has been for demand for gas to grow as Figure 7 shows. Fast growing emerging countries like China are demanding gas to fuel their economies. In developed countries, gas is being substituted for coal to produce electricity. Gas is a cleaner fuel than coal and produces fewer greenhouse gas emissions. The supply of gas has been growing too, particularly from Middle East producers such as Saudi Arabia.

The high cost of developing gas fields and transporting gas has tended to push up world gas spot prices over time as Figure 8 shows. However, gas prices in the USA have fallen on average over the past few years because of fracking. This is a relatively new technology which involves pushing water at high pressure into gas bearing rocks and collecting the gas released.

If there were no costs involved in the transportation of gas, gas prices in different parts of the world would be the same, all other things being equal. However, in the USA, transportation infrastructure has not kept up with growth in gas production. There are not enough pipelines or plants to convert gas into a liquid for transportation by ship to get more gas onto world

markets. The gas therefore has to be sold relatively locally in the USA. This has increased supply relative to demand, pushing down gas prices in the USA at a time when gas prices in other markets, such as Japan or Europe, have been rising.

In the long term, countries like the UK, Poland and Russia would like to extract gas through fracking. In the short term, however, the USA is the only country with a sizeable fracking sector. Low gas prices are likely to persist in the USA over the next ten years whilst gas prices in other markets are likely to be much higher.

Figure 7

World production and consumption of gas by region

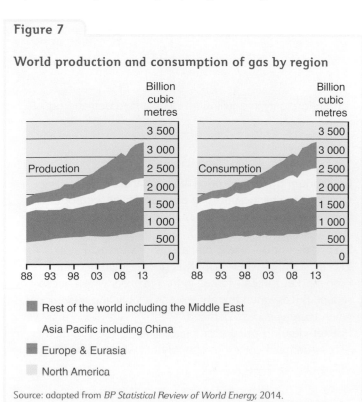

- Rest of the world including the Middle East
- Asia Pacific including China
- Europe & Eurasia
- North America

Source: adapted from *BP Statistical Review of World Energy*, 2014.

Figure 8

World gas prices

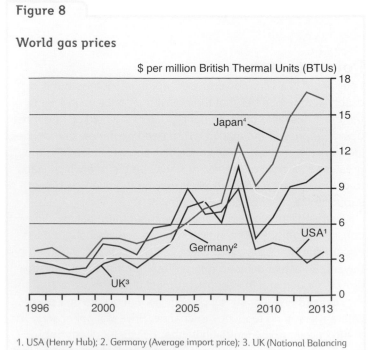

1. USA (Henry Hub); 2. Germany (Average import price); 3. UK (National Balancing Point); 4. Japan (Liquified Natural Gas)

Source: adapted from *BP Statistical Review of World Energy*, 2014.

Data Response Question

Cocoa bean prices

The raw ingredient for the chocolate we buy in the shops is cocoa beans. The world's largest producer of beans is Ivory Coast in Africa, although the cocoa tree is native to Central and South America. Most traders and buyers in the cocoa bean market agree that there will be supply shortages of beans in the next few years. Demand is rising rapidly in emerging markets such as China and India. Over the past five years, India has seen sales more than double from 54 700 tonnes to 129 200 tonnes, while China's rose 41 per cent to 192 500 tonnes. Demand is also recovering in the rich developed world after the prolonged recession following the 2008 financial crisis.

Cocoa beans can be stored from year to year. Rising prices will encourage those holding stocks to sell into the market. Rising prices will also encourage farmers to plant more cocoa trees but these take four to five years to grow before they will yield their first harvest. In the short term, supply is therefore crucially dependent on weather conditions. Recent good harvests in Ivory Coast as well as release from stocks have helped increased supply.

However, this has not been enough to stop a rise in prices.

Analysts are expecting demand to exceed supply for the next few years with the balance being met by sales from stocks. This will inevitably put upward pressure on prices.

Source: adapted from www.imf.org; the *Financial Times* 29.1.2014, All Rights Reserved.

Q

1. Identify two significant features of the change in cocoa bean prices between 2007 and 2014.

2. Explain, using demand and supply diagrams, three factors which are likely to affect the price of cocoa beans from 2014 onwards.

3. Evaluate whether cocoa farmers should be planting new cocoa trees from 2014.

Evaluation

In your answer, using demand and supply analysis, explain what would have to happen for extra production to be profitable, or not to be profitable, for farmers. Weigh up which of these is most important and which is most likely to occur.

Figure 9

Cocoa price

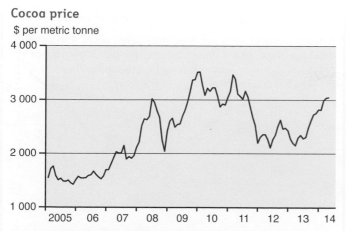

Source: adapted from Thomson Reuters Datastream; © the *Financial Times* 29.1.2014, All Rights Reserved.

Figure 10

Cocoa supply and demand balance

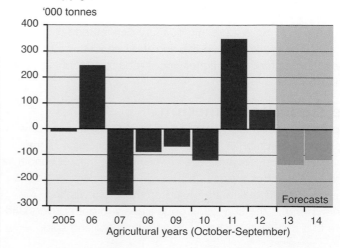

Note: + indicates excess supply, - indicates excess demand

Source: adapted from Thomson Reuters Datastream; © the *Financial Times* 29.1.2014, All Rights Reserved.

13 The price mechanism

Key points

1. Prices have three main functions in allocating resources. These are the rationing, signalling and incentive functions.

Starter activity

It is the end of December and it is sales time in the shops. Prices of your favourite purchases have been cut in half. What signals does this send to you? How have your incentives to buy changed? What do low prices say about the scarcity of the product?

The price mechanism

The price mechanism in a market economy allocates resources between conflicting uses. In a market, there are buyers who demand goods and sellers who supply goods. The interactions of demand and supply fix the price at which exchange takes place. The forces of demand and supply also determine how much is bought and sold and by whom.

Price has three important functions in allocating resources in a market: a **rationing function**; a **signalling function**; and an **incentive function**.

The rationing function

Consumer wants are infinite, but we live in a world of scarce resources. Somehow, those scarce resources need to be allocated between competing uses. One function of price in a market is to allocate and ration those resources. If many consumers demand a good, but its supply is relatively scarce, then prices will be high. Limited supply will be rationed to those buyers prepared to pay a high enough price. If demand is relatively low, but supply is very high, then prices will be low. The low price ensures that high numbers of goods will be bought, reflecting the lack of scarcity of the good. This can be shown on a diagram. In Figure 1, there is a fall in supply of a good from S_1 to S_2. As a result, quantity demanded falls from OB to OA. The movement up the demand curve shows the effect of the rationing function. Higher prices lead to a rationing of the good to buyers.

The signalling function

The price of a good is a key piece of information to both buyers and sellers in the market. Prices come about because of the transactions of buyers and sellers. They reflect market conditions and therefore act as a signal to those in the market. Decisions about buying and selling are based on those signals. In Figures 1 and 2, the change in price signals to both buyers and sellers that they should change quantity bought and sold.

Incentive

Prices act as an incentive for buyers and sellers. Low prices encourage buyers to purchase more goods. For consumers, this is because the amount of satisfaction or utility gained per pound spent increases relative to other goods. Higher prices

Figure 1

The rationing and signalling function of price

A fall in supply leads to higher equilibrium prices. This signals that buyers and sellers should change their behaviour. High prices also ration the good amongst buyers, shown by the movement up the demand curve to a new equilibrium.

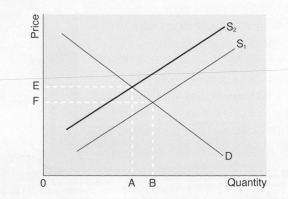

discourage buying because consumers get fewer goods per pound spent. On the supply side, higher prices encourage suppliers to sell more to the market. Firms may have to take on more workers and invest in new capital equipment to achieve this. Low prices discourage production. A prolonged fall in prices may drive some firms out of the market because it is no longer profitable for them to supply. This can be shown on a diagram. In Figure 2, there is a rise in demand for a good from

Figure 2

The signalling and incentive function of prices

A rise in demand leads to higher equilibrium prices. This signals that buyers and sellers should change their behaviour. Higher prices also act as an incentive for sellers to supply. They will increase the amount they supply to the market.

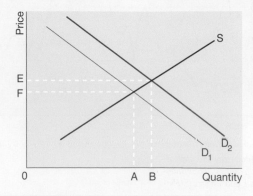

D_1 to D_2. As a result, quantity supplied rises from OA to OB. The movement up the supply curve shows the effect of the incentive function. Higher prices are an incentive for firms to increase supply.

To illustrate how these functions help allocate resources, consider two examples.

Example 1 Assume that the demand for fur coats falls because of lobbying from animal welfare groups. The demand curve for fur coats therefore shifts to the left. At the old price, more is supplied than is now demanded, i.e. there is excess supply. The equilibrium price will then fall. The lower price is a **signal** to manufacturers of fur coats that market conditions have changed for the worse. The lower price reduces incentives for fur coat manufacturers. Lower prices indicate that their profits will fall. Hence, they will make fewer fur coats, shown by the movement down the supply curve.

Example 2 Assume that the supply of oil falls. The supply curve for oil therefore shifts to the left. At the old equilibrium price, there is excess demand. The equilibrium price will then

rise with less oil being supplied and demanded. The higher price is a **signal** to buyers and sellers that market conditions have changed. The new higher price also **rations** oil amongst buyers shown by the movement up the demand curve for oil. Some consumers of oil will be priced out of the market altogether. Others will cut back on their purchases of oil.

Thinking like an economist

Motor cars

The history of the UK motor car industry in recent decades is a good example of how markets allocate resources. In the 1950s and 1960s, the British market was insulated to a great extent from foreign competition. The British motorist bought cars made in British factories, even if some of these factories were owned by foreign companies, such as Ford. It was largely a sellers' market, with demand constrained by the ability of consumers to obtain credit for the purchase of cars.

The 1970s and 1980s, however, were disastrous for the British car industry. British-made cars tended to be both of inferior quality in production and design to foreign made,

Figure 3

Annual production and sale of cars, UK (millions)

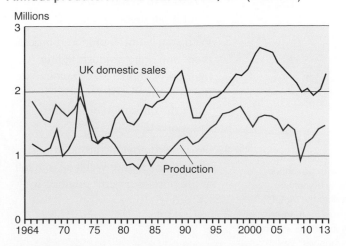

Source: adapted from Economic & Labour Market Review, Office for National Statistics; Motor Industry Facts 2012, Society of Motor Manufacturers and Traders (SMMT).

imported cars. High costs of production, due to high wages, a lack of investment and inefficient working practices, led to low profits or losses for UK car plants. The result, as Figures 3 and 4 show, was falling production, falling exports and increased imports. The market was signalling that the UK was a poor location to make cars. Low profits and losses provided an incentive for UK car factory owners to reduce production or close plants.

The turning point came in the mid-1980s with the arrival of Japanese manufacturers in the UK. Honda, Nissan and Toyota all set up new car plants. By using the same production methods as in Japanese factories, cars were produced at internationally competitive costs and quality. This new competition forced US and European car manufacturers in the UK market to change the way in which they designed and built cars. Today, there is no UK-owned mass manufacturer of vehicles. However, there is a number of foreign-owned car plants in the UK that are highly successful. Nissan's Sunderland car plant, for example, has one of the highest productivity (output per worker) levels in the world.

Figures 3 and 4 show both production and sales of cars in the UK fell significantly when the world economy went into recession in 2008. A shift to the left in the demand curve for cars led to both a fall in production and a fall in the average price of cars sold. The fall in demand signalled to car manufacturers that they should cut back production. The movement down the supply curve, with falling profits, was the incentive for firms to cut production both in the UK and worldwide.

Source: adapted from Thomson Reuters Datastream; © the *Financial Times* 24.7.2014, 18.12.2014, All Rights Reserved.

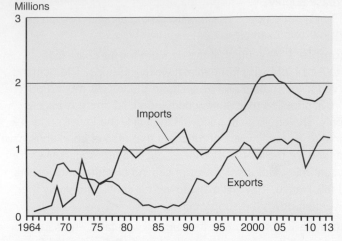

Figure 4

Annual exports and imports of cars, UK (millions)

Source: adapted from Economic & Labour Market Review, Office for National Statistics; Motor Industry Facts 2012, Society of Motor Manufacturers and Traders (SMMT)

Data Response Question

Organic farming in decline

The amount of land used for organic products is still in decline. A quarter of organic pig and lamb producers said prices for their products were 'definitely not' high enough to sustain organic production according to a survey carried out by the Organic Research Centre. Producers of other organic meat and dairy products too have been complaining about the prices they receive. One major problem to hit organic farmers has been the high prices they have to pay for animal feeds, which have contributed to falling profits.

The body which represents organic farmers, warned that rising demand for organic dairy and meat products by consumers coupled with falling output risked increasing the amount of organic food which was imported into the UK.

Source: adapted from © the *Financial Times* 13.3.2014, All Rights Reserved.

Figure 5

Organically managed land in the UK ('000 hectares)

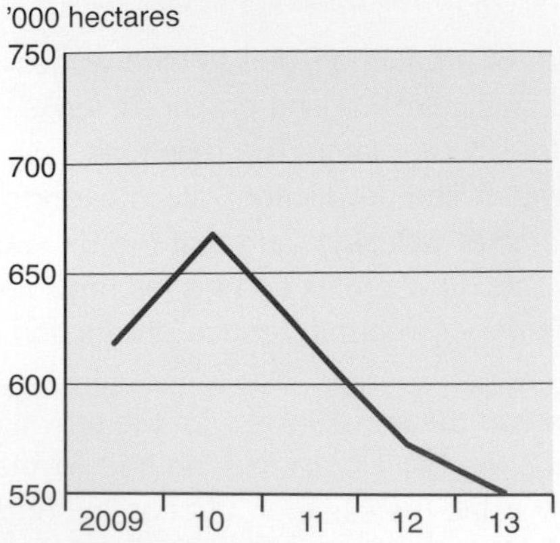

'000 hectares

Source: adapted from www.gov.uk.

Evaluation

For question 4, start by analysing the data using demand and supply diagrams. Are the increased imports happening with no change in UK output? Or are potentially higher UK prices for organic produce providing a signal to overseas buyers and an incentive for them to sell into the UK? Are imports the result of price changes or the cause of price changes? Weigh the different possibilities for your evaluation.

Q

1. What has happened to the amount of land used for organic farming in the UK in recent years? Give evidence from the data to support your answer.

2. Explain, using a diagram, how the signalling and incentive functions have acted to change the allocation of resources in the market for organic pig meat.

3. With supply of UK-produced organic meat and dairy products falling, their prices should rise. Explain how the rationing function will then affect the allocation of resources in this market.

4. Discuss whether increased imports of organic produce will lead to a fall in the price of organic products in UK shops.

14 Indirect taxes and subsidies

Key points

1. Indirect taxes can be either ad valorem taxes or specific taxes.
2. The imposition of an indirect tax is likely to lead to a rise in the unit price of a good which is less than the unit value of the tax.
3. The incidence of indirect taxation is likely to fall on both consumer and producer.
4. The more elastic the demand curve or the more inelastic the supply curve, the greater will be the incidence of tax on producers and the less will be the incidence of tax on consumers.
5. Tax revenues from an indirect tax will be greater the more inelastic the demand for the product.
6. Subsidies will lower the price of a good for consumers, but not all of the subsidy will be received by consumers because some will be received by producers.

Starter activity

The government announces a new sugar and fat tax that will increase the standard rate of Value Added Tax (VAT) on selected products from its current 20 per cent to 30 per cent. These products include fizzy drinks and chocolate bars. What is Value Added Tax and how is it calculated? By how many per cent do you think the price of these products will increase in shops? Will it have any impact on consumption of these items?

Indirect taxes and subsidies

An indirect tax is a tax on expenditure. The two major indirect taxes in the UK are VAT and excise duties.

VAT is an example of an **ad valorem tax**. The tax levied increases in proportion to the value of the tax base. In the case of VAT, the tax base is the price of the good. Most goods in the UK carry a 20 per cent VAT charge. Excise duties, on the other hand, are an example of a **specific** or **unit** tax. The amount of tax levied does not change with the value of the goods but with the amount or volume of the goods purchased. So the excise duty on a bottle of wine is the same whether the bottle costs £5 or £500, but the VAT is 100 times more on the latter compared to the former. The main excise duties in the UK are on alcohol, tobacco and petrol. They should not be confused with customs duties which are levied on imports.

A **subsidy** is a grant given by government to encourage the production or consumption of a particular good or service. Subsidies, for instance, may be given on essential items such as housing or bread. Alternatively, they may be given to firms that employ disadvantaged workers such as the long-term unemployed or people with disabilities. They may also be given to firms manufacturing domestically produced goods to help them be more competitive than imported goods.

Question 1

The price of a litre of unleaded petrol at the pumps is made up as follows.

	Pence
Petrol cost before tax	57.0
Excise duty	58.0
	115.0
VAT @20%	23.0
Price at the pumps	138.0

For each of the following changes, calculate the new price of petrol. For each change, assume that the price at the pumps is initially 138p.

(a) An increase in the cost of crude oil pushed up the cost of petrol before tax from 57p to 62p.

(b) The government increased excise duty from 58p to 62p.

(c) VAT was reduced from 20 per cent to 15 per cent.

(d) The government removed both excise duties and VAT on petrol and instead introduced a subsidy of 2p a litre.

Figure 1

The incidence of a specific tax

The imposition of an indirect tax of £1 per unit on wine will push up the supply curve from S_1 to S_2. The vertical distance between the two supply curves at any given output is £1. As a consequence, equilibrium price will rise from £3.30 to £4.00. The consumer therefore pays an extra 70p per bottle of wine. The other 30p of the tax is paid by the producer because the price it receives per bottle before tax falls from £3.30 to £3.00.

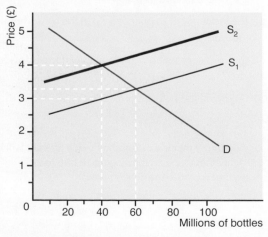

73

The incidence of tax

Price theory can be used to analyse the impact of the imposition of an indirect tax on a good. Assume that a specific tax of £1 per bottle is imposed upon wine. This has the effect of reducing supply. Sellers of wine will now want to charge £1 extra per bottle sold. In Figure 1, this is shown by a vertical shift of £1 in the supply curve at every level of output. However many bottles are produced, sellers will want to charge £1 more per bottle and therefore there is a parallel shift upwards and to the left of the whole supply curve from S_1 to S_2.

The old equilibrium price was £3.30, at which price 60 million bottles were bought and sold. The introduction of the £1 tax will raise price and reduce quantity demanded. The new equilibrium price is £4, at which price quantity demanded falls to 40 million bottles.

This result might seem surprising. The imposition of a £1 per bottle tax has only raised the price of a bottle by 70p and not the full £1 of the tax. This is because the incidence of tax is unlikely to fall totally on consumers. The **incidence of tax** measures the burden of tax upon the taxpayer. In this case the consumer has paid 70p of the tax. Therefore the other 30p which the government receives must have been paid by producers.

Question 2

Table 1 Demand, supply and tax

Price (£)	Quantity demanded	Quantity supplied
4	16	4
6	12	6
8	8	8
10	4	10
12	0	12

(a) Draw the demand and supply curves from the data in Table 1.

(b) What is the equilibrium quantity demanded and supplied?

The government now imposes a specific tax of £3 per unit.

(c) Show the effect of this on the diagram.

(d) What is the new equilibrium quantity demanded and supplied?

(e) What is the new equilibrium price?

(f) What is the incidence of tax per unit on (i) the consumer and (ii) the producer?

(g) What is (i) the tax per unit and (ii) total government revenue from the tax?

(h) By how much will the before tax revenue of producers change?

> **Maths Tip**
>
> Draw your diagram so that it is at least half a side of A4. It will help you get the right information on the diagram. It also helps examiners see that you have the right answers.

Figure 2

The incidence of an ad valorem tax

The imposition of an ad valorem tax will push the supply curve upwards from S_1 to S_2. The following gives the key facts about the change:
(a) original equilibrium price and quantity, OG and OB;
(b) new equilibrium price and quantity, OF and OA;
(c) incidence of tax per unit on consumers, GF;
(d) incidence of tax per unit on producers, HG;
(e) tax per unit in equilibrium, HF;
(f) total tax paid by consumers, GKEF;
(g) total tax paid by producers, GHJK;
(h) total tax revenue of government, FHJE;
(i) change in producers' revenue, OBCG - OAJH;
(j) change in consumers' expenditure, OBCG - OAEF.

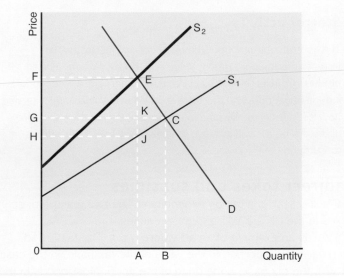

Tax revenues

Using Figure 1 we can also show the change in total expenditure before and after imposition of the tax as well as the amount of tax revenue gained by the government. The government will receive total tax revenue of £1 x 40 million (the tax per unit x the quantity sold); hence tax revenues will be £40 million. Consumers will pay 70p x 40 million of this, whilst producers will pay 30p x 40 million. Consumers will therefore pay £28 million of tax whilst producers will pay £12 million. Total spending on wine will fall from £198 million (£3.30 x 60 million) to £160 million (£4 x 40 million). Revenues received by producers will fall from £198 million (£3.30 x 60 million) to £120 million (£3 x 40 million).

Ad valorem taxes

The above analysis can be extended to deal with ad valorem taxes. The imposition of an ad valorem tax will lead to an upwards shift in the supply curve. However, the higher the price, the greater will be the amount of the tax. Hence the shift will look as in Figure 2. Consumers will pay FG tax per unit whilst the incidence of tax on producers per unit will be HG.

Subsidies

A subsidy on a good will lead to an increase in supply. At any given quantity supplied, the price will be lower. This is because

Figure 3

The effect of a subsidy

The government giving a subsidy on a good will push the supply curve to the right from S_1 to S_2. The following gives the key facts about the change:

(a) original equilibrium price OH and equilibrium quantity OA;
(b) new equilibrium price OJ and equilibrium quantity OB;
(c) subsidy per unit received by consumers JH;
(d) subsidy per unit received by producers HG;
(e) total subsidy per unit in equilibrium JG;
(f) total subsidy received by consumers JCEH;
(g) total subsidy received by producers HEFG;
(h) total subsidy given by government JCFG;
(i) change in producers' revenue (consumers' expenditure plus government subsidy) OBFG - OAKH;
(j) change in consumers' expenditure OAKH - OBCJ.

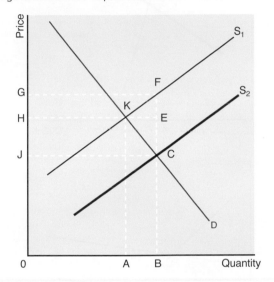

the price charged by suppliers will be higher than the price paid by consumers. The difference is the subsidy given by the government. The supply curve will therefore shift downwards and to the right, as shown in Figure 3.

The equilibrium price before the subsidy was given was OH and OA was demanded and supplied. With the subsidy, the equilibrium price is OJ and the equilibrium output is OB. The subsidy is the vertical distance between the two supply curves. At the equilibrium output of OB, the subsidy per unit is CF (or JG). This is the difference between the cost of production to firms of BF (or OG) and the price that consumers pay, BC (or OJ).

However, as with indirect taxes, the full subsidy per unit is not passed on completely to consumers. They see a fall in price of JH, but this is less than the subsidy paid of JG. Firms appropriate HG of the subsidy per unit. So some of subsidy goes to consumers, but some also goes to producers.

The total cost to the government of the subsidy is the quantity bought multiplied by the subsidy per unit. It is OB x JG which is the area JCFG.

Taxes and elasticity

The extent to which the tax incidence falls on consumers rather than producers depends upon the elasticities of demand and

The betting industry received both good and bad news in the 2014 Budget, sources suggested. On the one hand, the Chancellor announced a halving of the duty on bingo from 20 per cent to 10 per cent, estimated to cost the government £40 million a year. Cutting this ad valorem tax will bring relief to the bingo industry which in recent years has been in sharp decline.

On the other hand, the Chancellor announced a rise in duty on digital betting terminals from 20 per cent to 25 per cent, estimated to raise £90 million in tax. Digital betting terminals are machines which play a variety of fixed odds games, the most popular of which is roulette. They are found in almost all betting shops in the UK and are highly profitable for bookmakers such as William Hill and Ladbrokes. The price of shares in Ladbrokes fell 14 per cent in one day following the news.

Source: adapted from © the *Financial Times* 20.3.2014, All Rights Reserved.

(a) Explain, using a diagram, the effect of the changes in tax in the 2014 Budget on quantity and price of (i) bingo betting and (ii) digital betting terminal betting.

(b) Given that the government is cutting 10 per cent in tax on bingo but only increasing tax on digital betting terminals by five per cent, analyse why the government will increase its estimated net tax take by £50 million a year.

supply. Figure 4 shows situations where either the supply curve is perfectly elastic or the demand curve is perfectly inelastic. In both cases, the vertical shift in the supply curve, which shows the value of the tax per unit, is identical to the final price rise. Therefore, all of the tax will be paid by consumers.

Figure 5, on the other hand, shows two cases where the incidence of tax falls totally on the producer. Producers will find it impossible to shift any of the tax onto consumers if the demand curve is perfectly elastic. Consumers are not

Figure 4

Where the incidence of tax falls wholly on the consumer

If supply is perfectly elastic or demand perfectly inelastic, then it can be seen from the graphs that the incidence of tax will fall wholly on consumers.

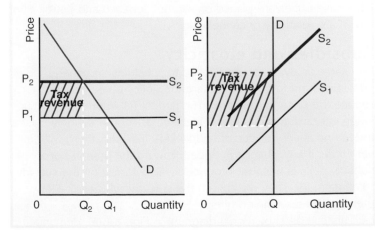

Figure 5

Where the incidence of tax falls wholly on the producer

If supply is perfectly inelastic or demand perfectly elastic, then it can be seen from the graphs that the incidence of tax will fall wholly on producers.

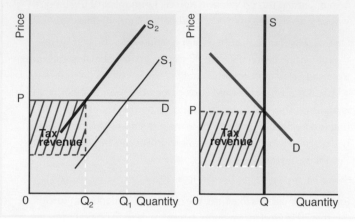

Figure 6

Elasticities and subsidies

The more price inelastic is demand or price elastic is supply, the more of a subsidy will benefit consumers rather than producers. Given a subsidy of HF per unit, HG per unit is received by consumers, but only GF by producers.

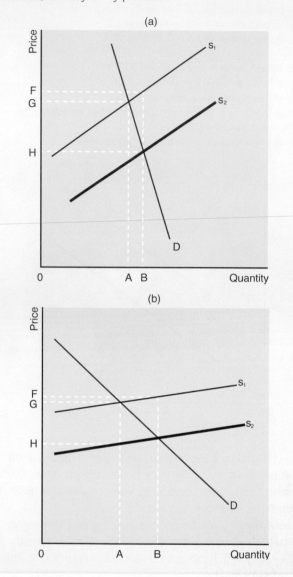

prepared to buy at any higher price than the existing price. If the supply curve is perfectly inelastic, then the supply curve after imposition of the tax will be the same as the one before. Equilibrium price will therefore remain the same and producers will have to bear the full burden of the tax.

Generalising from these extreme situations, we can conclude that the more elastic the demand curve or the more inelastic the supply curve, the greater will be the incidence of tax on producers and the less will be the incidence of tax on consumers. So far as the government is concerned, taxation revenue will be greater, all other things being equal, the more inelastic the demand for the product taxed. For instance, if demand were perfectly elastic, the imposition of an indirect tax would lead to quantity demanded falling to zero and tax revenue being zero. At the opposite extreme, if demand were perfectly inelastic, consumers would buy the same quantity after imposition of the tax as before. Hence revenue will be equal to the tax per unit times the quantity demanded before imposition. If the price elasticity of demand lies between these two extremes, the imposition of a tax will lead to a fall in quantity demanded. The higher the elasticity, the larger will be the fall in quantity demanded and hence the lower will be the tax revenue received by government. Hence, it is no coincidence that in the UK excise duties are placed on alcohol, tobacco and petrol, all of which are relatively price inelastic.

Subsidies and elasticity

The same analysis can be applied to subsidies. In general, subsidies tend to be given where the policy objective is to reduce the price of the good. The largest fall in price will occur when either demand is highly inelastic or supply is highly elastic. If demand is very elastic or supply very inelastic, there will be very little, if any, change in price following the granting of a subsidy. This is because producers will not pass on the subsidy to consumers. They will absorb the subsidy, which will allow them to increase their profits.

This can be shown on a diagram. In Figure 6(a), demand

is inelastic over the quantity range AB. A subsidy shifts the supply curve to the right, from S_1 to S_2. As a result, equilibrium price falls from OG to OH. Given that the subsidy is HF per unit, only FG per unit of this is appropriated by producers. Almost all of the subsidy per unit is received by consumers. The same analysis applies when supply is elastic as in Figure 6(b).

Key Terms

Ad valorem tax - tax levied as a percentage of the value of the good.
Incidence of tax - the tax burden on the taxpayer.
Specific or unit tax - tax levied on volume.
Subsidy - a grant given which lowers the price of a good, usually designed to encourage production or consumption of a good.

Thinking like an economist

The French film industry

The French government has, for a long time, believed that its film industry should be protected. It believed that without aid the French film industry would die, swamped by US imports of English language films. Protecting the survival of a vibrant French film industry has mainly taken the form of a variety of subsidies to French film projects, currently around €1 billion per year. By subsidising costs of production, the French government has shifted the supply curve of French films to the right. This has resulted in considerably more films being produced compared to the free market level.

Some of the subsidies are paid for by indirect taxes on ticket sales at cinemas and on sales of DVDs. These indirect taxes shift the supply curve for cinema tickets and DVDs to the left, raising their price and lowering the quantity bought. However, demand for both products is relatively inelastic and the taxes relatively small.

Part of the tax is paid by producers rather than consumers anyway. So the fall in quantity demanded is relatively small. The gain in subsidies is much greater than any loss from fewer sales.

In 2014, a government-funded report suggested a further tax of one per cent on sales of Internet-connected devices such as smartphones and tablets. The report argued that the impact on sales of smartphones and tablets would be minimal. Not only is one per cent a small number, but sellers would probably absorb almost all the tax themselves rather than pass them on to consumers. The tax would be 'fair' because owners of digital devices can view French films without necessarily paying for them directly.

Source: adapted from © the *Financial Times* 9.1.2014, All Rights Reserved.

Data Response Question

Alcohol

Alcohol is a major problem in the UK. Despite alcohol consumption per person falling, the numbers of people affected by alcohol-related illnesses is rising steeply. In the space of less than a decade, the number of alcohol-related admissions to hospitals has doubled. Problems are concentrated amongst a minority of heavy alcohol users, often drinking cheap alcohol promoted either by pubs and clubs or supermarkets.

The government could intervene in a number of ways. One is to increase the duty on alcohol. By putting this indirect tax on drink, it would raise its per unit price. The impact of this on alcohol consumption depends whether the alcohol is bought in a pub or club (on-trade) or for home consumption in a supermarket or off-licence (off-trade). It depends too on which type of alcohol is being targeted. A 20 per cent increase in duties on off-trade cider should have a bigger percentage impact on cider consumption than a 20 per cent increase in duties on off-trade wine on wine consumption. It also depends on how much of the increase in duty is paid by alcoholic drink manufacturers and retailers and how much is passed on to consumers.

Alcoholic drink manufacturers are lobbying fiercely behind the scenes to stop any government imposed increase in the price of drinks. In public, they say

that an increase in the price of alcohol will impact most on the 70 per cent of customers who drink responsibly. Health professionals argue that increasing the price, particularly of cheap alcoholic drink, is the only way to stop further rises in drink-related illnesses.

Source: adapted from © The *Financial Times*, 9.3.2012.

Table 2 Estimated price elasticities of demand for alcoholic drinks: on-licence and off-licence

	On-trade (e.g. pubs, clubs)	Off-trade (e.g. supermarkets, off-licences)
Beer	-0.77	-1.11
Wine	-0.46	-0.54
Cider	-0.85	-1.34
Spirit	-1.15	-0.90
Ready to drink (e.g. Alcopops)	-0.91	-0.93

Source: adapted from *Econometric Analysis of Alcohol Consumption in the UK*, HM Customs and Excise

2014 Budget measures

In the 2014 March Budget, the Chancellor of the Exchequer, George Osborne, announced that the tax on a typical pint of beer would be cut by 1p. The tax on whisky and cider would be unchanged. However, the tax on a typical bottle of wine would go up by 6p.

There would be an increase in alcohol consumption compared to the previous policy. This would support jobs in the pub industry and other retailers of alcohol and help household budgets.

Source: adapted from www.gov.uk.

Q

1. Define (a) an indirect tax and (b) price elasticity of demand.

2. Using a diagram, explain the impact of a rise in excise duty on wine on both the price and equilibrium output of wine.

3. Using the data in Table 2 and two diagrams, explain the different impacts of a rise in excise duty which increased the price of off-trade cider and off-trade wine by 20 per cent.

4. Discuss whether or not the measures announced in the March 2014 Budget would benefit consumers.

Evaluation

In your answer, you need to break 'consumers' down into different groups, such as beer drinkers, wine drinkers, non-drinkers and consumers who have a job in the drinks trade. How will the tax changes affect each group? Use Table 2 to help you deepen your analysis. Also analyse how big a change in the price of alcohol is taking place. Think not just about the immediate impact on the cost of spending but also long-term effects on health. In your conclusion, weigh up the possible costs and benefits to consumers.

15 Alternative views of consumer behaviour

Key points

1. Consumers may not behave rationally because of the influence of other people's behaviour, their own habits and weakness at computation.

Starter activity

Are you a rational human being out to maximise your own welfare? Give two examples of your own behaviour in the past when you have adopted a course of action knowing that it will not maximise your own welfare. Do you have habits which you find very difficult to break and which you know, rationally, are leading to negative welfare for you?

Rationality vs behavioural economics

It was explained in Unit 7 that neo-classical economics assumes that consumers are rational. They aim to maximise their own utility or economic welfare. They do this by buying a bundle of goods with their limited income. The bundle of goods is constructed so that it achieves maximum utility for the buyer. This then has implications for consumer behaviour. For example, consumers will always prefer to buy the same good at a lower price than a higher price. If they are offered a bundle of goods, with an additional good, X, they would prefer to buy it compared to just the bundle of goods without X.

Some economists, however, argue that the picture of **homo-economicus** offered by neo-classical economics of economic actors is incorrect. Economic agents, such as consumers, are not rational. For example, they often don't buy at the cheapest price and their choices can be manipulated. This view is explored by a branch of economics called **behavioural economics**.

Reasons why consumers may not behave rationally

There is a number of reasons why behavioural economists argue that consumers may not behave rationally, including the following.

Consideration of the influence of other people's behaviour Rationality assumes that economic actors act individually in a way which will maximise their own benefits. However, evidence suggests that individuals often do not make free and independent choices. Instead, they make choices which are influenced by social norms. These are beliefs held by a group of people about how to behave. For example, a group of university students might be on a night out where the social norm is that everyone drinks heavily. One individual doesn't want to drink. The social norm for the group is likely to make that one individual drink more than they might want. Or a teenager might insist that their parents buy very expensive branded trainers rather than unbranded trainers because the teenager wants to 'fit in' with a peer group.

The importance of habitual behaviour Habits are extremely important when making decisions. Habits may represent short cuts in decision-making. For example, using a rule of thumb saves time and effort. A rule of thumb is a quick way of assessing a situation that doesn't give an exact answer, but most of the time is sufficiently accurate to justify using it. Equally, consumers, as a habit, often don't gather together all the information they need to make a good decision 100 per cent of the time. This is because they know that good decisions can be made most of the time with only part of the information required. It isn't worth the time and effort to get all the information needed. Everyone has habits, which firms learn to exploit. Supermarkets, for example, know that shoppers tend to concentrate on products that are displayed at eye level. They exploit this habit by tending to place high-profit goods at eye level and low-profit goods at the bottom and top of shelves. Habits can be particularly destructive when they become addictions. Most people who are addicted to alcohol, tobacco or food know that it is in their long-term interests to control their addiction. However, they lack the self-control to give up or moderate a particular form of behaviour. Few people, for example, when they are overweight have enough self-control to change their diet, take exercise and lose weight. Lack of self-control then leads to economic agents making decisions that will not maximise their benefits.

Consumer weakness at computation Consumers are not always willing or able to make comparisons between prices and different goods on offer. Prices and offers are often presented in ways where consumers find it difficult to do the mathematics required for a comparison. Some firms deliberately exploit this weakness by presenting information in a disjointed way or simply not giving enough information to make a rational choice. For example, a shopper might want to buy some baked beans. On the shelves are individual cans and packs of six. The individual cans are priced at 47p. The pack of six is priced at £2.99. Past experience tells the shopper that multipacks are usually cheaper than individual items. So, because the shopper can't or won't make a calculation and habitually buys multipacks, it is the pack of six which goes into the shopping trolley. But it is actually 17p cheaper to buy six individual cans. 47p x 6 is not an easy calculation to make. Many consumers simply can't multiply 47 by 6 in their heads. Most of the rest, arguably, can do it, but will not try because it requires some mental effort. Yet, according to neo-classical economists, the supermarket will not sell any six packs of baked beans at these relative prices because consumers are rational.

Thinking like an economist

Payday loans

In 2014, the *World Development Report* discussed a US field trial, which demonstrated the power of information in decision-making. The trial was about payday lenders. Payday lenders offer very short-term loans at very high effective rates of interest, mainly to poorer people who are unable to access alternative sources of credit. It is commonly assumed that those who take out loans underestimate the cost of these loans, partly because payday lenders can make it difficult for borrowers to work out how much they are being charged.

The trial split the participants into two groups. One group received the standard paperwork from the payday lender, including the cash in an envelope. The envelope stated the amount due and the due date as shown in Figure 1. The second group also received a cash envelope. However, it showed how the fees accumulated if the money was borrowed for a longer period of time. It also showed the comparable fees for borrowing the same amount with a credit card as shown in Figure 2.

The trial found that those who received the envelope on which the costs of the loan were reframed in Figure 2 were 11 per cent less likely to borrow from the payday lenders in the four months following the intervention. Neo-classical economics would assume that there should be no difference because credit card interest rates are readily available information. However, most payday borrowers are unlikely to make the comparison because they don't seek the information. Also, seeing the two

costs side by side gives a nudge to show that either there are cheaper forms of borrowing and that payday lender rates are very high.

Figure 1

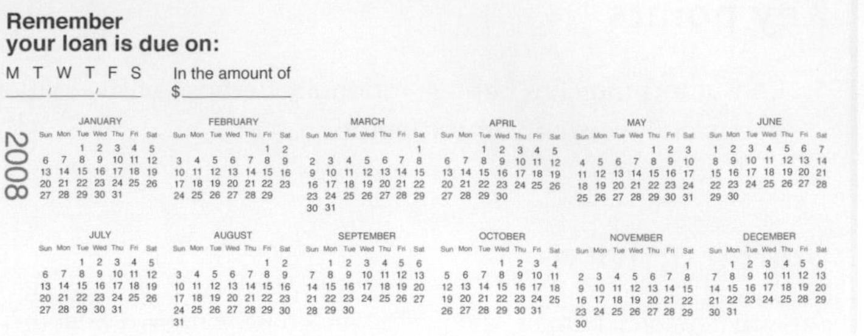

Remember your loan is due on:

M T W T F S In the amount of $ _____

2008
[calendar for year 2008]

Figure 2

How much it will cost in fees or interest if you borrow $300			
PAYDAY LENDER (Assuming two-week fee is $15 per $100 loan) If you repay in:		**CREDIT CARD** (Assuming a 20% APR) If you repay in:	
2 Weeks	$45	2 Weeks	$2.50
1 Month	$90	1 Month	$5
2 Months	$180	2 Months	$10
3 Months	$270	3 Months	$15

Source: adapted from the World Bank, *World Development Report* 2015; *Mind, Society and Behaviour.*

Data Response Question

Microfinance initiative

In India, a study was conducted of individuals who borrowed small sums of money through a microfinance initiative. One group of individuals met weekly to discuss how they were getting on. The other group met monthly, which was the norm for the scheme. Two years after the loans had been repaid, it was found that the individuals who met weekly had more informal social contact with each other than the individuals who met monthly. They were more willing to pool risks and were three times less likely to default on their second loan.

Source: adapted from the World Bank, *World Development Report* 2014.

Peso loans

Low income individuals from Mexico City were invited to choose the best one-year 10 000 peso loan product from a list of loan products typical of those available locally. Only 39 per cent of people could identify the lowest-cost product when given the information in the form of brochures designed by banks for their customers. In contrast, 68 per cent could pick out the lowest-cost product when using a user-friendly summary sheet designed by the Consumer Financial Credit Bureau of Mexico.

Source: adapted from the World Bank, *World Development Report* 2014.

Tesco

In 2015 Tesco became the first of the 'big four' supermarkets to ban sweets and chocolates from checkouts in all of its stores. The UK's biggest grocer will stop selling confectionery next to the tills from December as it tries to nudge its customers into healthier eating.

Source: adapted from © the *Financial Times* 22.5.2014, All Rights Reserved.

1. What is meant by rationality in economics?

2. Illustrating your answer from the data, explain why consumers might not behave rationally because (a) they are influenced by other people's behaviour; (b) of habitual behaviour; (c) of weaknesses in computation.

16 Types of market failure

Starter activity

The photograph shows a nuclear power plant. What are the costs to electricity generating firms of building and operating a nuclear power plant? Are there any costs which they don't pay, but are still costs to society? Do we know all the costs of nuclear power generation and can we put a price on them? Should the UK government encourage the building of more nuclear power plants in the future?

Market failure

The role of markets is to allocate scarce resources. In many cases, markets are an extremely efficient way of doing this. However, in some cases, markets fail in one of two ways:

- markets may lead to the overproduction or underproduction of goods; this is known as **partial market failure**;
- much more rarely, markets may not exist (known as **missing markets**), leading to no production of a good or service; this is known as **complete market failure**.

There is a number of types of **market failure**, briefly explained in the rest of this unit and then more completely explained in subsequent units.

Externalities

Prices and profits should be accurate signals, allowing markets to allocate resources efficiently. In reality, market prices and profits can be misleading because they may not reflect the true prices and profits to society of economic activities. These differences are known as the externalities of an economic activity. For instance, in Brazil it makes commercial sense to cut down the rain forest to create grazing land for cattle sold to the West as meat for hamburgers. However, this could lead to economic catastrophe in the long term because of global warming. The market is putting out the wrong signals, leading to a misallocation of resources.

Under-provision of public goods

The market, for a variety of reasons, may fail to provide certain goods and services, or may underprovide them. One example of this is in the provision of **public goods**. These are goods such as defence, street lighting and policing. One key reason for the under-provision of public goods is that it is relatively easy to gain the benefits from the good without having to pay for it. There is then a large incentive for individuals not to pay for the good in the hope that someone else will pay for its provision. The result is that public goods are under-provided if left to free market forces.

Information gaps

In an efficient market, both buyers and sellers have good knowledge of the product. Sometimes, though, information is imperfect. For example, a consumer buying a soft drink is likely to have tried out a variety of drinks before. The drink being bought is likely to be something the consumer likes and so the consumer has good information about the product. However, what about the purchase of a washing machine which the consumer might only make every eight years? In this case, the consumer might have imperfect information and make the wrong choice. Other examples relate to the problem of **asymmetric information**. This is when either the buyer or seller has more information than the other party. One example is private dentists. If a dentist recommends treatments when patients are not in any pain, how do patients know that the treatments are really in their best interests? Could it be that the dentist is recommending far more work than is necessary and is more interested in gaining a fee than in treating the patients properly? Another common example given is second hand cars. Some cars are 'lemons'. They constantly break down and require large repairs. Other cars of the same make and model are very reliable. The owner of the car for sale knows whether the car is a 'lemon' or not. However, the buyer does not have this information. Should the buyer offer a high price for the car on the assumption it isn't a 'lemon' or should the buyer offer a low price, assuming it will have problems?

Key Terms

Complete market failure - when a market fails to supply any of a good which is demanded, creating a missing market.
Market failure - where resources are inefficiently allocated due to imperfections in the working of the market mechanism.
Missing market - a market where the market mechanism fails to supply any of a good.
Partial market failure - when a market for a good exists but there is overproduction or underproduction of the good.

Thinking like an economist

Road congestion

Congestion on Britain's roads is a major cost to road users. For example, research by the Centre for Economics and Business Research suggests that drivers in London waste 82 hours a year in traffic jams. The estimated direct and indirect annual costs to the UK of congestion were £12 billion a year in 2013.

Congestion is a direct cost to road users because it creates longer journey times. For road hauliers, for example, that can be measured in terms of extra wages for lorry drivers or extra lorries needed to carry a given amount of freight. For motorists, there is an opportunity cost. It could be an extra half hour in bed, more time spent with the family or more time working.

There are also indirect costs. For example, congestion influences where people live and where they work. The greater the congestion, the more likely it is that workers will take a job in their local area. This might mean taking a lower paid job. It also reduces the pool of potential workers for businesses outside of that local area.

These costs create externalities for road users. The market price of a road journey includes the fuel used as well as average

maintenance costs of the vehicle and its depreciation. However, other motorists impose costs on the road user because they slow down the journey time. This cost is not reflected in the market price and so is an example of an externality.

Source: with information from © the *Financial Times* 18.10.2014, All Rights Reserved.

Data Response Question

Heathrow expansion

Heathrow Airport has been expanding for decades. It wants to build a third runway. Airlines too want to see extra capacity at the airport. However, governments have repeatedly refused to allow proposed schemes including building a third runway or extending an existing runway.

The problem is that Heathrow is situated in West London. Expanding Heathrow would lead to more planes using the airport. This would create both noise and air pollution for local residents. Hillingdon Borough Council, the local authority in which Heathrow is situated, has criticised Heathrow for contributing to poor air quality locally. A recent study in the *British*

Medical Journal linked aircraft noise to an increase of 10-25 per cent in stroke and cardiovascular diseases. Expanding Heathrow would also increase congestion on roads around Heathrow. An estimated 30 per cent of the road traffic on main roads in the local area is already airport-related traffic.

Both proponents and critics of the expansion make assumptions in making their case. For example, critics assume that aeroplanes and motor vehicles will remain both noisy and air polluting in the future. Proponents assume that both aeroplanes and motor vehicles will become less noisy and more fuel efficient, cutting down on air pollution.

Source: adapted from © the *Financial Times* 25.8.2014, 31.10.2014, All Rights Reserved.

Q

1. Briefly explain two costs that the owners of Heathrow Airport would have to pay if they were to build a third runway.

2. Explain two costs to society that it would not have to pay if a third runway were built.

3. Using your own knowledge and the data, evaluate whether the benefits of expanding Heathrow Airport would outweigh the costs.

Evaluation

Analyse the benefits of expanding Heathrow to its owners, airline passengers, businesses, workers and tourists. Analyse the costs including the building and maintenance costs and the costs to the local community. Weigh up whether the costs to the local community outweigh the benefits to everyone else. In your answer, use the terms market failure, externalities and information failure.

17 Externalities

Key points

1. Externalities are created when social costs and benefits differ from private costs and benefits.
2. The greater the externality, the greater the likelihood of market failure.
3. Market failure occurs when marginal social cost and marginal social benefit are not equal at the actual level of output. There will be a welfare loss or welfare gain at this level of output shown by the 'welfare' triangle on a marginal social and private cost and benefit diagram.

Starter activity

The media has reported that the inhabitants of the hamlet of Lower Thorpe Mandeville in Northamptonshire may have a problem. It is proposed that the UK's second high speed rail line, HS2, linking London with Birmingham and then Manchester and Leeds, will go through the village. What costs do you think the villagers will suffer, which will not be included in the building and operating costs of the line? What benefits might a citizen of Leeds gain even though they never travel on the high speed rail line?

Private and social costs and benefits

A chemical plant may dump waste into a river in order to minimise its costs. Further down the river, a water company has to treat the water to remove dangerous chemicals before supplying drinking water to its customers. Its customers have to pay higher prices because of the pollution.

This is a classic example of **externalities** or **spillover effects**. Externalities arise when private costs and benefits are different from social costs and benefits. A **private cost** is the cost of an activity to an individual economic unit, such as a consumer or a firm. For instance, a chemical company will have to pay for workers, raw materials and plant and machinery when it produces chemicals. A **social cost** is the cost of an activity not just to the individual economic unit which creates the cost, but to the rest of society as well. It therefore includes all private costs, but may also include other costs. The chemical manufacturer may make little or no payment for the pollution it generates. The difference between private cost and social cost is the externality or spillover effect. If social cost is greater than private cost, then a **negative externality** or **external cost** is said to exist.

However, not all externalities are negative. A company may put up a building which is not just functional but also beautiful. The value of the pleasure which the building gives to society over its lifetime (the social benefit) may well far exceed the benefit of the building received by the company (the private benefit). Hence, if social benefit is greater than private benefit, a **positive externality** or **external benefit** is said to exist.

This is often the case with health care provision (an example of a merit good). Although one individual will benefit from inoculation against illness, the social benefit resulting from the reduced risk of other members of society contracting the illness will be even greater. Positive externalities could also result from education and training. An individual may benefit in the form of a better job and a higher salary but society may gain even more

Question 1

Why might each of the examples in the photograph and cartoon give rise to positive and negative externalities?

from the benefits of a better trained workforce.

Activities where social benefit exceeds private benefit are often inadequately provided by a market system. In many cases this results in either state provision or a government subsidy to encourage private provision.

Externalities of production and consumption

Production externalities arise when the social costs of production differ from the private costs of production.

- **Negative externalities of production (or negative production externalities)** occur when social costs are greater than private costs in production. An example is when a factory pumps sewage into a river at no cost to itself.
- **Positive externalities of production (or positive production externalities)** occur when social costs are less than private costs in production. An example would be a supermarket which redeveloped a derelict industrial site for a new store but at the same time cleaned up pollution on the site, improved the roads around the site and subsidised the construction of some social housing next to the new store. **Consumption externalities** arise when the social benefits of consumption differ from the private benefits of consumption.
- **Positive externalities of consumption (or positive consumption externalities)** occur when social benefits are greater than private benefits in consumption. For example, when a child is immunised against chickenpox, it makes it less likely that another unimmunised child in the local area will get chickenpox.
- **Negative externalities of consumption (or negative consumption externalities)** occur when social benefits are less than private benefits in consumption. For example, with passive smoking, a person who smokes in their home harms the health of others in the home.

Market failure

The price mechanism allocates resources. Output is fixed where demand equals supply at the point where private costs equal private benefits. However, a misallocation of resources will occur if market prices do not accurately reflect the costs and benefits

to society of economic activities. There will only be a social optimum position if output occurs where social costs equal social benefits.

The greater the externality, the larger will be the divergence between private costs and benefits and social costs and benefits. The greater the externality, the greater the market failure and the less market prices provide accurate signals for the optimal allocation of resources.

Marginal costs and benefits

The difference between social costs and social benefits changes as the level of output changes. This can be shown using **marginal analysis**. The margin is a possible point of change. So the marginal cost of production is the extra cost of producing an extra unit of output. The marginal benefit is the benefit received from consuming an extra unit of output.

The marginal cost of production is likely to change as output increases. In Figure 1, it is shown as at first falling and then rising. Marginal costs fall at first because producing more can lead to greater efficiencies. However, then they start to rise. This could be because a firm is having to pay higher prices to obtain more factors of production: to employ more workers it might have to pay higher wages, for example. Or production might be less efficient if a firm is operating beyond its optimum capacity of production.

In contrast, the marginal benefit of consumption of a product falls as consumption increases. Each extra unit of consumption brings less benefit to the consumer. The marginal benefit curve is the same as the demand curve. This is because the demand curve also shows the value of the benefit put on the consumption of the product by a buyer.

Assume that the marginal cost curve and marginal benefit curves in Figure 1 are the costs and benefits to society. Then welfare would be maximised at a quantity level of OA and a price of OB. What if production and consumption are not at OA?

If quantity produced and consumed were greater than OA, the extra cost of production would be greater than the extra benefit from consumption. Welfare would be improved by reducing production and consumption. So this would lead to an inefficient allocation of resources.

If quantity produced and consumed were less than OA, then the marginal benefit of production would be greater than the marginal cost of production. Welfare could be increased if production and consumption were increased.

Note that when this diagram is usually drawn, only the upward sloping part of the marginal cost curve is shown as in Figure 2. This is because it is assumed that the marginal benefit curve will cut the marginal cost curve when marginal cost is increasing.

Welfare losses with production externalities

In many markets, social costs and private costs differ. So too do social benefits and private benefits. Figure 2 shows a situation where there are **negative externalities of production**. At every level of output, the **marginal social cost of production** is higher than the **marginal private cost**. So the marginal social cost

---

Figure 1

The optimal level of production and consumption

Welfare is maximised when the marginal cost of production equals the marginal benefit of consumption. This is at the output level OA and a marginal price or cost of OB.

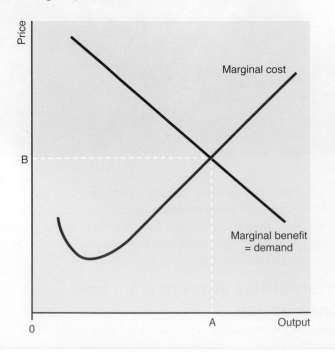

Figure 2

Free market and optimal levels of production

In a free market, production will take place at OB where MPC = MPB. However, the socially optimal level of production is OA where marginal social cost and marginal social benefit are the same.

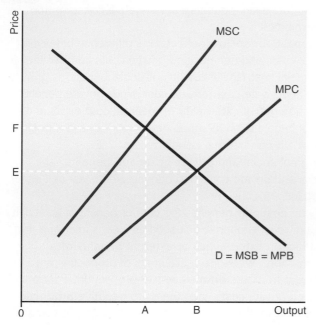

Figure 3

Welfare loss triangle from negative production externalities

If production takes place at the free market level of output of OB, then there will be a deadweight loss of welfare to society of GJK.

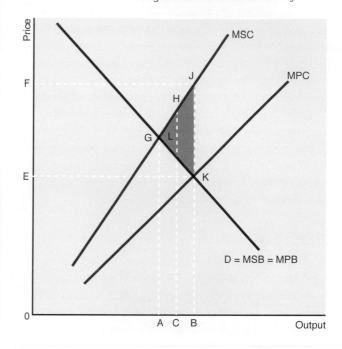

curve, the MSC curve, is higher and to the left of the marginal private cost curve, the MPC curve. It is assumed here that the marginal social benefit (MSB) and marginal private benefit (MPB) are the same. So the demand curve is also the MSB and MPB curves.

The market equilibrium is where the marginal private cost equals the marginal private benefit. This is at an output level of OB and a price of OE. If the price were higher than OE, consumers would buy less than OB because the demand curve shows the value or utility placed by consumers on the product. If the price were lower than OE, producers would not be prepared to supply OB because they would make a loss on the last or marginal units produced.

However, the socially optimum level of production is lower than OB. It is OA where marginal social cost equals marginal social benefit (MSC = MSB). The price of OF is higher than the free market price of OE. This reflects the fact that the free market price does not include the production externality generated by the good.

If production and consumption take place at OB, then there is a welfare loss to society. The loss is the difference between the marginal social cost and the marginal private benefit shown in Figure 3. On the last unit produced, the OBth unit, this is JK. On the OCth unit, the welfare loss is HL. So the total welfare loss is the sum of the vertical distances between the MSC curve and MSB curve between the output levels of OA and OB. This is the triangle GJK, sometimes called the **welfare loss triangle** or the **deadweight loss triangle**.

Figure 4

Welfare triangle with positive consumption externalities showing potential gain from increasing output

If production takes place at the free market level of output of OA, then the triangle GHK shows the welfare gain that could be achieved if output rose to the socially optimal level of output of OB.

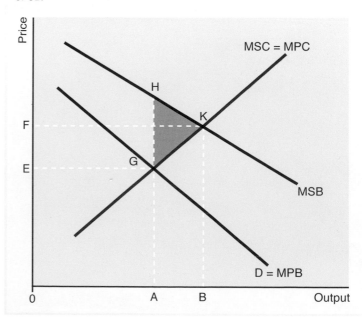

Welfare losses with consumption externalities

The same analysis can be applied to when there are **consumption externalities** or **externalities of consumption**. Figure 4 shows a situation where the **marginal social benefit** is greater than the **marginal private benefit**. This means that there are positive externalities. For example, if some individuals pay to go to the gym to keep fit, it benefits others because they are less likely later in life to suffer health problems. In Figure 4, it is assumed that the marginal social cost and marginal private cost are the same. The free market equilibrium is at an output level of OA where MPC = MPB, the marginal private cost of production is equal to the marginal private benefit of consumption. However, the socially optimum level of output is OB where MSC = MSB, the marginal cost equals the marginal social benefit. If the output were at OB, an extra GHK of welfare could be gained. There is therefore a loss of welfare of GHK compared to the socially optimal level of production.

Question 2

In 2014 media sources reported that tap water was cut off for the day in the Chinese city of Jingjiang. It followed detection of an unknown pollutant in the city's water supplies. Jingjiang, a city on the river Yangtze, is a centre for shipbuilding and textiles, and it was thought that either industry could have been the source of the pollution. Photos posted online showed residents filling buckets from an emergency reservoir in a local public park.

China is investing $536 billion in wastewater treatment and purification plants during the five years to 2015, but one quarter of its citizens still do not have access to clean drinking water.

Source: adapted from © the *Financial Times* 10.5.2014, All Rights Reserved.

(a) Explain how the shipbuilding or textile industry in Jingjiang may have created an externality.

(b) Using a diagram, explain why there has been a misallocation of resources.

Key Terms

Consumption externalities or **external benefits of consumption** - when the social costs of consumption are different from the private costs of consumption. If social benefits exceed private benefits, then there are **positive consumption externalities**. If social benefits are less than private benefits, then there are **negative consumption externalities**.

Externality or **spillover effect** - the difference between social costs and benefits and private costs and benefits. If net social cost (social cost minus social benefit) is greater than net private cost (private cost minus private benefit), then a **negative externality** or **external cost** exists. If net social benefit is greater than net private benefit, a **positive externality** or **external benefit** exists.

Marginal social and private costs and benefits - the social and private costs and benefits of the last unit either produced or consumed.

Private cost and benefit - the cost or benefit of an activity to an individual economic unit such as a consumer or a firm.

Production externalities or **external benefits of production** - when the social costs of production are different from the private costs of production. If social costs exceed private costs, then there are **negative production externalities**. If social costs are less than private costs, then there are **positive production externalities**.

Social cost and benefit - the cost or benefit of an activity to society as a whole.

Thinking like an economist

Mosquito nets

The fight against malaria has had some success over the past 15 years. Sources stated that deaths from malaria fell by 42 per cent between 2000 and 2013 and incidence of the disease has come down by a quarter. In large part this is due to an increase in international financial support for anti-malaria efforts, from just $100 million in 2000 to $1.84 billion in 2012. An estimated 3.3 million lives have been saved over the period. The hunt is still on for a wonder drug which will cure all malaria infections quickly, a vaccine or an effective way of eradicating the parasite that causes malaria.

However, in the meantime, a low-technology, low-cost solution has contributed much to the reduction in malarial infections. It is a sleeping net impregnated with insecticide. These nets have both private benefits and positive externalities in consumption. They protect the people who sleep under the net. However, the insecticide ensures that any mosquitos landing on the net will be killed. This benefits those under the net but it also reduces the number of mosquitos in a local area like a small village. The more mosquitos killed, the fewer will be alive to reproduce and bite humans. Hence people who are not sleeping under the net also benefit.

Private benefits are reduced when nets become torn through use. Positive externalities in consumption disappear when the net loses all its insecticide. Externalities also disappear when mosquitos evolve to become resistant to pyrethroid, the insecticide used. Although resistance has been detected in 64 countries, or nearly two thirds of countries affected by malaria, there are currently no acceptable alternatives to pyrethroid. For the time being, pyrethroid-impregnated nets remain the only way forward in the fight against malaria.

Source: adapted from © the *Financial Times* 25.4.2014, All Rights Reserved.

Data Response Question

Sugar

It has long been suggested that many people in developed countries eat too much sugar. Medical evidence points to sugar being a cause of obesity, diabetes, heart disease and cancer.

The sugar industry claims the problem lies not with excessive consumption of sugar but sedentary lifestyles. Whilst sugar consumption has been slowly declining in the UK, there has been a significant drop in the amount of physical exercise taken. Children, for example, instead of playing outside, spend far more time indoors watching television or playing computer games.

UK pressures groups, however, like Action for Sugar are campaigning for food manufacturers to cut sugar in drinks and foods - such as soups, pasta sauces, baked beans and bread - by 30 per cent over three to five years. This would particularly help low income households which consume above average proportions of their calorie intake from processed foods.

Source: adapted from © the *Financial Times* 6.2.2014, All Rights Reserved; The *Guardian* 21.05.2011.

Maths Tip

The answer to question 1 is not 11 (i.e. 24-13). You need to put the starting number into the percentage formula, which is

$$100 \times \frac{change}{start\ value}$$

Remember that giving a simple number like 11 is incorrect. The number must have % after it, like 11%.

1. Calculate to one decimal place the percentage increase in obesity for men over the period 1993 to 2012.

2. Explain using a diagram why current UK consumption levels of sugar may lead to negative externalities.

3. Discuss whether sugar consumption is the main market failure resulting in a rise in obesity in the UK.

Evaluation

Using a diagram, explain why sugar consumption might lead to market failure. Then consider other factors which might be contributing to a rise in obesity. The data suggests one factor. From your own knowledge, you should know that excessive consumption of other forms of carbohydrates apart from sugar and also fats contribute to obesity. Is there market failure in the markets for computer games and takeaway pizzas? Conclude by weighing up whether sugar is the **main** market failure leading to the rise in obesity.

Figure 7

Sugar content in common food products, grams per serving

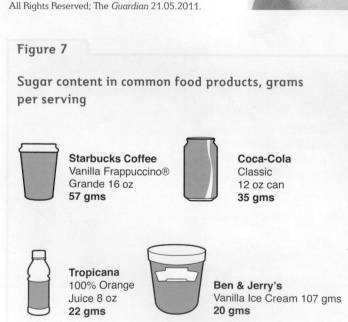

Starbucks Coffee
Vanilla Frappuccino® Grande 16 oz
57 gms

Coca-Cola
Classic
12 oz can
35 gms

Tropicana
100% Orange Juice 8 oz
22 gms

Ben & Jerry's
Vanilla Ice Cream 107 gms
20 gms

Source: adapted from © the *Financial Times* 6.2.2014, All Rights Reserved.

Figure 8

Obesity in adults, % of population (England)

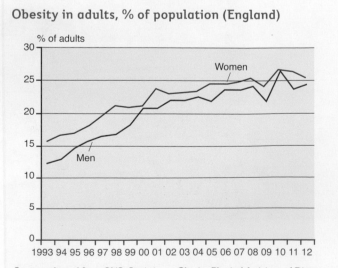

Source: adapted from ONS, *Statistics on Obesity*, Physical Activity and Diet: England 2014

Key points

1. Public goods possess the characteristics of non-rivalry and non-excludability.
2. The free-rider problem means that free markets will not provide enough or indeed any public goods, leading to market failure.
3. To correct this market failure, governments tend to provide or organise the production of public goods.

Starter activity

An individual approaches you, pulls out a knife and demands your mobile phone, which you give him. Two days later, he is caught by the police. You want him to go to prison for the robbery. The police say that they will try him in court if you pay £5 000 for the police and court costs. If you want him to go to jail for a year, that will cost you another £25 000. Is justice something that can be sold like an online film or a can of beer? Why might people argue that everyone should pay for upholding justice whether or not they have been a victim of crime? Why should online films or cans of beer not be provided free by the state, like the police, the courts or prisons?

Public goods

Nearly all goods are **private goods** (not to be confused with goods produced in the private sector of the economy). A private good is **rivalrous**. It is a good where consumption by one person results in the good not being available for consumption by another. For instance, if you eat a bowl of muesli, then your friend can't eat it; if a firm builds a plant on a piece of land, that land is not available for use by local farmers. Private goods are also **excludable**. Once provided, it is possible to prevent others from using it. For example, football clubs can prevent fans from seeing a game at their stadium by allowing only ticket holders to enter.

A few goods, however, are **public goods** or **pure public goods**. These are goods which possess the opposite characteristics to private goods.

- **Non-rivalry** - consumption of the good by one person does not reduce the amount available for consumption by another person; sometimes this is also known as **non-diminishability** or **non-exhaustibility**;
- **Non-excludability** - once provided, no person can be excluded from benefiting; equally, no person can opt out of receiving the good, which is known as **non-rejectability**.

Public goods are also different from private goods because the marginal cost (the extra cost) of providing a unit of the good is zero.

There are relatively few examples of pure public goods, although many goods contain a public good element. Clean air is a public good. If you breathe clean air, it does not diminish the ability of others to breathe clean air. Moreover, others cannot prevent you from breathing clean air. Defence is another example. An increase in the population of the UK does not lead to a reduction in the defence protection accorded to the existing population. People in Manchester cannot reject the 'benefits'

Question 1

Explain why lamp posts might be classed as a public good.

of defence protection even if they were to object to current defence policy, prefer to see all defence abolished and refuse to pay to finance defence. Also, the marginal cost of providing defence for one extra citizen is zero. For example, the cost of Britain's nuclear submarines does not increase when Britain's population increases by 50 000.

Goods which can be argued to be public goods are:

- defence;
- the judiciary and prison service;
- the police service;
- street lighting.

Many other goods, such as education and health, contain a small public good element.

The free rider problem

If the provision of public goods were left to the market mechanism, there would be market failure. This is because of the **free rider** problem. A public good is one where it is impossible to prevent people from receiving the benefits of the good once it has been provided. So there is very little incentive for people to pay for consumption of the good. A free rider is someone who receives the benefit but allows others to pay for it. For instance, citizens receive benefits from defence expenditure. But individual citizens could increase their economic welfare by not paying for it.

In a free market, national defence is unlikely to be provided. A firm attempting to provide defence services would have difficulty charging for the product since it could not be sold to benefit individual citizens. The result would be that no one would pay for defence and therefore the market would not provide it. The only way around this problem is for the state to provide defence and force everyone to contribute to its cost through taxation.

In practice, there are often ways in which providers of public goods can exclude consumers from benefiting from the public good. The problem of free riding can to some extent be solved for these **non-pure** or **quasi-public goods**. For example, motorists can be made to pay a toll for using a road. Television viewers can be forced to buy subscriptions because reception is encoded. Ships entering a port can be forced to pay taxes for the upkeep of local lighthouses. However, quasi-public goods possess the second characteristic of pure public goods. They are non-rival. So for most roads, for example, one motorist travelling along the road does not exclude another motorist from travelling along the same road. When goods are non-rival, it is unlikely that the free market mechanism will provide enough of the good. How many country roads would private firms provide if they were tolled? The answer is very few because the tolls collected would not cover the building and maintenance of the road. Hence, there is a very strong case for government providing this quasi-public good.

Key Terms

Free rider - a person or organisation which receives benefits that others have paid for without making any contributions.
Non-excludability - once provided, it is impossible to prevent any economic agent from consuming the good.
Non-rejectability - once provided, it is impossible for any economic agent not to consume the good.
Non-rivalry, non-diminishability or non-exhaustability - consumption by one economic agent does not reduce the amount available for consumption by others.
Private good - a good which possesses the characteristics of rivalry (once consumed, it cannot be consumed by any one else) and excludability (it is possible to prevent someone else from consuming the good).
Public good or pure public good - a good which possesses the characteristics of non-rivalry (or non-diminishability) and non-excludability (which includes the characteristic of non-rejectability).
Quasi-public good or non-pure public good - a good which does not perfectly possess the characteristics of non-rivalry and non-excludability and yet which also is not perfectly rival or excludable.

Thinking like an economist

Lighthouses

Public goods are goods which possess the two properties of non-excludability (once provided, it is impossible to prevent others from benefiting) and non-rivalry (benefit by one does not diminish the amount by which others can benefit). Lighthouses possess both these characteristics. Once the lighthouse is working, it is impossible to prevent any ship in the area benefiting. The fact that one ship sees the lighthouse doesn't prevent other ships from seeing it as well.

Economists from Adam Smith onwards have argued that public goods need to be provided by the public sector because there is no economic incentive for the private sector to provide them. Non-excludability would mean that there would be large numbers of free-riders - individuals or firms which benefited but did not pay. For instance, how could ships be made to pay for lighthouses?

In the UK, government doesn't provide lighthouses. They are provided by Trinity House, a private corporation. However, the government has given it the right to build lighthouses. In return, the government allows it to charge each ship which visits a British port a 'light charge'. This is collected by Revenue and Customs, part of the government. Trinity House has to submit its budget to both the government and representatives of the shipping industry each year, where it has to justify the scale of its charges. So in this case, whilst the government doesn't provide the public good, it is involved at every stage and crucially in forcing ships to pay charges for the upkeep of lighthouses.

It is in fact difficult to think of any public good for which the government doesn't provide or regulate its private provision. However, the example of lighthouses shows that a public good is not necessarily one directly provided by the government.

Data Response Question

Television viewing

Watching television is one of the UK's favourite occupations. Almost all households have a television and, on average, we watch almost four hours a day.

Television first became widely available in the UK in the 1950s, when the BBC offered one channel. To receive broadcasts legally, households have to buy a television licence. Some people argue that the licence fee is effectively a tax, as all of the monies raised are used to fund the BBC.

Sending out unscrambled television signals means that anyone with an aerial and a television set can receive television broadcasts, whether or not they have paid their licence fee. However, there are alternatives to the licence fee. Most commercial broadcasters in the UK, such as ITV, fund themselves through broadcasting advertising. Sky broadcasts its channels from a satellite. The signals can only be decoded by purchasing a viewing card from Sky. Alternatively, viewers can watch television via cable wires to their home. Companies such as Virgin Media offer cable services for a monthly fee.

Q

1. Explain the difference between a 'public good' and a 'private good'.

2. Why might BBC channels be classified as a public good?

3. To what extent are Sky satellite and Virgin Media cable services private goods?

Evaluation

In your answer to question 3, examine Sky and Virgin Media against the characteristics of a private good. Weigh up whether they perfectly match these characteristics. Do they have public good elements?

19 Information gaps

Key points

1. Market failure may be caused by information gaps including asymmetric information in a market.
2. Principal-agent problems, adverse selection and moral hazard all occur because of asymmetric information in markets such as education, pensions, drugs, health care, financial services and advertising.

Starter activity

What is your attitude to alcoholic drink? Can you name ten brands of alcoholic drink? Can you give three long-term medical problems that might arise from continued excessive drinking? Do you know what is meant by 'a unit of alcohol'? Do you know how many units are recommended safe limits per week for an 18-year-old male and female, according to government guidelines? Do you suffer from information failure about alcohol and how this might lead to a welfare loss?

Imperfect market information

In a perfect market, buyers and sellers have potential access to the same information. There is symmetric information. However, many decisions are based on **imperfect information**. Both buyers and sellers don't find out the information they need to make the decision that maximises their welfare. There is then **information failure** or an **information gap**.

Information gaps also occur when either the buyer or the seller has more information than the other. There is then a situation of **asymmetric information**. The buyer or seller with more information can exploit that information gap to their benefit.

Figure 1

Imperfect information

Buyers possess imperfect information, overestimating the benefits of buying a good. The result is that the actual demand curve is to the right of the demand curve where they have perfect information. AB too much is bought, leading to a misallocation of resources.

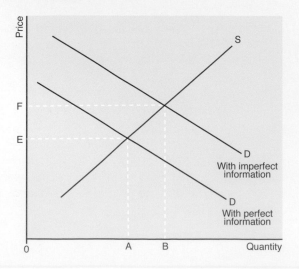

Information failure can be illustrated using a diagram. In Figure 1, welfare would be maximised where demand with perfect information equals supply at output OA and a price of OE. However, buyers in practice suffer information failure. They overestimate the benefits of the product and are therefore prepared to pay a higher price for a given level of output than it they enjoyed perfect information. Hence, the actual demand curve for the good is to the right of the one where buyers have imperfect information. The result is that OB is bought at a price of OF. There is a misallocation of resources because AB too much is bought compared to a situation where buyers had perfect information.

If buyers underestimate the benefits of buying a good because of information failure, then the actual demand curve will be to the left of the demand curve with perfect information. Too little will be bought at too low a price. The same analysis applies to suppliers. If they underestimate the benefits to themselves of selling a product, then the supply curve will be to the left of the supply curve where they possess perfect information. If they overestimate the benefits, the supply curve will be to the right.

The market for second-hand cars

The problem of asymmetric information was first outlined by the Nobel Prize-winning economist, George Akerlof. In 1970, he published a paper in which he used the example of second-hand cars to discuss the problem of asymmetric information. He argued that buyers of second-hand cars don't know whether any individual second-hand car is a good car or whether it is a 'lemon', a very poor quality car with significant defects. Buyers therefore have to guess whether or not a second-hand car is of good quality. Because they don't know, they are only prepared to offer to pay average prices for better than average quality cars. Owners of better than average quality cars therefore tend not to sell them because they can't get a high enough price. But then second-hand cars for sale become mainly average or below-average quality. Buyers therefore are not prepared to pay average prices for a second-hand car and therefore start to offer below-average prices. Owners of average quality cars then feel that they are not getting a high enough price for their car and so stop selling them in the market. George Akerlof argued that the final outcome was the disappearance of the market for second-hand cars. Asymmetric information has led to the collapse of the market.

In practice, second-hand car markets do exist. This is because buyers have more information that Akerlof's model assumes. For example, consumer protection laws in the UK state that car dealers must sell cars which at minimum are road worthy. Second-hand car dealers may offer a short guarantee period of, say, three months. Consumers can make some judgements about the second-hand car dealer by the state of their premises and the number of cars they are selling. The price of the car is also determined by its age and mileage. Consumers can find an approximate guide to the price of the car by buying a car price guide or looking on the Internet. However, it remains true that the price of a day old second-hand car is, for the most part, significantly below the price of a new car. That difference in price in part reflects the discount in the market because of asymmetric information.

Market examples

Asymmetric information can lead to a misallocation of resources and market failure, as the example of second-hand cars shows. There is a number of important markets where this occurs.

Education Education provides an example of the principal-agent problem. The principal is the individual or organisation which benefits or loses from a set of economic decisions. The agent is an individual or organisation which makes decisions on behalf of the principal. In education, the principal is the child or student. The agents are the parents and guardians of the child and society in general represented in the UK by government agencies such as the school and the courts. A child suffers from asymmetric information. It, typically, does not see the long-term benefits of education. Therefore it may act in ways, such as truanting from school or failing to work to its potential, which act to harm its long-term interests. If allowed, it will devote too few resources to education and so there will be a misallocation of resources. Agents for the child, therefore, have to act in a way which will foster and encourage the child to participate fully in the educational process.

However, the principal-agent problem occurs when parents and guardians collude with the child to avoid education. In a developing country, where parents may have to pay even for primary education, there is a financial incentive not to send children to school. This incentive is increased if the child can be kept at home and put to work. In the UK, there is a minority of parents for whom the emotional and financial cost of supporting their children in education is too high. They therefore could be said to be 'colluding' with their children in allowing them to be disruptive in school and in truanting. They may also not support their children beyond the age of 16 if they wish to go to college or university. The state has an incentive to see all children reach their full potential. This is the reason why the state, as agent, encourages young people to stay on as long as possible in education and to perform to their potential.

Pensions Many argue that young workers today are paying too little into pensions and instead spending the money on everything from houses to cars to holidays. This is because of asymmetric information. Many 25-year-olds may not be able to imagine what it will be like to live as a 70-year-old. As a result, they may ignore the loss of welfare that will come from having a low income at 70 to boost their current spending and immediate gratification.

Governments step in to remedy at least part of this misallocation of resources by forcing workers to save for their retirement. In some countries, workers have to save through pension schemes tied to their work. In others, such as the UK, occupational pension schemes are encouraged through tax breaks. But the government forces saving through a national retirement scheme. Workers have to pay National Insurance contributions and other taxes which pay for the state retirement pension and means-tested benefits.

Drugs Drugs, such as alcohol, tobacco and heroin, cause a misallocation of resources partly because of asymmetric information. Individuals are sometimes unaware of the long-term costs of drug use. For example, individuals are usually unaware of the medical risks to binge drinking. Individuals also typically fail to recognise that taking drugs can cause drug dependence. One decision can create an addict for life. Manufacturers of legal drugs such as alcohol and tobacco are far more aware of the risks than most of their customers. However, it is not in their interests to disclose the research evidence available to them. They gain by emphasising the positive aspects of drug use. During the 1950s, 1960s and 1970s, for example, tobacco companies consistently denied the evidence they had of the link between smoking and cancer. Asymmetric information, therefore, leads to overconsumption of drugs.

Financial services Financial institutions often have more information about the products they sell than their customers. For example, following the financial crisis that developed from 2008 onwards, it became clear that a wide range of financial institutions and their employees had abused their relationships with their customers. In the USA, some bank employees were incentivised in the years leading up to 2008 to sell mortgages to low income households. The bank employees had enough information to know that these households would not be able to repay those mortgages once introductory low rates of interest had expired. Banks were then bundling up their mortgages and then selling them on to third parties as if they were low risk products. When it became clear in 2008 that these households were defaulting on their debts in large numbers, it led to the largest financial crisis since the 1920s. There was information failure and **moral hazard**.

Moral hazard occurs when an economic agent, like a bank or banker, makes a decision in their own best interest knowing that there are potential adverse risks and that, if problems result, the cost will be partly borne by other economic agents. The bank employees who sold mortgages to risky customers knew that these were high risk loans, but they were paid on how many mortgages they sold, not on whether the mortgages were likely to be repaid. A collapse of a mortgage was a problem for their bank, not for them. Equally, senior bankers engaged in risky behaviour, assuming that if the bank failed, the state would bail it out. They would keep the pay, bonuses and pensions that they had earned from engaging in risky behaviour, whilst taxpayers picked up the bill for the huge losses created by risky transactions that went badly wrong.

Advertising Some advertising, such as small ads in newspapers or notifications for sale on sites such as eBay, increases information for buyers. It makes them aware of what is on offer in the marketplace. However, most advertising is persuasive advertising. It is designed to change attitudes on the part of the buyer. As such, it attempts to increase information failure on the part of the buyer to the benefit of the seller. For example, a soap powder advert might attempt to persuade buyers that a particular brand is better at cleaning clothes than another. A car advert might link owning the car with increased status for its owner. A tobacco advert might try to link smoking a particular brand with being 'cool'.

Key Terms

Asymmetric information - where buyers and sellers have different amounts of information, with one group having more information than the other.
Imperfect information or imperfect market information - where buyers or sellers or both lack information to make an informed decision.
Information failure or information gap - where buyers or sellers or both don't have the information that is available to make a decision.
Moral hazard - when an economic agent makes a decision in their own best interest knowing that there are potential adverse risks, and that if problems result, the cost will be partly borne by other economic agents.
Principal-agent problem - occurs when the goals of principals, those standing to gain or lose from a decision, are different from agents, those making decision on half of the principal. Examples include shareholders (principals) and managers (agents), or children (principals) and parents (agents).

Thinking like an economist

Payment protection insurance (PPI)

Payment protection insurance (PPI) is a financial product that should be designed to help customers who take out loans. For a small premium, the loan will be repaid if the customer dies, becomes disabled, suffers long-term illness, or loses their job.

In the UK, by 2000, it had become clear to banks that PPI was a highly profitable product. The cost or premiums on PPI for customers were high, but payouts were very low. It could easily be sold to customers taking out new credit cards. Customers failed to understand that the likelihood of them being able to make a claim was small because of the way in which the conditions attached to the policy were framed. A significant minority of customers didn't even know that they had been sold PPI by the banks because the banks in many cases had simply added the insurance to the credit card automatically. Banks failed to check whether PPI would be suitable for a customer. For example, self-employed people were sold PPI despite the fact that they couldn't make any claims under the loss of jobs part of the policy.

In economic terms, there was significant information failure. There was asymmetric information in the market, with banks possessing far more information than their customers. By 2008, there were 20 million PPI contracts in existence in the UK and the banks were selling them at a rate of 7 million a year as

customers took out new credit cards. PPI premiums could equal up to 50 per cent of the value of the interest on a loan and typically they were at least 25 per cent.

Following the financial crisis of 2008, banks came under much greater scrutiny about the products they offered and the way in which they conducted their business. It became apparent quite quickly that PPI was, in general, a product that offered little or no value for money to customers. In 2011, the banks admitted defeat in their legal battle to prevent customers from gaining compensation for having mis-sold them PPI products.

By 2014, banks had paid out £16 billion on 13 million customer complaints accepted. That made the average compensation per complaint as £1 230. Claims for compensation were still coming in and banks had set aside another £7 billion for future compensation claims.

PPI is an example of market failure on a significant scale. Given that there were only 26 million households in the UK in 2014, it meant that on average over half of all households had been sold a product which had been virtually useless at an average cost of over £1 000 by UK banks.

Source: adapted from © the *Financial Times* 3.2.2014, 9.4.2014, 19.5.2014, 31.7.2014, 3.8.2014, 30.8.2014, 3.9.2014, 7.1.2015, All Rights Reserved.

Data Response Question

Smoking

In 2014, the Campaign for Tobacco-Free Kids, an anti-smoking pressure group, published a report about the 'Be Marlboro' campaign. Marlboro is the world's best selling cigarette brand. The report pointed out that tobacco kills nearly 6 million people worldwide every year. New smokers are typically children or young people 'who are attracted to tobacco products through expensive marketing campaigns that use images that are highly appealing to young people around the globe'.

According to the report, *You're the Target*, the 'Be Malboro' campaign, 'draws on youth orientated images and themes that suggest to young people that they should Be a Marlboro smoker'. The campaign was launched in 2011 in Germany and has spread to more than 50 countries. In October 2013, a German court banned 'Be Marlboro' advertisements 'on the grounds that the campaign was designed to encourage children as young as 14 years of age to smoke, which is in violation of Germany's advertising law'.

Source: adapted from tobaccofreekids.org; *You're the Target*, March 2014, The Campaign for Tobacco-free Kids.

In the UK, there are taxes on cigarettes. All tobacco advertising is banned, as is smoking in public places. From April 2016, cigarettes will be sold in plain packaging, where the only distinguishing feature of each brand on the packet would be the name of the cigarette. Anti-smoking campaigners want the government to further increase tobacco taxes.

Table 1 Cigarette smoking by age – percentage of age group, GB

			%
	1978	1998	2013
16-19	34	31	15
20-24	44	40	30
25-34	45	35	25
35-49	45	31	22
50-59	45	28	19
60+	30	16	11

Table 2 Percentage of pupils age 15 who are regular smokers, England

		%
1982	1998	2013
25	23	8

Source: adapted from *Smoking Statistics*, October 2014, ASH.

Q

1. Give two significant features of the change in cigarette smoking over time shown in the data in Tables 1 and 2. Back up your statements with evidence.

2. Explain why there might be (a) asymmetric information in the tobacco market and (b) a misallocation of resources because of the sale of tobacco products.

3. Using the data and your own knowledge, discuss whether the most effective way of reducing the misallocation of resources due to tobacco consumption is to increase information about the health aspects of smoking.

Evaluation

Make sure this is an A level economics answer rather than a general studies answer. You need to focus your answer on asymmetric information and information failure. The data show who is most likely to smoke and Table 2 gives figures for illegal smoking. The data also describe an advertising campaign by a tobacco company. Can health education about smoking make information symmetric to all ages of smokers? Would other policies to reduce smoking be more effective?

20 Government intervention in markets

Key point

1. Governments attempt to correct market failure in a number of different ways including indirect taxes, subsidies, maximum and minimum prices, trade pollution permits, state provision of public goods, provision of information and regulation.

Starter activity

Litter in the streets is always a problem. People drop finished cigarettes or beer bottles, or throw away the wrapping from their chips or hamburgers. What might be the best way to deal with this? Introducing laws or regulations banning littering, subject to a fine? Taxing cigarette and drink manufacturers and using the money to clean up the litter? Running information campaigns about litter? Accepting that it will always be a problem and getting local authorities and taxpayers to pay to clean up the streets?

Government intervention to correct market failure

There is a variety of types of market failure that include externalities, provision of public goods and information failure. Governments can intervene in a number of different ways to correct market failure. Total welfare will be increased if any costs incurred in intervention are less than the benefits gained from intervention.

Indirect taxes

One way in which governments can correct market failure is through imposing indirect taxes. For example, assume that there is environmental market failure. Firms are emitting too many pollutants into the atmosphere. This results in negative externalities. The government could impose a tax on production. Firms would respond by producing less because their costs of production have now risen due to the tax. The level of the tax needs to be set so that negative externalities are eliminated and the marginal social cost of production equals the marginal social benefit.

This is shown in Figure 1. The free market level of output is OA where the marginal cost to firms, the marginal private cost, is equal to their marginal private benefit. The free market price is OF. However, the optimal level of output is OB where the marginal social cost is equal to the marginal social benefit. To achieve this level of output, a government could impose a tax of EG per unit. This would shift the marginal private cost curve up to equal the marginal social cost curve at output OB.

In Figure 1, the MPC and MSC lines diverge as output increases. This shows that the negative externality per unit increases as output increases. It is then appropriate to impose an ad valorem indirect tax like VAT where the amount of tax paid in money terms rises as price rises. In Figure 2, the MPC and MSC lines are parallel. It is appropriate here to impose a specific tax, like duty on petrol in the UK. The amount of tax per

Figure 1

Imposition of an ad valorem tax

With an optimal level of output of OB, a tax of EG per unit needs to be imposed to maximise welfare.

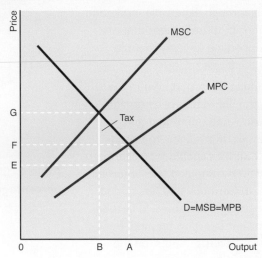

unit stays the same as the price of the good increases. As in Figure 1, the socially optimal level of output is OB and a specific tax of EG should be imposed to correct the market failure.

Figure 2

Imposition of a specific tax

With an optimal level of output of OB, a tax of EG per unit needs to be imposed to maximise welfare.

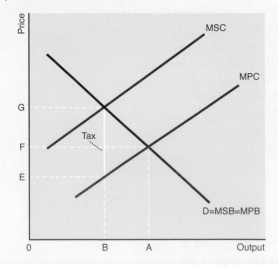

Indirect taxes can have problems.

- They may be difficult to target. So the tax may be too large or too small to correct the market failure exactly. Partly, this may be due to information failure on the part of government: it doesn't know the exact size of the market failure or it may not know the impact a tax will have on the market.

- Governments may use indirect taxes to raise revenues as well as reduce market failure. The two objectives can then conflict when decisions are made about the size of the tax.

- Taxes are unpopular. In the 1990s, the UK government was forced to abandon a plan to raise the rate of VAT on gas and electricity because of political opposition. It claimed it wanted to raise the rate of VAT partly to reduce greenhouse gas emissions.

Question 1

Air Passenger Duty, introduced in 1994 in the UK, is a specific tax on passengers flying out of the UK. It was introduced partly as an environmental measure: to discourage flying in order to reduce carbon emissions from aircraft. In 2015, the government reduced Air Passenger Duty on long-haul flights. Economy class passengers would see their tax reduced from up to £97 to £71 whilst those flying premium class would see a fall from up to £194 to £142. The government estimated the change could cost it up to £920 million over four years to 2019. While £985 million in tax would be lost through lower taxes, £65 million in tax would be gained because of increased ticket sales.

Source: adapted from © the *Financial Times* 20.3.2014, All Rights Reserved.

Explain, using a diagram, how:

(a) Air Passenger Duty could help correct an environmental market failure;

(b) the 2015 changes to Air Passenger Duty could increase market failure.

Subsidies

Another way in which governments can correct market failure is through the provision of subsidies. For example, assume that there are positive externalities in consumption from historic buildings. The private benefit to the owner of the historic building is less than benefit to society of the historic building. Then a government could provide subsidies, for example for the upkeep of this historic building or for its repairs.

This can be shown in Figure 3. If left to the market mechanism, there would be OA historic houses because this is where MPB = MPC. However, the marginal social benefit is higher than the marginal private benefit. The optimal level of historic houses is therefore OB where MSB = MSC. To achieve this, the government has to give a subsidy of EG per unit to owners of historic houses.

Subsidies can be used where there are positive externalities. They can also be used to correct information failure. The government could subsidise the provision of information to those suffering from a lack of information.

Subsidies can have problems.

- They may be difficult to target. As with taxes, the subsidy may be too large or too small to correct the market failure

Figure 3

Impact of a subsidy to correct market failure

With an optimal level of output of OB, a subsidy of EG per unit is needed to maximise welfare.

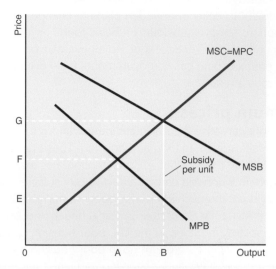

exactly. Partly, this may be due to information failure on the part of government: it doesn't know the exact size of the market failure or it may not know the impact a subsidy will have on the market.

- There can be conflict with other policy objectives. Someone must pay the subsidies. If it is government, this can conflict with objectives about low taxes or reducing government deficits. Subsidies can also be provided by firms. In the case of the UK electricity industry, government regulations force electricity generators to buy a certain percentage of their power from renewable sources. The prices paid are above the prices for conventional coal or gas generation. To make a profit, electricity generators then charge their customers a higher price. So customers are subsidising renewable energy by paying higher prices than they would otherwise have

Question 2

In 2014, the government announced that it was scrapping a subsidy scheme for large solar farms. Under the scheme, electricity was produced from solar panels deployed on a large scale at an individual site (nicknamed a 'solar farm'). The price of the electricity produced was then guaranteed into the future. The government said that the subsidy had been so popular that it would cost too much in future subsidies if the scheme were to be continued. In future, solar energy projects would have to compete with other sources of renewable energy, such as wind power, for subsidies under a different subsidy scheme.

Source: adapted from © the *Financial Times* 20.3.2014, All Rights Reserved.

(a) Explain, using a diagram and solar energy as an example, how a subsidy increases output of a product.

(b) Analyse, using a diagram, how the popularity of the subsidy scheme for solar energy, scrapped in 2014, could 'cost too much' for the government.

done. This can increase inflation. It can also impact on fuel poverty and the ability of low income households to heat their houses.

- Subsidies can be difficult to remove. Those who receive the subsidies effectively receive an increase in their income. If the subsidy is lowered or removed, they can lobby government to delay or abandon plans to change the subsidy. Attempts to remove subsidies on basic foods or fuel in countries like Iran, Venezuela or India have caused major riots in the past. In some cases, governments have even been toppled as a result.

Maximum prices

Market failure can arise if consumers cannot afford to buy basic necessities such as food and housing. These goods can have positive externalities in consumption. For example, if poor parents in Indonesia cannot afford to buy sufficient food for their children, those children may become malnourished. This may permanently affect their physical health and ability to function in society in future. In the UK, poor housing can also cause ill health. Children brought up in poor housing may suffer physically. It could affect their schooling and limit their ability to gain qualifications.

Imposing maximum prices for these goods will make them more affordable. In Figure 4, the free market rent for housing is OG and OB is demanded and supplied in equilibrium. The socially optimal level of housing is OC. If the government imposes a maximum rent or price of OF, then housing becomes more affordable and OC is demanded.

A problem with this policy is that if prices are forced down to make goods more affordable, then the quantity supplied falls. In Figure 4, at a price of OF, quantity supplied falls to OA. There is then excess demand of AC. Those able to buy OA are better off than before, but some of the consumers who want to buy AC are worse off because the good is not available.

Figure 4

Maximum prices

OG is the free market price. If the government sets a maximum price of OF, quantity demanded will increase to OC, whilst quantity supplied will fall to OA. The result will be excess demand of AC.

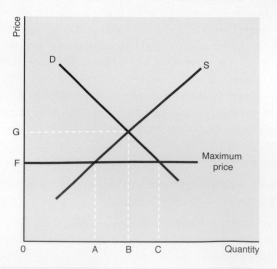

Maximum prices often lead to black markets. For example, some of the goods bought at price OF by consumers are resold on the black market at a higher price. Equally, producers may sell directly onto the black market to get higher prices.

Note that if the maximum price is set above the free market price, at more than OG in Figure 4, there will be no effect on the market. The equilibrium price in the market will remain where the quantity demanded equals the quantity supplied and equilibrium output will remain at OB.

Question 3

In September 2013, the leader of the Labour Party, Ed Miliband, said he would freeze the price of electricity and gas to households and firms if Labour won the next election in 2015. The freeze would last 20 months and, according to the Labour Party, save the average household £120 a year. Critics said energy companies would cut investment in new power plants, leading to power shortages and lost jobs.

In May 2014, Ed Miliband proposed also putting a cap on annual rent increases for households renting property. Critics said it would discourage landlords from renting out their properties and harm those looking for a property to let.

Source: adapted from © the *Financial Times* 25.9.2013, 2.5.2014, All Rights Reserved.

(a) Assume that the free market price of gas, electricity and rents on housing would have risen in 2015 and 2016. Explain, using a diagram, why the government putting a freeze on their prices in 2015 might lead to 'power shortages' and fewer properties to rent.

(b) (i) Explain, using a diagram, whether a price freeze in the short term would have any effect on output if supply were perfectly inelastic. (ii) Suggest two reasons why the supply of gas, electricity and housing is highly inelastic in the short run.

Minimum prices

Some goods, such as cigarettes and alcohol, have significant negative externalities in consumption. Governments may attempt to correct the resulting market failure by raising their price to a level where marginal social cost and marginal social benefit are equal. One way of doing this is to set a minimum price for the good.

In Figure 5, the free market equilibrium price is OF and output is OB. The government can then set a minimum price of OG above the free market price. This reduces the quantity demanded from OB to OA. However, it also increases the quantity supplied from OB to OC. The result is excess supply of AC.

Excess supply becomes a problem if it finds its way back onto the market. In the case of cigarettes and alcohol, minimum prices tend to create black markets where cigarettes and alcohol are sold at less than the minimum price.

Note that if the minimum price is set below the free market price at less than OF in Figure 5, there will be no effect on the market. The equilibrium price in the market will remain where the quantity demanded equals the quantity supplied and equilibrium output will remain at OB.

Figure 5

Minimum prices

OF is the free market price. If the government sets a minimum price of OG, supply will increase from OB to OC, whilst demand will fall to OA. The result will be excess supply of AC.

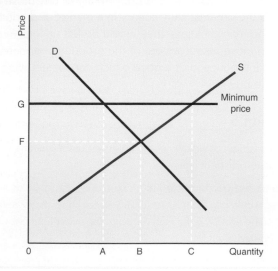

Regulation

Regulation is widely used to correct market failure. For example, regulation could be used to close information gaps. Airlines could be forced to disclose all the charges for an airline ticket at the start of the booking process rather than the end. Banks are forced to tell customers the rate of interest on a loan. Regulation is also widely used to control externalities. The government could lay down maximum pollution levels or might even ban pollution-creating activities altogether. For instance, in the UK, the Environmental Protection Act 1990 laid down minimum environmental standards for emissions from over 3 500 factories involved in chemical processes, waste incineration and oil refining. There are limits on harmful emissions from car exhausts. Cars that do not meet these standards fail their MOT tests. Forty years before these MOT regulations came into force, the government banned the burning of ordinary coal in urban areas.

Regulation is easy to understand and relatively cheap to enforce. However, it is a rather crude policy. First, it is often difficult for government to fix the right level of regulation to ensure efficiency. Regulations might be too lax or too tight. The correct level would be where the economic benefit arising from a reduction in externality equalled the economic cost imposed by the regulation. For instance, if firms had to spend £30 million fitting anti-pollution devices to plant and machinery, but the fall in pollution was only worth £20 million, then the regulation would have been too tight. If the fall in pollution was worth £40 million, it implies that it would be worth industry spending even more on anti-pollution measures to further reduce pollution and thus further increase the £40-million worth of benefits.

Moreover, regulations tend not to discriminate between different costs of reducing externalities. For instance, two firms might have to reduce pollution emissions by the same amount. Firm A could reduce its emissions at a cost of £3 million, whilst it might cost Firm B £10 million to do the same. However, Firm A could double the reduction in its pollution levels at a cost of £7 million. Regulations which set equal limits for all firms will mean that the cost to society of reducing pollution in this case is £13 million (£3 million for Firm A and £10 million for Firm B). However, it would be cheaper for society if the reduction could be achieved by Firm A alone at a cost of £7 million.

Trade pollution permits

Externalities caused by pollution can be reduced through the use of **trade pollution permits**, a key element of **cap and trade schemes**. To understand how they work, assume that the government wishes to control emissions of carbon, a greenhouse gas responsible for global warming. It has set a limit or cap on the amount of carbon to be emitted over a period of time, for example, like a year. This cap acts as the target for carbon emissions and is likely to be lower than current levels of carbon emission. The government then allocates permits to emit carbon, the total of which equals the cap. It could issue these, for example, by giving them to firms which currently emit carbon. The permits are then tradable for money between polluters. Firms which succeed in reducing their carbon emissions below their permit levels can sell their permits to other producers who are exceeding their limits. The higher the price of the permits, the greater the incentive for carbon-emitting firms to reduce their carbon emissions.

The main advantage of trade pollution permits over simple regulation is that costs in the industry and therefore to society should be lower than with regulation. Each firm in the industry will consider whether it is possible to reduce emissions and at what cost. Assume that Firm A, with just enough permits to meet its emissions, can reduce emissions by 500 tonnes at a cost of £10 million. Firm B is a high polluter and needs 500 tonnes worth of permits to meet regulations. It calculates that it would need to spend £25 million to cut emissions by this amount.

- If there was simple regulation, the anti-pollution costs to the industry, and therefore to society, would be £25 million. Firm B would have to conform to its pollution limit whilst there would be no incentive for Firm A to cut pollution.
- With permits, Firm A could sell 500 tonnes of permits to Firm B. The cost to society of then reducing pollution would only be £10 million, the cost that Firm A would incur. It might cost Firm B more than £10 million to buy the permits. It would be prepared to spend anything up to £25 million to acquire them. Say Firm A drove a hard bargain and sold the permits to Firm B for £22 million. Society would save £15 million, distributed between a paper profit of £12 million for Firm A and a fall in costs from what otherwise would have been the case for Firm B of £3 million.

State provision of public goods

Public goods are goods such as defence, the judiciary and prison service, the police service and street lighting. Because of their characteristics of non-rivalry and non-excludability, they will either not be provided by the market mechanism or will only be provided in small quantities. The result is market failure. In Figure 6, the socially optimal level of output of a public good is 0A. However, the maximum amount that is demanded in a free market is 0B and this is when the price is zero. Governments tend to respond to this by providing these goods directly and paying for them via taxes. In Figure 6, state provision is shown by the vertical supply curve (Supply).

Direct provision can have disadvantages. It may lead to inefficient production, particularly if the government produces

Figure 6

Direct provision of a public good

Assume this is the market for defence. To prevent market failure, 0A should be produced. However, there is no price on the demand curve at which 0A would be demanded. The government therefore steps in and provides 0A whatever the price of defence.

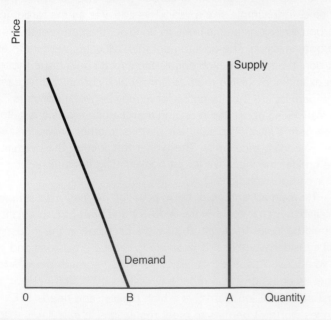

the good itself. This is because employees of the state, whether providing the good or buying it in, may have no incentive to cut costs to a minimum. It may also be inefficient because the wrong mix of goods is produced, especially if the goods are provided free of charge to taxpayers. The government may provide too many soldiers and too few hospital beds, for example. Markets, in contrast, give consumers the opportunity to buy those goods which give the greatest satisfaction. In a market, if producers supplied too many soldiers, they would be left unsold. Firms would then move resources out of the production of defence and into the production of a good which consumers were prepared to buy.

Question 5

There is a variety of ways in which the government could deal with the provision of street lighting.

(a) It could leave it completely to market forces. Households and firms would pay the full cost for any street lights they wanted, including providing the land on which the street lights would be erected.

(b) It could subsidise households and firms wishing to provide street lighting on their land but not provide any street lighting itself.

(c) It could provide street lighting directly and pay for it through levying taxes.

Discuss the relative merits of each of these options.

Provision of information

Information failure occurs because one party to a transaction does not have the information that is available to make a decision. A government can step in to provide the information itself. For example, it might run advertising campaigns to deliver messages about not smoking or the dangers of drinking and driving. Or it might force parties to a transaction to release information. Forcing cigarette manufacturers to put messages about the dangers of smoking on cigarette packets is an example.

Key Terms

Cap and trade schemes - schemes which set a limit on a particular type of pollution, and then issue pollution permits to the total of that limit which can be bought and sold between firms which pollute.
Trade pollution permit or pollution permit or pollution credit - a permission issued, usually by a government, to allow a fixed amount of pollution to be created; this permit can be used by the owner or sold to another firm.

Thinking like an economist

China's pollution problems

China's economy has been growing at 10 per cent per annum on average since the 1980s. Its national income has been doubling roughly every seven years. However, this increase in spending power has come at a severe price. Many Chinese people live and work in highly polluted environments. Growth of manufacturing and heavy industry such as steel works has led to high levels of air, soil and water pollution.

Local authorities and the government in China have been accused of tackling the problems half-heartedly. They know that pollution is a side effect of ever-increasing output, jobs and prosperity. They also know that tackling the complex issues will be costly. However, Chinese citizens are becoming ever more concerned about the effects of pollution on their health.

The most commonly used measure to control pollution is regulation. In the late 1990s, for example, the use of polystyrene boxes for takeaway food was banned. In the early 2000s, China phased out an extremely polluting aluminium smelting process. The province of Hebei, surrounding the capital Beijing, shut down polluting smaller steel mills to reduce air pollution in the capital. There are numerous regulations about the amount of pollution that individual plants can emit but these are often ignored by firms and by local authorities in charge of enforcing the regulations.

Subsidies have been used to reward polluters that reduce emissions. Subsidies have been given also for the installation of cleaner technology and the retrofitting of pollution-controlling equipment to some power stations.

China has also been experimenting with pollution permits for carbon emissions. These permits are given out to firms creating carbon emissions. If they fail to use their allocation, they can sell them to another firm that is exceeding its allowed carbon emissions. The idea is to issue fewer carbon emission permits than there are currently carbon emissions, thus lowering emissions.

Even though China is not a democracy, political leaders are being forced to address the issue of pollution because of the concerns of Chinese citizens. However, progress is likely to be slow and it could take 100 years for China to reduce its pollution levels to those currently seen in the UK.

Source: adapted from © the *Financial Times* 27.2.2014, 14.5.2014, All Rights Reserved.

Data Response Question

Carbon dioxide emissions from motor vehicles

Motor vehicles are a significant source of carbon dioxide (CO_2) emissions, which contribute to the growth of greenhouse gases in the atmosphere and global warming.

Governments in the European Union (EU) are committed to reducing CO_2 emissions. For example, high levels of VAT (an ad valorem tax) and excise duties (a specific tax) on fuel raise the cost of motoring and so reduce the number of miles travelled. In the UK, Vehicle Tax, a flat rate tax on ownership of a vehicle payable every 6 or 12 months, is lower on small engine, more fuel-efficient cars than on larger, less fuel-efficient engines.

At a European level, the EU has set emission targets for motor vehicles. Between 2011 and 2021, car manufacturers must cut emissions from the cars they sell by approximately 50 per cent. If they fail to do so, they

will be fined €95 per gram of CO_2 that their fleet is over the 95g limit multiplied by the number of cars they sold that year. According to the 2014 annual report by Transport & Environment, four of Europe's largest car manufacturers are predicted to miss these targets: General Motors, BMW, Fiat and Hyundai. All four companies denied they would fail to meet the 2021 deadline. They said that future engines and vehicle designs would speed up their rate of emissions reduction in the coming years.

Source: adapted from © the *Financial Times* 26.5.2014, All Rights Reserved.

Q

1. Distinguish between ad valorem taxes and specific taxes, using motor fuel as an example.

2. Explain, using a diagram, how taxes on fuel reduce CO_2 emissions.

3. Using your own knowledge and the data, evaluate whether regulations are always a better way of correcting market failure than indirect taxation.

Evaluation

Analyse the different ways in which regulations and indirect taxation work to reduce market failure. What are their advantages and disadvantages? Weigh these up, taking the issue of CO_2 emissions from motor vehicles as an example.

21 Government failure

Starter activity

In 2013, the Labour Party promised to freeze the price of gas and electricity to households if it won the next general election. Would that result in a net benefit to society or a loss? For example, would households be better off in the short term and in the long term? Would it encourage gas and electricity companies to invest in new equipment and power plants? Are gas and electricity companies simply making too much profit?

Government failure

Markets may fail. They may underprovide public goods. They may overprovide private goods which have negative externalities. They may cause prices to be too high because of asymmetric information. One response is for governments to intervene to correct these market failures. However, if markets can fail, so too can government. **Government failure** occurs when it intervenes in the market but this intervention leads to a net loss of economic welfare rather than a gain. So government failure arises when the total social costs arising from intervention are greater than the total social benefits which are created by that intervention. There is a number of reasons why government failure may occur.

Distortion of price signals

Some types of government intervention change price signals in the market. For example, many governments intervene in their domestic agricultural markets to support farmers. One way is to impose tariffs (taxes) on a product like wheat or rice being imported into the country. This allows high cost farmers who would otherwise be forced out of production by cheaper imports to stay in business and make a profit. However, it means that domestic consumers have to pay higher prices for the product. It also means that farmers are growing a crop on land that could be more efficiently used for something else if there were no price distortions. If the losses to consumers and to efficiency are greater than the gains to farmers, then there is government failure.

There are many examples of changes in price signals in the labour market that potentially can lead to government failure. For example, the government may want to raise income levels for the poor by setting a high minimum wage. However, this may be so high that employers shed low-paid workers, putting out of work large numbers of people whom the government wanted to protect. Similarly, the government may sharply raise unemployment benefit to help the unemployed. This may

discourage them from looking for work if they are now better off on benefits than working. This increases the numbers of unemployed.

Unintended consequences

Some interventions by government create unintended consequences. For example, when member countries of the European Union first implemented a Common Agricultural Policy (CAP) in 1962, they did not foresee what a boost it would give to agricultural production. The result was that in the 1970s and 1980s, most of the EU budget was spent on CAP and EU consumers paid much higher prices for food than if CAP had not existed. Another unintended consequence of CAP was that it depressed world prices of certain agricultural products. Under CAP, the EU bought up certain agricultural products at a minimum price. It then disposed of the produce by selling it below that price onto world markets. Farmers in rich countries like the USA and New Zealand suffered lower prices for their produce as a result. But so too did some farmers in developing countries round the world who couldn't compete with the low EU prices.

Excessive administrative costs

Sometimes, the administrative cost of correcting market failure is so large that it outweighs the welfare benefit from the correction of market failure. For instance, the government may put into place a scheme to help the unemployed back into work. During a year, 100 000 pass through the scheme. Of those, 50 000 would have found jobs anyway but simply use the scheme because it is advantageous for them or their employer to do so. 10 000 find a job who would otherwise not have done so. 40 000 remain unemployed. It may cost £3 000 per person per year on the scheme, giving a total cost of £300 million. This means that the cost per worker who would otherwise not have got a job is £300 million ÷ 10 000 or £30 000 per worker. This is an enormous cost for the benefit likely to be gained by the 10 000 workers. Indeed, almost certainly they would have preferred to have been given the £30 000 rather than gain a job. Another example would be the payment of welfare benefits. If it costs £1 to pay out a £3 benefit, is this likely to improve economic welfare?

Information gaps

Governments, like any economic agents, rarely possess complete information on which to base a decision. In some cases, the information available is positively misleading. It is not surprising, then, that governments may make the wrong policy response to a problem. For example, a government may decide to spend millions of pounds building a new road bridge between the mainland and a small island with a population of 10 000. It may justify the cost by projecting a number of benefits such as more jobs, more tourism to the island and lower cost of travel to and from the island. However, projections of costs and benefits like these are often wrong. Costs, such as the cost of building the bridge, may be underestimated whilst benefits, such as the number of extra tourists, may be overestimated. The result can be government failure.

Conflicting objectives

Governments often face conflicting objectives. For instance, they may want to cut taxes but increase spending on defence. Every decision made by the government has an opportunity cost. Sometimes, a decision is made where the welfare gain from the alternative foregone would have been even higher. In the case of education, contrast two systems. In one, there are selective (or grammar) schools and secondary schools for everyone who failed to pass the 11 plus test. In the other, every child, whatever their ability, goes to the same comprehensive school. Assume that those receiving a selective education in grammar schools receive a better education than if they were in a comprehensive school. In contrast, assume that those who fail to get into a selective school achieve less than they would have done if all children, whatever their abilities, had gone to the same school. There is now a conflict of objectives about which system to implement. Are the needs of those who would be selected for grammar schools more important than those of the rest of the school population, or vice versa? Governments may make the wrong policy decision when there are such conflicts of objective, choosing the option which gives lower economic welfare rather than higher economic welfare. They may do this because of lack of information, or they may act on their own political beliefs, ignoring information which goes contrary to these beliefs.

Politicians maximising their own welfare

Much of economics assumes that governments will act in a way that maximises the welfare of their citizens. **Public choice theory** suggests that politicians act in a way that maximises their own utility whether or not this leads to improved welfare for the citizens they are supposed to represent. For example, politicians in office who are fighting to get re-elected may implement policies which benefit their own electors at the expense of the welfare of all other citizens. Or they adopt policies which will produce benefits in the run-up to an election but which in the long term will lead to a net loss of economic welfare. Politicians may also engage in **rent-seeking** behaviour. This is where those in power manipulate the distribution of resources to benefit themselves without creating any extra wealth for society. For example, politicians may receive bribes from companies to make sure they win a government contract. Or a politician may be bribed to vote in a certain way on an issue.

Question 1

In 1861, Mrs Beeton, then the authority on cookery and household management and the Victorian equivalent of Delia Smith, wrote that her readers should always make their own vinegar. This was because shop-bought vinegar of the day tended to consist of diluted sulphuric acid.

Today, food manufacturers and retailers are so strictly controlled by government regulations that this could not happen. Some argue, though, that such regulations are excessive. They suggest that government red tape restricts the opening and running of new businesses and that consumers have to pay higher prices for their food because it costs firms money to conform to government regulations. For example, a report commissioned by the EUWEP, the EU trade association for egg packers, traders and processors, found that egg production in the EU was amongst the most expensive in the world in 2012. Fifteen per cent of the costs of producing eggs in the EU were the result of conforming to EU legislation, including higher animal welfare legislation. Major world egg producers such as Argentina, India and Ukraine had no specific animal welfare legislation, while in the USA, there were only voluntary guidelines.

Source: adapted from Isabella Beeton, *Beeton's Book of Household Management*, S. O. Beeton Publishing, 1861; *Farmers Weekly*, 11.11.2012.

(a) Explain why markets fail according to the data.

(b) Discuss whether there is government failure in the market for food in the UK.

Market vs government failure

In economic theory, it is often assumed that market failure should be corrected by governments. If markets fail to provide public goods, then the government should ensure their provision. If a monopolist is exploiting the consumer, then the government should regulate or abolish the monopoly. If a polluter is damaging the environment, then the government should act to limit the actions of those responsible. However, government intervention may lead to a loss of economic welfare rather than a gain in economic welfare and so government failure will exist. At one extreme, there are those who argue that government failure is so large and frequent that governments should only rarely intervene in markets. This tends to be associated with right wing political viewpoints. At the other extreme, there are those who argue that market failures are so large and frequent that the government must intervene in all the key workings of a market economy, either by regulating markets or by abolishing them altogether and having state provision of goods. This tends to be associated with left wing political viewpoints.

The evidence would suggest that the truth lies somewhere in between these two positions. Market failure is widespread and markets do need controlling by governments to some extent. However, markets often perform a better job of allocating resources than government, even when market failure is present.

Key Terms

Government failure - occurs when government intervention leads to a net welfare loss compared to the free market solution.
Public choice theory - theories about how and why public spending and taxation decisions are made.

Rent-seeking - the use of political power by an economic agent to manipulate the distribution of resources for their own benefit at the expense of others without creating any extra wealth for society.

Thinking like an economist

Venezuela in crisis

Commentators argue that Venezuela should be a rich and prosperous country. It has some of the world's largest oil reserves, an educated workforce, a modern industrialised economy and is well located for foreign trade. However, figures suggest that it has had economic problems for decades, arguably caused by poor governance. Between 1999 and 2013, the country was run by President Hugo Chavez, a socialist who was determined to redistribute income in favour of the poor. Economists would argue that his policies led to significant distortions and inefficiencies in the economy.

One example of government failure was a policy which saw large subsidies on petrol and gas. In 2013, Venezuela was earning $100 billion in oil revenues and selling petrol at approximately 1p a litre to Venezuelan motorists. The subsidy was costing the government $12 billion a year. In most countries, petrol is taxed, not subsidised. This subsidy had two negative effects. One was that large amounts of subsidised petrol were being smuggled illegally across the border to Colombia where it could be sold for profit. In 2014, this was estimated at 140 000 barrels of oil per day. Venezuelan citizens were effectively subsidising Colombian motorists. The other negative effect was high inflation of over 50 per cent a year. The government depended for almost all its revenues on oil rather than taxes on citizens and non-oil businesses. By 2013, it was running a large government deficit, including the $12 billion in fuel subsidies, and financing that through printing money. The result was high inflation.

Another example of government failure occurred in 2013. The government fixed the exchange rate of the currency, the bolívar, at 6.3 bolívars to the US dollar. Purchases of foreign currency at banks was strictly regulated. This was necessary because the black market exchange rate was seven times that amount. One loophole was that anyone buying an airline ticket to fly abroad could get up to $3 000 at the official exchange rate. Venezuelans exploited this by buying an airline ticket, exchanging bolívars at the official exchange rate of 6.3 bolívars to the US dollar and then exchanging the dollars back into bolívars on the black market. The airline ticket would be thrown away, unused. So long as the airline ticket was less than the profit made on the currency, speculators would make a profit at the expense of everyone else. Airlines flying out of Venezuela were also doing good business at the government's expense.

Government subsidies cover all basic items, from food to toilet paper. However, shortages were widespread because

the government placed maximum prices on goods. The maximum price was too low for importers to make a profit on goods bought abroad. It was also too low to prevent domestic producers from refusing to supply and closing down. One response of government was to nationalise companies. In response to shortages of toilet paper, for example, the government took over the largest manufacturer of toilet paper in September 2013. However, Venezuelans have to queue at shops, often for hours, to get basic essentials. In 2014, the government introduced fingerprint scanners at supermarkets to stop Venezuelans from stocking up on too many cheap items. At the same time, 27 000 government inspectors were checking shop prices to ensure that they were 'fair' and that shops were not profiteering.

Shortages, queues and refusal to supply impose heavy costs on an economy. If the Venezuelan government wanted to help the poorest people in the country, it would be far more efficient simply to pay a welfare benefit to those on low incomes and allow them to buy what they want.

Source: adapted from © the *Financial Times* 11.8.2013, 30.9.2013, 26.1.2014, 25.6.2014, 2.12.2014, All Rights Reserved.

Data Response Question

Government failure

In 2009, the European Union set a target for 10 per cent of transport fuel to be met from biofuels. It also set a target for member countries to generate a fifth of their energy from renewable sources by 2020. Governments have spent large amounts of money in subsidies to create a market for biofuels.

However, there was widespread criticism when farmers both in Europe and the USA began to plant large amounts of crops for conversion into biofuels. It was argued that it was a waste of prime farmland which should be used to grow food. This could potentially drive up world food prices because of the fall in supply, making it more difficult for the poor to feed themselves.

There was also criticism of the use of wood products to generate electricity. For example, in the UK, the Drax power plant in Yorkshire burns wood pellets to generate electricity. It is argued that burning wood pellets is better than burning coal because wood is a renewable resource and that carbon emissions from burning wood are absorbed by newly-planted trees. The pellets for Drax are bought mainly from the southern United States. They are meant to come from sawdust, offcuts or forest thinnings rather than healthy trees. However, critics say that regulation in the USA is very weak and that too much of the wood comes from whole trees specifically cut down to create wood pellets. They also say that it is difficult to monitor that trees are being replaced.

Source: adapted from © the *Financial Times* 16.4.2014, 5.5.2014, All Rights Reserved.

In January 2014, the media reported that the Australian government gave approval for a consortium to create the world's largest seaport for the export of coal, at Abbot Point. Its backers argued that it would unlock tens of billions of dollars of coal reserves in Queensland and provide a boost for the Australian economy. However, the plans were fiercely opposed by conservationists because they involved the dumping of three million cubic metres of dredged mud near the Great Barrier Reef, which already faces threats from environmental factors such as global warming. Two million tourists a year visit the Great Barrier Reef. UNESCO had already warned that it may place the reef on its list of sites in danger this year before the announcement of the Abbot Point development was made.

Source: adapted from © the *Financial Times* 1.2.2014, All Rights Reserved.

Evaluation

In your answer to question 3, you need to analyse the different sources of government failure, applying economic theory to the examples in the data and other examples you may have. Each source of market failure should be given a separate paragraph. Alongside the analysis, evaluate whether or not this is an important source of government failure with particular reference to the examples you have included. In a concluding paragraph, weigh up the evidence to come to a conclusion.

Q

1. Explain the difference between market failure and government failure.

2. Explain how increasing the output of bio-fuels could (a) help solve the problem of market failure in the market for fuels; (b) create an example of government failure.

3. Using the data and your own economic knowledge, evaluate whether the main source of government failure arises from information gaps on the part of government.

Measures of economic performance

Key points

1. The macroeconomic performance of an economy can be judged on its rate of economic growth, rate of unemployment, rate of inflation and its current account balance on the balance of payments.

Starter activity

Find out the current rate of economic growth, the rate of unemployment, the inflation rate and the level of the current account deficit on the balance of payments for the UK, France and the United States. Which is currently performing best do you think?

Microeconomics and macroeconomics

Microeconomics is the study of individual markets within an economy. For instance, microeconomics is concerned with individual markets for goods or the market for labour. Housing, transport, sport and leisure are all mainly microeconomic topics because they concern the study of individual markets.

In contrast, **macroeconomics** is concerned with the study of the economy as a whole. For instance, macroeconomics considers the total value produced of goods and services in an economy. The price level of the whole economy is studied. Total levels of employment and unemployment are examined. Housing becomes a macroeconomic issue when, for instance, rises in house prices significantly affect the average level of all prices in the economy.

National economic performance

One of the reasons why macroeconomics is useful is because it tells us something about the performance of an economy. In particular, it allows economists to compare the economy today with the past. Is the economy doing better or worse than it was, say, 10 years ago? It also allows economists to compare different economies. Is the Japanese economy doing better than the US economy? How does the UK compare with the average in Europe?

An economy is a system which attempts to resolve the basic economic problem of scarce resources in a world of infinite wants. An economic system is a mechanism for deciding what is to be produced, how production is to take place and who is to receive the benefit of that production. When judging the performance of an economy, one of the criteria is to consider how much is being produced. The more that is produced, the better is usually considered the economic performance. Another criterion is whether resources are being fully utilised. If there are high levels of unemployment, for instance, the economy cannot be producing at its potential level of output. Unemployment also brings poverty to those out of work and therefore affects the living standards of individuals. The rate at which prices rise is important too. High rates of price rises disrupt the workings of an economy. A national economy must also live within its means. So over a long period of time, the value of what it buys from

other economies must roughly equal what it sells. In this, it is no different from a household which cannot forever overspend and accumulate debts.

Economic growth

One of the key measures of national economic performance is the rate of change of output. This is known as **economic growth**. If an economy grows by 2.5 per cent per annum, output will double roughly every 30 years. If it grows by seven per cent per annum, output will approximately double every 10 years. At growth rates of 10 per cent per annum, output will double every seven years.

There is a standard definition of output based on a United Nations measure which is used by countries around the world to calculate their output. Using a standard definition allows output to be compared between countries and over time. This measure of output is called **gross domestic product** or GDP. So growth of three per cent in GDP (adjusted for inflation) in one year means that the output of the economy has increased by three per cent over a 12-month period.

Economic growth is generally considered to be desirable because individuals prefer to consume more rather than fewer goods and services. This is based on the assumption that wants are infinite. Higher economic growth is therefore better than lower economic growth. Periods when the economy fails to grow at all, or output shrinks as in a recession or depression, are periods when the economy is performing poorly. The depression years of the 1930s in Europe and the Americas, for instance, were years when poverty increased and unemployment brought misery to millions of households. In contrast, a boom is a period when the economy is doing particularly well with economic growth above its long run average.

Unemployment

Unemployment is a major problem in society because it represents a waste of scarce resources. Output could be higher if the unemployed were in work. It also leads to poverty for those who are out of work. So high unemployment is an indicator of poor national economic performance. Conversely, low unemployment is an indicator of good national economic performance.

Economic growth and unemployment tend to be linked. Fast-growing economies tend to have low unemployment. This is because more workers are needed to produce more goods and services. Low levels of economic growth tend to be associated with rising levels of unemployment. Over time, technological change allows an economy to produce more with fewer workers. If there is little or no economic growth, workers are made redundant through technological progress but fail to find new jobs in expanding industries. If growth is negative and the economy goes into recession, firms will lay off workers and unemployment will rise.

Fast economic growth, then, will tend to lead to net job creation. More jobs will be created than are lost through the changing structure of the economy. So another way of judging the performance of an economy is to consider its rate of job creation.

Inflation

Inflation is the increase in average prices in an economy. Low inflation is generally considered to be better than high inflation. This is because inflation has a number of adverse effects. For instance, rising prices mean that the value of what savings can buy falls. If a person had £50 in savings and the price of a T-shirt went up from £10 to £25, then they would be worse off because their savings could only now buy two compared to five before. Another problem with inflation is that it disrupts knowledge of prices in a market. If there is very high inflation, with prices changing by the month, consumers often don't know what is a reasonable price for an item when they come to buy it.

Today, inflation of a few per cent is considered to be acceptable. When inflation starts to climb through the five per cent barrier, economists begin to worry that inflation is too high. Inflation was a major problem for many countries including the UK in the 1970s and 1980s. In the UK, inflation reached 24.1 per cent in 1975, for instance. Today, some countries in the industrialised world are faced with the opposite problem: **deflation**, or falling prices. Japan, for example, has had bouts of deflation for the past 20 years. Deflation makes it more difficult for a country to grow its GDP. Hence deflation and recessions are linked.

The current balance

A household must pay its way in the world. If it spends more than it earns and takes on debt, then at some point in the future it must repay that debt. Failure to repay debt can lead to seizure of assets by bailiffs and the household being barred from future borrowing. The same is true of a national economy. A nation's spending on foreign goods and services is called the value of its imports. It earns money to pay for those imports by selling goods and services, known as exports, to foreigners. If the value of its imports is greater than the value of its exports then this must be financed, either through borrowing or running down savings held abroad. The economic performance of a country is sound if, over a period of time, its exports are either greater than or approximately equal to its imports. However, if its imports are significantly greater than exports, then it could face difficulties.

Where exports of goods and services are greater than imports, there is said to be a current account surplus. Where imports exceed exports, there is a current account deficit. Deficits become a problem when foreign banks and other lenders refuse to lend any more money. A 'credit crunch' like this occurred, for instance, in Mexico in 1982 and Thailand in 1998. Countries have to respond to restore confidence. This is likely to involve cutting domestic spending, which leads to less demand for imports. Cutting domestic spending, though, also leads to reduced economic growth and rising unemployment. So the current account position of a country is an important indicator of performance.

Thinking like an economist

The Irish economy

In the 1990s and early 2000s, Ireland was nicknamed a 'tiger economy'. The rate of growth of GDP averaged 4-5 per cent and unemployment was low. By 2007, income per head in Ireland was higher than in the UK. That all changed in 2008.

Figure 1

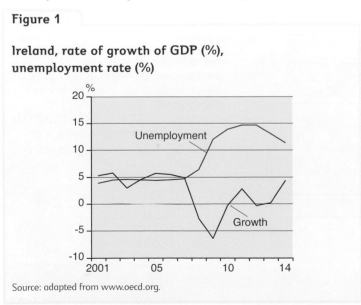

Ireland, rate of growth of GDP (%), unemployment rate (%)

Source: adapted from www.oecd.org.

Figure 2

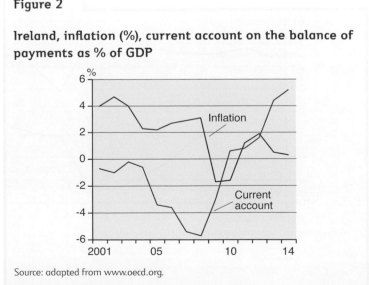

Ireland, inflation (%), current account on the balance of payments as % of GDP

Source: adapted from www.oecd.org.

High economic growth in the Irish economy had been fuelled by a booming property market. Irish banks had lent recklessly to property developers, builders and households. The worldwide financial crash of 2008 led to the implosion of the two main Irish banks, Allied Irish Bank and Bank of Ireland, as well as a number of smaller banks. They were bailed out by the Irish government at a cost of €62.8 billion.

The crisis had a direct impact on Ireland's main economic indicators, as Figures 1 and 2 show. The economy shrank in size, led by the construction industry. Unemployment soared. It would have been even worse had many younger Irish workers not emigrated. Prices fell due to lack of demand for goods and services. The current account on the balance of payments improved because falling incomes hit the ability of households and firms to spend on imports. In 2014, the economy showed signs that a long-term recovery was taking place, six years after the disastrous events of 2008.

Source: with information from www.oecd.org

Data Response Question

Spain 2001-2014

Figure 3

Spain, rate of growth of GDP (%), unemployment rate (%)

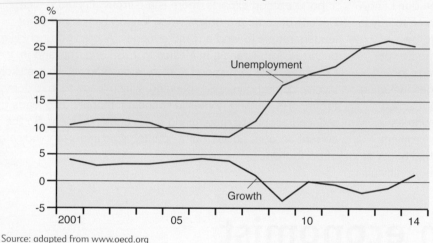

Source: adapted from www.oecd.org

Figure 4

Spain, inflation (%), current account on the balance of payments as % of GDP)

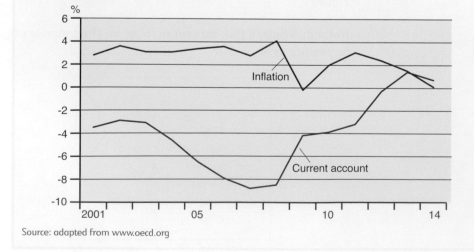

Source: adapted from www.oecd.org

Q

1. Consider the two periods 2001-2007 and 2008-2014. In which period was Spain doing better economically, judging by economic growth and unemployment? Justify your answer with statistics.

2. In 2008, like many countries around the world, Spain suffered a large financial crisis and its property market collapsed. Explain why this might have caused the change in unemployment seen in Figure 3.

3. In 2013 and 2014, Spain exported more than it imported, shown by the positive numbers in Figure 4. Discuss whether this showed that Spain had staged a full recovery from the financial crisis of 2008.

Evaluation

Look carefully at economic growth and unemployment. Do the numbers for 2014 suggest that Spain was in good economic shape in 2014?

23 The characteristics of aggregate demand

Key points

1. The aggregate demand curve is downward sloping. It shows the relationship between the price level and equilibrium output in the economy.
2. A movement along the aggregate demand curve shows how real output will change if there is a change in the price level.
3. A shift in the aggregate demand curve is caused by a change in variables such as consumption and exports at any given price level.

Starter activity

How would you calculate total spending in the UK economy? What is household spending called? What do firms spend? What does government spend? What do foreigners spend on UK goods and services?

Aggregate demand

Demand for an individual good is defined as the quantity that is bought at any given price. In this unit, we will consider what determines **aggregate** demand. 'Aggregate' in economics means a 'total' or 'added up' amount. **Aggregate demand** is the total of all demands or expenditures in the economy at any given price. National expenditure is one of the three ways of calculating national income, usually measured as GDP. National expenditure is made up of four components.

- **Consumption (C)**. This is spending by households on goods and services.
- **Investment (I)**. This is spending by firms on investment goods.

Figure 1

The aggregate demand curve

A rise in the price level will lead, to a fall in the equilibrium level of national income and therefore of national output. Hence the aggregate demand curve is downward sloping.

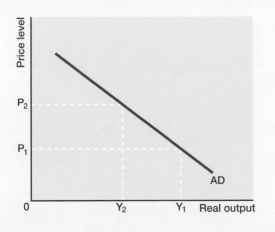

- **Government spending (G)**. This includes current spending, for instance on wages and salaries. It also includes spending by government on investment goods like new roads or new schools.
- **Exports minus imports (X - M)**. Foreigners spend money on goods produced in the **domestic economy**. Hence it is part of national expenditure. However, households, firms and governments also spend money on goods produced abroad. For instance, a UK household might buy a car produced in France, or a British firm might use components imported from the Far East in a computer which is sold to Germany. These imported goods do not form part of national output and do not contribute to national income. So, because C, I, G and X all include spending on imported goods, imports (M) must be taken away from C + I + G + X to arrive at a figure for national expenditure.

National expenditure or aggregate demand (AD) can therefore be calculated using the formula:

$$AD = C + I + G + X - M$$

The aggregate demand curve

The **aggregate demand curve** shows the relationship between the price level and the level of real expenditure in the economy. Figure 1 shows an aggregate demand (AD) curve. The price level is put on the vertical axis whilst real output is put on the horizontal axis.

The **price level** is the average level of prices in the economy. Governments calculate a number of different measures of the price level. In the UK, for instance, the most widely quoted measure is the **Consumer Prices Index**, figures for which are published every month and are widely reported in the news. A change in the price level is **inflation**.

Real output on the horizontal axis must equal real expenditure and real income. This is because, in the circular flow model of the economy, these are three different ways of measuring the same flow. The aggregate demand curve plots the level of expenditure where the economy would be in an equilibrium position at each price level, all other things being equal.

Demand curves are nearly always downward sloping. Why is the aggregate demand curve the same shape? One simple answer is to consider what happens to a household budget if prices rise. If a household is on a fixed income, then a rise in average prices will mean that they can buy fewer goods and services than before. The higher the price level in the economy, the less they can afford to buy. So it is with the national economy. The higher the price, the fewer goods and services will be demanded in the whole economy.

A more sophisticated explanation considers what happens to the different components of expenditure when prices rise.

Consumption Consumption expenditure is influenced by the **rate of interest** in the economy. When prices increase, consumers (and firms) need more money to buy the same number of goods and services as before. One way of getting more money is to borrow it and so the demand for borrowed funds will rise. However, if there is a fixed supply of money available for borrowing from banks and building societies, the price of borrowed funds will rise. This price is the rate of interest. A rise in interest rates leads to a fall in consumption, particularly of durable goods such as cars which are commonly bought on credit.

Another way a rise in the price level affects consumption is through the **wealth effect**. A rise in the price level leads to the real value of an individual consumer's wealth being lower. For instance, £100 000 at today's prices will be worth less in real terms in a year's time if average prices have increased 20 per cent over the 12 months. A fall in real wealth will result in a fall in consumer spending.

Investment As has just been explained, a rise in prices, all other things being equal, leads to a rise in interest rates in the economy. Investment is affected by changes in the rate of interest. The higher the rate of interest, the less profitable new investment projects become and therefore the fewer projects will be undertaken by firms. So, the higher the rate of interest, the lower will be the level of investment.

Government spending Government spending in this model of the economy is assumed to be independent of economic variables. It is exogenously determined, fixed by variables outside the model. In this case, it is assumed to be determined by the political decisions of the government of the day. Note that government spending (G) here does not include transfer payments. These are payments by the government for which there is no corresponding output in the economy, like welfare benefits or student grants.

Exports and imports A higher price level in the UK means that foreign firms will be able to compete more successfully in the UK economy. For instance, if British shoe manufacturers put up their prices by 20 per cent, whilst foreign shoe manufacturers keep their prices the same, then British shoe manufacturers will become less competitive and more foreign shoes will be imported. Equally, British shoe manufacturers will find it more difficult to export charging higher prices. So a higher UK price level, with price levels in other economies staying the same, will lead to a fall in UK exports.

Hence, aggregate demand falls as prices rise, first, because increases in interest rates reduce consumption and investment and, second, because a loss of international competitiveness at the new higher prices will reduce exports and increase imports.

110

Question 1

In 1975, inflation rose to a peak of 24.1 per cent. Real GDP fell in both 1974 and 1975. In 1980, inflation rose to a peak of 18.0 per cent and real GDP fell in 1980 and 1981. In 1990, inflation rose to a peak of 9.5 per cent. GDP fell in 1991 and 1992. In 2008, inflation rose to a peak of 3.6 per cent when GDP fell by 4.3 per cent in 2009.

How might economic theory account for this?

Shifts in the AD curve

The aggregate demand (AD) curve shows the relationship between the price level and the equilibrium level of real income and output. A change in the price level results in a **movement along** the AD curve. Higher prices lead to falls in aggregate demand.

Shifts in the aggregate demand curve will occur if there is a change in any other relevant variable apart from the price level. When the AD curve shifts, it shows that there is a change in real output at any given price level. In Figure 2, the shift in the AD curve from AD_1 to AD_2 shows that at a price level of P, real output increases from Y_1 to Y_2. There is a number of variables which can lead to a shift of the AD curve. Some of these variables are real variables, such as changes in the willingness of consumers to spend. Others are changes in **monetary variables** such as the rate of interest.

Consumption A number of factors might increase consumption spending at any given level of prices, shifting the AD curve from AD_1 to AD_2 in Figure 2. For instance, unemployment may fall, making consumers less afraid that they will lose their jobs and more willing to borrow money to spend on consumer durables. The government or central bank might reduce interest rates, again encouraging borrowing for durables. A substantial rise in stock market prices will increase consumer wealth which in turn may lead to an increase in spending.

Figure 2

A shift in the aggregate demand curve

An increase in consumption, investment, government spending or net exports, given a constant price level, will lead to a shift in the aggregate demand curve from AD_1 to AD_2.

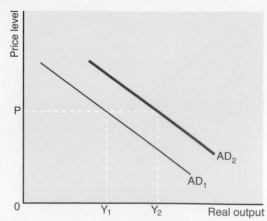

A reduction in the relative numbers of high saving 45-60-year-olds in the population will increase the **average propensity to consume** (the proportion of total income that is spent) of the whole economy. New technology which creates new consumer products can lead to an increase in consumer spending as households want to buy these new products. A fall in income tax would increase consumers' disposable income, leading to a rise in consumption.

Investment One factor which would increase investment spending at any given level of prices, pushing the AD curve from AD₁ to AD₂ in Figure 2, would be an increase in business confidence - an increase in 'animal spirits', as John Maynard Keynes put it. This increase in business confidence could have come about, for instance, because the economy was going into boom. A fall in interest rates ordered by the government would lead to a rise in investment. An increase in company profitability would give firms more retained profit to use for investment. A fall in taxes on profits (corporation tax in the UK) would lead to the rate of return on investment projects rising, leading to a rise in investment.

Government spending Government spending can change automatically because of previous government spending commitments, or the government can announce changes to its spending. A rise in government spending with no change in taxation will lead to a fall in its budget surplus or a rise in its deficit. This will increase aggregate demand, pushing the AD curve to the right from AD₁ to AD₂ in Figure 2. A fall in government spending with no change in taxation will lead to a shift to the left in the aggregate demand curve.

Exports and imports A number of factors can affect the balance between exports and imports. For example, a rise in the exchange rate is likely to lead to lower exports but higher imports. Exports minus imports will therefore fall, reducing aggregate demand. This is shown by a shift in the aggregate demand curve to the left. In contrast, an improvement in innovation and quality of UK manufactured goods is likely to lead to a rise in exports. This will increase aggregate demand and shift the aggregate demand curve to the right from AD₁ to AD₂ in Figure 2.

Important notes

Changes and shifts in AD Aggregate demand and aggregate supply analysis is more complex than demand and supply analysis in an individual market. You may already have noticed, for instance, that a change in interest rates could lead to a movement along the aggregate demand curve or lead to a shift in the curve. Similarly, an increase in consumption could lead to a movement along or a shift in the curve. To distinguish between movements along and shifts in the curve it is important to consider what has caused the change in aggregate demand.

If the change has come about because the price level has changed, then there is a movement along the AD curve. For instance, a rise in the price level causes a rise in interest rates. This leads to a fall in consumption. This is shown by a movement up the curve.

If, however, interest rates or consumer spending have changed for a different reason than because prices have changed, then there will be a shift in the AD curve. A government putting up interest rates at a given price level would lead to a shift in the curve.

Levels and changes As with any economic analysis, it is important to distinguish between absolute changes and rates of change. For example, a fall in the level of investment will lead to a fall in aggregate demand, all other things being equal. However, a fall in the rate of change of investment, when this rate of change is positive, means that investment is still rising. If growth in investment has fallen from five per cent to three per cent, investment is still increasing. So a fall in the rate of growth of investment will lead to an increase in aggregate demand and a shift of the AD curve to the right.

Question 2

Explain, using a diagram, the likely effect of the following on the aggregate demand curve for the UK.

(a) The 3.5 per cent fall in real household consumption expenditure between 2007 and 2011.

(b) The fall in bank base interest rates from 5.5 per cent in 2007 to 0.5 per cent in 2010.

(c) Rises in taxes in the 2011 and 2012 budgets.

(d) The 40 per cent fall in London Stock Exchange prices between October 2007 and February 2009.

(e) The rise in the household saving ratio from 5.6 per cent in 2008 to 11.0 per cent in 2010.

(f) The fall in real government spending between 2011 and 2014 and forecast to continue to 2018.

(g) The 23 per cent fall in the average value of the pound against other currencies between 2007 and 2011.

Key Terms

Aggregate - the sum or total.
Aggregate demand - the total of all demands or expenditures in the economy at any given price.
Aggregate demand curve - shows the relationship between the price level and equilibrium national income. As the price level rises the equilibrium level of national income falls.
Domestic economy - the economy of a single country.

Thinking like an economist

Aggregate demand

Aggregate demand (AD) is made up of private sector consumption (C), private sector investment (I), government spending (G) and exports (X) minus imports (I). Figure 3 shows the composition of UK aggregate demand in 2013. In that year, 65 per cent of GDP was made up of private consumption expenditure, the largest single component of aggregate demand. Private sector investment was the smallest component at 15 per cent of GDP. 23 per cent was government spending on current spending such as teachers' salaries and investment such as new road building. Exports were 30 per cent of GDP but the overall balance of X - M was negative because imports

were even higher at 32 per cent of GDP. The contribution of net exports (exports minus imports) to aggregate demand is extremely small. Between 1997 and 2013, net exports varied from +0.7 per cent to -4.2 per cent of aggregated demand.

Figure 4 shows how aggregate demand and its components have changed over time at constant prices. The period 1997 to 2007 saw a significant rise in aggregate demand. However, the financial crisis of 2008 brought growth to a halt. Between 2008 and 2013 the UK suffered the longest period of stagnation since the 19th century, greater even than the Great Depression of the 1930s.

Figure 3

GDP and its components, 2013

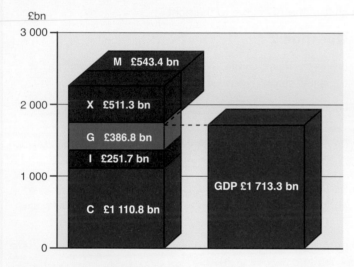

Source: adapted from www.ons.gov.uk.

Figure 4

Aggregate demand and its components, £bn at 2011 prices

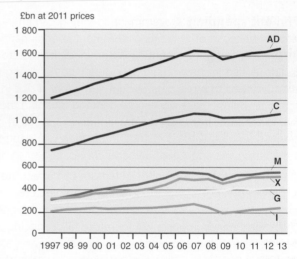

Source: adapted from www.ons.gov.uk.

Data Response Question

Optimism rises for the Spanish economy

Spain has been through difficult times since the world financial crisis of 2008. Aggregate demand in 2014 has still not reached its 2007 level. However, it has been suggested that recently there have been encouraging signs. 2013 saw a significant rise in exports, partly due to the falling prices of Spanish goods. The following year, consumption and investment began to increase after several years of negative growth.

Although government spending continued to fall in 2014, this should be more than outweighed by growth in private sector domestic spending.

Table 1 Spain: aggregate demand and its components[1]

	Euros bns	Annual percentage change				
	2010	2011	2012	2013	2014	2015
Aggregate demand (GDP)	1 046	0.1	-1.6	-1.2	1.2	1.6
Private consumption	605	-1.2	-2.8	-2.1	1.2	1.6
Government consumption	225	-0.5	-4.8	-2.3	-0.3	-1.5
Investment by private sector and government	239	-5.4	-7.0	-5.1	0.6	2.9
Exports	286	7.6	2.1	4.9	3.7	5.9
Imports	309	-0.1	-5.7	0.4	4.3	5.2

1. 2014 and 2015 are forecast data.

Source: adapted from OECD Economic Outlook (2014), No.95, Vol. 2014/1, updated and INE (2014), Contabilidad Nacional de España, INEbase, Insituto Nacional de Estadistica.

Q

1. Explain, using Table 1 for examples, what is meant by 'aggregate demand'.

2. Analyse the contribution of net exports to Spain's aggregate demand between 2010 and 2015.

3. Discuss whether Spain can recover from its recession without a large increase in domestic consumption.

Evaluation

Start by defining recession and aggregate demand. Analyse how increases in the different components of aggregate demand can help Spain recover, using examples from the data. Use this analysis to argue whether or not a rise in the other components of AD apart from consumption (or fall in the case of imports) can lift AD without a large increase in C. You will need to work out the approximate relative sizes of the annual increases in I, G and X-M from the annual increases in Table 1 to support your evaluation.

24 Consumption

Key points

1. Consumption can be divided into spending on durable goods and non-durable goods.
2. The consumption function shows the relationship between consumption and its determinants, the main one being income.
3. Consumption is also affected by changes in interest rates, consumer confidence, wealth, the availability of credit, inflation and the composition of households.

Starter activity

What is most important factor determining how much you spend? An allowance or pocket money given to you by parents? Wages from a paid job? Access to borrowed money? Your wealth in the form of savings? Confidence about your future income and wealth? The prices of goods you buy? Taking advantage of a special offer?

Defining consumption and saving

Consumption in economics is spending on consumer goods and services over a period of time. Examples are spending on chocolate, tablets or mobile phones, or buying a car. Consumption can be broken down into a number of different categories. One way of classifying consumption is to distinguish between spending on goods and spending on services. Another way is to distinguish between spending on **durable goods** and **non-durable goods**. Durable goods are goods which, although bought at a point in time, continue to provide a stream of services over a period of time. A car, for instance, should last at least six years. A television set might last 10 years. Non-durable goods are goods and services which are used up immediately or over a short period of time, like an ice cream or a packet of soap powder.

Saving is what is not spent out of income. For instance, if a worker takes home £1 000 in her wage packet at the end of the month, but only spends £900, then £100 must have been saved. The saving might take the form of increasing the stock of cash, or an increase in money in a bank or building society account, or it might take the form of stocks or shares. Income in this case is **disposable income**, income including state benefits such as child benefit and interest on, say, building society shares, but after deductions of income tax and National Insurance contributions.

Consumption and income

There is a number of factors which determine how much a household consumes. The relationship between consumption and these factors is called the **consumption function**. The most important determinant of consumption is disposable income. Other factors, discussed in sections below, are far less important but can bring about small but significant changes in the relationship between consumption and income.

Assume that one year a household has an income of £1 000 per month. The next year, due to salary increases, this rises to £1 200 per month. Economic theory predicts that the consumption of the household will rise.

How much it will rise can be measured by the **marginal propensity to consume** (MPC), the proportion of a change in income that is spent:

$$MPC = \frac{\text{Change in consumption}}{\text{Change in income}} = \frac{\Delta C}{\Delta Y}$$

where Y is income, C is consumption and Δ is 'change in'.

If the £200 rise in income leads to a £150 rise in consumption, then the marginal propensity to consume would be 0.75 (£150 ÷ £200).

For the economy as a whole, the marginal propensity to consume is likely to be positive (i.e. greater than zero) but less than 1. Any rise in income will lead to more spending but also some saving too. For individuals, the marginal propensity to consume could be more than 1 if money was borrowed to finance spending higher than income.

The **average propensity to consume** (or APC) measures the average amount spent on consumption out of total income. For instance, if total disposable income in an economy were £100 billion and consumption were £90 billion, then the average propensity to consume would be 0.9. The formula for the APC is:

$$MPC = \frac{\text{Consumption}}{\text{Income}} = \frac{C}{Y}$$

In a rich industrialised economy, the APC is likely to be less than 1 because consumers will also save part of their earnings.

The theory that income is the most important determinant of consumption is called the Keynesian theory of consumption. John Maynard Keynes was one of the greatest economists working in the first half of the twentieth century. He was the founder of modern macroeconomics. 'Keynesian' means that an idea is linked to an idea first put forward by Keynes. Keynesians suggested that as incomes rose, households would prefer to save more and so the average propensity to consume would decline. Also, higher income households would save a larger proportion of their income than poorer households. Redistributing income from high income earners to those on low incomes would therefore increase total consumption in the economy.

Other determinants of consumption

There is a number of other determinants of consumption apart from disposable income.

Interest rates Households rarely finance expenditure on **non-durables** such as food or entertainment by borrowing money. However, much of the money to buy **durables** such as cars, furniture, kitchen equipment and hi-fi equipment comes from credit finance. An increase in the rate of interest increases the monthly repayments on these goods. This means that, effectively, the price of the goods has increased. Households react to this by reducing their demand for durables and thus cutting their consumption.

Many households also have borrowed money to buy their houses. Increased interest rates lead to increased mortgage repayments. Again, this will directly cut spending on other items and perhaps, more importantly, discourage households from borrowing more money to finance purchases of consumer durables.

It has already been explained above that a rise in the rate of interest reduces the value of stocks on stock markets and thus reduces the value of household wealth. This in turn leads to a fall in consumption.

Consumer confidence Purchases of consumer durables and non-essential items like holidays are affected by consumer confidence. If consumers expect their situation to be the same or better in the future, they will tend to maintain or increase their spending. If they expect it to get worse, they are likely to hold back on purchases of non-essential items. Consumer confidence deteriorates during a recession. Some workers worry that they might lose their jobs. Others worry that their take home pay will fall because they will work less overtime or their bonuses will be cut. They might also worry that banks will refuse to lend them money and so they don't apply. In a boom, consumer confidence increases, boosting spending.

Wealth effects The wealth of a household is made up of two parts. Physical wealth is made up of items such as houses, cars and furniture. Monetary wealth is comprised of items such as cash, money in the bank and building societies, stocks and

shares, assurance policies and pension rights.

If the wealth of a household increases, consumption will increase. This is known as the **wealth effect**. There are two important ways in which the wealth of households can change over a short time period.

- A change in the price of houses. If the real price of houses increases considerably over a period of time, as happened in the UK from the mid-1990s to 2007, then households feel able to increase their spending. They do this mainly by borrowing more money secured against the value of their house.
- A change in the value of stocks and shares. Households react to an increase in the real value of a household's portfolio of securities by selling part of the portfolio and spending the proceeds. The value of stocks and shares is determined by many factors. One of these is the rate of interest. If the rate of interest falls, then the value of stocks will rise. So consumption should be stimulated through the wealth effect by a fall in the rate of interest.

Question 1

Table 1 Real consumption and household disposable income

£bn at 2011 prices		
	Consumption	Disposable income
1997	703.7	786.2
1998	734.8	809.3
2001	842.9	934.0
2002	876.5	959.0
2005	973.1	1 018.6
2006	994.2	1 037.4
2009	982.5	1 079.3
2010	987.0	1 088.6
2012	1 000.9	1 084.6
2013	1 017.3	1 082.1

Source: adapted from www.ons.gov.uk.

(a) Using the data, explain the relationship between consumption and disposable income.

(b) (i) Calculate the MPC and APC for 1998, 2002, 2006, 2010 and 2013. (ii) What happened to saving during these years?

Question 2

The share of new cars being purchased with credit has hit a record high of 75 per cent, compared to a pre-recession norm of about 50 per cent. Partly, booming car sales have been down to car manufacturers cutting the prices of their cars to levels which consumers can afford. However, the availability of credit and very low interest rates have also been very important drivers of new car purchases. The car manufacturers have been forced to offer very attractive credit deals to customers to get them to buy. Growing consumer confidence as the economy begins to grow again after the worst recession in 100 years has helped car sales too. However, the situation is not sustainable. Interest rates are likely to rise over the next two years, pushing up the monthly repayments borrowers will need to make. Also, car manufacturers are not making enough profit on each car sold to sustain long-term production. Car manufacturers can't afford to offer such attractive deals in the long term.

Source: adapted from © The *Financial Times* 4.10.2013, 11.8.2014, All Rights Reserved.

(a) Explain why a car is a consumer durable.

(b) Suggest why cars are mainly bought through loans.

(c) Explain why a rise in interest rates could lower car sales.

(d) Why might low interest rates raise consumer confidence in the car market?

The availability of credit The rate of interest determines the price of credit. However, the price of credit is not the only determinant of how much households borrow. Governments in the past have often imposed restrictions on the availability of credit. For instance, they have imposed maximum repayment periods and minimum deposits. Before the deregulation of the mortgage market in the early 1980s in the UK, building societies rationed mortgages. They often operated queueing systems and imposed restrictive limits on the sums that could be borrowed. When these restrictions are abolished, households increase their level of debt and spend the proceeds. Making credit more widely available will increase consumption.

Inflation Inflation, a rise in the general level of prices, has two effects on consumption. First, if households expect prices to be higher in the future they will be tempted to bring forward their purchases. For instance, if households know that the price of cars will go up by 10 per cent the next month, they will attempt to buy their cars now. So expectations of inflation increase consumption and reduce saving.

However, this can be outweighed by the effect of inflation on wealth. Rising inflation tends to erode the real value of money wealth. Households react to this by attempting to restore the real value of their wealth (i.e. they save more). This reduces consumption.

The composition of households Young people and old people tend to spend a higher proportion of their income than those in middle age. Young people tend to spend all their income and move into debt to finance the setting up of their homes and the bringing up of children. In middle age, the cost of homemaking declines as a proportion of income. With more income available, households often choose to build up their stock of savings in preparation for retirement. When they retire, they will run down their stock of savings to supplement their pensions. So if there is a change in the age composition of households in the economy, there could well be a change in consumption and savings. The more young and old the households, the greater will tend to be the level of consumption.

The determinants of saving

Factors which affect consumption also by definition must affect saving (remember, saving is defined as that part of disposable income which is not consumed). The **savings function** therefore links income, wealth, inflation, the rate of interest, expectations and the age profile of the population with the level of saving. However, because a typical **average propensity to save** (the APS - the ratio of total saving to total income calculated by Saving ÷ Income) is 0.05 to 0.2 in Western European countries, income is far less important in determining saving than it is in determining consumption. Factors other than income are therefore relatively more important. The **marginal propensity to save** (the proportion that is saved out of a change in income calculated by Change in saving ÷ Change in income) is equally unstable for these reasons.

Confusion sometimes arises between 'saving' and 'savings'. Saving is a flow concept which takes place over a period of time. Saving is added to a stock of savings fixed at a point in time. A household's stock of savings is the accumulation of past

savings. For instance, you might have £100 in the bank. This is your stock of savings. You might then get a job over Christmas and save £20 from that. Your saving over Christmas is £20. Your stock of savings before Christmas was £100 but afterwards it was £120. The savings function explains the relationship between the flow of savings and its determinants. It attempts to explain why you saved £20 over Christmas. It does not explain why you have £100 in the bank already.

Question 3

Table 2 Saving and disposable income, £ billion

Year	Saving £bn	Disposable income £bn	Average propensity to save	Marginal propensity to save
1	7.5	100		
2	7.9	102		
3	8.0	103		
4	8.3	106		
5	8.9	111		
6	9.0	112		

Calculate, to three decimal places, the average propensity to save and the marginal propensity to save for each year shown in the table.

Key Terms

Average propensity to consume - the proportion of total income spent. It is calculated by $C \div Y$.

Average propensity to save - the proportion of a total income which is saved. It is calculated by $S \div Y$.

Consumption - total expenditure by households on goods and services over a period of time.

Consumption function - the relationship between the consumption of households and the factors which determine it.

Disposable income - household income over a period of time including state benefits, less direct taxes.

Durable goods - goods which are consumed over a long period of time, such as a television set or a car.

Marginal propensity to consume - the proportion of a change in income which is spent. It is calculated by $\Delta C \div \Delta Y$.

Marginal propensity to save - the proportion of a change in income which is saved. It is calculated by $\Delta S \div \Delta Y$.

Non-durable goods - goods which are consumed almost immediately like an ice cream or a packet of washing powder.

Savings function - the relationship between the saving of households and the factors which determine it.

Saving (personal) - the portion of households' disposable income which is not spent over a period of time.

Wealth effect - the change in consumption following a change in wealth.

Thinking like an economist

Determinants of UK consumption

Consumption and income

Total real consumption increased over five times between 1948 and 2013 in the UK. Keynesian theory suggests that income is the major determinant of consumption. This is supported by the fact that, over the same period, household disposable income rose over five times too.

The relationship between real household consumption and real disposable income between 1997 and 2013 is shown in Figure 1 whilst the average propensity to consume (APC, which is consumption ÷ income) is shown in Figure 2. Figure 1 shows there is a close correlation between consumption and income over the period. However, the correlation is not perfect. The APC rose over the period 1997 to 2008, then fell sharply in 2009 before beginning to rise again.

Other determinants of consumption

If disposable income were the only determinant of consumption, then the APC in Figure 2 would be constant. The variation in the APC must mean that other factors affected consumption between 1997 and 2013.

Two important factors were the availability of credit and consumer confidence. There was a large increase in lending by banks to households between 1997 and 2007 which greatly increased household indebtedness. This coincided with growing household incomes shown in Figure 1. Growing income led to increased consumer confidence and a willingness to take on more debt.

The financial crisis of 2007-08 destroyed that consumer confidence. Increases in income came to a halt and unemployment rose. Many households experienced falls in their income. There was also a negative wealth effect. The value of houses fell in most regions of the UK with some households experiencing negative equity: the value of their house falling to below the level of the mortgage still left to pay. Households responded by cutting their spending. Not only did they cut spending on consumer durables, but they also cut spending on non-durables such as food. Very low interest rates, with the Bank of England base rate at 0.5 per cent from 2009, failed to have much impact on consumer spending.

By 2013, there were signs that consumer confidence was beginning to recover. Households had experienced the worst of the recession and were beginning to become more optimistic about the future. Many households, however, were still being affected by cuts in government spending on benefits and tax credits. New jobs were being created in the economy but many were low paid minimum wage jobs. The newly employed were getting very little more income in work than when they were unemployed and receiving benefits. The recovery in consumer spending was therefore fragile.

Figure 1

Real consumption expenditure and disposable income, £billion

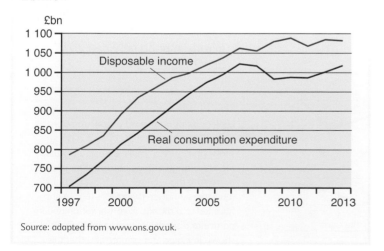

Source: adapted from www.ons.gov.uk.

Figure 2

The average propensity to consume (APC)

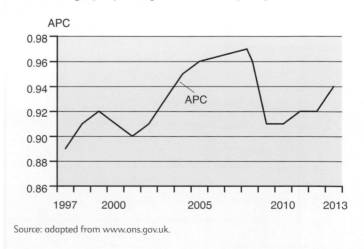

Source: adapted from www.ons.gov.uk.

Data Response Question

Consumption

The Bank of England has reported that growth in consumption expenditure has been accelerating over the past year. This rise has been driven, in part, by households' willingness to increase their spending more than the increase in their incomes.

One reason for this is increased consumer confidence. Survey evidence suggests that households have become much less concerned about the prospect of unemployment. Households have also become more confident about their own financial prospects.

Another reason has been an easing in household credit conditions. Survey evidence suggest that fewer households have been put off spending because of fears they would be refused credit by banks. In addition, increased consumer confidence has encouraged some households to spend money they have saved in case of problems such as working less overtime or being made redundant.

Consumption growth is expected to level off in the near future, as the effects of improved consumer optimism and easier credit conditions begin to fade.

Source: adapted from Bank of England, *Inflation Report*, November 2014.

1. Estimate the (a) percentage growth in consumer spending and (b) disposable income between the start and end of the periods shown in Figure 3 to one decimal place.

2. Explain the implications for the marginal propensity to consume if households 'increase their spending more than the increase in their incomes'.

3. Assess whether fear of unemployment was the main factor determining the change in consumption between 2011 and 2013.

Evaluation

Look at what happened to consumption expenditure between 2011 and 2013 shown in Figure 3. Make sure you calculate the percentage change because the graph makes the change look much bigger than it really was. Analyse the factors that might have led to a change in consumption and in particular disposable income which is also shown in Figure 3. Evaluate whether the data are sufficient to determine the main factor causing change in consumption. What is likely to have caused it and is the most likely factor fear of unemployment?

Figure 3

Real consumption expenditure and disposable income, quarterly, £ billion, seasonally adjusted

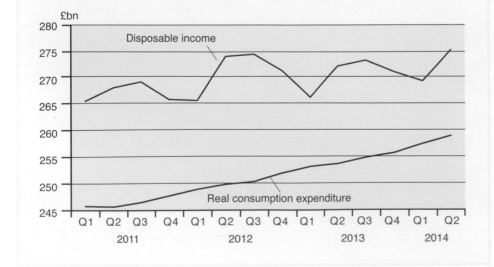

25 Investment

Key points

1. Investment is the purchase of capital goods which are then used to create other goods and services. This differs from saving, which is the creation of financial obligations.
2. The level of investment is determined by a number of variables, including the rate of interest, changes in national income, costs, business expectations and confidence, the state of the world economy, access to credit, retained profit, government policy and regulation.

Starter activity

An international chain of coffee shops is investigating opening a coffee shop in your local area. It will cost £700 000 to open and it will borrow the money to finance the deal. What do you think might be the factors which will influence whether or not it goes ahead with the investment?

A definition of investment

Economists use the word **investment** in a very precise way. Investment is the addition to the **capital stock** of the **economy** - factories, machines, offices and stocks of materials, used to produce other goods and services.

In everyday language, 'investment' and 'saving' are often used to mean the same thing. For instance, we talk about 'investing in the building society' or 'investing in shares'. For an economist, these two would be examples of saving. For an economist, investment only takes place if real products are created. To give two more examples:

- putting money into a bank account would be saving; the bank buying a computer to handle your account would be investment;

Question 1

Using the photograph, showing the interior of a UK bank, give examples of:

(a) past investment in physical capital;

(b) past investment in human capital;

(c) saving;

(d) capital consumption.

- buying shares in a new company would be saving; buying new machinery to set up a company would be investment.

A distinction can be made between **gross investment** and **net investment**. The value of the capital stock depreciates over time as it wears out and is used up. This is called **depreciation** or **capital consumption**. Gross investment measures investment before depreciation, whilst net investment is gross investment less the value of depreciation. Depreciation in recent years in the UK has accounted for about three-quarters of gross investment. So only about one quarter of gross investment represents an addition to the capital stock of the economy.

Another distinction made is between investment in **physical capital** and in **human capital**. Investment in human capital is investment in the education and training of workers. Investment in physical capital is investment in factories etc. and is the subject of this unit. It is physical investment which is the investment component, I, in aggregate demand.

Investment is made both by the public sector and the private sector. Public sector investment is constrained by complex political considerations. In the rest of this unit, we will consider the determinants of private sector investment in physical capital.

The rate of interest

One variable that affects the level of investment is the rate of interest. This works in two ways.

- Some investment is financed by firms borrowing money from banks or the money markets. Interest paid on a loan is then part of the cost of an investment project. The higher the rate of interest, the lower will be the profit that can be made from any investment, all other things being equal. At some point, the rate of interest will be so high that an investment project will become unprofitable. A rise in interest rates will therefore reduce the number of profitable investment projects and so firms will invest less. The lower the rate of interest, the more investment projects will be profitable and so there will more investment.
- Some investment is financed by **retained profit**. This is the savings that firms keep and do not distribute to their owners. The higher the rate of interest that banks and money markets offer on savings, the more attractive it is for firms to save money rather than invest it in physical capital. The lower the rate of interest, the greater the incentive for firms to run down their savings and use them to buy investment goods.

The rate of economic growth - the accelerator theory

If the same products and the same amount is being produced in an economy year after year, the level of investment will remain the same. Firms will invest to replace physical capital, such as machines, that have worn out and can no longer be used profitably. But there will be no need to increase investment beyond this replacement level.

In contrast, if the economy is expanding, firms will need to increase their investment to have the capital equipment to produce more goods and services.

If the economy is shrinking in size, as in a recession, firms will not need to replace all their investment goods which have become worn out. With lower output, they will need less capital equipment. So investment will fall when the rate of economic growth is negative.

The idea that investment is linked to changes in output or income in the economy is called the **accelerator theory**. The simplest form of the accelerator theory can be expressed by the equation

$$I_t = a \ (Y_t - Y_{t-1})$$

where:
- I_t is investment in time period t;
- $Y_t - Y_{t-1}$ is the change in real income during year t;
- a is called the **accelerator coefficient** and is the **capital-output ratio**.

The capital-output ratio is the amount of capital needed in the economy to produce a given quantity of goods. So if £10 of capital is needed to produce £2 of goods, then the capital-output ratio is 5. With a capital-output ratio of 5, an increase in income or output in the economy of £1 billion will lead to an increase in investment of £5 billion (5 x £1 billion).

Question 2

$I_t = 2 \ (Y_t - Y_{t-1})$

(a) In year 0 income was £100 million. In subsequent years, it grew by 5 per cent per annum. Calculate the level of investment in years 1 to 5.

(b) Compare what would happen to investment in each year if income grew instead by (i) 10 per cent and (ii) 2.5 per cent.

Costs

Private sector firms need to make a profit. They have to be able to sell the products made from an investment. They also have to keep their costs per unit below the selling price. Increases in costs, such as increases in wages or raw materials, will reduce the profitability or rate of return on an investment, all other things being equal. Costs and predictions about what will happen to costs over the lifetime of the investment are therefore important to firms considering whether or not to invest.

Business expectations and confidence

If firms expect their sales to increase, they are more likely to invest in new capital equipment. In a boom in the economy, for example, investment is likely to rise. If firms lose confidence and expect sales to fall in the future, they are likely to cut back on their investment plans.

John Maynard Keynes, writing in the 1930s, used the phrase 'animal spirits' to describe the mood of managers and owners of firms. Keynes argued that animal spirits, or confidence, was not something that could easily be measured. It was a feeling on the part of those who made decisions about investment as to whether the future was going to be better or worse. Moods can change. If enough firms feel confident in the future, investment will increase sufficiently to raise income and output in the whole economy. Equally, if decision makers are pessimistic about future output, that in itself can lead to economy-wide falls in output and income.

The world economy

If the world economy is booming, demand for exports is likely to increase. This in turn should lead to a rise in domestic investment. Conversely, a worldwide recession will reduce the demand for exports. So exporting firms are likely to cut back their investment. This will have a knock-on effect on other firms in the economy, reducing their sales and reducing their willingness to invest.

Access to credit

Some investment is financed through borrowing. The amount of money that is available for borrowing within the financial system varies. For example, in the years before the financial crisis of 2008, it was relatively easy for firms to borrow money from banks. After the financial crisis, banks became more risk averse. This meant they were less willing to give loans because they feared that firms would not be able to pay the money back with interest. So firms may want to borrow money to buy capital equipment but they may be turned down by banks as being too risky a customer.

Retained profit

About 70 per cent of industrial and commercial investment in the UK is financed from **retained profit**. This is profit which is kept back by firms and not distributed to shareholders. Some economists argue that firms, particularly small firms, tend not to consider the opportunity cost of investment - the interest lost from lending it out. Firms can also be risk averse, not wanting to borrow money in case the investment fails to make a profit. If the money is available, firms will invest. If retained profit is low, firms will tend not to invest. So retained profit becomes a determinant of the level of investment in the economy.

The influence of government and regulations

Governments can influence investment across the economy and in particular sectors. For example, some economists argue that cutting the tax on profits, known as corporation tax in the UK, will increase investment. This is because cutting taxes on profits effectively cuts costs for a firm on its investments. This raises the rate of return or profitability. Governments can target the cut in profits tax better by allowing any investment made by firms to be offset against the profits tax they pay. Another way that governments can encourage investment is by guaranteeing loans made by banks to firms for investment. If the firm fails to pay back the money, the government pays the bank instead.

This encourages banks to lend money on higher risk projects. Regulations can also affect investment. Some economists argue that highly regulated economies discourage investment. This is because regulation tends to increase costs for firms and so reduces their profitability. Regulation can also directly prevent a firm investing in a project because it is not permitted by regulations. For example, a firm may want to build a new factory on a site that it owns but is not allowed to because of planning regulations.

Key Terms

Accelerator coefficient - the capital-output ratio.
Accelerator theory - the theory that the level of investment is related to past changes in income.
Animal spirits - business confidence: the mood of managers and owners of firms about the future of their industry and the wider economy.
Capital-output ratio - the ratio between the amount of capital needed to produce a given quantity of goods and the level of output.
Depreciation (of the capital stock) or capital consumption - the value of the capital stock which has been used up or worn out.
Gross investment - the addition to capital stock, both to replace the existing capital stock which has been used up (depreciation) and the creation of additional capital.
Investment - the addition to the capital stock of the economy.
Net investment - gross investment minus depreciation.
Retained profit - profit kept back by a firm for its own use which is not distributed to shareholders or used to pay taxation.

Thinking like an economist

Investment in the UK

The composition of investment

Gross investment is called **gross fixed capital formation** (GFCF) in UK official statistics. Figure 1 shows the composition of investment in 1997 and 2013. Significant changes in this composition are apparent from the data.

Figure 1

Gross fixed capital formation by type of asset: 1997 and 2013 (£bn at 2011 prices)

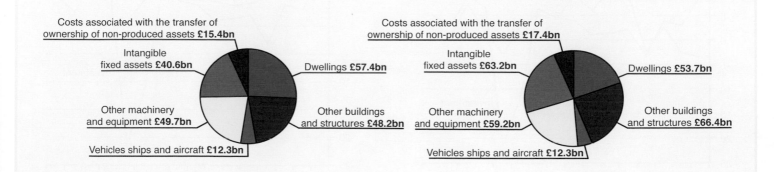

1997
Total investment £223.6bn
GDP at market prices £1 210.3bn
Investment as a percentage of GDP 18.5%

Costs associated with the transfer of ownership of non-produced assets **£15.4bn**
Intangible fixed assets **£40.6bn**
Dwellings **£57.4bn**
Other machinery and equipment **£49.7bn**
Other buildings and structures **£48.2bn**
Vehicles ships and aircraft **£12.3bn**

2013
Total investment £272.2bn
GDP at market prices £1 656.5bn
Investment as a percentage of GDP 16.4%

Costs associated with the transfer of ownership of non-produced assets **£17.4bn**
Intangible fixed assets **£63.2bn**
Dwellings **£53.7bn**
Other machinery and equipment **£59.2bn**
Other buildings and structures **£66.4bn**
Vehicles ships and aircraft **£12.3bn**

Source: adapted from Blue Book, 2014; www.ons.gov.uk.

- In real terms, investment in housing has barely changed. However, as a percentage of total investment, it has fallen from 26 per cent to 20 per cent.
- Investment in 'other new buildings and structures', which includes new factories and offices, has increased by one third. This is approximately equal to the percentage growth in real GDP over the period.
- Investment in vehicles, ships and aircraft has remained the same over the period.
- Investment in 'other machinery and equipment' has increased by 19 per cent. This investment ranges from milking machines to machine lathes to computers and desks.

- Intangible fixed assets, which are assets such as patents, copyright and goodwill, have increased significantly by 56 per cent. This reflects the growth of a knowledge-based economy.
- Costs associated with the transfer of ownership of non-produced assets are costs such as taxes and legal costs associated with the buying and selling of assets. They are counted as part of investment because firms sometimes need to pay these costs when they invest. These costs account for less than five per cent of total investment.

The determinants of investment

Economic theory suggests that there may be several determinants of private sector investment including past changes in income (the accelerator theory), profits earned by private sector companies and the rate of interest.

Figures 2 and 3 show the percentage change in income (GDP), private sector investment (gross domestic fixed capital formation) and private sector profits between 1998 and 2013. The fall in GDP in 2008 and 2009 coincided with a fall in both profits and investment. This would suggest that these three variables are linked.

Figure 4 shows the percentage change in investment with the rate of interest, measured by the Bank of England base rate. What the data show is that there seems to be little correlation between two variables. In particular, the very low interest rates of 2009-2013 did not lead to a consistently high rate of change of investment. If there is a correlation between the two variables, much more sophisticated statistical techniques would be needed to show it.

Figure 2

Annual percentage change in investment (GFCF) and income (GDP at market prices), UK

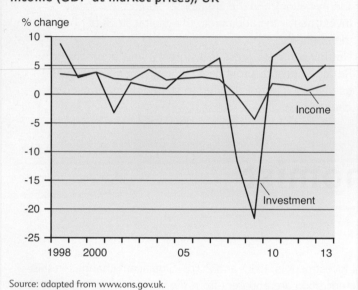

Source: adapted from www.ons.gov.uk.

Figure 3

Annual percentage change in investment (GFCF) and profits (private sector), UK

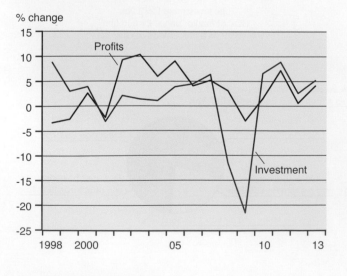

Source: adapted from www.ons.gov.uk.

Figure 4

Annual percentage change in investment (GFCF) and the rate of interest (Bank of England base rate)

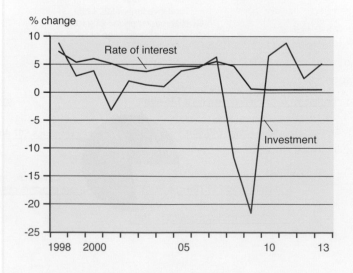

Source: adapted from www.ons.gov.uk.

Data Response Question

Little appetite for investment

Firms are reluctant to invest. The 100 largest firms listed on the London Stock Exchange (excluding financial companies) are currently holding between them £55.3 billion of cash reserves. In normal times, part of these reserves would have been spent on investment projects or buying other companies. However, firms are worried about the future and don't see the opportunities for profitable investment. For example, currently there is political turmoil in the Middle East and a low level war in the Ukraine. Low or zero economic growth in European economies is holding back investment. So too are weak growth figures from emerging countries such as China and Brazil.

Strong economic growth in the UK over the past year has failed to raise the animal spirits of business owners because firms are not convinced that the growth will continue.

Central banks in the UK, Europe, Japan and the United States have kept interest rates at historically low levels over the past five years. This has been aimed at encouraging households and firms to borrow money. Governments want households to borrow and buy goods and services in order for their economies to begin to grow again. Governments want firms to borrow to invest in new capital equipment. However, households have been reducing their borrowings because so many got into financial difficulties by over-borrowing before the financial crisis of 2008. Firms have been

reluctant to borrow and invest partly because they are pessimistic about future household spending.

1. Explain, using examples, what is meant by 'investment'.

2. Analyse two reasons why firms were reluctant to invest in 2014.

3. Discuss whether continued high economic growth in the UK after 2014 would inevitably lead to an increase in UK investment.

Evaluation

You need to outline the main causes of investment, building on your answer in question 2. Consider whether economic growth will inevitably lead to an improvement in other variables which affect investment. Under what circumstances could there be a situation where firms don't increase investment despite economic growth? In your conclusion, weigh up whether strong economic growth in the UK would overcome all other negative influences on UK investment.

26 Government expenditure and net trade

Starter activity

On what does government spend money in your local community? Why does it spend this money? What do you buy that is made abroad? Why do you buy these goods rather than goods made in the UK?

Reasons for government spending

Government plays a crucial role in modern economies. One way in which they intervene is by spending money on a wide variety of goods and services. For example, they provide public goods such as defence and the judiciary. They also provide goods such as education and health care.

The size of government spending varies from country to country. In a modern economy, the government will fund defence, the police and judiciary, roads and education. There are then wide divergencies between economies. In a free market economy like the United States, the private sector is expected to provide goods such as health care, housing and social care. In a mixed economy, the state will provide many of these goods. Some mixed economies, like Sweden, have much higher state involvement than countries like the UK.

Much of government spending is fixed from year to year. Schools must be funded. Warships must be fuelled. Pensions must be paid. However, governments vary what they spend their money on and how much they spend from year to year. Government announcements about changes in spending are made in **budgets**. Decisions about government spending, together with taxes and government borrowing, are called the **fiscal policy** of the government.

Typically, changes in government spending reflect changing priorities about how to spend money. A government might choose to spend more on education and less on defence next year, for example.

However, changes in government spending can also be made deliberately to affect total spending in the economy. Higher government spending can boost total spending and so affect variables such as unemployment and inflation. In particular, during the recession phase of a trade cycle, when unemployment is rising, governments may choose to increase government spending. This should reduce unemployment and boost demand in the economy. If the economy is in boom, the government may choose to reduce government spending. This should reduce demand in the economy and so reduce inflation.

Government spending will also rise automatically during a recession. In a recession, unemployment rises and some workers will earn less. These will then be a rise in government spending on unemployment benefits and benefits to support those on low or no incomes.

The impact of changes in government spending on total spending in the economy depends on levels of taxation. If the government raises taxes by the same amount as a rise in its spending, then there might be little impact on total spending in the economy. On the other hand, a rise in total spending with no change in taxation will have more impact.

Government spending can be greater than government receipts such as taxation. When this happens there will be a **budget deficit**. When government spending is less than government receipts such as taxation, there will be a **budget surplus**. A rise in government spending with no change in taxation will either reduce a budget surplus or increase a budget deficit.

Exports and imports

Exports are goods and services sold to foreigners. Imports are goods and services bought from foreigners. **Net exports** or **the net trade balance** are exports minus imports. Exports are an important part of total demand in an economy like the UK. The demand for exports and imports is influenced by a number of factors.

Price Buyers make decisions partly on the price of a good. The higher the price, the lower the quantity demanded. The price itself depends upon a variety of supply factors including costs. Over the past 15 years, production of low and medium technology manufactured goods has gone from high wage economies like the UK to low wage economies like China. So imports into the UK from China have increased because UK domestic producers can no longer compete.

Real income in the domestic economy If the economy is doing well and real incomes of households are rising, then they spend more. Part of this spending will be on imported goods and services. So rising real incomes suck in more imports. Conversely, if the economy is doing badly and is in recession, real incomes will fall and so too will imports.

The exchange rate The exchange rate is the price at which one currency is sold for another. A rise in the value of the pound means that it costs foreigners more to buy pounds with their local currency. This makes exports from the UK less price competitive and hence UK exports are likely to fall. Equally, a rise in the value of the pound means that UK buyers can buy foreign currency more cheaply with pounds. So imports become more price competitive to UK buyers. A fall in the value of the pound leads to the opposite result. UK exports become more price competitive to foreign buyers. In contrast, UK buyers find that imports become less price competitive.

State of the world economy If the UK's main trading partners are doing well economically, then UK exports are likely to rise. By far the largest export market for the UK is the rest of the European Union (EU). Recession in the EU could lead to a fall in UK exports whereas fast EU economic growth will boost UK exports.

Degree of protectionism Almost all countries limit in various ways goods and services coming into their economies. For example, they may put quotas on goods, which are physical limits on the amount that can be imported. Or they may put tariffs on imports. A tariff is a tax on imports. The greater the

degree of protectionism internationally, the more difficult it will be for UK firms to export. The great advantage for the UK of being part of the EU is that barriers to trade are very low for exports to countries such as France and Germany. Equally, though, other EU countries can sell into the UK without facing protectionist barriers.

Non-price factors Exports and imports may be bought solely on price. This is particularly true where goods are of standard quality. Copper, steel or wheat, for example, are standard commodities which tend to be traded on price. However, many products are unique in quality. They may have a unique design protected by patents. It may be a unique service, such as next day delivery. So a whole range of non-price factors affects the competitiveness of exports and imports.

> ### Key Terms
>
> **Net exports or the net trade balance** - exports minus imports

Thinking like an economist

French cuts in government spending

In 2014, various sources in the media reported that the French government led by Francois Hollande, from the Socialist party, was caught in a dilemma. On the one hand, the French economy was stagnant. Increasing government spending would be one way to increase demand in the economy and stimulate economic growth.

On the other hand, government spending was already very high as a percentage of the output of the French economy measured by Gross Domestic Product (GDP). France was spending over 10 per cent more of its GDP on government compared to the largest economy in Europe, Germany, as can be seen from Figure 1.

Moreover, the difference between government spending and tax revenues in France was more than three per cent, the maximum level set by the European Union for countries using the euro as their currency. There was therefore strong pressure on the French government to cut its spending.

The government was in fact committed to cutting public spending by €50 billion between 2015 and 2017 following a €15 billion cut in 2014. However, making cuts is always difficult especially when the government is made up of socialist politicians. Economists pointed out that the government could maintain services but save large amounts of money by making public spending more efficient. For example, an estimated €5 billion could be saved if French hospitals increased the proportion of outpatient surgery from current 40 per cent levels to the European norm of 80 per cent. The savings would come

from not having patients staying overnight in hospitals when they had a minor operation.

However, making the French state more efficient won't help boost total spending in the economy. French businesses need to be investing more to create both jobs and output. More private sector spending is needed to make up for the cuts in public sector spending.

Figure 1

Government spending as a percentage of GDP

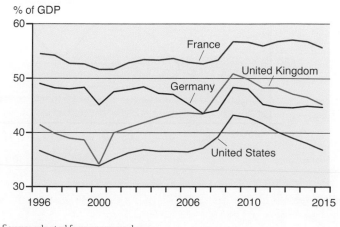

Source: adapted from www.oecd.org.

Data Response Question

UK trade deficits

The UK's trade deficit widened again in July. Net trade was in deficit by £3.3 billion, up from £2.5 billion the previous month.

Exports to Eastern Europe and Russia were hit by the continuing low level war in the Ukraine. The EU, the UK's main trading partner, is also in economic difficulties with little or no growth in income in many countries. Exports have also not been helped by the recent rise in the value of the pound against other currencies.

On the other hand, the UK economy has seen economic growth over the past three months. Firms and consumers have been buying more imported goods.

Source: adapted from © the *Financial Times* 10.9.2014, All Rights Reserved.

Figure 2

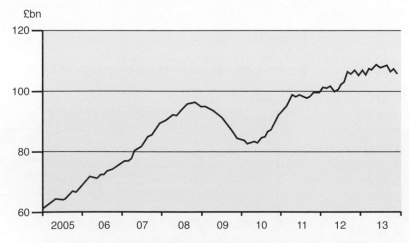

Deficit on trade in goods, sum over previous 12 months (£bn)

£bn

Source: adapted from Thomson Reuters Datastream; © the Financial Times 10.9.2014, All Rights Reserved.

Q

1. Identify one significant feature of the UK's net trade shown in Figure 2. Support your comment with statistics from the data.

2. Explain two reasons why the UK's trade deficit widened in July 2014.

27 Aggregate supply

Key points

1. The aggregate supply curve shows the level of output in the whole economy at any given level of average prices.
2. In the short run, it is assumed that the prices of factors of production, such as money wage rates, are constant. Firms will supply extra output if the prices they receive increase. Hence in the short run, the aggregate supply curve is upward sloping.
3. An increase in firms' costs of production will shift the short-run aggregate supply curve upwards, whilst a fall in costs will shift it downwards.
4. In the long run, it is assumed that the prices of factors of production are variable but that the productive capacity of the economy is fixed. The long-run aggregate supply curve shows the productive capacity of the economy at any given price level.
5. The long run aggregate supply curve shows the productive capacity of the economy in the same way that a production possibility frontier or the trend rate of growth shows this productive capacity.
6. Shifts in the long-run aggregate supply curve are caused by changes in the quantity or quality of factors of production or the efficiency of their use.
7. In the long run, it is assumed that the prices of factors of production are variable but that the productive capacity of the economy is fixed. The long-run aggregate supply curve shows the productive capacity of the economy at any given price level.

Starter activity

Find out the current level of national income (GDP). Think of two factors which could lead to an increase in GDP over the next year. What do you think would happen to total spending in the economy if inflation were very high?

The short-run aggregate supply curve

In Unit 11, it was argued that the supply curve for an industry was upward sloping. If the price of a product increases, firms in the industry are likely to increase their profits by producing and selling more. So the higher the price, the higher the level of output. The supply curve being talked about here is a microeconomic supply curve. Is the macroeconomic supply curve (i.e. the supply curve for the whole economy) the same?

The macroeconomic supply curve is called the **aggregate supply curve**, because it is the sum of all the industry supply curves in the economy. It shows how much output firms wish to supply at each level of prices.

In the short run, the aggregate supply curve is upward sloping. The short run is defined here as the period when money wage rates and the prices of all other factor inputs in the economy are fixed. Assume that firms wish to increase their level of output. In the short run, they are unlikely to take on extra workers. Taking on extra staff is an expensive process. Sacking them if they are no longer needed is likely to be even more costly, not just in direct monetary terms but also in terms of industrial relations within the company. So firms tend to respond to increases in demand in the short run by working their existing labour force more intensively, for instance through overtime.

Firms will need to provide incentives for workers to work harder or longer hours. Overtime, for instance, may be paid at one and a half times the basic rate of pay. Whilst basic pay rates

remain constant, earnings will rise and this will tend to put up both the average and marginal costs per unit of output. In many sectors of the economy, where competition is imperfect and where firms have the power to increase their prices, the rise in labour costs will lead to a rise in prices. It only needs prices to rise in some sectors of the economy for the average price level in the economy to rise. So in the short term, an increase in output by firms is likely to lead to an increase in their costs which in turn will result in some firms raising prices. However, the increase in prices is likely to be small because, given constant prices (e.g. wage rates) for factor inputs, the increases in costs (e.g. wage earnings) are likely to be fairly small too. Therefore **the short-run aggregate supply curve** is relatively price elastic. This is shown in Figure 1. A movement along the curve, caused by an increase in real output, from Y_1 to Y_2, leads to a small rise in the average price level from P_1 to P_2.

If demand and real output fall in the short run, some firms in the economy will react by cutting their prices to try to stimulate extra orders. However, the opportunities to cut prices will be limited. Firms will be reluctant to sack workers and their overheads will remain the same, so their average cost and marginal cost will barely be altered. Again, the aggregate supply curve is relatively price elastic. The movement along the curve,

Question 1

Using a short-run aggregate supply curve, explain the likely effect on the price level of the following, assuming that the prices of all factor inputs are fixed.

(a) In 2007, output in the UK economy was booming. Real GDP rose by 2.6 per cent.

(b) In 2009, there was a recession in the UK economy and output fell. Real GDP fell by 4.3 per cent.

Figure 1

The short-run aggregate supply curve

A change in real output, for examle from Y_1 to Y_2, will lead to a movement along the short-run aggregate supply curve. The slope of the SRAS line is very shallow because, whilst it is assumed that in the short run wage rates are constant, firms will face some increased costs, such as overtime payments, when they increase output.

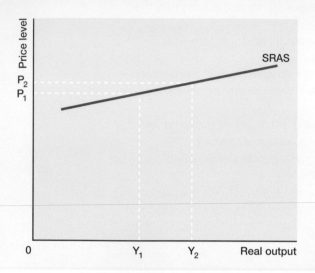

Figure 2

Shifts in the short-run aggregate supply curve

The short-run aggregate supply curve is drawn on the assumption that costs, in particular the wage rate, remain constant. A change in costs is shown by a shift in the curve. For instance, an increase in wage rates would push $SRAS_1$ up to $SRAS_2$ whilst a fall in wages rates would push the curve down to $SRAS_3$.

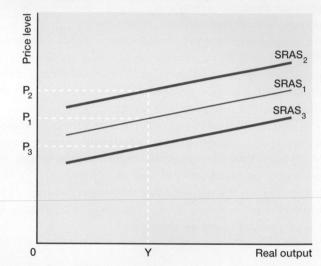

caused by a fall in real output from Y_2 to Y_1, leads to a small fall in the average price level, from P_2 to P_1.

Shifts in the short-run aggregate supply curve

The **short-run aggregate supply curve** shows the relationship between aggregate output and the average price level, assuming that money wage rates in the economy are constant. A change in real output will lead to a movement along the short-run aggregate supply curve and a change in the price level. But what if wage rates do change, or some other variable which affects aggregate supply changes? Then, just as in the microeconomic theory of the supply curve, the aggregate supply curve will shift.

Wage rates An increase in wage rates will result in firms facing increased costs of production. Some firms will respond by increasing prices. So at any given level of output, a rise in wage rates will lead to a rise in the average price level. This is shown in Figure 2 by a shift in the short-run aggregate supply curve from $SRAS_1$ to $SRAS_2$.

Raw material prices A general fall in the prices of raw materials may occur. Perhaps world demand for commodities falls, or perhaps the value of the pound rises, making the price of imports cheaper. A fall in the price of raw materials will lower industrial costs and will lead to some firms reducing the prices of their products. Hence there will be a shift in the short-run aggregate supply curve downwards. This is shown in Figure 2 by the shift from $SRAS_1$ to $SRAS_3$.

Taxation An increase in the tax burden on industry will increase costs. Hence the short run aggregate supply schedule will be pushed upwards, for instance from $SRAS_1$ to $SRAS_2$ in Figure 2.

Exchange rates If the exchange falls, the price of imported goods is likely to rise. This will lead to an increase in prices throughout the economy. So a fall in the exchange rate will shift the short-run aggregate supply curve up from $SRAS_1$ to $SRAS_2$ in Figure 2. Conversely, a rise in the exchange will lead to a fall in the price of imported goods. This will lead to a fall in prices throughout the economy. So a rise in the exchange rate will shift the short-run aggregate supply curve downwards, from $SRAS_1$ to $SRAS_3$ in Figure 2.

Productivity Productivity is output per unit of input employed. So labour productivity is output per worker. Capital productivity is output per unit of capital employed. Increases in productivity over time, for example because of a better-educated workforce or improved technology, will lead to an increase in long-run supply. However, it will also reduce costs of production in the short run, so shifting the short-run aggregate supply curve downwards.

When there is a large change in wage rates, raw material prices or taxation, a **supply-side shock** is said to occur. A

Question 2

Using diagrams, show the likely effect of the following on the short-run aggregate supply curve.

(a) Real national output in the third quarter of 2013 was approximately the same as in the 1st quarter of 2008 but average prices measured by the CPI had risen 11 per cent over the period.

(b) The price of Brent Crude oil rose from $46 a barrel in the first week of 2009 to £110 a barrel in the first week of 2013.

(c) Between 2000 and 2013, average weekly earnings rose by 50 per cent in the UK economy.

Figure 3

The classical long-run aggregate supply curve

Classical economics assumes that in the long-run wages and prices are flexible and therefore the LRAS curve is vertical. In the long run, there cannot be any unemployment because the wage rate will be in equilibrium where all workers who want a job (the supply of labour) will be offered a job (the demand for labour). So, whatever the level of prices, output will always be constant at the full employment level of income.

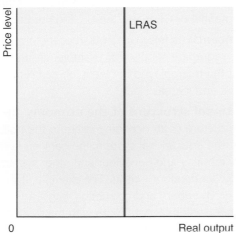

supply-side shock, like a doubling of the price of oil, can have a significant impact on aggregate supply, pushing the short-run aggregate supply curve upwards.

The long-run aggregate supply curve

In the short run, changes in wage rates or the price of raw materials have an effect on the aggregate supply curve, shifting the SRAS curve up or down. Equally, a rise in real output will lead to a movement along the SRAS curve.

In the long run, however, there is a limit to how much firms can increase their supply. They run into capacity constraints. There is a limit to the amount of labour that can be hired in an economy. Capital equipment is fixed in supply. Labour productivity has been maximised. So it can be argued that in the long run, the aggregate supply curve is fixed at a given level of real output, whatever the price level. What this means is that the long run aggregate supply curve is vertical on a diagram showing the price level and real output.

Figure 3 shows such a vertical **long-run aggregate supply curve** or **LRAS curve**. The long-run aggregate supply curve shows the productive potential of the economy. It shows how much real output can be produced over a period of time with a given level of factor inputs, such as labour and capital equipment, and a given level of efficiency in combining these factor inputs. It can be linked to three other economic concepts.

- The LRAS curve is the level of output associated with production on the production possibility frontier of an economy. In Figure 4, any point on the boundary AB is one which shows the level of real output shown by the LRAS curve.
- The LRAS curve is the level of output shown by the trend or long term average rate of growth in an economy. When output is above or below this long term trend level, an output

Figure 4

A production possibility frontier

Any point on the production possibility frontier AB shows the potential output of the economy when all resources are fully utilised. The long-run aggregate supply curve also shows the potential output of the economy. At any point in time, if the economy is operating on its long-run aggregate supply curve, then it will be operating at one of the points along the production possibility frontier.

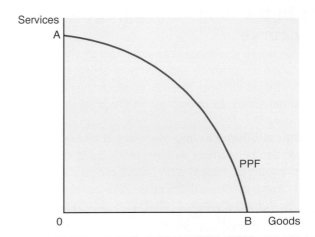

gap is said to exist. In Figure 5, the economy is growing along the trend rate of growth of AB. There are short term fluctuations in actual output above and below the trend rate. This shows that actual output can be above or below that given by the long-run aggregate supply curve. When actual output is above the trend rate on Figure 5 in the short run, and so to the right of the LRAS curve in Figure 3, economic forces will act to bring GDP back towards its trend rate of growth. Equally, when it is below its trend rate of growth, and

Figure 5

The trend rate of growth for an economy

At any point in time, the level of output shown by the long run aggregate supply is on the line of the trend rate of growth of output.

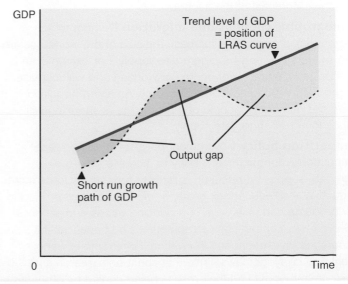

so to the left of the LRAS curve in Figure 3, the same but opposite forces will bring it back to that long-run position.

- The LRAS curve shows the level of **full capacity** output of the economy. At full capacity, there are no underutilised resources in the economy. Production is at its long-run maximum. In the short run, an economy might operate beyond full capacity, creating a positive output gap. However, this is unsustainable and the output in the economy must fall back to its full capacity levels.

Shifts in the long-run aggregate supply curve

The long-run aggregate supply curve is likely to shift over time. This is because the quantity and quality of economic resources changes over time, as does the way in which they are combined. These changes bring about changes in the productive potential of an economy.

Technological advances Improvements in technology allow new products to be made or existing products to be produced with fewer resources. Increases in capital productivity (output per unit of capital employed) shift the LRAS curve to the right.

Changes in relative productivity to competing economies An increase in UK productivity of a good relative to other world economies will encourage production of that good in the UK. Firms will invest, shifting the LRAS curve to the right. The LRAS of the world economy will increase if there is increased specialisation between economies, allowing production to be located in the cheapest and most efficient place in the world economy.

Changes in education and skills Improvements in education and skills of workers will raise their productivity (output per worker), so increasing long-run aggregate supply.

Changes in government regulations Changes in government regulations can lead to an increase in long-run aggregate supply. For example, making it simpler to set up a company could encourage more entrepreneurs to create companies, output and jobs. Imposing regulations on supermarkets to deal fairly with their suppliers could reduce the number of suppliers going into administration and reducing the productive potential of the economy.

Demographic changes and migration Demographic (population) changes that increase the size of the workforce are likely to increase long-run aggregate supply. For example, an increase in immigration of people of working age will increase the productive potential of the economy. An aging population where the number of people of working age is shrinking will reduce long run aggregate supply.

Competition policy Government policies which increase competition amongst firms is likely to increase long-run aggregate supply. Competition is likely to force firms to be more productive and reduce their costs, or more innovative producing new products and new ways of producing goods and services. However, less competition can sometimes be beneficial if it encourages investment and innovation. For example, without patent and copyright laws, firms that spent on research and development would find their results being copied by other firms.

Enterprise and risk taking Economies where enterprise and risk taking are encouraged are likely to see increases in their long-run aggregate supply. The creation of new firms will increase output now and in the future when some of them grow in size. Enterprise and risk taking also encourage competition which in itself might increase LRAS.

Factor mobility Increases in factor mobility are likely to increase long run aggregate supply. For example, in the European Union, movements of workers from Poland or Estonia to work in Germany or the UK are likely to increase the productive potential of Germany, the UK and the EU.

Economic incentives Improvements in economic incentives can increase aggregate supply. For example, giving tax incentives for the unemployed to take a job can reduce unemployment and increase output.

The institutional structure of the economy The institutional structure of an economy refers to the political system, laws, the educational system, the banking system, the framework of morality and behaviour and other systems which determine how an economy works. For example, if there is a strong tradition of bribery and corruption within an economy, then making the system accord more with the rule of law is likely to increase long-run aggregate supply. Equally, if the banking system is weak, saving and borrowing will be affected. A stronger banking system can encourage households to save and make funds more available to firms, again increasing long-run aggregate supply.

Figure 6 shows how a growth in potential output is drawn on an aggregate supply diagram. Assume that the education and skills of the workforce increase. This should lead to labour becoming more productive, in turn leading to an increase in the productive potential of the economy at full employment. The

Figure 6

A shift in the long-run aggregate supply curve

An increase in the productive potential in the economy pushes the long-run aggregate supply curve to the right, for instance from $LRAS_1$ to $LRAS_2$. A fall in productive potential, on the other hand, is shown by a shift to the left of the curve, from $LRAS_1$ to $LRAS_3$ for instance.

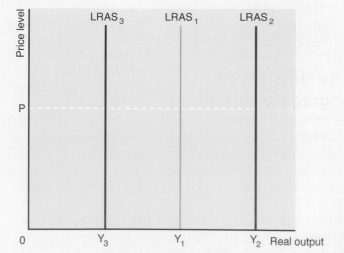

long run aggregate supply curve will then shift from LRAS$_1$ to LRAS$_2$, showing that at a given level of prices, the economy can produce more output. A fall in potential output, caused for instance by a fall in the size of the labour force, would be shown by a leftward shift in the curve, from LRAS$_1$ to LRAS$_3$.

A shift to the right in the LRAS curve shows that there has been economic growth. On a production possibility frontier (PPF) diagram, it would be represented by a movement outwards on the boundary. In Figure 5, it would be shown by a movement up along the trend rate of growth line. A shift to the left in the LRAS curve would show that the productive potential of the economy has fallen. On a PPF diagram, the boundary would shift inwards. On a trend rate of growth diagram, there would be a movement down the trend rate of growth line to the left.

Question 3

Figure 7

Output gap estimate

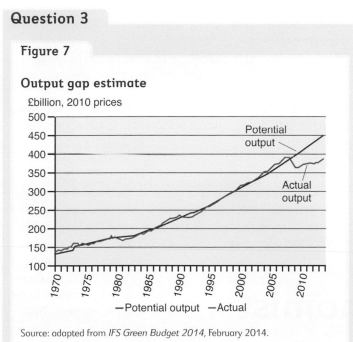

Source: adapted from *IFS Green Budget 2014*, February 2014.

In 2014, the Institute for Fiscal Studies made the estimate of the UK output gap shown in Figure 7. The output gap shows actual output less trend output at 2010 prices.

(a) Give one year when the economy was operating on its long-run aggregate supply curve.

(b) Over what period was the economy operating to the left of its long-run aggregate supply curve?

(c) The UK experienced a deep and long recession from 2008 onwards. Explain how this is shown on Figure 7.

The classical and Keynesian long-run aggregate supply curves

The vertical LRAS curve is called the classical long-run aggregate supply curve. It is based on the classical view that markets tend to correct themselves fairly quickly when they are pushed into disequilibrium by some shock. In the long run, product markets like the markets for oil, cameras or meals out, and factor markets like the market for labour, will be in equilibrium. If all markets are in equilibrium, there can be no unemployed resources. Hence, the economy must be operating at full capacity on its production possibility boundary.

Figure 8

The Keynesian long-run aggregate supply curve

Traditional Keynesian economists argue that, even in the long run, unemployment may persist because wages don't necessarily fall when unemployment occurs. When there is mass unemployment, output can be increased without any increases in costs and therefore prices. As the economy nears full employment, higher output leads to higher prices. At full employment, the economy cannot produce any more whatever prices firms receive.

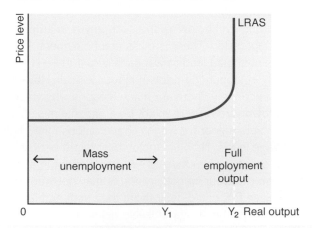

Keynesian economists, however, point out that there have been times when markets have failed to clear for long periods of time. Keynesian economics was developed out of the experience of the Great Depression of the 1930s when large-scale unemployment lasted for a decade. If it had not been for the Second World War, it could be that high unemployment would

Question 4

High unemployment in the UK should push down wages, but at the bottom end, a minimum level of wages is fixed by the National Minimum Wage, a legal minimum wage fixed at £6.50 an hour for 2014-15. However, many argue that the minimum wage is too low for workers to give them a basic standard of living. For this reason, it has been reported that some employers have been paying their workers a 'living wage'. This, for 2014-15, is fixed at £9.15 an hour in London and £7.85 outside of London. About 35 000 workers have benefited from the living wage rate since it was introduced in 2005 by some employers, but over five million are paid less than the living wage. Some companies, such as accountants KPMG, argue that paying the living wage to their lowest paid workers improves motivation, reduces absence due to sickness and helps retain staff. However, other employers argue that they must have the flexibility to pay lower wages to remain competitive. Paying higher wages could force them to employ fewer workers or even see them going out of business.

Source: adapted from © The *Financial Times*, 28.10.2012, 6.11.2012, 3.11.2014 All Rights Reserved.

(a) Explain why a 'living wage' might (i) prevent the labour market from clearing and (ii) lead to a long-run aggregate supply curve (LRAS) which is not vertical.

(b) Discuss whether the living wage in the UK in 2014 was, in practice, likely to prevent the LRAS curve from being vertical.

have lasted for twenty or thirty years. John Maynard Keynes famously said that 'in the long run we are all dead'. There is little point in studying and drawing vertical long-run aggregate supply curves if it takes 20-30 years to get back to the curve when the economy suffers a demand side or supply side shock.

Keynesian economists therefore suggest that the long-run aggregate supply curve is the shape shown in Figure 8.

At an output level of Y_2, the LRAS curve is vertical as with the classical LRAS curve. Y_2 is the full capacity level of output of the economy. It is when the economy is on its production possibility boundary.

At an output level below Y_1, the economy is in a deep and prolonged depression. There is mass unemployment. In theory, unemployment should lead to wages falling. If there is too much supply of labour, the price of labour will fall. However, in a modern economy, there are many reasons why wages are sticky downwards. There might be a national minimum wage which sets a floor for wages. Trade unions might fight to maintain wage levels. High unemployment might persist in one area of the country when there is full employment in another area because of labour immobility. Firms may not want to lower wages because this could demotivate their staff and lead to lower productivity. So at output levels below Y_1, markets, and in particular the labour market, fail to clear. Firms can hire and fire extra workers without affecting the wage rate. Wages are stuck and there is persistent disequilibrium in the long run. Hence, there is no pressure on prices when output expands.

At an output level between Y_1 and Y_2, labour is becoming scarce enough for an increase in demand for labour to push

Key Terms

Aggregate supply curve - the relationship between the average level of prices in the economy and the level of total output.

Full capacity - the level of output where no extra production can take in the long run with existing resources. The full capacity level of output for an economy is shown by the classical long run aggregate supply curve or the vertical part of a Keynesian aggregate supply curve.

Long-run aggregate supply curve - the aggregate supply curve which assumes that wage rates are variable, both upward and downwards. Classical or supply side economists assume that wage rates are flexible. Keynesian economists assume that wage rates may be 'sticky downwards' and hence the economy may operate at less than full employment even in the long run.

Short-run aggregate supply curve - the upward sloping aggregate supply curve which assumes that money wage rates are fixed.

Supply-side shocks - factors such as changes in wage rates or commodity prices which cause the short run aggregate supply curve to shift.

up wages. This then leads to a higher price level. The nearer output gets to Y_2, the full employment level of output, the greater the effect of an increase in demand for labour on wages and therefore the price level.

Thinking like an economist

The case of oil

Oil price changes and inflation

Between 1970 and 2014, there were three periods when the price of crude oil on world markets jumped significantly as can be seen from Figure 9. The first two were caused by political events. In 1973, a war between Israel and its Arab neighbours saw Arab oil producing countries restrict supplies to Western countries that supported Israel. It was also the first time that OPEC, the oil cartel, used its market power to restrict supply and raise prices. In 1978, a revolution in Iran brought to power a Shia Muslim government that was anti-Western. Iran was a major oil producer at the time. When it severely restricted supplies of oil to the market, the oil price increased dramatically. Finally, there was a significant rise in the price of oil from 2003 to 2012. The first two oil shocks were caused by a sudden fall in the supply of oil. The last was caused by increased demand for oil, particularly from China. In the early 2000s, Chinese demand for commodities such as oil saw a large increase fuelled by its average 10 per cent growth rate per year. As Figure 9 shows, there was sharp fall in the price of oil in 2008 and 2009 as the Europe and the USA suffered recessions due to a banking crisis. Their demand for oil fell.

Figure 9

Spot crude oil price[1], US$ per barrel at current and constant (2011 US$) price

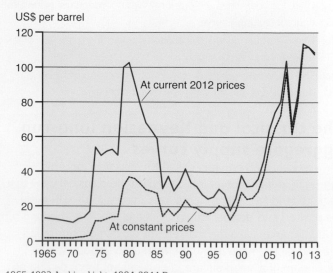

1. 1965-1983 Arabian Light, 1984-2011 Brent.

Source: adapted from *BP Statistical Review of World Energy*, 2014.

However, demand from fast-growing emerging countries such as China and India continued to grow. By 2010, oil prices had recovered significantly before falling again in 2013 as growth in China fell.

The impact on the short-run aggregate supply curve

The three periods of sharp oil prices all had an important effect on the short run aggregate supply curve of the UK economy. Oil price rises increase the costs of firms. So at any given level of output, firms need to charge higher prices to cover their costs. As a result the short-run aggregate supply curve shoots upwards as shown in Figure 11. The oil price rises of 1973-75 and 1979-81 were a major contributor to the inflation in those periods shown in Figure 10. However, the large increases in the oil price between 2003 and 2007 and then 2009-2012 had far less impact on inflation. One reason was that the average amount of oil used to generate £1 of GDP was far less between 2003 and 2012 than in 1975 or 1981. Greater energy efficiency and the decline of manufacturing industry were the main reasons for this. Another reason for the small impact of the oil price was that UK firms found it much more difficult to pass on price rises to their customers than in 1975 or 1981.

The economic climate was more competitive and firms tended to absorb oil price rises rather than pass them on. The severe and prolonged recession and weak recovery of 2009 to 2012 also meant that firms found it hard to pass on oil prices rises to customers.

The impact on the long-run aggregate supply curve

Many economists argue that the oil price rises of 1973-75 and 1979-81 also reduced the productive potential of the UK economy, shifting the long-run aggregate supply curve to the left, as shown in Figure 11. The rise in the oil prices meant that some capital equipment that was oil intensive became uneconomic to run. This equipment was mothballed and then scrapped, leading to a once-and-for-all fall in the amount of capital in the economy.

Because the economy was far less oil dependent by 2003, this scrapping of equipment was less significant. Firms had become reluctant to invest in equipment using oil when there were good substitutes because they were afraid of a large rise in oil prices.

Figure 10

Economic growth and inflation (RPI) year on year (%), in three periods of oil shocks

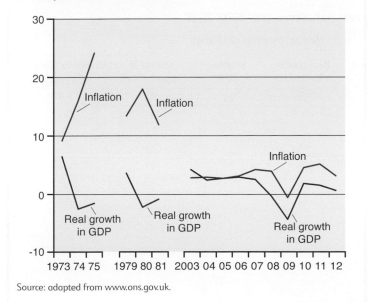

Source: adapted from www.ons.gov.uk.

Figure 11

The effect of steep rises in oil prices on aggregate supply

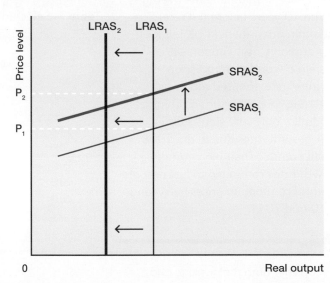

Data Response Question

Aggregate supply 2007-2013

Figures and economists suggest that 2008-2013 were difficult years for the UK economy. In 2007, the economy was enjoying its sixteenth year of positive growth and Gordon Brown, the Chancellor of the Exchequer and soon to be Prime Minister, was boasting in his Budget statement that because of his sound policies the economy 'will never return to the old boom and bust'.

In 2008, his prediction proved terribly wrong. A worldwide banking crisis, the 'credit crunch', saw the UK economy plunge into the longest downturn within living memory. Real GDP was still marginally lower in 2012 than it was in 2007, as was investment. Despite very weak demand, prices continued to rise at rates more than double the average for the 10 years before the recession. The main driver behind UK inflation was arguably rising import prices. Despite a worldwide recession in major industrialised countries, emerging countries, such as China and India, only saw small falls in their growth rates due to the 2008 'credit crunch'. Their high economic growth rates continued to fuel a boom in world commodity prices between 2010 and 2011.

Table 1 Selected economic indicators, UK, 2007-2013

| | Annual percentage change | | | | |
	Real growth in GDP	Real growth in investment	Inflation (RPI)	Change in import prices	Change in average earnings
2007	2.6	6.3	2.3	0.1	4.9
2008	-0.3	-11.6	3.6	12.9	3.5
2009	-4.3	-21.3	2.2	1.9	0
2010	1.9	6.5	3.3	3.9	2.3
2011	1.6	8.8	4.5	7.1	2.4
2012	0.7	2.5	2.8	-0.8	1.3
2013	1.7	5.1	2.6	1.0	1.3

Source: adapted from www.ons.gov.uk.

1. Consider both the passage and the table carefully. Analyse, using diagrams, what happened in the period 2008 to 2013 to (a) short-run aggregate supply and (b) long-run aggregate supply.

28 National income

Starter activity

Get a sheet of paper and put your name in a box. Put arrows into the box showing your sources of income. Put arrows out of the box showing what you do with your income. Group all spending under one category, 'expenditure'. Now think of how your outgoings are is linked to your income, perhaps through the wages of your parents, the taxes they pay which is spent by government or even through the international economy.

Income, output and expenditure

Macroeconomics is concerned with the economy as a whole. A key macroeconomic variable is the level of total output in an economy, often called **national income**. There are three ways in which national income can be calculated. To understand why, consider a very simple model of the economy where there is no foreign trade (a **closed economy** as opposed to an **open economy** where there is foreign trade) and no government. In this economy, there are only households and firms which spend all their income and revenues.

Households own the **wealth** of the nation. They own the stock of land, labour and capital used to produce goods and services. They supply these factors to firms in return for **income**.

These incomes are rents, wages, interest and profits - the rewards to the factors of production. They then use this money to buy goods and services.

Firms produce goods and services. They hire factors of production from households and use these to produce goods and services for sale back to households.

The flow from households to firms is shown in Figure 1. The flow of money around the economy is shown in colour. Households receive payments for hiring their land, labour and capital. They spend all that money on the goods and services produced by firms (consumption). An alternative way of putting this is to express these money payments in real terms, taking into account changes in prices. The real flow of products and factor services is shown in black. Households supply land, labour and capital in return for goods and services. The **circular flow of income model** can be used to show that there are three ways of measuring the level of economic activity.

National output (O) This is the value of the flow of goods and services from firms to households. It is the black line on the right of Figure 1.

National expenditure (E) This is the value of spending by households on goods and services. It is the red line on the right of the diagram.

Figure 1

The circular flow of income in a simple economy

Households supply factors of production to firms in return for rent, wages, interest and profit. Households spend their money on goods and services supplied by firms.

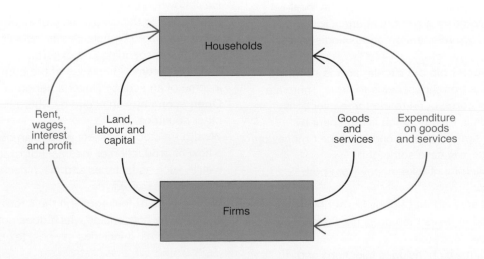

Figure 2

Injections and withdrawals and the circular flow

Investment, government spending and exports are injections into the circular flow. They raise spending. Saving, taxes and imports are withdrawals and reduce spending.

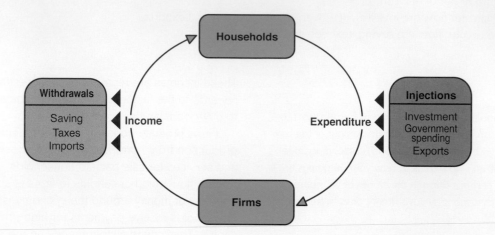

National income (Y) This is the value of income paid by firms to households in return for land, labour and capital. It is the blue line on the left of the diagram.

So income, expenditure and output are three ways of measuring the same flow. To show that they must be identical and not just equal, we use the ' ≡ ' sign.

$$O \equiv E \equiv Y$$

Injections and withdrawals

The simple circular flow of income model in Figure 1 can be made more realistic by adding **injections** and **withdrawals**. An **injection** into the circular flow is spending which does not come from households. There are three injections.

- Investment is spending by firms on new capital equipment like factories, offices and machinery. It is also spending on stocks (or inventories) of goods which are used in the production process.
- Government spending is spending by central and local government as well as other government agencies.
- Exports is spending by foreigners on goods and services made in the UK.

A withdrawal or leakage from the circular flow is spending which does not flow back from households to firms. There are three withdrawals which correspond to the three injections.

- Saving by households is money which is not spent by households. Equally, firms do not spend all of their money on wages and profits but may save some of it.
- Taxes paid to the government take money from both households and firms.
- Imports from abroad are bought both by households and firms. The money paid in taxes then does not flow back round the circular flow.

A circular flow diagram which includes injections and withdrawals is shown in Figure 2.

In equilibrium, when there is no tendency to change, injections must equal withdrawals. When this happens output, expenditure and income flowing round the circular flow remain the same. When injections are greater than withdrawals, national income will rise to reflect the greater spending. Equally, when injections are less than withdrawals, spending will fall. For example, a rise in investment will increase spending in the economy. A rise in saving will reduce spending.

Key Terms

Circular flow of income - a model of the economy which shows the flow of goods, services and factors and their payments around the economy.

Closed economy - an economy where there is no foreign trade.

Income - rent, interest, wages and profits earned from wealth owned by economic actors.

Injections - in the circular flow of income, spending which is not generated by households including investment, government spending and exports.

National income - the value of the output, expenditure or income of an economy over a period of time.

Open economy - an economy where there is trade with other countries.

Wealth - a stock of assets which can be used to generate a flow of production or income. For example, physical wealth such as factories and machines is used to make goods and services.

Withdrawals or leakages - in the circular flow of income, spending by households which does not flow back to domestic firms. It includes savings, taxes and imports.

Thinking like an economist

Increasing investment

In 2008 and 2009, published figures suggested that the UK economy had slid into a deep recession and, between 2010-13, growth in national income was very weak. This was despite unemployment climbing to 1.6 million in 2012. It was reported that some economists, including those from the opposition Labour Party, argued that government policy was misguided. The coalition of Conservatives and Liberal Democrats under the Chancellor George Osborne had decided as a priority to cut the budget deficit - the difference between government spending and taxation. The government raised taxes and cut government spending. The circular flow model shows that this policy will shrink the size of income, output and expenditure flowing round the economy. The economy only expanded slightly in size in 2010-13 because of small increases in investment and exports.

These critical economists argued that a better policy would have been to increase government spending on investment goods, because building more social housing, road building or improving rail infrastructure could have been achieved quickly. This would have injected money into the circular flow, increasing

national output, income and expenditure and, according to them, would have got the UK out of recession and stagnation more rapidly.

Data Response Question

Circular flow of income

The figures in Table 1 represent the only income payments received by households. There are no savings, investment, government expenditure and taxes or foreign trade in the economy.

Table 1

	£bn
Rent	5
Wages	75
Interest and profit	20

Q

1. Draw a circular flow of income diagram. Label it at the appropriate place with the value of: (i) income, (ii) output and (iii) expenditure.

2. How would your answer be different if wages were £100 billion?

3. Now assume that there are injections into and withdrawals from the circular flow. Investment is £10 billion, government spending £20 billion and exports £30 billion. Savings are £15 billion and taxes are £15 billion. (i) What must be the equilibrium level of imports? (ii) Show these injections and withdrawals on your circular flow diagram.

29 Equilibrium levels of real national output

1. The economy is in equilibrium when aggregate demand equals aggregate supply.
2. In the short run, equilibrium occurs when aggregate demand equals short run aggregate supply.
3. In the classical model, where wages are completely flexible, the economy will be in long run equilibrium at full employment. In the Keynesian model, where wages are sticky downwards, the economy can be in long run equilibrium at less than full employment.
4. In the classical model, a rise in aggregate demand will in the short run lead to an increase in both output and prices, but in the long run the rise will generate only an increase in prices. In the Keynesian model, a rise in aggregate demand will be purely inflationary if the economy is at full employment, but will lead to an increase in output if the economy is below full employment.
5. A rise in long run aggregate supply in the classical model will both increase output and reduce prices. Keynesians would agree with this in general, but would argue that an increase in aggregate supply will have no effect on output or prices if the economy is in a slump.
6. Factors which affect aggregate demand may well affect aggregate supply and vice versa, although this may occur over different time periods. For instance, an increase in investment is likely to increase both aggregate demand and aggregate supply.

Starter activity

Price and equilibrium output in a market are fixed by the forces of demand and supply. So in the whole economy, price and output are fixed by the aggregate demand (AD) and aggregate supply (AS). Give two factors that are currently in the news which affect either AD or AS. Explain what impact these are having on overall prices and output in the economy as a whole.

Equilibrium output in the short run

Units 23 and 27 outlined theories of aggregate demand and aggregate supply. Both Keynesian and classical economists agree that in the short run the aggregate demand curve is downward sloping whilst the aggregate supply curve is upward sloping. The equilibrium level of output in the short run occurs at the intersection of the aggregate demand and aggregate supply curves. In Figure 1, the equilibrium level of income and output is OY. The equilibrium price level is OP.

An increase in aggregate demand will shift the aggregate demand curve to the right. Aggregate demand is made up of consumption, investment, government spending and export minus imports. So an increase in aggregate demand will result from an increase in one of these components. For example:

- a fall in interest rates will raise both consumption and investment;
- a fall in the exchange rate will boost exports and reduce imports;
- a lowering of income tax will raise consumption because households will now have higher disposable income.

Figure 2 shows the impact of a rise in aggregate demand on equilibrium output and the price level. The aggregate demand curve shifts from AD_1 to AD_2. Equilibrium output then rises from OY_1 to OY_2 whilst the price level rises from OP_1 to OP_2. A rise in

Figure 1

Equilibrium output

The equilibrium level of national output is set at the intersection of the aggregate demand and supply curves at OY. The equilibrium price level is OP.

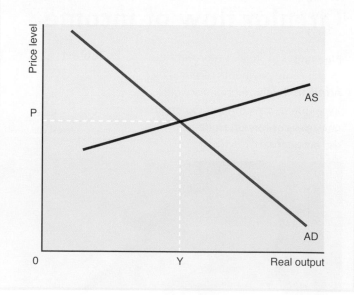

aggregate demand therefore increases both real output and the price level in the short run. The opposite is also true. A fall in aggregate demand will lead both to a fall in real output and a fall in the price level.

A fall in short-run aggregate supply will shift the SRAS curve upwards and to the left. A variety of factors could bring about a fall in short run aggregate supply. For example:

- wages of workers might rise;
- raw material prices might go up;

Figure 2

A rise in aggregate demand in the short run

A rise in aggregate demand, shown by the shift in the aggregate demand curve from AD_1 to AD_2, leads to a rise in both equilibrium real output from OY_1 to OY_2 and the price level from OP_1 to OP_2.

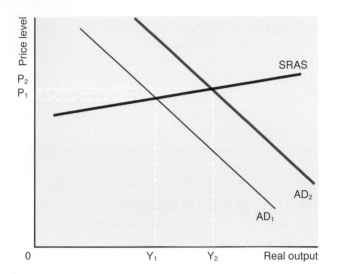

Question 1

What would be the effect on equilibrium income in the short run if the workers in the photograph were (a) successful and (b) unsuccessful with their demands?

- taxes on goods and services might be raised by the government.

Figure 3 shows the impact of a fall in aggregate supply on equilibrium output and the price level. The SRAS curve shifts from $SRAS_1$ to $SRAS_2$. Equilibrium output then falls from OY_1 to OY_2. At the same time, the price level rises from OP_1 to OP_2. A fall in short run aggregate supply therefore leads to a fall in output but a rise in the price level in the short run. The opposite is also true. A rise in aggregate supply, shown by a downward shift to the right of the SRAS curve, will lead to a rise in equilibrium output and a fall in the price level.

Equilibrium output in the long run

In the long run, the impact of changes in aggregate demand and supply are affected by the shape of the long-run aggregate supply curve. Classical economists argue that in the long run the aggregate supply curve is vertical, as shown in Figure 4. Long-run equilibrium occurs where the long-run aggregate

Figure 3

A fall in aggregate supply in the short run

A fall in short-run aggregate supply, shown by the shift in the SRAS curve from $SRAS_1$ to $SRAS_2$, leads to a fall in equilibrium real output from OY_1 to OY_2 and a rise in the price level from OP_1 to OP_2.

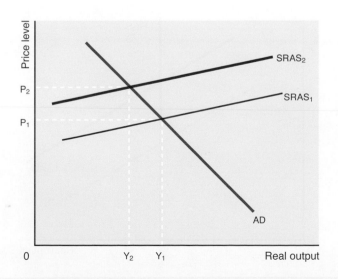

Figure 4

Long-run equilibrium in the classical model

Long run equilibrium output is OY, the full employment level of output, since wages are flexible both downwards as well as upwards.

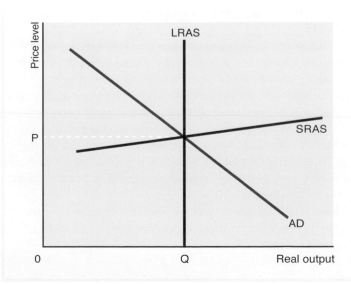

Figure 5

Long-run equilibrium in the Keynesian model

Long-run equilibrium output OY_1 may be below the full employment level of output OY_2 because real wages may not fall when there is unemployment.

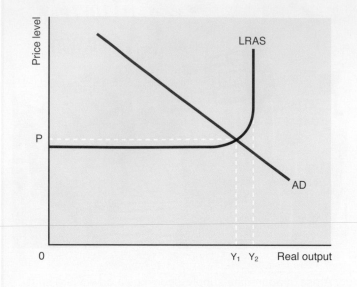

supply curve (LRAS) intersects with the aggregate demand curve. Hence equilibrium output is OY and the equilibrium price level is OP. Associated with the long run equilibrium price level is a short-run aggregate supply curve (SRAS) which passes through the point where LRAS = AD. The long-run aggregate supply curve shows the supply curve for the economy at full employment. Hence there can be no unemployment in the long run according to classical economists.

Keynesian economists argue that the long-run aggregate supply curve is as shown in Figure 5. The economy is at full employment where the LRAS curve is vertical at output OY_2 - a point of agreement with classical economists. However, the economy can be in equilibrium at less than full employment. In Figure 5 the equilibrium level of output is OY_1 where the AD curve cuts the LRAS curve. The key point of disagreement between classical and Keynesian economists is the extent to which workers react to unemployment by accepting real wage cuts.

Classical economists argue that a rise in unemployment will lead rapidly to cuts in real wages. These cuts will increase the quantity demanded of labour and reduce the quantity supplied, returning the economy to full employment quickly and automatically. Keynesian economists, on the other hand, argue that money wages are sticky downwards. Workers will refuse to take money wage cuts and will fiercely resist cuts in their real wage. The labour market will therefore not clear except perhaps over a very long period of time, so long that it is possibly even not worth considering.

Having outlined a theory of equilibrium output, it is now possible to see what happens if either aggregate demand or aggregate supply changes.

Question 2

In his Budget of 1981, with unemployment at 3 million and still rising, the Chancellor of the Exchequer, Geoffrey Howe, raised the level of taxes and significantly reduced the budget deficit in order to squeeze inflationary pressures. In a letter to *The Times*, 364 economists protested at what they saw as the perversity of this decision.

(a) Geoffrey Howe was influenced by classical economic thinking. Using a diagram, explain why he believed that his policy (i) would help reduce inflation and (ii) not lead to any increase in unemployment.

(b) The economists who wrote the letter to *The Times* could broadly be described as Keynesian. Using a diagram, explain why they believed that it was folly to increase taxes at a time when the economy was in the grip of the worst recession since the 1930s.

A rise in aggregate demand

Assume that there is a rise in aggregate demand in the economy with long run aggregate supply initially remaining unchanged. For instance, there may be an increase in the wages of public sector employees paid for by an increase in the money supply, or there may be a fall in the marginal propensity to save and a rise in the marginal propensity to consume (as explained in Unit 30). A rise in aggregate demand will push the AD curve to the right. The classical and Keynesian models give different conclusions about the effect of this.

The classical model A rise in aggregate demand, in the classical model, will lead to a rise in the price level but no change in real output in the long run. In Figure 6, the aggregate demand curve shifts to the right from AD_1 to AD_2. This could

Figure 6

A rise in aggregate demand in the classical model

A rise in aggregate demand in the long run will shift the aggregate demand curve from AD_1 to AD_2. The equilibrium price level will rise from OP_1 to OP_2 but there will be no change in equilibrium real output, Y.

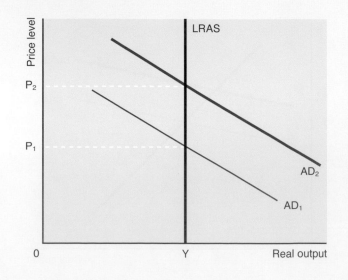

Figure 7

The classical model in the short and long run

A rise in aggregate demand shown by a shift to the right in the AD curve will result in a movement along the SRAS curve. Both output and prices will increase. In the long run, the SRAS curve will shift upwards with long run equilibrium being re-established at C. The rise in demand has led only to a rise in the price level.

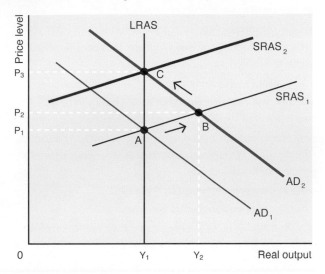

have been caused by a fall in interest rates, for example. The equilibrium price level rises from OP₁ to OP₂ but equilibrium real output remains the same at OQ. In the classical model, no amount of extra demand will raise long run equilibrium output. This is because the long run aggregate supply curve shows the maximum productive capacity of the economy at that point in time.

The movement from one equilibrium point to the next can also be shown on an AD/AS diagram. Assume there is a rise in aggregate demand, which shifts the aggregate demand curve from AD₁ to AD₂. In the short run, this will result in a movement up the SRAS curve. In Figure 7, output will rise from OY₁ to OY₂ and this will be accompanied by a small rise in the price level from OP₁ to OP₂. This will move the economy from A to B.

However, the economy is now in long run disequilibrium. The full employment level of output is OY₁, shown by the position of the long run aggregate supply curve. The economy is therefore operating at over-full employment. Firms will find it difficult to recruit labour, buy raw materials and find new offices or factory space. They will respond by bidding up wages and other costs. The short run aggregate supply curve is drawn on the assumption that wage rates and other costs remain constant. So a rise in wage rates will shift the short run aggregate supply curve upwards. Short run equilibrium output will now fall and prices will keep rising. The economy will only return to long run equilibrium when the short run aggregate supply curve has shifted upwards from SRAS₁ to SRAS₂ so that aggregate demand once again equals long run aggregate supply at C.

The conclusion of the classical model is that increases in aggregate demand will initially increase both prices and output

(the movement from A to B in Figure 7). Over time prices will continue to rise but output will fall as the economy moves back towards long run equilibrium (the movement from B to C). In the long term, an increase in aggregate demand will only lead to an increase in the price level (from A to C). There will be no effect on equilibrium output. So increases in aggregate demand without any change in long run aggregate supply are purely inflationary.

The Keynesian model In the Keynesian model, the long run aggregate supply curve is shaped as in Figure 8. Keynesians would agree with classical economists that an increase in aggregate demand from, say, AD₄ to AD₅ will be purely inflationary if the economy is already at full employment at OY₄.

But if the economy is in deep depression, as was the case in the UK during the early 1930s, an increase in aggregate demand will lead to a rise in output without an increase in prices. The shift in aggregate demand from AD₁ to AD₂ will increase equilibrium output from OY₁ to OY₂ without raising the price level from OP as there are unused resources available.

The third possibility is that the economy is a little below full employment, for instance at OY₃ in Figure 8. Then a rise in aggregate demand from AD₃ to AD₄ will increase both equilibrium output and equilibrium prices.

In the Keynesian model, increases in aggregate demand may or may not be effective in raising equilibrium output. It depends upon whether the economy is below full employment or at full employment.

Figure 8

The Keynesian model

If the economy is already at full employment, an increase in aggregate demand in the Keynesian model creates an inflationary gap without increasing output. In a depression, an increase in aggregate demand will increase output but not prices. If the economy is slightly below full employment, an increase in aggregate demand will increase both output and prices.

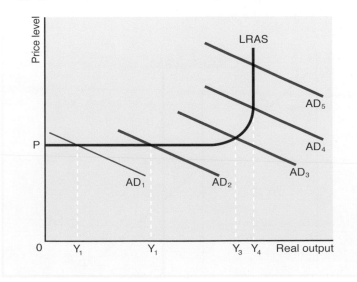

A rise in long-run aggregate supply

A rise in long-run aggregate supply means that the potential output of the economy has increased. Rises in long-run aggregate supply which are unlikely to shift the aggregate demand curve might occur if, for instance, incentives to work increased or there was a change in technology.

The classical model In the classical model, an increase in long-run aggregate supply will lead to both higher output and lower prices. In Figure 9 a shift in the aggregate supply curve from $LRAS_1$ to $LRAS_2$ will increase equilibrium output from OY_1 to OY_2. Equilibrium prices will also fall from OP_1 to OP_2. Contrast this conclusion with what happens when aggregate demand is increased - a rise in prices with no increase in output. It is not surprising that classical economists are so strongly in favour of supply side policies.

The Keynesian model In the Keynesian model, shown in Figure 10, an increase in aggregate supply will both increase output and reduce prices if the economy is at full employment. With aggregate demand at AD_1, a shift in the aggregate supply curve from $LRAS_1$ to $LRAS_2$ increases full employment equilibrium output from Y_E to Y_F. If the economy is at slightly less than full employment, with an aggregate demand curve of AD_2, then the shift to the right in the LRAS curve will still be beneficial to the economy, increasing output and reducing prices. However, Keynesians disagree with classical economists that supply side measures can be effective in a depression. If the aggregate demand curve is AD_3, an increase in aggregate supply has no effect on equilibrium output. It remains obstinately stuck at Y_D. Only an increase in aggregate demand will move the economy out of depression.

Question 3

In June 1995, a new French government unveiled a stiff budget designed to reduce high unemployment levels by 700 000 and bring down a high budget deficit from 5.7 per cent of GDP to 5.1 per cent of GDP within the fiscal year. The measures included:

- a substantial French Franc 19 billion cut in government spending affecting all ministries apart from justice and culture, with defence bearing nearly 50 per cent of the cuts;
- a rise in corporation tax from 33.3 per cent to 36.6 per cent;
- a rise in the standard rate of VAT from 18.6 per cent to 20.6 per cent;
- a 10 per cent rise in wealth tax;
- a 40 per cent cut in employment taxes paid by firms on employment of workers at or near the minimum wage level;
- new programmes targeted particularly at youth in difficulties, offering training, apprenticeship and other policies to bring people into the workforce;
- a rise in the minimum wage by 4 per cent;
- a rise in state pensions by 0.5 per cent;
- measures to stimulate the housing market, particularly focused on lodgings for people on lower incomes.

Using diagrams, explain what effect these measures would have on aggregate supply according to:

(a) classical or supply-side economists,

(b) Keynesian economists.

Figure 10

An increase in aggregate supply in the Keynesian model

The effect of an increase in long-run aggregate supply depends upon the position of the aggregate demand curve. If the economy is at or near full employment, an increase will raise output and lower prices. However, if the economy is in depression at Y_D, an increase in LRAS will have no impact on the economy.

Figure 9

An increase in aggregate supply in the classical model

A shift to the right of the LRAS curve will both increase equilibrium output and reduce the price level.

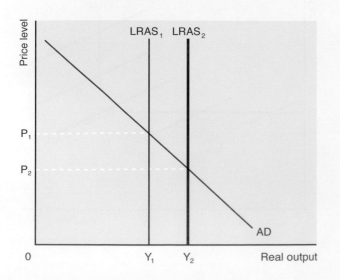

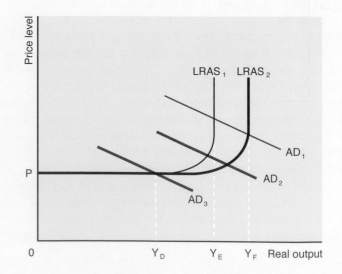

It is now possible to understand one of the most important controversies in the history of economics. During the 1930s, classical economists argued that the only way to put the millions of unemployed during the Great Depression back to work was to adopt supply side measures - such as cutting unemployment benefits, reducing trade union power and cutting marginal tax rates and government spending. John Maynard Keynes attacked this orthodoxy by suggesting that the depression was caused by a lack of demand and suggesting that it was the government's responsibility to increase the level of aggregate demand. The same debate was replayed in the UK in the early 1980s. This time it was Keynesians who represented orthodoxy. They suggested that the only quick way to get the millions officially unemployed back to work was to expand aggregate demand. In the Budget of 1981, the government did precisely the opposite - it cut its projected budget deficit, reducing aggregate demand and argued that the only way to cure unemployment was to improve the supply side of the economy.

Increasing aggregate demand and supply

In microeconomics, factors which shift the demand curve do not shift the supply curve as well and vice versa. For instance, an increase in the costs of production shifts the supply curve but does not shift the demand curve for a good (although there will of course be a movement along the demand curve

Figure 11

An increase in investment expenditure

An increase in investment will increase aggregate demand from AD_1 to AD_2, and is likely to shift the long-run aggregate supply curve from $LRAS_1$ to $LRAS_2$. The result is an increase in output and a small fall in prices.

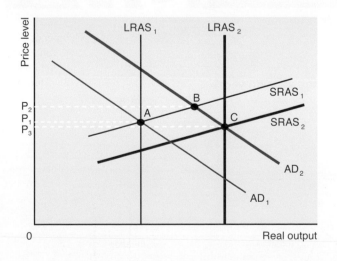

Question 4

Using a classical model of the economy, explain the effect of the following on: (i) aggregate demand; (ii) short-run aggregate supply; (iii) output and prices in the long run.

(a) A 10 per cent rise in earnings.

(b) An increase in real spending by government on education and training.

(c) An increase in the average long term real rate of interest from three per cent to five per cent.

as a result). However, in macroeconomic aggregate demand and aggregate supply analysis, factors which shift one curve may well shift the other curve as well. For instance, assume that firms increase their planned investment. This will increase the level of aggregate demand. However, in the long run it will also increase the level of aggregate supply. An increase in investment will increase the capital stock of the economy. The productive potential of the economy will therefore rise. We can use aggregate demand and supply analysis to show the effects of an increase in investment.

An increase in investment in the classical model will initially shift the aggregate demand curve in Figure 11 to the right from AD_1 to AD_2. There will then be a movement along the short-run aggregate supply curve from A to B. There is now long-run disequilibrium. How this will be resolved depends upon the speed with which the investment is brought on stream and starts to produce goods and services. Assume that this happens fairly quickly. The long-run aggregate supply curve will then shift to the right, say, from $LRAS_1$ to $LRAS_2$. Long-run equilibrium will be restored at C. Output has increased and the price level fallen slightly. There will also be a new short-run aggregate supply curve, $SRAS_2$. It is below the original short-run aggregate supply curve because it is assumed that investment has reduced costs of production.

Not all investment results in increased production. For instance, fitting out a new shop which goes into receivership within a few months will increase aggregate demand but not long-run aggregate supply. The long-run aggregate supply curve will therefore not shift and the increased investment will only be inflationary. Equally, investment might be poorly directed. The increase in aggregate demand might be greater than the increase in long-run aggregate supply. Here there will be an increase in equilibrium output but there will also be an increase in prices. The extent to which investment increases output and contributes to a lessening of inflationary pressure depends upon the extent to which it gives a high rate of return in the long run.

Thinking like an economist

Demand and supply side shocks in four recessions

Supply side shocks

Figures suggest that over the past 40 years, the UK has experienced four major recessions. The first two, in 1974-75 and 1980-81, shown in Figure 12, were caused mainly by supply side shocks. Sharp rises in world oil prices helped fuel UK inflation. Industrial unrest also saw large wage increases for workers. The result was a substantial shift upwards in the short-run aggregate supply curve. As Figure 13 shows, this led to a change in short run equilibrium for the economy from A to B. The price level was higher and output lower - a situation known as 'stagflation'. The economy was stagnating, unemployment was rising, output was falling but inflation was increasing. In Figure 12, this is shown by the two lines moving apart as the recession deepens.

Demand side shocks

The second two recessions of the past forty years were mainly caused by demand side shocks. Between 1986 and 1988, the Chancellor of the Exchequer, Nigel Lawson, helped fuel a boom with low interest rates and income tax cuts. The Lawson boom saw rising inflation. To combat this, the government raised interest rates from 7.5 per cent in May 1988 to 15 per cent in 1989 and kept them at this level for nearly a year. Combined with a high value of the pound, aggregate demand fell. As shown in Figure 14, this led to a recession with falling output and downward pressure on prices as the economy moved from A to B. All other things being equal, the economy would have returned to long-run equilibrium at C.

Figure 12

Inflation and economic growth in four recessions (percentage change year on year)

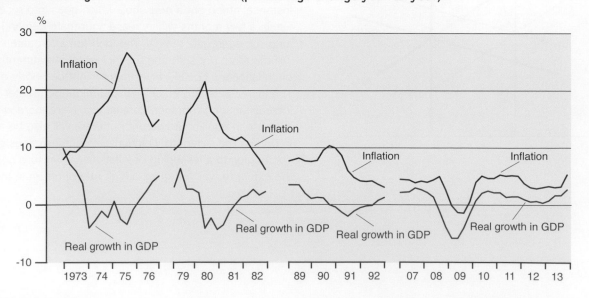

Source: adapted from www.ons.gov.uk.

Figure 13

Stagflation caused by supply-side shocks

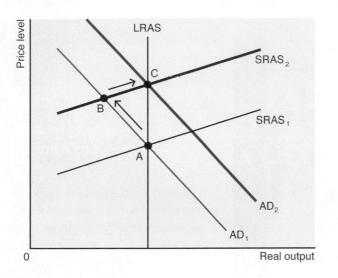

Figure 14

Recession caused by a demand-side shock

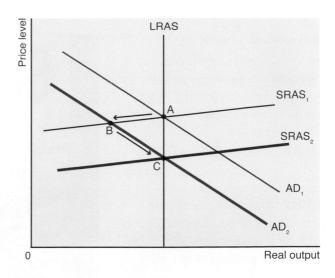

The downturn of 2008-13 was caused by a banking crisis in 2007-08. Fuelled by low interest rates and a banking system which over-lent to high-risk customers, many banks in the UK, the rest of Europe and the USA came close to collapse. The banking system had to be bailed out by governments. However, lending by banks fell sharply. There was also a fall in confidence by consumers and businesses that led to lower spending. The result was a sharp fall in aggregate demand. The situation was made worse by a backdrop of rising world commodity prices since the early 2000s.

China and other emerging countries were growing fast and world demand for raw materials had been rising. The 'credit crunch' banking crisis of 2007-08 saw a fall in world growth rates but by 2010 demand for commodities by countries such as China was again pushing up commodity prices and causing imported inflation to the UK. In the UK, weak growth in aggregate demand in 2011 and 2012 (shown by a small shift to the right in the AD curve) combined with a rising short-run aggregate supply curve due to imported inflation led to stagnating real output with relatively high inflation. Weak growth in aggregate demand was partly caused by weak growth in Europe, our main trading partner. UK government policy to cut public spending also contributed significantly to lower aggregate demand. Consumer spending was depressed too as many households attempted to pay off debt contracted before 2008. Rising unemployment and rises in taxes also hit household spending in 2010-11.

The last two recessions are shown in Figure 12. The demand side nature of both recessions can be seen from how the two lines broadly move together. As the economy moves into recession, inflation falls at the same time as economic growth.

Effects on long-run aggregate supply

Some economists argue that deep recessions lead to a permanently lower level of actual output from what it would otherwise have been had there been no recession. The long-run aggregate supply curve is shifted to the left. Once the economy recovers, it never catches up the lost economic growth. This is because capital equipment is scrapped as firms close. Workers become long-term unemployed, deskilled and demotivated, some never to work again.

There is evidence that this happened in all four major recessions of the past 40 years. Long-term unemployment first became an issue in the UK following the 1974-75 recession and has never disappeared. In all of the recessions, workers under 25 and over 50 have been particularly affected by long term unemployment and deskilling. Investment has been cut back. In the downturn of 2008-12, both economists and governments were dismayed to find that the economy failed to bounce back as in previous recessions. It could be that the UK economy will see sluggish growth for the next decade due to the severe damage done to the economy by the banking sector.

Data Response Question

The UK economy: stagnation 2010-13

Disappointing growth

Economists would suggest that the economy should have grown rapidly between 2010 and 2013 if it had performed in a similar way to previous recessions.

Instead, after an initial bounce back in 2010, figures showed that the rate of economic growth fell in both 2011 and 2012. At several points during this period, there was even a threat of a technical recession - two successive quarters of negative growth.

The main cause was disappointing growth in aggregate demand. Consumers were reluctant to increase spending as they paid off debts accumulated before the credit crunch of 2008. Higher taxes also hit consumer pockets, whilst the threat of unemployment reduced consumer confidence. Businesses too, despite having large reserves of profit, were reluctant to increase

investment spending when the economy was so depressed. However, at least consumption and investment rose between 2010 and 2013. Net exports too were higher in 2013 compared to 2010. In contrast, government spending was marginally lower in 2013 than in 2010, the result of government policy to cut the budget deficit. In previous recessions, government spending

increased as the economy came out of recession.

Continued problems with inflation

With real GDP lower in 2012 than it was in 2007, economists would argue that inflation should have been zero if not negative due to weak aggregate demand. However, inflation in 2012 was still above the Bank of England target of two per cent because of supply side factors. A combination of higher import prices and continued increases in domestic prices, such as fuel bills and university tuition fees, were pushing up prices.

Q

1. Using the data in Figure 15, estimate the change in aggregate demand over the period 2010 to 2013.

2. Outline (a) the demand side factors and (b) the short-run supply side factors that influenced the equilibrium level of national output and price level between 2010 and 2013.

3. Using an aggregate demand and short run supply diagram, evaluate whether changes in the world economy were the main factors causing UK equilibrium output to stagnate over the period 2010 to 2013.

Figure 15

Change to AD and components of AD in each year compared to 2010, £ billion at 2011 prices[1,2,3]

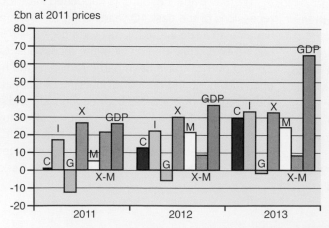

1. The graph shows the change from that year compared to 2010. For example, 2012 consumption shows the difference in consumption in £ billion between 2012 and 2010. So consumption was £12.6 billion higher in 2012 compared to 2010. 2013 GDP shows the difference in GDP in £ billion between 2010 and 2013. So GDP was £65 billion higher in 2013 compared to 2010.
2. I is private sector investment.
3. G is government current spending and government investment.

Source: adapted from www.ons.gov.uk

Evaluation

Build on your answer to question 2. Explain how demand and supply side factors shifted the AD and SRAS curves to achieve equilibrium. Then, using the data in Figure 15 and the text, analyse how the different components of AD contributed to the overall weak growth in GDP. Which of the components had the weakest growth? Was the international economy significant on the supply-side of the economy? Come to an overall conclusion.

30 | The multiplier

Key points

1. An increase in investment or any other injection will lead to an even greater increase in income. This is known as the multiplier process.
2. The multiplier can be calculated from the marginal propensities to consume, withdraw, save, tax and import.
3. The multiplier will cause aggregate demand to increase by more than the initial increase in investment, government spending or exports.

Starter activity

A supermarket chain has decided to build a small local store in your area. Draw a chart showing five ways in which this investment in your local community leads to further spending in the economy. For example, one way could be: construction workers spend their wages→spending on food→increased output by food processors→ more output by farmers.

This illustrates what is known in economics as the multiplier process.

The multiplier

If there is an increase in, say, investment of £1, what will be the final increase in national income? John Maynard Keynes argued in his most famous book, *The General Theory of Employment, Interest and Money*, published in 1936, that national income would increase by more than £1 because of the **multiplier effect**.

To understand why there might be a multiplier effect, consider what would happen if firms increased spending on new factories by £100 million. Firms would pay contractors to build the factories. This £100 million would be an increase in aggregate demand. The contractor would use the money in part to pay its workers on the project. The workers would

spend the money, on everything from food to holidays. This spending would be an addition to national income. Assume that £10 million is spent on food. Food manufacturers would in turn pay their workers who would spend their incomes on a variety of products, increasing national income further. Keynes argued that this multiplier effect would increase jobs in the economy. Every job directly created by firms through extra spending would indirectly create other jobs in the economy.

This process can be shown using the **circular flow of income model**. Assume that households spend 90 per cent of their gross income. The other 10 per cent is either saved or paid to the government in the form of taxes. Firms increase their spending by £100 million, money which is used to build new factories. In Figure 1, this initial £100 million is shown in stage 1 flowing into firms. The money then flows out again as it is distributed in the form of wages and profits back to households. Households spend the money, but remember that there are **withdrawals** of 0.1 of income because of savings and taxes. So only £90 million flows back round the economy in stage 2 to firms. Then firms pay £90 million back to households in wages and profits. In the third stage, £81 million is spent by households with £19 million leaking out of the circular flow. This process carries on with smaller and smaller amounts

Figure 1

The circular flow of income

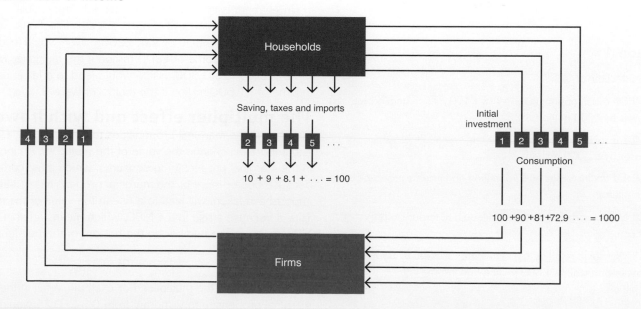

being added to national income as the money flows round the economy. Eventually, the initial £100 million extra government spending leads to a final increase in national income of £1 000 million. In this case, the value of the **multiplier** (or **national income multiplier** or **Keynesian multiplier** or **real multiplier**) is 10.

If leakages from the circular flow in Figure 1 had been larger, less of the increase in investment would have continued to flow round the economy. For instance, if leakages had been 0.8 of income, then only £20 million (0.2 x £100 million) would have flowed round the economy in the second stage. In the third stage, it would have been £4 million (0.2 x £20 million). The final increase in national income following the initial £100 million increase in investment spending would have been £125 million.

The multiplier model states that the higher the leakages from the circular flow, the smaller will be the increase in income which continues to flow round the economy at each stage following an initial increase in spending. Hence, the higher the leakages, the smaller the value of the multiplier. Leakages are what is not spent. So, another way of saying this is that the multiplier is smaller when the ratio of consumption to income is lower.

The multiplier effect works too when investment, government spending or exports fall. If government spending, for example, falls by £3 billion and the multiplier is 2, then the final fall in national income will be £6 billion.

Maths Tip

A multiplier example
Assume the following
MPC = 0.4
MPS = 0.1
MPT = 0.2
MPM = 0.3
The marginal propensity to withdraw (which is MPS + MPT + MPM) is therefore 0.6.
The value of the multiplier (1 ÷ MPW) is therefore 1 ÷ 0.6 or 1.66.
Alternatively it can be calculated from 1 ÷ (1 - MPC) which is 1 ÷ (1 - 0.4) or 1.66.
So if injections increase by £100 million, the final increase in national income is £166 million (£100 million x 1.66).

Question 1

Calculate the value of:

(a) the MPC if consumption increases by £100 million and income increases by £200 million;

(b) the MPS if saving increases by £200 million and income increases by £2 000 million;

(c) the MPT if tax increases by £50 million and income increases by £150 million;

(d) the MPM if imports fall by £300 million and income falls by £1 billion;

(e) the MPW if savings fall by £100 million, taxes fall by £300 million, imports fall by £600 million and income falls by £2.5 billion.

Calculating the multiplier

The value of the multiplier can be calculated by using a formula involving a number of variables (C or consumption; S or saving; T or taxation, M or imports, W or total withdrawals) and their marginal propensities.

- The marginal propensity to consume (MPC), which is the increase in consumption (ΔC) divided by the increase in income (ΔY) that caused it (i.e. $\Delta C \div \Delta Y$).
- The **marginal propensity to save (MPS)**, which is the increase in saving divided by the increase in income that caused it (i.e. $\Delta S \div \Delta Y$).
- The **marginal propensity to tax (MPT)**, which is the increase in tax revenues divided by the increase in income that caused them (i.e. $\Delta T \div \Delta Y$).
- The **marginal propensity to import (MPM)**, which is the increase in imports divided by the increase in income that caused them (i.e. $\Delta M \div \Delta Y$).
- The **marginal propensity to withdraw (MPW)**, which is the increase in withdrawals from the circular flow ($S + T + M$) divided by the increase in income that caused them (i.e. $\Delta W \div \Delta Y$); this the same as the sum of the marginal propensity to save, tax and import (MPS + MPT + MPM).

The formula for the multiplier is:

$$\frac{1}{1 - MPC}$$

which is equal to

$$\frac{1}{(MPS + MPT + MPM)}$$

or

$$\frac{1}{MPW}$$

The multiplier effect and injections

Investment is an injection into the circular flow. The multiplier effect shows the impact on aggregate demand and income of a **change** in an injection. So if the multiplier were 2, then a £100 million increase in investment would lead to an increase in national income of £200 million.

Investment is not the only injection into the circular flow. Government spending and exports are also injections. So a rise in government spending of, say, £200 million would lead to a rise in national income of £800 million if the multiplier were 4. A fall in exports of £500 million would lead to a fall in national income of £1 500 million if the multiplier were 3.

The multiplier effect and withdrawals

Changes in the marginal propensities to consume, save, tax and import will change the value of the multiplier. An increase in the marginal propensity to consume, which must come about because one or more or the marginal propensities to save, tax or import have fallen, will lead to a rise in the value of the multiplier. This is because a rise in the MPC, which means a fall in the MPW, reduces the number on the bottom of the fraction:

$$\frac{1}{1 - MPC} \quad \text{or} \quad \frac{1}{MPW}$$

used to calculate the multiplier. For example, a fall in the marginal propensity to withdraw from 0.5 to 0.25 would

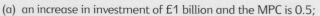

Figure 2

The multiplier effect on aggregate demand

An increase in exports of Y_1Y_2 leads to a final increase in equilibrium output of Y_1Y_3 due to the multiplier effect.

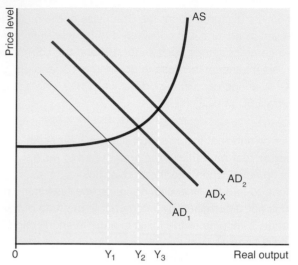

increase the value of the multiplier from 2 $(1 \div 0.5)$ to 4 $(1 \div 0.25)$.

Conversely, a fall in the MPC, which must be associated with a rise in the MPW, will lead to a fall in the value of the multiplier.

The multiplier and the aggregate demand curve

An increase in investment, exports or government spending of, for example, £1 billion will increase aggregate demand by £1 billion. The multiplier effect, assuming the multiplier is greater than 1, will lead to a further increase in aggregate demand. If the multiplier is 1.5, then the final increase in aggregate demand will be the £1 billion increase in I, X or M plus an additional £0.5 billion, making a total of £1.5 billion.

Figure 2 shows an initial aggregate demand curve of AD_1 with a Keynesian aggregate supply curve. An increase in exports

Question 3

Explain, using a diagram, the likely effect of the following on the aggregate demand curve for the UK.

(a) The 4 per cent fall in real household consumption expenditure between 2007 and 2011.

(b) The fall in bank base interest rates from 5.5 per cent in 2007 to 0.5 per cent in 2010.

(c) Rises in taxes in the 2011 and 2012 budgets.

(d) The 40 per cent fall in London Stock Exchange prices between October 2007 and February 2009.

(e) The rise in the household saving ratio from 1.7 per cent in 2007 to 6.6 per cent in 2011.

(f) The fall in real government spending forecast between 2011 and 2018.

(g) The 9 per cent rise in the average value of the pound against other currencies between March 2010 and September 2012.

Question 2

Calculate (i) the value of the multiplier and (ii) the change in income if there is:

(a) an increase in investment of £1 billion and the MPC is 0.5;

(b) a fall in government spending of £10 billion and the MPW is 0.8;

(c) an increase in exports of £5 billion and the MPC is 0.6;

(d) a fall in investment of £20 billion and the MPW is 0.25;

(e) a fall in exports of £7 billion and the MPS is 0.1, the MPT is 0.2 and the MPM is 0.2;

(f) a fall in government spending of £20 billion and the MPS is 0.2, the MPT is 0.3 and the MPM is 0.2;

(g) a rise in government spending of £10 billion and the MPS is 0.2, the MPT is 0.3 and the MPW is 0.7;

(h) a fall in investment of £30 billion and the MPS is 0.1, the MPM is 0.3 and the MPC is 0.5.

of Y_1Y_2 initially shifts the aggregate demand curve to AD_X. The multiplier effect then leads to a further increase of aggregate demand of Y_2Y_3, shifting the aggregate demand curve to AD_2. The total increase in aggregate demand is Y_1Y_3.

A fall in investment exports or government spending will lead to a shift to the left of the AD curve. The size of the fall in equilibrium national income will be the value of the fall in withdrawals times the multiplier.

Effects of the economy on the multiplier

The value of the multiplier is determined by the marginal propensities to consume, save, tax and import. These marginal propensities can change in value if other variables in the economy change.

Any change in a factor that affects the proportion of income spent will change the value of the multiplier. For example, the marginal propensities to consume and save are likely to change if there is a significant change in interest rates. A large rise in interest rates is likely to discourage consumption and encourage saving, leading to a fall in the MPC and a rise in the MPS. Consequently a large rise in interest rates is likely to lead to a fall in the value of the multiplier. Equally, a rise in household wealth is likely to raise the marginal propensity to consume and so lead to a rise in the value of the multiplier.

Government changes to taxes paid by households will affect the multiplier. A rise in taxes, that increases the proportion of income paid in tax at the margin, will increase the MPT. Hence the value of the multiplier will fall. A fall in marginal tax rates will lead to a rise in the value of the multiplier.

Any factor apart from income that changes imports will also change the value of the multiplier. For example, an improvement in the quality of imported goods, which encourages households to buy more imports, will increase the MPM and so reduce the value of the multiplier.

Governments and the multiplier

Governments in the past have used changes in government spending to influence national income and macroeconomic

149

variables such as unemployment and inflation. It would be very helpful if governments knew that an extra £1 in government spending would produce an extra, say, £2 in national income. However, in practice, it is not so simple.

- It is difficult to measure the exact size of the multiplier. Sophisticated econometric models have to be used which describe the workings of the economy. They are not completely accurate. Equally, changes can happen in an economy which can alter the size of the multiplier from one period to the next.

- The multiplier effect is not instantaneous. A £100 increase in government spending today does not increase national income by £200 today. It takes time for the money to flow round the circular flow. So there are time lags between the increase in the government spending and the final increase in national income.

- Economists disagree about the exact size of the multiplier. However, in general it is considered to be relatively low in high income countries such as the UK and the USA at around 0.5. This means an increase in government spending (G) of £100, or an increase in exports (X) of £100, only generates an extra £50 in GDP (Y).

Key Terms

Marginal propensity to import (MPM) - the increase in imports divided by the increase in income that caused them (i.e. $\Delta M \div \Delta Y$).

Marginal propensity to save (MPS) - the increase in saving divided by the increase in income that caused it (i.e. $\Delta S \div \Delta Y$).

Marginal propensity to tax (MPT) - the increase in tax revenues divided by the increase in income that caused them (i.e. $\Delta T \div \Delta Y$).

Marginal propensity to withdraw (MPW) - the increase in withdrawals from the circular flow (S + T + M) divided by the increase in income that caused them (i.e. $\Delta W \div \Delta Y$); this the same as the sum of the marginal propensity to save, tax and import (MPS + MPT + MPM).

Multiplier or national income multiplier or Keynesian multiplier or real multiplier - the figure used to multiply a change in an injection into the circular flow, such as investment, to find the final change in income (assuming the injection is not determined by income). It is the ratio of the final change in income to the initial change in an injection. It can be calculated as

$$\frac{1}{1 - MPC} \quad \text{or} \quad \frac{1}{(MPS + MPT + MPM)} \quad \text{or} \quad \frac{1}{MPW}$$

Multiplier effect or process - an increase in investment or other injection will lead to an even greater increase in income (assuming the injection is not determined by income).

Thinking like an economist

IMF encourages investment in infrastructure

European countries, including the UK, face major infrastructure problems. In the UK, for example, underinvestment in new or upgraded road and rail links is increasing journey times and transport costs for firms. A failure to invest sufficiently in new housing is one cause of house price inflation. In Europe, transport links too are a major problem. The German Institute for Economic Research (DIW Berlin), estimated that Germany spent 40 per cent less on transport infrastructure between 2006 and 2011 than needed to maintain the existing system in good working order. The fall in investment can be seen in Figure 3. Extra investment of €10 billion a year would be needed to make up the shortfall. Energy is another area suffering from lack of investment. In the UK, a failure to invest in new electricity sources such as gas-fired power stations or renewable energies means that the margin needed to prevent blackouts at peak demand times in winter is now dangerously small. In Europe, building new transmission lines between countries could radically reduce electricity costs for consumers and firms. Spain and Italy are ideally suited to produce solar-powered electricity. The north of Germany is ideally suited to produce wind energy. But getting that electricity to middle Europe needs investment in new transmission lines.

The IMF argued in 2014 that infrastructure spending increases national output by $3 for every $1 of investment.

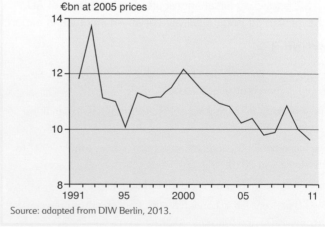

Figure 3

Falling investment in roads and bridges in Germany

€bn at 2005 prices

Source: adapted from DIW Berlin, 2013.

By borrowing money at current very low rates of interest, governments in Europe and the USA can provide a fiscal stimulus, which will increase both aggregate demand and aggregate supply. Infrastructure spending will in part use resources that are currently unemployed, such as unemployed or underemployed workers. It will increase economic growth both in the short term and the long term. Extra infrastructure spending in itself will increase the rate of growth of GDP in the year in which the money is spent. It will also increase growth in the long term because the productive capacity of the economy will have grown.

Currently, many governments are committed to reducing government spending and raising taxes to reduce their budget deficits. John Maynard Keynes argued in the 1930s that such policies at times of high unemployment were self-defeating. Cutting government spending leads to cuts in national income magnified by the multiplier effect. National income at best stagnates as do tax revenues. At worst, both income and tax revenues fall making the situation worse. Many economists today believe that austerity is recreating the problems of the 1930s. The solution is for governments in Europe and the USA to spend more on infrastructure and create economies that can grow at the rates seen in previous decades.

Source: adapted from IMF, *World Economic Outlook* October 2014; © the *Financial Times*, 10.7.14, 9.9.14, 7.10.2014, All Rights Reserved.

Data Response Question

The multiplier

Around the world, governments are struggling to get their budget deficits down to three per cent of GDP or less. Yet countries like Greece and Portugal are finding that austerity budgets are so depressing GDP that their ratio of the budget deficit to GDP is hardly changed.

Source: adapted from © The *Financial Times*, 12.10.2012, All Rights Reserved.

1. 'The value of the multiplier is around 0.5.' Explain what this means.

2. Analyse the impact of a cut in government spending of £10 billion if the multiplier is 1.5 rather than 0.5.

3. Discuss whether the best way for the UK government to cut its budget deficit would be for it to raise its spending and cut taxes.

Western governments and international bodies like the IMF (International Monetary Fund) have in recent years assumed that the value of the multiplier was around 0.5. However, in a recent piece of research by the IMF, its chief economist Olivier Blanchard, suggested that this was too low. 'Actual multipliers may be higher, in the range of 0.9 to 1.7' he argued.

The research was based on looking at the effects of the cuts in government spending and rise in taxes in a range of countries since 2010. Most governments of high-income countries have been forced to cut their budget deficits after they increased following the financial crisis of 2008. In the UK, for example, the Chancellor of the Exchequer, George Osborne, argued in 2010 that cutting the budget deficit would not prevent a recovery in GDP in 2011 and 2012. In fact, the UK economy has grown sluggishly since

with economic growth forecast to be perhaps one per cent in 2013. In countries like Greece and Portugal, sharp falls in GDP were expected in both 2012 and 2013 following austerity government budgets which sharply cut government spending and increased taxes.

If the IMF research is correct, countries would be better off promoting economic growth than cutting government spending and increasing taxes to solve their budget problems. For example, in the UK, if the government increased spending on infrastructure and the multiplier were 1.5, then £1 billion extra spent on, say, building social housing for rent would result in an increase in GDP of £1.5 billion. This would lift taxation revenues. The government budget deficit in monetary terms would rise but as a percentage of GDP - the crucial measure - it would fall because the percentage rise in GDP would be larger than the percentage rise in the budget deficit.

Evaluation

The key to answering question 3 is to question what is meant by a 'budget deficit'. Is an absolute amount in, say, billion pounds, or is it to be measured as a percentage of GDP? The budget deficit can grow in billion pounds and at the same time fall as a percentage of GDP, because the percentage growth in GDP is higher than the percentage growth in the budget deficit. In your answer, explain this, using the concept of the multiplier. The evaluation comes from comparing absolute amounts and percentages of GDP in a budget deficit. It also comes from comparing different values of the multiplier and the effect they have on budget deficits.

31 Economic growth

Key points

1. The most commonly used measure of national income is Gross Domestic Product (GDP).
2. National income can be measured in real or nominal terms and as a total or per capita.
3. National income statistics are used by academics to formulate and test hypotheses. They are also used by policymakers to formulate economic policy. They are often used as a proxy measure for the standard of living and to compare living standards within a country over time and between countries.
4. National income statistics can be inaccurate because of statistical errors, the existence of the hidden economy, of non-traded sectors and difficulties with valuing public sector output.
5. Problems occur when comparing national income over time as a measure of living standards because of factors such as inflation, changes in population, the quality of goods and services and changes in income distribution.
6. Further problems occur when comparing national income between countries. In particular, an exchange rate has to be constructed that accurately reflects different purchasing power parities.
7. There is only a partial correlation between levels of national income and levels of national happiness.

Starter activity

If you are studying in the UK, think about a student in Pakistan, who is of the same age and intelligence as you, studying for the equivalent of A level. What do you think the student in Pakistan might be earning in ten years' time in comparison with you? Twice as much? Half as much? One tenth as much? How would you compare your incomes given that the UK uses pounds sterling and Pakistan uses rupees? Would your standard of living be greater or lower than that of a student in Pakistan? What might that depend on? Would you be happier than the student in Pakistan? What might that depend on?

Measures of national income

One of the most important economic statistics is national income, which measures the size of an economy. Calculating national income is difficult and no measure of national income exactly captures the size of an economy and how it is changing.

The accounting standard used in the UK today is based on European System of Accounts 2010, which in turn is based on the United Nations' System of National Accounts 2008. Most countries today either have introduced this accounting standard or are in the process of revising their national income statistics to conform to these accounting standards.

The key measure of national income used in the UK is **gross domestic product (GDP)**. This is the total market value of all goods and services produced over a period of time. GDP is measured at market prices, which means it is a measure of national income that includes the value of **indirect taxes** (taxes on expenditure) like VAT. Indirect taxes are not part of the output of the economy, so this measure inflates the actual value of national income. There are other measures of national income.

Gross value added (GVA) at basic prices This is GDP minus indirect taxes plus subsidies on goods. Indirect taxes minus subsidies is called the basic price adjustment.

Gross national product (GNP) and gross national income (GNI) at market prices These are very similar measures of the domestic output of the country (as measured

by GDP) plus earnings from overseas. More precisely, **gross national income (GNI)** is the value of the goods and services produced by a country over a period of time (GDP) plus net overseas interest payments and dividends (factor incomes). **Gross national product (GNP)** is the market value of goods and services produced over a period of time through the labour or property supplied by the citizens of a country, both domestically (GDP) and overseas.

Net national income at market prices Each year, the existing capital stock or physical wealth of the country depreciates in value because of use. This is like depreciation on a car as it gets older. If individuals run down their savings to finance spending, their actual income must be their spending

Question 1

Figure 1

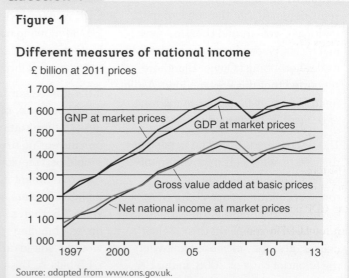

Different measures of national income

£ billion at 2011 prices

Source: adapted from www.ons.gov.uk.

(a) Briefly explain the difference between each measure of national income shown on the graph.

(b) 'Changes in GDP at market prices broadly reflect changes in other measures of national income over time.' To what extent do the data support this?

minus how much they have used from their savings. Similarly with a country, its true value of income is gross (i.e. before depreciation has been taken into account) national income minus depreciation. This is **net national income**.

GDP at market prices is the main headline figure used for national income because the data to calculate it is most quickly available. When comparing over time and between countries, movements in GDP at market prices are broadly similar to movements in other measures of national income. So it is a good guide to what is happening in the economy and can be used to judge the performance of the economy. In particular, the rate of growth of real GDP is the main indicator of the economic growth of an economy.

Real or volume vs nominal or value

It was explained in Unit 2 that data such as national income statistics can be measured either in real values or nominal values. Using nominal values means measuring data at the prices of the day, not taking into account the effect that inflation might have on the data. For example, in 1900, the typical rent for a house might have been 50p a week. Today it might be £300 a week. In nominal terms, rents are 600 times the level today they were in 1900. However, between 1900 and today, prices have increased considerably. To make a comparison in **real terms**, the data must be adjusted for inflation over the period. If prices have increased 600 times over the period, then at today's prices the rents are exactly the same. If prices increased 300 times, then today's rents are twice those of 1900.

When measuring national income, the real value of national income can also be described as measuring the **volume of national income**. It is the basket of goods and services that can be bought with a given amount of money. When comparing national income in 1900 with that of today in real terms, what is

Question 2

Table 1 GDP (£billion), population (millions) and prices (Year 1 = 100)

Year	GDP (£bn)	Population (millions)	Price index Year 1 = 100
1	100	1.00	100
2	120	1.20	100
3	150	1.25	200
4	200	1.25	250

The table gives data for GDP (at nominal prices), population and prices for 4 years. Calculate:

(a) GDP per capita at nominal prices;

(b) total GDP at real Year 1 prices;

(c) GDP per head at Year 1 prices.

Maths tip

How to calculate real GDP from nominal GDP is covered in Unit 2. To calculate numbers at Year 1 prices, divide nominal GDP by the ratio of the change in prices over the period. For example, prices increased 2.5 times (250 ÷ 100) between Year 1 and Year 4. So real GDP in Year 4 at Year 1 prices was £200 billion ÷ 2.5.

being measured is the relative size of that basket of goods and services. In contrast, the **value of national income** measures the monetary cost of the basket of goods and services at a given level of prices. The value is the equal to the volume times the current price level.

Total and per capita

The national income of the USA is approximately the same as that of China today and seven times that of the UK (at PPPs). However, this measure compares total national income of those economies. To compare living standards or the productivity of workers, it is better to compare national income **per person** or **per head** or **per capita**. This means dividing national income by the size of the population.

Measuring national income per capita considerably alters the comparison between these three countries. The USA has a population of approximately 320 million, China 1.4 billion and the UK 64 million. As a result, national income per capita of the USA is approximately 4.5 times that of China and 1.4 times that of the UK.

Transfer payments

Not all types of income are included in the final calculation of national income. Some incomes are received without there being any corresponding output in the economy. For instance:
- the government pays National Insurance and Social Security benefits to individuals, but the recipients produce nothing in return;
- children receive pocket money and allowances from their parents;
- an individual selling a second hand car receives money, but no new car is created.

These incomes, called **transfer payments**, are excluded from final calculations of national income. For instance, government spending in national income is **public expenditure** minus spending on benefits and grants.

Why is national income measured?

National income is a measure of the output, expenditure and income of an economy. National income statistics provide not only figures for these totals but also a breakdown of the totals. They are used in a number of different ways.
- Academic economists use them to test hypotheses and build models of the economy. This increases our understanding of how an economy works.
- Government, firms and economists use the figures to forecast changes in the economy. These forecasts are then used to plan for the future. Government may attempt to direct the economy, making changes in its spending or its taxes at budget time. Groups such as trade unions or the CBI will make their own recommendations about what policies they think the government should pursue.
- They are used to make comparisons over time and between countries. For instance, national income statistics can be used to compare the income of the UK in 1950 and 2016, or they can be used to compare France's income with that of the UK. Of particular importance when making comparisons over time is the rate of change of national income (i.e. the rate of economic growth).

- They are used to make judgements about economic welfare. Growth in national income, for instance, is usually equated with a rise in the **standard of living**.

The accuracy of national income statistics

National income statistics are inaccurate for a number of reasons.

Statistical inaccuracies National income statistics are calculated from millions of different returns to the government. Inevitably mistakes are made: returns are inaccurate or simply not completed. The statistics are constantly being revised in the light of fresh evidence. Although revisions tend to become smaller over time, national income statistics are still being revised decades after first publication.

The hidden economy Taxes such as VAT, income tax and National Insurance contributions, and government regulations such as health and safety laws, impose a burden on workers and businesses. Some are tempted to evade taxes and they are then said to work in the **hidden, black or informal economy**. In the building industry, for instance, it is common for workers to be self-employed and to under-declare or not declare their income at all to the tax authorities. Transactions in the black economy are in the form of cash. Cheques, credit cards, etc. could all be traced by the tax authorities. Tax evasion is the dominant motive for working in the hidden economy but a few also claim welfare benefits to which they are not entitled. The size of the hidden economy is difficult to estimate, but in the UK estimates have varied from seven to 15 per cent of GDP (i.e. national income

statistics underestimate the true size of national income by at least seven per cent).

Home produced services In the poorest developing countries in the world, GDP per person is valued at less than £100 per year. It would be impossible to survive on this amount if this were the true value of output in the economy. However, a large part of the production of the agricultural sector is not traded and therefore does not appear in national income statistics. People are engaged in subsistence agriculture, consuming what they produce. Hence the value of national output is in reality much higher. In the UK, the output of the services of housewives and househusbands is equally not recorded. Nor is the large number of DIY jobs completed each year. The more DIY activity, the greater will be the under-recording of national output by national income statistics.

The public sector Valuing the output of much of the public sector is difficult because it is not bought and sold. This problem is circumvented by valuing non-marketed output at its cost of production. For instance, the value of the output of a state school is the cost of running the school. This method of valuation can yield some surprising results. Assume that through more efficient staffing the number of nurses on a hospital ward is reduced from 10 to eight and the service is improved. National income accounts will still show a fall in output (measured by a drop in the two nurses' incomes). In general, increased productivity in the public sector is shown by a fall in the value of output. It looks as though less is being produced when in fact output remains unchanged.

Comparing national income over time

Comparing the national income of the UK today with national income in the past presents problems.

Prices Prices have tended to increase over time. So an increase in national income over the period does not necessarily indicate that there has been an increase in the number of goods and services produced in the economy. Only if the rate of increase of national income measured in money terms (the nominal rate of economic growth) has been greater than the increase in prices (the inflation rate) can there be said to have been an increase in output. So when comparing over time, it is essential to consider real and not **nominal** changes in income.

The accuracy and presentation of statistics National income statistics are inaccurate and therefore it is impossible to give a precise figure for the change in income over time. Moreover, the change in real income over time will also be affected by the inflation rate. The inevitable errors made in the calculation of the inflation rate compound the problems of inaccuracy. The method of calculating national income and the rate of inflation can also change over time. It is important to attempt to eliminate the effect of changes in definitions.

Changes in population National income statistics are often used to compare living standards over time. If they are to be used in this way, it is essential to compare national income per capita (i.e. per person). For instance, if the population doubles whilst national income quadruples, people are likely to be nearer twice as well off than four times.

Question 3

In 2014, the size of the UK's official GDP rose by £10 billion as prostitutes and drug dealers were included for the first time. Before 2014, these black economy workers were not included in the official figures. The Office for National Statistics (ONS), responsible for calculating GDP, estimated that there were 38 000 heroin users in the UK. Sales of heroin were worth £374 million at a street price of £37 per gram. Heroin is just one illegal drug. The ONS estimated that the total value of illegal drug sales were £4.4 billion.

Also included for the first time is the value of self-builds. These are individuals who build their own houses but whose time had not been included in the GDP statistics. They will add £4 billion to the revised GDP figures.

Some economists, however, are concerned that the size of the black economy has grown in recent years. The financial crisis and the following recession has increased the numbers of self-employed by half a million between 2007 and 2013.

Source: adapted from www.ons.gov.uk; © the *Financial Times* 30.5.2014, All Rights Reserved.

(a) Suggest what financial incentives there might be for drug dealers to work in the black economy, rather than the official recorded economy.

(b) Why should self-builds be included rather than excluded from official GDP figures?

(c) Why might a half million growth in self-employment make GDP figures less reliable?

Quality of goods and services The quality of goods may improve over time due to advances in technology but they may also fall in price. For instance, cars today are far better than cars 80 years ago and yet are far cheaper. National income would show this fall in price by a fall in national income, wrongly implying that living standards had fallen. On the other hand, pay in the public sector has tended to increase at about 2 per cent per annum faster than the increase in inflation. This is because pay across the economy tends to increase in line with the rate of economic growth rather than the rate of inflation. Increased pay would be reflected in both higher nominal and real national income but there may well be no extra goods or services being produced.

Defence and related expenditures The GDP of the UK was higher during the Second World War than in the 1930s, but much of GDP between 1940 and 1945 was devoted to defence expenditure. It would be difficult to argue that people enjoyed a higher standard of living during the war years than in the pre-war years. So the proportion of national income devoted to defence, or for instance to the police, must be taken into account when considering the standard of living of the population.

Consumption and investment It is possible to increase standards of living today by reducing investment and increasing consumption. However, reducing investment is likely to reduce standards of living from what they might otherwise have been in the future. As with defence, the proportion of national income being devoted to investment will affect the standard of living of the population both now and in the future.

Externalities National income statistics take no account of **externalities** such as pollution produced by the economy. National income statistics may show that national income has doubled roughly every 25 years since 1945. However, if the value of externalities has more than doubled over that time period, then the rate of growth of the standard of living has less than doubled. There has been some work on developing a measure called **green GDP** which takes away the environmental costs of production from GDP. Environmental costs include loss of biodiversity, pollution and resource depletion.

Income distribution When comparing national income over time, it is important to remember that an increased national income for the economy as a whole may not mean that individuals have seen their income increase. Income distribution is likely to change over time, which may or may not lead to a more desirable state of affairs.

Comparing national income between countries

Comparing national income between economies is fraught with difficulties too for many of the same reasons that it is difficult to compare national income over time.

- Countries may use different accounting conventions to calculate national income.
- The quality of national income data gathered varies enormously. For example, a poor country like Tanzania spends far less on gathering data than a rich country like the UK.
- The size of the unrecorded part of the economy differs between countries. Italy and Greece, for example, have much larger hidden economies than Sweden or the UK.
- National income figures must be adjusted for the size of the population. So GDP per capita rather than GDP itself is the variable which must be used to make comparisons.
- The quality of goods and services differs. For example, countries differ significantly in the speed and coverage of broadband and yet national income statistics will only record how much is being spent on broadband.
- Countries spend different proportions of their GDP on defence and related expenditures but these expenditures do not necessarily contribute to the standard of living of citizens.
- National income statistics take no account of externalities created by different economies.
- Income distributions differ between economies and so, for example, low income earners are likely to be better off in Denmark or Sweden than in the USA, which has a much higher GDP per capita.
- Geography distorts comparisons. For example, Italians have lower heating bills than Swedes. So the fact that more is spent per capita on domestic fuel in Sweden does not indicate they have a better standard of living. Equally, France is four times the size of England with a similar population. The fact that France has to build and maintain more roads

---

Question 4

Table 2

Year	Nominal GDP at market prices (£bn)	Index of prices (GDP deflator) 2013=100	Population (millions)
1948	11.6	4.3	48.7
1958	23.3	5.2	51.7
1968	44.9	7.1	55.2
1978	175.2	21.6	56.2
1988	511.7	48.2	56.9
1998	923.3	71.3	58.9
2008	1 518.7	90.0	61.8
2013	1 713.3	100.0	64.1

Source: adapted from www.ons.gov.uk.

(a) Calculate the value of (i) nominal GDP per head of the population and (ii) real GDP at 2013 prices per head of the population for three years: 1948, 2008 and 2013.

(b) To what extent is it possible to judge from the data whether living standards increased over the periods (i) 1948 and 2013; (ii) 2008 and 2013?

Maths tip

How to calculate real GDP from nominal GDP is covered in Unit 2. To calculate numbers at 2013 prices, multiply nominal GDP by the ratio of the change in prices over the period. For example, prices increased 23.26 times (100 ÷ 4.3) between 1948 and 2013. So real GDP in 1948 at 2013 prices was £11.6bn x 23.26.

doesn't give them a better standard of living than the English.

- Market exchange rates don't reflect purchasing power. So simple comparisons using market exchange rates may give a distorted picture of living standards between countries. A way round this is to use purchasing power parities.

Purchasing power parities

The day-to-day market exchange rate can bear little relation to relative prices in different countries. So prices in some countries like Sweden or Germany can be much higher at official exchange rates than in the USA, China or India. Therefore if national income statistics are to be used to compare living standards between countries, it is important to use an exchange rate that compares the cost of living in each country. These exchange rates are known as **purchasing power parities**. For instance, if a typical basket of goods cost €2 in France and £1 in the UK, then national income should be converted at an exchange rate of €2 to £1, even if the market exchange rate gives a very different figure.

Purchasing power parities often differ significantly from market exchange rates when comparisons are made between rich and poor countries. For example, it might be possible to survive on £2 a day in Kenya or Vietnam when £2 is converted at the market exchange rate into the local currency. In contrast, it is not possible to survive on £2 a day in the UK. However, £2 buys far more in Kenya or Vietnam than £2 would buy in the

UK. The market exchange rate undervalues the value of the local currency in Kenya or Vietnam when it comes to buying a basket of goods on which people can survive.

Income and wealth

National income tends to be correlated with national wealth. Wealth is a **stock** of assets which produce a **flow** of income over time. Countries with high levels of wealth, which includes both human wealth and non-human wealth, tend to produce higher levels of income than countries with low levels of wealth. The wealthiest nation in the world, the USA, also has the highest national income. A poor country like Tanzania with relatively little wealth also has a low national income. Wealth can be mismanaged and used poorly. So there is not a perfect correlation between wealth and income.

National income, economic welfare and happiness

National income is often used as a proxy measure for economic welfare or the standard of living. Income is also used often as a measure of 'happiness': the higher the income, the happier the individual. However, there are many other factors apart from income and GDP which contribute to the standard of living of an individual or an economy. These are exemplified in the National Well-being programme discussed in the 'Thinking like an economist' section of this unit.

Economists have been interested in the concept of 'happiness' for nearly 200 years. Jeremy Bentham, a philosopher working in the first half of the 19th century, famously said that human beings should act in a way that would cause 'the greatest happiness of the greatest number'. One of the key problems with this as a moral philosophy was how individuals could measure happiness both for themselves and for others.

Psychologists have long conducted surveys on happiness, simply asking respondents how happy they felt. These surveys, when compared, produce a consistent response. Respondents do seem to be able to say whether or not they are happy on a particular day. This has been backed up by neuroscience. During the 1990s it was discovered that happiness was associated with measurable electrical activity in the brain. This could be picked up by MRI scans. So it is possible to tell physiologically whether or not someone is telling the truth when they say they are happy.

One key finding dates back to the 1970s. Using surveys from across the world (cross sectional surveys), it was found that happiness and income are positively related at low levels of income but higher levels of income are not associated with increases in happiness. This is called the Easterlin Paradox, after Richard Easterlin, an economist, identified this problem in a 1974 research paper. The conclusion from his research is that an increase in consumption of material goods will improve well-being when basic needs are not being met, such as adequate food and shelter. But once these are being met, then increasing the quantity of goods consumed makes no difference to well-being. Having a new high-definition television, or a new car when you already have a reasonable functioning TV and car doesn't increase your well-being in the long term. What this means is that average levels of happiness in the UK,

Question 5

Figure 2

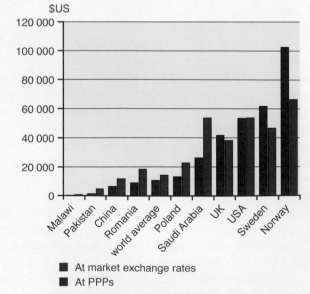

Gross national income per head at market exchange rates and PPPs 2013, US$

Source: adapted from www.worldbank.org.

(a) Explain the difference between income per head measured at market exchange rates and at purchasing power parities. Illustrate your answer with examples from the data.

(b) Explain what Figure 2 suggests about comparative living standards in the countries shown.

which already enjoys a high standard of living, will not increase if GDP doubles.

Some economists have disputed this finding. Reworking survey evidence, they suggest there is a correlation between income and happiness. Even if they are correct, the idea that happiness is caused by a wide variety of factors and not just income would suggest that GDP and happiness are likely to be only weakly correlated.

There is, however, a caveat to this debate about changes in absolute incomes. Survey evidence suggests that within a population, there is a positive correlation between **relative** income and happiness. Surveys across countries consistently show that those with above average incomes tend to have higher levels of happiness than those with below average incomes. So if incomes for every individual in the UK doubled, there would be no increase in happiness. But if an individual worker had their pay doubled, they would be happier because their income relative to everyone else has increased. Equally, the top 10 per cent of income earners in Bolivia might have half the income of the top 10 per cent of income earners in the UK. But they both have the same level of happiness because their income is higher than the other 90 per cent in their populations. Alternatively, if everyone owns an HD television, there is no increase in happiness compared to a situation where no one owns an HD television. But if you buy an HD television and 80 per cent of the population don't own one, then your happiness increases.

There are two suggested explanations for the correlation between relative income and happiness. One is that income is a symbol of social status. Psychologically, we are happier if we feel we have more status. This competitive streak is 'hard-wired' into our brains and comes from our biological roots. The second explanation is that above average incomes are correlated with a number of other factors which are associated with happiness. For example, those on above average income tend to enjoy better health and live longer. They have more control over their environment and are less likely to perform short repetitive tasks. They are less likely to be unemployed.

Key Terms

Green GDP - a measure of GDP which takes account of the environmental costs of production such as pollution and resource depletion.

Gross domestic product (GDP) - a measure of the output or value added of an economy which does not include output or income from investments abroad or an allowance for the depreciation of the nation's capital stock.

Gross national income (GNI) - the value of the goods and services produced by a country over a period of time (GDP) plus net overseas interest payments and dividends (factor incomes).

Gross national product (GNP) - the market value of goods and services produced over a period of time through the labour or property supplied by citizens of a country both domestically (GDP) and overseas.

Hidden, black or informal economy - economic activity where trade and exchange take place but which goes unreported to the tax authorities and those collecting national income statistics.

Net national income - a measure of national income which includes both net income from investments abroad and an allowance for deprecation of the nation's capital stock.

Per person or per head or per capita - per individual in a population.

Purchasing power parities - an exchange rate of one currency for another which compares how much a typical basket of goods in one country costs compared to that of another country.

Standard of living - how well off is an individual, household or economy, measured by a complex mix of variables such as income, health, the environment, participation in society and political freedoms.

Transfer payments - income for which there is no corresponding output, such as unemployment benefits or pension payments.

Value and volume of national income - the value of national income is its monetary value at the prices of the day; the volume is national income adjusted for inflation and is expressed either as an index number or in money terms at the prices in a selected base year.

Thinking like an economist

UK National Well-being programme

Economists have long pointed out that GDP and living standards are not necessarily correlated. In 2010, the government launched the National Well-being programme to 'start measuring our progress as a country, not just by how our economy is growing, but by how our lives are improving; not just by our standard of living, but by our quality of life'.

The programme has developed a number of indicators of well-being grouped into key areas.

- **The economy** considers net national disposable income, public sector net debt and inflation.
- **Personal finance** considers median household income and wealth, the proportion of households on less than 60 per cent median income, satisfaction with income and reported difficulty with finances.
- **Where we live** considers crimes against the person, feeling safe walking after dark, access to the natural environment, neighbourhood belonging, transport access to services and satisfaction with accommodation.
- **What we do** considers the unemployment rate, satisfaction with your job and your leisure time, volunteering, engagement with arts/culture and sport participation.
- **Health** considers healthy life expectancy at birth, illness and disability, satisfaction with health and mental ill health.

- **Our relationships** considers satisfaction with family life and social life and having someone to rely on.
- **Personal well being** considers very high life satisfaction, very high worthwhile rating, medium/high happiness yesterday, very low anxiety yesterday and population mental well-being.
- **The national environment** considers greenhouse gas emissions, protected areas in the UK, renewable energy consumption and recycling rates.
- **Government** considers voter turnout and trust in government.
- **Education and skills** considers human capital and the percentage of persons with five or more GCSEs and with no qualifications.

Most of the indicators are objective measures, such as net national disposable income, but a few are subjective. Subjective measures are ones where individuals are asked about their feelings or opinions. For example, a subjective measure would be a question about whether an individual felt they have low anxiety yesterday, or whether they felt a median level of happiness or a high level of happiness yesterday.

The programme does not attempt to aggregate the different indicators. There is no single measure of National Well-being. The great advantage of using GDP as a proxy measure of the standard of living is that it is one simple statistic which has been measured in the UK since 1948 and which is a standard measurement across countries. Whilst economists would agree that GDP is a flawed measure of living standards, it is likely to remain the most important indicator of national well-being in the future because of the problem of aggregation.

Source: with information from www.gov.uk; www.neighbourhood.statistics.gov.uk

Data Response Question

Living standards

Table 3 National income and population indicators, 2013

	PPP estimates of gross national income per capita, $	Population, millions	Gross national income, $ billion at market exchange rates	Gross national income per capita, $ at market exchange rates	Population, % of population aged 0-14
Tanzania	1 760	49	30	630	45
Kenya	2 780	44	52	1 160	42
Pakistan	4 840	182	247	1 360	34
Indonesia	9 270	250	895	3 580	29
China	11 850	1 357	8 905	6 560	18
Colombia	11 960	48	367	7 950	28
Malaysia	22 530	30	310	10 430	26
Russian Federation	23 190	144	1 988	13 850	16
Czech Republic	26 740	11	199	26 740	15
Spain	32 700	47	1 396	29 920	15
UK	38 160	64	2 672	41 680	18
USA	53 750	316	16 903	53 470	20

Source: adapted from www.worldbank.org.

Table 4 Health indicators[2]

	Life expectancy at birth, years, 2012	Under-five mortality rate, per thousand of the population, 2013	Prevalence of malnutrition, % of population, 2012	Access to improved water source, % of population, 2012	Improved sanitation facilities, % of population, 2012
Tanzania	61	52	33	53	12
Kenya	61	75	26	62	30
Pakistan	66	86	17	91	48
Indonesia	71	29	9	85	59
China	75	13	11	92	65
Colombia	74	17	11	91	80
Malaysia	75	9	5	100	96
Russian Federation	70	10	-	97	71
Czech Republic	78	4	-	100	100
Spain	82	4	-	100	100
UK	82	5	-	100	100
USA	79	7	-	100	100

Source: adapted from www.worldbank.org.

Table 5 Education[1,2]

	Youth literacy, % of females aged 15-24, 2005-13	School enrolment, % gross, 2012		Primary completion rate, total % of relevant age group, 2012	Ratio of girls to boys in primary and secondary education, % 2012
		Primary	Secondary		
Tanzania	73	93	35	81	100
Kenya	82	-	-	-	-
Pakistan	63	93	37	72	82
Indonesia	99	109	83	105	101
China	100	128	89	-	101
Colombia	99	107	93	-	93
Malaysia	98	-	67	-	-
Russian Federation	100	101	95	97	99
Czech Republic	-	100	97	102	100
Spain	99	103	131	102	100
UK	-	109	95	-	100
USA	-	98	94	98	99

Source: adapted from www.worldbank.org.

Table 6 Selected indicators[1]

	Paved roads, % of total, 2005-11	Mobile phone subscribers, per 100 people, 2013	Internet users, per 100 people, 2011	Electric power consumption, kWh per capita, 2011	High technology exports, % of manufactured exports, 2012
Tanzania	15	56	4	92	10
Kenya	7	71	39	155	6
Pakistan	73	90	11	449	2
Indonesia	57	122	16	680	7
China	64	89	46	3 298	26
Colombia	-	104	52	1 123	5
Malaysia	91	145	67	4 246	44
Russian Federation	-	153	62	6 486	8
Czech Republic	-	131	74	6 289	16
Spain	-	107	72	5 530	7
UK	100	124	90	5 472	22
USA	68	96	84	13 246	18

Source: adapted from www.worldbank.org.

1. Dashes in the tables indicate the data were unavailable from national government.
2. School enrolment and primary completion rates can be greater than 100 per cent. For school enrolment, the percentage is calculated by the number of children in primary school divided by the number of children of primary school age. In countries like Spain, children can be kept back to repeat a year of education if they fail to reach the right standard. So some 12 year olds are still in primary school even though primary school age is up to 11. Spain also has large numbers of 19 and 20 years in secondary school despite secondary school age being counted as up to 18. This also accounts for primary completion rates being above 100 per cent. 12 year olds completing primary school add to the numbers on top of the fraction but they are excluding from the bottom of the fraction because this is up to 11.

Q

Countries in the four tables have been ranked according to their gross national income per capita at purchasing power parity rates.

1. Explain the difference between gross national income, gross national income per capita and PPP estimates of gross national income per capita, using Table 3 to illustrate your answer.

2. Discuss whether countries with low incomes per capita have a lower standard of living than those with high incomes per capita.

Evaluation

There is an abundance of data to use to illustrate your answer to question 2. First, outline what is meant by standard of living. Then look for evidence to support the idea that greater income per capita leads to a higher standard of living. Then look for evidence which contracts this. In your conclusion, weigh up whether the evidence for is greater than the evidence against.

32 Causes of economic growth and the trade cycle

Key points

1. Economic growth is the change in potential output of the economy shown by a shift to the right of the production possibility frontier. Economic growth is usually measured by the change in real national income.
2. The trade cycle is the fluctuations of economic activity around the trend rate of growth.
3. A positive output gap exists when the economy is in boom and GDP is above its long-term trend value. A negative output gap exists when the economy is in recession and GDP is below its long-term trend value.
4. Economic growth is caused by increases in the quantity or quality of land, labour and capital and by technological progress which lead to a rise in long run aggregate supply.
5. Aggregate demand can be important in determining economic growth. Export-led growth can be a stimulant to rises in the long run potential output of the economy.

Starter activity

What is the current rate of growth of the UK economy? How does this compare to Germany, the USA and China? Is the UK economy in boom or in recession or neither? Why is the most important event in recent UK economic history the financial crisis of 2008?

Economic growth

Economies change in size over time. For example, the Chinese economy doubled the value of its production roughly every seven years between 1990 and 2010. The UK economy has seen its production grow at an average of 2.5 per cent per annum for the past 60 years.

Growth in the quantity of goods and services produced is measured by the percentage change in GDP. This is the **actual growth** of the economy. However, the actual level of GDP may be different from the productive potential of an economy. The productive potential is determined by the factors of production available to an economy, such as labour and capital. The productive potential of an economy is shown by the long-run aggregate supply curve, or the production possibility frontier (PPF). The actual level of output may be within the PPF if some factors of production are unemployed or are being used inefficiently. **Potential growth** is the change in the productive potential of the economy over time. It is shown on a diagram by the shift to the right in the LRAS curve or the PPF. The phrase **economic growth** can mean either actual growth or potential growth. Which of these two it refers to depends on the context in which the phrase is being used.

The trade cycle

It is not possible to measure the productive potential of an economy directly because there is no way of producing a single monetary figure for the value of variables such as machinery, workers and technology. Instead, economists use changes in GDP, the value of output, as a proxy measure.

The problem with using real GDP is that, in the short term, GDP fluctuates around the long-term **trend growth path of output**. These fluctuations are known as the **trade cycle** or

business cycle or economic cycle. All **trade** cycles are slightly different. However, they tend to have four main phases. These are illustrated in Figure 1.

- **Peak or boom.** When the economy is at a **peak** or is in a **boom**, national income is high. It is likely that the economy will be working at beyond full employment. **Overheating** is therefore present (although the economy could be at less than full employment, according to Keynesians, if there are bottlenecks in certain industries in the economy). Consumption and investment expenditure will be high. Tax revenues will be high. Wages will be rising and profits increasing. The country will be sucking in imports demanded by consumers with high incomes and businesses with full order books. There will also be inflationary pressures in the economy.
- **Downturn.** When the economy moves into a **downturn**, output and income fall, leading to a fall in consumption and investment. Tax revenues begin to fall and government expenditure on benefits begins to rise. Wage demands moderate as unemployment rises. Imports decline and inflationary pressures ease.

Figure 1

The traditional business cycle

The economy moves regularly from boom through recession to slump before recovering again.

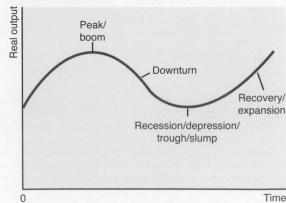

- **Recession or depression or trough or slump**. At the bottom of the cycle, the economy is said to be in a **recession** or **depression** or **trough** or **slump**. Economic activity is at a low in comparison with surrounding years. High unemployment exists, so consumption, investment and imports will be low. There will be few inflationary pressures in the economy and prices may be falling (ie there will be **deflation**).

- **Recovery or expansion**. As the economy moves into a **recovery** or **expansion** phase, national income and output begin to increase. Unemployment falls. Consumption, investment and imports begin to rise. Workers feel more confident about demanding wage increases and inflationary pressures begin to mount.

There is no standard way used by textbooks, newspapers and governments to describe or define the phases of the cycle. For example, sometimes the economic cycle is simply reduced to two phases - boom and recession, or alternatively expansion and contraction. Sometimes 'recession' and downturn' are used interchangeably. Some economists define recession in terms of a range of indicators including unemployment and investment rather than using GDP alone.

In the UK, the government defines recession as where real GDP falls in at least two successive quarters (i.e. where there is negative growth of real GDP quarter on quarter for two successive quarters). For example, the UK economy fell into recession following the banking crisis of 2008.

Question 1

Table 1 Economic indicators and the trade cycle

	Growth of real GDP	Investment	Unemployment	Exports - imports
	(%)	(£ billion at 2011 prices)	(millions)	(£ billion at 2011 prices)
1987	5.5	195.4	2.9	7.8
1988	5.9	225.7	2.4	-12.4
1989	2.5	236.6	2.1	-17.9
1990	0.5	230.6	2.0	-8.5
1991	-1.2	212.3	2.5	0.9
1992	0.4	208.8	2.8	-3.6
1993	2.6	210.4	2.9	-1.2

Source: adapted from www.ons.gov.uk.

Identify the four phases of the trade cycle from the data shown for the UK economy.

Two types of trade cycle

Figure 1 shows a trade cycle where GDP actually falls in the recession phase. However, there are milder trade cycles where GDP does not fall. Instead, the economy fluctuates around its long-run real GDP growth path but real GDP continues to rise even in a downturn even if the rise is relatively small. This type of trade cycle is shown in Figure 2. For example, growth of real GDP may fluctuate between one per cent and five per cent around a growth path averaging three per cent.

Figures 1 and 2 are not strictly mathematically accurate. The trend level of real GDP line should be gently curving upwards showing the effects of compound growth in real GDP. However,

Figure 2

A mild trade cycle

Peaks and troughs occur when economic growth is high or low respectively.

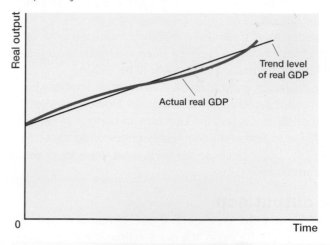

it is conventional at A level to draw the level of real GDP line as a straight line to make it easier to draw the diagram.

Causes of the trade cycle

There are many different reasons why the short run rate of growth of real GDP may fluctuate around its long-term trend. But they can be classified into two main types: **demand-side shocks** and **supply-side shocks**.

Demand-side shocks are shocks which affect aggregate demand. Examples of demand-side shocks include the following.

- A housing market bubble may burst. This occurs when house prices rise to too high a level and suddenly there is a collapse in demand for housing and a sharp fall in house prices. This erodes consumer confidence, leading to less consumer spending and few new houses being built which affects output and employment.

- The stock market may crash. Perhaps stock market prices are too high. A stock market crash reduces the wealth of individuals. They are then likely to cut back on their spending and save more to rebuild their wealth. This reduces aggregate demand causing the recession.

- The central bank may sharply raise interest rates perhaps to combat rising inflation. This reduces consumer spending on durables and investment spending, sending the economy into recession.

- The government may sharply raise taxes or cut government spending, perhaps to combat rising inflation or balance its budget. This leads to lower aggregate demand and a recession.

- The world economy may go into recession, hitting UK exports sharply and so sending the UK into a recession too.

- There may be a sharp rise in the value of the pound against other currencies. This reduces the competitiveness of the UK economy sending exports down and imports up. The subsequent fall in aggregate demand sends the economy into recession.

Supply-side shocks are shocks which affect aggregate supply. Examples of supply-side shocks include the following.

● A large rise in world commodity prices could both raise the price level in the UK and lead to a rise in import values if demand for the commodity is price inelastic. The rise in import costs will reduce aggregate supply leading to lower output.

● An outbreak of trade union militancy could see large wage increases which will raise the price level substantially and reduce aggregate supply leading to recession.

The examples given above are all negative shocks which could move the economy into recession. However, a shock can also be positive, causing the economy to boom. For example, a sharp fall in oil and other commodity prices could cause the UK economy to boom because the UK is a net importer of oil and other commodities.

The output gap

The difference between the actual level of real GDP and its estimated long term value at a point in time is known as the **output gap**. In Figure 3, the straight line is the trend rate of growth in real GDP over a long period of time. It is assumed that this shows the level of real GDP associated with the productive potential of the economy. The actual level of real GDP varies around the trend growth line. This fluctuation is the trade cycle. When the economy is in recession and there is high unemployment and deflation, the actual level of real GDP will be below the trend line. A **negative output gap** is then said to exist. This means there is **spare capacity** in the economy, with factories, offices and workers lying idle when they could be producing goods and services. In an inflationary boom, the actual level of real GDP is likely to be above the trend line. A **positive output gap** then exists.

Output gaps can also be illustrated using an aggregate demand and aggregate supply curve diagram. In Figure 4, the long-run equilibrium output of the economy is OY₁. This is shown

Figure 4

A positive output gap

The positive output gap is Y₁Y₂, shown by the difference between the actual level of output of Y₂ and the long-run potential output of the economy at Y₁.

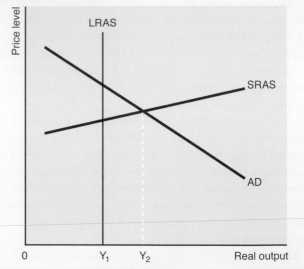

by the vertical long-run aggregate supply curve. However, in the short run, equilibrium is higher at OY₂, because this is where short-run aggregate supply and aggregate demand are equal. There will therefore be a positive output gap in the economy of Y₁ Y₂. This positive output gap will be filled either through long-run economic growth moving the LRAS curve to OY₂, or through a recession shifting aggregate demand downwards and the SRAS shifting upwards, or some combination of both.

Figure 5 shows a negative output gap. Long-run aggregate supply is to the right of the short-run equilibrium output level of OY₁. The negative output gap is therefore Y₁ Y₂. To close the

Figure 3

The output gap

The trend rate of growth of GDP approximates the growth in productive potential of the economy. When actual GDP falls below this or rises above it, there is said to be an output gap. When actual GDP growth falls below this, there is a negative output gap. When actual GDP growth rises above it, there is a positive output gap.

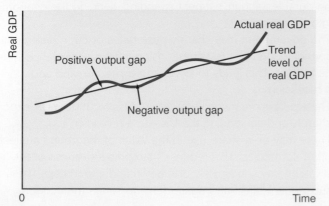

Figure 5

A negative output gap

The negative output gap is Y₁Y₂, shown by the difference between the actual level of output of OY₁ and the long-run potential output of the economy at OY₂.

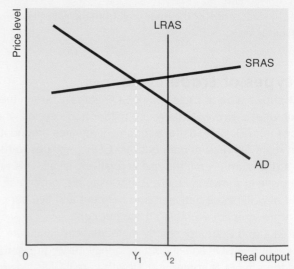

gap, aggregate demand is likely to rise faster than the long-run growth in the economy shown by the shifts to the right of the AD and LRAS curves.

It might seem that the size of any output gap is easy to estimate. In practice, it can be difficult to gauge. This is mainly because economists do not know exactly the position of the long run aggregate supply curve. For example, following the lengthy recession and very low recovery rate in the UK between 2008 and 2013, economists revised downwards their estimates for the long run rate of growth of the economy. By 2014, the negative output gap on the average 2008 estimate of the trend rate of growth was above 15 per cent of GDP. By reducing the trend rate of growth, this had been revised down to a few per cent in 2014 estimates. The other problem in estimating the output gap is that initial estimates of GDP, showing where short run aggregate supply and demand are equal, are almost always inaccurate. GDP figures are constantly revised. There can be quite major changes to figures one or two years after the period being measured. Some economists believe that output gaps are so difficult to measure that they are not a valid concept to use for the purpose of economic policy.

Question 2

Figure 6

Cyclical indicator estimates of the output gap

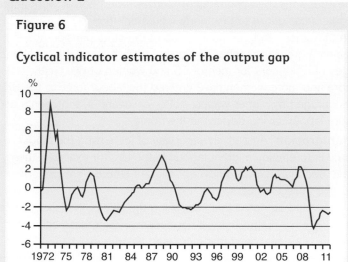

Source: adapted from *Estimating the UK's historical output gap* by Tom Pybus, Office for Budget Responsibility, 2011.

Explain, using an aggregate demand and supply diagram, whether there was a positive or a negative output gap in (a) 1981 and (b) 2007.

Hysteresis

Figure 3 might suggest that there is little cost associated with fluctuations in the level of activity. Output lost in a recession is regained during a boom, leaving the economy no better or worse off in the long term. However, there are possible other costs.

- Those made unemployed during a recession, however mild, suffer a loss in their income even if the majority of workers are unaffected.
- Those on fixed incomes suffer in a boom if inflation rises. Their spending power is eroded because of higher prices.

Figure 7

Hysteresis

The trend rate of growth of an economy can shift downwards if there is a deep recession because of permanent losses of human and physical capital.

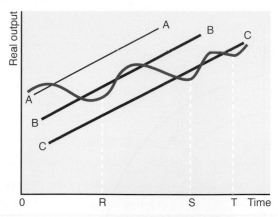

- Some economists argue that in a deep recession, economies do not bounce back to their previous trend level of growth. This is an example of **hysteresis**. Instead, the economy remains at a lower level of output, albeit still growing at its previous trend rate. In Figure 7, the economy starts off on a trend growth path of AA. However, a deep recession with its trough at OR means that the economy only booms at a level consistent with a lower growth path of BB. The economy then suffers another deep recession with a trough at OS. The trend line of growth shifts down to CC. After this, the business cycle is much shallower and actual output fluctuates around the trend line of CC. One reason why an economy may fail to recover fully from a deep recession is that there is a permanent loss of human capital. In a recession, millions can lose their jobs. Some take early retirement, with a consequent loss of output for the economy. Others suffer long periods of unemployment and become deskilled. They are therefore less productive than before. Another reason is that there can be a permanent loss of physical capital. In a recession, firms cut back on their investment. If they fail to make this up in the next boom, there is less physical capital in the economy than would otherwise have been the case. Potential output must then fall.

The production possibility frontier

Production possibility frontiers (PPFs) can be used to discuss economic growth. The PPF shows the maximum or potential output of an economy. When the economy grows, the PPF will move outward as in Figure 8. A movement from A to C would be classified as economic growth. However, there may be unemployment in the economy. With a PPF passing through C, a movement from B (where there is unemployment) to C (full employment) would be classified as **economic recovery** rather than economic growth. Hence, an increase in real national income does not necessarily mean that there has been economic growth. In practice it is difficult to know exactly the location of an economy's PPF and therefore economists tend to treat all increases in real GNP as economic growth.

Figure 8

Production possibility frontiers

A movement from A to C would represent economic growth if there were a shift in the production possibility frontier from PPF$_1$ to PPF$_2$. A movement from B to C would represent economic recovery if the production possibility frontier was PPF$_2$.

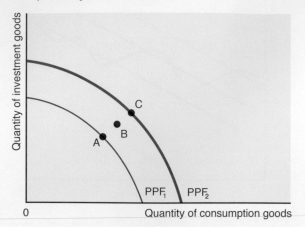

Figure 8 can also be used to show the conflict between investment and consumption. One major source of economic growth is investment. All other things being equal, the greater the level of investment the higher will be the rate of growth in the future. However, increased production of investment goods can only be achieved by a reduction in the production of consumption goods if the economy is at full employment. So there is a trade off to be made between consumption now and consumption in the future. The lower the level of consumption today relative to the level of investment, the higher will be the level of consumption in the future.

The causes of long-run economic growth

Fluctuations in the level of real GDP around the trend rate of growth are caused by demand and supply side shocks. However, what explains why the productive potential of the economy increases over time?

All economists would agree that an increase in long-run aggregate supply will increase the potential level of output in an economy. Long-run aggregate supply can increase if there is an increase in the quantity or quality of the inputs to the production process. Output can also be increased if existing inputs are used more efficiently. This can be expressed in terms of a **production function**:

Output = f (land, labour, capital, technical progress, efficiency)

Each of these factors will now be considered.

Land

Different countries possess different endowments of land. Land in economics is defined as all natural resources, not just land itself. Some countries, such as Saudi Arabia, have experienced large growth rates almost solely because they are so richly endowed. Without oil, Saudi Arabia today would almost certainly be a poor developing country. Other countries have received windfalls. The UK, for instance, only started to exploit its oil and gas resources in the mid 1970s. However, most economists argue that the exploitation of raw materials is unlikely to be a significant source of growth in developed economies, although it can be vital in developing economies.

Labour

Economic growth is likely to occur if there is either an increase in the **quantity of workers** in the economy or there is an increase in the **quality of labour**.

Increases in the labour force can result from changes in the birth rate, increases in participation rates and increases in immigration.

Changes in demography Today's birth rate has a knock-on effect on the size of the labour force in 20 years' time. Countries that have a high birth rate, such as many African countries, have increasing numbers of workers. In Europe, the birth rate has been relatively low in recent decades. This has reduced the size of the current labour force from what it would otherwise have been.

Changes in participation rates Participation rates are the proportion of the population of a certain age who are either in work or seeking work. Increases in the proportion of young people staying on in education have reduced the size of the UK labour force over the past few decades. At the opposite end of the age range, two contradictory forces have been at work. More workers can afford to take early retirement than 30 years ago. On the other hand, the pushing up of the state pension age is seeing a growing number of workers work beyond the traditional ages of retirement for men of 65 and women of 60. Lastly, more and more women have entered the labour force in the UK, encouraged by higher wages, better childcare arrangements and more labour saving devices in the home.

Immigration A relatively easy way of increasing the labour force is to employ migrant labour. In the UK, for example, there have been large inward flows of migrant labour from Eastern Europe in recent years.

It should be noted that increasing the size of the labour force may increase output but will not necessarily increase economic welfare. One reason is that increased income may have to be shared out amongst more people, causing little or no change in income per person. If women come back to work, they have to give up leisure time to do so. This lessens the increase in economic welfare which they experience.

Increasing the size of the labour force can increase output but increasing the **quality** of labour **inputs** is likely to be far more important in the long run. Labour is not **homogeneous** (i.e. it is not all the same). Workers can be made more productive by education and training. Increases in **human capital** are essential for a number of reasons.

- Workers need to be sufficiently educated to cope with the demands of the existing stock of capital. For instance, it is important for lorry drivers to be able to read, personal assistants to use computer software and shop workers to operate tills. These might seem very low grade skills but it requires a considerable educational input to get most of the population up to these elementary levels.
- Workers need to be flexible. On average in the UK, workers are likely to have to change job three times during their

lifetime. Increasingly workers are being asked to change roles within existing jobs. Flexibility requires broad general education as well as in-depth knowledge of a particular task.

- Workers need to be able to contribute to change. It is easy to see that scientists and technologists are essential if inventions and new products are to be brought to the market. What is less obvious, but as important, is that every worker can contribute ideas to the improvement of techniques of production. An ability of all workers to take responsibility and solve problems will be increasingly important in the future.

Capital

The stock of capital in the economy needs to increase over time if economic growth is to be sustained. This means that there must be sustained investment in the economy. However, there is not necessarily a correlation between high investment and high growth. Some investment is not growth-related. For example, it is often argued that investment in new housing does not lead to future increases in real GDP. Investment can also be wasted if it takes place in industries in projects which fail to be commercially successful.

Technological progress

Technological progress increases economic growth in two ways.

- It cuts the average cost of production of a product. For instance, a machine which performed the tasks of a simple scientific calculator was unavailable 100 years ago. 50 years ago, it needed a large room full of expensive equipment to do this. Today calculators are portable and available for a few pounds.
- It creates new products for the market. Without new products, consumers would be less likely to spend increases in their income. Without extra spending, there would be less or no economic growth.

Efficiency

The way in which the factors of production are used together is vital for economic growth. Increased efficiency in the use of resources in itself will bring about rises in output.

In a market economy, competition should lead to greater efficiency. Firms which use more efficient production techniques will drive less efficient firms out of the market. Firms which develop new, better products will drive old products out of the market. So economic growth can come about because of government policies which promote competition and protect innovation. For example, policies such as privatisation, deregulation and control of monopolies should increase competition. Laws which protect patents and copyright will encourage innovation.

Markets promote efficiency but they can also fail. So government may have to step in to redress market failure. In the past, some have argued that market failure is so widespread that the government should own most, if not all, of industry. This socialist or communist view is mostly rejected today. The problem was that in communist countries like Russia, government failure became so great that it outweighed any benefits from the correction of market failure. However, some countries today are more interventionist than others. France

Figure 9

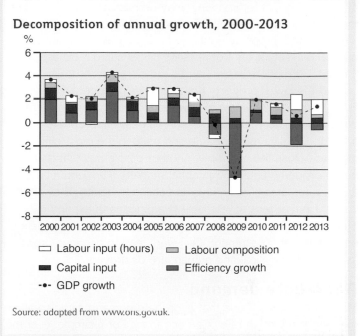

Decomposition of annual growth, 2000-2013

Source: adapted from www.ons.gov.uk.

Figures from the Office for National Statistics (ONS) show the main drivers of growth over the period 2000-2013. Throughout the period, the impact of a better-educated workforce, shown by 'Labour composition' in Figure 9, has made a positive contribution to economic growth. For the most part, so too has the number of hours worked. On the whole, this has not come from individual full-time employees working longer hours. It has come from an expanding labour force particularly due to immigration from the EU, and from part-time workers increasing their hours perhaps to full time.

Capital input too has made a positive contribution to growth. This is made up of new investment, but also past investment in capital goods, buildings and infrastructure.

Worryingly, however, since the recession, which started in 2008, the efficiency (called multi-factor productivity by ONS) with which the factors of production are combined has tended to be negative. The worst-performing sector of the economy in terms of efficiency has been North Sea oil where aging oil fields have made it harder to extract oil despite greater capital investment, and the employment of more and better-qualified workers.

The ONS estimates that before 1997, Britain's growth was driven by a more rapidly growing capital stock. Since 1997, the most important driver for growth has been the improvement in the education of the labour force.

Source: adapted from © the *Financial Times* 26.1.2015, All Rights Reserved, www.ons.gov.uk.

(a) Using the data, explain why GDP fell in 2009.

(b) How can (i) more workers and (ii) a better educated workforce contribute to economic growth?

(c) If firms invested more in North Sea oil production, discuss whether this would raise the rate of economic growth for the UK.

and Germany, for example, intervene more in markets than, say, the USA.

In low and middle income countries, many of the features of a functioning market economy may be missing. Resources are then combined inefficiently. For example, laws may not exist which protect property rights, or laws may exist but the state may take assets away from private citizens and businesses through corruption, bribery and a judiciary which doesn't uphold the law. If property rights are not protected, citizens and firms have little incentive to save and invest in the long term. Widescale bribery leads to resources being appropriated by a few individuals rather than being used in the most efficient manner across the economy. Another problem is that there may be no properly functioning capital markets. Farmers in rural areas, for example, may have no access to banks. They are then cut off from access to relatively cheap loans to expand their businesses. At worst, there may be civil war and a complete breakdown of government. Civil wars lead to negative growth as assets, both physical and human, are destroyed.

Aggregate demand

Many economists argue that aggregate demand can also affect the long run growth rate of an economy. For example, over the past 70 years, many politicians and economists in the UK have advocated **export-led growth**. They have seen the success of Germany, Japan and China and linked that to the strength of their exports. A rise in exports will initially increase aggregate demand rather than aggregate supply. However, a permanent increase in exports, all other things being equal, will force UK firms to invest in equipment and lead to a rise in the demand for labour to satisfy the increased demand. The rise in investment will lead to a rise in the productive potential of the economy and hence impact on economic growth. The other impact of export-led growth is on competitiveness and efficiency. To export, UK firms have to have a competitive advantage over domestic firms in foreign markets. For example, their prices have to be lower, or the goods have to better designed or of better quality. Becoming more export orientated therefore forces firms to become more efficient. Greater efficiency leads to an increase in long run aggregate supply and economic growth.

Some economists also argue that increases in aggregate demand in general, through its influence on investment, impacts on aggregate supply. When an economy goes into a moderate to severe recession, firms react by cutting their investment. Lower output means they don't need as much capital as before. Lower sales also reduce the amount of cash firms have to use for investment. If the economy bounces back quickly, firms will tend to overinvest in the next boom, making up for the loss of investment in the recession. However, in a prolonged recession, the loss of investment and the fall in human capital can lead to long run aggregate supply being permanently lower. This is the problem of hysteresis described above.

What if the economy fails to recover even within, say, 20 years and runs permanently below its productive potential?

This is an important current issue because of the experience of Japan and a number of countries in the eurozone such as Italy. In a number of eurozone countries, for example, there are unemployment rates of 10-25 per cent that have persisted over a number of years. Supply-side economists would argue that this shows that supply-side reforms need to be implemented in the labour market. Reducing workers' rights in areas such as the ability of employers to sack workers will encourage employers to take on more workers and so solve the problem. Other economists would argue that there will be no extra jobs if aggregate demand remains depressed. Government policies of fiscal austerity, for example, which reduce aggregate demand are contributing to low or zero growth rates in the economy. This would suggest that a necessary condition of economic growth is that there is adequate aggregate demand to stimulate investment and employment of unutilised resources.

Four distinctions

Economic growth is typically measured by the rate of change of output or GDP. When measuring GDP, four important distinctions should be made.

- Economic growth is typically measured by the rise in the output of goods and services over time. Economic growth is changes in **real** GDP and not changes in **nominal** GDP which also includes increases in prices. Real GDP over time has to be measured using one year's prices. So, for example, in 2015, real economic growth was measured by the UK statistical service, the Office for National Statistics, using 2011 prices.

- Real GDP is a proxy measure of the **volume** of goods and services produced. It is equal to the quantity produced in an economy. The **value** of goods and services produced is volume times the average price. So a proxy measure of the volume of goods produced can be calculated by taking the nominal value of GDP and dividing it by the price level.

- **Total GDP** is the total amount of GDP produced in an economy. However, when comparing living standards, it is often more important to compare **GDP per capita** or total GDP divided by the size of the population. Similarly, growth in GDP per capita, which takes into account both change in GDP and the change in population, is often more useful when comparing living standards than simply using growth in total GDP.

- Falling economic growth does not mean that the level of real GDP itself is falling. China grew at 10 per cent per annum between 1980 and 2010. If its growth rate fell to two per cent per annum, its GDP would still be rising by two per cent each year. A falling rate of growth simply means that GDP is not rising as fast as before. So it is very important to distinguish between the **level of GDP** and the **rate of growth of GDP**. Only if the rate of growth of GDP became negative would GDP be falling.

Key Term

Actual growth - economic growth as measured by recorded changes in real GDP over time.

Boom or peak - period of time when the economy is growing strongly and is operating above its productive potential.

Demand-side shock - a sudden and large impact on aggregate demand.

Depression or slump - a period of the trade cycle when there is a particularly deep and long fall in output.

Downturn - a period of the trade cycle when either economic growth or GDP itself is falling.

Economic growth - a rise in output in an economy which can be either actual growth or potential growth.

Economic recovery - the movement back from where the economy is operating below its productive potential to a point where it is at its productive potential.

Export-led growth - a rise in aggregate demand caused by a rise in exports.

Hysteresis - the process whereby a variable does not return to its former value when changed. In terms of the trade cycle, it is used to describe the phenomenon of an economy failing to return to its former long term trend rate of growth after a severe recession.

Output gap - the difference between the actual level of GDP and the productive potential of the economy. There is a **positive output gap** when actual GDP is above the productive potential of the economy and it is in boom. There is a **negative output gap** when actual GDP is below the productive potential of the economy.

Potential growth - economic growth as measured by the changes in the productive potential of the economy over time.

Recession - a period of the trade cycle when output or growth in output falls. The technical definition now used by the UK government is that a recession occurs when growth in output is negative for two successive quarters (i.e. two periods of three months).

Spare capacity - for a whole economy, this exists when long run aggregate supply is greater than aggregate demand and so there is a negative output gap.

Supply-side shock - a sudden and large impact on aggregate supply.

Trade or business or economic cycle - regular fluctuations in the level of economic activity around the productive potential of the economy. In business cycles, the economy veers from recession, when it is operating well below its productive potential, to booms when it is likely to be at or even above its productive potential.

Thinking like an economist

Economic growth in the UK economy

In his 1999 Pre-Budget Report, the Chancellor of the Exchequer at the time, Gordon Brown, who later on went on to become Prime Minister, said that 'under this government, Britain will not return to the boom and bust of the past'. He came to regret those words.

As can be seen from Figure 10, the UK economy performed well between 2000 and 2007. The world economy suffered no

Figure 10

Economic growth, quarterly (% change in GDP at market prices at 2011 prices, year on year)

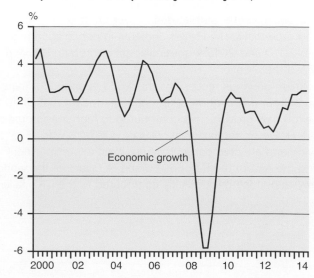

Source: adapted from www.ons.gov.uk

major shocks, which could have led to a demand-side shock for the UK economy. Positive economic growth encouraged UK firms to invest. Education standards improved whilst many UK firms, particularly large firms, became more efficient in the face of international competition.

However, the period also saw major market failure in the banking sector. Banks over lent to customers, seeking to grow and gain market share. Households in the UK increased their indebtedness as a proportion of their income. Banks also engaged in riskier and riskier activities in a search for profit. The catalyst for the financial crisis of 2007-08 came from the USA. Banks there had given large numbers of mortgages to low-income households (so called 'sub-prime' borrowers) on deals which fixed low repayments for a few years. When they came to pay the full rate of interest on their loans, many couldn't afford the repayments. The bad loans that resulted exposed the risky lending practices of many banks across the world. The result was a near collapse of the world banking system. Governments were left to bail out the banks. In the UK, banks cut back their lending and there was a sharp fall in housing prices. The demand-side shock led the economy into recession.

In previous recessions, the UK economy had bounced back strongly within two or three years. This recession shown in Figures 10 and 11, however, was different in a number of different ways.

First, households were highly indebted at the start of the recession. They were reluctant to increase their borrowing and kick start a recovery through increased consumer spending. Their income was also hit by tax rises from 2010 and relatively high inflation due to increases in world commodity prices between 2010 and 2013. Finally, depressed demand meant that employers were reluctant to give any pay increases to workers. The government itself imposed a general pay freeze on public sector workers between 2010 and 2014.

Second, firms cut back their investment. This is normal in a recession. However, lack of domestic demand and lack of growth in the UK's main export market meant that investment stayed depressed for a longer period of time than usual.

Third, a new government elected in 2010 prioritised cutting the large public sector budget deficit over other objectives including growth. Rises in taxes and cuts in public spending between 2010 and 2012 in particular cut aggregate demand and stalled the recovery.

Fourth, in previous recessions the world economic climate was much better. Growth in other countries meant that UK exports too saw growth. This contributed to higher aggregate demand. However, the financial crisis of 2007-08 was worldwide and affected particularly our main export partners including the rest of the European Union. A failure of the world economy to bounce back quickly contributed to the UK's failure to recover.

Figure 11

Real GDP, £ billion at 2011 prices, quarterly

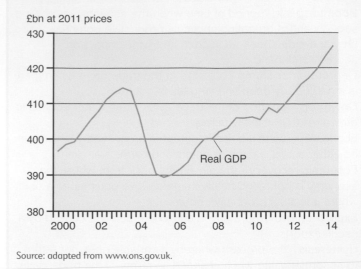

Source: adapted from www.ons.gov.uk.

Quarterly real GDP in the UK peaked in the first quarter of 2008. It wasn't till the third quarter of 2013 that GDP returned to that level. Historically, this was an exceptionally long period of time for a UK recovery.

Source: with information from www.ons.gov.uk; *Pre-Budget Report 1999*; www.gov.uk.

Data Response Question

Poland, Portugal and the eurozone

Figure 12

Economic growth (annual % change in GDP)

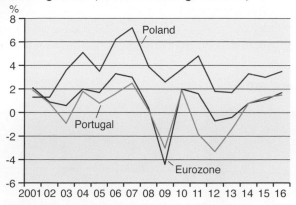

Figure 13

Unemployment rate (%)

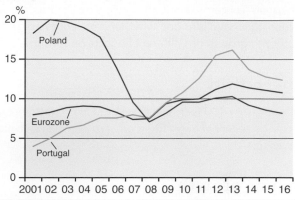

Figure 14

Inflation rate (annual % change in prices)

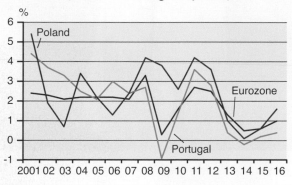

Figure 15

Investment (real total gross fixed capital formation, annual % change)

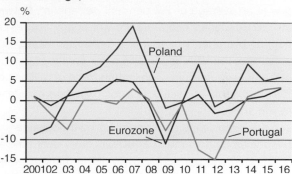

Figure 16

Output gap (deviation of actual GDP from potential GDP as % of potential GDP)[1,2]

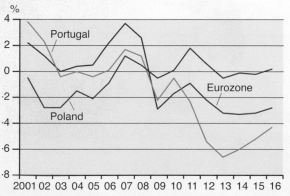

1. The eurozone is the group of EU countries which has adopted the euro as their currency, including Portugal, Germany, France and Ireland but excluding Poland and the UK.
2. 2015 and 2016 are forecast data.
Source: adapted from www.oecd.org

Q

1. Giving examples from the data, explain what is meant by a recession.

2. Explain, using examples from the data, the link between investment and growth in the potential output of an economy.

3. Discuss whether Poland's economic performance was better than that of either Portugal or the eurozone over the period shown in the data.

Evaluation

Start by defining economic performance. Then compare trends for the three economies for each economic variable. Look at the performance at the beginning of the period, the middle of the period and the end of the period. Weigh up the evidence for your evaluation. What variables are not present in the data but which are important for judging the economic performance of an economy? How does their absence affect your overall judgement?

33 The impact of economic growth

Key points

1. Economic growth gives rise to significant increases in GDP over time.
2. Economic growth is associated not just with increasing material prosperity but also increases in longevity, quality of housing, educational attainment and other socioeconomic variables.
3. There are concerns about economic growth including whether it is sustainable, whether it leads to widening inequalities and whether it increases living standards or happiness.
4. Economic growth has different impacts on consumers, firms, the government and living standards.

Starter activity

What was life like 100 years ago in the UK? Find 10 facts that relate to people's standard of living 100 years ago. Were people better off then than now?

Economic growth

The rate of economic growth of the world economy has accelerated, historically, in recent decades. Even 500 years ago, most people would have seen little change in incomes over their lifetimes. In Victorian England, the economy grew at about one per cent per annum. Between 1948 and 2014, UK real GDP grew at an average of 2.7 per cent per annum. Between 1979 and 2014, China's economy grew at nearly 10 per cent per annum on average. Growth in the developed world, in Western Europe, the USA, Japan and other countries, has led to enormous affluence. In China, whilst hundreds of millions of its 1.3 billion inhabitants are still very poor, many are now leading 'western' life styles.

To see the importance of economic growth, consider Table 1. It shows by how much £100 will grow over time at different rates. At one per cent growth per annum, income will roughly double over the lifetime of an individual. At two per cent, it will quadruple over a lifetime. At three per cent, it is doubling every 25 years. At five per cent, it only takes about 14 years to double income. At 10 per cent, it only takes about seven years to double income.

If the UK could grow at its long run rate of post-war growth of around 2.7 per cent, average British workers in 30 years' time will earn, in real terms, twice what they are earning today. When they are in their 70s, they can expect workers to earn four times as much as workers in the year that they were born.

Table 1 Compound growth rate of £100 over time

| Year | Annual growth rates | | | | |
	1%	2%	3%	5%	10%
0	100	100	100	100	100
5	105	110	116	128	161
10	110	122	134	163	259
25	128	164	209	339	1 084
50	164	269	438	1 147	11 739
75	211	442	918	3 883	127 189
100	271	724	1 922	13 150	1 378 061

Question 1

The photographs show a modern kitchen and a kitchen at the start of the 20th century. To what extent do they show that economic growth has been desirable?

The benefits of economic growth

For individuals as consumers, economic growth in the short term is likely to bring benefits. If nothing else, consumers can buy more goods and services. Between 1955 and 2013, for example, UK consumption per person per year in real terms increased from £6 224 in 1955 to £20 090 in 2013, a more than three-fold increase. However, economic growth can bring more fundamental changes.

- Life expectancy tends to be associated with income. So life expectancy in the UK in 1900 was approximately 49 years. Today it is 82 years.
- People have enough to eat and drink, which was not true in the UK in 1900. What we eat and drink is nearly always fit for human consumption. In fact, UK consumers are now so rich that overeating is a major problem.
- Housing standards today in the UK are very high. There is some inadequate housing but this is only a very small percentage of the housing stock. Relatively few houses that people lived in, in 1900, would be considered adequate today.
- Nearly everyone can read and write in the UK. Standards of education are much higher on average than 100 years ago when most children left school at 12.
- Health tends to be better. Not only are people living longer on average, but the quality of their life in old age has increased because of better health.

Despite the apparent benefits, the goal of economic growth is questioned by some economists and environmentalists.

Growth is unsustainable

Perhaps the most serious anti-growth argument is that growth is unsustainable. **Sustainable growth** can be defined as growth in the productive potential of the economy today which does not lead to a fall in the productive potential of the economy for future generations. Consider again Table 1. If a country like the UK grows at an average three per cent per annum, then in 25 years' time national income will be twice as large as it is today; in 50 years' time, it will be over four times as large; in 75 years' time, it will be nine times as large; and in 100 years' time it will be 19 times as large. If the average wage in the UK today of a full-time employee is £27 000 per annum, then in 100 years' time it will have risen to £518 940 per annum in real terms at an annual growth rate of three per cent.

Each extra percentage increase in national income is likely to use up **non-renewable resources** such as oil, coal and copper. It is argued that the world will soon run out of these resources and there will then be economic collapse. Increases in national income are also argued to be associated with greater pollution. The greatest threat we currently face is from global warming. The worst case scenario is that within 100 years, the earth will be so warm and sea levels will have risen to such an extent that much of the world will be uninhabitable. Again, a collapse in the world economy is forecast.

Economic theory suggests that the future may not be as bleak as this picture makes out. In a market economy, growing scarcity of resources, such as oil, results in a rise in price. Three things then happen. First, demand and therefore consumption falls - the price mechanism results in conservation. Second, it becomes profitable to explore for new supplies of the resource. Third, producers and consumers switch to substitute products. For example, it is likely that within the next 50 years, electric or hydrogen-powered cars will have replaced vehicles powered by scarce and more polluting oil.

Governments too respond to pressures from scientists and the public. The activities of industry are far more regulated today in the western world than they were 30 years ago. Individual governments, for example, have introduced strict controls on pollution emissions and regulated disposal of waste. Western European governments have also introduced strict greenhouse gas emission limits.

What is worrying, however, is that the market mechanism and governments are frequently slow to act. Governments and markets are not good at responding to pressures which might take decades to build up but only manifest themselves suddenly at the end of that time period. Some scientists have predicted that global warming is now already irreversible. If this is true, the problem that we now face is how to change society to cope with this. There is no clear consensus as to how we could reverse economic growth, consume less, and cope with the coming catastrophe, without creating an economic nightmare with mass starvation.

Increasing inequalities

Some economists have argued that economic growth is increasing inequalities in income and wealth. Karl Marx, the founder of communism in the 19th century, argued that workers would live on subsistence wages whilst all the benefits of economic growth would go to the owners of capital. The history of the 20th century in rich countries like the UK and the USA seemed to disprove this Marxist view. Inequalities broadly narrowed and both manual workers and the rich enjoyed rising incomes. Equally, since the 1990s, there has been a narrowing of income differentials between developing countries and rich western countries. For example, with China growing at up to 10 per cent per year and western economies at 2.5 per cent, the narrowing has been quite dramatic. Today, many developing countries are targeting growth rates of five or six per cent, whilst the developed world considers itself lucky if it can achieve 2.5 per cent.

However, certainly in the UK and the USA, inequalities have been growing in recent decades. In the case of the USA, the average (median) worker has seen almost no growth in income over the past 25 years at a time when the US economy has been growing on average by 2.5 per cent per year. One explanation is that the average worker today is competing for jobs not within an economy, but globally. A worker in UK manufacturing is competing for a job with a worker in China or Bangladesh. Technology gives the UK worker some competitive advantage. But often using state of the art technology is not enough to make the UK competitive. In the non-traded sector, workers, such as healthcare assistants or hotel staff, are competing with a steady supply of new immigrant labour. In the UK, this might mean other European workers. In the USA, it might be migrants from Central America. At the top of the pay scale, demand is pushing up wages for what are seen as the best workers. In the middle and the bottom, increases in the supply of workers are leading to stagnating wages. The benefits of economic growth are therefore being appropriated by the highest earners, particularly the top one per cent. None of the benefits is being seen by middle and lower income households. Whether this continues into the future remains to be seen.

Growth and happiness

Some economists argue that higher average incomes do not necessarily make individuals happier. Using psychological surveys from across the world (cross-sectional surveys), they have found that happiness and income are positively related at low levels of income but higher levels of income are not associated with increases in happiness. The idea that increases in GDP do not lead to increases in happiness is called the **Easterlin Paradox**, after Richard Easterlin, an economist who identified the problem in a 1974 research paper. The argument is that an increase in consumption of material goods will improve well-being when basic needs are not met, such as adequate food and shelter. But once these needs are being met, then increasing the quantity of goods consumed makes no difference to well-being. Having a new high-definition television, or a new car when you already have a reasonable, functioning TV or car doesn't increase your well-being in the long term.

Rather than concentrate on increasing GDP, governments of high-income countries such as the UK should concentrate on factors which contribute to happiness. These include improving the quality of human relationships, working fewer hours, ensuring adequate health care for all and giving all citizens a minimum income.

The anti-growth lobby

One point to note is that supporters of the anti-growth lobby tend to be people who are relatively well off. Cutting their consumption by 25 per cent, or producing environmentally friendly alternative technologies, might not create too much hardship for them. However, leaving the mass of people in the developing world today at their present living standards would lead to great inequality. A small minority would continue to live below the absolute poverty line, facing the continual threat of malnutrition. A majority would not have access to services such as education and health care which people in the West take for granted. Not surprisingly, the anti-growth lobby is stronger in the West than in the developing world.

The impact of economic growth

The impact of economic growth is felt by a number of different groups and on different issues.

Consumers Economic growth should allow households to see rising incomes over time. They can then afford to buy more goods and services. However, if the economic benefits of economic growth are appropriated by only the most well off in society, then average households will see no gain. This has been the experience of US households for the past 30 years.

Also, there is debate about whether buying more goods and services leads to rising living standards and rising levels of happiness. If the Easterlin Paradox is correct, economic growth will bring no benefits to consumers in terms of happiness in rich industrialised countries.

Firms Economic growth may provide opportunities for existing firms to increase sales as buyers have rising incomes. However, economic growth is accompanied by changes in the structure of the economy. Changing technologies mean that some firms will find their markets disappearing. Economic growth also provides opportunities for new firms to establish themselves.

The government Rising incomes means that government tax revenues should rise. Rising private sector spending also tends to lead to demands for similar rises in public sector spending. After all, if consumers are going on more holidays, buying more computer equipment or going out to restaurants more often, they also want to see better education for their children, better roads on which to drive their cars or better health care for themselves. However, the response to rising tax revenues depends upon parties in power. Right-wing governments are more likely to reduce rates of tax and reduce government services than left-wing governments.

The environment In rich developed countries, economic growth is likely to lead to less pollution and a cleaner environment. Economic actors are likely to spend on technologies and projects to improve the environment. In developing countries, growth in primary and secondary industries is likely to increase pollution and degrade the environment. China, for example, has a serious pollution problem because of the growth of its heavy industries in recent decades. However, further growth should lead to a cleaning up of the environment in these countries.

The economy Growth in GDP results in a larger economy. The possible impact on consumers, firms and government has already been described. In terms of jobs, growth may result in more jobs being created or there may be fewer if existing workers become more productive.

Current and future living standards The impact of economic growth on current living standards depends on who receives the benefit of that economic growth. If it is only the richest in society, then it will have no impact on the majority of households. However, in developing countries, everyone in society is more likely to benefit from economic growth. The debate about the link between rising GDP and living standards must also be taken into account. The weaker the link, the less economic growth will benefit households and individuals.

Key Term

Sustainable growth - growth in the productive potential of the economy today which does not lead to a fall in the productive potential of the economy for future generations.

Thinking like an economist

The standard of living in the UK since 1900

GDP is often used as the major economic indicator of welfare. Table 2 shows that, on this basis, living standards in the UK rose considerably last century. Between 1901 and 1931 GDP rose 26 per cent and between 1901 and 2013 it rose 727 per cent. Population has increased too, but even when this has been taken into account, the rise in income per person is impressive.

It is possible to chart a multitude of other ways in which it can be shown that the standard of living of the British family has improved. For instance, 14.2 per cent of children in 1901 died before the age of one. In 2013, the comparable figure was 0.4 per cent. In 1901, the vast majority of children left school at 12. From 2015, all children will stay on in school or full-time education to the age of 18. In 1901, few people were able to afford proper medical treatment when they fell ill. Today, everyone in the UK has access to the National Health Service.

Table 3 illustrates another way in which we are far better off today than a family at the turn of the century. It shows the weekly budget of a manual worker's family in a North Yorkshire iron town, estimated by Lady Bell in her book *At The Works*. The family lived off 7½ home-made loaves of 4lb (1.8kg) each thinly scraped with butter, 4lb (1.8kg) of meat and bacon, weak tea, a quart of milk and no vegetables worth mentioning. In 2013, whilst average consumption for five people of bread was 3.0kg a week, and sugar and jam 0.62kg, on the other hand meat consumption was 4.7kg, fresh and processed potato consumption was 3.4kg, and butter, margarine, and low fat spreads consumption was 0.86kg. Moreover, today's diet is far more varied and ample, with fruit and vegetables apart from potatoes playing a major part. Malnutrition, not uncommon in 1900, is virtually unknown in the UK today.

The budget also says a great deal about the very restricted lifestyle of the average family in 1908. Then, a family would consider itself lucky if it could take a day trip to the seaside. In comparison, individuals took an estimated 37.6 million holidays abroad in 2013.

Table 3 Family budget in 1908

Source: adapted from *At the Works: A Study of a Manufacturing Town*, Lady Bell, Edward Arnold, 1907.

Family budget in 1908 Income 18s 6d, family of five	s.	d.
Rent	5	6
Coals	2	4
Insurance	0	7
Clothing	1	0
Meat	1	6
14lb of flour	0	5
3½ lb of bread meal	1	4½
1lb butter	1	1
Half lb lard	0	2½
1lb bacon	0	9
4 lb sugar	0	8
Half lb tea	0	9
Yeast	0	1
Milk	0	3
1 box Globe polish	0	3
1lb soap	0	3
1 packet Gold Dust	0	9
3 oz tobacco	0	3
7lb potatoes	0	1
Onions	0	1
Matches	0	2
Lamp oil	0	3
Debt		
Total	18	6

In 1908, houses were sparsely furnished. The main form of heating was open coal fires; central heating was virtually unknown. Very few houses were wired for electricity. Table 3 shows that the typical house was lighted by oil. All the electrical household gadgets we take for granted, from washing machines to vacuum cleaners to televisions, had not been invented. The 1lb of soap in the 1908 budget would have been used to clean clothes, sinks and floors. Soap powders, liquid detergents and floor cleaners were not available. 'Gold Dust' was the popular name for an exceptionally caustic form of shredded yellow soap notorious for its ability to flay the user's hands. Compare that with the numerous brands of mild soaps available today.

Workers worked long hours, six days a week with few holidays, whilst at home household chores were a drudgery, with few labour-saving devices. Accidents were frequent and old age, unemployment and sickness were dreaded and, even more so, the workhouse, the final destination for those with no means to support themselves.

Ecologically, the smokestack industries of industrial areas such as London, the Black Country and Manchester created large-scale pollution. The smogs which are found in many cities such as Mexico City and Los Angeles today were common occurrences in turn-of-the-20th century Britain. The urban environment was certainly not clean 100 years ago.

Socially and politically, women, who formed over half the population, were not emancipated. In 1900, they did not have the vote, their place was considered to be in the home, they were often regarded as biologically inferior to men, and they were debarred from almost all public positions of influence and authority. In many ways, the standard of living of women improved more than that of men during the 20th century because of the repressive attitude held towards women over 100 years ago.

Overall, it would be very difficult to look back on 1900 and see it as some golden age. The vast majority of those in Britain today have much higher living standards than their counterparts in 1900. However, whilst there might be little absolute poverty today, it could be argued that there is considerable relative poverty. It could also be argued that the poorest today are probably still worse off than the top five per cent of income earners in 1900.

Source: with information from www.gov.uk; www.ons.gov.uk.

Table 2 GDP, GDP per head and population, 1901-2013

	GDP (£bn at 2013 prices)	Population (millions)	GDP per head (£ at 2013 prices)
1901	176.9	38.2	4 631
1911	203.0	42.1	4 822
1921	182.8	44.0	4 155
1931	222.9	46.1	4 835
1951	360.2	50.2	7 175
1961	465.9	52.7	8 841
1971	597.0	55.5	10 757
1981	698.6	55.1	12 679
1991	913.1	57.4	15 908
2001	1 212.5	59.1	20 516
2011	1 430.4	63.2	22 633
2013	1463.8	64.1	22 836

Note: GDP is at market prices.
Source: adapted from www.ons.gov.uk; www.bankofengland.co.uk.

Data Response Question

Comparative living standards in the UK

Table 4 UK, selected indicators

	1971	2013
GDP, £bn at current prices, UK	60.9	1 713.3
Price Index, GDP deflator (1971=100), UK	100	113.6
Population, millions, UK	55.5	64.2
Percentage of households, UK, owning		
Central heating	30	96
Dishwasher	0	42
Telephone	35	89
DVD player	0	85
Home computer	0	83
Number of workers, millions, UK		
Men in work	15.5	16
Women in work	9.0	14
Unemployed (LFS)	1.1	2.5
Motorway motor vehicle traffic, yearly vehicle kilometres, bn, GB	9.7	101.9
Percentage of males born 80 years previously and still alive, UK	24.9	57
Percentage of dwellings owner occupied, UK	50	63

Source: adapted from www.ons.gov.uk; www.gov.uk.

Table 5 UK, selected indicators

Percentage of adults smoking, GB	1974	2013
	46	19
Percentage of adults obese, England	1978	2012
	6	25
Number of marriages, England and Wales	1971	2012
	404 737	262 240
Number of students obtaining (first) university degrees, UK	1970	2012-13
	51 189	303 510
Mortgage payments as % of average (mean) take home pay, first time buyers, UK	1983Q1	2014Q3
	28.5	34.3

Source: adapted from www.ons.gov.uk; www.nationwide.co.uk; www.hesa.ac.uk.

Q

1. Compare real GDP per capita in 1971 with 2013.

2. Using the data, explain (a) three ways in which the average person was better off in 2013 than in previous decades and (b) one way in which the average person was worse off.

3. Discuss whether rising real GDP per person was sufficient to ensure that every citizen of the UK was better off in 2013 than in 1971.

Evaluation

The simple answer to this question is no. Look at the data and draw out examples where standards of living have fallen. You could also use your own examples. However, most of the data does suggest that people are better off. Give some examples when you write about this. Then weigh up the two sides to come to a conclusion. In your conclusion, you could also query whether higher consumption of goods and services leads to any greater happiness. Were people less happy in 1971 because no one had online streaming of films or music, for example?

Figure 1

Emissions of selected air pollutants, UK (1970=100)

Index (1970=100)[1]

- Ammonia
- Nitrogen Oxides
- Non-methane volatile organic compounds
- PM₁₀
- PM₂₅
- Sulphur Dioxide

1. Ammonia (1980 = 100)
Source: adapted from www.defra.gov.uk.

Figure 2

Index of volume of domestic household expenditure on goods and services (at 2011 prices), 1971=100

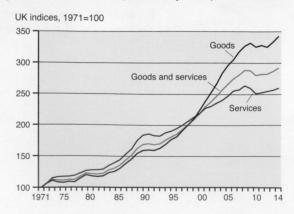

UK indices, 1971=100

Source: adapted from www.ons.gov.uk.

34 Inflation

Key points

1. Inflation is a general sustained rise in the price level.
2. Inflation is measured by calculating the change in a weighted price index over time. In the UK, the two main measures are the Consumer Prices Index and the Retail Prices Index.
3. A price index only measures inflation for average households. It also cannot take into account changes in the quality and distribution of goods over time.
4. Inflation may be demand-pull or cost-push depending on whether it is caused by excess demand or rising costs.
5. Inflation is generally considered to give rise to economic costs to society.
6. Deflation, falling prices, tends to lead to depressed demand in an economy.

Starter activity

In 1923, Germany suffered a catastrophic bout of hyperinflation. Find out what caused it and what effect it had on German citizens and firms. Contrast this with Japan in the 1990s and 2000s. It suffered deflation. Find out what caused this and what effect it has had on the Japanese economy.

Inflation, deflation and disinflation

Inflation is defined as a sustained general rise in prices across an economy. The opposite of inflation is **deflation**. This is defined as a sustained general fall in prices across an economy. **Disinflation** is defined as a fall in the rate of inflation.

For example, if prices in general are rising by three per cent per annum, there is inflation. If prices in general are falling by

Question 1

Figure 1

Angola: annual inflation, %

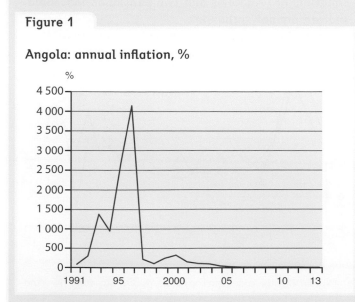

Source: adapted from http://data.worldbank.org.

(a) Describe the changes in prices in the African country of Angola shown in the data.

(b) To what extent could Angola be said to have experienced hyperinflation during the period shown?

one per cent per annum, there is deflation. If the rate of inflation falls from four per cent to two per cent, there is disinflation. Note that if there is disinflation, it means there is inflation in the economy, but the rate of inflation is falling.

A general rise in prices may be quite moderate. Creeping inflation would describe a situation where prices rose a few per cent on average each year. **Hyperinflation**, on the other hand, describes a situation where inflation levels are very high. There is no exact figure at which inflation becomes hyperinflation. However, annual inflation rates of 50 per cent or more would be classified as hyperinflation by most economists.

The term **reflation** is used to describe the rise in GDP which occurs following a recession. **Stagflation** is the term used to describe a period when inflation is rising or is very high at a time when the economy is in recession. The economy is stagnating but there is also inflation. **Deflationary policies** are policies pursued by governments. They are designed to reduce the rate of economic growth. If successful, they will almost certainly also reduce the rate of growth of inflation. However, deflationary policies are almost never aimed at bringing about negative inflation. So deflationary policies, designed to reduce the rate of economic growth are not usually linked to deflation, a fall in the price level.

Measuring inflation

The inflation rate is the change in average prices in an economy over a given period of time. The price level is measured in the form of an index. So if the price index were 100 today and 110 in one year's time, then the rate of inflation would be 10 per cent. In the UK, there are two widely used measures of the price level: the **Consumer Prices Index (CPI)** and the **Retail Prices Index (RPI)**.

Calculating a price index is a complicated process. Prices of a representative range of goods and services (a **basket** of goods) need to be recorded on a regular basis. In the UK, the basket is calculated from the results of the Living Costs and Food Survey. Each year, a few thousand households are asked to record their expenditure for one month. From these figures, it is possible to calculate how the average household spends its money. (This average household, of course, does not exist except as a statistical entity).

Table 1 Weights and inflation

Commodity	Proportion of total spending	Weight	Increase in price	Contribution to increase in CPI
Food	75%	750	8%	6%
Cars	25%	250	4%	1%
Total	100	1 000		7%

For example, the Survey might find that the average household spends an average £2 a week on beef mince and £0.40 on men's trousers.

With this information, surveyors are sent out each month to record prices for the mix of goods and services that the Living Costs and Food Survey has shown is bought by UK households. Prices are recorded in different areas of the country as well as in different types of retail outlets, such as corner shops and supermarkets. These results are averaged out to find the average price of goods and this figure is converted into **index number** form.

Changes in the price of food are more important than changes in the price of, say, tobacco. This is because a larger proportion of total household income is spent on food than on tobacco. Therefore the figures have to be **weighted** before the final index can be calculated. For instance, assume that there are only two goods in the economy, food and cars, as shown in Table 1. Households spend 75 per cent of their income on food and 25 per cent on cars. There is an increase in the price of food of eight per cent and of cars of four per cent over one year. In a normal average calculation, the eight per cent and the four per cent would be added together and the total divided by two to arrive at an average price increase of six per cent. However, this provides an inaccurate figure because spending on food is

more important in the household budget than spending on cars. The figures have to be weighted. Food is given a weight of ¾ (or 0.75 or 750 out of 1 000) and cars a weight of ¼ (or 0.25 or 250 out of 1 000). The average increase in prices is eight per cent multiplied by ¾ added to four per cent multiplied by ¼ (i.e. six per cent + one per cent). The weighted average is therefore seven per cent. If the CPI were 100 at the start of the year, it would be 107 at the end of the year.

The accuracy of price indices

It is important to realise that any price index is a weighted average. Different rates of inflation can be calculated by changing the weightings in the index. For instance, the Consumer Prices Index calculates the average price level for the average household in the UK. However, it is possible, again using data from the Living Costs and Food Survey, to calculate price indices for pensioner households or one-parent households. One major difference between these households and the average household is that they spend a larger proportion of their income on food. So a 10 per cent rise in the price of food compared to a five per cent rise in the price of all other items will result in a higher rate of inflation for pensioners and one-parent households than for the average household. In fact each individual household will have a different rate of inflation. The Consumer Prices Index only measures an average rate of inflation for all households across the UK.

The household spending patterns upon which the index is based also change over time. For instance, food was a far more

Question 2

Table 2 Price index weights

Year	Weights			% annual increase in prices	
	Food	All other items	Total	Food	All other items
1	300	700	1 000	10	10
2	250	750	1 000	5	10
3	200	800	1 000	4	6
4	150	850	1 000	3	2
5	125	875	1 000	4	4
6	120	880	1 000	6	4
7	120	880	1 000	5	7
8	110	890	1 000	8	10

Table 2 shows the price index weights given to food and to all other items in each of eight years. It also shows the percentage annual increase in prices of those items.

(a) Calculate the rate of inflation (i.e. the percentage increase in prices) in each year 1 to 8.

(b) What would the price index in years 2-8 be if the price index were 100 in year 1?

Question 3

Figure 2

Inflation: RPI All items and Two pensioner household indices, annual % change

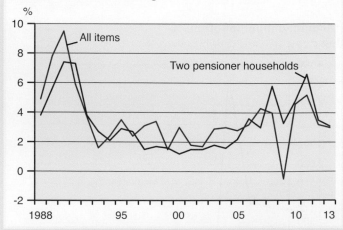

Source: adapted from www.ons.gov.uk.

(a) Explain why the change in the All Items RPI may differ from the change in the Two-Pensioner Household RPI.

(b) A two-person pensioner household where the pensioners retired in 1988 receives pensions linked to the All Items Index of Retail Prices. In which years would it, on average, have seen (i) an increase and (ii) a decrease in its real purchasing power? Explain why this occurs.

important component of price indices 30 years ago than it is today because spending on food was then a higher proportion of total spending. The index cannot indicate changes in the quality of goods. Cars might increase in price because their specifications improve rather than because there has been an inflationary price rise. The weights for the Consumer Prices Index are changed annually to take account of changes in spending patterns. However, this does not get round the fact that the average 'basket' or 'bundle' of goods purchased in 1950 and upon which the prices index was calculated was very different from the average bundle of goods purchased today.

The causes of inflation

Inflation can be caused by two main factors: too much demand in the economy or rising costs.

Demand-pull inflation In the market for oil, a significant rise in demand for oil with no increase in supply will lead to a rise in the price of oil. The same occurs at a macroeconomic level. If aggregate or total demand rises and there is no increase in aggregate supply, then **demand-pull inflation** is likely to occur. Demand-pull inflation is caused by excess demand in the economy. When there is too much demand, the **price level**, (or average level of prices in the economy) will rise. Excessive increases in aggregate demand in the UK can come about for a variety of reasons.

- Consumer spending may rise excessively. Interest rates could be low and consumers are spending large amounts on their credit cards, or consumer confidence could be rising because house prices are rising.
- Firms may substantially increase their spending on investment. Perhaps they are responding to large increases in demand from consumers and need extra capacity to satisfy that demand.

- The government might be increasing its spending substantially, or it could be cutting taxes.
- World demand for UK exports may be rising because of a boom in the world economy.

Demand-pull inflation may also be caused by growth of the money supply. Both central banks, like the Bank of England, and the banking system can influence the amount of borrowing and lending in the economy. If banks increase their lending to customers, the money supply will grow. Customers are likely to spend the money they have borrowed. The result will be increased aggregate demand. This can cause inflation. The most famous inflation caused by an increase in the money supply was Germany in 1923 when there was hyperinflation. Most examples of hyperinflation occur because the central bank lends money to the government which uses it to pay its bills rather than raise taxes.

Figure 3 shows how an increase in aggregate demand in the short run leads to inflation. Aggregate demand increases from AD_1 to AD_2. The price level increases from P_1 to P_2, showing the inflationary impact of this increase in aggregate demand.

Cost-push inflation Inflation may also occur because of changes in the supply side of the economy. **Cost-push inflation** occurs because of rising costs. There are four major sources of increased costs.

- Wages and salaries account for about 50 per cent of national income and hence increases in wages are normally the single most important cause of increases in costs of production.
- Imports can cause a rise in price. A boom in the world economy, for example, may push up commodity prices such as oil, copper and wheat. It will also push up the price of finished goods. This will lead to higher import prices for the UK.

Figure 3

A rise in aggregate demand leads to demand-pull inflation

A rise in aggregate demand from AD_1 to AD_2 leads to an increase in prices of P_1P_2.

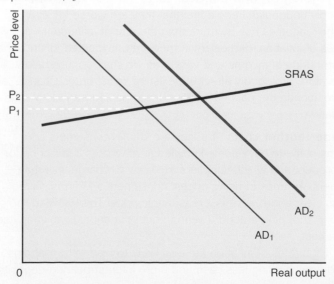

Figure 4

A rise in short-run aggregate supply leads to cost-push inflation

A shift upwards in short-run aggregate supply curve from $SRAS_1$ to $SRAS_2$ leads to an increase in prices of P_1P_2.

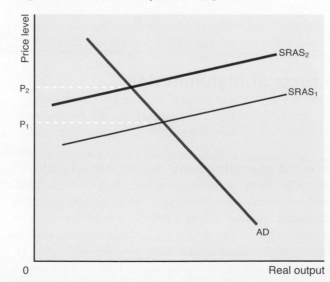

- Profits can be increased by firms when they raise price to improve profit margins. The more price inelastic the demand for their goods, the less will such behaviour result in a fall in demand for their products.
- Government can raise indirect tax rates or reduce subsidies, thus increasing prices.

Firms will try to pass on increases in their costs to customers. For example, if a firm gives a five per cent pay rise to its workers, and wages account for 80 per cent of its costs, then it will need to increase prices by four per cent (80 per cent of five per cent) to maintain its profit margins. Competition in the market may mean that it finds it difficult to pass on these price rises and maintain sales. However, if costs are rising over time, firms will have to increase their prices and this leads to inflation.

Figure 4 shows how a rise in short-run aggregate supply will lead to inflation. The short-run aggregate supply curve is pushed up from $SRAS_1$ to $SRAS_2$, for example, by a rise in wage rates or a rise in import prices. The price level increases from P_1 to P_2, showing the inflation impact of this increase in SRAS.

Sometimes, inflation may be primarily demand-pull in nature. In other time periods, it may be mainly cost-push. In a stable but growing economy with no demand-side or supply-side shocks, inflation is likely to be caused by a mix of the two factors.

Question 4

In December 2014, the Office for Budget Responsibility forecast that inflation in 2015 would be below two per cent. Sharp falls in the price of oil in late 2014 would work their way through the economy as would the effects of a rise in the value of the pound against other currencies. Gas and electricity prices would be stable or even fall. At the same time, there was no evidence of any significant rise in wage inflation. The economy was predicted to grow by 2.4 per cent in 2015. However, inflationary pressures would be weak because both falling government spending and weak exports were forecast to exert downward pressure on aggregate demand. The economy was also operating below its long run potential.

Source: adapted from ONS, *Economic and fiscal outlook*, December 2014, Office for Budget Responsibility.

(a) Explain two factors mentioned in the data which might cause a fall in cost-push inflation.

(b) Explain one factor mentioned in the data which would suggest that demand-pull inflationary pressures are very weak.

The costs of high inflation

A sustained rise in the price level is generally considered to be a problem. The higher the rate of inflation the greater the economic cost. There is a number of reasons why this is the case.

Growth and unemployment High inflation is typically unpredictable. Both consumers and firms find it hard to predict what will be the rate of inflation next month or next year. This **unanticipated inflation** makes it difficult, if not impossible, for consumers and firms to plan for the future. Firms, for example, may reduce their investment because they are less willing to take risks in an unstable macroeconomic climate. Consumers may bring forward or reduce their purchases depending on what

they think might be in their best interests. But this then disrupts patterns of spending in the whole economy, making it difficult for firms to supply goods. Economic disruption is likely to lead to lower levels of output and spending than would otherwise be the case. Lower economic growth or falling GDP then leads to higher unemployment.

Competitiveness High inflation can lead to a balance of payment effect. If inflation rises faster in the UK than in other countries, and the value of the pound does not change on foreign currency markets, then exports will become less competitive and imports more competitive. The result will be a loss of jobs in the domestic economy and lower growth.

Redistributional costs Inflation can redistribute income and wealth between households, firms and the state. This redistribution can occur in a variety of ways. For instance, anybody on a fixed income will suffer. In the UK, many pensioners have received fixed pensions from private company pension schemes which are not adjusted for inflation. If prices double over a five year period, their real income will halve. Any group of workers which fails to be able to negotiate pay increases at least in line with inflation will suffer falls in its real income too.

If real interest rates are negative as a result of inflation, there will be a transfer of resources from lenders to borrowers. With interest rates at 10 per cent and inflation rates at 20 per cent, a saver will lose 10 per cent of the real value of saving each year whilst a borrower will see a 10 per cent real reduction in the value of debt per annum.

Taxes and government spending may not change in line with inflation. For instance, if the Chancellor fails to increase excise duties on alcohol and tobacco each year in line with inflation, real government revenue will fall whilst drinkers and smokers will be better off in real terms assuming their incomes have risen at least by as much as inflation. Similarly, if the Chancellor fails to increase personal income tax allowances (the amount which a worker can earn 'tax free') in line with inflation, then the burden of tax will increase, transferring resources from the taxpayer to the government.

Psychological and political costs Price increases are deeply unpopular. People feel that they are worse off, even if their incomes rise by more than the rate of inflation. High rates of inflation, particularly if they are unexpected, disturb the distribution of income and wealth as we shall discuss below, and therefore profoundly affect the existing social order. Change and revolution in the past have often accompanied periods of high inflation.

Shoe-leather costs If prices are stable, consumers and firms come to have some knowledge of what is a fair price for a product and which suppliers are likely to charge less than others. At times of rising prices, consumers and firms will be less clear about what is a reasonable price. This will lead to more 'shopping around' (wearing out your shoes), which in itself is a cost.

High rates of inflation are also likely to lead to households and firms holding less cash and more interest-bearing deposits. Inflation erodes the value of cash, but since nominal interest rates tend to be higher than with stable prices, the opportunity cost of holding cash tends to be larger, the higher the rate of inflation. Households and firms are then forced to spend more time transferring money from one type of account to another or putting cash into an account to maximise the interest paid. This time is a cost.

Menu costs If there is inflation, restaurants have to change their menus to show increased prices. Similarly, shops have to change their price labels and firms have to calculate and issue new price lists. Even more costly are changes to fixed capital, such as vending machines and parking meters, to take account of price increases.

Some of these costs can be reduced if inflation can be predicted. **Anticipated inflation** allows economic actors to plan for the future and adjust their decision to take inflation into account. One way of doing this is through **indexation**. This is where economic variables like wages or taxes are increased in line with inflation. For instance, a union might negotiate a wage agreement with an employer for staged increases over a year of two per cent plus the change in the Retail Prices Index. The annual changes in social security benefits in the UK are linked to the Retail Prices Index.

Economists are divided about whether indexation provides a solution to the problem of inflation. On the one hand, it reduces many of the costs of inflation although some costs such as shoe leather costs and menu costs remain. On the other hand, it reduces pressure on government to tackle the problem of inflation directly. Indexation eases the pain of inflation but is not a cure for it.

Moreover, indexation may hinder government attempts to reduce inflation because indexation builds in further cost increases, such as wage increases, which reflect past changes in prices. If a government wants to get inflation down to two per cent a year, and inflation has just been ten per cent, it will not be helped in achieving its target if workers are all awarded at least 10 per cent wage increases because of indexation agreements.

Question 5

In 2012, the Consumer Prices Index rose by 2.8 per cent and in 2013 by 2.6 per cent. How might the following have been affected in real terms by the change?

(a) A pensioner on a fixed income.

(b) A bank deposit saver, given that the rate of interest on a bank deposit saving account was 0.5 per cent in both 2012 and 2013.

(c) A worker whose personal income tax allowance was £8 105 between April 2012 and March 2013 and £9 440 between April 2013 and April 2014.

(d) A parent with one child who received £20.30 per week in child benefit in both 2012 and 2013.

The costs of deflation

Over the past 50 years, the main problem that countries have faced is high rates of inflation. However, there can also be problems associated with deflation, falling price levels. For example, between 1995 and 2014, Japan experienced nine years of falling prices. This might seem insignificant but it had a serious impact on the Japanese economy. Falling prices were caused mainly by a lack of demand in the economy. However, they also caused demand to be depressed.

With falling prices, consumer confidence tends to be low. Consumers are concerned about the future and know that if they don't buy today, they might be able to buy at a cheaper price tomorrow. A lack of consumer confidence then feeds into a lack of business confidence and lower investment. Although interest rates tend to be very low with deflation, the real cost of borrowing is higher. If prices fall by, say, one per cent, then the real cost of borrowing is the actual or nominal interest rate plus one per cent.

The other major problem with deflation is the effect on asset values. Savers can see the real value of their savings grow even if they only receive one or two per cent interest. If prices fall by two per cent and they receive one per cent interest, then the real rate of return on their savings is three per cent. Deflation encourages households to save rather than spend and this leads to low or negative rates of economic growth. For borrowers, deflation leads to the real value of their debt increasing. This will discourage households and firms from borrowing and spending and so reduce aggregate demand.

The benefits of low inflation

Many central banks today set a target for inflation of around two per cent. This is a very low rate of inflation but it is still a positive increase in prices.

The reason why two per cent is considered desirable is because this isn't deflation but nor is it a significant rate of inflation. An inflation rate of two per cent avoids the problems associated with high inflation and deflation. It gives policy makers, such as central banks and governments, room to adjust the economy if inflation goes higher or lower. If annual inflation is 0.5 per cent, it is a signal that the rate of growth of aggregate demand needs to increase lest price growth become negative. If inflation is four per cent, it is a signal that growth in aggregate demand needs to decrease lest the inflation rate increase even further.

Another reason why two per cent is considered desirable is because of its effect on assets prices. At two per cent, the real value of borrowing falls gradually over time. This is seen as desirable because it makes it easier for those who borrow to finance consumption or investment to repay their borrowings. It also doesn't impact much on the incentive to save because it is argued that savers don't take the real erosion of their savings into account. They suffer from money illusion, thinking that inflation is zero.

Key Terms

Anticipated inflation - increases in prices which economic actors are able to predict with accuracy.
Consumer Prices Index (CPI) - a measure of the price level used across the European Union and used by the Bank of England to measure inflation against its target.
Cost-push inflation - inflation caused by increases in the costs of production in the economy.
Deflation - a fall in the price level.
Demand-pull inflation - inflation which is caused by excess demand in the economy.
Disinflation - a fall in the rate of inflation.
Hyper-inflation - large increases in the price level.

Indexation - adjusting the value of economic variables such as wages or the rate of interest in line with inflation.
Inflation - a general rise in prices.
Price level - the average price of goods and services in the economy.
Retail Prices Index (RPI) - a measure of the price level which has been calculated in the UK for over 60 years and is used in a variety of contexts such as by the government to index welfare benefits.
Unanticipated inflation - increases in prices which economic actors like consumers and firms fail to predict accurately and so their decisions are based on poor information.

Thinking like an economist

The Retail Prices Index and Consumer Prices Index

The Retail Prices Index

In the UK, there is a wide variety of different measures of inflation. The two most commonly used are the Retail Prices Index (RPI) and the Consumer Prices Index (CPI).

The RPI is the traditional measure of the price level in the UK. Apart from informing economists and economic agents, such as government or firms, of the rate of inflation, it is also used for the indexation of state benefits and index-linked gilts (a form of long term government borrowing). Trade unions and firms may use the RPI in wage agreements and property companies may use it for calculating increases in leases (rents) on property. Utility regulators, which set prices for firms in industries such as telecommunications and water, may impose restrictions on price increases, or set price falls in terms of the RPI.

There are different measures of the RPI. The headline RPI measure is the All Items RPI. It measures the average price of the typical 'basket of goods' bought by the average household. It therefore measures average consumer prices. However, the RPI is also calculated for different types of goods and services such as food, motoring expenditure or leisure services. It is also calculated for one-pensioner households and two-pensioner households.

The Consumer Prices Index (CPI)

The CPI is a more recent measure of the price level and inflation. It has been calculated in the UK since 1996 with estimates going back to 1988, and so this limits its use in making historical judgements about inflation in comparison with the RPI. However, it is the measure which is used in all EU countries to measure inflation. Since 2003, it has been used by the Bank of England to measure inflation against its target rate of inflation, currently two per cent. It is therefore now the key indicator for monetary policy. It is also increasingly being used to index pensions. For example, public sector pensions are now indexed with the CPI rather than the RPI. There is also discussion of using it to index welfare benefits.

Comparing the RPI and CPI

The RPI tends to be above the CPI, as shown in Figure 5. One reason is the method of calculating both indices. The RPI uses the Carli index, a type of arithmetic mean, to average out

Figure 5

The RPI inflation rate compared to the CPI inflation rate

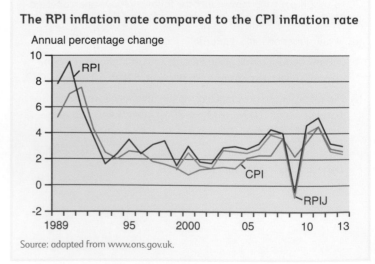

Annual percentage change

Source: adapted from www.ons.gov.uk.

different prices. The CPI uses a geometric mean. In 2013, a report by the Office for National Statistics (ONS) stated that the use of the Carli index meant that inflation was consistently overstated and the CPI represented a more accurate measure of actual inflation. In the same report, the ONS announced that it would be producing an additional RPI measure called the RPIJ which would use the same data and weights as the RPI but it would be calculated using the Jevons index, a type of geometric mean. RPIJ from 1999 can be seen in Figure 5. It follows the pattern of change of the CPI rather than the RPI because both it and the CPI are calculated using geometric means.

Another reason why the RPI and the CPI differ is that the CPI excludes a number of items relating to housing, including mortgage interest rate payments and Council Tax, whereas they are included in the RPI. Since the CPI was first calculated, housing costs in most years have risen faster than other items. Since the CPI excludes many housing costs, it has tended to show lower inflation than the RPI.

The RPI also covers a different sample of the population than the CPI. The RPI excludes the top 4 per cent of income earners and low income pensioners, on the basis that these are not typical households. The CPI covers all households and all incomes.

Calculating the RPI and CPI

The RPI and the CPI are calculated from the same data which is collected through monthly surveys. Two types of survey are carried out.

Prices are recorded in 141 different areas of the UK. These locations are chosen through a random sampling method. 100 000 prices are collected per month of a typical 'basket of goods' bought by consumers. Around 650 items are included in the basket. Over time, what is included in the basket is changed to reflect changes in consumer spending. For example, rabbits were taken out of the index in 1955, whilst condoms were added in 1989. In 2014, DVD recorders and wallpaper paste were taken out while DVD rental/video-on-demand subscription services and fresh fruit snacking pots were put in.

In addition, a further 80 000 prices are collected centrally each month for items where local sampling would be inappropriate. Prices of goods in catalogues, utility (gas, electricity and telephone) prices, internet prices, road tolls, and mortgage interest payments are examples.

The typical basket of goods is constructed from another survey, the Living Costs and Food Survey. This survey asks around 11 500 households chosen randomly, of whom around 5 500 agree to participate, keeping diaries of what they spend over a fortnight. A spending pattern for the average family can then be worked out. The RPI and CPI are weighted to reflect the importance of different expenditures within the total. So the price of gas carries more weight in the index than the price of processed fruit because households spend more on gas. Figure 6 shows how weights have changed between 1962 and 2014. The proportion spent on food in the average budget has been declining over time as incomes have risen (food has a very low positive income elasticity of demand). Travel and leisure and housing and household expenditure, on the other hand, have been rising. The impact of the 2008 financial crisis can clearly be seen from the basket. With average incomes no higher in 2014 than they were in 2007, spending patterns have remained broadly similar.

The validity of inflation indices

All price indices suffer from a major flaw. The assumption is that from year to year, the prices of the same sort of goods and services are being compared. However, over time, the quality of goods and services tends to improve. A car from the 1950s, for example, was far less comfortable and reliable than a car made in the 2010s. Moreover, new products become available or are invented. In the 1950s, the UK population did not have access to fast-food takeaways or mobile phones. Critics argue that inflation indices overestimate inflation because they fail to take account of a falling cost of living to purchase today's improved goods and services.

Figure 6

Change in the basket of goods used to calculate the RPI 1962-2014

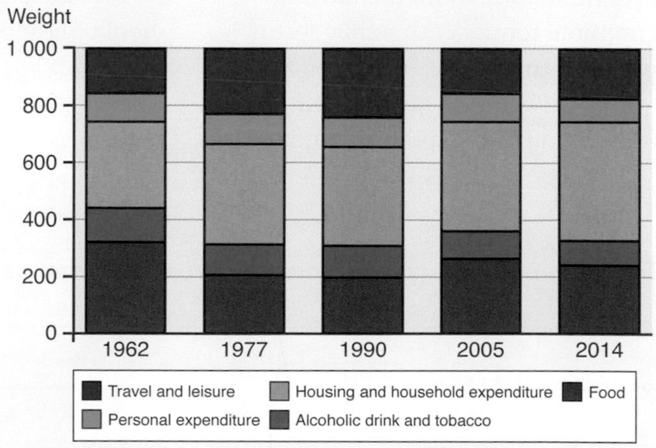

Source: adapted from www.ons.gov.uk.

Data Response Question

Inflation in Brazil

Before the conquest of hyper-inflation in Brazil in 1994, both Brazilian retailers and shoppers behaved in ways which seem strange today. Workers would be paid either at the end of the week or the end of the month. With prices going up every day, consumers would rush out with their pay packets and spend as much as they could afford. So retailers became used to sharp peaks in spending at the end of each week and a very large peak at the end of the month. There was little shopping around by consumers because they found it so difficult to keep up with changing prices. They had little or no idea what was a good price and what was expensive on any single shopping expedition.

As for retailers, they often made their profit not from sales but from getting free credit. They would receive goods on credit, sell them immediately, but only have to pay in 30 or 60 days' time. In the meantime, they could put the money in the bank and earn interest linked to the rate of inflation. In a good month, with inflation of, say, 100 per cent, they could double their money.

Source: adapted from *Economics*, 5th edition, Alain Anderton, Pearson.

Deflation in Spain

Spain is at risk of sliding into persistent deflation. Already, there have been months when prices have fallen. Spain could suffer badly if deflation becomes more permanent. When prices fall, it becomes harder to service debts, which are fixed in in nominal terms. With public sector debt close to 100 per cent of national income, the Spanish government remains one of the most indebted governments in Europe. Deflation could also threaten Spain's recovery from a deep recession. 'Once people start expecting deflation, they start postponing consumption because they think they will get more bang for their buck later on', said Professor Garicano from the London School of Economics.

Source: adapted from © the *Financial Times* 3.4.2014, All Rights Reserved.

Q

1. Using examples from the data, explain the difference between deflation and hyperinflation.

2. Analyse why consumers might bring forward or postpone spending and firms investment when there is hyperinflation and deflation.

3. Using examples from the data and your own knowledge, evaluate whether hyperinflation is more damaging to an economy than deflation.

Evaluation

Explain the different ways in which both hyperinflation and deflation can damage an economy, illustrating your answer with examples from the data and your own knowledge. As you do so, evaluate which is the more important. In your evaluation, remember that the percentage change in prices is likely to be far more with hyperinflation than deflation. In your conclusion, come to an overall judgement about the relative effects.

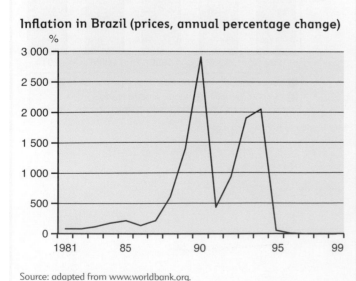

Figure 7

Inflation in Brazil (prices, annual percentage change)

Source: adapted from www.worldbank.org.

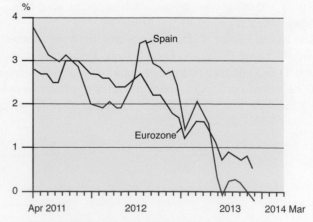

Figure 8

Inflation: Spain vs the eurozone (prices, annual percentage change)

Source: adapted from Thomson Reuters Datastream; © the *Financial Times* 3.4.2014. All Rights Reserved.

35 | Employment and unemployment

Key points

1. The labour force is made up of the self-employed, part-time workers, full-time workers and the unemployed.
2. Some workers who have jobs are under-employed.
3. The causes of unemployment can be classified as structural, frictional, seasonal, cyclical or real wage unemployment.
4. Changes in the rates of employment, unemployment and inactivity can have significant effects on the economy, as can migration and the skills level of the population.
5. Unemployment impacts on workers, firms, government and society.

Starter activity

Find out the local unemployment rate in your area. How does it compare to the national average? Think of two reasons why people might be unemployed. What effect does that unemployment have on the local community?

Definitions

In the UK, over 30 million people are in **employment**, defined as being in paid work. The majority of workers are **employees**, which means they are **employed** by another individual or a firm. A minority are **self-employed**, working for themselves and not as part of a company structure. Most are in **full-time** work, meaning that they work the hours and the days which are the norm for a particular job. A minority are **part-time workers** who work for a proportion of the hours of **full-time workers**. Some of those part-time workers are **underemployed**. They would prefer to work longer hours and some would prefer to have full-time rather than part-time jobs or be employees rather than self-employed.

Underemployment also covers those who are in jobs which do not reflect their skill level. For example, a university graduate who, unable to find a graduate job, works as a bartender would be considered underemployed.

Those in employment form part of the **labour force** which also includes the unemployed, those seeking work. The labour force, also known as the **active population**, includes most but not all of the **population of working age**. The population of working age is all people within a certain age range, typically between the statutory age for leaving school and the state retirement age. This could, for example, be 16-65. Some people of working age don't work and are not seeking work. They are **inactive**. This includes students, parents who stay at home to look after children, retired people within the age bracket and those who are unable to work because of sickness and disability.

The unemployed are those not in work but actively seeking work. **Unemployment** in the UK, as explained in more detail in the 'Thinking like an economist' section, is measured either through a monthly survey of the population or by counting the

number of people claiming benefits and able to work.

The number of people unemployed is measured at a point in time, like the 30th of each month. If unemployed is calculated monthly, it won't capture those who become unemployed on 1 December but get a new job by 29 December.

Question 1

Figure 1

Full-time jobs, part-time jobs and self-employment

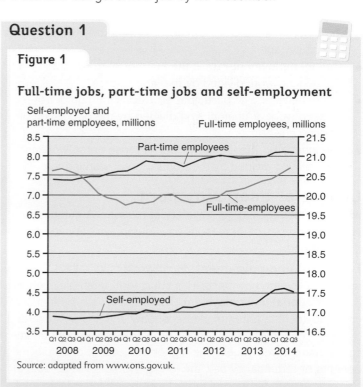

Source: adapted from www.ons.gov.uk.

(a) Compare the trend in full-time employment with that for self-employment and part-time employment over the period shown in the data. Use statistics to illustrate your answer.

(b) Calculate the number of people in employment in the Q3 2014.

(c) Explain which of the three categories of employment shown in the data might be part of hidden unemployment.

Maths Tip

Be very careful to identify which line goes with which vertical scale. Don't make the mistake of thinking that there are more part-time employees than full-time employees in the UK.

In fact, the flows of people becoming unemployed and getting new jobs are very large. For example, an estimated 2.3 million people in the UK in 2013 moved from being unemployed to being employed. Most of these will have been the **short-term unemployed**. The **long-term unemployed**, defined in the UK as being those out of work for more than 12 months, find it much more difficult to get jobs.

Some of those who are inactive in the population are, in fact, part of the **hidden unemployed**. When workers lose their jobs, they may become discouraged and not actively seek a new job. They may consider the costs of seeking work are not worth the likely chance of finding something suitable. However, if a suitable job came up and they were to get the job at little cost to themselves, then they would take it. Another group of the hidden unemployed are those who stay on in education rather than leaving and seeking work.

Again, if the employment situation were better, some in education would leave to take a job. A third group of the hidden unemployed are those who are underemployed as described above.

There are four important ratios, expressed as percentages, which are frequently quoted by economists and governments.

- The **employment rate** is the number of those in work (employees and the self-employed) divided by the population of working age.
- The **unemployment rate** is the number of those not in work but seeking work divided by the labour force.
- The **activity rate** or **participation rate** is the number of those in work or unemployed divided by the population of working age.
- The **inactivity rate** is the number of those not in work and unemployed divided by the population of working age.

Causes of unemployment

Unemployment occurs for a variety of reasons. A number of different types of, or reasons for, unemployment can be distinguished.

Frictional unemployment Most workers who lose their jobs move quickly into new ones. This short-term unemployment is called **frictional unemployment**. There will always be frictional unemployment in a free market economy and it is not regarded by most economists as a serious problem. The amount of time spent unemployed varies. The higher the level of unemployment benefits or redundancy pay, the longer workers will be able to afford to search for a good job without being forced into total poverty. Equally, the better the job information available to unemployed workers through newspapers, Jobcentre Plus etc. the shorter the time workers should need to spend searching for jobs.

Seasonal unemployment Some workers, such as construction workers or workers in the tourist industry, tend to work on a seasonal basis. **Seasonal unemployment** tends to rise in winter when some of these workers will be laid off, whilst unemployment falls in summer when they are taken on again. There is little that can be done to prevent this pattern occurring in a market economy where the demand for labour varies through the year.

Structural unemployment Far more serious is the problem of **structural unemployment**. This occurs when the demand for labour is less than its supply in an individual labour market in the economy. One example of structural unemployment is **regional unemployment**. Throughout the post-war period, the South of England has tended to be at full employment while regions such as Northern Ireland have consistently suffered unemployment. This has occurred because of a lack of mobility of factors of production between the regions. Another example is **sectoral unemployment**. The steel and shipbuilding industries in the UK declined sharply in the late 1970s and early 1980s leaving a considerable number of skilled workers unemployed. Unfortunately, their skills were no longer needed in the economy and without retraining and possible relocation, they were unable to adapt to the changing demand. **Technological unemployment** is another example of structural unemployment. Groups of workers across industries may be put out of work by new technology. Again, without retraining and geographical mobility, these workers may remain unemployed.

Cyclical or demand-deficient unemployment Economies tend to experience business cycles. These are movements from boom to recession over time. **Cyclical** or **demand-deficient unemployment** is unemployment which occurs when the economy is not in boom. It is when there is insufficient aggregate demand in the economy for all workers to get a job. In a recession, it is not just workers who are unemployed. Capital too is underutilised. So factories and offices can remain empty. Machinery and equipment can lie unused.

Real wage unemployment Real wage unemployment or **classical unemployment** exists when real wage rates are stuck at a level above that needed to reduce unemployment any further. Real wage rates are inflexible downwards. One cause of real wage unemployment is minimum wages. Unemployed

Question 2

The economy is currently in recession and the following workers are unemployed. Explain under which type of unemployment their circumstances might be classified.

(a) Katie Morris is a 30-year-old in Devon with a husband and two children. She works in the local hotel trade in the summer months on a casual basis but would like to work all the year round.

(b) John Penny, aged 22 and living in London, was made redundant a couple of weeks ago from a furniture store which closed down. He is currently seeking work in the retail sector.

(c) Manus O'Brien lives in Belfast in Northern Ireland. Aged 56, he last had a job 12 years ago working in a local factory.

(d) Nayara Jimenez, aged 31, lost her job six months ago working as a surveyor for an estate agent in Guildford in the south east of England. She is currently looking for another surveyor's job but the local housing market is very depressed.

(e) Khairul Fahmi, aged 40, has been out of work for 18 months. A former manager of a factory in the West Midlands, he is seeking a similar job within travelling distance of where he currently lives.

workers might be prepared to work for less than the minimum wage. Employers might be prepared to take on more workers but only if they could pay workers less than the minimum wage. However, the fact that employers are legally not allowed to pay workers less than the minimum wage means that those unemployed workers cannot get a job. Another cause of real wage unemployment is unemployed workers refusing to take low paid jobs because they can receive more in welfare benefits than working.

Cyclical unemployment is caused by a lack of demand in the economy. Frictional, seasonal, structural and real wage unemployment are caused by supply side factors. For example, if labour markets were more efficient, workers would move from job to job more quickly. So the time taken to get a new job would be shorter. In the case of frictional unemployment, an increase in the amount of information of jobs available to jobseekers would reduce the time they spent searching for a job. In the case of structural unemployment, making it easier to get cheap rented accommodation in areas of low unemployment would help workers in areas of higher unemployment to move. Better retraining of workers would also help reduce structural unemployment.

Using diagrams to illustrate unemployment

Unemployment can be illustrated using a variety of diagrams. Figure 2 shows a production possibility diagram. The economy is operating at its productive potential when it is somewhere on the production possibility frontier such as at point A. There are unemployed resources when the economy is operating within the frontier such as at point B.

Aggregate demand and supply analysis can be used to distinguish between demand side and supply side causes of unemployment. In Figure 3, the economy is in short run equilibrium at an output level of Y₁. However, what if the LRAS

Figure 2

The production possibility frontier

At any point on the production possibility frontier, there is no unemployment due to a lack of demand. At point B, there is cyclical unemployment.

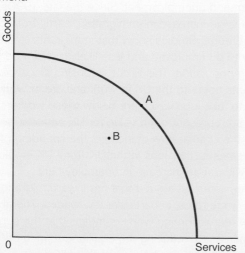

Figure 3

Cyclical unemployment

The economy is in equilibrium in the short run at an output level of OY₁. This is below the level of OY₂, shown by the long-run aggregate supply curve, where there would be no demand-deficient unemployment.

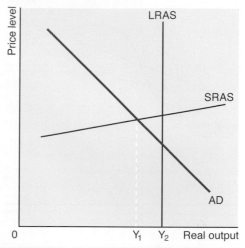

curve is to the right of this point? Then there must be cyclical or demand-deficient unemployment. The economy is in recession. Output at OY₁ does not represent the productive potential of the economy which is higher at OY₂. However, if there is an increase in aggregate demand, shown in Figure 4 by the shift in the aggregate demand curve from AD₁ to AD₂, full employment can be restored.

The same point can be illustrated using the concept of the output gap. The trend growth of the economy is shown by the upward sloping straight line in Figure 5. At point A, there is a negative output gap and the economy is in recession. So there is cyclical unemployment. An increase in demand will move the economy to B and eliminate demand-deficient unemployment.

Figure 4

Eliminating cyclical unemployment

Cyclical unemployment in the economy at the short-run equilibrium of OY₁ can be eliminated by raising aggregate demand, shown by the shift in the aggregate demand curve from AD₁ to AD₂.

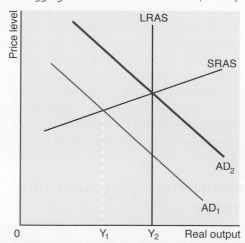

Figure 5

Unemployment and the output gap

Cyclical unemployment occurs if the actual level of income is below its long-run trend level, for example at A.

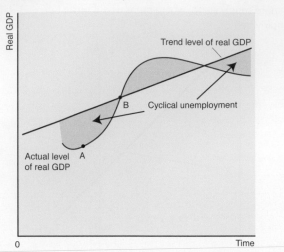

Supply-side causes of unemployment include frictional, seasonal and structural unemployment. In Figure 4, there is likely to be some frictional, seasonal and structural unemployment at an output level of OY_2. This is because the long-run aggregate supply curve is drawn on the assumption that there are limited resources and markets may work imperfectly. For example, some workers may be structurally unemployed because they do not have the right skills for the jobs on offer in the market. This lack of skills is taken into account when drawing the long run aggregate supply curve. If through training they acquire new skills and then get jobs, this leads to a rightward shift of the long run aggregate supply curve. A fall in frictional, seasonal and structural unemployment is shown by a rightward shift of the long run aggregate supply curve.

In Figure 5, the long-run trend line of growth is drawn assuming the gradual shift to the right in the long-run aggregate supply curve shown in Figure 4. If the long-run trend rate of growth is 2.5 per cent, then in Figure 4, the LRAS curve is shifting to the right by 2.5 per cent per year on average. So the trend rate of growth assumes there will be supply side improvements to the economy over time. This may or may not include supply-side improvements which reduce frictional, seasonal or structural unemployment. However, past evidence would suggest that existing structural unemployment tends to fall over time. Of course, there may be new supply-side shocks which lead to new structural unemployment. If the long run trend rate of growth could be raised, say from 2.5 per cent to three per cent, there is a greater likelihood that structural unemployment will fall. A rise in the long-run trend rate of growth would be shown by a shift upwards in the trend growth line in Figure 5.

Employment, unemployment and activity rates

Governments attempt to achieve full employment in their economies. Unemployment represents a significant cost and so

reducing unemployment rates is seen as economically desirable.

Some governments are also committed to increasing employment rates and reducing inactivity rates. Three main groups tend to be targeted.

- Women tend to have lower activity rates than men in rich industrialised economies. This is mainly due to women still being far more likely than men to give up their jobs to look after their children. Bringing more women into the labour force increases recorded GDP and so increases growth rates, a goal of governments. It increases tax revenues. It can also reduce welfare benefits where women are living in low income households. However, staying at home and looking after children in itself is a benefit to society even if it is not recorded in GDP. Not everyone agrees that encouraging mothers to go to work, particularly those with young children, brings overall benefits to society.

- Older workers, particularly over the age of 60, have lower activity rates. Many have retired even before they reach the state retirement age. Governments in Europe have been raising the retirement age in order to reduce the amount of government spending on pensions. At the same time, they have been encouraging workers to stay in work or get a new job rather than retire. They want to prevent individuals from claiming benefits because they have little or no income. So raising activity rates is part of the same policy of raising retirement ages in order to reduce the welfare benefit bill.

- Many governments in the past, including the UK government, have reduced politically sensitive unemployment rates by reclassifying some of the long-term unemployed as being unable to work due to disability. The result has been a significant increase in the amount spent on welfare benefits and lost output for the economy. Currently, some governments are attempting to reverse the process in order to cut the benefit bill. However, it is very difficult to get this group of people back into work. Many are genuinely unable to hold down a job because of physical or mental disabilities. Others have become so deskilled that they require a large amount of basic and costly training to help them to become employable.

Migration

Significant levels of migration can have an important impact on employment and unemployment. Since the late 1990s, the UK has seen a large increase in immigration, partly from countries in Eastern Europe. Studies show that immigrants to the UK are more likely to be employed and less likely to claim benefits than the existing population. This is not surprising since the majority of immigrants come to the UK to work and are of working age. They tend to take jobs which are below these workers' skill levels and so represent good value for UK employers.

Due to the circular flow of income, the spending of these workers creates further jobs in the UK. Total UK employment increases without an increase in unemployment.

However, it can be argued that net inward migration depresses wage rates, in particular low wages. The ability of UK firms to recruit foreign workers means that the supply of labour is increased, reducing the equilibrium price of labour, the wage rate. It can also be argued that UK workers with few skills are most affected by inward migration. This is because they are competing in the job market with migrants who are well motivated, have work skills and are prepared to work for low wages. UK workers who have low motivation to work, few skills and prefer to receive welfare benefits rather than work for the minimum wage can find themselves at a disadvantage when there is a plentiful supply of immigrant workers.

Question 3

Immigrants from the EU made a net contribution to government finances of £2 732 per year in the decade to 2011. In total, EU inward migration added £22bn to tax revenues over the whole ten year period. These figures come from a report published by the Migration Advisory Committee. It found that the employment rate of UK-born workers has been 'practically unchanged' despite the influx of 500 00 migrants from central and eastern Europe after EU expansion in 2004. In contrast, non-European migrants only contributed a net £162 per person per year to public finances in the decade to 2011. One in six of Britain's 13 million low-skilled jobs are now held by migrants. Some migrants are exploited by their employers and are paid less than the minimum wage. In a separate study, the Organisation for Economic Co-operation and Development (OECD) found that immigration leads to higher pay for native workers. Immigrants are in general more educated than native workers. Immigration is 'likely to create more opportunities for the receiving economy', wrote the researchers.

Source: adapted from © the *Financial Times* 9.7.2014, 30.9.2014
All Rights Reserved.

(a) Explain two advantages to the UK of inward migration of workers.

(b) Analyse what impact the fact that migrants are generally 'more educated than native workers' might have on (i) native UK workers and (ii) UK firms.

Skills

Economies become progressively more complex over time. Fifty years ago, it was still possible to find a large number of jobs in the UK where workers had no need to read or write, for example.

Today, the average skill level required by workers is much higher and will increase in the future. For the UK economy to maintain its employment levels in a competitive global market, it has to increase the skills of its workforce over time.

Problems occur when skills required by jobs are not matched by those of job seekers. UK engineering companies, for example, frequently complain they are unable to recruit skilled workers even though there are unemployed workers in the local area. This is an example of structural unemployment. If firms won't train workers, the government has to step in to correct this market failure. Training, however, is costly. The result is that many unemployed workers become long-term unemployed because their skills are not good enough to take jobs on offer.

The costs of unemployment

Long term unemployment is generally considered to be a great social evil. This is perhaps not surprising in view of the following costs of unemployment.

Costs to the unemployed and their dependants The people who are likely to lose the most from unemployment are the unemployed themselves. One obvious cost is the loss of income that could have been earned had the person been in a job. Offset against this is the value of any benefits that the worker might receive and any value placed on the extra leisure time which an unemployed person has at his or her disposal. For most unemployed people, it is likely that they will be net financial losers.

The costs to the unemployed, however, do not finish there. Evidence suggests that unemployed people and their families suffer in a number of other ways. One simple but very important problem for them is the stigma of being unemployed. Unemployment is often equated with failure both by the unemployed themselves and by society in general. Many feel degraded by the whole process of signing on, receiving benefits and not being able to support themselves or their families. Studies suggest that the unemployed suffer from a wide range of social problems including above average incidence of stress, marital breakdown, suicide, physical illness and mental instability, and that they have higher death rates compared with those in employment.

For the short-term unemployed, the costs are relatively low. Many will lose some earnings, although a few who receive large redundancy payments may benefit financially from having lost their job. The social and psychological costs are likely to be limited too.

However, the long-term unemployed are likely to be major losers on all counts. The long-term unemployed suffer one more cost. Evidence suggests that the longer the period out of work, the less likely it is that the unemployed person will find a job. There are two reasons for this. First, being out of work reduces the human capital of workers. They lose work skills and are not being trained in the latest developments in their occupation. Second, employers use length of time out of work as a crude way of sifting through applicants for a job. For an employer, unemployment is likely to mean that the applicant is, to some extent, deskilled. There is a fear that the unemployed worker will not be capable of doing the job after a spell of unemployment. It could show that the worker has personality problems and might be a disruptive employee. It could also be an indication that other employers have turned down the applicant for previous jobs and hence it would be rational to save time and not consider the applicant for this job. The long-term unemployed are then in a catch-22 situation. They can't get a job unless they have recent employment experience. However, they can't get recent employment experience until they get a job.

Costs to local communities Costs of unemployment to local communities are more difficult to establish. Some have suggested that unemployment, particularly amongst the young, leads to increased crime, violence on the streets and vandalism. Areas of high unemployment tend to become run down. Shops go out of business. Households have no spare money to look after their properties and their gardens. Increased vandalism further destroys the environment.

Costs to the government The cost of unemployment to the taxpayer is a heavy one. On the one hand, government has to pay out increased benefits. On the other hand, government loses revenue because these workers would have paid taxes if they had been employed. For instance, they would have paid income tax and National Insurance contributions on their earnings. They would also have paid more in VAT and excise duties because they would have been able to spend more. So taxpayers not only pay more taxes to cover for increased government spending but they also have to pay more because they have to make up the taxes that the unemployed would have paid if they had been in work. Governments also provide help to the unemployed to get a job. They might provide information about available jobs, such as through Job Centres in the UK. They may provide training schemes or subsidise employers who take on unemployed workers.

Costs to the economy as a whole Taxpayers paying money to the unemployed is not a loss for the economy as a whole. It is a transfer payment which redistributes existing resources within the economy. The actual loss to the whole economy is two-fold. First, there is the loss of output which those workers now unemployed could have produced had they been in work. The economy could have produced more goods and services which would then have been available for consumption. Second, there are the social costs such as increased violence and depression which are borne by the unemployed and the communities in which they live.

Costs to consumers The unemployed as consumers lose out because they are able to spend less. Consumers in areas of high unemployment also lose out because local shopping centres tend to be run down and don't offer the range of shops available to those in areas of low unemployment.

Costs to firms Firms suffer because unemployment represents a loss of demand in the economy. If there were full employment, the economy would be more buoyant and there would be more spending. Long-term unemployment also reduces the pool of skilled workers that a firm could hire.

Question 4

A report by Sheffield Hallam University has found that the south Wales valleys are still suffering the effects of large scale mine closures 30 years ago. In the Welsh valleys, 17 per cent of all adults of working age were on benefits compared to a national figure of 11 per cent. The rate of disability allowance claimants was 10.7 per cent, double the national average. One in five of the working age population had no qualifications and about 44 per cent of those in work were employed in unskilled manual jobs, compared to 36 per cent nationally. Average wages and average output per head of the population were lower than the national average.

Source: adapted from © the *Financial Times* 20.6.2014, All Rights Reserved.

Explain the likely costs of high unemployment in the south Wales valleys to (a) workers and those seeking work; (b) local communities; (c) government.

Key Terms

Active population - those in work or actively seeking work; also known as the labour force.
Activity rate or participation rate - the number of those in work or unemployed divided by the population of working age expressed as a percentage.
Cyclical or demand-deficient unemployment - when there is insufficient demand in the economy for all workers who wish to work at current wage rates to obtain a job.
Employed - the number of people in paid work.
Employees - workers employed by another individual or firm.
Employment - those in paid work.
Employment rate - the number of those in work divided by the population of working age expressed as a percentage.
Frictional unemployment - when workers are unemployed for short lengths of time between jobs.
Full-time workers - workers who work hours and the days which are the norm for a particular job.
Hidden unemployed - partly those in the population who would take a job if offered, but are not in work and are not currently seeking work; and partly those who are underemployed.
Inactive - the number of those not in work and not unemployed.
Inactivity rate - the number of those not in work and not unemployed divided by the population of working age expressed as a percentage.
Labour force - those in work or actively seeking work; also know as the active population.
Long-term unemployed - in the UK, those unemployed for more than one year.

Part-time workers - workers who only work a fraction of the hours and the days which are the norm for a particular job.
Population of working age - the total number of people aged between the statutory school leaving age and the state retirement age.
Real wage or classical unemployment - when workers are unemployed because real wages are too high and inflexible downwards, leading to insufficient demand for workers from employers.
Seasonal unemployment - when workers are unemployed at certain times of the year, such as building workers or agricultural workers in winter.
Self-employed - workers who work on their own account and are not employees.
Short-term unemployed - in the UK, those unemployed for less than a year.
Structural unemployment - when the pattern of demand and production changes leaving workers unemployed in labour markets where demand has shrunk. Examples of structural unemployment are regional unemployment, sectoral unemployment or technological unemployment.
Underemployed - those who would work more hours if available or are in jobs which are below their skill level.
Unemployed - those not in work but seeking work.
Unemployment - occurs when individuals are without a job but are actively seeking work.
Unemployment rate - the number of those not in work, but seeking work, divided by the labour force expressed as a percentage.

Thinking like an economist

Measuring unemployment

In economic theory, unemployment is defined as those without a job but who are seeking work at current wage rates. Measuring the number of unemployed in an economy, however, is more difficult than economic theory might suggest. In the UK, there are two ways in which unemployed is calculated: the claimant count and the Labour Force Survey (LFS) measures.

The claimant count

The claimant count measures unemployment by counting the number of people claiming benefits for being unemployed. It was the main measure of UK unemployment until 1997. However, it was open to political manipulation. In the 1980s and 1990s, the UK government introduced over 30 different changes to the way in which its was calculated to reduce the politically sensitive headline unemployment figure. The claimant count is also not an internationally recognised way of measuring unemployment. Hence it cannot be used to compare UK unemployment levels with those in other countries.

LFS (or ILO) unemployment

LFS (or ILO) unemployment is calculated using Labour Force Survey statistics. Each month 44 000 households with over 100 000 individuals are surveyed. The questionnaire used covers economic activity as well as household size and structure, accommodation details, and basic demographic characteristics such as age, sex, marital status and ethnic origin. To be classified as unemployed, an individual has to be without a paid job, be available to start a job within a fortnight and has either looked for work at some time in the previous four weeks or been waiting to start a job already obtained.

This measure of unemployment is based on an international standard set by the International Labour Organization (ILO). The UK is required by EU law to measure unemployment according to this definition. It then provides a way in which unemployment can be compared between countries.

LFS unemployment compared to the claimant count

Figure 6 shows that LFS unemployment figures differ significantly from claimant count figures. LFS unemployment tends to be above claimant count unemployment and since 1994, there has been a growing divergence between the two.

LFS unemployment is likely to be above the claimant count figure because the claimant count excludes a number of key groups of unemployed workers.

- Many female unemployed workers are actively looking for work (and are therefore included in LFS unemployment) but are not entitled to benefits for being unemployed. For instance, they might not have built up sufficient National Insurance contributions to qualify for unemployment benefit, a National Insurance benefit. They may also be living in a household where the husband or partner is earning too high a wage for them to qualify for means-tested benefits.

Figure 6

LFS and claimant count measures of unemployment

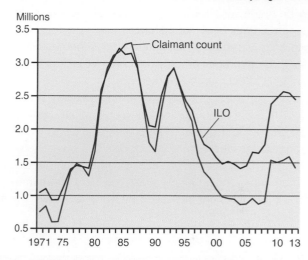

Source: adapted from www.ons.gov.uk.

- Older, particularly male, workers in their 50s and 60s may be collecting a pension from their previous employer or be supported financially by their spouse. They are therefore not entitled to benefits but may be actively seeking work.
- Workers are not entitled to register as unemployed with the DWP until they have been out of work for a number of weeks. However, anyone interviewed for the LFS count who is unemployed and is looking for work is counted as unemployed regardless of how long they have been unemployed.

Figure 7

Employment and unemployment, LFS measures, millions

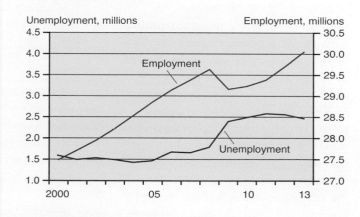

Source: adapted from www.ons.gov.uk.

The claimant count, however, may include some unemployed who would not be included in the LFS count. For instance, those working in the **hidden economy** may claim benefits for being unemployed but actually be in work, usually as a self-employed worker.

Over and underestimations of unemployment

Both the LFS and claimant counts could be argued to underestimate overall unemployment.

- They do not include part-time workers who are actively seeking full-time work, for instance.
- Those on government training and work schemes who would prefer to be in proper employment are not included. This particularly affects young workers.
- There are some out of work who are not actively seeking work or receiving benefits for being unemployed but who would take a job if offered. This mainly applies to women bringing up families. Figure 7 supports this point. Between 2008 and 2013, despite the economy falling into recession and then experiencing a very weak recovery, the number of people in employment increased by 400 000. Over the same period, unemployment increased by 700 000.

- Some unemployed workers in the 1980s and 1990s were moved from the unemployment registers onto sickness and disability benefits. Between 1979 and 2004, the numbers on sickness and disability benefits rose from 750 000 to 2.6 million. Today, areas of the country with high unemployment rates also have above average rates of people on sickness and disability benefits. Governments are now attempting to get some of these people off benefits and back into work. However, currently they are not counted as unemployed.

However, both measures of unemployment could be argued to overestimate unemployment. Some of those out of work find it almost impossible to get a job. Those with physical and mental disabilities, some ex-criminals or some with no qualifications find the job market very difficult. Some economists would argue that these workers are unemployable and therefore should not be counted as unemployed. A minority of those working in the hidden economy may claim benefits and may declare on surveys that they are out of work and seeking work.

Data Response Question

Unemployment rates

Normally, in a recession, unemployment rises and the number of people in work falls even more as some of those unemployed disappear from the labour force. The recession that started in 2008 was different. Between 2008 and 2012, measured unemployment did rise by over a million people but there was little change in the number of people in work. Unemployment would have been much worse, but for many of those losing their full-time jobs getting new jobs on a part-time basis or becoming self-employed. By the end of 2013, 900 000 more people were in work than at the start of the recession in 2008. But 200 000 fewer people were in full-time work, there were 500 000 more part-time workers and 600 000 extra self-employed workers. On average, part time workers and the self employed earn much less per hour worked than full time employees.

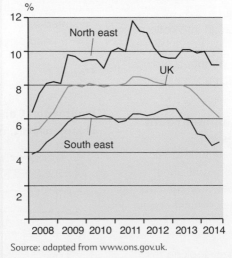

Figure 8

Regional unemployment rates

Source: adapted from www.ons.gov.uk.

This was one factor which contributed to average real household income being six per cent lower in 2012-13 compared to 2006-07.

Source: adapted from www.ons.gov.uk.

Q

1. Using Figure 8, analyse why, between 2008 and 2013, it is likely that (a) the North East suffered structural unemployment and (b) the UK economy suffered cyclical unemployment.

2. Evaluate whether the economic costs of the rise in hidden unemployment were greater than the rise in measured unemployment between 2008 and 2014.

Evaluation
Analyse the difference between hidden unemployment and measured unemployment in an introductory paragraph. Then analyse the costs for hidden unemployment, and do the same measured unemployment. Weigh up the relative costs of the two types of unemployment. Indicate what extra information you would need to make a more informed decision.

36 Balance of payments

Key points

1. Economies are interconnected through international trade.
2. The balance of payments accounts are split into two main parts. The current account records payments for the exports and imports of goods and services. The capital and financial accounts record saving, investment and speculative flows of money.
3. The balance of payments accounts must always balance. However, component parts of the accounts may be positive or negative. If there is a deficit on the current account, then the inflows on the capital and financial accounts must be greater than outflows.
4. A balance on the current account of the balance of payments is a macroeconomic objective of governments. For the UK, this may conflict with objectives to reduce unemployment and increase short-term economic growth.
5. A current account deficit on the balance of payments is most unlikely to be financed by government. The public sector deficit is different from a current account deficit.

Starter activity

Do you own a mobile phone? Where have it and its components been manufactured? To find out something about this, do an Internet search. If world trade stopped tonight, list 10 things you would not be able to buy in the future.

The interconnectedness of economies

Over time, the world economy has been growing more interconnected. There are four key ways in which this process of globalisation has been taking place.

- The proportion of output of an individual nation economy which is traded internationally is growing.
- There is ever-increasing ownership of physical and financial assets, such as companies or shares or loans in one country by economic actors in another country.
- Individuals are migrating in increasing numbers from one country to another.
- Technology is being shared between countries on a faster basis.

In the UK, for example, approximately one quarter of all output is exported. Despite producing more cars for export than we import, all the car manufacturing plants in the UK of any size are owned by foreign companies. In the 12 months to June 2014, 583 000 people came as immigrants to the UK, whilst 323 000 emigrated out of a population of 64.1 million.

The balance of payments account

Governments keep records of the numerous ways in which economies are interconnected. One important record is the **balance of payments account**. This is a record of all financial dealings over a period of time between economic agents of one country and all other countries. Balance of payments accounts can be split into two components:

- the **current account** where payments for the purchase and sale of goods and services are recorded;

- the **capital** and **financial accounts** where flows of money associated with saving, investment, speculation and currency stabilisation are recorded.

Flows of money into the country are given a positive (+) sign on the accounts. Flows of money out of the country are given a negative (-) sign.

The current account

The current account on the balance of payments is itself split into several components.

Trade in goods Trade in goods is often called trade in **visibles**. This is trade in raw materials such as copper and oil, semi-manufactured goods such as car components and finished manufactured goods such as cars, tablets or mobile phones. Visible exports are goods which are sold to foreigners. Goods leave the country, whilst payment for these goods goes in the opposite direction. Hence visible exports of, say, cars result

Question 1

A country has the following international transactions on current account: exports of manufactured goods £20 billion; imports of food £10 billion; earnings from foreign tourists £5 billion; interest, profits and dividends paid to foreigners £4 billion; purchase of oil from abroad £8 billion; earnings of nationals working overseas which are repatriated £7 billion; sale of coal to foreign countries £2 billion; payments by foreigners to domestic financial institutions for services rendered £1 billion.

(a) Which of these items are: (i) visible exports; (ii) exports of services; (iii) primary income and secondary income credits; (iv) visible imports; (v) imports of services; (vi) income and current transfer debits.?

(b) Calculate: (i) the balance of trade; (ii) the balance on all invisibles; (iii) the current balance.

(c) How would your answers to (b) be different if it cost the country £3 billion to transport its exports (i) in its own ships and (ii) in the ships of other countries?

in an inward flow of money and are recorded with a positive sign on the balance of payments account. Visible imports are goods which are bought by domestic residents from foreigners. Goods come into the country whilst money flows out. Hence visible imports of, say, wheat are given a minus sign on the balance of payments. The difference between the value of visible exports and visible imports is known as the **balance of trade**.

Trade in services A wide variety of services is traded internationally, including financial services such as banking and insurance, transport services such as shipping and air travel, and tourism. Trade in services is an example of trade in **invisibles**. These are intangible services. Exports of invisibles are bought by foreigners. So an American tourist paying for a stay in a London hotel is an invisible export. So too is a Chinese company buying insurance in the City of London or a Taiwanese company hiring a UK owned ship. With invisibles, money flows into the UK, as it would if a French company bought a machine manufactured in the UK, a visible export for the UK. Hence, on the official UK balance of payments accounts, invisible service exports are called export credits in services. Imports of services for the UK are services which are bought from other countries. A holiday taken by a UK national in Spain would be an invisible import for the UK. So too would be a UK firm hiring a private jet from a German company. With invisible imports, money flows abroad. Hence they are called debits on the official UK balance of payments accounts.

Primary and secondary income Not all flows of money result from trade in goods and services. **Primary income** results from the loan of factors of production abroad. For the UK, most of this income is generated from interest, profits and dividends on assets owned abroad. Equally, interest, profits and dividends on UK assets owned by foreigners have to be paid out. For some countries, their main income comes from the repatriation of earnings from national workers in foreign countries. For example, a Pakistani national may work in Kuwait and send back income to support his family in Pakistan. **Secondary income** is a range of mainly government transfers to and from overseas organisations such as the European Union. Primary and secondary income are examples of invisibles along with trade in services.

The **current balance** is the difference between the value of exports and total imports. It can also be calculated by adding the balance of trade in goods with that of services, income and current transfers.

The current account balance can be in surplus or deficit.

- A **current account surplus** occurs when exports are greater than imports. The monies flowing into the country from trade in goods and services, as well as primary and secondary income, are greater than monies flowing out of the country from these transactions.
- A **current account deficit** occurs when imports are greater than exports. The monies flowing out of the country from trade in goods and services, as well as primary and secondary income, are greater than monies flowing into the country from these transactions.

Current account imbalances and macroeconomic objectives

Governments have four major macroeconomic objectives. These are to achieve:

- low unemployment, achieving full employment;
- low and stable inflation, avoiding deflation;
- economic growth on a par with similar economies;
- balance of payments equilibrium, including equilibrium on the current account.

For the UK, there are potential conflicts in achieving these objectives. High economic growth tends to be associated with low unemployment but increased inflationary pressures. Unlike some other economies, high economic growth in the UK in recent decades has never been caused by a boom in exports. Instead, it tends to arise from increases in consumption spending or government spending, leading to a rise in aggregate demand. The rise in consumption and government spending leads to increased demand for imports. Hence, high economic growth is linked, for the UK, with a deterioration in the current account on the balance of payments. When the economy has gone into recession, with aggregate demand falling, the demand for imports has tended to fall. Inflation tends to fall and unemployment rises. The current account on the balance of payments tends to improve.

Governments would like to see export-led growth. This is a rise in economic growth due to a rise in exports. This would reduce unemployment and improve the current account balance on the balance of payments. The economic cost might be higher inflation. However, despite frequent export initiatives, successive UK governments have never achieved this.

Government deficits and balance of payments deficits

One common mistake is to assume that any current account deficit is paid for by the government. Another common mistake

Key Terms

Balance of payments account - a record of all financial dealings over a period of time between economic agents of one country and all other countries.

Balance of trade - the value of visible exports minus visible imports.

Capital and financial accounts - that part of the balance of payments account where flows of savings, investment and currency are recorded.

Current account - that part of the balance of payments account where payments for the purchase and sale of goods and services are recorded.

Current balance - the difference between the value of total exports (visible and invisible) and total imports.

Current account deficit or surplus - a deficit exists when imports are greater than exports; a surplus exists when the value of exports are greater than imports.

Invisibles - trade in services, transfers of income and other payments or receipts.

Visibles - trade in goods.

is to assume that government borrowing is the same as the current account deficit. The current account is made up of billions of individual transactions. Each one is financed in a different way. So a UK firm importing machinery will use different finance from a family taking a holiday in France. A Chinese firm buying specialist car parts from a UK company will finance this in a different way from a German firm buying insurance from a broker at Lloyds of London. If a current account deficit has been caused mainly by excessive government spending, then the government is likely to have borrowed at least some of the money from abroad. However, a current account deficit may be caused mainly by private consumers and firms buying too

many imports and borrowing the money from abroad to pay for them. The relationship between the current account deficit, private sector borrowing and government borrowing is therefore complex and depends upon individual circumstances.

Governments may choose to attempt to correct current account deficits or surpluses. They have a variety of ways in which they could attempt this, which have various advantages and disadvantages. These are discussed later. However, governments may choose to do nothing and allow free market forces to correct any imbalances. The last time the UK government and the Bank of England attempted to influence the current account directly was in the 1970s.

Thinking like an economist

The parts of the current account

The Office for National Statistics divides the UK current account into four parts, shown in Table 1.

- Trade in goods. Exports of goods minus imports of goods is equal to the balance of trade in goods.
- Trade in services. The main services traded are transport (such as shipping or air transport), travel and tourism, insurance and other financial services, and royalties and licence fees.
- Primary income. Some countries, such as Pakistan or Egypt, earn substantial amounts from the repatriation of income from nationals working abroad. For the UK, such income is relatively unimportant. Nearly all income in the UK balance of payments accounts relates to UK investments abroad and to foreign investments in the UK (investment income).

- Secondary income. The two largest components of secondary income are transfers related to the UK's membership of the EU such as agricultural subsidies or regional grants and non-life insurance payments.

Visibles in the account are the trade in goods. Invisibles are the trade in services, primary income and secondary income. In terms of relative size, invisibles outweigh visibles. Table 1 shows that the UK's current balance is crucially dependent not just on trade in goods and services, but also on income from foreign investments. Comparing this to a household, it is as if the financial soundness of the household is dependent not just on wage earnings and spending, but also very much on interest and dividends on savings and also on payments of interest on loans.

Table 1 The current balance, 2013 (£m)

Trade in goods		
Export of goods	306 810	
Import of goods	417 006	
Balance on trade in goods		- 110 196
Trade in services		
Export of services	204 465	
Import of services	126 369	
Balance of trade in services		78 096
Balance on trade in goods and services		- 32 100
Primary income		
Credits	161 756	
Debits	174 890	
Balance		- 13 134
Secondary income		
Credits	17 621	
Debits	44 783	
Balance		- 27 162
Current balance[1]		- 72 395

1. Balances may not add up due to rounding.
Source: adapted from The Pink Book, 2013, *The United Kingdom Balance of Payments*, Office for National Statistics.

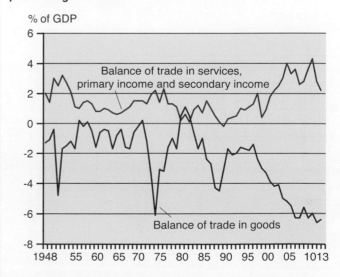

Figure 1

The balance of trade in goods and the balance of trade in services, primary income and secondary income, as a percentage of GDP

Source: adapted from www.statistics.gov.uk.

The current account over time

Since the Second World War, there has been a number of consistent trends on the UK current account.

- The balance of trade in goods has been negative, as can be seen from Figure 1. Visible exports have tended to be less than visible imports.
- The overall balance on trade in services, primary income and secondary income has been positive. Invisible credits have been greater than invisible debits.
- Breaking down invisibles, the balance of trade in services has nearly always been positive - more services have been sold abroad than have been bought from abroad. The primary balance has usually been positive too. The main reason is that investment income earned abroad has tended to be greater than investment income paid to foreigners. However, the primary balance fluctuates more from year to year than the balance of trade in services. Secondary incomes since the 1960s have always been negative. Since joining the EU in 1973, approximately half of the negative balance has been due to the UK paying more into EU coffers than receiving in grants.

The size of the current account balances

In the 1950s and 1960s, the current account posed a major problem for the UK. At the time, the value of the pound was fixed against other currencies. In years when the current account went into deficit, currency speculators tended to sell pounds sterling in the hope that the government would be forced to devalue the pound, i.e. make it less valuable against other currencies. Quite small current account deficits as a percentage of GDP, as in 1960 or in 1964, thus presented large problems for the government of the day.

From the 1970s, the pound was allowed to float, changing its value from minute to minute on the foreign exchange markets. Figure 2 shows that since 1984, the current account has

consistently been in deficit. It could be argued that this should pose long-term problems for the UK. If the UK is consistently spending more than it is earning abroad, this will lead to a long term build-up of debt. Just as households which consistently borrow more and more money should get into financial difficulties, so too should a country.

Figure 3

Balance of trade in services, primary income and secondary income

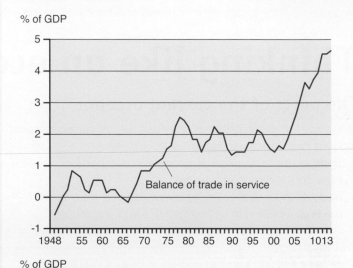

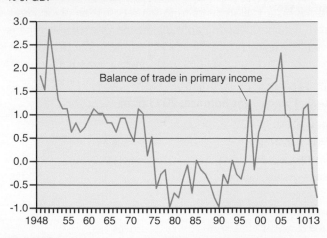

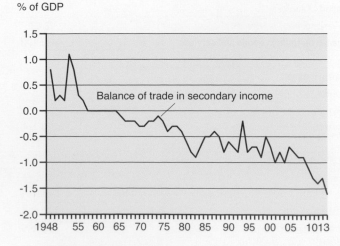

Source: adapted from www.statistics.gov.uk.

Figure 2

The current balance as a percentage of GDP

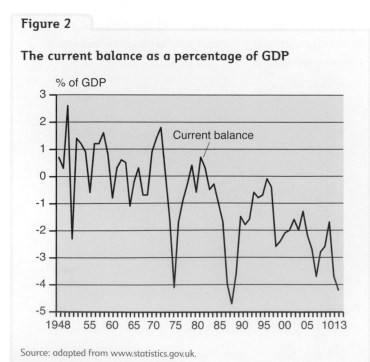

Source: adapted from www.statistics.gov.uk.

There are two reasons which might explain why the UK has not encountered problems relating to its persistent current account deficits since the 1970s. One is that the deficits are manageable given the economy's average growth rate of around 2.5 per cent over the period. For a household, so long as income is rising faster than debt, there should be no debt problem. Certainly, the financial markets have not shown any particular concern about the UK's current account deficits. Foreign lenders have not refused to lend UK borrowers any more money as they did, for example, to countries such as Mexico, South Korea or Poland when they had debt crises over the past 30 years.

The other reason is that the current account deficit is not the main determinant of the net debt owed by UK citizens, businesses and government to foreigners. The main determinant is changing asset values, such as stock market prices in New York or bond prices in Frankfurt. As Figure 4 shows, since 1966, the net assets of the UK, the difference between what UK households, businesses and government own abroad and what they owe to foreigners, has varied from plus 21.1 per cent of GDP in 1986 to minus 19.7 in 1999. Such huge swings are accounted for in small part by deficits and surpluses on the current account but mainly by changes in asset values of investments.

Figure 4

UK net international assets as a percentage of GDP

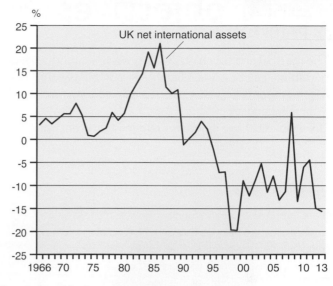

Source: adapted from www.statistics.gov.uk.

Data Response Question

UK exports

UK exports to Chile, China and the United Arab Emirates grew faster than those to any other countries last year, according to published figures. Exports to Chile rose by 72 per cent. This was driven largely by deliveries of North Sea oil, but there was also a rise in sales of machinery, mostly for the copper mining industry. Exports of cars, food and drink were also up. Waitrose, the supermarket group, has been exporting to Chile for just over a year to supply the Unimarc store chain. It sells into 300 shops, with a third offering more than 70 Waitrose products from mayonnaise to tea.

John Cridland, director-general of the CBI employers' group, said Britain needed a 'national export crusade' to lift exports. He said that Germany had been the best export performer over the past decade by selling capital goods such as machinery to emerging economies like China, India and

Brazil. But Britain could take the lead because its companies were capable of selling consumer goods and services to the emerging middle classes of these countries. He said: 'The focus has shifted from capital to consumer. They want British insurance, British coats, British handbags, British music, British architects, British cars, a whole range of consumer goods and products and we've got them.'

Source: adapted from © the *Financial Times* 20.7.2014, All Rights Reserved.

Q

1. John Cridland gave a list of six possible British exports from insurance to cars. Explain which of these would be classified as exports of goods and which would be exports of services.

2. Explain, using examples from the data, how countries are interrelated through international trade.

3. Evaluate whether a 'national export crusade' to lift exports would benefit the UK economy.

Evaluation

Analyse the possible benefits to the UK economy of increased exports using your understanding of macroeconomic objectives of government. Then analyse the possible costs to the UK economy of increased aggregate demand arising from increased exports. Evaluate the relative importance of benefits to costs.

Possible macroeconomic objectives

Key points

1. The macroeconomic objectives of government include high economic growth, low unemployment, low and stable inflation and a balance of payments equilibrium on current account.
2. Macroeconomic objectives also include limiting fiscal deficits and might include objectives about income inequality.
3. Governments have objectives relating to the environment.

Starter activity

Find out the current rate of economic growth, the rate of unemployment, the inflation rate and the level of the current account deficit on the balance of payments. Why might a high rate of economic growth benefit you and the household in which you live? Why might a high rate of inflation impose costs on you and your household? Why might a high rate of unemployment affect you in the future?

Government objectives

Governments attempt to manipulate the economy so as to improve its economic performance. Different economies perform in different ways. So what is possible for the UK economy might be very different from what is possible for the Chinese economy, the Afghan economy or the Serbian economy. However, typically governments have macroeconomic objectives relating to four variables: economic growth, unemployment, inflation and the current account on the balance of payments. They will also have objectives in relation to government budgets, the environment and income inequality.

Economic growth

All other things being equal, governments attempt to maximise the growth rate of their economies. For low and middle income countries like China, Uganda or Brazil, it may be possible to reach annual growth rates of up to ten per cent or even more. For high income countries such as the UK, the USA or Germany, an annual growth rate of 2.5 per cent might be possible. High rates of growth in low and middle income countries can be achieved, for example by moving large numbers of workers from low-productivity agriculture to higher-productivity manufacturing. Using modern technology can also significantly increase output per worker.

High income countries, however, have already been through an industrialisation process and are at the forefront of technological developments. Moreover, a number of high income countries, including Japan and Italy, face a rapidly ageing population, where the number of workers in the economy is falling. Achieving even a 2.5 per cent growth rate is now seen as challenging in these circumstances.

Unemployment and employment

Governments would like to see unemployment as low as possible without there being inflationary pressure in the economy. It is impossible to have zero unemployment in a market economy because there is always frictional and seasonal unemployment. The UK government has no official target for UK unemployment. Unemployment rates in the 1950s and 1960s, an era of full employment, were around 1.5 per cent. Over the past 20 years, the best unemployment figure was a 4.8 per cent rate achieved in 2004. Under present circumstances, a five per cent rate would be seen as a considerable policy achievement.

Recent governments have also been keen to expand employment. Higher employment should increase tax revenues and reduce welfare benefits to the unemployed and those on low incomes. Getting people out of unemployment and off benefits has been a major policy objective in recent years.

Inflation and deflation

Central banks and governments in the industrialised world have tended to set inflation targets of around two per cent. This is low but positive inflation. Higher inflation is seen as undesirable, particularly because of the fear that inflation will then increase even further. On the other hand, governments want to avoid deflation. Deflation is seen as being linked to recession and low or negative economic growth.

The balance of payments on current account

Governments aim for the balance of payments on current account to be broadly in balance over time. Economies where the current account is persistently in surplus are seen to be 'strong' economies whilst those running persistent deficits are seen to be 'struggling' or 'weak' economies. However, the reality is far more complex than these initial judgements. Countries can run persistent surpluses, for example, and have low economic growth rates. Other countries can run persistent deficits and grow very fast over time without significant economic problems.

Very large current account deficits, measured as a percentage of GDP can, however, be very dangerous. If borrowers in these countries reach a point where they can no longer repay their loans, as Argentina did in 2001 or Greece in 2009, then there will be an economic crisis and a sudden large fall in GDP.

Government budgets

Since the financial crisis of 2008, the importance of fiscal (i.e. government) budget deficits as a major economic objective has grown. If a country is growing at around 2.5 per cent per year and there is two per cent inflation and low interest rates, then a fiscal deficit of around three per cent per year will probably maintain a stable level of national debt (the sum total of all outstanding government borrowing) as a percentage of GDP.

Following the financial crisis of 2008, a number of countries including the UK, the USA, Greece and Spain saw their fiscal deficits grow to over 10 per cent of GDP. These levels are unsustainable in the long term because it means that governments have to borrow far more money than they expect to repay with interest in the future. In the short term, however, large fiscal deficits which increase the national debt from, say, 40 per cent of GDP to 100 per cent of GDP, are sustainable so long as the fiscal deficit is reduced to manageable levels over time.

Economists disagree about the path to long-term equilibrium. Some argue that fiscal deficits should be cut as quickly as possible even if this means negative economic growth and significant increases in unemployment. Others argue that cutting fiscal deficits at a slower pace is better because it allows the economy to grow faster, leading to a quicker rebound in tax revenues and fall in welfare payments to the unemployed.

The environment

There is no simple measure of the impact of economic activity on the environment. Governments therefore have a wide variety of objectives in relation to the environment. These might range from global warming to pollution on beaches to air quality in cities. There is a range of opinion about whether economic growth is good or bad for the environment.

Environmentalists tend to be anti-growth, arguing that any increased economic activity will damage the planet. Pro-growth economists tend to argue that increases in output and improvements in technology allow economies to clean up their environments and reduce pollution.

Income distribution

Economists and politicians disagree about income distribution policies. Very broadly, right-wing economists and politicians tend to argue that inequality is positive because it increases incentives to work and to take economic risks. This increases economic growth rates, raising incomes for all in society. They therefore are against policies which reduce inequalities, particularly increases in taxes on higher earners and businesses.

Left-wing economists and politicians tend to argue that, on principles of fairness, everyone in society should have access to a certain standard of living and that free markets lead to high levels of inequality. Therefore, governments need to intervene to reduce inequality. They can intervene in markets, for example, by setting minimum wages or maximum prices for essential goods. They can also provide goods such as health care and education free to every citizen and fund this through raising taxes, particularly on high earners. They can also transfer income directly through taxes and benefits. Left-wing economists would tend to argue that high levels of inequality are not correlated economic growth. Individuals will work and take risks even if marginal rates of tax are high.

There are many variations on these views. So whilst economists and politicians would on the whole agree, for example, that fiscal deficits need to be contained over time or that low unemployment is desirable, there is no consensus about objectives for income inequality.

Thinking like an economist

A tale of four economies

The USA, Germany, Japan and the UK are four of the largest economies in the world. Their governments are all committed to securing a high rate of economic growth for their economies.

Figures 1 and 2 show how well they have achieved that over the period 2001 to 2014. Looking at the data, it is clear that none of the four economies was able to avoid the impact of the 2008 financial crisis. In 2009, for example, the US economy contracted by 2.8 per cent whilst the German economy contracted by 5.6 per cent.

Figure 3 shows the percentage change in GDP at purchasing power parities over the whole period 2001-2008. This shows that over these eight years, the performance of the UK and US economies were significantly better than Japan or Germany. Japan faced particular problems. An ageing population, a high savings rate and prices at times falling rather than rising (deflation) served to dampen the growth of domestic demand.

Growth in exports, the main driver of the Japanese economy in the 1960s, 1970s and 1980s, was disappointing as Japanese companies lost competitive advantage to lower cost countries

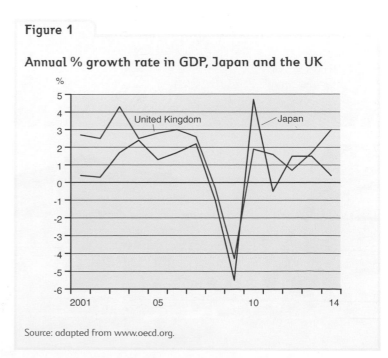

Figure 1

Annual % growth rate in GDP, Japan and the UK

Source: adapted from www.oecd.org.

Figure 2

Annual % growth rate in GDP, Germany and the USA

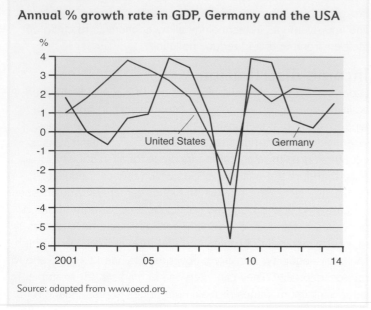

Source: adapted from www.oecd.org.

Figure 3

Percentage growth in real GDP (at PPPs) over the periods 2001-2008 and 2009-2013

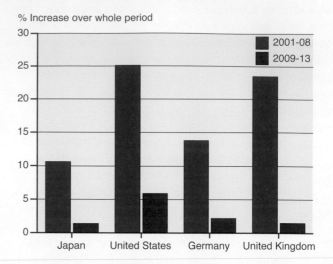

Source: adapted from www.oecd.org.

such as China and South Korea. Germany, in the early 2000s, was still suffering from the costs of the reunification of East and West Germany in 1990.

However, Figure 3 shows the disastrous cost of the 2008 financial crisis. In five years, 2009-2013, the four economies barely achieved what might have been one year's growth in the period 2001-2007. It also shows the poor relative performance of the UK economy compared to the US economy. In the USA, the government adopted a much looser fiscal policy than the

UK in order to increase demand and reduce unemployment. The UK, from 2010, saw significant government spending cuts and rises in taxes designed to reduce the government budget deficit. However, it had the effect of reducing demand in the UK economy and lowering economic growth. The UK government chose to prioritise cutting its budget deficit over its aim to achieve the long-term growth rate for the economy.

JAPAN

GERMANY

UK

USA

Data Response Question

Missed objectives

In March 2007, Gordon Brown, the Chancellor of the Exchequer, said: 'In this, my 11th Budget, my report to the country is of rising employment and rising investment; continued low inflation and low interest and mortgage rates; and this is a Budget to expand prosperity and fairness for Britain's families - and it is built on the foundation of the longest period of economic stability and sustained growth in our country's history. I can report the British economy is today growing faster than all the other G7 economies - growth stronger this year than the euro area, stronger than Japan and stronger even than America. Our forecast and the consensus of independent forecasts agree that looking ahead to 2008 and

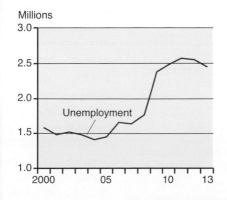

2009 inflation will also be on target. Mr Deputy Speaker, six months ago when we published the Stern report on climate change, we set a framework for environmental action combining a call to personal and social responsibility, with European and international co-operation. Since then we have secured support for a strengthened European carbon trade scheme on the road to a global scheme.'

Source: excerpts from The Budget Speech, March 2007.

Q

1. Using Figures 4 and 5, identify two significant points of comparison over the period shown between changes in the rate of economic growth and the level of unemployment.

2. Explain why 'low inflation' and 'strong growth' might be objectives of the UK government.

3. Evaluate how well the UK government met its probable economic objectives over the period 2008-2013 compared to 2000-2007.

Evaluation

First, outline briefly the probable economic objectives of government over the whole period 2000 to 2013. Take each objective and comment on how well this was achieved in the two periods 2000-2007 and 2008-2013. In your conclusion, make an overall judgement as to whether 2008-13 was a more successful period than 2000-2007. Identify areas where you might not have enough evidence to come to a conclusion (which might include any environmental objectives).

Figure 4

Economic growth, %; the current balance on the balance of payments as % of GDP

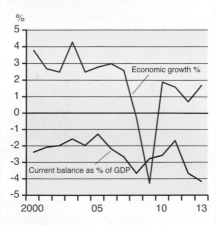

Figure 5

Unemployment, millions

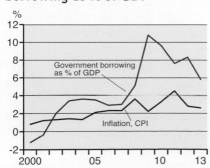

Figure 6

Inflation (CPI), %; government borrowing as % of GDP

When Gordon Brown, the Chancellor, stood up to make his Budget speech in 2007, he had not foreseen the disaster that would descend on the UK and world economies just one year later. Banks in the USA, the UK and other countries had lent recklessly, created far too many high-risk assets and engaged in fraudulent practices. This created a financial crisis in 2008 which threatened to lead to worldwide economic collapse. At a cost of trillions of millions of pounds, the world's banking system was bailed out by governments. But it led to years of recession and high unemployment.

Source: adapted from www.ons.gov.uk.

Key points

1. Monetary policy is the manipulation by government of variables such as the money supply and interest rates whilst fiscal policy is the manipulation of government spending and tax revenues.
2. Monetary policy instruments include interest rates and quantitative easing.
3. Monetary policy is administered by the Bank of England in the UK.
4. Fiscal policy instruments include government spending, tax and government borrowing.
5. A fiscal deficit occurs where government spending is greater than government revenues whilst a surplus occurs when government spending is less than revenues.
6. Governments levy both direct and indirect taxes.
7. Demand-side policies have strengths and weaknesses.

Starter activity

Aggregate demand is equal to consumption plus investment plus government spending plus net exports (X-M). How, in theory, could the government attempt to increase each individual component of aggregate demand? Use the Internet to find out one way in which the government has attempted to increase consumption, investment and net exports over the past two years.

Monetary and fiscal policies

Governments have a number of key macroeconomic and microeconomic objectives. At a macroeconomic level, these include promoting economic growth, securing low inflation and unemployment and achieving a sustainable balance on the current account of the balance of payments. At a microeconomic level, these include reducing market failures, such as environmental externalities.

To achieve these objectives, governments use monetary and fiscal policies.

- **Monetary policy** is the manipulation by government of monetary variables, such as interest rates and the money supply, to achieve its objectives.
- **Fiscal policy** is the use of taxes, government spending and government borrowing to achieve its objectives.

Monetary policy

Governments can, to some extent, control the rate of interest and the amount of money circulating in the economy. They can also influence the amount of borrowing or credit available from financial institutions like banks and building societies.

The variables which the government is attempting to control are known as the **instruments of policy**. So interest rates, the money supply, tax rates or government spending on roads are all examples of instruments of policy.

In recent years, the UK government, through the Bank of England, the **central bank** of the UK, has used two main monetary policy instruments to influence the economy as a whole: interest rates and quantitative easing. They have been used to get the economy out of the deep and prolonged recession that occurred after the financial crisis of 2008.

Interest rates as a monetary policy instrument

The **rate of interest** is the price of money. Lenders expect to receive interest if money is supplied for loans to money markets. Equally, if money is demanded for loans from money markets, borrowers expect to have to pay interest on the loans.

The rate of interest affects the economy through its influence on aggregate demand (AD). The higher the rate of interest, the lower the level of aggregate demand. There is a variety of ways in which interest rates affect the AD curve.

Consumer durables Many consumers buy consumer durables such as furniture, kitchen equipment and cars on credit. The higher the rate of interest, the greater the monthly repayments will have to be for any given sum borrowed. Hence, high interest rates lead to lower sales of durable goods and hence lower consumption expenditure.

The housing market Houses, too, are typically bought using a mortgage. The lower the rate of interest, the lower the mortgage repayments on a given sum borrowed. This makes houses more affordable. It might encourage people to buy their first house or to move house, either trading up to a more expensive house or trading down to a smaller property. There are three ways in which this increases aggregate demand. First, an increase in demand for all types of housing leads to an increase in the number of new houses being built. New housing is classified as investment in national income accounts. Increased investment leads to increased aggregate demand. Second, moving house stimulates the purchase of consumer durables such as furniture, carpets and kitchens. This increases consumption. Third, moving house may release money which can be spent. A person trading down to a cheaper house will see a release of equity tied up in their home. Those trading up may borrow more than they need for the house purchase and this may be used to buy furniture or perhaps even a new car.

Wealth effects A fall in rates of interest may increase asset prices. For instance, falling interest rates may lead to an increase in demand for housing, which in turn pushes up the price of houses. If house prices rise, all homeowners are better off because their houses have increased in value. This may encourage them to increase their spending. Equally, a fall in interest rates will raise the price of government bonds.

Governments issue bonds to finance their borrowing. They are sold to individuals, assurance companies, pension funds and others who receive interest on the money they have loaned to government. Like shares, bonds can go up and down in value. Rises in the price of bonds held by individuals or businesses will increase their financial wealth, which again may have a positive impact on consumer expenditure.

Saving Higher interest rates make saving more attractive compared to spending. The higher the interest rate, the greater the reward for deferring spending to the future and reducing spending now. This may lead to a fall in aggregate demand at the present time.

Investment The lower the rate of interest, the more investment projects become profitable. Hence the higher the level of investment and aggregate demand. Equally, a rise in consumption which leads to a rise in income will lead, in turn, to a rise in investment. Firms will need to invest to supply the extra goods and services being demanded by consumers.

The exchange rate A fall in the interest rate is likely to lead to a fall in the value of the domestic currency (its exchange rate). For the UK a fall in the value of the pound means that foreigners can now get more pounds for each unit of their currency. However, UK residents have to pay more pounds to get the same number of US dollars or Japanese yen. This in turn means that goods priced in pounds become cheaper for foreigners to buy, whilst foreign goods become more expensive for British firms to buy. Cheaper British goods should lead to higher exports as foreigners take advantage of lower prices. In contrast, more expensive foreign goods should lead to fewer imports as British buyers find foreign goods less price competitive. Greater export levels and fewer imports will boost aggregate demand.

Question 1

Inflation has hit a 15-year low of 0.5 per cent. The fall was almost all due to the fall in the world price of oil. Mark Carney, the Governor of the Bank of England, predicted that inflation might fall even further as the oil price effect worked its way through the economy.

Economic forecasters had predicted that the Bank of England would raise interest rates last year as economic growth recovered and demand-pull inflation rose. However, growth has not been particularly strong and inflation has fallen below the two per cent target for the Bank of England. As a result, economic forecasters are now predicting that the Bank of England will only increase interest rates in 2016. 'Good deflation' gives the Bank of England more room to keep interest rates low to boost economic growth this year and next.

Source: adapted from © the *Financial Times* 14.1.2015, All Rights Reserved.

(a) Explain the impact of a rise in the rate of interest on economic growth.

(b) Why does inflation falling below two per cent mean that the Bank of England can delay increasing interest rates?

Quantitative easing

In response to the financial crisis of 2008, governments through their central banks, including the UK and the USA, pushed interest rates to their minimum levels. However, historically low interest rates failed to stimulate aggregate demand sufficiently. Central banks then introduced a policy of quantitative easing. This is a monetary policy instrument where the central bank buys financial assets in exchange for money in order to increase borrowing and lending in the economy.

For example, a commercial bank in an economy might hold (i.e. own) bonds. Bonds are loans issued either by governments or by firms. With **quantitative easing**, the central bank buys bonds from banks in exchange for money. The commercial bank now holds fewer bonds, or loans, and more money. It can then lend out that money to customers. Those customers might be firms wanting to borrow to invest in new equipment. It might be households wanting to buy a car or a new kitchen. Higher investment and higher consumption then increases aggregate demand.

Quantitative easing also has the effect of lowering interest rates further and so encouraging borrowing. Central banks, like the Bank of England, have a headline rate of interest that is meant to influence other rates of interest in the economy. In the UK, this is called the **base rate**. It is the rate of interest that the Bank of England charges if a bank borrows money from it overnight. There is a large number of different interest rates in the economy, some of which are highly influenced by base rate and others which have little connection to base rate. Quantitative easing lowers interest rates for any type of financial asset that the central bank buys as part of its policy of quantitative easing. For example, in the UK it lowers interest rates on bonds issued by government and firms because the Bank of England effectively has increased demand for these bonds. It also indirectly influences other interest rates. For example, it allows commercial banks to offer very low interest deals to their borrowing customers because the Bank of England is providing them with so much cash to lend out.

Question 2

Quantitative easing seems to have succeeded at boosting growth and lifting inflation. Martin Weale, a member of the Bank of England's interest-rate setting Monetary Policy Committee, has found that asset purchases worth one per cent of national income boosted UK gross domestic product by about 0.18 per cent and inflation by 0.3 per cent.

Quantitative easing has been a monetary policy tool used by Japan, the United States and the UK. The European Central Bank has now decided to launch quantitative easing too. It has announced it will buy €1.1 trillion worth of bonds to combat low economic growth and the threat of deflation in the eurozone.

Source: adapted from © the *Financial Times* 21.1.2015, 23.1.2015, All Rights Reserved.

(a) Explain how quantitative easing might have boosted UK gross domestic product.

(b) Why might quantitative easing by the European Central Bank combat the threat of deflation in the eurozone?

There is also an effect on the exchange rate. By lowering interest rates, the exchange rate of a country falls. For example, if the UK engages in quantitative easing, interest rates in the UK fall. This encourages international investors to switch their money out of UK assets and into other assets in other countries. This leads to a fall in demand for the pound and a rise in its supply, so causing a fall in the price of the pound against other currencies. A lower exchange rate will make exports more competitive and imports less competitive.

The role of the Bank of England

In the UK, the elected government does not directly control monetary policy. Instead, this is delegated to the Bank of England, which operates monetary policy on an independent basis.

The most important decisions about monetary policy are made by the Monetary Policy Committee (MPC) of the Bank of England. This is a group of nine people. Five are from the Bank of England, including the Governor of the Bank of England. The other four are independent outside experts, mainly professional economists. The Committee sets the **Bank of England base rate** at its regular meetings. It also decides how quantitative easing is to be managed.

The main target of the Monetary Policy Committee is the UK inflation rate as measured by the CPI. In 2015, this target was 2.0 per cent. If inflation exceeds three per cent or is less than one per cent, the Governor of the Bank of England has to write to the Chancellor of the Exchequer to explain the reasons for this and outline what actions, if any, the Bank of England is taking to bring the inflation rate back to its target of two per cent. Assuming that the inflation rate is under control, the Monetary Policy Committee may also use monetary policy to achieve other government objectives, such as economic growth and employment.

In normal times, rises in the rate of inflation would indicate excess demand in the economy. The Monetary Policy Committee would then increase interest rates to reduce aggregate demand. If the rate of inflation fell towards zero, the MPC would cut interest rates to boost aggregate demand and nudge inflation back up to its target level.

From March 2009, however, the Monetary Policy Committee kept base rates at record low levels of 0.5 per cent. It recognised that any inflation above two per cent was most unlikely to be caused by excess demand. This was because unemployment was high and economic growth very weak. Monetary policy became focussed on the objectives of boosting economic growth and reducing unemployment. Interest rates would only be raised once the negative output gap in the economy had been eliminated and the economy was growing strongly.

Fiscal policy

Aggregate demand can also be affected by government fiscal policy. The UK government has been responsible for between 40 and 50 per cent of national expenditure over the past 20 years. The main areas of public spending are the National Health Service, defence, education and roads. In addition, the government is responsible for transferring large sums of money around the economy through its spending on social security and National Insurance benefits. All of this is financed mainly through taxes, such as income tax and VAT.

In the post-war era, governments have rarely balanced their budgets (i.e. they have rarely planned to match their expenditure with their receipts). In most years, they have run **budget deficits**, spending more than they receive. As a result, in most years governments have had to borrow money. In the UK, the borrowing of the public sector (central government, local government and other state bodies such as nationalised

---

Question 3

Figure 1

Public sector net borrowing and the National Debt[1], UK

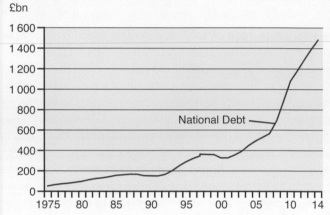

£bn

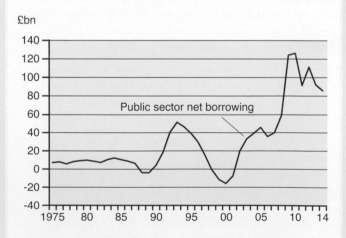

£bn

1. Different measures of the National Debt are used for 1975-1997 compared to 1997-2014.

Source: adapted from www.ons.gov.uk.

(a) (i) What is meant by public sector net borrowing? (ii) In which years did the government have a budget surplus?

(b) Using examples from the data, explain the link between public sector net borrowing and the National Debt.

(c) If a government wanted to pay off its National Debt over a number of years, how could it achieve this?

industries) over a period of time is called **public sector net borrowing (PSNB)**. In three fiscal periods over the past 50 years, between 1969-70, 1988-89 and 1998-2001, the UK government received more revenue than it spent. The normal budget deficit was turned into a **budget surplus**. There is then a negative PSNB. A budget surplus allows the government to pay off part of its accumulated debt. This debt, called the **National Debt**, dates back to the founding of the Bank of England in 1694. The official name of the National Debt in the UK is the **public sector net debt**. The government may have neither a budget deficit or surplus. Government receipts could equal government spending. In this case, there will be a **balanced budget**.

The government has to make decisions about how much to spend, tax and borrow. It also has to decide on the composition of its spending and taxation. Should it spend more on education and less on defence? Should it cut income tax by raising excise duties? These decisions about spending, taxes and borrowing are called the fiscal policy of the government.

There are two key dates in the year for fiscal policy. One is the day of the **Budget** which occurs in March. In the Budget, the Chancellor gives a forecast of government spending and taxation in the coming financial year. Changes in taxation are also announced. The other key date occurs in November or December with the Chancellor's **Autumn Statement**. In this report, the Chancellor gives another forecast of government spending and taxation and announces the government's spending plans for the year. The financial year in the UK starts on 6 April and runs until 5 April the following year.

Direct and indirect taxes

Taxes can be classified into two types. A **direct tax** is a tax levied directly on an individual or organisation. For example, income tax is a direct tax that individual income earners have responsibility for paying. The other main direct tax levied on individuals is National Insurance contributions which, like income tax, is levied on earnings. Corporation tax is a direct tax paid by companies. It is levied on company profits.

An **indirect tax** is a tax on a good or service. For instance, value added tax is an indirect tax because it is a 20 per cent tax on most goods and services. Excise duties on goods such as petrol, drink and tobacco, are indirect taxes levied on the volume of goods bought. Council tax is an indirect tax paid by homeowners on the notional value of a property whilst business rates, paid by firms, is an indirect tax on the notional rent of a property.

Fiscal policy and aggregate demand

Both fiscal policy and monetary policy can be used to influence aggregate demand, C + I + G + X - M.

With constant tax revenues, a rise in government spending will increase aggregate demand. In the formula for aggregate demand, a rise in G leads directly to a rise in AD. The rise in AD is shown by a rightward shift in the AD curve in Figure 2 leading to a high equilibrium level of national output at OY_2.

If government spending is kept constant but tax rates fall, equally there will be a rise in AD. If the government cuts income tax, the disposable income of households will increase which

Figure 2

Expansionary demand-side policies and aggregate demand

Expansionary policies, such as a rise in government spending or a fall interest rates, will shift the aggregate demand curve to the right from AD_1 to AD_2. In the short run, equilibrium output will rise from Y_1 to Y_2 but there will also be an increase in the price level from P_1 to P_2.

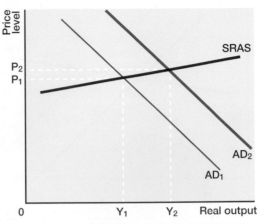

will lead to an increase in consumption, although there will also be a rise in imports. If the government cuts VAT or excise duties, prices of consumer goods should fall again, leading to a rise in consumption. If governments cut taxes on company profits, this might encourage firms to increase investment.

The government could also increase aggregate demand by raising both government spending and taxes but raising taxes by less than the increase in government spending. Equally, a cut in taxes but a smaller cut in government spending will lead to a rise in AD.

In general, a rise in the budget deficit or a fall in the budget surplus is likely to increase AD. This would be called **expansionary fiscal policy**. Fiscal policy is said to loosen as a result. In contrast, **contractionary fiscal policy** occurs when there is a fall in the budget deficit or a rise in the budget surplus. Fiscal policy is said to tighten as a result. In Figure 3, if the shift to the left in the aggregate demand curve were caused by tighter fiscal policy, equilibrium real output would fall from OY_1 to OY_2. So the **fiscal stance** or **budget position** of the government could be expansionary or contractionary. It could equally be neutral. **Neutral fiscal policy** is when changes to government spending and taxation leave the overall budget surplus or deficit unchanged and have no effect on aggregate demand.

Question 4

Explain, using a diagram, the probable effect the following would have on aggregate demand, all other things being equal:

(a) a rise in income tax rates;

(b) a cut in council tax rates;

(c) a cut in spending on education;

(d) a rise in VAT rates combined with an increase in spending on the NHS.

Figure 3

Contractionary demand-side policies and aggregate demand

Contractionary policies, such as a fall in government spending or a rise in interest rates, will shift the aggregate demand curve to the left from AD_1 to AD_2. In the short run, equilibrium output will fall from Y_1 to Y_2 but there will also be a fall in the price level from P_1 to P_2.

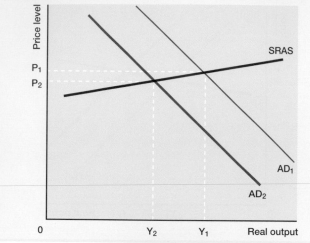

A rise in government spending will not just increase aggregate demand by the value of the increase in G. There will be a multiple increase in aggregate demand. This **multiplier effect** will be larger, the smaller the leakages from the circular flow. In a modern economy, where leakages from savings, taxes and imports are a relatively high proportion of national income, multiplier values tend to be small. However, Keynesian economists argue that they can still have a significant effect on output in the economy if the economy is below full employment.

Monetary policy and aggregate demand

Monetary policy can be used to influence aggregate demand. **Expansionary monetary policy**, or a **loosening** of monetary policy works, for example, through lowering interest rates or increasing quantitative easing. **Contractionary monetary policy**, or a **tightening** of monetary policy works, for example, through raising interest rates or reducing quantitative easing.

In Figure 2, a fall in the rate of interest leads to a rise in consumption and investment. This increase in aggregate demand is shown by a shift to the right in the AD curve. Equilibrium output increases from OY_1 to OY_2. In Figure 3, a rise in the rate of interest leads to a fall in consumption and investment, causing a fall in aggregate demand. This is shown by a shift to the left in the AD curve. Equilibrium output falls from OY_1 to OY_2.

Strengths and weaknesses of demand-side policies

Economists are divided about the effectiveness of demand-side policies and their strengths and weaknesses. Keynesian economists tend to favour the use of both fiscal and monetary demand-side policies when the economy is in recession or is growing so fast that inflation begins to increase. Classical economists tend to argue that fiscal policies are ineffective and

governments should rely solely on monetary policy to influence aggregate demand, if at all.

Speed of adjustment Economists are divided about how quickly an economy can revert to long-run equilibrium. Keynesian economists tend to argue that an economy could be in short-run disequilibrium for years and even decades because of a lack of demand. If consumers, firms and governments all spend less than is needed to get the economy to full employment, then the economy can remain depressed for a long time. Classical economists tend to argue that economies adjust very quickly. If there is long-term unemployment, for example, with no economic growth, this is not because there is recession in the economy. It is because there are supply-side problems in the economy. Using demand-side policies to get a stagnant economy moving again will have no effect.

Conflicting policies If there is high unemployment and the economy is in recession, Keynesian economists would argue that governments should use both expansionary fiscal and monetary policies to get the economy back to growth. However, since 2008, some economists have argued that fiscal policy should be contractionary, whilst monetary policy should be expansionary. This is because they argue that the costs of increasing the National Debt from expansionary fiscal policy are greater than any benefits to aggregate demand that might result. Some might go further and argue that fiscal policy has no impact on aggregate demand and so raising taxes and cutting government spending is not contractionary.

The National Debt In a recession, expansionary fiscal policy can be used as a demand-side policy to increase aggregate demand. However, it will increase the size of the national debt. Some economists argue that the benefit of increased aggregate demand in the short term is outweighed by the negative impact of increasing the National Debt. Keynesian economists argue the contrary. So long as a government can print money to finance its deficit without fuelling inflation or borrow money from the financial markets, then the National Debt is not a problem in the short term. Nearly all economists, however, would argue that, in the long term, large National Debts can be a problem, particularly if they are financed mainly by borrowing money from foreigners.

The rate of interest In a recession, economists agree that the central bank should cut interest rates to stimulate aggregate demand. However, following the financial crash of 2008, many central banks effectively reduced interest rates to zero and found it had little impact on aggregate demand. It was because of this that they resorted to quantitative easing. So interest rates have limitations on their effectiveness.

Quantitative easing Economists disagree about the effectiveness of quantitative easing. Some economists argue that it significantly boosts aggregate demand because households and firms borrow to spend on real goods and services. Other economists argue that it mainly pushes up asset prices such as houses or stocks and shares. Households and firms borrow money but instead, for example, of buying or building new houses, they instead buy second-hand houses, pushing up their price but not increasing aggregate demand.

The size of the multiplier Economists disagree about the size of the multiplier. Classical economists tend to argue that it is virtually zero even in the short term. They argue that extra government spending crowds out (or forces out) private sector spending. Cuts in tax financed by government borrowing mean that the private sector can borrow less money. An increase in the budget deficit financed by printing money only leads to inflation, not extra output.

Keynesian economists, on the other hand, argue that the multiplier is positive and can be large if government spending and tax charges are carefully targeted. For example, if there is large-scale unemployment in the construction industry, extra government spending on building new social housing could work its way quickly through the economy to increase aggregate demand.

Time lags Demand-side policies can have significant time lags. For example, if the UK government announces plans to build new motorways, high speed rail links or nuclear power stations to revitalise a stagnant economy, then the policy will fail. This is because there is inevitably at least a five-year time lag between announcement and spending taking place on big infrastructure projects. By the time the project is under way, the economic situation is likely to have changed significantly. Demand-side policies need to be focussed on changing aggregate demand within a very short period of time to be effective in responding to problems in the economy today.

Fine-tuning In the 1950s and 1960s, Keynesian economists thought that demand-side policies could nudge the economy to a very precise level of national income. Today, most economists agree that such fine-tuning is impossible. There are too many small, or indeed large, random shocks to the economic system and too little precision about the tools of demand-side policy for this to work.

Question 5

Economists polled by the *Financial Times* have said that a massive quantitative easing programme by the European Central Bank would fail to revive the eurozone economy. Dario Perkins, economist at Lombard Street Research, said it would help lift inflation expectations and reduce the value of the euro against other currencies but would not be a 'total game changer'. Several respondents said government bond buying would not prevent lacklustre growth. The biggest impact would come if governments at the same time were allowed to start a deficit-financed investment programme. However, borrowing to fund new roads, railway links and housing is unlikely to 'ever happen in the euro area' according to Carsten Brzeski of ING DiBa, a bank.

Source: adapted from © the *Financial Times* 5.1.2015, All Rights Reserved.

(a) The European Central Bank wants to raise growth in eurozone countries through quantitative easing. The economists polled by the *Financial Times* think this is unlikely to work. Put forward one argument which would support the European Central Bank view and one argument to support the view of the economists polled by the *Financial Times*.

(b) Why might a deficit-financed investment programme help economic growth?

Key Terms

Balanced budget - a statement of spending and income plans by government where spending is equal to its receipts, mainly tax revenues.

Bank of England base rate - the rate of interest charged by the Bank of England to banks to borrow money overnight. It is the most important interest rate in the UK financial system because it influences other interest rates in the UK such as savings rates and rates of interest on loans by banks.

Budget - a statement of the spending and income plans of an individual firm or government. The Budget is the yearly statement on government spending and taxation plans in the UK.

Budget deficit - a deficit which arises because government spending is greater than its receipts. Government therefore has to borrow money to finance the difference.

Budget surplus - a government surplus arising from government spending being less than its receipts. Government can use the difference to repay part of the National Debt.

Contractionary fiscal policy - fiscal policy which leads to a fall in aggregate demand.

Contractionary monetary policy - monetary policy which leads to a fall in aggregate demand.

Direct tax - a tax levied directly on individuals or companies such as income tax or corporation tax.

Expansionary fiscal policy - fiscal policy which leads to an increase in aggregate demand.

Expansionary monetary policy - monetary policy which leads to a rise in aggregate demand.

Fiscal policy - the use of taxes, government spending and government borrowing by government to achieve its objectives.

Fiscal stance or budget position - whether fiscal policy is expansionary, contractionary or neutral.

Indirect tax - a tax levied on goods or services, such as value added tax, excise duties or council tax.

Instrument of policy - an economic variable, such as the rate of interest, income tax rate or government spending on education, which is used to achieve a target of government policy.

Monetary policy - the manipulation by government of monetary variables, such as interest rates and the money supply, to achieve its objectives.

National Debt - the total accumulated borrowing of government which remains to be paid to lenders.

Neutral fiscal policy - when changes to government spending and taxation leave the overall budget surplus or deficit unchanged and have no effect on aggregate demand.

Public sector net borrowing (PSNB) - the official name given to the difference between government spending and its receipts in the UK.

Public sector net debt (PSND) - the official name given to the national debt in the UK.

Quantitative easing - a monetary policy instrument where the central bank buys financial assets in exchange for money in order to increase borrowing and lending in the economy.

Rate of interest - the price of money, determined by the demand and supply of funds in a money market where there are borrowers and lenders.

Thinking like an economist
The Great Depression and the Global Financial Crisis

The Great Depression

In the 1930s, the world experienced a severe depression, commonly called the Great Depression. World GDP fell and unemployment rose. In the UK as a whole, unemployment rose to over 15 per cent in 1932 as Figure 4 shows. In the United States, it rose to 24.9 per cent at its worst in 1933, as can be seen from Figure 5. However, national unemployment rates masked large differences in regional rates of unemployment. In parts of the North East of the UK, for example, unemployment rates rose to over 70 per cent.

The areas that were worst affected in the UK were those dependent upon primary industry and heavy manufacturing industry such as coal, steel and shipbuilding. This was because these products were traded internationally. The collapse of world trade during the Great Depression meant that industries and countries that were dependent on exports tended to suffer the most.

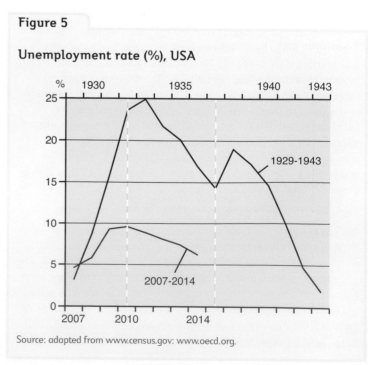

Possible causes of the Great Depression

Most economists agree that the Wall Street crash of 1929 was a defining point in the history of the Great Depression. The Wall Street crash was a sharp fall in share prices on the New York Stock Exchange, located on Wall Street. In October 1929, share prices dropped by 40 per cent. Economists differ in their opinion, however, about what caused the subsequent Great Depression.

Loss of consumer and business confidence One view is that the Wall Street crash knocked consumer and business confidence. Shareholders lost money in the crash. Others were worried about what would happen and so became more cautious in their spending. Firms cut back on investment. The result was a downward spiral in aggregate demand that only reversed itself in 1933.

The banking system Another view is that the Wall Street crash was part of a wider problem with the US banking system. It was not robust enough to cope with bad debts and lack of confidence following the Wall Street crash. It could also be argued that banks had been allowed to lend too much money in the 1920s creating an unsustainable credit boom. Following the events of 1929, the US authorities allowed a number of banks to fail, further creating insecurity. Loans to businesses and consumers fell sharply. All this reduced consumption and investment creating a downward spiral.

Figure 4

Unemployment rate (%), UK

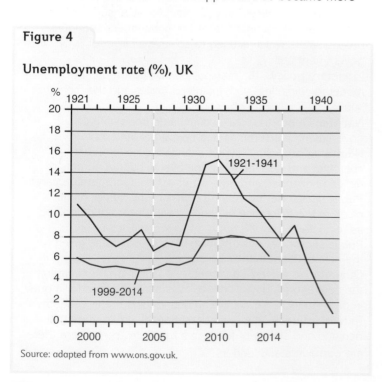

Source: adapted from www.ons.gov.uk.

Figure 5

Unemployment rate (%), USA

Source: adapted from www.census.gov: www.oecd.org.

Protectionism The Wall Street crash coincided with, and was perhaps partly caused by, attempts in the Houses of Congress to pass a law which would sharply raise tariffs (taxes) on imported goods. The Smoot-Hawley Tariff Act, which was eventually passed in 1930, reduced imports to the USA. But it also helped depress worldwide demand because imports to the USA were another country's exports. It also produced tit-for-tat responses by other countries that retaliated by raising their tariffs. The result was a shrinking of world trade by more than half in the 1930s. This was disastrous for the USA and the UK, which both had large export industries. It fed into loss of consumer and business confidence. It also directly caused bank failures in the USA because businesses involved in exports were no longer able to pay their loans.

The gold standard In the UK, a contributing factor to the initial slump was the fact that the country was on the gold standard. This meant that the pound was fixed against the price of gold. This then fixed its exchange rate with other countries. Britain had abandoned the gold standard in 1914 at the start of the First World War. It went back on the gold standard in 1925 at its 1914 level and value. Given that the value of the pound had fallen since 1914, this meant a sharp appreciation in the value of the pound. Exports fell because they became more expensive to foreigners. Firms reacted by cutting wages and this was partly responsible for the General Strike of 1926, when millions of workers, including miners, came out on strike against cuts in pay. The UK went into the Great Depression with an overvalued exchange rate.

How the Great Depression developed

The downturn in the US economy quickly spread through the world economy. In the UK, unemployment rose from 1.5 million to 2.5 million by the end of 1930. Exports fell by 50 per cent. Like in the USA, the British government believed that balancing the government budget was key to recovery. If the government

borrowed money, this was money which the private sector could not borrow. On the 10th September 1931, the British government introduced an emergency budget which cut public sector wages and unemployment benefit by 10 per cent and income tax was raised from 22.5 per cent to 25 per cent. This deflationary budget reduced aggregate demand at a time when aggregate demand needed to increase. It can be argued that it delayed the recovery from depression.

The Bank of England also needed to defend the value of the pound fixed through the gold standard. The pound came under attack from speculators who believed the UK would be forced out of the gold standard. Balancing the government budget would mean that the government did not have to borrow from abroad, helping to prop up the high exchange rate. The Bank of England also introduced high interest rates to defend the high exchange rate which simply deepened the recession. However, on 21st September 1931, following continual speculation against the pound, the government was forced to take the country off the gold standard. The value of the pound against other currencies fell by 25 per cent. The Bank of England cut interest rates to 2.5 per cent. The fall in interest rates helped increase domestic borrowing, whilst the fall in the exchange rate helped increase exports.

Figure 6 would suggest that the recovery for the UK from the bottom of the recession was rapid and strong. Certainly for London and the South East, where there was a house-building boom, this was true. But in the heartlands of heavy industry in Wales, the north and Scotland, unemployment remained persistently high because there was little recovery in steel, shipbuilding and coal. It wasn't until 1941, two years into the Second World War, that full employment returned to these regions. The Second World War and the large increase in government spending for the war effort is often seen by Keynesians as proof that fiscal expansion can get an economy out of recession and into full employment.

In the United States, the depression reached its worst in 1932-33, as can be seen from Figure 7. Presidential elections in 1932 saw the election of a new president, Franklin D Roosevelt. He promised to get the country out of the depression and launched the New Deal. This was a package of measures which included a fiscal stimulus as well as increased public sector investment and work schemes for the unemployed. As in the UK, it took the Second World War to get the economy back to full employment. The USA entered the war two years later than the UK, in 1941, and it was not until 1943 that full employment was restored. Roosevelt's New Deal can be argued to be an example of a Keynesian expansionary fiscal policy. It was partially successful at getting the unemployed back to work but can be criticised for not being large enough to get the USA back to full employment.

The Global Financial Crisis of 2008

There are many parallels between the Great Depression of the 1930s and the global financial crisis of 2008. It can be argued, for example, that the 2008 financial crisis originated in the USA, just as the Wall Street Crash had been followed by a US banking crisis in the 1930s. As in the 1930s, a US downturn then had worldwide repercussions both through the world's

Figure 6

Economic growth (%), UK

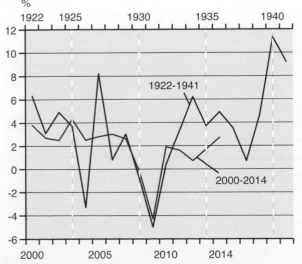

Source: adapted from www.ons.gov.uk.

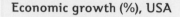

Figure 7

Economic growth (%), USA

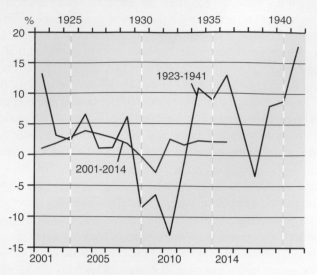

Source: adapted from www.census.gov: www.oecd.org.

banking systems and through foreign trade. The economic repercussions lasted many years unlike milder recessions experienced in the intervening period. However, as Figures 4-7 show, the financial crisis of 2008 was considerably milder than the Great Depression of the 1930s in terms of change in GDP and unemployment.

The 2008 financial crisis was sparked off by a crisis in mortgage lending in the USA. In the early 2000s, with government encouragement, many relatively poor people in the USA were encouraged to take out mortgages to buy their own homes. These 'sub-prime' borrowers were given introductory deals where interest rates on the loans in the first few years were very low. Salespeople in banks and estate agents were given bonuses for selling more mortgages. When the introductory deals ended, many sub-prime borrowers were no longer able to afford to keep up with their now much higher repayments. Houses began to be repossessed, fewer people were buying houses and house prices began to fall. This meant that the value of the loans taken out on mortgaged houses now began to exceed the value of the house in too many cases, a situation known as 'negative equity'. Whilst this was happening, banks which had given mortgages were bundling mortgages together and selling packages of mortgages to other banks or other investors. In the bundle would be mortgages from 'prime' borrowers who were almost certainly going to repay their loan and mortgages from sub-prime borrowers who were likely to default. But the banks were selling these bundles as if all the mortgages were prime mortgages. Selling these mortgages on was meant to reduce risk in the financial system. No one bank would be highly dependent on risky mortgages. But instead, it increased risk in the whole world financial system because so many institutions were now holding assets that were worth less than the price at which they had bought.

As the financial crisis unfolded, confidence collapsed. It became apparent that banks had created many types of highly

risky financial instruments, which had been sold to buyers as if they were relatively low risk. Banks stopped lending between themselves, afraid that they might lose the money if the other bank were to collapse. It became apparent that the problem of risky lending on property was not confined to the USA. The UK, Ireland, Spain and Portugal were just some of the other countries affected. In the UK, the Northern Rock Building Society was the first casualty in 2007 with too many of the loans it had made not being repaid. Northern Rock savers started to withdraw their money from the building society. The UK government was forced to nationalise it and guarantee savers their money. In the USA, the authorities allowed Lehman Brothers, an investment bank, to fail in 2008. This caused widespread panic and some feared that, just as in the 1930s, bank after bank would be allowed to collapse leading to losses for savers and a collapse in lending. It proved a turning point because governments realised that they had two alternatives. Either they propped up the banking system, if necessary by buying the banks themselves and making good the losses they had incurred. Or they could allow the banking system to shrink in a disorderly way and cause chaos in the real economy. They chose to prop up the banking system. In the UK, the government, having bought Northern Rock, proceeded to buy most of Royal Bank of Scotland and part of Lloyds Bank. In Ireland, the government was forced to buy the two main Irish banks. By the time the Irish government had pumped money into the banks to cover their losses, it had cost the Irish taxpayer €56 billion.

Financial instability and a fall in lending by banks led to a fall in consumer spending and investment spending by firms. GDP fell and unemployment rose. Some countries were particularly badly hit by the crisis. Countries like Spain, Portugal and Greece before the recession had seen their governments borrow money to finance their spending. The recession led to a sharp fall in tax revenues, whilst government spending increased due to an increase in benefits related to unemployment. It became apparent that these governments were in danger of not being able to repay their debts. It became difficult for them to borrow money in the financial markets. They were then forced to turn to institutions such as the European Union or the IMF to give them the loans they needed. These loans came with strings attached. Governments would have to cut their spending, raise taxes and introduce supply-side reforms to stimulate their economies. These 'austerity' measures remain highly controversial. Keynesian economists would argue that cutting government spending and raising taxes will only deepen any recession.

Policy responses in the UK and the USA

Both the UK and the USA went into recession in 2008 and both economies bottomed in 2009. But the US economy recovered faster than the UK economy, as Figure 8 shows. This could have been caused by a large number of different factors. However, in terms of demand-side policies, there were two significant similarities and one significant difference between the two countries.

Both countries bailed out their banking systems at enormous cost. They didn't allow a general bank collapse which would have led to a significant fall in aggregate demand. Both countries also implemented expansionary monetary policies. Interest rates were

Figure 8

GDP, 1st quarter 2008 = 100, USA and UK

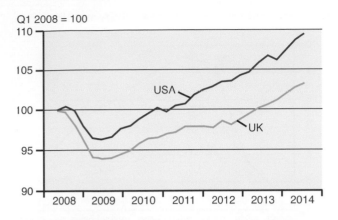

Source: adapted from Capital Economics.

Figure 9

Government budget balance, USA and UK, percentage of GDP

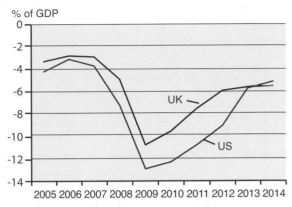

Source: adapted from www.oecd.org.

driven to historically low levels and both countries introduced quantitative easing. On the monetary side, it is difficult to see what else either country could have done to stimulate the economy and increase aggregate demand.

However, in terms of fiscal policy, the US government pursued a looser fiscal policy than the UK. Figure 9 shows the US government budget deficit was larger as a percentage of GDP than that of the UK throughout 2008 to 2012. Keynesian economics would suggest that this larger fiscal stimulus would lead to higher growth. Barack Obama wanted to continue a higher fiscal stimulus into 2013 and 2014 but was forced to cut public spending by his political opponents in the Houses of Congress. He argued that the recovery was going to suffer

without the extra fiscal stimulus. They argued that the US National Debt was getting too large. Figure 7 would suggest that Barack Obama might have been right because US economic growth flattened in 2013-14. In the UK, a decision was made by the incoming government in 2010 to prioritise cutting the fiscal deficit in order to control the National Debt. On Keynesian grounds, cutting government spending and raising taxes, as happened in 2011, will have reduced economic growth. It therefore took the UK much longer to recover from the recession than the USA because the UK government was implementing fiscal austerity measures.

Source: adapted from © the *Financial Times* 2.2.2015, All Rights Reserved.

Data Response Question

Germany rejects spending increase

Germany's finance minister, Wolfgang Schäuble, has said that his government would not increase public spending. He said that calls 'for the use of more and more public money and the acceptance of higher deficits and debts is leading us astray.' He went on: 'Growth and jobs don't come about via higher deficits, as if that were the case, we (in Europe) really wouldn't have any problems at the moment. Only innovation, structural reforms, investment and reliable (investment) conditions and, above all, trust in the sustainability (of public finances) will help.' The German

government has pledged to balance its budget from next year for the first time since 1999.

There has been rising pressure on Germany to increase public spending in order to combat high unemployment, low growth and high negative output gaps in other countries in the eurozone. Mario Draghi, president of the European Central Bank, signalled last month that countries in a better fiscal position could spend more to create a more 'growth-friendly overall fiscal stance for the euro area'.

Source: adapted from © the *Financial Times* 10.9.2014, All Rights Reserved.

Figure 10

GDP, 1st quarter 2008 = 100, Germany, USA and UK

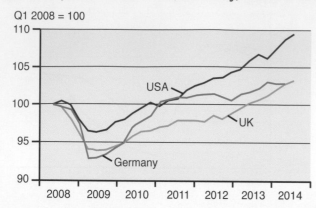

Source: adapted from Capital Economics.

Figure 11

Government budget balance, Germany, USA and UK, percentage of GDP

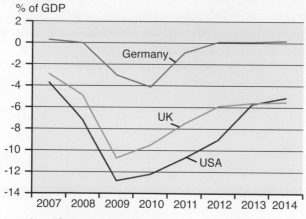

Source: adapted from www.oecd.org.

Figure 12

Unemployment rate (%), Germany, USA and UK

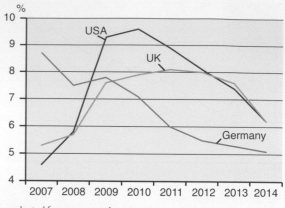

Source: adapted from www.oecd.org.

Figure 13

Output gap (deviation of actual GDP from potential GDP as a percentage of potential GDP), Germany, USA and UK

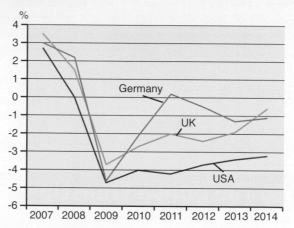

Source: adapted from www.oecd.org.

Q

1. Using Figure 10, compare how Germany, the USA and the UK recovered from the financial crisis of 2008.

2. Using the data in Figures 10, 11 and 12 and the concept of the multiplier, explain how increased government spending can help a country recover from recession.

3. 'Growth and jobs don't come about via higher (fiscal) deficits'. Evaluate whether in a recession governments should attempt to balance their budgets.

Evaluation

One way to answer question 3 is to question what is meant by economic growth in the short term compared to the long term and to contrast demand-side policies with supply-side policies. To what extent do the data support the view that higher fiscal deficits have no effect on GDP and unemployment in the short term? As an output gap closes, what should be the right mix of demand-side and supply-side policies?

39 Supply-side policies

Starter activity

You are offered a part-time job for £20 an hour, working three evenings a week for four hours and a Sunday for five hours. Would you take the job? If you were taxed at 20 per cent on your earnings would you still take the job? Taxed at 50 per cent? Would you still take the job if you were taxed at 80 per cent? If there were no tax and the job meant working from home, would you take the job? What if it took you two hours to travel there and back, plus £15 in transport each time, would you take the job? Would you take the job if it were £7 an hour, plus an hour's travel each day, plus £8 in transport costs each time? What is the minimum rate of pay, travel time and travel cost that would persuade you to take on a part-time job whilst you were working for your A levels?

Supply-side policies

Supply-side economics is the study of how changes in long run aggregate supply will affect variables such as GDP. The long run aggregate supply curve shows the productive potential of the economy. At any point in time, there is only so much that an economy can produce from a given set of resources.

Over time, there are likely to be **supply-side improvements**. Firms will invest, for example, and there will be innovation through technological progress, which will allow capital to produce more goods and services from a given input. The quality of labour is likely to increase as education and training standards improve. The productivity of labour is likely to rise due to higher capital stock and better skills. These supply-side improvements can be illustrated by a rightward shift in the long-run aggregate supply curve, as shown in Figure 1, from LRAS₁ to LRAS₂. They can also be shown as a movement outwards of the production possibility frontier on a PPF diagram. Alternatively, Figure 2 shows the impact of successful supply-side policies, assuming a Keynesian aggregate supply curve.

Supply-side improvements often originate in the private sector, independently of government. However, governments can attempt to further increase output through **supply-side policies**. These are government policies designed to increase the rate of economic growth. They may act broadly across the whole economy. They may also act specifically in certain markets to remove **bottlenecks** that prevent the economy from growing faster.

Figure 1

Supply-side policies

Effective supply-side policies push the long-run aggregate supply curve to the right. This increases economic growth and reduces inflationary pressures. It may also bring about a reduction in unemployment and lead to higher exports and lower imports.

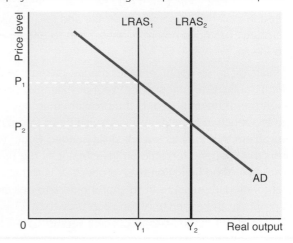

Figure 2

Supply-side policies and the Keynesian aggregate supply curve

Assuming a Keynesian aggregate supply curve, successful supply-side policies will shift the aggregate supply curve to the right, from LRAS₁ to LRAS₂. In equilibrium, real output will rise from Y₁ to Y₂ whilst the price level will fall from P₁ to P₂.

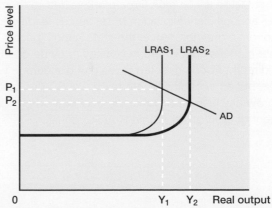

Supply-side policies mainly work through their impact on individual markets. The policies therefore are aimed to improve the microeconomic performance of different individual markets.

These, in turn, improve the macroeconomic performance of the economy.

Market based and interventionist approaches

Supply-side policies can be split into two types.

- **Market-based policies** are policies designed to remove barriers to the efficient working of free markets. These barriers limit output and raise prices. For example, in the labour market, they might reduce the willingness of workers to take jobs or to take risks. In the goods market, they might lead to inefficient production, high prices or a lack of innovation.

- **Interventionist policies** are policies designed to correct market failure. This means the government intervening in free markets to change the outcome from that which it would otherwise have been. For example, free markets may underprovide education and so the government has to step in and provide education. Firms may be short-termist, only interested in maximising short run profits and failing to invest for the future. The government might step in to encourage firms to invest.

Economists disagree about whether market-based policies or interventionist policies are most effective. For example, workers might be long-term unemployed. Is the problem that they are being paid too much in benefits to incentivise them to get a job? Or is the problem that they lack work skills needed to get them a job? Firms might spend too little on investment. Is the problem that they are taxed too highly on their profits? Or is it that they are subject to intense pressure from shareholders to deliver short-run profits at the expense of long-run growth?

The debate about market-based policies versus interventionist policies is part of a wider disagreement about the role of the state. Free market economists tend to argue that the state should be as small as possible. Rules and regulations (sometimes called **red tape**) governing markets should be light. As many goods and services as possible should be provided by the private sector rather than the public sector. Taxes should be as low as possible. Taxes discourage work and enterprise and reduce the productive potential of the economy.

Economists who support interventionist approaches argue that market failure is common. Free markets, left to themselves, will create an inefficient allocation of resources leading to lower economic growth. Hence, the state needs to intervene to regulate markets and, where necessary, provide goods and services directly. Poorly directed taxes can discourage work and enterprise, but an economy where taxes are 50 per cent of GDP will not grow any less quickly than an economy where taxes are 30 per cent of GDP, all other things being equal.

We will now consider a range of supply-side policies designed to improve the performance of the economy.

Increasing incentives

Proponents of market-based policies argue that incentives are vital for markets to function effectively. If incentives are too small, or even worse, encourage the wrong economic decisions, then long run aggregate supply will suffer. There is a number of key variables that affect incentives to work and invest.

Taxes on income   In the UK, there are two taxes on income: income tax and National Insurance contributions paid by employers, employees and the self-employed. High taxes on income will discourage individuals from working. This could mean taking a job, or working extra hours or working hard at a job. High taxes for employers will discourage them from hiring workers. The key variable is not average tax rates, but marginal tax rates. If workers work an extra hour, how much will they be taxed on the earnings from that extra hour and how much will they take home after tax? If the marginal rate of income tax is 60 per cent, and a worker is paid £10 an hour, then £6 will go in tax and £4 will be left. If the marginal tax rate is 20 per cent, then £2 goes in tax and £8 will be left.

Free market economists believe that the elasticity of supply of labour is high. Cutting the marginal rate of tax from 20 per cent to 15 per cent will lead to a significant increase in the desire to work. Other economists argue that small changes in marginal tax rates will have little effect on incentives. They point out that many workers are paid salaries and don't receive either overtime payments or bonuses. These workers cannot respond to changes in marginal tax rates except in the long term by changing jobs or leaving the workforce. For those who are not on a fixed salary, a change in tax from £2 to £2.30 or £1.50 on £10 earned will have almost no effect on incentives.

Question 1

In 2014, the French government launched a bid to revitalise its economy by promising a €30-billion payroll tax cut for French companies. France has very high taxes paid by employers on the wages of their staff. These taxes, or social charges, are used to fund the French welfare system. The €30-billion cut would reduce the wage bills for employers including social charges by 5.4 per cent on average. The government would also seek to reduce tax paid on profits and tackle France's notorious red tape and onerous labour regulations. The French President, François Hollande, called on businesses to commit to increase employment in return for these cuts in labour costs, taxes and red tape.

Source: adapted from © the *Financial Times* 15.1.2014, All Rights Reserved.

Explain why the measures announced by the French government might lead to (a) a rise in employment and (b) an increase in long-run aggregate supply.

Welfare benefits Incentives to work will be low if welfare benefits received by those not in work are too high in relation to the wages they could receive if they took a job. Hence, welfare benefits can reduce the level of aggregate supply because more workers remain unemployed. One solution is to cut state unemployment benefits to encourage workers to take on, typically, low-paid jobs. This can mean cutting rates of benefit paid to increase the ratio of pay to benefits. Or it could mean stopping benefits altogether if those out of work fail to seek work actively or take on jobs that are offered.

Poverty and unemployment traps The combination of marginal rates of income tax and withdrawal of benefits can lead to poverty and unemployment traps. The **poverty** or **earnings trap** occurs when a low income working individual or household earns more, for example by gaining promotion, getting a better paid job or working more hours, but the net gain is little or even negative. It occurs because as income increases, welfare benefits are withdrawn. Equally, the individual or household might start to pay tax. For example, if an individual loses 50p in benefits when earning an extra £1, and then pays income tax and National Insurance contributions at 30 per cent, then the net gain from earning the extra £1 is only 20p (£1 - 50p - 30p). The effective marginal rate of tax here is 80 per cent. If the benefit lost were 90p in the pound, the individual would be 20p worse off. The effective marginal rate of tax here would be 120 per cent. The poverty trap is a major disincentive for those working and receiving benefits to work harder or increase their skills. The **unemployment trap** occurs when an individual is little better off or is even worse off getting a job than staying unemployed because of loss of benefits and taxation. The unemployment trap, where it occurs, is a major disincentive for the unemployed to find work. One solution to both kinds of trap is to lower welfare benefits but this increases poverty. The other solution is to reduce taxes on income and the rate of welfare benefit withdrawal as incomes increase. This is a more expensive solution for the government and the taxpayer.

Subsidising workers One way to incentivise workers to take on work or work extra hours is to subsidise them for working. In the UK, low-paid workers can claim income tax credits. Instead of paying income tax, they receive tax rebates from the government. These are designed to reduce the effective marginal tax rates that occur when low-paid workers pay tax and lose benefits. They help reduce the impact of the poverty trap.

Taxes on profit In the UK, firms which are incorporated as companies have to pay a tax on their profits called corporation tax. Free market economists argue that high marginal rates of taxes on profits discourage firms from investing and from being successful. Tax taken from a company is not available to be reinvested in the firm to help it to survive and grow. High rates of tax also encourage firms to distribute profits to shareholders rather than invest for the future. This is because future profits after tax will be low and so the rate of return on investment made now will be lower than if taxes were lower. As with income tax, critics of this view would argue that there would be little or no effect on incentives to invest if the marginal rate of tax were 30 per cent or 20 per cent. If marginal tax rates were 80 per cent, then there could be some impact if they were

brought down to 20 per cent. So large changes could have some impact, but small changes will have little, if any, impact.

Research and development Spending on research and development (R&D) can lead to technological progress when that R&D gives rise to more efficient ways of making, or creates new types of, goods and services. A market-based approach to increasing R&D spending would be to cut taxes on company profits or give government subsidies to all types of R&D. For example, it is common for governments to allow firms to offset their R&D spending against taxes on profits. If a company made £100 million in profit and spent £20 million on R&D, then they would only pay the profits tax on £80 million. An interventionist approach would be for the government to undertake R&D itself, perhaps by giving funding to universities for research or by setting up its own research institutes. It could also give subsidies to firms but choose which R&D to subsidise. Government would then be claiming that it could pick the best R&D projects.

Promoting competition

Markets can fail because of a lack of competition. Typically this means there will be higher prices for goods because firms will exploit customers and earn higher profits. Output will be lower because customers will buy less at the higher price. There will also be less innovation if existing firms prefer to distribute profits to shareholders rather than spend on R&D and new equipment. There is a number of different supply-side policies that governments use to promote competition.

Privatisation Privatisation is the sale of government organisations or assets to the private sector. Over the past 50 years, the UK government privatised many previously state-owned organisations, including airline companies, gas companies, prisons and hospitals. Free market economists argue that government-run organisations have little incentive to cut costs or innovate. There is therefore government failure. Selling assets to the private sector enables those assets to be used more efficiently by private sector firms that are incentivised by the profit motive. Critics would argue that private firms put profit before providing a good or service.

Deregulation Deregulation is the process of removing government controls from markets. For example, a local council might remove restrictions on the number of taxis for hire in their area. The government might allow any bus company to offer services along a route. The government might relax planning controls on the building of new houses. The aim is to encourage more firms to provide goods and services. This will increase output and lower prices. A major problem with deregulation is that it encourages 'creaming' of markets. This means firms only providing services in the most profitable areas of the market. For example, in the postal market, Royal Mail is against deregulation because it argues that competitors will undercut the price it charges for providing postal services in urban areas, taking away revenue and profit that effectively subsidise postal services to rural areas.

Competition policy Competition policy is designed to increase competition in markets, reducing the power of monopolies and making cartels and price fixing agreements illegal. By reducing prices and increasing output, competition policy should raise output in the economy and so increase aggregate supply.

Industrial policy Industrial policy is government policy to promote and support individual firms that it considers are important for the growth of the economy. It is an example of interventionist policy. Before 1979, UK industrial policy was mainly focused on subsidising loss-making industries that were large employers. Shipbuilding, mining, the motor manufacturing industry and steel were all examples of industries that received government subsidies. Free market economists would argue that governments are poorly placed to pick industry 'winners'. UK industrial policy was more to do with managing the decline of these industries and firms than with promoting economic growth. However, countries such as Japan and South Korea have, arguably, in the past seen their governments successfully pick out firms that have contributed strongly to the growth of their economies.

Reforming the labour market

The level of long-run aggregate supply is determined in part by the quantity of labour supplied to the market and the productivity of that labour. For example, all other things being equal, an economy with ten million workers will produce less than an economy with 20 million workers. Equally, an economy where workers have little human capital will have a lower output than one where there are higher levels of human capital. There are a number of supply-side policies which will affect the labour market.

Improving labour market flexibility Labour market **flexibility** is the degree to which demand and supply in a labour market respond to external changes and return to a new market equilibrium. More flexible labour markets, such as in the UK and the USA compared to many EU countries, are associated with lower unemployment and a higher participation rate with a larger proportion of the population working. However, they are also associated with lower average wages. There are more jobs, but those in work, on average, are paid less. There are many different types of flexibility.

- Geographical flexibility refers to the willingness of workers to move area to get a job, or the willingness of firms to relocate to take advantage of a more advantageous labour market. For example, can workers easily locate from a high-unemployment region like the north east to a low-unemployment region like the south east of England? One major barrier in the UK to geographical flexibility for workers is housing. The cost of renting or buying a house in low-unemployment areas can be too high, particularly for low-wage workers wanting to move. Individuals in social housing in high-unemployment areas pay relatively low rents. To move into expensive private rented accommodation in a low-unemployment area often makes little financial sense.

- External numerical flexibility refers to the ability of firms to adjust their workforce according to their needs. For example, in some EU countries like Spain and Italy, it is very difficult to sack permanent workers, even when they are no longer needed by a firm. Firms get around this by hiring workers on a temporary basis or replacing workers by capital equipment.

- Internal numerical flexibility refers to the ability of firms to adjust the working hours of staff to suit their needs. In the UK, for example, there is a growing trend for firms to offer zero hour contracts, where workers are employed by a firm, but are not guaranteed any work. Effectively, they become perfectly flexible, working only as and when the firm needs them. Another trend is to sign contracts with self-employed workers or contractors rather than taking on permanent

Question 2

Figure 3

Italy unemployment rate (%)

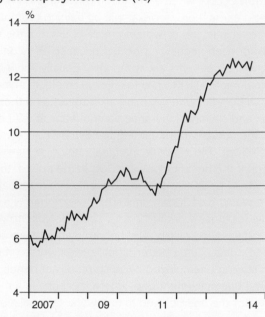

In 2014, the Italian Prime Minister, Matteo Renzi, was planning to reform the country's labour laws. Workers on permanent contracts had huge benefits, including rights that made it difficult for employers to make them redundant. In contrast, those on temporary contracts had almost no employment rights. Not surprisingly, very few young workers had permanent contracts. The government planned to establish a single contract for new workers that would gradually replace the old system. The new contract would have few protections in the first years of employment, but more in later years. There would also be a move to an unemployment insurance system that compensated laid-off workers for their lost salaries rather than keeping them technically employed at their old company with no hours and a fraction of their wages. Further, there would be tight links between unemployment benefits, job training and job searches.

(a) Explain why Italian employers in 2014 might have been reluctant to take on workers on permanent contracts.

(b) Explain why the Italian government's proposals might reduce unemployment in the long term.

members of staff. If they are not needed, self-employed workers and contractors can simply not be given any more work. With permanent staff, it is much more costly to make them redundant.

- Functional flexibility occurs when a firm can redeploy a worker from one job to another. Functional flexibility requires workers to be multi-skilled. This often requires firms to train workers. The cost of training has to be offset against the gains from more flexible working on the part of workers.
- Wage flexibility occurs when firms are able to adjust wages up and down according to the forces of demand supply in the labour market. In practice, most workers are on fixed wage contracts. However, wage flexibility can be achieved if bonuses form part of a worker's remuneration package. Equally, the weaker the power of any trade unions in a firm, the more likely it is that a firm could impose pay cuts.

Trade unions The purpose of a trade union is to organise workers into one bargaining unit. The trade union then becomes a monopolist, a sole seller of labour, and prevents workers from competing amongst themselves in the job market. Economic theory predicts that if trade unions raise wage rates for their members, then employment and output will be lower in otherwise competitive markets. So free market economist argue that government must intervene to curb the power of trade unions. In the UK, the power of trade unions was considerably reduced in the 1980s. Margaret Thatcher's government at the time curtailed the ability of trade unions to strike and outlawed arrangements where workers were forced to be trade union members at a place of work. The 1980s also saw a considerable shrinkage of heavy industry (including coal mining) and manufacturing, which were heavily unionised. The composition of the workforce changed with a much larger proportion of women in work. Women traditionally are less likely to be in a union than men. Today, the most powerful unions represent public sector workers. Free market economists argue that the ability of trade unions to strike should be curtailed even further. However, certainly in the UK, it could be argued that trade unions have little industrial power. Curbing their power further would then have almost no impact on improving the efficiency of the labour market.

Migration In recent years, there has been significant net migration into the UK of people of working age. Net inward migration of working age people increases the potential size of the labour force. With increased supply of labour, wage rates should be lower than they would otherwise have been. If the economy is at full employment, this helps reduce inflationary pressures. However, the exact impact on wages in individual occupations and on economic growth as a whole is more difficult to determine. For example, if all the immigrants were plumbers who settled in London, there would be a downward pressure on the earnings of plumbers in the London area but there would be little impact elsewhere in the economy.

Some have argued that the UK could benefit more from net immigration by targeting particular types of immigrants. This type of policy is used in countries such as the USA and Canada where those applying for visas to work in the country are more likely to be granted a visa if they have desirable skills and qualifications. This might mean skills and qualification in occupations where there is a shortage of workers; or it might mean high levels of skills, such as having a university degree. In a rich developed economy, supply-side benefits are more likely to come having well-educated and highly skilled workers than having low-skilled workers.

Minimum wages In many countries, there is a national minimum wage. In the USA, individual states can also set a higher minimum wage for their state than the national minimum wage set in Washington, the capital. It would be equivalent to paying a different minimum wage in London than in the rest of the UK. Free market economists argue that minimum wages create unemployment and tend to argue that they should be abolished. The higher the wage rate, the less demand there will be for workers from employers. Other economists argue that the impact on employment depends on the level at which the minimum wage is set. For the UK, there is little evidence to suggest that minimum wage levels create any significant unemployment. There is also an argument that a higher minimum wage can lead to supply-side improvements. Higher minimum wages encourage employers to train their low paid workers to be more productive in order to justify the expense of employing them. It also encourages firms to invest in physical capital to replace low-paid workers. If the economy is at full employment, higher investment will lead to higher economic growth.

Improving the skills and quality of the labour force

A more productive workforce with higher levels of human capital will raise the level of long run aggregate supply. Over time, the human capital of workers can be raised through education and training.

Education In the UK, as in most countries, education up to 18 is mainly provided by the state. Increasing educational levels of students can be affected by the amount of money spent on education. One reason why average attainment levels in the UK are higher than in, say, Kenya or India is because education is far better funded. Equally, the length of time students spend in full-time education is likely to affect educational attainment. A population where the majority have studied to 21 are more likely, all other things being equal, to be better educated than one where only a small minority study beyond 18. However, education standards are also affected by what students learn and how they are taught. An interventionist approach is for the government to set a curriculum, prescribe teaching methods and then set targets. A free market approach within a state-funded system is for the government to allow schools to compete for pupils, set their own curriculum and decide on their own teaching methods.

Training Training may give rise to market failure. Firms are responsible for training their own workers. This is a cost to the firm and they may provide less training than the socially optimal level of training for the whole economy. For this reason, governments tend to intervene in the training market. A market-based approach would be for government to give subsidies to firms for training. An interventionist approach would be for government to provide training itself, for example through further education colleges. It could also set up training schemes working in cooperation with firms.

Immigration One way to improve the average skills level of the workforce is to encourage immigration of individuals with above average skills as explained above.

Question 3

Six months after becoming Prime Minister, David Cameron said that its was 'perfectly possible' to halve net migration without damaging companies or the economy. Companies were sceptical at the time and new figures suggest they were right. In the two years since tougher visa restrictions were introduced, the number of highly skilled migrants from outside Europe has dropped by more than a third. At a key point in the economic recovery, companies are facing a potential shortfall in skilled workers. Those who are being recruited are coming from a considerably smaller pool of international talent. John Cridland, Director-General of the CBI employers' group, said: 'CBI members with shortages of engineers … would say the only thing that's keeping the wheels on the bus are eastern European engineers.' Barbara Roche, a former Labour Party immigration minister and chair of the Migration Matters Trust, said: 'The choice Britain faces is this: either we maintain a sensible migration policy, tackle the skills shortages holding back the economy and safeguard the recovery, or we leave the EU, slash immigration and tip Britain back into recession.'

Source: adapted from © the *Financial Times* 3.7.2014, All Rights Reserved.

Figure 4

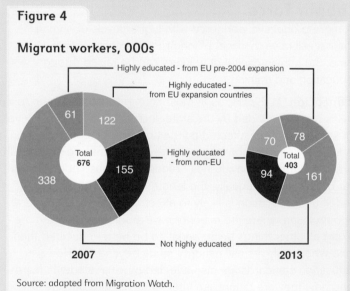

Migrant workers, 000s

Source: adapted from Migration Watch.

Explain how reducing the immigration of skilled workers could reduce growth in long run aggregate supply for the UK economy.

Improving infrastructure

Infrastructure is important to promoting economic growth. Poor roads, for example, lead to longer journey times for goods being transported and for workers getting to work. This adds costs to firms, making them less internationally competitive and creates labour immobility. A lack of good school buildings can harm education. Poor hospitals lead to more illness and deaths of workers, destroying the human capital of the economy.

Infrastructure spending tends to be the responsibility of government. They have to set priorities for spending, deciding which projects will go ahead and which will be shelved.

In the UK, there are, arguably, two key issues. One is the amount spent on infrastructure which as a percentage of GDP tends to be lower than many EU countries. The other is the geographical allocation of spending. Those living in London and the South tend to argue that it is only right that the majority of funds should be spend in their region. Over half the population lives in the South and output per worker is higher justifying higher levels of infrastructure spending. Those in the North argue that the North-South divide will only grow if the North is starved of funds for new roads, railways and other types of infrastructure. Reducing inequality in the UK means that the North should have greater amounts per capita spent on infrastructure than in the South.

Question 4

At a time when the Mayor of London, Boris Johnson, is saying that London needs £1 300 billion of infrastructure spending, five of Britain's northern cities have put forward a £15-billion plan for new road and rail links. The cities of Liverpool, Manchester, Leeds, Sheffield and Newcastle have put forward proposals for investment in extra road capacity, a new high-speed rail link across the Pennines and better access to Manchester airport. They said this would create a 'connected region' that would challenge London. George Osborne, the Chancellor, said the public expenditure choice facing the UK was between investment in big infrastructure projects and 'continuing to spend money on welfare payments that are not generating a real economic return'. London and the southeast have received the lion's share of infrastructure spending in past decades. That trend has been exacerbated by significant new investments in London such as Crossrail, the new £16-billion east-west railway line that is the largest construction project in Europe. According to KPMG, the capital spends as much on infrastructure every two days as Manchester does in a year.

Source: adapted from © the *Financial Times* 6.8.2014, All Rights Reserved.

(a) Explain why spending £15 billion on improved transport links in the North might increase long run aggregate supply.

(b) In 2014, London and the South were growing at a faster rate than the rest of the UK. Suggest two causes for this.

(c) Discuss whether welfare benefits cannot generate 'a real economic return'.

Encouraging the growth of small and medium-sized businesses

Small and medium-sized businesses are important in the economy because they can provide new jobs and become the big businesses of tomorrow. Governments tend to encourage the setting up of new businesses through various schemes such as providing training or benefits to those who become self-employed. 'Red tape' is often less than for large firms. Government may also directly or through the banking system offer loans at better than commercial terms to small and medium-sized businesses.

Strengths and weaknesses of supply-side policies

Supply-side policies have an effect on the macroeconomic performance of an economy but they have both strengths and weaknesses.

Economic growth Supply-side policies are designed to maintain or increase the rate of growth of the economy. Figure 5 shows a growing economy. Without supply-side policies, the productive potential of the economy would grow from $LRAS_1$ to $LRAS_2$ because of supply-side improvements occurring in the private sector such as use of better technology. However, with successful supply-side policies, the productive potential of the economy grows from $LRAS_1$ to $LRAS_3$. Extra output of Y_2Y_3 can be obtained through successful supply-side policies. The extra productive potential is dependent on the success of the policies in place. Individual supply-side policies may not work and, at worst, could reduce the growth rate.

Figure 5

The impact on growth of supply-side policies

Supply-side improvements push the LRAS curve from $LRAS_1$ to $LRAS_2$. The movement from $LRAS_2$ to $LRAS_3$ shows the additional impact of supply-side policies.

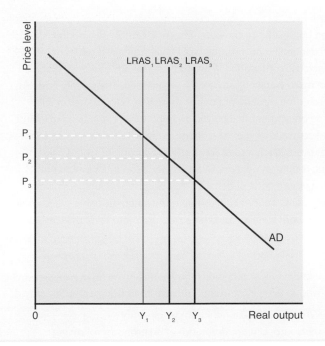

Inflation Figure 5 shows that successful supply-side policies have the effect of reducing the price level. This assumes that aggregate demand is constant. In a growing economy, however, aggregate demand will be increasing too. Figure 6 shows an economy where over time aggregate demand is growing shown by the rightward shift in the AD curve from AD_1 to AD_2 and AD_3. In this economy, there will be no inflation if long run aggregate supply is also increasing from $LRAS_1$ through to $LRAS_3$. To maintain a two per cent inflation rate, the inflation target for the Bank of England, supply-side policies need to be pushing the LRAS curve to the right at a slightly slower pace than the increase in aggregate demand, as shown in Figure 7.

Figure 6

Long-run aggregate supply and aggregate demand growing by the same amount

Supply-side improvements push the LRAS curve from $LRAS_1$ to $LRAS_2$. The movement from $LRAS_2$ to $LRAS_3$ shows the additional impact of supply-side policies.

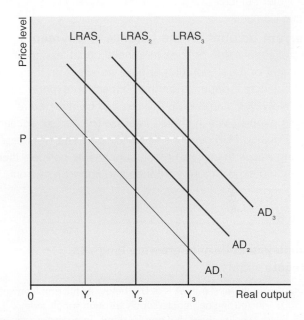

Figure 7

Achieving a small positive rate of inflation

If aggregate demand grows slightly more than long-run aggregate supply then there will be a small increases in the price level over time and so there will be low inflation.

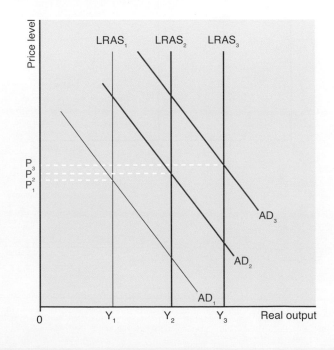

Unemployment Many supply-side policies are aimed at reducing unemployment and encouraging employment. However, supply-side policies on their own cannot guarantee low unemployment. Figure 8 shows an economy where, in the short run, output is OY_1 because this is where aggregate demand equals short-run aggregate supply. This is below the full employment output of long-run aggregate supply of OY_2. Increasing long run aggregate supply will not reduce unemployment unless there is a larger increase in aggregate demand.

The current account on the balance of payments
Successful supply-side policies in general could lead to an improvement or a deterioration or have no effect on the current account balance. It depends on their impact on exports and imports. However, supply-side policies can be directed at increasing exports, which should improve the current account balance. Equally, if UK supply-side policies are more successful at lowering prices than, say, French supply-side policies, then the UK should export more to France and import less from

France. The same would be true if supply-side policies led to greater technological advances in the UK.

Distribution of income Some market-orientated, supply-side policies lead to a widening of the distribution of income. For example, abolishing minimum wages, cutting welfare benefits to the unemployed and reducing trade union power whilst at the same time cutting marginal rates of tax for the top 10 per cent of income earners are all supply-side policies but will lead to a growing gap between high-income and low-income earners. Privatisation and deregulation too tend to lead to growing inequality because workers in the industries affected tend to see their wages fall in real terms after privatisation and deregulation have taken place. Free market economists would argue that rises in GDP caused by supply-side policies will benefit everyone. There will be more jobs and higher incomes. However, recent UK and US experience suggests that many of the new jobs will be low paid. At the same time, those on very high incomes tend to appropriate most of the increase in GDP, leaving those on low and middle incomes with almost no increase. Technically everyone benefits, but very high-income earners benefit disproportionately.

Figure 8

Unemployment despite growing long-run aggregate supply

If short-run equilibrium output is at OY_1 below its full employment level of OY_2, increasing aggregate supply through supply-side policies will not help achieve full employment. To do this, aggregate demand must rise faster than long run aggregate supply.

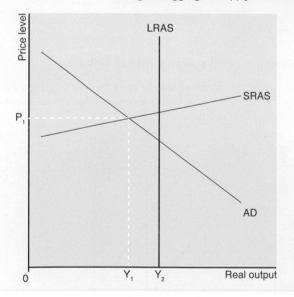

Question 5

Further cuts in real wages in countries whose labour markets have been hardest hit by the economic crisis would risk creating deflation and deepening poverty, the OECD has warned. It said that reforms to increase competition in product and service markets, rather than more wage adjustments, were needed. The priority now was to foster the creation of not just more jobs but also better jobs. Wage adjustment had played an important part in helping labour markets weather the deep downturn by improving competitiveness and reducing job losses. Any further reduction of wages risks being counter-productive because then economies would run into a vicious circle of deflation, lower consumption and lower investment. Policies such as minimum wages, progressive taxation and in-work benefits could help to share more fairly the costs of economic adjustments.

Source: adapted from © the *Financial Times* 4.9.2014, All Rights Reserved.

(a) Explain why supply-side adjustments in the labour market could lead to a fall in consumption, investment and economic growth.

(b) Why might higher minimum wages improve the macroeconomic performance of an economy following a deep and prolonged recession?

Key Terms

Bottlenecks - supply-side constraints in a particular market in an economy which prevent higher growth for the whole economy.
Deregulation - the process of removing government controls from markets.
Industrial policy - government policy to promote and support individual firms which it considers are important for the growth of the economy.
Interventionist policies - government policies designed to correct market failures that are reducing the growth rate of the economy.
Labour market flexibility - the degree to which demand and supply in a labour market respond to external changes (such as changes in demand for a product or in population size) to return the market to equilibrium.
Market-based policies - government policies designed to promote economic growth by reducing barriers to the efficient working of free markets.
Minimum wage - the least amount an employer can pay one of its workers, usually expressed as an hourly wage rate.
Poverty or earnings trap - occurs when an individual is little better off or even worse off when gaining an increase in wages because of the combined effect of increased tax and benefit withdrawal.

Privatisation - the sale of government organisations or assets to the private sector.
Red tape - rules and regulations issued by government which firms must adhere to operate legally.
Supply-side economics - the study of how changes in aggregate supply will affect variables such as national income; in particular, how government microeconomic policy might change aggregate supply through individual markets.
Supply-side improvements - changes in individual markets, such as investment by firms or improvements in the skills of workers which lead to an increase in long run aggregate supply without necessarily the intervention of government.
Supply-side policies - government policies designed to increase the productive potential of the economy and push the long run aggregate supply curve to the right.
Unemployment trap - occurs when an individual is little better off or even worse off when getting a job after being unemployed because of the combined effect of increased tax and benefit withdrawal.

Thinking like an economist

North east England

North east England has had higher unemployment than the national average since the 1930s. It was dependent on heavy industry, such as steel manufacturing, shipbuilding and coal mining. These industries have almost all gone today and the region has had to recreate itself economically.

Supply-side policies, designed to improve the performance of the whole UK economy, have had a positive impact on the north east but they do little to close the gap between the north east and the rest of the UK. What is needed are supply-side policies, particularly interventionist policies, targeted at the north east.

One of the north east's major problems is its geographical isolation from the UK's main markets. London and the south are the areas in the UK with the highest population and income per capita. The EU is the UK's main trading partner. Any geographical area so far away from major markets is going to struggle. For this reason, business leaders have long argued that improved transport links are essential to improve the supply side performance of the north east. In particular, they want major improvements to the A1, the main road running through the region from London in the south to Edinburgh in Scotland. The A1 in the north of the region is still a single carriageway road, often causing delays to road users going to and from Scotland. The government has promised to spend more than

£700 million on road upgrades in the north east. However, promised spending on transport over the next 20 years is £246 per person for the north east compared to £4 893 for London according to IPPR North, a think-tank.

Disproportionate spending on London's infrastructure is not the only threat the north east faces. High Speed 2, the new high-speed rail link from London to the north will only extend as far as Leeds. This will do little to help the north east become more competitive. Equally, the proposed Northern Hub, a £600-million rail upgrade programme connecting major northern cities such as Manchester and Leeds, will tend to favour the M62 corridor region to the south of north east England. Again, this could take firms and jobs away from the north east.

The north east could also lose out to a more aggressive devolved Scotland. Some Scottish politicians have proposed, for example, reducing or abolishing air passenger duty, a tax on passengers flying into and out of the UK. This supply-side reform might benefit Scottish airports, but it could take away passengers from the main airport in the north east, Newcastle International airport. The danger would be that Newcastle airport would lose so many passengers that airlines would stop using Newcastle airport.

Source: with information from © the *Financial Times* 11.3.2014, All Rights Reserved.

Data Response Question

Boosting engineering skills and research

The car-making and aerospace sectors will lose out to international rivals unless the government tackles a shortage of engineering skills and boosts research spending, a report has warned. A review by Jaguar Land Rover Executive Director Mike Wright said that Britain needs to strengthen advanced manufacturing - companies that use innovative technology, typically in the life sciences, automotive and aerospace sectors.

Advanced manufacturers are at a disadvantage to international rivals who benefit from better government support, the report said. The JLR director suggested expanding the number of manufacturing-related degrees taken by students and doubling the number of engineering apprentices qualifying at an advanced level to address a skills shortage that many businesses believe is the biggest curb on manufacturing growth.

While the number of engineering first degrees awarded in the UK rose 3 100 over the nine years to 2011-12, non-EU students accounted for three quarters of the increase. Companies have often warned that Britain risks losing its core manufacturing base and smaller supply chain companies unless the issue is tackled.

More spending on science and technology is another recommendation. The UK spends less on research and development as a share of GDP than Slovenia and Estonia, whilst China spends more than 10 times as much as the UK each year in absolute terms. Although the government has started to invest in business innovation in an attempt to help turn scientific breakthroughs into commercial successes, spending is low compared with other countries. The Technology Strategy Board, the government's innovation centre, had a budget of £444 million in 2013,

compared to the £1.6 billion spent by Germany's equivalent, the Fraunhofer Institute.

Source: adapted from © the *Financial Times* 27.6.2014, All Rights Reserved.

Q

1. In absolute terms, the USA is the largest spender on research and development in the world. Explain why, then, it is only ranked 5th in Figure 9.

2. Explain two ways in which government support for advanced manufacturing could lead to higher UK long-run aggregate supply.

3. Discuss whether advanced manufacturing in the UK would be better supported by market-orientated supply-side policies such as abolishing the national minimum wage, reducing unemployment benefits and cutting top rates of income tax rather than interventionist methods advocated in the report by Mike Wright.

Evaluation

Explain the difference between market-orientated policies and interventionist policies. Identify the problems that advanced manufacturing has in the UK from the data. Analyse the impact that market-orientated reforms might have on these problems. Then do the same for interventionist policies. Weigh up which are the better solutions. Part of your evaluation could be to point out that many supply-side policies are directed at the economy as a whole rather than the needs of a particular industry.

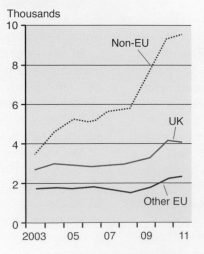

Figure 9

Expenditure on research and development, % of GDP, 2011

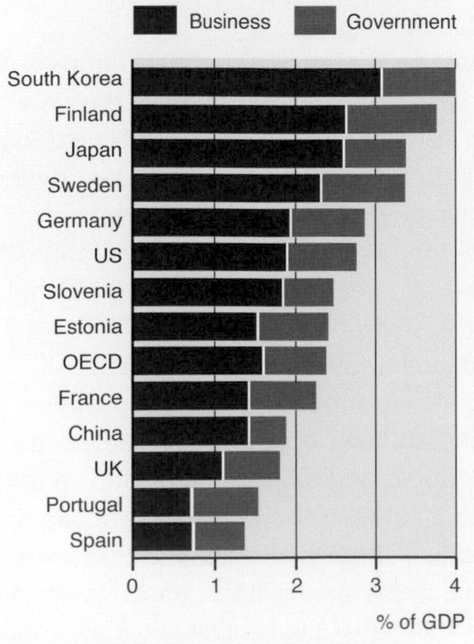

Source: adapted from OECD; *Engineering UK Report*, 2014, 'The State of Engineering'.

Figure 10

Postgraduate degrees (excluding doctorates) in engineering from UK universities by domicile of student

Source: adapted from OECD; *Engineering UK Report*, 2014, 'The State of Engineering'.

40 Conflicts and trade-offs

Key points

1. There are potential conflicts and trade-offs between macroeconomic objectives.
2. The short-run Phillips curve shows there is a trade-off between inflation and unemployment.
3. There are potential conflicts and trade-offs between different economic policies.

Starter activity

Should the government's top macroeconomic priority be the reduction in its fiscal deficit? What impact does cutting government spending and raising taxes have on aggregate demand? Use the Internet to find out what impact government austerity measures have had in countries such as Portugal, Spain and Greece.

Macroeconomic objectives

The government has a number of macroeconomic objectives, which were explained in Unit 37. These include:

- high and sustainable economic growth;
- low unemployment;
- low inflation;
- a sustainable current account equilibrium on the balance of payments;
- a sustainable fiscal position;
- environmental objectives, such as reducing pollution and greenhouse gas emissions;
- objectives relating to income and wealth equality.

Figure 1

A growing economy with low inflation

The shift from 0A to 0B can show a successful economy growing over time with full employment and mild inflation.

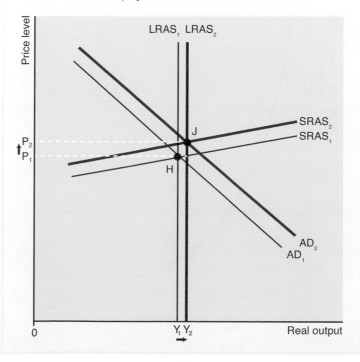

A successful sustainable economy

What might a successful economy look like for a developed country such as the UK, where the government was achieving all its macroeconomic objectives?

Consider Figure 1. At the point H, the economy is in both short-run and long-run equilibrium. Aggregate demand is equal to short-run and long-run aggregate supply. At OY, there may be structural unemployment, but here we will assume that there is full employment in all regions and all industries in the economy. The economy is growing at 2.5 per cent per year, the average for developed countries before the 2007-08 financial crisis. Over time, aggregate demand is increasing, shown by the shift in the aggregate demand curve to the right. This is matched by an increase in both short-run and long-run aggregate supply. At J, there is a new equilibrium. Output is higher. There is also very mild inflation, shown by the increase in the price level from OP_1 to OP_2. This is caused by aggregate demand rising slightly faster than short-run and long-run aggregate supply. Figure 1 can't be used to show that there is a sustainable fiscal equilibrium or that there is a sustainable current account equilibrium on the balance of payments. Again, assume that these two equilibria exist. Nor can Figure 1 say anything about income and wealth inequality. However, assume that growth in the economy is partly being used to finance environmental improvements, such as a shift towards renewable energy.

Conflicts between macroeconomic objectives

Macroeconomic objectives can conflict, particularly when the economy is in disequilibrium. Examples of how they can conflict include the following.

Inflation is too high Assume that the rate of inflation is too high. One way to reduce the rate of inflation is to reduce aggregate demand for example by cutting consumer spending or government spending. However, reducing aggregate demand is likely to lead to a recession and cyclical unemployment. A recession means that the rate of economic growth will become negative.

Growth is too low Assume that the rate of economic growth is too low. One way to increase it in the short term is to raise aggregate demand. This will lower unemployment but it will also increase inflation. It is also likely to lead to a rise in imports because increased incomes will lead to extra demand for imported goods. A rise in imports will lead to a deterioration in the current account position on the balance of payments. Another way of raising economic growth is to raise the growth of long-run aggregate supply. However, many of the methods advocated to raise long-run aggregate supply will lead to a fall in wage rates for many workers. For example, reducing trade union power, making wages more flexible and making it easier for firms to sack workers are all likely to put downward pressure on wages. So inequalities in income could grow. This is a problem if a government wishes to reduce inequalities. Equally, supply-side reforms might mean looser environmental controls on firms. This could conflict with environmental objectives.

Unemployment is too high If unemployment is too high, one way of reducing it is to raise aggregate demand. However, this might then conflict with objectives about inflation and the current account. Another way of reducing unemployment might be through supply-side reforms. However, more jobs might mean greater inequality if most of the jobs created are very low paid. Equally, more jobs might come at the expense of environmental objectives. A factory built on agricultural land might harm the environment for example.

The current account on the balance of payments is deeply in the red If imports are far greater than exports, there might be difficulties for a country in financing this deficit. Cutting imports by reducing domestic consumption and investment will lead to higher unemployment. This is because a fall in aggregate demand will also hit demand for domestically produced goods.

The fiscal deficit is too high If the government is borrowing too much as a percentage of GDP, then it may attempt to correct this through cutting its spending and raising taxes. However, these austerity measures will raise unemployment and, certainly in the short term, lower the rate of economic growth. If the fiscal austerity measures are great enough, the economy will fall into deep recession, as the recent examples of Greece, Portugal and Spain have shown.

Inequalities in income and wealth are too great

Correcting inequalities may involve direct government intervention by redistributing income through taxes and government spending. Direct provision of better educational outcomes for low-achieving students should lead, in the long term, to them being able to earn higher wages. Correcting inequalities may also involve intervening in markets, for example, by setting minimum wages or giving trade unions more power. Economists disagree about the outcomes of these measures. However, reducing inequality, for example by large rises in benefits for the unemployed is likely to have some disincentive effect to work and this then raises long-term unemployment and reduces long-term growth. Equally, a failure to correct inequalities in education between children from rich and poor households is likely to reduce long-term economic growth.

The environmental situation is deteriorating If environmental indicators are deteriorating, the government can introduce policies to reverse these trends. As with inequalities, economists disagree about the impact of policies designed to correct environmental failures. However, investing in cleaner technologies might lead to lower economic growth because investment resources are being diverted into resources that don't contribute to economic growth. Tightening environmental

regulation might discourage investment, leading to lower growth and high unemployment. On the other hand, investing in, say, wind farms or pollution-reducing equipment might lead to an increase in investment and therefore aggregate demand. This might raise growth and reduce unemployment.

The short-run Phillips curve

One example of a trade-off between two macroeconomic objectives is the short-run Phillips curve. A W Phillips was an economist who published a paper in 1958 showing that there was a statistical relationship between the rate of unemployment and the rate of change of money wages between 1861 and 1957 in the UK. This relationship, called the Phillips curve is shown in Figure 2. The money wages paid to workers are the most important single cost of production in the UK economy. When money wages go up faster than the increase in output per worker (their productivity) then costs increase for firms. They respond by putting up prices. The rate of increase in money wages is, therefore, a good proxy variable for the rate of increase in the price level i.e. the rate of inflation.

So the Phillips curve shows that there is a trade-off between unemployment and inflation. The lower the rate of unemployment, the higher the inflation rate. This trade-off can be seen on an aggregate demand and supply curve diagram. In Figure 3, the economy is at OA in short-run equilibrium. There is an increase in aggregate demand from AD_1 to AD_2. Real output rises from OA to OB. Higher output means more jobs and less unemployment. But the fall in unemployment comes at a cost

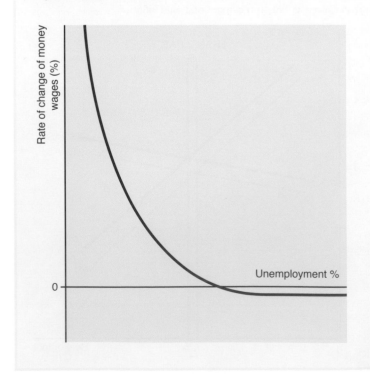

Figure 2

The short-run Phillips curve

The short-run Phillips curve shows there is a trade-off between high unemployment rates and higher rates of change of money wages, a proxy measure for inflation.

Figure 3

The trade-off between unemployment and inflation

The movement up the short-run aggregate supply curve leads to higher real output, lower unemployment but higher prices.

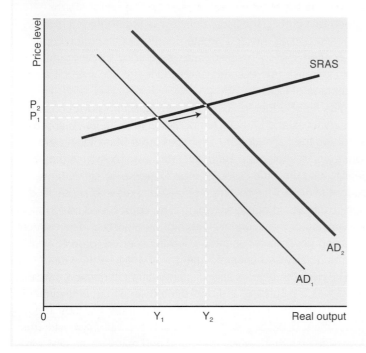

of a rise in the price level of EF. In the long run, with a vertical long-run aggregate supply curve, there is no trade-off between unemployment and inflation because, in the long run, there is no unemployment.

This trade-off is a short-run trade-off. It results from a movement up or down the short-run aggregate supply curve.

Conflicts and trade-offs between economic policies

Different economic policies typically have a number of different effects. These can conflict with other policies or lead to conflicts between economic objectives. Examples of how they can conflict include the following.

Expansionary and contractionary fiscal and monetary policy Expansionary fiscal and monetary policy will lead to an increase in aggregate demand. This should increase the short-term rate of economic growth and reduce unemployment. However, it is likely to lead to higher inflation and a deterioration on the current account of the balance of payments. This is because an increase in demand for goods and services will be partly met by an increase in imports. The reverse is also true. Contractionary fiscal and monetary policy is likely to reduce inflation and improve the current account position but lead to lower economic growth and higher unemployment.

Changes in interest rates The government might use interest rates as part of monetary policy to influence aggregate demand and hence inflation and unemployment in the short term. However, persistently high interest rates could damage long-term investment and hence reduce long-term growth. Equally, persistently high interest rates are likely to raise the

value of the currency against other foreign exchange currencies. For the UK, a high value of the pound could damage its international competitiveness and weaken its ability to export, whilst making imports more competitive. Interest rates also influence the distribution of income and wealth. Low interest rates benefit borrowers including those with mortgages. Younger people are more likely to have mortgages than older people. So low interest rates benefit younger people. High interest rates benefit savers and lenders. Older people, including pensioners, are more likely to have savings and so they are more likely to benefit from higher interest rates. Interest rates can also influence the distribution of wealth. Quantitative easing, which reduces interest rates to very low levels, encourages the better-off to borrow money to buy assets such as houses for rent. It also leads to rises in the price of assets such as shares and houses, because of higher demand financed by cheap borrowing. So quantitative easing arguably increases wealth inequalities.

Supply-side policies Supply-side policies should increase the productive potential of the economy, pushing the long-run aggregate supply curve to the right. In the long run they should reduce inflationary pressures. However, supply-side policies that encourage investment in physical capital will lead to higher aggregate demand in the short term if investment does increase. This increases inflationary pressures in the short term. Supply-side policies designed to reduce trade union power, make wages more flexible or reduce minimum wages are likely to increase income inequalities because wages at the bottom of the income distribution are likely to fall. Cutting unemployment benefits to encourage people to work is also likely to increase income inequalities at least in the short term.

Fiscal deficits Countries with fiscal deficits which are too high may attempt to reduce this by cutting government spending and raising taxes. This, then, will almost certainly lead to higher unemployment and lower growth in the short term. The higher the fall in output as a result of austerity measures and the higher the fall in tax revenues as a result, the more ineffective the policy will be. Austerity budgets that cut government spending and raise taxes are likely to widen inequalities in income and wealth. Those who lose their jobs or young people unable to get their first job will be particularly affected.

Environmental policies As explained earlier in this unit, environmental policies can lead to lower long-run aggregate supply and hence lower economic growth. This is because environmental policies may increase costs of production and reduce investment. However, in some cases, environmental policies can force inefficient firms to become more efficient, for example by recycling more of their waste or forcing them to think about whether it would be more profitable to replacing aging equipment. Environmental policies can also increase long-run aggregate supply from what it might otherwise have been if the cost of those environmental policies is less than the costs arising from environmental market failure that would otherwise have occurred. For example, assume it costs £20 billion to implement environmental policies. Then assume the environmental cost of doing nothing is £30 billion. Environmental policies have then gained the economy £10 billion.

Thinking like an economist

UK policy conflicts 2010-14

In 2010, a new coalition government came into office. The UK economy was still suffering from the effects of the 2007-08 financial crisis. In 2009, the economy had shrunk in size with a 4.3 per cent fall in GDP. Unemployment had risen from 1.6 million in 2007 to 2.4 million. Public sector borrowing was £124 billion, up from £40 billion in 2007. The current account on the balance of payments was in deficit at 2.8 per cent of GDP, although this was not a particularly high amount in recent historical terms. At least inflation was low at 2.2 per cent.

The 2010 general election campaign had been fought with two different views about future economic policy.

Figure 4

Real average weekly earnings (total pay adjusted by CPI); 1 January 2008 = 100

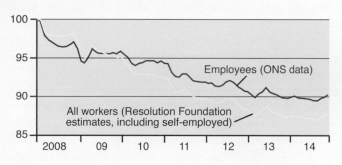

Source: adapted from Thomson Reuters Datastream; © the *Financial Times* 16.10.2014, All Rights Reserved; The Resolution Foundation; ONS.

Figure 5

Public sector budget balance (rolling 12 month sum), £bn

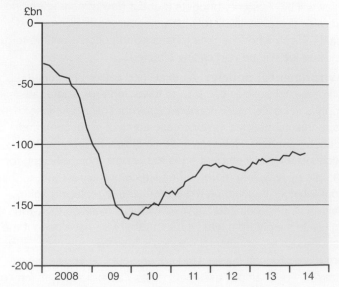

Source: adapted from Thomson Reuters Datastream; © the *Financial Times* 16.10.2014, All Rights Reserved.

The Conservative Party argued that cutting the fiscal deficit quickly was the most important priority. The Labour Party agreed that cutting the fiscal deficit was important but it proposed cutting it over a greater length of time in the hope that economic growth would increase quickly. Higher growth would increase tax revenues and reduce the fiscal deficit as a percentage of GDP.

In its first Budget in 2010, the new coalition government of Conservatives and Liberal Democrats prioritised its objective of cutting the fiscal deficit. 'The most urgent task facing this country is to implement an accelerated plan to reduce the deficit', said the Chancellor, George Osborne, in his 2010 Budget speech. The government raised taxes and announced significant cuts in public spending. The coalition called for a rebalancing of the economy with higher exports and investment replacing government spending. If this occurred, growth would resume quickly and unemployment would fall.

The next three years saw disappointing economic growth. There was a surprising and unexpected growth in employment and a fall in unemployment. In terms of numbers of jobs, the government could argue that it had achieved its objective. The downside was that wages stagnated and many of the new jobs created were either low-earning, self-employed jobs or minimum wage jobs. By 2014, average real earnings for workers were 10 per cent lower than they were at the start of 2008, as Figure 4 shows. As for GDP, it took until 2014 for GDP to equal its 2007 level. Inflation had been surprisingly high between 2010 and 2013. In 2011 it hit 4.5 per cent, compared to the Bank of England target of two per cent. The inflation, however, was cost-push in nature. Higher world commodity prices were a main factor in driving inflation higher. Certainly there were no significant demand-pull factors driving prices higher. By 2015, with falling world commodity prices, the economy was in danger of slipping into deflation.

Figure 6

Forecasts for tax receipts and other current revenues (% of GDP)

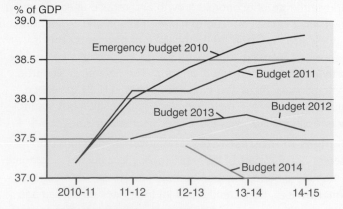

Source: adapted from ONS; HM Treasury; OBR; IFS.

As for the fiscal deficit, by 2014, it had only shrunk by one third in money terms compared to 2010, as Figure 5 shows. Significant government spending cuts had taken place. However, tax revenues remained very weak as Figure 6 shows despite some economic growth over the period. In his 2010 budget, George Osborne had predicted that 'public sector net borrowing will decline to 1.1 per cent of GDP in 2015-16' through government spending cuts, tax rises and strong economic growth. However, cutting aggregate demand through cutting government spending and raising taxes conflicted with the aspiration to see strong economic growth. As a result, the 1.1 per cent prediction is likely to be missed by a very wide margin.

Data Response Question

Bank of England's inflation target

The Bank of England is committed to a target of two per cent inflation. However, the Governor of the Bank of England, Mark Carney, said that a period of deflation would be 'unambiguously good' for the economy. He argued that falling prices in the economy overall due to falling world oil prices would raise incomes and spending. He said there were no signs yet of 'bad deflation' with consumers and firms putting off spending because of a persistent and generalised fall in prices.

With rapid spending growth and falling unemployment, there is a general expectation that the Bank

of England will raise interest rates from their current level of 0.5 per cent. Predicting 2.9 per cent growth in 2015 and real household post tax incomes rising 3.5 per cent, the Bank of England expects consumer spending to continue rising quickly this year. The only blot on the landscape was a reduction in the business investment forecast, which the governor said was entirely owing to weaker expectations of oil-related capital spending in the North Sea. The Monetary Policy Committee thinks that the output gap - the slack in the economy which can be used up without generating inflationary pressures - has fallen to roughly 0.5 per cent of gross domestic product.

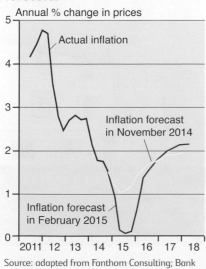

Figure 7

Bank of England inflation (CPI) forecasts

Source: adapted from Fanthom Consulting; Bank of England.

Q

1. Explain what is meant by a macroeconomic objective, using the inflation rate as an example.

2. Analyse, using a diagram, why an objective of raising the rate of economic growth might conflict with an objective to maintain low inflation.

3. Evaluate whether a prolonged period of deflation would conflict with the government's ability to achieve its other macroeconomic objectives.

Evaluation

To evaluate, you must first outline the macroeconomic objectives of government and then analyse how these objectives might or might not conflict when the economy is suffering from a prolonged period of deflation. When do they conflict and when do they not? Overall, do they mostly conflict or are they mostly compatible?

41 Business growth

Key points

1. Small firms exist because economies of scale may be limited, barriers to entry to an industry low and the size of the market may be very small.
2. In large firms, there may be divorce of ownership from control.
3. Organisations may be in the private or public sector and may be for profit and not-for-profit.
4. Businesses may grow organically or through vertical, horizontal or conglomerate integration.
5. Constraints on business growth include the size of the market, access to finance, owner objectives and regulation.
6. Demergers can impact on businesses, workers and consumers.

Starter activity

Use the Internet to find out about a recent merger or takeover. What did the two (or more) firms produce? What were the reasons given for the merger? Is it likely to create a business with a higher value measured by its share price?

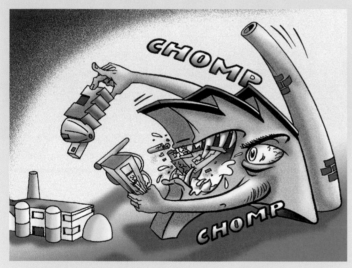

The size of firms

Although production in the UK is dominated by large firms, there are many industries where small and medium-sized enterprises play a significant role.

Large firms exist for two main reasons. First, economies of scale (explained in Unit 44) in the industry may be significant. Only a small number of firms, producing at the minimum efficient scale of production (explained in Unit 44), may be needed to satisfy total demand. The industry may be a natural monopoly (explained in Unit 55) where not even one firm can fully exploit potential economies of scale. Second, barriers to entry (explained in Unit 46) may exist which protect large firms from potential competitors. Conversely, small firms survive for the opposite reasons.

Economies of scale may be very small relative to the market size A large number of firms in an industry may be able to operate at the minimum efficient scale of production. Small firms may also be able to take advantage of the higher costs of larger firms in the industry caused by diseconomies of scale (explained in Unit 44). Changing technology such as

the Internet can allow small firms the same cost advantage as large firms in reaching out to customers especially in small niche markets.

The costs of production for a large scale producer may be higher than for a small company In part, this may be due to productive inefficiency - a large firm operating within its average cost curve boundary (explained in Unit 54). For

Question 1

(a) Why can small firms survive successfully in the hotel industry?

(b) What economic forces might favour hotel chains in the future?

instance, larger firms may be poorly organised in what they see as small unimportant segments of the market (called **market niches**). Or X-inefficiency (explained in Unit 54) may be present. Equally, the average cost curve of a large producer may be higher in certain markets than for a small producer. For instance, a large firm may be forced to pay its workers high wages because it operates in formal labour markets. A small firm may be able to pay relatively low wages in informal labour markets. Indeed, owners of small companies can work exceptionally long hours at effective rates of pay which they would find totally unacceptable if in a normal job. Or a small producer, like a corner shop sole proprietorship, may be prepared to accept a much lower rate of return on its capital employed than would a large company.

Barriers to entry may be low The cost of setting up in an industry, such as the grocery industry or the newsagents' market, may be small. Products may be simple to produce or sell. Finance to set up in the industry may be readily available. The product sold may be relatively homogeneous. It may be easy for a small firm to produce a new product and establish itself in the market.

Small firms can be monopolists A monopolist (explained in Unit 50) offers a product for sale which is available from no other company. Many small firms survive because they offer a local, flexible and personal service. For instance, a newsagent may have a monopoly on the sale of newspapers, magazines, greetings cards, toys and stationery in a local area. Consumers may be unwilling to walk half a mile extra to buy greetings cards at a 10 per cent discount or travel 10 miles by car to a local superstore to buy a £2 toy at a 25 per cent reduction. Or the newsagent may double up as a grocery store and off-licence, opening till 10 o'clock at night and all day Sunday, again offering a service which is not offered anywhere else in the locality. A small shop could be the only place locally where informal credit is offered, or where it is possible to buy a single item instead of a pack of six. Equally in the case of some products, such as cricket balls or croquet mallets, the size of the market is so small that one or two very small firms can satisfy total demand.

The divorce of ownership from control

In small firms, the owner is also likely to be running it on a day-to-day basis. The larger the firm, though, the more likely it is that the owners will take no part in the running of the firm. Instead, they appoint directors and managers to run the business. For example, the vast majority of the 100 largest companies quoted on the London Stock Exchange (the FTSE 100 companies) have no owners who are involved in running the business directly.

So, for large companies, there is a **divorce of ownership from control** of the day-to-day running of the business. In a large company in the UK, there will be a board of directors, which will include a chair of the board and the chief executive. Most of the board of directors will be part-time and themselves will have no involvement in the day-to-day running of the company. They and the chair of the board are there to represent the shareholders, the owners of the company. The board of directors oversees the work of the chief executive and the senior managers of the company. It is the chief executive and the

senior managers who work full time for the company and control day-to-day decision making.

The divorce of ownership from control is an example of the principal-agent problem explained in Unit 19. The principal-agent problem occurs when one group, the agent, is making decisions on behalf of another group, the principal. In theory, the agent should maximise the benefits for those whom they are looking after. In theory, therefore, directors and senior managers of companies should always put the interests of shareholders first. In practice, agents always have the temptation to maximise their own benefits at the expense of the principals. In the case of companies, directors and managers have an incentive to appropriate part of the profit or potential profit of the company. They can do this, for example, by awarding themselves large pay packages and bonuses. They can grow the company to maximise its size but at the expense of profit. Salaries and bonuses tend to depend on size of the company rather than its profitability. If there is a takeover bid for the company, there is a temptation for directors to accept or reject the bid according to what will most benefit them rather than what will benefit the shareholders.

Shareholders do have some control over directors through the Annual General Meeting (AGM) of the company. They have the power to vote directors onto or off the board of directors. They can pass resolutions. However, the AGM is a very ineffective tool for controlling directors. Only a minority of shareholders are likely to vote and, at best, only a few per cent might attend. Directors ensure they have blocks of votes ready to cast for the resolutions they have put to the meeting, to ensure that these resolutions pass. The main power shareholders have over directors is through the buying and selling of shares. If share prices drop significantly, this can put pressure on the board of directors to change its strategy.

Public sector and private sector organisations

Public sector organisations are organisations that are owned and controlled by the state. There is a wide variety of different public sector organisations in the UK including:

- civil service departments like the Ministry of Defence;
- local authorities like Westminster City Council;
- public corporations like the BBC;
- trusts like National Health Service trusts or education trusts which run acadamies;
- regulators like OFWAT, which regulate some private sector companies.

The purpose of public sector organisations is to provide a service to the UK citizen. Some are able to make profits and losses because of the way they are structured financially. However, making a profit is not generally the main aim of a public sector organisation.

Private sector organisations are organisations that are owned by individuals or companies and not the state. Almost all private sector organisations aim to make a profit. Exactly how much profit depends on the objectives of the organisations themselves. For example, a self-employed businessperson may want to maximise profits. Equally, the businessperson may prefer to make less profit and work fewer hours. In the case of large companies, the divorce of ownership from control means that making a profit is important, but whether it is the maximum profit or something less depends very much on the motivations of directors and managers.

Question 2

Fitness First, the chain of 377 fitness centres, has announced it was hiring 250 personal trainers to help drive its shift into the premium health and fitness market. It wants to get out of the mid-market because its revenues and profits are under attack from low-cost gyms.

It is investing £86 million in rebranding and new openings, mainly in Asia. £18 million will be spent in its 77 UK clubs to create new gym space and recruit 400 floor staff, fitness managers and sales consultants, and 250 personal trainers. About 20 clubs have already been revamped. On average they have increased their revenues by four per cent and their profit by ten per cent.

Source: adapted from © the Financial Times 12.1.2015, All Rights Reserved.

(a) 'Fitness First is attempting to grow organically.' Explain what this means using examples from the data.

(b) Suggest and explain one reason why Fitness First might want to grow.

(c) Suggest why it is most unlikely that Fitness First would want to grow through either backward or forward integration.

There are a few private sector organisations that are **not-for-profit organisations**. They are organisations that do not have making a profit as a goal but use any profit or surplus they generate to support their aims. These include charities that can range from a national charity like the NSPCC (National Society for the Prevention of Cruelty to Children) to a local charity like a food bank or a local church. Charities in the UK are regulated by The Charity Commission. Being granted charitable status gives tax advantages. However, there are many more local community organisations which are not large enough to be official charities but which are still not-for-profit organisations.

How businesses grow

Firms may grow in size in two ways:
- by **organic** or **internal growth**;
- by external growth through **merger, amalgamation** or **takeover**.

Organic growth simply refers to firms increasing their output, for instance through increased investment or an increased labour force. A merger or amalgamation is the joining together of two or more firms under common ownership. The boards of directors of the two companies, with the agreement of shareholders, agree to merge their two companies together. A takeover implies that one company wishes to buy another company. The takeover may be amicable. Company X makes a bid for company Y. The board of directors considers the bid and finds that the price offered is a good price for the shareholders of the company. It then recommends the shareholders to accept the offer terms. However, the takeover may be contested. In a hostile takeover the board of directors of company Y recommends to its shareholders to reject the terms of the bid. A takeover battle is then likely to ensue. Company X needs to get promises to sell at the offer price of just over 50 per cent of the shares to win and take control.

Economists distinguish between three types of merger.
- **Horizontal integration** or a **horizontal merger** is a merger between two firms in the same industry at the same stage of production, for instance, the merger of two building societies or two car manufacturers or two bakeries.
- **Vertical integration** or a **vertical merger** is a merger between two firms at different production stages in the same industry. **Forward production integration** involves a supplier merging with one of its buyers, such as a car manufacturer buying a car dealership, or a newspaper buying newsagents. **Backward vertical integration** involves a purchaser buying one of its suppliers, such as a drinks manufacturer buying a bottling manufacturer, or a car manufacturer buying a tyre company.
- **Conglomerate integration** or a **conglomerate merger** is the merging of two firms with no common interest. A tobacco company buying an insurance company, or a food company buying a clothing chain would be conglomerate mergers.

Reasons for growth

It is suggested that profit maximising companies are motivated to grow in size for a number of reasons.
- A larger company may be able to exploit economies of scale more fully. The merger of two medium-sized car

manufacturers, for instance, is likely to result in potential economies in all fields, from production to marketing to finance. Vertical and conglomerate mergers are less likely to yield scale economies because there are unlikely to be any technical economies. There may be some marketing economies and more likely there may be some financial economies.

- A larger company may be more able to control its markets. It may therefore reduce competition in the market place in order to be better able to exploit the market.
- A larger company may be able to reduce risk. Many conglomerate companies have grown for this reason. Some markets are fragile. They are subject to large changes in demand when economies go into boom or recession. A steel manufacturer, for instance, will do exceptionally well in a boom, but will be hard hit in a recession, so it might decide to diversify by buying a company with a product which does not have a cyclical demand pattern, like a supermarket chain. Other industries face a very uncertain future. It became fashionable in the 1970s and early 1980s for tobacco companies to buy anything which seemed to have a secure future, from grocery stores to insurance companies.
- Where there is a divorce of ownership from control, a larger company may justify higher salaries and bonuses to directors and managers. Since it is directors and managers who run the firm, they can take decisions about the size that will benefit them, but not necessarily bring any benefit to shareholders.

Advantages and disadvantages of different types of growth

There are advantages and disadvantages to firms growing organically or through different types of integration.

Organic growth Almost all growth of firms is organic. This is because almost all firms are small. Vertical, horizontal and conglomerate integration through mergers and takeovers is associated with medium-sized and large firms. Merging with or taking over another firm is expensive and time-consuming. Mergers and takeovers are high risk and evidence suggests that most fail in the sense that they reduce the long-term share price of the company. It also means there has to be some sort of strategy for development which would require a merger or takeover to succeed. Taking on an extra worker, renting the shop next door to expand premises or buying an extra machine are much easier than targeting another firm for expansion. Even with medium-sized and large firms, organic growth is the norm and integration through mergers and takeovers is the exception.

However, sometimes another firm has a market or an asset that it would be difficult or impossible to gain through organic growth. For example, a European company may wish to expand into the Asian market but has no expertise in this market. It might be cheaper and far less risky to buy a company selling into the Asia market rather than try to achieve this through organic growth. Organic growth may also be too slow for directors and managers who wish to maximise their salaries and bonuses from the business. The easiest way to expand rapidly and justify higher remuneration is through mergers and takeovers.

Vertical integration There are several possible advantages of vertical integration.

- There may be cost savings. Integrating a supplier or a buyer into the firm may make the firm more efficient.
- Vertical integration may also reduce risk. For example, a supplier might have a technology that it could offer to rival firms and give them a competitive advantage. A supplier might unexpectedly refuse to sell its product to the firm. A buyer could decide to buy from another firm.
- Forward vertical integration could give a firm more control over its market. For example, if a firm owned another firm that bought its products, it could decide at what price to sell the product and in what markets. It could better control branding of the product.

There is a number of disadvantages to vertical integration.

- A firm making a vertical acquisition may have little expertise in that particular industry. For example, a motor manufacturing company over many years might have developed a deep knowledge of motor manufacturing. However, if it buys a chain of car dealerships, selling its cars to the public, it is unlikely that it will have that same level of knowledge in selling cars. The result is that the car dealership part of the business performs much less well than the core motor manufacturing business. The more distinct parts to a business, the less likely it is that senior management will be able to get the best out of every part of the business.
- Firms often pay too much for the firm they take over and the share price of the firm falls rather than rises.
- There can be difficulties in merging the two firms together into one firm. Either the costs of creating a single firm from two separate firms are too great or the two firms fail to integrate, but costs rise because extra layers of management are needed to control the new, larger firm.
- Many of the key workers in the firm that has been taken over may leave, taking with them much of the expertise that made it successful.

Horizontal integration Most mergers and takeovers are examples of horizontal integration. At the small firm level, an example would be a hairdresser buying a second hairdressing business. At an international level, it might be one pharmaceuticals company buying another pharmaceuticals company.

Horizontal integration has a number of advantages for the firm.

- It may allow reductions in average costs due to economies of scale.
- It can reduce competition in the market by taking out a competitor.
- It can allow one firm to buy unique assets owned by another company like a new drug or operations in another part of the world.
- It allows a business to grow in a market where it already has knowledge and expertise. This is likely to make the merger more successful.

Despite the many advantages of horizontal integration, evidence suggests that most horizontal mergers are not successful. As with vertical integration, firms often pay too much

Question 3

Robert Forrester is chief executive of the fast-growing UK motor dealer, Vertu. He learnt about the business of selling cars by being a group finance director for Reg Vardy, the Sunderland based motor dealer. In 2006, Reg Vardy was taken over by Pendragon and Mr Forrester lost his job.

He decided to set up his own car dealer company. He realised that he could not challenge the big, long-established companies in the sector by setting up just another small, privately owned, dealership. Instead, his strategy was to grow through buying up existing businesses. He assembled a team of former Reg Vardy executives and persuaded City investors to invest £25 million in a new, publicly quoted company. Mr Forrester himself invested £400 000. Vertu Motors floated on AIM, the stock market, in December 2006.

Its first deal was the £40 million acquisition of Bristol Street Motors Group, which had sales of £576 million. The purchase was funded through the initial £25 million raised a year earlier and a further £26 million sale of shares.

When the recession struck in early 2008, car values dropped five per cent in a month. With £20 million worth of stock, the company suffered an overnight loss of £1 million on the value of the cars it held. However, the company survived. The recession also provided a good buying opportunity for Vertu. Car dealerships fell in price and Vertu accelerated its acquisition-buying programme. In 2009, it raised a further £300 million by selling new shares to fund more purchases.

Today, Vertu has 3 600 employees and 104 dealerships. Sales are expected to exceed £1.6 billion this year with pre-tax profit approaching £16 million.

Source: adapted from © the *Financial Times* 8.1.2014, All Rights Reserved.

(a) Explain what is meant by horizontal integration, using Vertu as an example.

(b) Explain two constraints on business growth that Vertu might have experienced.

(c) Discuss whether Vertu would have been more successful if it had grown organically rather than through acquisitions.

for the firm they are buying. Integration of the two firms is too often poorly managed and many of the key workers may leave following the acquisition.

Conglomerate integration There are several advantages of conglomerate integration.

- One advantage is to reduce risk. Buying another firm operating in a completely different market means that a firm is not so dependent on the ups and downs of one market.
- A conglomerate may find it easier to expand compared to a situation where the companies or operations were independent. Size gives a conglomerate more options to obtain finance to expand the business. Successful senior managers can be transferred from company to company depending on their need.
- It could be an opportunity for asset stripping. Some companies specialise in buying other companies which they see as having more valuable individual assets than the buying

price of the company. For example, a company might be bought for £100 million. It is then broken up. Most of its land holding might be sold for £60 million. A part of the company is sold for £30 million. Some patents are sold for £20 million. What is then left of the company might be kept, sold on or simply closed down.

One disadvantage of conglomerate integration is that firms do not have expertise in the market into which they buy. As with vertical integration, a lack of specialist understanding of the market can reduce performance. As for asset stripping, it provides a quick profit for the asset stripper. It doesn't benefit workers, customers or local economies. Workers lose their jobs. Customers might find they are no longer able to buy products which they value. Local economies can end up with lost jobs and derelict industrial sites. As with vertical integration, firms engaging in conglomerate integration often pay too much for the firm they are buying. Integration of the two firms is too often poorly managed and many of the key workers may leave following the acquisition.

Constraints on business growth

There is a number of different constraints on business growth including the following.

Size of the market Markets vary in size. Some local markets are very small. Take the example of a butcher in a large village in rural Wales. The local market may be able to support the business adequately with customers coming from surrounding villages. However, expanding the business, for example by opening a new shop in the next village, may fail because there are not enough customers in the market in the two villages. Equally, national and international markets can be relatively small. The market for cricket balls for example is much smaller than the market for coffee. The opportunities for expansion in the cricket ball market are very limited in comparison to the coffee market.

Access to finance To expand, firms need access to finance. Most firms expand by using the profit they have made in previous years and putting this back into the business. However, firms also commonly use loans and overdrafts from banks to finance their expansion. This depends on banks being willing to give them a loan. For medium-sized and large firms, they may be able to obtain equity funding. In a limited company, new shares are sold to investors. If the company is a public limited company, second-hand shares will be bought on a stock exchange, like the London Stock Exchange or AIM (the Alternative Investment Market based in London). However, this is a relatively unimportant way of getting access to finance overall.

Owner objectives Not every owner wants to grow a firm. Owners can have many objectives. They may be content with the profit they are currently making and not wish to have the extra work or the extra risk that comes from growing the business.

Regulation Most firms are able to expand their businesses without any interference from government. However, government regulation can be an important factor in a few cases. For example, in the UK, government regulates the number of pharmacies in a local area. An existing pharmacy, looking to expand, can only do this by buying another pharmacy. For large companies, competition law can restrict the scope for takeovers and mergers. Any merger which creates a company with a market share of 25 per cent or more must be reported to the Competition and Markets Authority. It can investigate the merger and has the power to forbid the merger.

Reasons for demergers

A **demerger** occurs when a firm splits itself into two or more separate parts to create two or more firms. The two or more new firms may be of roughly equal size. Sometimes, though, the term is used to describe the sale of a small part of a business to another business.

Demergers occur for a variety of reasons.

Lack of synergies Management may feel that there are no **synergies** between the parts of the firm. This means that one part of the firm is having no impact on the more efficient and profitable running of the other part of the firm. Where there are no synergies, there could even be diseconomies of scale because senior management are having to divide their time between two or more businesses which have little to do with each other.

Price The price of the demerged firms might be higher than the price of the single larger firm. For example, a firm may be valued at £300 million on a stock exchange. But if it split into two, the two new firms might be valued at £150 million and £250 million. Investors in companies base valuations on a variety of different factors but one of them is the growth prospects of a firm. If a firm has a part which is growing fast, it will be worth more than another part of equal size which is growing more slowly. The relatively poor performance of one part of a company can drag down the share price of the whole company despite the fact that other parts are performing well. Financial markets talk about 'creating value' by splitting up companies like this.

Focussed companies In the 1970s, it was fashionable to create conglomerates to diversify risk. In recent years, it has become fashionable to create firms which are highly focussed on one or just a few key markets. The argument is that management can deliver higher profits and growth by concentrating their energies on getting to know and exploiting a limited range of markets. Evidence also suggests that being the market leader in terms of sales tends to be relatively more profitable than being, say, number three or four in the market, so companies therefore divest themselves of (i.e. sell off) parts which don't fit in with their core activities. Sometimes, a firm will sell off a part cheaply which goes on to be very successful. It could be argued that the firm's management sold the part too cheaply. Equally, it can be argued that it shows that a company has only limited management resources. The part sold off would never have been successful within that particular firm because management did not have the time or expertise to make it flourish.

Impact of demergers

Demergers can have an impact on businesses, workers and consumers.

Businesses Firms will benefit from a demerger if the increased specialisation that results leads to greater efficiency. If firms are able to cut costs or develop new and innovative products, then their profits should rise. Greater efficiency will also enable firms to survive greater competition in their markets. Firms will lose out if the demerger leads to more inefficiency. If the demerged firms are run less well than when they were one single firm, then profits are likely to fall.

Workers Workers may benefit or lose out following a demerger. Senior managers may gain promotion. For example, one firm only needs one senior financial director. If it splits into two, each firm will need their own senior financial director. On the other hand, some workers may lose their jobs following a demerger. If each firm becomes more efficiently run as a result of the demerger, then some jobs losses are likely.

Consumers Consumers may benefit or lose out following a demerger. They will gain if the demerged firms become more efficient, cut costs and offer lower prices. They could also gain if the demerged firms invest more and develop new and innovative products. Consumers will lose out if the demerged firms become more focussed on increasing profit in their businesses through raising prices or reducing their product ranges.

Question 4

eBay, the company which owns eBay the online auction site, PayPal, a payments business, and eBay Enterprise, a company which helps other companies to sell online, is to be split into three companies.

For some time, it has come under pressure from some shareholders to sell PayPal. They argued that eBay and PayPal would be worth more as two separate companies than staying together as one company. This is because the two businesses have different growth rates and profit rates. PayPal is the star performer, with revenue up 20 per cent last year. eBay is highly profitable but it is forecast to grow only between zero and five per cent next year. The third business, eBay Enterprises, also saw double-digit growth last year. It is a combination of GSI Commerce, bought by eBay for $2.4 billion in 2011 and Magento, bought in 2011 for more than $100 million.

Some analysts have questioned whether eBay, the auction site, will be as profitable without PayPal. Currently, eBay uses information about customer purchases made from other Internet sites when these purchases are made using PayPal. Without PayPal, it will have less information about the buying behaviour of its customers. This will make it more difficult to target eBay users with information about what they could buy on the site.

Source: adapted from © the *Financial Times* 30.9.2014, 1.10.2014, 22.1.2015, All Rights Reserved.

(a) Explain why eBay is demerging PayPal and eBay Enterprises.

(b) Discuss whether the demerger will lead to high growth for each of the three businesses.

Key Terms

Backward vertical integration - a joining together into one firm of two or more firms where the purchaser mergers with one or more of its suppliers.

Conglomerate integration or merger - a joining together into one firm of two or more firms producing unrelated products.

Demerger - when a firm splits into two or more independent businesses.

Divorce of ownership from control - occurs when the managers and directors of a business are a different group of people from the owners of the business.

Forward vertical integration - a joining together into one firm of two or more firms where the supplier mergers with one or more of its buyers.

Horizontal integration or horizontal merger - a joining together into one firm of two or more firms in the same industry at the same stage of production.

Market niche or niche market - a small segment of a much larger market.

Merger, amalgamation, integration or takeover - the joining together of two or more firms under common ownership.

Not-for-profit organisations - organisations that do not have making a profit as a goal but use any profit or surplus they generate to support their aims.

Organic or internal growth - a firm increasing its size through investment in capital equipment or an increased labour force.

Private sector organisations - organisations that are owned by individuals or companies and not the state

Public sector organisations - organisations that are owned and controlled by the state.

Synergy - when two or more activities or firms put together can lead to greater outcomes than the sum of the individual parts.

Vertical integration or vertical merger - a joining together into one firm of two or more firms at different production stages in the same industry.

Thinking like an economist

Primark's expansion into the US market

Primark, the low-price fashion clothes retailer, announced in 2014 that it was going to open a store in Boston, USA. George Weston, Chief executive of AB Foods, the owner of Primark, said he was confident that Primark would succeed in the US market. 'We think what Primark does, the combination of up-to-date fashion at great prices, will be attractive to American shoppers too,' he said. This is an example of organic growth. Primark is not buying a US company to expand. It is setting up its own store financed out of the profit it makes in the UK and other European countries.

UK retailers have not had much success in expanding into the USA. In the 1990s, Marks & Spencer bought a men's up-market clothing retailer called Brooks Brothers, an example of horizontal integration. It hoped to use the retailer to launch Marks & Spencer products into the US. However, the purchase was a disaster and Marks & Spencer sold the company in 2001.

More recently, Tesco bought a chain of food stores in the USA and converted them into a chain called Fresh & Easy. The chain failed to make a profit despite hundreds of millions of pounds of investment from Tesco. In 2013, Tesco closed the chain and sold off the assets.

The problem with both attempts at expansion was that they failed to understand the US market and US customers. Primark is hoping that its attempt at breaking into the US market will be different. It points to the fact that it has already successfully expanded into nine European countries. It also can point to Topshop, the UK fashion retailer which has successfully built a chain of stores in the USA. Both Primark and Topshop have chosen to grow organically which limits the losses from any failure.

Source: with information from © the *Financial Times* 13.9.2013, 24.4.2014, 24.7.2014, All Rights Reserved.

Data Response Question

Celgene

Pharmaceutical companies spend billions of pounds researching and developing new drugs. The problem is that very few of those drugs ever make it to market. Either they don't work well enough or they have significant side effects.

Large pharmaceutical companies may then be forced over the 'patent cliff'. Many pharmaceutical companies rely on just one or a few 'blockbuster' drugs for most of their sales. Celgene, for example, a biotech company with a market value of almost $100 billion, is heavily reliant on sales of one drug, Revlimid. The drug accounts for 65 per cent of annual sales of the company. In 2019, it faces its own patent cliff when patents on Revlimid begin to expire. This means that any pharmaceutical company will be able to produce its own 'generic' copy of Revlimid and sell it to customers, usually for a fraction of the price of the original drug. Celgene could then see its sales fall dramatically in value and billions could be knocked off its share value.

Celgene has responded to this threat by buying up companies completely or in part, or entering into agreements with companies to share the costs and revenues of promising new drugs. For example, Celgene has spent $7.2 billion buying Receptos, a biotech company specialising in treatments for multiple sclerosis and inflammatory bowel conditions. In April, it paid $710 million to Nogra Pharma, a privately held Irish biotech company, to access its drug for Crohn's disease, a bowel disorder. The drug is still at the clinical trial stage and Celgene is taking a gamble that it will make it to market. Other stakes it has acquired include a 10 per cent share of Juno, a company specialising in immunotherapy for blood cancers and solid tumours, and a five per cent share of Mesoblast, which specialises in stem cell therapies for cancer.

In all, over the past six and a half years, Celgene has taken minority stakes or struck agreements with more than 30 companies, as well as taking over two companies completely: Receptos for $7.2 billion and Abraxis for $2.9 billion.

George Golumbeski, senior vice-president of business development at Celgene, says the company has been pursuing what it calls a 'distributive model or research and development'. 'We consciously decided not to perpetually grow R&D internally and that we would work as closely and actively as we could with smaller companies, who have an exquisite focus, a leanness and a superior, efficient output'.

It is unlikely that all of Celgene's bets will pay off, given that so many waged on early-stage science. However, it only needs one or two to deliver a blockbuster drug to prevent its sales from falling once Revlimid begin to go out of patent after 2019.

Source: adapted from © the *Financial Times* 17.7.2015, All Rights Reserved.

1. Using pharmaceutical companies as an example, explain what it means for a firm to grow internally.

2. Analyse two possible reasons why Celgene has chosen to grow through a process of horizontal integration rather than to grow internally.

3. Discuss whether it would be better for pharmaceutical companies, such as Celgene, to become conglomerates, rather than remaining narrowly focussed on selling pharmaceuticals products.

Evaluation

Evaluation will come from comparing the advantages and disadvantages of conglomerates using pharmaceutical companies as an example. Evaluation could also come from a discussion of the meaning of 'better'. What are the possible objectives of pharmaceutical companies and how might this affect their decisions?

42 | Revenue

Starter activity

A Gucci handbag might cost you £2 000. A Primark handbag might cost £8. What determines how much revenue Gucci and Primark make from selling handbags? If Gucci sold handbags for £8 and Primark sold them for £2 000, what would happen to their revenues and why? What has price elasticity of demand got to do with this?

Table 1 Total, average and marginal revenue

Sales	Average revenue £	Total revenue £	Marginal revenue £
1	5	5	
			5
2	5	10	
			5
3	5	15	
			5
4	5	20	
			5
5	5	25	

Total, average and marginal revenues

A firm's revenues are its receipts of money from the sale of goods and services over a time period such as a week or a year. Revenues can be either total revenue, average revenue or marginal revenue.

- **Total revenue** (TR) is the total amount of money received from the sale of any given level of output. It is the total quantity sold (Q) times the average price (P) received (TR = QP). For example, if a company sold 100 machines at an average price of £1 million each over a year, then its total revenue would be £100 million.
- **Average revenue** (AR) is the average receipt per unit sold. It can be calculated by dividing total revenue by the quantity sold.

$$AR = \frac{TR}{Q}$$

For example, if total revenue for a company is £50 million and it sold 50 machines over a year, then its average revenue would be £1 million. If all output is sold at the same price, then average revenue must equal the price of the product sold.

- **Marginal revenue** (MR) is the receipts from selling an extra unit of output. It is the difference between total revenue at different levels of output.

$$MR = TR_X - TR_{X-1}$$

It is therefore equal to the change in total revenue (ΔTR) divided by the change in total output (ΔQ).

$$MR = \frac{\Delta TR}{\Delta Q}$$

For example, if total revenue were £900 million when 70 machines were sold but £910 million when 71 machines were sold, then the marginal revenue from the last machine sold is £10 million.

Revenue curves

Different revenue curves can be drawn given different assumptions about average revenue. One assumption is that a firm receives the same price for each good sold. This is shown in Table 1. The price is £5. As the price is the same however many are sold, this must also be equal to the average revenue. The total revenue increases as total sales increase. The marginal revenue, the additional revenue from each unit sold, is also £5 at all levels of sales.

This data can be illustrated on a diagram. Figure 1 shows the total revenue curve. Figure 2 shows the average and marginal revenue curves. Note that because the price of the good remains the same, the average and marginal curves are

Figure 1

Total revenue when price is constant

The total revenue curve is upward sloping as sales increase.

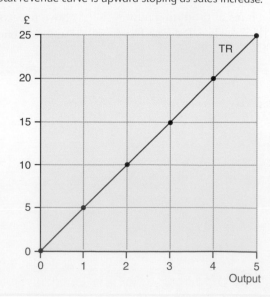

Figure 2

Average and marginal revenue when price is constant

Average and marginal revenue are constant when sales increase.

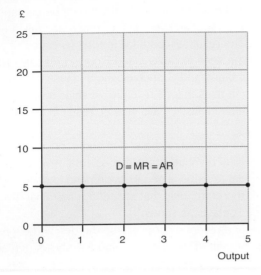

Figure 3

Total revenue when price is falling

The total revenue curve shows that total revenue at first increases and then begins to fall as sales increase and price falls.

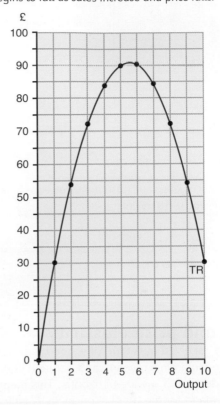

identical. The line is also horizontal, showing that whatever the level of output, average and marginal revenue remain the same at £5. The average revenue curve is the demand curve because it shows the relationship between average price and quantity sold. So at any quantity sold, marginal revenue equals average revenue equals demand.

Table 2 shows a situation where a firm has to lower its price to achieve higher sales. So the average revenue, or average price, is falling as sales get larger. Table 2 shows that when sales reach six units, total revenue begins to fall. The loss in revenue from having to accept a lower price more than outweighs the increase in revenue from extra sales. As a result, marginal revenue becomes negative. Each extra unit sold brings in negative extra revenue.

Figures 3 and 4 show the total, average and marginal revenue curves derived from the data in Table 2. The total revenue curve at first rises and then falls. The average revenue curve is downward sloping. The marginal revenue curve is also downward sloping. It slopes more steeply than the average revenue curve. Mathematically, the slope is twice as steep and, measuring the distance horizontally on the graph, marginal

revenue is always exactly half average revenue. The average revenue curve is also the demand curve because it shows the relationship between average price and quantity sold. So average revenue equals demand.

Figure 4

Average and marginal revenue when price is falling

The average and marginal revenue fall as sales increase. The average revenue curve is also the demand curve for the good because it shows the average price received at each level of sales.

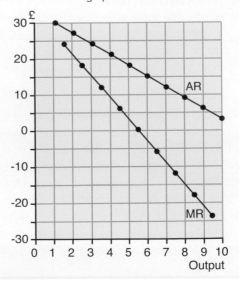

Table 2 Total, average and marginal revenue

Sales	Average revenue £	Total revenue £	Marginal revenue £
1	30	30	
			24
2	27	54	
			18
3	24	72	
			12
4	21	84	
			6
5	18	90	
			0
6	15	90	
			-6
7	12	84	
			-12
8	9	72	
			-18
9	6	54	
			-24
10	3	30	

Question 1

Table 3 Average, total and marginal revenue

Sales (million units)	Average revenue (£)	Total revenue (£)	Marginal revenue (£)
1	20		
2	18		
3	16		
4	14		
5	12		
6	10		
7	8		
8	6		
9	4		
10	2		

Calculate (a) total revenue and (b) marginal revenue at each level of sales from 1 million to 10 million.

Maths Tip

Put the marginal revenue figures 'in between' the lines to show that it is the difference between two numbers.

Revenue and price elasticity

When the price received by a firm for a good is constant, the average revenue, marginal revenue and demand curves for the good are identical. They are horizontal. This means that price elasticity of demand for the good is perfectly elastic. Whatever the percentage change in the price of the good, there is no change in quantity demanded.

However, when the price of a good declines as sales increase, there is likely to be a change in price elasticity of demand along the average revenue curve. In Unit 9, it was explained that if demand was price inelastic, a rise in price would bring about a rise in total spending by consumers, which is the same as a rise in total revenue for a firm or firms. If the percentage fall in quantity demanded is less than the percentage rise in price, then total revenue will increase. Conversely, if demand is price elastic, then a percentage rise in price will bring about an even larger percentage fall in quantity demanded. The result will be a fall in total revenue.

This can be seen in Table 2 and Figure 3. At sales levels up to six units, demand is price elastic because falls in price are resulting in rises in total revenue. At sales levels above this, demand is price inelastic. Falls in price result in falls in total revenue.

In terms of marginal revenue, demand is price elastic so long as marginal revenue is positive i.e. total revenue is rising. When marginal revenue is negative, demand is price inelastic. In Figure 4, therefore, only that part of the marginal revenue where price is elastic is shown.

The average revenue curve is also the demand curve for the good. The top half of the curve in Figure 4 shows demand as being price elastic. The bottom half of the curve shows demand being price inelastic.

Price elasticity of demand is 1 or unitary when total revenue is maximised. This is when marginal revenue is zero.

Key Terms

Average revenue - the average receipts per unit sold. It is equal to total revenue divided by quantity sold.
Marginal revenue - the addition to total revenue of an extra unit sold.
Total revenue - the total money received from the sale of any given quantity of output.

Thinking like an economist

Revenue maximisation

In 2014, Ryanair was offering a flight from London to Gdansk in Poland for £17.99 on its website. This is far below the average total cost per passenger carried of the flight. How can it make commercial sense for a firm like Ryanair to sell tickets below cost?

There is a range of industries where maximum profits are likely to be achieved if total revenues are maximised too. This is because in these industries there are very large fixed costs and relatively small variable costs. The additional cost or marginal cost of extra orders is therefore relatively small. Short run profits therefore become crucially dependent on how much revenue is gained. Examples of such industries and firms include airlines, trains, passenger ferries, the Channel Tunnel and hotels.

Maximising total revenue requires a highly flexible pricing structure. Demand for a service like an aeroplane flight differs according to the time of the day, the day of the week, the week of the year and from year to year. Different groups of passengers are also prepared to pay different fares for fairly small differences in levels of service. For example, an airline might be able to charge double or treble the fare to a business person by allowing them to go straight to the front of the check-in queue at the airport, allowing them to sit in a special curtained-off section at the front of the plane and giving them a few free sandwiches and drinks on board.

Another way of saying this is that the price elasticity of demand for the product varies considerably between customers. For a business person having to get to a meeting by 10 o'clock in the morning, the price elasticity of demand is low. For a pensioner couple who have no time commitments and are prepared to travel to an out of the way airport at any time of the day or night, price elasticity of demand is high.

Maximising total revenue means that marginal revenue will be almost zero on some sales. Taking airlines as an example, companies like Ryanair attract some customers by offering headline cheap deals. However, the number of seats offered at these very low prices is very small. They represent only a tiny fraction of the number of seats sold over a whole year. They are also used mainly as part of marketing to generate interest from passengers who go on to buy flights at higher prices. However, economic theory would suggest that for airline companies, getting a passenger onto a plane who has paid almost nothing for the flight is better than having an empty seat which generates no revenue.

Data Response Question

Finchfield Cycles

Finchfield Cycles is a UK company based in Leeds which sells bicycles. In recent years, with a growing trend towards healthier living, exercise and cycling to work, demand for its bicycles has grown considerably. Five years ago, sales were 10 000 a year. Today they are 20 000. Despite selling at £1 000 each, there is a long waiting list for the bicycles due to bottlenecks in production.

The company's sales director has been researching different pricing strategies. He estimates they could sell 25 000 cycles a year and not have to drop their prices. To push sales beyond 25 000 a year would require some easing of prices. He estimates that the company could sell 30 000 a year at £900 but a move to 35 000 a year would have to see prices drop to £800. To sell 40 000 cycles a year would probably need a price of £700.

An alternative strategy would be to segment the market. Currently around half of all sales go overseas and they are sold at the same price per unit as home sales. The overseas sales, the sales director believes, are more price sensitive.

He estimates that over the sales range 10 000 to 20 000, price elasticity of demand is 4. In contrast, price elasticity of demand for home sales he estimates is 2 for the equivalent sales range.

1. (a) From the data, assuming no bottlenecks in production and no differential pricing, what does the sales director believe would be total sales at a price of (i) £1 000; (ii) £900; (iii) £800; (iv) £700?

    (b) From this data, draw an accurate (i) total revenue curve; (ii) average revenue curve; (iii) marginal revenue curve. You would find this easier if you used graph paper.

    (c) Calculate the price elasticity of demand between the four price points, assuming that the higher price is the initial price.

2. If prices were cut by different amounts for overseas sales compared to home sales to get higher sales, which prices should be cut the most? Explain your answer.

43 Production

Key points

1. The short run is defined as that period of time when at least one factor of production cannot be varied. In the long run, all factors can be varied, but the state of technology remains constant. In the very long run, the state of technology may change.
2. If a firm increases its variable inputs in the short run, diminishing marginal returns and diminishing average returns will eventually set in.
3. Constant returns to scale, or economies and diseconomies of scale, may occur in the long run when all factors are changed in the same proportion.

Starter activity

You want to employ cleaners to clean your house. They won't bring their own cleaning equipment. Instead, they will use only the cleaning equipment (vacuum cleaners, brooms, mops, dusters, polish etc.) that you have. What would happen if you employed one person for four hours? Compare that to two people working together for four hours. What about a team of four people working together for four hours? A team of 10? A team of 100?

The short run and long run

Economists make a distinction between the short run and the long run. In the **short run**, producers are faced with the problem that some of their factor inputs are fixed in supply. For instance, a factory might want to expand production. It can get its workers to work longer hours through overtime or shift work, and can also buy in more raw materials. Labour and raw materials are then variable inputs. But it only has a fixed amount of space on the factory floor and a fixed number of machines with which to work. This fixed capital places a constraint on how much more can be produced by the firm.

In the **long run**, all factor inputs are variable. A producer can vary the amount of land, labour and capital if it so chooses. In the long run, the firm in the above example could move into a larger factory and buy more machines, as well as employ more labour and use more raw materials.

In the long run, existing technologies do not change. In the **very long run**, the state of technology can change. For instance, a bank would be able to move from a paper-based system with cheques, bank statements and paper memos to a completely electronic paperless system with cards, computer terminal statements and memos.

The way that the short run and the long run are defined in the theory of production means that there is no standard length of time for the short run. In the chemical industry, a plant may last 20 years before it needs replacing and so the short run might last 20 years. In an industry with little or no permanent physical capital, the short run may be measured in months or even weeks. The short run for a market trader, who hires everything from the stall to a van and keeps no stock, may be as short as one day, the day of the market when she is committed to hiring equipment and selling stock.

The short run: diminishing returns

In the short run at least one factor is fixed. Assume for example that a firm uses only two factors of production: capital, in the form of buildings and machines, which is fixed, and labour, which can be varied. What will happen to output as more and more labour is used?

Initially, output per worker is likely to rise. A factory designed for 500 workers, for instance, is unlikely to be very productive if only one worker is employed. But there will come a point when output per worker will start to fall. There is an optimum level of production which is most productively efficient. Eventually, if enough workers are employed, total output will fall. Imagine 10 000 workers trying to work in a factory designed for 500. The workers will get in each other's way and result in less output than with a smaller number of workers. This general pattern is known as the **law of diminishing returns** or the **law of variable proportions** or the **law of diminishing marginal productivity**.

Total, average and marginal products

The law of diminishing returns can be explained more formally using the concepts of total, average and marginal products.

- **Total product** is the quantity of output produced by a given number of inputs over a period of time. It is expressed in physical terms and not money terms. (Indeed, economists often refer to total physical product, average physical product and marginal physical product to emphasise this point.) The total product of 1 000 workers in the car industry over a year might be 30 000 cars.
- **Average product** is the quantity of output per unit of input. In the above example, output per worker would be 30 cars per year (the total product divided by the quantity of inputs).
- **Marginal product** is the addition to output produced by an extra unit of input. If the addition of an extra car worker raised output to 30 004 cars in our example, then the marginal product would be four cars.

  Now consider Table 1. In this example capital is fixed at 10 units whilst labour is a variable input.
- If no workers are employed, total output will be zero.
- The first worker produces 20 units of output. So the marginal product of the first worker is 20 units.
- The second worker produces an extra 34 units of output. So the marginal product of the second worker is 34 units. Total output with two workers is 54 units (20 units plus 34 units). Average output is 54 ÷ 2 or 27 units per worker.

Table 1 Total, average and marginal products[1]

| Capital | Labour | Physical product as labour is varied | | Units |
		Total	Average	Marginal
0	0	0	0	
				20
10	1	20	20	
				34
10	2	54	27	
				46
10	3	100	33	
				51
10	4	151	38	
				46
10	5	197	39	
				33
10	6	230	38	
				21
10	7	251	36	
				-17
10	8	234	29	

1. Rounded to the nearest whole number.

- The third worker produces an extra 46 units of output. So total output with three workers is 100 units (20 plus 34 plus 46). Average output is 100÷3 or approximately 33 units per worker.

Initially, marginal product rises, but the fifth worker produces less than the fourth. **Diminishing marginal returns** therefore set in between the fourth and fifth worker. Average product rises too at first and then falls, but the turning point is later than for marginal product. **Diminishing average returns** set in between five and six workers.

The law of diminishing returns states that if increasing quantities of a variable input are combined with a fixed input, eventually the marginal product and then the average product of that variable input will decline.

Figure 1

Total, average and marginal product

The curves are derived from the data in Table 1. Note that diminishing marginal returns set in before diminishing average returns. Note too that the marginal product curve cuts the average product curve at its highest point, whilst the total product curve falls when the marginal product curve cuts the horizontal axis.

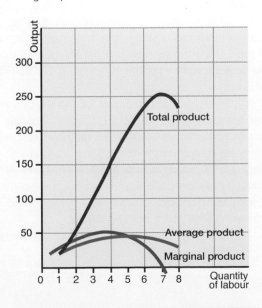

Question 1

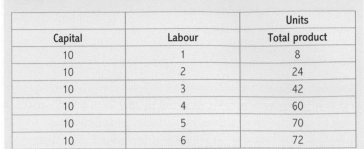

Table 2

| | | Units |
Capital	Labour	Total product
10	1	8
10	2	24
10	3	42
10	4	60
10	5	70
10	6	72

Table 2 shows the change in total product as the quantity of labour increases and all other factor inputs remain constant.

(a) Calculate the average and marginal product at each level of labour input.

(b) Draw the total, average and marginal product curves on a graph.

(c) At what level of output do (i) diminishing marginal returns and (ii) diminishing average returns set in?

It is possible to draw total, average and marginal product curves. The curves in Figure 1 are derived from the data in Table 1. All three curves first rise and then fall. Marginal product falls first, then average product and finally total product.

The long run: returns to scale

The law of diminishing returns assumes that firms operate in the short run. In the long run, firms can vary all their factor inputs. What would happen to the output of a firm if, for instance, it were to increase all its inputs by the same proportion? There are only three possibilities.

- **Increasing returns to scale** occur if an equal percentage increase in inputs to production leads to a more than proportional increase in output. If a firm doubles its land, labour and capital inputs, but as a consequence trebles its output, then increasing returns to scale have occurred. For instance, if as in Table 3, one unit of capital and one unit of all other factors of production are used, then 20 units of output are produced. Doubling the inputs to two units of capital and two units of all other factors more than doubles output to 50 units. An increase in inputs by 50 per cent from two to three units of all factors increases output by more than 50 per cent from 50 units to 80 units. Therefore the firm is operating under conditions of increasing returns to scale.

Table 3 Increasing returns to scale

| | | Units of capital | | |
		1	2	3
Units of all other factors of production	1	20	35	45
	2	30	50	65
	3	35	63	80

- **Constant returns to scale** occur if an equal percentage increase in inputs to production leads to the same percentage increase in output. For example, if a firm doubles its inputs and this leads to a doubling of output, then constant returns to scale occur.

- **Decreasing returns to scale** occur if an equal percentage increase in inputs to production leads to a less than proportional increase in output. So decreasing returns to scale occur if a firm trebles its inputs but only doubles its output.

Key Terms

Average product - the quantity of output per unit of factor input. It is the total product divided by the level of output.
Law of diminishing returns or variable proportions or marginal productivity - if increasing quantities of a variable input are combined with a fixed input, eventually the marginal product and then the average product of that variable input will decline. Diminishing returns are said to exist when this decline occurs.
Long run - the period of time when all factor inputs can be varied, but the state of technology remains constant.
Marginal product - the addition to output produced by an extra unit of input. It is the change in total output divided by the change in the level of inputs.

Returns to scale - the change in percentage output resulting from a percentage change in all the factors of production. There are increasing returns to scale if the percentage increase in output is greater than the percentage increase in factors employed, constant returns to scale if it is the same and decreasing returns to scale if it is less.
Short run - the period of time when at least one factor input to the production process cannot be varied.
Total product - the quantity of output measured in physical units produced by a given number of inputs over a period of time.
Very long run - the period of time when the state of technology may change.

Thinking like an economist

Increasing returns at petrol stations

The production function
Petrol stations provide a service to their customers. They buy in fuel and other merchandise in large quantities, store it and then sell it in smaller quantities to customers when they want to make their purchases. Other inputs apart from stock to this production process include the land on which the petrol station is built, capital in the form of buildings and equipment, and labour.

Changing product mix
Petrol stations tended originally to be attached to garages which repaired and perhaps also sold cars. Garages aimed to provide a complete service to the motorist. Increasingly, however, petrol stations were built without the provision of other garage services. This enabled them to benefit from specialisation.

By the 1970s, petrol stations started to undergo another change. New petrol stations began to be built by the supermarket chains. They were able to undercut existing petrol station prices by selling large volumes of petrol and by buying at lowest prices on the world oil markets. While there were few supermarket petrol stations in a region, this posed little threat to traditional suppliers. By the late 1980s, however, supermarket petrol stations could be found in most localities. Traditional petrol stations started to close under the fierce price competition.

In 1990, there were around 20 000 petrol retail sites in the UK but this had more than halved to 8 613 by 2013. The number of supermarket sites had increased over the same period from 360 to 1 347. But the number of petrol retail sites owned by the major oil companies had declined from 6 500 to 1 927 whilst the number of independent retailers had gone from 13 000 to 5 339. The supermarket price discounters had won a decisive victory over more expensive oil company and independent sites.

Increasing returns
Petrol stations rarely operate at maximum capacity. Most could supply petrol to more customers without having to increase the size of their site or install new pumps. So more petrol sales could be achieved by combining existing capital with more petrol.

Petrol companies have also realised for many years that other goods could be sold from petrol stations. Typically, this started off with confectionery and a few motor products like oil. However, they have increasingly turned petrol station kiosks into mini convenience stores. By combining groceries, snack foods, motor products and newspapers, they have again been able to achieve increasing returns to scale, selling more products without increasing their stock of fixed capital.

Source: with information from UKPIA, using data from the Energy Institute 1990 - 2005; Catalist from 2006 onwards.

Data Response Question

Overfishing

In the early 1950s, the world fish catch was a little over 20 million tonnes. By 2012 it had risen to nearly 80 million tonnes. But there were warning signals coming from different fisheries around the world that overfishing was destroying the industry as early as the 1960s. From Newfoundland to the Mediterranean to the North Sea, fish stocks were reaching critical levels. Off Newfoundland, the fishing industry destroyed the fish stock in the 1980s. In Europe, the EU and member governments were forced to introduce a quota scheme to restrict fish catches, much to the anger of the fishing industry which had been expanding dramatically. The problem is that fish stocks are not infinite. If the fish population is not kept at a critical level, fish stocks will decline over time and eventually will completely collapse. The United Nations Food and Agriculture Organisation (FAO) in 2014 estimated for 2011 that 28.8 per cent of the world's fish stocks are over exploited and 61.3 per cent were fully exploited, defined as being fished to their maximum biological productivity. Putting more boats into these areas would produce hardly any additional output. Only 9.9 per cent of the world's fisheries are underexploited and could sustain moderate increases in fishing.

Source: with information from Food and Agriculture Organization of the United Nations, *The State of World Fisheries and Aquaculture*, 2014, Rome, Italy. Reproduced with permission.

Q

1. Outline the problem of overfishing.

2. Giving examples from the data, explain why fishing was subject to diminishing returns both in the UK waters and worldwide.

3. Four possible solutions to the problem of overfishing include tightening existing quotas on fish catches, banning all fishing in a particular fishery, reducing the number of boats licensed to fish and increasing taxes on fish sales. Discuss these solutions, evaluating whether they would help solve the problem and who might benefit and lose out from their implementation.

Figure 2

Size of UK fishing fleet[1]

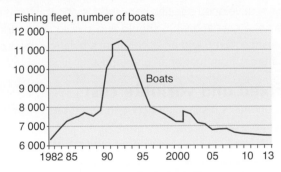

Source: adapted from *Annual Abstract of Statistics*, Office for National Statistics; www.marinemanagement.org.uk

1. There was a change of definition in number of boats in 2001.

Figure 4

World catch of seawater fish

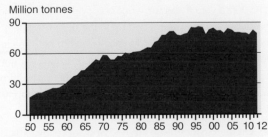

Source: adapted from Food and Agriculture Organization of the United Nations, *The State of World Fisheries and Aquaculture*, 2014, Rome, Italy. Reproduced with permission.

Figure 3

Percentage of fish stocks around the UK that are fished at a sustainable level[1]

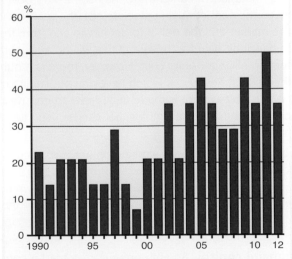

Source: adapted from *UK Sea Fisheries Statistics*, 2013, www.marinemanagment.org.uk.

1. Sustainability is defined as fishing at a level where fish are reproducing sufficiently highly to allow a good probability of stock replenishment.

Evaluation

Analyse each of the four options in turn. Use diagrams to illustrate your answer where possible. Compare who might benefit and who might lose out in your analysis. Use this analysis to weigh up benefits and costs of each option. Then in a concluding paragraph, compare the effectiveness of each option and their benefits and costs.

44 Costs

Key points

1. Economists use the word 'cost' of production in a way different from its general usage. Economic cost is the opportunity cost of production.
2. There is a difference between total, average and marginal costs as well as fixed and variable costs.
3. The short run average and marginal cost curves are U-shaped because of the law of diminishing returns.
4. The long run average and marginal cost curves are U-shaped too because of economies and diseconomies of scale.
5. There is a difference between internal and external economies of scale.
6. The long run average cost curve of a firm is an envelope for the firm's short run average cost curves.

Starter activity

Sanjeet and William start up a company making ready meals. Their first three months are spent working from the kitchen of William's parents' house. List ten possible costs they face. How would they calculate their total costs, average cost per ready meal sold and marginal cost of an extra ready meal? Do you think their average costs would rise or fall if they moved production to a factory unit?

The economic definition of cost

Economists use the word 'cost' in a very specific sense. The **economic cost** of production for a firm is the opportunity cost of production. It is the value that could have been generated had the resources been employed in their next best use.

For instance, a market trader has some very obvious costs, such as the cost of buying stock to sell, the rent for her pitch in the market and the petrol to get her to and from the market. Money will be paid for these and this will be an accurate reflection of opportunity cost. However, there is a number of hidden costs. Resources which have an opportunity cost but for which no payment is made must have an **imputed cost**. There is a number of examples that can be used to illustrate imputed cost.

Labour A market trader working on her own account may calculate that she has made £50 'profit' on a day's trading. However, this may not include the value of her own time. If she could have earned £40 working in another job for the day, then her economic profit is only £10. Hence, the opportunity cost of her labour must be included as an economic cost of production.

Financial capital An entrepreneur may start a company with his own money investing, say, £50 000. The economic cost of production must include the opportunity cost of that start-up capital. If he could have earned 10 per cent per annum in an alternative investment, then the economic cost (the opportunity cost) is £5 000 per year.

Depreciation The **physical capital** of a company will deteriorate over time. Machines wear out, buildings need repairs, etc. Moreover, some capital will become obsolete before the end of its physical life. The economic cost of depreciation is the difference between the purchase price and the second-hand value of a good. A car, for instance, which lasts for eight years does not depreciate at 12½ per cent each year. In the first

year, cars depreciate on average by 40 per cent. Therefore a company paying £10 000 for a new car which depreciates by 40 per cent over its first year only has an asset worth £6 000 at the end of the year. £6 000 is the monetary value of the opportunity cost of keeping the car rather than selling it at the end of that year.

Goodwill A firm trading over a number of years may acquire a good reputation. It may produce branded goods which become household names. The goodwill of these brands has an opportunity cost. They could be sold to a rival company. Therefore the interest foregone on the potential sale value of these must be included as an economic cost.

Economists differ in their use of the word 'cost' from accountants, tax inspectors, businesses and others. Accountants have developed specific conventions about what is and what is not a cost and what should and should not be included on a balance sheet, and an accountant's balance sheet may be very different from that of an economist.

Fixed and variable costs

Economists distinguish between two types of cost: fixed and variable cost.

A **fixed cost** (also called an **indirect** or **overhead cost**) is a cost which does not vary directly with output. As production levels change, the value of a fixed cost will remain constant.

Question 1

A woman runs her own business. Over the past 12 months, she has paid £18 000 for materials and £9 000 in wages to a worker whom she employs. She runs the business from premises which her parents own. These premises could be rented out for £10 000 a year if she were not occupying them. She has £40 000 worth of her own capital tied up in the business. She is a trained teacher and at present works exactly half of her time in a school earning £15 000. She could work full time as a teacher (earning £30 000 a year) if she didn't run the business. The current rate of interest is five per cent. The total revenue of her business over the past 12 months was £60 000.

(a) On the basis of these figures, what were the costs she actually paid out and what were her economic costs?

(b) Did she make a profit last year?

242

For instance, a company may rent premises. The rent on the premises will remain the same whether the company produces nothing or produces at full capacity. If a firm pays for an advertising campaign, the cost will be the same whether sales remain constant or increase. Costs commonly given as examples of fixed costs are capital goods (e.g. factories, offices, plant and machinery), rent and rates, office staff and advertising and promotion.

A **variable** (or **direct** or **prime**) **cost** is a cost which varies directly with output. As production increases, so does variable cost. For instance, a steel maker will use iron ore. The more steel produced, the more iron ore will be needed, so the cost of iron ore is a variable cost. Raw materials for production are the clearest example of variable costs for most firms. It is not always easy to categorise a cost as either fixed or variable. Many costs are **semi-variable costs**. Labour is a good example. Some firms employ a permanent staff, which could be classified as a fixed cost. They might ask the permanent staff to do overtime when necessary, or employ temporary labour. These costs would be classified as variable. However, permanent staff could be seen as a variable cost if a firm were willing to hire and fire staff as its output changed. In practice, firms do adjust staff numbers with output, but the adjustment is sluggish and therefore the cost of labour is neither variable nor fixed - it is semi-variable.

In the **short run**, at least one factor input of production cannot be changed. Therefore, in the short run, some costs are fixed costs whilst others will be variable. In the long run, all factor inputs can vary, so in the long run, all costs will be variable costs.

Question 2

Rachel Hughes owns a whole food vegetarian restaurant. Explain which of the following costs would be most likely to be fixed costs, variable costs or semi-variable costs for her business: rice; rent; wages of casual staff; interest payments on a loan; electricity; cooking oil; pots and pans; her own wage; VAT.

Total, average and marginal cost

It is important to distinguish between the total, average and marginal costs of production. The **total cost** (TC) of production is the cost of producing a given level of output. For instance, if a manufacturer produces 100 units a week and its weekly costs come to £1 million, then £1 million is the total cost of production. Increased production will almost certainly lead to a rise in total costs. If the manufacturer increased output to 200 units a week, it would need to buy more raw materials, increase the number of workers, and generally increase its factor inputs.

This is illustrated in Table 1. At an output level of one unit per week, the total cost of production is £400. If output were two units per week, total costs would rise to £500.

The total cost of production is made up of two components:
- **total variable cost** (TVC) which varies with output;
- **total fixed cost** (TFC) which remains constant whatever the level of output.

So in Table 1, total variable cost increases from zero to

Table 1 Total costs of production

(1)	(2)	(3)	(4)
Output (per week)	Total variable cost (£)	Total fixed cost (£)	Total cost (columns 2+3) (£)
0	0	200	200
1	200	200	400
2	300	200	500
3	600	200	800
4	1 200	200	1 400
5	2 000	200	2 200

£2 000 as output increases from zero to five units per week, whilst total fixed costs remain constant at £200 whatever the level of output. Total variable costs when added to total fixed costs are equal to total cost. Mathematically:

$$TVC + TFC = TC$$

The **average cost** of production is the total cost divided by the level of output. For instance, if a firm makes 100 items at a total cost of £1 000, then the average cost per item would be £10. If a firm made 15 items at a cost of £30, then the average cost of production would be £2. Mathematically:

$$AC = \frac{TC}{Q}$$

where AC is average cost, TC is total cost and Q is quantity or the level of output.

Average cost, like total cost, is made up of two components.
- **average variable cost** (AVC) is total variable cost divided by the level of output.
- **average fixed cost** (AFC) is total fixed cost divided by the level of output.

The average costs of production for the example in Table 1 are given in Table 2.

Table 2 Average costs of production[1]

(1)	(2)	(3)	(4)
Output (per week)	Average variable cost (£)	Average fixed cost (£)	Average total cost (columns 2+3) (£)
1	200	200	400
2	150	100	250
3	200	67	267
4	300	50	350
5	400	40	440

1. Rounded to the nearest pound.

Marginal cost is the cost of producing an extra unit of output. For instance, if it costs £100 to produce 10 items and £105 to produce 11 items, then the marginal cost of the eleventh item is £5. If it costs £4 to produce two items but £10 to produce three items, then the marginal cost of the third item is £6. Mathematically, marginal cost (MC) is calculated by

243

Table 3 Marginal costs of production

(1) Output (per week)	(2) Total cost (£)	(3) Marginal cost per unit of output (£)
1	400	
		100
2	500	
		300
3	800	
		600
4	1 400	
		800
5	2 200	

dividing the change in total cost (ΔTC) by the change in total output (ΔQ).

$$MC = \frac{\Delta TC}{\Delta Q}$$

The marginal costs of production for the figures in Tables 1 and 2 are given in Table 3.

Diminishing returns and short-run costs

In the short run a firm will be faced with employing at least one factor input which can not be varied. For instance, it might have a given number of machines or a fixed quantity of office space. If it were to increase output by using more of the variable factor inputs, diminishing marginal returns and then diminishing average returns would set in eventually.

Diminishing returns are a technical concept. Therefore, they are expressed in terms of physical inputs and physical product (the output of the firm). However, it is possible to express physical inputs in terms of costs. For example, a firm which employed five workers at a wage of £200 per week, and had no other costs, would have total weekly costs of £1 000. If each worker produced 200 units of output, then the average cost per unit of output would be £1 [£1 000 ÷ (5 x 200)]. The marginal cost of the 200 units produced by the fifth worker would be that worker's wage (£200), and so the marginal cost per unit of output would be £1 (£200 ÷ 200).

Question 3

Table 4 Output and costs

Units Output	Total fixed cost	Total variable cost	Total cost	Average fixed cost	Average variable cost	Average cost	Marginal cost £
0	40						
1		6					
2		11					
3		15					
4			60				
5			66				

Complete Table 4, calculating the missing figures.

Short-run cost schedules

Having looked at inputs, it is now possible to see how the law of diminishing returns affects short-run costs. Table 6 is an example of how this can be done. It is assumed that the firm can employ up to eight workers at identical wage rates (i.e. the supply of workers over the range one to eight is perfectly elastic). The price of capital per unit is £100 and the price of labour is £200 per unit.

Capital is the fixed factor of production. Therefore whatever the level of production, total fixed cost will be £1 000 (10 units x £100). Total variable cost will increase as more and more labour is added. Therefore, the total variable cost of producing 20 units is £200 (1 unit of labour x £200), of 54 units it is £400 (2 units of labour x £200), and so on.

Total cost is total fixed cost plus total variable cost. Once the three measures of total cost have been worked out, it is possible to calculate average and marginal costs. Alternatively, it is possible to calculate marginal cost per unit by finding the cost of the additional labour and dividing it by the marginal physical product. In our example, the cost of hiring an extra worker is a constant £200. Therefore, the marginal cost of producing, say, an extra 34 units once 20 have been made is £200 (the cost of the second worker). The marginal cost per unit is then £200 ÷ 34. Average variable cost can be calculated in a similar manner.

Question 4

Table 5

Workers	Total physical product	Total fixed costs	Total variable costs	Total costs	Average fixed costs	Average variable costs	Average total costs	Marginal cost £
1	20							
2	45							
3	60							
4	70							

Table 5 shows how total physical product changes as the number of units of labour changes with a fixed amount of capital. The cost of the capital employed is £200. The firm can employ any number of workers at a constant wage rate per unit of labour of £50. Calculate the different costs shown in Table 5 as the number of workers increases from one to four units of labour.

Short-run cost curves

The cost schedules in Table 6 can be plotted on a graph (Figure 1) to produce cost curves.

Total cost curves The total fixed cost (TFC) curve is a horizontal straight line, showing that TFC is constant whatever the level of output. The total cost (TC) and total variable cost (TVC) curves are parallel because the vertical distance between the two (the difference between TC and TVC) is the constant total fixed cost. The inflections in the TC and TVC curves are caused by the change from increasing returns to diminishing returns.

Table 6 Marginal costs of production

£

Capital	Labour	Total physical product (output)	TVC	TFC	TC	AVC	AFC	ATC	MC
			Total cost[1]			**Average cost**[2]			**Marginal cost**
10	0	0	0	1 000	1 000	0	–	–	
									10.0
10	1	20	200	1 000	1 200	10.0	50.0	60.0	
									5.9
10	2	54	400	1 000	1 400	7.4	18.5	25.9	
									4.3
10	3	100	600	1 000	1 600	6.0	10.0	16.0	
									3.9
10	4	151	800	1 000	1 800	5.3	6.6	11.9	
									4.3
10	5	197	1 000	1 000	2 000	5.1	5.1	10.2	
									6.1
10	6	230	1 200	1 000	2 200	5.2	4.3	9.6	
									9.5
10	7	251	1 400	1 000	2 400	5.6	4.0	9.6	
									22.2
10	8	260	1 600	1 000	2 600	6.2	3.8	10.0	

1. Assuming that capital costs £100 per unit and labour costs £200 per unit.
2. The three measures of average cost have been calculated to the nearest decimal from total figures. ATC therefore does not always equal AVC+AFC because of rounding.

Average cost curves The average fixed cost (AFC) curve falls as output increases because fixed costs represent an ever-decreasing proportion of total cost as output increases. The average cost (AC) curve and average variable cost (AVC) curve fall at first and then rise. They rise because diminishing average returns set in. The vertical distance between the AC and AVC curves is the value of average fixed cost. This must be true because average cost minus average variable cost is equal to average fixed cost.

Marginal cost curve The marginal cost (MC) curve at first falls and then rises as diminishing marginal returns set in.

Points to note

U-shaped AC and MC curves The MC and AC curves in Figure 1 are 'U-shaped'. This is a characteristic not just of the sample figures in Table 6, but of all short run MC and AC curves. They are U-shaped because of the law of diminishing returns. The lowest point on the MC and the AVC curves shows the point where diminishing marginal returns and diminishing average returns set in respectively.

Product and cost curves The marginal and average cost curves shown in Figure 1 are mirror images of the marginal and average product curves that could be drawn from the same data in Table 6. Marginal and average physical product rise when marginal and average cost fall, and vice versa. This is what should be expected. If marginal physical product is rising, then the extra cost of producing a unit of output must fall, and similarly with average physical product and average variable cost. For instance, when the second worker produces 34 units, the third worker 46 units and the fourth worker 51 units, the marginal cost of production must be falling because the increase in output is rising faster than the increase in cost. When marginal physical product is falling, the extra cost of producing a unit of output must rise for the same reason. However, the cost and product curves will only be mirror images of each other if there are constant factor costs per unit. If, for instance, we assumed that the unit cost of labour rose as more workers were employed, so that the average wage of three workers was higher than the average wage of two, then the product and cost curves would not be mirror images.

MC curve cuts AC curve at its lowest point In Figure 1, the marginal cost curve cuts the average cost curve and average variable cost curve at their lowest points. To understand why

Figure 1

The shape of short-run cost curves

The shape of the average and marginal cost curves is determined by the law of diminishing returns. The curves are drawn from the data in Table 6. Assuming constant factor prices, diminishing marginal returns set in at an output level of 145 when the marginal cost curve is at its lowest point. Diminishing average returns set in at the lowest point of the average variable cost curve at an output of 210 units.

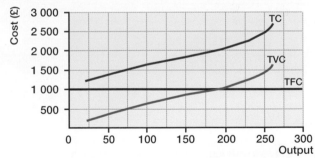

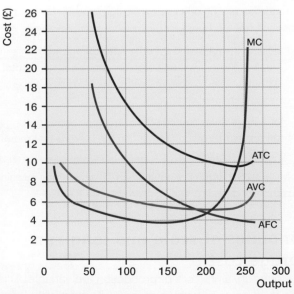

245

this must be so, consider the example of a group of students whose average height is six feet. A new student (the marginal student) arrives in the group. If the student is above six feet then the average height of the group will now rise. If the student is less than six feet, the average height of the group will fall. If the student is exactly six feet tall, then the average height of the group will stay the same. Now apply this to average and marginal cost. If the average cost curve is falling, then the cost of an extra unit of output (the marginal cost) must be less than the average cost. If average cost is rising, it must be true that the cost of an extra unit of output is even higher than the average cost. When average cost is neither rising nor falling, marginal cost must be the same as average cost. Hence we know that:

● the average cost curve is above the marginal cost curve when average cost is falling;
● the average cost curve is below the marginal cost curve when average cost is rising;
● average cost and marginal cost are equal for all levels of output when average cost is constant; if the average cost curve is U-shaped, this means that marginal cost will be equal to and will cut the average cost curve at its lowest point.

The same chain of reasoning applies to the relationship between the average variable cost curve and the marginal cost curve.

Question 5

Table 7 Capital, labour and total product

		Units
Capital	Labour	Total product
10	0	0
10	1	8
10	2	24
10	3	42
10	4	60
10	5	70
10	6	72

Table 7 shows the change in total product as more labour is added to production and all other factor products remain constant. The price of capital is £1 per unit whilst labour is £2 per unit.

(a) Calculate the following over the range of output from zero to 72 units: (i) total fixed cost; (ii) total variable cost; (iii) total cost; (iv) average fixed cost; (v) average variable cost; (vi) average total cost; (vii) marginal cost.

(b) Plot each of these cost schedules on graph paper, putting the total cost curves on one graph and the average and marginal cost curves on another.

(c) Mark on the graph the point where (i) diminishing marginal returns and (ii) diminishing average returns set in.

Economies of scale and long-run average cost

In the long run, all factors of production are variable. This has an effect on costs as output changes. To start with, long-run

Figure 2

Economies of scale

The long-run average cost curve is U-shaped because long run average costs:
• at first fall over the output range OA showing economies of scale;
• then are constant over the output range AB;
• then rise when output exceeds OB showing diseconomies of scale.
Over the output range AB, the minimum cost level of production, the firm is said to be at its optimum level of production.

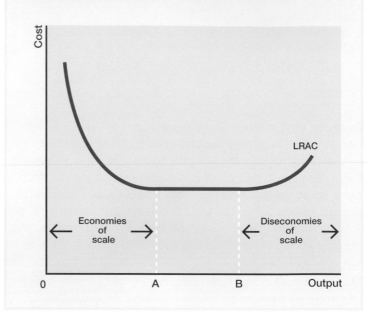

costs fall as output increases. **Economies of scale** are then said to exist. For instance, a firm quadruples its output from 10 million units to 40 million units. However, total costs of production only increase from £10 million to £20 million. The average cost of production consequently falls from £1 per unit (£10 million ÷ 10 million) to 50p per unit (£20 million ÷ 40 million).

Empirically (i.e. from studying real examples of the costs of firms), economists have found that firms do experience economies of scale. As firms expand in size and output, their long run average costs tend to fall. At some point, which varies from industry to industry, long run average costs become constant. However, some firms become too large and their average costs begin to rise. They are then said to experience **diseconomies of scale**. For instance, if a firm doubled its output, but as a result its costs were four times as high, then the average cost of production would double.

This pattern of falling and then rising long run average costs is shown in Figure 2. At output levels up to OA, the firm will enjoy falling long run average costs and therefore experience economies of scale. Between output levels of OA and OB, long run average costs are constant. To the right of OB, long run average costs rise and the firm faces diseconomies of scale.

LRAC in Figure 2 is drawn given a set of input prices for costs. If the cost of all raw materials in the economy rose by 20 per cent, then there would be a shift upward in the LRAC curve. Similarly, a fall in the wage rates in the industry would lead to a downward shift in the LRAC curve.

The optimum level of production

Productive efficiency is said to exist when production takes place at lowest average cost. If the long run average cost curve is U-shaped, then this will occur at the bottom of the curve when constant returns to scale exist. The output range over which average costs are at a minimum is said to be the **optimal level of production**. In Figure 2 the optimal level of production occurs over the range AB.

The output level at which lowest cost production starts is called the **minimum efficient scale (MES) of production**. In Figure 2, the MES is at point A. If a firm is producing to the left of the MES, then long run average costs will be higher. To the right, they will either be the same (if there are constant returns) or will be increasing (if there are diseconomies of scale).

Sources of economies of scale

Economies of scale occur for a number of reasons.

Technical economies Economies and diseconomies of scale can exist because of **increasing** and **decreasing** returns to scale. These economies and diseconomies are known as **technical economies**. They arise from what happens in the production process. For instance, many firms find that they need equipment but are unable to make maximum use of it. A small builder may use a cement mixer on average only three days a week. If he were able to take on more work he might be able to use it five days a week. The total cost of the cement mixer is the same whether it is used for three days or five days a week (apart from possible depreciation) but the average cost per job done will be lower the more it is used. This is an example of an **indivisibility**. The larger the level of output, the less likely that indivisibilities will occur.

Technical economies arise too because larger plant size is often more productively efficient. For instance, because an oil tanker is essentially a cylinder, doubling the surface area of the tanker (and therefore doubling the approximate cost of construction) leads to an approximately three-fold increase in its carrying capacity. It is generally cheaper to generate electricity in large power stations than in small ones. The average cost of production of a car plant making 50 000 cars a year will be less than that of one making 5 000 cars a year.

So far, it has been assumed that unit costs are constant. However, unit costs may change as a firm changes in size. Other factors, apart from technical economies, can then lead to economies and diseconomies of scale.

Managerial economies Specialisation is an important source of greater efficiency. In a small firm, the owner might be part time salesman, accountant, receptionist and manager. Employing specialist staff is likely to lead to greater efficiency and therefore lower costs. The reason why small firms don't employ specialist staff is because staff often represent an indivisibility.

Purchasing and marketing economies The larger the firm the more likely it is to be able to buy raw materials in bulk. Bulk buying often enables these firms to secure lower prices for their factor inputs. Large firms are also able to enjoy lower average costs from their marketing operations. The cost of a sales force selling 40 different lines of merchandise is very much the

same as one selling 35 lines. A 30-second TV commercial for a product which has sales of £10 million per annum costs the same as a 30 second TV commercial for one which has sales of only £5 million per annum.

Financial economies Small firms often find it difficult and expensive to raise finance for new investment. When loans are given, small firms are charged at relatively high rates of interest because banks know that small firms are far more at risk from

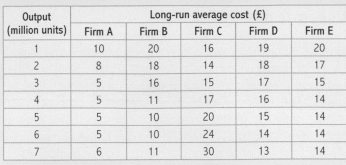

Question 6

Table 4

Output (million units)	Long-run average cost (£)				
	Firm A	Firm B	Firm C	Firm D	Firm E
1	10	20	16	19	20
2	8	18	14	18	17
3	5	16	15	17	15
4	5	11	17	16	14
5	5	10	20	15	14
6	5	10	24	14	14
7	6	11	30	13	14

For each firm, A to E, give:

(a) the range of output over which there are: (i) economies of scale; (ii) diseconomies of scale;

(b) the optimum level or range of output;

(c) the minimum efficient scale of production.

Question 7

In 2011, the Spanish airline company Iberia merged with the UK airline, British Airways (BA). Iberia's operating costs were higher than those of BA and so there were plenty of opportunities for the new group called International Airlines Group (IAG) to cut these closer to industry norms. However, the merger also gave savings in other areas. For example, significant savings were made by combining all or part of 'back-office' functions such as administration, IT services and support services for planes. At individual airports, one set of staff instead of two could deal with everything apart from desk service. Where BA and Iberia flew the same routes before the merger in competition with each other, flight services could be combined when planes were less than full. Marketing too could be made more cost-effective. The group could save on marketing by advertising BA and Iberia flights together. By directing BA passengers onto Iberia flights where BA did not fly a route also reduces the cost per passenger of a flight. In 2014, IAG raised its full-year profit forecast after reporting a 22 per cent jump in earnings in the 3rd quarter. Partly, the rise in earnings was due to continued cost cutting in its Spanish operations. In December 2014, AIG made a takeover bid for the Irish airline, Aer Lingus, in part hoping that a larger airline would reduce average costs.

Source: adapted from © the *Financial Times*, 7.12.2012, 1.11.2014, 18.12.2014, All Rights Reserved.

What economies of scale might IAG enjoy compared to BA, Iberia and Aer Lingus as independent airlines?

bankruptcy than large firms. Large firms have a much greater choice of finance and it is likely to be much cheaper than for small firms.

Diseconomies of scale

Diseconomies of scale arise mainly due to management problems. As a firm grows in size it becomes more and more difficult for management to keep control of the activities of the organisation. There is a variety of ways of dealing with this problem. Some companies choose to centralise operations with a small, tightly-knit, team controlling all activities. Sometimes a single charismatic figure, often the founder of the company, will keep tight control of all major decisions. In other companies, management is decentralised with many small subsidiary companies making decisions about their part of the business and head office only making those decisions which affect the whole group. However, controlling an organisation which might employ hundreds of thousands of workers is not easy and there may come a point where no management team could prevent average costs from rising.

Geography too may lead to higher average costs. If a firm has to transport goods (whether finished goods or raw materials) over long distances because it is so large, then average costs may rise. Head office may also find it far more difficult to control costs in an organisation 1 000 miles away than in one on its door step.

Movements along and shifts in the long-run average cost curve

The long run average cost curve is a boundary. It represents the minimum level of average costs attainable at any given level of output. In Figure 3, points below the LRAC curve are

unattainable. A firm could produce above the LRAC boundary, but if it were to do this it would not use the most efficient method to produce any given level of output. Thus a firm could, for instance, produce at the point A, but it would be less efficient than a firm producing the same quantity at the point B.

An increase in output which leads to a fall in costs would be shown by a movement along the LRAC curve. However, there is a variety of reasons why the LRAC might shift.

External economies of scale The economies of scale discussed so far in this unit have been **internal economies of scale**. Internal economies arise because of the growth in output of the firm. **External economies of scale** arise when there is a growth in the size of the industry in which the firm operates. For instance, the growth of a particular industry in an area might lead to the construction of a better local road network, which in turn reduces costs to individual firms. Or a firm might experience lower training costs because other firms are training workers whom it can then poach. The local authority might provide training facilities free of charge geared to the needs of a particular industry. The government might assist with export contracts for a large industry but not a small industry. External economies of scale will shift the LRAC curve of an individual firm downwards. At any given level of output, its costs will be lower because the industry as a whole has grown.

Taxation If the government imposes a tax upon industry, costs will rise, shifting the LRAC curve of each firm upwards. For instance, if the government increased employers' National Insurance contributions, a tax upon the wage bill of a company, the total cost of labour would rise, pushing up average costs.

Figure 3

The LRAC as a boundary

The LRAC curve is a boundary between levels of costs which are attainable and those which are unattainable. If a firm is producing on the LRAC curve, then it is producing at long-run minimum cost for any given level of output, such as at point B. If long-run production is inefficient, cost will be within the LRAC boundary such as at point A.

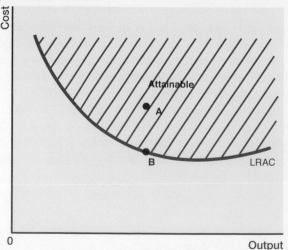

Question 8

'Motorsport valley' is centred around Silverstone, the grand prix racing track in Northamptonshire and Buckinghamshire. The area is home to a network of 3 000 small engineering companies focused on supplying the motorsport industry. Largely because of this expert supply chain, several of the eleven Formula 1 racing teams have their headquarters in the UK, although most are foreign owned. Formula 1 racing supports 5 000 jobs directly and generates £2 billion worth of sales of goods and services to meet the tight delivery schedules of its racing team customers. The wider business community employs close to 40 000 and is worth £9 billion to the UK economy, according to the Motorsport Industry Association.

The network of engineering companies contains specialised manufacturing capability which the racing teams need to win. Being close to the headquarters of the Formula 1 teams means that parts can be delivered at very short notice as cars are built and prepared for grand prix races. Face to face contact between engineers is vital, according to Tim Angus of Motorsport Research Associates. 'It's what we call the tacit knowledge and it's another reason the UK supply chain will continue to thrive'.

Source: adapted from © the *Financial Times* 18.3.2014, 5.7.2014, All Rights Reserved.

Explain the possible sources of external economies of scale for engineering companies in 'Motorsport valley'.

Technology The LRAC curve is drawn on the assumption that the state of technology remains constant. The introduction of new technology which is more efficient than the old will reduce average costs and push the LRAC curve downwards.

External diseconomies of scale These will shift the long-run average cost curve of individual firms in the industry upwards. They occur when an industry expands. Individual firms are then forced to compete with each other and bid up the prices of factor inputs such as wages and raw materials.

The relationship between the short-run average cost curve and the long-run average cost curve

In the short run, at least one factor is fixed. Short-run average costs at first fall, and then begin to rise because of diminishing returns. In the long run, all factors are variable. Long-run average costs change because of economies and diseconomies of scale.

In the long run, a company is able to choose a scale of production which will maximise its profits. Assume in Figure 4 that it decides to produce in the long run at point A. It buys factors of production such as plant and machinery to operate at this level. Later it wishes to expand production by PQ but in the short run it has fixed factors of production. Expanding production may well lead to lower average costs as it does in Figure 4. Diminishing average returns have not set in at point A.

Figure 4

The long-run average cost curve

In the long run, all factors are variable. Points A, D and G show long run cost curves at different levels of production. If the firm in the short run then expands production, average costs may fall or rise to B, E or H respectively. But they will be above the long-run costs, C, F and J, for those levels of output because the cost of production with at least one fixed factor is likely to be higher than the cost if all factors were variable.

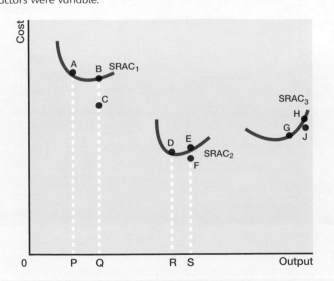

Figure 5

The long-run average cost curve envelope

The long-run average cost curve is an envelope for all the associated short run average cost curves because long-run average cost is either equal to or below the relevant short run average cost.

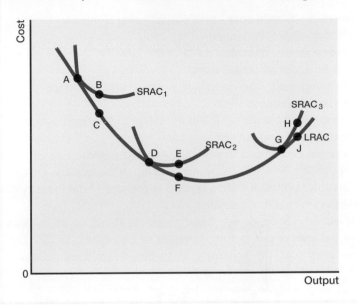

However, production must be less cost-efficient at B compared to the long run situation where the firm could have varied all its factors of production and produced at C. At B, the firm is working with plant and machinery designed to work at optimum efficiency at a lower output level OP. At C, the firm is working with plant and machinery designed to produce at C.

Similarly, if D and F are long run cost positions, a firm producing at E with plant and machinery designed to produce at D must be less cost-effective than a firm operating at F with a factory designed to produce OS of output.

A, C, D, F, G and J are least cost points in the long run. Combining these, as in Figure 5, we get a long run average cost curve. For each point on this curve there is an associated short run average cost curve, such as AB. If the firm operates in the short run at the point where the short run cost curve just touches (is tangential to) the long run cost curve, then it is operating where the company thought it would operate when it was able to vary all its factor inputs.

If short run output is different from this position, then its short run costs will be higher than if it could have varied all its factors of production. However, it could be higher or lower than the tangency point depending upon whether diminishing returns have or have not set in.

The long run average cost curve is said to be the envelope for the short run average cost curves because it contains them all.

Key Terms

Average cost - the average cost of production per unit, calculated by dividing the total cost by the quantity produced. It is equal to average variable cost + average fixed cost.

Average fixed cost - total fixed cost divided by the number of units produced.

Average variable cost - total variable cost divided by the number of units produced.

Diseconomies of scale - a rise in the long run average costs of production as output rises.

Economic cost - the opportunity cost of an input to the production process.

Economies of scale - A fall in the long run average costs of production as output rises.

External economies of scale - falling average costs of production, shown by a downward shift in the average cost curve, which result from a growth in the size of the industry within which a firm operates.

Fixed or indirect or overhead costs - costs which do not vary as the level of production increases or decreases.

Imputed cost - an economic cost which a firm does not pay

for with money to another firm but is the opportunity cost of factors of production which the firm itself owns.

Internal economies of scale - economies of scale which arise because of the growth in the scale of production within a firm.

Marginal cost - the cost of producing an extra unit of output.

Minimum efficient scale (MES) of production - the lowest level of output at which long run average cost is minimised.

Optimal level of production - the range of output over which long run average cost is lowest.

Semi-variable cost - a cost which contains within it a fixed cost element and a variable cost element.

Total cost - the cost of producing any given level of output. It is equal to total variable cost + total fixed cost.

Total fixed cost - the value of the cost of production which does not vary however many units are produced.

Total variable cost - the overall cost of those factors of production that vary directly with the amount produced.

Variable or direct or prime costs - costs which vary directly in proportion to the level of output of a firm.

Thinking like an economist

Cost in the shipping industry

Over the past decades, ships have been getting larger and larger. This is because of economies of scale. Doubling the surface area of a ship, and therefore roughly its cost to build, leads to a three-fold increase in carrying capacity. What's more, a ship which has double the carrying capacity of another ship does not have double the short-term costs of operation. In 2014, the world's largest container ship to date, the CSCL Globe, had its maiden (first) voyage. It was able to carry 19 000 standard container units (TEUs). Two 9 500 TEU capacity ships will have larger combined operating costs. The smaller ships between them will have more crew, cost more in fuel per mile, have higher insurance premiums and more docking charges.

However, large ships are not necessarily profitable. Following the financial crisis of 2008, the shipping industry faced a worldwide slump as growth in world trade slowed considerably. Worldwide trade slumped 10 per cent in 2009 and growth to 2013 was sluggish. At the same time, ships ordered in 2007 and before were still being delivered to shipping companies. They have also carried on ordering very large ships because it gives them an extra competitive advantage in terms of costs. The result has been a glut of shipping and a collapse in the rates received by shipping firms for transporting goods.

Shipping companies have a stock of ships and they are therefore in a short run position. Faced with rock bottom revenues per journey, they have responded in a variety of ways. One way is to move down the short run average cost curve of running a ship. Fuel costs can be saved, for example, by slowing down the speed of a ship. Another way for a shipping company to minimise short run costs is simply to lay up their

most inefficient ships, i.e. anchor them in a safe place and not use them. By using the most efficient ships in their fleet, they can save on costs such as fuel and crew. By adopting these strategies, they may be operating above their long run average cost curves, but they are at least on their short run average cost curve.

Data Response Question

Ocado vs the rest

Online supermarket shopping has been growing at a much faster pace than shopping from 'bricks and mortar' supermarkets. In the UK, two different models have sprung up. In 2002, Ocado started trading as a business to deliver groceries from dedicated warehouses. It started in partnership with the supermarket chain, Waitrose, offering Waitrose own branded products as well as branded products from manufacturers such as Nestlé and Proctor & Gamble. Initial costs were high because Ocado not only had to build its warehouse distribution centres but also because it designed sophisticated computer systems to deal with every point along the supply chain, from ordering from suppliers to picking in the warehouse to orders from customers.

Tesco, Asda and Sainsburys had been offering limited Internet shopping since the 1990s. In the 2000s, their services were expanded nationally. However, all three supermarket chains decided that the Ocado model of distribution from dedicated warehouses could not be profitable in the short term. Instead, they chose to distribute from their existing stores, employing 'pickers' to take items from supermarket shelves just like ordinary shoppers. This considerably reduced their initial costs, but meant that their 'picking' costs were higher.

Morrisons, the fourth largest supermarket chain, waited till 2014 to offer Internet shopping. It chose to

sign a deal with Ocado to licence Ocado's technology and to buy a warehouse from Ocado to distribute its groceries. Due to high initial costs and missed targets for sales, Ocado only expected its first profit in 2015.

Source: with information from © the *Financial Times* 18.3.2013, 15.1.2015, All Rights Reserved.

Evaluation

In your answer, you need to distinguish between the various types of costs - total, average or marginal. Would they have lower fixed costs, variable costs, short run costs or long run costs? Would costs be lower if they set up their own warehouse distribution system or attempted to use another firm's distribution system like Morrisons has done with Ocado? You could use the diagram showing the long run average cost as an envelope for short run cost curves to analyse the situation.

Q

1. Explain the difference between fixed costs and variable costs for firms, using Internet grocery shopping as an example.

2. Explain the possible economies of scale that supermarket chains might experience in Internet grocery shopping.

3. Discuss whether supermarkets would all have lower costs if they used a centralised warehouse distribution model for online grocery services.

45 Profit

Key points

1. Profit is the difference between revenue and costs.
2. Profit is maximised at a level of output where the difference between total revenue and total cost is greatest.
3. At this profit maximising level of output, marginal cost = marginal revenue.
4. An increase in costs will lower the profit maximising level of output.
5. An increase in revenues will raise the profit maximising level of output.
6. In the short run, profit maximising firms will operate so long as their revenue is greater than their variable cost.

Starter activity

What is profit? When you leave full-time education, you could get a job with a starting salary of £25 000 a year. Or you could set up your own business. You don't pay yourself a salary. You also use £20 000 left to you by a relative to establish the business, money which had been earning three per cent interest a year in a bank account. What would have to be true about the relationship between costs and revenues in the business for you to be better off setting up your business (a) in the first year and (b) in the long term?

Profit

Profit is the difference between revenue (the receipts of the firm) and costs (the monies paid out by the firm). A firm will make the most profit (or maximum profit) when the difference between total revenue and total cost is greatest.

This is shown in Table 1. Total revenue is shown in the second column whilst total cost is in the third column. Profit is the difference between the two. At low levels of production, the firm will make a loss. The **break-even point**, where total revenue equals total cost, is reached at an output level of three units. Thereafter profit increases as output increases.

Normal and abnormal profit

Cost for an economist is different from that for an accountant or business period. The economic cost of production is its opportunity cost. It is measured by the benefit that could have been gained if the resources employed in the production process had been used in their next most profitable use.

If a firm could have made £1-million profit by using its resources in the next best manner, then the £1-million profit is an opportunity cost for the firm. In economics this profit, which is counted as an economic cost, is called **normal profit**.

If the firm failed to earn normal profit, it would cease to produce in the long run. The firm's resources would be put to better use producing other goods and services where a normal profit could be earned. Hence, normal profit must be earned if factors of production are to be kept in their present use.

Abnormal profit (also called **pure profit**, or **economic profit** or **supernormal profit**) is the profit over and above normal profit (i.e. the profit over and above the opportunity cost of the resources used in production by the firm). It is important to remember that the firm earns normal profit when total revenue equals total cost. However, total revenue must be greater than total cost if it is to earn abnormal profit.

In Table 1, there are two levels of output where profit is highest at £27. However, the profit separated out in the table is abnormal profit. Normal profit is included as part of total cost. Therefore the firm will choose to produce at the higher of the two levels of output, at seven units. The 7th unit of output does not increase abnormal profit because this is zero on the 7th unit. But it increases the amount of normal profit. Therefore producing seven units rather than six units will increase total normal profit.

Table 1

Output	Total revenue (£)	Total cost (£)	Profit (£)
1	25	35	-10
2	50	61	-11
3	75	75	0
4	100	90	10
5	125	106	19
6	150	123	27
7	175	148	27
8	200	182	18
9	225	229	-4

Question 1

Liam leaves his £70 000 a year job to set up a company from which he draws a salary of £30 000 in its first year, £50 000 in its second year and £70 000 in its third year. He puts £50 000 of his own savings into the company as start-up capital which previously had been invested and could earn a rate of return of ten per cent per annum. Accountants declare that the costs of the firm over the first 12 months were £250 000, £280 000 in the next 12 months and £350 000 in the third year. Revenues were £270 000 in the first year, £310 000 in the second year and £450 000 in the third year.

For each year, calculate the firm's:

(a) accounting profit; (b) economic profit; (c) normal profit.

Profit maximisation: the MC = MR rule

Marginal cost and marginal revenue can also be used to find the profit maximising level of output. Marginal cost is the addition to total cost of one extra unit of output. Marginal revenue is the increase in total revenue resulting from an extra unit of sales.

Table 2 shows the marginal cost and marginal revenue figures derived from Table 1. Marginal revenue minus marginal cost gives the extra profit to be made from producing one more unit of output. The firm makes a loss of £10 on the first unit, and £1 on the second. The third unit of output yields a profit of £11, the fourth £10 and so on. So long as the firm can make additional profit by producing an extra unit of output, it will carry on expanding production. However, it will cease extra production when the extra unit yields a loss (i.e. where marginal profit moves from positive to negative). In Table 2, this happens at an output level of seven units. The seventh unit contributes nothing to abnormal profit.

However, as explained above, cost includes an allowance for normal profit and therefore the firm will actually produce the seventh unit. The eighth unit yields a loss of profit of £9. The firm will therefore not produce the eighth unit if it wishes to maximise its profit.

Economic theory thus predicts that profits will be maximised at the output level where marginal cost equals marginal revenue.

Cost and revenue curves

These same points can be made using cost and revenue curves. The revenue curves in Figure 1 are drawn on the assumption that the firm receives the same price for its product however much it sells (i.e. demand is perfectly price elastic). So the total revenue curve increases at a constant rate. The marginal revenue curve is horizontal, showing that the price received for the last unit of output is exactly the same as the price received for all the other units sold before.

The total revenue and total cost curves show that the firm will make a loss if it produces between 0 and B. Total cost is higher than total revenue. B is the break-even point. Between B and D the firm is in profit because total revenue is greater than total cost. However, profit is maximised at the output level C where the difference between total revenue and total cost is at a maximum. If the firm produces more than D, it will start making a loss again. D, the second break-even point on the diagram, is the maximum level of output which a firm can produce without making a loss. So D is the sales maximisation point subject to the constraint that the firm should not make a loss.

Now consider the marginal cost and marginal revenue curves. It can be seen that the profit maximising level of output, OC, is the point where marginal cost equals marginal revenue. If the firm produces an extra unit of output above OC, then the marginal cost of production is above the marginal revenue

Table 2

Output	Marginal revenue (£)	Marginal cost (£)	Addition to total profit (£)
1	25	35	-10
2	25	26	-1
3	25	14	11
4	25	15	10
5	25	16	9
6	25	18	7
7	25	25	0
8	25	34	-9
9	25	47	-22

Figure 1

The profit maximising level of output

Profit is maximised at the level of output where the difference between total revenue and total cost is at its greatest, at OC. This is the point where marginal cost equals marginal revenue. OB and OD are break-even points.

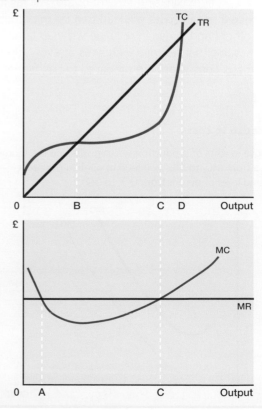

Question 2

Table 3

Output (million units)	Total revenue (£ million)	Total cost (£ million)
1	10	8
2	20	14
3	30	20
4	40	30
5	50	50
6	60	80

(a) Calculate the total profit at each level of output.

(b) What is the profit maximising level of output?

(c) Calculate the marginal revenue and marginal cost of production at each level of output.

(d) Explain, using the data, why MC = MR at the profit maximising level of output.

received from selling the extra unit. The firm will make a loss on that extra unit and total profit will fall. On the other hand, if the firm is producing to the left of OC the cost of an extra unit of output is less than its marginal revenue. Therefore the firm will make a profit on the extra unit if it is produced. Generalising this, we can say that the firm will expand production if marginal revenue is above marginal cost. The firm will reduce output if marginal revenue is below marginal cost.

It should be noted that there is another point in Figure 1 where MC = MR. This is at the point A. It isn't always the case that the marginal cost curve will start above the marginal revenue curve at the lowest level of output. However, if it does, then the first intersection point of the two curves, when marginal cost is falling, is not the profit maximising point. The MC = MR rule is therefore a **necessary** but not **sufficient** condition for profit maximisation. A second condition has to be attached, namely that marginal cost must be rising as well.

Question 3

(a) From the data in Table 3, draw two graphs showing
   (i) total revenue and total cost curves and (ii) marginal revenue and marginal cost curves. Draw the graphs one underneath the other using the same scale on the output axis.

(b) Mark on each of the graphs (i) the break-even levels of output and (ii) the profit maximising level of output.

Shifts in cost and revenue curves

It is now possible to analyse in greater depth the effects of changes in costs or revenues on output. Assume that costs, such as the price of raw materials, increase. This will mean that the marginal cost of production at every level of output will be higher. The marginal cost curve will shift upwards as shown in Figure 2. The profit maximising level of output will fall from OQ_1 to OQ_2. Hence a rise in costs will lead to a fall in output.

On the other hand, a rise in revenue will lead to an increase in output. Assume that revenue increases at every given level of output. Perhaps consumers are prepared to pay higher prices

Figure 2

An increase in costs

An increase in costs of production which pushes up the marginal cost curve from MC_1 to MC_2 will lead to a fall in the profit maximising level of output from OQ_1 to OQ_2.

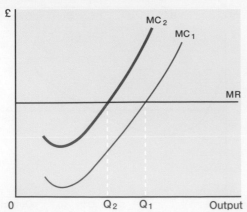

Figure 3

An increase in revenue

An increase in revenue at any given level of output will push the marginal revenue curve upwards from MR_1 to MR_2. This will lead to a rise in the profit maximising level of output from OQ_1 to OQ_2.

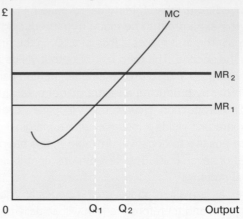

because their incomes have increased, or the good has become more fashionable to purchase. This will push the marginal revenue curve upwards as shown in Figure 3. The profit maximising level of output will then rise from OQ_1 to OQ_2.

Shut down points in the short and long runs

Firms are not always able to operate at a profit. They may be faced with operating at a loss. Neo-classical economics predicts that firms will continue in production in the short run so long as they cover their variable costs.

Consider Table 4. The company would lose £20 million in any period in which it shut down its plant and produced nothing. This is because it still has to pay its fixed costs of £20 million even if output is zero. Total fixed costs represent the maximum loss per period the company need face.

The table shows that the firm is facing a steadily worsening trading situation. Its costs remain the same throughout, but each period its revenue declines. In period 1, total revenue exceeds total costs. The firm makes a profit of £10 million if production takes place. In period 2, it makes no profit by operating its plant (although it should be remembered that cost includes an allowance for normal profit).

However, this is better than the alternative of shutting down and making a £20 million loss. So too is producing in

Table 4

					Profit or loss		£ million
Period	Total variable cost	Total fixed cost	Total cost	Total revenue	If production takes place	If plant is shut down	
1	30	20	50	60	+10	-20	
2	30	20	50	50	0	-20	
3	30	20	50	40	-10	-20	
4	30	20	50	30	-20	-20	
5	30	20	50	20	-30	-20	

Figure 4

Short-run and long-run shut down points

In the short run, a firm will shut down if the price it receives falls below OC. Below OC, the price will not even cover its variable costs. In the long run, when all costs are variable, the shut down price is OD.

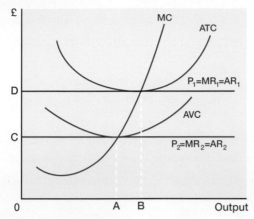

period 3. Although the company makes a loss of £10 million, it will continue to produce because the alternative to not producing is a loss of £20 million. In period 4, the company is on the dividing line between whether to produce or not. In period 5, the company will clearly not produce. Its operating losses would be greater than if the plant were shut down.

So short run profit maximisation implies that a firm will continue to produce even if it is not fully covering its total costs. It will only shut down production when its total revenue fails to cover its total variable cost.

This can be shown on a diagram. In Figure 4, short-run average cost and revenue curves are shown. The average fixed cost is the vertical distance between the average variable and average total cost curves. Price is assumed to be constant however many units are sold. Because of profit maximisation, the firm will produce where MC = MR.

- If price, P_1, were OD, the firm would cover its costs and make normal profit on output OB.
- If price were higher than OD, it would produce more than OB and earn abnormal profit.
- If price were between OC and OD, it would not cover both its variable and fixed costs. However, the price would be higher than variable cost. Hence, in the short run, sales would make a contribution to paying fixed costs.

Question 4

Consider the data in Table 3. What is the new profit maximising level of output if:

(a) marginal revenue falls to £6 million at each level of output;

(b) marginal revenue increases to £20 million at each level of output;

(c) marginal cost increases by £4 million at each level of output;

(d) total cost increases by £5 million at each level of output;

(e) total revenue doubles at each level of output?

Question 5

A profit maximising company has fixed costs of £10 million. Its variable costs increase at a constant rate with output. The variable costs of production of each unit is £1 million. Explain whether it will produce:

(a) 10 units if total revenue is £30 million;

(b) 15 units if total revenue is £25 million;

(c) 20 units if total revenue is £22 million;

- OC is the lowest price at which the firm will produce in the short run. At price P_2, or OC, no contribution is made to paying fixed costs but the firm is earning the normal profit element included in costs.
- Below a price of OC, the firm will shut down. Its losses from continuing in production would be greater than the losses made by shutting down. Not only is it not covering its fixed costs but it is not even covering its variable costs.

Point A is called the short-run shut down point. If Figure 4 showed long run costs, the long run shut down point would be OB. In the long run, all costs are variable and so the average total cost curve is the same as the average variable cost curve. Price would have to be at least OD for the firm to produce.

The same analysis can be used if the average revenue curve or demand curve is downward sloping. In Figure 5, the average total cost and average variable cost curves are drawn. Five different possible average revenue or demand curves are also drawn.

Figure 5

Different average revenue curves will give different profit outcomes

The position of the average revenue curve in relation to average cost curves will determine whether the firm makes abnormal profit (AR_1), normal profit (AR_2), or a short-run loss (AR_3). The shut down point is along AR_4 and the firm would not produce with AR_5.

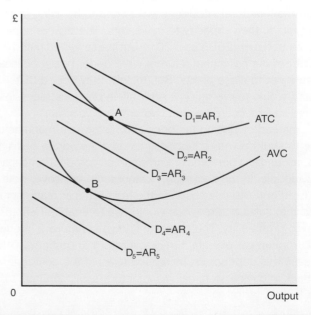

- Along AR_1, there are many levels of output where average revenue is greater than average cost. The firm will definitely produce somewhere along this line because it will be able to make abnormal profit.
- Along AR_2, there is just one point, A, where average revenue equals average cost. This will be the profit maximising point for the firm. It will earn normal profit, but not abnormal profit. The point A, where the AR and AC curves are tangential, is the long-run shut down point. If AR were below this, it would not produce in the long run.
- Along AR_3, at every level of output, average total cost is greater than average revenue. So it will always make a loss. But there are many levels of output where average revenue is greater than average variable cost. In the short run, it will therefore continue to produce, because at least it is making some contribution to paying fixed costs.

Key Terms

Abnormal profit - the profit over and above normal profit.
Break-even point - the levels of output where total revenue equals total cost.
Normal profit - the profit that the firm could make by using its resources in their next best use. Normal profit is an economic cost.

- Along AR_4, there is just one point, B, where average revenue equals short-run average cost. This is the short-run shut down point. If average revenue were any lower, the firm would not even cover its average variable cost and so it would not produce.
- Along AR_5, there is no point where average revenue even covers average variable costs, let alone average total cost. So the firm would not produce if faced with this average revenue line.

Question 6

A firm has total fixed costs of £900 and variable costs of £1 per unit.

(a) What will be the price per unit if it sets out to manufacture 300 units a week and make a 25 per cent profit over costs?

(b) Demand is not as great as the company hoped. If it maintains its price, what is the minimum number of units that must be sold per week if the company is to break even?

(c) Demand is 150 units per week. The company is offered an order for an extra 350 units a week if it drops its price on all units sold to £3 per unit. However, it believes that demand will slowly increase in the future to the planned 300 units a week if the original price is maintained. Should the firm accept the order?

Thinking like an economist

Difficult times for European car manufacturers

The financial crisis of 2008 was a disaster for European car manufacturers. Between 2008 and 2014, they made heavy losses on their European operations. The crisis saw a sharp fall in demand for new cars as consumers and firms cut back on their spending. With high fixed costs and much lower total revenues, car manufacturers slumped into the red.

Car manufacturers could have responded by axing factories and reducing their capacity to make cars. There were some closures between 2008 and 2014 but these were limited. Partly it was because car manufacturers were under heavy political pressure not to close plants. But, mainly, they hoped that demand would revive quickly. After all, in previous recessions demand had recovered within two or three years.

So instead of closing factories completely, car manufacturers chose to shut down production lines on a temporary basis. In 2014, around 30 per cent of European car production capacity was lying idle. In the short run, revenues did not cover both their fixed and variable costs. In the long run, car manufacturers hoped that sales and revenue would rise to enable them to return to profitability. The estimate shown in Figure 6 suggests that European car manufacturers will return to profit in 2015. However, this depends on increased sales. If the eurozone falls back into recession, car manufacturers will continue to make losses.

Source: with information from © the *Financial Times* 21.7.2014, All Rights Reserved.

Figure 6

Car manufacturers' capacity utilisation[1]

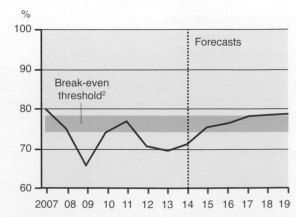

1. Capacity utilisation is the number of cars actually produced divided by the maximum number of cars that could be produced given existing factories and machines, expressed as a percentage.
2. The break-even threshold on the diagram is the capacity utilisation needed for car manufacturers to at least break even. Note that break-even here is defined in accounting terms. It does not include normal profit. It is a range because different car manufacturers have different break-even thresholds.

Source: adapted from IHS Global; © the *Financial Times* 21.7.2014, All Rights Reserved.

Data Response Question

The European steel industry

The years before 2008 were boom years for the European steel industry. Prices and sales rose as the European economy experienced a period of sustained growth. Able to earn abnormal profit, steel firms expanded their European production facilities. Net steel imports from the rest of the world almost fell to zero, as Figure 7 shows.

Figure 7

European steel: demand and supply (Million tonnes)[1]

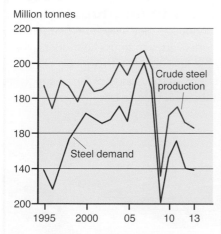

Source: adapted from World Steel Association.
1. Production is greater than demand because the balance is exported from Europe to other world markets. The graph shows that Europe was a net exporter of steel over the period.

It all came to an end in 2008 as the failures of the world banking system pushed the world into recession. Demand for steel in Europe fell from over 200 million tonnes in 2007 to nearly 120 million tonnes in 2009 as prices plummeted. Steel producers initially reacted by cutting production but keeping their plants open. This quickly became unsustainable and steel producers began to shut their most loss- making plants completely.

However, European governments fought fiercely to prevent steel plant closures.

Even today, steel plants across Europe are producing on average only 75 per cent of their potential output and profitability is patchy. European steel plants are having to rely on sales to the rest of the world to survive because European demand is too weak. With energy costs high in Europe and steel prices still depressed, some commenters argue that more European steel plants will be forced to close in the future.

Source: adapted from © the *Financial Times* 10.4.2014, All Rights Reserved.

Q

1. Explain, using the steel industry as an example, what is meant by 'profit'.

2. Explain why, in the short run, a steel manufacturing firm might keep on producing despite making losses.

3. Evaluate whether further closures of steel plants in Europe in 2014 were inevitable.

Evaluation

Explain why steel plants in Europe would be forced to close using the concepts of costs, revenues and shut down points, and a diagram. Then explain what would have to happen if existing steel plants were to remain open in terms of costs and revenues. Is it inevitable that these events would never happen? Weigh up the likelihood that supply and demand conditions will change in the European steel market.

46 Market structure

Key points

1. Market structures are the characteristics of a market which determine firms' behaviour within the market
2. The number of firms within a market may vary from one (as in monopoly), to several (as in oligopoly), to a large number (as in monopolistic competition or perfect competition).
3. Barriers to entry prevent potential competitors from entering a market.
4. Industries may produce homogeneous or differentiated (branded) goods.
5. Perfect knowledge or imperfect knowledge may exist in an industry.
6. Firms may be independent or interdependent.

Starter activity

What are the characteristics of the mobile phone market (for sending and receiving data rather than the handsets) in the UK? Look at the opening paragraph in this unit to help you describe these characteristics.

- the ease or difficulty with which these new entrants might come in;
- the extent to which goods in the market are similar;
- the extent to which all firms in the market share the same knowledge;
- the extent to which the actions of one firm will affect another firm.

Market structure

Market structures are the characteristics of a market which determine firms' behaviour. Economists single out a small number of key characteristics:

- the number of firms in the market and their relative size;
- the number of firms which might enter the market;

The number of firms in an industry

The number of firms in an industry may vary from one to many. In the UK market for letter deliveries to household doors, the Post Office is essentially the sole supplier. In agriculture, on the other hand, there are tens of thousands of farms supplying potatoes and carrots to the market in the UK.

Question 1

(a) How many firms are there in each of the industries shown in the photographs?

(b) In which of these industries do a few large firms dominate?

- A **monopoly** is said to exist where there is only one supplier in the market.
- In a market dominated by a few large producers, the market structure is **oligopolistic**. In an oligopolistic market there may be a large number of firms, but the key characteristic is that most are small and relatively unimportant, whilst a small number of large firms produces most of the output of the industry.
- In **perfect competition** or in monopolistic competition there is a large number of small suppliers, none of which is large enough to dominate the market.

The degree to which large firms dominate an industry is known as **market concentration**. This can be measured using a **concentration ratio**, which considers the **market share** of the leading firms in an industry. This is explained in detail in the 'Thinking like an economist' section in this unit.

Barriers to entry

Market structures are not only affected by the number of firms in an industry and their relative output, but also by the potential number of new entrants to the market. Firms in an industry where there are unlikely to be any new entrants may behave differently from firms in an industry where there are many strong potential competitors.

There is a number of **barriers to entry** which prevent potential competitors from entering an industry.

Capital costs Buying a local corner shop is relatively cheap and therefore the entry cost to most forms of retailing is low. Buying a car plant or an aluminium smelter, on the other hand, is extremely expensive. Entry costs to these industries are very high and only large companies on the whole can pay them. Capital costs therefore represent a very important barrier to entry and vary from industry to industry.

Sunk costs Sunk costs are costs which are not recoverable. For instance, a woman may set up a gardening business, buying a lawnmower, a van, garden tools and paying for advertising. If the business folds, she will be able to get some money back by selling the van, the tools and mower, but she won't be able to get any of the money back from the advertising. The cost of advertising and the difference between the purchase price and resale price of the capital equipment would be her sunk costs. High sunk costs will act as a barrier to entry because the cost of failure for firms entering the industry will be high. Low sunk costs, on the other hand, will encourage firms to enter an industry because they have little to lose from failure.

Scale economies In some industries, economies of scale are very large. A few firms operating at lowest average cost (the **optimum level of production**) can satisfy all the demand of buyers. This will act as a barrier to entry because any new firm entering the market is likely to produce less and therefore have much higher average costs than the few established producers. In some industries, it could be that a few firms supplying the whole industry are still unable to exploit fully the potential economies of scale. A **natural monopoly** is then likely to result, with just one firm surviving in the industry, able to beat off any new entrants because it can produce at lowest cost.

Natural cost advantages Some producers possess advantages because they own factors which are superior to others and which are unique (i.e. have no close substitutes). For instance, a petrol station site on a busy main road is likely to be superior to one in a sleepy country village. A stretch of desert in Saudi Arabia with oil underneath may be superior for oil production to the most beautiful of the Derbyshire Dales. The Victoria and Albert Museum should be able to attract more visitors because of its wide collection than a small provincial

Question 2

Compare and contrast the barriers to entry to the UK food retailing industry, the international oil industry and the UK banking industry.

town museum. As a result, they will either be able to produce at lower cost or be able to generate higher revenues than their potential competitors.

Legal barriers The law may give firms particular privileges. Patent laws can prevent competitor firms from making a product for a given number of years after its invention. The government may give a firm exclusive rights to production. For instance, it may give broadcast licences to commercial television companies or it may make nationalised industries into monopolies by legally forbidding private firms to set up in the industry.

Marketing barriers Existing firms in an industry may be able to erect very high barriers through high spending on advertising and marketing. The purpose of these is to make consumers associate a particular type of good with the firm's product, creating a powerful **brand** image. One example of this from 50 years ago was the success of the Hoover company with its vacuum cleaner. Even today, many people still refer to vacuum cleaners as 'hoovers'. In the UK detergent industry, a national launch of a new brand of soap or washing powder will cost in excess of £10 million. Soap and washing powders are low technology products whose costs of production are relatively low. Marketing barriers, however, make the industry almost impossible to enter.

Limit pricing Firms in an industry may choose to set lower prices than they would charge if they maximised their short run profits. They do this to keep out new entrants. If they only earn normal profit, new firms will not be attracted into the industry. This strategy is known as **limit pricing**. The strategy helps the firms to maximise long run profits. If new firms did enter the industry, this could lead to existing firms losing their abnormal profits anyway. They would also lose sales and so their normal profit would be lower. It is better to accept lower profits in the short run to preserve profit in the long run. Limit pricing is a barrier to entry because it keeps new entrants out of the industry.

Question 3

Dyson was founded in 1993 and is most famous for its innovative vacuum cleaner. Its bagless vacuum technology shook up the vacuum cleaner market and quickly established the Dyson brand as representing leading edge technology. The company has just announced the launch of a robotic vacuum cleaner that has taken 16 years to develop. The Dyson 360 Eye will probably sell for around £750, at the high end of the price range within the vacuum cleaner market.

Dyson has moved into several categories in recent years and now makes heaters and fans as well as products using its Airblade technology, including a unique tap with an inbuilt hand dryer.

Source: adapted from © the *Financial Times* 5.9.2014, All Rights Reserved.

(a) Explain what is meant by a 'brand' using Dyson as an example.

(b) Vacuum cleaners can be bought for less than £100. To what extent do consumers benefit from being offered branded vacuum cleaners such as the Dyson 360 Eye?

Anti-competitive practices Firms may deliberately restrict competition through restrictive practices. For instance, a manufacturer may refuse to sell goods to a retailer which stocks the products of a competitor firm. A manufacturer may refuse to sell a good, when it has a monopoly in production, unless the buyer purchases its whole range of goods. Firms may be prepared to lower prices for long enough to drive out a new entrant to the business.

These barriers to entry may be divided into two groups. Some occur inevitably. These are known as **innocent entry barriers**. Most cost advantages fall into this category. However, other barriers are created by firms in the industry **deliberately** to keep out potential competitors. Marketing barriers limit pricing and anti-competitive practices are examples of these.

The extent to which there is freedom of entry to a market varies enormously. Manufacturing industries, with high capital costs and with extensive marketing power, tend to have higher barriers than service industries. However, many service industries have high barriers too. Banking, for instance, has a high capital cost of entry, legal permission is required, and marketing barriers are high. In the professions, like law, architecture and accountancy, new entrants are kept out by enforcement of minimum qualification levels, qualifications which are impossible to obtain except through working in the profession itself.

Barriers to exit

In most industries, **barriers to exit** are low. Barriers to exit are barriers which prevent a firm from leaving an industry quickly and at little cost. Barriers to exit include the cost and time of making employees redundant, selling premises and stock or notifying customers and suppliers. Barriers to exit increase when employment laws make it more difficult to make staff redundant. However, there may be other barriers to exit. A firm may be locked into a contract to supply another firm to which, if it breaks the contract, it will have to pay a large penalty. Or it may have leased premises where the individual owner has to continue paying the lease even if the business is closed down. In these circumstances, the firm may make a smaller loss by staying in the industry than by closing down.

Product homogeneity and branding

In some industries, products are essentially identical whichever firm produces them. Coal, steel and potatoes are examples. This does not mean to say that there are not different grades of coal or types of steel, but no producer has a monopoly on the production of any such grade or type. Goods which are identical are called **homogeneous** goods.

Firms find it much easier to control their markets if they can produce goods which are **non-homogeneous**. Differentiating their product from those of their competitors (called **product differentiation**) and creating brands allows them to build up brand loyalty. This in turn leads to a reduction in the elasticity of demand for their product. A branded good may be physically no different from its competitors, or it may be slightly different, but branding has value for the firm because consumers think that the product is very different, so different that rival products are a very poor substitute for it. This perception is built up

Question 4

In the market for bank current accounts, the three biggest challengers are on track to open at least two million accounts this year. TSB, Nationwide and Santander are trying to take away customers from the top four high-street banks including Lloyds Banking Group, Barclays, Royal Bank of Scotland and HSBC. Current accounts are important because it is easier to sell mortgages, savings accounts and credit cards to current account customers. With a fixed pool of savings and credit card borrowing, for example, one bank's extra customer can easily be another bank's loss.

Source: adapted from © the *Financial Times* 2.6.2014, All Rights Reserved.

Explain, using the example of banks, what is meant by interdependence in a market.

through advertising and marketing and enables firms to charge higher prices without losing very much custom (i.e. demand is relatively inelastic).

Knowledge

Buyers and sellers are said to have **perfect knowledge** or **perfect information** if information about prices, output and products is readily available. Therefore, if one firm were to put up its prices, it would lose all its customers because they would buy from elsewhere in the industry. Hence, there can only be one price in the market.

Perfect knowledge also implies that a firm has access to all information which is available to other firms in its industry. In UK agriculture, for instance, knowledge is widely available. Farmers can obtain information about different strains of seeds, the most effective combinations of fertilizers and pesticides and when it is best to plant and reap crops.

Perfect knowledge does not imply that all firms in an industry **will** possess all information. An inefficient farmer might not bother to gather relevant information which is readily available. In the short term, the farmer might survive, although in the longer term the farm will be driven out of business by more efficient competitors. Equally, perfect information does not imply that all firms know everything about their industry and its future. Farmers do not know if in 6 months' time a drought will destroy their crops. They have to work on the basis of probability. Perfect knowledge only means that all firms have the same access to information.

Firms have imperfect knowledge where, for instance, there are industrial secrets. Individual firms may not know the market share of their competitors or they may be unaware of new technology or new products to be launched by rival companies. Information could then act as a barrier to entry, preventing or discouraging new firms from entering the industry.

There is **asymmetric information** in a market when there is imperfect knowledge in the market and some firms have more information than others. Firms with more information are likely to be better decision makers and this will give them a competitive advantage. There may also be asymmetric information between firms and customers leading to market failure. When firms have more information than customers, there can be a misallocation of resources when firms exploit this information gap to their advantage.

Interrelationships within markets

There are two possible relationships between firms in an industry. Firms may be independent of each other. This means that the actions of any one firm will have no significant impact on any other single firm in the industry. In agriculture, for instance, the decision of one farmer to grow more wheat this season will have no direct impact on any other farmer. It will not affect his next door neighbour. This **independence** is one reason why perfect knowledge exists to some degree in agriculture. There is no point in keeping secrets if your actions will not benefit you at the expense of your competitors.

If firms have **interdependence** then the actions of one firm will have an impact on other firms. An advertising campaign for one brand of soap bar, for instance, is designed mainly to attract customers away from other brands. Firms are more likely to be interdependent if there are few firms in the industry.

Interdependence implies **uncertainty**. One firm in the market does not know how other firms will react if it makes a change to, say, the price of a product or spending on an advertising campaign.

Competition and market structure

The neo-classical theory of the firm recognises a number of market structures derived from the characteristics above. In later units these market structures will be considered in greater detail. Here, however, the key features are summarised. In neo-classical theory, there are three main types of market structure.

- **Perfect competition**. A large number of firms, each producing a homogeneous good, compete in the industry. None of the firms is large enough to have a direct impact on any other firm or on the market price of the good. There is freedom of exit and entry to the industry.
- **Monopoly**. There is only one firm in the industry. Barriers to entry make it impossible for new firms to enter.
- **Imperfect competition**. **Imperfect competition** exists where there are at least two firms in the industry, and the industry is not perfectly competitive. For instance, non-homogeneous goods may be produced, there may be imperfect knowledge or firms may be interdependent, or some combination of these.

Firms in imperfectly competitive industries can compete in a number of ways. For instance, they can compete on:
- **price** - offering a lower price should attract more orders;
- **quality** - consumers are likely to prefer a better quality good;
- **after-sales service**;
- **delivery date** - a buyer may look elsewhere if a firm cannot deliver quickly and on time;
- **image** - building a strong brand image through advertising and other forms of marketing is likely to be a major factor in determining demand for the product.

In perfect competition, firms are not in direct competition with each other. One firm can expand output without affecting either the price received by or the sales of another firm. Each firm is a price taker, facing a perfectly elastic demand curve. However, competition is 'perfect' because any firm which charges a higher price than its competitors, or sells an inferior product, will lose all its sales as perfectly informed consumers buy elsewhere in the market. The discipline of the market is so

strong in a perfectly competitive industry that, in the long run, productive inefficiency (production at above minimum cost) cannot exist.

Key Terms

Barriers to entry - factors which make it difficult or impossible for firms to enter an industry and compete with existing producers.

Barriers to exit - factors which make it difficult or impossible for firms to cease production and leave an industry.

Brand - a name, design, symbol or other feature that distinguishes a product from other similar products and which makes it non-homogeneous.

Concentration ratio - the market share of the largest firms in an industry. For instance, a five firm concentration ratio of 60 per cent shows that the five largest firms in the industry have a combined market share of 60 per cent.

Homogeneous goods - goods made by different firms but which are identical.

Imperfect competition - a market structure where there are several or a relatively large number of firms in the industry, each of which has the ability to control the price that it sets for its products.

Independence - in market theory, when the actions of one firm will have no significant impact on any other single firm in the market.

Interdependence - in market theory, when the actions of one firm will have an impact on other firms in the market.

Limit pricing - when a firm, rather than short run profit maximising, sets a low enough price to deter new entrants from coming into its market.

Market concentration - the degree to which the output of an industry is dominated by its largest producers.

Market share - the proportion of sales in a market taken by a firm or a group of firms.

Market structures - the characteristics of a market which determine the behaviour of firms within the market.

Natural monopoly - where economies of scale are so large relative to market demand that the dominant producer in the industry will always enjoy lower costs of production than any other potential competitor.

Non-homogenous goods - goods which are similar but not identical made by different firms, such as branded goods.

Perfect knowledge or information - exists if all buyers in a market are fully informed of prices and quantities for sale, whilst producers have equal access to information about production techniques.

Product differentiation - aspects of a good or service which serve to distinguish one product from another such as product formulation, packaging, marketing or availability.

Sunk costs - costs of production which are not recoverable if a firm leaves the industry.

Uncertainty - in market theory, when one firm does not know how other firms in the market will react if it changes its strategy such as changing its price.

Thinking like an economist

Industry and concentration ratios

What is an industry or market?

How many firms are there in an industry or market (here we will assume that the two terms can be used interchangeably)? The answer to this question will depend on how we define the market or industry. For instance, the economy could be split up into three very broad market classifications - the market for primary goods, the market for secondary goods and the market for tertiary goods. There is a large number of firms operating in each of these markets. At the other extreme, one could ask how many UK firms produce balls for use in professional cricket, an extremely narrow market.

It should be obvious that the more narrowly a market is defined, the more likely it is that there will be relatively few producers. In the transport market, there are bus companies, rail companies, airlines, etc. In the air transport market, there will be fewer companies. In the market for direct air travel from Birmingham International to the Isle of Man, there was only one company in 2015.

The Standard Industrial Classification

The Office for National Statistics (ONS) conducts regular censuses of production in the UK. The statistics record production levels in different industries using the Standard Industrial Classification 2007. This is a classification system which subdivides industry into broad divisions. For instance, Section B comprises mining and quarrying. Section C is manufacturing, whilst Section K is financial and insurance activities. Each section is then divided into sub-sections. Sub-section C10, for example, is manufacture of food products. Section C11 is manufacture of beverages. The ONS classification is one way of grouping firms into individual industries, each sub-section representing an industry or group of industries.

Concentration ratios

Having classified firms into industries, it is possible to see how many producers there are in the industry. The number of producers is likely to be less important in studying the behaviour of the industry than the economic power of individual producers within the industry. One way of measuring this potential power is to calculate their market share. This measure is then called a **concentration ratio**.

A three-firm concentration ratio would be the total share of the market held by the three largest producers in the industry; a four-firm concentration ratio would be the total share of the market held by the four largest producers.

Figure 1 shows the concentration ratios of food retailers in the UK in June 2014. One firm, Tesco, had 28.8 per cent of the food retail market by sales. The top three firms (Tesco, Asda and Sainsbury's) had 62.2 per cent. The top four firms (Tesco, Asda, Sainsbury's and Morrisons) had 73.2 per cent of the market. This means that other supermarket chains, such as The Cooperative and Waitrose, only had 26.8 per cent of the market.

Concentration in food retailing has been growing over time. There are considerable economies of scale to be achieved in food retailing, which large supermarkets pass on to their customers in the form of lower prices. Large supermarkets are also able to offer their customers one-stop shopping, very important when many consumers work and have limited time to

Figure 1

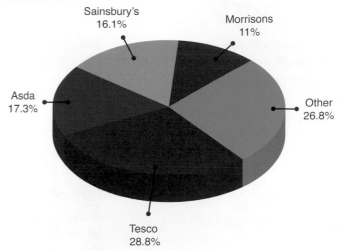

UK grocery sector by market share, 12 weeks to October 2014

Sainsbury's 16.1%
Morrisons 11%
Other 26.8%
Asda 17.3%
Tesco 28.8%

spend on activities such as shopping. Finally, they offer a much wider range of choice than small, independent, local grocery stores. However, since 2010, the four largest supermarket chains have lost some market share to two 'hard discounters', Lidl and Aldi. These two supermarket chains offer a limited range of products but at lower prices than the big four supermarkets.

The large supermarket chains in the UK would claim that the high concentration ratios found in the industry do not prevent the industry from being highly competitive. Critics would argue that, in practice, competition is limited. The top four supermarkets have such enormous economies of scale and so many retail outlets that they can withstand competition at the margins of their business from hard discounters. Competition at this level is imperfect with supermarkets competing on quality of products and customer experience as well as on price.

Data Response Question

Eurostar

November 1994 saw the first Eurostar train pass through the Channel Tunnel with fare-paying passengers from London to Paris. Since then, Eurostar has gradually been gaining market share on the London to Paris route against rival airline services and coach services. By 2013, Eurostar had gained around an 80 per cent share of the travel market between London and Paris, and London and Brussels. Airlines were struggling with the competition from Eurostar which typically gave faster journey times from central London to central Paris including check-in times.

Eurostar offers a fast, reliable, efficient and comfortable service between the two capital cities. The potential competition from airlines means that it has to keep its fare relatively low. In June 2015, for example, the cheapest return fare was £72, whilst the most expensive Business Premier return ticket was £490. Some would argue that its cheap fares have been massively subsidised by bond and shareholders in Eurotunnel, the group that built the Channel Tunnel and was forced to write off billions of pounds in debt. The charge made by Eurotunnel to Eurostar for allowing trains to pass through the tunnel is only a fraction of the sunk costs of the tunnel itself.

Competition doesn't just come from airlines. People can drive to Paris. Alternatively, they can go by coach. For tourists, other destinations also provide competition. If tourists didn't like Eurostar's services to Paris, they

might choose to fly to Rome or Prague for their holiday. Business travellers, in contrast, have no such choice. If they have to get to a meeting in Paris, they have to use some form of transport to make the meeting.

The Eurostar phenomenon is part of a wider pattern of changes in transport. High speed trains have devastated airline passenger numbers between cities where connections have opened up. For example, when the Paris to Marseille high speed train route was opened in 2002, rail only held 22 per cent of the market. By 2006 it was 69 per cent. The shorter the journey time by train, the greater the market share of the train compared to airlines.

Source: with information from © the *Financial Times* 13.11.2014, All Rights Reserved.

Q

1. Explain what is meant by market share, illustrating your answer with examples from the data.

2. Analyse the market structure of the London to Paris route.

3. Discuss whether Eurostar will eventually gain 100 per cent market share on the London to Paris route.

Evaluation

First define market share and then point out that this could have different meanings in this context. Is it just rail versus air or does it include coach travel or travellers using their own motor cars? Is it likely that Eurostar will get 100 per cent of the market if this just includes rail and air travel? Have they achieved that since 1994? What is the likelihood that they will be able to achieve that in the future? Is it more or less likely that they could get 100 per cent market share for all forms of transport?

47 Perfect competition

Key points

1. In a perfectly competitive market it is assumed that there is a large number of small firms that produce a homogeneous product. Firms are price takers. There are no barriers to entry or exit and there is perfect knowledge.
2. The demand curve facing an individual firm is perfectly elastic because the firm is a price taker. This means that price = AR = MR.
3. The short run supply curve of the firm is its marginal cost curve above its average variable cost curve.
4. If firms in the short run are making abnormal profits, new firms will enter the industry, increasing market supply and thus reducing price. This will continue until only normal profits are being made.
5. If production is unprofitable, firms will leave the industry, reducing market supply and increasing price. This will continue until only normal profits are being made.
6. In long run equilibrium, AR = AC because no abnormal profits are made.

Starter activity

You are a wheat farmer in East Anglia. What is the structure of the market in which you operate? How many buyers and sellers are there? How easy is it to enter or exit wheat farming? Is there perfect knowledge? Do you produce a homogeneous good? Can you dictate prices to your customers? All other things being equal, what will happen to prices if there is a bumper harvest of wheat world wide, or to your profits if the price of fertilizer increases significantly?

Assumptions

The model of **perfect competition** describes a market where there is a high degree of competition. The word 'perfect' does not mean that this form of competition produces ideal results or maximises economic welfare; in other words, the word 'perfect' should not have any **normative** overtones.

A perfectly competitive market must possess four characteristics.

- There must be many **buyers** and **sellers** in the market, none of whom is large enough to influence price. Buyers and sellers are said to be price takers. This type of market has many relatively small firms that supply goods to a large number of small buyers.
- There is **freedom of entry to and exit** from the industry. Firms must be able to establish themselves in the industry easily and quickly. Barriers to entry must therefore be low. If a firm wishes to cease production and leave the market, it must be free to do so.
- Buyers and sellers possess **perfect knowledge** of prices. If one firm charges a higher price than the market price, the demand for its product will be zero as buyers will buy elsewhere in the market. Hence the firm has to accept the market price if it wishes to sell into the market (i.e. it must be a price taker).
- All firms produce a **homogeneous** product. There is no branding of products and products are identical.

There are relatively few industries in the world which approximate to this type of market structure. One which might is agriculture. In agriculture there is a large number of farmers

supplying the market, none of whom is large enough to influence price. It is easy to buy a farm and set up in business. Equally it is easy to sell a farm and leave the industry. Farmers on the whole possess perfect knowledge. They know what prices prevail in the market, for instance from the farming press. Finally, farmers produce a range of homogeneous products. King Edward potatoes from one farm are indistinguishable from King Edward potatoes from another.

In Europe and in many countries around the world, farming is in certain instances not a perfectly competitive market. This is because governments may interfere in the market, buying and

Question 1

Cotton prices have fallen by more than 25 per cent this year. Hundreds of thousands of cotton farmers worldwide might be fearful of where the price could go in the future. The upside is that lower cotton prices will encourage garment manufacturers worldwide to use more cotton in the clothing they make. Cotton had a 27.5 per cent share of the global fibre market last year compared to a historical norm of 40 per cent.

Figure 1

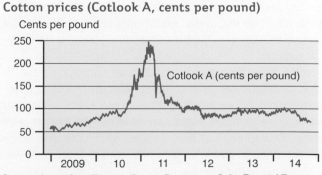

Cotton prices (Cotlook A, cents per pound)

Discuss why producers in the world cotton market might be said to operate in a perfectly competitive market.

Figure 2

The effect of an increase in supply by one firm in a perfectly competitive industry

An increase in supply by one firm from S₁ to S₂ will have such a small effect on total supply that equilibrium price will remain at OE.

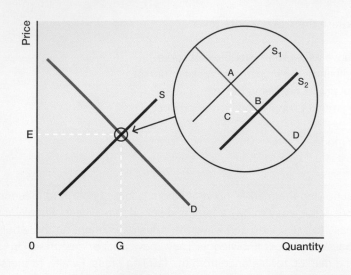

Figure 3

The demand curve facing a firm in perfect competition

A change in output by the firm will have no effect on the market price of the product. Therefore the firm faces a perfectly elastic demand curve. This is also the firm's average and marginal revenue curve.

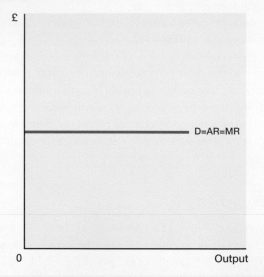

selling to fix a price. In some markets in the UK, there is a small number of very large buyers, such as supermarkets. Again, these markets would not be classified as perfectly competitive.

Demand and revenue

It is an assumption of the model of perfect competition that there is a large number of sellers in the market. Assume that one of these firms decides to double output. Industry supply will increase, pushing the supply curve to the right. However, the increase in supply is necessarily very small because the firm is small. In fact it will be so small that the resulting movement along the demand curve will be impossible to distinguish and the price will not change.

This can be seen in Figure 2. The area around the existing equilibrium point has been enlarged. An increase in supply by one firm has shifted the supply curve from S₁ to S₂, reducing equilibrium price by AC and increasing equilibrium quantity demanded and supplied by CB. However, AC is so small that it has no effect on the overall equilibrium price of OE and it is impossible to draw two supply curves thinly enough to show this shift in supply.

In agriculture, for instance, it would be surprising if the decision of one farmer to double wheat output were to have any perceptible influence on equilibrium price. His or her extra output is so insignificant that it cannot affect the market price for wheat. Of course, if all farmers were to double their wheat output, the price of wheat would collapse. However here we are interested only in the effect on price of the production decisions of a single farm.

A firm in perfect competition can therefore expand output or reduce output without influencing the price. Put another way, the firm cannot choose to raise price and expect to sell more of its product. It can lower its price but there is no advantage

in this since it can sell its entire output at the higher market price. The demand curve for an individual firm is therefore horizontal i.e. perfectly elastic as in Figure 3. (Note that if a firm expanded output sufficiently its demand curve would become downward sloping, but then the industry would be made up of one large firm and many small firms and would no longer be perfectly competitive.)

The perfectly elastic demand curve facing a perfectly competitive firm also means that it is a **price taker**. It has no choice about what price it receives for its product. Either it accepts the market price or it can choose not to sell. At a cattle

---

Question 2

Table 1 Market demand and supply

Quantity demanded (million units)	Quantity supplied (million units)	Price (£)
1 000	6 000	10
3 000	4 000	8
5 000	2 000	6

(a) Draw the market demand and supply curves on graph paper.

(b) There are 1 000 firms in the industry each producing the same quantity. One firm now doubles its output.

   (i) Show the effect of this on market demand and supply.

   (ii) On a separate graph draw the demand curve facing the firm.

(c) All firms in the industry now double their output.

   (i) Show the effect of this on market demand and supply.

   (ii) What will be the effect on the demand curve for the individual firm?

Figure 4

The firm's supply curve

The marginal cost of production is the lowest price at which a profit maximising firm will sell a marginal unit of production. Therefore the marginal cost curve is the supply curve for the firm. However, in the short run the firm may stay in production so long as it can cover its average variable costs. Hence the short run supply curve is the marginal cost curve above average variable cost as in Figure 4(a). In the long run a firm will leave the industry if it makes a loss. Hence, the supply curve in the long run is the marginal cost curve above the average cost curve as in Figure 4(b).

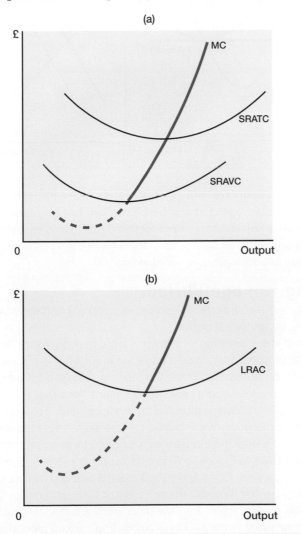

- The marginal cost of production is the lowest price at which a firm would be prepared to supply an extra unit of output. For instance, if the marginal cost were £3 when price received was £5, then the firm would be able to make £2 abnormal profit (profit over and above the normal profit included in cost on that unit). The firm would definitely produce this marginal unit. If marginal cost were £3 when price were £3 it would still produce this marginal unit because it would earn normal profit on it. However, if marginal cost were £3 when price was £2 it would not produce the extra unit because it would make a £1 loss on it.

- In the short run, a firm will not necessarily shut down production if it makes a loss. A firm has fixed costs which it has to pay whether it closes down and produces nothing or whether it continues to operate. Any revenue over and above variable cost will make some contribution towards paying its fixed costs. Therefore it will only close down (i.e. cease to supply) if average revenue or price is below average variable cost.

The firm's short-run supply curve will therefore be that part of the marginal cost curve above its average variable cost curve - the 'solid' portion of the marginal cost curve in Figure 4(a).

In the long run there are no fixed costs and the average total cost and average variable cost curves are one and the same. The firm will not produce unless it can cover all its costs. Therefore in the long run, the firm's supply curve is the marginal cost curve above its average cost curve as shown in Figure 4(b).

The supply curve for the industry can be constructed by horizontally summing the individual supply curves of each firm.

Short-run equilibrium

In perfect competition it is assumed that firms are short-run profit maximisers. Therefore the firm will produce at that level of

auction, for example, farmers can choose either to sell at the auction price or take their cattle home.

The demand curve facing a perfectly competitive firm is also the firm's average and marginal revenue curve. If a firm sells all its output at one price, then this price must be the average price or average revenue received. If a firm sells an extra or marginal unit, it will receive the same price as on preceding units and therefore the marginal price or revenue will be the same as the average price or revenue.

Cost and supply curves

In a perfectly competitive market, the supply curve of the firm will be its marginal cost curve.

Question 3

Table 2

Units						£
Output average	Total fixed cost	Total variable cost	Total cost	Average variable cost	Average total cost	Marginal cost
2	100	100				40
3						30
4						40
5						60
6						
7						1 000

Table 2 shows the costs of production of a firm.

(a) Calculate for levels of output from two to seven units: (i) total fixed cost (ii) total variable cost; (iii) total cost; (iv) average variable cost; (v) average total cost.

(b) Plot the firm's short run supply curve on a graph.

(c) Would a firm cease production (1) in the short run and (2) in the long run if the sales price per unit were: (i) £80; (ii) £70; (iii) £60; (iv) £50; (v) £40; (vi) £30?

Figure 5

Short-run profit maximisation

The firm produces at its profit maximising equilibrium level of output OQ where MC = MR. Because AR is greater than AC, it makes an abnormal profit of EFGH.

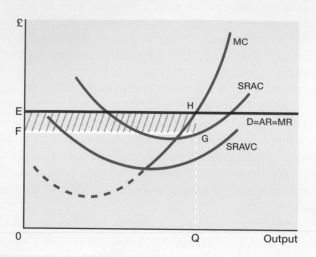

Figure 7

Long-run equilibrium following short run losses

If losses are being made in the short run firms will leave the industry, pushing the supply curve from S_1 to S_2. At S_2 there will no longer be any pressure for firms to leave because they will be able to make normal profits on their operations.

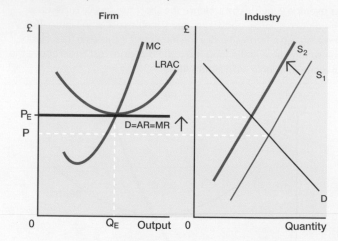

output where marginal cost equals marginal revenue (the MC= MR rule). The price it charges is fixed by the market because the individual firm is a price taker.

Figure 5 shows one possible short run equilibrium situation. The demand curve is perfectly elastic at a price of OE. The marginal cost curve cuts the marginal revenue curve at H and hence the equilibrium, profit maximising level of output for the firm is OQ. At this level of output, average revenue (QH) is higher than average cost (QG) and so the firm will make an abnormal profit. This is given by the shaded area EFGH and is average profit (EF) multiplied by the quantity produced (FG).

Figure 6 gives another possible situation. Here the firm is making a loss at its equilibrium, profit maximising (or in this case

Figure 6

Short-run operation at a loss

The firm produces at its profit maximising equilibrium level of output OQ where MC = MR. In this case, because AR is less than AC, it will make a loss shown by the shaded area EFGH. This is the minimum loss it will make if AR is greater than AVC.

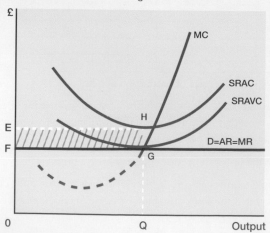

loss minimising) level of output OQ where MC = MR. Price OF is lower than average cost and hence the firm makes a total loss of EFGH. The firm will stay in production if this loss is smaller than the loss it would make if it shut down (i.e. so long as average revenue is above average variable cost).

Long-run equilibrium

In the long run, a perfectly competitive firm will neither make losses nor abnormal profits.

Consider a situation where firms were making losses. In the long term, some firms would leave the industry. It is pointless carrying on production in the long term at a loss. If firms leave the industry, total supply will fall. The more firms that leave the industry, the greater will be the fall in supply and the greater will be the rise in price of the product. Firms will continue to leave the industry until the industry as a whole returns to profitability. This is shown in Figure 7. When the supply curve is S_1 the firm is making a loss. Firms leave the industry, pushing the supply curve to the left. With S_2, the price is just high enough for firms to make normal profit. If on the other hand a firm were making abnormal profit in the short run, other firms would enter the industry eager to gain high profits. This is shown in Figure 8. At a price of P, firms are making abnormal profit. This encourages new entrants to the industry, increasing supply from S_1 until with S_2 the price is just low enough for firms to make a normal profit.

In the long run, then, competitive pressures ensure equilibrium is established where the firm neither makes abnormal profits or losses. This means that in equilibrium, average revenue equals average cost (AR = AC). It should also be remembered that MC = MR because the firm is profit maximising and that AR = MR because the demand curve is horizontal. Putting these three conditions together, it must be true that for a firm in long run equilibrium in a perfectly competitive market:

$$AC = AR = MR = MC$$

Long-run cost curves

One interesting point to note is that the model of perfect competition predicts that all perfectly competitive firms will have identical costs in the long run. Assume a firm discovers some new technique of production which enables it to reduce costs and increase profits in the short run. Other firms will respond by copying this technique. They can do this because there is perfect knowledge in the industry and therefore there can be no industrial secrets. Firms will then start to cut prices, hoping to be able to expand their sales. If a firm fails to adopt the new techniques, it will start to make a loss when other firms expand supply and undercut its price. Eventually it will be forced either to leave the industry because it is uncompetitive, or to adopt the latest production techniques.

Alternatively, a firm may possess some unique factor of production. It may have an exceptional manager, or find that it

Question 4

Iron ore prices are plunging. After a decade of rapidly rising prices, which saw the spot price of iron ore rise fifteen fold, prices have halved since their peak in 2010. The rise in iron ore prices in the 2000s saw a large increase in investment in new mines. Supply expanded rapidly. However, growth in demand for iron ore has slowed considerably over the past few years. The growth in supply has outstripped the growth in demand, leading to excess supply. Investment is now being sharply cut back. High-cost producers are leaving the industry. Firms with deeper pockets are operating some of their mines at a loss. Production has fallen by 85 million tonnes already this year and predictions are that it will fall a further 125 million tonnes by the end of the year.

Source: adapted from © the *Financial Times* 30.9.2014, All Rights Reserved.

Figure 9

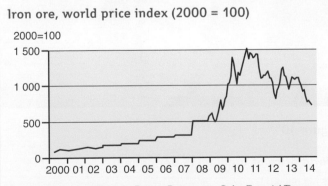

Iron ore, world price index (2000 = 100)

Source: adapted from Thomson Reuters Datastream; © the *Financial Times* 30.9.2014, All Rights Reserved.

(a) Using a perfect competition diagram alongside a demand and supply diagram, explain how supply increasing faster than demand has lead to a fall in the price of iron ore.

(b) Explain, using a perfect competition diagram, why some iron ore producers are 'leaving the industry'.

(c) Using the concepts of fixed and variable costs, explain why some iron ore mining companies are prepared to operate their mines at a loss in the short run.

Figure 8

Long-run equilibrium following short run abnormal profit

If abnormal profits are being made in the short run, firms will enter the industry, pushing the supply curve from S_1 to S_2. At S_2 firms will no longer be attracted into the industry because they will only be able to make normal profits on their operations.

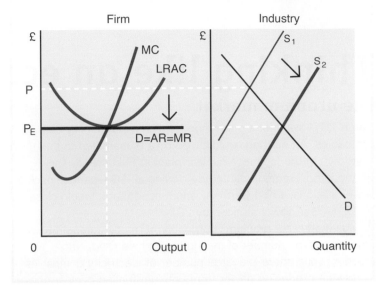

is far better sited than other firms. In a perfectly competitive world, the manager will be able to demand increases in salary which match the extra profit that she is generating for the firm. If the firm fails to pay this, she will be headhunted by another

Question 5

Josh Hampton has been looking for premises to set up a flower shop. In his local market town, the main street is High Street which has on it multiples such as Boots, TopShop and Next. There is a vacant property on High Street, currently a charity shop, with a lease of £50 000 a year. Just round the corner in a side street is another vacant property, almost identical in size, with a lease of £20 000 a year.

Use the theory of perfect competition to explain the difference in annual lease payments between the two properties.

firm which realises the potential of the manager to create profits. As for the better site, the firm could sell it to another firm in the industry for a much higher price than those sites owned by competitors. Therefore the opportunity cost of the site is much higher than other sites and it is the opportunity cost, not the accounting cost, that is shown in economists' cost curves.

Thinking like an economist

The uranium market

March 2011 was not a good month for uranium mining companies. An earthquake followed by a tsunami led to the meltdown of the Japanese nuclear plant at Fukushima. The Japanese government reacted by closing all 50 Japanese nuclear power stations, whilst Germany announced that it would close all its 17 nuclear power stations by 2020.

The market for uranium is arguably perfectly competitive. There is a large number of mining companies producing uranium whilst there is a large number of electricity companies worldwide producing power from uranium-fuelled nuclear power stations. Following the Fukushima incident, the price of uranium fell from a high in early 2011 of $72 a pound to $35 a pound in 2014.

Uranium is a homogeneous product and there is freedom of entry and exit to the uranium mining industry. Assume there is perfect knowledge in the market. On the spot market, mining companies are price takers for the ore.

Economic theory would suggest that a large fall in the price of uranium would lead to a fall in output as uranium mines became loss making. This is what happened with some high-cost producers shutting their mines. Others carried on producing even though they were making losses. One estimate suggested that in 2014, half of all production was loss making. In the short run, mining companies will continue in production so long as they are at least covering their variable costs. Low prices also led to mining companies cutting their plans to expand existing mines or open new mines.

However, demand for uranium is likely to rise in the future. Japan is likely to reopen its 50 nuclear reactors. In 2014, there were also 71 nuclear reactors under construction, 40 per cent of them in China. There were a further 486 either planned or proposed. Industry experts expect the price of uranium to rise in the future as a result. This will allow low-cost uranium miners to earn abnormal profits. This will incentivise mining companies to expand their operations.

Source: with information from © the *Financial Times* 13.2.2014, All Rights Reserved.

Figure 10

World price of uranium ($ per pound)

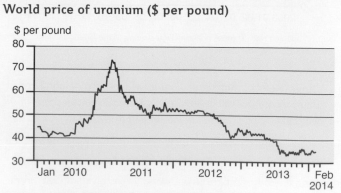

Source: adapted from Thomson Reuters Datastream; © the *Financial Times* 13.2.2014, All Rights Reserved.

Data Response Question

Coal

Coal is demanded worldwide mainly by coal-fired electricity power stations owned by thousands of different electricity generating companies. It is supplied by thousands of mining companies worldwide. Demand for coal is growing. However, the supply of coal has been growing at an even faster rate. The result has been that the price of coal has been falling on world markets since 2011.

For the next two years, supply will continue to grow as major new mines come on stream. However, the fall in prices has led to a cut back in investment in new mines, the effects of which will be felt from 2016 onwards. In the long term, demand for coal could also fall. Coal burnt in power stations is a major source of greenhouse gas emissions. Already, curbs on greenhouse emissions have seen the amount of coal burnt fall in countries such as the UK. At the

same time, costs for solar and wind energy are falling and reducing the cost competitiveness of coal.

Source: adapted from © the *Financial Times* 21.8.2014, All Rights Reserved.

Figure 11

World price of coal (shipped from Australia, $ per tonne)

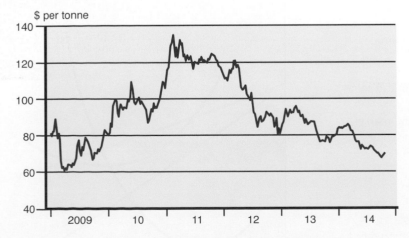

Source: adapted from Glencore; © the *Financial Times* 21.8.2014, All Rights Reserved.

Q

1. Why might the world coal market be perfectly competitive?

2. Using a perfect competition diagram, explain the impact of the change in world coal prices in 2012-14 on an individual coal mining firm.

3. Discuss whether there will be any firms operating coal mines in 50 years' time.

Evaluation

It is important throughout your answer to use economic concepts. For there to be no coal mines in 50 years, either there would have to be no coal left to mine or there would have to be no demand at the market price. The data gives no indication that long term supply is a problem. However, it does suggest that environmental concerns and the growth of renewable energy will cut demand. Will these cut it to zero? What is likely to happen to the demand for electricity worldwide over the next 50 years as countries such as India and China continue to grow? Use a perfect competition diagram to analyse under what circumstances firms would cease to produce in the long run. In a concluding paragraph, weigh up the likelihood that coal will have no place in the energy mix in 50 years' time.

Key points

1. In a monopolistically competitive market, there is a large number of relatively small buyers and sellers, no barriers to entry or exit, firms sell non-homogeneous goods but their market power is weak.
2. In the short run, firms can earn abnormal profit or make losses but, in the long run, they will earn only normal profit.

Starter activity

How many ladies' or gents' hairdressers are there within a three-mile radius of either your school/college or your home? How do they compete with each other? What do you think are the limits on the prices they can charge their customers?

Imperfect competition

Perfect competition and monopoly are at either end of a spectrum of market structures. There are relatively few industries which conform to the strict characteristics of these two models. Most industries fall somewhere in between. In most industries:

- competition exists because there are at least two firms in the industry;
- competition is imperfect because firms sell products which are not identical to the products of rival firms.

The neo-classical theories of perfect competition and monopoly were first developed during the latter half of the 19th century. At the time, it was not unreasonable to suggest that many industries were made up of a large number of small firms producing identical or homogeneous products. In the 20th and 21st century fewer and fewer industries can be said to be perfectly competitive, so a number of theories of **imperfect competition** have been advanced to explain the behaviour of firms. One important model, the model of **monopolistic competition**, was developed by Edward Chamberlain, an American economist, in the 1930s, and his work was mirrored by an English economist, Joan Robinson, at the same time.

Assumptions

The theory of monopolistic competition makes almost the same assumptions as that of perfect competition, namely:

- there is a large number of buyers and sellers in the market, each of which is relatively small and acts independently;
- there are no barriers to entry or exit;
- firms are short run profit maximisers.
  However, one assumption is different:
- firms produce differentiated or non-homogeneous goods.

It can be argued that relatively few industries possess these characteristics. Most industries have concentration ratios which would suggest they were oligopolistic in character. However, examples might be the hotel trade, coach travel or furniture making.

The downward sloping demand curve

If a firm produces a product which is slightly different from that of its competitors, then it has a certain amount of market power.

It will be able to raise price, for instance, without losing all its customers to firms which have kept their prices stable. So it is not a **price taker** like a perfectly competitive firm. However, because there is a large number of firms in the industry producing relatively close substitutes, its market power is likely to be relatively weak. Small changes in price are likely to result in relatively large changes in quantity demanded as consumers switch to close substitutes (i.e. demand is likely to be relatively elastic). The demand curve facing the firm is therefore downward sloping but elastic (i.e. it will operate on the upper portion of its demand curve). The firm's revenue and costs curves are shown in Figures 1 and 2. The reasons why the marginal revenue curve is below the average revenue curve and the cost curves are U-shaped are explained in more detail in Unit 50 on monopoly.

Figure 1

Short-run equilibrium for a monopolistically competitive firm earning abnormal profit

A firm will produce where MC = MR in equilibrium. Because average revenue is above average cost at the equilibrium level of output of 0A, it will earn abnormal profit of BEFG.

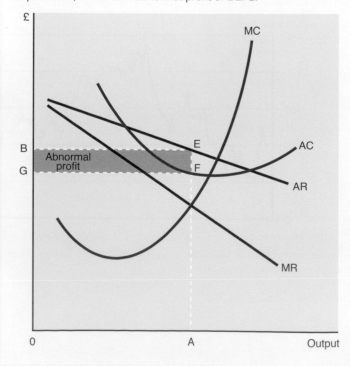

Short-run equilibrium

In the short run, firms in a monopolistically competitive industry can earn abnormal profit or they can make losses. Figure 1 shows a firm making abnormal profits. The firm will produce where MC = MR because it is a profit maximiser. This means that it will produce at an output level of OA. It will charge a price based on its demand or average revenue curve, in this case OB. The average price, or average revenue, will be above the average cost. It will therefore make abnormal profits per unit of EF and a total abnormal profit of BEFG.

Figure 2 shows a firm making a loss. It will produce where MC = MR in order to minimise its losses. It will charge a price based on its demand or average revenue curve, in this case OG. The average cost will be above the average price, or average revenue. It will therefore make a loss of EF per unit sold and a total loss of BEFG.

Long-run equilibrium

Long-run equilibrium is shown in Figure 3. The firm will produce where MC = MR, the profit maximising level of output. It will charge a price based on its demand or average revenue curve, in this case OB.

The firm in the long run will not be able to earn abnormal profit. This is because there is freedom of entry to the market. If the firm is making abnormal profit in the short run, then firms will come into the industry attracted by the high level of profits. This will increase supply in the market. As a result, each firm will see a fall in demand for its product, shifting the average revenue

Figure 2

Short-run equilibrium for a monopolistically competitive firm making a loss

A firm will produce where MC = MR in equilibrium. Because average cost is above average revenue at the equilibrium level of output of OA, it will make a loss of BEFG.

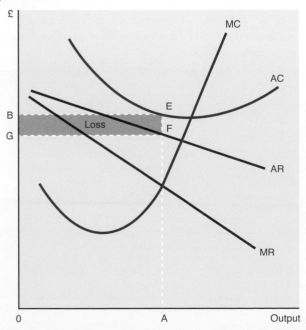

Figure 3

Long-run equilibrium for a monopolistically competitive firm

A firm will produce where MC = MR. As there are no barriers to entry, the firm will be unable to earn abnormal profits in the long run. Therefore it must also be true that AC = AR at the equilibrium level of output. This occurs when the AC curve is tangential to the AR curve.

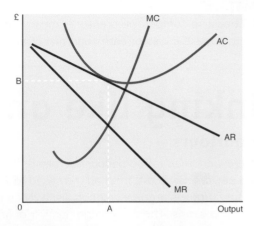

Question 1

Lucy Reynolds opened her nightclub four years ago. Although her local town had plenty of pubs, there was nowhere to go if you wanted good music, a dance and a drink. It was a runaway success. She recouped her investment within six months and after that, the profits simply rolled in. However, it came to an end when another nightclub opened just a few doors away. Her club is still just about profitable enough for her to carry on trading, but if another club came to town, she would probably sell up and move on.

Figure 4

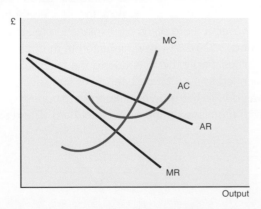

(a) Two years after opening, the marginal cost and revenue costs for Lucy's club were as in Figure 4. Copy out Figure 4 and show on the diagram her abnormal profit.

(b) (i) On the same diagram, draw in new revenue curves showing her position after the new club opened. Label the profit maximising level of output.

(ii) Explain why the revenue curves have shifted and why she is no longer earning abnormal profit.

273

curve downwards to the point where average revenue is just equal to average cost.

If firms in the industry are making losses in the short run, then firms will leave the industry. This will reduce market supply. Each remaining firm will see an increase in demand for their product, shifting the average revenue curve upwards to the point where average revenue is just equal to average cost.

Therefore, in monopolistic competition two conditions must hold in long-run equilibrium:

- MC = MR because the firm is a profit maximiser;
- AC = AR because competitive pressures mean that a firm cannot either make a loss or earn abnormal profit.

This means that at the profit maximising output, the average cost curve is tangential to the average revenue curve as shown in Figure 3.

Thinking like an economist

Tattoo parlours

In 2009, there were 402 tattoo parlours across Britain's 650 largest town centres. By 2014, this had increased to 1 014. The market for tattoos is arguably monopolistically competitive in large cities and towns. There is a large number of firms in the market. No firm is large enough to be able to set prices. In one sense, they are selling a homogeneous product, a tattoo. However, each tattoo parlour has some control over its market. Location is an important factor. No one in Birmingham is likely to make a special trip to get a tattoo in Leeds, for example. Equally, if there are several tattoo parlours competing in a local area, they may be able to establish a reputation for reliability or quality, which could give them some pricing advantage.

Tattoos did become much more popular over the period 2009-2014. However, the percentage growth in sales was less than the percentage growth in the number of tattoo parlours. On average, the number of tattoos completed per parlour fell over the period. This could indicate that tattoo parlours in 2009 were earning abnormal profit and this attracted new entrants into the market. However, a more plausible explanation relates to costs.

The period 2009-2014 saw high streets throughout the UK in difficulties. Partly this was due to the financial crisis of 2008, which led to a prolonged period of stagnation in incomes. Partly it was due to the growth of Internet shopping which hit retailers with premises on the high street hard. The result was

that many retailers closed their high street shops. Vacancy rates for high street premises significantly increased. Shop owners were forced to reduce the rents they charged. This led to a fall in costs for firms renting premises. A fall in costs with no fall in average revenues will lead to an increase in output. So the number of tattoo parlours increased. On average, sales per tattoo parlour fell but they could still earn normal profit because their costs had also fallen.

Data Response Question

The decline of the pub

The traditional English pub is in decline. Hundreds of pubs are closing every year. The problem facing pubs is three fold. First, drinkers have been deserting pubs in favour of drinking at home. The price of supermarket and off-licence beer and spirits is much lower than the prices charged in the local pub. Second, pubs have faced spiralling costs. The tax on beer keeps on increasing. The minimum wage, which most bar staff earn, goes up each year. Rising rents are also a problem, particularly for city centre pubs. Third, many pubs are worth far more if they can be demolished and replaced by housing or a local supermarket than their sale value as a pub.

Customer loyalty is very weak across the industry. Major pub chains attempt to brand the service they provide but with limited success. A few pub chains have made a success by going back to basics: offering beer and other drinks at very low prices, but not offering much else. Most successful pub chains today combine drink sales with food, turning pubs into a type of restaurant. The advantage of offering food is that it appeals to another group of customers. It increases the average spend per customer because each customer not only eats but orders at least one drink. Profit margins on food are also on average higher than on drinks.

Q

1. Explain why the pub market might be seen as monopolistically competitive.

2. Using a monopolistic competition diagram, explain why 'hundreds of pubs are closing every year'.

3. Using diagrams, discuss whether or not there will be any pubs left open in 30 years' time.

Evaluation

Explain why pub closures indicate that in the short run, many pubs are either making profits but these are below normal profits, or they are making losses. Do you think that every pub in the UK is unprofitable in an economic sense? If not, there must be some long run equilibrium point for the pub industry. What factors will determine where this long run equilibrium point will be in terms of revenues and costs? Can individual pubs create customer loyalty and if so how? In your conclusion, weigh up how significant are the negative forces currently hitting the UK pub industry.

49 Oligopoly

Key points

1. Oligopolistic markets are characterised by high concentration ratios and interdependence of firms. There may also be high barriers to entry and exit and product differentiation but there are some oligopolistic markets where these characteristics are not present.
2. Oligopolistic firms have a strong incentive to engage in collusive behaviour, such as being members of a cartel or accepting price leadership in a market.
3. Game theory is one way to explain the behaviour of firms in an oligopolistic market.
4. There are many types of price competition including price wars, predatory pricing and limit pricing.
5. Examples of non-price competition include branding and promotion.

Starter activity

Make a list of 15 different chocolate bars. Who owns and produces these chocolate bars? Does the price of these chocolate bars go up and down like the price of petrol? How do manufacturers of chocolate bars compete with each other?

The importance of oligopoly

Most markets could be said to be imperfectly competitive. A few are monopolistically competitive but the majority are **concentrated markets**, dominated by a few suppliers. Therefore the theory of **oligopoly** is arguably the most important of the theories of the firm. Yet there is no single dominant model of oligopoly within economics. Rather there is a number of competing models which make different assumptions and draw different conclusions.

In the rest of this unit, we will consider **market conduct**. This is how oligopolistic firms behave in order to achieve their objectives.

Market structure

For an industry to be called 'oligopolistic', there must be two key characteristics of its market structure.

- Supply in the industry must be concentrated in the hands of relatively few firms. For instance, an industry where the three largest firms produce 80 per cent of output would be oligopolistic. Note that alongside a few very large producers there may also be a much larger number of very small firms, so an industry with 100 firms, where the three largest firms produced 80 per cent of the output, would still be classed as oligopolistic.
- Firms must be interdependent. The actions of one large firm will directly affect another large firm. In perfect competition, firms are independent. If one farmer decides, for instance, to grow more wheat, that will have no impact on price or sales of other farmers in the industry. In oligopoly, if one large firm decides to pursue policies to increase sales, this is likely to be at the expense of other firms in the industry. One firm is likely to sell more only by taking away sales from other firms. Interdependence means that firms will face uncertainty. They don't know how other firms will react if they change their competitive strategy, such as changing their price or their mix of products.

Economists are also interested in two other characteristics of oligopolistic markets.

- Are there barriers to entry to the market? Unit 52 will explore markets where barriers to entry might be low. In this unit, we will assume that oligopolistic markets have high barriers to entry and exit.
- Are products differentiated? If there is product differentiation, then each firm sells slightly different products. For example, car manufacturers all sell cars but each produces unique models of car which normally cannot be bought from another manufacturer. However, in some highly concentrated oligopolistic markets where firms are interdependent, they sell identical, homogeneous products. In this unit, we will explore oligopolistic markets where there is product differentiation.

Collusion

Oligopolistic firms may compete amongst themselves. When this occurs, **non-collusive** or **competitive oligopoly** is said to exist. However, there is a very strong incentive for oligopolistic

Question 1

Coca-Cola is the largest soft drinks manufacturer in the world. It sells over 500 different brands of sparkling and still drinks, including Coca-Cola itself, the original drink which started the company. In the USA, Coca-Cola had 42 per cent of the cola market compared to 31 per cent for Pepsi Cola in 2013. Traditionally, Coca-Cola and Pepsi have engaged in a fiercely competitive fight for market share both in the USA and worldwide. Market share gained by Pepsi has come at the expense of market share lost by Coca-Cola and vice versa. However, both companies in recent years have come under pressure from manufacturers of what are sold as healthier soft drinks from water to fruit juices to vitamin drinks. Both companies have responded by bringing out their own 'healthier' drinks brands or by buying up small rising companies. For example, in 2014, Coca-Cola launched Coca-Cola Life, a product with natural sweeteners and containing two thirds of the calories of a regular Coke.

Source: with information from © the *Financial Times* 11.6.2014, All Rights Reserved.

Explain why the soft drinks market might be categorised as oligopolistic by discussing (a) concentration (b) interdependence; (c) barriers to entry; (d) product differentiation.

Table 1

Million units			£ millions
Output (a)	Average revenue (b)	Average cost (including normal profit) (c)	Total abnormal profit (b - c) x a
1	10	5	5
2	9	5	8
3	8	5	9
4	7	5	8
5	6	5	5
6	5	5	0

firms to **collude**. This means they make agreements amongst themselves so as to restrict competition and maximise their own benefits. **Collusive oligopoly** is said to exist when oligopolistic firms collude.

To understand the benefits of **collusion**, consider Table 1. It shows the average costs and revenues for each firm in an oligopolistic market. Assume that all firms face identical average costs and revenues and they are all producing identical products. If they competed against each other, prices (or average revenues) are likely to be low. The lowest quantity at which they would be prepared to supply in the long run is six million units each. This is where their average costs, including normal profit, equalled their average revenue. However, if they colluded, they could fix output at a level that maximised their profit. If each firm only produced three million units, then each could earn £9 million in abnormal profit. Collusion, by restricting output, leads to higher prices and higher profits.

Overt or **formal collusion** exists when firms make agreements amongst themselves to limit competition. For example, two firms in a market may share out new contract work between themselves or agree not to sell in certain geographical areas. They may come to a **price agreement** where they fix prices for their products.

When there is a wide-ranging agreement amongst several firms in a market, a **cartel** is said to exist. In this type of overt collusion, firms typically agree to limit their output in order to raise prices. Production limits need to be agreed. Regular meetings to discuss issues and problems are another feature of cartels. The most famous cartel today is not made up of firms but of countries. OPEC (Organization of the Petroleum Exporting Countries) is a group of oil-producing countries that today sell less than half of world output of oil but have more than half of the world's known oil reserves. OPEC attempts to manipulate the world price of oil by restricting supply. Countries are given production quotas that are renegotiated every six months at OPEC meetings.

For a cartel to function effectively, a number of conditions must apply.
- An agreement has to be reached. This is likely to be easiest in oligopolistic industries where only a few firms dominate the market; the larger the number of firms, the greater the possibility that at least one key participant will refuse to collude. It is also likely to be easiest in stable, mature industries where no single firm has recently been able to gain

advantage by pursuing aggressive competitive strategies. For instance, collusion is far more likely in a mature industry like steel manufacturing or cement making than in a rapidly changing industry like the computer industry.
- Cheating has to be prevented. Once an agreement is made and profitability in the industry is raised, it would pay an individual firm to cheat so long as no other firms do the same. For instance, it would pay a small cartel producer with 10 per cent of the market to expand production to 12 per cent by slightly undercutting the cartel price. The profit it would lose by the small cut in price on the 10 per cent is more than offset by the gain in profit on the sale of the extra two per cent. However, if every producer does this, the market price will quickly fall to the free market level and all firms will lose the privilege of earning abnormal profit.
- Potential competition must be restricted. Abnormal profits will encourage not only existing firms in the industry to expand output but also new firms to enter the industry. Firms already in the industry which don't join the cartel may be happy to follow the policies of the cartel in order to earn abnormal profits themselves. To prevent this, cartel firms could agree to drive other firms which compete too aggressively out of the market. Cartel firms could also agree to increase barriers to entry to the industry.

Sometimes a distinction is made between overt and covert collusion. Both then become types of formal collusion. Overt collusion occurs when the collusion is open for everyone to see. OPEC, for example, is an example of overt collusion. However, collusion is illegal in most countries including EU countries and the USA. For this reason, firms wanting to create a cartel or collude in some other way have to collude covertly, or in secret. Covert collusion is designed to be hidden from legal authorities. Most formal collusion today is covert rather than overt.

Tacit or **informed** collusion exists when there is still collusion but firms do not make any formal agreements about cooperating together. Instead, firms monitor each other's behaviour closely. Unwritten rules are developed which become custom and practice, defining ways in which firms may or may not compete.

One form of tacit collusion is **price leadership**. This is when one firm in the market sets a price that other firms in the market follow. The **price leader** is often the largest firm (the **dominant firm**) in the market and the **price followers**, the smaller firms in the market. The firms in the industry effectively collude to maximise their profits. The price leader sets a price that allows it to earn abnormal profit but at the same time also allows price followers to earn a higher profit than would be the case if competition broke out in the market.

Tacit collusion can take many forms apart from price leadership. For example, an unwritten rule in a market may be that firms do not try to take away existing customers from other firms. Or there may be an understanding that advertising expenditure should be kept low.

Question 2

The De Beers diamond cartel was one of the oldest cartels operating in the world. De Beers in the 20th century was the world's largest diamond producer, producing diamonds mainly from its mines in Africa. Until 2000, through its Central Selling Organisation (CSO), it attempted to buy up all the world's diamond production. It then sold these uncut diamonds to customers at regular sales. It attempted to regulate the price by selling fewer diamonds when prices were falling and selling more when prices were rising. In 1999, it held a stockpile of unsold diamonds of $5.2 billion.

However, in 2000, CSO announced that it would cease to act as a cartel. There was a number of reasons for this. One was that an increasing proportion of world diamond production was being sold outside of the Central Selling Organisation. Producers in countries such as Russia were finding it more profitable to sell directly to the market rather than sell to the CSO because they could get better prices. Another problem was the rising cost to De Beers of buying diamonds from other producers. It was also attempting to mop up diamonds which were being mined illegally in war torn countries such as Angola and the Democratic Republic of Congo. These diamonds came to be called 'blood diamonds' because their sale often passed through guerrilla and insurgent groups which used the money to buy arms. De Beers feared that the image of diamonds as a whole would become tainted in the same way that the fur trade had acquired a bad reputation. A further reason was growing worldwide demand for diamonds, particularly from India and China. In the USA, selling De Beers diamonds was illegal under anti-trust laws. Abandoning the cartel would enable De Beers to sell into the US market directly.

Source: adapted from Alain Anderton, *Economics*, 5th Edition, Pearson.

(a) Explain how De Beers' Central Selling Organisation might have raised prices and profits for diamond producers in the cartel before 2000.

(b) Why was there an incentive for producers outside the cartel to cheat?

(c) Why might De Beers have considered it in its best interests to dismantle its cartel because of (i) rising demand for diamonds and (ii) the mining of diamonds in war torn areas of the world?

Game theory and collusion

One way to understand why collusion, whether formal or tacit, benefits all firms in the market is to use **game theory**. Game theory is a theory which can be used in many subject disciplines, not just economics. Game theory considers what would be the outcomes if two or more players were interdependent and made certain choices.

The most famous example of game theory is the **prisoner's dilemma**. Two individuals have committed a crime together and have been arrested. They are kept in separate cells. Each prisoner knows that there is enough evidence to convict them on a related minor charge for which they can expect to serve six months in jail. However, they have been arrested for a more serious offence. The police offer each prisoner a deal. If

Table 2 A payoff matrix which shows that two firms have an incentive to collude

		Firm B	
		Raise price	Leave price unchanged
Firm A	Raise price	£100m/£70m	£30m/£40m
	Leave price unchanged	£40m/£20m	£50m/£30m

they confess and implicate their fellow prisoner, they will get a reduced suspended sentence, which means they don't have to go to jail. But their fellow prisoner will get five years in jail. However, if both confess, then they will both get two years in jail. If they could get together and collude, they would choose to plead their innocence and both would get six months on the minor charge. But in isolation, neither trusts the other. So they both choose to plead guilty and both get two years in jail.

In an oligopolistic market, there are a few interdependent dominant firms. Typically, if they can collude, they can raise prices and their profits at the expense of customers. But they need to be able to trust each other. Consider Table 2 which shows a **payoff matrix**. There are just two firms in the industry (it is a **duopoly**). Each firm has two strategies. It can either raise the price of its product or leave it unchanged. The figures in the box represent the payoffs from the interaction of strategies by the two firms. In this case, they are the profits for Firm A (in black) and Firm B (in red) which would result from each strategy.

Which strategy should firm A use? Firm A is better off raising its price if Firm B also raises its price. Instead of earning £50 million in profit if prices are left unchanged, it could earn £100 million. But if Firm B chose to leave its price unchanged when Firm A raised its price, Firm A would be worse off, earning only £30 million profit.

Similarly, Firm B would be better off if both firms raised their prices. But like Firm A, if it chooses to raise its price when Firm A leaves its price the same, it will be worse off.

The safe option to choose for both firms is to leave their prices unchanged. However, if both firms colluded by both agreeing to raise prices, they would both be better off. In this market, there is a strong incentive for firms to collude.

Question 3

In 2005, 50 of Britain's top fee paying schools were astonished to receive notification from the Office of Fair Trading (OFT) that they were in breach of competition law and faced fines possibly totalling millions of pounds. Schools from Ampleforth College, Eton College, Millfield School and Westminster College to Worth School had, from 1997 on, taken part in a survey, known as the 'Sevenoaks Survey'. Between February and June each year, the schools concerned gave details of their intended fee increases and fee levels for the academic year beginning in September. Sevenoaks School then collated that information and circulated it, in the form of tables, to the schools concerned. The information in the tables was updated and circulated between four and six times each year as schools developed their fee increase proposals in the course of their annual budgetary processes. The Office for Fair Trading deemed that 'this regular and systematic exchange of confidential information as to intended fee increases was anti-competitive and resulted in parents being charged higher fees than would otherwise have been the case'. Parents sending their children to these fee-paying public schools are unlikely to make choices on the basis of a difference of a few hundred pounds in school fees when yearly fees for boarders now typically exceed £30 000. However, schools often justify fee increases by pointing out that similar schools are charging £X more this year. With demand highly price inelastic, not to increase fees by at least the average fee increase for similar schools is to lose revenue unnecessarily.

Following a full investigation, the OFT fined the schools £10 000 each and in addition they agreed to pay collectively £3 million into a trust for the benefit of pupils attending the schools during the period involved.

Source: adapted from www.oft.gov.uk.

Use game theory to suggest why the 50 schools found it in their interest to exchange information about their proposed level of fees for the forthcoming academic year. In your answer, compare a situation where a school increased its fees by the average for other schools and one where it increased its fees by less than the average.

It is not always the case that firms are better off colluding to raise prices. Table 3 shows a market where there is instability. There is no set of strategies which would make both firms better off. If, for example, both were to raise their prices, Firm B would earn higher profits of £15 million but Firm A would earn lower profits of £40 million. In this market, game theory would predict that both firms will be constantly adjusting their prices to attempt to take advantage of the decisions of the other firm.

Table 3 A payoff matrix which shows an unstable market

		Firm B	
		Raise price	Leave price unchanged
Firm A	Raise price	£40m/£15m	£30m/£25m
	Leave price unchanged	£10m/£35m	£50m/£10m

Types of price competition

Firms in an oligopolistic market can engage in a variety of types of price competition. Three examples are price wars, predatory pricing and limit pricing.

Price wars Typically, **price wars** occur in markets where non-price competition is weak. For example, goods may only be weakly branded. Consumers may be highly price conscious and advertising may fail to persuade them that one firm's product is better than another. They also occur in markets were firms find it difficult to collude either formally or tacitly. Price wars tend to drive prices down to levels where firms are frequently making losses. In the short run, firms stay in the market because they are at least covering their variable costs of production and making some contribution to fixed costs. In the long run, prices must rise perhaps because supply falls as firms leave the market or because demand rises.

Predatory pricing Predatory pricing occurs when an established firm in a market is threatened by a new entrant. The established firm responds by setting such a low price that the new entrant cannot make a profit. The aim of the established firm is to drive the new entrant out of the market. Once this is achieved, the existing firm then puts its prices back up to their previous levels. Predatory pricing can also be used by one firm in a market against another firm. If the one firm judges that the other firm is gaining too much of a competitive advantage and gaining market share, it may defend its share by cutting prices. This may take away market share from the other firm or even force it out of the market.

Limit pricing Limit pricing occurs when firms set a low enough price (the limit price) to deter new entrants from coming into the market. For example, assume that there is tacit collusion in a market with four firms. They all charge around £10 for a good that they make. If £10 is a very high price and allows the firms to earn high levels of abnormal profit, then new entrants are likely to come into the market. By charging a lower price, they can gain market share and still make at least normal profit. It would be better for existing firms to charge a lower price than £10. The price has to be high enough for them to make at least normal profit but low enough to discourage any other firm from entering the market. The limit price will be greater the higher the barriers to entry to the market. This is because the higher the barriers to entry, the less likely it is that a new entrant will come into the industry. For example, there might be large initial costs that could not be recovered if the new entrant left the industry (i.e. there are high sunk costs). If sunk costs are high, a firm is unlikely to risk entering the industry unless there are large profits to be made.

Types of non-price competition

In a perfectly competitive market, firms producing homogeneous goods compete solely on price. In the short run, factors such as delivery dates might assume some importance, but in the long term price is all that matters. In an imperfectly competitive market (i.e. monopolistic competition or oligopoly), price is often not the most important factor in the competitive process. Firms decide upon a **marketing mix** - a mixture of elements which form a coherent strategy designed to sell their products to their market. The marketing mix is often summarised in the '4 Ps'. Firms produce a **product** which appeals to their customers. The product may or may not be differentiated from rivals' products. A **price** needs to be set but this could be above or below the price of competing products depending upon the pricing strategy to be used. For instance, a high price will be set if the product is sold as a high-quality product. A low price will be set if the firm wishes to sell large quantities of a standard product. **Promotion** (advertising and sales promotion) is essential to inform buyers in the market that the good is on sale and to change their perceptions of a product in a favourable manner. A good distribution system is essential to get the product to the right place at the right time for the customer.

Many markets are dominated by **brands**. A branded good is one which is produced by a particular firm and which appears to possess unique characteristics. These may be real characteristics, such as a unique formulation or a unique design. A Mars bar or a Rolls Royce car, for instance, are unique products, but often more important than the real characteristics are the imagined characteristics of the product in the mind of the buyer. This image is likely to have been created by advertising and promotion, so it is possible for the same baked beans or the same breakfast cereal to be packaged differently and sold on the same supermarket shelves at different prices. Often the higher-priced, branded product will sell far better than the lower-priced, unbranded product despite the fact that the product itself is the same.

Question 4

Today, Apple is one of the most recognised brands in the world. At the core of its current success is the iPhone, a smartphone. In 2014, it had a world market share for smart phones of 12 per cent. In some geographical markets, it was much higher than this. In the US market, for example, it had a market share of around 33 per cent.

Its main competitor in 2014 was Samsung with its Galaxy range of smart phones. In 2014, Samsung enjoyed a higher market share than Apple worldwide. Arguably it achieved this because it was significantly cheaper than the iPhone. However, Apple is able to compete successfully on a number of fronts. Its phone and the software it carries is unique and widely recognised as amongst the best in the market. Very importantly, its technology has a loyal customer base willing to upgrade to new iPhone products as they come onto the market. It promotes its products. It also has strong distribution channels with iPhones selling in all major world markets including China.

Source: adapted from © the *Financial Times* 30.1.2015, All Rights Reserved.

Explain how Apple competes in the smartphone market.

Key Terms

Cartel - a formal agreement between firms to limit competition in the market, for example by limiting output in order to raise prices.

Collusion - collective agreements, either formal or tacit, between firms that restrict competition.

Collusive oligopoly - a market with a high concentration ratio where a few interdependent firms cooperate, either formally or tacitly, to restrict competition.

Concentrated market - a market where most of the output is produced by a few firms and where therefore the concentration ratio is high.

Duopoly - an industry where there are only two firms.

Game theory - the analysis of situations in which players are interdependent.

Market conduct - the behaviour of firms, such as pricing policies, promotion of products, branding and collusion with other firms.

Marketing mix - different elements within a strategy designed to create demand for a product and profits for a firm.

Non-collusive or competitive oligopoly - when firms in an oligopolistic industry compete amongst themselves and there is no collusion.

Oligopoly - a market structure where there is a small number of firms in the industry and where each firm is interdependent with one another, creating uncertainty. Barriers to entry are likely to exist.

Overt or formal collusion - when firms make agreements among themselves to restriction competition, typically by reducing output, raising prices and keeping potential competitors out of the market; cartels are one example of formal collusion.

Payoff matrix - in game theory, shows the outcomes of a game for the players given different possible strategies.

Predatory pricing - a pricing strategy where a firm lowers its prices when a new entrant comes into the market in order to force the competitor out of the market, and then putting prices back up again once this objective has been achieve.

Price agreement - a type of formal collusion where two or more firms arrange to fix prices of their products.

Price follower - a firm which sets its price by reference to the prices set by the price leader in a market.

Price leadership - when one firm, the **price leader**, sets its own prices and other firms in the market set their prices in relationship to the price leader.

Price war - a situation where several firms in a market repeatedly lower their prices to outcompete others firms; the objective may be to gain or defend market share.

Prisoner's dilemma - a game where, given that neither player knows the strategy of the other player, the optimum strategy for each player leads to a worse situation than if they had known the strategy of the other player and been able to co-operate and co-ordinate their strategies.

Tacit or informal collusion - when firms collude without any formal agreement having been reached and where there is no explicit communication between firms and strategies; an example is price leadership.

Thinking like an economist

The UK new car market

The UK car market is fiercely competitive. There are 45 manufacturers selling cars into the market. Some, however, are very small. In 2014, for example, Lotus sold 235 cars, whilst Aston Martin sold 864. Compare this to the market leader, Ford, which sold 326 643 cars. The four firm concentration ratio was 40 per cent made up of Ford, Vauxhall, Volkswagen and Audi as is shown in Figure 1.

Each large manufacturer sells a range of differentiated products. So Ford, for example, sells different cars in all significant segments of the market from SUVs to family cars to mini cars. Branding is reinforced by heavy advertising. There is a regular cycle of model replacements to encourage customers to change their cars frequently and to gain market share over rivals.

Barriers to entry to the market are relatively high despite there being 45 manufacturers present in 2014. Marketing is a major barrier to entry. Cars need to have brand recognition if they are to sell well. Manufacturers also need a network of dealers to sell their cars. Setting up dealerships is expensive. Persuading independent dealers to become a franchised dealer selling a make of car implies that the dealer thinks the cars will sell well.

Firms are interdependent. The market grows and shrinks according to economic conditions. Although 2014 was a record year for UK car sales, 2009-2013 had been very difficult as the economy suffered the effects of the financial crisis of 2008. Within that market, however, a car sold by Ford is one not sold by Vauxhall or Volkswagen.

It could be argued, therefore, that the car manufacturing market in the UK is oligopolistic. There is one feature of the market, though, that distinguishes it from many other oligopolistic markets. This is price competition. In a typical oligopolistic market, firms avoid price competition because it erodes their profits. The problem with car manufacturing is that companies have significant fixed costs. In the short run, selling an extra car at below total average cost makes sense. So long as the price is above the marginal cost of production, then the extra sale makes a contribution to paying fixed costs. However, in a depressed market, too many cars are sold below total average cost and car manufacturers slip into losses. This is what happened in 2009-2013. Even in 2014, record car sales in the UK were only achieved because of intense price competition and not all manufacturers made profits despite significant increases in sales.

Source: with information from © the *Financial Times* 22.3.2014, All Rights Reserved.

Figure 1

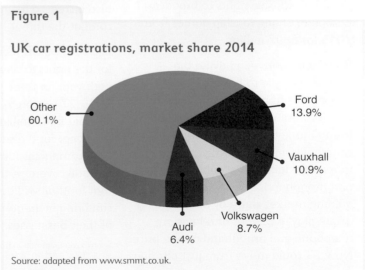

UK car registrations, market share 2014

Other 60.1%
Ford 13.9%
Vauxhall 10.9%
Volkswagen 8.7%
Audi 6.4%

Source: adapted from www.smmt.co.uk.

Data Response Question

Broadcast football

BSkyB is a commercial television company. Its success has been very much linked to football. When the Premier League was first created for the 1992-93 season, BSkyB acquired the exclusive rights to broadcast its matches for a fee of £304 million. In 2007, BSkyB's monopoly was broken when a company called Setanta bought the rights from Premier League to broadcast exclusively a small number of matches. However, Setanta failed to sell enough subscriptions to its channels and went out of business in 2009. In 2013, more serious competition for BSkyB emerged when British Telecom bought the rights to broadcast 38 matches a year for £246 million per year until 2015. BSkyB was forced to pay £767 million per year for the right to broadcast 116 games per year, a considerable increase on its pre-2013 payments. BSkyB suffered a further blow when BT won the exclusive rights to broadcast European Championship games from 2015 for £897 million.

BT's main motive in paying the Premier League to broadcast its games was to help its main business of telecommunications. It had been losing market share to a number of companies, including BSkyB, in its market for landline telephone services and broadband. BSkyB had been gaining market share by offering 'triple play' packages of television, telephone and broadband at one price. Now BT could move from just offering

telephone and broadband services to its own triple play package. For BT, it was a successful strategy in 2013-14. It gained a majority of new customers for broadband. In the meantime, BSkyB experienced the lowest number of new broadband customers since 2006. BSkyB also increased its marketing spending to combat the threat from BT.

In 2015, BSkyB paid £4.176 billion for the rights to screen 126 matches each year for three years from the 2016-17 season to the 2018-19 season. BT paid £960 million for 42 matches each year for the same period. With both companies losing money on their football coverage, they have gambled that football will be the loss leader that can bring in greater profits in other areas of their businesses.

Source: with information from © the *Financial Times* 17.5.2014, 27.7.2014, 11.2.2015, All Rights Reserved.

Q

1. Explain why the market for broadcast Premier League football matches was oligopolistic in 2014.

2. Discuss whether or not BT's decision to enter the television market will be seen in 10 years' time as having been a successful strategy.

Evaluation

What does 'success' mean for BT? From an A level perspective, it is probably profit, the difference between revenues and costs. Explore what might happen to these in the long term compared to a situation where BT had not entered the television market. Point out that is impossible to come to a firm prediction because this depends on how BSkyB reacts – there is uncertainty in the market. A sophisticated answer could use game theory to explore this issue.

50 Monopoly

Key points

1. A monopolist is the sole producer in an industry.
2. The demand curve faced by the monopolist is the market demand curve.
3. The monopolist's demand curve is also its average revenue curve.
4. The marginal revenue falls twice as steeply as the average revenue curve.
5. The profit maximising monopolist will produce where MC = MR and price on its demand curve.
6. The monopolist is likely to be able to earn abnormal profit because average revenue will be above average cost at the equilibrium level of output.
7. A monopolist may be able to price discriminate and further increase abnormal profit.
8. There are three different degrees of price discrimination.

Starter activity

Find out how much it costs to travel from London to Brighton by train. Is there just one price? If there is more than one price, what do the different prices depend on? Why does the train operator charge different prices to different customers?

Assumptions

The neo-classical theory of **monopoly** assumes that a monopoly market structure has the following characteristics:

- there is only one firm in the industry - the **monopolist**;
- barriers to entry prevent new firms from entering the market;
- the monopolist is a short run profit maximiser.

There are many industries in the world economy which possess most or all of these characteristics. In the UK, for instance, there are examples of monopolies in the gas, electricity, telecommunications, rail transport and water supply industries. In a **pure monopoly**, there is only one firm in the market. However, in many markets, there is a number of firms which have **monopoly power**. This occurs when a firm is able to control the price it charges for its product in a market. Firms in a monopolistically competitive market or an oligopolistic market have monopoly power for example.

Sources of monopoly power

Monopolies acquire and maintain power over their markets for a variety of reasons.

Barriers to entry Monopolists are protected from new entrants by barriers to entry. These include legal barriers, sunk costs, capital costs, scale economies, natural cost advantages, anti-competitive practices and marketing barriers including advertising. By keeping out new entrants, monopolists can then control the market. The higher the barriers to entry, the stronger the power of the monopolist over its market. For example, in the UK, legal barriers prevent firms from setting up new pharmacies in local areas. Planning permission regulations give large supermarket chains monopoly powers in some local areas in the UK.

Product differentiation and the number of near competitors Some monopolists sell products which are clearly differentiated from rival products. For example, households

Question 1

British Gas was created by the Labour government of 1945-51 from a network of local gas companies, some owned by local authorities. As a nationalised industry, it was the sole supplier of piped gas in the UK. In 1986, the industry was privatised as one company, retaining the legal power to be the sole supplier of gas. Then the government decided that there would be considerable efficiency gains if the gas market were to become competitive. In 1988, the company was forced to allow other gas companies to supply gas to industrial customers using British Gas pipelines. In 1996, British Gas was split into two parts. Transco owned the gas pipeline network and would earn revenues from charging other gas companies to transport gas into homes and business premises. British Gas, renamed Centrica, retained the gas supply business. However, in 1997-98, the gas market to domestic users was opened up to other companies. Now, both homes and businesses could choose which supplier to use, although all the gas was transported through Transco pipelines. Following the entry of a number of companies into the residential gas supply market, the market share of British Gas by 2015 had fallen significantly. However, given previous trends, it is unlikely that British Gas will lose substantial market share in the future.

Source: adapted from Alain Anderton, *Economics*, 5th edition, Pearson.

(a) To what extent was British Gas a monopoly supplier of gas in the UK in (i) 1986; (ii) 1990; (iii) 2015?

(b) To what extent was the gas industry a monopoly in 2015?

have to buy electricity from an electricity distributor. Gas, oil or batteries are very poor substitutes for electricity. Similarly, on the Manchester to London route, the railway has a strong monopoly because airline flights or road transport are much more inconvenient and the journey time can be much longer. The higher the degree of product differentiation, the stronger the monopoly power. The lower the degree of product differentiation, the larger the number of competitors the monopolist faces in practice. For example, Mars Foods has a monopoly on the production of Mars bars, but the monopoly is very weak because a number of competitors produce similar chocolate bars.

Figure 1

The revenue curves of a monopolist

A monopolist, being the sole supplier in the industry, faces a downward sloping demand or average revenue curve. Marginal revenue falls at twice the rate of average revenue and becomes zero when total revenue is maximised.

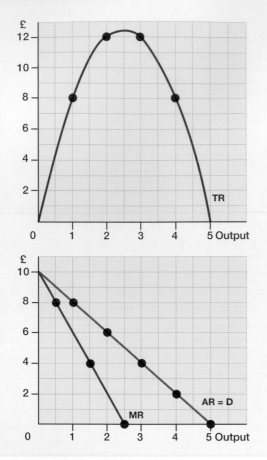

Table 1

Quantity	Average revenue or price £	Total revenue £	Marginal revenue £
0	0	0	
			8
1	8	8	
			4
2	6	12	
			0
3	4	12	
			-4
4	2	8	
			-8
5	0	0	

£200 (£20 x 10 units) to £209 (£19 x 11 units), so marginal revenue on the eleventh unit is £9 (£209 - £200) whilst the average revenue on selling 11 units is £19 (£209 ÷ 11 which is, of course, the price).

Table 1 gives a further example of falling marginal and average revenues. Note that the fall in marginal revenue is twice as large over any given change in quantity as the fall in average revenue. This is true of all straight line average revenue curves. Plotting these figures on a diagram, we arrive at Figure 1. The marginal revenue figures, as with all marginal figures, are plotted half way between 'whole' output figures, so the marginal revenue of the second unit is plotted half way between one and two units. It can be seen that at any given level of output, average revenue is twice marginal revenue. Total revenue is maximised when marginal revenue is zero. If marginal revenue (the addition to total revenue) becomes negative then total revenue will automatically fall. Total revenue is zero if average revenue, the price received per unit of output, is zero too.

Revenue curves

A monopoly firm is itself the industry. As the industry faces a downward sloping demand curve, so too must the monopolist. It can therefore only increase sales by reducing price, or increase price by reducing sales. It can set either price or output but not both.

The demand curve shows the quantity bought at any given price. For instance, a water company might sell two billion gallons of water at 1p per gallon. This price is the same as its average revenue; on average it will receive 1p per gallon, so the downward sloping demand curve facing the firm is also the average revenue curve of the firm.

If average revenue is falling, marginal revenue must be falling too and at a faster rate. For example, assume a firm sells 10 units at £20 each. To sell an eleventh unit, it needs to lower its price, say to £19. Not only will it have to lower its price on the eleventh unit, but it will also have to lower its price on the other 10 units. This is because it cannot charge a higher price to some consumers than others (although we will see later on in this unit that it is possible in limited cases). There is a loss of revenue not just of £1 on the sale of the eleventh unit but of a further £10 on the first 10 units. Total revenue increases from

Question 2

Table 2

Output (units per week)	Marginal revenue £
0	
	10
1	
	7
2	
	4
3	
	1
4	
	-2
5	

(a) Calculate (i) total revenue and (ii) average revenue at output levels 0 to 5 units.

(b) (i) Draw the axes of a graph with revenue from £0 to £10 and output from 0 to 10. (ii) Plot the marginal and average revenue curves. (iii) Extend the average revenue curve to the output axis assuming that average revenue continues to fall at the same rate as in the table.

(c) What is the value of marginal revenue when total revenue is at a maximum?

Equilibrium output

The neo-classical theory of the firm assumes that a monopolist will be a short run profit maximiser. This means that it will produce where MC = MR.

Figure 2

Profit maximising output

The monopolist will maximise profits by producing where MC = MR at OA. It will base its prices on its average revenue curve, charging OE. It will be able to earn abnormal profit of EFGC because average revenue is greater than average cost at this level of output.

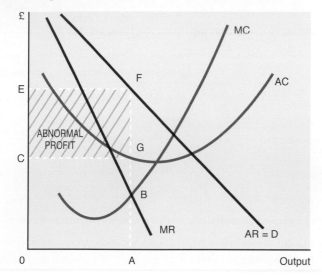

Figure 3

The appropriation of consumer surplus

A monopolist can appropriate ABEG of consumer surplus by price discriminating selling OK output to those consumers prepared to pay a minimum OB, and selling KH to other consumers only prepared to pay a minimum OA.

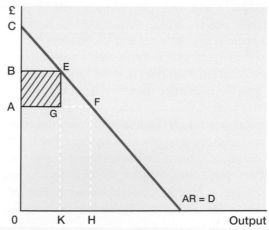

Figure 2 adds the traditional U-shaped average and marginal cost curves to the average and marginal revenue curves outlined above.

- The **equilibrium profit maximising level of output** is OA where MC = MR.
- **The price** will be OE. Buyers are prepared to pay OE for this output. We know this because the average revenue curve is also the demand curve and the demand curve shows the maximum price buyers will pay for any given level of ouput.
- **Abnormal profit** of EFGC will be made. The abnormal profit per unit (GF) is the difference between the average revenue received (AF) and the average cost incurred (AG). OA units are sold. Therefore total abnormal profit is OA x FG, or the area EFGC.

Note that EFGC is abnormal profit because economic cost includes an allowance for normal profit. Note also that price is not equal to the intersection of the MC and MR curves (i.e. price is not AB). This is because the firm, although deciding on the level of output by the MC = MR condition, fixes its price on the average revenue or demand curve. Also abnormal profit is not the area EF x FB (i.e. it is not the area between the average revenue curve and the marginal revenue and cost curves). Profit per unit is the difference between average revenue and average cost.

Discriminating monopoly

Some buyers in the market will almost certainly be prepared to pay a higher price for a product than other buyers. For instance, a rail commuter is likely to be prepared to pay more for a journey at 8 o'clock in the morning to take her to work than would a shopper. A millionaire faced with the need for heart surgery is likely to pay more than a person on a low income with the same complaint. This can be illustrated on a monopoly diagram. In Figure 3, the profit maximising output

for a monopolist is assumed to be OH and OA is therefore the profit maximising price. OA represents the maximum price that the marginal consumer is prepared to pay. Other consumers are prepared to pay a higher price. If output were only OK, the marginal consumer would be prepared to pay OB. The area ACF represents the area of consumer surplus when price is OA, the difference between what consumers are prepared to pay in total for a good and what they actually pay.

A monopolist may be able to split the market and **price discriminate** between different buyers. In Figure 3, the monopolist may be able to charge OB for OK of output, and then charge a lower price of OA for KH of output. In this way, the monopolist appropriates ABEG of consumer surplus when price is OB in the form of higher profit (i.e. higher producer surplus).

There is a number of different ways in which a monopolist may choose to discriminate.

- Time. It may charge a different price at different times of the day or week, as do the electricity distribution companies or rail companies.
- Place. It may vary price according to the location of the buyer. The same car can be bought at different prices in different countries of the EU, for instance.
- Income. It may be able to split up consumers into income groups, charging a high price to those with high incomes, and a low price to those with lower incomes. Examples of this can be found in medical practice and amongst lawyers. Hairdressers (who may be local monopolists) offering reduced rates to pensioners are likely to be price discriminating according to income too.

Three conditions must hold if a monopolist is to be able to price discriminate effectively.

- The monopolist must face different demand curves from separate groups of buyers (i.e. the elasticity of demand of buyers must differ). If all buyers had the same demand curve, then the monopolist could not charge different prices to buyers.

- The monopolist must be able to split the market into distinct groups of buyers, otherwise it will be unable to distinguish between those consumers prepared to pay a higher price and those prepared to a pay a lower price.
- The monopolist must be able to keep the markets separate at relatively low cost. For instance, it must be able to prevent buyers in the high priced market from buying in the low price market. If a German car company sells its cars at 25 per cent less in Belgium than in the UK, then it must be able to prevent UK motorists and UK retailers from taking a day trip to Belgium to buy those cars. Equally, it must be able to prevent traders from buying in the low price market and selling into the high price market at a price which undercuts that of the monopolist.

Price discrimination can be analysed using the concepts of marginal cost and marginal revenue. Assume that the monopolist is able to divide its markets into two, Market A and Market B. Without any price discrimination, the equilibrium marginal revenue is higher in Market A than in Market B. Further assume that the costs of production are identical in both markets. Given these assumptions, the firm could increase its total revenue from a given output by switching goods from B to A. Marginal revenue in market B will now rise because it can charge a higher price if it sells less. Marginal revenue in market A will fall because it has to lower price to sell more. For instance, if marginal revenue in market A were £10 when it was £6 in market B, then the firm could gain an extra £4 of revenue by switching the marginal unit of production from market B to market A. It will carry on switching from market B to A until there is no more advantage in doing so, which occurs when the marginal revenues are the same.

In Figure 4, the demand curves in markets A and B are drawn first. From these demand or average revenue curves, the marginal revenue curves in each market can then be calculated. The average and marginal revenue curves for the total market can be calculated by summing horizontally the average and marginal revenue curves in each market. The profit maximising monopolist will produce where MC = MR across the whole market, at output level OT. This output (OT) is then split between the two markets (OR and OS) so that the marginal revenue is equal in both individual markets (OE). In each market, a firm's price will be based on the average revenue curve. A price of OG can be charged in market A, and a price of OH can be charged in market B. Average cost of production is OF and the abnormal profit earned in each market is shown by the shaded areas on

Figure 4

Price discrimination

By charging a different price in two markets, a monopolist is able to earn higher profits than it would if it charged the same price.

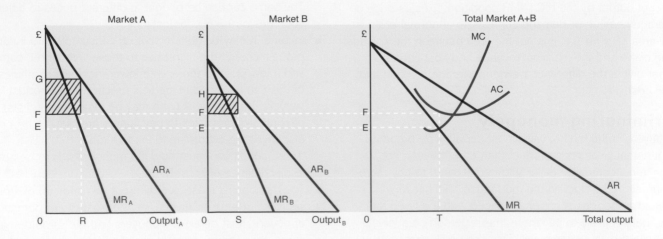

the diagram. This will be higher than the abnormal profit the firm would have made if it had not discriminated.

Costs and benefits for producers and consumers from price discrimination

Firms benefit from price discrimination because it increases their profits. They can appropriate as producer surplus some of what would otherwise be consumer surplus. Their costs of production may be higher because of price discrimination. But this is not important so long as their revenues are even higher.

Consumers are likely to lose out because many will pay higher prices. They will lose some of their consumer surplus to producers. However, there are two ways in which consumers can sometimes benefit from price discrimination.

- Some customers will be winners from price discrimination and others losers. Take the example of a monopolist which, without price discrimination, would set a price of £10 per unit to maximise its profits. When price discriminating, it sets two prices, one £15 and the other £8. Customers who pay £15 lose out, but customers who pay only £8 are gainers. Some of these customers are ones who would otherwise have paid £10. Others are customers who would not have bought the product at all at a price of £10. Price discrimination not only results in cheaper prices for some customers but it also expands the market.
- In some cases, a monopolist would not supply at a profit maximising single price because it would make a loss. Its average revenue curve would be above its average cost curve at every level of output, but by price discriminating, it might be able to raise revenues to a point at which average cost at least equalled average revenue. At this point it would produce because it would be earning normal profit.

Four technical points

Degrees of discrimination Price discrimination under monopoly is often split into three types. Third-degree price discrimination is the type of discrimination described above. First degree price discrimination occurs when a firm is able to charge each customer a different price. That price is the maximum price the customer will pay. Second degree price discrimination is when a monopolist charges customers according to how much they buy. For example, an electricity company may charge a high price for the first 100 units consumed per quarter and a lower price for anything above that amount.

Absence of a supply curve in monopoly In perfect competition, the supply curve of the firm is its marginal cost curve above average cost in the long run. In monopoly, there is no supply curve which is determined independently of demand. Look back at Figure 2. The firm will produce at output OA because that is the output where MC = MR. Now assume that demand changes in such a way that the marginal revenue curve is much steeper but still passes through the point B. If the MR curve is steeper, so too will be the AR curve. The firm will now be able to charge a much higher price than OE for its product. For each differently sloped MR curve that passes through the point B, the firm will charge a different price to the consumer. The firm is prepared to supply OA output at a variety of different

prices, depending upon demand conditions, so no supply curve for the monopolist can be drawn. (Contrast this with the firm in perfect competition. Falls in demand which reduce prices received by the firm will result in a fall in quantity supplied as the firm moves down its supply curve.)

A monopolist will produce only where demand is elastic Look back to Figure 1. It should be obvious that the firm will not produce more than 2½ units of output. If it produces three units, it will almost certainly have higher costs than if it produces 2½ units but total revenue will fall. Profit therefore is bound to fall. 2½ units is the output where marginal revenue is zero. It is also the point where price elasticity of demand is unity because we are now half way along the demand or average revenue curve. To the left, elasticity is greater than 1, to the right less than 1. Since the firm will only produce to the left of 2½ units, it must produce where demand is elastic. An alternative explanation is to remember that a fall in price (needed to increase quantity sold) will only increase revenue if demand is elastic. Therefore a monopolist would not increase sales to the point where demand became inelastic.

Short-run and long-run operation So far no distinction has been made between the short run and the long run. A firm will produce in the short run if total revenue is greater than total variable cost. In the short run, a monopolist may therefore operate at a loss but it will close down if it cannot cover its variable costs. In the long run, a monopolist will not operate if it cannot cover all costs of production. Such a situation is shown in Figure 5. To maximise profits or minimise losses, it will produce where MC = MR, but at this level of output average cost is greater than average revenue. As the monopolist is the sole supplier in the industry, long-term losses will mean that no firm will supply and hence the industry will cease to exist.

Figure 5

An industry where no firm will produce

The figure shows an industry in the long run. Because LRAC is greater than AR, no firm will be prepared to operate and therefore no goods will be produced.

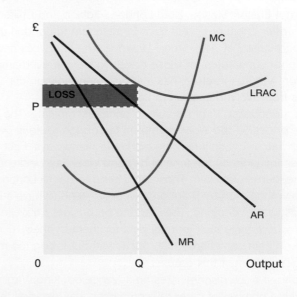

Question 4

Draw two diagrams showing the change in equilibrium output of a profit maximising monopolist if:

(a) its marginal revenue increases;

(b) its marginal cost increases.

Key Terms

Monopolist - a firm which controls all the output in a market.
Monopoly or pure monopoly - market structure where one firm supplies all output in the market without facing competition because of high barriers to entry to the market.
Monopoly power - exists when firms are able to control the price they charge for their product in a market.
Price discrimination - charging a different price for the same good or service in different markets.

Thinking like an economist

Virgin Wolverhampton to London

When British Rail was broken up in 1996, Virgin won the franchise to operate trains on the West Coast line. This included taking over the Wolverhampton to London line. In one respect, this was a monopoly service. No other train operator has the legal right to run express services from Wolverhampton through Birmingham New Street Station and Milton Keynes down to London Euston. The terms of the franchise issued by the government in 1996 therefore constituted a legal barrier to entry to this market.

However, travellers have alternatives. There are three train operators running from Birmingham to London: Virgin, London Midland and Chiltern Railways. Wolverhampton passengers can therefore travel to Birmingham and change to either London Midland or Chiltern. London Midland only runs stopping trains to London Euston with a typical journey time one hour longer than Virgin. The rolling stock itself is suburban carriages designed for short journeys rather than the InterCity rolling stock of Virgin. The journey is therefore far less comfortable. As for Chiltern, it operates out of different stations from Virgin. At Birmingham, it runs out of Snow Hill Station. Most trains into Birmingham, including Virgin trains, go to Birmingham New Street. Making a connection between New Street and Snow Hill requires a two minute walk. In London, Chiltern Railways goes to Marylebone Station, not Euston Station. Both London Midland and Chiltern Railways offer cheaper tickets from Birmingham to London than Virgin, particularly at peak times. However, their services have proved poor substitutes for those travelling from Wolverhampton to London. Virgin, therefore, has a strong monopoly on rail journeys from Wolverhampton to London.

As a monopolist, Virgin is able to price discriminate. The range of prices on the Wolverhampton to London route is shown in Table 4. It splits up the market in many ways. First, it price discriminates by the time of day and weekday/weekend when the journey is taken. Those who need to get to London from Wolverhampton by 9 am on a weekday tend to have a low price elasticity of demand. They tend to be business travellers, many of whom have their journey paid for them by their employer. Virgin can charge high prices without losing too many passengers amongst this group.

Second, it price discriminates on advance booking. Virgin, along with a number of other rail companies, has decided that

Table 4 Virgin Trains Wolverhampton - London return fares[1]

	1995 £	2015 £	1995-2015 Percentage increase
First class open[2]	82.00	318.00	288
Standard class open[2]	57.00	230.00	304
Cheap day return (1995)/ Off-peak return 2015)[2]	19.50	53.60	175
Cheapest pre-booked fare[3]	15.00	15.0	0

1. 1995 prices are British Rail fares prior to the takeover of the route by Virgin.
2. Ticket bought on day of travel at Wolverhampton Station
3. Ticket can only be bought by booking at least one day in advance.

Source: adapted from www.virgintrains.co.uk.

it is in its interests to encourage as much advance booking as possible. It improves cash flow because tickets are paid for in advance. It locks passengers into travelling when, on the day, they might otherwise have chosen not to travel by Virgin or travel at all. It also spreads passenger loads. Passengers unable to book a ticket to travel at the most popular times may switch to a less popular time. Advance booking allows passengers to book a seat, which is important if there is likely to be overcrowding on the train, but also the cheapest tickets on the Wolverhampton to London route are only available by booking in advance for a specifically timed journey. They are likely to be bought by passengers with the highest price elasticity of demand: those who would otherwise not travel if the price were much higher. Only a very small proportion of seats on a train are available at the cheapest price and many trains have no value tickets allocated to them, so Virgin can advertise low prices without losing too much revenue. It can also offer the bargain hunter travel at a less crowded and popular time, allowing Virgin to spread travel numbers during the day.

Virgin has a large number of other ways in which it price discriminates. It encourages children and families to travel by offering reductions for children and Family and Friends Rail Cards. Young people can get reductions by buying a 16-25 Railcard. Those aged 60 and over are offered a similar reduced tariff card, the Senior Railcard.

Virgin's pricing policy over time would suggest that it has a keen understanding of price elasticity of demand. Its lowest cost fares have not changed between 1995 and 2015, as Table 4 shows. In contrast, Virgin has significantly increased its 'open' fares which have no restrictions on when the passenger can travel. The cost of travelling to London first class has increased by 288 per cent and standard class by 304 per cent. By charging higher prices, it has been able to appropriate the consumer surplus of business customers and turn this into profit or producer surplus for itself. At the bottom end of the market, it has encouraged larger numbers of private customers to travel at less popular times of the day. Every extra passenger that would otherwise not have travelled on these services is nearly 100 per cent profit for Virgin because the marginal cost of taking them is virtually zero.

Data Response Question

Motorway service stations

The British motorway service station is an example of a local monopoly. Protected by government from competitors setting up a service station next door, they have been a feature of motorway travel since the first motorways were built in the 1960s, but the legal monopoly comes at a price for their owners. The government lays down stringent conditions about the operation of the service stations. For example, they have to be open 24 hours a day, 365 days a year. They must provide a range of services including free toilets. This is very important when surveys show that the vast majority of people who go to a motorway service station head for the toilet first. Motorway service stations cannot by law be a meeting place for more than 12 people to prevent them becoming conference centres. Alcohol cannot be sold. There are also other restrictions on what they sell, to prevent them becoming retail or leisure parks. Some of the restrictions force the motorway service stations to provide services which motorway motorists might need. Some of the restrictions are designed to prevent the service station becoming a 'destination in its own right'. To recoup their relatively high cost of operation, motorway

service stations typically charge higher than average prices for goods and services sold on site.

For decades, service stations have been seen as infrastructure assets, offering their owners steady but unspectacular profit growth in a regulated environment with limited competition, but over the past few years, motorway service owners have become more aggressive in their search for profit. One key development has been the signing of partnerships between established brand names and service stations. McDonald's, Burger King, Costa Coffee and Marks & Spencer are just some of the retail brands that have appeared. Well-known brands help lift sales of products. Customers are more likely to buy a McDonald's hamburger than an unbranded motorway service station hamburger. Equally, customers are unlikely to buy the evening meal they are going to eat when they get home from a motorway service

branded shop, but they will do if the shop is a Marks & Spencer outlet. The goal is to leverage the selling space at motorway service stations so that when customers have a toilet or coffee stop, they spend more than they would otherwise. Tired motorists in a hurry are prepared to pay higher prices for their favourite branded goods than they would on the high street.

1. Explain why a motorway service station has a 'local monopoly'.

2. Motorway service stations tend to charge higher prices for products than a supermarket which might be sited just off a motorway junction. Using a monopoly diagram, explain why motorway service station prices might be higher.

3. Discuss whether expanding sales at motorway service station outlets will benefit consumers.

Evaluation

Weigh up the potential benefits and costs to consumers of buying from a greater range of retailers at motorway service stations. Are consumers being exploited or are they being given greater choice?

51 Monopsony

Key points

1. Monopsony can lead to lower prices being paid to suppliers and a fall in quantity demanded and supplied as monopsonists exploit their monopsony power.
2. Monopsony is likely to lead to lower profits and output from suppliers. Customers may benefit from lower prices if lower prices are at least in part passed on by the monopsonist.
3. In a bilateral monopsony situation, output and prices are likely to be higher in the market than where one buyer faces many sellers.

Starter activity

Five years ago, your small firm had a lucky break. A large supermarket chain agreed to stock two of your products. Today, the supermarket order for those two products account for 80 per cent of your sales. But over the five years, the supermarket has progressively imposed harsher and harsher terms on your firm, effectively cutting the price you receive. Today, you are making a small loss on the sales. Should you carry on supplying or cancel the contract? What factors should you take into account when making your decision?

Monopsony

A **monopsony** exists when there is only one buyer in the market. There are very few pure monopsonists in the UK but there is a number of markets where one buyer dominates the market. For example, Network Rail in the UK dominates the market for the purchase of rail track maintenance. The government dominates the market for the hiring of teachers.

For a market to be **monopsonistic**, it also has to possess the same characteristics as a monopolistic market apart from the difference between buyers and sellers. So sellers in the market must not be able to sell their product to other firms outside the market. Monopsonists may have a variety of business objectives but in this unit, it will be assumed that they are profit maximisers.

Equilibrium price and output under monopsony

Economic theory suggests that monopsonists will pay lower prices to their suppliers than if the market were competitive. But this means that suppliers will also supply less to the market. With monopsony, equilibrium price and quantity will be lower than if the market were perfectly competitive.

Figure 1 shows the market for organic parsnips. If a market were perfectly competitive, the equilibrium price would be set where demand equals supply. Equilibrium price would be OF and equilibrium output would be OB.

However, this would be different if there were a monopsonistic supermarket chain that bought all the market output of organic parsnips from farmers. It would be in the interests of the supermarket chain to beat down the price it paid to farmers for organic parsnips. By reducing the price, the supermarket chain could increase its profits on parsnips. So, the supermarket chain is only prepared to pay OE. But at this lower price, fewer farmers wish to supply organic parsnips.

So equilibrium output falls to OA. Where there is a monopsonist, economic theory suggests that both the price paid by and the amount supplied to the monopsonist will fall compared to a perfectly competitive market.

The exact amount that a profit maximising monopsonist will buy is determined by the marginal cost = marginal revenue rule. If the supply curve is upward sloping, it means that the monopsonist has to pay a higher average price if it wants to buy more from the market. But the marginal cost of buying more is higher than this average price.

For example, assume that the supermarket chain buying organic parsnips is currently buying one million tonnes as shown in Table 1. The price is £2 per tonne. If it then wants to buy twice as much, two million tonnes, the price rises to £4 per tonne. At three million tonnes, the price is £6. So the supply curve is upward sloping with prices rising as quantity

Figure 1

Equilibrium under perfect competition and monopsony

In a perfectly competitive market, equilibrium output would be where demand equals supply at OB. But if there is a monopsonist in the market, it will seek to buy at a lower price of OE. But at this price, sellers will not want to supply as much as under perfect competition. Equilibrium quantity supplied therefore falls to OA. Under monopsony, both prices and quantity supplied are lower compared to a competitive market.

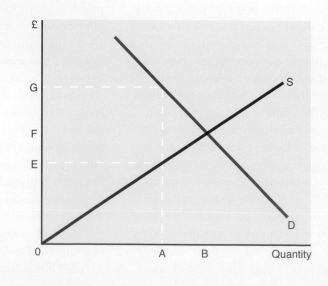

Table 1

Quantity of organic parsnips Million tonnes	Average price or cost £	Total cost £ million	Marginal cost per unit £
0	0	0	
			2
1	2	2	
			6
2	4	8	
			10
3	6	18	

supplied increases. However, the increase in price leads to large increases in total costs for the supermarket. Buying one million tonnes gives a total cost of £2 million (1 million x £2). But buying two million tonnes sees total cost rising to £8 million (2 million x £4) and three million tonnes sees total costs at £18 million (3 million x £6). The marginal cost per unit therefore rises from £2 for the first one million units to £6 for the second million units and £10 for the third million units.

Table 1 shows that marginal cost rises much faster than average cost. If the monopsonist is profit maximising by buying where marginal cost equals marginal revenue, it will then buy less than if the market were perfectly competitive and equilibrium was set where demand equals supply.

Costs and benefits

There is a variety of potential costs and benefits of monopsony to both firms and consumers.

The monopsonist The monopsonist gains higher profits by being able to buy at lower prices. This reduces its costs of production and is likely to lead to an increase in overall output because of a shift downwards in its marginal cost curve. Note that whilst overall output is likely to increase, supply of inputs over which the firm has monopsony power will fall.

Suppliers Suppliers are likely to lose out from a monopsony. Prices paid for their goods or services will fall. If it is farmers supplying a supermarket chain, they will see their prices fall. If it is workers supplying their services to a monopsony buyer of their labour, they will see their wages fall. Low prices will lead to less being supplied. In the case of farmers supplying a monopsonist supermarket chain, some farmers will switch out of producing one product and into another. Some farmers may be forced out of the market altogether.

Customers The impact on customers depends on a variety of factors. Part of the lower costs for the monopsonist is likely to be passed on to customers in lower prices. On the other hand, there may be restrictions in supply. The extent to which supply to customers will fall depends upon the price elasticity of supply in the market in which the monopsonist is the buyer. For example, if supply is highly price inelastic, there will be little fall in supply.

Employees The impact on employees is uncertain. For the monopsonist, its purchase costs will be lower compared to a competitive market. However, it will purchase less of the good. It is therefore unclear as to whether more, fewer or the same number of employees will be employed by the monopsonist. For the seller, they will sell less. Therefore they will employ fewer workers.

Bilateral monopoly

So far, it has been assumed that the monopsonist is able to buy from a large number of suppliers. But it could be the case that the monopsonist faces a monopolist in its market. In this case there is only one buyer and one seller in the market. A bilateral monopoly is then said to exist where there is countervailing power in the market. The example most explored by economists is when a single buyer of labour, such as the government for teachers, faces a single seller of labour, such as a trade union which represents all teachers. In this case, economic theory predicts that prices and quantity demanded and supplied will be higher than in a market a monopsonist faces many sellers. This suggests there will be greater allocative efficiency in the market.

Monopsony power

A pure monopsony exists when there is only one buyer in the market. This is relatively rare in practice. However, there are many more examples of firm that have monopsony power. This means that they are a large enough buyer in the market to be able to change the price at which they buy from suppliers.

The more a firm buys as a percentage of total sales in the market, the more monopsony power it is likely to have. For example, a firm that buys 60 per cent of all products in a market is likely to have greater monopsony power over the market than a firm which buys 20 per cent of all products. Equally, the more a firm buys from a single supplier, the greater its monopsony power. For example, if 100 per cent of Firm A sales are to Firm B, then Firm B is likely to have a high degree of monopsony power over Firm A.

When a firm has weak monopsony power over the market, suppliers are to some extent likely to be able to resist the demands of the monopsonist. Suppliers, for example, can sell to other firms if the monopsonist won't buy its products. However, the greater the monopsony power, the less able are suppliers to find other customers.

Key Term

Monopsony - exists when there is only one buyer in the market.

Thinking like an economist

Monopsony market power

In 2014, the Federation of Small Businesses published a report which provide 'alarming evidence' of the mistreatment of suppliers by their business customers. Out of 2 540 members contacted, 17 per cent said that they been bullied by the businesses they supplied over the past two years. The businesses surveyed said there was a number of common practices. One was 'pay to stay' fees. These are amounts of money the supplier must give to their business customer simply to continue supplying their goods. For example, a supermarket chain may charge a supplier a fixed amount to stock the product on the supermarket shelves. Another practice is excessively long payment terms. Goods are delivered, but the customer might not pay for three or six months. Discounts for prompt payment mean that a customer expects a discount if it pays on time (which could be 90 days after delivery) rather than paying after the money is due. Retrospective pricing occurs when a customer informs its supplier that it will be paying less than any money owed. This is typically justified by the supplier as a contribution to marketing costs. Many businesses also regularly pay their suppliers after the due date by which payment is due. Research by BACS suggested that in July 2014, total late payment debt by UK businesses was £46.1 billion.

The reason why suppliers put up with these practices is because buyers have varying degrees of monopsony power over them. Suppliers could, for example, simply refuse to supply firms which don't pay on time or demand pay to stay fees. However, suppliers don't want to lose customers, particularly if a customer accounts for a large share of its sales. For the big supermarket chains, for example, a small supplier might be highly dependent on its purchases. If 60 per cent of output is going to one customer, losing that customer is likely to be very damaging.

Large buyers justify their actions by saying that it is simply normal practice in the market. When Premier Foods, a large manufacturer of processed food, was criticised for 'pay to stay' conditions in 2014, its chief executive, Gavin Darby, said that the company's policies had been 'widely misunderstood and misinterpreted. Most companies look for value from their suppliers and will commonly negotiate discounts or lump sums wherever they can. This is standard business practice.'

Source: adapted from © the *Financial Times* 8.12.2014, 11.12.2014 All Rights Reserved.

Data Response Question

Suppliers' fees

The chief executive of Halfords said that suppliers who refused to pay the retailer a fee would 'reduce their likelihood of doing business with us'. Halfords is a UK chain that sells bicycles and motor products and services. Recently, it has implemented a turnaround plan at a cost of £100 million to increase sales and profits. It has invested heavily in staff training and in changing the format of its stores to make them more customer-friendly.

Matthew Davies, Chief Executive, made clear that suppliers who failed to pay as much as 10 per cent of annual sales made through the retailer would not be looked on favourably. 'We are not a charity' said Mr Davies. 'Our strategy is about driving top-line sales growth. Our suppliers are benefiting from that growth. That growth does not come free: there is significant investment. We are asking our suppliers to support that investment.' He added: 'Suppliers that want to work with us in partnership are going to be better placed than those who don't want to be part of Halfords.'

The comments came as Halfords reported very strong growth in cycle sales. These rose 19.4 per cent for the year to March 2014, partly due to the continued popularity of cycling following the 2012 London Olympics.

Halfords is the latest retailer to demand that suppliers either provide a discount or pay a fee. Debenhams and Mothercare, which have struggled with falling sales in the UK, have both recently asked suppliers for a handout.

Source: adapted from © the *Financial Times* 23.5.2014, All Rights Reserved.

Q

1. Explain why is meant by a 'monopsonist', using Halfords as a possible example.

2. Explain, using a diagram, why monopsonists are able to lower prices paid to their suppliers compared to a market where there are many buyers.

3. Discuss whether firms which insist that their suppliers pay a fee for supplying them benefit their customers and their suppliers.

Evaluation

Analyse why customers might benefit from these fees. Why might they lose out? For example, under what circumstances might suppliers simply stop supplying? What are the advantages and disadvantages to suppliers of carrying on with contracts at lower prices? Weigh up the costs and benefits to customers and suppliers. Use the data throughout to illustrate your answer.

52 Contestability

Key points

1. In a contestable market, barriers to entry and exit (including sunk costs) are low and there is perfect knowledge.
2. Firms in a contestable market are likely to earn only normal profit because any abnormal profit made will attract hit and run competitors.

Starter activity

How easy is it to set up as a coffee shop? How easy is it to set up as a car manufacturer? How much of your initial investment might you get back if you closed the coffee shop you had opened? Would that differ from a car manufacturer closing?

Contestable market theory vs neo-classical theory

Many, if not most, markets in the UK and in other industrialised economies are dominated by a few producers. **The neo-classical theory of oligopoly** assumes that oligopolistic markets feature **high barriers to entry**. However, there is also evidence to suggest that many oligopolistic markets have low barriers to entry. Therefore, firms in the industry are likely to behave in a different way from that predicted by neo-classical theory. The theory of contestable markets explores the implications of low barrier to entry markets.

Assumptions

The theory of **contestable markets** makes a number of assumptions.

- The number of firms in the industry may vary from one (a monopolist) having complete control of the market, to many, with no single firm having a significant share of the market.
- In a contestable market, there is both freedom of entry to and exit from the market. This is a key assumption of the model. Its implications are discussed below.
- Firms compete with each other and do not collude to fix prices.
- Firms are short run profit maximisers, producing where MC = MR.
- Firms may produce homogeneous goods or they may produce branded goods.
- There is perfect knowledge in the industry.

Normal and abnormal profit

The theory of contestable markets shows that in a contestable market:

- abnormal profits can be earned in the short run;
- only normal profit can be earned in the long run.

Assume that firms in a contestable market were making abnormal profit in the short run. Then new firms would be attracted into the industry by the abnormal profit. Supply would increase and prices would be driven down to the point where only normal profit was being made. This is the same argument that is used in the theory of perfect competition. Equally, if a firm

is making losses, it will eventually leave the industry because in the long run it cannot operate as a loss-making concern.

Entry to and exit from the industry

The ability of firms to enter and leave the industry is crucial in a contestable market and is not necessarily linked to the number of firms in the industry as in neo-classical theories of the firm. In neo-classical theory, low barriers to entry are linked with a large number of firms in an industry (perfect competition and monopolistic competition) whilst high barriers are linked with few firms in the industry (oligopoly or monopoly). Perfectly competitive and monopolistically competitive industries are contestable because an assumption of both these models is that

Question 1

To what extent do (a) clothing manufacturers and (b) clothing retailers operate in contestable markets?

Question 2

Explain whether the following would make it more likely or less likely that there would be potential entrants to an industry.

(a) The inability of firms in the industry to lease capital equipment for short periods of time.

(b) Very high second-hand prices for capital equipment.

(c) Heavy advertising by existing firms in the industry.

(d) The existence of a natural monopolist which was highly inefficient and had high costs of production.

(e) Patents held by an existing firm in the industry which were crucial to the manufacture of the product.

(f) Government legislation which gave monopoly rights to a single producer in the industry.

there are low barriers to entry. But what of oligopolies and monopolies?

Some barriers to entry are natural (sometimes called **innocent entry barriers**). For instance, the industry may be a natural monopoly as in Network Rail. Alternatively, there may be very high capital entry costs to the industry, as in car manufacturing. Neo-classical theory would predict that firms in these industries would earn abnormal profits. Contestable market theory suggests that this depends to a large extent on the costs of exit from the industry.

For instance, assume that the natural monopolist is charging high prices and earning abnormal profit. A competitor then enters the industry and takes market share by charging lower prices. The natural monopolist reacts by cutting prices and the competitor leaves the industry, unable to compete on these new lower prices because its costs are too high. So long as the cost of leaving the industry is small, it still makes sense for the competitor to have earned profit in the short run by entering the industry. The costs of exit are the sunk costs of operating in the industry (i.e. the fixed costs of production which cannot be recovered if the firm leaves the industry). Money spent on advertising would be an example of a sunk cost. So too would capital equipment which had no alternative use. If the sunk costs are low - the firm has done little advertising and capital equipment has been leased on a short-term basis, for instance - then the firm has lost little by entering and then leaving the industry. However, in the meantime, it has earned profit at the expense of the existing firm in the industry.

Some barriers to entry, however, are erected by existing firms in the industry. In the soap powder market, soap powder producers spend large amounts of money advertising and branding their products. It may still be worth a firm entering this industry if the new entrant can charge a high enough price to cover the cost of entering and then possibly being forced to leave the industry. For instance, a firm might seek to earn

£10 million profit over 12 months. It is then forced to leave the industry because existing firms drive down prices or increase their advertising budget. If it earned £15 million operating profit but lost £5 million in leaving the industry, it would still be worthwhile for the firm to have entered and operated for a year.

Potential competition

In a contestable market, firms are able to enter and leave the industry at relatively little cost. So far, we have implied that, in the short run, existing firms in a contestable market may well be earning abnormal profit. However, contestable market theory suggests that, in practice, established firms in a contestable market earn only normal profit even in the short run (i.e. they behave as if they operated in a perfectly competitive market).

Assume that a monopolist is the established firm in an industry. If it charges prices which would lead to it earning abnormal profit, then another firm may enter the industry charging lower prices. The new entrant will remain so long as the existing firm is earning abnormal profit, taking market share away from it and reducing its overall profits. To force the new entrant out, the monopolist would have to lower its prices. If it did this, and the new entrant left, and then the monopolist put up its prices again, all that would happen is that another firm would enter the industry. The only way to prevent this **hit and run competition** would be for the existing firm to price at a level where it only earned normal profit.

Hence, the ability of firms to earn abnormal profit is dependent on the barriers to entry and exit to the industry, not on the number of firms in the industry as neo-classical theory would imply. With low barriers, existing firms will price such that AR = AC (i.e. no abnormal profits are being earned) because they are afraid that otherwise hit-and-run entrants to the industry will come in and damage the market for them. They are also afraid that new entrants may stay on a permanent basis, reducing the market share of existing firms in the industry.

Degrees of contestability

It can be argued that no market is perfectly contestable. There are always some barriers to entry and exit which have a deterrent effect on hit and run competitors, for example. However, some markets are more contestable than others. The lower the barriers to entry and exit, the more contestable a market is likely to be. Hence, there are degrees of contestability across markets. Some markets are highly contestable, others are only weakly contestable.

Key Terms

Contestable market - a market where there is freedom of entry to the industry and where costs of exit are low.
Hit and run competition - when firms can enter a market at low cost attracted by high profits and then leave the market at low cost when profits fall.

Thinking like an economist

The air passenger market

The air passenger market is often given as an example of a contestable market. In the market, there are a relatively few number of companies flying on particular routes. Up until the 1990s, airlines tended to charge high prices. Those that were well run were able to make abnormal profit. Many, though, were poorly run, with very high costs and sometimes operating on routes that would always struggle to be profitable. Some were owned by governments, more concerned with national prestige than losses.

In the 1990s, deregulation and privatisation in Europe led to the growth of low-cost airlines. They took away significant market share from more established airlines on short-haul routes. Very quickly, a number of low-cost, budget airlines were set up, many of which disappeared within a few years of operation because they were not able to make a profit.

One of the key factors for the contestability of the air passenger market is the ability of airlines to hire both staff and equipment. A new entrant can, for example, hire an aircraft for a short period of time like six months and, if necessary, on a flight by flight basis. Cabin crew and airport staff can be hired from companies specialising in providing services to airlines. Landing and take-off slots can be negotiated from most airports on a short-term basis. The sunk costs are therefore relatively low given the nature of the industry. Internet price comparison sites also making it easy for price-conscious travellers to see the lowest cost flight, making it relatively easy for new entrants to sell tickets.

There is a number of factors which make the air passenger market less than perfectly contestable. For example, there are still aviation laws which prevent foreign companies from flying

to and from many destinations in the world. In the UK, Heathrow is so congested that no new entrant is likely to gain landing and take-off slots. This is one of the reasons why companies like easyJet fly from Luton airport rather than Heathrow.

Overall, though, what could be an oligopolistic market with firms making abnormal profits is instead a contestable market where keen price competition allows firms to earn only normal profits.

Data Response Question

The bus market

Local bus services in the UK are provided by a large number of different bus companies. However, the majority of local bus routes in the UK are serviced by just one company, which enjoys a monopoly on the route. Outside London, the largest five firms have a market share of approximately 70 per cent. These are Stagecoach, FirstGroup, Arriva, Go-Ahead and National Express. In London, seven firms have 99 per cent of the market.

Most routes only have one bus provider operating the route. However, it is relatively easy for a competitor to offer an alternative service on the route. Setting up a bus company can cost as little as £100 000. Approval needs to be given by the local traffic commissioner, who will issue a PSV (Public Service Vehicle) Operator Licence. Most start-ups buy very old second-hand buses. A garage to keep and maintain the buses can be rented. The buses need to be maintained properly or the traffic commissioner will revoke the operating licence. Insurance is one of the overheads. Drivers need to hold a valid driving licence.

A minority of bus routes are subsidised by local authorities. Fares taken don't cover operating costs. If they were not subsidised, bus companies wouldn't operate the route. Local authorities typically invite bus companies to tender to operate the route. The bus company accepting the lowest subsidy wins the contract and receives the subsidy for the length of the contract.

Competition on routes occurs on those with the highest number of passengers. These routes are most likely to provide sufficient revenues for the bus companies to survive.

Source: with information from www.gov.uk.

Q

1. Explain what is meant by a 'monopoly', using bus services as an example.

2. Analyse the barriers to entry and exit in the local bus passenger market.

3. To what extent are bus companies likely to earn abnormal profit?

Evaluation

Outline the theory of contestable markets. To what extent are bus routes contestable? What is likely to happen if a company is earning abnormal profit on a bus route?

Figure 1

UK bus market share outside of London

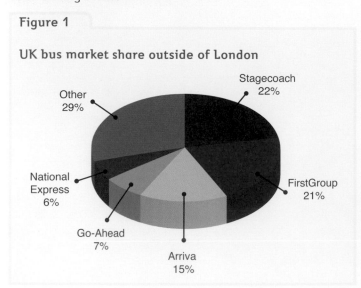

Stagecoach 22%
Other 29%
FirstGroup 21%
National Express 6%
Go-Ahead 7%
Arriva 15%

Figure 2

London bus market share

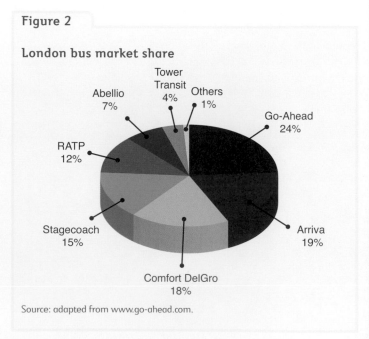

Tower Transit 4%
Abellio 7%
Others 1%
Go-Ahead 24%
RATP 12%
Arriva 19%
Stagecoach 15%
Comfort DelGro 18%

Source: adapted from www.go-ahead.com.

Key points

1. Shareholders, managers, workers, government, consumers, pressure groups and others can influence decision making in a firm.
2. Firms may pursue a variety of objectives including profit maximisation, revenue maximisation and sales maximisation.
3. Firms which pursue other objectives than profit maximisation are likely also to pursue an objective of profit satisficing in order to survive in the long term.

Starter activity

Identify a good or a service that you buy frequently. Who makes the product? What do you think might be their business objective or objectives? Which business objective is the most important do you think?

Control

The question of what motivates a firm in its actions can only be answered if there is a clear understanding of who controls the decision-making process. This control is likely to lie with one or more of the firm's stakeholders. In a UK context these are as follows.

The owners or shareholders It might seem obvious to state that it is the owners or shareholders of a company who control it. This is perhaps true for small businesses where the owner is also the director or manager of the business. The owner of a small local corner shop, for instance, who also runs the shop will make the decisions about the business. However, it is less obvious that owners control the business they own when there is a very large number of shareholders.

Directors and managers Shareholders in a public limited company elect directors to look after their interests. Directors in turn appoint managers who are responsible for the day to day running of the business. Therefore there may be a divorce between ownership and control. The only way in which owners can influence decision making directly is by sacking directors at the Annual General Meeting (AGM) of the company. In practice, the company needs to be in serious difficulties for this to happen. Shareholders can also sell their shares, forcing the share price down and making the company more vulnerable to a takeover bid. If there is a takeover the directors and managers may well lose their jobs and hence there is pressure on managers to perform well.

The workers The workers, particularly through their trade unions, may be able to exert strong pressure on a company. They do not have the power to run the company in the way that shareholders or managers might be able to do. However, they can have an important influence on matters such as wages (and therefore costs), health and safety at work and location or relocation of premises.

The state The state provides an underlying framework for the operation of the company. Legislation on taxation, the environment, consumer protection, health and safety at work, employment practices, solvency and many other issues force companies to behave in a way in which they might otherwise not do in an unregulated environment.

The consumer The consumer, through organisations such as the Consumers' Association or various trade organisations, can bring pressure to bear on companies in an attempt to make them change their policies. This form of influence is often rather weak. **Consumer sovereignty** - the power of consumers to allocate resources according to their own preferences through their spending decisions - is more important. In a free market, consumers cast their spending votes amongst companies.

Question 1

Yesterday, McDonald's Chicago headquarters was picketed by more than 400 protestors as, inside the building, its annual shareholder meeting took place. The day before, 100 people were arrested for trespassing after up to 1 500 protestors called for a $15 an hour minimum wage and a trade union for fast-food workers. McDonald's has become the main target of those wishing to raise the minimum wage in the US. At the annual shareholders' meeting, the theme was touched on in a question that has come to dominate its recent shareholder meetings - the contribution McDonald's makes to childhood obesity. While the company spends billions on marketing 'to hook more kids on junk food and increase executive compensation, many of your employees can barely make ends meet on poverty wages', said Sriram Madhusoodanan of Corporate Accountability International, a public health and human rights watchdog.

Don Thompson, McDonald's chief executive, replied by saying that 60 per cent of its employees were under age 24 in company owned-US restaurants and nearly 70 per cent were part-time workers, 'many of whom are just starting out'. He said that 'offering opportunity is a part of the McDonald's heritage' and 'we continue to believe that we pay fair and competitive wages.'

Critics contend that workers would like to work more hours, but are limited because the company does not to offer the benefits full-time employment requires. According to a 2013 study by the pro-labour National Employment Law Project, US government programmes subsidise the incomes of about 700 000 McDonald's employees.

Source: adapted from © the *Financial Times* 23.5.2014, All Rights Reserved.

Identify six different stakeholders of McDonald's mentioned in the data and briefly explain their possible objectives.

Theme 3 - Unit 53

Companies which do not provide the products that consumers wish to buy will go out of business whilst companies which are responsive to consumers' needs may make large profits. According to this argument, it is the consumer who ultimately controls the company. This assumes that consumer sovereignty exists. In practice, firms attempt to manipulate consumer preferences by marketing devices such as advertising. Firms are therefore not the powerless servants that theory implies.

Pressure groups Pressure groups, like Friends of the Earth or Oxfam, are groups which attempt to influence others to advance a particular cause or viewpoint. Friends of the Earth, for example, is an environmental pressure group, whilst Oxfam is a charity concerned with global poverty. Only large firms are likely to be targeted by pressure groups. However, pressure groups have the power to change company policies. For example, pressure groups highlighting the use of child or slave labour in a company's supply chain might be able to force the company to review all its buying policies. Equally, environmental groups might be able force companies to abandon projects or modify their work practices.

Short-run profit maximisation

In neo-classical economics it is assumed that the interests of owners or shareholders are the most important. Just as consumers attempt to maximise utility and workers attempt to maximise their rewards from working, so shareholders will be motivated solely by maximising their gain from the company. Therefore it is argued that the goal of firms is to **profit maximise**.

Question 2

Vinyl records are making a comeback. Audiophiles - lovers of high-quality music - believe that vinyl records give a better recording quality than digital formats such as the CD. Adam Teskey runs the UK's largest vinyl pressing plant in Hayes, Middlesex. It is based on the site of the old EMI factory, where records by the likes of The Beatles and Jimi Hendrix were pressed. In the 1960s, about 14 000 people worked there, pressing vinyl records; today there are just 22. For Adam Teskey, the future is premium, high profit margin releases, such as the collaboration The Vinyl Factory undertook with the Pet Shop Boys last year: five records inside a transparent, fluorescent acrylic box. Only 350 were made and every copy was signed. At £500 each, they sold out in less than 48 hours.

Mr Teskey describes his strategy as the difference between a Fiat 500 car and a Rolls Royce. One is built for mass-market, the other for luxury. Put simply, it is more profitable than pressing thousands of albums for mass release and leaves Mr Teskey less exposed to the vagaries of commercial pressing requirements. 'You know what I really hate. I really hate the word profit being a dirty word in the UK. I don't get it,' he says.

Source: adapted from © the *Financial Times* 15.10.2014, All Rights Reserved.

(a) What is the most likely objective of The Vinyl Factory?

(b) Explain why a 'Rolls Royce' strategy might help Adam Teskey achieve his objective more than a 'Fiat 500' strategy.

Neo-classical economics assumes that it is short-run profits that firms maximise. They equate marginal cost and marginal revenue in the short term to decide on their level of production. In markets where there is heavy branding, such as soap powders, prices are likely to be stable. However, in commodity industries where firms are producing homogeneous goods like copper, paper or wheat, prices are likely to be unstable. Short-run profit maximisation implies that firms will be prepared to supply even if they make a loss in the short run so long as price is above the average variable cost of production. In the long run, firms must cover all their costs or they will leave the market.

Profit maximisation occurs at the output where the difference between total revenue and total cost is the greatest, as explained in Unit 45. Another way of expressing this is to say that a firm maximises profits when marginal cost equals marginal revenue (MC = MR).

Long-run profit maximisation

Neo-Keynesian economists believe that firms maximise their long-run profit rather than their short-run profit. This is based upon the belief that firms use **cost plus pricing** techniques. The price of a product is worked out by calculating the average total cost of operating at full capacity and adding a profit mark-up. The price set and therefore the profit aimed for is based upon the long run costs of the firm.

Short-run profit maximisation implies that firms will adjust both price and output in response to changes in market conditions. However, according to neo-Keynesians, rapid price adjustments may well damage the firm's position in a market. Consumers dislike frequent price changes. Price cuts may be seen as a sign of distress selling and large buyers may respond by trying to negotiate even larger price reductions. Price increases may be interpreted as a sign of profiteering, with consumers switching to other brands or makes in the belief that they will get better value for money. Price changes also involve costs to the company because price lists need to be changed, sales staff informed, advertising material changed, etc. Therefore it is argued that firms attempt to maintain stable prices whilst adjusting output to changes in market conditions.

This may mean that a firm will produce in the short run even if it fails to cover its variable cost. If it takes the view that in the long run it may make a profit on production of a particular good, it may prefer to produce at a loss rather than disrupt supplies to the market. Equally, it may cease production in the short run even if it can cover its variable costs. It may prefer to keep prices above the market price in the short run and sell nothing if it believes that price cutting in the short run would lead to a permanent effect on prices and therefore profits in the long run.

Divorce of ownership from control

In small firms, the owner or owners are likely to work in the firm. This is still true of many medium-sized businesses. However, in large businesses, owners are likely to appoint directors and managers to run the firm on their behalf. When this happens, there is a divorce of ownership from control. Most large firms are listed companies. Their shares are traded on stock exchanges. Sometimes, the original founders of the firm have a large

298

holding of shares. However, the older the company, the more likely it is that the original founders will have sold most or all of their shares. Shareholdings are then likely to be fragmented with the largest shareholder holding no more than 10 per cent of the shares.

The owners of a large firm are likely to want to maximise the returns on their investment in the company. Short-run profit maximisation is likely to achieve this.

However, it is far from obvious that directors and managers will share this objective. As employees of the company, neo-classical economic theory would predict that they would attempt to maximise their own rewards. These will include their own pay and bonuses. Fringe benefits, such as pension entitlements, company cars and free private medical care, are important too. So are less tangible rewards, such as power, the ability to distribute resources or government honours, such as knighthoods.

Making a profit must remain an important objective for directors and managers. They have to be seen to be efficient enough to make profits to justify their remuneration packages. Criticism from shareholders at shareholders' meetings or through the press has to be avoided. If profits are not high enough, there is the threat of a takeover by another company. If the firm makes losses, these could be high enough to force the company into liquidation. Directors and managers would then lose their jobs.

So directors and managers have to make enough profit to satisfy the demands of shareholders and the markets. Making enough profit, but not maximising profit, is known as **profit satisficing**. Once directors and managers have profit satisficed, they are then free to maximise their own rewards from the company.

In recent decades, the trend has been for companies to attempt to change the behaviour of directors and managers by rewarding them for achieving set outcomes. Bonuses can be linked to sales targets, profit targets or share price targets, for example. However, it is the directors and managers of companies who devise these schemes. This is the equivalent of allowing workers to set their own rates of pay. Not surprisingly, the result has been a growing gap between the remuneration packages for senior managers and directors and the average wages of workers in the company.

The divorce of ownership from control is an example of the principal agent problem explained in Unit 19. The principal-agent problem occurs when one group, the agent, is making decisions on behalf of another group, the principal. In theory, the agent should maximise the benefits for those whom they are looking after. In practice, agents always have the temptation to maximise their own benefits at the expense of those of the principals.

Revenue maximisation

One theory that uses the concept of divorce of ownership from control is the theory of **revenue maximisation**. In this theory, it is assumed that the objective of managers is to maximise total revenues for the firm, subject to a profit satisficing constraint. The larger the sales revenue of the firm, the higher is likely to be the pay and prestige of senior managers. A company that has twice the value of sales of another competing company would

presumably pay its directors and managers more than its smaller rival. Revenue maximisation and the size of the company is, therefore, a way for managers to justify their rewards.

Total revenue will be maximised when marginal revenue is zero. Assume the firm is a monopolist and that the minimum level of profit which will satisfy shareholders is the level of normal profit. With a downward sloping marginal revenue curve, shown in Figure 1, selling an extra unit above OB will result in negative marginal revenue and therefore a fall in total revenue. So OB is the revenue maximising output of the firm. This compares to the profit maximising level of output of OA, where MC = MR.

The price it charges will be determined by the demand curve facing the firm, which is also the average revenue curve. So it will charge OF. This is lower than the profit maximising price of OE. This is what should be expected. Facing a downward sloping demand curve, the firm can only sell more by lowering its average price.

At OB, the firm is making both normal and abnormal profit. It is making normal profit because this is included as part of costs, shown by the marginal and average cost curves. It is also making abnormal profit of HF per unit. HF is the difference between the average revenue at output OB and average cost, OH. It therefore makes abnormal profit of FKMH. This is smaller than the abnormal profit it would have made had it profit maximised, which is EJNG.

Figure 1

Maximisation alternatives

The profit maximising firm will produce at OA and price at OE. The revenue maximising firm will produce at OB and price at OF. The sales maximising firm will produce at OC and price at OG.

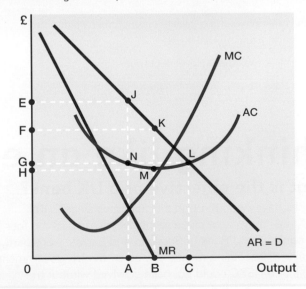

Table 1

	Level of output (assuming the firm profit satisfices where it just makes normal profit) occurs when:
Profit maximiser	MC = MR
Revenue maximiser	MR = 0
Sales maximiser	AC = AR or TC = TR

This analysis is also applicable to oligopolistic firms where firms can make abnormal profits in the long run. It doesn't apply to firms in either perfect competition or monopolistic competition in the long run. In these market structures, firms can only earn normal profit in the long run. If we assume that normal profit is the profit satisficing level of output, then firms cannot operate at any other point but the profit maximising level of output.

Sales maximisation

An alternative theory is that firms **sales maximise**: they maximise their sales volumes, the number of products they sell. As with revenue maximisation, it can be argued that sales volume is a measure of the size of a firm. Managers and directors can then justify the rewards they take from the firm by pointing to the sales they have achieved.

Assume that earning normal profit will satisfy the needs of the owners of the firms. Also assume that the firm is a monopoly or an oligopoly which can make abnormal profits both in the short and long runs. The level of production where sales are maximised is where average costs = average revenue (which is the same as where total costs = total revenue). In Figure 1, this is at the output OC where the AC curve cuts the AR curve. At this level of output, the firm makes normal profit because normal profit is part of cost. Any output beyond OC will be loss making because AC is above AR. So at any output level beyond OC, the firm will not even make normal profit breaking the profit satisficing assumption. Output is higher than the revenue maximisation output at OB and higher than that profit maximising output of OA.

The price at which the firm sells its good is OG. This is below both the revenue maximising price of OF and the profit maximising price of OE. At output OC, the firm makes no abnormal profits, compared to FKMH abnormal profits for the revenue maximiser and EJNG for the profit maximiser.

Question 3

Table 2

Output	Total revenue £000	Total cost £000
1	50	23
2	90	48
3	120	63
4	140	83
5	150	99
6	150	116
7	140	140
8	120	175

Table 2 shows the output, total revenues and total costs for a firm. The firm is a profit satisficer, wanting at least to earn normal profit on its output. Subject to this constraint, explain, using a diagram, what would be:

(a) the profit maximising level of output (profit which is both abnormal and normal profit);

(b) the sales maximising level of output;

(c) the sales revenue maximising level of output.

Key Terms

Consumer sovereignty - exists when the economic system allocates resources totally according to the preferences of consumers.

Cost-plus pricing - the technique adopted by firms of fixing a price for their products by adding a fixed percentage profit margin to the long-run average cost of production.

Profit maximisation - occurs when the difference between total revenue and total cost is greatest.

Profit satisficing - making sufficient profit to satisfy the demands of owners, such as shareholders.

Revenue maximisation - occurs when total revenue is highest and when marginal revenue equals zero.

Sales maximisation - occurs when the volume of sales is greatest; when the objective of a firm, this is usually subject to a profit satisficing constraint.

Thinking like an economist

What is the objective of a UK bank?

UK banks have been through difficult times since 2007. In 2007-08, they came close to insolvency. Two of the four major banks, Royal Bank of Scotland and Lloyds, were partly nationalised, becoming mostly owned by the UK government. Barclays and HSBC could not have survived without the government, through the Bank of England, injecting large amounts of money into the banking system.

The banks are public limited companies, owned by shareholders. Shareholders appoint directors to supervise the running of the company, which is then given over to its managers.

Economic theory suggests that those shareholders want to see their returns maximised. This means some combination of

Figure 2

Total UK bonus payments, year of April to end March (£bn)

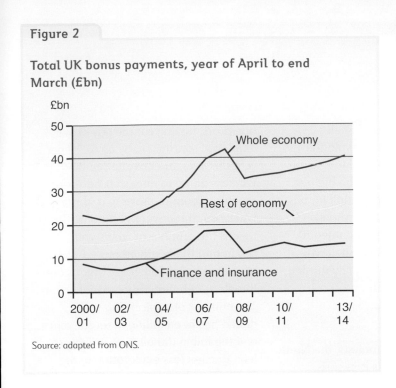

Source: adapted from ONS.

Figure 3

Bonuses as share of total pay, year of April to end March (%)

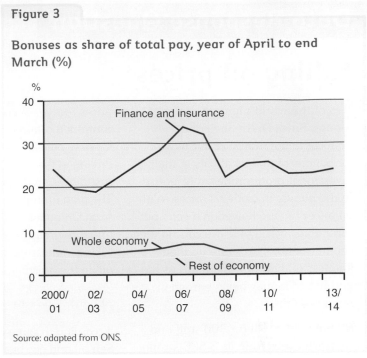

Source: adapted from ONS.

maximum dividends (the shareholders' share of the profits) and maximum growth in the share price. However, any shareholder buying bank shares at the start of 2007 will have suffered a large loss. For example, Barclays' share price on 1 January 2007 was 659p. On 1 January 2015, it was 244p.

Economic theory also suggests that the principal-agent problem can prevent shareholders maximising their returns. The principal-agent problem in this case is that the directors and managers, whom shareholders appoint to run the company on their behalf, will seek to maximise their own returns at the expense of shareholders. Two interlinked examples of the ability of employees of the bank to maximise their own returns can be found in bank bonuses and bank scandals.

The higher the level of basic pay, the more likely it is that the employee will be in receipt of a bonus. So the bank cleaner won't receive a bonus, but the chief executive will be entitled to a bonus typically worth millions of pounds a year. As Figures 2 and 3 show, bonuses are a particularly important part of total pay in UK finance and insurance. Bonuses are justified as a reward for success. However, throughout the banking crisis of 2008-09 and beyond when banks were loss-making, bankers were still being paid large bonuses. So a different argument was used to justify the bonuses. It was argued that if they weren't paid, employees would leave the bank and get a job elsewhere, losing the bank even more money. Employees of the banks, therefore, were still able to reward themselves significantly, even when the shareholders, the owners, were suffering very large losses.

Another example of employees maximising their own returns at the expense of shareholders was the widespread use of illegal practices at banks. Since 2007, the UK banking industry has been hit by revelations of a series of scandals relating to illegal activities, dating at least back into the 1990s. For example, customers were sold products they didn't need, such as PPI, payment protection insurance. Interest rates and currency rates were rigged to benefit bank dealers. Banks, such as HSBC, offered clients opportunities to evade UK taxes. In the short term, managers who encouraged the mis-selling of PPI products or packages that allowed customers to evade paying tax were rewarded with higher bonuses. In the long term, with customers receiving over £20 billion in compensation for the mis-selling of PPI and banks being fined by government authorities tens of billions of pounds for successive scandals, it is the shareholders who have lost out.

Bank executives might argue that their objective is to maximise profits for shareholders. The evidence suggests that they maximise sales or sales revenue, whichever will give them the greatest returns. It is easier to justify bonuses if banks are making a profit. But as events since 2007 have shown, huge losses have not prevented UK banks giving out thousands of millions of pounds in bonuses to their staff.

Source: with information from © the *Financial Times* 12.1.2015, 5.3.2015, All Rights Reserved; www.barclays.com.

Data Response Question

Falling oil prices

Two of the world's largest energy groups, Royal Dutch Shell and ConocoPhillips, have set out plans for billions of dollars of cuts in their investment programmes in response to the plunge in crude oil prices. With oil prices having halved in a year, oil companies worldwide are cutting their capital spending to shore up their finances and protect dividends as the amount of money being earned in revenues falls.

BP has said it will cut 300 staff and contractor jobs from its 3 500-strong North sea business and freeze salaries in an attempt to cut costs. French company Total announced this month that it planned to reduce capital spending by 10 per cent this year and speed up billions of dollars in sales of assets.

Ben van Beurden, Shell's chief executive, stressed that the company was 'taking a prudent approach. We must be careful not to overreact to the recent fall in oil prices'. He went on to say that over time, supply and demand would come back into balance and

prices recover. As a sign of Shell's continued commitment to exploring for new oilfields, he pledged to resume drilling in the Artic, one of the highest cost places on the planet to drill for oil. The plan prompted a fierce response from Greenpeace, the environmental pressure group, which said Shell was taking 'a massive risk doggedly chasing oil' in the 'pristine' Arctic.

Source: adapted from © the *Financial Times* 30.1.2015, All Rights Reserved.

According to some oil analysts, the North Sea oil and gas business is in crisis. Tony Craven Walker, chief executive of Serica Energy, said: 'Smaller companies like ours are losing their ability to raise finance and reward shareholders. It is a slow death by attrition.' He said that the plunge in oil prices from $115 a barrel last summer to around $60 now, a tax system that deterred investment and a failure by producers to cooperate could lead to a wave of early closures of oil and gas fields.

Already, North Sea oil and gas companies have been cutting costs in response to the fall in price. Several

operators, having cut the pay of self-employed contractors by up to 15 per cent this year, are now demanding workers agree to new shift patterns, requiring them to move to a 'three weeks on, three weeks off' rota. This means the number of crews will be cut and those still employed will spend more days offshore. Unions are threating to ballot for industrial action. The number of exploration wells drilled has been falling in recent years and the fall in the oil price is likely to lead to even less exploration in the North Sea.

The effects of this fierce cost-cutting, lower prices and less exploration will be felt well beyond Scotland. Suppliers such as OGN in the northeast of England, which makes oil and gas platforms, fear job losses will follow. 'The company has work into next year but little beyond that', said Alexander Temerko, deputy chairman.

Source: adapted from © the *Financial Times* 26.2.2015, All Rights Reserved.

Q

1. Describe the trend in exploration shown in Figure 4, giving evidence from the data to support your statement.

2. Explain why falling oil prices should lead to cutbacks in investment by oil companies.

3. Using evidence from the data, discuss whether or not oil companies are profit maximisers.

Figure 4

UK continental shelf: number of exploration wells drilled

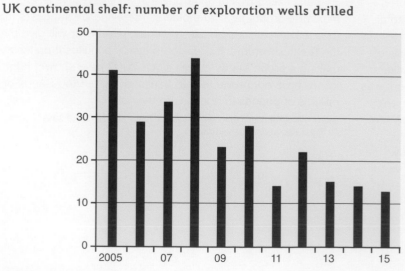

Source: adapted from Oil & Gas UK.

Evaluation

Outline other objectives of the firm apart from profit maximisation. What evidence is there from the data that firms are pursuing any of these objectives, including profit maximisation? What other information would you need apart from what is in the data to make a better evaluation?

54 Efficiency

Starter activity

Name a firm from which you buy goods or services. It could be a local shop, the local bus company or an Internet provider. Do you think it is run efficiently? If not, why do you think it isn't run efficiently? If you think it is, what might it do to be labelled inefficient in some area of its business? In your answers, think about costs and whether it provides what customers want to buy.

Efficiency

The market mechanism allocates resources, but how well does it do this? One way of judging this is to consider how **efficiently** it resolves the three fundamental questions in economics of how, what and for whom production should take place. Efficiency is concerned with how well resources, such as time, talents or materials, are used to produce an end result. In economic terms, it is concerned with the relationship between scarce inputs and outputs. There is a number of different forms of efficiency which need to be considered.

Static vs dynamic efficiency

Static efficiency exists at a point in time. An example of static efficiency would be whether a firm could produce one million cars a year more cheaply by using more labour and less capital. Another example would be whether a country could produce more if it cut its unemployment rate. Productive and allocative efficiency (discussed below) are static concepts of efficiency. Economists use them to discuss whether more could be produced now if resources were allocated in a different way. These concepts can be used, for instance, to discuss whether industries dominated by a monopoly producer might produce at lower cost if competition were introduced into the industry or whether a firm should be allowed to pollute the environment. **Dynamic efficiency** is concerned with how resources are allocated **over a period of time**. For instance, would there be greater efficiency if a firm distributed less profit over time to its shareholders and used the money to finance more investment? Would there be greater efficiency in the economy if more resources were devoted to investment rather than consumption over time? Would an industry invest more and create more new products over time if it were a monopoly than if there were perfect competition?

Productive efficiency

Productive efficiency exists when production is achieved at lowest cost. There is productive inefficiency when the cost of production is above the minimum possible given the state of knowledge. For instance, a firm which produces one million units at a cost of £10 000 would be productively inefficient if it could have produced that output at a cost of £8 000.

Question 1

Table 1

Output	Units	
	Minimum input levels	
	Labour	Capital
10	4	1
20	8	2
30	11	3
40	14	4
50	16	5

(a) Firm A uses 21 units of labour and 6 units of capital to produce 60 units of output. A competing firm uses 19 units of labour and 6 units of capital to produce the same output. Explain whether Firm A is more technically efficient than the competing firm.

(b) Firm B uses 24 units of labour and 7 units of capital to produce 70 units of output. Firm B pays £10 000 to employ these factors. A competing firm employs the same number of factors to produce the same level of output but only pays £8 000 for them. Explain whether Firm B is more productively efficient.

(c) Now look at Table 1. From the table, which of the following combinations are:

(i) technically efficient and

(ii) productively efficient if the minimum cost of a unit of labour is £100 and of a unit of capital is £500?

(1) 8 units of labour and 2 units of capital to produce 20 units of output at a cost of £1 800.

(2) 15 units of labour and 4 units of capital to produce an output of 40 units at a cost of £3 500.

(3) 4 units of labour and 1 unit of capital to produce 10 units of output at a cost of £1 000.

Figure 1

Productive efficiency

For a firm, productive efficiency only occurs when production takes place at lowest average cost. In this case it is at an average cost of OE and an output level of OA. There is X-inefficiency if the firm produces at a cost within the average cost boundary such as at the point H.

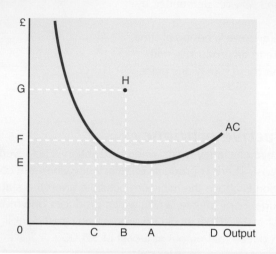

Productive efficiency will only exist if there is **technical efficiency**. Technical efficiency exists if a given quantity of output is produced with the minimum number of inputs (or alternatively, if the maximum output is produced with a given number of units). For instance, if a firm produces 1 000 units of output using 10 workers when it could have used nine workers, then it would be technically inefficient.

However, not all technically efficient outputs are productively efficient. For instance, it might be possible to produce 1 000 units of output using nine workers. But it might be cheaper to buy a machine and employ only two workers. Equally, Firm A might be using a machine and two workers to produce a given output. However, if it is paying £100 000 a year for this, whilst a competing business is paying only £80 000 a year for the same factor inputs, then Firm A is productively inefficient.

This can be illustrated on an average cost curve diagram. Figure 1 shows the average cost for a firm. It is productively efficient if it is producing OA at an average cost of OE. If it produces OD at an average cost of of OF, it is productively inefficient, producing too much because OF is not the lowest average cost possible. The same argument applies if it produces at output OC and an average cost of OF. In this case, however, it is producing too little to be productively efficient.

There will also be productive inefficiency if the firm produces within its average cost curve boundary. If the firm is operating at point H, then output is OB and average cost is OG. It is then productively inefficient for two reasons. First, at point H, it is not achieving the lowest average cost possible as shown by the average cost curve. Second, even if it were producing on the average cost boundary, production of OB would be too low to achieve minimum average cost.

In Figure 1, OA is the productively efficient level of output whether the average cost curve is the short-run average cost

curve or the long-run average cost curve. A firm is productively efficient in the short run if it is operating on the bottom of its short run average cost curve. It is productively efficient in the long run, if it is operating on the bottom of its long-run average cost curve.

For an economy as a whole, there is productive efficiency if it is operating on its production possibility frontier. To understand why, consider what would be the case if one competitive firm in the economy were productively inefficient. Then it would use up too many resources to produce its output. Either by expanding or contracting output, or closing down and its production being taken over by other firms in the industry, average costs could be reduced to a minimum, so releasing resources to be used elsewhere in the economy. There is no possibility of gaining any extra production in the economy if all firms are producing at lowest cost. Hence, there must be productive efficiency only when the economy is operating on its production possibility boundary.

X-inefficiency

X-inefficiency or **organisational slack** is a specific type of productive inefficiency. It occurs when a firm is not producing at the lowest possible cost for a given level of output.

X-inefficiency is present when a firm is operating within its average cost curve and not on the boundary. In Figure 1, if a firm is producing OB but its average cost is OG, then it is X-inefficient because it is operating within the average cost boundary. In contrast, if it produces at OC and its average cost is OF, then there are no X-inefficiencies. However, the firm is still productively inefficient because it is not operating at the lowest point on its average cost curve at output OA.

X-inefficiencies can occur for a large number of reasons. One is that management of a firm is poor at controlling costs. It doesn't, for example, get the cheapest possible prices on its supplies. It employs too many workers or has too many production sites. It doesn't employ the most efficient and profitable capital equipment. Another reason is that stakeholders within the firm are able to extract benefits that are greater than the firm needs to pay. For example, directors and managers might pay themselves and take bonuses in excess of what is needed to keep them employed in the firm. Trade unions might be able to negotiate higher rates of pay than the market wage rate. Environmental groups might put pressure on a firm to adopt stricter environmental standards than cost minimisation would dictate.

Allocative efficiency

Allocative or **economic efficiency** measures whether resources are allocated to those goods and services demanded by consumers. For example, are there enough foreign holidays being sold? Are too many shoes being produced in the economy but not enough jumpers? Should there be more caviar and lobster on supermarket shelves and less white bread? The basic economic problem is that resources are scarce whilst wants are infinite. There is allocative efficiency when scarce resources are used to produce a bundle of goods that satisfies consumer preferences and maximises their welfare.

Economic theory suggests that there will be allocative

efficiency in a market when the marginal benefit received from consumption is equal to the marginal cost of production. The marginal benefit is shown by the price consumers are willing to pay for the last good consumed. It is shown by the demand curve for a good. So there is allocative efficiency when the price of the product is equal to its marginal cost of production (P = MC).

This argument can be developed using demand and cost curves. Demand and marginal cost have a particular significance in **welfare economics**, the study of how an economy can best allocate resources to maximise the utility or economic welfare of its citizens.

- The demand curve shows the value that consumers place on the last unit bought of a product. For instance, if a utility maximising consumer bought a pair of tights at £2, then the pair of tights must have given at least £2 worth of value (or **satisfaction** or **utility**). If total demand for a product is 100 units at a price of £10, then the value placed by consumers on the hundredth unit must have been £10. The value placed on each of the other 99 units bought is likely to be above £10 because the demand curve slopes back upwards from that point. The marginal (or extra) value of a good to the consumer (i.e. the marginal utility) is given by the price shown on the demand curve at that level of output.
- The marginal cost curve shows the cost to firms of producing an extra unit of the good. 'Cost', we will assume here, is the cost of production to society as well as to firms. In practice, the **private cost** of production of the firm may differ from the **social cost** because of **externalities**, and this has important implications for allocative efficiency.

In Figure 2, two markets are shown. In the wheat market, current output is OB. The market price is £1 per unit, but farmers receive £3 per unit, for instance because the government subsidises production. In the gas market, output is OE. The price is £6 but gas suppliers receive only £4, for instance because the government imposes a £2 tax per unit.

Figure 2

Allocative efficiency

Transferring resources from the wheat market where price is below marginal cost to the gas market where price is above marginal cost will lead to allocative efficiency.

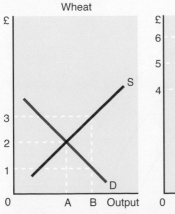
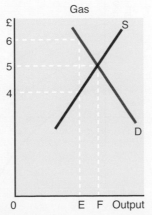

In the wheat industry, price is below marginal cost (P < MC). This means that the value that consumers place on the product is less than the cost to society of producing the product. Consumers value the last unit produced at OB at £1 (shown on the demand curve). The cost to society of producing the last unit is £3 (shown on the marginal cost curve). Therefore consumers value the last unit of wheat purchased at £2 less than it cost to produce.

In the gas market, price is above marginal cost (P > MC). This means that the value consumers place on the last unit produced is more than the cost to society of its production. Consumers value the last unit produced at OE at £6 whilst its cost to society is only £4. Hence consumers value the last unit of gas purchased at £2 more than it cost to produce.

This suggests that scarce resources would be more efficiently allocated if less wheat and more gas were produced in the economy, but how much wheat and gas should be produced? If price is equal to marginal cost in both markets (P = MC), then consumers value the last unit consumed of both wheat and gas as much as it costs to produce those commodities. If the price of wheat in Figure 2 were £2 and gas £5, then it would be impossible to reallocate resources between the two industries to the advantage of consumers.

Hence allocative efficiency will exist if price is equal to marginal cost in each industry in the economy. This is a very important conclusion but we shall see in the next unit that it needs to be very heavily qualified.

Allocative efficiency also does not mean that incomes are distributed equitably or fairly. For every combination of income distribution in a society, there will be a distribution of resources that is allocatively efficient. A society that is highly unequal will have a different allocatively efficient distribution of resources from one that is highly equal.

Question 2

In some areas of the country, some state schools are over-subscribed. This means that there are more children wanting to come to the school than there are places available. In such circumstances schools have to choose their children according to admission rules. Typically, these are based on catchment areas. Children who live close to the school get in. Those who live further away do not. This might not be the most efficient way of allocating places. Some economists have advocated giving each child in the country a voucher worth £x which is handed over to their school and then cashed in to pay for the expenses of running the school. Oversubscribed schools could charge fees over and above the value of the voucher. The size of the fee would be fixed to limit the number of entrants to the school to the number of places offered. Just as in, say, the market for second-hand cars, if some cars are more popular than others then car sellers can charge higher prices, so would be the case in the education market. Resources will thus be efficiently allocated.

(a) Why might it be argued that there is allocative inefficiency in areas where some schools are oversubscribed?

(b) What might be the advantages and disadvantages to introducing a voucher and fee system in education?

Dynamic efficiency

There is dynamic efficiency in an economy when resources are allocated efficiently over time. Productive and allocative efficiency, in contrast, are examples of static efficiency. This is efficiency at a point in time.

One example of dynamic efficiency concerns the rate of investment. Firms invest either to cut costs or to make new products. Investment can be in research and development, in machinery or buildings or in training workers. The rate of investment by firms is determined by a number of typically short run considerations like levels of demand in the economy, interest rates and their past profitability. Dynamic inefficiency can occur if firms fail to take into account all the future costs and benefits of investment. With research and development, which can have very long term pay-offs, firms may take no account of revenues to be received after, say, five years because they regard these benefits as too uncertain, but if all firms do this, there will be underinvestment in the economy as a whole in long-term research and development. This will reduce the socially optimal rate of technological change over time. With the training of workers, firms may choose to 'poach' workers from firms that have good training programmes for their workers, rather than increase their costs by training them themselves. If all firms do this, there will be underinvestment in training in the economy.

Another example of dynamic efficiency concerns sustainable growth. Production uses up non-renewable resources and creates waste. Future generations face the exhaustion of some non-renewable resources like oil and natural gas. They might also be paying to clean up waste created by us today, for example from nuclear power stations. There is no exact link in economic theory between dynamic efficiency and sustainable growth. However, markets are unlikely to be dynamically efficient if their activities leave future generations considerably worse off.

Efficiency and the production possibility frontier

The various concepts of efficiency can be illustrated using a production possibility frontier (PPF). A production possibility frontier shows combinations of goods that could be produced if all resources were fully used (i.e. the economy were at full employment).

Any point on the boundary in Figure 3 is productively efficient. Points A, B, C and D, for example are productively efficient. This is because each point shows the maximum combination of goods that could be produced. If there were inefficiencies in production, then the firm or the economy would produce within the PPF, say at E.

If there is allocative efficiency, then production must take place again on the boundary. If production took place at E, it would be possible to have both more goods and services. This would benefit consumers. Hence E is allocatively inefficient. However, there is only one point on the boundary that is allocatively efficient. This is the point where the preferences or utility of consumers are maximised. It is the point where the right combination of goods is produced to maximise the satisfaction of consumers. For example, the point D is on the boundary. However, producing here would mean that no food

Figure 3

Productive and allocative efficiency

Productive and allocative efficiency occur when the economy operates on its boundary, for example at A or B. However, there is only one point on the boundary which is allocatively efficient, showing the preferences of consumers for a given combination of goods.

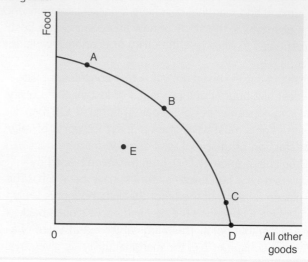

was produced. This is unlikely to maximise consumers' welfare and hence D is unlikely to be allocatively efficient.

Dynamic efficiency is shown by the movement of the PPF to the right. In Figure 4, an economy moves from the point A to B to C over time. Dynamic efficiency will be achieved if the preferences of present consumers and future consumers are realised. Individuals face this problem when they are young and deciding whether to save for their retirement. If they spend all their income when they are young, saving nothing, will this

Figure 4

Dynamic efficiency

Dynamic efficiency occurs when consumer preferences for present versus future consumption are met. There is dynamic efficiency when the boundary is moving outwards in accordance with those preferences.

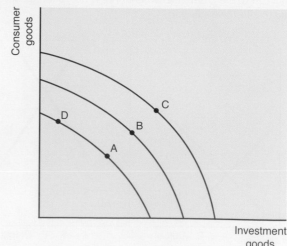

optimise their welfare over their lifetime when they are left poor as pensioners?

An economy could, for example, produce and consume at D rather than A in Figure 4. At D, the economy is producing far more consumer goods than at A but far fewer investment goods. This means that present consumption is higher than, say, at A. However, less investment is likely to mean that growth in the future will be lower than if the economy were at A. What if starting at the point D the economy grew to reach the PPF boundary on which B is located? In contrast, if the economy started at A, could it have reached C in the same time? Which is

the best outcome depends on the value that consumers put on present and future consumption.

Key Terms

Allocative or economic efficiency - occurs when scarce resources are used to produce a bundle of goods which satisfies consumer preferences and maximises their welfare.
Dynamic efficiency - occurs when resources are allocated efficiently over time.
Productive efficiency - achieved when production is achieved at lowest average cost.
Static efficiency - occurs when resources are allocated efficiently at a point in time.
Technical efficiency - achieved when a given quantity of output is produced with the minimum number of inputs.
Welfare economics - the study of how an economy can best allocate resources to maximise the utility or economic welfare of its citizens.
X-inefficiency or organisational slack - inefficiency arising because a firm or other productive organisation fails to minimise its average costs of production at a given level of output.

Thinking like an economist

The misallocation of resources in transport

It is widely argued that public transport is underutilised, whilst private modes of transport, mainly the car, are overused. Partly, this view is held because cars create externalities. However, it is also true that the pricing structure of private and public transport leads directly to a misallocation of resources.

When travellers consider what mode of transport to use, they will look at a number of factors. These include whether or not a journey can be made by public transport, the time it takes and the comfort experienced on the journey.

Another important factor, though, is cost. Decisions are made at the margin. How much will it cost to undertake this extra journey? For the motorist, the marginal cost is the variable cost of motoring. This is petrol plus any car parking fees. The fixed costs of motoring, which include purchase, insurance and road tax, do not enter into the decision making process for a single journey. These costs have already been paid and do not change if an extra journey is made.

In contrast, the price of public transport includes both fixed and variable cost. For instance, when the train passenger buys a ticket, it includes the fixed cost of the payment to Network Rail for the use of the infrastructure and the cost of the train. On top of that is the variable cost of the train driver and the fuel. How much of the fixed cost the passenger pays depends on the pricing policy of the rail company. The tendency is for the train companies to load most of the fixed cost onto passengers travelling at peak times.

Therefore the price that travellers pay excludes fixed costs in private motoring but, particularly for peak-time travellers, includes it in public transport. Not surprisingly, this tends to make private motoring seem cheap for any single journey compared with public transport. This is particularly true if there is more than one passenger travelling in the car because the marginal cost of carrying an extra passenger is zero.

The result is that there is a misallocation of resources. In public transport, price tends to be set above the marginal cost of a single journey, whereas in private motoring, it is equal to marginal cost. The result is that too many car journeys are made and too little use is made of public transport.

Source: adapted from Alain Anderton, *Economics*, 5th edition, Pearson.

Data Response Question

Outsourcing

Traditionally, airlines have kept their services in-house. Budget airlines, however, realised that this was costly. By outsourcing, they could cut costs and offer lower ticket prices. For example, everything from check-in staff to baggage handlers to cleaning and maintenance of aircraft to catering and security can be outsourced to specialist companies. 'We outsource everything that we can outsource' said Warwick Brady, Chief Operations Officer at budget ailine easyJet. 'As long as we can manage it and control it, it gets outsourced.' Only staff in easyJet's core functions, such as its crew and its pilots, are employed directly by the company.

In 2013, the German airline Lufthansa outsourced maintenance and support for its ticketing and reservations booking system. It saved money and was a more efficient use of resources. Workers would be on hand when needed rather than being in-house and on standby at all times. In 2012, Lufthansa pushed through a cost-cutting strategy that eliminated 3 500 jobs.

The aviation market is set to grow at about five per cent a year, according to industry estimates. Outsourcing companies are hoping to achieve growth even higher than this. John Menzies, for example, the world's second-biggest provider of airport

services, is targeting 10-15 per cent growth in its aviation division, which covers cargo and ground handling as well as check-in and aircraft preparation services.

Source: adapted from © the *Financial Times* 22.4.2014, All Rights Reserved.

Q

1. Name two different types of static efficiency and explain how they might be affected by the outsourcing of services by airline companies.

2. Given worries about climate change and pollution caused by aircraft, discuss whether dynamic efficiency will be achieved if the aviation market grows 'at about five per cent a year'.

Evaluation

For question 2, use a PPF diagram to illustrate your answer. Explain what is meant by dynamic efficiency and apply it in the context of the aviation market. Why might a growth in passenger and cargo aviation transport satisfy the wants of consumers? What alternative spending could take place by consumers? What damage might it cause? Overall, weigh up whether consumers will benefit from aviation growth rather than growth in other areas of consumer expenditure. Will consumers suffer more harm than benefits because of its growth in the long term?

Key points

1. Firms in perfectly competitive markets and contestable markets will be statically efficient in the long run, unlike firms in imperfectly competitive markets.
2. There is no incentive for perfectly competitive firms to innovate and hence perfectly competitive markets are not dynamically efficient. Imperfectly competitive firms do have an incentive to innovate and hence there are some dynamic efficiencies.
3. Profit maximising monopolies are neither productively or allocatively efficient, but there can be dynamic efficiencies if monopolists use some of their profit to innovate.
4. Natural monopolies will produce nearer the productively efficient level of output than if the market were supplied by competing firms.
5. Different market structures, such as a monopoly, have costs and benefits to owners, consumers, employees and suppliers.

Starter activity

You want to buy a packet of crisps. Write down 10 different firms within a three-mile radius of your school or home where you could buy the packet. Now think of a situation where every grocery and newsagent store was owned by just one company. What might be the advantages and disadvantages to you as the customer of there being a monopoly in grocery retailing?

Competition

In economics, competition is generally seen as more desirable than monopoly. Firms can compete amongst themselves in a variety of different ways. They can compete:

- on price, offering the lowest price to customers;
- on the formulation or design of a product, offering non-homogeneous products which differ from their rivals;
- on quality, reliability and customer service, offering products and services which are better made, last longer or are easier to buy;
- on availability of a product, at a point in time and in a particular geographical area;
- through promotion such as advertising.

In Business Studies, this is summarised as the four Ps: price, product, promotion and place.

Perfect competition, monopolistic competition and oligopoly are three different market structures in which there is an element of competition between firms. In perfect competition, there is mainly price competition because it is assumed that firms make homogeneous (i.e. identical) products. In monopolistic competition, not only is there competition on price, but also products are non-homogeneous. Firms therefore compete on product too. In oligopoly, there may be price competition but firms are likely to find it in their best interests to avoid price competition. This is because they can make abnormal profit in the long run, as there are barriers to entry to the market. Instead, they compete mainly on production, promotion and place. In a contestable market, firms have to compete as if there were competitors in the market. This is because too high a price,

leading to abnormal profits, will lead to new firms entering the market, cutting prices to the point where only normal profit is made.

Perfect competition, contestable markets and static efficiency

In perfect competition, firms in the long run cannot earn abnormal profit. If they earn abnormal profit in the short run, new firms will enter the market increasing output and lowering price until the abnormal profit is eliminated.

The long run equilibrium position for a firm in perfect competition is shown in Figure 1. Equilibrium output is at Q_E where MC = MR. This is the profit maximising level of output. Equilibrium price is P_E.

Figure 1

Competition and efficiency

A perfectly competitive firm is productively efficient in the long run because it operates in equilibrium at the bottom of the average cost curve. It is allocatively efficient because it operates where price = marginal cost.

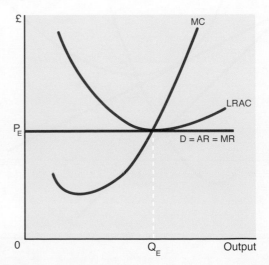

In equilibrium, the firm produces at the lowest point on its long run average cost curve. Hence, the firm is productively efficient. It also produces where price, shown by the horizontal demand curve, equals the marginal cost of production (P = MC). Hence the firm is allocatively efficient. A perfectly competitive market in the long run, therefore, is statically efficient.

Firms in strongly contestable markets with low barriers to entry and exit are also under pressure to be productively and allocatively efficient. To understand why, assume a firm in a contestable market was not operating at the bottom of its average cost curve. Then a new entrant would be able to establish itself, producing at the bottom of its average cost curve. It could then price at this level, undercutting the price of the existing firms within the market. Hence, firms in the long run, in a contestable market, must be productively efficient. They must also be allocatively efficient. Firms in a contestable market can only earn normal profit in the long run. Hence average revenue must equal average cost (AR = AC). If firms are producing at the bottom of their average cost curve, then marginal cost must equal average cost (MC = AC). This is because the marginal cost curve cuts the average cost curve at its lowest point. Hence, since equilibrium output will be where AR = AC and where MC = AC, it must be true that firms produce where AR (which is price) = MC. This is the condition for allocative efficiency.

Imperfect competition and static efficiency

Imperfect competition covers both monopolistic competition and oligopoly. Figure 2 shows a monopolistically competitive market

in the long run. A monopolistically competitive firm cannot make abnormal profit in the long run because there is freedom of entry and exit to and from the market. Hence average revenue must equal average cost in equilibrium. Equilibrium output is at OA at an output level where MC = MR, the profit maximising condition. Equilibrium price is OB. The firm is not producing at the bottom of its average cost curve (point C) and hence it is not productively efficient. Nor is it allocatively efficient because it is not producing at F, where price = marginal cost. Marginal cost, AE, is lower than price OB at the equilibrium level of output.

Figure 3 shows an oligopolistic firm. Assume it is able to make abnormal profit in the long run because of high barriers to entry. At its profit maximising equilibrium level of output of AO, it is not productively efficient. This is because its average cost is higher than the lowest average cost possible at the point C. Nor is it allocatively efficient because the price of OB is higher than the marginal cost of AE.

Hence, both monopolistic competition and oligopoly lead to some degree of market failure.

Competition and dynamic efficiency

In a competitive market, it might seem that firms will inevitably compete by producing new innovative products. If they develop a new product, they can gain a competitive advantage which, at least in the short run, will allow them to make abnormal profit. This might be true of oligopolistic or monopolistically competitive markets, but it is unlikely to be true of perfectly competitive markets.

Figure 2

A monopolistically competitive firm is neither productively or allocatively efficient at its long-run equilibrium point.

At the profit maximising output of OA, the firm is neither productively efficient (output is not at lowest average cost) or allocatively efficient (where P = MC).

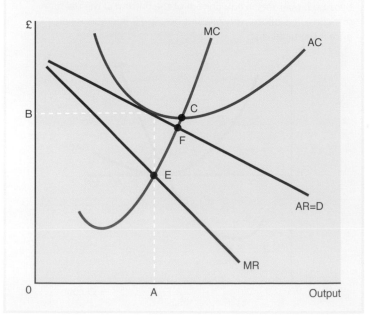

Figure 3

An oligopolistic firm is neither productively or allocatively efficient at its long-run equilibrium point.

At the profit maximising output of OA, the firm is neither productively efficient (output is not at lowest average cost) or allocatively efficient (where P = MC).

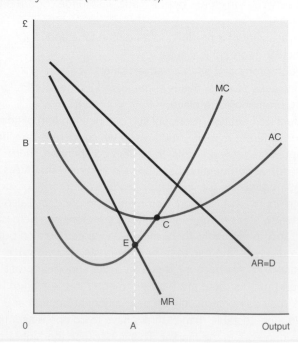

In perfect competition, there is a large number of small firms operating in the market. No one firm will have large enough funds available for research and development. Small firms in general find it more difficult to raise finance for growth and expansion than large firms, and banks are likely to be unsympathetic if borrowed money is to be used on risky research projects. Moreover, perfect knowledge is assumed to exist in the market. The invention of one firm will quickly be adopted by other firms, so there is little or no incentive to undertake research and development.

Patent laws and copyright laws can protect the inventions of small firms, providing some encouragement to innovate. However, in markets where patent and copyright laws exist, the markets are likely to be monopolistically competitive or oligopolistic because of the assumption of perfect knowledge in perfect competition. Patent and copyright laws also create barriers to entry, so patent and copyright laws create branded, non-homogenous goods.

Question 1

In 2006, the postal services market was opened to full competition. Previously, Royal Mail had a monopoly in the collection and delivery of small letters. In October 2007, Postcomm, the independent regulator for postal services, published the results of a survey of businesses into the changes they had seen in the market.

The market research revealed that, although Royal Mail remained the dominant operator, one in five small and medium mailers and more than a third of large mailers were using more than one mail company. One in five respondents had explored alternatives to mail and had moved some of their mail to other media in the past 23 months. This confirmed the need for all postal operators to place more emphasis on customer service and innovation.

More than half of respondents agreed that competition had improved choice and more than a third believed competition had improved Royal Mail's quality of service. 15 per cent of respondents believed that competition had resulted in significantly lower prices.

Source: adapted from Alain Anderton, *Economics*, 5th Edition, Pearson.

Outline the benefits that increased competition in the postal market might have had in terms of (a) productive efficiency; (b) allocative efficiency; (c) dynamic efficiency.

Evaluating competition

The degree of competition differs from market to market. Perfect competition and pure monopoly can be seen as the two extremes of a spectrum of competitiveness. There are markets that approximate to perfect competition and monopoly. Many agricultural markets and commodity markets have many features of perfect competition. Pure monopolies exist in the UK, say, with the rail infrastructure controlled by Network Rail or the electricity transmission system owned by National Grid.

Some argue that perfect competition is not a useful model because most markets are imperfectly competitive. Others argue that the perfect competition model acts as a paradigm. By understanding its market characteristics and market conduct, it provides a benchmark against which to judge imperfectly competitive markets.

In perfect competition, there is a trade off between static and dynamic efficiency. There is both productive and allocative efficiency. Costs and prices are kept to a minimum in the long run because firms cannot make abnormal profit. Firms respond to changing buyer preferences through the signalling effect of prices and profits. Consumer surplus is maximised because prices are kept to a minimum. However, there is no incentive for firms to innovate.

With imperfect competition, equilibrium prices are higher and output is lower than with perfect competition. Firms are productively and allocatively inefficient. However, although there is static inefficiency, there are some dynamic efficiencies. Firms have an incentive to innovate. In monopolistic competition, innovation could lead to abnormal profits being earned in the short run but not in the long run. In theories of oligopoly, where there are barriers to entry, innovation may lead to abnormal profits being made in the long run. The question is then whether the benefits to society from innovation are worth the cost of abnormal profits being earned by the firm.

In the few perfectly competitive industries that might be argued to exist, innovation is often provided not by individual firms but by government-funded or government-organised research institutions. In agriculture, for instance, major advances in crop strains in developing nations have been developed by

Question 2

Tesco is to close its ebook-selling service, blinkbox Books. It had been looking to sell the loss-making operation but failed to find a buyer. Ebooks are a fast growing market with some predicting that more ebooks will be sold than physical books over the next few years. In the UK, the market is dominated by Amazon, which has around 90 per cent of the market. Tesco had been hoping to gain a share of this market when it bought Mobcast, the digital book service, in September 2012 for £4.5 million. However, the service has been loss making. It made a pre-tax loss of £2 million on sales of just £70 000 for the year to February 2013.

Source: adapted from © the *Financial Times* 14.11.2014, 13.1.2015, 27.1.2015, All Rights Reserved.

Explain why the closure of blinkbox Books might show that the ebook market was an efficient market in 2015.

state-funded universities and research institutes. This is an example of government correcting market failure. Alternatively, new crops, like GM varieties, have been developed not by farmers but by farming suppliers. These industries are oligopolistic and not perfectly competitive.

Monopoly

In a pure monopoly, there is no competition. One firm produces all the output of the industry. If the monopolist is a profit maximiser, then it will be both productively and allocatively inefficient and hence there will be market failure.

Consider Figure 4. The profit maximising monopolist will produce where MC = MR at output OA. It will price on its demand curve or average revenue curve at OH. Output at OA is neither productively efficient or allocatively efficient. Productive efficiency occurs at the point L where average cost is at its lowest. Allocative efficiency occurs where price = marginal cost. This is at the point K where the marginal cost curve intersects the demand or average revenue curve. So the profit maximising level of output is below the productively efficient level of output at OB and below the allocatively efficient level of output at OC. The profit maximising price of OH is above the allocatively efficient price of OF and the productively efficient price of OG.

The deadweight loss associated with production at the profit maximising output of OA and the allocatively efficient output of OC is shown in Figure 5. The total deadweight loss is LHJ. This can be broken down into a loss of consumer and producer surplus.

Figure 4

Monopoly and efficiency

A profit maximising monopolist will produce at output OA. This is lower than the productively efficient level of output of OB and also lower than the allocatively efficient level of output of OC.

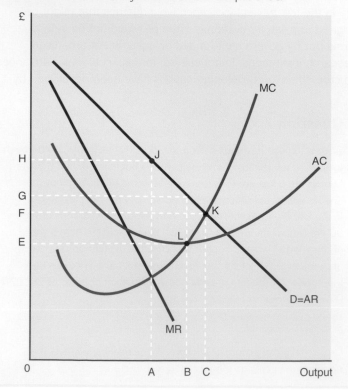

- Consumer surplus would have been TRJ if output was at OC, the allocatively efficient level of output. It now falls to SRH. So consumer surplus falls by TSHJ.
- Producer surplus would have been VTJL if output was at OC, the allocatively efficient level of output. It now rises to VSHL. Note that the monopolist has gained TSHM of producer surplus, which would have been consumer surplus if output had been at OC.

Total consumer and producer surplus at the allocatively efficient level of output OC is therefore the area VRJL. At the profit maximising level of output, it falls to VRHL. The loss of consumer and producer surplus, the deadweight loss of welfare due to monopoly, is therefore the triangle LHJ. This deadweight loss of welfare is made up of a loss of consumer surplus of MHJ and producer surplus of LMJ. Why would the monopolist produce at OA if it loses producer surplus of LMJ as a result? The answer is because it gains part of the surplus which consumers lost of TSHM and converts this into producer surplus. For the monopolist, the gain in producer surplus of TSHM outweighs the loss of producer surplus of LMJ.

Figure 5

Deadweight loss associated with monopoly

Compared to the allocatively efficient point of production at J, there will be a deadweight loss of welfare of LHJ if a monopolist produces at OA, the profit maximising level of output. Comparing output at OC with OA:
- consumer surplus falls by TSHJ;
- producer surplus rises by TSHM - LMJ;
- LMJ is a deadweight loss of producer surplus;
- MHJ is a deadweight loss of consumer surplus.

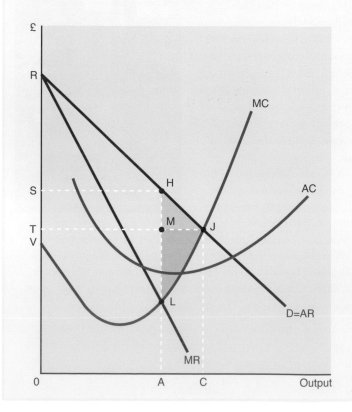

Natural monopoly

Pure monopolies arise for a number of reasons. One is that no single producer is able to exploit fully the potential economies of scale in the market. Hence, the single firm in the industry is always able to undercut any potential competitor in price and force them out of the industry if it so chooses. A monopoly arising from economies of scale is called a natural monopoly. Examples would be Network Rail or the electricity transmission system owned by National Grid.

A natural monopoly is shown in Figure 6. The monopolist will produce where MC = MR at output OB and earn abnormal profit by pricing at OF. However, making the industry more competitive would result in lower efficiency. Splitting the industry in two, for example, with each firm producing OA (half of OB), would increase the average cost of production from OE to OG. More competition in the industry would result in a loss of productive efficiency, not a gain. Also, producing at the allocative efficient level of output where price = MC would result in a loss for the firm. At output OC, average revenue is less than average cost. In the long run, a firm must at least make normal profit to stay in the industry. Hence in the long run, no firm in this industry would produce at the allocatively efficient level of production.

Multi-plant monopolists

A natural monopoly occurs when no single product is able to exploit fully the potential economies of scale in a market. However, monopolies can exist for a number of other reasons. For example, one firm might have bought up all the other firms in a market and then prevents new firms from entering the market through heavy advertising and other forms of promotion. Or it may have acquired a patent on a product or manufacturing process. If the monopolist is operating a large number of

different sites, each one of which is operating at the bottom of its average cost curve, then it is known as a **multi-plant monopolist**. This type of monopolist could be broken up by government to create a perfectly competitive industry.

If, in the long run, the multi-plant monopolist wished to expand output, it would do so not by expanding an existing plant but by building a new one. It would operate the plant at its most efficient scale, at the bottom of the plant's average cost curve. If it wanted to contract output in the long run it would close down a plant rather than maintain the same number of plants each producing at less than the most efficient scale of production. Hence, the long run average cost curve for a multi-plant monopolist is horizontal. It can increase or reduce output in the long run at the same minimum average cost.

The demand curve for the monopolist is downward sloping. The marginal cost curve will be the same as the average cost curve if the AC curve is horizontal (for the same reasons that AR = MR if average revenue is constant). Hence, the cost and revenue curves facing the multi-plant monopolist are as shown in Figure 7.

If the industry were perfectly competitive, it would produce where demand equals supply (i.e. where price is equal to marginal cost). If it is a monopoly, the firm will produce at its profit maximising position where MC = MR, and price on its demand or average revenue curve. Hence, under perfect competition, output will be at OB whilst price will be at OE. If the industry were a monopoly, long run output would fall to OA and price would rise to OF. This leads to the conclusion that output will be lower and price will be higher in monopoly than under perfect competition. The multi-plant monopolist is **allocatively inefficient**.

Figure 6

Natural monopoly

In a natural monopoly, economies of scale are so large that not even a single producer could fully exploit them. Competition would be highly inefficient, raising the average cost of production. The profit maximising level of output for the monopolist is OB, but output would be greater at OC where price = MC.

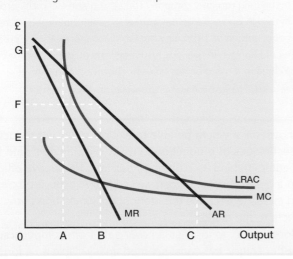

Figure 7

Deadweight loss if a perfectly competitive industry becomes a monopoly

If the industry were producing under conditions of perfect competition, price and output would occur where price = MC, at output OB and price OE. If the industry were a monopoly, output would be where MC = MR at OA whilst price would be on the demand curve at OF. Price is higher and output lower in the monopoly industry. The welfare loss is the shaded triangle.

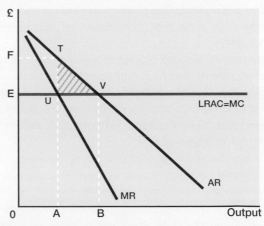

The welfare cost or deadweight loss associated with monopoly compared to perfect competition can be shown on the diagram. It is assumed that there are no externalities. The demand curve shows the marginal social benefit received by consumers of the product. The marginal cost curve is the marginal social cost curve, the cost to society of producing an extra unit of output. Consumers were prepared to pay OF for the extra unit at OA whilst it would only have cost OE to produce. Therefore the net social cost (the difference between social benefit and social cost) on the last unit of output is EF. Similarly the vertical distance between the demand curve and the average cost curve shows the net social cost of each unit not produced between OA, the monopoly output, and OB, the output under perfect competition. Hence the net social cost to society of multi-plant monopoly production compared to production under conditions of perfect competition is the shaded triangle TUV. This deadweight loss is a loss of consumer surplus. The rest of the consumer surplus lost, EFTU, is appropriated by the monopolist as increased producer surplus.

The net social cost might be even greater than this triangle for two reasons.

- The monopolist might have to create and maintain barriers to entry to keep potential competitors out of the industry. For instance, it might have to spend large sums of money on advertising or other promotions. This will increase its average and marginal cost in the long run. Output will then be even lower and price even higher than if it operated under the same cost conditions as perfect competition.
- The firm may be able to shelter behind barriers to entry and as a consequence inefficiency may result. X-inefficiency is the term used to describe inefficiencies which occur in large organisations which are not under pressure to minimise cost. Average costs will therefore be higher than under perfect competition, resulting in even lower output and even higher prices.

Innovation

So far, the analysis has been static. Perfect competition and monopoly have been compared at a point in time. However, there are also important **dynamic** considerations. The Austrian economist Joseph Schumpeter (1883-1950) argued that monopoly might be far more efficient over time than perfect competition.

Perfect competition is unlikely to be dynamically efficient because there is no incentive to innovate. Low entry barriers and perfect knowledge mean that competitors can quickly copy any innovation made.

Innovation could also be lacking in a monopoly market. A monopolist, safe behind high entry barriers, may choose to take the easy life. Sleepy and inefficient, it exploits the market and earns enough profits to satisfy shareholders. Research and development, which imply potential change, are unlikely to be a high priority for this type of firm.

Schumpeter, however, argued that the reverse was likely. The monopolist would have the resources from its abnormal profits to spend on research and development. In the UK, for instance, about 70 per cent of all investment is funded from retained profit. The monopolist would also have an incentive to spend

on innovation. It would be able to exploit any new products or new techniques of production to its own advantage, safe from competitors behind its high entry barriers. Productive efficiency would increase because costs would fall. Allocative efficiency would increase because the monopolist would bring new products to the market.

Moreover, a monopolist is never safe from competition. In the 18th century, the canal seemed unassailable as a form of

Table 1 Profits of PowerGen and National Power, £ million

	PowerGen	National Power
1991	£267m	£427m
1992	£326m	£525m
1993	£449m	£599m
1994	£477m	£734m

In 1991, the government privatised the electricity generation industry. When the industry had been owned by the government, it had operated as a single corporation. When the government sold it off, it was split into a considerable number of different companies including area companies selling electricity to local consumers and a single company which owned the national grid. Electricity generation - making electricity from fuels such as coal or nuclear power - was a multi-plant monopoly when it was a state-owned business. It was split at privatisation. Nuclear power remained in government control as did the Scottish generating company. However, the mainly coal-fired electricity power stations in England and Wales were split between two new companies, PowerGen and National Power.

After privatisation, the profits of the two generating companies soared as shown in Table 1.

Source: adapted from Alain Anderton, *Economics*, 5th Edition, Pearson

(a) Assume that, before privatisation, the electricity industry priced its product as if it were a perfectly competitive industry, earning only normal profits. Assume too that it was X-efficient (producing at the lowest cost possible). Using a diagram, explain (i) where the industry would have produced and (ii) whether this would have resulted in an efficient allocation of resources.

(b) Assume that after privatision, costs in the industry remain constant. (i) What do the figures in Table 1 indicate about normal and abnormal profit? (ii) Are resources now efficiently allocated?

(c) Assume that PowerGen and National Power were making abnormal profits in 1994 but that the industry had been X-inefficient when it was government owned before 1991. Assume also that PowerGen and National Power had succeeded in reducing costs considerably between 1991 and 1994. Would the industry have been more or less efficient in 1991 compared to 1994?

(d) In the long run, any company can become an electricity producer in the UK and sell into the market. If abnormal profits were being earned in 1994, (i) what would economic theory predict would happen in the next few years and (ii) would this be likely to lead to a more or less efficient allocation of resources?

Source: adapted from Alain Anderton, *Economics*, 5th Edition, Pearson.

industrial transport. Yet during the 19th century, the monopoly of canals and the monopoly profits of canal owners were destroyed by the coming of railways. In the 20th century, the same process turned railways into loss-making concerns as railway monopolists saw their markets taken away by the motor car and lorry. In the 21st century, broadband and the mobile phone have destroyed traditional monopolies over fixed line telephone connections. Schumpeter called this 'the process of **creative destruction**'. High barriers mean that potential competitors have to produce a substitute product which is radically better than the old. It is not good enough to add some fancy packaging or change the colour of the product or add a few gadgets. Therefore monopoly encourages fundamental rather than superficial progress. So Schumpeter argued that a system of monopoly markets was far more likely to produce efficiency over a period of time than perfect competition.

Evaluating monopoly

Profit maximising monopolists are neither productively nor allocatively efficient. They produce too little and charge too high a price. As a result, they are able to earn abnormal profit at the expense of customers. Consumer surplus is lower and producer surplus is higher than if the monopolist produced where price = MC, the allocatively efficient point of production.

However, productive and allocative efficiency is affected if the monopolist is a natural monopolist. If it is a natural monopolist, then potentially it can produce at lower average cost than if the industry contained two or more competing firms. Hence the natural monopolist will be more productively efficient than firms in competition. There will also be no attainable allocatively efficient level of output in the long run because at the point where price = marginal cost, the monopolist will make a loss.

However, monopolists may or may not be more dynamically efficient than an industry where there are competing firms. If investment is higher leading to more innovation, then there will be greater dynamic efficiency. However, the monopolist may choose not to invest more than is necessary to ensure short run profit maximisation. Instead, it may choose to reward its owners for example by paying out high dividends to shareholders. In this case, monopoly leads to no greater dynamic efficiency than a competitive industry.

The costs and benefits of monopoly can also be evaluated by looking at different stakeholders affected by monopoly.

Monopolist firms and their shareholders If monopolists profit maximise, then they will maximise the rewards for their owners, the shareholders. However, monopolists may not profit maximise for a number of reasons. They may be X-inefficient because of lack of competitive pressures and managers may profit satisfice. Monopolists could choose to revenue maximise or sales maximise because managers gain greater rewards from this strategy than profit maximisation. Equally, if the market is contestable, the monopolist may choose to earn only normal profit to discourage new entrants to the industry.

Employees A profit maximising monopolist will produce at a lower output than either an allocatively efficient level of output or one where competing firms would produce if the monopolist could be split up into a number of different firms. If it produces

Trademarks are an important way for businesses to defend their intellectual property. Trademarks such as Coca-Cola, Apple and Chanel are worth millions if not billions of pounds because of their associations with consumers. Defending trademarks is therefore very important to any company whose trademarks are recognisable to their customers. Several high-profile international businesses have recently successfully defended their trademarks from incursions by rival businesses. Among them is luxury fashion designer Giorgio Armani, which stopped the registration of the trademark 'Benjamin Armani' by a retailer of baby buggies, high chairs and children's car seats. Another, Syco Entertainment, Simon Cowell's TV production company and owner of the X-Factor reality television show, also successfully challenged a trademark application by jewellery retailer SGI Jewellery for the registration of the trademark 'Little Mix' - the name of one of the show's winning acts. In sport, Chelsea Football Club was challenged by menswear retailer Chelsea Man for the use of the trademark Chelsea for its sport-clothing apparel.

Source: adapted from © the *Financial Times* 16.6.2014, All Rights Reserved.

Discuss whether a system of trademarks, where businesses are given monopoly rights to use a brand name, benefits firms, employees and consumers.

at a lower level of output, it will employ fewer workers.

On the other hand, assuming a divorce of ownership from control, directors and senior managers may choose to produce at a higher level of output and profit satisfice rather than profit maximise. Directors and senior managers would then be able to take higher pay and bonuses from the company than if it were profit maximising. More workers would also be employed at a higher level of output. Employees could also benefit if the firm were run inefficiently. If this inefficiency took the form of paying higher wages than the market rate, then employees would be better off.

Consumers If the monopolist profit maximises, then output will be lower and prices higher compared to a competitive industry. So consumers will pay higher prices. Some consumers could be better off, however, if the monopolist price discriminates as explained in Unit 50, although other consumers could be even worse off. If the monopoly is a natural monopoly, consumers could benefit even if the monopolist maximises profits. Splitting the firm into two or more competing firms might produce such high marginal and average costs of production that prices are higher under competition than under a profit maximising monopolist. Whether or not consumers would be better off depends on the shape of the cost and revenue curves: how much abnormal profit will the profit maximising monopolist make compared to the cost of less efficient production in an industry with competing firms?

Suppliers For suppliers, the impact of a monopolist will depend on the extent to which the monopolist is also a monopsonist. For example, a supplier might sell to a monopolist but these sales could be only a fraction of its total sales. If it lost sales to the monopolist, then revenues could fall but it would be relatively insignificant. In this situation, the monopolist can exert little pressure on a supplier to reduce prices and its profits. On the other hand, the monopolist might be the most important customer of the supplier or be the only customer. If the monopolist is also a monopsonist, then it can exert downward pressure on prices to suppliers, transferring profit that suppliers could have made to its own profits.

This analysis has concentrated on short term costs and benefits to do with prices, output and profit. In the long term, costs and benefits will depend on the ability of monopolists to innovate. If they fail to innovate and completely new products remove their monopoly, then all the stakeholders will lose out. For example, the displacement of rail travel by car travel in the 20th century led to lower profits for railway companies, many lines closed, fewer jobs in the industry, fewer orders for suppliers and remaining rail customers being offered fewer choices of destination. Successful innovation, however, will tend to benefit all stakeholders. Shareholders will continue to earn profits, employees will see their jobs safeguarded, consumers will get new products and suppliers will keep supplying the monopolist.

Evaluating monopoly against competition is even more complicated because of the theory of the second best.

The theory of the second best

An economy will be economically efficient if all markets are perfectly competitive. Therefore it might seem like common sense to argue that economic efficiency will be increased in an economy where there are many instances of market failure, if at least some markets can be made perfectly competitive and market distortions removed.

In the late 1950s, Richard Lipsey and Kelvin Lancaster (1956-7) published an article entitled 'On the General Theory of the Second Best'. They assumed an economy where some firms were not pricing at marginal cost. They then showed that a move towards marginal cost pricing by one firm might lead to an an increase in efficiency, but equally it could lead to a decrease in efficiency. The radical conclusion was that introducing marginal cost pricing could lead to efficiency losses rather than efficiency gains.

For instance, consider Figure 8. It shows two industries. The food industry is assumed to be monopolistic. Output is set at OA where MC = MR (the profit maximising condition) and price is then set at OP on the average revenue or demand curve. The entertainment industry is perfectly competitive. Output is at OF where marginal cost equals price. Assume that resources were transferred from the entertainment industry to the food industry such that output in the food industry rose to OB whilst output in the entertainment industry fell to OE. The welfare gain in the food industry, shown by the difference between demand and marginal cost, is the shaded area on the graph. This is larger than the welfare loss in the entertainment industry, shown by the shaded triangle. Hence in this case there is a net welfare gain if there is a move away from perfect competition in the entertainment industry.

Figure 8

Resource allocation in an imperfect market

If some markets are imperfectly competitive or a monopoly, there could be efficiency gains if resources are transferred from a perfectly competitive market to the imperfectly competitive market or the monopoly. The loss of efficiency in the entertainment market, shown by the shaded area, is less than the gain in welfare in the food market in this example.

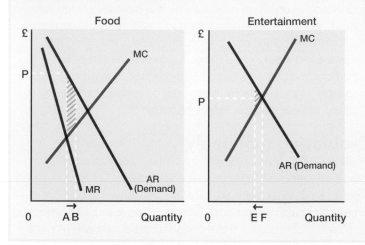

It can be shown that, in general, efficiency can be increased by transferring resources to industries where price is far in excess of marginal cost from industries where it is less so or where demand is less than marginal cost. Efficiency is likely to be achieved where the difference between price and marginal cost is the same throughout an economy.

This is a very important conclusion. Every economy suffers from market failure. It will never be the case that marginal cost can equal price across all sectors of the economy. Therefore simple rules or slogans such as 'competition good, monopoly bad' are unlikely to lead to good economic policy making. What the theory of the second best suggests is that distortions within an economy need to be evened out as far as possible. Eliminating them in some markets but allowing them to remain high in others could well lead to less efficiency overall than decreasing them in markets where they are high but actually increasing them in markets where distortions are low.

Key Terms

Creative destruction - a process where firms produce or create innovative new products that replace or destroy existing products in the market; for example the internet has led to a significant shift of spending from bricks and mortar high street shops to online shopping.

Multi-plant monopolist - the sole producer in an industry but where production takes place at a number of different sites or plants, each of which could be sold off to provide competition in the industry.

Thinking like an economist

Eating out

Demand for food and drink consumed outside the home is booming. The market is crowded with suppliers. There are chains like McDonald's, Pret, Costa Coffee or JD Wetherspoon. But equally there are thousands of small firms serving local markets. Enzo Moschetta, for example, began selling his French bread and pastries in Brick Lane market in 2009. It was a down-market location for an up-market product, but it was a success. In 2013, he expanded to take a pitch in nearby Bow at the Roman Road street market.

It could be argued that this is an example of a monopolistically competitive market. Barriers to entry are low. Enzo Moschetta, for example, had to buy the equipment to make his French bread and pastries but he didn't have the costs of renting or buying premises to sell his produce. A market stall was enough. So financial barriers are low. There are many small firms in the market and even big chains like McDonald's only have a few per cent of the UK market. Each firm is selling a slightly different product and so has some control over the price at which they sell. However, that market power is weak.

Would consumers be better off if the market were perfectly competitive, an oligopoly or a monopoly? If it were perfectly competitive, each firm would sell an identical product. Consumers would lack choice which, arguably, is highly valued in the eating-out market. A hamburger is not a good substitute for a French pastry. Consumers might get slightly lower prices because economic theory suggests that monopolistically competitive firms are not productively efficient, i.e. do not produce at the bottom of their average cost curve. However, choice is arguably more important than a slightly lower price. Also, big chains like McDonald's or JD Wetherspoon are highly cost-efficient. They have to be to offer the low prices that are part of their attraction to customers.

If the market were an oligopoly, there would be choice. However, prices would probably be higher because oligopolistic firms would seek to use their market power to earn abnormal profit. Choice, too, probably would be more restricted. If a national chain, for example, could gain 25 per cent of the market, they would service it by opening more outlets, not by offering more choice.

If the market were a monopoly, again prices would be higher because of abnormal profit and choice would be restricted. Given the costs involved to firms in the eating-out market, it is likely that economies of scale are fairly limited. If they were very large, a firm like McDonald's would have driven local fish and chip or burger shops out of the market a long time ago. So, large chains, whilst enjoying some cost advantages over small independent outlets, do not have such a big cost advantage as to drive small firms out of the market.

It can also be argued that there is dynamic efficiency. One way in which food outlets compete is through innovation, providing a product which is new and differentiated from rivals. That might mean a better food product, or better service or a better design for the outlet itself. Enzo Moschetta, for example, is providing competition to G Kelly on Roman Road. G Kelly was opened in 1937 providing traditional pie and mash. For decades, it was one of the only dining-out options in the area. Today, with competition from the likes of Enzo Moschetta and outlets in the giant Westfield shopping mall close by, competition is fierce. Sue Venning, the owner of G Kelly, said: 'In the 1970s our shop was one of the very few takeaway shops and we were extremely busy. Now there is more choice.'

Source: with information from © the *Financial Times* 12.7.2014, All Rights Reserved.

Data Response Question

King of the castle

When Lego decided to launch an online game, it spent years planning and perfecting Lego Universe until its launch in 2010. But the game quickly fell flat and was killed off 18 months later, at a cost of about 115 jobs. Around the same time, Markus Persson, a Swedish games developer, put out a test version of a game that he had developed in his spare time. That game became Minecraft, a game which allows users to build whatever they want using digital building blocks. Minecraft is the biggest-selling PC game in history.

In its 2013 annual report, Lego estimated that if all the world's Lego were shared out between the Earth's population, every person would have 94 bricks.

Figure 9

Lego sales

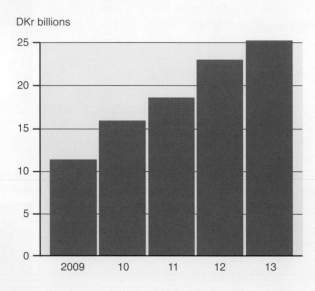

Figure 10

Lego profit (operating income)

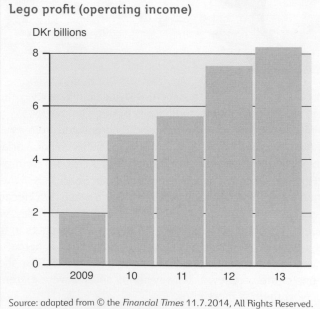

Figure 11

Lego: number of employees

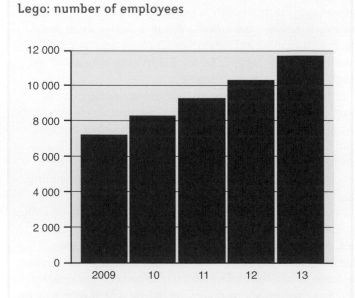

The Lego formula appears simple: take plastic costing less than $1 per kilogramme and transform it into sets based on *Star Wars*, *Legends of Chima* or *The Hobbit* and sell the plastic for about $75 per kilogramme. However, reality is much more complex. A look at the recently released Simpsons House, based on the cartoon television series, shows why. The $200 set includes mini figures of the entire family, including mother Marge with her distinctive blue beehive. 'The big blue hair. That is a bit of a costly element to manufacture to be quite honest but it is also a very special element', says Jørgen Knudstorp, Chief Executive of Lego. So the designer is basically told: 'You get that, but in the rest of the set we want to see a fairly standard execution.' That means the designer needs to use bricks from other sets to keep costs down. Professor Robertson, of the University of Pennsylvania's Wharton School, says DK1m ($182 600) is the 'magic number' for bricks. If a single element - say a red brick with two rows of four studs - makes more than DK1m in all the sets it is in, the profit rises almost exponentially over that sum: if it sells less than that, a loss is guaranteed.

In 2004, Lego was in deep crisis. Children were turning away from playing with physical toys to spend more time playing computer games. New product launches were not particularly successful whilst costs were rising. By 2014, the company had been transformed. Annual sales growth between 2008 and 2014 averaged 20 per cent. Its new range launches had proved much more successful. For example, its *Friends* range, aimed at girls (traditionally Lego is played more by boys than girls), was a big seller. Its Ninjago and *Legends of Chima* ranges proved

a big hit with customers. It also altered its previous policy to produce ranges tied in with characters whose copyright was owned by other companies. For example, it launched ranges centred round *Star Wars*, *Harry Potter* and *The Hobbit*.

Jørgen Knudstorp became Chief Executive of Lego in 2004. He has transformed the company, partly by being open to different ways of gaining sales revenue for Lego. Traditionally, Lego attempted to keep everything in-house, refusing, for example, to make ranges linked to characters whose copyright was owned by other companies. Today, it recognises that it has great expertise in making and selling physical bricks but not necessarily in inventing characters, producing computer games or making films. Jørgen Knudstorp said in 2014: 'What we're finding is that if you are very good at writing books, you are not necessarily the best to turn that book into a great movie. You need somebody who makes movies … and in our case we need partners who can translate the physical Lego experience into the digital experience.' Lego has teamed with TT Games, a British games developer, to make video games from Lego ranges such as *Star Wars* and *Chima*. Many have become best sellers and Lego has had success too with online games. It also partnered with Warner Bros to make *The Lego Movie*, which was the seventh highest grossing film of 2014, generating close to $500 million in sales globally.

The digital layer is making Lego's product launches more complex. When *The Lego Movie* was released, Lego had to organise the design and production of physical construction sets, a video game and a website. These merchandising tie-ins have long been a highly profitable part of film releases by film companies such as Disney and DreamWorks.

1. Explain the link between copyright and monopoly, giving examples from the data.

2. Explain, using a diagram and examples from the data, whether a monopoly can be both productively and allocatively efficient.

3. Using the data and your own knowledge, discuss the extent to which monopolies benefit their customers.

Evaluation

In your answer, you need to analyse the advantages and disadvantages for customers of monopolies, including diagrams. The evaluation will come partly from giving examples of each of these advantages and disadvantages for individual products and firms and illustrating their relative importance. Are the advantages and disadvantages the same, for example, for a toy manufacturer and a gas pipeline company?

56 Government intervention and product markets

Starter activity

Every year, households in the UK receive a bill from their local water company to pay for water and sewage treatment. The water company is a monopoly supplier - households don't get any choice about the company from which they buy these services. Government regulates water companies. If there were no regulation, how might water companies behave economically? If there is regulation, how could government regulate private sector water companies, given that it needs them to provide a vital service to households?

Controlling monopolies

Figure 1 shows the cost and revenue curves of a monopolist. A profit maximising monopolist would produce at output OA. This is neither productively efficient nor allocatively efficient. Productive efficiency would be achieved at the output OB, where the firm is producing at the bottom of its average cost curve. Allocative efficiency would be achieved at the output OC, where price = marginal cost. Profit maximising monopolists earn abnormal profit at the expense of their customers, reducing consumer surplus and expropriating some of it as increased producer surplus. Producing below the allocatively efficient level of output also produces a deadweight welfare loss.

It can therefore be argued that governments should control monopolies or firms with significant monopoly power. There is a variety of different possible ways in which this could be done.

Price controls or price regulation One method would be to introduce price controls. The maximum price that a monopolist could charge would be set equal to the marginal social cost of production. Thus there would be allocative efficiency in the market (P = MC). The effect of price controls is shown in Figure 2. Without price controls, the monopolist faces a normal downward sloping demand (= average revenue) curve and a normal downward sloping marginal revenue curve. Its profit maximising level of output is OA and its profit maximising price is OF. There is allocative efficiency if the price were OE which is where P = MC. So OE is the maximum price that the government must impose on the monopolist to ensure there is allocative efficiency in the market. At output levels from O to B,

the average revenue curve, which is the price curve, becomes horizontal. The marginal revenue curve between O and B is the same as the average revenue curve because each additional unit sold is sold at the same maximum price of OE. The monopolist can sell more than OB but then the price it receives will fall because the demand curve is downward sloping. There is a discontinuity for the marginal revenue curve at output OB because selling an additional unit of output means that all output of OB plus the extra unit will have to be sold at a lower price. Hence the marginal revenue of the OB plus one unit is much lower than the marginal revenue of the OBth unit sold at the maximum price.

Price controls are one of the main methods used by the UK government to regulate privatised monopolies. In 2015, for example, there were price controls on some train fares and on

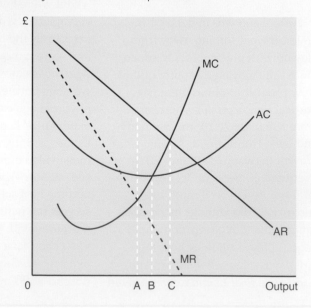

Figure 1

A monopoly

A profit maximising monopolist would produce at output OA. But this is below the productively efficient level of output of OB and the allocatively efficient level of output of OC.

Figure 2

Price controls in a monopoly industry

Fixing a maximum price for a monopolist makes the average and marginal revenue curves horizontal for part of these curves. It results in higher output at 0B and a lower price of 0E compared to the profit maximising outcomes, of 0A and 0F respectively.

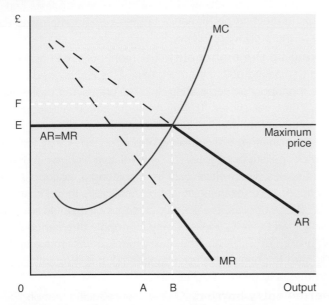

water supply. However, critics argue that it is difficult for the government to know where the cost and revenue curves lie and what is the allocatively efficient level of output. Price controls can also lead to dynamic inefficiency. If the monopolist were prepared to increase investment if they were allowed to operate at the profit maximising level of output, then future output might be higher or be at a lower price if investment increased future productive efficiency.

Profit controls or profit regulation Another method of controlling monopolists is to fix a maximum level of profit that they can earn. The government should set a level of profit such that the monopolist makes no more profit than if the industry were perfectly competitive. In practice, this is done by calculating what should be the operating costs of the monopolist and adding a rate of return (or rate of profit) on capital employed.

Rate of return regulation has been extensively used in the USA to control utility companies such as electricity and water companies. There is a number of problems, however, with the approach.

- It requires regulators to have a good understanding of costs and rates of return in the industry. The monopolist has an incentive to predict to regulators that future costs will be higher. The monopolist therefore attempts to create a situation where there is asymmetric information: the monopolist has more information than the regulator. If the regulator accepts industry forecasts, then the monopolist will be allowed to earn more profit than it would if it had accurately predicted costs.
- Monopolists have little incentive to minimise costs. If they are allowed to cover their costs and earn a profit on capital

Question 1

Ofwat, the water regulator, has confirmed details of agreements with 18 water companies across England and Wales. Average bills over the next five years have been set at the rate of inflation (RPI) minus five per cent. So bills in real terms will fall, but in nominal terms they may raise depending on the rate of inflation. Thames Water, the country's biggest water company, had wanted Ofwat to allow it to increase its bills by three per cent plus inflation. This was rejected by Ofwat. In fixing prices, Ofwat has lowered the estimated rate of profit on capital employed that water companies will earn from 3.85 per cent to 3.74 per cent.

The promise of lower prices in real terms follows criticism from politicians and consumer groups that many privately owned water companies have profited unfairly from much lower than expected borrowing costs during the current five-year settlement, running from 2010-14. Tony Smith, chief executive of the Consumer Council for Water, the independent body representing water customers, said: 'It's been the best process for the customer than any price review since privatising. Ofwat has been generous to the sector over several previous reviews.'

Thames Water customers are still expected to be hit during the period with additional price increases to pay for the building and financing costs of the Thames 'super-sewer', a £4.2-billion project designed to prevent regular overflows of untreated sewage into the capital's river. The cost of that project could eventually add £80 annually to Thames Water customer bills.

Source: adapted from © the *Financial Times* 12.12.2014, All Rights Reserved.

(a) Water companies in England and Wales are monopoly private sector suppliers of water and sewage services to households. Explain why they might need regulating.

(b) Ofwat fixes prices for households by allowing water companies to change their bills on an RPI plus or minus formula. Using the data, explain what this means.

(c) Why might water companies earn abnormal profit even though their prices are being regulated?

employed, then it doesn't matter to the monopolist whether costs are £100 million or £110 million. The costs will be covered by the customer.

- Monopolists have an incentive to employ too much capital. If they are being awarded a percentage rate of return on capital, the more capital employed, the higher the amount of profit earned. For example, if the monopolist is allowed to earn a 10 per cent return on capital employed, it will earn twice the profit if it has capital employed of £2 billion than if it has only £1 billion employed.

Quality standards A profit maximising monopolist is focussed on profit and not quality. Monopolists that provide high-quality products only do so because this allows them to maximise profits. If the way to maximise profits is to produce poor-quality products, then the customer will receive poor-quality products. Where quality is an issue, governments can intervene by setting quality standards. For example, in the

UK the Post Office has a legal obligation to deliver letters on a daily basis to rural areas despite the fact that deliveries to rural areas are loss making. Electricity generators may be forced to have enough capacity to prevent blackouts occurring.

It is in any monopolist's interests to resist the imposition of quality standards. One way for them to do this is to suggest self-regulation, discussed below. Another is to lobby hard to water down any quality standards so compliance becomes much less costly. Monopolists will also argue that they will be providing products with quality standards in the future and so regulation now is unnecessary. Governments need to have both political will and an understanding of the industry to impose meaningful quality standards on a monopolist that is only interested in making profit.

Performance targets Performance targets are similar to quality standards. Government sets targets for a variety of different outputs from a firm. This could be about prices charged, the quality of the product or degrees of customer choice, for example. It could set targets for costs of production. Performance targets are used in the UK for rail travel, for example. Train companies are given targets for the percentage of trains that arrive on time. Monopolists will resist the imposition of performance targets, especially if not meeting them results in bad publicity and regulatory fines. Where performance targets are imposed, monopolists will attempt to find ways to 'game the system'. For trains, for example, one way of increasing the percentage of trains arriving on time is to change the train timetable so that train journeys become officially longer. If the target doesn't cover intermediate stations on a journey but only the start and finish stations, train companies can increase the journey time just for the last leg of the journey. Adding five minutes to travel time between the last two stations on a journey might significantly improve punctuality data, even if trains are frequently late arriving at the other stations on the journey. As with quality standards, it requires considerable political will and understanding of the industry to successfully impose performance targets. Performance targets might also have to be changed frequently as monopolists find ways round meeting performance targets without improving the quality of the product provided.

Breaking up the monopolist The monopolist can be broken up into competing units by government. This is designed to reduce monopoly power leading to lower prices and profits and greater customer choice. This might be an effective solution for a multi-plant monopolist with a large number of plants, where the minimum efficient scale of production is very low, but most monopolists or oligopolists have relative high minimum efficient scales. The welfare gain from splitting a monopolist into a duopoly, for example, might be negligible. In the case of natural monopolies, breaking up a monopolist would almost certainly lead to welfare losses. Any monopoly threatened with being broken up will lobby the government, other firms and the public hard to prevent this from happening. It is often difficult for governments to resist this pressure.

Lowering entry barriers One way of reducing monopoly power is for the government to reduce barriers to entry in the hope that other firms will enter the market and overturn the monopoly. If there are legal barriers, governments can remove these (this is called deregulation and is discussed below). If there are marketing barriers, governments can restrict a firm's ability to market. For example, with medical drugs, governments can forbid doctors from attending conferences in holiday destinations where drug companies pay all the doctors' expenses for the trip. If there are financial barriers, the government can help to organise finance for new entrants. However, if the monopoly is a natural monopoly, the government cannot do anything about the nature of costs in the industry.

Windfall taxes Where monopolists make particularly large abnormal profits, governments can impose windfall taxes. These are taxes that are imposed after the event has occurred. Windfall taxes tend to be arbitrary and therefore are not a good long-term solution to regulation of profit maximising monopolies. If windfall taxes become a feature of the economic and political system, firms such as banks, that suffer, will attempt to reduce their reported profits artificially.

Privatisation and nationalisation If the monopolist is state owned, the firm can be **privatised**. This means that it is sold off to private sector owners. Privatisation in itself does not lead to the break-up of a monopoly or any extra competition in the market. However, free market economists might argue that privatisation in itself will increase efficiency. This is because, although a privatised monopoly might substantially increase profits, it is also likely to reduce costs. For free market economists, this is because nationalised industries are always productively inefficient. Privatisation will lead to reduced costs of production as the monopolist seeks to raise profit. The monopolist will then offer lower prices to customers and a

Question 2

Train punctuality has fallen to its worst level in five years, according to ORR, the regulator for the rail industry. In a damning report on the performance of Network Rail, which owns the rail infrastructure in the UK, it said that in the first seven months of a new five-year funding period beginning in April, 50 000 more trains were late than there should have been. Overall punctuality at a national level was 89.1 per cent, 0.7 per cent short of target and a drop of 1.5 per cent from levels a year ago. Punctuality is defined as a train arriving at its terminating stop within five minutes of schedule for commuter services and 10 minutes for long-distance services.

Network Rail is planning to invest £35 billion in the five years to 2019. ORR said Network Rail had missed 11 out of 44 regulated milestones for improvement. The regulator said this raised 'serious questions as to how the company will deliver the ambitious programme expected in the next five years, particularly the electrification projects.'

Thirteen out of 18 franchised operators, the companies running the trains, were exceeding targets for cancellations and severe lateness.

Source: adapted from © the *Financial Times* 21.11.2014, All Rights Reserved.

Discuss, using examples from the data, whether the quality of services provided by monopolists can be controlled by setting them performance targets.

better-quality product because the efficiency savings they make far outweigh any extra profit they earn.

The argument can be reversed. Interventionist economists might argue that private sector monopolies will always damage the interests of their customers because they charge too high prices and produce too little. **Nationalisation**, the taking into state ownership of private assets, will solve this problem. A nationalised monopolist will be able to operate for the benefit of customers and not private shareholders. Prices can fall and output can increase. Costs need not rise so long as government places the right management in charge of the nationalised company.

Deregulation Deregulation is the process of removing government controls from markets.
- The government may allow private firms to compete in a market which is currently being supplied by a state monopoly. An example of this would be if the government allowed private firms to compete with letter delivery against a state-owned postal service.
- The government may lift regulations which prevent competition between private firms. For instance, the government may limit the number of premises in a local area which can be used for the sale of pharmaceutical drugs. Deregulation could then lead to the abolition of this licensing system, with any retailer free to sell drugs from its premises.
- The government may lift regulations when an industry is privatised. For instance, when coal was privatised in the UK, the regulation that no private coal mine could employ more than 10 workers was abolished.

Deregulation attempts to improve economic efficiency through the promotion of competition. This, it is argued, will lower costs (leading to greater productive efficiency) whilst reducing prices and increasing output (increasing allocative efficiency). A major problem with deregulation is that it encourages 'creaming' of markets (firms only providing services in the most profitable areas of the market). For instance, in the bus industry, deregulated in the 1980s, bus firms concentrated on providing bus services on profitable urban routes into town centres, arguably to the detriment of country passengers.

Subsidies Economic theory suggests that one way of creating allocative efficiency in a monopolistic market is to subsidise the monopolist. At any given level of output, the government could subsidise production, reducing marginal cost. If the government wishes the monopolist to produce where MC = price, it will need to find out the level of output where the marginal cost curve cuts the average revenue curve before a subsidy is given. In Figure 3, this occurs at output level OB where MC_1 = AR. The size of the subsidy required on the last unit of output is EF. This shifts the marginal cost curve to MC_2. The monopolist produces OB because this is now the level of production where MC = MR, and society benefits because production is at a level where the true cost to society, MC_1, is equal to price. The government can recoup that subsidy by taxing away the profits made by the monopolist.

This seems an ideal solution. Unfortunately there is a number of practical problems. First, giving subsidies to private sector monopolists is likely to be politically impossible for any

Figure 3

Subsidising a monopolist to improve efficiency

A profit maximising monopolist will produce at OA where MC_1 = MR and price is OG. Output under perfect competition would be at OB, where price = MC_1. A subsidy of EF on the last unit of output would shift the marginal cost curve downwards from MC_1 to MC_2. The monopolist would now produce at the perfect competition level of output. The government could recoup the subsidy by a tax on profits.

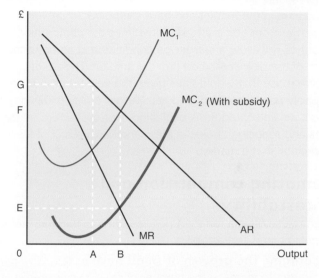

government. It is difficult enough for governments to subsidise nationalised industries. Second, the policy requires an accurate knowledge of cost and revenue curves. When the policy is first imposed, there is some chance that a reasonable guess can be made. However, subsidies distort the market so that in the long term it becomes very difficult to guess where hypothetical points on the curves might be. Third, it has already been discussed in detail whether allocative efficiency would increase by moving to a price = MC level of output in one industry. Imposing subsidies assumes that there is clear understanding of what the efficiency maximising level of output and price might be.

Self-regulation When monopolists come under threat of regulation by government, they tend to suggest that self-regulation would be a far better solution to any concerns the government may have. Self-regulation means that firms establish their own standards or **codes of practice** and promise to keep to those standards and codes. There may also be some 'independent' body that has the power to investigate breaches of regulation and even impose fines. Self-regulation is relatively common. In the UK for example, there are codes of practice in the food manufacturing industry, production of alcoholic drink and the newspaper industry. From a government viewpoint, it means that there is no need to pass legislation and industries police themselves rather than the government having to pay workers to enforce regulations. However, self-regulation tends to be very weak in terms of influencing firms. They have every incentive to 'game the system'. For example, independent bodies set up to investigate breaches of the code will be staffed by workers employed by the firms that are being investigated.

Codes of practice will be drawn up with vague wish lists but few enforceable policies. Where defined courses of action are agreed to, these will be as minimal as possible. The ideal code of practice for a firm is one where it does not require it to change its behaviour.

Merger policy Another way of controlling monopolies is to prevent their creation in the first place. All developed countries now have laws and regulations which cover the mergers between two or more firms. Competitions authorities will investigate large mergers which will significantly reduce competition in the market and have the power to prevent the merger from going ahead. Sometimes the competition authorities will allow a merger on condition that some of the assets of the new combined firm are sold off. The assets sold are those that would have given the new firm too much monopoly power in given markets. Merger policy is designed to prevent amalgamated firms exploiting their customers by raising prices and reducing choice in the market as a result of less competition in the market.

Promoting competition and contestability

Governments have a range of policies open to them to promote competition and contestability.

Encouraging the growth of small businesses Government can attempt to increase the number of small businesses in order to increase competition in the market. For example, government can give training and grants to potential new entrepreneurs. It can threaten to withdraw welfare payments for unemployed workers who fail to get a job unless they become self-employed (the self-employed are workers who run their own one-person business). Governments can also encourage the growth of existing small businesses by giving tax incentives or subsidies. For example, small businesses may pay a lower rate of tax on profits than larger businesses.

Anti-competitive practices Firms have a long history of engaging in anti-competitive practices. These are arrangements that seek to limit competition in a market. For example:

- a number of firms may create a cartel, colluding to fix high prices for contracts and allocate those contracts between themselves;
- firms may refuse to supply a product to a customer unless the customer buys other products at a high price from the firm;
- a monopolist may engage in predatory pricing, lowering the price of its product if a new entrant comes into the market: the low price means that the new entrant makes a loss; when the new entrant leaves the market, the monopolist puts back its prices to their old levels;
- a manufacturer may refuse to supply retailers that seek to sell those products at low prices; the aim is to prevent the manufacturer's profit margins being eroded by suppliers who want to negotiate lower priced contracts for the goods from the manufacturer.

Anti-competitive practices are illegal in both the EU and the USA. However, anti-competitive practices are quite common because firms believe they will not be found out or prosecuted. Equally, if the fine for engaging in anti-competitive practices is a fraction of the extra profit that can be made from such practices, then there is a strong financial incentive for firms to engage in illegal activities. Strengthening laws, prosecuting offenders more and imposing larger fines therefore can increase competition in an industry. This should lower prices and increase consumer choice.

Deregulation Deregulation, explained above, is a way of removing monopoly power. It is also, therefore, a way of increasing competition in an industry.

Lowering other barriers to entry Government regulations are a legal barrier to entry to a market. Deregulation is therefore a way of reducing legal barriers to entry. However, government can also lower other entry barriers through their policies. For example, if finance is a barrier to entry, the government could set up a scheme where it guaranteed loans by banks to small businesses setting up. If marketing is a barrier to entry, the government could set up training courses to help small businesses market their products better. Lowering barriers to entry should put downward pressure on prices and increase choice for customers.

Competitive tendering The government has to provide certain goods and services because they are public goods such as defence or goods which have significant positive externalities in consumption such as education. However, this does not imply that the state has to be the producer of all or part of these goods and services. For instance, in the UK, the

Question 3

In December 2012, Cineworld, the operator of 79 cinemas in the UK, announced it was buying Picturehouse, the owner of 21 cinemas, for £47 million. Cineworld tends to operate multiplexes with screens showing the latest Hollywood blockbusters. Picturehouse tends to show lower-budget independent and foreign movies.

Cineworld argued that there was no overlap between the two chains. Each was showing different films. However, the merger was investigated by the Competition Commission (now the Competition & Markets Authority). Alasdair Smith, deputy chairman of the Competition Commission, said, following the investigation, that 'when setting the price of tickets, exhibitors (cinemas) take account of the prices of competing cinemas operating in their local area'. The Competition Commission allowed the merger to take place but ordered that Cineworld sell either a Cineworld or Picturehouse cinema in three locations (Aberdeen, Bury St Edmunds and Cambridge) where there was an existing Cineworld cinema.

After arguing against the ruling, Cineworld sold the three required cinemas in 2014 and 2015.

Source: adapted from www.gov.uk/government/news/; © the *Financial Times* 20.8.2014, All Rights Reserved.

(a) Explain, using the data as an example, why a merger might give the newly created firm greater monopoly power.

(b) Why might this greater monopoly power harm customer interests?

Question 4

German sausage makers have been fined €388 million. Germany's federal cartel authority has found that some of the country's most successful sausage producers have colluded for decades to fix prices of sausages and related products. The cartel has been called the Atlantic Circle - named after Hamburg's Hotel Atlantic where the sausage producers first met. According to the cartel authority, 21 producers and 33 individuals will share the fine. The cartel office said it was tipped off about the price fixing. Eleven companies co-operated with the investigation, which helped reduce their fines. Other companies face individual fines running to the higher millions of euros. The country's largest sausage producer, ZUER-Mühlen-Gruppe, which owns the Böklunder and Könecke brands, said yesterday it planned to contest the fines and denied the allegations.

Source: adapted from © the *Financial Times* 16.7.2014, All Rights Reserved.

Explain, using a diagram and the data as an example, (a) what is meant by a cartel and (b) how a cartel might fix higher prices in the market.

state has not made the sheets that are in NHS hospitals, or the tanks that are used in the British army. They are produced by private sector firms and sold to the public sector. In theory, a government could contract out provision of all goods and services provided. It could employ private firms to operate everything from roads to hospitals to the army. **Contracting out** in itself will not necessarily increase competition in a market. If the government contracts out a good or service to the same firm every time, then the firm effectively becomes the monopoly supplier to the government for that good or service. This may occur, for example, where there is only one supplier in a country and the government does not want the contract to go to a foreign company, perhaps for security reasons or because it wants to maintain jobs and incomes in the country. However, it can introduce competition through **competitive tendering** of contracts. This is where the government draws up a specification for the good or service and invites private sector firms to bid for the contract to deliver it. The firm offering the lowest price, subject to quality guarantees, wins the contract.

Privatisation Privatisation in itself does not necessarily increase competition in a market. For example, a nationalised firm could be privatised as a single firm and legal barriers to entry to the market could remain high. Privatisation will only increase competition if either the nationalised firm is split up into competing firms or if barriers to entry are lowered sufficiently to encourage new entrants into the market.

Government intervention to protect suppliers

Some firms have monopsony powers. They are a significant buyer or perhaps the sole buyer of products from a supplier. This means they have considerable market power to reduce the prices they pay to their supplier. To prevent exploitation of suppliers, governments have a number of possible policies.

- They can pass anti-monopsony laws which make certain practices illegal.

- They can appoint an independent regulator which has powers to force monopsonists to change their buying practices through a code of practice, possibly with the threat of large fines.
- They can encourage monopsonists to regulate themselves, drawing up their own code of practice.

Self-regulation is by the far the weakest of these three options. Monopsonists are likely to draw up a code of practice which allows them to continue to exploit their suppliers. Independent regulators are potentially a far better solution. However, to be successful, independent regulators must be genuinely independent: not, for example, run by monopsonist representatives. They must be able to force monopsonists to hand over information about their relations with suppliers. They must also be able to impose large enough fines for them to be a deterrent to misbehaving in future.

Government intervention to protect employees

Employees of firms are vulnerable to exploitation. Profit maximising firms, for example, wish to pay the lowest possible wage, give as few benefits as possible and spend as little as possible on the working environment. The market itself will provide some protection to employees. Workers can choose not to be employed by firms with a poor reputation on issues such as wages or health and safety. However, it has long been recognised that workers need government protection from employers. This can be achieved in a number of different ways.

- Legal protection is extensive under both UK and EU law. This includes legislation on health and safety at work, employment contracts, maximum hours at work, redundancy procedures and the right to belong to a trade union. Firms can be prosecuted for breaking the law whilst individual employees in the UK can sue for compensation in industrial tribunals.
- Trade unions give their members significant protection from employers. The role of government is to create a legal framework within which trade unions can operate.
- Government can encourage firms to draw up codes of conduct relating to employment practices. As with all voluntary codes of conduct, this is a very weak way of attempting to protect employees.

The effectiveness of government intervention

Government intervention in product and factors markets is designed to:
- lower prices to customers;
- reduce abnormal profits of firms achieved by firms expropriating consumer surplus and turning it into producer surplus;
- increase productive, allocative and dynamic efficiencies;
- increase the quality of the product where quality is an issue;
- increase customer choice both of supplier and of product.

Government intervention, in practice, can be limited and ineffectual. This is because firms themselves have significant political power. A small business employing a couple of workers is unlikely to be able to influence the policy or practice of

Question 5

Christine Tacon, the government Groceries Code Adjudicator, has launched a formal investigation into Tesco. The probe would 'consider the existence and extent of practices which have resulted in delay in payments to suppliers'. Tesco faces a series of allegations, including the bullying of suppliers, demanding rebates in exchange for prominent positioning on the shelves, invoicing discrepancies and deductions for unknown or unagreed items between June 2013 and February this year.

The Chartered Institute of Procurement & Supply said Britain was suffering from a culture of late payment that extended beyond the supermarkets to the food industry as a whole. The most controversial was Premier Foods, maker of Kipling cakes and Hovis bread, which had told suppliers last year that they could lose the chance of new contracts unless they made cash payments. It later backed down, saying it would revert 'to a more conventional type of discount negotiation'. Last week, Diageo, the world largest distiller and owner of Johnnie Walker scotch whisky, said it would in future look to new contract terms and take 90 days to pay suppliers instead of 60. Other food and drinks manufacturers, including Heinz, the banked beans and ketchup company, and 2 Sisters Food Group, the UK's biggest Christmas pudding maker, have all sought to extend new payment terms.

Source: adapted from © the *Financial Times* 6.2.2015, All Rights Reserved.

(a) Give two examples from the data as to how a monopsonist might exploit its power over its suppliers.

(b) Why might monopsonists change their behaviour in the face of government regulation?

government. However, a large firm employing thousands of people could have some influence. A major industry, like the newspaper industry, food manufacturers, the alcoholic drinks industry or the tobacco industry is likely to be even more powerful compared to a single firm.

Firms or groups of firms use a number of ways to influence government.

- They can lobby government or MPs on issues concerning the industry. For example, they can request meetings with government. They can provide 'information' packs that carry their message. They can set up and fund pressure groups that attempt to influence government and public opinion. In many countries round the world, firms simply bribe ministers and parliamentary members to pursue policies that are favourable to them. Firms can also attempt to intimidate governments, for example by threatening to take them to court to get government decisions declared illegal or to gain significant amounts in compensation. The tobacco industry has been attempting to sue governments for billions of pounds in compensation following the introduction of plain packaging for cigarettes.

- Where there are regulatory bodies, firms can attempt to alter the decisions of regulators in their favour. This is known as **regulatory capture** and is an example of government failure. For example, firms can attempt to develop a favourable relationship with the regulator. In some countries, this simply means bribing the regulator. In countries like the UK, the approach has to be more subtle. Alternatively, firms can attempt to bully the regulator, for example by constantly threatening to take the regulator's decisions to court. Releasing the minimum amount of unfavourable information to the regulator is also common practice. This results in **asymmetric information**. The regulator has less information than the firms. The regulator then makes decisions which are more favourable to firms than if it had all the relevant information. Some regulators are paid for by the firms they are regulating. This makes the regulator particularly vulnerable to intimidation by firms. If cases go against them, the firms can threaten to withdraw from the regulatory scheme. The staff at the regulator could then lose their jobs. So they make decisions that favour the firms. Equally, there are regulators where many of the senior personnel come from the firms they are supposed to be regulating. Inevitably, the regulator then favours firms.

- Where there are voluntary codes of conduct, firms will draw these codes up in such a way as to minimise the cost of compliance. If government puts pressure on firms to make the code more rigorous, firms will then put counter pressure on government to get their own way. Firms anyway normally have an advantage in any negotiations with government because of asymmetric information. They are better informed than government about how to minimise the impact of any code to which they agree.

Key Terms

Competitive tendering - introducing competition among private sector firms which put in bids for work which has been contracted out by the public sector.

Contracting out - getting private sector firms to produce the goods and services which are then provided by the state for its citizens.

Deregulation - the process of removing government controls from markets.

Regulatory capture - an example of government failure, it occurs when firms in an industry are able to influence to their advantage a regulatory body which is supposed to be regulating the behaviour of those firms.

Nationalisation - the transfer of firms or assets from private sector ownership to state ownership. It is the opposite of privatisation.

Privatisation - the transfer of organisations or assets from state ownership to private sector ownership. It is the opposite of nationalisation.

Thinking like an economist

UK and EU competition policy

UK competition policy is based on European Union competition policy in Articles 101 and 102 of the *Treaty of the Functioning of the European Union*. These articles prohibit the abuse of a dominant position in a market by a firm when this affects cross-border trade.

In the UK, competition policy is based upon the *Competition Act 1998* and the *Enterprise Act 2002*, as amended by the *Enterprise and Regulatory Reform Act 2013*. These laws seek to curb practices that would undermine or restrict competition to the detriment of consumers. This covers

- the abuse of a dominant market position by a firm;
- anti-competitive agreements between firms;
- mergers or takeovers which, if allowed, would result in a substantial lessening of competition.

The UK regulatory framework

The regulatory framework in the UK is shown in Figure 4.

Regulators In the UK, there are six regulators:

- the Office of Rail and Road (ORR);
- the Water Services Regulation Authority (Ofwat);
- the Office of the Gas and Electricity Markets (Ofgem);
- the Office of Communications (Ofcom);
- the Civil Aviation Authority (CAA)
- the Utility Regulator (UR) - the regulator for gas, electricity and water in Northern Ireland.

Figure 4

The UK regulatory framework

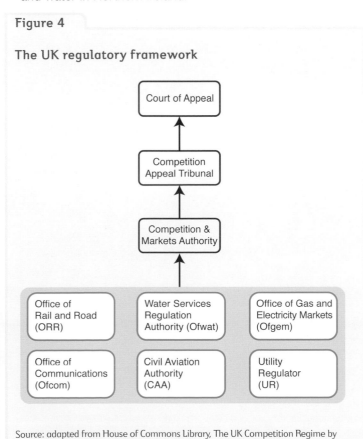

Source: adapted from House of Commons Library, The UK Competition Regime by Antony Seely.

These regulatory bodies oversee markets which were formally nationalised industries and which have since been privatised. Firms in these industries have 'dominant market positions' i.e. they are either monopolies or have monopoly powers. Regulatory bodies have the power to investigate suspected competition abuses by companies in their industry. Some also have the power to fix prices. For example, Ofwat sets the maximum price that water companies can charge their residential customers. CAA fixes the landing charges that airports can charge airlines for using an airport.

The Competition & Markets Authority (CMA) The CMA is the main body responsible for investigating competition issues such as mergers which restrict competition, anti-competitive practices such as the operation of a cartel and the abuse of customers by companies with monopoly powers. If it believes there is an issue, it has the power to investigate the problem. It may investigate a whole industry, such as the grocery industry. It may investigate individual firms if it believes that the firms are engaged in anti-competitive practices. It also can investigate a merger where it believes that the new enlarged firm will have the potential to restrict competition.

Under EU and UK law, holding a 'dominant position' (i.e. having monopoly power) is not illegal. What is prohibited in law is a firm abusing that dominant position. Having a dominant position is not linked to any fixed level of market share. Rather it is judged on whether firms, in theory, could sustain prices five to 10 per cent above what would be a competitive level in that market. In terms of market share, a firm having 25 per cent of the market, for example, may or may not hold a dominant position in the market. However, the European Court has stated that any firm having 50 per cent of the market can be presumed to have a dominant position, unless there is evidence to the contrary. The CMA considers it unlikely that a firm will be individually dominant if its share of the market is below 40 per cent.

Anti-competitive practices cover a wide range of activities by firms such as refusing to sell to certain suppliers or forcing customers to buy a range of products exclusively from that one firm. 'Hard core' anti-competitive practices that are likely to lead to large fines include cartels and refusal to supply. These practices are judged to be particularly damaging to the interests of consumers.

The CMA reviews significant proposed mergers in the UK. There will be an automatic review if one of the following is true.

* The merger involves a takeover of a firm with more than £70 million of assets worldwide.
* The mergers would create a firm with 25 per cent or more of the market;
* The merger involves a firm with an existing 25 per cent or more market share.
* The firms are in the newspaper or water industries.

If the CMA judges that the merger will not harm the interests of consumers, the merger will be allowed to go ahead. The CMA could judge that, in general, the merger will not affect competition, but there are small detailed competition issues. For example, if two supermarkets merged, the new supermarket chain may be forced to sell off supermarkets in those local areas of the country where it would face little competition. Lastly, the CMA could judge that the merger was against the public interest and refuse to allow it to occur.

The Competition Appeal Tribunal Firms may appeal against decisions made by the CMA to the Competition Appeal Tribunal. This is a court of law. The Competition Appeal Tribunal can uphold the decisions of the CMA or reject them.

Court of Appeal Firms can appeal against decisions made by the Competition Appeal Tribunal to the Court of Appeal. This very rarely happens.

The EU regulatory framework The EU intervenes in competition policy when it involves cross-border trade. A firm that sells products in several EU countries, for example, could be investigated by the EU for anti-competitive practices. The body within the European Commission responsible for competition policy is the Directorate General for Competition. It is headed by the European Commission for Competition. A firm can appeal to the European Court of Justice against any ruling made by the Directorate General for Competition.

For example, in the 2000s, the European Directorate for Competition was involved in a long investigation of Microsoft. It resulted in Microsoft being fined €561 million in 2013 for failing to carry undertakings it had made to give consumers a choice of browser within its Windows operating system. The Directorate General for Competition launched investigations into Google in 2015 for allegedly using its search engine to drive users to sites from which Google could make a profit. It also launched an investigation into Gazprom, the Russian gas producer, for charging different prices for gas to different customers in different EU countries.

Source: with information from *Abuse of a dominant position*, Office of Fair Trading, 2004; House of Commons Library, *The UK competition regime by Antony Seely*; europa.eu rapid/press-release; © the Financial Times 16.4.2015, 27.4.2015, All Rights Reserved.

Data Response Question

Controlling monopoly power

European regulators have fined Servier of France and several other drugmakers $428 million for blocking the introduction of cheaper generic competition to an expensive branded medicine. Servier had struck 'pay-for-delay' deals.

Drugs are only protected by patent for 20 years in the EU. After that period, other drug manufacturers can sell copies of the drug and these are called 'generic' drugs. One way round this is for drug companies with patents expiring on a drug to pay other companies not to produce generic versions of the drug.

However, regulators have decided to take a hard line on such deals. 'Servier had a strategy to systematically buy out any competitive threats to make sure that they stayed out of the market,' said Joaquin Almunia, the European competition commissioner. 'Such behaviour is clearly anti-competitive and abusive.' He said that agreements that postponed the entry of cheaper medicines to the market 'directly harm patients, national health systems and taxpayers. Pharmaceutical companies should focus their efforts on innovating and competing rather than attempting to extract extra rents from patients.'

In the US, the Federal Trade Commission has also stepped up scrutiny of pay-for-delay deals after a US Supreme Court ruling in June 2013 backed the regulator's right to challenge such deals.

The Civil Aviation Authority, the UK regulator that sets prices for landing charges at UK airports, has shocked the owners of Heathrow Airport. The CAA has said the airport's landing charges should rise by inflation minus 1.5 per cent each year between 2014 and 2019. Heathrow had proposed its charges should increase by inflation plus 4.6 per cent over the period. The airport has some of the highest landing changes in the world. These have been rising well above inflation since 2003. The CAA said that this settlement for 2014-19 should lead to lower prices for passengers.

Heathrow, Europe's busiest airport, denounced the regulator's move as 'draconian'. Heathrow threatened last July to reduce its planned capital spending between 2014 and 2015 from £3 billion to £2 billion if the regulator imposed a tough financial settlement.

In 2012, Eurotunnel, the company operating the undersea rail link between the UK and France, bought the assets of Seafrance which had gone into administration. Seafrance operated a cross-channel ferry service from Dover to Calais in competition with two other companies, P&O Ferries and Denmark's DFDS. The ferry service was renamed as MyFerryLink.

In 2014, the UK Competition and Markets Authority (CMA) ordered Eurotunnel to sell off its MyFerryLink business. It said that Eurotunnel 'should be barred from operating its MyFerryLink service from Dover' because the company controlled more than half the cross-channel market. If one of the other two Dover-Calais ferry operators were to fold, its market share could rise even more.

Eurotunnel said that it would struggle to find a buyer for MyFerryLink. It could be faced with simply selling the assets of the company – mainly its two ferries, leaving the Dover-Calais route serviced by just two companies. The move would create a 'de facto duopoly in the maritime sector which will lead to an increase in prices for consumers and a reduction in revenues for the ports of Dover and Calais', Eurotunnel said.

Q

1. Explain how a drug patent can confer monopoly power to a drug manufacturer.

2. Using examples from the data and diagrams, explain two ways in which firms with monopoly power can exploit customers.

3. Using examples from the data and your own economic knowledge, discuss the advantages and disadvantages of different methods of controlling firms with monopoly power.

Evaluation

There are many ways that firms with monopoly power can be controlled. If you discuss too many, you will end up with too much description and far too little evaluation. Concentrate on the methods described in the data. Weigh up the possible advantages and disadvantages to customers supporting your evaluation with evidence from the data and your own economic knowledge.

57 Demand for labour

Key points

1. In the long run, the demand curve for labour is downward sloping because capital can be substituted for labour.
2. In the short run, the downward sloping demand curve for labour can be explained by the law of diminishing returns.
3. The marginal revenue product curve of labour is the demand curve for labour. This is true whether the firm operates in a perfectly competitive or imperfectly competitive market.
4. The elasticity of demand for labour is determined by time, the availability of substitutes, the elasticity of demand for the product and the proportion of labour costs to total costs.

Starter activity

Vihaan owns and runs a village café and coffee shop. His business is booming, but there are times of the day when he knows that customers feel annoyed that it is taking so long to be served. He is considering employing another person at a cost of £400 per week to work for 40 hours per week, in addition to the six staff he already employs. From a financial viewpoint, how would Vihaan calculate whether to take on the extra employee if he were a profit maximiser?

The downward sloping demand curve

Firms need workers to produce goods and services. The demand curve for labour shows how many workers will be hired at any given wage rate over a particular time period. A firm, for instance, might want to hire 100 workers if the wage rate were £2 per hour but only 50 workers if it were £200 per hour.

Economic theory suggests that the higher the price of labour, the less labour firms will hire.

- In the long run, other things remaining equal, firms can vary all factors of production. The higher the wage rate, the more likely it is that firms will substitute machines for workers and hence the lower the demand for labour.
- In the short run, firms are likely to have an existing stock of capital. They will have to produce with a given amount of factory or office space and with a fixed amount of plant, machinery and equipment. The more workers that are added to this fixed stock of capital, the less likely it is that the last worker employed will be as productive as existing employees. Hence the wage rate would have to fall to encourage the employer to take on an extra worker.

So the demand curve for labour is likely to be downward sloping both in the long run and the short run. Why do the long run and short run demand curves slope downward and what determines the elasticity of demand for labour?

The long-run demand for labour

In the long run, all factors of production are variable. A firm has complete freedom to choose its production techniques. In the developing world, where labour is cheap relative to capital, firms tend to choose labour intensive methods of production. In the developed world, labour is relatively expensive and hence more capital intensive techniques of production are chosen. So

in agriculture in the developed world, far more use is made of tractors and other machinery, whilst in the developing world, far more workers per acre are employed.

The short-run demand for labour

In the short run, at least one of the factors of production is fixed. Assume that all factors are fixed except labour. The **law of diminishing returns** states that marginal output will start to decline if more and more units of one variable factor of production are combined with a given quantity of fixed factors. One common example is to imagine a plot of land with a fixed number of tools where extra workers are employed to cultivate the land. Diminishing returns will quickly set in and the eleventh worker, for instance, on a one-acre plot of land will contribute less to total output than the tenth worker.

Table 1

						Per week
1	2	3	4	5	6	7
Labour input	Total output	Marginal physical product	Price of product	Marginal revenue product (3 x 4)	Wage rate per worker	Contribution (5 - 6)
(workers)	(units)	(units)	£	£	£	£
1	8	8	10	80	70	10
2	17	9	10	90	70	20
3	25	8	10	80	70	10
4	32	7	10	70	70	0
5	38	6	10	60	70	-10
6	43	5	10	50	70	-20

This is shown in Table 1. Labour is assumed to be a variable factor of production whilst all other factors are fixed. As extra workers are employed, total output, or **total physical product**, increases. However, **marginal physical product**, the number of extra units of output a worker produces, starts to decline after the employment of the second worker. So diminishing marginal returns set in with the third worker. Assume that the firm is in a perfectly competitive industry and therefore faces a horizontal, perfectly elastic demand curve. This means that the firm can sell any quantity of its product at the same price per unit. In Table 1, it is assumed that the price of the product is £10. **Marginal revenue product** can then be calculated because it is the addition to revenue from the employment of an extra worker.

Question 1

Table 2

Number of workers employed	Total physical product per week	Total revenue product	Marginal revenue product
1	10		
2	24		
3	36		
4	44		
5	50		
6	53		

Table 2 shows the total physical product per week for a small firm as the number of workers employed varies. The price of the product sold is £10 per unit.

(a) Calculate total revenue product at each level of employment.

(b) Calculate marginal revenue product as employment increases.

(c) Explain how many workers the firm should employ if the weekly wage per worker were: (i) £60; (ii) £30; (iii) £120; (iv) £100.

For instance, the first worker produces eight units and so, at a price per product unit of £10, the marginal revenue product is £80 (£10 x 8). The marginal revenue product of the second worker is £90 (£10 x the marginal physical product).

It is now possible to calculate how many workers a firm will employ. The contribution to the payment of fixed costs and the earning of profit of each worker is the difference between the marginal revenue product of the firm and the cost to the firm of the worker. Assume that the firm is able to employ any number of workers at a wage rate of £70. The contribution of the first worker is £10, the worker's marginal revenue product minus the worker's wage (£80 - £70). The contribution of the second worker is £20 (£90 - £70). It can be seen from Table 1 that the first three workers each make a positive contribution. The fourth worker neither increases nor decreases total profit for the firm. The firm would definitely not employ a fifth worker because

that employment would result in a loss of £10 to the firm. The worker's wage of £70 would exceed the worker's marginal revenue product of £60. So marginal revenue product theory suggests that the firm will employ a maximum of four workers because this number maximises total profit (or minimises the loss) for the firm.

If the wage rate were to fall to £50, the firm would employ more workers. The fourth worker would now definitely be employed because the contribution would be £20. The fifth worker too would contribute a positive £10. The firm might also employ a sixth worker although the contribution is zero. Marginal revenue product theory therefore suggests that the lower the wage, the more workers will be employed.

The demand curve for labour

Figure 1 shows a firm's marginal revenue product curve for labour. It is downward sloping because marginal revenue product declines as output increases (as shown in Table 1. It is conventional to ignore the upward sloping part of the line at low levels of output.). If the wage rate is OF, the firm will employ OB units of labour. If the wage rate rises, the firm will cut back employment to OA. If, on the other hand, wage rates fall to OE, then the firm will take on extra workers and increase the labour force to OC. The marginal revenue product curve therefore shows the number of workers the firm will employ at any given wage rate, but this is the definition of the firm's demand curve for labour. Therefore the marginal revenue product curve is also the firm's demand curve for labour.

This is true for all factors of production. Figure 1 shows the familiar price/quantity diagram. The price of labour is the wage rate. Quantity is the quantity of labour employed. The downward sloping marginal revenue product curve gives us the familiar downward sloping demand curve.

Figure 1

The MRP curve is the demand curve for a factor

The MRP curve shows the maximum price a firm would be prepared to pay for an extra unit of a factor of production and therefore it is the demand curve for that factor.

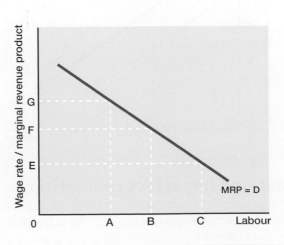

Question 2

Table 3

Number of workers employed	Number of units produced and sold per week	Price per unit £
1	10	£15
2	24	£14
3	36	£12
4	44	£11
5	50	£10
6	53	£9

The firm in Table 3 produces in an imperfectly competitive market. As output increases, the price falls.

(a) Calculate (i) the total revenue product and (ii) the marginal revenue product of labour as employment increases.

(b) How many workers would the firm employ if the weekly wage were: (i) £20; (ii) £40; (iii) £60; (iv) £80; (v) £100; (vi) £120?

Shifts in the the demand curve for labour

The demand curve for labour can shift to the left or right if the marginal revenue product of a given quantity of labour changes. There are two main reasons why marginal revenue product may change given that marginal revenue product equals marginal physical product x the price of the product.

- The physical productivity (physical output per worker) of labour may change. If car workers increase their output from four cars per day to five cars per day, their marginal physical product will increase and hence so too will their marginal revenue product. Employers will be prepared to pay more to workers who are more productive.

- The price of what is produced may change. If the market price of a car increases from £5 000 to £10 000, the marginal revenue product will double. Car manufacturers will then be prepared to pay more for labour.

An increase in labour productivity **(output per worker)** or an increase in the price of the product made will increase the demand for labour, shifting the demand curve to the right. Conversely, a fall in labour productivity or a fall in the price of the product will reduce the demand for labour, shifting the demand curve to the left. In Figure 2, the demand curve has shifted to the right. For any given quantity of labour, the marginal revenue product of labour has increased. So, for example, if OA labour were employed, its MRP before the MRP increase was OB. Now it is OC and so the demand curve has shifted from D_1 to D_2.

Figure 2

A rise in the demand for labour

A rise in the marginal productivity of labour at any given level of employment will lead to a shift of the MRP or demand curve for labour to the right.

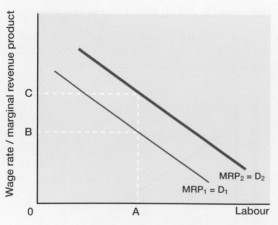

Perfect and imperfect competition

So far it has been assumed that the employer is supplying goods in a perfectly competitive market. This is because it has been assumed that the firm can supply any quantity of goods to the market at the same price per unit (i.e. the firm faces a horizontal demand curve). The marginal revenue product curve falls because of diminishing returns.

However, if the employer supplies goods in an imperfectly competitive market, then it faces a downward sloping demand curve for its product. If it expands output, price per unit sold will fall. Consider Table 1 again. The fall in marginal revenue product would be even greater than that shown if the price of the product did not remain at £10 per unit, but fell as output expanded. So the marginal revenue product curve for an imperfectly competitive firm falls not only because of diminishing returns but also because the price or average revenue of the product sold falls too as output expands.

Whether the firm is perfectly or imperfectly competitive, it is still true that the demand curve for labour is the marginal revenue product curve of labour.

Determinants of the elasticity of demand for labour

The **elasticity of demand for labour** is a measure of the responsiveness of the quantity demanded of labour to changes in the price of labour (i.e. the wage rate). For instance, if elasticity of demand for labour were two and wage rates increased 10 per cent then, all other things being equal, the demand for labour would fall by 20 per cent. If demand for labour fell by one per cent when wage rates rose by 100 per cent, all other things being equal, then elasticity of demand for labour would be 0.01 (i.e. highly inelastic).

There is a number of factors which determine the elasticity of demand for labour.

Time The longer the time period for adjustment, the easier it is to substitute labour for other factors of production or vice versa. In the short term, a firm may have little choice but to employ the same number of workers even if wage rates increase rapidly. Workers will have contracts of employment. There may be severe financial penalties in the form of redundancy payments if workers are sacked. Or a firm may not wish to lose skilled staff because they would be difficult to replace. In the longer term, the firm can buy new labour-saving machinery and carry out changes in its methods of work which will reduce the labour employed. Hence the longer the time period, the higher will tend to be the elasticity of demand for labour.

Question 3

Explain whether you would expect the elasticity of demand for labour for lorry drivers to be relatively high or low.

Availability of substitutes The easier it is to substitute other factors for labour, the greater will be the response by firms to a change in real wage rates. So the better the substitutes, the higher will tend to be the elasticity of demand for labour.

Elasticity of demand for the product Labour is **a derived demand**. It is only demanded because the goods that it produces are demanded. For instance, if there is a collapse in demand for steel, then there will also be a collapse in the demand for steel miners. This means that the elasticity of demand for labour in an industry is directly correlated with the elasticity of demand for the product made in the industry. If the elasticity of demand for the product is low, as for instance for gas or electricity, then a sudden rise in wages which pushes up gas or electricity prices will have little effect on demand for gas or electricity. There will be little effect on employment in the industry and hence the demand for labour will be low. If, on the other hand, elasticity of demand for the product is high, elasticity of demand for labour will be high. A steel company, for instance, faces highly elastic demand for many of its products. A rise in wages not matched elsewhere in the industry is likely to increase its prices and lead to a loss of orders and therefore jobs.

The proportion of labour cost to total cost A rise in **unit labour costs**, the cost of employing labour per unit of production, will reduce the supply of a product, shifting the supply curve upwards and to the left. This will lead to a reduction in quantity demanded. The bigger the shift, the larger the reduction in demand. If a group of workers gains a 50 per cent pay rise but these workers only account for one per cent of the total cost of production, then the supply curve of the product will hardly shift. There will be little fall in demand and hence little loss of employment in the firm. If, however, this group of workers accounted for 50 per cent of the costs of the firm, then a 50 per cent pay rise would have a dramatic effect on the supply curve and lead to a large decrease in quantity demanded of the product. This in turn would lead to a large fall in employment. Hence, the larger the proportion of labour cost to total cost, the higher the elasticity of demand for labour.

Key Terms

Elasticity of demand for labour - the responsiveness of the quantity demanded of labour to changes in the price of labour, the wage rate. It is measured by the formula

$$\frac{\% \text{ change in quantity demanded for labour}}{\% \text{ change in the wage rate}}$$

Marginal physical product - the physical addition to output of an extra unit of a variable factor of production.
Marginal revenue product - the value of the physical addition to output of an extra unit of a variable factor of production. In a perfectly competitive product market, where marginal revenue equals price, it is equal to marginal physical product times the price of the good produced.
Total physical product - the total output of a given quantity of factors of production.
Unit labour cost - cost of employing labour per unit of output or production.

Thinking like an economist

Executive pay

The average pay of the directors of the largest 100 companies quoted on the London Stock Exchange increased by 21 per cent in 2013. Over the same period, average pay in the UK rose by 2.2 per cent. Chief executives at some of Britain's biggest companies in 2013 earned 120 times more than an average full-time employee, compared with 47 times more in 2000. The Chief Executive of Burberry, Christopher Bailey, the luxury fashion brand, saw shareholders vote against his £20 million annual pay package in 2014. His predecessor, Angela Ahrendts, left Burberry to take on a job with the US technology company Apple for $60 million in her first year.

Economic theory would suggest that firms will pay the marginal worker the value of their marginal revenue product. There is only one chief executive in a firm. However, across the economy, there are many chief executives and so there is a market for chief executives. The marginal revenue product of a chief executive is the addition to revenue product that the employee brings to the company. If there were no chief executive, how much would total revenue product fall?

Chief executives could argue that their marginal revenue product is very high. A large company can easily see millions of pounds lost or gained in revenue in a single year. In 2013-14, Burberry's total revenue was £2 330 million, up from

£1 999 million in 2012-13. Christopher Bailey's proposed pay packet of £20 million was only a fraction of the increase in revenue.

However, this anecdotal evidence doesn't explain why there has been such a large increase in executive pay in the recent years. Why should the ratio of chief executive pay to that of the average full-time employee have risen from 47:1 to 120:1 between 2000 and 2013? It also doesn't explain why executive pay can rise when revenues and profits have fallen. For example, in 2014, there was controversy when Barclay's Bank announced that bonuses for some in its investment banking division would be increased by 10 per cent, despite the fact that the division's pre-tax profit had fallen by more than one third.

The marginal revenue product, the value that executives bring to a company, is clearly only one factor in determining their remuneration. In situations when pay rises when performance falls, it is clearly not a particularly important factor. Economic theory might help to explain this by pointing out the 'divorce of ownership from control' in large companies. What is best

for executives is not necessarily best for the owners, the shareholders. It should also be remembered that shareholders do not set executive pay: at best, they might be asked to vote on this at a shareholders meeting. It is directors who set the pay of other executives and directors. Over time, the statistics suggest directors and executives have taken an ever larger share of the profits of companies both in the UK and the USA whatever the value of their marginal revenue product to their employer.

Source: with information from © the *Financial Times* 6.3.2014, 12.7.2014, 13.10.2014, All Rights Reserved.

Data Response Question

North Sea oil and gas workers

Thousands of North Sea oil and gas workers face pay cuts of up to 15 per cent in 2015 in the face of plummeting oil prices. Oil prices have roughly halved since June 2014. BP said it remained 'firmly committed' to the North Sea, but added that 'costs have been rising and we must respond to these toughening market conditions'.

When oil prices were rising in 2012-13, the average pay of North Sea workers rose too. An annual pay survey by recruitment group Hays showed that average wages for North Sea workers rose from $87 100 in 2012 to $94 200 in 2013.

The cuts in pay are likely to be followed by job losses. Oil companies are cutting back on exploration and development in the face of the sharp fall in the price of oil. The North Sea is extremely vulnerable because oil production is already in decline despite investment in new projects recently hitting record levels. Soaring costs and a complicated tax system have made opening up smaller fields a riskier bet.

Source: adapted from © the *Financial Times* 31.12.2014, All Rights Reserved.

Q

1. Explain, using a demand for labour diagram and the concept of marginal revenue product, why some North Sea workers were facing pay cuts in 2015.

2. Discuss the extent to which the demand for North Sea oil workers is likely to be elastic.

Evaluation

For each factor that determines the elasticity of demand for labour, explain why it affects elasticity and then apply this to the North Sea example. Where there is insufficient information in the data, put forward different outcomes depending on what the conditions in the market for North Sea workers might be. Weigh up the arguments in your answer to come to an overall conclusion.

58 Supply of labour

Key points

1. The supply curve for an individual worker is backward sloping at high levels of income.
2. Backward sloping supply curves result because the negative income effect of a wage increase outweighs the positive substitution effect.
3. The supply curve of labour to a firm, to an industry and to the economy as a whole is likely to be upward sloping.
4. There can be market failure if labour is geographically or occupationally immobile.

Starter activity

Laketta leaves university at 21 and gets a job in the investment banking division of a large bank. By the age of 30, including bonuses, she is earning £800 000 a year. Aged 32, she is headhunted by another bank and given an introductory bonus of £1.2 million. Aged 45, she is earning £1 million a year including bonuses, but decides to retire to the farm in Sussex, which she bought in her early thirties. She no longer wants to work 60-80 hours a week.

Riley leaves school at 18. He has a variety of unskilled labouring jobs during his lifetime paying the minimum wage, but also experiences regular periods of unemployment. He retires age 68 when he is able to take his state retirement pension.

Why would Laketta withdraw her supply of labour to the market aged 45 when she is earning so much? Why doesn't Riley retire at 45?

The supply curve for an individual worker

A supply curve shows the quantity that will be supplied to the market at any given price. For an individual worker, the quantity supplied is the number of hours worked over a time period, such as a year. Neo-classical theory starts by assuming that a worker can decide how many hours to work per week and how many weeks' holiday to take per year. The price of labour is the wage per time period (i.e. the wage rate). The wage rate that determines supply is the **real wage rate** (the money or nominal wage rate divided by the price level). This is because the worker decides how many hours to work by relating it to what the wage will buy. For instance, a worker might take a job if a week's wages of £300 were to buy a television set, but she would be likely to turn it down if £300 were to only buy a newspaper.

Figure 1 shows a backward bending supply curve for labour. Between wages rates 0 and B a rise in real wage rates will lead to an increase in working hours supplied. For instance, the worker will offer to work DF extra hours if real wage rates increase from A to B. However, a rise in real wage rates above OB, for instance from B to C, will lead to a desire for shorter working hours.

To understand why this might be the case, consider a part-time factory worker. Initially she is low paid, as are nearly all part-time workers. The firm she works for then doubles her real wage rate. She is likely to respond to this by wanting to work longer hours and perhaps become a full-time worker. Further increases in real wage rates might persuade her to work overtime. However, there are only 24 hours in a day and 365 days in a year. Eventually it is likely that increases in wage rates will make her want to reduce her working week or increase her holidays. She will value increased leisure time more than extra money to spend. Put another way, she is choosing to buy leisure time by forgoing the wages she could otherwise have earned and the goods she could otherwise have bought. This is an example of the concept of opportunity cost.

This process can be seen at work over the past 100 years in the UK. Real wage rates have risen considerably but hours worked have fallen. The typical Victorian working week was 60 to 70 hours with few or no holidays. Today, average hours worked per week for full-time workers are down to about 40 hours with a typical holiday entitlement of four weeks per year. Workers have responded to increases in wage rates by supplying less labour.

Note that when wage rates increase, workers are likely to be able to both increase earnings and reduce hours worked. For instance, if real wage rates increase by 20 per cent from £10 per hour to £12 per hour, then workers can cut their hours worked by 10 per cent from 40 hours to 36 hours per week and still see an increase in earnings from £400 per week

Figure 1

The backward bending supply curve

The supply curve for an individual worker is assumed to be this shape because at high levels of income the worker will prefer to work shorter hours rather than receive the extra income the worker could have earned.

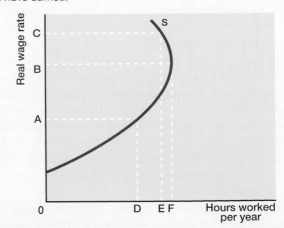

Question 1

Figure 2

Activity rates of 50-64 year olds by sex (percentage of total population aged 50-64 either in work or unemployed)

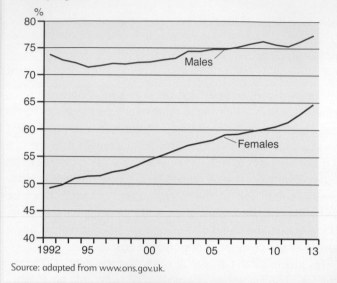

Source: adapted from www.ons.gov.uk.

Real wage rates in the UK increased between 1992 and 2009, after which they broadly remained stable. Unemployment was higher than average for the period between 1992 and 1996 and again between 2009 and 2013.

Do the data support the idea that the supply curve of labour for an individual worker is backward sloping?

(40 x £10) to £432 per week (36 x £12). Real wage rate increases in the neo-classical model give workers a choice between increased earnings or increased leisure time or some combination of the two.

Income and substitution effects

The backward bending supply curve occurs because of the interaction of **income** and **substitution** effects. An increase in real wage rates means that the reward for working, rather than not working and taking more leisure hours, increases. For instance, a worker receiving a pay rise of 10 per cent after tax and deductions can now buy 10 per cent more goods and services. The opportunity cost of not working therefore rises. Workers will therefore **substitute** work for leisure if the rate of pay increases.

However, work is arguably an **inferior good**. The higher the income, the fewer hours individuals will wish to work. For instance, it is pointless being able to buy tennis or squash equipment if you don't have the time to play. Earning more money has little use if you can't take the time off to have a holiday, go to the pub or go shopping. So the **income effect** of work tends to be negative for most individuals. The higher the income, the less work and the more leisure time is demanded.

At low levels of income, the positive substitution effect outweighs the negative income effect of a wage rise. Hence,

Figure 3

Substitution and income effects

Up to real wage rate OA, an increase in wages leads to an increase in the number of hours worked because the positive substitution effect of the wage rise outweighs its negative income effect. At real wage rate rises above OB, an increase in wages leads to a fall in hours worked, because the negative income effect outweighs the positive substitution effect.

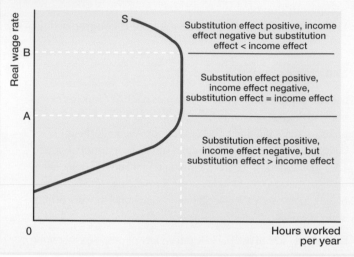

a rise in pay for these workers leads to an increase in the number of hours worked. At higher levels of income, the positive substitution effect is likely to be equally matched by the negative income effect. Wage increases then have neither an incentive nor a disincentive effect on working hours. But at high levels of income, the positive substitution effect of a wage increase is more than offset by the negative income effect. Hence the worker will choose to work fewer hours.

This can be shown in Figure 3. At wage rates up to OA, higher wage rates will lead to increased hours of work. Between A and B the supply curve is vertical, showing that increased wages have no effect on hours worked. Between A and B the negative income effect cancels out the positive substitution effect as wages rise. Above OB the supply curve slopes backward showing that the negative income effect of a wage rise more than offsets its positive substitution effect.

In the real world, many workers have little choice about how many hours they work. However, rising incomes have been associated with longer holidays and also a shorter working life. Those on higher incomes often want to retire as early as possible given that they have been able to save up enough over their working life to finance a reasonable pension. Many other workers do have the opportunity to work longer hours during the week by taking overtime. There is a limit, though, to the amount of overtime employees are prepared to work, showing the negative income effect in operation.

Monetary and non-monetary considerations

The supply of labour to a particular market is affected not just by **monetary** or **pecuniary** considerations. **Non-monetary** or **non-pecuniary** considerations can be important too. The trade-off between work and leisure has already been explained. But

other non-monetary considerations include:
- job satisfaction. Workers are prepared to accept lower wages if there is greater job satisfaction. Evidence suggests, though, that higher pay is associated with greater job satisfaction because higher paid jobs tend to give workers more control over their working environment.

- location. A job may be attractive to an individual worker, for example, because it is close to relatives and friends, or it is in London with its social life.
- friends and family. Some jobs are attractive because they involve working with friends and family.
- commuting. Time taken to travel to work, the pleasantness of the journey and its cost affect people's choices of jobs.

Question 2

Figure 4

Effective tax rate (%) for a couple with two children both earning the minimum wage and paying rent for their house under Universal Credit

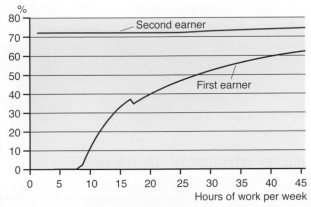

Source: adapted from Resolution Foundation, Universal Credit 2014, D Finch, A Corlett and V Alakeson.

The government is in the process of introducing Universal Credit. This will be a single welfare benefit that will replace six existing welfare payments and tax credits for the low paid in work. However, the roll out has been greatly delayed because of the complexity of the new system. The government claims that it will increase incentives to work compared to the present system and that '3 million households will be better off by an average of £177 a month'. However, the Resolution Foundation, a UK think-tank, has warned that Universal Credit could worsen incentives for some groups. Under Universal Credit, earnings for up to 26 hours of part-time work on the minimum wage will not be taken into account when calculating Universal Credit although workers will still be liable for National Insurance contributions and income tax. Figure 4 shows a situation where there are two earners both earning the minimum wage in a household with two children. The first earner sees their effective tax rate (tax rate plus withdrawal of benefits) rise to over 60 per cent when working 45 hours a week. The second earner starts at an effective tax rate of over 70 per cent when working just a few hours a week.

Source: adapted from © the *Financial Times* 9.9.2014, All Rights Reserved.

(a) Explain why higher net wage rates (after tax and benefits have been accounted for) might increase incentives to work.

(b) Using the example in Figure 4, explain whether the first earner or the second earner has the greater incentive to work.

(c) Using the concepts of income and substitution effects, explain whether the second earner has a greater incentive to work five hours a week or 40 hours or a week or not work at all.

Supply of labour to a firm

In a perfectly competitive market there are many buyers and sellers. In a perfectly competitive factor market, there are many firms hiring many individual workers. This means that an individual firm will be able to hire an extra worker at the existing wage rate.

Figure 5 (a) shows the supply curve of labour facing the firm. The firm is small and wants to expand its workforce from 20 workers to 21 workers. Figure 5 (b) shows the supply curve of labour for the industry to be upward sloping, as will be argued below. 100 000 workers are currently employed in the industry. The movement up the industry supply curve from 100 000 workers to 100 001 workers is so small that the firm can employ the extra worker at the ruling industrial wage rate. Therefore the supply curve facing the firm is horizontal (i.e. perfectly elastic).

Many industries, however, are either oligopolies or monopolies. Firms in these industries are therefore likely to be significant employers of particular types of labour. For instance, the government employs over 90 per cent of all UK teachers. If a firm is a monopsonist (i.e. is the sole buyer) in its labour market, then the supply curve of labour to the firm will also be the supply curve of labour to the industry. It will be upward sloping, showing that the firm has to offer increased wages if it wishes to increase its labour force.

The cost of employing an extra worker (the marginal cost) will be higher than the wage rate the firm has to pay the extra worker. This is because it not only has to pay a higher wage rate to the worker but it must also pay the higher wage rate to all its

Figure 5

Supply in a perfectly competitive market

The supply curve of labour facing a firm in a perfectly competitive factor market is perfectly elastic. The firm can hire new workers at the existing wage rate because their employment has an insignificant impact on the total supply of labour in the market.

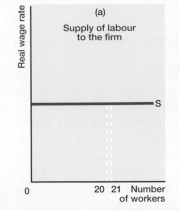 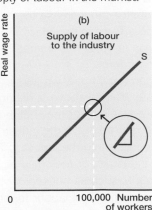

Table 1

Units of labour supplied	Cost per unit (£)	Total cost (£)	Marginal cost £
0	-	0	
			10
1	10	10	
			30
2	20	40	
			50
3	30	90	
			70
4	40	160	

other workers. In Table 1, for instance, the firm has to increase the wage rate as extra workers are employed. The wage rate needed to attract three workers to the industry is £30 per worker. However, the marginal cost of the third worker is £50; £30 for the third worker plus an extra £10 paid to each of the first two workers.

The supply curve of labour to the firm and the firm's marginal cost of labour derived from the data in Table 1 are shown in Figure 6. The marginal cost curve for labour for the monopsonist employer is higher than the supply curve of labour.

Figure 6

Supply curve and marginal cost curve of labour facing a monopsonist employer

The supply curve for labour facing a monopsonist employer is upward sloping. The marginal cost of hiring extra workers is more than the wage rate because the higher wage rate paid to the marginal worker needs to be paid to all existing workers.

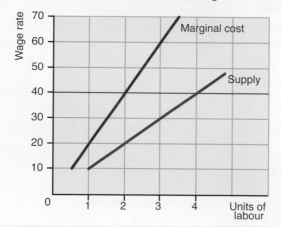

The supply curve of labour for an industry

An industry can increase the number of hours worked by its labour force in two ways:
- it can increase the number of hours worked by its existing labour force;
- it can recruit new workers.

As explained above, a rise in real wage rates, all other things being equal, may or may not increase the supply of labour by individual workers in the industry. However, it is likely to attract new workers into the industry. These new workers may be from other industries or they may be workers who previously did not hold a job, such as housepersons or the unemployed. Therefore, the supply curve of labour for an industry is likely to be upward sloping, the ability of firms to recruit new workers outweighing

Question 3

Table 2

Number of workers employed	Wage per week per workers (£)
100	200
200	220
300	240
400	260

The table shows the wage rates per week a firm has to offer to recruit workers.

(a) Draw (i) the supply curve of labour and (ii) the marginal cost curve of labour facing the firm. (Remember that the marginal cost of, for instance, the 100 workers employed between 300 and 400 is drawn at the 350 point.)

(b) How would the supply curve and marginal cost curve differ if the firm could recruit any number of workers at a wage rate of £200 per week?

any possible disincentive effect on existing workers. The higher the industry real wage rate, the more workers will want to enter that particular industry.

Elasticity of supply of labour

The elasticity of supply of labour is a measure of the responsiveness of the quantity supplied of labour to changes in the price of labour (i.e. the wage rate). The elasticity of supply of labour to an industry will depend upon a number of factors.

The availability of suitable labour in other industries
An engineering company wanting to recruit unskilled workers will be able to 'poach' workers relatively easily from other industries because there is a large pool of unskilled workers spread throughout industry. Schools will have more difficulty recruiting teachers because there is a limited number of workers with appropriate teaching qualifications to fill posts. So the elasticity of supply of a pool of workers spread across many industries is likely to be higher than that of a group of workers concentrated in the recruiting industry.

Time Elasticity of supply is likely to be lower in the short run than in the long run. For example, the education service might not be able to recruit large numbers of extra teachers tomorrow. But supply could be expanded over a 20-year period through increasing places on teacher training courses.

The extent of underemployment and unemployment
The higher the level of unemployment, the higher is likely to be the elasticity of supply. With high unemployment, firms are more likely to be able to recruit workers at the existing real wage rate from the pool of the unemployed.

Supply of labour to the economy

The supply of labour to the economy as a whole might seem to be fixed (i.e. perfectly inelastic). However, this is unlikely to be the case.
- In the UK, only about three-quarters of people aged 16-64 are in employment. The rest tend to be in education, at home looking after children, unemployed or have taken early retirement. This pool of people are potential workers and

some would enter the workforce if real wages rose.

- Some of the retired could be brought back to work if there were sufficient incentives for them.
- Immigration too could expand the domestic supply of labour. The supply of labour in the UK is currently being boosted by immigration from other EU countries.
- Some economists argue that increasing incentives to work through cutting taxes and cutting unemployment benefits will lead to a significant increase in the supply of labour.
- In the longer term, education and training can increase the supply of more skilled labour to the economy.
- Social trends, such as the change in attitudes towards women working over the past 100 years, can change the supply of labour.
- The power of trade unions in an economy can change the supply of labour. This is explained in the next unit.

So the supply of labour to the economy as a whole is likely to be upward sloping too. There is some evidence to suggest that it might also be backward sloping. Those who can afford it tend to take early retirement in their mid to late 50s. This tends to be workers who have had sufficiently high earnings to be able to afford to pay into a pension scheme. Effectively, they are choosing to work less over their lifetime because their earnings are high.

The mobility of labour

In a perfect labour market, there are no barriers to the supply of labour to any region or any occupation. Workers can move freely from one job to another in different regions and in different occupations. In practice, there are a wide variety of barriers to mobility of labour causing market failure. Labour can be highly immobile, unable to move from job to job despite high unemployment.

Geographical immobility of labour One type of labour immobility is geographical immobility. This is when workers find it difficult to move from one area to another. One reason for geographical immobility is search costs. Unemployed workers in Glasgow might find it difficult to find a job in London. They may not be aware of what jobs are available in London. They might only be able to find out by visiting London at high cost to themselves. Even if they could get a job in London, they may not wish to leave friends and family who provide a support network. Many workers are unwilling to leave their geographical area because they feel they have strong roots there. Housing can also be a major cause of geographical immobility. Workers who rent their accommodation from social landlords like the local council or a housing association may not be able to get a new house if they move elsewhere. Alternative private rented accommodation may be much more expensive or unsuitable. If workers own their own home, house prices in the area they wish to move to may be much more expensive. High house prices in London and the South East, for example, are a major barrier to mobility into these regions. Selling and buying a house is also a major cost in itself. On the whole, the lower the income of an individual, the greater is housing a barrier to mobility.

Occupational mobility Occupational mobility refers to the ability of workers to transfer from one occupation to another,

Question 4

High levels of unemployment should mean that firms can recruit workers easily, without increasing their rates of pay. However, despite relatively high unemployment nationally, firms are finding it difficult to recruit workers with the right skills. According to a survey of 400 job agencies by the Recruitment and Employment Confederation (REC) and KPMG, the professional services firm, the availability of candidates to fill permanent job vacancies fell at its sharpest rate for almost 17 years in May 2014. Starting salaries for permanent and temporary staff had increased in recent months. Kevin Green, the REC's chief executive repeated his call for the easing of visa restrictions so that more highly skilled workers could be recruited from overseas.

Source: adapted from © the Financial Times 6.6.2014, All Rights Reserved.

(a) Define elasticity of supply of labour.

(b) (i) Explain whether economic theory would predict that the elasticity of supply of labour would be high or low if there were high unemployment in an economy. (ii) Why might the elasticity of supply of labour have been higher than this in some occupations in 2014 in the UK?

(c) Explain what could happen to the elasticity of supply of labour if there were an 'easing of visa restrictions'.

such as a teacher to an accountant. Some jobs require only general work skills. So most workers could become office cleaners or car parking attendants. Most jobs, though, require particular knowledge and aptitude skills. Teachers, doctors and judges only get their jobs after years of education and training. In the short term, it is very difficult for workers to transfer from one occupation to another and in many cases it is impossible. In the longer term, it becomes more possible although the cost for the individual may be very high.

Key Terms

Activity or participation rates - the percentage or proportion of any given population in the labour force.

Economically active - the number of workers in the workforce who are in a job or are unemployed.

Net migration - immigration minus emigration.

Population of working age - size of the population aged between the school leaving age and the state retirement age.

Workforce or labour force or working population - those economically active and therefore in work or seeking work.

Workforce jobs - the number of workers in employment. It excludes the unemployed.

Thinking like an economist

The supply of labour in the UK

In 2014, the population of the UK was approximately 64.2 million. Not all were available for work. Those below the age of 16 were in full-time education whilst men and women over the age of 65, were officially counted as retired. The rest, those aged 16-65, are known as the **population of working age**. Figure 7 shows that the numbers in this age group have increased in recent decades. The precise definition of the population of working age can change over time. In the UK, the state pension retirement age for women has increased from 60 in 2010 to 65 in 2018. The state retirement age will then increase for both men and women to 66 in 2020 and to 68 between 2044 and 2046. Also all 16-18-year-olds will have to remain in full-time education or training to the age of 18 starting in 2015.

Not all of those of working age are **economically active** and part of the **workforce** (or **labour force** or **working population**). Many women choose to leave employment to bring up children. Young people too may stay on in education after the age of 18. Many over-50s takes early retirement. So the workforce is smaller than the population of working age.

Figure 7

Population of working age[1], economically active, total in employment and unemployment

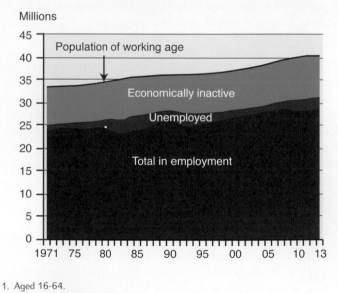

1. Aged 16-64.
Source: adapted from www.ons.gov.uk.

The workforce, made up of those who are economically active, is made up of two groups: those in work and those seeking work and who are therefore unemployed. Figure 8 gives a breakdown of those in work with **workforce jobs**. Most are **employees** who work for someone else, their **employer**. A minority who work for themselves are known as **self-employed**.

Figure 8

Workforce jobs

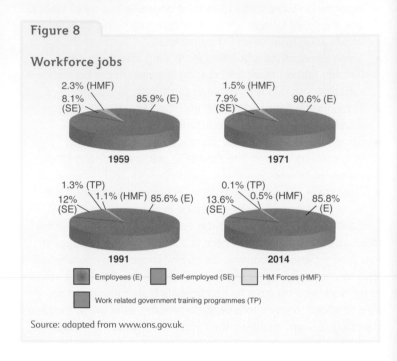

Source: adapted from www.ons.gov.uk.

Figure 8 shows that the workforce (those in a job and those officially unemployed) has tended to increase over time, from 25.1 million in 1971 to 31.5 million in 2013. The growth in workforce jobs has been less smooth than that of the workforce itself. Four major recessions, 1975-77, 1980-82 and 1990-92 and 2008-09, resulted in large increases in unemployment and falls in the number of people in work. In the recessions of 1980-82 and 1990-92, there was even a fall in the numbers of those economically active. Workers, particularly women, became discouraged from looking for work and disappeared from official counts of the unemployed.

Male and female employment

The workforce has grown at a slightly faster rate than the population of working age in recent times. Table 3 shows that whilst the total population of working age grew by 20.8 per cent over the period 1971 to 2013, the workforce grew by 25.5 per cent. The totals, however, mask a much larger change

Table 3 Labour force and population of working age[1], UK

	Economically active			Millions
	Males	Females	Total	Population of working age
1971	15.7	9.4	25.1	33.6
1981	15.8	10.7	26.5	34.9
1991	15.9	12.3	28.2	36.5
2001	15.6	13.1	28.7	37.6
2011	16.6	14.5	31.1	40.5
2013	16.8	14.7	31.5	40.6

1. Males and females aged 16-64.
Source: adapted from www.ons.gov.uk.

in the composition by gender of the labour force. The male workforce has increased by 1.1 million between 1971 and 2013. In comparison, the female workforce has increased by 5.3 million.

Another way of showing increased female participation in the labour force is to calculate the female **activity rate** or **participation rate**. This is the percentage of any given population that is in the labour force (i.e. the percentage of an age group either in work or officially counted as unemployed). Figure 9 shows how the activity rates of females have increased over time whilst those of males have declined. There is a number of reasons why an ever-larger proportion of females have gone out to work.

Figure 9

Economic activity rates by gender, 16-64

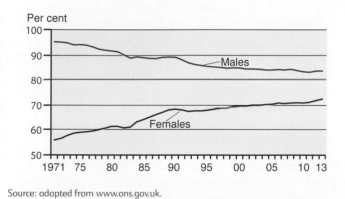

Source: adapted from www.ons.gov.uk.

- Real wages have increased over the period. Economic theory would predict that an increase in real wages will increase the supply of labour into the market.
- Through changes in social attitudes and legislation, women now have much greater opportunities in employment than in 1971 and far more than say in 1931 or 1901. Again this means that more women are getting higher paid jobs, attracting them to make careers for themselves.
- The opportunity cost of going out to work has fallen. A hundred years ago, women created a large number of household services, from cleaning the house to baking bread to making clothes. They had to spend large amounts of time each week doing this. Today, cheap and efficient machines do much of this work. What is more, the real price of washing machines, microwaves, etc. has tended to fall over time. Households have been able to afford to buy more and more of these gadgets. The result is that women have increasingly been able to combine a career with running a home. Moreover, changes in social attitudes over the past 20 years have meant that men have increasingly shared in domestic chores, again helping to create time for women to work in paid employment.
- Falls in the number of children in a family help explain why there was an increase in the number of women working over the period 1900 to 1970. However, the size of families with children has altered relatively little since 1970. What has changed is an increase in nursery education and in pre-school and childminding facilities. Women have found it

easier to get their children looked after at an affordable cost since 1970.

Male activity rates, in contrast, have fallen. In 1971, virtually all males aged 16-65 were in the labour force. Only a minority stayed on in education, aged 16-18, for example, and only about 10 per cent of the age cohort would go on to university or other full-time education, aged 18-21. It was also rare for males to take early retirement. There were far fewer long-term sick males of working age. Many males who are long-term sick today would have been dead in 1971 because medical care was not as good.

Table 4 Percentage of those in employment working in each occupation group by sex, April to June 2013, UK[1]

		Percentage
	Males	Females
Managers and senior officials	13.1	7.3
Professional occupations	18.5	20.7
Associate professional and technical occupations	14.9	12.5
Administrative and secretarial occupations	4.9	18.2
Skilled trades occupations	18.1	2.3
Caring, leisure and other service occupations	3.1	16.1
Sales and customer service occupations	5.6	10.6
Process, plant and machine operatives	10.6	1.5
Elementary occupations	11.2	10.6
All occupations	**100.0**	**100.0**

1. Figures do not add up to exactly 100 because of rounding.

Source: adapted from www.ons.gov.uk.

The distribution of men and women between different occupations is very different, as Table 4 shows. For example, administrative and secretarial occupations are dominated by women, whilst process, plant and machine operatives are dominated by men. If you call a plumber (part of skilled trades occupations) you will almost certainly get a man. If you are looked after in a care home (caring, leisure and other service occupations), you will almost certainly be cared for by a woman. Nearly twice the number of managers and senior officials are men compared to women.

There is a number of possible reasons which might explain this. Traditionally, males have taken jobs which require heavy manual labour. Women, in contrast, have been associated with the caring professions such as nursing. Secretarial and clerical work is another area which has traditionally been female dominated over the past 100 years. Women are also disproportionately represented amongst occupations where there are large numbers of part-time workers. Due to child care commitments, many women prefer to work part-time rather than full time and therefore occupations which offer opportunities for part-time work are likely to attract more female workers.

Sexual equality is a relatively recent phenomenon and females are still disproportionately represented in higher paid jobs such as managers and senior officials. This could be due to discrimination against women. However, it must also reflect the fact that women are far more likely than men to take a career break to bring up children. Even a few years out of the labour force has a considerable impact on promotion prospects. Finally, the differences in Table 4 may simply reflect occupational preferences between males and females. Males, perhaps, may

341

Figure 10

Immigration and emigration, thousands

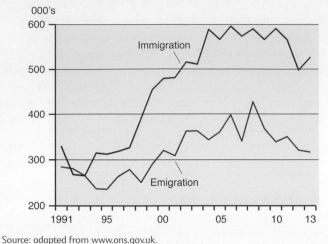

Source: adapted from www.ons.gov.uk.

prefer to mix concrete rather than act as a receptionist. This might suggest that the supply curve for any occupation is different between men and women.

Employment by age

Not only has the balance of the labour force changed between the sexes, it has also changed by age as Table 5 shows. Over time, the number of 16-24 year olds working has fallen. This is mainly due to increased participation in full-time education both aged 16-18 and then at university. At the other end of the age range, the number of over 65-year-olds in work is rising. The UK government aims to raise the state pension retirement age for women to 65; then for both men and women to 66 and then 68. Many workers have occupational pensions, linked to their work, which allow them to retire earlier. However, public sector pension schemes, such as for teachers and local authority workers, are increasing their retirement ages. By 2050, the age at which most will be able to take their pension is likely to be in the late 60s. A few workers have always wanted to work beyond 65. Either they enjoy working or they feel they need to earn money. Most of the increase in future, however, will be from workers who would prefer to retire but are forced to keep on working because they cannot draw their pension.

The average age of those in work is rising for 25-64-year-olds. This has been caused by changes in the number of births over time. The number of births increased from the end of the Second World War to the mid-1960s. They then fell to 1978, rose again to 1990, fell to 2002 and are now rising

Table 5 Employment by age, millions UK

					Millions
	18-24	25-34	35-49	50-64	65+
1971	5.1	5.3	7.9	5.8	0.4
1984	5.1	5.3	8.0	5.6	0.4
1992	4.5	6.6	9.1	5.0	0.5
2002	4.1	6.5	10.4	6.5	0.5
2013	3.7	6.8	10.7	7.8	1.0

Source: adapted from www.ons.gov.uk.

again. These rises and falls create bulges of workers in the age distribution of the labour force. People born from the end of the Second World War in 1945 to the mid-1960s are called 'baby boomers'. These baby boomers have gradually pushed their way through the age range of the working population and many have now retired.

Employment by ethnic group

Statistics for the employment of different ethic groups in the population can be found in the data question in this unit. In general, the employment statistics of those of non-white origin seem less favourable than those of the white population but there are significant exceptions to this.

Employment by industry and region

The supply of workers to different industries and different regions has changed considerably over the past 50 years. Broadly, there has been a major shift of workers from the primary and secondary sector of the economy to the tertiary sector. Consequently, regions heavily dependent upon coal mining and heavy manufacturing saw losses of jobs and population to regions which have traditionally specialised in light manufacturing and services. London has grown in importance economically over the past 20 years. This and proximity to mainland Europe has meant that the south of England has outperformed the south west, the midlands, the north of England and Scotland, Wales and Northern Ireland.

Other factors affecting the labour force

There are factors other than the increased participation of women, birth rates, education and the age of retirement which affect the labour force.

Migration If immigration is larger than emigration, then the workforce is likely to increase. During the 1950s, the UK encouraged immigration from new Commonwealth countries to fill an acute labour shortage. In the 1960s and 1970s, following the 1961 Immigration Act, **net migration** (immigration minus emigration) tended to be negative. Since the 1980s, it has tended to be positive. Part of the reason for this is the free flow of labour within the European Union. Since the late 1990s, as Figure 10 shows, there has been a significant increase in immigration, in part due to increased immigration from Eastern European countries. Some argue this increased supply has helped depress UK wage rates in the middle and bottom end of the wage spectrum.

Part-time work The numbers and proportion of part-time workers in the workforce have been growing over the past 30 years. Figure 11 shows that there was an increase of 31 per cent in the number of female part-time workers between 1984 and 2013. The number of male part-time workers increased by 259 per cent. At the same time, the numbers in full-time work increased by 13 per cent.

There were 3.4 times as many female part-time workers compared to male part-time workers in 2013. The main reason for this is that women are still the main carers for children. The trend is for more women to combine either a part-time job or a full-time job with looking after their children.

The growth in male part-time employment is due to a variety of factors. There is a rise in the number of men who are looking

Figure 11

Full-time and part-time employment by gender

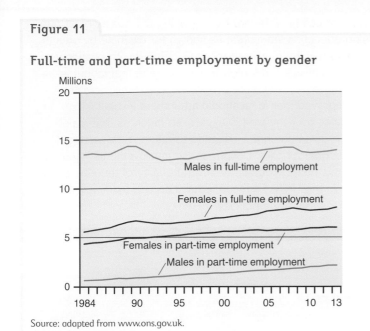

Source: adapted from www.ons.gov.uk.

Figure 12

Self-employment

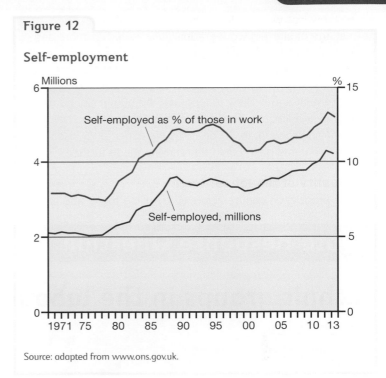

Source: adapted from www.ons.gov.uk.

after their children. More men cannot find full-time jobs and so take part-time jobs. Also the growing number of men working beyond retirement age are tending to work part-time rather than full-time.

Self-employment As Figure 12 shows, both the number of people self-employed and the proportion of self-employed in those in work has grown over time. Growth in self-employment tends to be correlated to unemployment. The high unemployment period of the 1980s saw a large increase in self-employment as did the difficult economic times following the financial crisis of 2007-08. Between the first quarter of 2008 and the third quarter of 2014, employment rose by 1.1 million. Of this, 732 000 were self-employed and only 339 000 found jobs as employees. Some people who become self-employed do so because they want to run their own business. However, at times when jobs are difficult to get, self-employment becomes an acceptable alternative to unemployment.

Temporary work Figure 13 shows that there was a growth of temporary employment in the 1990s and again following the financial crisis of 2007-08. Most temporary workers

would prefer a permanent job. For employers, however, hiring temporary workers reduces risks should there be a fall in output. The decline in temporary workers in the early 2000s probably reflected the growing confidence of employers in the economy and a stronger labour market where workers could more easily find permanent jobs.

Hours of work and holidays Hours of work have changed little since the early 1970s. On average, full-time male workers have worked 41 hours per week throughout the period. Figure 14 shows how the hours of work of male and female workers have changed since 1997. It shows that full-time men work slightly longer hours than full-time women. Yearly hours of work have tended to fall over time because of higher holiday entitlement. In 1961, for example, workers were entitled by law to just two weeks paid holiday per year plus bank holidays. By 2014, this had risen to four weeks paid holiday a year plus bank holidays. During the second half of the 20th century, there was

Figure 13

Temporary workers

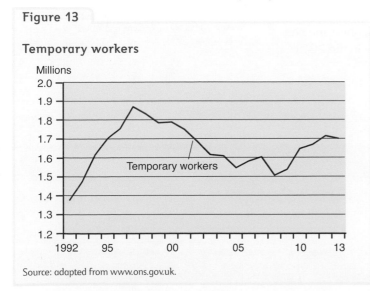

Source: adapted from www.ons.gov.uk.

Figure 14

Mean weekly paid hours of work for full-time workers including overtime

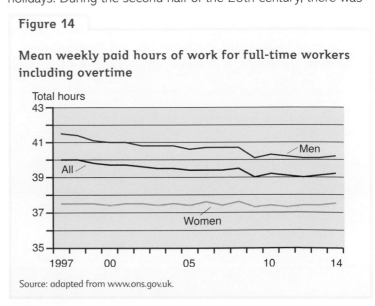

Source: adapted from www.ons.gov.uk.

a trend towards working fewer hours over a lifetime. The normal age of starting work gradually increased as more and more stayed on in education. There was also a growing trend at the end of the period for some to take early retirement. However, at the start of the 21st century, the pushing back of the retirement age is likely to lengthen the number of hours worked over a lifetime. Those born in 2000 could well be facing having to work to 70 or 75 as life expectancy rises and governments push back the retirement age further.

The quality of the labour force

Greater production can be achieved by using more labour.

Equally, it can be achieved by improving the quality of labour. Rising education standards, as shown for example by greater numbers gaining qualifications at GCSE, A level, vocational level and university degrees, would suggest that labour is becoming potentially more productive over time. Females have improved their educational attainment levels faster than males over the past 30 years, so much so that male underachievement in the education system is now a target for government policy. Despite these improvements, there is an intense political debate about the quality of the education system in the UK. As a result, education and training remain a focus for supply-side policies.

Data Response Question

Ethnic groups in the labour force

Inactivity

Why are men and women aged 16-64 inactive, i.e. not in work or unemployed? According to the 2011 Census, the main reasons for men being economically inactive was because they were a student (37 per cent) or sick and disabled (27 per cent), whereas the main reason for women was because they were looking after the family and home (31 per cent). High proportions of ethnic minority men were economically inactive due to being a student which is consistent with the younger age profile of these groups. Chinese men (83 per cent) and women (64 per cent) were the most likely to be economically inactive due to being a student. Women who were Bangladeshi (54 per cent), Pakistani (52 per cent) and Arab (39 per cent) had the highest economic inactivity because of looking after the family or home. Retirement is more dominant

for White British men and women than minority ethnic groups largely because of the older age profile of these groups. White British had the highest median age of all ethnic groups in the 2011

Census (53 and 42 years of age respectively).

Source: adapted from ONS, Ethnicity and the Labour Market, 2011 Census, England and Wales, 13 November 2014.

Characteristics of ethnic groups in employment

The 2011 Census collected information about the jobs people held both according to the type of work undertaken and the industry in which they worked.

Overall, 37 per cent of men in employment worked in low-skilled occupations. However, over half of the men who were of Pakistani (57 per cent), Black African (54 per cent) and Bangladeshi (53 per cent) ethnicity worked in low-skilled jobs. Men who were the least likely to work in low-skilled occupations were Chinese (24 per cent), closely followed by White Irish (29 per cent).

Overall, almost 6 in 10 (59 per cent) women in employment worked in low skilled jobs in the 2011 Census. Women most likely to work in low skilled jobs were Gypsy or Irish Traveller (71 per cent), Bangladeshi

(67 per cent) and White and Black Caribbean (66 per cent). Like men, women least likely to work in low-skilled jobs were Chinese (42 per cent) and White Irish (45 per cent).

Certain ethnic groups were concentrated in particular industries. Men from the Asian/Asian British groups were highly concentrated across the 'Accommodation and food service activities' (for example working in restaurants and hotels) and 'Wholesale and retail trade' (for example, shops). Over a third of Bangladeshi men (36 per cent) worked in the 'Accommodation and food service industries'. Women from the Black ethnic minorities and Other Asian were highly concentrated within the 'Human health and social work activities'. Black African women had nearly 4 in 10 (38 per cent) working in this sector.

Overall, around 16 per cent of men in employment worked part-time in the

2011 Census. With the exception of White Irish and White Other, men in ethnic minority groups were more likely than average to work part-time. Over half (54 per cent) of Bangladeshi men worked part-time and just over 1 in 8 worked 15 hours a week or less (12 per cent). Overall 44 per cent of women in employment worked part-time (30 hours or less) in the 2011 Census. Bangladeshi (56 per cent), Gypsy or Irish Traveller (54 per cent) and Pakistani (52 per cent) women were the most likely to work part-time. Bangladeshi and Pakistani women had the highest proportion, working less than 15 hours a week (23 per cent and 20 per cent respectively). Overall one in five (19 per cent) men worked 49 hours or more.

Source: adapted from ONS, Ethnicity and the Labour Market, 2011 Census, England and Wales, 13 November 2014.

Figure 15

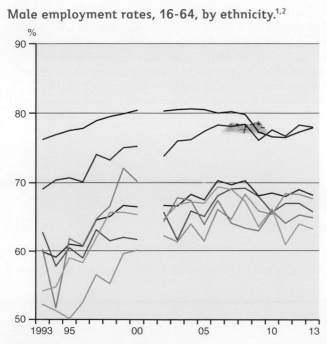

Male employment rates, 16-64, by ethnicity.[1,2]

Figure 16

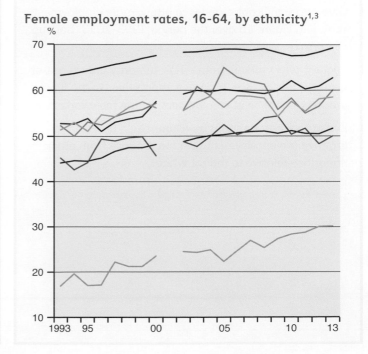

Female employment rates, 16-64, by ethnicity[1,3]

—White
—Black
—Mixed or multiple
—Indian
—Pakistani/Bangladeshi
—Chinese & Other
—All ethnic minorities

1. There is a discontinuity in 2001.
2. Percentage of men aged 16-64 in work out of the total population of men aged 16-64.
3. Percentage of women aged 16-64 in work out of the total population of women aged 16-64.

Source: adapted from www.ons.gov.uk.

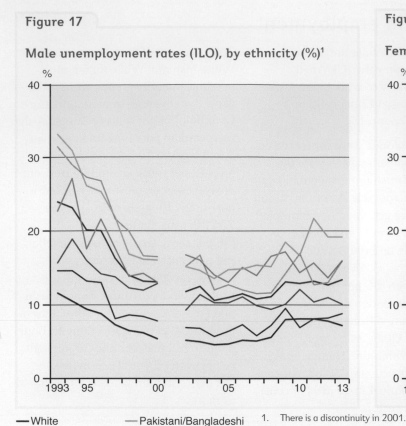

Figure 17

Male unemployment rates (ILO), by ethnicity (%)[1]

Figure 18

Female unemployment rates (ILO), by ethnicity (%)[1]

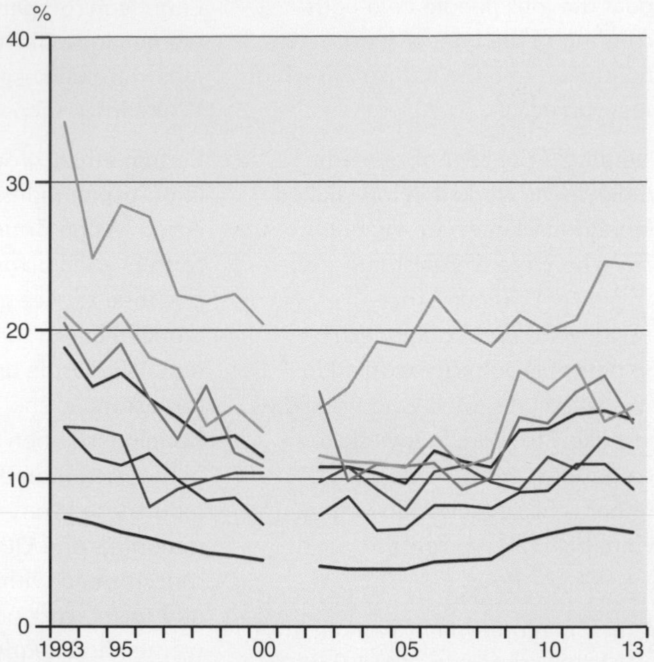

— White   — Pakistani/Bangladeshi
— Black   — Chinese & Other
— Mixed or multiple — All ethnic minorities
— Indian

1. There is a discontinuity in 2001.
Source: adapted from www.ons.gov.uk.

Q

1. Give two significant changes to ethnic male employment shown in Figure 15 over the period 1993-2013. Back up you answer with statistics.

2. Suggest why workers from ethnic minority groups are, on average, less likely to (a) supply themselves to the labour market and (b) be in employment than white workers.

3. Evaluate what economic measures could be taken to improve the employment position of those from ethnic minorities relative to that of whites.

Evaluation

Analyse how and why those from ethnic minorities seem to be disadvantaged relative to whites. For example, there are issues about low pay, higher unemployment, lower activity rates and part-time working. Having identified an issue, suggest some solutions, such as better educational attainment or better childcare facilities. As part of your evaluation, point out that crude statistics don't tell the full story. For instance, inactivity amongst Chinese men and women is mainly caused by them being in full-time education rather than being discouraged workers.

59 Wage determination

Key points

1. The wage rate of labour is determined by the demand for labour and the supply of labour and their relative elasticities.
2. In an economy where labour is homogeneous and all markets are perfect, wage rates would be identical for all workers.
3. Wage differentials are caused partly by market imperfections and partly by differences in individual labour characteristics.
4. In a perfectly competitive market, individual firms face a horizontal supply curve and will hire labour up to the point where the wage rate is equal to the marginal revenue product of labour.
5. In an imperfectly competitive market, either the firm is a monopsonist or there is a monopoly supplier of labour, such as a trade union, or both. A monopsonist drives down wage rates and employment levels, whilst a monopoly supplier increases wage rates.

Starter activity

Why don't all workers earn the same amount per year?

How wage rates are determined

Prices are determined by demand and supply. So the price of labour, the real wage rate, is determined by the demand for and the supply of labour.

The demand curve for labour in an industry is the marginal revenue product curve of labour. This is downward sloping, indicating that more labour will be demanded the lower the real wage rate. The supply curve of labour to an industry is upward sloping, indicating that more labour will be supplied if real wage rates increase. This gives an equilibrium real wage rate of OA in Figure 1. OB units of labour are demanded and supplied.

The demand and supply curves for labour can shift for a variety of reasons, giving new equilibrium real wage rates and levels of employment in the industry. The demand curve for labour will move to the right showing an increase in the demand for labour if the marginal revenue product of labour increases. This might occur if:

- productivity improves, perhaps due to changing technology or more flexible working practices, increasing output per worker;

Figure 1

Equilibrium wage rate in an industry

The equilibrium real wage rate is OA whilst the level of employment in equilibrium is OB.

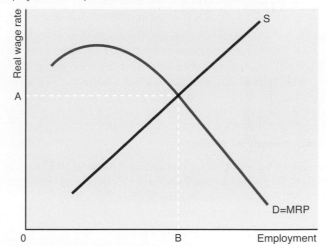

- there is a rise in the selling price of the product, increasing the value of the output of each worker;

Question 1

(a) On a diagram, draw a demand and supply curve for labour in the DVD production industry.

(b) Mark on the diagram the equilibrium wage rate and the equilibrium level of employment.

(c) Show how the demand curve or the supply curve might shift if there is:
   (i) a fall in labour productivity;
   (ii) an increase in wage rates in all other labour markets in the economy;
   (iii) a fall in demand for DVDs;
   (iv) an introduction of new labour-saving technology;
   (v) a fall in the number of 16-25-year-olds in the population as a whole.

- the price of capital increases, leading to a substitution of labour for capital.

The supply curve might move to the right, showing an increase in supply, if:

- there is an increase in the number of workers in the population as a whole, perhaps because of changing demographic trends, or because government alters tax and benefit levels, increasing incentives to work;
- wages or conditions of work deteriorate in other industries, making conditions relatively more attractive in this industry.

Elasticities of demand for and supply of labour

The elasticities of demand for and supply of labour affect what happens to the real wage rate and employment in a market or an economy when demand and supply change.

Figure 2 shows a labour market when supply is highly inelastic. If there is an increase in demand for labour, shown by the shift in the demand for labour curve from D_1 to D_2, then there will be very little increase in employment but a large increase in the real wage rate. All other things being equal, the lower the elasticity of supply for labour, the greater will be the change in the real wage rate and the less will be the change in employment as a result of a change in demand for labour.

Figure 3 shows a labour market where demand is highly inelastic. If there is an increase in the supply of labour, shown by the shift in the supply curve from S_1 to S_2, then there will be very little increase in employment but a large fall in the real

Figure 2

Inelastic supply of labour

With inelastic supply of labour, an increase in demand for labour from D_1 to D_2 leads to a large increase of EF in real wage rates but only a small increase in employment of AB.

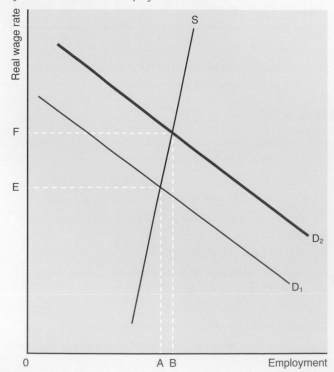

Figure 3

Inelastic demand for labour

With inelastic demand for labour, an increase in supply for labour from S_1 to S_2 leads to a large fall of EF in real wage rates but only a small increase in employment of AB.

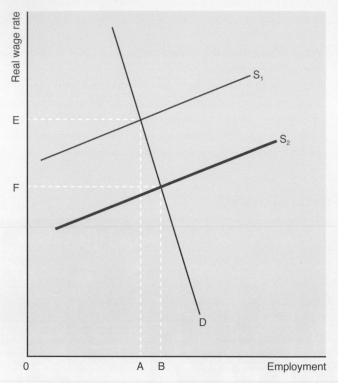

wage rate. All other things being equal, the lower the elasticity of demand for labour, the greater will be the change in the real wage rate and the less will be the change in employment as a result of a change in supply for labour.

A labour market where all workers are paid the same

Consider an economy which has the following labour market characteristics.

- Labour is homogeneous (i.e. all workers are identical, for instance in age, skill and sex).
- There is perfect knowledge in the labour market. For example, a worker in Scotland is as aware of job opportunities in London as a Londoner.
- There is perfect mobility of labour. Workers can move at no cost between jobs in the same industry, between different industries and between geographical areas. Equally, there are no costs to firms in hiring and firing workers.
- All workers and employers are price takers. There are no trade unions or monopsonist employers.
- There are no barriers which prevent wages rising and falling to accommodate changes in the demand for and supply of labour.
- Firms aim to maximise profit and minimise costs of production, whilst workers aim to maximise their wages.

In this perfect labour market, all workers would be paid the same wage rate. To show that this must be true, consider two markets where wages rates are different. We have to assume that there are no costs in moving jobs and that rents and property prices are the same in the two areas of the country. In the Manchester catering market, wages are higher than in the catering market in Wales. Welsh catering workers would know this because there is perfect knowledge in the market. They would apply for jobs in the Manchester catering market. They would be prepared to work for less than existing Manchester catering workers so long as the wage rate was higher than their existing wage rate in Wales. Manchester employers, seeking to minimise costs, would then either sack their existing workers and replace them with cheaper Welsh workers, or offer to continue employing their existing workforce but at a lower wage. Meanwhile, Welsh catering firms would be threatened with a loss of their workers. To retain them, they would need to put up their wage rates. Only when the two wage rates are equal would there be no incentive for Welsh catering workers to move to Manchester.

Why wage rates differ

In the real world, wage rates differ. One important reason is because labour is not homogeneous. Each worker is a unique factor of production, possessing a unique set of employment characteristics such as:

- age - whether young, middle aged or old;
- sex - whether male or female;
- ethnic background;
- education, training and work experience;
- ability to perform tasks - including how hard they are prepared to work, their strength and their manual or mental dexterity.

For instance, a manager of a company is likely to be paid more than a cleaner working for the same company. On the one hand, the marginal revenue product of the manager is likely to be higher. Her education, skills and work experience are likely to provide greater value to the company than the cleaner's. On the other hand, the supply of managers is lower than the supply of cleaners. Most workers in the workforce could be a cleaner, but only a few have sufficient qualities to be managers. Greater demand and less supply lead to higher wage rates for managers than cleaners.

Wage rates also differ because workers do not necessarily seek to maximise wages. Wages are only part of the net benefit workers gain from employment. Workers whose jobs are dangerous, unpleasant, tedious, where there is little chance of promotion, where earnings fluctuate and where there are few or no fringe benefits, may seek higher wages than workers whose jobs possess the opposite characteristics. Market forces will tend to lead not to equality of wage rates but to equality of net benefits to workers.

Labour is not perfectly mobile. Hence there can be unemployment and low wages in Scotland whilst employers offering much higher wages are crying out for labour in London. Part of the reason why there is a lack of mobility is the absence of perfect knowledge within the labour market. Workers in Scotland may be unaware of job opportunities in the south of England. There are also many other imperfections in the market which prevent wage rates rising or falling in response to market pressures.

Question 2

Name	Petra Ellis
Age	29
Occupation	Personnel assistant
Location	Chester
Earnings	£25 000 per year

Name	Addo Tower
Age	45
Occupation	Finance director
Location	London
Earnings	£120 000 per year

Name	Mike Sellers
Age	19
Occupation	Sales assistant
Location	Tenby, West Wales
Earnings	£10 700 per year

Name	Geena Miles
Age	33
Occupation	Civil engineer
Location	Birmingham
Earnings	£48 000 per year

Why do the earnings of these workers differ?

Perfectly competitive labour markets

In a perfectly competitive factor market, there is a large number of small firms hiring a large number of individual workers. For the individual firm operating in such a market:

- the demand curve for labour, the marginal revenue product curve of labour, is downward sloping;
- the supply curve of labour is perfectly elastic and therefore horizontal; the firm can hire any number of workers at the existing industry wage rate.

How many workers should this type of firm employ? If a worker costs £200 per week, but increases revenue net of all other costs by only £150, then he should not be employed.

Putting this theoretically, the firm will hire workers up to the point where the marginal cost of labour is equal to the marginal revenue product of labour. If the marginal cost were higher than marginal revenue product, for instance at OC in Figure 4, the firm would make a loss on the output produced by the marginal worker and hence it would cut back on employment of labour. If the marginal revenue product of labour were higher than the marginal cost of labour, for instance at OA, then it would hire more workers because these workers would generate a profit for the firm.

Hence, in Figure 4 the equilibrium level of employment by the firm is OB. This is the point where the marginal cost of labour (the supply curve) is equal to the marginal revenue product of labour (the demand curve). The equilibrium real wage rate is OW. This is the ruling equilibrium wage rate in the industry as a whole.

Imperfectly competitive labour markets

An imperfectly competitive labour market is one where:

- the firm is a dominant or monopoly buyer of labour and is therefore a **monopsonist**, but where there are many individual workers;

Figure 4

Equilibrium employment and wage rates for a firm in a perfectly competitive factor market

In a perfectly competitive factor market, the supply curve for labour facing the firm is horizontal. The equilibrium real wage rate, OW, is set by the industry as a whole. The firm will then employ OB workers in equilibrium.

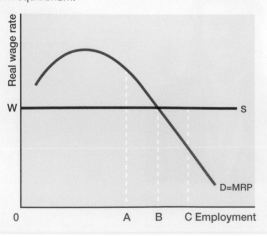

Question 3

Table 1

Number of workers employed	Total revenue product (£ per month)
1	700
2	1300
3	1 800
4	2 200

The data show the monthly total revenue product of a profit maximising manufacturing company in a perfectly competitive industry.

(a) Plot the marginal revenue product curve on graph paper (remembering to plot the MRP half way between whole numbers on the employment axis).

(b) What would be the maximum number of workers the firm would employ if the monthly wage per worker were:
(i) £600; (ii) £400; (iii) £425; (iv) £800; (v) £525?

- the firm is faced with a monopoly supplier of labour, which is most likely to be a trade union;
- a firm is a monopoly buyer of labour and is faced with a monopoly supplier of labour.

Each of these three types of imperfectly competitive labour market will now be considered.

A monopoly buyer of labour

If a firm is the sole buyer of labour, it is called a monopsonist. The state, for instance, employs over 90 per cent of teachers in the UK and therefore is essentially a monopsonist. A monopsonist is able to exploit market power and therefore common sense would suggest that the monopsonist would use this power to force down wage levels.

The marginal cost of employing an extra unit of labour is higher for the monopsonist than the average cost or wage. This is because the firm has to raise wage rates to attract extra labour into the industry. So the cost of employing an extra unit of labour is not just the higher wage paid to that unit but also the extra wages that now need to be paid to all the other workers in the industry.

In Figure 5, the demand and supply curves for labour are drawn. The firm will employ workers up to the point where the marginal cost of an extra worker is equal to the worker's marginal revenue product. Therefore the monopsonist will employ OA workers, the intersection of the marginal cost curve and the marginal revenue product or demand curve. The firm does not then need to pay a real wage rate of OG to each worker. It only needs to pay a real wage rate of OE to attract OA workers to the industry.

If the market were perfectly competitive, employment would be OB and the equilibrium wage rate would be OF. So economic theory suggests that a monopsonist drives down wages and reduces employment levels compared to a perfectly competitive factor market. Note that this is similar to the perfect competition/monopoly analysis in a goods market where it is argued that a monopolist reduces output and raises prices compared to a perfectly competitive market.

Figure 5

Monopsony in the labour market

A monopsonist will hire labour to the point where MC = MRP (i.e. up to the point OA). It will then pay labour the lowest wage rate possible which is OE. If the industry had been perfectly competitive then both the equilibrium wage rate OF and the equilibrium level of employment OB would be higher than under monopsony.

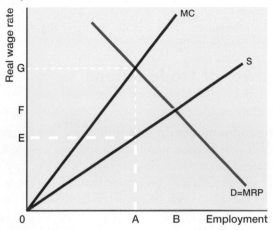

Figure 6

Trade unions in a competitive market

The entry of a trade union to a competitive factor market is likely to 'kink' the supply curve of labour. OB is the union-negotiated wage rate in an industry. Employment will fall from OF to OE whilst wage rates will rise from OA to OB. At a wage of OB, there is now EG unemployment.

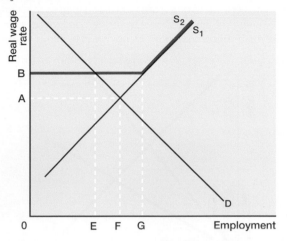

Question 4

Teachers' pay in the UK is currently determined by the findings of a School Teachers' Review Body (STRB). This takes evidence from the government, which generally wishes to keep wage increases to a minimum, and from trade unions, which want to see high increases in wages. The government can choose either to accept the recommendations of the STRB or to impose its own, invariably lower, pay deal. The government is effectively a monopsonist employer for teachers because only nine per cent of teachers work in private sector schools.

(a) Draw a diagram to show the situation of the government facing trade unions in the market for teachers.

Assume the government decides to impose work place bargaining in teaching, with individual teachers negotiating with each school in which they are employed.

(b) Using a diagram, compare the wages and level of employment this system might create to the current system of national bargaining.

A monopoly seller of labour – trade unions

A trade union is an organisation of workers who combine together to further their own interests. Within a company organisation, an individual worker is likely to be in a relatively weak bargaining position compared to his or her employer. The employer possesses far greater knowledge about everything from safety standards to the profitability of the firm than an individual worker. Moreover, the loss of an individual worker to a firm is likely to be far less significant than the loss of his or her job to the employee.

So workers have organised themselves in unions to bargain collectively. Instead of each individual worker bargaining with the firm on a wide range of wage and employment issues, workers elect or appoint representatives to bargain on their behalf. From an economic viewpoint, trade unions act as monopoly suppliers of labour.

Trade unions act to further the interests of their members. One of the key ways in which they do this is to press for higher wages. In economic terms, they attempt to fix a minimum price for the supply of labour. This produces a kinked supply curve.

In Figure 6 the non-union demand and supply curves for labour in an industry are D and S_1 respectively. A union agreement to raise wages from the free market wage of OA to the unionised wage rate of OB means that employers in the industry cannot hire workers below a wage rate of OB. The supply curve therefore is perfectly elastic (i.e. horizontal) over the employment range OG. The union agreement does not prevent employers paying higher wages than the negotiated wage. Employers would need to pay higher wage rates if they wished to hire more workers than OG. Above OG the new supply curve S_2 is the same as the old supply curve S_1. The new equilibrium wage rate is OB, the wage rate that the union negotiated. However, employment in the industry falls from OF (the equilibrium in a non-unionised market) to OE.

Neo-classical micro-economic theory therefore suggests that trade unions increase wages for their members, but also cause unemployment in the industry. Wages would be lower and employment higher if the industry were non-unionised.

Bilateral monopoly

Many trade unions operate in factor markets where there are monopsony employers. A sole seller of labour (the trade union) faces a sole buyer of labour (the monopsonist). This is called a bilateral monopoly.

Trade union vs a monopsonist employer

A monopsonist facing a large number of employees in an industry will force wage rates down to OE and restrict employment to OA. The entry of a trade union to the industry which sets a minimum wage of OF will 'kink' the supply curve of labour and produce a discontinuity in the marginal cost curve for labour. The monopsonist has a profit incentive to hire extra workers so long as the marginal revenue product of labour, shown by the demand curve, is greater than the marginal cost of labour. Hence it will employ OB workers.

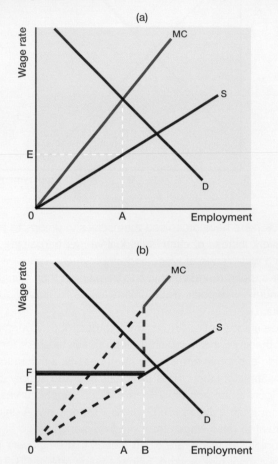

(a)

(b)

revenue product of labour, shown by the demand curve, is greater than the marginal cost of labour. Hence it will employ OB workers.

Why should a monopsonist buy more labour at a higher wage rate from a union than it would otherwise? It should be remembered that a firm bases its decision on how much labour to hire not on the wage rate (the average cost of labour) but on the marginal cost of labour. It can be seen from Figure 7 that the marginal cost of unionised labour is lower between employment levels A and B than it would have been if labour had been non-unionised. In the former case it is flat at OF, whilst in the latter it is rising steeply above OF.

The power of trade unions

There is a variety of factors which make trade unions more or less powerful.

Trade union membership and militancy A union which has 100 per cent membership in an industry is likely to be stronger than a union which only represents 10 per cent of potential members. It could be argued that the RMT is far more powerful in the railway industry than the Unite union is in the hairdressing industry. Equally, unions are more likely to call for industrial action if union members are militant. The more militant the union membership, the more costly a dispute is likely to be for an employer.

The demand curve for labour is relatively inelastic A rise in wage rates will have far less impact upon employment in the industry if the demand for labour is relatively inelastic than if it is elastic. Hence, there will be far less cost to the union of a wage rate increase in terms of lost membership and to its members in terms of lost employment.

Profitability of the employer A trade union is unlikely to be able to negotiate large wage increases with an employer on the verge of bankruptcy. It is likely to be in a stronger position with a highly profitable firm. This implies that trade unions will be stronger in monopolistic and oligopolistic industries, where firms are able to earn abnormal profit, than in perfectly competitive industries where only normal profit can be earned in the long run.

Efficiency

Neo-classical economic theory suggests that trade unions operating in competitive industries reduce employment levels and raise wage rates. If all industries but one were perfectly competitive then a trade union in that one industry would mean that the economy as a whole was not efficient.

However, most industries in the UK are imperfectly competitive. A trade union facing a monopsonist will redress the balance of power in the industry and lead to a level of employment and a wage rate which will be nearer to the free market price of labour. It could well be that the presence of a trade union increases economic efficiency in an imperfectly competitive market. Hence the effect of trade unions on economic efficiency depends on the structure of markets in an economy.

A further important argument needs to be considered. Some economists have suggested that trade unions raise economic

Economic theory suggests that a trade union will increase both wages and employment compared to a factor market where a monopsony employer negotiates with a large number of individual employees. Figure 7(a) shows the wage and employment levels in an industry with a monopsonist and many individual employees. Employment is OA and the equilibrium wage rate is OE. Figure 7(b) shows the entry of a trade union to the industry. Assume that the trade union forces the wage rate up to OF. This produces a kinked supply curve. The monopsonist cannot pay a wage rate lower than OF because of its union agreement. However, it is free to pay higher wage rates if it wishes to employ more than OB workers. This produces a kink in the marginal cost of labour to the firm. Up to OB, the marginal cost of labour is the same as the union negotiated wage rate. The employer can hire an extra unit of labour at that wage rate. If it employs more than OB workers, the wage rate will rise, resulting in a jump in marginal cost at OB. The monopsonist has a profit incentive to hire extra workers so long as the marginal efficiency because they lower costs of production to the firm. The trade union performs many of the functions of a personnel department within a firm. It deals with workers' problems and obviates the need for the firm to negotiate pay with each and every worker. More importantly, it can be a good vehicle for negotiating changes in working practices. A firm may wish to implement changes which will lead to less pleasant working conditions for its workers. Perhaps it wishes to increase the speed of the assembly line, or force workers to undertake a variety of tasks rather than just one. It may find it difficult to implement these changes on a non-unionised workforce because some workers may take unorganised industrial action or do their best to disrupt any changes being introduced. A union may help the firm to persuade workers that changes in working practices are in their own interest. The union will usually demand a price for this co-operation - higher wage rates for its members. But it still leads to an increase in economic efficiency because the firm is able to make higher profits whilst workers receive higher wage rates. According to this view, trade unions increase productivity in the economy.

Key Terms

Bilateral monopoly - when a single buyer faces a single seller in a market. In a labour market, this is most likely to occur when government is the single buyer of a type of labour and the workforce is unionised, so that the trade union acts as a single seller.

Question 5

Table 2

Units of labour employed	Wage rate per worker, £		Marginal cost of employing one extra worker, £		Marginal revenue product of labour, £
	With no trade union	With a trade union	With no trade union	With a trade union	
2	4	8	4	8	16
3	5	8	6	8	14
4	6	8	8	8	12
5	7	8	10	8	10
6	8	8	12	8	8
7	9	9	14	14	6
8	10	10	16	16	4

The table shows wage rates, marginal employment costs and MRPs facing a monopsonist employer of labour.

(a) (i) What is the maximum number of workers the firm would employ if the labour force were non-unionised?
(ii) What would be the equilibrium wage rate?

(b) What is the maximum number of workers the firm would employ if workers belonged to a trade union and it had negotiated a minimum wage rate of £8?

(c) Explain why trade unions might increase rather than decrease the level of employment in an industry.

Thinking like an economist

Wage determination

Wage structure by occupation
Economic theory would suggest that wage rates would be the same if all labour was homogeneous and all jobs possessed the same characteristics. In the real world, workers are not identical. They differ, for instance, in where they are prepared to work, their hours of work and their levels of human capital. Jobs differ too. In particular, the marginal revenue product curve for each type of job is different.

For example, Figure 8 shows that in 2014 the average weekly earnings of full-time health professionals, such as doctors and teachers, was £711. This compares with full-time workers in sales occupations who earned on average £332 a week.

Figure 8

Medium full-time gross weekly earnings by major occupational group, April 2014

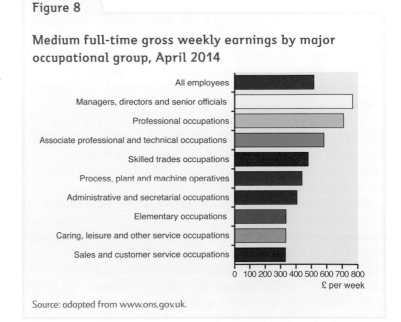

Source: adapted from www.ons.gov.uk.

Table 3 Highest and lowest paid occupations, April 2014, UK

Occupation	Earnings per year
Highest paid	
Aircraft pilots and flight engineers	£90 420
Chief executives and senior officials	£81 521
Air traffic controllers	£79 874
Medical practitioners	£71 141
Marketing and sales directors	£70 742
Information technology and telecommunications directors	£64 511
Financial managers and directors	£61 108
Senior police officers	£57 896
Financial institution managers and directors	£53 621
Senior professionals of educational establishments	£50 367
Lowest paid	
Other elementary services occupations	£14 575
Nursery nurses and assistants	£14 305
Cleaners and domestics	£14 164
Playworkers	£14 023
Retail cashiers and check-out operators	£13 911
Launderers, dry cleaners and pressers	£13 767
Kitchen and catering assistants	£13 396
Hairdressers and barbers	£13 373
Bar staff	£12 948
Waiters and waitresses	£12 507

Source: adapted from www.ons.gov.uk.

Figure 9

Hourly pay distribution percentiles: ratio of real hourly pay, full-time and part-time workers, 2013 compared to 1975

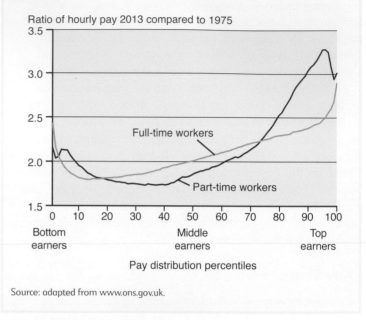

Source: adapted from www.ons.gov.uk.

Neo-classical economic theory suggests that such differences are due to differences in the demand for and supply of different types of labour.

On the supply side, there are potentially far more workers with the ability and training to become manual workers than non-manual workers.

In Table 3, aircraft pilots and flight engineers earning £90 420 a year could become a waiter or waitress earning £12 507 a year, but the waiter or waitress could not necessarily become a successful aircraft pilot or flight engineer. Occupations which are unpleasant or dangerous, or where earnings can fluctuate greatly, are likely to attract fewer workers than others where the non-pecuniary (i.e. non-monetary) advantages are much greater. Hence, earnings in construction and mining are likely to be higher than average, all other things being equal, because of the danger of the job. In general, the larger the potential supply of labour to an occupation, the lower is likely to be the level of earnings.

On the demand side, non-manual jobs are likely to carry a higher marginal revenue product than manual jobs. Without an effective manager, a company may lose thousands and perhaps millions of pounds of potential revenue or suffer high costs of production. But the company could get by without an effective office cleaner. Hence professional workers in management and administration are paid more highly than workers in catering, cleaning and hairdressing because their revenue product is greater.

So far we have assumed that labour markets are perfectly competitive and that they are in equilibrium. In practice, many of the differences in wages between occupations may be accounted for by trade unions or monopsony employers. For instance, miners saw their trade union power decline when their strike in 1984-85 was broken by the government under Margaret Thatcher.

Alternatively, the market may be in disequilibrium. It could be argued that wage rates in low-skilled jobs in parts of manufacturing are depressed today because of the continued shrinkage of manufacturing industry. On the other hand, earnings in occupations related to computers have been buoyant over the past 15 years as the industry has expanded.

Wage structure by distribution

Over time, there have been large changes in the relative pay of different occupations. Some occupations, for example in web design, didn't exist 30 years ago. Others, such as coal mining, have seen a dramatic decline.

There has also been a significant increase in inequality of earnings. Figure 9 shows the percentage change in real hourly pay for full-time and part-time workers across the income scale between 1975 and 2013. Full-time workers who made up the top 95th percentile on the pay scale (almost at the top of the pay range) saw their real hourly pay increase by 150 per cent. So for every £1 this one per cent group earned in 1975, the equivalent group in 2013 earned £2.50. This can be compared to the 49th percentile income group (in the middle of the pay scale). For every £1 they earned in 1975, the equivalent group in 2014 earned £2.00. The worst performers over the period were in the 13th and 14th percentile (towards the bottom of the pay range). For every £1 they earned in 1975, the equivalent group in 2013 earned £1.79. In general, the higher the real hourly pay, the higher has been the increase between 1975 and

Figure 10

FTSE 350 chief executives and full-time employees, index of earnings growth, 2000-2013 (2000=100)

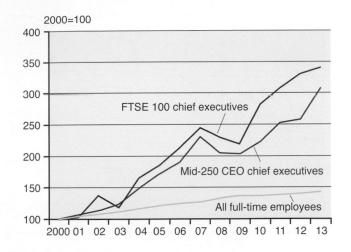

Source: adapted from Executive remuneration in the *FTSE 350 - a focus on performance-related pay*, October 2014, A report for the High Pay Centre From Incomes Data Services.

2013. Inequality in earnings has been rising over time. The only exception to this is the bottom few per cent of income earners. Their relative gain has been entirely due to the introduction of the minimum wage in 1997.

Figure 9 shows that the top five per cent of wage earners have gained the most since 1975. This, in fact, underestimates the relative gain for this group. This is because these workers are the most likely to receive bonuses which are not captured in hourly wage rates. This top five per cent of wage earners include very senior company executives, investment bankers and top lawyers as well as Premier League footballers. To some extent, they are a group of workers who have been able to influence how much they have been paid in ways which other workers, such as waiters or teachers, have not been able to do. The bonuses of investment bankers, for example, are not decided by bank shareholders but by other bankers who also receive large bonuses.

Figure 10 shows how the earnings of the lead or chief executives of the largest 350 companies quoted on the London Stock Exchange (the FTSE 350) have changed since 2000 in money terms (i.e. not adjusted for inflation). For chief executives of the 100 largest companies (FTSE 100), their earnings have increased nearly 3.5 times. For the next 250 companies (Mid-250), their earnings have more than trebled. In contrast, average full-time workers have seen less than a 50 per cent rise in earnings.

There is a number of possible reasons for these trends towards growing inequality in wages.

Decline of primary and secondary industries
Since 1970, there has been a relative decline of primary and secondary industries in the UK as the service sector has expanded. Well-paid manual jobs were concentrated in manufacturing industry and primary industries such as mining and tended to be occupied by men. The number of manual jobs in service industries has grown, but traditionally these have been low-paid jobs done by women.

Decline of trade union membership
Union membership before 1980 was heavily concentrated amongst males in primary and secondary industries, and public sector workers. Trade unions were able to secure higher wages than the free market rate in many cases. Anti-union legislation in the 1980s weakened the power of trade unions at a time when there was considerable shrinkage in the number of jobs in primary and secondary industries. This dealt a double blow to relatively well-paid male manual workers.

Globalisation
Globalisation has put added pressures on poorly skilled low-paid workers. There has been an ever-increasing trend for work requiring high-labour, low-skill inputs to go to the developing world where wages are a fraction of what even low-paid workers earn in the UK. In contrast, the long-term trend for UK manufacturing and services in areas which are internationally traded is for the UK to specialise in producing ever-more sophisticated technological products. This requires high-skill labour inputs and therefore increases the demand for workers who are already better educated, better trained and better paid.

Immigration
The other side of globalisation has been immigration. The UK operates a restrictive immigration policy, but workers from other EU countries are free to enter the UK labour market. In the 2000s, it can be argued that immigration has expanded the supply of workers willing to take low-paid jobs and has been a factor in depressing wage rates.

Technology
Improved technology has resulted in greater productivity of workers. However, the impact of technology has differed between different groups of workers. Some workers have lost their jobs as technology has replaced human workers. Over the past 30 years, information technology in particular has revolutionised the ways in which many goods and services are produced. The introduction of new technology has particularly affected middle and low-skilled workers. For example, banking and finance have cut thousands of processing jobs through automation. This has put downward pressure on wage rates for middle and low-income workers. In contrast, there has been a growth in demand for workers who can successfully use more sophisticated technology. So the wages of better-educated and better-skilled workers have tended to rise.

'Winner takes all'
A very few workers are able to take advantage of 'winner takes all' labour markets. One example is Premier League football. The wages of the very top footballers are now hundreds of thousands of pounds per week. The demand for their services is so great, and the budgets of football clubs are so large, that they can negotiate these very large salaries. Chief executives (CEOs) of large companies can also be seen as being in this category. However, unlike top footballers, there is no evidence to link the performance of companies with the pay given to their chief executives. In contrast, directors of companies responsible for setting salaries and bonuses argue that there is a limited pool of talent for CEOs and therefore they need to be given ever-increasing remuneration packages either to retain them or replace them.

Government policy Wage inequality differs between rich industrialised countries. The US and the UK have relatively high levels of inequality. Countries like Norway and Italy have relatively low levels of wage inequality. Partly this can be explained by government policy. Since the 1980s and the 'Thatcher revolution', successive UK governments have created conditions which encourage growing wage inequality. Policies that have exerted a downward pressure on wages include the considerable weakening of trade union power and measures to make labour markets more 'flexible'. At the same time, some governments have positively encouraged workers to strive for the highest earnings possible. Margaret Thatcher, Prime Minister between 1979 and 1989, for example, equated high earnings with a successful economy. Her government cut the top rate of income tax from 83 per cent to 40 per cent, arguing that high-income earners needed extra incentives to earn even more. In countries like Norway, government policies are designed to encourage much lower wage inequalities. This means increasing the wages of low-paid workers whilst putting downward pressure on the earnings of top-wage earners. In the UK, the only recent government measure to counter growing inequality was the introduction of the minimum wage in 1997. This had a significant impact on the wages of the very lowest-paid workers.

Wage structure by gender

Females have traditionally earned less than men. Economic reasons can be put forward for this. In the past, women were denied the same educational opportunities as men and were thus unable to acquire the same level of human capital. Equally, they were denied access to all but a narrow range of jobs.

Today, possibly the most important factor causing inequality in earnings between the sexes in the UK is the unequal burden of child care. It is still more likely that women will take primary responsibility for bringing up children. Many take a career break after their first or second child or drop down to part-time work. Having taken a career break, some take up low-paid, part-time work which fits in to their primary role as child-carers.

Taking a career break is enormously costly in terms of human capital. Those who continue in employment will not only receive formal training, but will build up informal knowledge and understanding of new work methods, new technology, and new products. In contrast, taking ten years out of the workforce to look after children will leave a worker with outdated skills. This is reflected in the fact that a worker's earnings potential drops every year they are out of work. The time when women choose to leave their careers is also important. It is traditional for workers to make their most important career progressions between the ages of 20 and 40, precisely the time when many women are out of the workforce. Although illegal because it is contrary to equal opportunities legislation, employers may respond to less stable work patterns of women by offering less training to female employees. Women may also be passed over for promotion. At the top, a 'glass ceiling' may exist beyond which male bosses may refuse to promote female workers. To see the glass ceiling in action, it is only necessary to look at the very small numbers of women who make it onto the boards of UK publicly quoted companies.

Figure 11

Ratio of women's to men's earnings: median hourly earnings[1,2]

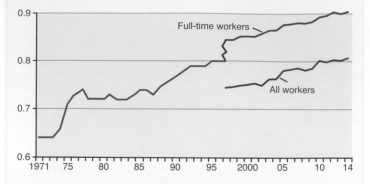

1. Employees on adult rates, pay unaffected by absence. Figures represent the difference between men's and women's hourly earnings as a percentage.
2. Discontinuity in 1997 was caused by the introduction of a new way of calculating average earnings.

Source: adapted from www.ons.gov.uk.

Figure 11 shows the relative hourly earnings of full-time females to males. During the first half of the 1970s, the gap between male and female earnings narrowed. This was mainly the result of the passing of the Equal Pay Act 1970 and the Sex Discrimination Act 1975. The 1970 Act made it illegal to pay women less than men if they were doing the same job. The 1975 Act guaranteed women equality of opportunity. Figure 11 would suggest that this was a once and for all gain. Relative earnings then hardly changed for a decade. Since the mid-1980s, however, there has been a steady narrowing of pay differentials. By 2014, the pay gap was only nine per cent. A number of factors may have caused this.

- The growing proportion of well-qualified women in the workforce may have exerted upward pressure.
- If the 1970s saw an upward trend in relative pay for legal reasons, perhaps from 1987 onwards there was growing social and business awareness that discrimination against women was not acceptable.
- Female workers are far more likely to work part-time than male workers. Average part-time hourly earnings are less than average full-time hourly earnings. Hence the ratio of average hourly earnings of all women workers, both full and part-time, compared to all male workers is lower than for full-time workers alone as can be seen from Figure 11.
- Since the 1990s, the proportion of male workers belonging to trade unions has fallen but the proportion of female workers belonging to trade unions has remained roughly constant. If trade union membership does lead to higher wages as economic theory suggests, male wage rates should have fallen relative to female wage rates.

However, there are still reasons why the earnings of female workers will continue to be less than for males.

- Women on average work fewer hours, and therefore even if hourly pay was the same, women would earn less per week than men.

Figure 12

Median full-time gross weekly earnings by sex and age group, UK, April 2014

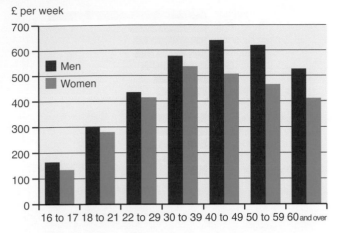

Source: adapted from www.ons.gov.uk.

Figure 13

Employees in London in low-paid work by ethnicity

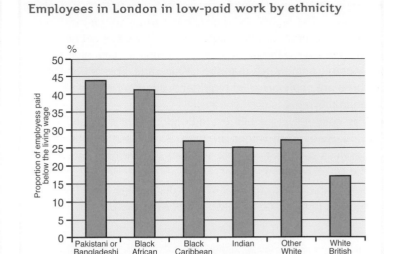

Source: adapted from www.ons.gov.uk.

- Many occupations, such as secretarial work, are dominated by females. It could be that the marginal revenue product of occupations traditionally filled by women is lower than that of occupations which are traditionally male dominated.

Wage structure by age

Age is an important determinant of pay as Figure 12 shows. Economic theory would suggest that older workers would receive higher rates of pay because of higher levels of human capital due to education, training and experience. To offset this, older workers in their 40s, 50s and 60s may be less physically strong and agile, important for manual work, or less adaptable, important for any job. Figure 12 provides some support for this. Weekly earnings in 2014 peaked in the 40-49 age group and then fell for those aged 50 and over.

Part-time and full-time working

Part-time workers in the UK are likely to hold less responsible jobs within an organisation. Mainly for this reason, as Table 4 shows, they earn on average far less per hour than full-time workers. Most part-time workers are women. In April 2013, female part-time workers earned 31 per cent less per hour than female full-time workers. The hourly pay gap was even higher for men. Male part-time workers earned 42 per cent less per hour than male full-time workers.

Wages by ethnic group

On average, white British workers in the UK have higher hourly

Table 4 Median gross hourly earnings (excluding overtime), UK, April 2013

	Full-time	Part-time	All
Men	13.60	7.95	12.86
Women	12.24	8.40	10.33
All	13.03	8.29	11.56

Source: adapted from www.ons.gov.uk.

earnings than the rest of the working population. As the data for London in Figure 13 shows, white British workers are less likely to be low paid than other ethnic minority workers.

There is a number of factors which cause workers from ethnic minority groups to earn less than white workers. First, workers from ethnic minorities, on average, tend to be less qualified than white workers. This means workers from ethnic backgrounds are more likely to be in manual jobs than white workers, and also less likely to be in managerial posts. Second, workers from ethnic minorities are more likely to work in distribution (including shops), hotels, catering and in the health service than white workers. For example, according to the 2001 Census, nearly half of all Bangladeshi men, 40 per cent of Chinese men and one third of Chinese women in employment had jobs in hotels and restaurants. Nearly 40 per cent of black Caribbean women were employed in education, health and social work compared to 30 per cent for white women. Some jobs in these sectors are well paid and workers from an Indian background are disproportionately represented amongst doctors, for example. However, on average workers from ethnic minorities are more likely to be employed in industries where low pay is a prominent feature. Finally, there is evidence that pay discrimination against workers from ethnic minorities takes place, despite equal pay legislation. There is also discrimination against ethnic minority workers when it comes to recruitment, selection, promotion and training.

Wages by region

Average wages differ between UK regions. The highest average wage in April 2014 was paid in London whilst the lowest average wage was in Northern Ireland as Figure 14 shows. There are differences in wages between regions for a number of different reasons, many of which are interlinked.

- Labour productivity (output per worker) is highest in London and lowest in Northern Ireland. The higher the labour productivity, the higher tends to be the wage rate.
- London has the most-skilled workforce in the UK measured

357

by educational qualifications. Higher skills tend to feed into higher labour productivity.

- Employment and unemployment rates are indicators of labour scarcity. The higher the employment rate and the lower the unemployment rate, the higher wages tend to be. London, despite having the highest wages, tends to have higher unemployment rates than the UK average. This is because there are some areas of high deprivation in London where unemployment is concentrated.
- The cost of living is highest in London. This is caused in part because average wages are high. So costs of production of services such as transport or meals out are high. However, the reverse is also correct. Employers have to pay higher wages in order to retain staff and discourage them from moving to lower cost of living regions in the UK.

Figure 14

Median full-time gross weekly earnings by region, UK, April 2014

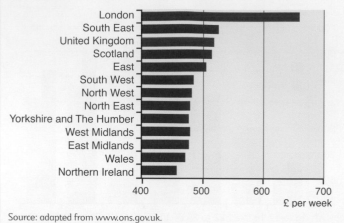

Source: adapted from www.ons.gov.uk.

Data Response Question

UK car manufacturing

Ten years ago, the UK car industry seemed in terminal decline, but today prospects have been transformed. Revived brands, such as Jaguar Land Rover, are racking up the profits from their West Midlands plants, whilst Nissan's Sunderland factory continues to swell production of SUVs for buyers across Europe.

But those on the shop floors are missing out on the full benefits. Real wages for the lowest-paid 30 per cent of workers have fallen by 7.5 per cent since 2009 while average salaries at five of the UK's six largest carmakers remained flat in the three years to 2013. Over the same period, production at UK car, bus and truck factories has risen by almost half whilst the average salaries of the highest-paid directors at the UK's six largest carmakers have soared by 34 per cent in real terms. The squeeze for those on the shop floor is set to continue. New recruits, for example, at General Motors Vauxhall plant at Ellesmere Port from 2015 will only receive 70 per cent of standard salary

Figure 15

Employment and pay in the car industry

Number of employees

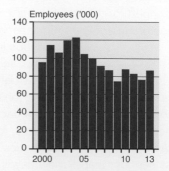

Change in real pay (2009-13) by income deciles

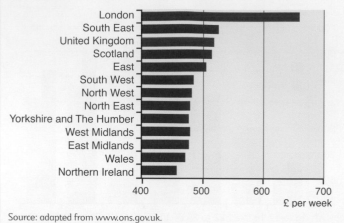

Total pay adjusted for inflation

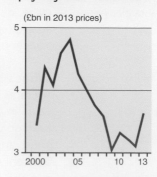

Index of total pay of directors

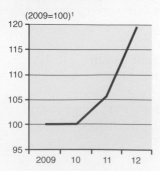

Source: adapted from Thomson Reuters Datastream; © the *Financial Times* 17.2.2014, All Rights Reserved; ONS.

1. At JLR, Vauxhall, Nissan, Honda, Toyota and BMW UK.

for the first four years, while pension benefits will be less generous.

Total annual pay at UK automotive manufacturers today stands at £3.6bn. This is more than £1bn lower than a historical high in 2004. Despite production inching back up to levels seen that year, fewer people today operate more productive factory lines.

Manufacturers such as Vauxhall say the wage freezes were essential to protect UK jobs and factories from the plant closures seen elsewhere in Europe. Car workers in the USA have had to make similar compromises. For example, at the General Motors' Lake Orion plant near Detroit, trade unions have had to agree to a two-tier workforce. New recruits are paid less and get fewer benefits. However, General Motors says that without such a deal, production of smaller cars would have been shifted to Mexico.

Trade unions agreed to these deals to keep the jobs of their members. However, with demand for UK vehicles continuing to grow, UK unions want a better deal. 'Companies that can are simply getting away with it,' says Roger Maddison of the Unite Union.' We're prepared to make difficult choices … but carmakers do need to give something back now the situation is brighter.'

Source: adapted from © the *Financial Times* 17.2.2014, All Rights Reserved.

Evaluation

In question 3, build on your answer to question 2 to explore how the forces underlying the demand for and supply of labour in car manufacturing might change over the next ten years. A good source of evaluation is to question the probabilities of events happening. For example, what is the probability that car manufacturers will continue to be attracted to open new plants in low wage cost economies like Mexico or Eastern Europe? How likely is it that executive pay will stop growing at a much faster rate than for ordinary workers? Also, pointing out information that you don't have but would be relevant to answer the question can form part of your evaluation.

Q

1. Compare the growth in pay for the different income groups shown in the data.

2. Analyse, using a demand and supply for labour diagram, why car workers in the UK saw little change in their real pay over the period 2010-2013.

3. Car manufacturing operates within a global economy. Discuss whether, over the next 10 years, directors of UK car companies will see large increases in their pay whilst their workers will barely seen any increase.

60 Government intervention in labour markets

Key points

1. Governments may impose a minimum or maximum wage that may have an impact on employment.
2. Wage setting in the public sector may differ from wage setting in the private sector.
3. Government may use a variety of policies to tackle labour market immobility.
4. Current labour market issues include skills shortages, young people and education, older workers and retirement, temporary work, zero-hour contracts, migration, and wage inequality.

Starter activity

A cleaner at a bank in London is paid the minimum wage of £6.70 an hour. He is on a zero-hours contract and would like to work 35 hours a week. His actual hours vary from five hours to 30 hours. The CEO (Chief Executive Officer) of the bank for which he works earned £7.2 million last year including bonuses. The CEO is on a permanent contract and works on average 60 hours a week. Is this both an efficient and equitable distribution of income? To answer this, think of 10 different issues that might be used when coming to a conclusion.

Minimum wages/the living wage

Many workers in the world economy work for very low wages. One way that governments can intervene to raise the wage rates of the lowest earning workers is to impose a **minimum wage**. Employers then have to pay a minimum wage rate per hour or risk legal and financial penalties. Economic theory would suggest that minimum wages will benefit some workers but disadvantage others.

Figure 1 shows the demand and supply curves for labour in an industry. The equilibrium wage rate is OE whilst the equilibrium level of employment is OB. The government now imposes a minimum wage of OF, forcing industry wage rates to rise to OF. Firms demand AB less labour whilst BC more workers wish to gain jobs in the industry. The result is AC unemployment.

Existing workers have not necessarily benefited. OA workers have gained higher wages. But AB workers have lost their jobs as a result of the legislation. What is more, the workers who have lost their jobs are likely to be the least employable. Firms will have fired their least productive employees.

Minimum wage legislation can also prevent the market from clearing when there is an increase in unemployment. In Figure 2, D_1 and S are the original demand and supply curves respectively. Assume that the minimum wage is set at OF. Then the equilibrium market wage rate is equal to the minimum wage rate and there is no unemployment. Now assume that the economy goes into recession. Demand for the industry's product falls and so the demand for labour in the industry falls (remember, labour is a derived demand). The new demand curve is D_2. If the market had been free, wage rates would have

Figure 1

Minimum wage legislation

A minimum wage of OF will result in higher wage rates in the industry. However, AB workers will lose their existing jobs whilst a total of AC unemployment will be created.

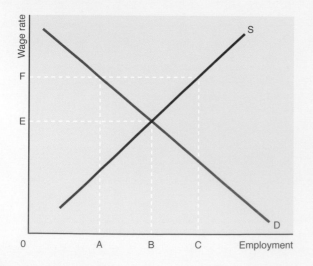

Figure 2

Minimum wages can cause unemployment

A fall in demand for labour from D_1 to D_2 should lead to a fall in wage rates from OF to OE. However, a minimum wage of OF will prevent this and will cause unemployment of AC to arise.

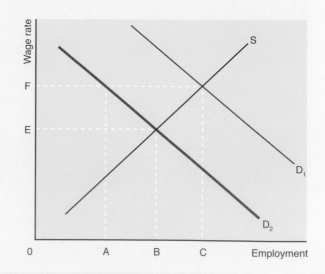

fallen to OE and any transitional unemployment in the market would have disappeared. However, with a minimum wage of OF, unemployment of AC is created. So it is argued that minimum wage legislation can cause unemployment.

The extent to which minimum wages lead to a rise in unemployment depends crucially on three factors.

- The first relates to the difference between the new rights and existing free market rights. For instance, if the market wage rate is £12 per hour and a minimum wage is set at £9 per hour, the minimum wage will have no effect. It won't raise wages in the market or create unemployment. If the minimum wage is set at £9 when market clearing rates are £8.25 per hour, there will be a small increase in average wages but equally it is unlikely that much unemployment will be created. A minimum wage of £18 with market clearing rates of £6 per hour, on the other hand, will give substantial benefits to workers employed but is likely to create substantial unemployment.

- Second, the amount of unemployment created depends on the relative elasticities of demand and supply for labour. Consider Figure 3 and compare it to Figure 1. Both diagrams relate to the introduction of a minimum wage. The market clearing wage is OE and the minimum wage set is OF. Unemployment of AC is created by the introduction of the minimum wage. In Figure 1, the demand and supply curves are relatively elastic between OE and OF. The unemployment created is large. In Figure 3, the demand and supply curves are relatively inelastic between OE and OF. The unemployment created is relatively small. Indeed if the demand for labour is perfectly inelastic, a rise in wages will have no effect on the demand for labour.

Figure 3

Inelastic demand and supply curves for labour

The more inelastic the demand and supply curves for labour, the less unemployment is created when minimum wages are introduced.

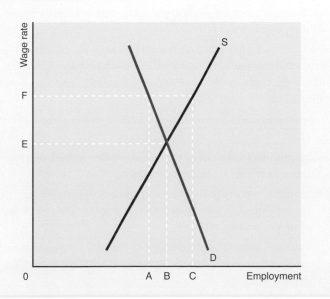

- Third, what might be true for a single industry might not be true for the economy as a whole. For instance, minimum wage legislation in the hairdressing industry might result in unemployment amongst hairdressers. However, minimum wage legislation across all industries might have little or no effect on unemployment. In economics, it is not possible to conclude that the economy as a whole will behave in the same way as an individual market.

Question 1

Professor Sir George Bain, founding chair of the Low Pay Commission, which recommends the amount that should be paid as the minimum wage, said that it had been successful, but had 'pretty much run its course'. When it was first introduced in 1999, predictions of heavy job losses were not borne out by what actually happened. However, today, although there are only just over a million workers on the minimum wage, many more workers earn just above the minimum wage. In some sectors, such as parts of the retail industry, the minimum wage had become the going rate. Around five million workers are low paid today, defining low paid as earning two-thirds of the typical hourly wage. He said that the first objective of government should be to get people into jobs. The second was to ensure that those jobs paid workers sufficiently so workers can maintain a decent standard of living. One way of raising the minimum wage without causing unemployment would be to raise it at a higher rate than the growth in average earnings at a time of sustained economic expansion or when unemployment was low or falling.

Source: adapted from © the *Financial Times* 21.2.2014, All Rights Reserved.

(a) Using a diagram, explain why the introduction of a minimum wage might have caused 'heavy job losses'.

(b) Using another diagram, explain why the introduction of the minimum wage in the UK in 1999 did not cause significant job losses.

(c) Why would raising the minimum wage above the rate of increase of average earnings 'at a time of sustained economic expansion or when unemployment was low or falling' be less likely to cause unemployment than if these conditions did not apply?

Maximum wages

Most developed countries set minimum wages. However, maximum wages are relatively uncommon.

- In the 1970s, the UK government set maximum wage increases that workers could receive in an attempt to control inflation.
- More recently, some economists have suggested setting a maximum wage for chief executives of companies. Typically this is set at a ratio of chief executive pay to the pay of the lowest wage rate earner in the company. The call for maximum wages for chief executives has come because their pay has been increasing very much faster than that of their workers.
- Governments can set maximum pay limits for public sector workers in an attempt to keep down public sector spending.

Figure 4

Maximum wages

Setting a maximum wage of W_{Max}, below the free market wage of W_1, will lead to excess demand for workers. Fewer workers want to work at the lower wage rate whilst employers want to employ more workers.

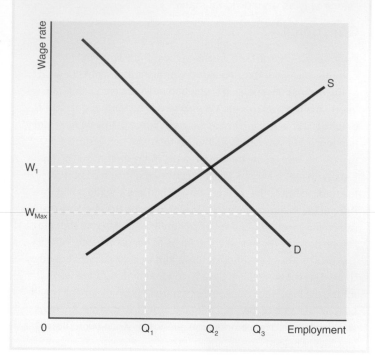

Figure 5

Inelastic demand and supply curves with a maximum wage

The free market wage rate is W_1 with $0Q_1$ being demanded and supplied. Setting a maximum wage rate of W_{Max} leads to $0Q_2$ equilibrium employment, barely changing the free market equilibrium employment level.

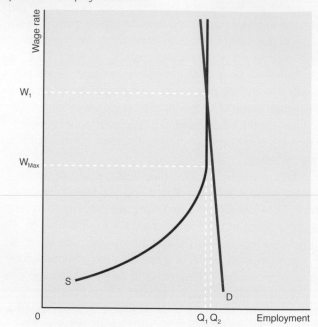

Figure 4 shows the impact of a maximum wage in a competitive market. The market clearing wage rate is W_1. The imposition of a maximum wage of W_{Max} leads to excess demand in the market of Q_1Q_3. This is because $0Q_3$ is now demanded by employers, whilst $0Q_1$ is supplied. In terms of chief executives, it could be argued that fewer workers will want to put themselves forward because the rewards for the job don't match the stress and responsibilities of the job. Equally, in the UK, it could be that chief executives will move abroad to take posts in other countries, reducing supply.

However, as with minimum wages, the impact of a maximum wage depends on relative elasticities of demand and supply. It could be argued that the number of people capable of being chief executives is very small and that their supply is highly wage inelastic. Equally, the demand is very wage inelastic. Companies only need one chief executive but their remuneration is a relatively small part of total cost even if it increases by 20 or 50 per cent.

Figure 5 shows a situation where the supply curve is perfectly inelastic at Q_1 employed and the demand curve is highly inelastic. The vertical part of the supply curve shows that the same number of chief executives are prepared to work whatever the wage rate they receive above W_{Max}. The equilibrium wage rate is W_1. If a maximum wage is imposed of W_{Max}, there will be excess demand of Q_1Q_2. However, this is very small in relation to the number of chief executives employed. In this case, imposing a maximum wage will have almost no effect on the market.

Question 2

Ministers should consider forcing companies to cap executive pay at a fixed multiple of their lowest-paid employee, a lobby group has urged. The High Pay Centre said in a report that, since the late 1990s, executive pay had grown from 60 times that of the average UK worker's pay packet to nearly 180 times. Radical action was needed if the gap was to return to more proportionate levels.

Investors in luxury group Burberry on Friday voted down a £20-million pay deal for new chief executive Christopher Bailey. This followed other pay revolts by shareholders at FTSE companies including Barclays and HSBC.

The High Pay Centre said the perception of an executive elite reaping all the reward from economic growth was damaging trust in business, while the threat of widening inequality could also cause political and economic instability.

Source: adapted from © the *Financial Times* 14.7.2014, All Rights Reserved.

(a) Using a diagram, explain the possible effect on pay and employment if the pay of top executives was capped 'at a fixed multiple of their lowest-paid employee'.

(b) Using the concept of the divorce of ownership and control, explain how chief executives can reap much of 'the reward from economic growth'.

(c) Discuss whether chief executives of FTSE 100 companies would be less effective at their jobs if they were paid half as much as at present.

Public sector wage setting

The public sector in developed economies employs millions of workers. The government therefore has a major influence on wage rates both for public sector workers and private sector workers. In countries where public sector trade unions are weak, such as the UK, the government can effectively make whatever settlements it decides in the short term using its market power as a monopsonist buyer of labour. In the UK for example, public sector workers were subject to a pay freeze between 2010 and 2015 as the government sought to reduce public sector spending. In countries where public sector trade unions are strong, such as France, it is much more difficult for government to unilaterally decide on pay. Public sector unions in France are more aggressive and have much more sway over public opinion.

In the short term, pay freezes in the public sector are likely to exert downward pressure on pay in the private sector. Private sector workers are less likely, all other things being equal, to seek jobs in the public sector if there is a public sector pay freeze. This will keep the supply of private sector workers stable. Also, a public sector pay freeze will limit average pay rises in the whole economy. This will reduce expectations of pay rises by both private sector employers and employees. For example, private sector employers will be able to use this data in negotiations to limit pay rises for their employees.

In the long term, if private sector employees are receiving regular pay increases with a public sector pay freeze, then shortages will develop of public sector workers. Government will find it difficult to recruit workers with the right skills and qualifications. Eventually, these shortages will become unsustainable and the government will have to concede pay rises. Over long periods of time, the wages of public and private sector workers tend to rise by the same percentage, but in the short term, they can rise by different rates.

Policies to tackle labour market immobility

Labour market immobility occurs when workers are not flexible enough to move from job to job according to the needs of the market. As a result of labour market immobility, workers might find themselves, for example:
- unemployed when employers are reporting a shortage of workers;
- in temporary employment or self-employment when they would prefer to be in full-time employment with an employer;
- in a job which fails to use their skills and talents.
  Governments can employ a variety of policies to improve labour market flexibility and reduce immobility which were explained in detail in Unit 39. These could include:
- improving education and training to increase the functional flexibility of workers, allowing them to move more easily from one type of job to another;
- providing specific training for workers to target skills shortages in the economy;
- subsidising employers who take on unemployed individuals from groups in the labour market who have above average unemployment rates, such as young workers or those with disabilities;

- providing relocation subsidies to workers who have to move house to get a job;
- providing help with housing for workers who get jobs outside of their local area;
- increasing knowledge of job opportunities, for example by running jobcentres;
- helping workers with job applications, for example by giving them training or paying travel costs for interviews;
- reforming the tax and benefits system or increasing the minimum wage to increase the ratio of take home pay in a job to the benefits received from being unemployed;
- reducing discrimination in the labour market which reduces the ability of certain groups, such as women, those from ethnic minorities or those with disabilities to gain a job.

Labour market issues

There is a number of ways in which one could judge a labour market.
- Is everyone who wants a job in employment?
- Is everyone working the hours they want to work?
- Are the skills and talents of workers being used to their full potential?
- Are workplaces safe environments where, for example, there are no accidents and where employees are safe from harassment, bullying and discrimination?

More controversially, the following could be asked.
- Should workers be forced to spread their income over their lifetimes by saving for a pension and at what age should workers expect to retire?
- Should a country allow workers from outside the state borders to take up jobs in the country?
- Are the wages of low paid workers sufficiently high to be deemed as a 'fair wage'?
- Are increasing wage inequalities acceptable to society?

These questions relate to a number of labour market issues that currently face the UK economy.

Skill shortages The UK faces skill shortages both geographically and by industry. For example, there are skill shortages in London and in the IT industry. At the same time, there are workers unemployed or underemployed because they don't have the right skills. Equally, they may have the right skills but be geographically immobile for example because they live in social housing. Skill shortages can be addressed through more focussed education and training by government and by firms. However, geographical immobility particularly if it is caused by shortage of housing in low unemployment areas is much more difficult to solve in the short term.

Young workers Young workers aged 17-24 were particularly badly affected by the 2007-08 financial crisis. In the subsequent recession and very weak recovery due to fiscal austerity, employers tended to keep their existing workers but not employ new workers. This hit young workers entering the labour force hard. Unemployment amongst young workers was much higher than the average. Many who did get jobs were forced to take jobs below the level that might be expected from their qualifications. They also were paid less than previous young workers because supply exceeded demand and average wage rates for young workers fell. The impact on young workers was fairly similar to young workers starting out following the recessions of 1980-81 and 1990-91. If the economy continues to recover, subsequent cohorts of young workers will face much better employment prospects. However, the history of previous recessions suggests that young workers coming into the labour market between 2008 and 2014 will always have lower lifetime earnings than cohorts of young workers who enter the labour force in better times.

Raising the length of time spent in full-time and part-time education Over the past 150 years, the statutory age for leaving full-time education has progressively risen. At the same time, the proportion of young people staying on to do further studies at college or university has risen significantly. This reflects the increasing demands from employers for a skilled labour force. On average, the higher the qualifications of an individual, the higher is likely to be their lifetime earnings and the less likely they are to be unemployed. Over time, the level of education required even to do very low-skilled work has risen. Fifty years ago, many manufacturing unskilled jobs required no ability to read or write. In a modern service economy, the picker in a supermarket collecting items for a home delivery certainly needs to be literate. Education and training make workers more productive. Therefore, for the sake of future prosperity, it is very important for government to ensure that schools and universities are continuing to raise standards. Ensuring that spending on education rises in real terms over time is likely to be a necessary condition for this to happen.

Retirement Life expectancy has been rising for the past 200 years. When the UK state retirement pension was introduced in 1908 for those over 70 on low incomes, the average life expectancy was around 50. Today, average life expectancy for men is 79 and 83 for women and it is forecast to carry on rising. There is also a rise in the number of people reaching retirement because the newly retired individuals are 'baby boomers', born between 1945 and 1964 when the number of children born peaked. This has major implications for government spending on the state pension. State pensions are already over 50 per cent of the total welfare budget. Governments have responded by raising the retirement age. Under UK plans, the state retirement age will rise to 66 between 2018 and 2020 rising to 68 between 2044 and 2046. The growing number of state pensioners means that either those in work will have to pay higher taxes over time or other areas of government spending will have to be cut. A greater proportion of those in their 50s and 60s will stay in work because they cannot afford to retire. If they keep their jobs, it could become more difficult for young people to gain promotion or even a job. An alternative scenario is that many workers in their late 50s and 60s will not be able or will not want to keep their existing jobs. Demanding physical jobs become more difficult with age. Equally, workers may choose to give up positions of responsibility to work part-time as they approach retirement. Almost certainly, the percentage of people aged 67 in 2044 in work will be lower than the percentage of 50 year olds. The government also wants workers to save for their retirement so they have an income over and above the state pension. However, UK government policy on private occupational pensions has been inconsistent since the 1980s. Given that saving for a pension takes 40 or more years, to be changing schemes and tax incentives on a regular basis has meant that workers, particularly in the private sector, have not seen pension saving as a reliable or secure way to provide for their old age.

Temporary work Most jobs are permanent and full time. Workers want a full-time job and the security that goes with a permanent contract. Equally, employers value full-time employees and want to know that workers will be turning up for work every week. Using temporary workers gives employers flexibility. In certain industries like tourism, where work can be highly seasonal, employers don't want to employ permanent workers when there is very little work for them to do. Equally, in the construction industry, there is a long history of workers being employed on a temporary basis on particular construction projects. However, using temporary workers in other industries allows firms to cope with peak demands of work. In recessions, employing temporary workers rather than permanent workers is a way for employers to minimise the risk of employing an extra person. Some workers prefer temporary work to permanent work. It gives them greater flexibility about when to work and for whom to work. However, the sharp rise in temporary workers following the recession of 1990-91 and the recession following the financial crisis of 2007-08 was employer driven. Most of those extra temporary workers would have preferred permanent work.

Zero-hours contracts In recent years, there has been a large increase in zero-hour contracts. Workers are given a permanent contract but the employer does not give the workers any minimum number of hours to be worked. Equally, the worker

Question 3

Women will take two thirds of the high-skilled jobs created during the next six years as men fall further behind in qualifications, says the government-backed UK Commission for Employment and Skills (UKCES). It forecasts that 49 per cent of working-age women would have degree-level qualifications by 2020 compared with 38 per cent now. It said men's qualification levels were also set to rise, but more slowly than women's, with the percentage of men with degree-level skills reaching 44 per cent by 2020. However, despite a reduction in the number of people with low or no qualifications, the proportion the UK population with low skills levels is also likely to remain relative high. Frances O'Grady, the general secretary of the Trades Union Congress and a UKCES commissioner, said: The increased disparity between men's and women's skills levels is concerning for both sexes. Men are finding it harder to get skilled jobs, whilst for many women their higher qualifications are not leading to better pay and jobs. Tackling inequality - in skills, qualifications and pay for both sexes - is essential if we are to have a prosperous and stable future.'

Source: adapted from © the *Financial Times* 5.9.2014, All Rights Reserved.

Explain the possible advantages and disadvantages to the UK economy of the trends in qualifications and skills mentioned in the data.

Question 4

In April 2015 whilst campaigning during the General Election, David Cameron, UK Prime Minister, said that 'we are living through a jobs miracle brought to you by a Conservative government'. That month, unemployment reached a seven year low. However, critics argued that the UK was experiencing low-wage growth.

Source: adapted from © the *Financial Times* 5.9.2014, 6.5.2015, All Rights Reserved.

Figure 6

Change in employment, UK, May 2008 to June 2014, (000s of persons)

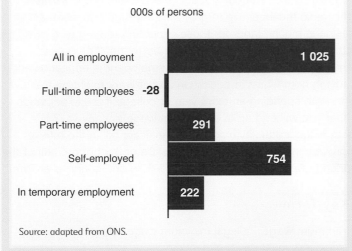

Source: adapted from ONS.

Figure 7

Index of real and nominal earnings and the price level (CPI), January 2008 = 100

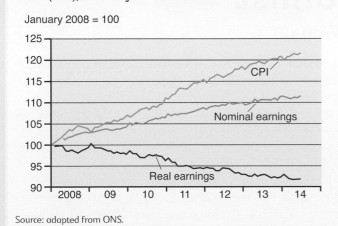

Source: adapted from ONS.

(a) Using Figure 6, explain what happened to employment between 2008 and 2014.

(b) Using Figures 6 and 7, suggest why real earnings fell between 2008 and 2014.

(c) Explain why the evidence from the employment market led to different views about the strength of the recovery from the 2007-08 financial crisis.

---

does not have to work any minimum of hours. If an employer has no work for an employee in a week, then the worker receives no pay and does no work. It gives employers complete flexibility over the use of those workers on zero-hour contracts. In some cases, zero-hour contracts work to the benefit of both

Question 5

Zero-hours contracts are controversial. Some employers, including McDonald's, Cineworld and Sports Direct, use them for nearly all their staff. McDonald's, which has used zero-hour contracts in the UK since it opened its first restaurant in 1974, says that it benefits its employees. Many of them are parents or students who are looking to fit flexible, paid work around childcare, study and other commitments. Frances O'Grady, general secretary of the Trades

Figure 8

Proportion of businesses using zero-hour contracts

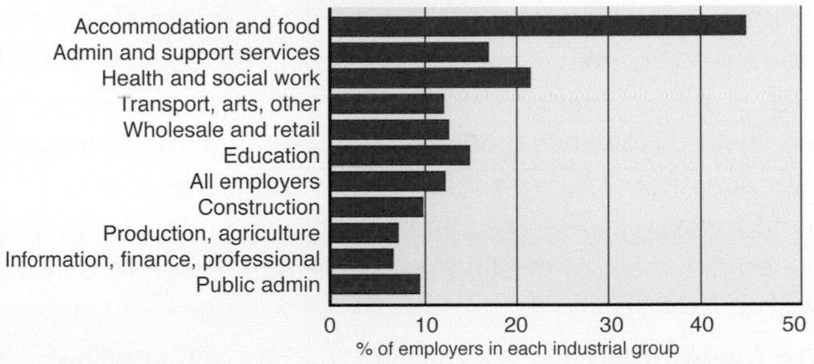

Source: adapted from ONS.

Union Congress, has an opposing view. She said: 'Insecure work with no guarantee of regular paid hours is no longer confined to the fringes of the jobs market. It is worrying that so many young people are trapped on zero-hours contracts, which can hold back their careers and make it harder to pay debts like student loans.'

The Chartered Institute of Personnel and Development estimates the number of people on zero-hours contracts at 1 million, or 3.1 per cent of the workforce. Their use is thought to have increased sharply since the recession and some economists see it as a factor in the UK's poor productivity performance.

John Philpott, director of the Jobs Economist consultancy, said: 'The ready supply of workers for low-paid, low-skilled jobs means employers are able to operate on a business model that has a high turnover of staff and compete on low cost and low value. But this model is holding back productivity and the economic recovery.'

Source: adapted from © the *Financial Times* 5.9.2014, 6.5.2015, All Rights Reserved.

(a) (i) Which industry has the largest proportion of its employees working on zero-hours contracts? (ii) Suggest why this benefits employers in that industry.

(b) Suggest why zero-hours contracts have 'increased sharply since the recession'.

(c) What are the possible advantages and disadvantages to employees of being on a zero-hours contract?

employers and employees. For example, an employer might need 50 to 100 staff at any one time. Workers are free to pick and choose when to work knowing that they can get enough work each week if they sometimes compromise on when they work. However, many zero hour contract workers are employed by firms who provide highly variable periods of work and give little or no notice of when workers will be required. Not knowing whether any money will be earned in a week is very difficult. Equally, being expected to turn up for work at an hour's notice is highly disruptive.

Migration Immigration has always been a controversial topic. Over the past 60 years, the UK has used immigration to solve labour supply problems. For farmers today, this means being able to recruit eastern European workers to work at minimum wages. For multinational companies in the UK, it is about being able to bring in staff from other countries to work for a time in the UK operation. For the NHS, it is about recruiting doctors and nurses from overseas because not enough medical staff have been trained in the UK. For employers, in general, immigration allows them to recruit from a larger pool of workers than if they had to rely solely on existing UK labour. Increased supply would suggest that this would put downward pressure on wages paid by employers. However, those workers create demand for goods and services from UK firms. This in turn creates an increased demand for labour. The exact impact on wage rates, employment and unemployment of existing UK workers is therefore difficult to assess.

Wage inequality It was explained in Unit 59 that wage inequality has been growing over the past 50 years. For example, between 1975 and 2013, the real income of the 15th centile of full-time workers rose 80 per cent. For the 50th centile of workers, it rose 101 per cent. For the 99th centile, it rose by 189 per cent. After direct taxes and benefits, the earnings gap is reduced. However, both gross earnings and post-tax and benefits earnings show that inequalities are widening over time. These trends give rise to questions about equity. Is it fair that the higher the earnings, the larger will be the percentage increase in those earnings over time? It also raises issues about efficiency. Free market economists could argue that these trends are the result of efficient labour markets. Growing inequalities also raise incentives for workers on low incomes to gain the skills to get more highly paid jobs. However, a contrary argument is that inequality reduces economic growth. This is because the incentive to gain skills through education and training is much higher for those expecting to earn high incomes than those on low incomes. For the bottom half of income earners, the rate of return on extra time spent in education and studying both whilst in education and at work might be too low. Is it worth spending an extra year at college if the expectation is that you will end up in a minimum wage job anyway? If rising wage inequality leads to a significant fall in the rate of improvement in the education and skills of the bottom half of the working population, this will act as a drag on economic growth.

> **Key Term**
>
> **Minimum wage** - a legal minimum wage rate per hour which employers must pay their workers.

Thinking like an economist

The National Minimum Wage and the Living Wage

Minimum wage statistics

In April 1999, the UK government introduced a National Minimum Wage (NMW) of £3.60 per hour for adults aged 22 and over. By 2015-16, it had risen to £6.70. In 1999, an estimated 2 million workers were paid below the minimum wage. In 2014, the number of workers being paid the minimum wage was 1.4 million, which, as can be seen from Figure 9 was 5.3 per cent of all jobs in the economy. Over 11 per cent of all part-time jobs were minimum wage jobs, most of these being female part-time workers. Only three per cent of full-time jobs were paid at the minimum wage.

Low paid jobs are spread unevenly through the economy as Figure 9 shows. In the whole economy, minimum wages are more likely to be paid to:

- temporary workers rather than those on permanent contracts;
- workers who have been in their post for less than 12 months rather than those who have been with the same employer for more than 12 months;
- private sector workers than public sector workers;
- workers employed by very small (micro) firms rather than larger firms;
- workers in occupations which have low average earnings;
- workers in industries where workers on average have low earnings.

Although the minimum wage is paid to only 5.3 per cent of workers, it has an effect on the bottom 30-40 per cent of wage rates paid. This is because income differentials need to maintained. So if the minimum wage is increased by two per cent, it is likely that wages slightly above that level will also increase. This then pushes up wages above that level and so on. Eventually, as the wage rate rises, the impact becomes minimal. However, changes in the minimum wage do have an impact on low wage earners in general.

The level of the minimum wage paid in the UK is comparable to levels paid in other EU countries. Figure 10 shows the minimum wage paid in different countries both in monetary terms (euros per hour) and as a percentage of the full-time median wage in October 2011. In euros, the UK minimum wage is higher than in Spain, Greece, Portugal and Romania but equally, GDP per capita in the UK is higher than in these countries. As a percentage of the full-time median wage, it is broadly similar.

Arguments against raising the minimum wage

There is a debate about whether the level of the minimum wage in the UK is too high or too low. Groups representing businesses tend to argue that the minimum wage is either at the right level, is too high or should be abolished. Figure 9 showed that a disproportionate number of minimum wage jobs are in very small firms (micro firms) or (other) small firms. A hairdresser or an independent coffee shop or café would be typical examples of these firms. The argument is that the minimum wage increases costs for these firms disproportionately because the majority of the staff are on the minimum wage. Also, staffing represents a very high proportion of total costs. Cutting the minimum wage or abolishing it altogether would allow more small firms to be created and for existing firms to grow, taking on more staff. The debate centres round whether the demand for labour at the minimum wage is wage elastic or wage inelastic. Proponents of a wage cut would tend to suggest that it is wage elastic.

Figure 11, however, shows that in the slow recovery from the 2007-08 financial crisis, low paying sectors where there are a disproportionate number of minimum wage jobs were creating jobs at a faster percentage rate than the economy as a whole. This suggests that the minimum wage was not an obstacle to job creation in that period.

Arguments in favour of raising the minimum wage

Groups representing the low paid, including trade unions, argue that the minimum wage is too low. They put forward a number of arguments.

- Rises in the minimum wage will reduce inequality and increase 'fairness'. This is especially important when, as now, free market forces are tending to increase the gap between the wage rates paid to high-income and low-income earners.
- Demand for labour at the minimum wage is wage inelastic. The minimum wage could rise by, say, 10 per cent over a

Figure 9

Characteristics of minimum wage jobs, UK, 2014

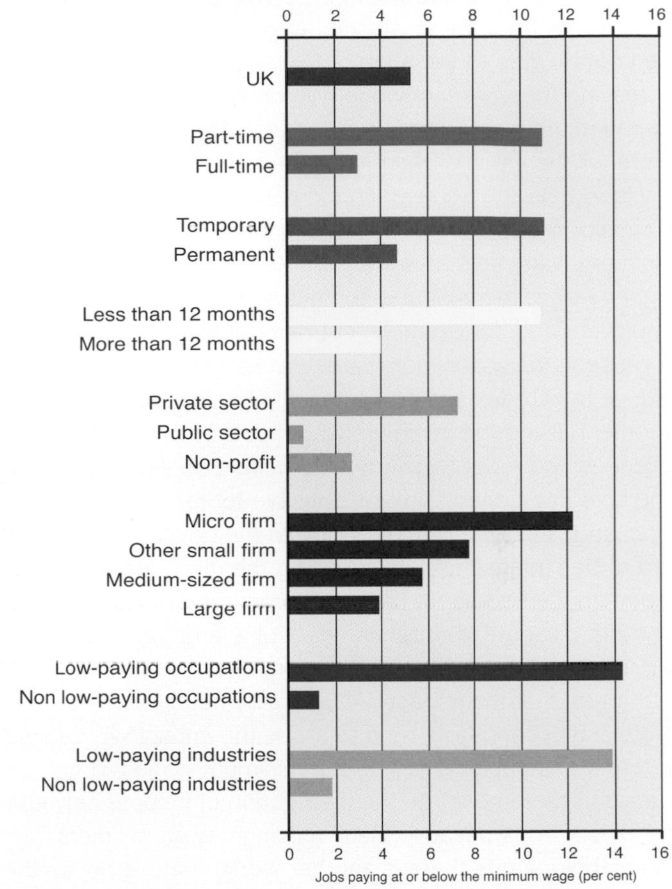

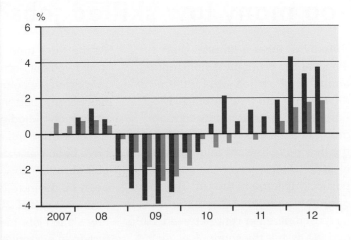

Source: adapted from *National Minimum Wage*, Low Pay Commission Report 2015.

Figure 10

Minimum wages in selected EU countries, October 2011

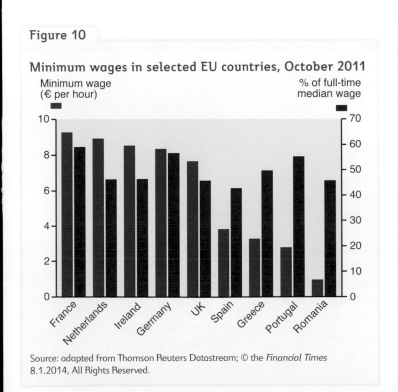

Source: adapted from Thomson Reuters Datastream; © the *Financial Times* 8.1.2014, All Rights Reserved.

Figure 11

Percentage change in the number of employee jobs on a year earlier

Source: adapted from © the *Financial Times* 8.1.2014, All Rights Reserved.

five year period all others things being equal and the impact on employment would be small. The overall welfare gain to minimum wage workers and those above them in the wage distribution of a significant increase would outweigh the welfare loss from the small number of workers who would then not be able to get a job.

- Increasing the minimum wage will force employers to make their workers more productive to justify their increase wages. There will be much greater incentive to train them and to buy labour-saving equipment. Increased labour productivity is a major factor in determining economic growth. Too low a minimum wage acts as a drag on the UK growth rate.

- Higher wages increase the commitment of workers to their employers and, for example, cut rates of absenteeism.

- At present, many minimum wage workers pay no tax and receive tax credits and other benefits because of their low income. Raising the minimum wage would increase tax revenues and reduce government welfare spending.

The Low Pay Commission responsible for recommending yearly changes in the minimum wage to the government has tended to be cautious about increasing the minimum wage. It has been concerned about the employment issue. However, economists disagree about the impact of a large rise on employment and unemployment. Free market economists tend to argue that the impact will be highly negative whilst interventionist economists tend to argue the impact will be small.

In terms of inequality, raising the minimum wage will not have a significant impact on the distribution of income between households. This is because many minimum wage workers live in a household where there is another worker who is not on the minimum wage. Equally, many low-income households, such as retired households, have no workers in them.

There would be a positive impact on government finances of raising the minimum wage. However, the government itself is an employer of minimum wage workers even if, as Figure 9 shows, the vast majority of minimum wage workers are found in the private sector. The impact on government finances is therefore not as simple as it might at first seem.

The Living Wage

In 2001, a group of parents in East London put forward the idea of the 'Living Wage'. This was a minimum level of pay above that of the minimum wage that would allow workers on low wages to provide effectively for themselves and their families. The Living Wage Foundation campaigns for individual employers to sign up to paying the Living Wage to their workers. In 2015, the Living Wage was set at £7.85 an hour for the UK but £9.15 an hour for London workers, reflecting the higher cost of living in London. Over 1 000 employers had signed up to paying the Living Wage by 2015 but less than 100 000 workers were covered by these pledges.

The Living Wage campaign highlights the problem of low pay, especially in London. Minimum wage workers are worse off in London than, in say, Leeds or Cardiff because the cost of living is so much higher. Companies which sign up to paying the Living Wage can get positive publicity for being an 'ethical' company.

However, the Living Wage campaign highlights the problems of any voluntary scheme. The vast majority of firms will either not sign up to it or will attempt to minimise its impact on them. Comparisons can be made with Voluntary Codes of Practice and monopolies along with self-regulation by firms and industries. It can also be compared to the Fair Trade movement where the percentage of goods traded in the world that are 'Fair Trade' is less than 0.1 per cent. The business community in the UK on the whole expresses enthusiasm about the Living Wage but, statistically, virtually no employers sign up to it. Voluntary schemes are never a substitute for legally enforceable measures such as the UK minimum wage.

Source: with information from *National Minimum Wage*, Low Pay Commission Report 2015; www.livingwage.org.uk; © the *Financial Times* 30.6.2014, All Rights Reserved.

Data Response Question

Too many low skilled jobs?

Britain has more graduates than ever, yet the economy is not creating enough high-skilled jobs for them all, according to new research. Most European countries produced more graduates than high-skilled jobs in the decade before the financial crisis of 2007-08. However, the gap was particularly large in the UK. The share of graduates in the UK workforce increased nine per cent between 1996 and 2008, but the share of high-skilled jobs increased only four per cent over the same period.

At the same time, technology has 'hollowed out' jobs in the middle producing an 'hour glass' economy which has become bottom heavy with low-skilled jobs. Middle-skilled jobs, such as secretaries and machine operators have been squeezed by technology and globalisation. Low-skilled jobs have been on the increase especially since the financial crisis of 2007-08. Examples of low-skilled jobs include shop assistants, fast-food operatives and cleaners.

The author of the research, Craig Holmes of Oxford University, says that between 1996 and 2008, Britain has shifted more towards low-skilled jobs than most of its neighbours in Europe.

Since 2010, unemployment in the UK has been falling but many of the jobs created have been in lower-paid, lower-skilled sectors. This has hurt income tax revenues and hampered the government's attempt to repair the public finances.

Mr Holmes said that one reason the UK might have created more low-skilled jobs between 1996 and 2008 was because it was less costly to create them: flexible employment laws make it more attractive to hire people, and the minimum wage is lower than in many other parts of Europe. He also found a correlation between countries with strong trades union membership, such as Denmark, and higher growth in high-skilled roles.

Lesley Giles, deputy Director of the UK Commission for Employment and Skills, a government-funded body, said it was still problematic than many highly educated UK workers were not in suitably skilled jobs. 'Whilst we have the most qualified workforce we've ever had, and therefore you could say 'skilled', we do have this growing phenomenon of underutilisation of skills, which does seem to be higher than other countries,' she said. This suggested that Britain needed more vocational training to equip workers with the skills that employers needed, she argued.

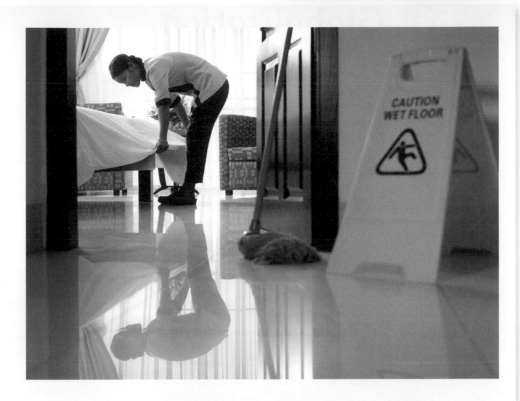

David Cameron, the prime minister, has called Britain the 'jobs factory of Europe' as employment rates in the UK reached near-record levels.

1. According to World Bank data, Switzerland in 2013 had a significantly higher income per capita at purchasing power parities than any EU country. Using Figure 12, suggest one factor that might have caused this.

2. Explain, using examples from the data, what is meant by a 'skills gap'.

3. Discuss whether the focus of government policy should be on job creation whatever the type of job created rather than concentrating solely on the creation of high skilled jobs.

Evaluation

What are the advantages and disadvantages of creating different types of jobs in an economy? Is it better to concentrate on creating high skilled jobs particularly if the education system is creating individuals with the capacity to hold those jobs? Does it matter whether a job is high skilled or low skilled in terms of its benefits to the economy? Is a low skill job economy a desirable way forward for the UK?

Figure 12

Changes in employment share, 1996-2008

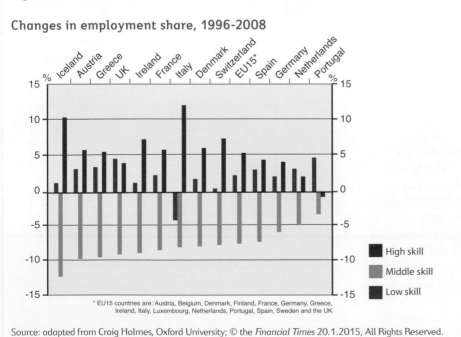

* EU15 countries are: Austria, Belgium, Denmark, Finland, France, Germany, Greece, Ireland, Italy, Luxembourg, Netherlands, Portugal, Spain, Sweden and the UK

61 Globalisation

Key points

1. The characteristics of globalisation include increased trade, and movements of labour, capital and technology between countries leading to greater specialisation and interdependence in the world economy.
2. Globalisation is being driven by factors such as price competition, improved transport links, liberalisation of trade, multinational companies and international flows of capital.
3. Globalisation and multinational companies have an impact on individual countries, governments, consumers, producers, workers and the environment.

Starter activity

Make a list of 10 items in the environment in which you are currently sitting which reflect the way the UK is integrated into the world economy. For example, are there any products around you which have been made abroad? Which products have been made and distributed by multinational companies? Where has the technology on your mobile phone come from? Do any of your relatives work for foreign or multinational companies? Do you have family relations who have emigrated? Is anybody in the room a first or second generation immigrant? Do you have an account with a foreign bank, like HSBC or Santander? Have you taken foreign holidays and, if so, where and how frequently?

The characteristics of globalisation

Globalisation, from an economic perspective, can be defined as the ever-increasing integration of the world's local, regional and national economies into a single international market. Economic integration can be broken into four main areas:

- free trade across national boundaries of **goods and services** so that, for example, it becomes as easy for a firm in London to sell to a firm in Poland or Vietnam as it is to sell to a firm in Birmingham, Manchester or Belfast;
- free movement of **labour** between countries, in the same way that there is currently free movement of labour within the UK or within the EU;
- free movement of **capital** between countries, so that a UK pension company might invest in China, or the Chinese central bank use some of its foreign currency reserves to invest in the USA, or a US company buy a UK company;
- free interchange of **technology** and **intellectual capital** across national boundaries; so that, for example, a South African company can license technology from the USA on exactly the same terms as a US company; or a US firm can protect its patents in China on the same terms as it can in the USA; or a UK company can use its own patented technology in a factory in Brazil in the same way that it could in one of its UK factories.

A world where there are no boundaries to trade in goods and services and there is perfect free movement of labour, capital and technology is at one end of a spectrum. Given the many boundaries that exist today, the world is nowhere near this position. At the other end of the spectrum is a world which is narrowly localised. In this world, people live in villages or small towns. Trade is the exception and people do not move from village to village. There is no exchange of capital or technology. This is a world which to some extent existed in the past in Britain and still exists in some parts of the developing world.

The term 'globalisation' is a relatively new term and only became part of everyday economic language in the 1980s. Some argue that globalisation is simply a new term for the internationalisation of economies. Internationalisation has been taking place since trade first began thousands of years ago. In Roman times, for instance, goods were traded in Europe which had originated in Africa, India and China. In the 17th and 18th centuries the East India Company, owned by British shareholders, developed strong trade links between Britain and India. The period 1870-1913 is sometimes called the first wave of globalisation because of the significant increase in the percentage of world GDP being traded between countries. Trade then fell back between 1914 and 1950 due to two world wars and the Great Depression of the 1930s when states adopted

Question 1

Figure 1

World GDP per capita (2005 international dollars) and exports of goods and services as percentage of world GDP

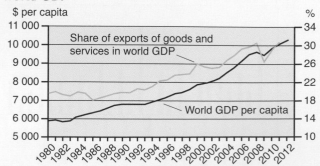

Source: adapted from *World Trade Report 2014*, World Trade Organisation.

(a) Identify two significant features of the data in Figure 1, backing up your answer with statistical evidence.

(b) Suggest why changes in world GDP per capita might be both a cause and an effect of changes in world exports.

protectionist policies. Since the 1950s the rate of economic integration between world economies has accelerated. An ever-larger share of world GDP is exported to other countries.

The causes of globalisation

Globalisation is being caused by a complex mix of factors, none of which on their own can account for the process of globalisation. Many of the factors are interlinked. For example, trade liberalisation is causing an increase in world trade. Equally, the growth in world trade has created groups of consumers and firms which stand to benefit from further liberalisation. They then put pressure on governments to lower protectionist barriers further. Some of the causes of globalisation can be categorised in the following way.

Trade in goods For rich, developed countries, goods are increasingly being manufactured abroad, many for the first time in developing countries such as China and India. This trade is occurring because developing countries are acquiring the capital equipment and the know-how to produce manufactured goods; there are efficient modes of transport to get goods to markets; and developing countries have a cost advantage in the form of very cheap labour.

Trade in services Trade in services is growing. For instance, growth in tourism is taking large numbers of visitors abroad. Call centres for customers in developed countries are being located in developing countries. India has become a world leader in writing software and then selling these skills to companies in developed countries.

Trade liberalisation Trade in goods and services is growing partly because of trade liberalisation. In the 1930s, international trade collapsed as the world went into the Great Depression and individual countries misguidedly tried to boost domestic demand by adopting fierce protectionist policies. Since 1945, protectionist barriers have gradually fallen. Lower protectionist barriers have encouraged growth in world trade.

Multinational companies Multinational (or transnational) companies have grown in number and size. In some industries, like car manufacturing or the oil industry, this is because only large multinational companies have the economies of scale and technological knowledge to make products that are both cheap and technologically advanced. In other industries, multinational companies, particularly in food and household products, have used highly successful marketing techniques to create global brands. Coca Cola, McDonald's hamburgers, Magnum icecreams and Snickers chocolate bars are available in all five continents. Multinational companies have also acquired market and political power. Many have monopoly power in many markets. They may engage in illegal anti-competitive practices. They also are able to influence the decisions of governments across the world. Partly, this is because they have the skills and the money to lobby governments. Partly, it is because governments are influenced by promises of large investments or threats of disinvestment in their countries. Partly, it is because multinationals have a record of using bribery to influence government decisions.

International financial flows International financial flows are becoming far greater. Countries such as China and Malaysia have financed part of their fast economic growth from inward flows of international capital.

Foreign ownership of firms Foreign ownership of firms is increasing. Many large multinational companies, for example,

Question 2

China is now the world's largest car market, overtaking the USA this year. However, less than 40 per cent of the cars sold in China are Chinese branded. Over 60 per cent are foreign branded, the market leaders being Germany's Volkswagen and General Motors of the USA. This doesn't mean that ownership and manufacturing are all foreign. Under the rules that allow foreign car companies to sell into the Chinese market, foreign car companies have to have a Chinese partner. Many of the foreign-badged cars sold are also made in China in plants owned jointly between the foreign company and a Chinese company.

Chinese consumers are voting with their wallets to buy foreign-badged cars. However, there is some controversy about the high prices they have to pay. A China Central Television broadcast in May reported on the high cost of imported BMWs relative to other international markets. BMW and other foreign car-makers say prices reflect market demand and, where cars are imported rather than being made in China, on the tariffs (taxes) imposed by the Chinese government.

'Market demand' effectively means that foreign car-makers can charge high prices because there is excess demand for foreign cars. This is reflected in the profits made. In the first quarter of this year, General Motors' Chinese joint venture made a profit of $595 million compared to just $100 million for General Motors operations in all other countries round the world. For Volkswagen, its Chinese joint venture allowed it to earn €9.6 billion last year. Its profits in all its other operations worldwide were €11.7 billion.

Figure 2

Annual China car sales (rolling 12 month average), millions

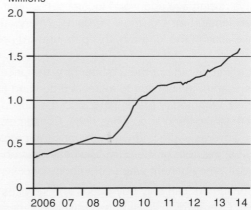

Discuss whether Chinese consumers benefit from buying foreign-badged cars.

have invested in factories and companies in China. French firms have bought US firms. A company which started in India is now one of the world's largest steel producers after buying a number of steel companies in the developed world. Some oil rich states like Dubai, Qatar or Norway have state investment funds which buy stakes in foreign companies or purchase them outright.

Communications and IT Developments in communications and information technologies have shrunk the time needed for economic agents to communicate with each other. In industries such as software production, programmers are effectively just as near to a client's office located in, say, London if they themselves are located in India or in Kent.

Impact on consumers

Globalisation has an impact on consumers across the world.

Consumer choice The availability of goods and services has considerably increased with globalisation leading to greater consumer choice. The number of different products available in high streets, shopping centres and supermarkets is larger than it was 20 years ago. In the services market, Blackpool and Southend struggle as tourist destinations when people can go to Spain, Turkey or the Caribbean. Some argue that goods have become more homogenised. A holiday in Spain is the same as a holiday in Peru apart from the scenery. The food is 'international food', the hotels provide the same rooms and facilities, and sightseeing is packaged to suit western tastes. Equally, the same skirt made in China may end up being bought by a girl in the UK, the USA or Japan.

Prices The relative price of goods and services is changing. Globalisation is leading to a fall in the price of some goods and services because production is being switched from high-cost locations to low-cost locations. For example, switching production of television sets from Wales to China will lead to a fall in labour costs because Chinese workers are prepared to work for a fraction of the wages of Welsh workers. Equally, the globalisation of technology means that a Chinese factory can employ the most advanced machines and methods of production to ensure lowest cost. However, globalisation is leading to a rise in price in some goods and services. This is because globalisation is raising average world incomes. Higher income means higher demand for individual products. Where supply is not perfectly elastic in the long run, this puts upward pressure on prices.

During the first decade of the 21st century, the price of commodities soared, mainly due to increased demand from China. However, commodity prices have since collapsed as China's growth slowed and supply has risen. Consumers round the world are adversely affected when the price of petrol increases by 50 per cent or the price of wheat goes up by 30 per cent. Equally, they benefit when commodity prices slump.

Incomes Consumers can only buy goods and services if they have incomes. Overall, globalisation has raised incomes round the world. Consumers are therefore able to buy more goods. However, not every consumer has gained. A worker in South Wales who has lost his job because production has moved to China is likely to be worse off. Equally, some argue that globalisation is a cause of stagnant incomes of below average earnings workers in countries like the USA.

Impact on workers

Workers have been affected by the forces of globalisation in different ways.

Employment and unemployment Globalisation has seen both winners and losers in terms of employment and unemployment. For example, the transfer of much of manufacturing from western Europe and the USA to countries such as China and Poland has led to large scale losses of jobs in these sectors in the developed world whilst there has been an increase in employment in the developing world. In western Europe and the USA, many workers made unemployed have found new jobs, particularly in the service sector of the economy but not necessarily at the same rate of pay as before. Some have simply remained unemployed. Structural unemployment in traditional manufacturing areas has therefore occurred. These changes, however, are not new. Throughout the Victorian era, there was a large transfer of workers from rural areas to towns and from agriculture to manufacturing and services. Globalisation might be speeding up the rate of change, but there would have been change anyway.

Migration Increased migration is a characteristic of globalisation. Many migrants are forced to move from their homes because of war and persecution. However, many are economic migrants, moving because they think they can enjoy a better standard of living for themselves and their families in a new country. Immigration is almost always controversial in countries receiving immigrants. On the one hand, first generation economic immigrants tend to be successful in gaining jobs and increasing their incomes. They can fill skill gaps in the economy and so raise the productivity of existing workers. By creating businesses, some immigrants also create jobs. On the other hand, they are competing in the job market with workers from the host country. Native workers can then perceive immigrants as taking 'their jobs' or lowering wages rates because of competition in the labour market. Immigration can also place strains on housing, education and health care. The exact impact of immigrants varies from country to country. However, in an ever-increasing global economy, migration is likely to increase over time. In UK terms, obstacles for workers from Sunderland to move to London to work are an example of market failure. Obstacles preventing a worker in Delhi moving to Birmingham for work could be seen as government failure.

Wages In a perfect labour market where all workers are homogeneous (identical), all workers will earn the same wage rate. Globalisation is shifting workers to different locations round the world. It is also shifting places of work from one country to another. Fifty years ago, an unskilled worker in a factory in the UK making television sets was only competing for a job with other unskilled workers in the local area or in the long run in the rest of the UK. Today, an unskilled factory worker in the UK is competing not just with workers who have moved into the area or the UK, but with factory workers in China or Vietnam. A multinational electronics company is likely to base their production operations in countries with low wage costs. So workers in the UK have to match the wage levels of workers in other countries if they want to keep their jobs. In practice, what has happened is that a large proportion of manufacturing in the high-cost developed world has shut down and production has moved to low-cost developing countries. However, international competition has tended to depress the wages of unskilled and low-skilled workers in developed countries as a result. The impact on high-skilled workers has been the reverse. In a global market place, their skills are in high demand because there are relatively few workers with these skills in developing countries. For developing countries, the wages of low-skilled workers are tending to increase. Demand for workers has increased, pushing up wage rates. The result is that in global terms, inequalities are being reduced as low-income workers in developing countries earn better wages. For developed countries, however, globalisation is tending to increase inequality as there is downward wage pressure on low-skilled workers and upward pressure on high-skilled workers.

Multinationals Multinationals create jobs wherever they set up operations. They are sometimes criticised for only creating low level jobs for local employees whilst importing more highly skilled labour from abroad. A French hotel chain in the UK, for example, may employ local British labour for cleaning but in practice always has a French worker as the manager of each hotel. However, increasingly multinational companies recognise that creating an international employment base leads to greater productivity. Training local workers to take high-level jobs within the company is an investment which strengthens the company. Training given to employees also spills over into the local economy. It raises the level of human capital. Employees leave multinationals to take jobs elsewhere in the economy and sometimes to set up their own businesses.

Impact on producers

Globalisation is affecting producers worldwide in a variety of ways.

Specialisation and economic dependency Globalisation comes about through increased specialisation and trade. Economic agents, including firms, are increasingly dependent upon each other. A fault at a manufacturing plant in Thailand can impact on a firm in the UK buying its products, for example. Equally, the imposition of trade sanctions on Russia can destroy a market for a UK firm selling into Russia. Increased specialisation inevitably increases some risks when trade links break down. Equally, it reduces risks because firms are able to source products from a wider variety of countries and sell into more countries.

Costs and markets Globalisation allows firms to source products from a wider variety of countries and firms. The wider the supplier network, the lower is likely to be the price at which a firm can buy. Key to lower costs is being able to use lower-paid workers, often in the developing world. Equally, globalisation opens markets. Firms in the UK, for example, can sell to countries which previously were closed to trade or had insufficient incomes to buy their goods.

Footloose capitalism Firms which operate in several countries (i.e. multinationals) have the power to move production from country to country, creating and destroying jobs and prosperity in their wake. They do this to maximise their profits. For instance, they might close a production facility in a high-cost country like the UK or the USA and move it to a low-cost country like India or Thailand. Globalisation is inevitably leading to a shifting of production from the developed world to the developing world. This is one key way in which the poor developing countries of the world can increase their living standards. However, multinationals are not the prime cause of this shift in production. Rather, they are responding to market forces in exactly the same way that national companies are so doing. Over the past 30 years, domestic UK companies have increasingly sourced goods from overseas to take advantage of better prices. They have closed their own manufacturing operations, or forced previous UK suppliers to close down through loss of orders. Multinationals are part of this trend which is exploiting **comparative advantage**.

Tax avoidance Firms which operate in several countries (i.e. multinationals) have the possibility to engage in tax avoidance. There are three main ways in which they do this.

- One is based on genuine production and **transfer pricing**. A firm produces good X in country A and then transports to country B to make into good Y which it then sells. Country A has high taxes on profits and country B has low taxes on profits. The multinational can reduce its total profits tax by putting a very high artificial notional price on the product made in country A before sending it to country

Question 3

Investment is pouring into Poland as companies in other developed countries outsource work. Poland is becoming a hub, for example, for the back-office functions of banks. Credit Suisse, UBS and BNY Mellon are planning to add 3 000 workers to their Polish operations over the course of the next eight months. Multinational companies in other industries too are relocating to Poland. Already, Royal Dutch Shell runs more than $1 trillion of cash transactions each year through its offices in Krakow in southern Poland. Similarly, Proctor & Gamble runs its entire logistics and supply chain operations for Europe from Warsaw.

In the 1990s, companies realised that huge cost savings could be made by moving call centres to India. However, companies now want their outsourced operations to perform more complex tasks. Poles are better educated, boast more professional skills and have a wider European language proficiency than their Asian rivals. They are also much cheaper to employ than university graduates in Germany, the UK or the USA. Jacek Levernes, president of Poland's Association of Business Service Leaders commented: 'It is actually more expensive to set up a team that can, say, speak, 10 different languages and handle complex projects in Bangalore or Gurgaon than Wrocław or Kraków.'

Source: adapted from © the *Financial Times* 23.1.2015, All Rights Reserved.

(a) What has been the impact of outsourcing on Indian and Polish workers?

(b) Why might a firm want to outsource part of its operations to another country?

B. Profits are then reduced in country A and increased in country B. Overall the multinational makes a tax saving.

- A second way is to set up an office in a low-tax country like Ireland, Luxembourg or the Bahamas. Ownership of a key production element like a patent, copyright or sales is then assigned to that country. A significant proportion of costs is then assigned to that key production element which at best eliminates all profit made in other countries. The revenues are then taxed in Ireland, Luxembourg or another tax haven at virtually zero per cent. As a result the multinational avoids tax.
- A third way is to transfer production facilities to a low tax country. Ireland has attracted many firms, for example, because it has very low taxes on profits compared to other EU countries.

Multinationals would argue that they pay exactly the right amount of tax according to the tax laws of every country. Critics would argue that they artificially create structures in order to avoid paying tax.

Impact on governments

Globalisation presents both opportunities and threats for governments. Globalisation can both create prosperity and bring economic problems. For example, a multinational moving a car plant from the UK to China is an opportunity for China but leaves the UK with fewer jobs, fewer exports and less tax revenues. Governments therefore have to adopt policies which will capture as large a share as possible of the benefits of globalisation and minimise the losses. This might mean lowering taxes on profit for companies or giving subsidies to multinationals setting up manufacturing facilities in the country. It could also mean increasing spending on education and research and development in order to give the country a competitive edge in a global market place.

Governments have become increasingly aware of the ability of multinationals to avoid paying taxes on their activities in a country. Some have responded by lowering their tax rates in order to encourage multinationals to relocate to their tax jurisdiction. However, this issue remains a major problem for most governments.

As explained above, governments are also prone to bribery and corruption. Multinational companies have a long history of gaining contracts or control of resources through bribing government officials or politicians. This is likely to distort development and leads to lower income for countries. This is not particularly a problem for countries like Norway or Finland where there is very little corruption. It has been a major problem for many African, South American and Asian countries where corruption can be endemic.

Impact on the environment

Rising world production inevitably has an impact on the environment. If world production of wooden furniture rises, then there must be an increase in logging of trees. If world food production rises, then this must impact on the amount of land in cultivation and farming practices. If every Chinese and Indian household is to own a refrigerator, then there must be an increase in the production of iron ore and electricity.

Extra demand for raw materials and increased emissions and waste have, so far, had an overall negative impact on the world environment. For example, greenhouse gas emissions continue to rise. However, environmental degradation is not inevitable and economic growth can be environmentally sustainable. Rich countries, like the UK and Sweden, have made considerable progress in many areas by using some of the proceeds of economic growth to reverse environmental degradation.

Multinationals also have an impact on the environment. A number of multinationals dominate world extraction industries, such as oil or gold mining. These industries are inevitably particularly destructive of the environment. Other multinationals, such as motor manufacturers or even service companies, have also been accused of destroying the environment, for instance in the way in which they source their raw materials. However, any form of production could be argued to be undesirable from an environmental viewpoint. Moreover, multinational companies often have better environmental records than smaller national companies. They not only have the financial resources to be able to minimise their impact on the environment; they also have the technical knowledge and ability to innovate, which can lead to minimising environmental problems.

Question 4

Ireland has responded to EU pressure and will shut its so-called 'double Irish' corporate tax loophole next year to new companies and from 2020 for existing companies. The tax loophole exploited differences in Irish and US rules about residency. Under US law, a company registered in the USA has to pay tax on its profits in the USA. However, a US-registered company can own a company abroad. This second company is then not taxed in the USA under US law unless it sends profits back to its parent company in the USA. Under Irish law, a company registered in Ireland pays taxes on its profits from the country from which they are run. So, an Irish registered company can run part of its company from a tax haven like Bermuda where taxes on profits are zero, and not pay any tax in Ireland on that company.

US companies like Microsoft, Google, Apple and Facebook have exploited the 'double Irish' loophole to minimise the tax they pay on their operations outside the USA. For example, the Irish subsidiary of Google funnelled €8.8 billion of royalty payments through a subsidiary company in Bermuda. This was €8.8 billion which was not taxed in Ireland and not taxed in the USA. The tax saving is greater because a number of companies push European sales through Ireland. Google, eBay and Amazon, for example, had sales in the UK of $13 billion in 2012. But only $2.8 billion of this was recorded for tax purposes in the UK because the sales were routed through Ireland. The $2.8 billion was commission on sales and marketing services according to the companies. The result is that profits are pushed into low-tax Ireland and away from higher-tax countries like the UK.

Source: adapted from © the *Financial Times* 4, 1, 2014, 15.10.2014, All Rights Reserved.

Explain how multinationals can avoid tax, using the data for examples.

Impact on individual countries

Countries can both benefit and lose out from the process of globalisation. They benefit economically if globalisation leads to rising incomes, more and better quality jobs, lower prices and more consumer choice. They lose out if globalisation leads to loss of industries, higher unemployment and lower wages.

The process of globalisation can lead to major economic change over a relatively short period of time with profound long term consequences. For example, in the UK, globalisation and competition from the Far East in the 1950s, 1960s and 1970s decimated the UK's textile and shipbuilding industries. This had knock-on effects on the steel industry and the coal industry. Regions such as Wales, Scotland, Northern Ireland, the North East and the North West are arguably still recovering today from the loss of those industries.

In countries like China, the benefits from rapid growth in incomes have to be offset against the very large negative impact that the growth of heavy industry has had on the environment. Equally, there has been a massive internal migration of people from rural areas to cities which brings its own benefits but also has costs in terms of dislocation of family ties.

Non-economic impact of globalisation

Globalisation is not just an economic phenomenon. It is a political, social, technological and cultural phenomenon too. One non-economic impact is on culture. On the one hand, globalisation weakens native cultures. In particular, US culture, as seen through US films and television programmes shown throughout the world, is replacing some aspects of native culture. On the other hand, partly through migration, native cultures are spreading round the globe. Multicultural Britain today is very different from the Britain of the 1950s.

Politics too is affected by globalisation. Nation states have lost sovereignty, which is the ability to make choices about how their affairs are conducted. Partly, this is because they have signed international treaties which limit their sovereignty. Partly, it is because the forces of globalisation have become so strong that nation states cannot resist them. For example, it is difficult for a nation state to impose complete censorship on its people in the age of satellite broadcasting, the Internet or the video and DVD.

The costs and benefits of globalisation

Economists disagree about the exact costs and benefits of globalisation. For example, what are the benefits in terms of increased income; what are the environmental costs; and do the benefits of increased income outweigh these environmental costs?

Equally, there is no agreement about the extent to which it is globalisation that is bringing about these costs and benefits. For example, if the UK economy grew by 3.0 per cent last year, what proportion of this was due to globalisation? Or what proportion of the environmental degradation in Brazil is being caused by globalisation?

Arguments for and against globalisation tend to be linked to a number of other economic debates, discussed elsewhere in this book.

- Does economic growth lead to an increase in economic welfare?
- Is economic growth unsustainable from an environmental standpoint?
- Does protectionism rather than free trade promote economic growth?
- Do multinational companies have more power over economies than most nation states and act purely to gain profit for their shareholders?
- To what extent are developing countries lifting themselves out of poverty? Is there any evidence to suggest that developing countries are catching up with developed countries?
- Is the rich developed world exploiting the poor, developing world?
- Are organisations, like the World Trade Organization or the IMF, which support or promote trade liberalisation, controlled by the rich countries of the world and do they act against the interests of poorer countries?

Key Terms

Globalisation - from an economic perspective, the ever-increasing integration of the world's local, regional and national economies into a single international market.
Multinational company or multinational corporation or transnational corporation - a company with significant product operations in at least two countries.
Transfer pricing - an account technique used by multinational companies for reducing taxes on profits by selling goods at a low price internally from a high-tax country to another part of the company in a low-tax country.

Thinking like an economist

The UK and globalisation

The UK, like almost every country round the world, has been experiencing globalisation for decades. Three aspects of this process are growing integration in trade, the movement of workers and financial capital.

Exports and imports Figure 3 shows exports of goods and services as a percentage of GDP. In 1948, exports of goods and services accounted for 20.9 per cent GDP. By 2013, this had risen to 33.8 per cent. The rise has not been uniform. Exports of goods and services as a percentage of GDP, for example, declined in the mid-1960s and late 80s. However, the trend has been broadly upwards over time, showing the UK's increasing integration into the world trading economy.

Migration Figure 4 shows trends in migration since 1970. Immigration in the UK has been controlled since 1963. However, the UK is a member of the European Union and one of the core principles of the EU is freedom of movement of labour. A worker

in one country can move to another country to work. The large increase in migration from 1995 coincided with strong economic growth in the UK economy which lasted until the financial crisis of 2007-08. British citizens also have the right to settle in any EU country. Over time, the UK population is likely to become more diverse, again showing the impact of globalisation.

Wealth Figure 5 shows the overseas assets and liabilities of the UK as a percentage of UK GDP. Assets are the value of wealth owned by UK citizens, firms and the government overseas. Money held in a Swiss bank account or a UK firm owning shares in a foreign company would be examples. Liabilities are the value of what UK citizens, firms and the government owe to foreigners. In an increasingly globalised economy, it is to be expected that ownership of wealth will be less and less confined to nation states and more and more spread across the world. This is what Figure 5 shows. It also shows the damage done to wealth by the financial crisis of 2007-08.

Figure 3

UK exports of goods and services as a percentage of GDP

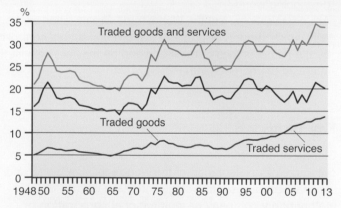

Source: adapted from www.ons.gov.uk.

Figure 4

UK immigration and emigration

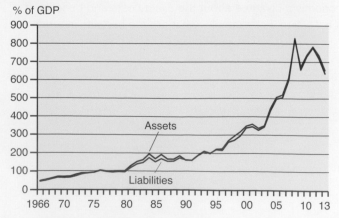

Source: adapted from www.ons.gov.uk.

Figure 5

UK international assets and liabilities as a percentage of UK GDP

Source: adapted from www.ons.gov.uk.

Data Response Question

China

For three decades from 1980, China's economy grew at around 10 per cent per year. It went from being a poor, relatively backward country economically, to being the world's largest economy at PPP exchange rates in 2014.

Gerhard Flatz, general manager of an Austrian factory in Heshan in China that makes high-end skiwear for European brands, is a victim of this success story. He cannot find enough skilled seamstresses for his factory even though top performers can earn $1 500 a month, about eight times the local minimum wage. Heshan is just one of many cities in the Pearl River Delta, part of the province of Guangdong, that has transformed this area into the factory of world.

The Pearl River Delta has a population of 56 million and produces everything from bicycles to jeans to iPads. Another city in the Pearl River Delta is Dongguan. Its factories alone made about 30 per cent of the toys delivered over Christmas round the globe, 20 per cent of the sweaters and 10 per cent of the running shoes worn by consumers.

However, the local economy is coming under strain from the very prosperity that it has created. Workers are harder to find, wages are rising rapidly, and raw material and land prices are going up. The obvious challenge to the region is labour costs. Roger Lee, chief executive of TALK, a Hong Kong company with 11 factories in Asia that produces clothes for dozens of global brands, says wages have doubled over the past five years. In 2008, its Dongguan factories made clothes at half the cost of its facilities in Malaysia and Thailand but that gap has since disappeared.

Some companies are responding to the rising wages by shifting production to other countries in South East Asia. Others are moving to cheaper parts of China. Samsonite, the luggage maker, which outsources about 65 per cent of its production to Chinese companies, has seen many of its suppliers move to provinces around Shanghai. 'About 80 or 90 per cent of the people we were working with were based in southern China' says Tim Parker, chief executive of Samsonite. 'Now probably the majority... we purchase comes from eastern China.'

Despite rising labour costs, any decision to leave the Pearl River Delta is not easy for foreign companies and their local manufacturers. Its ecosystem - everything from clusters of suppliers to road and rail infrastructure to access to ports in Shenzhen and Hong Kong - is hard to match elsewhere without sparking other cost increases. Nick Debham, Asia head of consumer markets at KMPG, says textile manufacturers, for example, can shift lower-skilled production to countries such as Bangladesh and Cambodia relatively easily, although wages in these countries are also rising. But other industries, such as toy manufacturing, which is concentrated in south China,

are less mobile as they rely on concentrated clusters of suppliers. 'There are so many ancillary bits and pieces that need to be in place, it is difficult to move the whole thing lock, stock and barrel out of China', he says.

Source: adapted from © the *Financial Times* 23.1.2014, All Rights Reserved.

1. Explain what is meant by 'globalisation', illustrating your answer with examples from the data.

2. Analyse why globalisation is taking place, providing evidence from the data.

3. Discuss whether globalisation is having a positive impact on both the UK and the Chinese economies.

Evaluation

In your answer, you need to identify examples of globalisation having a positive effect and a negative effect. You also need to identify whether globalisation is a win-win process for both China and the UK or a win-lose situation where positive impacts such as more jobs and higher wages in China might be causing job losses and lower wages in the UK. In your conclusion, weigh up the arguments.

62 Specialisation and trade

Key points

1. International trade takes place for a number of reasons including differences in factor endowments, price and product differentiation.
2. Patterns of trade are influenced by factors including comparative advantage, the growth of emerging economies, growth or trading blocs and changes in relative exchange rates.
3. If one country has lower costs of production for a good than another country, then it is said to have an absolute advantage in the production of the good.
4. International trade will take place even if a country has no absolute advantage in the production of any good. So long as it has a comparative advantage in the production of one good, international trade will be advantageous.
5. There are both advantages and disadvantages to countries specialising in the production of some goods for trade with other countries.

Starter activity

In three minutes, Drishya can throw a tennis ball into a waste paper basket which is four metres away and collect the ball (the ball doesn't have to stay in the basket when thrown so long as it goes in first) on average 10 times. Madison is not as good and gets the ball into the basket on average seven times. Drishya can catch a tennis ball thrown to her from four metres, run to return it to the thrower and then back to base ready to catch again, 15 times on average in three minutes. Madison can catch the ball eight times on average in three minutes. If they worked as a team and were allowed to specialise in throwing and catching, would they catch and throw more balls between them if (a) they divided throwing and catching equally between them or (b) Drishya spent all the time throwing, whilst Madison spent all the time catching or (c) Madison spent all the time throwing, whilst Drishya spent all the time catching? This is a question about comparative advantage.

Reasons for international trade

Many goods and services are traded internationally. For instance, there are international markets in oil, motor vehicles and insurance. There is a number of reasons why international trade takes place.

Differences in factor endowments Countries have different factor endowments. Saudi Arabia has large reserves of oil whilst Japan has virtually none. Costa Rica has a tropical climate suitable for growing bananas whilst the UK has a temperate climate where bananas can only be grown in artificial conditions. The USA has a large stock of skilled workers. Sudan's workforce is comparatively unskilled. The UK has a larger stock of physical capital per capita compared to Bangladesh. These differences in factor endowments lead to trade between countries. Saudi Arabia exports oil whilst Costa Rica exports bananas. The UK and the USA export high technology equipment.

Price Some countries can produce goods at a relatively cheaper cost than other countries. This may be because of the availability of natural resources, the skills of the workforce or the quality of the physical capital in the economy. There are substantial gains to be made from specialisation. Much of this unit explains this in more detail.

Product differentiation Many traded goods are similar but not identical. For instance, a small hatchback car from one motor manufacturer is very much the same as another. It will, for instance, have four wheels, four seats and an engine. However, the differences mean that some consumers in one country will want to buy a car made in another country, even if domestically produced cars are available at exactly the same price. International trade allows consumers much wider choice about the product they buy. The same basic goods or services can differ in a wide variety of ways. Specifications might be slightly different. There may be different deals on finance available. Delivery times can vary. One product may be of better quality than another. Much of world trade is driven by a combination of these factors.

Political reasons Sometimes trade takes place or does not take place for political reasons. Countries sign trade deals with each other which lock their suppliers into doing business between each other. Or a country will place an embargo on trade with another country. For example, the USA has an embargo on most trade with North Korea.

Patterns of trade

There are many different factors that influence the pattern of trade between countries today and the change in this pattern of trade over time.

Comparative advantage Differences in costs of production between countries affect patterns of trade. This is explored below under the **theory of comparative advantage**.

Impact of emerging economies Countries today rarely stay the same size. On the whole, they grow although countries like Syria where there is civil war can see their economies shrink. However, countries don't grow at a uniform rate. Some are currently growing very rapidly, whilst others are growing very slowly. When a country grows, it is likely to import more goods and services than before. It also needs to export more to pay for these imports. So growth will affect patterns of trade internationally. Over the past 50 years, for example, China has gone from barely trading with the rest of the world to being one of its leading exporters today. Emerging economies, middle income countries which have high rates of growth, are disrupting existing trade patterns as their share of world exports and imports grow.

Growth of trading blocs and bilateral trading agreements
Recent decades have seen the proliferation of trading blocks and bilateral trading agreements. These are discussed in greater detail in Unit 64. Trading blocs and bilateral trading agreements are designed to increase trade between participating countries at the expense of other countries. Hence they change the pattern of trade.

Changes in relative exchange rates
The exchange rate of one currency for another affects the relative prices of goods between countries. For example, if the value of the Japanese yen falls in relation to the US dollar, then Japanese exports will become cheaper for US buyers but the price of imported goods for Japanese buyers will rise. So changes in relative exchange rates affect patterns of trade. This is discussed in more detail in Unit 71.

Absolute advantage
Economists in the 18th and 19th centuries developed theories centred round why differences in costs led to international trade. Adam Smith, in his famous example of a pin-making factory, explained how specialisation enabled an industry to increase the production of pins from a given quantity of resources. In an economy, specialisation exists at every level, from the division of labour in households to production at international level.

Consider Table 1. Assume that there are only two countries in the world, England and Portugal. They produce only two commodities, wheat and wine. Labour is the only cost, measured in terms of worker hours to produce one unit of output. Table 1 shows that it costs more in worker hours to produce a unit of wine in England than in Portugal. Portugal is said to have an **absolute advantage** in the production of wine. It can produce both goods but is more efficient in the production of wine. On the other hand, it costs more in worker hours to produce wheat in Portugal than in England, so England has an absolute advantage in the production of wheat. It is clear that it will be mutually beneficial for England to specialise in the production of wheat and for Portugal to specialise in the production of wine and for the two countries to trade.

Table 1

	Cost per unit in worker hours	
	Wheat	Wine
England	10	15
Portugal	20	10

The same conclusion can be reached if we express relative costs in terms of absolute output. If Portugal could produce either five units of wheat or 10 units of wine, or some combination of the two, the relative cost of wheat to wine would be 2:1 as in Table 1. If England could produce either nine units of wheat or six units of wine, the relative cost would be 3:2 as in Table 1. Hence, Portugal could produce wine more cheaply and England could produce wheat more cheaply.

Question 1

Table 2

	UK			France		
	Cars		Computers	Cars		Computers
(a)	10	OR	100	9	OR	108
(b)	5	OR	10	4	OR	12
(c)	20	OR	80	25	OR	75
(d)	5	OR	25	4	OR	30
(e)	6	OR	18	8	OR	16

Two countries with identical resources, UK and France, using all these resources, can produce either cars or computers or some combination of the two as shown above. Assuming constant returns to scale, state which country has an absolute advantage in the production of (i) cars and (ii) computers in each of (a) to (e) above.

Comparative advantage
David Ricardo, working in the early part of the 19th century, realised that absolute advantage was a limited case of a more general theory. Consider Table 3. It can be seen that Portugal can produce both wheat and wine more cheaply than England (i.e. it has an absolute advantage in both commodities). What David Ricardo saw was that it could still be mutually beneficial for both countries to specialise and trade.

In Table 3, a unit of wine in England costs the same amount to produce as two units of wheat. Production of an extra unit of wine means forgoing production of two units of wheat (i.e. the **opportunity cost** of a unit of wine is two units of wheat). In Portugal, a unit of wine costs 1½ units of wheat to produce (i.e. the opportunity cost of a unit of wine is 1½ units of wheat in Portugal). As relative or comparative costs differ, it will still be mutually advantageous for both countries to trade even though Portugal has an absolute advantage in both commodities. Portugal is relatively better at producing wine than wheat: so Portugal is said to have a **comparative advantage** in the production of wine. England is relatively better at producing wheat than wine: so England is said to have a comparative advantage in the production of wheat.

Table 3

	Cost per unit in worker hours	
	Wheat	Wine
England	15	30
Portugal	10	15

Table 4 shows how trade might be advantageous. Costs of production are as set out in Table 3. England is assumed to have 300 worker hours available for production. Before trade takes place it produces and consumes four units of wheat and

Table 4

	Production before trade		Production after trade	
	Wheat	Wine	Wheat	Wine
England	4	8	20	0
Portugal	15	10	0	20
Total	19	18	20	20

eight units of wine. Portugal has the same labour resources as England available for production. Before trade takes place it produces and consumes 15 units of wheat and 10 units of wine. Total production between the two economies is 19 units of wheat and 18 units of wine.

If both countries now specialise, Portugal producing only wine and England producing only wheat, total production is 20 units of wheat and 20 units of wine. Specialisation has enabled the world economy to increase production by one unit of wheat and two units of wine. The theory of comparative advantage does not say how these gains will be distributed between the two countries. This depends upon the wheat/wine exchange rate, a point discussed below.

This is shown on the two production possibility frontiers in Figure 1. Portugal has an absolute advantage in production of both wine and wheat, shown by the fact that with same resources it can produce more wine and wheat than England. However, wine is relatively cheaper to produce in Portugal than in England and vice versa for wheat. With the same resources, twice as much wine (20 ÷ 10) can be produced in Portugal as in the England, but only one and half times as much wheat (30 ÷ 20) can be produced in Portugal as in England.

The theory of comparative advantage states that countries will find it mutually advantageous to trade if comparative costs of production differ. If, however, comparative costs are identical, there can be no gains from trade. Table 5 shows the maximum output of two countries, A and B, of two products, X and Y. The Table shows that country A, for instance, can either produce

Figure 1

Production possibility frontiers and trade

The PPF for Portugal shows that it can either produce 30 units of wine or 20 units of wheat or some combination of these. With the same inputs, England can only produce 20 units of wine of 10 units of wheat or some combination of these. Portugal has an absolute advantage in the production of both wine and wheat but it only has a comparative advantage in the production of wine, whilst England has a comparative advantage in wheat.

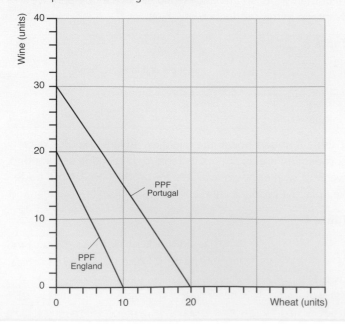

Table 5

	Output		
	Good X		Good Y
Country A	20	OR	40
Country B	50	OR	100

20 units of good X or 40 units of good Y or some combination of both. The comparative cost or the opportunity cost of production is identical in both countries: one unit of X costs two units of Y. Hence there can be no gains from trade.

Question 2

Table 6

	Cost per unit in worker hours	
	Meat	Bread
UK	5	10
France	3	4

(a) Which country has a comparative advantage in the production of (i) meat and (ii) bread?

(b) The UK has a total of 300 worker hours available for production whilst France has a total of 200. Before any trade took place, the UK produced and consumed 38 units of meat and 11 units of bread. France produced and consumed 20 units of meat and 35 units of bread. How much more could the two countries produce between them if each specialised and then traded?

(c) How would the answer to (a) be different, if at all, if the cost of meat and bread in France were: (i) 4 and 4; (ii) 3 and 7; (iii) 3 and 6; (iv) 6 and 12; (v) 6 and 15; (vi) 1 and 3?

The assumptions of the theory of comparative advantage

The simple theory of comparative advantage outlined above makes a number of important assumptions.

- There are no transport costs. In reality, transport costs always exist and they will reduce and sometimes eliminate any comparative cost advantages. In general, the higher the proportion of transport costs in the final price to the consumer, the less likely it is that the good will be traded internationally.
- Costs are constant and there are no economies of scale. This assumption helps make our examples easy to understand. However, the existence of economies of scale will tend to reinforce the benefits of international specialisation. In Table 4 the gains from trade will be more than one unit of wheat and one unit of wine if England can lower the cost of production of wheat by producing more and similarly for Portugal.
- There are only two economies producing two goods. Again this assumption was made to simplify the explanation. But the theory of comparative advantage applies equally to a world with many economies producing a large number of traded goods. Table 7 shows that Chile has no absolute advantage in any product. However, it has a comparative advantage in

Table 7

	Cost per unit in worker hours			
	Apples	Wine	Wheat	Copper
England	10	15	20	50
Portugal	15	10	30	60
Chile	20	20	50	70

the production of copper. Portugal has a clear comparative advantage in the production of wine whilst England has a comparative advantage in the production of apples. Exactly what and how much will be traded depends upon consumption patterns in all three countries. For instance, if neither Portugal or Chile consume apples, England will not be able to export apples to these countries.

- The theory assumes that traded goods are homogeneous (i.e. identical). Commodities such as steel, copper or wheat are bought on price. However, a Toyota car is different from a Ford car and so it is far more difficult to conclude that, for instance, the Japanese have a comparative advantage in the production of cars.
- Factors of production are assumed to be perfectly mobile. If they were not, trade might lead to a lowering of living standards in a country. For instance, assume the UK manufactured steel but then lost its comparative advantage in steel making to Korea. UK steel-making plants are closed down. If the factors of production employed in UK steel making are not redeployed, then the UK will be at less than full employment. It might have been to the UK's advantage to have kept the steel industry operating (for instance by introducing quotas) and producing something rather than producing nothing with the resources.
- There are no tariffs or other trade barriers.
- There is perfect knowledge, so that all buyers and sellers know where the cheapest goods can be found internationally.

Question 3

Table 8

	Cost per unit in worker hours			
	DVDs	Sweaters	Beefburgers	Chocolate
England	20	10	8	20
Portugal	30	8	12	30
Chile	40	8	4	25

(a) Which country has an absolute advantage in the production of
(i) DVDs; (ii) sweaters; (iii) beefburgers; (iv) chocolates?

(b) Which country has a comparative advantage in the production of
(i) DVDs; (ii) sweaters; (iii) beefburgers; (iv) chocolates?

The terms of trade

In Table 4, it was shown that England and Portugal could benefit from trade. Whether trade takes place will depend upon the **terms of trade** (explained in more detail in Unit 63) between the two countries. From the cost data in Table 3, England could produce two units of wheat for every one unit of wine. It will only trade if it receives more than a unit of wine for every two

Figure 2

The terms of trade

England will find it advantageous to trade only if its terms of trade are at least one unit of wine for every two units of wheat exported. Portugal will only trade if it can receive at least two units of wheat for every 1⅓ units of wine exported. Therefore the terms of trade between the two countries will lie somewhere in the shaded area on the graph.

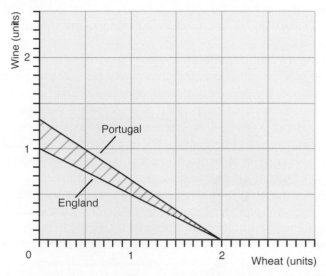

units of wheat. Portugal on the other hand can produce two units of wheat for every 1⅓ units of wine. It will only trade if it can give England less than 1⅓ units of wine for two units of wheat. Hence trade will only take place if the terms of trade are between two units of wheat for one unit of wine and two units of wheat and 1⅓ units of wine (i.e. between 2:1 and 2:1⅓).

This is shown in Figure 2. The cost ratios of wine for two units of wheat are drawn. England will only gain from trade if the international price of wine for wheat is to the right of its existing domestic cost line. Portugal on the other hand will only gain if the international price is to the left of its domestic cost line. Hence trade will only be mutually advantageous if the terms of trade are somewhere between the two lines, the area shaded on the graph.

Question 4

Look again at the data in Table 6.

(a) Show on a graph the price ratios of meat for bread in the two countries before trade.

(b) Would both countries find it mutually advantageous to trade if the international trade price ratio were 1 unit of meat for:
(i) 4 units of bread; (ii) 3 units of bread; (iii) 1¹/₂ units of bread;
(iv) 1 unit of bread; (v) ¹/₂ unit of bread; (vi) 2 units of bread;
(vii) 1¹/₃ units of bread?

Why comparative advantage exists

David Ricardo believed that all costs ultimately could be reduced to labour costs. This belief is known as the **labour theory of value**. Hence the price of a good could accurately be measured in terms of worker hours of production. Following on from this, he argued that differences in comparative costs reflected differences in the productivity of labour.

There is an element of truth in this idea. The theory suggests that high labour productivity countries would have a comparative advantage in the production of sophisticated high technology goods whilst low labour productivity countries would have a comparative advantage in the production of low technology goods. Looking at the pattern of world trade, it is true for instance that developing countries export low technology textiles whilst developed countries export high technology computer equipment.

However, neo-classical price theory suggests that labour is not the only source of differing opportunity costs of production. For instance, the price of a piece of agricultural land can increase several times overnight if planning permission is given for residential building. This increase in value has little to do with worker hours of production. Prices and costs are, of course, linked to quantities of labour inputs, but they are also linked to forces of scarcity which can drive prices up or down.

Heckscher and Ohlin, two Swedish economists working in the inter-war period, suggested that different costs were the result not just of different labour endowments between countries but also of different capital and land endowments. If an economy, such as India, has a large quantity of unskilled labour but little capital, then the price of capital relative to labour will be high. If, on the other hand, an economy like the USA has a large stock of capital relative to labour, then capital will be relatively cheap. Hence India will have a comparative advantage in the production of goods which can be made using unskilled labour. The USA will have a comparative advantage in the production of goods which require a relatively high capital input. Saudi Arabia is much more richly endowed with oil than France. France, on the other hand, has a rich abundance of skilled labour and capital equipment in the defence industry. Hence the theory would suggest that Saudi Arabia will specialise in producing oil, France in producing defence equipment and that the two countries will trade one product for the other.

Non-price theories of trade

The theory of comparative advantage provides a good explanation of world trade in commodities such as oil, wheat or copper. Countries with relatively rich endowments of raw materials or agricultural land specialise in the production of those commodities. It also provides a good explanation of the pattern of trade between First and Third World countries. Third World countries tend to export commodities and simple manufactured goods whilst importing more technologically sophisticated manufactures and services from the First World. However, the theory does not account for much of that half of world trade which occurs between the rich developed economies of the world.

Commodities are **homogeneous** products. There is nothing to choose between one grade of copper from Chile and the same grade from Zambia. Therefore the main determinant of demand is price. Manufactured goods and services tend to be **non-homogeneous**. Each product is slightly different. So when a consumer buys a car, price is only one amongst many factors

that are considered. Reliability, availability, image, colour, shape and driving performance are just as important, if not more so. There is a wide variety of cars to choose from on the market, some produced domestically but many produced abroad. **Preference similarity theory** suggests that many manufactured goods are imported not because they are relatively cheaper than domestic goods but because some consumers want greater choice than that provided by domestic manufacturers alone. Domestic manufacturers, however, should have a competitive edge because they should be more aware of the needs of their domestic customers. This limits the extent to which foreign manufacturers can penetrate the home market.

The benefits of trade

Economists today tend to favour **free trade** between countries. Free trade occurs when there are no barriers to trade, such as taxes on imported goods or bans on imports. Free trade is beneficial for a number of reasons.

Specialisation The theory of **comparative advantage** shows that world output can be increased if countries specialise in what they are relatively best at producing. It makes little point, for instance, for the UK to grow bananas given its climate when they can be grown much more cheaply in Latin America. Equally, it makes little sense for Barbados to manufacture motor vehicles given the size of the island, the relatively small population, the small domestic market and its geographical location.

Economies of scale Trade allows economies of scale to be maximised and thus costs reduced. Economies of scale are a source of comparative advantage. Small countries can buy in goods and services which are produced in bulk in other countries, whilst themselves specialising in producing and exporting goods where they have developed economies of scale.

Choice Trade allows consumers the choice of what to buy from the whole world, and not just from what is produced domestically. Consumer welfare is thus increased because some consumers at least will prefer to buy foreign goods rather than domestic goods.

Innovation Free trade implies competition. A lack of free trade often leads to domestic markets being dominated by a few firms who avoid competition amongst themselves. Competition provides a powerful incentive to innovate. Not only are new goods and services being put onto the market, but firms are also competing to find production methods which cut costs and improve the quality and reliability of goods. A few firms are at the forefront of innovation in their industries. In a competitive market, however, other firms copy this innovation to remain competitive. The few countries in the world which for political reasons have chosen to isolate themselves from trade and attempt to be self-sufficient, like North Korea, have found that over time their economies have tended to stagnate. On their own, they simply do not have the resources or the incentives to keep up with the pace of innovation in the outside world.

The costs of trade

Trade between countries can be beneficial, but it can also have costs.

Overdependence Countries can become overdependent on foreign trade. Small countries in particular can become dependent on exports of one or two commodities. If the prices of those commodities fall, or demand falls, then these countries can experience large falls in GDP. Trade also opens the risk that imports will be cut for political reasons. The first oil crisis of 1973-75, for example, was caused by the threat of a refusal by Arab states to supply oil to Western countries selling arms to Israel.

Jobs Changes in demand can lead to unemployment. For example, parts of the UK suffered structural unemployment during the second half of the 20th century as primary and manufacturing industries shrank in size due to competition from imports. The less mobile the workforce, the greater the likelihood that changes in demand due to trade will reduce output and employment over long periods of time.

Risk Trade exposes a country to many risks. Demand for a country's exports can suddenly fall or their prices can fall. Supplies can be cut by foreign countries. There can be credit crises which cut off finance for a country to pay for imports. The cost of borrowing to buy imports can suddenly rise.

Distribution of income Trade can lead to a less equal distribution of income. If the benefits of trade go mainly to other countries, then a country may find itself relatively less well off. Equally, trade alters patterns of demand within a country. The benefits of trade may go mainly to rich elites within a country and the poor may even end up worse off. This widens inequality within a trading country.

The environment Trade can lead to environmental degradation and unsustainable development. Demand for timber, for example, has led to large-scale deforestation in the developing world.

Loss of sovereignty Trade leads to nation states losing sovereignty. This means they lose the ability to make decisions about matters which affect them. The loss of sovereignty may be explicit because a government signs an international treaty. For example, the UK has lost sovereignty by joining the EU. Or it may be because the complex network of private trade gives power to foreign companies or foreign consumers.

Loss of culture Trade brings foreign ideas and products to an individual country. Some argue that this leads to a loss of rich traditional native culture.

Key Terms

Absolute advantage - exists when a country is able to produce a good more cheaply in absolute terms than another country.

Comparative advantage - exists when a country is able to produce a good more cheaply relative to other goods produced domestically than another country.

Theory of comparative advantage - countries will find it mutually advantageous to trade if the opportunity cost of production of goods differs.

Question 5

Manufacturing in the UK has been in decline for the past 30 years. Industries like clothes manufacturing and petrochemicals have seen their output fall as manufacturers overseas have outcompeted them on price. However, many people believe the future of UK manufacturing lies with so-called 'advanced manufacturing': the use of innovative technology to make distinctive products that are not made by other companies. The UK's aircraft and car industries have been two of the brightest spots for UK manufacturing growth, with output up 60 per cent and 40 per cent respectively compared to five years ago. Michael Straughan, who heads Bentley's manufacturing, believes the industry's revival has been a product-led recovery, boosted by foreign investment. 'The UK car industry (is) almost all entirely owned by a foreign company and each of those companies invested very heavily in product at a time when it was most difficult', he says. More than £2.6 billion was invested in the British car industry in 2013, as foreign-owned manufacturers such as Jaguar Land Rover and Bentley increased investment in factories and the wider supply chain.

Source: with information from © the *Financial Times* 13.3.2014, All Rights Reserved.

Using the data, explain the possible benefits and costs over the past 30 years of foreign trade to UK (a) manufacturing firms; (b) workers employed in manufacturing and (c) consumers of manufactured goods.

Thinking like an economist

The pattern of UK trade

Goods vs services
The UK trades in a wide variety of both goods and services. Over time, the pattern of trade for the UK has changed, as Table 9 shows. Over the past 60 years, the UK has increasingly had a comparative advantage in the production and export of services rather than goods. In 1955, for example, the UK exported approximately £15 of goods for every £5 of services. By 2014, this ratio had changed approximately to £15 of for every £10 of services.

Over the same period, foreign trade has increased as a proportion of national income. In 1955, exports of goods and services were 24 per cent of national income. By 2014, this had risen to 31 per cent.

The physical pattern of trade in goods
In the 19th century, the UK used to be the 'workshop of the world'. It imported raw materials and turned them into manufactured goods which it exported. Table 10 shows that this pattern of trade was still true to some extent for the UK 60 years ago in 1955. However, by 1995, the UK has lost much of its competitive advantage in manufactured goods. This is

Table 9 UK exports and imports of traded goods and services, national income (Gross value added at basic prices)

£ billion

| | Exports | | Imports | | |
	Goods	Services	Goods	Services	National Income
1955	3.1	1.0	3.4	1.0	17.6
1965	5.0	1.6	5.3	1.7	33.4
1975	19.5	7.7	22.8	6.0	102.8
1985	78.3	25.7	82.0	17.2	346.8
1995	153.6	59.1	166.6	42.9	703.6
2000	187.9	81.4	222.0	67.4	911.1
2005	212.7	128.9	282.4	94.0	1 189.2
2010	270.8	176.2	368.2	115.9	1 400.7
2014	292.2	207.7	412.1	122.6	1 593.4

Source: adapted from www.ons.gov.uk.

Table 10 Exports and imports by commodity (% of total value)

		1955	1975	1985	1995	2005	2014
Food, beverages and tobacco	Exports	6.0	7.1	6.3	7.3	5.2	6.5
	Imports	36.9	18.0	10.6	9.4	8.4	9.3
Basic materials	Exports	3.9	2.7	2.7	1.9	1.8	2.4
	Imports	29.0	8.4	6.0	3.9	2.4	2.9
Fuels	Exports	4.9	4.2	21.5	6.5	10.6	12.5
	Imports	10.6	17.5	12.8	3.7	9.4	12.6
Total food and raw materials	Exports	14.8	14.0	30.5	15.7	17.5	21.4
	Imports	76.5	43.9	29.4	17.0	20.2	24.8
Semi-manufactured	Exports	36.9	31.2	25.6	28.3	28.0	26.3
	Imports	17.9	23.9	24.8	27.3	22.8	23.3
Finished manufactured	Exports	43.5	51.0	41.2	54.8	53.6	50.5
	Imports	5.3	29.9	44.0	54.7	56.0	50.7
Total manufactured	Exports	80.4	82.2	66.8	83.1	81.6	76.8
	Imports	23.2	53.8	68.8	82.0	78.9	74.1
Unclassified	Exports	4.8	3.8	2.7	1.2	1.3	1.8
	Imports	0.3	2.7	1.8	1.0	1.0	1.2

Source: adapted from www.ons.gov.uk.

shown by the significant increase in imports in the proportion of manufactured goods to total imports from just 23.2 per cent in 1955 to 82 per cent by 1995. The 1970s and 1980s saw a process of deindustrialisation in the UK with the closure of significant proportions of its manufacturing industry, unable to compete with countries such as Germany and Japan.

The UK today has a significant oil sector due to North Sea oil. The first oil to be extracted commercially was in 1975. Between 1975 and 1985, exports of fuels including oil rose from 4.2 per cent of total exports to 21.5 per cent. Over the same period, imports of fuel as a percentage of total imports fell from 17.5 per cent to 12.8 per cent. North Sea oil is in decline today. By 2014, exports of fuels had fallen to 12.5 per cent of total exports. Oil remains, however, a significant export earner for the UK.

The pattern of trade in services

Table 11 shows the composition and change in trade in services since 1975. The data show that the UK has a comparative advantage in financial and insurance services. In 2013, one quarter of total exports of services were financial services. It also shows that the UK has a comparative disadvantage in

travel, which includes tourism. Far more UK citizens want to take holidays abroad than foreign citizens want to take a holiday in the UK.

The geographical pattern of trade in goods and services

Table 12 shows how the geographical pattern of UK trade has changed over time. In 1955, the UK was still to a great extent following trading patterns established during the Victorian era, buying raw materials from its colonies and ex-colonies in the developing world and selling them manufactured goods. By

Table 11 The composition of trade in services

£ billion

	1975	1985	1995	2005	2013
Exports					
Transport	3.4	6.1	10.2	18.5	24.2
Travel	1.2	5.4	13.0	16.9	26.2
Financial and insurance	2.9	12.1	7.9	29.9	46.7
Other	-	-	18.8	63.7	107.3
Total	7.5	23.6	49.9	128.9	204.5
Imports					
Transport	3.3	6.4	10.7	19.8	22.5
Travel	0.9	4.9	15.8	32.8	33.7
Financial and insurance	1.5	4.6	1.6	7.0	8.6
Other	-	-	13.4	34.4	61.5
Total	5.7	15.9	41.5	94.0	126.4

Source: adapted from www.ons.gov.uk.

Table 12 Trade[1] by area

| | | Percentage of total | | | | |
		1955	1975	1995	2005	2013
Europe	Exports	31.9	51.3	60.5	58.9	53.4
	Imports	31.0	53.8	63.3	65.2	62.4
of which EU[2]	Exports	26.8	41.1	49.5	51.9	54.3
	Imports	25.9	45.1	51.0	42.9	40.7
North America	Exports	11.3	12.1	15.6	18.3	19.5
	Imports	19.8	13.5	15.3	11.3	10.5
Other developed countries[3]	Exports	15.3	9.6	5.8	5.3	4.9
	Imports	12.4	8.0	7.0	5.5	3.9
of which Japan	Exports	0.5	1.6	3.0	2.4	1.9
	Imports	0.6	2.8	5.0	2.7	1.8
Rest of the World	Exports	41.5	27.0	19.1	17.5	29.0
	Imports	36.8	24.7	14.4	18.0	23.2
of which China	Exports	-	-	0.5	1.4	3.4
	Imports	-	-	1.0	3.7	6.5

Source: adapted from www.ons.gov.uk.

1 1955 and 1975 data are trade in goods only. 1995 and 2004 data are trade in goods and services.
2 Includes all 1995 EU countries in 1955 and 1975 percentages; 2005 and 2013 data are for the EU28 countries.
3 Australia, New Zealand, Japan, South Africa.

2013, UK trade had shifted dramatically. The UK's entry to the European Union in 1973 led to a significant increase in the proportion of exports being sold into Europe and imports being bought from Europe. Low growth in the EU following the 2007-08 financial crisis and policies of fiscal austerity implemented by many countries led to a fall in the proportion of exports going to Europe. Table 12 also shows the rapid increase in imports to the UK from China. Even so, China only accounted for 6.5 per cent of total imports of goods and services in 2013.

Figure 3 shows the UK's 10 largest export trading partners by country in 2013. Four of these are in the EU and six are non-EU. The UK's largest export market by country is the USA with 17.6 per cent of total UK exports in 2013. Exports to the EU, however, were three times as great. If the UK were to leave the European Union, there is a considerable risk that exports to the EU would fall. For every one per cent fall in EU exports, the UK would need to grow its exports to, for example, the USA by three per cent to compensate for this. Given the UK's traditional poor export performance, it is difficult to see how this sort of readjustment in the geographical pattern of UK trade could take place.

Figure 3

The UK's main trading partners; exports of goods and services to individual countries as percentage of total exports, 2013

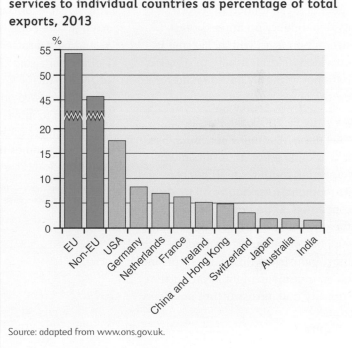

Source: adapted from www.ons.gov.uk.

Data Response Question

Impact of economic sanctions on Russia

Russia's aggressive foreign policy in annexing the Crimea and invading the Ukraine has led to the EU and the USA imposing sanctions. These sanctions limit trade with Russia.

Dmitry Medvedev, Russia's Prime Minister, told parliamentarians that faced with the threat of more sanctions, Russia had to reduce its dependency on imports and strengthen from within. He said it provided an opportunity to create a national economy based on domestic production.

As early as 2009, the Russian President, Vladimir Putin, said that it was a 'disgrace' that Russia was importing more than 40 per cent of its food and over half of all medicines consumed. Little has changed since then. Russia relies heavily on foreign supplies of manufactured goods across most industries. This is not surprising given that investment in production capacity and infrastructure has been

Russia's weakest spot. There is no sign that things are turning the corner. After stagnating in 2013, fixed-asset investment fell four per cent in the first quarter of this year.

Analysts warn that Moscow will struggle to prop up its stagnant economy by reducing economic integration. 'It is sensible for Russia to try and strength the domestic economy, but it would be a disaster if that resulted in isolationism' said Chris Weafer, a partner at MacroAdvisory, a Moscow-based consultancy. 'We only just saw Russia beginning to move in the right direction and starting to globalise its economy, and now, bang, comes this crisis, which could ruin it all.'

Q

1. Sanctions on Russian trade were imposed in 2014. Give two pieces of evidence that the Russian economy was struggling even before this.

2. Using the theory of comparative advantage, explain why creating a 'national economy based on domestic production' is likely to lead to a fall in output for Russia.

3. Discuss whether a policy of free trade would best suit the needs of Russian firms and consumers.

Evaluation

Very briefly, recap the comparative advantage argument which you have outlined in question 2 and apply this to its impact on firms and consumers. Then analyse and evaluate each argument for and against free trade for Russia. In your conclusion, weigh up these advantages and disadvantages.

Figure 4

Russian trade (sum over previous 12 months)

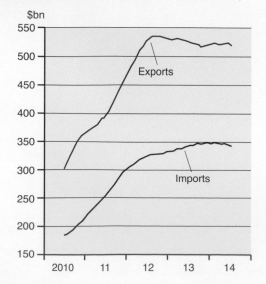

Figure 5

Russian GDP growth (% change on previous quarter)

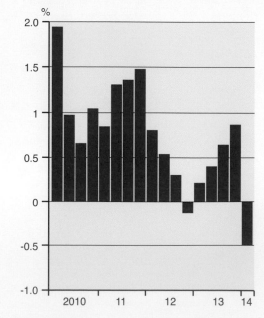

63 The terms of trade

Key points

1. The terms of trade are the ratio of export prices to import prices.
2. The terms of trade are influenced by a variety of factors including changes in the exchange rate, relative inflations and relative productivity levels.
3. The impact of changes in the terms of trade on the current account balance depends on the price elasticity of demand of exports and imports.
4. Changes in the terms of trade can affect GDP, inflation and the level of unemployment.

Starter activity

In 2014, the world price of crude oil approximately halved. For a few countries around the world, like Venezuela and Saudi Arabia, oil exports account for the vast majority of all their exports. For these countries, what happens to the amount of imports they can buy with each barrel of oil exports? Are they better off or worse off?

Calculating the terms of trade

The **terms of trade** is defined as the ratio between average export prices and average import prices.

$$\text{Index of terms of trade} = \frac{\text{Index of export prices}}{\text{Index of import prices}} \times 100$$

It is measured in the form of an index because it is calculated from the weighted average of thousands of different export and import prices. For example, the UK exports oil and Rolls Royce cars. The value of exports of UK oil from the North Sea is far greater than the value of exports of Rolls Royce cars. Therefore, a change in the price of oil is far more important when calculating the average price of exports than a change in the price of Rolls Royce cars. Changes in the price of oil are weighted more heavily when calculating the index or average of export prices than changes in the price of Rolls Royce cars.

The terms of trade are said to improve when its value increases, i.e. when export prices rise relative to import prices. There is a deterioration in the terms of trade when its value decreases, i.e. when export prices fall relative to import prices.

Question 1

Table 1 Index of export prices and index of import prices (Year 5 = 100)

Year	1	2	3	4	5	6
Index of export prices	105	99	95	97	100	110
Index of import prices	110	107	105	102	100	105
Index of terms of trade						

(a) Table 1 shows the index of export prices and the index of import prices for a country over six years. Copy out the table and calculate for each year the Index of the terms of trade in the bottom row.

(b) Between which years is there (i) and improvement and (ii) a deterioration in the terms of trade?

Factors influencing the terms of trade

The terms of trade for a country can change for a variety of reasons in the short run.

- A change in the exchange rate will change import and export prices. For example, a rise in the exchange rate is likely to lead to a fall in the price of imported goods. The terms of trade will therefore improve.
- If inflation is also occurring in the economies of a country's main trading partners, then a rise in inflation relative to other countries is also likely to improve the terms of trade.
- A change in demand for exports or imports, which leads to a change in their price, will change the terms of trade.

In the long term, there will be other factors at work which affect the terms of trade.

- A rise in productivity compared to a country's main trading partners should reduce the relative price of exports as higher productivity leads to lower costs of production. Hence a relative rise in productivity could lead to a deterioration in the terms of trade.
- Changing incomes will affect patterns of demand. As world incomes rise, for example, there has been an increase in demand for tourism. If this leads to a rise in prices in the tourist industry in, say, Turkey, then all other things being equal, there will be an improvement in Turkey's terms of trade.

Some countries are heavily dependent on exports of commodities such as oil or copper. Their terms of trade will be heavily influenced by changes in the world price of commodities. For example, a large rise in the price of oil will lead to significant rises in the terms of trade for oil-exporting countries such as Saudi Arabia and Venezuela.

Effects of changes in the terms of trade on the balance of payments

Changes in the terms of trade can have an effect on the balance of payments on current account depending upon the price elasticity of demand for exports and imports. This is summarised in Table 2. The current account balance is defined for this analysis as exports minus imports of traded goods and services.

Exports are price elastic Assume that exports are price elastic. This means that a rise in export prices leads to a larger proportionate fall in export quantities or volumes. The total value of exports is equal to average prices times volume. So a rise in export prices with price elastic demand for exports will lead to a fall in the value of exports. For example, assume that price elasticity of demand for exports is -3. A 10 per cent rise in export prices will then lead to a 30 per cent fall in export volumes (-3 = -30/+10). The total value of exports will therefore fall by approximately 20 per cent. A rise in export prices, all other things being equal, will lead to an increase in the terms of trade (export prices ÷ import prices) but a deterioration in the current account on the balance of payments (exports - imports). Conversely, a fall in export prices, all other things being equal, will lead to a fall in the terms of trade but an improvement in the current account.

Exports are price inelastic If exports are price inelastic, a rise in export prices which causes an improvement in the terms of trade will lead to a less than proportionate fall in export volumes. The value of exports will therefore rise. So a rise in export prices here will lead to an improvement in the terms of trade and an improvement in the current account position.

Imports are price elastic If imports are price elastic, a rise in import prices which causes a deterioration in the terms of trade will lead to a more than proportionate fall in import volumes. The value of imports will therefore fall. So a rise in import prices here will lead to a deterioration in the terms of trade and an improvement in the current account position.

Imports are price inelastic If imports are price inelastic, a rise in import prices which causes a deterioration in the terms of trade will lead to a less than proportionate fall in import volumes. The value of imports will therefore rise. So a rise in import prices here will lead to a deterioration in the terms of trade and in the current account position.

Changes in export prices and import prices can come about for a variety of reasons. For example, between 2000 and 2008, the prices of commodity products such as copper and wheat rose due to an increase in world demand particularly from the fast-growing Chinese economy. Commodities tend to be price inelastic. So countries which were highly dependent on exports of commodities tended to see both their terms of trade and current account balances improve.

Another factor affecting export and import prices is domestic inflation. A general rise in prices in the economy is also likely to be associated with a rise in the prices exporters charge their customers. Assume that import prices remain the same. Then the terms of trade will improve. However, the impact on the current account balance will depend on whether the demand for exports is price elastic or price inelastic.

Table 2 The effect of a change in export and import prices on the current account

	Elasticity	Price change	Terms of trade	Current account balance
Exports	Elastic	Rise	Improve	Deteriorate
		Fall	Deteriorate	Improve
	Inelastic	Rise	Improve	Improve
		Fall	Deteriorate	Deteriorate
Imports	Elastic	Rise	Deteriorate	Improve
		Fall	Improve	Deteriorate
	Inelastic	Rise	Deteriorate	Deteriorate
		Fall	Improve	Improve

Effects of changes in the terms of trade on the domestic economy

Changes in the terms of trade can have an impact on the domestic economy as well as on the balance of payments. An improvement in the terms of trade caused by a rise in export prices is likely to lead to a fall in the volume of exports sold. With less being produced in the export sector, this could lead to a fall in GDP and a rise in unemployment.

An improvement in the terms of trade caused by a fall in import prices is likely to lead to a rise in the volume of imports. Inflation is likely to fall because the fall in import prices will put downward pressure on prices throughout the economy. If there are few substitutes for the imports which have fallen in price and they are price inelastic, then extra spending on imports could displace spending on goods produced in the domestic economy. If motorists are having to pay higher prices for petrol because of a rise in crude oil prices, they may spend less on other goods and services. If there are good substitutes for the imports, then a fall in their price will make them more price competitive. Domestic producers will therefore lose market share. GDP will fall and unemployment will rise as a consequence.

Key Terms

Index of terms of trade - equal to:

$$\frac{\text{Index of export prices}}{\text{Index of import prices}} \times 100$$

Terms of trade - the ratio of export prices to import prices.

Thinking like an economist

Norway compared to the UK

Norway and the UK face each other across the North Sea. They share geological formations that in the 1970s proved to be rich in oil. However, there are differences. Norway also has oil reserves to its north, in the Barents Sea and in Arctic waters. Its oil reserves and oil production are much larger than those of the UK. In fact, Norway is currently Europe's largest oil producer. Norway also has a much smaller population than the UK. At five million compared to 64 million for the UK, its population is only eight per cent that of the UK. This means that the oil industry, the jobs it brings, the price of oil, and tax revenues are far more significant for Norway than the UK.

Figure 1 shows how the price of oil has changed since 1997. Between 1997 and 2012, the price of oil broadly rose apart from two sharp dips in 2001 and 2009. Figure 2 shows the annual percentage change in export and import prices for the UK. There is little correlation between these changes and the changes in the price of oil. Figure 2 also shows that import and export prices for the UK tend to move in the same direction and the same amount over time. This means that the UK's terms of trade were broadly stable over the period 1997 to 2013. It suggests that factors influencing export prices were broadly similar to the factors influencing import prices.

Figure 3 shows the annual percentage change in export and import prices for Norway. The change in export prices is significantly correlated to changes in the international price of oil in Figure 1. It reflects Norway's dependence on oil for exports. Unlike the UK, changes in import prices are not necessarily correlated to changes in export prices. Norway's imports are a very different basket of goods than its exports. So Norway will have experienced far more volatility in its terms of trade between 1997 and 2013 than the UK because export prices are moving independently of import prices and are highly dependent upon volatile oil prices.

Source: with information from www.eia.gov/countries/country-data.cfm?fips=no.

Figure 1

Annual percentage change in the price of Brent crude oil

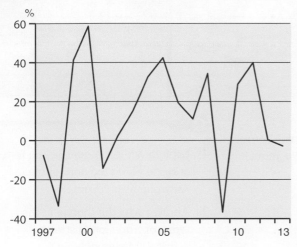

Source: adapted from BP, *Statistical Review of World Energy*, 2014.

Figure 2

UK: annual percentage change in export and import prices

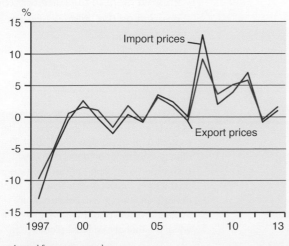

Source: adapted from www.oecd.org.

Figure 3

Norway: annual percentage change in export and import prices

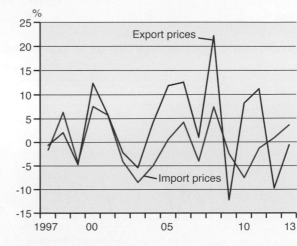

Source: adapted from www.oecd.org.

Data Response Question

Deterioration in Australia's terms of trade

Australia's terms of trade have fallen a quarter since peaking in late 2011. The reason is that the prices of the country's main exports, iron ore and coal, have slumped.

The fall in the terms of trade is having a big impact on incomes in Australia. Real wages are falling for the first time since the last official recession in Australia in 1991-92, and the unemployment rate has increased. The downturn is hitting young people hardest with the youth unemployment rate for those aged 15-24 at 13.8 per cent, the highest level since 2001.

The fall in commodity prices has led to the major mining companies cutting back on investment and production. This has quickly filtered through to the rest of the economy. Phil Ramondino, for example, is a self-employed construction worker. He says: 'Competition is very tough,

construction companies are going bust, leaving me unpaid, and my take-home pay is down 20 per cent in two years.'

Figure 4

Australia: annual percentage change in export and import prices

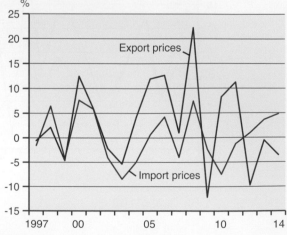

Source: adapted from www.oecd.org.

Q

1. Explain what is meant by the terms of trade, using the data about Australia as an example.

2. Analyse why the change in the terms of trade for Australia in 2012-14 should have led to unemployment and falling investment.

3. Discuss whether the changes in the terms of trade between 2012 and 2014 are likely to have led to an improvement in the current account position on the balance of payments for Australia.

Evaluation

Analyse the impact of a change in the terms of trade on exports and imports using the concept of price elasticity of demand. The data give information about changes in both export and import prices. Then weigh up the likely impact on total exports, total imports and the current balance. Your evaluation could also cover the time over which the changes will take place.

64 Trading blocs

Key points

1. Trading blocs are groups of countries which, at a minimum, have agreed to reduce some protectionist barriers to trade between themselves.
2. Trading blocs can take the form of preferential trading areas, free trade areas, customs unions, common markets and economic unions. Monetary unions can be a feature of any of these types of trading bloc.
3. Most trading blocs are created by bilateral agreements between two countries or trading blocs. A minority of trading blocs are created by multilateral agreements between three or more countries or trading blocs.
4. Trading blocs have advantages and disadvantages, but overall they are likely to bring less welfare gains than a situation where all trading countries signed a common trade agreement.

Starter activity

Use the Internet to find out about 10 different trading blocs. What are their names? How have they affected trade? Are there any plans for future development?

Trading blocs

A **trading bloc** is a group of countries that have signed an agreement to reduce or eliminate tariffs, quotas and other protectionist barriers between themselves. The agreement is called a **regional trade agreement**. The number of trading blocs has considerably increased over the past 40 years. Some countries belong to more than one trading bloc. Some trading blocs are relatively inactive and are unlikely to lead to deeper economic integration. A few, such as the European Union, are very active and it can be predicted with some certainty that in 10 or 20 years' time, the level of economic integration between member countries will be much deeper than it is today.

There are five main types of trading bloc.

- **Preferential trading areas** are where tariff and other trade barriers are reduced on some but not all goods traded between member countries. Member countries sign a **preferential trade agreement (PTA)** to create the preferential trading area.
- **Free trade areas** are where all tariffs and quotas are removed on trade in goods between member countries. However, each member country is able to impose its own tariffs and quotas on goods it imports from outside the trading bloc.
- **Customs unions** are where there is free trade within the trading bloc and a common external tariff on goods coming from outside the bloc.
- **Common markets** are customs unions where both labour and capital have freedom of movement within the area and where product standards and laws concerning free movement of goods and services are common between countries.
- **Economic unions** are where the economies of member countries are as fully integrated as different regions within a country. Economic union implies that there is some degree of **fiscal union**, with a central body having some powers over taxation and spending, and **monetary union**, where all member countries share a common currency.

Most regional trade agreements take the form of **bilateral agreements**. These are agreements between one single country and another single country, or in the case of the EU, between the EU and another single country. A minority of regional trade agreements are **multilateral** or **plurilateral agreements**. These are agreements between at least three countries. Monetary unions can be a feature of any type of trading blocs.

Advantages and disadvantages of trading blocs

Economic theory suggests that free trade can bring both static and dynamic benefits. Static benefits come from the gains from specialisation. Dynamic benefits come from increased competition and the transfer of resources. Regional trade agreements are a second best solution to complete free trade between all countries. They will bring static benefits if the net welfare gains from trade creation exceed the net welfare losses from trade diversion (explained in Unit 65). They will bring dynamic benefits if competition is sufficiently large between firms in member countries to bring increased efficiencies and transfers of resources.

In practice, trading blocs and regional trade agreements have a number of advantages and disadvantages.

- Creating and maintaining trading blocks can distract governments from the much larger gains that could be made by signing free trade agreements with all countries through the Word Trade Organization (WTO). The WTO is an organisation established to promote free trade between all member countries. In particular, bilateral trade agreements can bring very little gain to the two countries making the agreement but can take up significant government resources to get to the point of signing the agreement.
- Some regional trade agreements in practice distribute the gains from trade unequally. For example, bilateral agreements between the EU or the USA and developing countries may give little benefit to the developing country but open up their markets to significant imports from the EU and the USA.
- Many regional trade agreements are very weak because they cover free trade in a very limited range of goods. The economic benefits are therefore small.

- At worst, the creation of a trading bloc can lead to more trade diversion than trade creation. They therefore reduce overall economic output even if some members of the trading bloc are net gainers.
- Trading blocs lessen national sovereignty. Around the world, there is considerable debate about sovereignty. In the UK for example, UKIP (the United Kingdom Independence Party) would like to see the UK leave the EU because of loss of sovereignty to Brussels.

- Membership of trading blocs can bring dynamic grains if it lessens the international isolation of countries and brings improvements in government, the rule of law and state institutions. In the EU, for example, membership has helped countries like Bulgaria and Romania with relatively poor records of good governance to improve the quality of state institutions and the rule of law.

Key Terms

Bilateral trade agreement - a regional trade agreement between two countries.

Common market - a customs union where in addition both labour and capital have freedom of movement within the area and where product standards and laws concerning free movement of goods and services are common between countries.

Customs union - a group of countries between which there is free trade in products and which imposes a common external tariff on imported goods from outside the market.

Economic union - a group of countries where the economies of member countries are as fully integrated economically as different regions within a single country; for example, a single market will be combined with a fiscal and monetary union.

Fiscal union - a group of countries where a central body has some powers over government borrowing, government spending and setting uniform rates of taxation in member countries.

Free trade area - a group of countries between which there is free trade in goods and services but where member countries

are allowed to set their own level of tariffs against non-member countries.

Monetary union - a group of countries which share a common currency such as the euro.

Multilateral or plurilateral trade agreement - a regional trade agreement between three or more countries or trading blocs.

Preferential trade agreement - a treaty between two or more countries to lower or abolish some protectionist barriers such as tariffs on trade between members.

Preferential trading area - a group of countries that have signed a preferential trade agreement lowering or abolishing some protectionist barriers such as tariffs on trade between themselves.

Regional trade agreement - an agreement between at least two countries to reduce or eliminate tariffs, quotas and other protectionist barriers between themselves.

Trading bloc - a group of countries that have signed an agreement to reduce or eliminate tariffs, quotas and other protectionist barriers between themselves.

Thinking like an economist

Trading blocs

As of 7 April 2015, some 612 notifications of RTAs (counting goods, services and accessions separately) had been received by the General Agreement on Tariffs and Trade (GATT)/World Trade Organization. Of these, 406 were in force.

Most regional trade agreements are bilateral agreements and are relatively unimportant. However, a few trading blocs have a significant impact on world trade.

The European Union The European Union is, arguably, the world's most important trading bloc. In 2015, it had 28 member countries and is in the process of transforming itself from being a customs union into a full economic union. It is discussed in more detail in Unit 65. Linked to the European Union is the European Free Trade Area (EFTA). This is a group of four countries, Norway, Iceland, Switzerland and Liechtenstein. The four countries, through various treaties, are part of the EU single market, which allows the free movement of goods, people and financial capital between countries.

North American Free Trade Agreement (NAFTA)

NAFTA is the world's largest trading bloc measured by the GDP of its three member countries - the USA, Canada and Mexico. Formed in 1994, it is a free trade area which covers trade in goods excepting agricultural products for which special provisions apply. Removal of tariff barriers has led to the relocation of many businesses to Mexico to take advantage of much lower wages. There has been a large increase in the number of Maquiladoras, Mexican factories which take in imported raw materials and produce goods for export. Associated with NAFTA are a number of other agreements between the three countries, including ones on the environment and labour. However, at this stage there are no serious political negotiations to move NAFTA from being just a free trade area to a customs union.

The Association of Southeast Asian Nations (ASEAN)

ASEAN was formed in 1992 between Brunei, Indonesia, Malaysia, Philippines, Singapore and Thailand. It now also includes Cambodia, Lao PDR, Myanmar and Vietnam. Part of ASEAN is an economic agreement which has created the ASEAN Free Trade Area (AFTA). In AFTA, each country is free to set its own tariffs on imports but there are no or minimal tariffs on goods which have an AWEAN 40 per cent content value. AFTA was due to be replaced by the ASEAN Economic Community (AEC), a common market with free movement of goods, labour, investments and capital by 2015. However, there is considerable doubt about whether AEC will come into existence by this date or when exactly it might be achieved. The delay shows the problems faced when countries attempt to create free trade areas and common markets. First, there is often considerable reluctance on the part of individual governments to concede sovereignty to new institutions. Second, it requires considerable resources to set up institutions to govern the workings of a common market.

Union of South American Nations (UNASUR)

The Union of South American Nations is a union of two South American trading blocs, the Andean Community of Nations (CAN) and Mercosur. Most South American countries belong to USAN. The aim of USAN is to create a single market between member countries but little progress has been made to date on this objective.

Source: with information from www.wto.org; www.asean.org; www.unasursg.org; www.nafta-sec-alena.org; www.efta.int.

Data Response Question

Regional trade agreements

The Committee on Regional Trade Agreements, a committee of the World Trade Organization, met on 8 April 2014 and reviewed the Chile-Malaysia Free Trade Agreement. The Malaysian representative said that this was its first regional trade agreement with a Latin American country. Trade between Malaysia and Chile had risen 76 per cent since the implementation of the regional trade agreement.

The committee went on to review the Canada-Panama Free Trade Agreement. Canada said that it views regional trade agreements as a means for establishing a level playing field for Canadian producers. It said that this regional trade agreement would allow Canadian companies to participate in government procurement in Panama, including construction projects related to the expansion of the Panama Canal. The Panamanian representative said that its trade with Canada had risen by 125 per cent since the entry into force of the regional trade agreements and that Canadian investment into Panama had risen by 31 per cent. He said that it had become one of the most dynamic countries in the region through its trade liberalisation policies.

Source: adapted from www.wto.org.

Q

1. Define, with the help of examples from the data, what is meant by a regional trade agreement.

2. Explain two ways in which firms in member countries could benefit from the regional trade agreements described in the data.

3. Using the data and your own economic knowledge, evaluate the costs and benefits of regional trade agreements.

Evaluation

In your answer, you can evaluate by pointing out that it is very difficult to be precise about the size of the costs and benefits. For example, trade between Malaysia and Chile might have grown by 76 per cent. But how much would it have grown anyway without the bilateral trade agreement?

65 Common markets and monetary unions

Key points

1. In a common market, there is free movement of goods and services, and factors of production. Goods and services imported from outside the common market face a common external tariff.
2. Free trade involves harmonisation in a wide range of areas, including product standards and taxation.
3. The formation of a common market will lead to trade creation and trade diversion. The greater the trade creation and the less the trade diversion, the greater will be the welfare benefits to member countries.
4. Dynamic gains from membership include economies of scale in production. Competition is likely to increase in the short run but mergers and takeovers are likely to lessen competition amongst firms in the long run.
5. Common market spending and taxation will lead to a redistribution of resources between member countries. Inevitably some countries will gain and others will lose from the common market budget.
6. There are advantages and disadvantages to member countries from a monetary union.
7. In an optimum currency area, there is free movement of products and factors of production between countries, fiscal transfers between regions and similar trade cycles.

Starter activity

How does the European Union affect you? Give 10 different ways in which it might impact on your present life and your life in the future.

A common market

A **common market** or customs union is a group of countries between which there is free trade and which impose a **common external tariff** on imported goods from outside the market. In theory, free trade between member countries involves goods and services as well as the factors of production.

- **Land.** There should be free trade in natural resources. In Europe, for instance, a British company should be free to buy land in Paris, whilst a French company should be free to own a licence to exploit North Sea oil.
- **Labour.** Workers should be free to work in any member country. For instance, an Italian should be able to work in London on exactly the same terms as a worker born in Birmingham.
- **Capital.** Capital should flow freely between countries. Of particular importance is **financial capital**. A Scottish firm should be free to borrow money in Paris to set up a factory in Italy, just as a London-based firm could borrow money from a Scottish bank to invest in Wales.

Imports from outside the common market present a problem. For instance, assume that the UK imposes a tariff of 10 per cent on imports of foreign cars whilst France imposes a tariff of 20 per cent. With free trade between France and the UK, foreign importers would ship cars intended for sale in France to the UK, pay the 10 per cent tariff, and then re-export them 'tariff-free' into France. There are two ways to get round this problem.

- One way is to impose a common external tariff. All member countries agree to change their tariff structures so as to impose the same tariff on imported items. In our example, France and the UK would have to change or **harmonise** their tariffs on cars to an agreed European Union (EU) figure.

- The other way is for member countries to impose tariffs on re-exports. In our example, France could impose a 10 per cent tariff on the original price of cars imported from non-member countries.

This second solution is a feature of **free trade areas**. A free trade area differs from a common market partly because of its different approach to dealing with non-member imports. It also differs because member countries are not committed to working towards closer economic integration. In a free trade area, the sole objective is free trade between member countries.

In a common market, the goal is to establish a single market in the same way that there is a single market within an individual

Question 1

- In 1994, a group of countries, including France, Germany, Holland and Belgium, dismantled all frontier posts between their countries.
- On 1 January 2002, euro notes and coins were issued in 11 countries of the European Union, followed shortly afterwards by the withdrawal of national currencies in those countries.
- Since the 1980s, the EU has suggested that tax rates between member countries should be harmonised (i.e. made the same). This would prevent, for instance, the large-scale smuggling of tobacco into the UK from France and Belgium, or the move of manufacturing plants from high labour taxed countries like Germany to low taxed countries like the UK.
- In 2004, the European Commission issued the Working Time Directive which limited workers' hours of work per week to 48 hours throughout the EU.
- In 2006, the European Parliament approved a new services directive which would increase the ability of service sector companies to compete throughout the EU. The service sector accounts for half of the EU's GDP and two thirds of jobs.

Source: adapted from Alain Anderton, *Economics*, 5th Edition, Pearson.

Explain why each of these illustrates how a common market works.

economy. Ultimately this involves a large number of changes including:

- no customs posts between countries; just as goods and people are free to travel between Manchester and London, so they should be free to travel between London and Milan;
- identical product standards between countries; the existence of individual national safety standards on cars, for instance, is a barrier to trade just as it would be if cars sold in London had to meet different safety requirements from cars sold in Bristol;
- harmonisation of taxes; if the tax on the same car is £2 000 more in the UK than in France, then UK residents will buy their cars in France and take them back to England, distorting the pattern of trade; equally if direct taxes on income are an average 15 per cent in France and 30 per cent in the UK, some UK workers may be tempted to go and work in France;
- a common currency; having to buy foreign exchange is a barrier to trade, especially if there are exchange rate movements; hence there should be a single common market currency just as there is a single currency in the UK.

Stages of economic integration

A Hungarian economist, Bela Balassa, put forward a theory in the 1960s of stages of ever-deeper economic integration. He suggested that a group of countries might go through six stages. These are summarised in Table 1.

- At the start, there would be a **preferential trading area**. This is where countries agree to reduce or abolish tariffs, quotas and other protectionist barriers on some goods being traded between them.
- This could develop into a **free trade area** where tariffs and quotas have been abolished between member countries. However, each member country may impose different tariffs and quotas on trade with countries outside the free trade area.
- In a **customs union**, there is free trade between member countries and a common external tariff.
- This might then develop into a **common market** where there is free trade not just in goods and services but also in factor markets. There is free movement of labour and capital. In the EU, the term 'single market' tends to be used to describe a common market today.
- A common market could lead onto **economic** and **monetary union**. In an economic union, there is a truly integrated

common market together with a single currency. Having a single currency means there will be a central bank for the union which controls monetary and exchange rate policy. There will also need to be some central control of fiscal policy within the union.

- There will be **complete economic integration** when the countries in a union operate in the same way as might counties, departments, regions or areas in a nation state. Economic integration implies some form of central government which controls a significant budget for spending and taxation across the union. Complete economic integration is therefore associated with a **political union**.

In practice, unions do not necessarily evolve in the way described in this model. The European Union, for example, was never a free trade area although there were preferential trading agreements between some member countries. However, the model helps to understand the depth of economic integration which can go from fairly shallow integration with preferential trade agreements to complete economic integration with an economic union.

Trade creation and trade diversion

The **theory of comparative advantage** shows that free trade between countries is likely to increase total world production. When a small number of countries form a common market, there will be gainers and losers.

Trade creation is said to take place when a country moves from buying goods from a high-cost country to buying them from a lower-cost country. For instance, country A might have imposed a 50 per cent tariff on imported cars. As a result, all cars sold in country A were produced domestically. It now joins a customs union. The common external tariff is 50 per cent but cars from member countries can be imported free of the tariff. Country A now buys some cars from common market countries because they are lower priced than those previously produced domestically. Consumers in country A have benefited because they are able to buy cars from a cheaper source.

Trade diversion takes place when a country moves from buying goods from a low-cost producer to buying them from a higher-cost producer. For instance, before entry to the European Union, the UK had low or zero tariffs on imported foodstuffs. It bought from the lowest-cost producers round the world such as New Zealand and the USA. After entry, the UK had to impose the much higher EU common external tariff. As a result it became cheaper to buy food from other EU countries such as France and Italy. France and Italy are higher-cost producers than the USA and New Zealand for many food items.

In general the higher the tariffs imposed by a country before entry to a common market, the more likely it is that trade creation rather than trade diversion will take place. It is also true that the net gains will tend to be larger, the greater the volume of trade between the countries in the common market.

Free trade vs customs unions

Customs unions can be seen as a 'second best' solution in a world where there is protectionism. Economic efficiency would be maximised if there were no barriers to trade between countries. Individual economies would also have perfectly

Table 1 Stages of economic integration

	Tariffs on trade between countries in the agreement	Common tariffs on imports from outside the agreement area	Free factor mobility within the area	Harmonisation of economic policies
Preferential trade agreeement	Reduced	No	No	No
Free trade agreement	Eliminated	No	No	No
Customs union	Eliminated	Yes	No	Possible
Common market	Eliminated	Yes	Yes	Desirable
Economic union	Eliminated	Yes	Yes	Yes

Source: adapted from UNCTAD secretariat.

competitive products and free labour and capital markets. In this theoretical world, comparative advantage would determine which countries produced what goods. This would be the 'first best' solution. In the real world, such conditions don't exist. Economic inefficiency arises because relatively high-cost producers can shelter behind protective barriers. A customs union brings down these barriers, at least between member states. Member countries may therefore be able to switch buying from a high-cost producer to a lower-cost producer. However, countries will only benefit if trade creation is greater than trade diversion. Consideration must also be taken of whether there will be dynamic gains or losses from the creation of a customs union.

Economies of scale

Gains from trade creation are static gains. They occur once and for all following the creation of, or entry to, a common market. Membership of a common market may also result in dynamic gains or losses - gains or losses which occur over a period of time. One important such gain comes from economies of scale. In a common market, the potential size of the customer market is inevitably larger than in a national market. For instance, the European Union has 503 million inhabitants compared to 65 million for the UK. This means that important economies of scale can be achieved by national companies if they carve out a market for themselves throughout the common market. This is no easy task given that each country is likely to have different consumer preferences. However, there are some products, such as basic chemicals, which are demanded by all countries. Other products, such as cars, are relatively easily sold across national boundaries. Other products, such as cosmetics, may need different packaging for different countries, but the basic product is the same.

Economies of scale will be achieved over a period of time as companies expand internally or merge with other foreign companies. The size of the potential gains will be greater, the more homogeneous the tastes of consumers within the market. For instance, the gains are likely to be higher for a market comprising France and the UK than for the UK and Iran. Economies of scale bring benefits to consumers because average costs of production fall, and therefore prices are likely to fall too.

Competition

Another possible dynamic gain arises from increased competition between firms. A common market should eliminate restrictions on trade between member countries. Domestic industries will therefore face greater competition than before from firms in other member countries. Competition will encourage innovation, reduce costs of production and reduce prices. There will therefore be gains in productive and allocative efficiency.

Although there is likely to be greater competition in the short run, evidence suggests that this competition will be reduced in the long run. Competition will drive the least efficient firms out of the market, as the theory of perfect competition predicts. Other firms will seek to maintain monopoly profits by re-establishing control over their markets. They will do this by merging with or taking over foreign firms within the common market. Over time,

the oligopolistic nature of competition in domestic markets will be recreated on a common market level. This may benefit the consumer through economies of scale but it certainly will not bring the benefits that free market economists suggest.

The Austrian School of Economics argues that competition is not necessarily beneficial to the consumer. Large international monopolies, earning considerable abnormal profit, will have the resources to devote to research, development and investment. If they fail to develop products that satisfy consumer wants, their monopoly will be lost through the process of creative destruction. Competitors will break their monopoly by creating new products. This constant development of new products is far more beneficial to consumer welfare than a few per cent off the price of existing products which might result from a perfectly competitive environment.

Transfers of resources

Common markets may differ in the size and power of their institutions. The European Union has a sizeable bureaucracy, a parliament and a large budget. Money is paid into a Union budget by member countries. The money is used to pay for administration and the implementation of Union-wide policies. Any budget of any size opens up the possibility that some member countries may pay more into the budget than they receive. There may therefore be a net transfer of resources from one country to another within a common market. These represent static losses and gains (i.e. once and for all losses and gains) for an individual country.

Perhaps more importantly, there can also be transfers of real resources from country to country. Countries in the common market which are particularly dynamic and successful are likely to attract inflows of labour and capital. Countries which have lower growth rates are likely to suffer net capital outflows and lose some of their best workers to other economies. This could heighten regional disparities, making the richer nations relatively even richer.

The process may be magnified if the successful countries are at the geographical centre of the common market whilst the less successful countries are on the fringe. Transport and communication costs tend to be lower for companies sited at the centre and higher for those at the periphery. Hence central countries tend to have a competitive advantage over fringe countries.

Neo-classical economic theory suggests that free market forces would equalise the differences between regions. An unsuccessful region will have cheap labour and cheap land. Firms will be attracted into the region to take advantage of these. In practice, this effect seems to be very weak. Cheap labour economies can easily become branch economies. Firms set up branches in these regions, employing cheap labour to perform low-productivity tasks. Tasks which have high value added are completed at headquarters in higher-cost areas. The result is growing economic divergence, with poorer regions losing the most skilled of their labour force to the richer regions and being left with less dynamic and less skilled workers to do less well paid jobs.

Monetary unions

A **monetary union** (or **currency union**) occurs when at least two countries share the same currency. The most important monetary union today is the Economic and Monetary Union (EMU) of the European Union. However, there have been other monetary unions in the past. For example, the Austro-Hungarian Empire at the start of the 20th century shared a single currency. In 2015, there were four monetary unions apart from EMU.

- The Economic and Monetary Community of Central Africa, made up of a number of ex-French colonies, uses the CFA franc.
- The West African Economic and Monetary Union is another group of ex-French colonies which uses a different CFA franc.
- The Overseas Issuing Institute issues the CFP franc to three overseas collectivities of France in the Pacific: French Polynesia, New Caledonia and Wallis and Futuna.
- The Eastern Caribbean Currency Union is a group of eastern Caribbean countries, including Dominica, Grenada and Saint Lucia, which uses the East Caribbean dollar.

There is also a number of other examples where countries use the currency of another country rather than issuing their own currency. For example, the South African rand is legal tender not just in South Africa but also in Swaziland, Lesotho and Namibia. The US dollar is used in Ecuador, El Salvador, Panama, the British Virgin Islands and the Turks and Caicos Islands.

Monetary union within the European Union has a long history

going back to the late 1960s. The first agreed plan for monetary union was put forward in the Werner Report in 1970. However, difficult economic conditions in the 1970s and 1980s meant that it wasn't until 1989, with the publication of the Delors Report, that the route to today's monetary union was set out. The process was completed in 2002 when on 1 January, euro notes and coins replaced national currencies in 13 EU countries. The UK, Denmark and Sweden decided not to join and retained their national currencies. The accession countries that joined the EU after 2004 all agreed to adopt the euro as their currency at some point in the future.

The European Central Bank (ECB)

Members of EMU have given control of monetary and exchange rate policy to the European Central Bank (ECB), which was set up in 1998 and is located in Frankfurt. The ECB has a number of functions.

- It is responsible for distributing notes and coins throughout the eurozone, the countries which have adopted the euro as their currency.
- As a central bank, it sets interest rates in the same way that the Bank of England sets interest rates in the UK. Like the Bank of England, decisions about interest rates are made to achieve an inflation target, which is currently to keep inflation below but close to two per cent. The ECB is independent of national governments in the same way that the Bank of England has independence on how to conduct policy from the UK government.
- It is responsible for maintaining a stable financial system. If banks within the eurozone get into difficulties, it is the ECB which is responsible for dealing with any problems.
- It manages the foreign currency reserves of the Economic and Monetary Union. It can use these to intervene in the foreign exchange markets to influence the value of the euro against other currencies, although in practice it allows the euro to float freely against other currencies.

Fiscal policy rules

When creating a monetary union, the EU recognised that there would be major problems if a member country were to behave in a fiscally irresponsible way. For example, if the governments of large countries like France or Germany borrowed large amounts of extra money to finance fiscal deficits, this could increase interest rates and threaten increased inflation in the eurozone. The EU also recognised that there could be problems if the government of a country borrowed so much that it could not repay its debts as they became due. For this reason, they devised the Growth and Stability Pact that was replaced in 2010 by the Fiscal Compact (the Treaty on Stability, Co-ordination and Governance). There are two main fiscal rules. Governments must:

- not exceed a fiscal deficit of more than three per cent of GDP;
- have a National Debt of no more than 60 per cent of GDP.

These fiscal rules have been tested to the limits since the financial crisis of 2007-08. This is because the governments of a number of countries including Greece, Spain and Portugal found themselves with fiscal deficits of over 10 per cent of GDP and rapidly increasing National Debts. The National Debt of the

Greece by 2014 was 175 per cent of GDP. The result was that financial markets were unwilling to lend to these countries for a period. In the case of Greece, this has proved catastrophic as will be explained below.

The advantages of monetary union for eurozone countries

Fixed prices When countries have their own currencies, there can be exchange rate fluctuations. In a floating exchange rate system, for example, exporters and importers don't know what the exchange rate will be in three months' time. A single currency creates fixed prices and eliminates the risks that would have arisen from exchange rate fluctuations between member countries.

Reduced exchange rate costs A single currency means that there are no exchange rate costs in making transactions. It is as costless for a French firm based in Calais to buy from a firm in Germany as from a firm in Paris. In contrast, a French firm buying from a British firm will still have the cost of changing currency. This is not just the commission and charges imposed by banks. It is also the costs arising from the risk factor of currencies changing in value from day to day in a floating exchange rate system.

Greater price transparency With many national markets and many different currencies, customers, whether firms or households, are likely to have imperfect information about prices across the whole area. A single currency makes it easy for customers to compare prices between different countries and buy from the cheapest source. Multinational producers are far less able to price discriminate between countries by charging higher prices in some than in others to earn monopoly profits. The result has been lower prices across the eurozone to the benefit of consumers.

More trade and greater economies of scale Reduced exchange rate costs and greater price transparency have led to more trade between member countries. There has been a wave of cross-border mergers and takeovers to create larger firms supplying across the eurozone rather than just a single national economy. This has led to greater economies of scale, further reducing prices to customers.

Inward investment Being inside the eurozone has given countries a competitive advantage compared to those outside the eurozone, such as the UK. The UK itself over the past 30 years has enjoyed considerable inward investment, for instance from Japanese and US companies. One advantage to the companies is that they avoid tariffs and quotas placed on goods coming from outside the EU. They are also nearer the European market, which gives them advantages when developing new products and in marketing. However, being located in a country outside the eurozone creates exchange rate risks and uncertainties. Companies such as Toyota have said quite explicitly that this is a negative factor in any decision about whether to expand in the UK. Conversely, one of the reasons why Eastern European countries want to join the euro is because they recognise that this will create an added incentive for multinational firms to locate in their country.

Price stability Some countries like Germany have had a long history of price stability since the Second World War. For Germany, with memories of 1923 and hyperinflation, price stability was a key macroeconomic goal. Other countries, such as Greece, Italy and Portugal, were more prone to periods of high inflation. A single currency where the central bank was not controlled by governments out to maximise short-term political gain was seen as positive. The euro has delivered price stability. This price stability is one of the key reasons why citizens in countries like Greece, Spain and Portugal did not want to leave the euro even when after 2007-08 their economies came under severe deflationary stress. They fear that if they abandoned the euro, any new currency they created would quickly fall in value, eroding their savings through high inflation.

The longer term agenda A monetary union is one step further along the road to complete economic and political union for EU states. For some, this is seen as positive. For eurosceptics, it is a reason for either not joining the euro or leaving the eurozone.

The disadvantages of monetary union for eurozone countries

Transition costs The creation of a single currency inevitably created transition costs. For instance, vending machines had to be changed to take the new coins. Some bank employees lost their jobs because foreign exchange departments were cut in size. Customers had to become used to using the new money.

Loss of policy independence In the United Kingdom, regions such as Wales or Northern Ireland do not have control over monetary policy or much of fiscal policy. These are managed from London for the whole of the UK. Similarly, a single currency, the euro, means that countries such as Portugal, Italy and Greece have no control over monetary policy or exchange rate policy. These are determined by the European Central Bank. Just as the Bank of England may set an interest rate which benefits southern England but disadvantages Northern Ireland, so the European Central Bank can set an interest rate which benefits Germany but disadvantages Portugal. This is an inevitable feature of any union. Countries also only have limited control over fiscal policy because of the Fiscal Compact.

Inability to change the value of a currency Sometimes, the best policy response for a country to its economic problems is to devalue its currency, i.e. let it fall against other currencies. In a currency union, by definition, a country cannot devalue its currency against those of other members of the union. This problem particularly applied to Greece after the financial crisis of 2007-08. It emerged with an unsustainable fiscal deficit and National Debt. If Greece had had its own currency, it would have dealt with this crisis partly through fiscal austerity and partly through devaluing its currency. Greek citizens would have suffered a loss of GDP, unemployment and inflation. However, because it could not devalue its currency, it was forced to take more extreme fiscal austerity measures. The positive side was that there was no inflation. But there was a larger fall in GDP and a larger rise in unemployment than with a devaluation.

Structural problems In a currency union, there will be regions which are better off than others. In the UK, for example,

GDP per head is higher in the South East of England than in Northern Ireland. Within the UK, there are transfers of resources from rich to poor regions through the tax and government spending system. On average, households in the South East of England pay more in tax than those in Northern Ireland, whilst government spending per head is higher in Northern Ireland than in the South East. In the EU, these transfers are much lower. If a country like Portugal had its own currency, it might push down its foreign exchange rate to stimulate exports and raise GDP. With a single currency, it does not have this policy option.

Break up of the monetary union A single currency can just as well be dissolved as created. In the past, monetary unions have tended to fail because of the political break up of a country or area. Examples include the Austro-Hungarian empire, which collapsed in 1918, the Soviet Union which collapsed in 1990 and Czechoslovakia which split into two countries in 1993. It is difficult to foresee what the main costs would be if the European Monetary Union collapsed. In 2015, when Greece was on the verge of being forced out of the eurozone by economic circumstances, there was widespread disagreement about whether this would be good or bad for Greece and the rest of the eurozone. However, there is agreement that the transition costs in any break-up would be significant.

Conditions necessary for the success of a monetary union

Some economists argue that the chances of success for a monetary union can be forecast from a given number of conditions. This is the theory of **optimum currency area**, a geographical area like the eurozone where efficiency would be maximised by sharing a common currency rather than having separate currencies. A good way of judging the success of the euro is to compare it with the United States and the US dollar. The US dollar is a common currency across the member states of the United States.

- There should be free movement of labour. There are far more barriers to the free movement of labour in the EU than in the USA. One, for example, is the language barrier which can prevent a worker getting a job in another EU country.
- There should be capital mobility associated with wage and price flexibility. So financial capital should be free to flow between member countries. Prices and wages should be free to adjust to changing patterns of demand and supply within regions. The US arguably has deeper capital mobility than the EU. Individual countries within the EU also have different minimum wage rates and can impose price restrictions. However, the same is true in the USA. Arguably, the EU is not far behind the USA on these criteria.
- There should be automatic fiscal transfers when individual countries are performing poorly. Fiscal transfers from the US federal government to individual USA states and their citizens are far higher than in the EU, where they are extremely limited. The refusal by rich countries like Germany to help crisis-ridden countries like Greece after 2007-08 shows that there is a lack of political will to deepen fiscal transfers in the EU. The EU scores poorly on this.

Question 3

Mark Carney, Governor of the Bank of England, has said that for the euro to be successful, member states need to be prepared to adopt some common tax and spending policies and allow more cross-border transfers of revenues. 'The currency union has been relatively timid in putting in place ... the institutions necessary to deliver sustainable prosperity for its citizens', he said. There were a number of options, he argued, that European policy makers could choose from for sharing fiscal risks. These included a full transfer union where public spending in individual countries is paid for in part by a eurozone treasury. This would be like government spending in Yorkshire being paid for out of taxes collected by central government in London. Or there could be a pooled employment insurance mechanism. Unemployment benefits in an individual country like Greece or Portugal would then by paid out of a pot of taxes collected by a eurozone treasury. Mark Carney added that such a scheme would have the advantage of combining the current push towards greater labour market reforms with the 'longer-term imperative to build elements of an efficient transfer union'.

Source: adapted from © the *Financial Times* 29.1.2015, 30.1.2015 All Rights Reserved.

Explain why a common fiscal policy might help create a successful monetary union.

- Countries should share the same trade cycle. For example, Germany should not be in boom when Spain is in recession and Bulgaria is recovering from a recession. Sharing the same trade cycle is important because otherwise monetary and fiscal policy will work for some countries but make problems worse for others. For example, the European Central Bank

Key Terms

Common external tariff - a common tariff set by a group of countries imposed on imported goods from non-member countries.

Common market - a group of countries between which there is free trade in products and factors of production, and which imposes a common external tariff on imported goods from outside the market.

Free trade area - a group of countries between which there is free trade in goods and services but which allows member countries to set their own level of tariffs against non-member countries.

Harmonisation - establishing common standards, rules and levels on everything from safety standards to tariffs, taxes and currencies.

Monetary union or currency union - a group of countries that share a common currency like the euro.

Optimum currency area - a group of countries where efficiency would be maximised by sharing a common currency.

Trade creation - the switch from purchasing products from a high-cost producer to a lower-cost producer.

Trade diversion - the switch from purchasing products from a low-cost producer to a higher cost producer.

raising interest rates to curb inflation in a booming Germany economy is not going to help Spain if it is in recession. Both the EU and the USA traditionally have regional areas which are out of phase with the main trade cycle, but, on the whole, in both, regions are dragged towards what is happening in the main part of the economy over time.

The main problem for the EU as an optimal currency area is arguably the lack of automatic fiscal transfers. These would have considerably eased the pain experienced by countries such as Greece, Spain and Portugal following the financial crisis of 2007-08. It would have reduced the risk of these countries leaving the euro.

Thinking like an economist

Advantages and disadvantages of Britain's membership of the EU

For the past 60 years, the UK has debated whether or not it should be part of the European Union. When the EU was first set up in the 1950s, the UK chose to stay out. It believed that its ties with its colonies and former colonies, as well as those with the USA, were more important than ties with a group of six European countries who were still recovering from the effects of the Second World War. By the early 1960s, many in Britain believed that this had been the wrong decision to make. However, the EU refused Britain entry in the 1960s. It was not until 1973 that Britain became a member. Since then, Britain has tended to resist further European integration. In 1992, for example, the UK secured an opt-out of some of the labour market provisions of the Maastricht Treaty. In 2001, it chose not to adopt the euro when most EU countries created a single currency. Successive governments, therefore, have tended to be 'eurosceptic'. What are the issues that make the UK better off or worse off as an EU member?

Trade in goods and services Being a member of the EU means that UK firms have access to a common market of over 300 million people. Economies of scale in production mean that the UK firms can enjoy lower costs whilst UK consumers can buy at lower prices. This assumes that there is more trade creation than trade diversion. Around the world, countries are signing regional trade agreements that show that larger integrated markets are considered to increase the welfare of individual countries. The trend is towards more free trade rather than protectionism. If the UK were to leave the EU, eurosceptics assume that the UK would be able to negotiate the same access to EU markets as it presently enjoys. If the EU, instead, chose to erect trade barriers against UK goods and services, this potentially could have a devastating effect on UK firms. Over 50 per cent of all UK exports of goods currently go to the EU.

Inward investment Flows of FDI to the EU disproportionately benefit the UK. Firms in countries like the US prefer to establish themselves in the UK or Ireland simply because of the language barrier. Equally, FDI (Foreign Direct Investment) from firms in the rest of the EU has been greater than FDI by UK firms into the rest of Europe. This has helped UK private sector investment.

Standards One aspect of the single market project is standardisation. This means having the same rules governing products and markets across the European Union. Standardisation is positive when it allows UK firms to export to the rest of the EU. It is also positive when it protects workers from exploitation by firms. However, eurosceptics tend to see standardisation as something that has a negative effect on the

UK. Rules and regulations become 'red tape'. This means they serve little purpose whilst imposing costs on firms. For example, under the EU 48 hours Working Time Directive, workers are not allowed to work more than 48 hours a week. Some see this as positive, preventing employers from exploiting their workers and getting them to work unreasonable hours. Eurosceptics see this as limiting the freedom of firms to use their workforce flexibly and adding to their costs.

Free movement of labour The single market is not just about creating one market for goods and services. It is also about creating a single market for factors of production including labour. This means that a worker from Poland can move to the UK to work in just the same way that a worker from Scotland can move to London. Until the early 2000s, the free movement of labour was not particularly an issue for the UK because on average as many workers from the UK moved to jobs in the rest of the EU as other EU nationals came to Britain. However, since then it has become central to the argument about whether or not the UK should remain part of the EU. This is because there has been a large increase in the number of workers coming from eastern Europe to work in the UK, attracted by the availability of jobs and higher pay than they could earn in their home country. This free market in labour is no different from an unemployed Welsh worker moving to London to find work or a Cumbrian worker moving to Edinburgh. This has raised issues about employment and unemployment, housing, schools and access to the welfare benefit system and the National Health Service. EU migration into the UK is almost all of working age individuals with their families coming to seek employment. There is little evidence to suggest that they are displacing resident UK workers from their jobs. By living in the UK and spending their income, they effectively create their own jobs. The number of jobs rises with no effect on unemployment. However, given that the UK is not building enough houses, there is added pressure on housing. Equally, with spending on education set to fall in real terms for the foreseeable future, there will also be pressure on schools. Employers tend to be in favour of the free movement of labour. It allows them to recruit from across the EU, giving them access to a much wider supply of labour.

Budget contributions The UK is a net contributor to the EU budget. It pays more in contributions than it receives in benefits from EU central funds. Traditionally, this was because the UK had a smaller agricultural sector than many other countries in the EU. In more recent times, the proportion of the EU budget going to agriculture has decreased significantly and there is more spending on structural funds aimed at raising incomes in poorer EU countries. The UK contribution is less than one per cent of UK GDP and so it is not a significant burden to the UK. Eurosceptics, however, argue that any net budget contribution is bad for the UK.

The political agenda Being a member of the EU limits the ability of the UK to make its own political decisions. The 'European project' is for ever-deeper economic and political ties within the EU. For eurosceptics, the transfer of power from Westminster to Brussels is unacceptable. However, in a world that is becoming more integrated, the ability of the UK to make its own decisions is also become more limited. Membership of organisations such as the World Trade Organization (WTO) and the United Nations limits the UK in its decision making for example. On a national scale, the 2014 Scottish referendum reflected these concerns. Scottish nationalists didn't want decisions about Scotland being made in London by a British parliament.

The debate about whether the UK should leave the EU today has the added dimension of risk. Eurosceptics, when arguing for leaving the EU, make a large number of assumptions about how the rest of the EU, non-EU countries and foreign firms will react if the UK were to leave. In the Scottish referendum, Scottish nationalists made a number of assumptions too. For example, they assumed that they could keep the pound, that supermarket chains would keep prices the same in Scottish and English supermarkets, that they would automatically become members of the European Union and that no firms would leave Scotland because it was out of the union. During the referendum, all these assumptions were challenged. In leaving the EU, there is a risk that the EU will put up trade barriers against UK exports. UK workers will not have freedom of movement in Europe. Multinational companies wanting to locate in the EU are unlikely to choose the UK as a place to set up a manufacturing unit. UK employers will find it much more difficult to recruit workers. Tax revenues per person in the UK may go down if there is an exodus of working-age EU nationals. What if a significant proportion of the two million UK nationals currently living in other EU countries were forced to return to the UK?

Overall, it is possible to argue both for staying in the EU and leaving it. This is because there are so many variables to consider and so many assumptions that need to be made when calculating costs and benefits. Because of the very large number of unknowns, the debate is likely to continue for decades.

Data Response Question

Should Britain leave the EU?

A new report by the Centre for European Reform sets out some of the costs if Britain were to leave the EU. It argues that EU membership has been a 'boon' for the UK economy, increasing its goods trade with other EU members by 55 per cent. It has generated increased inward investment. The City of London has also benefited. The UK has the largest proportion of foreign bank assets as a proportion of total banking assets in the EU.

Critics of the EU complain about rules and 'red tape'. The report says that Britain has the second most lightly regulated product market in the developed world. Levels of employment protection are only marginally more restrictive than in the US or Canada, and well below those in France or Spain. Some of the most controversial EU rules, such as the Working Time Directive, have had only a 'marginal effect' on the labour market. 'A bonfire of European rules would not transform Britain's economic prospects' according to the report. The idea that the UK would be freer outside the EU is based on a series of misconceptions.

If Britain were to leave the EU, it would have to negotiate a new treaty arrangement with the EU. Options include a Swiss-style deal based on bilateral agreements with the EU; a customs union of the kind Turkey has with the EU; or, like Norway, membership of the European Economic Area. All of these options would require the UK to abide by EU rules and regulations without giving it any negotiating power when new rules are set. It could find itself still paying into the EU budget. A Norwegian-style deal would only lower net contributions by 9 per cent whilst a Swiss arrangements would still leave the UK paying 45 per cent of its current contributions.

Source: adapted from © the *Financial Times* 9.6.2014, All Rights Reserved.

Figure 1

UK's main trading partners, % of total trade

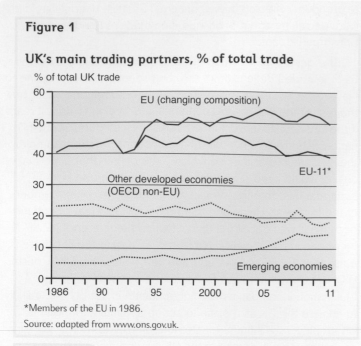

% of total UK trade

*Members of the EU in 1986.

Source: adapted from www.ons.gov.uk.

Figure 2

Source of foreign direct investment (FDI) in the UK ($bn)

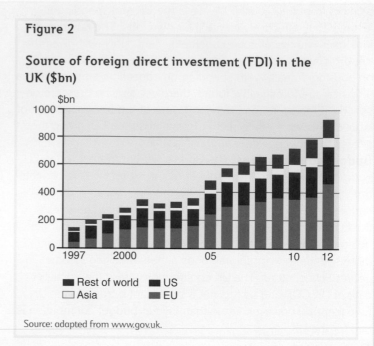

Source: adapted from www.gov.uk.

Figure 3

Foreign branch assets as a proportion of total banking assets (%), 2012

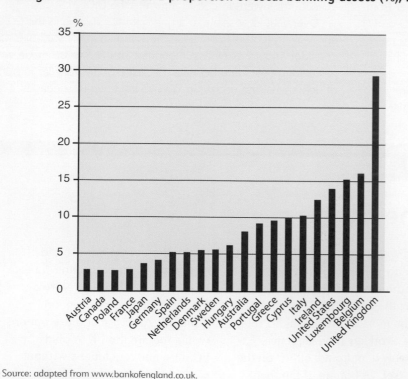

Source: adapted from www.bankofengland.co.uk.

Q

1. Using Figure 2, explain how foreign direct investment into the UK has changed over the period shown.

2. Explain one advantage and one disadvantage of EU 'red tape' regulations to the UK economy.

3. Discuss whether the UK should leave the EU.

Evaluation

There are plenty of issues raised in the data where the advantages and disadvantages of EU membership can be assessed. In your conclusion, you could point out that the data contains very little which would support the UK leaving the EU. To what extent is this bias or does it reflect reality?

A German study from the Bertelsmann Foundation, a leading German think tank, has said that the UK could lose 3 per cent of GDP by 2030 if it left the EU. The negative impact on the UK would be higher than the cost to the rest of the EU. If the UK decided to go for an 'isolationist' policy, the UK would lose favourable access to EU markets, becoming more like the US. It would also forfeit access rights for exports negotiated by the EU to 38 non-EU countries such as Mexico and Turkey. The report says the main saving to Britain - its net annual contribution to the EU budget of 0.5 per cent of GDP - would pale in comparison to a withdrawal. It also considers a more extreme scenario under which lost trade with the EU undermines British productivity because UK companies, facing less foreign competition, would cut investment and innovation. UK GDP could then shrink by up to 14 per cent by 2030.

Source: adapted from © the *Financial Times* 28.4.2015, All Rights Reserved.

66 The World Trade Organization

Key points

1. The World Trade Organization (WTO) was set up to promote the liberalisation of trade.
2. It does this mainly through attempting to get its member countries to reduce protectionist barriers and by providing a mechanism for the settlement of trade disputes.
3. It has proved difficult for the WTO to get member countries to conclude the Doha Round of talks, whilst at the same time the number of regional trade agreements has grown.
4. The WTO has become the focus for critics of free trade.

Starter activity

Use the Internet to find out three ways in which the World Trade Organization helps to reduce protectionist barriers.

World trade and GATT

Economic theory suggests that free trade is likely to benefit countries. By allowing each country to specialise, production will take place in locations which enjoy a comparative advantage. World trade expanded in the 19th century but the first half of the 20th century saw a fall in trade. This was partly caused by the economic disruption of two world wars. The Great Depression of the 1930s also led countries to adopt deeply protectionist policies. Governments mistakenly believed that by keeping foreign goods out, they could save domestic jobs. In practice, all countries adopted the same mix of measures. World trade collapsed, jobs were lost in export industries and consumers were left having to pay higher prices to inefficient domestic producers when before they could buy goods from overseas at cheaper prices.

After the Second World War, there was a general recognition that these protectionist policies had been self-defeating. The Bretton Woods system of exchange rates banned competitive devaluations, whilst 23 countries in 1947 signed the General Agreement on Tariffs and Trade (GATT). Under GATT rules, member countries were not allowed to increase the degree of protection given to their domestic producers. Also, under the most-favoured nation clause of the agreement, a country which offered a cut in tariffs to one country had to offer the same terms to all member countries.

GATT rules prevented protection increasing, but did nothing to reduce protectionism. For this reason, GATT, and its successor organisation, the World Trade Organization (WTO) have, over the years, organised a series of negotiations (called 'rounds') aimed at reducing tariffs and quotas.

By the end of the Tokyo Round of negotiations in 1979, the average tariff on industrial goods had fallen to 4.7 per cent. Between 1986 and 1994 an eighth round of negotiations, the Uruguay Round, was successfully completed. In this round, unlike previous rounds, agreements were made not just on trade of manufactures, but also agriculture and services.

- In agriculture, non-tariffs barriers, such as quotas, were dismantled and replaced by tariffs. This was intended to make the level of protectionism more transparent.
- In manufacturing, the single most important agreement was dismantling protectionist barriers in textiles and garments from 2005. This has led to a substantial increase in exports, particularly from China, since then.
- In services, copyright and royalty fee agreements were tightened up, and a start made in opening up highly protected services industries such as finance and telecommunications.

The various trade rounds have been a powerful influence in expanding trade in the post-war period.

World Trade Organization

The World Trade Organization (WTO) was set up in 1995 by the signatories to the Uruguay Round to replace GATT. The WTO has a broader range of functions than GATT. Its two main functions are:

- to encourage countries to lower protectionist barriers and thus increase trade between countries. So the WTO exists to bring about **trade liberalisation**. It does this mainly through the various rounds of talks, the Doha Round being the latest, which have occurred since the Second World War.
- to ensure that countries act according to the various trade agreements they have signed. Any country or group of countries can file a complaint with the WTO against the competitive practices of another country. The WTO attempts to resolve most complaints through negotiations between the two parties. Ultimately, though, the complaint can go to a panel of experts (effectively an international court), and this panel will deliver a judgment. Either side can then appeal against the judgment. However, ultimately they must accept the WTO ruling. If they reject the ruling, the country which

wins the ruling has the legal right to impose trade sanctions against the exports of the losing country to impose the same damage to trade that it is suffering. When this has occurred, the losing country has quickly gone back to the negotiating table.

The Doha Round
The World Trade Organization launched the 9th round of world trade talks in 2001. They are called the Doha Round because the first meeting took place in Doha, the capital city of Qatar. Talks have covered a wide variety of issues including the following:
- cutting protectionist measures on trade in agricultural goods;
- further reductions in tariffs on manufacturing goods;
- access to markets in services, such as allowing foreign companies to bid for government contracts;
- tightening intellectual property rights given problems of widespread piracy, such as the illegal copying and sale of films via DVD;
- giving the WTO more powers to settle trade disputes.

The Doha Round has become stalled because any new treaty requires the consent of all member countries. At any point in time, there has always been a country or group of countries that have refused to accept the outcome of negotiations on a particular issue like farming subsidies. Recently, the WTO has changed its negotiating strategy and aimed to get agreement on just a small part of its wider agenda. In 2014, it negotiated an agreement to ease customs procedures and to facilitate the move, release and clearance of goods, but at the last minute this was blocked by India and a small group of other countries including Cuba and Venezuela. The agreement only went forward when India was given the right to continue to subsidise wheat and rice production.

The problem facing the WTO is that any single country can veto any trade deal. What's more, such a veto can be politically motivated. A country may veto a trade deal because it wants to retaliate against the USA, for example, on some other completely unrelated issue.

A way forward is for future trade agreements to be signed on a plurilateral basis. For example, an agreement could be signed by 157 WTO members, with three members not signing the agreement. This would break a fundamental principle of the WTO that all member countries must agree to changes. However, it would allow the vast majority of countries to move forward with a lowering of trade barriers which would bring large economic gains for the world economy. The danger for the WTO is that it will become irrelevant in negotiations about lowering barriers to trade.

Multilateral vs regional trade agreements
If the WTO can't produce multilateral agreements between all member countries, then countries will resort to signing ever more regional trade agreements (RTAs). This has been happening for the past 20 years. RTAs don't need approval from the WTO.

However, RTAs don't produce anywhere near the economic gains that could be achieved by a world trade agreement between all countries. The economic gains from specialisation predicted by the theory of comparative advantage, combined with the losses because of trade diversion, mean that any RTA will almost certainly produce an inferior outcome to a multilateral agreement. An RTA is likely to be better than no agreement. But economists have criticised some RTAs for actually leading to a loss of economic welfare because the gains from trade creation have been outweighed by the losses from trade diversion.

Criticisms of the World Trade Organization
The WTO has come in for fierce criticism from the anti-globalisation, environmental and development lobbies. They argue that the WTO:
- allows rich countries to exploit developing countries' workers, paying them low wages and making them work in conditions which would be completely unacceptable in developed countries;
- is causing an environmental catastrophe in developing countries as richer countries plunder the national resources of the planet and give very little in return to poorer countries;
- forces poor countries to lower their barriers to trade whilst rich countries keep their barriers in place;
- is destroying native cultures and ways of life, and is replacing it with a shallow, materialistic American life-style;
- is leading to the impoverishment of developing countries whose economies are exploited by the rich countries of the world because free trade allows rich countries to force down prices of goods made in developing countries, whilst allowing their own technology-rich products to go up in price;
- gives ownership of the rules of the world trading system to a few rich countries and their multinational companies and strips power from poor countries and their citizens.

However, much of this criticism of the WTO is arguably unjustified because the WTO does not have the power to destroy cultures or force a Vietnamese worker to work for £1 a week. The WTO is there to encourage countries to negotiate rules of trade, which include mechanisms for ensuring that those rules are enforceable. It does have a pro-free trade bias but it cannot force poor countries to enter internationally binding agreements. Ultimately, the WTO is an organisation which helps develop freer trade between nations. The criticisms of the WTO are, in fact, criticisms first of free trade itself, the power of the market mechanism which does give richer countries more influence than poorer countries because they have more spending 'votes', and second the globalisation of culture.

Key Term
Trade liberalisation - the move towards greater free trade through the removal of protectionist barriers to trade.

Thinking like an economist

The Bali Agreement

The World Trade Organization (WTO) was set up in 1995 with high hopes for a 9th round of reduction in trade barriers, following on from the highly successful 8th Round, the Uruguay Round. However, negotiations produced nothing till 2013. The reason for the breakthrough was a change in negotiating tactics by the newly appointed head of the WTO, Roberto Azevêdo, who took up post in September 2013. He decided to go for a small change to international trading rules rather than a very large comprehensive settlement like the Uruguay Round.

At a meeting in Bali, countries agreed a 'Trade Facilitation Agreement'. This covered the easing of customs procedures to facilitate the move, release and clearance of goods This would reduce red tape for the transport of goods at national borders. Reducing journey times for exports and imports reduces costs and therefore encourage more trade.

However, the weakness of the WTO system was shown when India elected a new government in May 2014. The new government refused to sign the Bali agreement unless it won a concession from the WTO about its programme of food subsidies. Currently, India provides subsidies to rice and wheat farmers so that the price of rice and wheat is affordable to Indian consumers on low incomes. These subsidies are in breach of the Uruguay Round agreement but, at the time of signing, India won a reprieve to be allowed to continue the subsidies to 2017. In international trade terms, these subsidies give a competitive advantage to Indian farmers over farmers in, say, the US or Europe. The subsidies have also resulted in overproduction in India. The Indian government has periodically sold off excess stocks onto world markets depressing wheat and rice prices again hitting other world farmers. Rwanda, for example, has complained that cheap, subsidised rice imports from India are making it difficult for Rwandan farmers to compete. Nigerian farmers also have been affected. Nigeria responded by raising tariffs on imports of Indian rice. But this has had little effect because Indian rice is now imported to Benin, a neighbouring country, and smuggled across the border into Nigeria avoiding the high tariffs.

The final outcome after months of negotiations was that India gained the right to continue its subsidy programme indefinitely in return for agreeing to sign the Trade Facilitation Agreement. However, in the process, WTO member countries were forcibly reminded that getting agreement from all member countries could, in the future, be an impossible task. There could always be one country seeking to protect its farmers or a particular industry or group of workers that could veto an agreement. With 160 members in 2014, getting unanimous consent might be impossible. For this reason, the Doha Round may never be concluded. This would lead to lower growth in the world economy as protectionist barriers remained in place.

Source: with information from © the *Financial Times* 24.9.2014, 3.12.2014, All Rights Reserved.

Data Response Question

Trade disputes at the WTO

The US has requested formal talks at the World Trade Organization with China over its use of 'demonstration bases' or special government-supported industrial clusters. The request is the first stop in bringing a case at the WTO. The US alleges that China provides discount services and cash bonuses tied to export performance to businesses located in 179 'demonstration bases' in China. These amount to illegal export subsidies for a wide range of goods from agricultural to medical goods.

The US and Brazil have agreed to resolve a decade-long feud over cotton subsidies, making an end to one of the highest-profile disputes in the history of the World Trade Organization. Under the agreement, the US will pay a lump sum of $300 million to Brazilian cotton farmers and change its support for cotton produced by US farmers.

The case was first filed at the WTO dispute resolution arm in 2002 and was decided in 2004. A panel ruled that US direct payments, crop insurance and export credit programmes for cotton farmers was illegal under the WTO agreement.

The World Trade Organization has ruled against the US in a dispute over tariffs it imposed on steel and other imports from China and India. The US has tried for years to build a case against Chinese and Indian state-owned companies, saying they benefited from both overt and hidden subsidies. These unfairly lowered their costs of production. It argued those amounted to government subsidies to China's and India's exports, which are banned by the WTO.

A three-judge WTO panel tried the cases. They said that state-owned companies were not necessarily 'public bodies'. If public bodies gave subsidies to exports, then that would be unlawful because public bodies represent the state or government. But in this case, state-owned Chinese and Indian exporters should not be equated with the Chinese and Indian governments. Therefore, the Chinese and Indian governments had not given subsidies to these firms and so it was not illegal under WTO rules.

Trade disputes between countries are relatively common. If the dispute is serious enough, governments can resort to retaliation. For example, in response to Indian subsidies to rice farmers, Nigeria has increased tariffs on imported Indian rice. Argentina, in response to being reported to the World Trade Organization in 2012 following its nationalisation of the Spanish energy company Repsol, imposed a range of trade restrictions including limiting the imports of lemons from the USA. The United States imposed higher tariffs on imports of steel from China after accusing the Chinese government of illegally subsidising exports of steel.

1. Explain, using examples from the data, what is meant by a 'subsidy'.

2. Analyse, using a diagram, how Indian rice subsidies might harm Rwandan and Nigerian farmers.

3. Discuss the advantages and disadvantages to countries like the USA or China of agreeing to settle trade disputes through the WTO rather than being free to impose trade restrictions as a retaliatory measure.

Evaluation

Weighing up the relative importance of different advantages and disadvantages will lead to evaluation. What information do you not have which might influence your final conclusion?

67 Restrictions on free trade

Key points

1. There is a wide variety of ways in which governments can restrict foreign trade, such as tariffs, quotas, domestic subsidies or giving their firms a competitive edge such as export subsidies.
2. Protectionist measures can be used in attempts to nurture infant industries, protect jobs, retaliate against other countries adopting protectionist measures and alter the terms of trade.
3. Protectionist policies can impact on consumers, firms, workers, governments, living standards and equality.

Starter activity

Over the past 60 years, the UK's textile industry has shrunk from being one of its most important industries by output and a major source of jobs to a fraction of its former size. The shrinkage has occurred mainly because of cheap foreign imports. Assume the UK could have banned all imports of foreign textiles. Make a list of the advantages and disadvantages of such a measure, identifying who might gain and who might lose out.

Restrictions on free trade

Free trade allows comparative advantage to maximise output between trading nations. However, every country uses protectionist policies to some degree. **Protectionism** is the use of economic policies deliberately to regulate trade between countries, mainly to reduce imports. On the whole, protectionist policies are designed to reduce imports, but some protectionist policies are designed to reduce exports or increase exports. There are many methods that can be used, including tariffs, **quotas**, subsidies, exchange rate manipulation and administrative barriers.

Tariffs

A **tariff** is a tax on imported goods. It is sometimes called an **import duty** or a **customs duty**. Tariffs can be used by governments to raise revenue to finance expenditure. However, they are most often used in a deliberate attempt to restrict imports. A tariff, by imposing a tax on a good, is likely to raise its final price to the consumer (although occasionally a foreign supplier will absorb all the tariff to prevent this from happening). A rise in the price of the good will lead to a fall in demand and the volume of imports will fall. A tariff should also help domestic producers. Some consumers will switch consumption from imported goods to domestically produced substitutes following the imposition of a tariff. For instance, if the UK imposed a tariff on sugar cane imports, British-produced sugar beet would become more competitive and demand for it would rise.

This is shown in Figure 1. D is the domestic demand for a good. $S_{Domestic}$ is the domestic supply curve of the product. With no foreign trade, equilibrium output would occur where domestic demand and supply were equal at OL. However, with foreign trade, world producers are assumed to be prepared to supply any amount of the product at a price of OP. Consumers will now buy imported goods because the world price OP is below the

domestic price of OR. Domestic supply will fall back along the supply curve to OJ. Demand for the good will rise to ON. Imports must be JN if demand is ON and domestic supply is OJ. Now assume that the government of the country imposes a tariff of PQ per unit. The price to domestic consumers will rise to OQ. Domestic producers will not pay the tariff. Therefore they find it profitable to expand production to OK. Higher prices cause demand to fall to OM. Hence imports will only be KM. Expenditure on imports will fall from JTWN (price JT times quantity bought JN) to KYZM. Of that area KYZM, KUVM will be the revenue gained by foreign firms. The rest, UYZV, is the tax collected on the imports and will therefore go to the government.

There is a deadweight welfare loss to the country associated with the imposition of a tariff. In Figure 1, imposing a tariff leads to a loss of consumer surplus of PQZW. This is because consumers buy less at a higher price. Domestic producers gain producer surplus of PQYT. They produce more at a higher price and so gain producer surplus. The loss of consumer surplus is greater than the gain of producer surplus by the area TYZW. Of this, the government receives UYZV in revenues from the tariff. So the deadweight loss to the country in welfare from the tariffs is the sum of the two triangles TYU and VZW.

Figure 1

Tariffs

If the world price of a good is OP, a tariff of PQ will shift the supply curve upwards from S_{World} to $S_{With\ tariff}$. Domestic consumption will fall by MN whilst domestic production will rise by JK. Imports will fall from JN to KM.

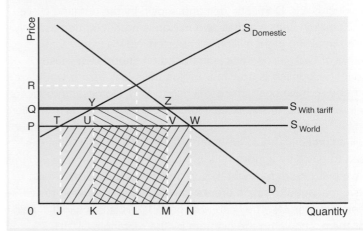

Question 1

Figure 2

Domestic demand and supply

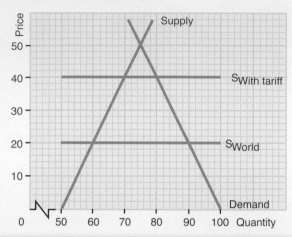

Figure 2 shows the domestic demand and supply curves for a good.

(a) What is the equilibrium price and quantity demanded and supplied domestically?

(b) The country starts to trade internationally. The international price for the product shown is 20. The country can import any amount at this price. What is:

(i) the new level of demand; (ii) the new level of domestic supply; (iii) the quantity imported?

(c) The government, alarmed at the loss of jobs in the industry, imposes a tariff of 20 per unit. By how much will: (i) domestic demand fall; (ii) domestic supply rise; (iii) imports fall?

(d) What would happen if the government imposed a tariff of 40 per unit?

Quotas

A quota is a physical limit on the quantity of a good imported. It is an example of a physical control. Imposing a limit on the quantity of goods imported into a country will increase the share of the market available for domestic producers. However, it will also raise the price of the protected product.

This is shown in Figure 3. The world supply price of a product is £8. Domestic demand shown by the demand curve D is 10 million units. Of that, two million is produced domestically. The remaining eight million is imported. Now assume that a quota of two million units is imposed on imports. Because quantity supplied is now four million units less than it would otherwise have been, price will rise to £10. Domestic production will rise to four million units. Domestic consumption is six million units. The rise in price has led to a reduction in demand of four million units. It should be noted that quotas, unlike tariffs, can lead to gains by importers. It is true in Figure 3 that foreign firms have lost orders for eight million units. But those firms which have managed to retain orders have gained. They used to sell their units for £8. They can now get £10. This is a windfall gain for them, shown on the diagram by the rectangle GLMH.

Figure 3

Quotas

If the world price of a good is £8, the introduction of a quota of two million units will reduce supply and raise the domestic price to £10. Domestic consumption will fall from 10 million units to six million units whilst domestic production will rise from two million units to four million units. Importers of the two million units subject to quota will make a windfall gain. Before the imposition of the quota they could only get a price of £8 per unit. After the imposition of the quota they can charge £10 per unit.

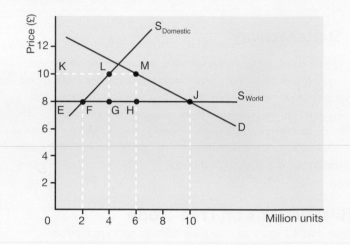

As with tariffs, there is a deadweight welfare loss associated with a quota. The imposition of the quota reduces consumer surplus by EKMJ. This is because consumers buy less at a higher price. Domestic firms gain producer surplus of EKLF because their production rises and is sold at a higher price. The difference between the loss of consumer surplus and the gain in producer surplus is the area FLMJ. Of this, GLMH is gained by foreign firms importing into the country. So the deadweight welfare loss to the country is the whole area FLMJ. The deadweight welfare loss to the world economy is the two triangles FLG and HMJ, the welfare loss to the country minus the welfare gain to foreign firms.

Subsidies

Subsidies can be used both to increase exports and reduce imports.

Export subsidies Subsidies can be given by the government to exports. These subsidies might only be given on goods that are exported. For example, many countries subsidise exports of agricultural produce. It increases exports and supports farm incomes. Or subsidies might be given to products, firms or industries where exports are a large proportion of output. For example, the US aircraft manufacturer Boeing has on many occasions accused European governments of subsidising Airbus, the European aircraft manufacturer. Certainly, European governments have given financial support to Airbus and European governments want to support a strong aircraft manufacturing base in Europe to create exports and jobs.

Subsidies to reduce imports Governments can reduce imports by giving subsidies to domestic firms that compete with

Question 2

Lee Sang-yu is a struggling South Korean rice farmer. South Korean consumers are eating less rice and prices have been falling. Mr Lee's earnings from his business fell to $35 000 last year from $45 000 in 2011. However, his problems are likely to get much worse in the future. South Korea traditionally has protected its rice farmers by imposing a quota on imported rice. This year, the quota was 408 700 tonnes, which was just eight per cent of national consumption. The other 92 per cent was produced by South Korean farmers. In a 2012 review, the World Trade Organization (WTO) argued that the import quota had pushed up the cost of rice in the country to 1.6 times the world average. Government financial support for farmers was 2.5 times the OECD average, amounting to two per cent of South Korean GDP.

Now South Korea is wanting to sign a number of trade agreements with foreign countries and it may be forced to abolish its rice quota. This has alarmed the farming community. The government has suggested that the quota could be replaced by a tariff. Imported rice already carries a tariff of five per cent. This could be increased to as high as 300 - 500 per cent. However, such punitive tariffs could strain relations with countries such as China and the USA that sell rice into the South Korean market.

Source: adapted from © the *Financial Times* 30.6.2014, All Rights Reserved.

(a) Explain, using a diagram, how quotas benefit South Korean rice farmers at the expense of South Korean consumers.

(b) Explain, using diagrams, how South Korean farmers could receive the same protection if the rice quotas were replaced by tariffs on imported rice.

imports. These subsidies are almost always indirect subsidies rather than direct subsidies on domestically produced goods that compete against imports. For example, governments are most unlikely to give subsidies on steel produced domestically. But the government could give cheap loans or tax breaks on investment to domestic steel producers to allow them to compete more effectively against steel imports.

Administrative barriers

There is a large number of different ways in which countries can put up administrative barriers to reduce imports or encourage exports. One common way is to impose product standards that differ from those in other countries. This raises the costs to importers because they have to adapt their products to the product standards set. Countries may simply put bans on imports because of a perceived problem with a product. When UK cows were infected with BSE, for example, many countries banned the import of UK beef. Some countries make it difficult for importers by putting large amounts of red tape on imports. Importers may have to get licences to import. Imports may only be allowed in via certain ports or airports. Officials may take months to clear paper work on imports. Shipments might be delayed for months at ports because customs officials have to check consignments. In some countries, importers may have to bribe officials to get consignments into the countries.

Exchange rate manipulation

Governments can use exchange rates as a form of protectionist policy. By lowering the exchange rate, exports will be become cheaper and imports more expensive. Today, most exchange rates are free floating. Governments do not target a particular value of the exchange rate of their currency. However, some governments peg their exchange rates in various ways. If the peg is used to artificially depress the value of the currency, it will increase exports and reduce imports.

Reasons for restrictions on trade

The theory of comparative advantage states that there are major welfare gains to be made from free trade in international markets. However, protectionism has always been widespread. What arguments can be put forward to justify protectionist policies?

The infant industry argument This is one of the oldest arguments in favour of protection. Industries just starting up may well face much higher costs than foreign competitors. Partly this is because there may be large economies of scale in the industry. A new low-volume producer will find it impossible to compete on price against an established foreign high-volume producer. Once it is sufficiently large, tariff barriers can be removed and the industry exposed to the full heat of foreign competition. There may also be a learning curve. It takes some time for managers and workers in a new industry to establish efficient operational and working practices. Only by protecting the new industry can it compete until the 'learning' benefits come through.

Some countries, such as Japan, have successfully developed infant industries behind high **trade barriers**. It is also true that many countries such as the UK have financial systems which tend to take a short view of investment. It is difficult, if not impossible, to find backers for projects which might only become profitable in 10 or even five years' time.

However, infant industries in general have not grown successfully behind trade barriers. One problem is that a government needs to be able to identify those infant industries which will grow successfully. Governments have a poor record of picking such 'winners'. Second, industries protected by trade barriers lack the competitive pressure to become efficient. Infant industries all too often grow up to be lame duck industries. They only carry on operating because they have become skilled at lobbying government to maintain high trade barriers. Third, it is usually more efficient to use other policy weapons if a government genuinely wishes to encourage the development of a new industry. Specific subsidies, training grants, tax concessions, or even the creation of state enterprises, are likely to be better ways of creating new industries.

Job protection Another argument is that protectionism can create or at least preserve jobs. If, for example, there is a large increase in quantity imported of steel, then domestic steel producers will see reduced orders. They will cut back production, cutting jobs and possibly closing plants. Protecting the local steel industry from foreign competition then means that the orders, jobs and plants are preserved. Workers and domestic producers benefit. However, customers lose out. Customers could have bought imported goods at a lower price. Or, if the imports had been better quality or differently designed products, then customers lose out on choice.

Dumping Dumping can be defined in a number of ways. Broadly speaking it is the sale of goods below their cost of production, whether marginal cost, average total cost, or average variable cost. Foreign firms may sell products 'at a loss' for a variety of reasons.

- They may have produced the goods and failed to find a market for them, so they are dumped on one country in a distress sale.
- In the short run, a firm may have excess capacity. It will then sell at a price below average total cost so long as that price at least covers its variable cost.
- Low prices could represent a more serious long-term threat to domestic industry. A foreign producer may deliberately price at a loss to drive domestic producers out of business. Once it has achieved this, it can increase prices and enjoy monopoly profits.

Goals of long-term domination by a foreign producer might justify trade barriers, although it might be more efficient to subsidise domestic industries. It is more difficult to say whether short-term distress dumping leads to a loss of domestic welfare. On the one hand, domestic producers and their workers may suffer a loss of profits and wages. The impact on employment should be limited if dumping is only a short-term phenomenon. On the other hand, consumers gain by being able to buy cheap goods, even if only for a limited period.

Cheap labour Countries which have plentiful sources of cheap labour are often accused of 'unfair competition'. High labour cost countries find it difficult if not impossible to compete against products from these countries and there is pressure from threatened industries to raise trade barriers. However, cheap labour is a source of comparative advantage for an economy. There is a misallocation of resources if domestic consumers are forced to buy from high-wage domestic industries rather than low-wage foreign industries. Resources which are used in high-cost protected industries could be used elsewhere in the economy to produce products for which the country does have a comparative advantage in production.

The terms of trade One argument in favour of tariffs for which an economic case can be made is the optimal tariff argument. In Figure 1 it was assumed that a country could import any amount at a given price because it was a relatively small buyer on the world market. However, if a country imports a significant proportion of world production, then it is likely to face an upward sloping supply curve. The more it buys, the higher the price per unit it will have to pay. At the extreme, the country may be a monopsonist (i.e. the sole buyer of a product).

If the country faces an upward sloping supply curve, the marginal cost of buying an extra unit will not only be the cost of the extra unit but also the extra cost of buying all other units. For instance, a country buys 10 units at £1. If it buys an 11th unit, the price rises to £11. The cost of the 11th unit is therefore £11 plus 10 x £1 - a total of £21. The decision to buy the 11th unit will be made by individual producers and consumers. The cost to them of the 11th unit is just £11 - the other £10 extra is

borne by the producers and consumers who bought the other 10 units.

Therefore the marginal cost to the economy as a whole of buying an extra unit of imports is greater than the marginal cost to the individual. But it is the individual who makes the decision about whether to buy or not. If the marginal cost of purchase is lower for the individual than for the economy as a whole, more imports will be bought than if the individual had to pay the whole cost of purchase (i.e. the cost including the increased price of previously purchased units). This would suggest that a tariff which increased prices to the point where the cost to the individual purchaser was equal to the cost borne by society as a whole of that decision would increase economic welfare.

Imposition of a tariff will reduce demand for imported goods, and this in turn will lead to a fall in the price of imported goods

Question 3

Between January and March, the US imported 8.8 million net tonnes of steel products, up from seven million net tons in the first three months of 2013. A Washington think tank, the Economic Policy Institute, declared it the 'worst crisis' for the US steel industry since the mid-2000s.

US steel producers and trade unions blame the increase on dumping of steel by countries such as South Korea, Mexico and India. Steel producers in these countries are currently suffering from a glut of overcapacity. US firms and trade unions want their government to impose anti-dumping duties on steel imports in retaliation for alleged dumping.

Source: adapted from © the *Financial Times* 14.5.2014, All Rights Reserved.

Figure 4

US imports of steel mill products

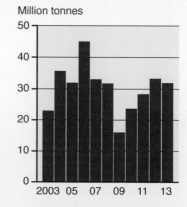

Source: adapted from American Iron and Steel Institute.

(a) Explain, giving an example from the data, of what is meant by 'dumping' in an international trade context.

(b) Using the concepts of fixed and variable cost, explain why a Mexican steel manufacturer might dump products onto the US market.

(c) Explain who might benefit and who might lose out if the US government imposed duties on imported steel.

(a tariff is an indirect, ad valorem or specific tax which shifts the supply curve for imported goods to the left, resulting in a fall in equilibrium price received by suppliers). Hence the terms of trade (the ratio between export prices and import prices) will rise in favour of the importing country. The importing country will be able to buy goods more cheaply. But it is important to remember that this gain will be at the expense of the exporting country. If, for instance, the UK imposed a tariff on tea, the price of tea might fall. The UK will gain but only at the expense of, say, India and Sri Lanka. Also, if the exporting country retaliates by imposing its own tariffs, both countries could be worse off than before.

Other arguments A number of other arguments are put forward in favour of trade barriers. It is sometimes argued that a country needs a particular domestic industry for defence purposes. A country may wish to preserve a particular way of life, such as preventing depopulation of remote rural areas heavily dependent upon a particular agricultural product. It may be felt that some imports are too dangerous to be sold domestically. 'Dangerous' could range from unsafe electrical products to toxic waste to drugs. Alternatively, a country may decide that it is too dependent upon one industry. Some small developing countries depend crucially upon one cash crop such as cocoa, bananas or sugar cane for their economic well being. These commodities are subject to large fluctuations in price on world markets. Falls in price can give rise to large falls in living standards in these economies. Diversifying, even if the newly established industries are uneconomic by world standards, could provide a valuable insurance policy against commodity price fluctuations. Trade barriers are one means of sheltering these industries from foreign competition.

Impact of protectionist policies

Protectionist policies have an impact on consumers, producers, workers, governments, livings standards and equality.

Consumers Protectionism tends to harm the interests of consumers. Either they are unable to buy imported goods at a lower price than goods produced domestically. Or they suffer restrictions on the range of goods being offered to them for sale. Their choice is therefore restricted. Protectionist policies also tend to raise the price of domestically produced goods. Goods and services in the supply chain of domestically produced goods may be subject to import restrictions. For example, if there are tariffs on the import of wheat, then the price of bread in the shops is likely to be higher. Equally, import restrictions limit competition for domestic producers. They have less incentive to become more efficient and lower costs or produce new innovative products. This is because domestic consumers have less choice about the products they buy with protectionism.

Producers Domestic firms can both gain and suffer from protectionism. If their domestic markets are threatened by imports, then protectionist policies can help keep out imports. This means higher output, higher sales and higher profits. Equally, if they benefit from measures to encourage exports, then their output and profits should be higher. However, some domestic firms could suffer. If tariffs are imposed on steel imports, for example, domestic car manufacturers will suffer

because they have to pay higher prices for steel. This could increase their costs and make them less price competitive compared to foreign car manufacturers.

Workers Protectionist policies are often justified as necessary to maintain jobs. If protectionist policies were not implemented, firms would shed jobs or close down altogether. This is a short-term gain. However, it could be argued that workers in the long term would be better off if production did close down as a result of foreign competition. The market would reallocate resources into industries where the country was able to compete. New jobs would be created which had greater job security.

Governments Governments tend to benefit in the short term from protectionist policies. If tariffs are imposed, they gain higher tax revenues. If jobs are protected, they don't lose the taxes paid by those workers that would have been made redundant. In the long term, however, governments can lose out if protectionist policies result in an inefficient economy where growth is restricted. Their tax revenues will be smaller and they may have to pay out more in welfare benefits if unemployment is higher or worker's wages are too low to support them.

Living standards Protectionism in the short term may protect living standards. However, if protectionism leads to a less efficient, slower growing economy in the long run, then there will be a negative impact on living standards.

Equality Trade unions are often in favour of protectionist policies. They want to protect their member's jobs against 'unfair competition' from abroad. Trade union membership tends to be associated with higher wages than would be the case if the firm or industry were not unionised. So protectionist policies may serve to create greater equality where unionised jobs are threatened. Equally, in farming, small farmers are often in favour of protectionism for their products. It raises their incomes that are often low because they are too small and inefficient. Again this might create a more equal distribution of income. However, these benefits are short-term benefits. If protectionism leads to lower growth, over time workers are likely to lose out in absolute terms even if in relative terms they have maintained their incomes.

Free trade vs protectionism

Over the past 70 years, protectionism has been in decline whilst free trade has increased. The main arguments in favour of free trade are that:

- it leads to a more efficient allocation of resources between countries allowing for specialisation;
- it encourages competition between producers, reducing costs of production and leading to innovation and greater choice for consumers; this leads to both static and dynamic efficiencies;
- selected protectionist policies can be successful in nurturing infant industries and creating successful firms as the examples of South Korea and China have shown;
- it can protect a country against dumping by producers in other countries in the short term;
- it can maximise welfare where an optimal tariff exists.

Countries have found it difficult to lower protectionist barriers because they are always seeking reciprocity. If the UK cuts protectionist barriers, it wants equal cuts in protectionist barriers from other countries. Raising protectionist barriers, however, always runs the risk that other countries will raise barriers in retaliation. This is called a **tit-for-tat** response. In the 1930s, what came to be called **beggar-thy-neighbour** policies proved disastrous for the world economy. Countries raised protectionist barriers to cut imports and protect their industries. They hoped that other countries would not respond. They could then take jobs away from these other countries harming their economies. However, other countries did retaliate and world trade collapsed. Everyone was worse off as a result of sheltering behind high tariff walls.

Thinking like an economist

Australian car industry

Australia once had ambitions to be a major car manufacturer. To protect its industry, it erected tariff and quota barriers. However, the cost of producing cars in Australia was high because manufacturing failed to achieve sufficient economies of scale. Protectionist barriers also led to X-inefficiencies in production. The lack of competition meant that local manufacturers were not under pressure to reduce costs to a minimum.

In the mid-1980s, the Australian government decided to bring down trade barriers to boost the efficiency of its car industry. By 2000, quotas had been abolished and tariffs had been reduced from more than 50 per cent to 15 per cent. Imports rose whilst domestic manufacturing shrank. By 2015, there was intense competition in the market with 67 brands selling 350 different models of car. There are more brands and models sold in Australia with an annual market of 1.1 million cars than in more protected markets such as the US with 17 million sales last year and China with 23 million sales.

A series of regional trade agreements with the US, Thailand, South Korea and Japan have now virtually eliminated tariffs on imported cars. There is still a five per cent tariff on EU imports but a trade deal is under discussion which would eliminate this.

Australian consumers have benefited from the abolition of protectionist measures in the car market. They now have unprecedented choice and price competition is fierce. Australia's motor vehicle production industry has suffered. Plants have closed. Toyota, Ford and Holden have all recently decided to close their remaining Australian car plants by 2017. For

international companies like Toyota and Ford, shifting production from Australia to one of their other factors round the world is not a major cost. However, car workers in Australia will lose their jobs. The Australian government will lose tax revenues from the Australian car manufacturing industry. But, assuming that the workers are employed elsewhere in the economy, this will only be a short-term loss. Overall, the Australian economy should gain as it shifts resources out of less competitive car manufacturing to more competitive industries such as mining.

Data Response Question

Shoe and textile tariffs

For companies such as Ricosta, a German family-run children's shoemaker, trying to export to the USA has proved almost impossible. Of the 2.2 million pairs of shoes it makes each year, it sells only about 10 000 to the US. The company's difficulties are typical in Europe's footwear and textiles industry where only about 10 per cent of exports go to the US. This is because US import tariffs can reach up to 40 per cent on some fashion items. Within the footwear sector, tariffs are lower for luxury brands that make shoes entirely of leather. But for more mainstream shoes manufacturers and sportswear makers who use synthetic materials, tariffs are much higher. Ricosta uses enough leather in its shoes to keep duties between 20 per cent but US footwear tariffs can rise as high as 37.5 per cent. The EU also hits US footwear imports with duties of up to 17 per cent. In clothing it can be even higher. The EU, for example, imposed a 26 per cent tariff on some jeans.

This could soon all change because the EU and the US are negotiating a bilateral trade deal which would free

up trade between the two. At a national level, an end to tariffs would particularly help Portugal, Spain, Italy, Romania and Bulgaria where textiles and shoemaking are important employers. US producers are also not opposing the change. This is because the US now imports 99 per cent of its shoes, with only two per cent of that coming from the EU. US consumer groups also say the high tariffs on children's shoes have increased the prices of shoes to hard-pressed US families.

However, abolishing tariffs is not enough according to Fabio Aromatici, director of the Italian shoes manufacturers' association. He warned that non-tariff barriers, such as complex paperwork and labelling requirements, were also barriers to the US market. EU companies would need to work harder at finding lawyers, agents and distributors in the US, an area where they have struggled in the past.

Source: adapted from © the *Financial Times* 20.2.2014, All Rights Reserved.

Q

1. Explain what is meant by 'protectionist barriers', using examples from the data to illustrate your answer.

2. Using a diagram, analyse how US tariffs on shoes imported from the EU affect trade.

3. Discuss whether economic welfare will increase if both the US and the EU abolish tariffs on clothes and footwear imported from each other.

Evaluation

Identify the gains and losses to different groups within the US and EU economies of an abolition of tariffs. Also identify any groups outside the US or EU who might benefit or suffer. Overall, will there be a net gain or a net loss in welfare? What extra information might you need to help you provide a more certain answer?

Figure 5

EU exports to the US, 2012

% of total exports of a product category sold to the US.

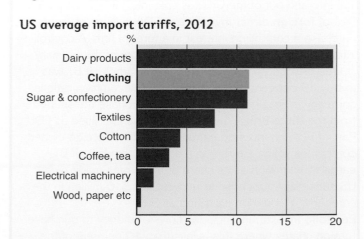

Source: adapted from Unctad, unctadstat.unctad.org, © 2015 United Nations. Reprinted with the permission of the United Nations.

Figure 6

US average import tariffs, 2012

Source: adapted from WTO, www.wto.org, World Tariff Profiles 2014, © 2014 United Nations. Reprinted with the permission of the United Nations.

Key points

1. The balance of payments is split into two main parts: the current account and the capital and financial accounts. Credits and debits on the balance of payments must always add up to zero because the money leaving the country must always equal the money entering the country.
2. There are many causes of deficits and surpluses on the current account including natural resources such as oil, underlying competitiveness of the economy, exchange rates, relative inflation rates, investment and long-term economic growth and spending by consumers and governments.
3. There is a number of different policies which a government can pursue to correct a current account deficit, including devaluation, deflation, supply-side policies, protectionism and currency controls.
4. Global trade imbalances can be a source of macroeconomic instability.

Starter activity

Tata Group is an Indian multinational company. In 2008, it bought the UK-based Jaguar and Land Rover companies from Ford, the US multinational motor company. In 2015, Land Rover announced it was to double the size of its new Wolverhampton plant, investing in extra capacity for its highly successful range of vehicles. Give 10 examples of foreign currency transactions that this activity might have generated.

Components of the balance of payments

In Unit 36, it was explained that the UK balance of payments accounts are split into two main parts.

- The current account is where payments for the purchase and sale of goods and services are recorded.
- The capital and financial accounts is where flows of money associated with saving, investment, speculation and currency stabilisation are recorded.

The **capital account** is relatively unimportant. The largest transfers recorded are those of immigrants and emigrants bringing financial capital to the UK or taking it abroad, and of government transfers such as debt forgiveness to developing countries or to and from the EU.

The **financial account** records almost all the flows of financial capital into and out of the UK. It is split into three main parts.

- Part of **foreign direct investment (FDI)** is flows of money to purchase a controlling interest in a foreign firm. A controlling interest is defined as 10 per cent or more of the ordinary shares or voting power of a firm. For example, if BT was to buy 15 per cent of the shares of a telecommunications company in Brazil, with cash for the purchase transmitted from the UK to Brazil, then this would be classified as FDI. Part of FDI is reinvested earnings: profits of foreign-owned companies which are reinvested in the company. If BT earned $10 million as its share of the profits made by a US subsidiary but chose to reinvest this $10 million in the company, it would be classified as FDI.
- **Portfolio investment** includes flows of money to purchase foreign shares where this is less than 10 per cent of the company. However, for the UK, over 90 per cent of portfolio investment is debt securities such as bonds, long-term loans, issued by governments and firms.

Table 1 UK current account, capital and financial accounts and the balancing item 2013, £ billions

£ billions	Credits	Debits	Balance
Current account	+690.7	+763.1	-72.4
Capital and financial accounts	-138.6	-201.7	+63.1
Balancing item			+9.3
Balance			0

Source: adapted from www.ons.gov.uk.

- 'Other investments' is investment other than direct and portfolio investment. It includes trade credit, loans, purchases of currency and bank deposits.

Table 1 shows the relationship between the current account and the capital and financial accounts. In 2013, the UK's current account was in deficit by £72.4 billion. This means that there were £72.4 billion more imports of goods and services and outflows of money on primary and secondary incomes, than there were exports of goods and services and inflows of money on primary and secondary incomes. If there is a deficit on the current balance, there must be a surplus on the capital and financial accounts. This is because the balance of payments must always balance and add up to zero. In 2013, there was a surplus on the capital and financial accounts of £63.1 billion. The difference between -£72.4 and +£63.1 billions is -£9.3 billion. This is known as the **balancing item**. It is the sum of all the transactions that fail to be officially recorded by the statisticians compiling the balance of payments account. Some of the items missed are because individuals and firms who should send in accurate information fail to do so because they want to avoid tax or because they are engaged in other illegal activities.

Table 2 gives a breakdown of inflows and outflows on the capital and financial accounts for 2013. One significant feature

Table 2 UK capital and financial accounts

£ billions	Net inflow	Net outflow	Balance
Capital account	+1.8	+1.3	+0.5
Financial account	-140.4	-203.0	+62.6
of which			
Direct investment	+27.4	-12.7	+40.1
Portfolio investment	+30.7	+1.2	+29.5
Other investment	+198.5	-210.5	+11.9

Source: adapted from www.ons.gov.uk.

of the 2013 numbers are the minus signs. Inflows are flows of money into the UK and outflows are flows of money out of the UK. In 2013, foreign direct investment outflows were -£12.7 billion. These are flows of money abroad by UK firms to purchase controlling interest in foreign firms. The minus sign shows there was disinvestment by UK firms abroad. UK firms sold £12.7 billion more assets abroad than they bought. Similarly with 'other investment', foreigners reduced their investments overall in the UK and UK citizens and firms reduced their overseas investments.

Reasons for international capital flows

World capital flows have been growing over time at a much faster rate than growth in world GDP. This has been one aspect of globalisation. International capital flows occur for a number of reasons.

- Speculators are looking for quick profits. Shifting capital round the world and buying and selling debt and shares, trying to spot which currency will appreciate in value and which will fall, are an inevitable part of the world capitalist system. International speculation is, in motivation, no different from the British pensioner who moves part of his savings from one bank account to another to take advantage of a higher rate of interest. Speculators occasionally perform an economic function because they help to bring adjustments in prices to reflect longer-term demand, supply and price conditions.
- Capital flows are an essential part of the finance of trade. A UK resident may take out a UK loan to buy a car. A UK firm may take out a loan from abroad to finance the purchase of a machine from abroad.
- Banks in one country are finding it increasingly profitable to lend to economic agents in another country on a short-term basis. A UK bank, for example, may decide to expand its operations in the French loan market.
- Individuals transfer funds abroad for a number of reasons. One is that they might have a holiday house in another country. UK residents who have holiday houses in Spain or France may transfer funds into a Spanish or French bank account. Tax evasion is another reason why UK residents might want to transfer funds into a foreign bank account.
- Foreign direct investment occurs because a firm in one country can see that it can make a profit by investing in the longer term in a firm in another country.
- Portfolio investment may occur for the same reasons as FDI or it may be more speculative in motivation.
- Part of portfolio investment is investment in government bonds, a form of long-term loan to governments. Governments may encourage foreigners to buy their bonds to increase the amount of credit available within a national economy.

Advantages and disadvantages of international capital flows

Growth in international capital flows is important for the world economy.
- It facilitates growth in world trade because it is helping to finance that growth.

- It provides capital for firms that would otherwise not be able to secure finance within their own countries. This is particularly important for developing countries where there may be a lack of financial capital for investment.
- Foreign direct investment also leads to a transfer of technology and information between countries. For developing countries, FDI is one way in which they can gain such technology from developed countries.

However, growth in international capital flows can have disadvantages.

- The 2007-08 financial crisis showed how vulnerable the world's financial systems were to problems in parts of the system. The initial problems in the US financial system spread and directly caused problems in weak points of financial systems in the rest of the world, including the UK.
- Foreign direct investment leads to national firms becoming owned by overseas firms. Some argue this leads to exploitation of countries by multinational companies. There can also be issues of national security. In recent years, a bid for the ownership of six major US seaports by an investment vehicle for the United Arab Emirates failed after an outcry in the US worried about national security. In the UK, a Russian company was forced to sell off the North Sea assets of a company it was taking over. Britain was concerned that the Russian company would shut down its North Sea operations in retaliation for increased UK sanctions against Russia over its aggressive stance towards its neighbours.
- Availability of international credit encourages governments, firms and individuals to overborrow. There have been recurrent world financial crises due to overborrowing. This included the devastating overborrowing by African countries in the late 1970s and early 1980s which lead to two decades of poor economic performance by some of the world's poorest countries as they struggled to repay debt.

Causes of surpluses and deficits on the current account

The current account balance of a country is never likely to equal zero. The current account is made up of millions of different transactions. So countries can expect surpluses and deficits to occur in the short term. In the long term, countries can be split into three groups:
- countries where the current account broadly is in balance such as France or Chile;
- countries which run persistent current account surpluses such as Norway, China, Germany and Switzerland;
- countries which run persistent current account deficits such as the UK, the US, Turkey, Poland and Australia.

There are a number of reasons why countries run persistent surpluses or deficits on their current accounts.

Natural resources Some countries are abundant in natural resources relative to the size of their population. For example, both Norway and Saudi Arabia are large oil producers but have small populations. They then tend to run large current account surpluses because there is little pressure to use the money from exported oil to fund imports.

Underlying competitiveness Some countries have acquired

Question 1

The USA has run a deficit on
its current account on the balance of payments for decades. USA
manufacturing has shed jobs as manufacturers have relocated to
countries with cheaper labour costs such as China. This 'off-shoring'
has taken place at the same time as USA manufacturers have
simply closed down due to price competition from the Far East.
These trends have put downward pressure on wages in the US. The
average US worker has seen little wage growth for the past
30 years. In contrast, wages in the Far East have been growing fast.
In China, average labour costs almost tripled over the 10 years to
2014. The result is that the US is slowly becoming more
cost-competitive. Over the past few years, this cost advantage has
been reinforced by falling US natural gas prices. This has been due
to the sudden expansion of the new technology of fracking: using
liquid to force open gas and oil bearing rocks to release them. Oil
fracking has benefited all countries because a large increase in the
domestic production of oil in the US has fed through to lower world
oil prices. However, gas is much more difficult to export. The result
is that gas prices in the US are now significantly lower than in many
countries around the world. In China, gas prices have doubled in the
10 years to 2014.

There has been a growing trend for 're-shoring': US manufacturers
bringing production back from overseas factories to the US. This
can save on transport costs as well as reducing lead times between
production and delivery. Quality can also be more easily monitored.

Source: with information from © the *Financial Times* 25.4.2014, All Rights Reserved.

(a) Explain one reason why the US has run a current
account account deficit for decades.

(b) What impact will 're-shoring' have on the US current account?

over time an underlying competitiveness which makes their
goods particularly attractive to foreign buyers. Germany, for
example, has developed expertise in machine tools. Low
and middle-income countries can benefit from having cheap
labour. Competitiveness may be based on quality and design
of goods and services. Firms in a country may have developed
a reputation internationally for quality and design which gives
them a competitive edge. Competitiveness may also be based
on labour productivity. If output per worker is relatively high, this
should give a country a cost advantage compared to countries
which have low labour productivity.

Poor competitiveness can be a cause of current account
deficits. For example, countries where it is difficult to set up
businesses and where there is widespread corruption are going
to find it difficult to have successful export industries. Equally,
countries whose firms in general produce goods with poor
quality and design, or where there is low labour productivity will
be at a competitive disadvantage.

Exchange rates Some governments deliberately keep their
exchange rates artificially low. This means that the prices of
their exports are lower than they would be if the exchange rate
were fixed by free market forces. It also means that imports are
more expensive to buy in local currency terms. Exchange rate
manipulation which depresses the exchange rate can then lead

to persistent surpluses on the current account. Equally, some
countries keep their exchange rates artificially high. This keeps
the price of imports low for consumers and firms giving them
an increase in their spending power. However, an artificially high
exchange rate makes exports more expensive to foreigners. With
more imports and fewer exports, these countries are likely to run
persistent current account deficits.

Inflation Relatively high rates of domestic inflation
compared to international competitors will quickly erode price
competitiveness of exports and of domestically produced
goods competing against imports. High inflation without a
corresponding fall in the exchange rate can therefore cause
growing current account deficits.

Investment and long-term economic growth Some
countries attract large amounts of foreign direct investment. In
the 19th century, for example, the USA tended to run current
account deficits because money was flowing in from other
countries to invest in the growth of firms in the US. Similarly,
some countries run surpluses because they are net exporters
of capital. The UK, for example, in the late Victorian and
early Edwardian era invested throughout the world in a wide
variety of business enterprises not just in the British Empire
but in countries like Argentina and Russia. Both inward and
outward investment tend to be seen as positive signs of strong
economies, either attracting funds from other countries or being
able to make profitable investments abroad. Both contribute to
long-term economic growth. But equally, long-term economic
growth can result in investment flows causing both current
account surpluses and deficits.

Spending by consumers and government Deficits can
be a sign that consumers and government are overspending.
In order to finance that consumption, they are borrowing funds
from abroad. When this borrowing reaches critical levels, it can
destabilise an economy. Countries from Argentina to Greece and
Portugal have all found, for example, that excessive government
borrowing abroad leads ultimately to a financial crisis when
foreigners decide that debts are too high and there is a strong
risk that the countries will not be able to pay off their debts.
Countries in this situation face a stark choice. If they default on
their debts, i.e. refuse to pay all of their debts, then they will be
cut off from the world financial system as Argentina found in
the 2000s after the Argentinian government defaulted in 2001.
Or domestic spending has to be cut back to create a current
account surplus which allows for the repayment of debt. This is
the situation that Greece and Portugal have found themselves in
since the financial crisis of 2008.

Measures to reduce imbalances on the current account

There is a variety of ways in which a government can affect the
current account of its economy.

Exchange rate changes If an economy is running a
persistent deficit on its current account, then a currency
devaluation or depreciation is likely to increase exports and
reduce imports. As explained in Unit 69, a fall in the value of
the currency should make exports cheaper to foreigners whilst

making imports more expensive for domestic buyers. This assumes that the combined elasticity of demand for exports and imports is greater than one, the Marshall-Lerner condition. In the short term, there may be a deterioration in the current account because of the J curve effect, explained in Unit 70, but in the long term the current account should improve. Depreciation or devaluation is an example of an **expenditure switching policy**. Expenditure is switched from higher priced imports to more price competitive domestically produced products. Expenditure is also switched from products for sale in the domestic market to exports (products for sale in foreign markets). Devaluation or depreciation will be more successful if:

- price elasticities of demand for exports and imports are relatively high. If exports and imports are mainly being bought on quality or because they are different from domestically produced goods, changing prices for exports and imports will have much less impact on demand.
- resulting cost-push inflation is low. Depreciation or devaluation will inevitably push up the prices of some imported goods including raw materials. If a cost-push spiral develops with workers receiving higher pay rises because inflation has increased, this will feed back into costs for firms, leading to them raising their prices, including exported goods and domestically produced goods which compete against imports. The higher the rise in domestic prices resulting from a depreciation or devaluation, the less will be the impact on the current account.

If an economy is running a persistent surplus, then raising the value of the currency should lead to a reduction in the current account surplus in the same ways that a fall in the value of the currency will reduce a current account deficit.

It should be remembered that devaluation of a currency means that the government has somehow fixed its value against other currencies. Many developing countries use different varieties of fixed exchange rates. However, developed countries such as the UK and the USA almost all have floating exchange rates. Their central banks can intervene in the market to change the value of the currency by buying and selling currency. However, their interventions are likely only to nudge the currency value up or down for a relatively short period of time. A more important way of depreciating or appreciating a currency is for the central bank to lower or raise interest rates. This affects investment flows across the foreign exchange markets. A cut in interest rates will lead to a fall in the value of the currency and should lead to a rise in exports and a fall in imports. However, a cut in interest rates will also lead to an increase in both consumption and investment because the cost of borrowing is lower. This will lead to a rise in imports. The overall impact on the current balance will depend on the relative importance of these rises and falls in exports and imports.

Deflationary policies These policies are aimed at aggregate demand in the economy, for example by raising interest rates or increasing taxes. Households will then have less money to spend and so they will reduce their consumption of domestically produced goods and imported goods. Equally, firms will cut back on investment including purchases of imported capital equipment. Imports therefore decline. Exports may also rise if domestic firms switch sales from the depressed domestic market to foreign markets. These policies are examples of **expenditure reducing** polices because they work by reducing aggregate demand.

Deflationary policies will be more effective if:

- the marginal propensity to import (MPM) is high. The MPM is the change in imports divided by the change in national income. The higher the fall in imports for every £1 fall in income, the greater will be the improvement on the current account.
- they lead to a significant fall in the domestic rate of inflation. A fall in the rate of inflation relative to other countries will give exports a competitive edge in terms of price. Equally, it will make imports less price competitive.

A government wanting to reduce a current account surplus could adopt reflationary policies. Higher spending will increase imports and should also lead to higher inflation, leading to a loss of international competitiveness.

Supply-side policies Supply-side policies aimed at reducing unit labour costs, increasing investment, increasing the skills of the labour force and improving the quality and design of products should lead to increased exports and reduced imports. The major problem with supply-side policies is that they are almost always long-term policies. Devaluing a currency or deflating the economy can affect the current account within a few years. Supply-side policies often take decades to improve the competitiveness of an economy.

Protectionism Increasing tariffs or quotas or other protectionist measures will reduce imports thus improving the current account position. Tariffs and quotas can both have a significant impact in the short term. However, protectionism is not much favoured by economists. First, the country is likely to find itself becoming even more internationally uncompetitive in the long run as its domestic industries have no incentive to improve their efficiency. Second, protectionism in one country invites retaliation from its trading partners. The country could find that the gains on current account from reduced imports are more than matched by losses of exports as a result of retaliation.

Increased protectionist measures are also forbidden except under certain specific circumstances by the WTO (the World Trade Organization). Membership of a trading bloc like the European Union severely limits the ability of individual countries to limit imports through protectionist policies.

Protectionist policies are an example of expenditure switching policies. They work by getting households and firms to change their spending from imports to domestically produced goods and services.

Currency controls A government may choose to impose or tighten currency controls or foreign exchange controls. These are controls on the purchase of foreign currency by domestic citizens and firms. Many countries today have currency controls including Pakistan, Russia and Venezula in 2015. By restricting the purchase of foreign currency, consumers and firms are limited on the amount of imports that can be bought. The tighter the currency controls, in theory, the lower will be the level of imports. In practice, black markets develop to get round the restrictions. Inefficiency results. Currency controls are often linked with or lead to corruption and bribery because some government officials can illegally divert scarce foreign currency to selected individuals or firms.

Question 2

China has long used an undervalued exchange rate as a way of boosting exports and reducing imports. Over the past 20 years, it has run a persistent current account surplus. However, as its economy has grown and become more integrated into the world financial system, the Chinese central bank, the People's Bank of China (PBoC) has found it more difficult to control the value of the Chinese currency, the renminbi.

Since 2005, the renminbi has been slowly appreciating in value against the US dollar. The PBoC has resisted this rise in the value of renminbi by intervening in the foreign currency markets, selling renminbi and buying US dollars. Currency controls have remained in place too. However, speculators have found ways to get round these controls. One popular method is to falsify export invoices on difficult-to-value goods such as electronic circuits. The PBoC then allows the exporter to sell more US dollars and buy more renminbi than is actually needed for the real transaction. The exporter then waits for the renminbi to go up in value against the US dollar and then sells the renminbi for US dollars, making a profit in US dollars.

The slow appreciation of the renminbi has led to the current account surplus falling. In 2007, the current account surplus peaked at 10.1 per cent of GDP. By 2013 this had fallen to two per cent of GDP.

Source: adapted from © the *Financial Times* 20.8.2014, All Rights Reserved.

(a) Giving examples from the data, explain how a country can use (i) changes in the value of its currency and (ii) currency controls to affect its current account balance.

(b) Why do currency controls tend to lead to fraud and black markets in the currency?

Global trade imbalances

Since the late 1990s, there have been concerns about global imbalances. These can be measured in two ways:
- imbalances on the current account of the balance of payments;
- imbalances in assets owned abroad or borrowing from abroad.

The two are linked. If a country consistently has a current account surplus, it will tend to build up a stock of assets abroad. If it has a persistent current account deficit, it will owe more and more to foreign creditors. This is no different from a household. If a household consistently spends £5 000 more per year than it earns, then after 10 years its borrowing, all other things being equal, will be £50 000 plus interest.

If imbalances are small, there is little problem. If a household earns £40 000 a year and spends £40 500, over a 10 year period it might have run up debts of £5 000 plus interest. But on an income of £40 000, this is not particularly significant. If imbalances are large, however, there can be major problems.

The most important debtor country is the USA. As Figure 1 shows, it has run a persistent current account deficit since 1990.

Figure 1

Current account surpluses and deficits[1]
(% of world GDP)

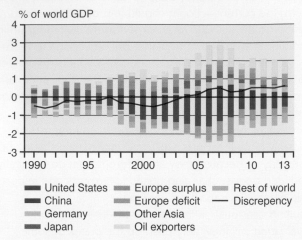

1. Discrepancy line shows the amount of current account items which are missing from world accounts. Missing items are the result of inadequate collection of statistics, tax evasion and criminal activities.

Source: adapted from www.imf.org.

So long as countries are prepared to lend to or invest in the USA, there is no problem from a global perspective. In recent years, the USA has decreased its current account deficit as a percentage of world GDP. This is because the financial crisis of 2008 initially reduced US GDP and imports. The financial crisis deflated the US economy and its current account position improved. Figures 1 and 2 show that there is not necessarily a connection between current account deficits and the value of net assets or liabilities for a country. If US investors can earn a higher rate of return on their investments overseas than

Figure 2

Net foreign assets[1,2] (% of GDP)

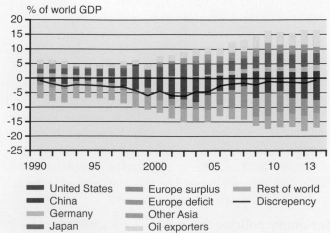

1. Difference between foreign assets owned by entities such as governments, firms and households in a country and what is owed by these entities to foreigners.

2. Discrepancy line shows the amount of assets and liabilities which are missing from world accounts. Missing items are the result of inadequate collection of statistics, tax evasion and criminal activities.

Source: adapted from www.imf.org.

Question 3

Consider Figures 1 and 2 and base your answers on the data in these two graphs.

(a) In what year did China first record a significant current account surplus?

(b) Suggest why oil exporting countries, such as Saudi Arabia and Norway have tended to record current account surpluses.

(c) In the 1990s, many predicted that Japan would cause major problems internationally because of its competitiveness. (i) Why might they have suggested this? (ii) Does Japan continue to pose a problem economically for the rest of the world?

(d) (i) Does the evidence show that United States runs persistent current account deficits? (ii) Is there a correlation between US current account deficits and its net foreign liabilities?

foreigners can on the US investments, then the net liabilities of the US will fall.

Financial crises

Problems do arise if foreign investors suddenly refuse to lend to a 'country'. This is the situation that a number of Asian countries faced in 1997. It is also the situation that faced Greece following the financial crisis of 2008 as well as Italy, Spain and Portugal.

It is important to remember that loans are not given to countries. They are given to institutions or individuals within countries. This could be central government, local government bodies, banks, firms or individuals for example. So if a Spanish firm found that it could not repay its loans that it had taken out in dollars, the firm would go into insolvency but the impact on the whole economy would not necessarily be too great. If a Spanish bank could not repay its loans, foreign lenders could well stop lending to all Spanish banks fearing that there would be 'contagion' - that other Spanish banks would have lent to the bank in trouble and so themselves be at risk of going under. If the Spanish government could not repay its loans, it would no longer be able to borrow money on the money markets. Spain would face a collapse in public services as pensions, teachers and civil servants could no longer be paid. This sort of collapse would be so catastrophic that institutions have been set up to lend to borrowers in difficulties.

- In the short term, central banks lend money to banks in difficulties as the 'lender of last resort'.
- If banks are insolvent because their bad debts are too great, then governments are likely to step in and prevent a bank collapse. This was what happened in the financial crisis of 2007-08.
- Local government bodies can be bailed out by central government.
- Governments can borrow money from the International Monetary Fund (IMF), an institution set up precisely to deal with these sorts of circumstances. Within the eurozone, governments can borrow money from the European Stability Mechanism (ESM), a fund set up to help eurozone governments that are unable to borrow money from the private money markets.

Default

Economic history can help us understand what happens when financial crises are not contained. Many governments over time have defaulted on their debts. This means they have refused or been unable to pay interest owed or the debt itself.

- Failure to pay debt means that governments will not be able to borrow money on international markets in the short to medium term.
- Those owed money will attempt through the courts to acquire any assets owned by that government overseas.
- Overseas firms may refuse to supply governments with goods and services because they are afraid they will not be paid for them. If the government runs the nation's health services, for example, this means that hospitals are likely to run short of essential medicines.
- There may be a refusal by international creditors to lend money to cover day-to-day imports. International trade is typically financed by firms sending out goods and buyers paying later, with insurance companies and factors guaranteeing payment. Importers may find they have to pay foreign companies before they receive the goods. This then puts a strain on the gold and foreign currency reserves of the country held by the central bank. As a result, imports are typically severely controlled by government to prevent those reserves running out. The outcome is a shortage of imported goods in the domestic market.

In the medium to long term, governments are likely to come to some agreement with their overseas creditors. A debt-restructuring agreement is likely to be made, where those owning the debt agree to a write down of the value of the money they are owed. So they might get £2 in every £10 that they are owed, for example.

Although the government now owes less money and is able to borrow again on international markets, interest rates on new loans could well be high as investors are reluctant to lend more money. Also, the turmoil created by the crisis in the domestic economy with disruptions to imports is likely to lead to much lower economic growth in the short to medium term. Countries that default pay a heavy economic price even though they reduce their debts.

Correcting imbalances

Countries with large current account deficits are generally seen as having a problem. Countries with large current account surpluses are generally seen as being successful. What if every country tried to have a large current account surplus? In practice, this could never happen. This is because one country's surplus is another country's deficit. The current accounts of all the countries in the world must add up to zero. If one country succeeds in turning a deficit into a surplus, this can only happen because other countries experience an equal and opposite movement in their current accounts.

Countries with large surpluses, therefore, are directly creating instability in the world's economic system just as much as those running large deficits. For example, a major cause of the US current account deficit over the past 15 years has been China's surplus. The US has bought large amounts of goods from China and found it more difficult to export its own goods because other countries too have been buying Chinese goods. The Chinese central bank has accumulated trillions of US dollars as a result, which it has lent back to the United States. This lending allows the US to carry on spending abroad.

One way for countries to attempt to correct their deficit is through a devaluation of their currency. However, surplus countries may consider this to a threat to their exports and devalue their currencies in return. 'Competitive devaluation' therefore can lead to no relative change in currencies. Putting up protectionist barriers is another option but equally this risks retaliation from other countries. If every country puts up protectionist barriers, every country is likely to lose out. Even highly successful supply-side policies need not necessarily bring about significant improvements in the current account. This is because other surplus countries may also be implementing successful supply-side policies which allow them to retain their competitive advantage.

In the 1970s, western developed countries adopted a system of floating exchange rates because the previous system of fixed exchange rates had proved impossible to maintain. Since then, governments of these countries have become much less concerned about running deficits. Countries like the UK and the US have had no problems financing these deficits and net borrowings have not built up in an unsustainable way. So deficit countries do not necessarily have significant problems. Countries that have got into problems tend almost always to have had governments which have overspent and financed through borrowing large proportions of this money from overseas investors in foreign currencies. It is when governments can't

repay their foreign currency debts that current account deficits tend to become a problem.

It should also be remembered that surplus countries pay a price for running large surpluses. They are foregoing the benefits that extra imports could bring them. For China, its citizens could enjoy a higher standard of living if imports were raised to matched exports. Equally, if the surpluses that countries like China earn are poorly invested, giving low returns or even negative returns, then they will receive little if any benefit in the future. Running a large surplus, therefore, is not necessarily a good policy to pursue.

Key Terms

Expenditure reducing - in a balance of payments context, government policies to reduce the level of aggregate demand in order to reduce imports and boost exports.
Expenditure switching - in a balance of payment context, government policies such as devaluation or protectionism designed to switch production currently being sold domestically to exports.
Foreign direct investment (FDI) - flows of money between countries where one firm buys or sets up another firm in another country. Technically, it is defined as purchasing a controlling interest in a foreign firm, defined as 10 per cent or more of the shares of a firm.
Portfolio investment - flows of money between countries to purchase foreign shares where this is less than 10 per cent of the company, or bonds.

Thinking like an economist

The problem of the UK current account balance

In the 19th century, the UK was once the 'workshop of the world' exporting finished manufactured goods and importing raw materials. In the 20th century, the UK frequently experienced continuing problems of international competitiveness. Governments have exhorted firms to export more but in the long term, whatever policies have been implemented, that underlying lack of competitiveness has persisted.

Figure 3 shows the current account as a percentage of GDP between 1985 and 2014. It was negative in every year ranging from a virtual balance in 1997 to nearly -5 per cent of GDP in 1989 and 2014. Over the period, the main factor causing the deficit was a deficit on trade in goods. The performance of the trade goods sector broadly deteriorated faster than other elements of the current balance after 1992. After the financial crisis of 2008, export earnings from the UK financial services sector also deteriorated whilst the net income the UK earns on its overseas investments deteriorated too.

The main policy used by the UK government over the period to increase exports, particularly of goods, has been a mix of supply-side policies. These supply-side policies might have been successful in raising exports from what they would

Figure 3

UK trade in goods balance and current account balance, as % of GDP

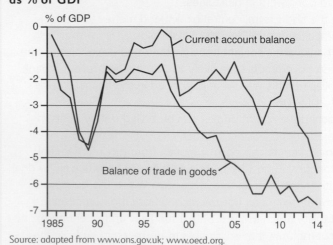

Source: adapted from www.ons.gov.uk; www.oecd.org.

otherwise have been. However, Figure 4 shows that they have not been good enough to prevent an overall loss of international competitiveness over the period.

Although the UK government has not deliberately used exchange rate policy to improve the current account, Figure 4 shows that there have been significant fluctuations in the value of the pound since 1985. The large fall in the value of the pound between 1991 and 1996 was associated with an improvement in the balance of trade in goods shown in Figure 4. Equally the appreciation in the value of the pound from 1997 to 2007 saw a steady decline in the balance of trade in goods. Rises and falls in the exchange rate in this period did seem to affect the ability of UK firms to compete in export markets and against imports in the domestic market. The financial crisis of 2007-08 saw a large fall in UK interest rates as the Bank of England attempted to stimulate the economy. The fall in interest rates led to a significant depreciation in the value of the pound. However, the balance of trade in goods was hardly affected.

The problem for UK exporters following the 2007-08 financial crisis was that economic growth in the UK's main export markets was depressed. Over 50 per cent of UK exports of goods go to other EU countries. Many EU governments adopted deflationary fiscal policies in a bid to reduce their fiscal deficits. This reduced demand for UK exports. From 2010, the UK government also adopted deflationary policies in a bid to reduce its fiscal deficit. This reduced economic growth and therefore reduced the demand for imports. Figure 5 shows that between 2011 and 2013, there was almost no change in either exports or imports. Deflationary policies clearly worked. However, it failed to improve the balance of trade in goods because deflationary policies in the UK were matched by deflationary policies in the UK's main trading partners.

The UK cannot use protectionist policies to improve its current account balance because of its treaty obligations both to the EU and the WTO. It also does not use currency controls. These were abandoned in the early 1980s as part of Margaret Thatcher's supply-side reforms.

Overall, UK export performance remains weak. At over five per cent of GDP, the current balance deficit in 2014 must be a major cause of concern. However, there is no clear indication that the problem of the current account deficit will improve in the near future.

Figure 4

Sterling effective exchange rate (Jan 2005=100), annual average

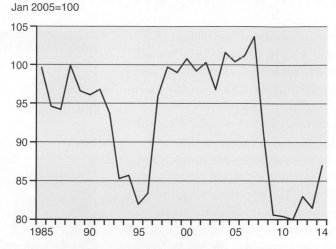

Source: adapted from www.bankofengland.co.uk.

Figure 5

Exports and imports of goods, £bn

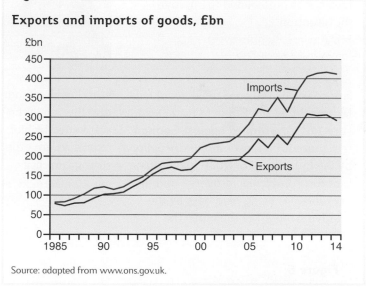

Source: adapted from www.ons.gov.uk.

Data Response Question

France: a deteriorating current account position

France has one of the highest GDPs per capita in the world. This is partly due to high labour productivity and a well-educated work force. However, the country in recent years has suffered from low economic growth due to supply-side weaknesses. These weaknesses are also a factor in the country's export performance. Since 2007, the country has run a current account deficit following a deterioration in its international competitiveness in the first half of the 2000s. Supply-side reforms such as reducing taxes on employing labour and simplifying regulation for businesses are needed to improve the situation.

Source: with information from OECD Economic Surveys, France, March 2015.

France wants the euro to be devalued, Manuel Valls, the Prime Minister said. Paris has long argued against German resistance for a looser monetary policy by the European Central Bank, arguing that the eurozone's recovery - and that of France - is being held back by the relative strength of the euro. The

euro has risen sharply against the dollar and the yen in the past year. Already weakened by high internal costs, French exporters are especially vulnerable to a strong currency.

Source: adapted from © the *Financial Times* 30.4.2014, All Rights Reserved.

Q

1. Explain, using France as an example, what is meant by a current account deficit on the balance of payments.

2. Explain how a devaluation of the euro in 2014 might have helped improve the French current account position on the balance of payments.

3. Discuss whether supply-side policies are always a better way to resolve current account deficits than other policies such as devaluation or deflation.

Evaluation

In this answer, you need to outline the advantages and disadvantages of different policies to resolve current account deficits, weighing up their relative costs and benefits. Think too about the short term and the long term. If there is an economic crisis today which is at least partly caused by a current account deficit, can supply-side policies help in the short term? Use France as an example and discuss whether France in 2014 had a significant current account problem which needed to be immediately addressed.

Figure 6

France: export performance[1]

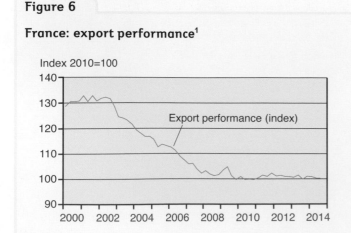

Source: adapted from OECD Economic Surveys, France, March 2015.

1. Difference between export growth and export market growth, in volume terms.

Figure 7

France: current account balance as % of GDP

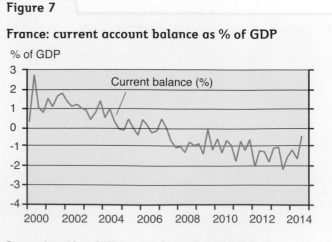

Source: adapted from OECD Economic Surveys, France, March 2015.

69 Exchange rate systems

Key points

1. The exchange rate is the price at which one currency is convertible into another.
2. In a free foreign exchange market, the equilibrium exchange rate is established where demand for a currency is equal to its supply.
3. The demand for and supply of pounds is influenced by exports and imports, investment transactions and speculation.
4. Exchange rate systems can be classified as free, managed and fixed exchange rate systems.
5. In a pure free floating system, there is no government intervention in the foreign exchange markets but in both managed and fixed exchange rate systems, central banks intervene to support the value of their currency.
6. Different exchange rate systems have different advantages and disadvantages.

Starter activity

Find out the value of the pound sterling against the euro yesterday or today. What was it a year ago? List three factors which might have caused the exchange rate to change.

The exchange rate

Different countries use different types of **money** or **currency**. In the UK, goods and services are bought and sold with pounds sterling, in France with the euro, and in the USA with the dollar.

The rate at which one currency can be converted (i.e. bought or sold) into another currency is known as the **exchange rate** or **bilateral exchange rate**. For instance, an Indian company may wish to purchase pounds sterling. If it pays 80 million rupees to purchase £1 million, then the exchange rate is 80 rupees to the pound.

Exchange rates are normally expressed in terms of the value of one single currency against another single currency - pounds for dollars for instance, or euros for yen. However, it is possible to calculate the exchange rate of one currency in terms of a group or basket of currencies. The **effective exchange rate** or **trade weighted exchange rate** or **exchange rate index** are calculations of the average movement of the exchange rate, usually on the basis of weightings determined by the value of trade undertaken with a country's main trading partners.

To illustrate how the trade weighted index is calculated, assume that the UK trades only with the USA and France.

70 per cent of UK trade is with the USA and 30 per cent is with France. The value of the pound falls by 10 per cent against the dollar and by 20 per cent against the euro (which, incidentally, means the euro has gone up in value against the US dollar). The trade weighted index will now have changed. The fall in the dollar contributes a seven per cent fall in the exchange rate (10 per cent x 0.7) whilst the fall in the euro contributes a six per cent fall (20 per cent x 0.3). The average fall is the sum of these two components (i.e. 13 per cent). If the trade weighted index started off at 100, its new value will be 87.

Foreign currencies can be bought today. The exchange rate, at the current point in time is known as the **spot exchange rate**. However, foreign currencies can also be bought today for delivery in one month's time, or six months' time. The rate of exchange for currency to be delivered at a future point in time is called the **forward exchange rate**. Forward exchange rates are

Question 1

Table 1

Original value of the trade weighted index	Change in exchange rate %		New value of the trade weighted index
	Country X	Country Y	
100	+10	+20	
100	+20	+10	
100	-10	+10	
100	+10	-10	
100	-6	-6	

Country A trades only with two countries. 60 per cent of its trade is with country X and 40 per cent with country Y.

(a) Complete the table by calculating the new value of the trade weighted index for country A following changes in its exchange rate with countries X and Y.

(b) What would be the values of the trade weighted index if country A had 90 per cent of its trade with country X and 10 per cent with country Y?

(c) Calculate the new values of the trade weighted index in (a) if the original value of the trade weighted index was not 100 but 80.

used, for example, by firms buying or selling goods in foreign currencies. A UK firm may agree to sell goods to a US customer for $100 000. The goods will be delivered in six months' time. In those six months, the exchange rate is likely to change. To guarantee the £ price, the UK firm can offer to sell today $100 000 for UK pounds to be delivered in six months' time. Forward exchange rates can therefore be used to reduce the exchange rate risk from export and import contracts. They are also used by speculators gambling on whether the exchange rate will go up or down.

Equilibrium exchange rates

Currency is bought and sold on the **foreign exchange markets**. Governments may buy and sell currencies in order to influence the price of a currency. Here we will assume that governments do not intervene and that currencies are allowed to find their own price levels through the forces of demand and supply. There are then three main reasons why foreign exchange is bought and sold.

- International trade in goods and services needs to be financed. Exports create a demand for currency whilst imports create a supply of currency.
- Long-term capital movements occur. Inward investment to an economy creates a demand for its currency. Outward investment from an economy creates a supply.
- There is an enormous amount of speculation in the foreign exchange markets.

The equilibrium exchange rate is established where the demand for the currency is equal to its supply. Figure 1 shows the demand and supply of pounds priced in dollars. The market is in equilibrium at an exchange rate of $2 = £1. Buying and selling is equal to £1 000 million each day.

The demand curve is assumed to be downward sloping. If the price of the pound falls against the dollar, then the price of British goods will fall in dollar terms. For instance, if the exchange rate falls from $2 = £1 to $1 = £1, then a British good costing £1 000 will fall in price for Americans from $2 000 to $1 000. Americans should therefore buy more British goods and demand more pounds to pay for them. So a fall in the price of the pound should lead to an increase in quantity demanded of pounds, giving rise to the downward sloping demand curve. Similarly the supply curve is upward sloping because a fall in the value of the pound will increase the price of foreign imports for the British, leading them to reduce their purchases of foreign goods and therefore of foreign exchange.

All other things being equal, a fall in the value of the pound from, say, $2 to $1 is likely to make the pound look cheap and this may attract speculative buying of the pound and discourage speculative selling. This would then produce downward sloping demand curves and upward sloping supply curves for the pound sterling.

Shifts in the demand and supply curves for a currency

The exchange rate will change if either there is a change in demand for or a change in supply of a currency. Figure 2 shows the market for pounds sterling, the currency of the UK. An initial equilibrium exchange rate of OB with OQ being bought and sold exists. Example of what might cause a shift in one of the curves includes the following.

A rise in UK exports If British exports to the USA increase, American firms will need to buy more pounds than before to pay for them. Hence an increase in the value of UK exports will

---

Figure 1

Floating exchange rate systems

In a free exchange rate market, the price of a currency is determined by demand and supply. Equilibrium price is $2 to the pound whilst equilibrium quantity demanded and supplied is £1 000 million per day.

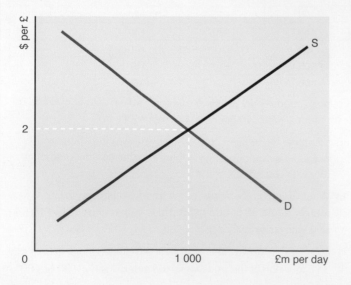

Figure 2

Changes in exchange rates

The equilibrium value of the pound will change if there is a change in either the demand for or supply of pounds (or both).

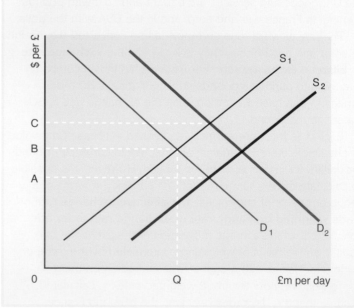

increase the demand for pounds, shifting the demand curve from D_1 to D_2. The exchange rate will therefore rise from OB to OC.

A rise in UK imports If imports from the USA increase, British firms will need to buy more dollars than before to pay for them. They will buy these dollars with pounds. Hence an increase in the value of UK imports will increase the supply of pounds. The supply curve will shift to the right from S_1 to S_2. The equilibrium value of the pound will fall from OB to OA.

A rise in UK interest rates If the rate of interest in the London money markets increases, US savers will switch funds into the UK. This is likely to be short-term money or hot money which flows from financial centre to financial centre attracted by the highest rate of return. An increase in these flows will increase the demand for pounds, shifting the demand curve from D_1 to D_2, and increasing the value of the pound from OB to OC.

An inflow of investment funds If there is an inflow of funds for long-term investment in the UK, again the demand for pounds will rise. For instance, Japanese investment in car plants

---

Question 2

Figure 3

The demand and supply of pounds

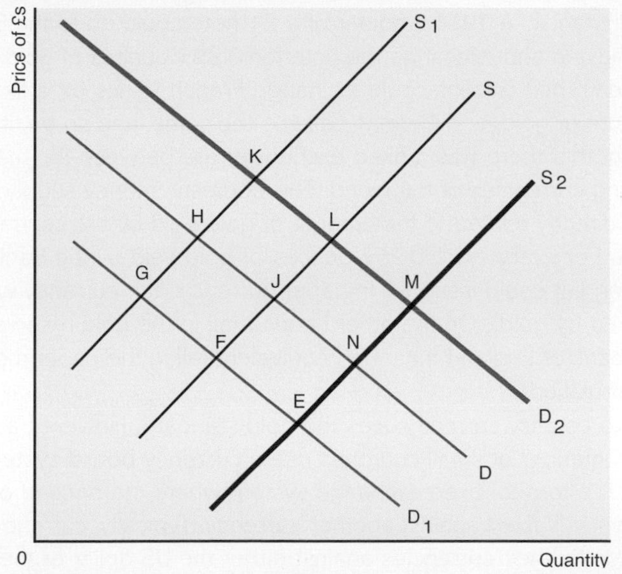

Figure 3 shows the demand and supply of pounds. D and S are the original demand and supply curves respectively.

(a) At which point (E to N) is the market in equilibrium?

(b) To which point will the market be most likely to move in the short term if there is: (i) an increase in exports; (ii) an increase in imports; (iii) a fall in interest rates in the London money markets; (iv) a rise in takeovers of US companies by British companies; (v) a belief that the value of the euro will rise in the near future; (vi) the discovery of a huge new oil field in the North Sea; (vii) bad summer weather in the UK which sharply increases the number of foreign holidays taken; (viii) a series of prolonged strikes in the UK engineering sector of the economy?

---

in the UK will raise the demand for pounds (and increase the supply of yen) shown by the shift in the demand curve from D_1 to D_2, raising the value of the pound from OB to OC.

A belief that the pound is going to fall in value
Speculation is the single most important determinant today of the minute by minute price of the pound. If speculators believe that the value of the pound is going to fall against the dollar, they will sell pounds and buy dollars. An increase in the supply of pounds on the market, shown by the shift in the supply curve from S_1 to S_2, will lead to a fall in the price of the pound from OB to OA.

Speculative activity

It is difficult to assess the level of speculative activity on the foreign exchange markets. Less than one per cent of daily foreign exchange transactions in London is a result of a direct buying or selling order for exports and imports or long-term capital flows. However, each order tends to result in more than one transaction as foreign exchange dealers cover their exposure to the deal by buying and selling other currencies. Even if every order were to result in an extra three transactions, this would still only account for at most four per cent of transactions, which would suggest that speculative deals form the majority of trading on a daily basis.

Thus, in the short term, the value of a currency is dominated by speculative activity in the currency. However, there is evidence to suggest that in the longer term, the value of a currency is determined by economic fundamentals - by exports, imports and long-term capital movements.

The purchasing power parity theory of exchange rates

Different countries have different inflation rates. The cost of living may also be different. The **nominal exchange rate**, which is the current market exchange rate, takes no account of this. However, **real exchange rates** can be constructed which use a comparison of the cost of living in one country with another country. As explained in Unit 31, this is done by measuring **purchasing power parities (PPPs)**. For example, if it costs £300 to buy a bundle of goods in the UK and $600 to buy the same bundle of goods in the USA, then the real exchange rate is £1 = $2.

At any point in time, the nominal exchange rate is unlikely to be the same as the real exchange rate. This is because nominal exchange rates reflect short-term day-to-day speculative activity on the foreign exchange rate markets. In contrast, the **purchasing power parity theory of exchange rates** states that exchange rates in the long-term change in line with inflation rates between economies. To understand why exchange rates might change in line with inflation rates, assume that the balance of payments of the UK is in equilibrium with exports equal to imports and capital outflows equal to capital inflows, but it is suffering from a five per cent inflation rate (i.e. the prices of goods are rising on average by five per cent per year). Assume also that there is no inflation in the rest of world. At the end of one year, the average price of UK exports will be five per cent higher than at the beginning. On the other hand, imports will be five per cent cheaper than domestically produced goods. At the end of the second year, the gap will be even wider.

Starting from a PPP rate of $2 = £1, this change in relative prices between the UK and the rest of the world will affect the volume of UK exports and imports. UK exports will become steadily less price competitive on world markets. Hence sales of UK exports will fall. Imports into the UK, on the other hand, will become steadily more price competitive and their sales in the UK will rise. The balance of payments on current account will move into the red.

A fall in the volume of UK exports is likely to lead to a fall in the value of exports (this assumes that exports are price elastic and therefore the demand for pounds will fall). A rise in the value of imports will result in a rise in the supply of pounds. A fall in demand and a rise in supply of pounds will result in a fall in its value.

So the purchasing power parity theory argues that in the long run exchange rates will change in line with changes in prices between countries. For instance, if the annual UK inflation rate is four per cent higher than that of the USA over a period of time, then the pound will fall in value at an average annual rate of four per cent against the dollar over the period. In the long run, exchange rates will be in equilibrium when **purchasing power** parities are equal between countries. This means that the prices of typical bundles of traded goods and services are equal.

The causes of inflation are complex. However, one fundamental reason why economies can become less price competitive over time is **labour productivity** (i.e. output per worker). If output per worker, for instance, increases at a rate of

two per cent per annum in the UK and five per cent per annum in Japan, then it is likely that the UK will become less competitive internationally than Japan over time. Wage costs are the single most important element on average in the final value of a product. In the UK, approximately 60 per cent of national income is made up of wages and salaries. Hence changes in labour productivity are an important component in changes in final costs.

Floating exchange rate system

An **exchange rate system** is any system that determines the conditions under which one currency can be exchanged for another. In a pure **floating** or **free exchange rate system**, exchange rates are solely determined by the free market forces of demand and supply. There are no government controls over how much foreign currency can be bought and sold. Nor does the government intervene in the market, buying and selling currency, in an attempt to influence the exchange rate.

Fixed exchange rate systems

A **fixed exchange rate system** is one where a currency has a fixed value against another currency or commodity. The best know example of such as system in the past was the **gold standard**, which operated in the 19th and 20th centuries.

Under the gold standard, the major trading nations made their domestic currencies **convertible** into gold at a fixed rate. For instance, in 1914 a holder of a £1 note could go to the Bank of England and exchange the note for 0.257 ounces of gold. Since French citizens could exchange French francs for a fixed amount of gold, and German citizens the same, and so on, it meant that there was a **fixed exchange rate** between the major trading currencies of the world. The domestic money supply was directly related to the amount of gold held by the central bank. For every extra 0.257 ounces of gold held by the Bank of England, it could issue £1 in paper currency (the currency was backed by gold). On the other hand, a fall in the gold reserves at the Bank of England meant an equivalent fall in the paper money in circulation.

No country currently uses the gold standard. However, a small number of small countries use a **currency board system**. This is a form of fixed exchange system where the price of one currency is fixed against another currency. Typically, currency boards fix their currencies against either the US dollar or the euro. The choice of which foreign currency to use is linked to foreign trade. For example, a number of very small states in Europe like the Vatican and Andorra link their currency to the euro. The central bank of the country is able to print domestic currency but the amount it can print is linked to the foreign currency reserves it holds. Confusingly, some writers classify currency boards as an example of a managed exchange rate system. Equally, the Bretton Woods system described below under managed exchange rate systems, is often classified as a fixed exchange rate system.

There are two other examples of currencies which are fixed in value against each other although technically they are not fixed exchange rate systems. This is because there is no currency to trade.

● Some small countries don't issue their own currency but

Question 3

Figure 4

Inflation differentials and the UK effective exchange rate[1]

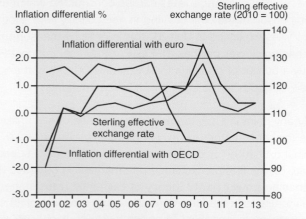

1. UK inflation rate (CPI) minus the inflation rate of euro countries and OECD countries. Approximately 50 per cent of the UK's trade is with eurozone countries and 70 per cent with OECD countries.

Source: adapted from www.oecd.org.

(a) Explain why differences in the UK inflation rate and that of other countries might affect the value of the pound.

(b) To what extent is this relationship supported by the data?

simply use the currency of another country. Panama in Central America, for example, uses the US$ as its currency. During the Scottish referendum on independence, one of the options was that Scotland would use the pound sterling as its own currency. In this system, the country using a foreign currency has no control of the central bank of the other country and so cannot influence its value.

- Some countries agree to set up a common currency. The best example of this is the euro. Independent national states therefore agree to give up their own currencies in favour of a single currency. This single currency, however, could be part of any type of exchange rate system. Each member country has some control over the central bank operating the currency. Currently, the European Central Bank operates a managed float against other currencies such as the US dollar. This was another option suggested for Scotland during its independence debate. The Bank of England would then have been controlled by both Scotland and the UK.

Managed exchange rate systems

Most countries currently use some form of **managed exchange rate system**, sometimes called a **hybrid** or **intermediate system**. In a managed exchange rate system, free market forces of demand and supply are one determinant of the exchange rate. However, government also plays some part in determining the exchange rate of the currency. It can do this either by intervening directly, buying and selling currency using the gold and foreign currency reserves held by its central bank. Or it can intervene indirectly, for example by raising or lowering

interest rates which then influence the free market demand for and supply of the currency. There are many forms of managed exchange rate systems some of which are, confusingly but not necessarily incorrectly, sometimes labelled as fixed exchange rate systems.

Adjustable peg systems An **adjustable peg system** is an exchange rate system where, in the short term, currencies are fixed or pegged against each other and do not change in value, whilst in the longer term the value of a currency can be changed if economic circumstances change. Sometimes, adjustable peg systems are classified as fixed exchange rate systems because the value of the currency is fixed at least in the short term. Between the end of the Second World War and the early 1970s, exchange rates were determined by an adjustable peg system called the **Bretton Woods system**. Under the system, each country fixed its exchange rate against other currencies. This was known as the par value for the currency. The exchange rate was allowed to fluctuate on a day-to-day basis within a very narrow band. If the exchange rate threatened to go below this band, the central bank of a country would intervene by buying up its currency. This would increase the demand for the currency and so raise its price. If it threatened to go above the band, then the central bank would sell its currency, increasing supply and so lowering the price.

This mechanism is shown in Figure 5. The central bank fixed the par value of the currency at OG, but it is allowed to fluctuate within a narrow band of FJ. If demand and supply are D and S, the equilibrium exchange rate is OH is within the band. The central bank therefore does not have to intervene. But assume the supply curve of the currency shifts from S to S_1. The equilibrium exchange rate is then OE below the bottom of the band. To bring the exchange rate back to OF, the minimum price of the currency, the central bank has to buy BC of the currency. BC is the difference between free market supply of OC and free market demand of OB.

Crawling peg systems A **crawling peg system** is a form of adjustable peg system,. A country fixes its currency against another currency or currencies within a band. However, there is a mechanism built into the system which allows the band to rise and fall regularly over time. For example, the band may be moved every three months. The central value could then be based on the average value of the currency in the previous three months.

Managed float or dirty float A **managed** or **dirty float** occurs when exchange rates are freely floating but governments and their central banks occasionally intervene to change the value of the currency. Central banks may intervene on a day-to-day basis to reduce volatility of the currency. This means they want to smooth out sudden sharp rises and falls in the currency that can be disruptive for foreign trade. They may also intervene to change the value of the currency because they feel this is in the national economic interest. For example, a central bank may sell its currency to reduce the exchange rate because it wants to help exporters and reduce imports. Managed floats are the single most important type of exchange rate system used today. The value of the US$, the euro, the British £ (£ sterling) and the Japanese yen are all determined under a managed float.

Figure 5

Central bank intervention in the foreign currency markets

If the central bank wishes to maintain a minimum price of OF for its currency, but the supply curve is S_1 and the demand curve is D, then it has to buy BC currency.

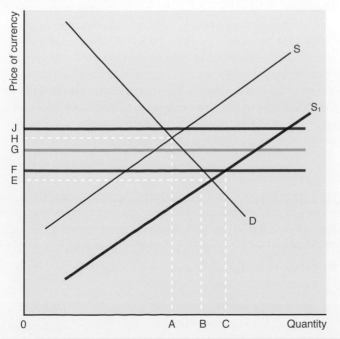

Question 4

Figure 6

The demand and supply of pounds

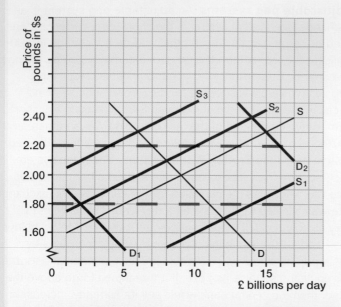

D and S are the free market demand and supply curves for pounds in dollars. The Bank of England is committed to keeping the dollar price of sterling between $2.20 and $1.80.

(a) What is the free market price of the pound?

(b) With a demand curve D, how much currency (in £) will the Bank of England have to buy or sell per day if the supply curve shifts from S to: (i) S_1; (ii) S_2; (iii) S_3?

(c) With a supply curve S, how much currency (in £) will the Bank of England have to buy or sell per day if the demand curve shifts from D to: (i) D_1; (ii) D_2?

Influencing the exchange rate under a managed exchange rate system

Under a managed float, governments have a variety of ways in which they can attempt to change the value of their currency against other currencies.

Buying and selling currency One way is to intervene in the market buying or selling currency. If the central bank wants to raise the value of the currency, it will buy its own currency in exchange for foreign currencies. If it wants to lower the exchange rate, it will sell its own currency into the market. Buying its own currency is only possible because the central holds **gold and foreign currency reserves**. This is monies owned by the central bank to be used to intervene in the markets. Central banks do not own infinite amounts of gold and foreign currency reserves. Today, they are only a small fraction of the total annual dealings of a currency on the foreign exchanges. So central banks find it difficult, if not impossible, to maintain a significantly higher exchange rate than the markets predict except in the short term. In 1992, for example, the Bank of England was defending a high value of the pound against

what would become the euro. Foreign exchange speculators bet against the pound, selling pounds, some of which the Bank of England had to buy to maintain the high exchange rate. Selling got so great that on 'Black Wednesday', 16 September 1992, the government and the Bank of England admitted defeat in its defence of the pound and stopped buying pounds. The value of the pound against other currencies fell by over 15 per cent. Speculators who had been selling pounds could buy back those pounds for less and in the process made profits of billions of pounds partly at the expense of the gold and foreign currency reserves of the Bank of England.

A central bank wishing to lower the value of its currency would sell the currency. Either it has to borrow the money it sells, or it can print the money. Printing the money could have an impact on inflation.

Changing the interest rate The central bank can affect the exchange rate through a change in interest rates. If it raises interest rates, this makes financial investments in the country more attractive. For the UK, foreigners will therefore buy pounds to invest. Also, existing holders of UK investments will be more reluctant to sell, reducing the supply of pounds onto the market. Greater demand for pounds and a reduced supply will then raise the value of the pound. There is a second way in which interest rates affect the value of a currency. For the UK, a rise in interest rates will reduce both consumption and investment, leading to lower GDP. Lower consumption and investment will lead to lower imports to the UK. Imports are paid for with pounds which are then exchanged into a foreign currency. So fewer imports mean a lower supply of pounds onto foreign exchange markets. This then leads to a rise in the value of the pound.

Currency controls Central banks can alter the supply and demand of a currency through **currency** or **exchange controls**. These are limits on the amount of foreign currency that can be bought. For example, under very strict currency controls, the

Question 5

Nigeria has devalued its currency by nearly 10 per cent and raised interest rates to record levels. In 2011, the Nigerian central bank had pegged the value of the naira (N), the Nigerian currency, at N155 to the US dollar (US$). The naira was allowed to fluctuate within a plus or minus 3 per cent band around the midpoint. Yesterday, the Nigerian central bank devalued the naira to N168 to the US$. The band was also increased to plus or minus 5 per cent around the midpoint, allowing a 10 per cent fluctuation before the central bank would intervene to stabilise the currency. The rise in the rate of interest was from 12 per cent to 13 per cent.

The naira has come under pressure because of the large fall in the price of oil, Nigeria's most import export. Nigeria is one of the world's largest oil producers. 90 per cent of its export earnings come from oil as well as 70 per cent of government revenues.

Source: adapted from © the *Financial Times* 26.11.2014, All Rights Reserved.

(a) Explain how a rise in Nigerian interest rates might help boost the value of the naira.

(b) Why would a fall in the price of oil lead to the naira falling in value against other currencies?

only place where a currency could be bought and sold would be the central bank. A firm wanting to import cars would have to buy the foreign currency from the central bank. A firm exporting textiles would have to sell any foreign currency it received to the central bank. By limiting the amounts of currency available, the central bank is able to fix the value of the currency. Often, central banks using currency controls will have several different exchange rates. For instance, it might have a low exchange rate for imports of consumer goods but a higher exchange rate for imports of investment goods. This reduces the price of imported investment goods and so encourages investment at the expense of consumption. Currency controls inevitably lead to black markets developing in a currency. They are also open to corruption because those getting hold of scarce currency at official rates can usually sell the currency at a higher black market rate, making a profit.

Borrowing from international institutions like the IMF A last resort for a country wanting to maintain a high exchange rate would be borrowing from an institution like the IMF (International Monetary Fund). The borrowed money can

then be used to buy up the currency and so raise its price. It is a last resort because borrowing like this is taken to be a sign of economic failure. Lenders like the IMF also will insist on economic reforms which are likely to be highly unpopular with the electorate in the country.

Devaluation and revaluation If a country has fixed its currency against another currency, as with an adjustable peg system, it can choose to devalue or revalue its currency. A **devaluation** means that the value of the currency officially falls. For example, when the UK devaluated its currency in 1967 under the Bretton Woods system, the value of the pound fell from $2.80 to $2.40. A **revaluation** means that the value of the currency officially rises. Devaluation and revaluation imply that the government is committed to maintaining the new official rate of exchange, for instance, through buying and selling in the market or through interest rate policy. Devaluation is different from depreciation. **Depreciation** of a currency is when it falls in value because of free market forces or intervention by the central bank. **Appreciation** of a currency is when its rises in values because of buying and selling in the market. A devaluation or revaluation can only occur when a country has pegged its currency to another currency or basket of currencies.

The advantages and disadvantages of different exchange rate systems

Over the past 200 years, a wide variety of exchange rate systems has been used. This would suggest that no system is perfect. A number of key issues determine the advantages and disadvantages of different exchange rate systems.

Volatility Under a fixed exchange rate system, there is no volatility in the value of the exchange rate. It remains fixed. This is good for encouraging international trade and for long-term international investment. Exporters, importers and investors know how much they will pay or receive in six months' time or in six years' time. In contrast, with a pure float, the exchange rate is changing minute by minute. There are many cases over the past 40 years when a currency has depreciated or appreciated by large percentages over just a few days. This volatility is a barrier to trade and international investment because every transaction carries an exchange rate risk. Currency can be bought forward to hedge against exchange rate risks. Governments will often guarantee the exchange rate on very large export orders where monies might only be paid in three or five years' time. Examples would be a contract to build a power station or deliver turbines to generate electricity. However, this is a second best solution compared to a fixed exchange rate.

Robustness Under a pure floating exchange rate system, there is no need for any government intervention. The market fixes the price of a currency on a second by second basis. As such, it is a highly robust system, i.e. it is unlikely to collapse. A managed or dirty float is also robust. Governments don't have to intervene in the market. When they do intervene, they can estimate the benefits if it is successful and compare this with the risk of not doing anything or of the intervention being a failure. In contrast, fixed and peg exchange rate systems are far less robust. This is because the gold and foreign currency reserves used to defend a currency are limited in comparison with the

Question 6

Figure 7

Annual percentage change in the euro (€)[1] vs US dollar ($)

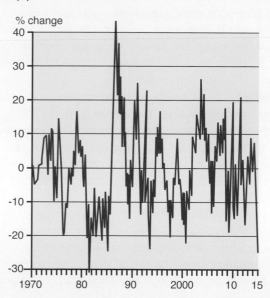

1. Reconstructed euro pre-1999.

Source: adapted from Thomson Reuters Datastream; © the *Financial Times* 22.3.2015, All Rights Reserved.

In the early 1970s, the Bretton Woods system collapsed and the price of currencies such as the dollar were fixed through a managed float system.

(a) To what extent is the exchange rate of the euro and the dollar volatile?

(b) Why might the pattern of changes shown in the data be a problem for European and US exporters and importers?

large amounts of speculative money that can be used to force a devaluation or revaluation of a currency. For example, the gold standard collapsed during the Great Depression of the 1930s. The Bretton Woods system collapsed in the early 1970s when speculative pressure became too great.

Economic costs of adjustment   What happens if the demand and supply for a currency are in disequilibrium? In a pure floating exchange rate system, the price of the currency adjusts automatically through the free market mechanism. For example, assume that there is disequilibrium because imports are greater than exports in the UK. Households, firms and government are spending too much on imported goods. If this happens, supply of pounds is greater than the demand for pounds on the foreign exchange markets. The result will be a fall in the price of the pound. This depreciation means that imports become more expensive and exports become cheaper for foreigners. Households, firms and government buying imports

are worse off because they can now buy fewer imported goods with their incomes. Any unemployment is likely to fall because UK firms will now be more competitive. However, there will be an increase in inflation because of imported inflation. Unless this is contained, it could be a major problem because it could set off a wage-price cost-push inflationary spiral.

In a fixed exchange rate system, the price of the currency cannot change. If there is disequilibrium because imports are greater than exports, this can only be resolved by households, firms and government buying fewer imports and exporting more. In the short term, the government could deflate the economy to achieve this. With less income, perhaps because of higher taxes, lower government spending or higher interest rates, households and firms will spend less on imported goods. However, the contractionary policies of government will have led to higher unemployment. In turn, this should put downward pressure on inflation and also wage rates. By cutting wage rates, firms will

Key Terms

Adjustable peg system - an exchange rate system where currencies are fixed in value in the short term but can devalued or revalued in the longer term.

Appreciation of a currency - when the value of a currency rises because of free market forces or with a dirty float, because of government intervention.

Bilateral exchange rate - the rate of exchange of one single currency for another single currency.

Bretton Woods system - an adjustable peg exchange rate system which was used in the post-Second World War period until its collapse in the early 1970s.

Crawling peg system - an adjustable peg system of exchange rates where there is an inbuilt mechanism for regular changes in the central value of the currency.

Currency board system - an exchange rate system where a country fixes the value of its currency to another currency. Notes and coins in the domestic currency can only be printed to the value of assets in the other currency held by the central bank.

Currency or exchange controls - limits on the purchase and sales of foreign currency, usually through its central bank.

Depreciation of a currency - when the value of a currency falls because of free market forces or with a dirty float, because of government intervention.

Devaluation of a currency - when a government or central bank officially fixes a new lower exchange rate for the currency in a fixed or pegged system of exchange rates.

Effective exchange rate or trade weighted exchange rate index - measure of the exchange rate of a country's currency, usually against a basket of currencies of a country's major trading partners.

Exchange rate - the value of one currency when traded for another currency.

Exchange rate systems - systems which determine the conditions under which one currency can be exchanged for another.

Fixed exchange rate system - a rate of exchange between at least two currencies, which is constant over a period time.

Floating or free exchange rate system - where the value of a currency is determined by free market forces and where the value of a currency changes from day to day.

Foreign exchange markets - trading arrangements where currencies are bought and sold for each other.

Gold and foreign currency reserves - gold and foreign currency owned by the central bank of a country and used mainly to change the foreign exchange value of the domestic currency by buying and selling currency on foreign exchanges.

Gold standard - an exchange rate system where the value of a currency was fixed against a weight of gold.

Managed exchange rate system or hybrid or intermediate system - an exchange rate system where free markets determine the value of a currency but where central banks intervene from time to time to change the value of their currency.

Managed or dirty float - where the exchange rate is determined by free market forces but governments intervene from time to time to alter the free market price of a currency.

Nominal exchange rate - the rate at which one currency is bought and sold on the foreign exchange markets for another currency.

Purchasing power parity theory of exchange rates - the hypothesis that long run changes in exchange rates are caused by differences in inflation rates between countries.

Real exchange rate - the ratio of the cost of a typical bundle of goods in one country compared to its cost in another country in the currencies of each country.

Revaluation of a currency - when a government or central bank officially fixes a new higher exchange rate for the currency in a fixed or pegged system of exchange rates.

become more competitive internationally. However, households will be worse off on average.

So the economic costs of adjustment if imports are greater than exports between floating and fixed exchange rates are different. Both leave households worse off. With floating exchange rates, inflation could become a problem as employment rises. With fixed exchange rates, unemployment in the short-term rises as inflation falls.

Financial discipline In the past, some governments have allowed inflation to rise because of imbalances in the economy. This is easy to do if the currency is floating freely against other currencies. For example, if the government is overspending or keeping interest rates too low, there will be an expansionary effect on the economy. This could be particularly attractive to the government if it is about to face a general election. In the long term, it is unsustainable. The exchange rate falls and this leads to higher inflation. In a fixed exchange rate system, major problems in the foreign exchange markets occur if the government attempts to reflate the economy when exports and imports are not in balance. So a fixed exchange rate system imposes financial discipline on any government tempted to overspend.

Question 7

In the late 1980s and early 1990s, the Argentinian economy was in deep trouble. Inflation peaked at 3 000 per cent in 1989 whilst GDP was 10 per cent lower in that year than in 1980. As part of a recovery plan, the Argentinian government introduced a currency board system in 1991. The Argentinian peso was pegged against the US dollar at an exchange rate of 1 peso to $1. Inflation fell to 3.4 per cent in 1994 but by this stage the peso was overvalued against the dollar and Argentina's main trading partners. The result was that the peg became a major source of deflation in the economy. A number of exchange rate crises in the 1990s culminated in the currency board being abandoned in 2002. The value of the peso fell by two thirds against the US dollar.

Estonia gained its independence from Russia in 1990. A period of rapid inflation was brought to an end when Estonia's central bank pegged its new currency, the kroon, against the German currency at the time (the mark) and created a currency board. When Germany adopted the euro in 2002, the kroon was pegged against the euro. Estonia is a relatively small country and has been dependent on trade with other countries for its prosperity. In 2004, it joined the European Union and adopted the euro in 2011. Stable prices created by a successful currency board have helped Estonia's rapid economic growth.

Source: adapted from Alain Anderton, *Economics*, 5th ed, Pearson.

Using the examples of Argentina and Estonia, explain (a) what is meant by a 'currency board'; (b) the advantages and disadvantages of currency boards.

Thinking like an economist

The Bretton Woods system

The Bretton Woods system, first devised in 1944, provided exchange rate stability. Hence, it can be argued that it encouraged the growth of world trade during the 1950s and 1960s.

It was intended that governments could choose how to resolve a current account deficit. They could deflate the economy, creating unemployment, reducing imports and reducing domestic inflation. This was the same adjustment mechanism as present under the gold standard. They could also devalue the currency. By changing the relative price of exports and imports, the economy could be made more internationally competitive without creating unemployment. However, there would be some cost in terms of imported inflation.

In practice, countries tended not to devalue except in a crisis. This was because devaluation, wrongly in the view of many economists, came to be associated with economic failure. Deficit countries tended to use deflation as the main policy weapon to deal with balance of payments problems, negating the flexibility of adjusting relative prices built into the system. The burden

of adjustment also fell solely on deficit countries. There was little pressure within the system for surplus countries to reduce their surpluses, for instance by revaluing their currencies. The result was that the system became increasingly brittle. Deficit countries like the UK tended to lurch from one foreign exchange crisis to the next whilst surplus countries like West Germany resisted pressures to take any action to reduce their surpluses.

Problems were compounded by the fall in the value of gold and currency reserves as a ratio of world trade during the 1950s and 1960s. To maintain exchange rate stability, central banks bought and sold currency. So long as the central banks were the main buyers and sellers in the market, they could dictate the price of foreign exchange. However, during the 1950s and 1960s world trade expanded at a much faster rate than gold and foreign currency reserves.

In an attempt to inject greater liquidity into the international financial system, the IMF issued Special Drawing Rights (SDRs) to member countries in 1969. SDRs are a form of international currency which can only be used by central banks to settle debts between themselves or with the IMF. When a country needs foreign currency to defend its own currency, it can buy it with the SDRs it holds. Whilst SDRs, effectively a handout of 'free' money, increased liquidity in the system at the time, the IMF failed to allocate further SDRs to member countries. The countries which control the IMF, the industrialised nations of the world, particularly the USA, were afraid that further creation of SDRs would encourage countries, particularly developing countries, to put off dealing with fundamental balance of payments problems by using newly distributed SDRs to finance their large current account deficits.

The Vietnam war from 1965 onwards made matters worse. To finance the war the USA ran a large current account deficit and therefore was a net borrower of money on its capital account. Individuals and firms were quite happy to lend their pounds, francs, deutschmarks and other currencies to the US and in exchange receive dollars because exchange rates were fixed to the dollar and dollars were seen to be as safe as gold itself.

By the late 1960s there was a large amount of money, particularly dollars, being held outside its country of origin. Americans were holding pounds, Japanese were holding deutschmarks, Germans were holding dollars, etc. This provided the base for large speculative activity on the foreign exchanges. It had become obvious that the United States would need to devalue the dollar if it were to return to a balance of payments equilibrium. On the other hand, it was obvious that Germany and Japan, two large surplus countries, would have to revalue their currencies. There was persistent selling pressure on the dollar and buying pressure on the deutschmark and yen. Central banks found it more and more difficult to match the speculative waves of buying and selling. In the early 1970s, after some traumatic devaluations and revaluations, one country after another announced that it would float its currency.

The Bretton Woods system provided a long period of exchange rate stability during which there was a significant expansion of world trade. The cost of adjustment to current account deficits was probably less than under the gold standard. Although deflation was widely used in response to this problem, countries also devalued their currency, trading off slightly higher imported inflation for less unemployment. However, the system was not sufficiently robust to prevent its collapse in the early 1970s.

Data Response Question

The Swiss franc and the Danish krone

The Swiss National Bank, the central bank of Switzerland, has abandoned its self-imposed peg against the euro. Introduced in 2011, the Swiss National Bank committed itself to maintaining a ceiling on the price of Swiss francs (SFr) at SFr1.20 to the euro. The ceiling was introduced because the Swiss were worried that a rising Swiss franc was making more and more of its industries uncompetitive.

Since 2011, the Swiss National Bank has been forced to buy SFr 237 billion of foreign currency to keep the price of the SFr at or below the ceiling. The foreign currency reserves of the Swiss National Bank have increased from SFr258 billion to SFr495 billion. These reserves now amount to 80 per cent of gross domestic product. In theory, there is no problem with maintaining a ceiling because the central bank can simply print more of its currency which is in demand to buy foreign currencies. However, open-ended money creation has lead to the Swiss monetary base quintupling to SFr400 billion. As a consequence, bank lending has risen by 25 per cent as a share of GDP to 170 per cent fuelling a rise in Swiss property prices.

The markets were stunned by the announcement and the SFr initially soared by 40 per cent against the euro and dollar, although it dropped back within two months to a 15 per cent increase. One possible reason why the Swiss National Bank has abandoned its ceiling is because of worries about the effects of quantitative easing in the eurozone. Quantitative easing, likely to be announced next week by the European Central Bank, will push eurozone interest rates down. That will make Swiss interest rates relatively more attractive, threatening to bring a shift of investment monies into the SFr and out of the euro.

Figure 8

Swiss franc against the euro

SFr per €

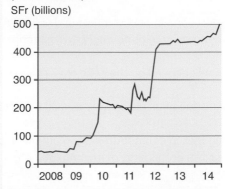

Currency speculators are looking for their next target after forcing Switzerland to abandon its defence of the Swiss franc. This target could be the Danish krone. Since 1999, Denmark's central bank, Nationalbanken, has pegged the krone (DKr) against the euro. Its monetary policy is aimed at keeping the krone within 2.25 per cent on either side of the currency peg of DKr7.46 to the euro. Following Switzerland's announcement, Nationalbanken has cut its deposit rate from minus 0.05 per cent to minus 0.20 per cent to discourage speculative buying of the krone. The interest rate cut was largely expected by economists because the krone has strengthened in recent days. Nationalbanken also said that it had bought foreign exchange in market.

Figure 9

Swiss foreign exchange reserves (SFr billions)

SFr (billions)

At the end of last year, the total balance sheet of Denmark's Nationalbanken was 27.6 per cent of gross national product compared with 85 per cent for the Swiss National Bank.

Evaluation

To evaluate, compare the importance of the advantages and disadvantages. Also evaluation points can be made in respect of possibilities. How likely is it that something will be correct or will happen?

Q

1. How volatile was the price of the Swiss franc against the euro between 2008 and 2015?

2. Explain, using diagrams, how the Swiss National Bank was able to maintain a ceiling on the price of the Swiss franc against the euro whilst the Danish Nationalbanken was able to peg the Danish krone against the euro.

3. Discuss the possible advantages and disadvantages to countries like Switzerland and Denmark of adopting currency ceilings and currency pegs.

The impact of changes in exchange rates

Key points

1. A change in the exchange rate will affect exports and import volumes and values. A fall is likely to lead to an improvement in the current account on the balance of payments whilst a rise is likely to lead to a deterioration.
2. The impact of a change in the exchange rate will depend on the price elasticities of demand for exports and imports.
3. Because of the J curve effect, a change in the value of an exchange rate will be different in the short term from the long term.
4. Other countries may retaliate if a country engages in a competitive devaluation of its currency.
5. Changes in exchange rates can have an impact on economic growth, employment and unemployment, the rate of inflation and FDI flows.

Starter activity

The exchange rate of the pound against other currencies falls by 15 per cent. Give five different ways in which you think this might affect you. Think of foreign holidays, for example, or the price of clothes or food.

Exports and imports

Changes in exchange rates affect the economy mainly through their impact on exports and imports. In most cases, a fall in the exchange rate (a depreciation in a floating exchange rate system or a devaluation in a fixed exchange rate system) will lead to:

- a rise in the value of exports;
- a fall in the value of imports;
- an improvement on the current account on the balance of payments.

A rise in the exchange rate, either an appreciation or a revaluation, will have the opposite effects. However, the change in the current account is dependent on the relative elasticities of exports and imports and whether the short term or the long term is being considered.

These effects will now be considered in more detail using the example of a fall in the value of the UK currency, the pound sterling. The opposite effects will occur if there is a rise in the value of the currency.

The effects of a fall in the value of the exchange rate

Assume that the pound falls in value against other currencies by 10 per cent. The price of imports will therefore rise in pounds sterling. With an exchange rate of $2 = £1, a US car sold to UK importers for $20 000 would have cost £10 000 in pounds sterling. With a 10 per cent devaluation of the pound, the new exchange rate will be $1.8 = £1. So the cost of a $20 000 US car will be £11 111 ($20 000 ÷ 1.8). At the new price, demand is likely to fall. The effect on the total value of imports will depend upon the elasticity of demand for US cars. If demand is elastic, the percentage rise in the price of US cars will be more than offset by a percentage fall in the demand for cars. Hence

the total sterling value of imported US cars will fall. (This is an application of the relationship between elasticity and revenue.) If demand is price inelastic, a rise in price will lead to a rise in expenditure on US cars and hence a rise in the sterling value of US car imports.

In summary, a fall in the value of the pound will:

- leave the US **dollar price** unchanged but increase the sterling price of imported goods;
- result in a fall in **import volumes**;
- lead to a fall in the **total sterling value** of imports assuming that domestic demand for imports is elastic; if demand is inelastic, there will be a rise in the sterling value of imports.

A fall in the value of the pound should have no effect on the sterling price of exports. A £10 000 car exported to the USA will still be £10 000 after the fall. But the price will have fallen in US dollars. If the value of the pound falls from $2 = £1 to $1.8 = £1, the £10 000 car will fall in price in the USA from $20 000 to $18 000. This should lead to a rise in demand for UK cars.

A fall in the value of the pound will therefore:

- leave the **sterling price** of exports unchanged but reduce the price in foreign currency terms;
- lead to a rise in **export volumes**;
- increase the **total sterling value** of exports.

Devaluation and elasticity

Overall, a fall in the value of the pound will increase the sterling value of exports, but may or may not lead to a fall in the value of imports depending upon the elasticity of demand for imports. It is likely that, even if import values increase, export values will increase even more. Hence a fall in the value of the pound will result in an improved current account position. The **Marshall-Lerner** condition states that, given very stringent conditions, a fall in the value of the pound will result in an improvement on current account if the combined elasticities of demand for exports and imports are greater than 1. If the combined elasticities for exports and imports are less than 1, then the correct policy response to a current account deficit should be a currency revaluation.

Question 1

Initially, the UK exports 100 units of goods (the export volume) at an average price of £1. The price elasticity of demand for exports is 0.8.

(a) What is the initial value in pounds of total exports?

(b) The pound is devalued by 20 per cent. (i) What is the new volume of exports assuming exporters keep their prices in pounds the same? (ii) What is the new value of total exports?

Initially, the UK imports 200 units of goods (the import volume) at an average price of £0.60. The price elasticity of demand for exports is l.5.

(c) What is the initial value in pounds of total imports?

(d) The pound is devalued by 20 per cent. As a result, importers have to pay on average 72p for each unit of imports. Explain why this is so.

(e) (i) What is the new volume of imports given a rise in their price of 20 per cent assuming that foreign companies don't change their prices in their own currencies? (ii) What is the new value of imports in pounds?

(f) (i) What was the initial balance of trade (exports minus imports) (ii) What is the new balance of trade after the devaluation?

(g) Give answers to (a) to (f) but assume that the price elasticity of demand for exports is 0.4 and for imports is 0.2.

Devaluation and pricing strategies

So far it has been assumed that UK exporters will choose to keep the sterling price of the products constant and change the foreign currency price, whilst importers will choose to keep the foreign currency price of their goods the same and change the sterling price. However, exporters and importers may choose a different strategy. A luxury car manufacturer, for instance, may price a model at $40 000 in the USA. If the value of the pound is $2 = £1, it will receive £20 000 per car. If the value of the pound now falls to $1 = £1, the manufacturer has a choice of strategies. It could keep the sterling price constant at £20 000 and reduce the dollar price to $20 000. However, a fall in price of a luxury car may give the wrong signals to US car buyers. They may assume that the cars are no longer luxury cars. They may think that the business is not doing well in the US and is having to reduce prices in order to maintain sales. The fall in the dollar price may generate few extra sales. So the manufacturer is likely to hold constant the dollar price of $40 000 and consequently increase its profit margins. When the value of the pound rises against the dollar, the manufacturer may again choose to hold constant the dollar price. A rise in the dollar price may lead to large falls in sales if the manufacturer is in a competitive market with other luxury car manufacturers.

If both exporters and importers adopt the strategy of leaving the prices they charge to their customers unchanged, a fall in the value of the pound will still improve the current account position. Assume the pound is devalued.

• The sterling value of exports will rise because exporters

have chosen to increase the sterling price of exported goods rather than reduce their foreign currency price. Export volumes will remain unchanged because the foreign currency price has remained unchanged. Therefore sterling export values will increase because of the sterling price increase.

• The sterling value of imports will stay the same. Foreign firms have chosen to keep the sterling price of their goods constant. Hence volumes will not change. Neither, therefore, will the sterling value of imports.

With export values increased and import values unchanged, there will be an improvement in the current account position.

Problems associated with devaluation

There are three major problems if governments and central banks use devaluation as a policy weapon to improve the current account position on the balance of payments.

The J curve The current account following devaluation is likely to get worse before it gets better. This is known as the J curve effect and it is shown in Figure 1.

Assume the UK has a current account deficit and the UK government attempts a devaluation of the pound. In the short run the demand for exports and imports will tend to be inelastic. Although the foreign currency price of UK exports will fall, it takes time before other countries react to the change. Hence, the volume of exports will remain the same in the short term, before increasing in the longer term. This means that in the short term, there will be no increase in sterling export values.

Similarly, although the sterling price of imports rises, in the short term UK buyers may be stuck with import contracts they signed before devaluation. Alternatively, there may be no alternative domestic suppliers and hence firms may have to continue to buy imports. Hence, in the short term, sterling import values will rise. In the longer term, contracts can be revised and domestic producers can increase supply, thus leading to a reduction in import volumes.

Overall, in the short term, import values will rise but export values will remain constant, thus producing a deterioration in the current account. In the longer term, export values will rise

Figure 1

The J curve effect

Devaluation will initially lead to a deterioration of the current account position before it improves in the longer term.

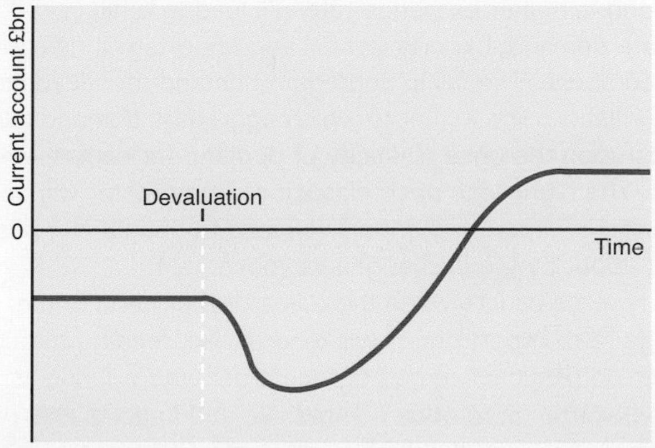

whilst import values might fall, producing an improvement in the current account position.

Cost-push inflation Devaluation generates imported inflation. This is not serious if there is a once and for all increase in prices. But if it starts up or fuels a cost-push **inflationary spiral**, then the increased competitiveness achieved by the devaluation will be quickly eroded. For this reason, devaluation is usually only successful in improving a current account position if it is part of a much wider package of measures designed to increase the competitiveness and performance of a deficit economy.

Competitive devaluation A country which deliberately devalues or depreciates its currency to gain a competitive advantage runs the risk that other countries will also devalue their currency. Where a country is running a persistent current account deficit, there will be an international recognition that this is likely to cause economic problems for the country concerned. Competitive devaluations are therefore unlikely to result. However, a country may have a current account surplus and still devalue. This could be because it wants to stimulate demand in its economy because it is experiencing low growth or high unemployment. Devaluation becomes a policy weapon to improve the domestic economic situation rather than the balance of payments. In this situation, countries are more likely to retaliate. The other situation where there is likely to be competitive devaluation is where two countries are economically highly interlinked. Denmark, for example, has its own currency but this is pegged to the euro. The eurozone is by far Denmark's largest export market. So when the euro falls in value, the Danish central bank will ensure that the Danish currency, the krone, falls by an equal amount. Effectively, Denmark is engaging in a policy of competitive devaluation with the eurozone.

Inflation, growth and unemployment

Changes in exchange rates can affect the performance of an economy.

Inflation A rise in the exchange rate is likely to moderate inflation for two reasons. First, a higher exchange rate will tend to lead to a fall in import prices, which then feeds through to lower domestic prices. As explained above, some importers will choose to keep their foreign currency prices the same in order to increase their profit margins. However, other importers will cut their foreign currency prices. The extent to which a rise in the exchange rate leads to a fall in domestic prices depends upon what proportion of importers choose to cut prices.

Second, a higher exchange rate will lead to a fall in aggregate demand. Exports will fall and imports will rise as explained above. The fall in aggregate demand then leads to a fall in inflation. The extent to which aggregate demand falls depends upon the price elasticity of demand for exports and imports. The higher the price elasticities, the greater will be the change in export and import volumes to changes in prices brought about by the exchange rate movement.

The reverse occurs when there is a depreciation of the exchange rate. Import prices will tend to rise, feeding through to higher domestic inflation. Aggregate demand will rise as exports become more price competitive and imports less price competitive. As a result, inflation will tend to increase.

Question 2

Switzerland has abandoned its three-year-old currency ceiling against the euro. The currency ceiling was designed to prevent an appreciation of the Swiss franc. Following the announcement by the Switzerland's central bank, the value of the Swiss franc against the euro soared by as much as 39 per cent before settling down at the end of trading to an appreciation of 13.8 per cent against the euro.

The rise in the value of the Swiss franc has important implications for Swiss companies. Economists said that Switzerland's economy was well diversified, both in terms of what it makes – with products ranging from pharmaceuticals and food to watches and machinery – and its export markets. However, some sectors are likely to be hit harder by the rise in the value of the currency than others, including the tourism industry which can do little to offset a strong Swiss franc. Machine makers will also be hit, according to Rudolf Minsch, chief economist at Economiesuisse, the Swiss business lobby. 'Switzerland's machinery industry sends a higher share of its exports to Europe than the pharmaceutical or watch industries, for example, so they will feel this much more than other more globally orientated companies,' he said. The impact on companies would also depend on the nature of the markets in which they operate, François Savary, an economist at Bank Reyl in Geneva, said. 'Swiss exporters have had a blow of about 10-12 per cent to their relative competitiveness. If they are in niche markets, without much competition, maybe they won't be too affected. But if they are a big player competing in global markets, this is going to hurt', he said. François Savary also said that if the appreciation settled down to around 10 per cent, then this was 'probably supportable'. If it were 20 or 30 per cent, then it would be 'very difficult indeed'.

Source: adapted from © the *Financial Times* 16.1.2015, All Rights Reserved.

(a) Explain why Swiss exporters in general would be affected by a rise in the value of the Swiss franc against the euro.

(b) Some Swiss companies are able to 'offset' possible rises in the price of their exports because they import a significant part of the final value of the goods they produce. Why are they less likely to be affected by the rise in the value Swiss franc than, say, firms in the tourism industry that 'can do little to offset a strong Swiss franc'?

(c) Explain why exporting firms 'in niche markets without much competition' will be affected less than other exporting firms.

(d) Why does the size of the appreciation matter for Swiss exports and imports?

Economic growth A change in the exchange rate may have an impact on long-term growth rates. A higher exchange rate which discourages exports and encourages imports may lead to lower domestic investment, and vice versa for a lower exchange rate. However, the main impact of a changing exchange rate will be felt on short-run output. A rise in the exchange rate will dampen output in the short term because exports fall and imports rise, leading to a fall in aggregate demand. A fall in the exchange rate will lead to rising exports and falling imports, raising aggregate demand and thus equilibrium output.

Unemployment A rise in the exchange rate will tend to increase unemployment. This is because an exchange rate rise will tend to lower aggregate demand and thus equilibrium output. A fall in the exchange rate will tend to reduce unemployment. Changes in unemployment will be felt unequally in different sectors of the economy. In those industries which export a significant proportion of output, or where imports are important, there will tend to be larger changes in employment

and unemployment as a result of exchange rate changes. In industries, particularly some service industries, where little is exported or imported, changes in the exchange rate will have little effect on employment and unemployment.

Foreign direct investment

A fall in the value of a currency, such as the pound, may lead to an increase in foreign direct investment (FDI). For an example, a US company may be considering a takeover of a UK company for £100 million. If the exchange rate is £1 = $2.00, then the cost to the US company is $200 million. Now assume there is a fall in the value of the pound so that £1 = $1. The takeover will now only cost the US company $100 million. So a fall in the value of the exchange rate should lead to an increase in FDI from abroad.

However, this may not occur if the value of a currency is continually falling. If the US company has bought the UK company for $100 million at an exchange rate of £1 = $1, it now has an investment worth £100 million. If the exchange rate falls to £1 = $0.50, that investment is now worth only $50 million all other things being equal. A fast falling exchange rate is an indication that an economy has serious economic difficulties. This is likely to discourage FDI.

Question 3

The pound, on a trade-weighted basis, appreciated by 10 per cent last year. However, its rise doesn't seem to be troubling the government or the Bank of England. Neville Hill, an economist at Credit Suisse, is among those arguing that a short-term rise in sterling might do more good than harm. It would bring down inflation and boost household's purchasing power. As for exports, changes in UK manufacturing with supply chains, offshoring of production and a shift to higher-tech products 'makes the impact of exchange rate movements on 'competitiveness' more ambiguous in the short run' he says. However, whilst the short-run impact might not harm the current account position too much, in the long run there could be a significant deterioration in the already large current account deficit.

Source: adapted from © the *Financial Times* 22.4.2014, All Rights Reserved.

(a) Explain how an appreciation in the value of the pound might
   (i) 'bring down inflation and boost household's purchasing power' and (ii) have little effect on the competitiveness of UK exports.

(b) Why might the appreciation in the value of the pound have a different impact in the short run than in the long run?

Key Terms

J curve effect - in the short term, a devaluation is likely to lead to a deterioration in the current account position before it starts to improve.
Marshall-Lerner condition - devaluation will lead to an improvement in the current account so long as the combined price elasticities of exports and imports are greater than 1.

Thinking like an economist

A missing J curve?

In the early 1990s, Japan suffered a financial crisis very similar to the one experienced by Europe and the USA in 2007-08. Following the crisis, Japan slipped in and out of recession. Economic growth was low whilst there were periodic bouts of falling prices. In 2012, the country elected a new prime minister, Shinzo Abe, who was committed to revitalising the economy. He wanted higher consistent economic growth and a return to mild inflation.

Part of his strategy for achieving this was a devaluation of the Japanese yen. In late 2012, foreign exchange markets pushed the value of the yen sharply downwards. They realised that the Bank of Japan would pursue more aggressive quantitative easing policies and would use its gold and foreign currency reserves to take the yen lower. So expectations of government intervention led the foreign exchange markets to push the yen downwards.

The depreciation in the yen made imports more expensive. The trade balance (exports of goods and services minus imports of goods and services), which was already in deficit,

deteriorated further. This is what the J curve would suggest. As Figure 2 shows, in the first half of 2013, the value of Japanese imports rose as importers had to pay higher prices in yen but were committed to buying goods and services they had ordered before the depreciation. However, what should then have happened is that imports should have fallen. But they failed to do so. One economist close to the Japanese government said 'There has been no J curve'.

One possible explanation for the absence of a J curve effect lies with the 2011 Fukushima nuclear disaster. In 2011, a tsunami seriously damaged the Fukushima nuclear power plant. Japan was heavily reliant on nuclear energy. Worries over the safety of Japan's many nuclear power stations led to them all being shut down. Japan then had to increase significantly imports of oil and gas. These had very low price elasticities of demand. So when the yen depreciated in 2012-13, Japan continued to buy oil and gas in almost the same quantities.

Another possible explanation lies with sales tax. The Japanese government has run a significant fiscal deficit over the past 20 years, attempting to stimulate the economy through Keynesian demand management techniques. It has run up the largest National Debt amongst developed countries. In 2014, according to the OECD, its National Debt as a percentage of GDP was 230 per cent. Compare that to Greece with 182 per cent and Germany with 79 per cent. It had no problem financing its debt because interest rates were virtually zero. Its debt repayments were 1.1 per cent of GDP compared to 4.2 per cent for Greece and 1.3 per cent for Germany. However, Shinzo Abe argued, probably correctly, that further growth in the National Debt increased future risk for the Japanese economy. Part of his plans was for sales tax (the equivalent of VAT) to rise from five to eight per cent to cut the fiscal deficit. Knowing that sales tax would rise in 2014, Japanese consumers brought forward spending into 2013 to avoid paying the higher tax. Higher spending meant higher imports, preventing an improvement in the current account.

A third explanation lies in off-shoring. Japanese multinational companies such as Sony and Toyota have moved significant amounts of manufacturing capability to other countries. They have wanted to take advantage of much cheaper labour costs in countries like China. They have also wanted to move production to where the sites occur. Toyota moving production of cars to the UK, for example, means there is far less risk to profits from changes in the exchange rate on cars that will be sold in the UK. But this limits the ability of Japanese exports to rise when a depreciation of the yen makes them more price competitive. It also makes Japan more dependent on imports of these goods.

So there may be a full J curve effect but the upturn may simply have been delayed. Naohiko Baba, chief Japan economist at Goldman Sachs, for example, expects 'a gradual improvement (in the trade balance) over time in line with the J curve effect. However, he also thinks there may have been a structural change to imports as Japanese buy not only more oil, gas and other products that have historically been bought from abroad but also goods such as electronics that used to be manufactured in Japan.

Figure 2

Japanese trade, rolling three-month sum, yen trillion

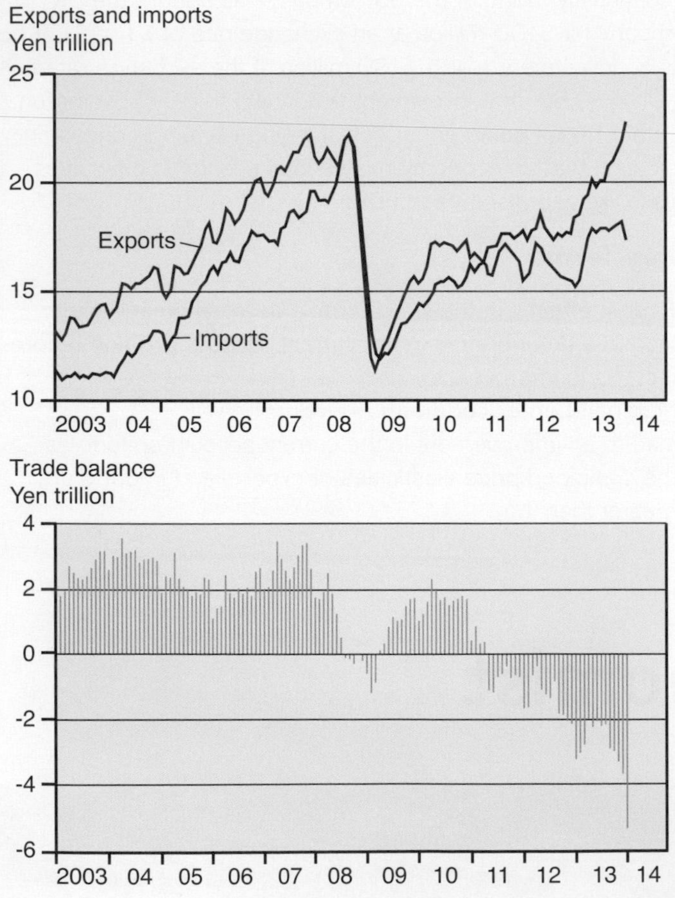

Source: adapted from Thomson Reuters Datastream; © the *Financial Times* 21.2.2014, All Rights Reserved.

Source: with information from © the *Financial Times* 21.2.2014, All Rights Reserved; www.oecd.org

Data Response Question

Appreciation of the pound, 1996-2001

The value of exports and imports, measured in £s, is the volume of exports and imports times their average price. In the data here, volume and price are measured as index numbers.

Between 1996 and 2000, there was a sharp appreciation in the value of the pound which affected both exports and imports. Two other factors also affected exports and imports at the time. One was the above trend rate of growth in GDP. The other was a fall in average world prices for traded goods, the result of increasing globalisation.

Figure 3

Exchange rate value of the pound: effective exchange rate, euro and dollar

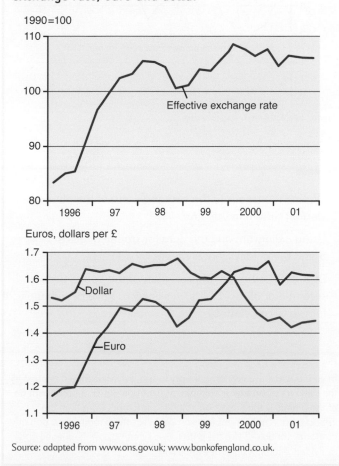

Source: adapted from www.ons.gov.uk; www.bankofengland.co.uk.

Figure 4

Balance of payments: balance of trade in goods, balance in traded services and current balance, £ billion

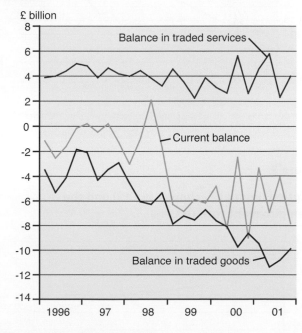

Source: adapted from www.ons.gov.uk.

Figure 5

Exports of traded goods by value (£ billion), volume (2002=100) and price (2002=100)

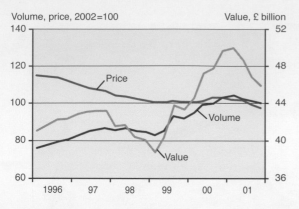

Source: adapted from www.ons.gov.uk

Figure 6

Imports of traded goods by value (£ billion), volume (2002=100) and price (2002=100)

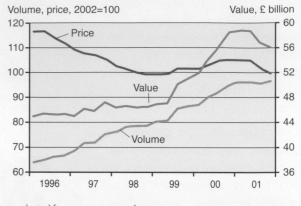

Source: adapted from www.ons.gov.uk.

Figure 7

Value of exports and imports of traded services (£ billion)

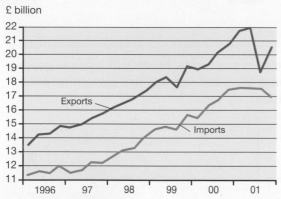

Source: adapted from www.ons.gov.uk.

1. Traded services do not include primary or secondary income, the other components of 'invisibles' on the current account.

Figure 8

Percentage growth in real GDP (year on year)

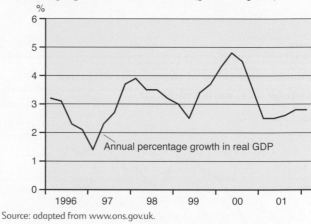

Source: adapted from www.ons.gov.uk.

Figure 9

Inflation (annual % change in CPI) and the unemployment rate (ILO %)

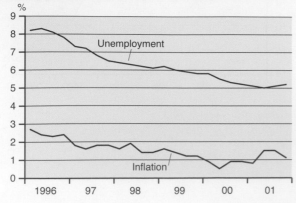

Source: adapted from www.ons.gov.uk.

Q

1. Outline the trends in the exchange rate of the pound sterling shown in the data.

2. Using a diagram and the data for traded goods in Figures 5 and 6, explain what is meant by a J curve.

3. Discuss whether the appreciation of the pound in the second half of the 1990s was likely to have been beneficial for the UK economy.

Evaluation

In your answer, use economic theory to suggest what should happen to the main macroeconomic variables following a significant appreciation of the pound. Is the impact on inflation more important than the impact on unemployment for example? Was there much impact on any economic variables? Use the data to see what actually happened and as evidence to back up your evaluation.

Key points

1. There is a number of different measures of international competitiveness, including relative unit labour costs and relative export prices.
2. Factors influencing competitiveness include the exchange rate, productivity, wage and non-wage costs, regulation, product quality and research and development.
3. The benefits of international competitiveness include higher economic growth, a better current account position on the balance of payments, higher employment and higher domestic purchasing power.
4. Countries over time can lose their international competitiveness if their costs rise too fast, their exchange rate rises or other countries impose protectionist barriers to their exports.
5. Government policies that can increase international competitiveness include supply-side policies, exchange rate policies and ensuring macroeconomic stability.

Starter activity

A UK firm manufactures clothing and sells to UK customers and to customers abroad. Make a list of eight factors that could make it more internationally competitive. Which one of these do you think is the most important and why?

Competitiveness

Many UK based firms compete in global markets. It could be a small UK firm exporting foundry products. Or it could be a UK factory of a Japanese multinational exporting motor vehicles. Or it could be a bed and breakfast in Edinburgh serving customers from the United States. Equally, many UK firms are affected by global markets. Much of UK manufacturing has disappeared over the past 40 years because it could not compete with imports from countries with much cheaper labour. Equally, the UK tourist trade has suffered because more UK citizens have chosen to take holidays abroad rather than holiday in the UK.

The competitiveness of individual firms and industries therefore changes over time. Competitiveness can be used in the context of national economies. For example, it could be argued that the Chinese economy is more internationally competitive than the Indian economy. In this unit, we will consider how competitiveness can be measured, what influences competitiveness and what policies the government can use to improve competitiveness.

Measures of competitiveness

There is a number of measures of international competitiveness which include the following.

Relative unit labour costs Unit labour costs are total wages divided by real output. It is the cost of employing labour divided by the amount labour produces. For example, if a firm employs 100 workers at £1 000 each, its total wage bill would be £100 000. If these workers produced 50 000 units of output, unit labour costs are £2 per unit. Unit labour costs for an economy are measured in index number form with one year chosen as a base year equal to 100. UK relative unit labour costs are unit labour costs compared to other countries. A rise in UK relative unit labour costs shows that labour costs per unit of output are rising faster in the UK than in other countries. Or

alternatively, UK unit labour costs are falling less fast than in other countries. Hence, a rise in UK relative unit labour costs shows that the UK is becoming less competitive. A fall in UK relative unit labour costs shows that the UK is becoming more competitive.

Relative export prices Relative export prices are the export prices of UK goods compared to the export prices of the UK's main trading partners, expressed as an index. A rise in relative export prices means that export prices of UK goods have risen faster or fallen less than those of the UK's main trading partners. Therefore a rise in relative export prices shows that there has been a fall in the UK international competitiveness. Conversely, a fall in relative export prices shows that there has been a rise in UK international competitiveness.

Export prices compared to import prices If UK export prices are rising significantly faster than UK import prices, the country is likely to be losing international competitiveness. Conversely, if UK import prices are rising significantly faster than UK export prices, there is a rise in international competitiveness. Export prices and import prices can change significantly if there are changes in the world price of commodities. For example, a large fall in the price of oil will lower average UK import prices but also lower average UK export prices because the UK exports some North Sea oil. A large fall in the value of the pound could lead to a large rise in UK import prices, whilst leaving export prices the same. However, there is an alternative scenario that reflects recent UK experience. A large fall in the value of the pound leads to importers, on average, cutting the prices they receive in their foreign currencies in order to keep the UK pound sterling price the same. This means they earn lower profits, but maintain their market share. UK exporters respond by raising the pound sterling price of their goods the same and keeping the foreign currency price the same. The result is no increase in quantity sold, but an increase in profit margins. If this happens, a large fall in the value of the pound will tend simply to increase both export and import prices by roughly the same amount, leaving price competitiveness unchanged.

Factors influencing competitiveness

There is a number of factors which affect international competitiveness which include the following.

Question 1

Figure 1

UK relative unit labour costs (manufacturing), 2010=100; sterling effective exchange rate, January 2005=100

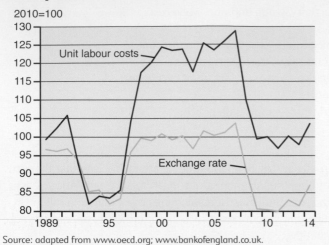

Source: adapted from www.oecd.org; www.bankofengland.co.uk.

(a) During which two periods did UK's relative unit labour costs most improve?

(b) Explain why there might be a link between UK relative unit labour costs and the sterling effective exchange rate.

Exchange rates The exchange rate affects the price at which products are bought and sold internationally. As explained in Units 38 and 70, a rise in the UK's exchange rates is likely to make UK goods less price competitive abroad and imports more competitive in UK markets. A fall in the UK's exchange rates is likely to make UK goods more price competitive abroad and imports into the UK less competitive. The extent to which there is a change in competitiveness depends in part on the price elasticity of demand for a good. The lower the price elasticity of demand, the less impact a change in price caused by a change in the exchange rate will have on quantity demanded. Also, the way in which firms respond to a change in the exchange rate will affect competitiveness. For example, if export firms respond by keeping foreign currency prices the same, there will be no change in price competitiveness, although there could be long run effects due to changes in profits and the impact this has on investment.

Productivity Rises in the UK's productivity relative to its main trading partners will increase the UK's competitiveness. For example, if a UK export firm is able to produce 20 per cent more goods with the same amount of labour, then labour productivity will have risen. This is likely to lead to the firm cutting its prices, making its goods more internationally price competitive if foreign firms have not achieved this rise in productivity. However, if foreign firms at the same time have increased their production by 30 per cent with the same amount of labour, the UK firm's relative productivity will have fallen, making it less competitive. This assumes that all other factors such as wage costs remain the same.

Wage and non-wage costs If UK wage and non-wage costs, such as company pensions or taxes on employment of workers, rise relative to its main trading partners, then the UK will become less internationally competitive. Increases in wage costs are likely to lead to increases in prices. So a 10 per cent rise in wages in the UK is likely to lead to some rise in export prices. The extent of the rise will depend on factors such as increases in labour productivity and whether firms are prepared to change their profit margins.

Regulation Increases in regulation of industry tend to increase costs of production for firms. For example, UK firms tend to have lower costs than firms in France and Germany because regulation is lighter in the UK. Hence, less regulation is likely to increase international competitiveness.

Quality Prices and costs are only one factor determining demand and supply. Quality of products is also an important determinant. Firms which produce better-quality products than their international rivals will have a competitive advantage. Much of the UK's manufacturing sector in recent years has only survived because it has avoided price competition with cheap labour countries and produced unique better-quality products.

Research and development Research and development influences the uniqueness of a product. The extent to which firms engage in research and development may influence their long-term international competitiveness. For example, in industries such as the aerospace and pharmaceuticals industry, R&D determines whether a firm will have unique products to sell in five, 10 and 20 years' time in international markets. R&D may also help to reduce costs of production if it leads to new labour and capital-saving equipment being introduced.

Taxation Firms argue that levels of company taxation are important to international competitiveness. Low taxes on profit encourage investment and innovation, which lead to improved international competitiveness. High taxes on profits lead to deteriorating international competitiveness.

Benefits of being internationally competitive

International competition produces winners and losers amongst firms, industries and countries. The winners are likely to be those that are most efficient. Either their costs of production are lower (productive efficiency) or they are producing goods that are more attractive to buy. For example, they may be better quality, better designed or incorporate the most recent technologies (allocative and dynamic efficiencies). This greater efficiency then creates a variety of benefits for the economy.

Current account surpluses Countries which are internationally competitive are likely to run current account surpluses on the balance of payments. This is because exports are likely to be larger than imports. A surplus frees them from the constraints that a country running a very large deficit may face.

International investment A current account surplus gives the country the opportunity to invest overseas and build up a surplus of assets overseas on which interest, profit and dividends can be earned. A competitive economy is also likely to attract inflows of foreign investment. Foreign companies might want to set up factories and offices in the country either to sell into the domestic market or use as an export base. Equally, foreign companies might want to buy domestic firms to exploit their competitiveness. Whichever option is chosen, there is likely to be a transfer of knowledge, skills and technology to domestic firms increasing their competitiveness.

Employment Being internationally competitive implies that exports are likely to be high in relation to imports. This creates jobs in the domestic economy and reduces any unemployment that might be present.

Economic growth Greater efficiency is likely to lead to higher economic growth. Greater demand for exports will lead to higher investment and will contribute to higher aggregate demand and long-run aggregate supply.

Wage growth For developing countries, a major source of their international competitiveness might be low wages which allow for low costs of production. Being internationally competitive should lead to higher exports and greater demand for workers. As a result, wage rates are likely to rise, benefiting workers.

Higher domestic purchasing power Consumers in the economy are likely to benefit. First, their incomes are likely to rise faster because of higher economic growth. Second, they will be able to buy goods and services that are lower in price and more attractive to buy than if the country were less internationally competitive.

Problems of sustaining international competitiveness

The problem with being internationally competitive is that this competitiveness can be lost.

- For low and middle-income countries, the competitive benefit of low wage costs are likely to be eroded as the country becomes more developed and wage rates rise at a relatively high rate.
- Other costs, such as the price of land or the materials bought from other domestic firms, are likely to rise as a country becomes more developed. Again this could erode international price competitiveness.
- A current account surplus could lead to a rise in the exchange rate, making exports more expensive to foreign buyers and imports cheaper for domestic buyers. This erodes competitive advantage.
- Less competitive foreign countries may impose trade barriers to protect their own less competitive industries. This will erode a country's competitive advantage.

However, international competitiveness is not inevitably lost as a country becomes more developed. Germany and Singapore are two examples of highly competitive economies that have retained their competitiveness over a long period of time.

Question 2

Figure 2

UK indices of export and import prices, 2011=100

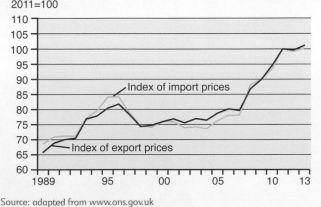

Source: adapted from www.ons.gov.uk

(a) To what extent does Figure 2 suggest that UK export and import prices change at different rates over time?

(b) Suggest why changes in export and import prices might be highly correlated for the UK.

Question 3

Figure 3

Index of GDP per hour worked, 2005=100

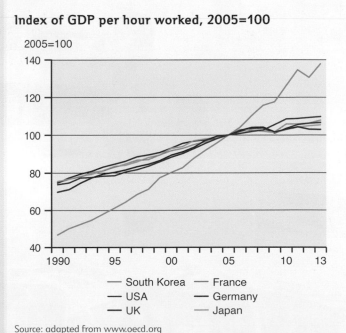

Source: adapted from www.oecd.org

(a) Which country had the highest growth in labour productivity over the period shown in Figure 3?

(b) Suggest and explain two reasons why rich developed countries like the USA, the UK and Germany find it difficult to increase their labour productivity at a significantly faster rate than each other when poorer developing countries like South Korea can see significant increases in productivity.

443

Government policy

Governments have a variety of policies which they can use to influence the international competitiveness of its firms.

Supply side policies Supply-side policies will increase international competitiveness. For example, improvements in education and training will in the long term lead to higher labour productivity. Tax incentives on investment will lead to more capital intensive production, which should reduce costs. Deregulation should lead to increased competition and lower costs.

Exchange rate policies The UK government through the Bank of England does not manipulate the exchange rate to influence international competitiveness. However, many countries do intervene in foreign currency markets to aid exporters. The

most important example in the recent past has been China where its central bank deliberately kept the Chinese currency, the renminbi, at an artificially low value to increase the export competitiveness of Chinese industry.

Control of inflation and macroeconomic stability
Countries which fail to control inflation tend to lose international competitiveness. High inflation leads to rising export prices. It also leads to further inflation as workers demand high wage increases to compensate them for their loss of earning power. Control of inflation is part of the broader issue of macroeconomic management. A stable macroeconomic environment encourages firms to invest and innovate, which will help export performance.

Thinking like an economist

Finland

Finland is a prosperous Nordic country. In 2013, its GNP per capita at PPPs was $39 860, five per cent higher than that of the UK at $37 970. However, in 2015 it was facing a crisis of competitiveness. In 2007-08, its economy suffered the effects of the world financial crisis and went into recession. It quickly

staged a recovery starting in 2009, but then in 2012 slipped back into recession.

It faces a number of major competitiveness problems. The first has been the growth of unit labour costs shown in Figure 4. From 2010, unit labour costs in Finland have been

rising at a much faster rate than its main trading partner, the rest of the eurozone. In 2015, labour costs were the same as in France, 20 per cent more than Germany and 15 per cent more than Sweden. To regain labour competitiveness, Finnish workers will either have to accept real wage cuts or taxes paid by firms on employing labour will have to fall.

Cutting taxes on employing staff faces a major obstacle. The 2007-08 financial crisis and the current recession have hit government finances. In 2014, Finland's government budget deficit was 3.4 per cent of GDP, above the three per cent allowed by the eurozone authorities. Finland's National Debt in 2015 was also forecast to pass the 60 per cent of GDP level fixed as the limit within the eurozone. So the government has limited room to cut taxes or boost government spending either to improve competitiveness or increase aggregate demand.

Workers themselves have become less productive. Between 2007 and 2014, labour productivity fell 4.4 per cent. It also fell relative to eurozone countries and to the USA. Figure 5 shows the difference between productivity changes in the eurozone and the USA and Finland. In most years this was negative, showing that Finland was becoming less competitive.

Productivity levels have almost certainly been hit by problems at Nokia. At its height, Nokia provided nearly a quarter of corporate tax in income in 2003 and half of Finland's growth in GDP in 2000. In 2007, Nokia was the world's largest mobile phone handset designer and manufacturer. However, it failed to innovate quickly enough to combat the growth of smartphones produced by competitors. In 2013, the company was sold to Microsoft, the US company. At its peak, Nokia employed more than 130 000 workers in Finland. By 2015, it only employed around 60 000. There have been some benefits from Nokia's

demise. It has released a large number of talented workers who have gone on to create their own companies. This has led to innovation and alternative sources of income for the Finnish economy. However, Finland would almost certainly have been better off today if Nokia had remained the world's number one seller of mobile phones.

Before the creation of the euro, a quick and easy solution to Finland's competitiveness problems would have been for Finland to devalue its currency. Rising import prices would have hit living standards in Finland, but exports would have been more price competitive. Within the eurozone, Finland cannot resort to this strategy.

Exactly how else Finland will deal with this crisis is difficult to foresee. However, there must be some element of improving relative unit labour costs. The Finnish public sector as a proportion of GDP is one of the world's largest at 58 per cent. Cutting public spending and using the proceeds to cut taxes on firms might lead to an improvement. Cutting public spending by increasing unemployment might also put downward pressure on wages. However, both measures would imply a cut in Finnish living standards. Increasing competitiveness through increased innovation would be beneficial, but there is no guarantee that Finland will be relatively more innovative over the next 5-10 years than its main international competitors. In short, in 2015, there were no easy solutions to Finland's deterioration in international competitiveness.

Source: with information from © the *Financial Times* 15.3.2014, All Rights Reserved; data.worldbank.org; www.oecd.org.

Figure 4

Unit labour costs (Q1 2007=100)

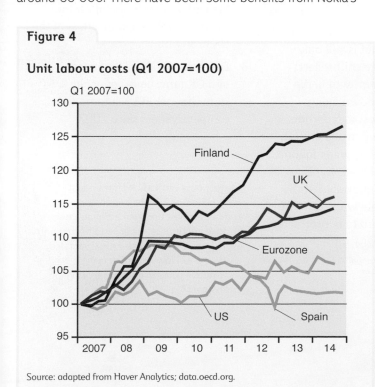

Source: adapted from Haver Analytics; data.oecd.org.

Figure 5

Relative change in labour productivity: Finland compared to the eurozone and the USA[1]

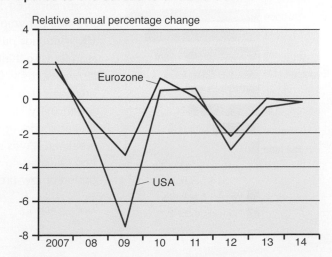

Source: adapted from www.oecd.org.

1. Lines show the annual change in labour productivity for Finland minus that for the eurozone and minus that for the US. For example, productivity growth in Finland in 2014 was +0.2% and in the eurozone was +0.4%. So the relative growth in Finland compared to the eurozone was 0.2% minus 0.4% or -0.2%.

Data Response Question

Hourly labour costs in the UK

It is now on average cheaper to hire a worker in the UK than in Spain. The average hourly cost of employing someone last year in the UK was €20.90 compared to €21.10 in Spain according to data from Eurostat, the statistical office of the EU. Both countries' labour costs were lower than the EU average of 23.70 and far below those of Germany, France, Italy and the Netherlands.

'I think this is part of the story of very strong job growth in the UK', said Michael Saunders, a Citi economist. 'The UK by western European standards is a relatively low cost country.'

The UK's average hourly labour costs in euros barely changed between 2008 and 2013, while the EU's climbed 10.2 per cent and Spain's rose 8.7 per cent. As well as wages and

bonuses, the figures include non-wage costs such as employers' social contributions, which are also lower in the UK.

Britain's divergence from its neighbours is the result of a fall in the value of sterling during the financial crisis from almost €1.50 in 2007 to less than €1.10 in 2009. Sterling has risen since then, particularly this year, but is still only worth about €1.25. The shift reflects five years of weak pay growth in the UK which has pushed down living standards to their lowest in a decade. However, the UK's weak wage growth has been accompanied by weak labour productivity. Ben Broadbent, the Bank of England's deputy governor, said at the weekend it was possible wage growth had adjusted downward to a 'protracted period of low productivity growth.'

Figure 6

EU labour costs, € per hour, 2013

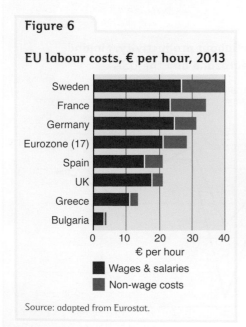

Source: adapted from Eurostat.

Q

1. Explain why, in 2013, the UK had lower labour costs than Spain despite having higher average wages and salaries.

2. Analyse how both labour costs and the exchange rate can affect the international competitiveness of the UK economy.

3. Evaluate whether UK workers and UK firms have benefited from changes in UK international competitiveness since 2007.

Evaluation

Identify how workers and firms might have gained or lost out by trends in competitiveness and then evaluate their relative importance. What extra information would you need to make a more rounded assessment? How important is the information you don't have to making the assessment?

Key points

1. In a market economy, there is a variety of reasons why the income and wealth of individuals and households differ, including differences in wages, economic activity and access to pensions.
2. A Lorenz curve and Gini coefficient can be used to show the degree of inequality in income in society.
3. Poverty can be characterised as either absolute poverty or relative poverty.
4. Equity or fairness can be either horizontal equity or vertical equity.

Starter activity

Joshua is 27 and works 25 hours a week on a minimum wage job. Is he poor? In the UK, are you poor if you cannot afford to rent a place of your own but have to live with your parents? Or go on holiday? Or afford a mobile phone? In Pakistan, are you poor if you cannot eat every day? Or afford to send you child to school? Or own a mobile phone?

Resource allocation, equality and equity

The chairperson of a large company may earn hundreds of millions of pounds per year. A pensioner might exist on a few thousand pounds per year. This distribution of income in the economy is the result of the complex interaction between the workings of the market and government intervention in the market. Markets are impersonal. They produce a particular allocation of resources which may or may not be efficient but is almost certainly not equal. In this unit, we will consider how the market allocates resources and then consider how the market may be judged on grounds of equality and equity (or fairness) in rich developed countries like the UK. Inequality and poverty in developing countries will be considered in Units 74-76.

The distribution of resources in a capitalist market economy

Individuals receive different incomes in a market economy. This is because it is based on the ownership of property. Individuals, for instance, are not slaves. They are able to hire themselves out to producers and earn income. They might own shares in a company and receive dividends, a share of the profits. They might own a house from which they receive rent. How much they receive depends upon the forces of demand and supply.

Workers with scarce skills in high demand, such as chairpersons of companies, can receive large salaries. Workers with few skills and in competition with a large number of other unskilled workers are likely to receive low wages. Workers who fail to find a job will receive no wage income through the market mechanism. These workers might be highly capable and choose not to take a job. On the other hand, they might be disabled or live in a very high unemployment region. Similarly, the market decides upon the value of physical assets and the income that can be earned from them through the market mechanism. If an individual inherits a house, all other things being equal, the house will be worth more if it is in central London than if it is in Doncaster. The rent on the house will be higher in central

London. Shares in one company will be differently priced from shares in another company, and the dividends will be different.

The owners of assets which have a high value are likely to earn a high income. The human capital of the chairperson of Barclays Bank is likely to be very high and therefore he or she will be able to command a high salary. The Duke of Westminster, the largest individual landowner in London, owns large amounts of physical capital. This too generates large incomes. Some individuals own large amounts of financial capital, such as stocks and shares. Again, they will receive a far larger income than the majority of the population, who own little or no financial capital.

In a pure free market economy, where the government plays only a small role in providing services, such as defence, those with no wealth would die unless they could persuade other individuals to help them. Usually, non-workers are supported by others in the family. In many societies, the family network provides the social security net. Charities too may play a small role.

In the UK, the government has made some provision for the poor since medieval times. In Victorian England, the destitute were sent to workhouses where conditions were made so unpleasant that it was meant to encourage people to work to stay out of these institutions. Since 1945, a welfare state has been created which goes some way towards altering the distribution of income to ensure greater equality. In other words, government has decided that the market mechanism produces an allocation of resources which is sub-optimal from an equality viewpoint and attempts to correct this situation.

Causes of inequality in income

There is a number of reasons why the **personal distribution of income** is unequal in a market economy.

Earned income Some workers earn more than others. The amount earned per month or per year or over a lifetime depends on a wide variety of factors. Educational attainment is one determinant for example. Those with a university degree on average earn more than those with lesser qualifications. Another determinant is the number of hours worked. A full-time worker on average earns more than a part-time worker.

Non-workers Not all people work. Non-workers are likely to receive lower incomes than those in work. For example, pensioners tend to receive lower incomes than workers. Parents who stay at home full time to look after their children will earn less than if they went out to work.

Physical and financial wealth Those in society who

own a great deal of physical or financial wealth will be able to generate a higher income from their assets than those who own little or nothing.

Household composition How income is measured can be important in determining inequalities. An individual may earn a high salary. However, if he or she has to support a large family, then the income per person in the household may be quite low. On the other hand, a household where there are two parent wage earners and four child wage earners may have a high income despite the fact that all six adults are individually 'low paid'. So inequalities differ according to whether they are being measured per individual or per household.

Government policy The extent to which government redistributes income through taxes and benefits will affect the distribution of income.

The degree of competition in product markets
Imperfectly competitive markets will result in a different distribution of income and wealth than perfectly competitive markets. Consider Figure 1. It shows the cost and revenue curves for an industry. If the industry were perfectly competitive, production would take place where price = MC at output level OB. If the industry now became a multi-plant monopolist, output would be at OA where MC = MR. EFG is the allocative loss to society. It is sometimes called a deadweight loss because the loss is not recoverable. However, there is also a transfer of income from consumers to the monopoly producer represented by the rectangle CDEF.

Figure 1

Allocative and distributive effects of monopoly

If the industry is perfectly competitive, it will produce at OB where price = MC. If it were a multi-plant monopolist, it would produce at OA where MC = MR. EFG is the deadweight allocative loss to society. CDEF is the total 'tax' of the monopolist on the consumer. It results in a redistribution of income from consumer to shareholder.

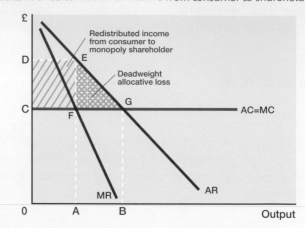

Causes of inequality in wealth for individuals

Wealth for an individual can take a number of forms.
- Property wealth is the value of houses together with any commercial property that an individual might own, such as farming land and commercial buildings.

Question 1

Figure 2

How sources of household gross income have changed, UK

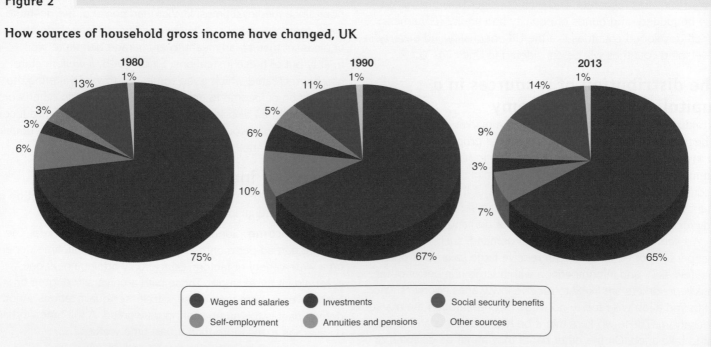

Source: adapted from *Family Spending*, Office for National Statistics.

(a) How have the sources of income for UK households changed between 1980 and 2013?

(b) Inequalities have increased over the 33 year period. Using the data, suggest why this has occurred.

- Physical wealth is the value of physical valuables apart from property. This includes personal property, such as antiques and furniture, as well as cars.
- Financial wealth is the value of monetary assets. These include personal savings, such as money saved in the bank or building society, and stocks and shares.
- Private pension wealth is locked up in pension funds. These could be pension funds linked to an occupation, like teachers' pensions or doctors' pensions, or they could be personal pensions.

Wealth is accumulated in a number of different ways. It can be built up through saving rather than consuming out of income. Wealth can increase through an increase in assets prices, like an increase in the price of a house or an increase in share prices. Wealth can also be inherited, mainly from parents.

These different ways of accumulating wealth can explain the main causes of inequality of wealth between individuals.

Income levels The higher the level of income, the more likely it is that the individual will be able to save and accumulate physical assets. So an individual earning £100 000 a year is likely to be putting aside more money into a savings account, a pension scheme or have a mortgage on a larger house than an individual earning £30 000 a year. At the bottom end of the income scale, it is unlikely that the individual will save anything and hence will accumulate no wealth.

Wealth levels On average, those owning high levels of wealth are able to make a higher return and therefore income as a percentage of their assets than those on low incomes. For example, those owning high levels of assets are more able to take on risk than those owning few assets. Riskier assets tend to earn higher rates of return. Equally, wealthy individuals have more access to potential high return assets than poor individuals. A wealthy individual today, for example, could buy a property to let in central London with the hope that London property prices will rise faster than the rest of the UK over the next ten years. An individual with £500 in savings can't invest in property at all.

Inheritance The more an individual inherits, the higher is likely to be their own wealth. Traditionally, much of the wealth of the UK was based on land. The landed aristocracy passed down their wealth through the generations. Today, the most valuable asset an individual can on average expect to inherit is their parents' house. At a more fundamental level, social mobility in the UK today is far less than it was 50 years ago. Parents pass down levels of education, work ethics and aspirations to their children. The result is that in the UK income and wealth levels are correlated between generations.

Chance There is a certain element of chance in the accumulation of wealth. For example, the owner of a house in Chelsea will have been luckier than the owner of a house in Wolverhampton over the past 20 years because house prices in Chelsea have increased much faster than in Wolverhampton. There is an element of chance in owning stocks and shares and other forms of financial wealth. There is also an element of chance in income levels. Choice of occupation and chance associated with career progression affect earnings and hence the amount of wealth accumulated. An individual starting out as

an investment banker in 1995 on average will have earned far more by 2015 than another individual starting out as a doctor. The investment banker is therefore likely to have owned far more than the doctor in 2015.

Measuring inequality

One common way to measure inequalities in income is to use a **Lorenz curve**. On the horizontal axis in Figure 3, the cumulative number of households is plotted, whilst the vertical axis shows cumulative income. The straight 45° line shows a position of total equality. For instance, the line shows that the bottom 20 per cent of households receive 20 per cent of total income whilst the bottom 80 per cent of households receive 80 per cent of income. Hence, each one per cent of households receives one per cent of income and there is complete equality of income.

Line 1 shows an income distribution which is relatively equal. The bottom 20 per cent of households receive 10 per cent of income. This means that they receive half the average income. The top 10 per cent of households (between 90 and 100 on the horizontal axis) receive 20 per cent of income (from 80 to 100 on the vertical axis). So they receive twice the average income.

Line 2 shows a very unequal society. The bottom 50 per cent of the population receive only 10 per cent of income. Therefore half of all households receive one fifth (10 ÷ 50) of average income. The top 10 per cent of income earners, on the other hand, earn 60 per cent of all income (from 40 to 100 on the vertical axis). That means the top 10 per cent earn six times the average income.

These two examples taken together show that the further the Lorenz curve is from the 45° line, the greater the income inequality in society.

Lorenz curves can also be constructed for the distribution of wealth.

Figure 3

Lorenz curves

A Lorenz curve shows the degree of inequality of income in a society. The further the curve is from the 45° line, the greater the degree of inequality.

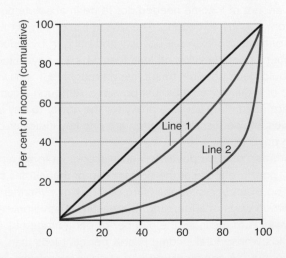

Question 2

Table 1 Distribution of disposable household income[1]

	Quintile groups of households				
	Bottom fifth	Next fifth	Middle fifth	Next fifth	Top fifth
1979	10	14	18	23	35
2002-03	7	12	17	24	40
2012-13	7	12	16	23	41

1. After direct taxes and benefits.
2. Figures may not add up due to rounding.

Source: adapted from www.ons.gov.uk; *Social Trends*, ONS.

(a) Construct three Lorenz curves from the data above.

(b) Has the distribution of income become more or less equal between 1979 and 2012-13?

One statistical measurement of the degree of inequality is the **Gini coefficient**. Mathematically, it is the ratio of the area between the 45 degree line and the Lorenz curve divided by the triangle representing the whole area under the 45 degree line. It has values between 0 and 1. The higher the Gini coefficient, the more unequal the distribution of income. If every person has equal income, the Gini coefficient is 0. There is perfect equality of income. If the Gini coefficient is 1, then one person has all the income whilst everyone else has no income. Sometimes the Gini coefficient is measured as an index out of 100. The Gini index is simply the Gini coefficient times 100.

Absolute and relative poverty

If there is inequality in society, there will inevitably be relative poverty but not necessarily any absolute poverty. **Absolute poverty** occurs when individuals are not able to consume sufficient necessities to maintain life. Individuals who are homeless or malnourished therefore suffer absolute poverty. In rich industrialised societies, levels of absolute poverty are very low because governments step in to provide resources for the poorest in society. Levels of absolute poverty tend to increase as average incomes of economies fall. So absolute poverty tends to be correlated with economic development.

The amount of income needed not to be in absolute poverty varies from country to country. The United Nations in 2015 has a target of reducing 'extreme poverty and hunger' by reducing the number of people living off less than $1.25 a day. In the UK, it would be impossible to survive on roughly £1 a day. In Tanzania or India, it would be just possible. Although income figures are used, they act as a proxy for the ability to buy basic necessities. Malnourishment figures are one key indicator of absolute poverty.

In contrast, **relative poverty** is always present in society. The relatively poor are those at the bottom end of the income scale. There is no exact accepted measure of this. However, there are two common ways of attempting to measure relative poverty.

One way is to measure the number or percentage of households whose total income is at X per cent less than median income. A commonly quoted statistic for relative

poverty used by both the UK and the EU is the number or proportion of households on less than 60 per cent of median household income and the total number of people living in those households. The argument for using this number is that households will find it difficult to participate effectively in society below this level. Exactly how income is defined, and whether it should be before or after housing costs have been taken out, are debated by economists and politicians.

Another way of defining relative poverty is to consider what necessities people might have to buy in order not to be considered poor. Adam Smith in the 18th century wrote that necessities were 'whatever the custom of the country renders it indecent for creditable people, even of the lower order, to be without'. So relative poverty existed if poor people could not afford to buy a minimum acceptable basket of goods for the society in which they live. Relative poverty therefore changes over time. 150 years ago, no one had an electric refrigerator. Today, it could be argued that not being able to afford to buy and run a refrigerator in the UK is a sign of relative poverty. 150 years ago, no one had a mobile phone. Is it a sign of relative poverty today if you cannot afford to own and run a mobile phone?

The causes of poverty

As there is no single definition of poverty, it is impossible to give a precise analysis of the causes of poverty. However, poverty tends to be associated with a number of causal factors, many of which are interlinked.

- A disproportionate number of people without jobs are in poverty. Without a job, they don't earn income and have to fall back on other means to survive. In the UK, being without a job explains why there are higher percentages of children, the elderly and women in poverty than the average.
- Lack of human capital - education and training - tends to be associated with poverty. With little human capital, workers can only sell their services in the market for low wages. There is a positive correlation both within countries and between countries of the number of years spent in education and the level of income of an individual.
- Lack of financial capital particularly hits those who are retired. Poverty amongst old people is high because they have inadequate savings to give them a pension or other income.
- Health problems affect an individual's ability to work and earn money. There could be a physical problem like Aids or a mental health problem.
- Being dependent on others for income tends to lead to poverty. For example, the percentage of children in poverty tends to be above the percentage of adults of working age in poverty. Equally, those dependent on unemployment benefits tend to be poor.
- Inheritance is very important if sometimes difficult to quantify. Those born into poor families have a disproportionate chance of being poor themselves. This is sometimes called the 'cycle of poverty'. It is true between countries. Someone born in Tanzania today is likely to remain poor for the rest of their lives compared to someone born today in the UK. Equally, it is true within countries. A child born into a low income family is likely to receive less education and to have a lower

educational achievement by the end of compulsory schooling than someone born into a middle or high-income family. They are more likely to suffer health problems. Their opportunities will be more limited.

- Between countries and regions, the amount of physical capital and intellectual capital like patents is an important determinant of poverty. You are far more likely to be living off less than $100 a year if you live in a country with relatively few paved roads, hospital buildings, airports or research facilities.

The effects of poverty

As with the causes of poverty, the effects of poverty depend upon how it is defined.

- With absolute poverty, a lack of the necessities of life, means that the effect will be ill health and possibly death.
- With relative poverty, ill health and death are still a hazard. Statistics show that those in relative poverty are more prone to ill health than the average and have a lower life expectancy. Partly this is because relative poverty can be associated with poorer housing, bad diets and in countries like the USA lack of access to health care. However, it is also the case that those with poor health tend to be relatively

Question 3

A clear link between the rapid expansion of food banks and cuts to welfare and other local services under the government has been identified in a study for the *British Medical Journal*. The number of local authorities with food banks operated by the Trussell Trust, a non-governmental body that co-ordinates food banks, jumped from 29 in 2009-10 to 251 in 2013-14.

The Conservative Prime Minister, David Cameron, has suggested that the increase in distribution of food parcels to those in need was owing to jobcentres publicising their availability to those seeking work. However, the research shows that food banks were more likely to open in areas of higher unemployment and greater welfare cuts. In a local authority that did not have government budget cuts in the previous two years, there was about a one in eight chance of a food bank opening. Where there had been spending cuts of three per cent, that chance increased to more than one in two.

Researchers also found that the number of food parcels given out was linked to the degree of local authority government cuts and the sanctions used by jobcentres and other authorities to get those without a job into work. Benefit claimants can have their benefits stopped if they fail to show that they are actively seeking work. Even minor infringements like turning up to an interview late can lead to benefits being stopped.

Source: adapted from © the *Financial Times* 24.2.2014, 16.4.2014, 9.4.2015, All Rights Reserved.

(a) Explain why food banks in the UK are helping to prevent absolute poverty.

(b) Explain why, in local authority areas where government cuts have been greater than others, there could be a greater need for individuals to resort to getting emergency food parcels from food banks.

poor. Relative poverty is associated with lack of access to physical goods and services, from cars to education to holidays. Those in relative poverty within a society can have low psychological well being. Their self-esteem can be low because they know they are poor in comparison with others. They tend to have less control of their lives. They can make fewer choices about how to organise their work if they have a job. Outside the workplace, they often can't choose where they live or how much income they receive. These factors affect the quality of life and mental well being.

Causes of changes in absolute and relative poverty

Absolute poverty tends to fall as GDP rises. In rich developed countries, there is very little absolute poverty. However, rising GDP is not in itself a guarantee of the elimination of absolute poverty. The free market might make most individuals and households better off because wages and other earnings rise. But there will also be groups who will never be able to work and earn money and who have no private sources of income. They then have to depend either on charity or on the state. For example, the elderly and those too ill to work are two vulnerable groups. The elimination of absolute poverty is then dependent on how well the state can reach those at risk and provide support. In the case of the elderly, having a well-funded state retirement pension scheme is crucial to the elimination of absolute poverty amongst this group. So too is a free health care service to prevent premature death. Provision of social housing for those too poor to afford to rent privately or own their own home is important too. To eliminate absolute poverty, the state has to work alongside the market mechanism to support vulnerable individuals and groups.

Relative poverty changes for two main reasons. First, the market mechanism may alter relative income including wages and relative wealth over time. These changes may push a larger number of individuals or households below a measure of relative poverty, such as below 60 per cent of median earnings. For example, a disproportionate growth in minimum wage jobs in the economy is likely to increase relative poverty. Second, government spending and taxation may change affecting relative incomes. Cuts in benefits combined with increases in Value Added Tax, for example, are likely to raise levels of relative poverty because they will affect those on low incomes the most. Government policy on income distribution is discussed in the next unit.

Horizontal and vertical equity

Inequalities are not necessarily unfair. For instance, assume one worker worked 60 hours per week and another, in an identical job, worked 30 hours per week. It would seem fair that the 60 hour per week worker should receive roughly twice the pay even though this would then lead to inequality in pay between the two workers. Similarly, many poor pensioners today are poor because they failed to make adequate pension provision for themselves whilst they were working. It seems only fair that a worker who has saved hard all her life through a pension scheme should enjoy a higher pension than one who has decided to spend all her money as she earned it. Nevertheless, there is an inequality in this situation. In economics, **equity** or fairness is defined in a very precise way in order to distinguish it from inequality.

Horizontal equity Horizontal equity is the identical treatment of identical individuals in identical situations. Inequitable treatment can occur in a number of different situations in our society today. An Asian applicant for a job may be turned down in preference to a white applicant even though they are the same in all other respects. A woman may apply to a bank for a business loan and be refused when a male applicant for exactly the same project may have been successful. A 55-year-old may be refused a job in preference to a 25-year-old despite identical employment characteristics. An 18-year-old may gain a place at university in preference to another solely because her father is much richer.

Vertical equity Everybody is different, from the colour of their hair to the size of their toes and from their intellectual capacities to their social background. **Vertical equity** is the different treatment of people with different characteristics in order to promote greater equity. For instance, if equity were defined in terms of equality, vertical equity would imply that everybody should have the opportunity to receive the same standard of education and the same standard of health care whatever their job, race, income or social background.

Key Terms

Absolute poverty - absolute poverty exists when individuals do not have the resources to be able to consume sufficient necessities to survive.
Equity - fairness.
Gini coefficient - a statistical measure of inequality of income. Its value ranges from 0, where there is perfect equality of income, to 1 where income is highly unequal with one person having all the income and everyone else having no income. The Gini index is the Gini coefficient times 100.
Horizontal equity - the identical treatment of identical individuals or groups in society in identical situations.
Lorenz curve - a graphical representation of the degree of income or wealth inequality in society.
Personal distribution of income - the distribution of the total income of all individuals.
Relative poverty - poverty which is defined relative to existing living standards for the average individual.
Vertical equity - the different treatment of individuals or groups which are dissimilar in characteristics.

Thinking like an economist

Trends in the distribution of income

For most of the 20th century, the long-term trend was for income differentials to narrow. High taxes and two world wars considerably reduced the wealth of the traditional land owning aristocracy whilst there was considerable upward mobility due to

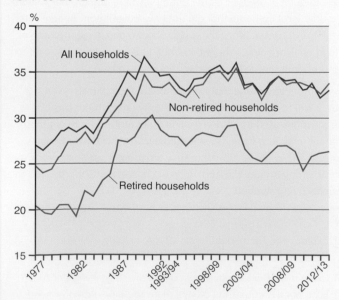

Figure 4

Index of household disposable income, 1977 to 2012-13; 1977=100

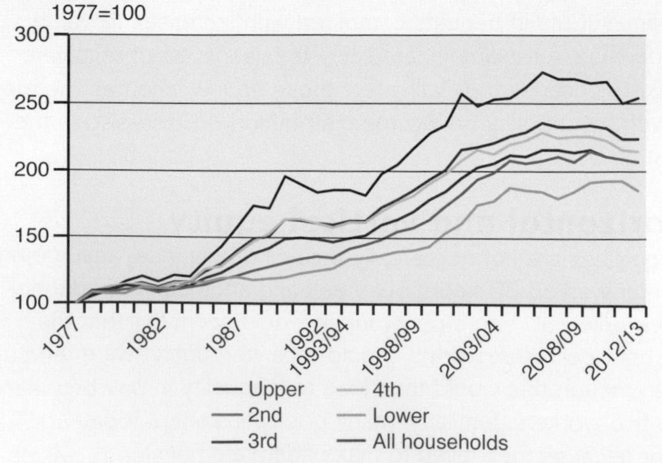

Source: adapted from ONS, *The effects of taxes and benefits on household income, 2012-13.*

Figure 5

Gini coefficients for the distribution of income, UK, 1977 to 2012-13

Source: adapted from ONS, *The effects of taxes and benefits on household income, 2012-13.*

Figure 6

Income shares of the top 10 per cent and top one per cent of workers, 1970-2011

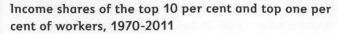
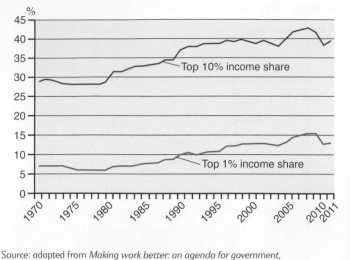

Source: adapted from *Making work better: an agenda for government,* by Ed Sweeney, The Smith Institute, 2014.

Figure 7

Aggregate total wealth, by deciles and components, Great Britain, 2010/12

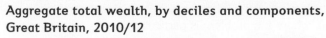
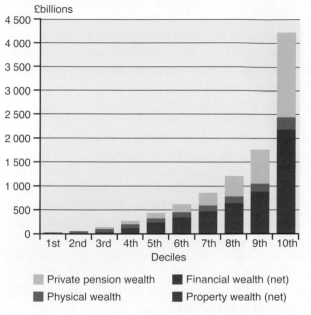

Source: adapted from ONS, *Wealth and Assets Survey.*

better education and more work opportunities.

Figure 4 shows trends in household disposable income (income after welfare benefits and direct taxes have been taken into account) for the period 1977 to 2012-13. Households have been split into quintile groups (fifths of all households) according to their disposable income. Inequalities grew sharply in the late 1980s, shown by a rise in the Gini coefficient in Figure 5. Partly this rise in inequality was due to large income tax cuts for high earners under the Prime Minister Margaret Thatcher. High unemployment and restraints on trade union power also restricted wage growth at the bottom end of the income scale. Since 1990, the distribution of disposable income between household quintiles has remained broadly the same.

Inequalities in disposable house income by quintile group might not have changed much since 1990. However, inequalities in earnings of workers have been growing over the period. Figure 6 shows the percentage share of all earnings of the top one per cent and top 10 per cent of income earners since 1970. By 2011, the top 10 per cent of income earners received nearly 40 per cent of total earnings. This means they earned nearly four times the average level of earnings. The top one per cent received 13 per cent of total earnings, meaning they earned 13 times average earnings. This was double their relative earnings in 1970.

The distribution of wealth

The distribution of wealth in the UK is far less equal than the distribution of income. Figure 7 shows the distribution of wealth for 2010-12 by decile groups for Great Britain. The top 10 per cent of households owned £4.2 trillion of assets, the single most important of which was money locked into private pension schemes. The second most important was property wealth, primarily the house in which the household lives. In contrast, the bottom 10 per cent of households owned just £3.9 billion between them. The top 10 per cent of households owned

1081 times the amount of wealth compared to the bottom 10 per cent.

Figure 8 shows Lorenz curves for total wealth and the components of wealth in Great Britain in 2010-12. Physical wealth such as furniture and cars is most equally distributed. Private pension wealth is less equally distributed.

Figure 8

Lorenz curves for wealth, Great Britain

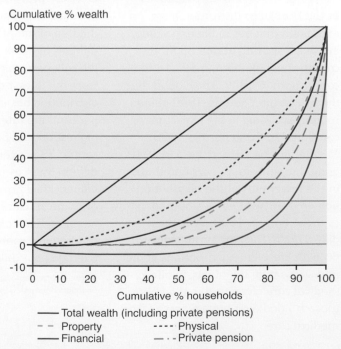

Source: adapted from ONS, *Wealth and Assets Survey.*

453

Absolute and relative poverty

Absolute poverty is rare in the UK. On possible indictor of absolute poverty is the number of people sleeping rough. In London, where the problem is particularly acute, local agencies reported 6 508 people sleeping rough at some point in 2013-14. The NHS admitted 5 500 people to hospital suffering from malnutrition in 2013 but there was no further information about causes. At least some would have been elderly people who were not able to look after themselves properly and had stopped eating properly.

However, by the very definition of the term, there is relative poverty in the UK. Figure 9 shows the percentage of different groups in relative poverty defined as at or below 60 per cent of median income. In 2012-13, for example, 21 per cent of all individuals in the UK suffered from relative poverty. For pensioners, 13 per cent of pensioners suffered from relative poverty whilst 17 per cent of children also suffered from relative poverty. Figure 9 shows that that there was a small decline in relative poverty for all individuals and children over the period 1998-99 to 2012/13. However, there was a large decline in relative poverty for pensioners in the first half of the period. This reflects higher state pensions and more pensioners retiring with a pension from their workplace.

Figure 9

Percentage of all individuals, pensioners and children in relative poverty (at or below 60 per cent of median income), 2012-13[1]

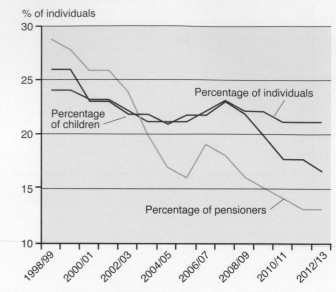

Source: adapted from ONS, Households below average income, 2014.

1.   All individuals and pensions after housing costs have been taken into account, but children before housing costs.

Data Response Question

Absolute and relative poverty

Barry Bosworth and his colleagues at the Brookings Institution have examined changes in life expectancy in the US starting at age 55 for the cohort of people born in 1920 and the cohort born in 1940. They found that the richest men born in 1940 gained roughly six years in life expectancy compared to those born in 1920. Middle-income earners born in 1940 gained roughly four years and those in the lower part of the distribution gained only two years compared to those born in 1920. Why these differences? They are more likely to do with lifestyle and variations in diet and stress than the ability to afford medical care given that in the US, those 65 and over have access to free medical care.

Over the past two generations the gap in education achievement between the children of the rich in the USA and the children of the poor has doubled. While the college enrolment rate of children from the lowest quarter of the income distribution has increased from 6 to 8 per cent, the rate for children from the highest quarter has risen from 40 per cent to 73 per cent. One crucial factor driving these trends is that the average affluent child now receives 6 000 hours of extracurricular education - such as being read to, taken to a museum, coached in a sport - more than the average poor child.

The typical American family earns less in real terms than in 1989, according to a September report by the US Census Bureau. The report also records that household incomes have fallen for the fifth consecutive year. At the same time, the share of wealth of the top one per cent has increased. In the three years to 2012, the top one per cent of incomes grew by 31 per cent while the rest rose by just 0.4 per cent.

Figure 10

US income inequality; average real income 2011

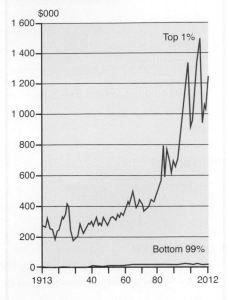

Source: adapted from Piketty and Saez;
Department of Health and Human Services.

Figure 11

US poverty rates, percentage of group[1]

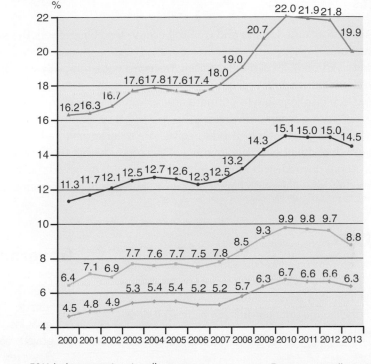

- 50% below poverty rate, all persons — Poverty rate all persons
- 50% below poverty rate, children under 18 — Poverty rate children under 18

1. In 2013, individuals were defined as poor if they lived in a household with an income of $23 834 or less. 50% below poverty means that individuals lived in a household with an income of $11 917. Median US household income in 2013 was $51 939.

Source: adapted from www.hhs.gov.

About 6.2 million people in Italy live in absolute poverty, one in ten of the population, a figure that has almost doubled in the past two years according to the country's national statistics agency Istat. In addition, four million are considered to suffer from hunger, of whom 10 per cent are children under five and 14 per cent are older than 65. Real incomes are lower than 15 years ago.

The cause has been Italy's economic stagnation that was a problem even before the financial crisis of 2007-08 hit the economy. The relatively prosperous north has been hit by thousands of businesses failing. Unemployment is now a record 13.4 per cent.

Source: adapted from © the *Financial Times* 13.1.2015, All Rights Reserved.

Q

1. Distinguish between absolute and relative poverty, using examples from the data.

2. Explain three main causes of poverty, using examples from the data.

3. Discuss whether children are most at risk from being in poverty today and whether children from poor households are likely to become poor themselves when they are adults.

Evaluation

Look at the evidence from the data about child poverty versus other groups in poverty to make a judgement. Identify any other data you would need to have to make a firmer conclusion. Then consider the cycle of poverty and make a judgement about how easy it is for a child from a poor background to break out of that bracket as an adult.

1. Governments redistribute income and wealth because they believe that this will increase economic welfare.
2. They can do this through fiscal means, raising taxes from the relatively well off to spend on services and benefits for the relatively less well off.
3. Governments can also legislate to promote greater equality, for instance through passing equal pay legislation or imposing minimum wages.
4. Some economists argue that redistribution gives rise to large welfare losses. These include lower economic growth and higher unemployment. They conclude that the poor would be better off in the long term without any redistribution of income and wealth by government. Other economists argue that reducing inequalities will lead to higher economic growth and lower unemployment.

Starter activity

You are currently receiving an education. Who benefits from free education? Is access to free education dependent on the income of parents? Who ultimately pays for the free education given to children? How is there a redistribution of income in the economy because of education?

The distribution of income and wealth

Free market forces give rise to a particular distribution of income and wealth in society. This distribution is unlikely to be either **efficient** or **equitable**. In previous units, we have looked at how government can correct a variety of **market failures**. This unit outlines how government might intervene to make the distribution of income and wealth in society more equitable.

The current distribution of income and wealth can be seen by government as undesirable for various reasons.

- **Absolute poverty** may exist in society. At the extreme, people may be dying on the streets for want of food, shelter or simple medicines.
- **Relative poverty** may be considered too great. The government may consider the gap between rich and poor in society to be too wide.
- **Horizontal equity** may not exist. For instance, men may be paid more for doing the same jobs as women. Workers from ethnic minority groups may be discriminated against in employment and housing.
- The current distribution may be seen to conflict with considerations of economic efficiency. For instance, it might be argued that income and wealth differentials need to be increased in order to provide incentives for people to work harder.

The first three of the above arguments suggest that income and wealth differentials should be narrowed. Some economists, however, have suggested that, if income differentials are too narrow, incentives will be too low for workers and risk takers and this could have a negative impact on economic growth rates.

How can governments change the distribution of income and wealth in society?

Government expenditure

Government expenditure can be used to alter the distribution of income. One obvious way is for government to provide monetary benefits to those requiring financial support. Social security and National Insurance benefits now account for over 30 per cent of UK government expenditure.

However, governments may wish to target help more precisely. For instance, an increase in the old age pension will not necessarily relieve absolute poverty amongst some old people. They may live in houses which are damp and cold and be unable or unwilling to pay considerable sums of money to remedy the situation, so the government may choose to spend money on housing for the elderly, for instance providing low-rent housing or offering renovation grants for owner-occupied property. Similarly, governments may choose to help children in need not by increasing child benefit for all children regardless of income, but targeting help to low-income families with children by offering free school meals, free nursery education or subsidised energy for heating.

Another important area of government activity is the provision of goods and services which give citizens equality of opportunity in society. The Beveridge Report of 1942 argued that citizens should have access to a minimum standard of health care, housing and education as well as minimum incomes and employment.

There are three positions that can be taken on this.

- The pure free market approach is to argue that education, housing and health care are no different from cars or holidays. If individuals have a high income, they should be able to buy better education for their children and better health care for themselves, just as they can buy better cars or more expensive holidays. Individuals who have no income simply won't have access to these goods or services.
- A middle position is that all individuals have a right to a minimum level of education, housing and health care. However, those on higher incomes can use the market mechanism to buy higher-quality services. So in education, every child is entitled to free education in a state school but

some households will choose to spend money on sending their children to private schools. In health, individuals can choose to buy private medical care although the state provides a health service for all. A key debate then becomes how much the state should spend on providing services such as education and therefore what quality are state-provided services compared to private sector services.

- An interventionist approach is to argue that all individuals should have equal access to some services such as education and health care. Private education and private health care should not be available to those who can afford to buy them. So private schools and private hospitals would be banned by law. This would lead to horizontal equity.

The extent to which governments should use its spending to redistribute income is highly controversial. In Nordic countries such as Sweden and Denmark, there is widespread agreement that the state should provide a comprehensive welfare state, equalising provision of many services for their citizens. In free market economies such as the USA, there is little consensus about the role of the state. However, government provision of welfare benefits and services is much less than in Nordic countries.

taxpayer rises. For instance, income tax would be progressive if a worker earning £4 000 a year were to pay five per cent of income in tax, but 25 per cent on income of £ 40 000.

A **regressive tax** is a tax where the proportion of income paid in tax falls as the income of the taxpayer rises. An extreme example of a regressive tax was the poll tax in the UK between 1990 and 1992. The amount paid in poll tax was identical for most poll tax payers. A person earning £8 000 per year and paying £400 a year in poll tax paid exactly the same amount as a person earning £40 000, so the proportion of tax paid was different - five per cent of income for the person earning £8 000 a year (£400 ÷ £8 000), but only one per cent for the person earning £40 000 a year (£400 ÷ £40 000).

A **proportional tax** is one where the proportion paid in tax remains the same while the income of the taxpayer changes (although the actual amount paid increases as income increases). For example, a taxpayer might earn £10 000 and pay £1 000 in tax. If tax increases to £2 000 when income rises to £20 000, then the tax is proportional over the income range £10 000 to £20 000.

Direct taxes on income tend to be progressive because of the way they are structured. Those on very low incomes pay no income tax whilst those on very high incomes pay a higher rate

Question 1

The Chancellor, George Osborne, has said he needs to cut spending on welfare by £12 billion a year as part of his drive to balance the government budget. It will require some difficult decisions since he has already promised to protect state pensions. The state pension accounts for just over half of all spending on welfare benefits. This means that most of the £12 billion will have to come from those under pension age. Working families could see almost £500 a year taken away from them on average as benefits are cut. George Osborne has already pledged to freeze benefits such as jobseeker's allowance, tax credits, universal credit, child benefit and income support. With no increase, the real value of these benefits will fall over time. Matthew Whittaker of the Resolution Foundation said the effect of the freeze would be similar to that of the one per cent uprating (i.e. benefits were increased by one per cent per year but because inflation was much higher, the real value of benefits fell) introduced by Mr Osborne in 2012 that had been 'pretty straightforwardly regressive'. With the sole exception of poorer pensioners, it had hit the bottom three deciles hardest, he said.

Source: adapted from © the *Financial Times* 7.1.2014, 30.9.2014, All Rights Reserved.

Explain why the £12 billion of cuts to welfare benefits promised by George Osborne are likely to be 'regressive' and lead to greater inequalities in incomes.

Taxation

The tax system can be used to redistribute income and wealth. Taxing those on high incomes or with high levels of wealth more than those on low incomes reduces after tax incomes and produces a more equal distribution of income.

Taxes can be classified according to their incidence as a proportion of income. A **progressive tax** is a tax where the proportion of income paid in tax rises as the income of the

Question 2

Figure 1

Taxes as a percentage of disposable income: by quintile grouping of households, 2012-13

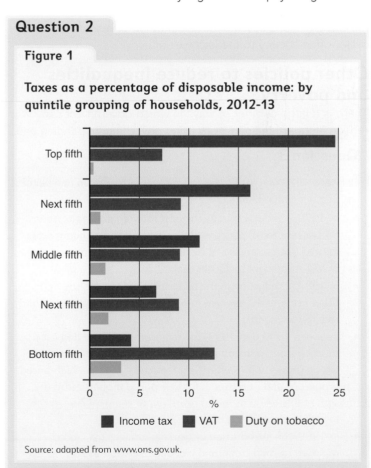

Source: adapted from www.ons.gov.uk.

(a) Explain what is meant by a progressive and regressive tax, using the data to illustrate your answer.

(b) If the government raised duty on tobacco, how would this affect the distribution of income after all taxes have been taken into account?

of tax than those on lower incomes. Indirect taxes, such as VAT, tend to be regressive. As incomes increase, households tend to spend less as a proportion of income and save more. The result is that taxes on spending fall as a proportion of income as income rises. Taxes on cigarettes and alcohol tend to be highly regressive because they form a much larger percentage of spending for low-income households than high-income households. So reducing rates of income tax and raising the same amount of revenue by increasing indirect taxes will lead to greater inequality.

There are two ways in which government can attempt to reduce inequalities in wealth. One is to impose inheritance taxes. The higher the rate of tax, the more difficult it becomes for individuals to pass on their wealth to the next generation. The main problem with inheritance taxes is that they are mainly avoidable through careful tax planning. The other way is to have very high taxes on high levels of income. Those with wealth can then be forced to spend some of their wealth in order to maintain a certain standard of living. As with inheritance taxes, very high rates of income tax encourage tax avoidance.

The distinction between progressive, regressive and proportional taxes is made because it is important in the study of the distribution of income and wealth. The more progressive the tax, the greater the link with ability to pay the tax and the more likely it is to result in a redistribution of resources from the better off in society to the less well off.

Other policies to reduce inequalities and poverty

There is a large number of ways in which government can reduce inequalities apart from using government spending and

taxation. Some of the most common include the following.
- Raising the minimum wage will raise incomes of the lowest paid workers.
- Maximum wages can be fixed. For example, in a company, the maximum wage payable to the highest-paid worker could legally be 20 times the wages of the lowest-paid worker.
- Employers can be forced to provide benefits free to their workers such as sickness benefits, pensions and medical care, effectively increased wages.
- Passing equal pay legislation. Certain groups may be discriminated against and be paid lower wages for doing the same work as others. Making it illegal to discriminate against women, people from ethnic minorities and those with disabilities is likely to reduce inequality.
- Passing trade union-friendly legislation. Trade unions on average raise the wage rates of their members because they are able to bargain collectively on behalf of their members. Lower-income earners benefit more as a proportion of their after tax income from such increases in wages rates.
- Price controls on essential goods and services can be imposed. For example, maximum rents can be fixed. Or a maximum price for bread, rice, petrol or electricity could be imposed. Private bus and train companies might have limits placed on their fares. These measures increase the spending power of those on low incomes.
- Private sector goods and services can be provided on the basis of income. For example, a new housing estate might be developed where only first-time buyers can buy housing under the planning permission terms given by government. Since first-time buyers are likely to be on relatively low incomes, this could reduce inequality.

The costs of redistribution: a free market perspective
Intervention in the economy may well lead to higher economic welfare for some, but it may also lead to lower economic welfare for others.

There is an obvious cost to those in society who lose directly from increased taxation. Some economists argue that any taxation results in a loss of freedom. The taxpayer loses the ability to choose how to allocate those scarce resources which are now being expropriated by the state. Therefore, in a free society, taxation should be kept to an absolute minimum.

Classical or free market economists would also suggest that redistribution involves heavy costs in terms of economic growth, employment and market inefficiencies.

Taxation Raising income tax rates lowers the incentives of those in employment to work, thus reducing the growth rate of the economy. Higher taxes paid by employers on the wages of their workers discourages them from employing labour. Higher taxes on company profits reduces incentives to make profit and invest. High tax rates on income and profits can lead to a flight of capital and labour from the country. Individual entrepreneurs may choose to emigrate, taking their money and skills with them. Firms may choose to locate abroad to take advantage of lower tax rates, leading to a loss of domestic jobs and income. Overall, the higher the tax rate, the more incentives there are for taxpayers to use legal loopholes to avoid paying tax or simply to use illegal methods to evade taxes.

Minimum and maximum wages High minimum wages may discourage employers from taking on workers. Low maximum wages may discourage workers from taking on more difficult and responsible jobs. Top companies and the City of London frequently argue that any limits on pay for top executives will simply lead to workers moving abroad and an inability to recruit workers of the right calibre to important positions.

Maximum prices Maximum prices may lead to shortages and queues. Black markets often develop where goods and services bought at low maximum prices are sold at a higher price. Maximum prices also discourage production and investment. For example, if bakeries cannot make a profit on the bread they make because of maximum prices on bread, they will cease production in the long term. If landlords receive low rents, there will be no incentive for them to renovate properties and keep them to an acceptable standard. The larger the gap between the free market price and the maximum price, the larger will be the inefficiencies created in the market.

Free market economists also use the concept of **trickle down**. This is the argument that income cascades down the chain of supply. So the cleaner in a luxury goods shop only has his or her job because high-income earners can afford to spend £2 000 on a handbag or £1 000 on a pair of shoes. The gardener employed on a country estate only has his or her job because the owner is rich enough to own and run the estate. The successful entrepreneur who creates a business employing 2 000 people has created prosperity for those 2 000 workers and their families. So everyone benefits when high-income earners earn and spend even more. To restrict the earnings of the highest paid would lead to unemployment and lower living standards for all.

Minimising the costs of redistribution

The free market view of the costs of income and wealth redistribution represents one perspective. Other views suggest that redistribution can be beneficial and costs can be minimised.

The law of diminishing marginal returns suggests that taking resources away from an affluent individual to give to a poor person will lead to an increase in the combined utility of the two individuals. This law states that the higher the spending of individuals, the less utility or satisfaction they get by spending an extra pound. For instance, an extra £10 a week to a poor family would give them more utility than getting an extra £10 a week having suddenly won £1 million on the lottery. The law implies, for instance, that £1 spent on a coffee by a high-income earner in the UK gives less utility than £1 spent on food by a poor individual in Bangladesh. The implication is that redistributing income from the rich to the poor increases total utility because the loss of utility by the rich person will be less than the gain in utility by the poor person. One of the problems with this approach is that the law of marginal utility refers specifically to spending changes by a single individual. One pound is worth less to an individual earning £1 million a year than if she were only earning £5 000 a year. The law in its strictest sense cannot be used to compare income changes between individuals

because it is not possible to make direct utility comparisons between individuals.

The free market view that redistribution of resources causes lower growth and gross market inefficiencies is also not born out by the evidence. Nordic countries such as Sweden and Denmark have enjoyed approximately the same rate of economic growth as the United States over the past 50 years. Yet there is far more redistribution of income and wealth in Nordic countries than in the USA. Also, governments are constantly interfering in individual markets. Some of these interventions prove successful and others are clearly failures. For example, the amount of unemployment created by the minimum wage in the UK has been very small. The disruption to supplies of basic necessities because of maximum prices in Venezuela over the past ten years has been considerable. In the UK, raising the top rate of income tax to 90 per cent would almost certainly have an impact on incentives to work for very high-income earners in the same way that it does for very low-paid workers caught in poverty and unemployment traps. However, raising the top rate of income tax from 45 per cent to 50 per cent might have little or no effect. This suggests that the costs of redistribution can be minimised.

As for trickle down theory, it is important to remember that a £2 000 handbag represents £2 000 worth of economic resources. Those resources could have been used, for example, to renovate a house with damp problems. If society chooses to produce £2 000 handbags, then workers will be employed in the supply chain to produce those handbags. But a house renovation also needs workers and a supply chain. For society, the question is about opportunity cost and distribution. If the economy produces £1 billion of luxury handbags, that is

£1 billion worth of resources that can't be used to renovate poor-quality housing. Greater inequality does not in itself produce a larger national income. As the examples of the Soviet Union in the 20th century or Venezuela in the 21st century show, a failure to create enough economic incentives to work and invest will lead to low or negative economic growth. But highly egalitarian economies such as Sweden and Denmark have shown that redistribution of resources can be achieved at the same time as maintaining the same economic growth rate as other economies with a far greater degree of inequality.

Key Terms

Progressive tax - a tax where the higher the income of the taxpayer, the larger the proportion of income is paid in tax.
Proportional tax - a tax where as the income of taxpayers increases, the same proportion of income is paid in tax.
Regressive tax - a tax where the higher the income of the taxpayer, the smaller the proportion of income is paid in tax.

Thinking like an economist

Reducing inequalities in the UK

Taxes and benefits

The Welfare State, whose foundations were laid down by the Labour government of 1945-51, was designed to ensure that every citizen of the UK enjoyed a minimum standard of living. To achieve this, higher-income earners are taxed more than lower-income earners. The revenue raise is used to provide a variety of benefits in cash or in kind.

Table 1 shows how this redistribution affected household income in 2012-13. The table splits the 26.6 million households in the UK into quintile groups (i.e. fifths). Each quintile group contains 5.3 million households grouped according to their disposable income per year. Disposable income is gross (or original) income plus welfare benefits minus direct taxes. The average gross income per year of the average household in the bottom quintile in 2012-13 was £5 536 compared to £81 284 for the top fifth of households. This means that before tax and benefits, the average income of the top fifth of households was 14.7 times that of the bottom fifth of households.

These sharp inequalities are reduced through the effects of the tax and benefit system. The single most important welfare benefit is the state pension. This together with other welfare benefits raise the incomes disproportionately of lower income households. After cash benefits have been taken into account, the yearly income of the average household in the bottom quintile rose in 2012-13 to £12 690 and for the top quintile was £83 950. After cash benefits but before tax, the income ratio of the top to the bottom quintile was therefore 6.6:1.

Direct taxes tend to be progressive: the higher the income, the higher proportion of income paid in tax. Once direct taxes are taken into account, the disposable income (gross or original income plus cash benefits minus direct taxes) for the average household in the bottom quintile was £11 434. For the top quintile, it was £63 628. The ratio of disposable income between the top and bottom quintiles was therefore 5.6 times.

Table 1 also shows the regressive nature of indirect taxes. As a proportion of disposable income, the average household in the bottom quintile paid 31 per cent of the income in indirect taxes such as VAT. The average household in the top quintile paid just 14 per cent.

On the other hand, poorer households receive more in money terms in benefits in kind than richer households. The average household in the bottom quintile received an estimated £7 646 yearly in direct benefits such as education. The top quintile household received slightly less at £5 403.

The benefits system

Table 2 shows the main welfare benefits in the UK. The single most important welfare benefit is the state pension, accounting for nearly 50 per cent of all spending on welfare benefits. Government policy is to increase the state pension by the rate of inflation or the real rate of growth of earnings, whichever is the greatest. The state retirement age is rising eventually to 68. However, people are also living longer. With a rising number of individuals over the pension age, the amount of money spent on the state pension is likely to rise in real terms.

Both the state pension and child benefit are, for the most part, not linked to income. The amount received across the income range is dependent on the number of pensioners and the number of children in each quintile group of households. Equally, disability living allowance is not linked to income.

The other benefits named in Table 2 are linked to income. They serve to redistribute income across the income range. For example, housing benefit is a particularly important benefit for low-income households.

Overall the welfare benefits system favours low-income households and helps reduce poverty and inequality. However, the top quintile of households is still receiving a significant amount of income from the welfare system mainly because of entitlement to state pensions.

Table 1 Redistribution of income through taxes and benefits, 2012-13

	Bottom	2nd	3rd	4th	Top	All households
Average per household (£ per year)						
Quintile groups of all households ranked by disposable income						
Wages and salaries	3 554	8 703	17 160	30 630	60 818	24 173
Imputed income from benefits in kind	25	30	89	292	866	260
Self-employment income	709	847	1 798	2 238	9 073	2 933
Private pensions, annuities	844	1 911	3 195	4 277	6 306	3 307
Investment income	190	243	426	881	3 809	1 110
Other income	214	218	402	380	412	325
Total original income	5 536	11 952	23 069	38 697	81 284	32 108
plus Direct benefits in cash						
State pension	2 523	3 747	3 362	2 652	1 767	2 810
All other benefits	4 631	5 070	3 260	2 039	899	3 180
Total cash benefits	7 154	8 817	6 622	4 691	2 666	5 990
Gross income	12 690	20 769	29 692	43 388	83 950	38 098
less Direct taxes and Employees' NIC	1 256	2 257	4 620	8 635	20 322	7 418
Disposable income	11 434	18 512	25 072	34 753	63 628	30 680
less Indirect taxes	3 488	3 986	5 029	6 474	9 140	5 623
Post-tax income	7 946	14 527	20 043	28 279	54 488	25 057
plus Benefits in kind						
Education	3 310	3 019	2 623	2 113	1 574	2 528
National health service	4 029	4 371	4 202	3 869	3 527	4 000
Housing subsidy	8	9	6	3	1	5
Rail travel subsidy	40	33	54	92	181	80
Bus travel subsidy	128	128	114	110	116	119
School meals and Healthy Start Vouchers	132	57	26	6	3	45
Total	7 646	7 617	7 026	6 193	5 403	6 777
Final income	15 592	22 143	27 069	34 472	59 890	31 834

Source: adapted from www.ons.gov.uk.

The tax system

Table 3 shows the main taxes in the UK. Income tax is the most progressive tax levied on households. The bottom quintile paid four per cent of their original income plus state benefits (excluding tax credits) in income tax. The top quintile paid 17 per cent. Employees' National Insurance contributions are also progressive. However, all other taxes are regressive. For example, the bottom quintile paid 11 per cent of their original income plus benefits or 12 per cent of their disposable income in VAT. This compares to five per cent and seven per cent respectively for the top quintile of income earners. For duty on tobacco, the bottom quintile of households paid more in absolute terms in tax than the top quintile of households.

Overall the bottom quintile of households paid 37 per cent of their original income plus benefits in tax compared to 35 per cent for the top quintile. Although higher-earning households pay more in tax than lower-earning households on average, as a proportion of income it is broadly similar. UK taxes taken as a whole are therefore broadly proportional.

Table 2 Cash benefits by quintile groups of households, 2012-13

	Average per household (£ per year)					
	Quintile groups of all households ranked by disposable income					
	Bottom	2nd	3rd	4th	Top	All households
Original (gross) income	5 536	11 952	23 069	38 697	81 284	32 108
Direct benefits in cash						
State pension	2 523	3 747	3 362	2 652	1 767	2 810
Child benefit	451	525	464	398	307	429
Disability living allowance	262	483	517	408	77	350
Income support and pension credit	686	664	404	172	20	389
Housing benefit	1 160	1 454	629	255	25	705
Job seeker's allowance (Income based)	275	74	9	7	1	73
Tax credits	1 051	1 127	596	139	18	586
Other	746	743	641	660	451	648
Total cash benefits	**7 154**	**8 817**	**6 622**	**4 691**	**2 666**	**5 990**

Source: adapted from www.ons.gov.uk.

Table 3 Taxes by quintile groups of households, 2012-13

	Average per household (£ per year)					
	Quintile groups of all households ranked by equivalised disposable income					
	Bottom	2nd	3rd	4th	Top	All households
Original income plus benefits	12 690	20 769	29 692	43 388	83 950	38 098
Direct taxes and Employees' NIC						
Income tax	462	1 189	2 605	5 157	14 576	4 798
less Tax credits	99	244	200	66	17	125
Employees' NI contributions	180	527	1 192	2,345	4 279	1 704
Council tax and Northern Ireland rates	1 051	1,049	1 143	1,260	1 502	1 201
less Council tax benefit/Rates rebates	338	263	120	61	18	160
Total direct taxes	1 256	2 257	4 620	8 635	20 322	7 418
Disposable income	11 434	18 512	25 072	34 753	63 628	30 680
Indirect taxes						
VAT	1 397	1 609	2 140	2 918	4 323	2 477
Duty on tobacco	355	331	374	340	262	332
Duty on beer and cider	67	83	118	155	201	125
Duty on wines & spirits	107	125	175	239	390	207
Duty on hydrocarbon oils	262	361	478	635	703	488
Other	1 300	1 477	1 744	2 187	3 261	1 994
Total indirect taxes	3 488	3 986	5 029	6 474	9 140	5 623
Total direct and indirect taxes	**4 744**	**6 243**	**9 649**	**15 109**	**29 462**	**13 041**

Source: adapted from www.ons.gov.uk.

Data Response Question

Growth and inequality

The gap between rich and poor is at its highest level in most OECD countries in 30 years. Today, the richest 10 per cent of the population in the OECD area earn 9.5 times more than the poorest 10 per cent. By contrast, in the 1980s the ratio stood at 7:1. The increase in income inequality is evident not just in a widening gap between the top and bottom income deciles but also in the Gini coefficient, shown in Figure 2. In OECD countries in the mid-1980s, the Gini measure stood at 0.29; by 2011/13 it had increased by three points to 0.32.

New OECD analysis suggests that income inequality has a negative and statistically significant impact on medium-term growth. Rising inequality by three Gini points would drag down economic growth by 0.35 per cent per year for 25 years. This is a cumulative loss in GDP at the end of the period of 8.5 per cent. Figure 3 shows by how much the GDP growth rate would have changed over

the period 1990-2010 had inequality not changed between 1985 and 2005. Rising inequality is estimated to have knocked more than 10 per cent off growth in Mexico and New Zealand, nearly nine per cent in the United Kingdom and seven per cent in the United States, Italy and Sweden.

The biggest factor for the impact of inequality on growth is the gap between lower-income households and the rest of the population: in particular gap between the bottom four deciles of the income distribution and the rest. Policy must not just be about tackling poverty, it also needs to be about addressing lower incomes more generally.

The most direct policy tool to reduce inequality is redistribution through taxes and benefits. The analysis shows that redistribution does not in itself lower economic growth. However, redistribution policies that are poorly targeted and do not focus on the most effective tools can lead to a waste or resources and generate inefficiencies.

The evidence strongly points to one theory about how inequality affects growth. Inequality hinders the growth of human capital. This is because income inequality undermines educational opportunities for disadvantaged individuals. It lowers social mobility and hampers skills development. OECD analysis

Figure 2

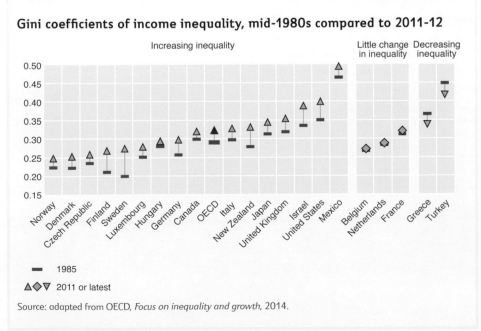

Gini coefficients of income inequality, mid-1980s compared to 2011-12

Source: adapted from OECD, *Focus on inequality and growth*, 2014.

Figure 3

Estimated consequences of changes in inequality (1985-2005) on subsequent cumulative economic growth (1990-2010)

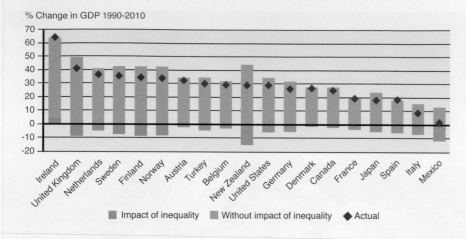

■ Impact of inequality ■ Without impact of inequality ◆ Actual

Source: adapted from OECD, *Focus on inequality and growth*, 2014.

1. Explain what is meant by a Gini coefficient, giving examples from the data to illustrate your answer.

2. Analyse, using diagrams, why rising inequality might lead to lower economic growth.

3. Evaluate whether the best way to increase the incomes of the bottom 40 per cent of the income distribution in the UK in order to increase long-term economic growth is to increase welfare benefits.

Evaluation

To make a judgement about the 'best', it is essential to identify alternatives to welfare benefits. Equally, there are many types of welfare benefits. Which welfare benefits might best help the goal of increasing growth? Identify which policies are likely to achieve this and which will not. For potentially successful policies, which are the most likely to be successful whilst at the same time minimising the costs of redistribution to markets and to the economy?

shows that the human capital of people whose parents have low levels of education deteriorate as income inequality rises. For those less well off, making them even more relatively poor reduces incentives to gain education and training and also reduces their resources to invest in their own education and training. In contrast, there is little or no effect for the human capital of people with middle or high levels of parental educational background.

The evidence challenges the view that there is a trade-off between promoting growth and addressing inequality. The evidence suggests that reducing inequality will increase economic growth in the long term.

Policy makers including governments need to be concerned about the economic performance of the bottom 40 per cent. This includes the vulnerable lower-middle class who are at risk of failing to benefit from future growth. Higher welfare benefits targeted at the bottom 40 per cent as well as increased access to high-quality education, training and health care are important social investments to create greater equality in the long run. Government policy also needs to confront the historical legacy of underinvestment by low-income groups in formal education. Strategies to foster skills development must include improved job-related training and education for the low skilled over their whole working lives.

Source: adapted from OECD, *Focus on inequality and growth*, 2014.

74 Measures of development

Key points

1. Countries can be classified into different groups according to their stages of development.
2. There are many different characteristics that can be used to compare the stage of development of an individual country, including GDP per capita, levels of human and physical capital, health and mortality, education, the structure of the economy and institutional structures.
3. Economic growth and economic development are interlinked but are different ways of judging the performance of a country over time.
4. Different indices have been devised to measure the level of economic development of countries including the Human Development Index, the Inequality-adjusted Human Development Index, the Multidimensional Poverty Index and the Genuine Progress Indicator.

Starter activity

Choose a developing country. It may be a country that you know about or even have visited. What do you think makes it different in terms of 'development' from the UK? You might want to start with income per capita and work out what it means to have an income per capita of, say, 10 per cent of that of the UK. Use the Internet to provide statistics of these differences.

Classification of countries

There are many countries spread across the four continents that can sustain human life. They differ in many ways, one of which is their level of economic development. Economists, politicians, government agencies and world organisations, such as the World Bank, the IMF and the OECD, classify countries and band them into groups. Examples of these classifications include the following.

High-income, middle-income and low-income countries

One simple way to classify countries is by their income. Countries differ in size of population. So the key indicator is income per capita. To eliminate exchange rate issues, income per capita can be measured in terms of purchasing power parities (PPPs). High-income countries are those in Western Europe, the USA and Canada, Australia and New Zealand and Japan. Middle-income and low-income countries are found throughout the rest of the world. A disproportionate number of low-income countries, however, are found in Africa.

Developed, developing and less developed countries

Developed countries are high-income countries, such as the UK and the US. Developing or less developed countries are broadly middle-income and low-income countries. Low-income countries are sometimes called least developed countries.

First, second and third world countries

This classification was based on the world as it was before 1990. First world countries are the rich-developed, high-income countries. Second world countries were communist countries, including the Soviet Union and eastern European countries, such as Poland. Third world countries were low-income and middle-income countries in the rest of the world.

Other classifications

There are many other terms used to describe countries.

- Emerging countries are middle-income countries which could become high-income countries over the next 20 or 30 years. Another term used to describe this group is newly industrialised countries (NICs).
- BRIC countries are four countries: Brazil, India, Russia and China. When the term was first used in the early 2000s, it was judged that these countries were very large, but also

Question 1

Table 1 Classification of countries 2014[1]

	GNI per capita at current prices $US	Examples of countries	GNI per capita $US 2013
Low-income	1 045 or less	Central African Republic	320
		Ethiopia	470
		Cambodia	950
		Bagladesh	1 010
Lower-middle-income	1 045 - 4 124	Pakistan	1 360
		India	1 570
		Egypt	3 140
		Armenia	3 800
Upper-middle-income	4 125 - 12 745	China	6 560
		Romania	9 050
		Mexico	9 940
		Brazil	11 690
High-income	12 745+	Lithuania	14 900
		South Korea	25 920
		United Kingdom	41 680
		United States	53 470
		Switzerland	90 680

1. World Bank categories for income per capita Atlas method, current US$. Actual data for individual countries is 2013.

Source: adapted from worldbank.org.

Explain in which group of countries (low-income, lower-middle-income, upper-middle-income, or high-income countries), shown in Table 1, you think you would put: (a) France; (b) Tanzania; (c) BRIC countries; (d) least developed countries; (e) first world countries; (f) newly industrialised countries?

they had high growth prospects. As such, their growth would be very important for the whole world economy.

- Tiger economies are economies with very high growth rates, such as have been experienced by South Korea, Singapore and Taiwan in the past.

Characteristics of developing countries

No two economies are the same. However, developing countries possess certain characteristics when compared to developed countries.

Lower per capita incomes Developing countries have lower per capita incomes than developed countries. Per person, their output measured in money terms is lower and the incomes received by citizens on average are lower.

Physical capital Developing countries have less physical capital per capita than developed countries. This means there is less infrastructure, such as roads, hospitals and schools per capita. There are fewer workplaces, such as factories and offices. The quality and quantity of machinery and equipment on average is lower per capita. In the home, there is less access on average to safe drinking water or to sanitation facilities.

Human capital Developing countries, on average, have lower levels of human capital. On average, the population is less well educated and trained than in developed countries. In poorer developing countries, for example, illiteracy rates might be high. Some developing countries have significant differences in literacy rates between men and women because of different social attitudes about who should receive an education.

Health and mortality Individuals in developing countries on average suffer poorer health and die younger than in developed countries. Health is crucially influenced by living conditions. In developing countries, individuals are more likely to have no access to safe drinking water, have no proper sanitation facilities, live in cramped conditions, not have enough to eat and have limited access to medical facilities. There is an enormous range of experiences within developing countries. Elites live a very similar life to individuals in developed countries. In relatively rich developing countries, many in the population live a 'first world' lifestyle. In poor countries, however, like Tanzania or Mozambique, the majority of the population suffer poverty. Affluence, in itself, can also bring problems. Some argue that mortality rates will rise in countries like the USA and the UK over the next 20 years because of the epidemic of obesity.

Population growth Population growth tends to be linked to average incomes. The higher the average income, the lower is likely to be the rate of population growth. One reason is that in low-income countries, children can be put to work and bring income into the family. They can also look after the parents in old age. In developed countries, children are a major cost to parents, including lost earnings of the main child carer in the family. Another reason for higher population growth is less access to family planning.

Unemployment and underemployment Less physical and human capital, combined with high population growth, can lead to large scale unemployment and underemployment. Unemployment occurs because there are simply not enough jobs in the economy. Underemployment occurs partly because workers are forced to work fewer hours than they would like or because they are overqualified for the jobs they undertake.

Structure of the economy As economies develop, typically they pass through the same restructuring of their economies. In less developed economies, the agricultural sector is large, whilst manufacturing is small. In middle-income countries, the agricultural sector has shrunk in relative size to be replaced by manufacturing. In developed countries, the agricultural sector tends to be a very small part of the economy, whilst the service sector can be 70-80 per cent of GDP.

Institutional structures Developed countries have a complex system of institutional structures. There is 'good' government, an independent judiciary, a strong set of laws that protect private property and a sophisticated financial system. Institutional structures in developing countries tend to be weaker. At worst, there can be civil war, which is highly destructive of both physical and human capital.

The environment A growing population, together with growth of agriculture, mineral extraction and manufacturing, mean that the environment is under greater pressure in developing countries than in developed countries. Developing countries are experiencing the process that developed countries went through in the 19th and 20th centuries with the Industrial Revolution and the mass migration of people from the countryside to the urban environment. In rich developed countries in the 21st century, there is sufficient income to protect the environment and make it cleaner. In poorer countries, the environment has a much lower priority.

Question 2

Table 2 Development indicators, 2013

	Ethiopia	Brazil	UK
GNI per capita, US$ at PPP	1 380	14 750	37 970
Internet users (per 1 000 people)	1.9	51.6	89.8
Literacy rate (% of adults aged 15 and over)	n.a.	91	99
Life expectancy at birth, years	64	74	81
Population growth, %	2.6	0.9	0.6
Unemployment, %	5.7	5.9	7.5
Agriculture, % of GDP	45	5.7	0.07
CO_2 emissions, metric tons per capita	0.1	2.2	7.9

Source: adapted from data.worldbank.org.

Using the data, compare the levels of development of Ethiopia, Brazil and the UK.

Growth vs development

In the 1950s and 1960s, there was an assumption amongst economists that economic growth and economic development were closely linked. High economic growth would lead to fast economic development and vice versa.

Economic growth is relatively simple to measure. It is the rate of change of national income, as measured, for example, by GDP or GNI. It captures changing output, expenditure and income in the economy.

Economic development, though, is a much wider concept. It includes the change in GDP. But it is also concerned with how that GDP is distributed. Economic development is limited if most of the growth in GDP is being taken by the top 10 per cent of income earners, for example. Economic development is also limited if there is widespread absolute poverty such as death from malnutrition or easily preventable diseases. Education,

social mobility, the relative positions of men and women, mortality rates, access to medical care and the environment are just a few of the indicators that can be used to discuss and measure economic development.

It can be argued that economic growth is the best single measure of economic development just as it can be argued that national income is the best single measure of the standard of living. However, there are some economists who argue that economic growth leads to lower economic development mainly because of environmental effects. Other economists argue that emphasising economic growth can distort economic development, at least in the short term, because it takes no account, for example, of absolute poverty or educational opportunity.

Measures of economic development

One important advantage of using growth in GDP as the indicator of development is that it is a single measure calculated using the same unit. That unit is money such as US dollars or pounds or euros. It isn't possible simply to add up GDP with access to mobile phones with energy consumption with school enrolment figures using a monetary unit. However, it is possible to calculate an index where different statistics are given particular **weightings**. This is the type of calculation used, for example, for the Retail Prices Index or the Consumer Prices Index, measures of inflation. There is a variety of development indices in use today.

The Human Development Index The United Nations calculates a measure of economic development called the **Human Development Index (HDI)**. This is an index based on three indicators of development:
- health, as measured by life expectancy at birth;
- education, as measured by two variables: the mean (i.e. average) years of schooling of adults aged 25 and over; and the expected years of schooling that current five-year-olds can expect to receive over their lives.
- income as measured by real gross national income (GNI) per capita at purchasing power parities.

Each of the three individual indicators is given equal weighting and a geometric mean is taken which gives a score of between 0 and 1. The higher the score, the greater the level of economic development. The Human Development Index gives a broader measure of economic development than just using national income statistics. However, it only uses four indicators to measure the three variables of health, education and income. This has its limitations. For example, in high-income countries, life expectancy at birth is relatively high. However, a growing proportion of the population have health problems which prevent them from leading a normal life. Alzheimer's and obesity are two examples of this. Years of education are not necessarily correlated to quality of education or educational outputs. GNI takes no account of income inequalities. The Human Development Index also takes no account of a large number of other variables such as housing, employment or the environment. However, the HDI is relatively easy to calculate because governments tend to collect the statistics used in the index. Also, it is only an indicator and not a precise measure.

Question 3

The Democratic Republic of Congo should be the economic powerhouse at the heart of Africa. Damning its river could solve the power problems of the continent. Its mining and farming potential could transform the nation, securing growth and stability for millions of potential consumers. 'Congo should be a Brazil, the engine of sub-Saharan Africa whether in hydro-power or farming or mining', says Aly Khan Satchu an investment adviser on east Africa.

Instead Congo is the second least-developed country in the world. Corruption, dysfunction and civil war have destroyed the economy and deterred investment. Average annual income stands at $390 per person. Eighty eight per cent of its 70 million people live in poverty.

Congo is Africa's largest producer of copper and the source of most of the world's cobalt. Copper production reached record levels in recent years following investment by international mining investors in assets owned by the Congo's state-owned mining company Gécamines. More than 95 per cent of Congo's exports come from extractive industries such as copper mining.

Source: adapted from © the *Financial Times* 21.1.2015, All Rights Reserved.

Figure 1

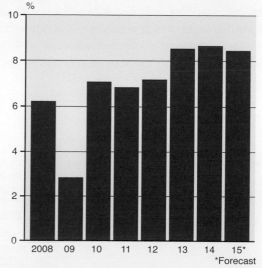

Congo: real GDP growth (annual % change)

Source: adapted from Thomson Reuters Datastream; © the *Financial Times* 21.1.2015, All Rights Reserved.

(a) Using Figure 1, describe the economic growth of the Congo between 2008 and 2015.

(b) Explain why strong economic growth might not have led to strong economic development in Congo in recent years.

The Inequality-adjusted Human Development Index

(IHDI) This index is a modification of the Human Development Index. It adds a fourth indicator of development: inequality. Each of the three measures of longevity, educational attainment and the standard of living are adjusted for degrees of inequality using the Atkinson index, a measure of inequality like the Gini coefficient. The greater the inequality in a country, the greater will be the negative impact on the IHDI score which, like the HDI, goes from 0 (least developed) to 1 (most developed). Inequality reduces the potential for human development and therefore higher inequality is considered to have a negative impact on economic development. IHDI is a broader measure of development than the HDI but like the HDI can be criticised for not taking into account more variables that affect development.

The Multidimensional Poverty Index (MPI) The

Multidimensional Poverty Index (MPI) measures the percentage of the population that is multidimensionally poor. Like the Human Development Index and the Inequality-adjusted Human Development Index, it uses data for health, education and the standard of living to provide an index number scoring. However, the MPI uses a broader range of indicators in each of these categories. In education, its uses years of schooling and child school attendance data; in health, it uses child mortality and nutrition data; in the standard of living it uses availability of electricity, improved sanitation and safe drinking water to households, whether or not the floor of a house is made of dirt, sand or dung, cooking fuel used and assets owned such as radio, telephone or refrigerator. By focussing on data linked to poverty, it produces different scorings to the Human Development Index and highlights countries which might be affluent in some respects, such as high average incomes, but where many in the population do not benefit from these high incomes. Because it uses more indicators, it is not possible to calculate the MPI for every country because these statistics are not necessarily collected or made available. In contrast, HDI scores are available for almost all countries. Like the HDI

and IHDI, it can be criticised for not taking into account other measures of economic development such as the environment.

The Genuine Progress Indicator The Genuine Progress Indicator attempts to give a more comprehensive measure of economic development than indicators like the HDI or the MPI. It is calculated from 26 different indicators grouped into three main categories: economic, environmental and social. In the economic category, for example, personal consumption data is used together with income inequality and the cost of unemployment. In the environmental category, the cost of pollution, loss of natural areas, CO_2 emissions, ozone depletion and depletion of non-renewable resources are accounted for. In the social category, 10 indicators range from the value of housework and parenting to the cost of crime and commuting to the value of volunteer work. The GPI attempts to capture an indication of economic sustainability. Economic growth or development is sustainable if the amount produced and consumed will not limit the amount produced and consumed by future generations. Indicators like the GPI tend to put high negative values on loss of the natural environment or resource depletion. This tends to result in high-income countries being credited with negative economic development over time. Environmentalists would argue that this shows today's generation is enjoying a higher standard of living at the expense of future generations. Economic growth is unsustainable and needs to be reversed. The contrary argument is that indices like the GPI are biased. They are constructed so as to prove the anti-growth case. This shows the importance of the individual indicators used to construct any index of economic development. GDP might be flawed as an indicator, but are indices like the GPI or the IHDI any less flawed at capturing what is meant by economic development?

Other measures There is a number of other indices which combine different variables compiled by agencies such as the United Nations. However, it is also possible to judge economic development by considering a variety of statistics on their own. For example, over a short period of time, changes in electricity

Question 4

Table 3 Selected indicators of development

	Multidimensional Poverty Index (MPI)	Inequality-adjusted HDI	Human Development Index (HDI) Value 2013	Life expectancy at birth (years) 2013	Mean years of schooling (years) 2012	Expected years of schooling (years) 2012	Gross national income (GNI) per capita (2011 PPP $) 2013
Norway	-	0.891	0.944	81.5	12.6	17.6	63 909
Chile	-	0.661	0.822	80.0	9.8	15.1	20 804
Mexico	0.024	0.583	0.756	77.5	8.5	12.8	15 854
India	0.282	0.418	0.586	66.4	4.4	11.7	5 150
Zimbabwe	0.41	0.358	0.492	59.9	7.2	9.3	1 307
Mozambique	0.39	0.277	0.393	50.2	3.2	9.5	1 011
Niger	0.584	0.228	0.337	58.4	1.4	5.4	873

Source: adapted from hdr.undp.org/en/data.

(a) Explain how each of the three indices in Table 3 are calculated.

(b) Discuss whether any of these three indices is a better indicator of development than GNI per capita.

production can sometimes be a better measure of the economic growth of a developing economy than changes in GDP. This is because electricity production is a relative simple statistic to collect accurately whereas GDP statistics are made up of millions of individual statistics and are often subject to significant change over time. Equally, the number of mobile phones per thousand of the population is a good indicator of connectivity of individuals and businesses within an economy.

Thinking like an economist

India and education

Comparisons have long been made between India and China. Both are developing countries with large populations and a large land mass. In 1980, it could be argued that both were at similar stages of economic development. Since then, China's performance has outstripped that of India by a large margin. There are many possible reasons for this difference in economic performance, but one is education. In 1980, China had a strong system of state schools. Since then, educational attainment has risen, keeping pace with the needs of its strongly growing economy. In contrast, India's education system has failed to develop sufficiently, leading to too many adults being illiterate. Its education system is hindering the economic development of India and is also impacting negatively on India's economic growth rate.

India in recent years has made significant progress in ensuring access to primary education. In the 1990s, less than 80 per cent attended primary school. Many rural families lived too far from the nearest school to easily send their children, especially girls. Equally, many rural families did not see much value to education because it didn't seem to add any value to their faming-centred lives. In 2002, the government passed a constitutional amendment declaring primary school education a 'fundamental right' for every child aged 6-14. Between 2005 and 2015, 350 000 new primary schools have been built and more than 95 per cent of villages have their own school. Almost every child now goes to school.

However, the quality of education leaves much to be desired. The national curriculum assumes that students will learn to read in their first year of school. This simply isn't happening. Part of the problem is absenteeism. Nearly all children may be enrolled at a school but their attendance can be erratic. Too many parents keep their children off school when there is work to be done on the family farm or in the family business. Teachers too are frequently absent. Surveys indicate that 15-25 per cent of teachers are absent on any given day. Teachers are on salaries and are not particularly held accountable if they fail to turn up to teach.

The result is low standards. According to the 2014 Annual Status of Education Report, a survey of 650 000 children organised by the non-government Pratham Education Foundation, more than half of rural India's fifth-year students cannot read a simple story from a year two textbook, while nearly 20 per cent of second year students cannot recognise numbers up to 9. Worryingly, results have declined considerably since the assessments began in 2005. Pratham estimates that, over the past decade, 100 million children completed primary school without attaining basic reading and maths skills. In 2009, India ranked 73 out of 74 countries in the OECD's triennial test of reading, maths and science skills of global 15-year-olds. India has refused to take part in subsequent OECD tests.

Poor education harms economic development. Part of that harm occurs because it impacts on jobs prospects. For the next stage of India's economic development, millions of people need to move from agricultural employment into secondary and tertiary industries. Most newly created jobs are in services, which require basic literacy and numeracy. Young people who lack these fundamental skills are likely to wind up in employment that barely pays enough to survive and keeps them in poverty.

Source: adapted from © the *Financial Times* 8.5.2015, All Rights Reserved.

Figure 2

India: percentage of pupils from the relevant age group completing primary school

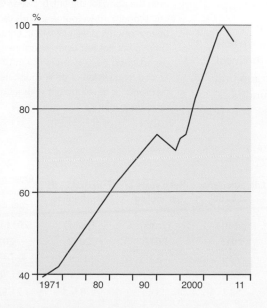

Source: adapted from World Bank.

Table 4 India and China: GNI per capita at current prices, US$ (Atlas method)

	GNI per capita at current prices (Atlas method) US$	
	1980	2 013
China	220	6 560
India	270	1 570

Source: adapted from data.worldbank.org.

Data Response Question

Equatorial Guinea

Equatorial Guinea has the highest level of per capita income in all sub-Saharan Africa. Per capita income is twice more than South Africa and nearly the same as Portugal. But three quarters of the population live below the poverty line because inequalities are so great.

The country has everything to be successful. It has big oil reserves, low government debt, fertile land and a small population of less than 800 000 people. However, it is also perhaps the world's best example of the resource curse: instead of creating prosperity, its oil output underpins a dictatorship, fosters corruption and undermines economic development. Human Rights Watch describes the problem bluntly, saying that 'corruption, poverty and repression continue to plague' the nation. 'Vast oil revenues fund lavish lifestyles for the small elite surrounding the president, whilst most of the population lives in poverty, their basic economic and social rights unmet.'

Oil was first produced in Equatorial Guinea in 1995. Oil output rose dramatically over the 10 years to 2005, when it hit a record high of 376 000 barrels per day. Since then, production has declined because of ageing fields and a lack of new discoveries.

Over the past five years, there has been a burst of public spending. The government has rebuilt airports and roads, and improved electricity and water supplies. But opposition activists say that it has benefited the local ruling class with lucrative government-funded contracts. The country has also spent lavishly on 'prestige' projects, including conference centres, luxury hotels and massive six-lane highways hardly used by the local population. Meanwhile, education and health services remain underfunded.

While the government is spending heavily, little is being invested in ways that would foster long-term development, foreign economists and local activists say. As a result, the economy is expected to contract in 2014. Negative economic growth is an oddity in sub-Saharan Africa where most economies are growing at 5-10 per cent per year.

Source: adapted from © the *Financial Times* 4.2.2015, All Rights Reserved.

1. Explain why Equatorial Guinea's Human Development Index score is significantly below that of South Africa despite have a GNI per capita which is nearly twice as high.

2. Using the data and your own economic knowledge, discuss whether rises in GNI automatically lead to an increase in the level of economic development of a country.

Evaluation

There is a number of issues here which can be evaluated. For example, is Equatorial Guinea the exception rather than the norm for the link between GNP and economic development? Has there been economic development in Equatorial Guinea but not just as much as one would expect given the very rapid rise in GNI? Over a long period of time, can there be economic development without any increase in GNI?

Figure 3

GDP growth

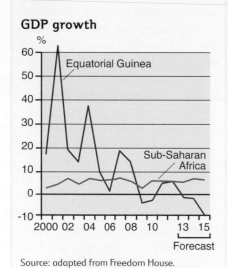

Source: adapted from Freedom House.

Figure 4

Rating on freedom

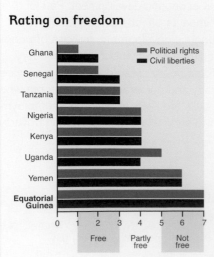

Source: adapted from Freedom House.

Table 5 Selected indicators

	Human Development Index (HDI)s	Life expectancy at birth	Mean years of schooling	Expected years of schooling	Gross national income (GNI) per capita
	(value)	(years)	(years)	(years)	(2011 PPP $)
	2013	2013	2012	2012	2013
Portugal	0.822	79.9	8.2	16.3	24 130.0
South Africa	0.658	56.9	9.9	13.1	11 788.0
Equatorial Guinea	0.556	53.1	5.4	8.5	21 927.0

Source: adapted from hdr.undp.org.

Factors influencing growth and development

Key points

1. A large number of factors influence growth and development. These include political and institutional factors, education and skills, infrastructure, technology, levels of absolute poverty, income distribution, access to credit and banking, demographic factors, international trade, commodities prices, savings, foreign aid, borrowing and debt, foreign direct investment and portfolio capital flows, remittances, gender issues, the environment and many non-economic factors, such as civil war.

Starter activity

In 2015, Syria was engaged in a prolonged civil war. List 10 factors which result from civil war that lead to economic development going backward.

Complexity

Economic development is complex. History suggests there is a number of different ways in which countries can develop. There is no single factor or single model that causes or explains economic development. However, there is a number of factors that influence development and these will be explored in this unit.

Political and institutional factors

Growth and development are fostered by good governance and the rule of law. Where the rule of law is weak, there is often an effective lack of property rights. Individuals and businesses are unable to use the law to defend their ownership of assets. The result is lower investment and lower output. Individuals and businesses are less willing to buy machinery, build factories or establish brands if powerful individuals or organisations within the state can effectively steal those assets. Linked to this is corruption. Where corruption is widespread, it is often better to seek positions where you can receive large amounts of bribes than ones where there is a genuine output of goods and services. This is a form of **rent seeking**. In authoritarian regimes, corruption tends to be endemic. Those in power use their positions to enrich themselves, their families or their ethnic group. Equally, corruption can be present in democracies. There is widespread corruption in India, for example, despite it being a democracy. Bureaucracy and regulation can be a problem. In some countries, it is very costly and time-consuming to set up a legal business because of the bureaucracy and regulation involved. Arbitrary application of tax laws can also deter business activity.

Education and skills

Education and skills have long been recognised as an important factor in economic development. Countries such as China and South Korea that invested heavily in education when they were still relatively poor, have benefited in the long term. Education raises the human capital of the population. It allows workers to be more productive. There is much debate, however, about what

sort of education is most important. Universal primary school education, for example, is almost certainly a higher priority than sending an extra five per cent of secondary students to university. There are also issues concerning over-education. If, for example, university graduates cannot get graduate-level jobs, does this show that the money spent on their education would be better spent on other development goals?

Question 1

The governor of the central bank of Nigeria, Lamido Sanusi, has alleged that massive fraud is taking place inside the state-owned Nigerian National Petroleum Corporation (NNPC). He says that more than $1 billion a month is going missing in revenues that are paid to the Nigerian government. In spite of consistently high international prices, Nigeria's income from oil has been declining sharply.

One area of alleged fraud is fuel subsidies. The NNPC claims that in the period January 2012-July 2013, it spent $8.49 billion on subsidising fuel to consumers including a subsidy on kerosene. However, the kerosene subsidy was abolished in 2009. Nowhere in Nigeria was kerosene sold at a subsidised rate during 2012-13. Lamido Sanusi estimated that $100 million a month has gone missing from these non-existent subsidies.

Another source of alleged fraud is crude oil swaps. The NNPC swaps crude oil (that is exported) for refined oil (that is imported) with international and local traders without any money changing hands. Lamido Sanusi believes that crude oil is being exchanged at too cheap a price with bribes and kick-backs being paid by oil traders to officials at the NNPC.

Oil revenues are the largest source of income for the Nigerian government. Fraud on the scale alleged by Lamido Sanusi would have a significant impact on the ability of the government to fund its spending and would put pressure on foreign currency reserves and the value of the currency, the naira.

Source: adapted from © the *Financial Times* 13.2.2014, All Rights Reserved.

(a) How might senior officials at a state owned oil company defraud the company?

(b) Explain two ways in which large-scale fraud at the Nigerian National Petroleum Corporation might harm the economic development of Nigeria.

Infrastructure

The built environment is vital for economic development. In a developed country like the UK, there is a complex network of buildings, roads, railways, airports, ports, utilities like water and gas pipes, telephone and electricity cables, and industrial plants. The greater the level of development, the higher tends to be the value of the built environment. Growth in physical capital is as important as growth in human capital if more goods and services are to be produced. However, growth of infrastructure can conflict with environmental goals. Building a new town or a new motorway will leave less land available either for agriculture or other uses.

Technology

A developed economy like the UK uses a wide range of technologies to produce goods and services. Some, like the flushing toilet, date back to the 19th century. Others, like graphene, were invented in the 21st century. Economic development requires countries to gain technologies and then apply them in the production process. It is about multiplying the use of existing technology: instead of having 1 000 factories making garments, it is about extending this to 10 000 factories making garments. It is also about introducing new technology. For example, firms can buy more up-to-date equipment that incorporates newer technology. Or firms can be set up to make machines or products which incorporate newer technology. The use of technology is linked to other factors. Individuals need to have sufficient human capital to use the technology. There needs to be support systems to repair machines and plant when they break down. The technology also has to be affordable.

Absolute poverty

Widespread absolute poverty is a severe restraint on economic development. Malnutrition, for example, which leads to death, destroys potentially productive human beings with whatever education and training they have gained. Malnutrition amongst babies and young children inhibits brain development, again leading to loss of human potential. Easily preventable diseases can kill or lead to long-term illness as do more complex

illnesses such as malaria and HIV/AIDS. In some countries in Africa both malaria and HIV/AIDS have had a severe impact on economic and social structures. Taking people out of absolute poverty should therefore be a high priority for governments and organisations such as the World Bank.

Income distribution

High levels of inequality are more likely to result in absolute poverty for some in society. High levels of inequality also reduce opportunity and incentives for the bottom deciles of the income distribution. In countries where families have to pay for the education of their children, fewer children will receive an education compared to a more equal society. Those at the bottom of the income range on average will receive less for working than if income were more equally distributed and this reduces incentives to work. It can be argued that greater inequality will encourage saving because the marginal propensity to save for an individual increases as their income rises. Higher saving then creates higher investment as explained below. However, those on low incomes will save to invest if the investment opportunities are there. Also, simply creating more saving will not necessarily lead to more investment. It could be absorbed by higher government spending or by high imports, for example.

Access to credit and banking including microfinance

In developed countries, individuals, firms and governments have access to sophisticated financial systems that allow them to save money with interest and to borrow money. Equally, there are systems for taking equity stakes in companies. There are banks, stock markets and insurance companies for example. The poorer the developing country, the less likely it is that individuals and businesses will have access to such financial institutions and markets. This restricts development because financial institutions provide ways to save now and spend in the future, or borrow now and pay back in the future at a reasonable cost. Poor families can resort to loan sharks to borrow money, but interest rates are punitive and often leave individuals permanently in

Question 2

Table 1 Selecting indicators of infrastructure and technology

	GNI per capita at PPs, US$	Electricity consumption per capita kWh 2011	Mobile phone subscriptions per 100 people 2013	% of urban population with access to an improved drinking water source 2012	% of rural population with access to an improved drinking water source 2012	% of population living in cities with more than one million inhabitants 2014
Angola	7 000	248	62	68	34	29
Brazil	14 750	2 438	135	100	85	40
Dominican Republic	11 630	893	88	83	77	27
India	5 350	684	71	97	91	14
Indonesia	9 270	680	125	93	76	10
Tanzania	2 430	92	56	78	44	10

Source: adapted from data.worldbank.org.

Discuss which country shown in the data is the most economically developed, based on the evidence given.

debt. Building a banking system that is accessible to all is therefore important for economic development. The importance of technology in development is shown by recent trends for individuals to gain access to financial systems via mobile phones. Instead of a physical network of branch banks, for example, some banking services, such as cash transfers, can be made using mobile phones. Another important development has been the growth of microfinance. Pioneered by NGOs (non-governmental organisations, some of which are charities), very small loans are given out to individuals who would otherwise not have access to borrowed money. Interest rates are reasonable and often lending is done within the context of a group, like a village. Peer pressure encourages people taking out loans to be responsible with how the money is spent and encourages repayments. Groups such as women, who often have less access to finance than men, may be targeted. Microfinance allows individuals to invest in the businesses they already own or start up new businesses.

Demographic factors

The changing structure of the population and its rate of growth can be important for development. In many developing countries, such as Italy and Japan, the population is ageing. This means the proportion of workers to dependents is falling. If the size of the population is static, output will fall, all other things being equal, because there are fewer workers. Ageing populations also place pressure on parts of the economy that serve the needs of the elderly such as health systems. Development tends to be linked to demography. The lower the level of development, the higher tends to be the birth rate. Young populations can be dynamic. However, there is a large burden on the education system to provide education and training for such a large number of young people. There also tends to be large amounts of unemployment and underemployment because economies cannot provide enough jobs for the large cohorts of young people joining the working population.

International trade

International trade is a powerful way in which developing countries can integrate themselves into the world economy. To export goods and services, firms in developing countries have to have some competitive advantage. This encourages efficiency. Importing goods and services allows them to access technology from developed countries. For example, developing countries over the past 50 years have destroyed most of the textile industry in developed countries. They have done this partly by buying textile machinery from developing countries such as Germany and Italy.

Countries that have either been excluded from international trade because of sanctions (for example Cuba) or excluded themselves for ideological reasons (such as North Korea) have suffered much lower economic growth than other developing countries. Economies with very high growth rates, such as China or South Korea have built their success on exports.

Commodities

Some developing countries are highly dependent on exports of commodities whilst others are high dependent on imports of commodities. These commodities range from agricultural products such as rice or soya beans, to mineral commodities such as copper or iron ore, to fossil fuels such as oil or coal. Dependency is related to the proportion of GDP that is accounted for by commodity exports, the proportion of exports that are commodity exports and the number of people employed in commodity production. Some commodities are highly labour intensive to produce, such as cocoa or coffee. Others, such as oil, tend to be highly capital intensive and can employ relatively few domestic workers. Commodities and natural resources should bring prosperity and increased rates of economic development to countries that are abundant in natural resources. However, there is a number of reasons why abundance of natural resources might lead to a **resource curse** where economic development is constricted.

One reason is fluctuating commodity prices. The more price inelastic the demand for the commodity, the greater are likely to be the fluctuations in price. Sudden price changes can mean large amounts of extra revenue being earned by an economy or large falls in revenue. This makes it difficult for firms and government to predict their revenues in the short and long term. This can discourage investment. However, when commodity prices rise over a number of years, there tends to be over-investment in the production of the commodity. Producers assume that prices will carry on rising or remain the same and can be caught out by large falls in price. The more dependent a country is on commodity exports, particularly one or two commodity exports, the greater the risk there will be sizeable changes in GDP when commodity prices change.

When commodity prices are declining, the terms of trade for commodity export dependent countries fall. They can afford to buy fewer goods and services from abroad with the revenues earned from sale of commodities. In the past, it has been argued that commodity prices will be in a permanent state of decline compared to all other goods such as manufactured goods. Commodities are argued to have a low-income elasticity of demand whilst manufactured goods and services have a high elasticity of demand. As world incomes rise, demand for manufactured goods and services will rise faster than for commodities. So commodity export dependent countries will grow relatively poorer to other countries. However, the experience of the world commodity boom from 2001 to 2013 shows that commodity prices can rise significantly over a long period compared to the price of all other goods. In the early 2000s, it was developed countries who were seeing their terms of trade decline compared to commodity export dependent countries. It was also true that commodity rich countries, ranging from Australia to Chile to Saudi Arabia, saw their growth rates exceed less resource-rich countries.

Another problem is what is known as the **Dutch disease**. Some countries become significant commodity producers in a relatively short space of time. The Netherlands in the 1960s became a significant producer of natural gas from a large offshore field in the North Sea. As a result, the Netherlands imported less energy and exported gas. This increased the demand for the Dutch currency and reduced supply leading to a significant rise in the Dutch foreign exchange rate. As a result,

Dutch agricultural and manufacturing products became less internationally price competitive and output in these two sectors fell from what they would otherwise have been. If the economic loss from closure of firms is greater than the gain from increased commodity revenues, the economy can become worse off as a result of the exploitation of a commodity. The non-oil sectors in countries like Nigeria and Venezuela have suffered because oil exports have pushed up the value of their currencies.

Another aspect of the resource curse occurs when commodity resources can be controlled by small groups that seek to maximise their own rewards at the expense of the rest of the population. An example might be the development of a gold mine. A multinational mining company wants to develop the mine and maximise its own profits. It therefore wants to pay as little to the government of the country as possible in licences, fees and taxes. It also wants to operate the mine as cheaply as possible. So it wants to be able to dispose of waste without worrying about environmental damage. It also wants to be able to recruit local workers at the lowest possible wage rate, preferably without any trade unions being involved. It therefore bribes local officials and politicians to secure a good deal. Members of government might be paid millions of dollars in bribes whilst local officials might be paid lesser amounts to disregard environmental damage. The police might be bribed too to control workers. It is now illegal for multinational companies based in countries such as the UK and the USA to pay bribes. However, every year, cases of multinational companies using bribery to secure sales orders or gain possession of assets are reported. Many more go undetected. The losers are local populations. Despite billions of dollars of commodities being extracted from their countries, they can receive little benefit compared to the multinational companies engaged in extraction.

The savings gap, foreign aid and the Harrod-Domar model

Development economics has a relatively short history. The first major work in this field of economics was done in the 1950s. The most important question which development economists first asked themselves was 'how can economic growth in an economy be raised?' Development economists initially used a widely accepted growth theory of the time called the **Harrod-Domar growth model**. This theory (shown in Figure 1) states that investment, saving and technological change are the key variables in determining economic growth. Increased investment in the economy pushes out the production possibility frontier. So too does the introduction of new physical capital where new, technologically advanced capital can produce more output than a unit of the old capital using less advanced technology. Saving is important because savings approximately equals investment in an economy.

The policy implications of the Harrod-Domar model are clear. Increasing the rate of economic growth is a simple matter of either increasing the savings ratio in the economy that will increase the amount of investment. Or it is about technological progress that allows more output to be produced from a single unit of that capital.

If a country is poor, it might seem obvious that savings will

Figure 1

The Harrod-Domar model of growth

The Harrod-Domar model can be expressed in simple algebraic terms. Savings (S) is a proportion (s) of national income (Y). So S = sY. Investment (I) is the change in the capital stock (ΔK). The amount of extra capital (ΔK) needed to produce an extra unit of output (ΔY) is called k, the capital-output ratio and is equal to $\Delta K \div \Delta Y$. Investment is roughly equal to savings in an economy, and so it can be said that S = I.

What then causes economic growth, which is measured by the change in output divided by the original level of output ($\Delta Y \div Y$)? The top of the fraction, ΔY can be found from the definition of the capital output ratio, k = ($\Delta K \div \Delta Y$). Rearranging this equation gives: $\Delta Y = (\Delta K \div k)$. The bottom of the fraction, Y, can be found from the equation S = sY, remembering that S = I and that I = ΔK. This gives us S = I = ΔK = sY. Rearranging the last part of this gives:

$$Y = \Delta K \div s$$

Δk can be found on both the top and bottom of this fraction for the growth rate of the economy and therefore cancel each other out. This leaves us with:

$$\text{The rate of growth} = \frac{\Delta Y}{Y} = \frac{s}{k}$$

be low. Households will be spending all their money simply to stay alive. Therefore poor developing countries will have insufficient levels of savings to finance investment. The result will be a cycle of low savings, low investment and low economic growth. One way out of this is for rich developed countries to give foreign aid. If used to boost investment, it fills the **savings gap**, the difference between actual savings and the level of savings needed to achieve a higher growth rate. Equally, foreign aid might be used to fill a **foreign exchange gap**. This is when exports from a developing country are too low compared to imports to finance the purchase of investment or other goods from overseas required for faster economic growth.

Economists are widely agreed that increasing savings and investment are likely to secure higher growth rates. However, these are not **sufficient** conditions for economic growth. Investment can be wasted. Building a new steel mill in a developing country might lead to nothing if workers are not able to run the mill, or if there aren't the ports to import iron ore, or the road to transport the finished product. There can be **capital flight**. This is when savings are sent abroad by citizens and firms of a country to another country which is either seen as being more secure or where the money can be hidden from government authorities. Foreign aid can be expropriated by local elites through bribery and corruption. Or it can be used to finance arms purchases rather than used for productive investment. Also, when opportunities for small-scale profitable investment projects arise, households will increase their saving to invest. Farmers, for example, will save more if they know that investing in more productive seeds or a new piece of equipment will be profitable.

Debt

Foreign currency debt was a major problem for many developing countries in the 1980s and 1990s. In the 1970s, the governments of developing countries had been encouraged by banks to borrow money at low rates of interest denominated in US dollars. The early 1980s, however, saw a rise in the value of the US dollar against other currencies and a rise in interest rates. It left the governments of many developing countries paying substantially more in their own local currencies simply to pay the interest on their foreign currency loans. One response was to borrow more money to keep up with interest payments. However, in 1982, the government of Mexico defaulted on its debts, i.e. it refused to make further payments on its debts. Banks took fright and were very reluctant to lend to many developing countries. This 'Third World debt crisis' led to examples of poor developing countries paying more in interest and debt to banks in developed countries than they received in loans and foreign aid. Money was therefore flowing from poor countries to rich countries, the opposite of what economic development needed.

The debt crisis was resolved by a combination of measures. Debt was written off or reduced. Economic growth in developing countries reduced the ratio of debt payments to GDP and so debt repayments became more affordable. Rising exports in developing countries released foreign currency to repay debt.

The debt crisis, however, hindered economic development in countries that were badly affected. The money that was borrowed was all too often squandered by governments. Some of it was simply appropriated by elites through corruption. Some of it was very badly invested in projects which gave little or no economic return. Some of it was spent on arms. It wasn't until the early 2000s that many countries resolved their debt problems through fast economic growth. Even today, a few countries, such as Argentina, are still suffering from the debt crisis through economic mismanagement.

Borrowing money to finance economic growth should in theory make sense. Firms, for example, borrow money to finance

Question 3

Mongolia is an upper middle-income landlocked country with a small population of three million people. In 2013, GNI per capita at PPPs was $8 810, a little higher than that for Jamaica and about a quarter of that of the UK. It has become one of the world's most highly commodity dependent countries. Its GDP is crucially dependent on mining. The mining sector, which is mainly controlled by multinational companies, has seen Mongolian GDP at PPPs rise two and half times between 2004 and 2013.

In 2014, the world price of copper fell significantly as demand from fast-growing countries such as China fell. Mongolia was part way through the development of the Oyu Togoi gold and copper mine in partnership with Rio Tinto, the Anglo-Australian multinational company. Rio Tinto has annual revenue five times the GDP of Mongolia measured in dollars at market prices. The output of the Oyu Togoi mine, once fully developed, is predicted to form one third of the total output of the Mongolian economy.

In 2014, Rio Tinto and the Mongolian government had fallen out over the next phase of development of Oyu Togoi. The first phase of the project had already cost more than $6 billion with significant cost overruns being incurred. The Mongolian government had initially agreed to take a 34 per cent stake in the mine, borrowing the money via Rio Tinto, to be repaid through its share of the profits from the mine. However, it was forecast that it would take 20 years for the Mongolian government to receive any revenues from its stake in the mine. Hence, the government had wanted to renegotiate the deal, getting Rio Tinto to pay royalties on output year by year rather than wait 20 years for profits. In 2015, the Mongolian government backed down and negotiated a settlement with Rio Tinto which included keeping to its 34 per cent stake. It needed the foreign direct investment to sustain its economy. Between 2017 and 2018, external debt of $1.08bn matures and will need repaying. Without continued foreign direct investment (FDI) in the country, GDP will fall as will living standards.

The difficult relationship the Mongolian government has with foreign investors can be seen from the case of Khan Resources. In 2009, the Mongolian government nationalised the Domod uranium

prospect declaring it to be a 'national resource'. The Canadian company owning the prospect took the Mongolian government to an international arbitration panel and in 2015 was awarded $100 million in damages. Payment will put pressure on Mongolia's reserves of foreign currency, counteracting the beneficial effects of FDI.

Source: adapted from © the *Financial Times* 6.4.2014, 3.3.2015, 13.3.2015, 6.4.2015 All Rights Reserved; data.worldbank.org.

Figure 2

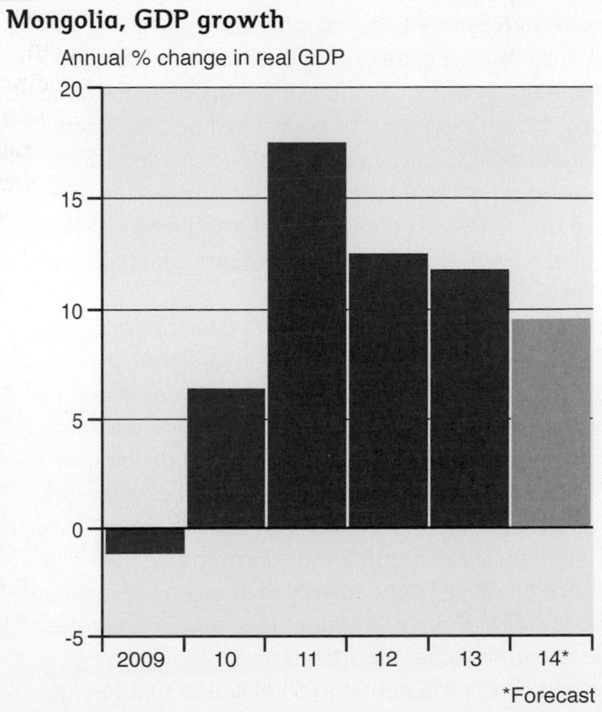

Mongolia, GDP growth

Source: adapted from Thomson Reuters Datastream; © the *Financial Times* 6.4.2015, All Rights Reserved.

Explain, using the data as an example, the advantages and disadvantages of a country relying heavily on foreign direct investment for its economic development.

their day-to-day activities and their investment plans. If the private sector in developing countries is borrowing money to finance its growth, this should increase the productive potential of the economy. Recent history suggests that the problem with debt in developing countries occurs when it is government that is taking on the debt and then spending that money badly.

Foreign direct investment (FDI) and portfolio capital flows

Foreign direct investment (FDI) is investment usually by one private sector company in one country into another private sector company from another country. Ford setting up a car manufacturing plant in China would be an example. Most FDI, though, is the purchase of existing assets. For example, Ford buying a local Chinese car manufacturing company would be FDI.

Investment capital is different from loan capital. A loan has to be repaid even if the investment that is made with the loan is not successful. The government of a developing country borrowing money to build a power station has to repay the loan whether the power station is built or not. However, if the power station is built and owned by a company from another country, then that company takes on the risk of failure. If it fails, the developing country does not owe any money to foreigners.

Investment capital also involves the transfer of some sort of knowledge from one country to another. For example, a US car component manufacturer may build a manufacturing plant in China. It will almost invariably import some machinery and equipment from the US. But it will also combine that with locally produced investment capital such as buildings. It will train staff. It will create a climate that ensures commercial success. This has large positive spin-offs for China. Extra goods for domestic consumption and for export will be produced, increasing GDP. Local workers will be able to absorb US production techniques, leading to the establishment of new local Chinese firms. The US company will also need suppliers in the local Chinese economy. There is therefore a multiplier effect on investment and output.

To counterbalance these advantages, a developing country accepting FDI flows will lose some of its sovereignty. It will become dependent to some extent on the activities of foreign firms. However, this is no different from FDI flows between individual countries in the developed world. The developing country will also have to allow the repatriation of profits - the equivalent of debt interest. Profit rates on capital are typically lower than interest rates on borrowed funds and so FDI investments are a relatively cheap way of acquiring investment capital. What is more, if the investment is relatively unsuccessful, there will be no profit to be repatriated to another country.

Developing countries accepting FDI may find that foreign companies 'exploit' the local economy by setting themselves lower safety standards or working their labour force longer hours for lower pay than similar operations in a developed country. However, it should be remembered that one of the main reasons why firms from developed countries are attracted to set up in developing countries is because of lower costs of production.

In the 1960s and 1970s, FDI was often viewed with suspicion by developing countries. They saw it as part of the way in which former colonial powers in the developed world could continue to exploit them. By the 1990s, it was obvious that FDI flows could be of significant benefit to developing countries. The challenge became one of how to attract FDI flows whilst at the same time ensuring that they created economic development in the developing country.

Remittances

Unemployment and underemployment is a major problem in many developing and developed countries. Some of those who are unemployed or underemployed will choose to find work abroad. In the EU, for example, there are flows of economic migrants from Eastern Europe to Western Europe. Ireland, traditionally an economy with not enough jobs for its growing population, has seen tens of millions migrate over the past 200 years. In developing countries, there are large migrant populations from countries such as Pakistan and Egypt working in the Gulf States and in Saudi Arabia. In Russia, there are millions of migrants from former Asian Soviet republics such as Turkmenistan.

Some of the migrants will settle in their new country. Some will want to settle but will be refused permission. For others, their work is temporary. They want to make enough money to go home and buy a house or have financial security for years to come. Many migrants send back money to their families whilst they are working abroad. These are called **remittances**. For some countries, remittances are a major export earner. On the balance of payments, they are an invisible export. They therefore add to GDP. According to the World Bank, the top five countries in terms of remittances as a percentage of GDP were Kyrgyz Republic (31.5 per cent), Nepal (28.8 per cent), Moldova (24.9 per cent), Haiti (21.1 per cent) and Armenia (21 per cent). Other countries with high remittances included Lesotho (19.8 per cent) Honduras (16.9 per cent) and Bangladesh (9.0 per cent). In contrast, remittances to the UK were 0.1 per cent of GDP.

Remittances are positive because they increase GDP and they allow otherwise unemployed workers to have a job. However, they are a second-best solution to those workers being employed in high value jobs in their countries. They can aid economic development but they are also a sign that there are major labour market problems in those countries.

Gender issues

On average, women in developing countries are disadvantaged compared to men. In many countries, for example, girls will complete fewer years of schooling than boys. They therefore will build up less human capital. They can also be excluded from many jobs and positions of authority. If food is scarce, women will often go hungry to feed the men in their family and their children. If they become widowed and have to find a job, then they face a labour market where women's wages for the same work tends to be lower than for males workers. High mortality rates from childbirth are also a problem faced by women in poorer developing countries. Overall, life expectancy of women can equal those of men in poorer developing countries. This can be compared to developed countries where life expectancy for females is several years higher than males.

Economic development therefore needs to address gender issues if it is assumed that women should have the same life chances as men. It also needs to be addressed because underutilising half the population has many negative effects. It reduces GDP from what it could otherwise be. It disempowers women and means they play a less effective role in whatever they are doing whether in the home or in the workplace. In terms of bringing up children, the more educated the mother, the more likely it is that her children will be educated to a similar standard too.

Question 4

26 years ago, the Delhi Development Authority (DDA) began encouraging a housing development on farmland, creating the middle-class satellite city of Dwarka on the western fringes of the Indian capital. Now with a population of half a million, the city is still growing. But it faces a major problem: lack of water. When the city first began, groups of residents would drill their own boreholes to provide for their water needs. Many of these have now run dry as the water table falls due to over-exploitation of ground water. Many residents of Dwarka are reliant on water that is brought in by tanker lorries. The DDA admits that it is only able to supply half of Dwarka's official demand of 40 million litres a day. Overexploitation of water resources has led to major problems with too many remaining water resources being contaminated or unfit to use. Dwarka's prosperous residents complain bitterly of official corruption and water theft by nearby communities and say they are fed up with having to pay what they call the 'water mafia' for their tanker suppliers.

Source: adapted from © the *Financial Times* 20.6.2014, All Rights Reserved.

Figure 3

Top 10 fresh water users, annual withdrawals, 2011

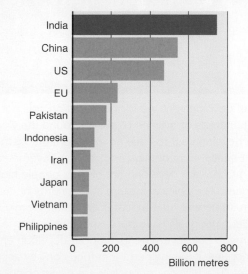

Source: adapted from OECD.

Explain why a lack of water supplies to homes and businesses may hinder economic development.

The environment

Economic development is partly about increasing GDP. Producing goods and services uses up resources, some of which are non-renewable. It also creates waste. In the UK, almost every household owns a refrigerator. Economic development is about almost every household in the world owning a refrigerator. This, however, will use up more non-renewable resources. The power source used to make the refrigerator work will today most likely come from non-renewable resources and create CO_2 emissions. Then the refrigerator will need to be disposed of at the end of its life.

The experience of the past 50 years indicates that developing countries harm the environment as they grow. Rich developed countries in contrast have reduced the environmental impact of every extra £1 of GDP produced it can be argued. This is because they are affluent enough to devote resources to reduce the environmental impact of production. It can be argued that developed countries have not done enough and that the net damage they have inflicted on the environment is higher than it was ten or 20 years ago. Unless the environmental cost per £1 of output has been at least halved, then the overall environmental damage will be higher if output is twice as high. This debate partly centres on what is considered to be damage to the environment and what value should be placed on the damage.

In developing countries, there are strong economic incentives for firms to create negative environmental externalities. Reducing pollution reduces profits in many cases. Governments are often more focussed on increasing economic growth and employment than on safeguarding the environment. Hence environmental

Key Terms

Capital flight - when savings are sent abroad by citizens and firms of a country to another country which is either seen as being more secure or where the money can be hidden from government authorities.

Dutch disease - in economics, where exploitation of natural resources leads to a rise in the exchange rate and the loss of international competitiveness of the country in the production of non-resource goods and services.

Foreign exchange gap - the difference between the actual level of exports and the level of exports needed to create higher economic growth for an economy.

Harrod-Domar growth model - a model which suggests that economic growth is dependent on the saving ratio and technological progress.

Rent seeking - behaviour which attempts to gain a share of an existing pot of income or wealth rather than creating higher income or wealth.

Resource curse - exists where an abundance of natural resources in a country is exploited, but where there is consequently little increase in economic development.

Savings gap - in development economics, the difference between the actual level of savings in an economy and the level of savings needed to finance the investment required for a higher rate of economic growth.

regulations tend to be lax and often not applied. However, as with developed countries, the question is what value should be put on damage to the environment in relation to rises in GDP. High values on environmental damage imply much less economic development has taken place than if low values are put on the damage.

Non-economic factors

There is a large number of non-economic factors that influence development. One major cause of negative development is war. Countries such as Syria, Iraq and Afghanistan have paid a very heavy price in recent years for continued war that has destroyed both physical and human capital. Poor governance has been a key factor in weak economic development. Diseases such as HIV/AIDS and malaria continue to have a heavy impact on affected countries. Geographical location is also important. Economic growth in China has been much faster in coastal regions with easier access to ports for exported goods than inland. Landlocked countries like Bolivia or Uganda have a natural economic disadvantage compared to countries with access to sea routes.

Thinking like an economist

Millennium goals

In 2000, world leaders at the United Nations headquarters in New York adopted the United National Millennium Declaration. This committed them to working for the eradication of extreme poverty in the world. A number of Millennium Development Goals were to be set with a deadline set for achieving these of 2015. These goals were:

1. to eradicate extreme poverty and hunger;
2. to achieve universal primary education;
3. to promote gender equality;
4. to reduce child mortality;
5. to improve maternal health;
6. to combat HIV/AIDS, malaria and other diseases;
7. to ensure environmental sustainability;
8. to develop a global partnership for development.

Each goal was then given more specific targets. For example, for the first millennium goal of eradicating extreme poverty and hunger, three targets were set:

- to halve between 1990 and 2015 the proportion of people whose income less than $1.25 a day;
- to achieve full and productive employment and decent work for all including women and young people;
- to halve between 1990 and 2015 the proportion of people who suffer from hunger.

By 2015, progress towards meeting the goals had been patchy. Some countries had made very little progress over the period 2000-2015. Others, such as China, had made very good progress on many indicators. In the case of China, the country with the world's highest population in 2015, this was mainly due to its very high economic growth rate over the period. High economic growth increased average incomes although it came at a high environmental cost.

Critics argued that the Millennium goals had little impact on development. This was because they were not constructed by individuals, organisations and governments which needed to make the most progress in these goals. Critics also said that the targets were far too few and didn't fully capture all the facets of economic development.

However, the Millennium goals were never meant to be a comprehensive list of targets needed for economic development. They were meant to be an easily understood list of some main

indicators of development. As for participation, it is not possible to get the hundreds of millions of groups round the world involved in development to have an input to the construction of targets. Equally, dictatorships and corrupt governments are never going to put the development of their people high on their list of priorities. The political system in a minority of countries is bound to frustrate attempts to foster economic development.

The Millennium goals have put a spotlight on key indicators of development. For governments that put development high on their list priorities, it has helped them focus on key aspects of development. The Millennium goals were never going to solve the problems of poverty in the world. But, arguably, they have made a contribution towards world economic development.

Source: with information from www.un.org/millenniumgoals, *Millennium Development Goals and Beyond, 2015*, © 2015 United Nations. Reprinted with the permission of the United Nations.

Data Response Question

Millennium goals

Goal: Achieve universal primary education

Target: Ensure that, by 2015, children everywhere, boys and girls alike, will be able to complete a full course of primary schooling

Fast facts

- Literacy rates among adults and youths are on the rise and gender gaps are narrowing.
- New national data show the number of out-of-school children dropped from 102 million to 57 million from 2000 to 2011.
- Primary education enrolment in developing countries reached 90 per cent in 2010.

Where we stand

Developing regions have made impressive strides in expanding access to primary education. From 2000 to 2011, the enrolment rate grew from 83 per cent to 90 per cent, and the number of out-of-school children dropped by almost half from 102 million in 2000 to 57 million in 2011. Achieving gains in education will have an impact on all Millennium Development Goals. Even after four years of primary schooling, as many as 250 million children cannot read and write, worldwide. Without these fundamental skills, the basis for all future learning is severely undermined. Going to school is not enough; improving learning is critical. Early school leaving remains persistent. Among the 137 million children who entered first grade in 2011, 34 million are likely to leave before reaching the last grade of primary school. This translates into an early school-leaving rate of 25 per cent - the same level as in 2000. Literacy rates are rising. The greatest rises in youth literacy rates between 1990 and 2011 were

in Northern Africa (from 68 to 89 per cent) and Southern Asia (from 60 to 81 per cent), where gender gaps narrowed. Poverty, gender and place of residence are key factors keeping children out of school. Children and adolescents from the poorest households are three times more likely to be out of school than children from the richest households. Even in the richest households, girls are more likely to be out of school than boys. Globally, 123 million youth aged 15 to 24 lack basic reading and writing skills; 61 per cent of them are young women. Progress in reducing the number of out-of-school children has come to a standstill as international aid to basic education in 2011 fell for the first time since 2002. This stalled progress, combined with reductions in aid, has put the chances of meeting the 2015 target at risk.

What's working?

Cambodia: Schools connect remote villages. Children in Tuol Pongro village can now continue their education after the Inter-Commune Cooperation project, with UNDP (United Nations Development Programme) support, built a local secondary school. The project is now reaching 54 of Cambodia's 171 districts, prompting the government to consider integrating it into national policies for local governance. Since 2006, more than 260 projects have built roads, bridges and schools in remote communities.

Brazil: Millions step out of poverty into school. A conditional cash transfer programme is making it easier for parents to send their children to school. Since 2003, Bolsa Família has lifted 50 million people out of poverty in 5,500 communities, with steady reports of improved school attendance and health conditions.

Guatemala: Potential unleashed among indigenous girls. Since 2004,

Abriendo Oportunidades has reached more than 4,000 girls from 45 Mayan communities in poor, isolated areas. The project is improving opportunities for girls, who often face a future of limited schooling and early marriage. Girls are building their self-esteem and literacy, staying in school and breaking the cycle of poverty.

Source: with information from www.un.org/millennium goals, Millennium Development Goals and Beyond, 2015, © 2015 United Nations. Reprinted with the permission of the United Nations.

1. Explain what is meant by 'youth literacy rates'.

2. Analyse why successfully completing education for both boys and girls is an important factor affecting growth and development.

3. Discuss whether it would be better for growth and development if the governments of developing countries, aid agencies and international bodies like the United Nations concentrated more on supporting business communities such as farmers, manufacturers or service industry firms and less on education.

Evaluation

Question 3 sets up an either/or scenario - if there is £100 to spend, should it go to supporting business or to education? One source of evaluation is to compare the impact of these choices on growth and then development in the short term. Could you get higher economic growth but less development if the money were spent on supporting businesses rather than education? Is the same correct in the long term? Would £100 spent on education today benefit businesses more in 20 years' time than £100 spent today on supporting businesses? The data mention the importance of education for girls. How important will their role be in business in 20 years' time if they have received an education today?

Strategies influencing growth and development

Key points

1. There are many different types of development strategy including market-orientated strategies and interventionist strategies.
2. Issues which must be decided by governments when considering economic development include protectionism, subsidies, exchange rates, infrastructure development, the financial sector, FDI and joint ventures, privatisation, buffer stock schemes, industrialisation, development of primary industries, tourism, fair trade schemes, foreign aid and debt forgiveness.
3. International organisations such as the World Bank and the IMF together with NGOs can impact on economic development.

Starter activity

Have you ever heard of fair trade products? Have you ever bought or consumed fair trade products? How might you buying fair trade products help those in developing countries?

Different types of development strategy

Economists and politicians differ about the most effective development strategies for any individual country or groups of countries. Some economists tend to advocate market-orientated strategies. These strategies rely upon free markets to deliver economic development. Examples of such strategies include:

- trade liberalisation;
- promotion of foreign direct investment (FDI);
- removal of government subsidies;
- freely floating exchange rates;
- microfinance schemes;
- privatisation.

Other economists tend to advocate interventionist strategies. These are strategies where government plays a leading role, regulating and manipulating markets or bypassing markets through direct provision of goods and services. Examples of interventionist strategies include:

- development of human capital through state-provided education;
- trade protection;
- managed exchanged rates;
- infrastructure development;
- promoting joint ventures with global companies;
- buffer stock schemes.

Other strategies for development include:

- industrialisation, the development of tourism and the development of primary industries;
- fair trade schemes;
- aid and debt relief.

These strategies will now be considered in more detail.

Trade liberalisation vs protectionism

During the 1930s, when the world economy was rocked by the Great Depression in the USA and Europe, many developing countries, like most developed countries, opted for a policy of **protectionism**. It was argued that the best way to protect jobs and promote the growth of domestic industry was to keep foreign goods out. This then led many developing countries to believe that their own development could best be promoted through a policy of **import substitution**, the deliberate attempt to replace imported goods with domestically produced goods by adopting protectionist measures.

Import substitution policies might create jobs in the short run, as domestic production replaces foreign production. However, economic theory would suggest that, in the long run, output and growth of output will be lower than it would otherwise have been. This is because import substitution denies the country the benefits to be gained from **specialisation**. The theory of comparative advantage shows how countries will gain from trade. Moreover, protectionism leads to dynamic inefficiency. Protected domestic producers have no incentive to reduce costs or improve products because there is a lack of foreign competition. Countries which have adopted import substitution strategies have tended to experience lower growth rates than other countries, particularly if they are small countries The larger the country, the more opportunities there are for specialisation within the country.

The opposite strategy to import substitution is that of **export-led growth**. Rather than becoming less dependent upon world trade, it is argued that growth can be increased by becoming more dependent. Removing trade barriers will force domestic industry either to close or to become as efficient as any world producer. Resources will be reallocated to those industries that produce goods in which the country has a comparative advantage in production. In a developing country, these are likely to be labour-intensive, low-technology industries. Countries wishing to diversify from exporting commodities can give short-term selective assistance to their manufacturing industries. The newly industrialised nations of Brazil and Mexico, and particularly Hong Kong, South Korea and Singapore, have enjoyed above-average growth by adopting such a strategy.

Government subsidies

The governments of many developing countries provide a wide range of subsidies. Many of these subsidies target essential items, such as food or fuel, that make up a disproportionate share of spending of low-income households. Other subsidies target agriculture and industry in a bid to increase output and investment.

Subsidising essential items, such as food and fuel, can be an effective way of minimising absolute poverty. It can ensure that prices are low enough for poor households to buy sufficient food and fuel to stay alive. They are an easily understood and politically popular method of government intervention.

However, there is a number of problems with subsidies.

- Subsidies are poorly targeted if everyone in the population can buy the subsidised goods. If everyone can buy subsidised rice, for example, rich households benefit even though they do not need the subsidies. Fuel subsidies that target motor fuels rather than heating fuels benefit those with motor vehicles. These are unlikely to be the poorest in the population.

- Economic theory would suggest that welfare would probably be higher if poor households were given cash payments rather than subsidies. The payments could be targeted, avoiding the problem of everyone being able to buy subsidised goods.

- Where subsidies are given to farmers or industry, government is saying that it is better at allocating scarce resources than free markets. This may be the case. For example, subsidising fertilisers for selected farmers may help them increase their incomes considerably. However, in general, the larger the subsidy, the larger the group that receives it and the longer the period of time that the subsidy is given, the less likely it is that the subsidy will increase economic development.

- Subsidies can easily become a significant proportion of total government spending. There is then a large opportunity cost in development terms. The money used for subsidies is money that is not available to spend on education, health care or building infrastructure.

- Subsidies can be a major source of corruption and criminality. For example, in Venezuela, subsidised fuel is smuggled across its borders and sold in neighbouring countries at a higher price.

- Removing subsidies can be very difficult politically. Governments have been thrown out of office, sometimes violently, for attempting to do this. There are too many people who have a vested interest in maintaining subsidies for it to be an easy option.

Figure 1 shows the effect on price and quantity of removing a subsidy. With a subsidy of EG per unit, quantity demanded and supplied is OB. Removing the subsidy shifts the supply curve to the left from S_1 to S_2. Quantity demanded and supplied falls to OA whilst price rises to OF. The government is now spending EGHK less in subsidies (the subsidy EG x the quantity bought OB). If the good is a necessity like a basic food, the demand curve is likely to be relatively inelastic. The more price inelastic is demand, the greater will be the impact of a subsidy on equilibrium price. Removing the subsidy will therefore lead to a larger increase in price than if the demand curve were more price elastic.

The best time for a government to remove a subsidy is when

Figure 1

Removing a subsidy

Removing a subsidy of EG per unit on a good leads to a rise in equilibrium price of EF and a fall in quantity demanded and supplied of AB.

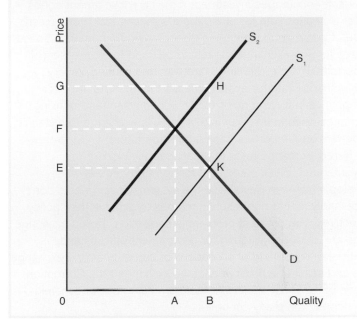

the free market price of the good is falling. In an ideal scenario, the free market price of a good falls, for example, by 20 per cent when the subsidy is also 20 per cent. Removing the subsidy then leads to no change in price.

Exchange rates

Most governments have a choice about which type of exchange rate system (explained in Unit 69) to use for its currency. The few that don't are countries that are part of a monetary union like the eurozone. Some countries use a floating exchange rate system. Market forces determine the value of the currency. The advantage of this is that governments don't have to intervene and don't have to worry about their gold and foreign currency reserves running out. There are two main disadvantages. One is that the value of the currency is likely to be volatile. This is true whether the country is a developed country like the UK or the USA or a developing country. Volatility makes it difficult for exporters and importers to make decisions about the future. The other disadvantage is that it can lead to swings in macroeconomic variables, such as economic growth, inflation and unemployment. Large rises in the exchange rate, for example, can lead to lower exports and higher imports. This reduces GDP and is likely to increase unemployment. On the other hand, inflation will fall. Not controlling the value of the currency means that a country is very vulnerable to exchange rate swings.

A more interventionist approach is to manage the exchange rate. One of the most interventionist types of policy is to fix a number of different exchange rates. For example, there might be a high exchange rate for imports of essential products. There might be a lower one for imports of other goods. There might be an even lower one for exports. Foreign currency is managed through the central bank. It controls how much foreign currency will be available, for example, for imports of essential goods and imports of all other goods. A high exchange rate for imports of essential products means that the domestic price of these goods is low. This helps relieve poverty if they are essential consumer goods. It encourages investment if they are investment goods. A lower exchange rate for other imports means that the domestic price of these goods is higher, discouraging their import. So less scarce foreign exchange is likely to be used for non-essential imports than if the exchange rate was free floating. A very low exchange rate for exports means that exports are price competitive in foreign markets. An added advantage of fixing exchange rates in this way is that there is exchange rate stability. Exporters and importers can plan for the future.

Tiered exchange rates in practice rarely work in the way intended. Black markets in foreign exchange always develop which can destabilise the system. Governments don't necessarily fix the right exchange rates to achieve their policy objectives. The greatest problem is corruption. Tiered exchange rates are an open invitation for government officials and politicians to get hold of allocations of currency at one exchange rate and sell it at a profit at another exchange rate. Corruption is one of the most significant factors holding back economic development in many countries.

Governments can choose to manage a single exchange rate, buying and selling currency to fix an exchange rate. However, speculation in currency markets is so large that countries find it very difficult to maintain an exchange rate even within a broad band over a number of years.

Infrastructure development

Infrastructure is essential for economic development. For example, a coastal country needs well-functioning ports if it is to export and import efficiently. A land-locked country needs good roads, railways and airports for trade and the movement of people. Schools and hospitals need to be built.

An interventionist approach to infrastructure development is for government to be the principal builder of infrastructure. In a country like the UK, for example, the government is responsible for building and maintaining roads, schools and hospitals. A more free market approach is for government to allow private sector companies to develop infrastructure. For example, many seaports and airports around the world are owned by private sector companies. The private sector can also build and operate hospitals and schools.

Who should provide infrastructure depends on a number of factors. One is profitability. The private sector will only build and operate infrastructure if it is profitable. A majority of infrastructure projects, like building and operating a new school or a new road, will never be privately profitable. However, there may be significant positive externalities and so there may be a significant social profit to be made. In this case, it is the government's responsibility to finance the infrastructure.

Another factor is efficiency. Free market economists argue that the private sector is more efficient in general than the public sector. For example, the total cost of building a new container port is likely to be lower if it is owned, built and operated by a private sector company than by government.

A third factor is availability of resources. A government may not have the resources from its budget to build a new port. However, allowing the private sector to fund the development may allow the project to go ahead.

Some large infrastructure projects in a number of developing countries have not given the benefits intended. They may have been poorly built and poorly maintained. In the case of dams, they have been criticised for creating large-scale environmental damage as well as displacing large numbers of people from their lands. Infrastructure projects are also often associated with bribery and corruption.

Developing a financial sector

Countries need a financial sector. Households, firms and government need to be able to save money and borrow money, transferring assets and liabilities from now into the future. They need services such as insurance. Poorer developing countries have relatively weak financial sectors. Providing banking services for low-income households and firms with small revenues is unlikely to be profitable for example.

Microfinance schemes, explained in Unit 75, are one way of reaching out to low-income households. Another is to deepen the services offered via mobile phones. In some developing countries, mobile phone penetration is relatively high. These can be used to offer basic banking services such as transfers of money.

Foreign Direct Investment (FDI) and joint ventures

Many developing countries compete for inflows of FDI as explained in Unit 75. This is because inflows of FDI add to the resources which can be given over to investment helping to close any saving gap or foreign currency gap. There is also

Question 1

Renault, the European automaker, has launched its Kwid hatchback, hoping to gain five per cent of the Indian market. The car will be built in India and costs 300 000 Rupees ($4 700). The Kwid will initially be manufactured at its existing Chennai facility in India which it shares with Nissan. Renault has already invested 45 billion Rupees ($705 million) in the Chennai facility. However, Renault plans to increase its investment in India and would consider either building a new factory or expanding the existing Chennai facility.

Much of the design and engineering for the Kwid has been done in India, a process some have hailed as an example of 'frugal innovation', whereby products are developed within the budgetary constraints of emerging markets and global car production.

Navi Radjouy, an expert on low-cost manufacturing and fellow at Cambridge Judge Business School, said that: In the next stage of globalisation, more companies will view countries such as India not just as new markets but bases for developing new products.'

Source: adapted from © the *Financial Times* 21.5.2015, All Rights Reserved.

Explain how Renault, a European company, can help the economic development of India.

frequently a transfer of knowledge that adds to a country's stock of human and physical capital.

However, FDI can also be associated with exploitation where foreign companies take far more from their investment than the country receives in benefits. It also reduces national sovereignty.

One way of reducing perceived exploitation is for a government to insist on major investment being set up as a **joint venture**. For example, the government of a developing country may allow a US car vehicle manufacturer to establish a car plant in its country. However, it may insist that US manufacturer find a local partner to create a jointly owned company for the car plant. Ownership may be 50:50, with the US company only owning half the company. By doing this, the government ensures that only half the profits of the car plant will go back to the US. The local partner is also likely only to provide finance rather than knowledge. However, once the car plant is established, there will inevitably be a transfer of knowledge to the local partner. It may use this to develop other activities or the knowledge may be diffused more widely in the local business community and amongst local workers.

Privatisation

In the 1960s and 1970s, many developing countries were influenced by socialist and Marxist theories of development. These theories advocated interventionist policies that included state ownership of many key industries. In the 1980s, that view was challenged by UK and US policies to reduce the size of the state in order to increase efficiency. The Thatcherite revolution in the UK, for example, saw the privatisation of companies from airlines to gas companies to coal mines. Privatisation is favoured by free market economists. They argue that the discipline of the market forces firms to cut their average costs to a minimum leading to productive efficiency. They also have to be allocatively efficient, giving customers what they want to buy. In contrast, nationalised industries have no incentive to be efficient.

Privatisation in developing countries can be a powerful way to increase efficiency. However, where nationalised industries are privatised as monopolies, then there are no competitive pressures. Hence the privatised monopoly can be as inefficient as it was when in state hands. Equally, privatisations in developing countries can easily be associated with corruption. An easy way for politicians or government officials to get rich is to sell a nationalised company at well below its market value to a family member or a friend. Equally, large bribes can change hands at the time of privatisation.

Buffer stock schemes

The price of commodities is volatile over time. This is a problem for developing countries reliant upon commodities for exports, jobs and government income. One way of stabilising commodity prices is to set up a **buffer stock scheme**. This is likely to be set up by a group of governments to fix world prices for a commodity. Equally, it could operate within a country assuming that exports and imports are controlled.

A buffer stock scheme that works effectively over a long period of time has a number of possible advantages.

- By stabilising prices, it encourages firms in the industry to invest. If it is an agricultural commodity like rice, it gives

farmers an incentive to plan for the long term.
- It prevents sharp falls in prices. If it is an agricultural commodity, it could prevent the poorest farmers sinking into absolute poverty.
- Consumers will also benefit from less price volatility.

Buffer stock schemes combine elements of both minimum and maximum prices. Typically a minimum price is set for the commodity. If the free market price threatens to go below the minimum price, then the buffer stock scheme will buy the commodity. This increases demand and raises prices. The buffer stock scheme may also set a maximum price where it will sell the commodity. This increases supply, reducing price.

The 'buffer stock' is a physical stock of the commodity held in warehouses. When the free market price is below the minimum price, stocks will be rising as the scheme buys in the market. When the free market price is above the maximum price, stocks will fall as the scheme sells in the market. For the scheme to work effectively over time, stocks must rise and fall. If they only rise, the scheme will run out of money to carry on buying. If they only fall, eventually there will be no stocks left to sell to reduce prices.

A buffer stock scheme can be shown diagrammatically. In Figure 2(a), the buffer stock agency has set a maximum price or ceiling price for the commodity of ON and a minimum price or floor price of OL. The equilibrium price of a commodity is currently OM whilst OG is demanded and supplied. The buffer stock agency does not have to intervene in the market because the price of OM is between the maximum and minimum prices. Now assume that supply increases to S_2 in Figure 2(b). The free market equilibrium price falls to OK. This is below the minimum price of OL. The buffer stock agency then buys HJ of the commodity, i.e. demand has to increase by HJ. This is just enough to raise the price to the minimum or floor price. Now assume that supply falls to S_3 in Figure 2(c). The free market equilibrium price is OR above the maximum price. So the buffer stock agency has to sell EF. This increases supply by EF and brings the price down to ON, the maximum price.

Buffer stock schemes are not common.
- A considerable amount of capital is needed to set them up. Money is required to buy produce when prices are too low. There are also the costs of administration, transport and storage of produce purchased. If the commodity is a food commodity, it may deteriorate in storage adding to costs.
- Those funding the buffer stock scheme must feel that it is benefiting them substantially because others may also benefit without incurring any of the costs. For example, a small group of countries whose farmers produce 60 per cent of world output in a commodity might set up a scheme to control world prices. There is nothing the scheme can do to prevent farmers in countries producing the other 40 per cent from benefitting from less volatile prices. Those 40 per cent become free riders on the scheme.
- The main reason why buffer stock schemes are not common, however, is because minimum prices tend to be set too high. In the short term, this benefits producers because they get higher prices than the free market price. In the long term, it is unsustainable. Stocks carry on building up and eventually

Figure 2

Buffer stock scheme

In (a), the maximum (ON) and minimum (OL) prices set by the buffer scheme are shown. The free market price of OM is between these limits and so there is no intervention. In (b), the free market price of OK is below the minimum price. So the buffer stock scheme has to increase demand by buying HJ to raise the price to OL. In (c), the free market price is above the maximum price. So the buffer stock scheme has to increase supply by selling EF to lower the price to ON.

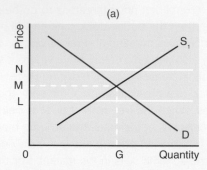
(a)

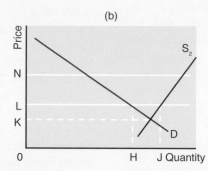
(b)

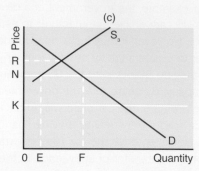
(c)

the buffer stock scheme runs out of money and collapses. Stocks are then sold off depressing the free market price. In this phase, producers are worse off because they are getting below what would otherwise be the free market price.

Where a buffer stock scheme is operated within a country or small group of countries, there are additional costs. The buffer stock scheme may be funded by taxpayers and operate at a loss. So taxpayers effectively subsidise commodity producers, usually farmers. If the minimum price is set too high, stocks will rise. A way of getting rid of some of these stocks is to sell them at a loss on world markets. This increases supply on world markets depressing prices. Commodity producers worldwide then receive less income. If it is an agricultural commodity like wheat or rice, it means that poor farmers in other countries become even poorer as the value of their crop falls.

Question 2

In 2011, a new Thai government implemented a rice subsidy scheme. The Thai government promised to buy rice from Thai farmers at a price that was well above world market prices for rice. It would be stored and then sold onto world markets when world market prices were higher.

The IMF severely criticised the scheme but the Thai government defended it saying that it benefited rural Thai rice farmers. However, a new Thai government elected in 2014 announced that it would end the scheme. World rice prices had fallen and the Thai government had accumulated large stocks of unsold rice. The government could no longer afford the estimated $4-$7 billion a year for the programme.

Rice stocks will prove difficult to sell. Some of the rice held in state warehouses is old. What is more, the government's intervention scheme did not encourage farmers to sell good-quality rice. The state warehouses could hold between 10 million and 15 million tonnes. This is just under half the total yearly amount of rice that is exported by all rice-exporting countries.

Source: adapted from © the *Financial Times* 12.2.2014, 14.4.2014, 27.4.2014, All Rights Reserved.

(a) Explain, using a diagram, how the Thai subsidy scheme raised the price of rice that Thai rice farmers received in Thailand.

(b) Why might the Thai scheme have succeeded if the world price of rice had risen?

(c) What was likely to happen to the world price of rice if the Thai government had sold a large proportion of its stocks in 2014?

The Lewis model

Developed countries have large service industries and very small agricultural sectors measured in terms of output and employment. To achieve this, they went through a stage where there was a rapid expansion of manufacturing industry before this shrank in relative importance. Industrialisation is therefore a key feature of economic development of mainly agricultural economies.

W Arthur Lewis was an economist who used this to focus on the role of migration in developing countries. He argued that growth could be sustained by the gradual transfer of workers from low-productivity agriculture (the **traditional sector**) to higher-productivity urban secondary and tertiary industries (the **modern sector**). The **industrialisation** of the economy, therefore, can be seen as an objective of development. He assumed that marginal workers in rural areas added nothing to the output of the rural economy (i.e. their marginal productivity was zero). Either they genuinely did not work (i.e. they were unemployed) or the work that they did could have been performed by existing workers, with no effect on total output (i.e. there was a large amount of underemployment in the rural economy). Workers could gradually be transferred into the urban higher-productivity sector. The rate of transfer depended on the rate of capital accumulation in the modern sector of the economy. The greater the investment, the faster the transfer. Eventually, nearly all workers will have been transferred from the traditional sector to the modern sector and the economy will have become developed.

Interventionist economists suggested that government should promote industrialisation in order to create economic development. However, there are many problems with the

Question 3

Guyana is situated on the coast in north east South America, next door to Venezuela and Brazil. It is a small country, an ex-British colony, with a population of just 750 000 and is the third poorest country in Latin America and the Caribbean. Recent elections have seen a change of government.

The new president, David Granger, has talked about a 'new era' and hopes are high about a recent oil find by ExxonMobil off the coast that the US company described as 'significant'. David Granger has said that he is 'friendly with foreign investment' and is willing to attract Brazilian infrastructure ventures. But he has also pledged to review certain contracts made during his predecessor's rule, including that of the recently opened $58-million Marriott hotel in central Georgetown, the capital. 'Too many of the contracts engaged by the previous administration are opaque,' he says.

The economy is heavily reliant on commodities, in the form of gold, bauxite, sugar and rice. Partly thanks to the commodities boom, over the past eight years the country's economy has been expanding at an average rate of around four per cent annually, according to the World Bank. However, it warns in its latest report that 'volatile commodity prices represent a significant risk'. If oil is eventually extracted, David Granger says he would seek to copy the Norwegian model and establish a sovereign wealth fund where 'the profits from that industry will go ... so that it will be looked after for future generations'. But he adds a cautionary note to those involved in extractive industries. 'Now we have Russians extracting bauxite, we have Chinese extracting timber and they are getting into other industries as well. I am not saying that foreign industries themselves are predatory, what I'm saying is that they need to be tightly controlled,' including Exxon.

Source: adapted from © the *Financial Times* 4.6.2015, All Rights Reserved.

(a) What might be the advantages and disadvantages to Guyana of relying on commodities?

(b) Why might the new president be concerned about the building of a $58-million luxury hotel?

Lewis model. One is about causality. If a government builds steel plants and car manufacturing facilities, will this cause economic development to happen? Some countries, such as South Korea, have prospered from governments favouring the growth of private manufacturing companies from shipbuilding to car manufacturing to electronics. In most countries, however, forced industrialisation has tended to lead to a waste of scarce resources because these industries have failed. There has been a steady drift of people from rural areas into cities throughout the developing world. However, marginal workers in cities can often have as low incomes and be as underemployed as marginal workers in the countryside. There is no simple relationship between poverty in the countryside and affluence in towns. Industrialisation can then be argued to be the result of economic development rather than a cause. Migration from the countryside to the town is the result of higher incomes and growth in urban jobs. Encouraging rural depopulation will simply lead to urban poverty, not increased affluence.

Development of primary industries

Countries such as Saudi Arabia, Chile, Australia and Norway have seen significant economic development because they have a comparative advantage in production of certain primary commodities. Oil, copper, coal and iron ore have created income and employment. However, as Unit 75 explained, commodities can be highly damaging to an economy as well as highly advantageous. It depends on the economic policies pursued by government.

Countries dependent on commodities for exports, such as coffee, cocoa, soya beans, rubber, oil and copper have to accept that their prices will fluctuate significantly. In the case of agricultural products, natural disasters such as disease or drought can have a heavy impact on the amount produced from year to year. Successful economic development in commodity-rich countries tends to result from the use of commodity revenues to diversify the economy. The smaller the proportion of GDP from commodities, the less vulnerable is an economy from commodity price fluctuations.

Government policy also needs to address the problem of too high an exchange rate destroying non-commodity local industries. Norway, for example, has a sovereign wealth fund. The government sets aside a significant portion of its oil revenues and invests these overseas. This increases the supply of the Norwegian currency, the krone, which offsets the demand for krone to buy Norwegian oil. This prevents Norwegian non-oil industries from being priced out of export markets and domestic markets due to a high value of the krone and thus avoiding Dutch Disease (explained in Unit 75).

Primary industries are also a major source of corruption in many countries, another aspect of the resource curse explained in Unit 75. The less corruption, the more likely it is that the country will benefit from the exploitation of primary commodities.

Tourism

Developing countries are increasing their exports of services over time. One example is tourism. Growth in tourism has been very high since the 1960s. This is not surprising since tourism has a relatively high-income elasticity of demand. In 2011, tourism was the first or second most important source of export earnings in 20 out the world's 48 least developed countries. In some developing countries, particularly small island states like the Maldives, tourism can account for over 25 per cent of GDP. In 2011, 46 per cent of total world tourist arrivals occurred in developing countries. This means that almost half of all tourist trips worldwide are to developing countries.

Tourism has a number of advantages for developing countries compared to, say, manufacturing.

- It makes use of natural assets such as a warm climate and beautiful landscapes and existing man-made assets such as historical sites.
- It is labour intensive and therefore creates a large number of jobs in relation to capital employed. Many jobs do not require much education or training and so are accessible particularly to the poor. Jobs are particularly available to women and young people who might otherwise find it hard to get a job.

485

- There can be a significant multiplier effect if the local tourist industry can supply locally made products for tourists to buy.

There are criticisms made of the impact of tourism on economic development. It can make local inhabitants feel inferior because they cannot afford the lifestyle on offer in the hotels to tourists from wealthier nations. It can degrade local people by turning them into characters from a theme park. There may also be a negative impact on the local environment as, for instance, the local shore line is irreparably damaged by the building of hotels. However, on balance, countries which have become tourist destinations have strongly welcomed the opportunity to gain export earnings and diversify their economies.

Fair trade

In recent years, there has been a considerable growth in sales of 'fair trade' products. There is a number of organisations internationally which certify products as being 'fair trade'. These international organisations monitor that what is being sold under the fair trade label conforms to a number of key principles. One is that producers should receive a 'fair price'. Typically this means that a buyer like a supermarket chain signs an agreement with a group of producers, such as farmers in a local area, to buy a guaranteed amount of produce over a period at a price which is above the market price when the agreement was signed. This gives producers some certainty about sales and price. It also raises their incomes from what it would otherwise have been. Fair trade is also linked to community development, fair working conditions and the environment. For example, child labour must not be used. Production must be sustainable and not take place at the expense of environmental degradation.

In 2013, fair trade sales were £4.4 billion worldwide. This is very small in relation to total world trade in goods. Over 1.5 million farmers and workers were in fair trade certified producer organisations, only a fraction of the developing world's working population. Fair trade was particularly significant in a few product categories, such as coffee and tea.

Critics of fair trade argue that its impact on the developing world is insignificant. It is a distraction from the real issues of development. For supermarkets, it is good marketing because it makes them appear ethical. For the consumers that buy fair trade products, it is a way of of pretending they are making a difference when the impact is minimal. Critics also point out that advantaging some producers can leave other producers worse off. When a supermarket decides only to sell fair trade bananas, growers of non-fair trade bananas see a fall in demand for their product. Moreover, raising the price of fair trade commodities may encourage producers to grow more, leading to falls in the price of non-fair trade products.

Advocates of fair trade argue that for millions of people, fair trade makes a difference. Not surprisingly, studies have shown that communities benefiting from fair trade agreements are better off on a wide range of development indicators than non-fair trade communities. Advocates, also say that fair trade is growing very fast. In 10 or 20 years' time, fair trade could be benefiting hundreds of millions of relatively poor people in the developing world. Ultimately, proponents of fair trade argue that

doing something, however small, is better than doing nothing in the face of global poverty.

Foreign aid

Commercial loans are one way of financing development. Foreign aid is another. Following the devastation of the Second World War, the Americans gave Marshall Aid to Europe to help in reconstruction. This became a model for later economic development for the developing world. The argument was persuasive.

- The citizens of developing countries, because they were so poor, would have a very high propensity to consume and a very low propensity to save. Hence, savings would be likely to be below the level of investment needed to generate high economic growth in the economy. Inflows of foreign capital, for instance supplied through foreign aid programmes, would help fill this **savings gap**.
- Foreign exchange would be extremely scarce. Export revenues would be limited and would be likely to be insufficient to cover imports of machinery and other capital equipment as well as imports of essential raw materials. Foreign aid would help cover this **trade gap**.
- Foreign aid reflects only part of capital flows from the developed world to the developing world. However, it can be directed at those countries which are in most need of development assistance. These countries may be very poor or they may find it difficult to attract private capital funding. On the other hand, they may be going through temporary difficulties and therefore need assistance at a point in time.

Foreign aid can take a variety of forms.

Grants The most generous form of aid is a grant. A donor country might, for instance, give a sum of money to a developing country for a development project, it might offer free technical expertise, or it might offer free university education for foreign students in the donor country. Humanitarian aid for natural disasters such as earthquakes and famine would also be an example of grant aid.

Loans Aid might take the form of a loan. The loan might be at commercial rates of interest, in which case the donor country is giving little if anything to the developing country borrower. Alternatively, the loan might be a soft loan, a loan which carries a lower rate of interest than the commercial rate of interest.

Tied aid Grants or loans might only be available if the recipient country was prepared to purchase goods and services with the money from the donor country. For instance, during the 1980s the UK government devoted some of its aid budget to backing British exports. UK loan aid was available if a developing country awarded a contract to a British company. Tied aid in now illegal in the UK under the International Development Act 2002.

Bilateral and multilateral aid Bilateral aid is given directly from one country to another. A UK loan to Kenya would be an example. Multilateral aid describes the situation when donor countries give money to an international agency, such as UNICEF (the United Nations Children's Fund), and the agency then disperses the aid. The most important multilateral aid agency is the International Bank for Reconstruction and Development (IBRD), more commonly known as the World Bank. Most bilateral aid is tied in one form or another whilst multilateral aid is generally not tied.

Foreign aid has undoubtedly helped millions in the developed countries achieve a better standard of living. However, foreign aid has been increasingly criticised by those in both developed countries and developing countries.

- It is implicitly assumed in the economic argument presented above that governments of developing countries desire to maximise the economic welfare of their citizens. However, this is not the case in many developing countries. Governments serve the interests of a narrow range of groups in society, often better-off urban dwellers. Foreign aid monies can be diverted into serving the needs of these groups rather than achieving genuine economic development, particularly for the poor in the developing world.
- 'Fashions' in foreign aid projects change over time. In the 1950s, large-scale projects, such as dams and steel mills, were seen as important in economic development. Many of these projects failed to yield a sufficiently high rate of return. Many large-scale manufacturing plant projects failed because of lack of infrastructure and lack of skilled workers and management. In the 1990s, aid to help large numbers of small-scale enterprises, particularly in rural areas, was fashionable. Equally, aid projects increasingly had to pass an environmental audit to prevent large-scale ecological disasters which occurred on some previous aid projects. The question that arises is whether western aid agencies, even now, know what are the best strategies for development.
- Foreign aid which takes the form of subsidised food or consumer goods is likely to be positively harmful to long-term economic development. Food aid in a famine situation can be helpful. However, long-term food aid, by increasing the supply of food on the local market, depresses local prices and therefore discourages local production of food. This increases the dependence of the country on imported food, uses up scarce foreign exchange and results in lower living standards for farmers.
- Tied foreign aid, especially in the form of loans, may result in developing countries getting a worse 'buy' than if they shopped around internationally for the cheapest product.
- Loans need to be repaid with interest. The repayment of loans has resulted in enormous problems for developing countries both in the past and in some cases still today.

With the recent fast growth of many developing countries, foreign aid has become less and less relevant to the development agenda for most developing countries. Foreign aid is therefore now focussed mainly on the poorest countries in the world.

Debt relief

In the 1970s and early 1980s, the governments of a number of developing countries borrowed money which later they were unable to repay or service the interest on the loans. They fell into the same debt trap that Greece faces today. The result for a number of countries was nearly two decades of low economic growth. These governments found it difficult, if not impossible, to borrow on international markets because they were already

so indebted. They were forced to adopt what today are called fiscal austerity policies. Their countries also had to export more than they imported in order to earn the foreign currency to make repayments on debts.

By the 2000s, most countries had recovered from the **debt crisis** of the 1980s. A number of low-income developing countries, however, (called Highly Indebted Poor Countries or HIPCs) were still constricted by debt and it was recognised by developed countries and multilateral agencies such as the IMF that debt relief should be given. Because of inflation, the amounts were extremely small compared to the GDP of developed countries. But for this small group of low-income developed countries, the debt could still be a burden. For this reason, most of this debt was **written off** by developed countries (also called **debt forgiveness** or **debt relief**).

Those arguing in favour of debt relief put forward a number of arguments.

- The debt was relatively small for the countries and agencies that were owed the money.
- The debt was limiting the growth of some of the poorest countries in the world.
- Interest payments on the debt had already exceeded the value of the original debt and therefore it was unfair to make poor countries pay more.
- The governments that had originally taken on the debt were often either foolish or corrupt and had been pressurised or lured into taking on the debt in the first place. Why should poor people today still be paying for the mistakes of a government in power 25 years ago?

However, there were some who argued against debt forgiveness.

- It created a dangerous precedent. There was moral hazard in debt forgiveness because every poor country would in future expect to receive debt relief on loans taken out today.
- Debt relief eased pressure on weak governments to adopt good and appropriate economic policies.

The role of international financial institutions and non-government organisations

International financial institutions have a variety of roles to play in development.

The International Monetary Fund (IMF) The IMF was one of a group of institutions founded after the Second World War to promote world development and stability. Its specific purpose is to 'promote international monetary co-operation, exchange rate stability, and orderly exchange rate arrangements; to foster economic growth and high levels of employment; and to provide temporary financial assistance to countries to help ease balance of payments adjustment' (IMF). It was not founded to promote economic development. Instead, its role is to ensure that exchange rate systems are working well. When there are international exchange rate crises, such as the Asian crisis of 1997 or the Greek crisis starting in 2010, it can provide temporary assistance in the form of loans to help countries affected. Where there are more deep-rooted problems such that a country cannot afford to pay its international debt out of its export earnings, the IMF can lend money in the short term. But it insists that the country makes macroeconomic reforms to resolve the problem. The IMF has attracted a great deal of criticism over the years from countries that have been forced to borrow money from the IMF and then sign up to agreements which give them some chance of repaying the loans and solving the problem which originally caused the crisis. Inevitably the reform programme is painful because it involves reducing imports and increasing exports and so reducing the amount of resources available for domestic consumption. However, countries are not forced to involve the IMF in their difficulties. They could, for example, simply default on their debts. The fact that few countries do this is because the cost to an economy of a government defaulting on its foreign currency debts is usually greater than signing up to an IMF reform programme. Defaulting on debts means that a country is unlikely to be able to borrow again on international markets in the short term. This could bring foreign trade to a virtual halt.

The World Bank The World Bank was founded, like the IMF, after the Second World War. Unlike the IMF, it was set up to promote economic development. It is made up of two institutions. The International Bank for Reconstruction and Development (IBRD) focuses on middle income and creditworthy poor countries. The International Development Association (IDA) focusses on the poorest countries in the world. The World Bank 'provides low-interest loans, interest-free credit and grants to developing countries for education, health, infrastructure, communications and many other purposes' (World Bank). The World Bank has its critics. They argue that the World Bank, like the IMF, is an agent of Western and in particular US imperialism, imposing faulty development policies on poor developing countries. The World Bank then becomes part of a set of international institutions designed to keep the people of developing countries in poverty.

The World Trade Organization The World Trade Organization promotes the liberalisation of trade. It does this in two ways. First it acts as a forum for governments to negotiate agreements. In particular, it conducts 'rounds', the latest of which is the Doha Round, a series of negotiations which lead to major agreements being signed to reduce trade barriers. Second, it settles disputes between member countries about the agreements that have been signed. Ultimately it acts like an international court for countries bringing trade disputes against each other. Like the IMF, the WTO attracts fierce criticism which was explained in Unit 66 on the World Trade Organization.

Private sector banks Private sector banks lend and borrow money internationally. They also help facilitate foreign direct investment and portfolio investment for their clients. Part of the cause of the 1980s debt crisis which hit many developing countries was overlending by private sector banks to governments particularly in Africa. Banks play a vital role both domestically and internationally because they act as a channel for saving and borrowing. Critics argue that they act irresponsibly and their actions lead directly to poverty in developing countries when borrowers, whether governments, firms or individuals, get into difficulties repaying loans. However, private sector banks are profit making institutions. They do

not exist explicitly to promote economic development. To criticise them when they put profit before development is to misunderstand the nature of private sector banks.

Non-governmental organisations (NGOs) NGOs are, as the name implies, organisations which are separate from government and are not commercial, profit making organisations. There is a wide range of NGOs from local community action groups to charities to pressure groups. NGOs are important for economic development in two ways. First, they may provide direct assistance in the form of project work. Charities like Oxfam, Christian Aid or Cafod run a large number of projects in developing countries, providing education, digging wells or giving health care assistance. Second, they may act as pressure groups, lobbying governments and other organisations to adopt what they see as more pro-development strategies. In the developing world, NGOs may be set up by people to benefit themselves. For example, the women in a village may set up an organisation to provide education for their children or a co-operative to sell their produce. Critics of NGOs say that,

---

Question 4

Jim Yong Kim is President of the World Bank. Last year, its board approved a $73-million project to help authorities in the Democratic Republic of Congo to conduct environmental and other feasibility studies for what could be the most important dam in the world. Situated at the mouth of the River Congo, the Grand Inga complex could, if built, generate half of current African production of electricity and twice the output of China's huge Three Gorges Dam.

The World Bank was founded 79 years ago alongside the IMF. It is a central force in global development. Last year, it gave more than $65 billion in loans, grants and other commitments to developing countries. It has more than 12 000 staff and almost 5 000 consultants in 131 countries working on everything from education to climate change and health policy to bridges and dams.

However, the World Bank faces competition. Increasingly, developing countries can go to the world's financial markets to borrow money for development projects. There will soon also be competition from the China-backed Asian Infrastructure Investment Bank. However, Jim Yong Kim believes the future of the World Bank lies not just in its ability to lend money but also in its expertise and vast pools of knowledge.

Whether the Grand Inga Complex ever gets off the ground remains an open question. Damning the Inga Rapids was first floated as an idea almost a century ago. Two dams were built in the 1970s and 1980s but they are in poor repair and operating well below their capacity. There are major environmental concerns about the project. Also the Democratic Republic of Congo is one of the poorest countries in the world measured by income per capita. It has been racked by civil war and poor government for decades that have led to negative economic development.

Source: adapted from © the *Financial Times* 17.4.2015, All Rights Reserved.

(a) Explain the role of the World Bank in economic development.

(b) Discuss whether economic development can be achieved by building a large dam.

whilst they do much good work, NGOs in themselves will never solve the development problem. Only governments can put in place the structures which will promote and maintain development. Taking a UK example, no number of medical charities could replace a properly funded National Health Service organised by government and paid for by everyone through their taxes. Critics of NGOs also point out that many NGOs are not impartial. They have developed an anti-capitalist agenda blaming governments of rich countries and organisations like the IMF and WTO for all the problems that face developing countries.

International financial institutions operate within the global capitalist system. This system has many faults and many mistakes have been made by governments and organisations like the IMF in the past. Global capitalism will continue to be an

imperfect system for economic development. Governments and international organisations will therefore need to continue to intervene in markets to improve their efficiency and produce a more equitable allocation of resources. However, the experience of the past 100 years suggests that alternatives to global capitalism would produce worse outcomes.

Thinking like an economist

India vs China

India and China have many similarities including having the world's largest populations of approximately 1.3 billion each. Both are developing countries. However, over the past 40 years, China's economy has grown at a considerably faster rate than India's. This has resulted in China overtaking India in GNI per capita as Figure 3 shows.

There are many possible explanations for this. However, one key difference has been China's increasing integration in the world economy. Since the early 1980s, it has become more and more export focussed as Figure 4 shows. Its fastest growing regions on the east coast of China have had much higher growth rates than its inland regions. Over time, it has moved from manufacturing low value products at cheap prices using low cost labour to manufacturing more sophisticated products, including electronic goods and motor vehicles. For a developing country, it had a relatively well-educated labour force in the 1980s and has continued to invest in education. Central government in China and local governments have used their

power to approve infrastructure projects despite the existence sometimes of local opposition. In recent years, investment has accounted for nearly half of GDP as Figure 5 shows. In the long run, this is unsustainable. There is already considerable evidence of over investment such as in empty housing projects or roads and bridges that connect relatively unimportant areas. However, if the Chinese economy can move from being highly export orientated and investment led to being more consumption led, living standards in China could increase rapidly in the future.

India, in contrast, was not particularly export focussed in the 1980s and 1990s although this has considerably changed as Figure 4 shows. Manufacturing has developed but much of the growth in the economy has come from shifting labour from agriculture to service industry jobs. India, for example, has developed a comparative advantage in IT. Investment in education was insufficient in the 1980s and the 1990s and even since then, with increased investment, the outputs have not been very satisfactory. India is a parliamentary democracy, unlike

Figure 3

Gross National Income per capita at PPPs, US$

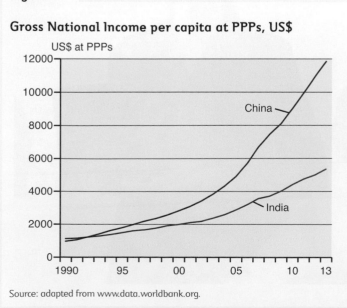

Source: adapted from www.data.worldbank.org.

Figure 4

Exports of goods and services as a percentage of GDP

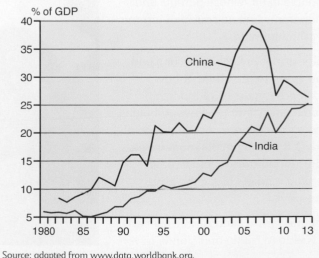

Source: adapted from www.data.worldbank.org.

China. Government has often found it difficult to implement change. For example, some very large infrastructure projects have been abandoned because of the opposition of local farmers not wanting to sell their land. Investment as a proportion of GDP has been significantly lower than in China as Figure 5 shows.

Growth rates in India have increased since 2000 whilst China's growth rate has been slowing. In 2015, however China was still growing faster than India. Over time, India is likely to catch up but this could take a hundred years.

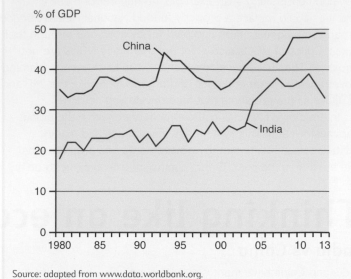

Figure 5

Gross domestic investment as a percentage of GDP

Source: adapted from www.data.worldbank.org.

Data Response Question

Development in India

Bheem Chandra Mahto has found an ingenious way to add to the income of the family tailoring business. He has plugged in a computer, added an Internet connection and started making about 200 rupees ($3) a day downloading and selling music, mostly folk songs, to walk-in customers. The shop in Kerowas, a village in West Bengal, helps supports four brothers and their children - 13 people in all, whose parents and grandparents had no source of income other than farming.

Similar stories are told from one end of the street to the other: of how subsistence famers have made a tentative entry into the lower echelons of India's middle class as the nation of nearly 1.3 billion people modernises, urbanises and tries to follow other emerging markets along the path to prosperity.

Companies from Hindustan Unilever and Nestlé to Nokia and Honda have

Figure 6

Indian GDP growth (annual % change)

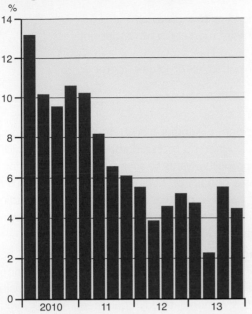

Source: adapted from Thomson Reuters Datastream; © the *Financial Times* 17.4.2014, All Rights Reserved; McKinsey & Co, *National Sample Survey*, McKinsey Global Analysis.

Figure 7

Estimated efficiency or effectiveness of government spending

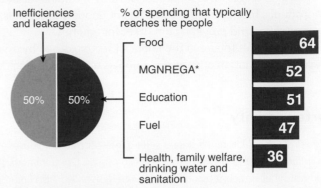

Inefficiencies and leakages

% of spending that typically reaches the people

Food	64
MGNREGA*	52
Education	51
Fuel	47
Health, family welfare, drinking water and sanitation	36

* Mahatma Gandhi National Rural Employment Guarantee Act.

Source: adapted from Thomson Reuters Datastream; © the *Financial Times* 17.4.2014, All Rights Reserved; McKinsey & Co, *National Sample Survey*, McKinsey Global Analysis.

long targeted the growing number of aspiring Indians as a market for everything, from toothpaste to scooters. In the past 10 years alone, mobile phone ownership across India has increased from seven per cent of the population to 82 per cent.

Yet such gains are fragile. In the absence of the type of large-scale manufacturing jobs that abound in China, Indians emerging from rural poverty must make their own way as petty entrepreneurs or service sector workers. They remain vulnerable to changes in government policy or misfortunes such as the sudden halving of economic growth that Indian has experienced in the past three years.

In India there is the added complication of heavy dependency on government subsidies. Take Mr Mahto. He and his family can buy rice at the subsidised price of Rs2 per kg, as well as cheap flour, oil, kerosene for cooking and fertiliser for their own rice paddy. Occasionally he has earned Rs130 a day labouring on local roads under a government

rural job creation scheme, although he and other residents of Kerowa say they have not been offered the full 100 days of work that are supposedly guaranteed by the government under the Mahatma Gandhi Rural Employment Guarantee Act (MGNREGA).

The subsidies have been credited with boosting rural incomes, creating a tentative shift out of extreme poverty that Indians are eager to sustain. Yet the $95 billion a year spent on subsidies and basic services are essential not only for the destitute but also for new entrants into the middle classes who are struggling to escape poverty. Unfortunately corruption is a major issue in India. Half of the $95 billion is estimated to be stolen or wasted.

A new study of India by the McKinsey Global Institute concludes that in addition to the 267 million Indians living below the poverty line, there are a further 413 million below the 'empowerment line': a line above which basic needs such as sanitation, school and housing are met.

Source: adapted from the *Financial Times* 17.4.2014, All Rights Reserved.

1. Describe the trend in economic growth shown in Figure 6.

2. Analyse the possible effects of a withdrawal of all subsidies in India.

3. Discuss whether the most effective way for India to promote economic development is to promote the growth of manufacturing industry.

Evaluation

There are many different facets of economic development that you could discuss in your answer including the difference between economic growth and economic development. Make sure you cover those that are mentioned in the article and data because this will give you evidence to support your evaluation. A key paragraph in your answer will be one about manufacturing. Here you could compare the development strategies of countries such as China and South Korea with India.

77 Financial markets

Key points

1. Financial markets have a number of roles, including facilitating savings, lending to businesses and individuals, facilitating the exchange of goods and services, providing forward markets in currencies and commodities and providing a market for equities.
2. There is market failure in the financial sector caused by asymmetric information, externalities, moral hazard, speculation and market bubbles and market rigging.

Starter activity

In the early 2000s, UK banks began selling interest rate derivatives (also called interest rate swaps) to small businesses. Use the Internet to find out what is meant by an 'interest rate derivative'. Also find out why most of these sales were inappropriate for the needs of small businesses. Why did banks sell these products to their customers?

Financial markets

A **financial market** is any convenient set of arrangements where buyers and sellers can buy or trade a range of services or assets that are fundamentally monetary in nature. Financial markets are different from product markets or factor markets. Product markets exist for the buying and selling of physical goods and services. Factor markets exist for the buying and selling of land, labour and capital.

Financial markets exist for two reasons. One is to provide services demanded by households, firms and government. For example, households want to be able to spend money using a credit card. Firms want to be able to pay their suppliers. Governments want to be able to borrow money. However, financial markets also exist because they allow participants to speculate and realise financial gains. Foreign exchange traders betting on which way a currency might move in the next few seconds are not providing a service to a customer. They are gambling in the hope of making a profit.

The combination of speculation and provision of genuine services means that financial markets are prone to regular crises that cause significant damage to the real economy. In this unit, we will look at the role of financial markets, the main types of financial markets and the main market institutions. We will also look at why market failure is such a pervasive aspect of financial markets. In the next unit, we will look at the role of central banks and how they can attempt to regulate financial markets which in the past have generally succeeded at getting round financial regulation.

The role of financial markets

Financial markets have a number of important roles to play in an economy. These include the following.

Saving Financial assets, such as money or stocks and shares, are a way of transferring spending power from the present into the future. For example, a worker is paid in July but wants to put aside some money to pay for Christmas presents in November

and December. Another worker is 25 and wants to save some money for when he is retired aged 68. A household, currently renting property, wants to save £1 000 a month for three years to put as a deposit on house. A firm has earned £6 million in profit. It wants to put that money aside in case trading falls and it has unexpected bills in the future. Facilitating saving is a key role of financial markets.

Lending Households, firms and governments all borrow money. For example, a household might borrow money on a credit card to finance the purchase of a new television. A firm might borrow money to buy equipment. A bank might borrow to lend more profitably to another financial institution. Or it may borrow to speculate on foreign currency. A government might borrow money to finance government spending which is not paid for by its receipts including taxes.

Facilitating the exchange of goods and services

Financial institutions play a vital role in creating payment systems for goods and services. Central banks, for example, mint coins and print paper money. Retail banks offer cheque services, debit cards and credit cards. More hidden from view are institutions which process trillions of cheque transactions per year. Visa, Amex and Mastercard are companies which offer credit card services to banks, retailers and individuals. Banks and bureau de changes buy and sell foreign currencies, exchanging notes, for example, or transferring money from one account into another bank account in a different country and a different currency. Firms might use a factor. This is a company which offers a variety of services, the most important being paying now for goods and services which have been delivered to another company and where the payment is only due in the future.

Providing forward markets Firms sometimes want to buy or sell forward. For example, farmers may want to sell the crop they are sowing at a guaranteed price. So they agree to sell 100 tones of a crop at $800 a tonne for delivery in six months' time. Food producers may want to even out price fluctuations by buying forward. A chocolate manufacturer, for example, may agree to buy 1 000 tonnes of cocoa beans at $3 000 per tonne for delivery in nine months time. Forward markets exist in food commodities such as wheat, cocoa and soya beans. They also exist in other commodity markets such as copper or nickel. Foreign exchange such as dollars or euros can be bought and sold forward too.

Providing a market for equities Equities are the shares of companies (in the US, shares are called 'stocks' - hence the name stock exchange). Issuing shares, or **equity** finance, can be an important way in which companies, particularly those that are growing in size, can finance their expansion. Those buying new shares will get a share of profits made by the company. However, few would buy new shares if they could never sell them again. Locking up money forever in shares would be a very large risk for a saver. Not being able to sell means that the shares would be completely illiquid. Stock markets provide a way in which owners of shares can sell them to others. They create liquidity in the market. The greater the number of shares issued, and the more buyers and sellers in the market, the greater the liquidity. Having markets for second-hand shares therefore encourages buyers to purchase new shares when they become available.

Providing insurance Life is full of risks. Some of these can be insured against. For example, households and firms take out insurance against the risk of fire or theft. In return for a premium, an insurance company will pay out the cost of damage if the event takes place. A key role for financial markets is to provide these insurance services.

Different types of financial institutions

There is a variety of financial institutions which provide financial services. It should be noted that in the UK, Europe and the United States, the largest banks are combined retail, commercial and investment banks. However, there are also independent retail, commercial and investment banks.

Retail banks Retail banks are banks which provide a variety of services to individuals. For example, most households in the UK have at least one member who has a bank account. Wages or benefits are paid into the account. Withdrawals can be made in cash, for example by taking money out of a cash machine. Regular bills can be paid using standing orders and direct debits. A variety of savings accounts will be offered giving interest. The retail bank will also provide a range of services from overdrafts, loans and mortgages to credit cards, foreign exchange and insurance. Retail banks make a profit out of borrowing money at low rates of interest or zero rates of interest and lending it out again at higher rates of interest. They also charge for their services. In the UK, building societies have traditionally offered a narrow range of services, taking in money from savers and lending it out again purely to purchase a house through a mortgage. Over the past 30 years, some building societies have become much more like retail banks.

Commercial banks Commercial banks are banks which provide a variety of services to businesses. They borrow from businesses, allowing them a secure place to put their funds. Commercial banks provide ways for firms to receive money, for example from customers, and to pay for supplies as well as wages. Firms can borrow money on overdraft or by taking out a loan.

Investment banks Investment banks are banks which engage in a variety of activities. Different investment banks provide a different range of services. They trade in foreign exchange, commodities, bonds and shares. They also trade in derivatives. There is a variety of financial instruments which base their values on prices of other financial instruments. One

example of a derivative that has been widely used for centuries is a forward contract to buy a commodity. In the run-up to the 2007-08 financial crisis, investment banks created a wide range of derivative products that contained risks that were little understood by some key buyers. Investment banks also advise companies on how to raise money, including the issuing of new shares. They also advise on mergers and takeovers of companies.

Saving vehicles There is a number of different types of financial institution whose primary function is to help individuals make a return on their savings.

- Pension funds organise long-term savings, mainly for workers saving for their retirement. They also provide a type of pension, called an annuity, in return for a cash sum.
- Assurance companies provide long-term saving, getting savers to save a regular amount each month and providing a lump sum typically after 10 or 25 years.
- Unit trust and investment trust companies invest savers' money mainly in shares.
- Private equity and hedge funds specialise in riskier investments in a variety of markets including stocks and shares but also currency and commodity markets.

Speculators One of the primary purposes of an investment bank is to engage in speculative behaviour. However, there is a large number of much smaller firms or sole traders whose sole purpose is to speculate on financial markets. They are called a variety of different names depending on the context in which they are being discussed. Hedgers, day traders, margin traders, arbitrageurs and dealers are some of the names used. It could be argued that hedge funds are part of this group too.

Insurance companies These provide insurance against risks by charging customers a premium.

Different types of markets

There is a number of different financial markets. These include the following.

Money markets A money market provides short-term borrowing and lending, usually defined as up to one year. For example, the UK government borrows short term by issuing Treasury Bills that are repayable after 91 days. Bills of exchange are a form of borrowing by companies. Essentially they are promises by companies to pay for goods and services they have already received, at a fixed point in the future such as 91 days. These then get traded by firms that have delivered the goods and want their money immediately. A very important money market is the interbank market where banks lend between themselves. At the end of every trading day, some banks will have a surplus of money whilst others will need to borrow money to balance their books.

Capital markets Capital markets provide longer-term financing, usually defined as being more than one year. The main assets traded on capital markets are bonds (called stocks in the UK) and shares (called stocks in the US). Bonds are long-term loans issued by firms and governments. The UK National Debt, for example, is mostly made up of bonds. A bond could be a 25 year bond paying five per cent interest per year and redeemable for £100. What this normally means is that the original buyer will receive £5 interest per year for 25 years and then be paid £100 in capital at the end. Bonds are a way for firms and governments to borrow long term. The advantage to those who buy bonds is that they can be traded second hand on bond markets. They can therefore sell their bonds before the date when the issuer will repay the money. There is a number of stock markets around the world where companies are listed. This means that their second-hand shares are traded on those stock markets. Over the past 20 years, bonds and shares have been increasingly traded outside official stock markets like the London Stock Exchange or the New York Stock Exchange located on Wall Street. Less than one per cent of all trading on capital markets is of new borrowing through bonds or new shares. Almost all trading is of second-hand bonds and shares. Of the second-hand trading, less than one per cent is from buyers and sellers who want to sell or buy bonds or shares to reduce or increase their savings. Almost all is speculative activity by financial institutions such as investment banks trying to make a short-term profit.

Foreign exchange markets Foreign exchange markets are where different currencies are traded. These could be spot markets where the currency is traded now. Or they could be forward markets where currencies contracts are made for some time in the future like three months. A very small fraction of the trades represent demand and supply for currency arising from physical transactions, such as the exports of goods or individuals buying foreign currency to go on holiday. There are also transactions that relate to transfers of money between countries, such as foreign direct investment. However, almost all dealings on foreign exchange markets are speculative with financial institutions like investment banks trying to make a short-term profit.

Commodity markets Commodity markets such as the London Metal Exchange or the Chicago Mercantile Exchange are where commodities are traded. Contracts may be spot or futures contracts. Some contracts are for delivery of real commodities. A contract, for example, may specify that 10 tonnes of nickel will be available for collection in six months' time. Other contracts are simply bets on future prices. As with capital and foreign exchange markets, most contracts are speculative in nature.

Derivatives markets Derivatives markets are markets which trade financial instruments based on the values of other financial instruments. Many capital market, foreign exchange and commodity market transactions are **derivatives**. For example. Derivate markets can in theory reduce financial risks in markets. The 2007-08 financial crisis showed that in practice they can be enormously destabilising. Clients of investment banks, for example, were being sold derivatives that they thought were low risk, when they were in fact high risk. Investment banks themselves were creating new types of derivative without fully understanding the possible risks they could create for markets.

Insurance markets Insurance markets are where individuals, firms and governments can buy insurance. Part of the insurance market is the reinsurance market. This market is where an insurer reduces its risks on the insurance it has sold. It does this by itself taking out insurance on the risk. For example, an insurer may sell 20 per cent of all the house insurance policies in Jamaica. This is a big risk because Jamaica is prone to natural disasters. So the insurer sells three quarters of the insurance liability to another 15 insurance companies. This way, no insurance company carries too much risk in case of a natural disaster.

Market failure

There has been market failure in financial markets for as long as financial markets have existed. The 2007-08 financial crash that caused trillions of pounds of damage to the real economies of the world was just the latest of a succession of financial crashes that have had a devastating impact. In the 17th and 18th century, for example, the Darien scheme in Scotland, the South Sea bubble in England and the Mississippi bubble in France all led to significant falls in the GDP of their respective countries. However, financial crashes are not the only symptom of market failure in financial markets. Down the centuries, financial institutions have consistently been defrauding their customers and each other, for example by overpricing products, selling products to customers that they don't need or rigging markets in their favour. There is a number of reasons why market failure is and will continue to be such an endemic and pervasive feature of financial markets.

Asymmetric information One problem is that financial institutions frequently have more knowledge than their customers or have more knowledge compared to other rival financial institutions. In the case of Payment Protection Insurance (PPI), UK banks in the 1990s and 2000s sold tens of millions of insurance contracts to customers who were taking out a loan, a mortgage or a credit card. Banks failed to find out whether the insurance was appropriate for most customers. Those customers didn't understand what they were being sold. Nor did they realise they could buy the same product for a fraction of the price from another insurer. Another example of asymmetric information was the securitisation in the USA of mortgages. A bank would give a mortgage to a home-owner. That mortgage would then be sold off to another financial company that would buy other mortgages to create a collection or pool or mortgages. The mortgages represented an asset to the financial company because homeowners owed it money and were making regular payments. So the financial company could sell the rights to that stream of income. There were various complex ways of doing this. However, some financial institutions sold these mortgage-backed securities as low risk products despite knowing that there were problems with some of the mortgages. This was because some of these mortgages were sub-prime mortgages, sold to customers who would have difficulties in making the repayments. By manufacturing complex products, sellers of the securities made it very difficult, if not impossible, for buyers to understand what they were buying. Mortgage-backed securities were a major cause of the 2007-08 financial crisis.

There can also be asymmetric information between financial institutions and regulators. Financial institutions have little incentive to help regulators understand their businesses. As with utility companies discussed in Unit 56, it is in their interests to get regulators to see their businesses from their point of view. What's more, financial institutions have proved to be very powerful and successful political lobbyists to ensure that the power of regulators is minimised. Financial regulation is discussed further in Unit 78.

Question 1

The PPI (Payment Protection Insurance) scandal occurred during the 1990s and 2000s. UK banks were selling very highly priced insurance to cover loan, mortgage or credit card debt against illness or unemployment. Many customers were unaware that they were even buying the product when they took out a credit card or a loan. For others, such as the self-employed, it was not explained that the insurance did not cover them if they could no longer gain an income. Some were told that they could not get a loan or credit card unless they bought the insurance. Very few customers realised that they could have bought the insurance at a fraction of the price from another supplier. In 2011, the banks lost their fight in the UK courts to prevent customers claiming compensation. By 2014, banks had paid out £16 billion in compensation on 13 million customer complaints accepted.

Source: adapted from © the *Financial Times* 3.2.2014, 9.4.2014, 19.5.2014, 31.7.2014, 3.8.2014, 30.8 2014, 30.9.2014, 7.1.2015, All Rights Reserved.

(a) Explain why banks were able to exploit asymmetric information to sell PPI.

(b) Explain why banks would want to sell their customers a product like PPI when they also wanted to be attractive to customers and sell them other financial products.

Moral hazard Moral hazard occurs when an economic agent makes decisions in their own best interest knowing that there are potential adverse risks, and that if problems result, the cost will be partly borne by other economic agents. One example of moral hazard in financial institutions relates to the taking of short-term risk. In investment banking, traders and senior executives can earn very large bonuses for generating profits for the bank. This encourages these workers to take excessive short-term risks without considering what might happen in the long term. If a senior executive can earn £1 million a year in pay and bonuses for five years, then at the end of that time they have earned £5 million. In year six, they cause a loss to the bank of £20 million and they are fired. Now assume they could have taken a less risky approach to their activities, generated pay and bonuses for themselves of £250 000 a year, made steady profits for the bank and kept their job. They would have needed to work for at least 20 years to earn the £5 million they earned taking more risk. In investment banking, there is widespread knowledge of risk. However, incentives tend to be structured to encourage the making of short-term profit rather than encouraging workers to take a long-term perspective.

In the 2007-08 financial crisis, moral hazard was used in the context of financial institutions themselves. Financial institutions, such as banks, were accused of pursuing short-term profit by taking excessive risk because they knew that if things went wrong, they would be bailed out by their governments. Again, take the example of chief executives, earning £20 million a year for eight years between 2000 and 2008 and then getting

sacked when the bank was nationalised. They are better off than earning £5 million a year for 20 years and running the bank more cautiously but also earning lower yearly profit.

Speculation and market bubbles Almost all trading in financial markets is speculative. This, in itself, creates problems including the creation of market bubbles. A market bubble occurs when the price of a particular asset is driven to an excessive high and then collapses. Market bubbles are often caused by herding behaviour. This occurs, for example, when investors see that prices of an asset are rising. Some decide that this is an indication that prices will rise even further and so they buy into the market. More and more investors become convinced that they too must buy. Eventually the price becomes too high. Enough investors decide that it is time to realise their profits and sell for the price to begin falling. Panic sets in and large numbers of investors try to sell too. The result is a price collapse. Herding behaviour exists because investors, instead of looking at the underlying value of an asset, base their actions on what other investors are doing. This is similar behaviour to animals in a herd.

In the UK, financial markets have helped create successive bubbles in the housing market, for example. By lending too much into the property market, financial institutions have created too much demand for houses. This has led to unsustainable increases in the price of housing. Then something happens to burst the bubble. It could be a large rise in interest rates, for example. This makes it more difficult for those with existing mortgages to make repayments and increases the number of households that are forced to default on their debts. It also reduces demand for new mortgages as some home buyers are priced out of the market. This leads to a fall in demand for houses and a fall in house prices. The fall in house prices leads to negative equity as some highly indebted households owe more on their mortgage than the new lower value of the house they have bought. This in itself can cause households to default. Banks are left with loans that are not going to be repaid in full. The collapse in house prices also leads to falls in real spending in the economy. Household wealth has fallen whilst households have less to spend because of increased mortgage payments due to higher interest rates. Less demand for houses means fewer new houses being built, less employment amongst housing and related services, such as estate agents.

The UK is particularly prone to housing bubbles partly because too few new houses are being built and partly because such a high proportion of households own their own houses. However, other countries have experienced housing bubbles too. In Japan, a housing bubble in the late 1980s and early 1990s was a major contributor to over two decades of low economic growth. In the US, it could be argued that the 2007-08 financial crisis was partly caused by a housing bubble.

Bubbles occur not just in housing, but in a variety of assets. In 1997-2000, there was a bubble, called the dot-com bubble, in stock market valuations of new Internet companies. A very famous bubble was the unsustainable rise in stock market prices in the USA that led to the Wall Street crash of 1929, often regarded as a major trigger of the Great Depression of the 1930s.

Market rigging Financial markets are prone to market rigging. This is where a group of individuals or institutions collude to fix prices or exchange information that will lead to gains for themselves at the expense of other participants in the market. Market rigging has always been present in financial markets because it is very difficult to detect and because participants have been likely to suffer few penalties if caught. This has been changing since the 2007-08 financial crisis. However, the rewards to individuals from market rigging are so large that it is likely to continue in the future.

An example of market rigging is insider trading. This is when an individual or institution has knowledge about something that will happen in the future (inside knowledge). This knowledge is not shared with other participants in the market. Based on that knowledge, an asset is bought or sold to make a profit. For example, an individual may know that in 24 hours' time, two firms will announce a merger that will push up their share prices. He or she buys shares in the companies today and 48 hours later sells them at a profit. Another example is of the director of a company who knows that her company will announce bad news tomorrow about profits that will cause the share price to fall. She owns shares in the company and so decides to sell them today at the higher price.

Market rigging can also refer to individuals or institutions fixing the price of a commodity, a currency or an asset. Sudden large trades in a currency, for example, can shift the value of a currency. The change in value doesn't need to be much for a trader to benefit by buying or selling related financial derivatives.

Externalities Financial markets create significant negative externalities. These are costs that are borne by other firms, individuals and governments but not financial markets themselves. For example, the cost to the UK taxpayer of

supporting UK financial institutions during the 2007-08 financial crisis was, at its peak, £1.162 trillion. With a UK population of 61.8 million in 2008, this meant that the financial markets were being supported with £18 803 per person in the UK. Most of this was temporary because it was guarantees given by the UK government. Even so, the UK government spent £133 billion nationalising a number of UK banks and building societies. This works out at £2 152 per person in the UK. Again, this money is expected to be repaid as the government sells off its shareholdings in UK banks. UK taxpayers were relatively lucky.

Question 3

Royal Bank of Scotland warned of a tough year ahead as it aims to clear the bulk of misconduct and litigation changes in an attempt to return the bank to profitability. The bank is 80 per cent owned by the government, having been taken into public ownership during the financial crisis of 2007-08. It has now had seven successive years of losses. It has been forced to set aside £856 million to cover the costs of fines relating to illegal market rigging in foreign exchange markets. Restructuring costs, as the bank shrinks its unprofitable operations, have been set at £453 million for the year. This includes the bank withdrawing from 25 of the 38 countries in which it operates. It will cut a significant number of employees in its investment bank based in London. Analysts at Barclays warn that a potential fine against RBS for mis-selling mortgage-backed debt is a major concern, noting that the ultimate settle could be 'substantially higher' than the £2 billion the bank has set aside to cover the problem.

Source: adapted from © the Financial Times 1.5.2015, All Rights Reserved.

(a) Explain what is meant by an 'investment bank'.

(b) How has Royal Bank of Scotland created significant externalities for the UK economy since 2007?

Question 2

Six global banks will pay more than $5.6 billion to settle allegations that they rigged foreign exchange markets, in a scandal the FBI said involved criminality 'on a massive scale'. The US Department of Justice said that between December 2007 and January 2013, traders at Citigroup, JP Morgan Chase, Barclays and Royal Bank of Scotland, who described themselves as The Cartel, used an exclusive chatroom and coded language to manipulate benchmark exchange rates 'in an effort to increase their profits'. One Barclays trader said in a November 5 2010 chat: 'If you aint cheating, you aint trying'. The revelation that traders colluded to move around currency exchange rates was particularly embarrassing for the banks because it occurred after they had paid billions of dollars to settle claims that their traders had tried to rig the London interbank offered rate (LIBOR). It has raised questions as to whether the industry had learnt any lessons from the previous scandal. 'The criminality occurred on a massive scale' said Ander McCabe, FBI assistant director. 'The activities undermined transparent market-based exchange rates that serve as a critical benchmark to the economy.'

Source: adapted from © the Financial Times 21.5.2015, All Rights Reserved.

Explain why individual traders and the financial institutions they work for have an incentive to rig markets.

Key Terms

Capital markets - financial markets which provide long-term borrowing and lending, usually defined as over one year.
Commercial banks - banks that provide services to businesses.
Derivatives - financial instruments based on the values of other financial instruments.
Equity - in a company, is the value of the assets owned by the shareholders.
Financial market - any convenient set of arrangements where buyers and sellers can buy or trade a range of services or assets that are fundamentally monetary in nature.
Investment banks - banks that engage in a variety of activities in different financial markets, such as the foreign exchange market, the money markets, the capital markets and the derivatives markets.
Money market - financial markets that provide short-term borrowing and lending, usually defined as up to one year.
Retail banks - banks that provide services to individuals.

In countries like Ireland and Greece, taxpayers will never recoup the full cost of their governments bailing out their financial institutions.

The worldwide cost of bailing out financial institutions, however, is just a fraction of the cost of lost output due to the financial crisis of 2007-08. In the UK, the long-term growth rate of the economy for the past 60 years has been 2.5 per cent per annum. In 2007, real GDP at 2011 prices was £1 637.4 billion. At a growth rate of 2.5 per cent per annum, it should have been £1 946.4 billion in 2014. The actual level of real GDP was £1 702.1 billion. The difference is £244.3 billion. With a 2014 population of 64.1 million, that is lost GDP over the seven years

of £3 811 per person. Calculating lost output due to the financial crisis is not as simple as these numbers make out. Other factors have contributed to slower economic growth in the UK and it could be argued that there was a positive output gap in 2007 (i.e. UK GDP was above its long run trend level). However, it would be difficult to argue that there was no significant loss of output due to the financial crisis. Other countries such as Greece and Ireland have suffered much more than the UK.

An explanation of the causes of the 2007-08 financial crisis and the way that it impacted on GDP, unemployment and fiscal balances is given in the Thinking like an economist section in Unit 38.

Thinking like an economist

Payday lenders

In the 2000s, there was a considerable growth in the number of payday lenders in the UK and the amount that was borrowed from them. A payday lender is a financial institution that specialises in providing very small loans to relatively poor customers. The name 'payday' comes from the fact that some of their business came from customers who had run out of cash to buy essentials like food and needed a small loan to tide them over until they received their next benefit payment or wage payment. They first emerged in the UK in the early 1990s following the passing of the Cheque Act that enabled consumers without a bank account to pay in a cheque in return for cash and a fee.

Payday lenders provide a genuine financial service. They allow customers who would otherwise not be able to get a loan to obtain one immediately. In 2013, around 1.6 million people borrowed a total of £2.5 billion. Each individual borrowed £260 on average for a period of 30 days.

However, as the number of payday lenders grew in the 2000s, it became more and more apparent that they exploited their customers. Payday lending is costly to provide. Lending £100 for two weeks, for example, is very costly to administer for the payday lender. They are also specialising in lending to a group (sub-prime borrowers) who are far more likely not to repay their money on time, if at all. Those costs need to be reflected in administration fees or high rates of interest on the loans. However, rates of interest on loans could sometimes exceed 6 000 per cent per annum. Payday lenders exploited the existence of asymmetric information in the market. They knew exactly what they were charging and the rates of interest that applied to loans. Customers, however, were deliberately confused by the way in which charges and interest rates were presented to them. Customers were also a highly unsophisticated group financially. Taking out a payday loan was a reasonable indication that an individual had poor financial skills.

Payday lenders made little effort to find out if their customers could afford the repayments on the loans. In 2014, the Chairman of Wonga, the largest UK payday lender admitted that, in the past, checks had not 'been strong enough or sophisticated enough' to assess properly whether borrowers could repay loans.

The best customers for payday lenders were those who rolled over their loans, preferably having missed payments. Payday lending should be about making small loans for a very short period of time. However, a customer who borrowed a few hundred pounds in 2012, missed a few payments, and rolled over the loan, could easily have ended up in 2014 owing thousands of pounds due to high interest rates and penalties on missed payments. Payday lenders encouraged rolling over of loans because they were highly profitable. Customers, for the most part, had little understanding of the exorbitant costs they were facing, another example of asymmetric information.

Payday lenders were not too fussy about the methods they used to collect payments from customers. In 2014, for example, Wonga was forced to compensate thousands of customers because it had sent them debt collection letters from made-up law firms. The idea was to add pressure to customers to get them to pay by pretending that Wonga had hired a law firm to pursue the claim. Again, this is an example of asymmetric information. Wonga knew that it, Wonga, was sending the letters. Customers thought they were being sent by law firms acting on behalf of Wonga.

Strong concerns about the behaviour of payday lenders and the way they were exploiting often vulnerable individuals were present throughout the 2000s. However, it wasn't until 2015 that the government, through the Financial Services Authority, imposed tough new regulations on payday lenders. The new regulations were predicted to result in the closure of nearly all of Britain's hundreds of payday lenders. The few that would survive would see their lending substantially cut and their profits fall as they were forced to behave in a way that would more benefit their customers.

It could be argued that payday lenders should have been subject to stronger regulation ten or even 20 years earlier. Allowing them to operate led to market failure. The market failure was particularly severe because payday lenders exploited a highly vulnerable group in society who should have been protected from unscrupulous lenders.

Source: with information from © the *Financial Times* 26.6.2014, 1.10.2014, 3.10.2014, 4.10.2014, All Rights Reserved.

Data Response Question

Financial institutions and market failure

Ian Hanman, the investment banker and former chairman of capital markets at JPMorgan, has lost his appeal against UK regulators who found that he engaged in market abuse by passing inside information to Ashti Hawrami, the Kurdish oil minister. In 2012, Ian Hannam was fined £450 000 by the UK regulatory authorities. The market abuse ruling was based on emails sent in 2008 when Ian Hannam offered an 'update on discussions' with a potential for Heritage Oil, an oil company. The second email referred to Heritage's chief executive having 'just found oil and it is looking good'.

Antony Jenkins is the current Chief Executive Officer of Barclays Bank. He replaced Bob Diamond, the former CEO, in 2012. Bob Diamond had been called the 'unacceptable face' of banking in 2010 by the then UK business secretary Peter Mandelson after reports that he had been awarded millions of pounds in bonuses when Barclays had been making large losses.

Antony Jenkins is committed to cleaning up the bank's culture after the period of office of Bob Diamond. He has said it will take a decade to change the culture at Barclays. This month, he told a conference: 'I recognise that what matters now is not public commitment to change but, rather, demonstrating it over time and earning the trust and permission to be believed – and we will do that'.

He faces a difficult task. For example, a lawsuit has just been filed by New York's attorney-general. It alleges that investors have been misled when they have used the LX dark pool, a new technology launched by Barclays

four years ago. 'Dark pools' are trading venues where deals are done away from traditional financial exchanges such as the London Stock Exchange or the New York Stock Exchange. Around 40 per cent of trading in US shares in now done outside of official stock exchanges, an increase from 16 per cent a few years ago. There are more than 40 dark pools in the US alone, many owned by big investment banks such as Goldman Sachs, Credit Suisse, UBS and Barclays. They are used because trading fees are lower than on traditional stock exchanges. Barclays owns the second largest dark pool in the world, operating not just in the US but also, for example, in the UK.

New York's attorney-general alleges that Barclays has encouraged high-speed traders to use its dark pool. These traders use sophisticated software based on algorithms to buy and sell in seconds or fractions of a second depending on factors such as how prices of shares are changing. By making large numbers of trades in a short period of time, high-frequency traders can make a profit. New York's attorney-general is arguing

that Barclays has favoured high-speed traders and misled other institutional investors. It alleges that Barclays was 'telling investors that they were diving into safe waters' while its dark pool 'was full of predators - there at Barclays' invitation'.

In 2011, Bob Diamond, Chief Executive Officer (CEO) of Barclays Bank appeared before the Treasury Select Committee of the House of Commons. He was grilled about financial markets and the role of Barclays Bank in those markets. In response to one question, he said: 'There was a period of remorse and apology for banks, that period needs to be over. We need banks to be able to take risk, working with the private sector in the UK.'

He was also questioned about risk.

Chair: If Barclays did get into trouble, how would you as the chief executive lose out?

Bob Diamond: I think it is clear that, if any banking institution got into trouble, where you look first is at the chief executive and at the risk management of the institution, and I think that has been the case when we've seen banks fail - whether it's here in the UK or around the world during this period.

Chair: Okay, but how would you lose out?

Bob Diamond: I would assume I would lose out by both losing my job and losing any shares that I had in the company.

Chair: This is under the claw-back agreement that you have signed and that is disclosed in the company accounts?

Bob Diamond: Yes, I think that is how the compensation programmes work. Correct.

Chair: The public's liability, though, is unlimited, but your liability is limited to the claw-back. Isn't that right?...

Chair: You do accept, though, that the risks to the senior executives are limited, whereas the risks to the taxpayer are unlimited?

Bob Diamond: Yes, and we also agree that it's not okay for taxpayers to have to bail out banks. Banks should be allowed to fail. If banks have bad management, then they should be allowed to fail. We completely agree.

Bob Diamond lost his job with Barclays in 2012.

Source: adapted from www.publications.parliament.uk.[1]

1. The above text had not been corrected by the witnesses nor Members at the time of printing.

Evaluation

This is a question about the benefits that financial institutions give to an economy and the size of market failure. Use the data to construct your evaluation. For example, should government be interfering in dark pools? Would it have been better, as Bob Diamond suggested, had financial institutions in the 2007-08 financial crisis been allowed to fail rather than being bailed out by governments?

1. Explain the following terms, using examples from the data to illustrate your answer:
   (a) asymmetric information;
   (b) moral hazard;
   (c) market rigging;
   (d) externalities.

2. In 2011, Bob Diamond, CEO of Barclays, said: 'There was a period of remorse and apology for banks, that period needs to be over.' Discuss whether financial institutions, such as banks, would fulfil their roles better if governments did not interfere in these markets.

Central banks and financial market regulation

Key points

1. Central banks have a number of key functions, including implementing monetary policy, acting as bank to the government and as banker to banks, including being the lender of last resort.
2. Central banks along with other government agencies have an important role in the regulation of their financial systems.

Starter activity

Use the Internet to find a story about a bank being fined for misconduct. This could be about misleading customers or rigging markets for example. Why did the bank engage in this activity? Why was it an example of market failure?

Central banks

All but the smallest countries round the world have **central banks**. For example:
- the Bank of England is the central bank for the UK;
- the Federal Reserve Bank is the central bank for the USA;
- the European Central Bank is the central bank for the eurozone group of countries;
- the Bank of Japan is the central bank for Japan;
- the People's Bank of China is the central bank for China.

Central banks have a number of roles including:
- the issuing of notes and coins;
- implementing monetary policy, explained in Unit 38;
- managing exchange rates and the gold and foreign currency reserves of the country, explained in Unit 69;
- acting as banker to the government;
- acting as banker to banks including being the **lender of last resort**;
- regulating the financial system;
- liaising with other central banks and international organisations such as the World Bank.
  Some of these functions will be considered in more detail.

Acting as banker to the government

Most central banks act as the banker to their governments. An exception is the European Central Bank, where there is no national European government for it to serve in this role. The exact nature of the services offered by central banks differs from country to country. In the UK, for example, the Bank of England was responsible for managing the national debt but this role was transferred in 1998 to a new body, the UK Debt Management Office. Central banks may handle the accounts of government departments and make short-term advances to government.

Acting as banker to other banks

Central banks tend to force the largest banks which operate in their country to deposit money with them. In some countries, this is used to balance the accounts of banks at the end of each day. So if Bank X owes Bank Y £50 million because Bank X's customers have paid a net £50 million more in cheques to Bank Y customers, this £50 million is debited from Bank X's account at the central bank and transferred to Bank Y's account.

The key role, though, of central banks in relation to other banks is to act as lender of last resort. Banks can face liquidity crises for two reasons.
- A bank at the end of a day's trading can run out of liquid assets to pay money it owes. For example, a bank may one day experience a withdrawal of £50 million more than it expected by its customers. It has more than enough assets to cover this but they are illiquid, i.e. difficult if not impossible to

Question 1

In 2014, Scottish people voted in a referendum on whether or not Scotland should become independent from the rest of the United Kingdom. The Scottish government argued in favour of independence. One of the assumptions it made was that Scotland would continue to use the pound sterling as its currency. On its pro-independence website, it had the following question and answer.

Question. Who will be the lender of last resort to Scottish financial institutions?

Answer. The Bank of England, as the institution responsible for financial stability, will continue to play its role in the effective functioning of the banking system using its operations under the Sterling Monetary Framework.

In the Sterling Area, lender of last resort arrangements for financial institutions will continue to operate on a common basis across Scotland and the rest of the UK. This will reflect the reality of our integrated financial system. The Bank of England, as the institution responsible for financial stability, will continue to play its role in the effective functioning of the banking system using its operations under the Sterling Monetary Framework.

Banks receive lender of last resort facilities from across the world, and it is normal for countries to act in a coordinated way to secure financial stability. For example, the RBS and Barclays received significant liquidity support from the US Federal Reserve at the height of the financial crisis.

Source: adapted from www.scotreferendum.com.

Why would a Scottish government want an English central bank to act as lender of last resort to Scottish banks in an independent Scotland?

sell immediately. It can turn to the central bank as the lender of last resort and either borrow the £50 million or sell it some of those illiquid assets. This is a short-term liquidity problem and does not mean that the bank is in fundamental trouble.

- The bank may face fundamental problems because too many of its assets have fallen in value. For example, it may have lent money to customers and too many of those loans turn into bad debts, never to be repaid. In the 2007-08 financial crisis, banks, for example, found that too many of their mortgage assets were in default. Poor lending combined with a housing bubble left many banks exposed to bad debts. The central bank then becomes the lender of last resort in the sense that it lends money to banks to prevent them from collapsing.

Some argue that acting as lender of last resort results in moral hazard. Banks know that they can engage in highly profitable, high-risk activities in the short term because if they ultimately make large losses, then the central bank will bail them out. On the other hand, if central banks didn't act as lender of last resort, banks could fail. One bank failing would almost certainly see customers of other banks trying to get their money out: this is known as a 'run on the banks'. The whole banking system could fail because banks only keep a small fraction of their assets in relatively liquid assets. There is no way that a bank like HSBC or Barclays could pay back in cash in one day every single pound deposited with it. The cost to the economy of a whole banking system failing would be far larger than the cost of a central bank bailing out one or a few banks which were in difficulties.

Regulator of the financial system

Different countries regulate their financial systems in different ways. In some countries, but not all, central banks are responsible for regulating the financial system of their economies. There are also international bodies and agreements that attempt to regulate parts of the world financial system.

Financial regulation is needed for three main purposes.

- Financial institutions need to be monitored because otherwise they would engage in a wide range of practices which would harm their customers. In the 19th century, it was common for bakers to adulterate their bread, putting in materials such as alum, chalk and plaster of Paris instead of more expensive flour. Food regulations stamped out this practice in the 20th century. Similarly with financial institutions, there are large incentives for them, for example, to sell products to customers that either give the customers no benefit or actually harm their financial interests.
- Financial institutions have an incentive to engage in risky activities which give them short-term profits, but could lead to their collapse. Since the cost of bailing out a financial institution are borne by those outside the financial sector, it is important that individual financial institutions are regulated to prevent them collapsing.
- The whole financial system needs to be regulated to prevent it from collapse. The risk of the whole system collapsing is called **systemic risk**.

From a historical viewpoint, regulation tends to go in cycles. There is a major financial crisis. Regulations are

tightened to prevent the financial crisis recurring. Two things then happen over time. First, financial institutions successfully lobby regulators and the government to have the regulations relaxed. Second, financial institutions find ways to get round the regulations. A major source of concern today is the growth of **shadow banking**. These are financial institutions, parts of financial institutions and financial markets that are either much less regulated than the mainstream financial system or are completely unregulated. Relaxation of regulation and growth of unregulated financial markets eventually leads to another financial crisis and the cycle restarts.

This pattern reflects regulatory capture. It should be remembered that financial institutions tend to be highly profitable and are well connected with government. They have the resources to influence government and their regulators. They are also constantly pushing at boundaries of regulation because it is so profitable to do so.

Types of regulation

There are many different types of regulation that can be used to control financial institutions. One is to issue rules about how financial institutions should behave and then fine them when they break those rules. For example, banks should not rig financial markets to their benefit. They should not sell unsuitable products to customers. Maximum interest rates on loans can be set. These rules are likely to grow as financial institutions find new ways to exploit their customers and other market participants.

Another main way is to make sure financial institutions have enough reserves of money to cover any losses they make. Table 1 shows a very simplified balance sheet for a newly set up bank in 2015. The assets of the bank must always equal (i.e. balance) its liabilities and this is shown on a balance sheet. It has assets of £100. These are mortgages, loans to customers for the purchase of property. They are assets because it owns this money. It then has £100 of liabilities. It has borrowed £90 from customers who have made deposits into their savings accounts at the bank. It then has £10 of shareholders' capital.

Table 1

2015	
Liabilities	
Customer deposits	£90
Shareholder capital	£10
Total liabilities	£100
Assets	
Mortgage loans	£100
Total assets	£100

Table 2

2016	
Liabilities	
Customer deposits	£90
Shareholder capital	£2
Total liabilities	£92
Assets	
Mortgage loans	£92
Total assets	£92

Table 3

2017 Insolvency	
Liabilities	
Customer deposits	£90
Shareholder capital	£0
Total liabilities	£90
Assets	
Mortgage loans	£89
Total assets	£89

This is money which shareholders, the owners of the bank, have put into the company to set up the bank. During 2015, a number of its mortgage customers fail to make repayments on their mortgages. The bank accepts that £8 of these mortgages will never be repaid and the money has been lost to the bank. It 'writes down' the value of its loans on its 2016 balance sheet by £8. The 2016 balance sheet is shown in Table 2. The £8 lost as assets must also show up as a £8 fall in liabilities. It still owes £90 to customers. So the value of shareholders' capital is now only £2. Shareholders took a risk when they invested in the bank. They have lost out because of the defaulting mortgages. In 2017, in Table 3, the bank loses another £3 on

its mortgage lending. At this point, the bank becomes insolvent, i.e. it fails. This is because it now only has £89 worth of mortgage loans as assets. But it owes £90 to its depositors. It owes more money than it owns. Why does it not also owe money to its shareholders? This is because shareholders have invested in the company knowing that they could lose some or all of their money if the company performs poorly. In this case, shareholders have seen their £10 investment wiped out completely by poor lending by the bank. Their shares are now worthless.

Tables 4 and 5 explain why, the higher the ratio of share capital to loans, the safer the bank. If the bank had £20 of share capital in 2015 and only £80 of customers' deposits as liabilities, as shown in Table 4, it would not have become insolvent in 2017. It would have had £80 of customers' deposits and £9 of shareholders capital as liabilities to match its assets of £89 of loans.

Table 4

2015	
Liabilities	
Customer deposits	£80
Shareholder capital	£20
Total liabilities	£100
Assets	
Mortgage loans	£100
Total assets	£100

Table 5

2017	
Liabilities	
Customer deposits	£80
Shareholder capital	£9
Total liabilities	£89
Assets	
Mortgage loans	£89
Total assets	£89

In the real world, there is a number of liabilities for a financial institution that act like the shareholders capital in Tables 1-5. These include shares, but can also include assets such as bonds. They are given a variety of names by regulatory authorities including 'capital' and 'reserves'. The ratio of these liabilities to total assets is also given a variety of names, including 'capital ratio' and 'leverage ratio'.

Banks and other financial institutions want these ratios to be as low as possible. To understand why, look at Table 1 again. Assume that the loans are paying five per cent interest per year but the bank is only giving one per cent to depositors. It therefore makes £5 on its loans (5 per cent x £100) but only pays out £0.90 to deposits (1 per cent x £90). The profit is £4.10. There is £10 worth of shares. So every £1 share is due a profit of £0.41 (£4.10 ÷ 10). Now consider a situation where the bank has to have £20 of share capital to £100 of loans. The cost of customer deposits falls to £0.80 because it only needs to have £80 of customer deposits as liabilities with £20 of shareholder capital. So the profit is higher at £4.20. But this needs to be shared out between twice as many shares. For each £1 share, the profit is now only £0.21 (£4.20 ÷ 20). So the lower the ratio of share capital to loans, the more profitable per share the bank will be. In the real world, the situation is more complex because different assets can act as reserves or capital. However, the underlying principle about capital ratios and profitability remains the same.

Key Terms

Central bank - the financial institution in a country or group of countries, typically responsible for the printing and issuing of notes and coins, setting short-term interest rates, controlling monetary policy, managing the country's gold and foreign currency reserves and issuing government debt.

Lender of last resort - usually a function of a central bank, it occurs when financial institutions can obtain money from the central bank to balance their accounts when they are unable to do this from the financial markets in which they operate.

Shadow banking - parts of the financial market that are either much less regulated than the norm or are completely unregulated.

Systemic risk - in the context of financial markets, the danger that the failure of parts of the financial system will lead to the collapse of the whole of the financial system.

Question 3

The Financial Policy Committee is considering what level should be set for the leverage ratio in the UK mortgage market. This ratio is the amount of equity capital a bank or building society will be forced to hold as a proportion of its total mortgage lending. Equity capital is financial assets that belong to the shareholders of the company on its balance sheet. If the bank makes a £1 billion loss, for example, then that will be paid for by a reduction in the equity capital owned by the shareholders on its balance sheet. The higher the ratio, the less risk there is that if customers default on their loans, the bank or building society will fail. Banks and building societies are worried that the Bank of England will set a leverage ratio of at least four per cent and possibly more than five per cent. It if sets it at a high level, banks and building societies will have two choices if they do not have enough capital compared to their mortgages to meet the ratio. They could sell more shares in the company. This is likely to lead to a fall in the share price because more shareholders will now have a claim on the profits of the company. This means dividends per share will fall. Or they could cut back on their mortgage lending that will lead to a fall in their profits.

Banks and building societies have lobbied against too high a ratio. They argue that it could cut mortgage lending which will lead to lower growth in the economy and prevent its recovery. They also argue that it will give banks an incentive to engage in riskier lending. If all loans, not just mortgage loans, have the same leverage ratio, then banks will be encouraged to lend at higher rates of interest on riskier loans than mortgages. This will increase risk in the whole financial system.

Source: adapted from © the *Financial Times* 13.10.2014, All Rights Reserved.

(a) Using the data as an example, explain why financial institutions lobby regulators and governments to prevent regulations being imposed upon them.

(b) Explain why the size of leverage ratio on mortgage lending might have an impact on economic growth and unemployment.

Thinking like an economist

Financial regulation

Before the 1980s, the UK financial markets were relatively tightly regulated. This did not prevent financial crises occurring. For example, between 1973 and 1975, there was what came to be called the 'Secondary Banking Crisis'. Secondary banks were relatively small banks that had expanded by lending to homeowners to buy their houses. There was a housing boom in the late 1960s and early 1970s with large increases in house prices. However, house prices fell in 1973 as the Bank of England sharply increased interest rates and the economy went into recession in 1974. The result was that some homeowners couldn't keep up their repayments and secondary banks were in danger of collapsing. The Bank of England stepped in and bailed out a number of these secondary banks.

In 1979, Margaret Thatcher was elected Prime Minister and she was committed to deregulating markets. This included the financial markets. In 1986, in a process known as 'Big Bang', a large number of financial regulations were abolished. The City of London reorganised itself as a result with a large number of mergers and takeovers creating much larger financial institutions. She encouraged risk taking. High salaries and bonuses were a sign that financial markets were doing well and creating wealth for the UK. 'Light touch regulation' came to be seen as the way forward, liberating financial markets and leading to high profits for financial institutions. Financial regulations were relaxed in many countries around the world, including the USA.

Worldwide, there was a number of major financial crises in the 1980s, 1990s and early 2000s but these had only a marginal impact on UK and US financial markets. The 2007-08 financial crisis, however, was a full-blown crisis for the UK and the USA. It was recognised that 'light touch regulation' was one of the reasons why the financial crisis was allowed to develop by the regulatory authorities. As a result, a much stricter regulatory regime emerged in developed countries.

In 2012, the UK parliament passed the Financial Services Act. This created three bodies responsible for financial regulation in the UK.

The Financial Policy Committee The Financial Policy Committee (FPC) is an independent committee of the Bank of England. According to the Bank of England, it is 'charged with a primary objective of identifying, monitoring and taking action to remove or reduce systemic risks with a view to protecting and enhancing the resilience of the UK financial system. The FPC has a secondary objective to support the economic policy of the Government.' It is responsible for taking an overview of the financial system to ensure that there are no systemic collapses. It has been responsible for ensuring that regular 'stress tests' are conducted on financial institutions. A stress test is a hypothetical scenario to see what would happen to a financial institution if certain events happened. For example, what would happen to a bank if interest rates rose to seven per cent and there was a 30 per cent fall in world stock market prices? What would happen to an insurance company if bond prices fell 40 per cent and there was a series of natural disasters worldwide within a six-month period? If a financial institution would collapse under moderate stresses, then it must be forced to strengthen its underlying financial position. This normally means it must hold much more capital. These are reserves that would be used to make up any losses.

The Prudential Regulation Authority The Prudential Regulation Authority (PRA), according to the Bank of England, 'is responsible for the prudential regulation and supervision of

around 1 700 banks, building societies, credit unions, insurers and major investment firms. It sets standards and supervises financial institutions at the level of the individual firm. The PRA's role is defined by three statutory objectives: i) to promote the safety and soundness of its firms; ii) specifically for insurers, to contribute to the securing of an appropriate degree of protection for policyholders; and iii) a secondary objective to facilitate effective competition.' The PRA is part of the Bank of England. It regulates individual financial institutions to ensure that they do not collapse.

The Financial Conduct Authority The Financial Conduct Authority (FCA) is responsible for ensuring that financial institutions provide consumers with appropriate products and services and that they act with integrity and fairness. The FCA has the power to fine financial institutions for misconduct such as market rigging.

In the wake of the 2007-08 financial crisis, regulation has been considerably tightened. However, history suggests that over time regulation will become lighter whilst larger and larger parts of the financial system will escape regulation altogether. There are concerns today about the continued growth of the 'shadow banking system' worldwide. These are financial institutions and financial markets that are not regulated. All the major investment banks have activities that are regulated today, but they also continue to engage in unregulated activities. There are trillions of dollars tied up in the shadow banking system and it was partly responsible for the 2007-08 financial crisis. History suggests that it is only a matter of time before financial institutions create another damaging crisis that imposes an enormous cost on real economies.

Source: with information from www.bankofengland.co.uk.

Data Response Question

Shadow banking

Shadow banking is on the increase in the United States. Shadow banks perform bank-like functions, such as lending, but are subject to lighter regulatory supervision because they are funded by a small number of professional investors rather than millions of bank customers who deposit relatively small amounts in their savings accounts with banks.

Shadow banks, such as Quicken Loans, PHH and loanDepot.com, provided the finance for 53 per cent of US government-backed mortgages in April. This is almost double their share in April 2013. They have been able to increase their market share because main stream bank lenders such as Wells Fargo, Bank of America and JPMorgan have been reducing their lending. They have been doing this because they have been forced by regulators to raise more capital to support their mortgage loans in case a more than expected number of these mortgage loans don't get repaid. This makes mortgage loans less profitable. They have also been subject to heavy fines imposed for mis-selling products to customers after the 2008 crisis.

The tightening grip on the mortgage lending market by shadow banks is causing concern in Washington. In April, the Department of Justice sued Quicken, the biggest non-bank lender, claiming that it knowingly broke rules when making loans backed by the Federal Housing Administration (FHA).

The shadow banks' rise is one of the 'unforeseen consequences' of five years of increasingly tough oversight of mainstream banks, said Marshall Lux, senior fellow at Harvard University's Kennedy School. While much of the competition from newer lenders is healthy, he said, there were 'concerning' signs of slipping

standards. Bob Walters, chief economist at Quicken, said that 'any implication that non-banks are doing riskier loans than banks is flat-out wrong'.

Seven years after the 2007-08 financial crash, the alarming fact is that financial regulators still know next to nothing about the true level of risk that big banks are exposed to. Everyone knows that there remain huge exposures to risk, especially in so-called shadow banking, the vast off-balance-sheet activities of banks and other financial companies. But no one knows where the risks are, or how big they are. Huge swathes of the financial system are still outside the control of the Federal Reserve Bank as well as its safety net. This includes money market mutual funds, overnight repurchase agreements, over-the-counter derivatives and loans to hedge funds.

It means that a central bank like the Federal Reserve Bank can never know when a major bank is insolvent and will fail. According to Andrew Haldane, the chief economist at the Bank of England, market data is 'partial and patchy' and 'large parts of the core of the international banking map remain, essentially, uncharted territory'. This should be a major concern for regulators. How can they 'oversee', 'supervise' or 'regulate' something that is 'essentially uncharted territory'?

For example, the US investment bank JPMorgan reports gross derivatives receivables of $1.2 trillion, which is about 45 per cent of its total assets. But what does that represent? It has 'notional' derivatives totalling $64 trillion, the largest of any US bank. The veteran investor Warren Buffett says that even with his decades of experience, he cannot understand JPMorgan's presentation of its derivatives positions.

One reason for the failure of regulators has been the authorities desire to keep banks lending. If banks cut back on their lending, the recession following the 2007-08 financial crisis would have been even longer and the recovery much weaker. Another reason for failure is the political power of the big financial institutions, in both American and Europe, which has blocked any serious attempt to make the financial system more transparent.

As Andrew Haldane and others have repeatedly said, the global finance system is fragile, by which is meant it is a system that is chronically prone to crash.

Q

1. Explain what is meant by 'shadow banking', using the data to give examples.

2. Analyse two reasons why financial markets need to be regulated, using examples from the data.

3. Discuss whether strong regulation can make the global financial system safe rather than being 'a system that is chronically prone to crash'.

Evaluation

The answer to this partly centres around whether regulation, however tight, can influence the behaviour of the global financial system. Will regulated banks for example follow regulations? Will the shadow banking system take an ever-larger share of financial markets? It also centres round whether governments can maintain tight regulation in the long term. Why do financial institutions have such a large incentive to get regulations reduced and why are they often so successful at changing regulation in the long term?

Key points

1. There is a number of reasons why governments should spend money on behalf of their citizens, including equity and efficiency and macroeconomic and microeconomic management of the economy.
2. Over time, the size and composition of public spending is likely to change depending on the stage of development of a country, its demographic profile and the ideological views of voters and governments.
3. A distinction can be made between current expenditure of government, which includes transfer payments, and capital expenditure.
4. Differing levels of government spending as a proportion of GDP have an impact on many variables including productivity and growth, living standards, crowding out, the level of taxation and equality.

Starter activity

Use the Internet to find out about the 'Nordic model' and then contrast that with a more free market model found in the United States. Why is the size of the state larger under the Nordic model than in the US? What effects does it have on economic variables such as levels of taxation, productivity and growth, equality and happiness?

The reasons for public expenditure

There is a number of reasons why governments should spend money on behalf of their citizens.

Efficiency and market failure Free markets can be less efficient in the production of some goods and services than the state. Market failure, for example, means that free markets will produce too few **public goods** and other goods where market failure occurs. The state therefore has to organise production of services such as defence, law, order and protective services and education. Production of too few goods and services is an aspect of allocative inefficiency. Free markets, though, can also be productively inefficient. It can be argued, for instance, that health care should be provided by the state because costs, for the same level of services, are higher when it is provided by the private sector. This is to do with economies of scale and the ability of a sole buyer (a monopsonist) to drive down prices of suppliers to the market such as doctors, hospitals and drugs companies. Free markets may also lead to dynamic inefficiencies. In the agricultural sector, perfectly competitive farmers have no incentive to engage in research and development. For this reason, governments round the world tend to have state owned and funded agricultural research institutions. Overall, where the state is more efficient than the private sector in providing goods and services, then there is a case for government spending.

Equity and equality Free markets can produce an inequitable and unequal distribution of resources. In health care, for instance, those likely to face the largest bills are the elderly, typically in the lower income brackets of income distribution. Unless the state provides assistance, many elderly people would not be able to afford health care. Similarly, if education had to be paid for, children from poor families would suffer most. Governments therefore can be argued to have an obligation to

spend in such a way as to reduce inequity and inequality.

Macroeconomic management Governments may want to use their spending to manage individual markets in the economy. Markets may overproduce or underproduce. For example, free markets are likely to overproduce cigarettes and underproduce green energy. Governments can spend money on anti-smoking advertising campaigns to reduce market failure in the cigarette market. It can give subsidies to producers of green energy in order to reduce greenhouse gas emissions.

Reasons for changing size and composition of public expenditure

Over time and between countries, the level and composition of government expenditure changes. For free and mixed economies, the lower the average income of the country, the lower is likely to be the percentage of GDP spent by the

Question 1

Cuts to bus funding are harming the UK economy and leaving people unable to get to work or the shops, campaigners have warned. Nearly a third of shoppers rely on buses as their only means of traveling to town centres, according to data compiled by Leeds University's Institute of Transport Studies. It found that almost a third of spending in city centres comes from bus users. A report by MPs found that people in urban and rural areas were being cut off from education, work and health services as bus subsidies were cut.

More big cuts are looming. The public spending squeeze means councils are looking to cut £23.3 million from a collective local authority transport budget of £260 million. Last year, councils cut funds for bus services by £17 million.

Bus routes not deemed profitable by bus companies receive support from local authorities. These tendered services make up about 15 per cent of business for the bus companies Arriva and Stagecoach. The bus industry points to a study by KPMG showing bus priority measures generate £3.32 of net economic benefit for every £1 spent.

Source: adapted from © the *Financial Times* 22.7.2014, All Rights Reserved.

Explain why government should subsidise bus transport, explaining the impact of subsidies on rural communities, town centres and low-income households.

government. This is partly because lower-income countries lack a tax base to raise revenues to pay for government spending. Taxes like income tax and VAT are difficult to administer and easy to evade in lower-income countries. Moreover, the higher the income of the country, the more its citizens will demand higher-quality goods and services of the sort that are typically provided by government, i.e. government provided goods and services are income elastic. Citizens demand better roads, better education and safety nets in the form of welfare benefits to guard against sickness, unemployment and old age as GDP rises. For example, technological advances in health care mean that more and more illnesses are now treatable. However, the additional nursing, the equipment and the drugs needed are all increasing the average cost of health care per person.

Amongst rich developed countries, however, there are significant differences in the size of the state. In 2014, for example, the USA had government spending including transfer payments of 38 per cent of GDP. At the other extreme, for Finland, it was 58 per cent. For all OECD countries, the average was 42 per cent whilst for the euro area it was 49 per cent. For the UK it was 44 per cent. These differences reflect ideological differences about the role of the state and the role of the market. The USA is far more market orientated. In 2014, for example, access to medical care for 16-65-year-olds was left mainly to free markets whereas in Europe, various different state-backed systems meant that everyone had access to free medical care.

For Europe and Japan, the next 30 years will see considerable upward pressure on government spending. This is because their populations are aging. With more elderly people in the population and fewer workers, demand for health care, pension payments and care home costs will rise at the same time as economic growth may fall because of fewer workers. Unless government spending as percentage of GDP grows, rises in spending on the elderly will have to come from cut backs in other areas of government spending.

In the short term, governments are still recovering from the effects of the financial crisis of 2007-08, which saw government spending rise at the same time as tax revenues fall. Some governments have chosen to react, or been forced to react, by cutting public spending through 'austerity budgets'. In some cases, the amount of interest paid on the national debt has increased, although for countries such as the UK and the USA, this increase has been relatively small because interest rates have fallen to historical lows. A few governments have even been able to borrow money at negative rates of interest. Where budget deficits and national debts as a percentage of GDP remain high, however, there will be constraints on any growth in public spending.

Current and capital expenditure and transfer payments

Total government spending is equal to current expenditure plus capital expenditure. This can be broken down as follows.

- **Capital government expenditure** is spending on investment goods. Examples are new motorways or roads, new schools, new hospitals or new street lights. These are items that will

be consumed over a period of time longer than a year.

- General government final consumption is spending on goods and services that will be consumed within a short time, like a year. Examples are the wages of teachers, heating and lighting for a hospital or grit used to de-ice roads in winter.
- **Transfer payments** are mainly welfare payments made to individuals, such as the state pension and child benefit. They are payments by government for which there is no corresponding output. Hence transfer payments are not included in the measurement of GDP.
- Debt interest is interest paid on the National Debt by government.
- **Current government expenditure** is general government final consumption plus transfer payments plus debt interest.

Budgets can be analysed in terms of current and capital expenditure. A government can have a budget deficit just on its current expenditure. Not only is it not raising taxes and other receipts to pay for capital expenditure, it is not even covering its day-to-day expenditure. This is generally considered to be undesirable because it will have to borrow to pay for current spending. Tomorrow's taxpayers will have to pay for today's expenditure. However, it is considered reasonable to borrow money to pay for capital expenditure. Taxpayers in the future will benefit from capital expenditure made now. So, it can be argued, they should be made to pay their share of capital expenditure made now.

Living standards and equality

Government expenditure can have a significant impact on living standards. If there were little or no government spending, there would be significant market failure. The private sector is likely

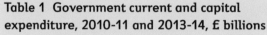

Question 2

Table 1 Government current and capital expenditure, 2010-11 and 2013-14, £ billions

	Debt interest	Net welfare benefits	General government final consumption	Capital expenditure	Public sector net debt at end of period (excluding banks)
	£bn	£bn	£bn	£bn	£bn
2010-11	46.6	178.8	415.4	59.0	1 101
2013-14	48.7	196.3	431.1	52.6	1 402

Source: adapted from ONS, *Public Sector Finances*, February 2015.

(a) Using the data in the table, calculate how (i) government current expenditure, (ii) government capital expenditure and (iii) total government spending have changed between 2010-11 and 2013-14.

(b) Analyse what might be the impact on future (i) growth of the UK economy and (ii) living standards of the changes in government capital expenditure over the period.

(c) (i) Calculate the percentage increase in the National Debt between 2010-11 and 2013-14. (ii) Explain why, despite this change, the amount of interest paid on the debt has barely increased.

to underprovide everything from roads to refuse collection to education. Even in quasi-free market economies like Singapore or the United States, the government steps in to provide these services.

Government expenditure is also vital in the prevention of absolute poverty. In low-income countries, governments do not have the resources to transfer income to those most in need. The result is malnutrition, insanitary drinking water and very poor-quality housing which can result in death. Again, even in quasi-free market economies in rich developed countries, there are government support mechanisms to prevent absolute poverty.

However, there is a debate about how much government can contribute to livings standards and the extent to which equality is a desirable economic objective.

The efficiency of government All economists agree that governments can be inefficient in the way they spend taxpayers' money. But, equally, private sector firms can be inefficient too. The debate centres around the extent to which government can ever be efficient, both statically and dynamically. On the one hand, it can be argued that government can be just as efficient at providing goods and services as the private sector. With the right controls and incentives in place, government can be a cost-effective provider (i.e. productively efficient), producing the level of goods or services consumers desire (i.e. allocatively efficient), whilst at the same time being innovative (i.e. dynamically efficient). On the other hand, some economists argue that government can never be as efficient as the private sector. This is because government lacks the profit motive. Private sector firms will drive down costs in order to maximise profit. They will produce the goods and services that consumers show that they wish to buy through the market mechanism. Private firms will also be innovative and seek out new products to sell. So private sector provision will always be better than public sector provision. If the inefficiency of government is greater than the benefits from correcting market failure, then government should be as small as possible.

Disincentive effects Being taxed at 98 per cent on income earned is likely to discourage individuals from working or saving. Being provided with high levels of benefit for not working is equally likely to discourage work. Free market economists tend to argue that the disincentive effects of taxation and welfare benefits are so large that they outweigh any benefits that might arise from high levels of government spending. Therefore the government should spend as little as a percentage of GDP as possible. The contrary view is that the tax and benefits system can be designed to minimise disincentive effects. For example, in Nordic countries, taxes are high and welfare benefits are generous. However, activity rates are also very high. Nordic countries also have similar rates of economic growth compared to lower tax and government spending countries such as the USA or the UK.

Utility Some economists argue that government spending should be as low as possible because of the principal-agent problem. Decisions are made by politicians and civil servants about how taxpayers' money should be spent. However, if left in the pockets of taxpayers, this money would be spent

Question 3

Margaret Thatcher, UK Prime Minister and Leader of the Conservative Party, said in an interview to *Woman's Own Magazine* in October 1987 that: 'I think we've been through a period where too many people have been given to understand that if they have a problem, it's the government's job to cope with it. "I have a problem, I'll get a grant." "I'm homeless, the government must house me." They're casting their problem on society. And, you know, there is no such thing as society. There are individual men and women, and there are families. And no government can do anything except through people, and people must look to themselves first. It's our duty to look after ourselves and then, also to look after our neighbour. People have got the entitlements too much in mind, without the obligations. There's no such thing as entitlement, unless someone has first met an obligation.'

Source: quoted in www.margaretthatcher.org; http://briandeer.com.

Using the data, discuss the view that government spending should always be as low as possible.

differently. Hence, there must be a loss of welfare or utility. The problem with this argument is that it assumes that individuals are best placed to make spending decisions to maximise their utility. If an individual can choose one pair of jeans rather than another, then utility is likely to be greater than where the state produces only one type of jeans. But individuals often do not make decisions that are in their own best interests. For example, they often fail to save during their working lives for their retirement. Equally, there may be missing markets. How would the market mechanism provide a comprehensive road network for example? As for the redistribution of income and wealth, this poses fundamental moral and philosophical questions. Margaret Thatcher, the UK Prime Minister between 1979 and 1989, said in 1987 that 'there is no such thing as society'. At one extreme, it can be argued that no one individual has any responsibility for any other individual. Therefore government should not be taxing individuals to benefit others. The contrary view is that society does exist and that certain spending decisions need to be made by a majority even if some disagree. The political system is the mechanism through which such decisions can be made.

Taxation

If government is spending a high proportion of GDP, this can only be sustainable in most cases if tax revenues are also a high proportion of GDP. There are exceptions to this, such as oil-rich countries, where revenues from oil pay for most of government spending. High levels of tax can have disincentive effects if taxes are poorly structured. However, countries such as Sweden and Denmark have both high government spending and high taxes without there being major disincentive effects.

Crowding out

If the economy is at full employment and on its production possibility frontier, it would seem logical to suggest that increasing government spending by £1 must lead to £1 less of private sector spending. In Figure 1, an increase in public sector spending of AB must lead to a fall in private sector spending of

Figure 1

Crowding out

If the economy is at full employment, producing on its production possibility frontier, then an increase in public sector spending of AB will crowd out CD of private sector spending. However, if there is unemployment and the economy is at G, a move to the PPF can give both extra public sector and private sector spending.

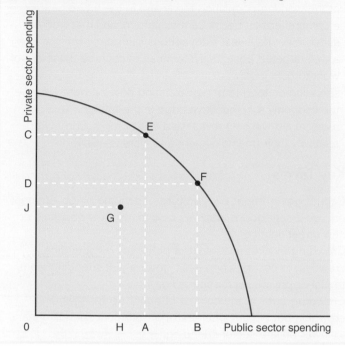

Unemployment If the economy is suffering from unemployment, then extra government spending could lead to **crowding in**. This means that extra government spending leads to high private sector spending through the multiplier effect. In Figure 1, if the economy is initially at G, higher government spending could lead to the economy moving to either E or F. If it moves to F, then an extra HB government spending crowds in JD of private sector spending.

Economic growth Government sector investment could also lead to higher private sector spending. In Figure 2, the economy is initially at E. The government increases its investment spending. As a result, the PPF of the economy moves outwards and the economy moves to the point F. Increased public sector spending then results in extra private sector spending.

Free market economists would tend to disagree with these arguments.

- Increased taxes, for examples on workers or company profits, to pay for higher welfare payments will discourage workers from working and companies from making profits. Therefore the economy will shrink in size reducing private sector spending. So increases in transfer payments by government leads to falling private sector spending.
- The multiplier is very low, if not zero. If the government attempts to increase its spending and borrows the money to do so, interest rates will rise and this will reduce private sector spending. If it prints the money to finance the extra spending, there will be higher inflation, which will cut real

CD. The movement along the PPF from E to F shows clearly that extra public spending will crowd out private sector spending. Taking the example of Sweden versus the USA, public sector spending in Sweden averaged approximately 54 per cent of GDP between 2000 and 2014; over the same period it averaged 38 per cent in the USA. In Sweden, government spent 16 per cent more of GDP on public sector provided goods and services compared to the US. In Sweden, therefore, there was resource **crowding out** by the public sector of private sector spending.

Crowding out can also occur at less than full employment, through the financial markets. Financial crowding out occurs when the public sector borrows extra money to fund increased public expenditure or reduced taxes. This extra borrowing increases interest rates because there is an increase in demand for borrowed funds. Higher interest rates discourage private sector borrowing both for consumption and investment. So private sector spending falls.

However, there are a number of reasons why public sector spending need not crowd out private sector spending.

Transfer payments £1 spent on transfer payments does not necessarily crowd out private sector spending. This is because there is no corresponding output associated with transfer payments. For example, if the government gives £1 billion extra to pensioners and pays for that by raising taxes on workers by £1 billion, there is not necessarily any crowding out. The private sector will continue to produce the same level of goods and services as before. It is just that it will produce an extra £1bn for sale to pensioners and £1 billion less to workers.

Figure 2

Crowding in

Assume the economy is at full employment on its production possibility frontier at E. Public sector investment increases the productive potential of the economy shifting the PPF rightwards and moving production to the point F. Increased public sector spending has crowded in both private sector and public sector spending.

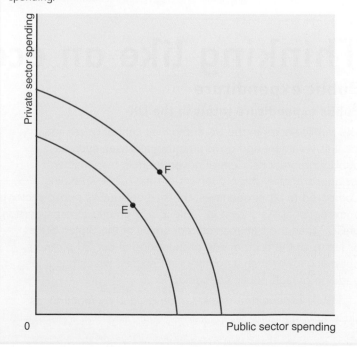

private sector spending. If there is high unemployment, the solution is to reduce government spending in order to reduce taxes. A reduction in taxes will incentivise workers to work harder and firms to produce more. The private sector will then increase employment and so unemployment will fall.

- Government spending on investment is often wasteful and badly targeted. The result is that the government wastes money and fails to increase the productive potential of the economy. The private sector is far better placed to seek out profitable opportunities that will increase the size of the economy. Less government spending and more private sector spending is therefore key to long-term economic success.

Productivity and growth

Economists are divided about the impact of government spending on productivity and growth. Free market economists argue that public sector spending is often wasteful and inefficient. Therefore, cutting public spending is likely to increase

productivity and growth if these resources are transferred to the more efficient private sector.

A contrary argument is that the public sector provides goods and services vital to productivity and growth which the private sector would otherwise not do. For example:

- an efficient road system encourages trade and specialisation and lowers costs for firms;
- a high quality education system increases the human capital of the working population today and in the future;
- a comprehensive health care system means that workers suffer fewer days lost from serious illness;
- a well targeted benefits system can encourage those out of work to gain jobs;
- spending on long term research and development will give the economy a competitive edge in the future;
- regional aid will help revitalise areas of the country with relatively high unemployment and increase GDP.

Question 4

How might households respond to a rise in interest rates? The Bank of England has used NMG Consulting to conduct a survey to see the reactions of different households. In the survey, each household was told what a two per cent rise in interest rates would imply for their interest income and payments, given their reported debt and deposits. 57 per cent of those with mortgages said they would cut their spending. In contrast, only 10 per cent of those with savings said they would increase their spending. 18 per cent of those with mortgages said they would increase their working hours to increase their income. Of those with particularly high levels of mortgage debt to their income, 24 per cent said they would work more hours.

Source: adapted from the Bank of England, Inflation Report, November 2014.

Assume that increased UK government borrowing increases interest rates in the UK financial markets. Explain, using the data, why this might lead to crowding out.

Key Terms

Capital government expenditure - spending by government on investment goods, such as new roads, new hospitals or new street lighting.
Crowding in - in the context of public sector spending, crowding in occurs when extra government spending leads to higher private sector spending.
Crowding out - in the context of public sector spending, crowding out occurs when extra government spending leads to lower private sector spending.
Current government expenditure - spending by government on goods and services which will be consumed in the short term, such as teachers' salaries or heating for government buildings; it also includes transfer payments and debt interest.
Transfer payments - spending for which there is no corresponding real output; in government expenditure, transfer payments are welfare payments such as the state pension or child benefit.

Thinking like an economist

Public expenditure

Public expenditure totals in the UK

The public sector in the UK comprises central government, local government and government enterprises such as public corporations. Central government is responsible for approximately three quarters of total public spending. Compared to other countries, the size of Britain's public sector is unexceptional. As shown in Table 2, it is greater as a proportion of GDP than the free market economies of the United States or Japan, at the bottom end of the range of our EU partners, but much lower than a country like Sweden which has a long tradition of high public spending.

Public expenditure totals can be divided by function, as illustrated in Figure 3.

- The largest single item of public expenditure is social protection shown in Figure 4. This covers **transfer payments** such as child benefit and Jobseeker's allowance. The most costly benefit is the state pension, received by over 12 million pensioners.
- Spending on **health** is the second largest category of expenditure. Most of this is accounted for by the cost of the National Health Service.
- **Education** covers local government spending on primary and secondary schools, and colleges of further education. Central government pays for higher education and research grants.
- **Personal social services** include expenditure by local authority social services departments and children's departments on social workers, home care assistants and placements for the elderly in residential homes.

Figure 3

Public sector spending by function, 2015-16

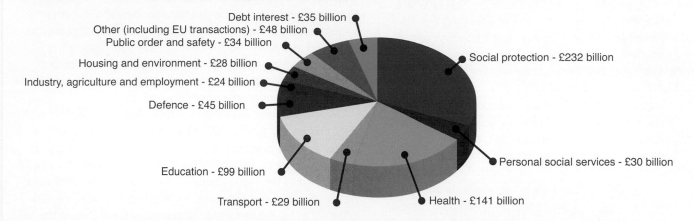

Debt interest - £35 billion
Other (including EU transactions) - £48 billion
Public order and safety - £34 billion
Housing and environment - £28 billion
Industry, agriculture and employment - £24 billion
Defence - £45 billion
Social protection - £232 billion
Personal social services - £30 billion
Education - £99 billion
Transport - £29 billion
Health - £141 billion

Source adapted from HM Treasury, *Budget* 2015.

- **Transport** includes roadbuilding and maintenance as well as subsidies for train and bus services.
- **Industry, agriculture, employment and training** includes grants and subsidies to promote growth of businesses, maintenance of farms, training of workers and measures such as the Work Programme to get the unemployed back to work.
- **Defence** spending is expenditure on the army, navy and airforce.
- **Public order and safety** covers spending on the police, the judiciary, prisons and the fire service.
- **Housing and the environment** covers grants to Housing Associations to build new homes and to local councils for the repairs and maintenance of their existing stock as well as expenditure on refuse collection, parks and environmental protection measures.
- **Debt interest** is the interest that the government has to pay on the money it has borrowed in the past - the National Debt.

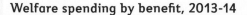

Table 2 Government expenditure as a percentage of GDP

	1960-67	1968-73	1974-79	1980-89	1990-99	2000-07	2008-14
France	37.4	38.9	45.0	49.9	52.8	52.2	56.2
Sweden	34.8	44.3	51.4	59.8	63.1	54.0	53.5
Italy	31.9	36.0	38.2	47.5	51.7	46.9	50.0
UK	34.7	39.5	44.2	43.0	39.8	39.8	45.8
Germany	35.7	39.8	47.5	47.8	43.5	45.8	45.1
Canada	29.3	34.7	39.8	45.4	47.5	39.6	41.3
Japan	18.7	20.5	30.2	32.9	35.0	37.2	41.2
US	28.3	31.0	34.6	36.7	36.9	36.1	40.6

Source: adapted from OECD, *Historical Statistics*, www.stats.oecd.org.

- **Other expenditure** includes expenditure on overseas aid, the arts, libraries and embassies abroad.

Figure 4

Welfare spending by benefit, 2013-14

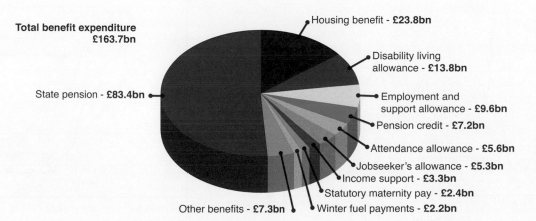

Total benefit expenditure £163.7bn
Housing benefit - £23.8bn
Disability living allowance - £13.8bn
State pension - £83.4bn
Employment and support allowance - £9.6bn
Pension credit - £7.2bn
Attendance allowance - £5.6bn
Jobseeker's allowance - £5.3bn
Income support - £3.3bn
Statutory maternity pay - £2.4bn
Other benefits - £7.3bn
Winter fuel payments - £2.2bn

Source: adapted from DWP; IFS.

Trends in public expenditure

Table 2 shows trends in public expenditure as a percentage of GDP for a number of rich, industrialised countries. As incomes rose in the 1960s and 1970s, so did the proportion of GDP spent by governments. Today, the range of spending lies approximately between 35 and 55 per cent for industrialised countries. Economists and politicians disagree about what might be the 'right' level of public expenditure. However, the lower the level of government spending as a percentage of GDP, the greater the inequalities there are likely to be amongst individuals and households. For example, the Gini coefficient for the US is significantly higher than that for Sweden or France.

Figure 5 shows how public spending as a percentage of GDP in the UK has changed over time. Total government spending, mainly spending by central and local government, is officially called total managed expenditure in the UK. There is a number of key periods in this history.

- The rise in public spending between 1939 and 1945 due to the Second World War.
- The creation of the welfare state between 1945 and 1951 which saw public spending settle down to a higher level that the inter-war period of 1919-1939.
- The fall in public spending between 1982 and 1989 as the Prime Minister Margaret Thatcher strove to reduce the size of the state and increase the size of the private sector.
- The rise in public spending under the Prime Minister Tony Blair between 2001 and 2007 which saw significant rises in spending on the National Health Service and education.
- The rise in public spending between 2008 and 2010 due to the financial crisis of 2007-08 and the resulting recession.
- The fall in public spending from 2011 onwards as the Prime Minister, David Cameron, oversaw large cuts in public

spending firstly to reduce the fiscal deficit but secondly to cut the size of the state in order to be able to cut taxes.

Capital and current expenditure

Public expenditure can be divided into capital and current expenditure. Capital expenditure over the past 40 years has averaged less than five per cent of total public spending whilst current expenditure has accounted for over 95 per cent. However, capital expenditure is important because it is a determinant of economic growth.

Figure 6 shows how public sector investment fell from the mid-1960s to around 2000. The gross fixed capital formation line shows the percentage of GDP spent by government on investment goods. The net investment line shows how much this added to the capital stock of the country. The difference between gross and net is depreciation: the value of capital goods that have been worn out and scrapped. Part of the fall in public sector investment between 1975 and 1985 was due to a slowdown in investment in new housing. The failure of the public sector to invest sufficiently in social housing over the past 30 years is one of the reasons why private sector house prices have increased dramatically. With too few new homes being built, demand for housing has exceeded supply pushing up prices.

Public sector investment increased between 2000 and 2008 as the government under Tony Blair invested heavily in new schools and hospitals. However, as part of fiscal austerity measures from 2010, the government cut gross public sector investment by a quarter. After depreciation is taken into account, net investment nearly halved. Keynesian economists would argue that the government should have increased public sector investment when the economy was stagnating and unemployment was high. With the cost of borrowing at virtually zero per cent, it would have given a multiplier boost to current GDP as well as increasing future potential output. It would also have increased private sector investment according to the accelerator theory of investment.

Figure 5

Total public sector spending and receipts as a percentage of GDP, UK

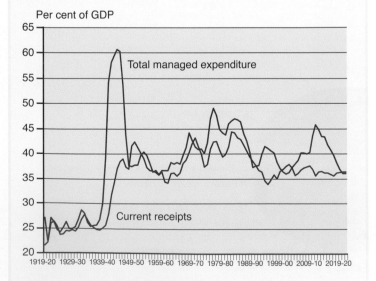

Source: adapted from Office for Budget Responsibility, *Economic and Fiscal Outlook*, March 2015.

Figure 6

Gross and net public sector investment, % of GDP (excluding banks)

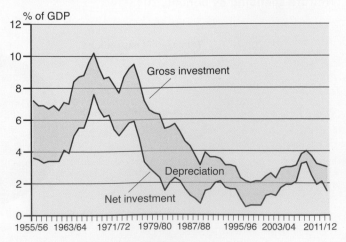

Source: adapted from ONS, *Longer-term trends - Public Sector Finance*, by A Jowett and M Hardie, 2014.

Figure 7 shows the composition of central government spending over time. In 2014, approximately 85 per cent of 'other expenditure' was current consumption with the remaining 15 per cent being government investment expenditure. Figure 7 shows that the proportion of GDP spent by central government on welfare benefits has been broadly stable since the mid-1990s at 11 per cent of GDP. Equally, interest paid on the National Debt as a percentage of GDP has remained under five per cent since 1955. Despite a doubling of the National Debt between 2009 and 2014, interest payments have barely risen. This is because interest rates in 2014 were at historic lows. The government was able to double the size of the National Debt at the same time as almost halving the average rate of interest paid on that debt. This indicates that at no time following the financial crisis of 2007-08 was there a problem for the UK government to finance its deficits.

Figure 7

Composition of central government spending, % of GDP, four quarter moving average[1]

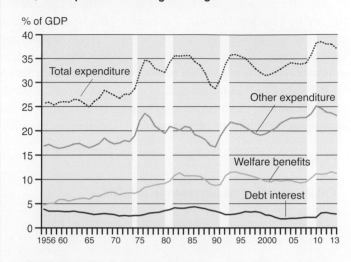

1. Vertical grey bars indicate periods of recession.
Source: adapted from ONS, *Longer-term trends - Public Sector Finance*, by A Jowett and M Hardie, 2014.

Data Response Question

Sweden

In 2014, Sweden held a general election in which the Social Democratic Party was returned to power. In the post-war period, the dominant political party had been the Social Democrats. They created a society which was one of the most egalitarian in the developed world. They achieved this through building a welfare state which gave high-quality public services, such as education and health care, as well as redistributing income from the better off to the less well off. Government spending peaked at 70 per cent of GDP in 1993 after a property and financial bubble burst in the early 1990s. Unemployment rose sharply at the time and the government responded by spending extensively on retraining programmes and unemployment benefits. There was general agreement that state spending of 70 per cent of GDP was

unsustainable. Over the next 15 years, with tight control of public spending and rising GDP, the ratio of public spending to GDP fell to 52 per cent in 2006.

In 2006, the Social Democrats lost the election to a centre-right coalition committed to boosting the private sector. Although public spending as a percentage of GDP did not fall under the new government, it set about increasing the proportion of government services that were supplied by private sector companies. However, outsourcing the provision of services has been controversial. There were allegations of cruelty in private equity-owned care homes and one private school group went bankrupt.

Magdalena Andersson, a senior Social Democrat, said in the 2014 election campaign that 'we want much stricter rules, when it comes to how (private

equity companies) can act within the sector'. She pointed to three areas that needed improvement: companies should be forced to take a longer-term perspective; there should be stiffer regulations on quality so that, for example, companies cannot increase profits merely by cutting the number of teachers; and companies would be forced to disclose their profit from each school, hospital or care home. Private companies need 'to understand that this is not selling toothpaste, this is taking care of our children', she said. Anders Borg, the finance minister in the centre-right government, said: 'The increased competition that we've seen in the welfare sector is a major factor why Sweden has been growing fast. We've seen a very strong increase of employment and number of companies in these sectors.'

There are many views about the success or otherwise of the 'Nordic model' - the societies that have been created by Sweden, Norway, Finland and Denmark through comprehensive welfare states. However, these countries regularly top global rankings for indicators such as happiness, competitiveness, the best place to be a woman and the best place to be born.

For example, the 2013 World Happiness Report produced by the United Nations ranked Denmark as the country with the happiest citizens in the world. Second was Norway, fifth was Sweden, 7th was Finland, whilst the USA was seventeenth. This was despite the US having the highest GDP per capita in the world amongst medium to large-sized countries. The UK came twenty-second.

Source: adapted from © the *Financial Times* 12.8.2014, 21.11.2014, All Rights Reserved; United Nations, *World Happiness Report*, 2013.

Q

1. Using Figure 9, compare how income inequality has changed both before and after direct taxes and benefits for Sweden and the USA.

2. Using Sweden and the USA as examples, analyse why higher levels of GDP as a proportion of GDP might lead to greater equality.

3. Using examples from the data and your own economic knowledge, discuss whether lower levels of public spending as a percentage of GDP will lead to higher economic growth and improved living standards.

Evaluation

Your answer needs to contain both contrasting theoretical arguments and evidence from the data and your own knowledge. Part of the evaluation will come from judging whether the evidence supports a particular theoretical view. Another part of the evaluation relates to whether economic growth and improved living standards both benefit from lower levels of public spending or whether it benefits one but not the other. To what extent are your conclusions limited by a lack of data?

Figure 8

Public spending as percentage of GDP[1]

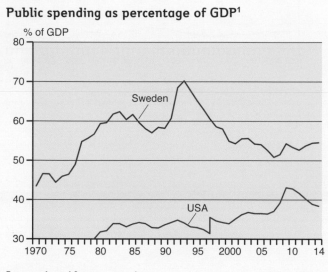

Source: adapted from www.oecd.org.

1. Discontinuity in 1997 for US because of change in way in which the ratio was calculated.

Figure 9

Inequality: Gini coefficients, before and after tax and benefits

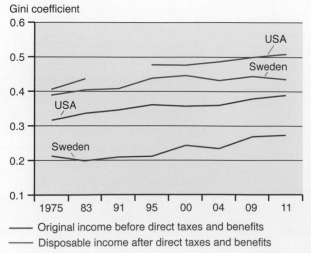

— Original income before direct taxes and benefits
— Disposable income after direct taxes and benefits

Source: adapted from www.oecd.org.

Figure 10

Index of GDP per hour worked, 1970=100

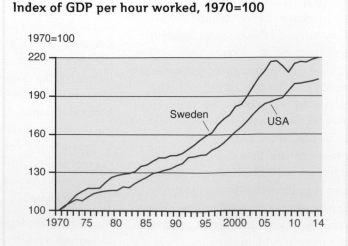

Source: adapted from www.oecd.org.

80 Taxation

Key points

1. Governments impose taxes for a variety of reasons, including to pay for government spending.
2. Taxes can be direct or indirect, or progressive, proportional or regressive.
3. The canons of taxation are a set of principles by which taxes can be evaluated.
4. Taxes and tax rates can have an impact on many economic variables including incentives to work, income distribution, real output and employment, the price level, the trade balance and FDI flows.

Starter activity

Currently, VAT in the UK is not charged on food or children's clothes. Make a list of eight different economic variables that might be affected by imposing VAT on these items at 20 per cent and briefly say what the effects would be.

The reasons for taxation

Governments use taxation for a number of purposes.

To pay for government expenditure Governments need to raise finance for their expenditure programmes. They can borrow a limited amount of money for this, but most of the finance must come from taxation if inflation is to be avoided.

To correct market failure such as externalities Governments can intervene in individual markets by changing taxes and thus changing demand. For instance, tobacco consumption can be reduced by raising taxes on cigarettes, pollution can be controlled by imposing pollution taxes, or sales of books can be increased by exempting them from VAT. Used in this way, taxation becomes a way of increasing economic efficiency.

To manage the economy as a whole Taxation can have an important influence on the macro-economic performance of the economy. Governments may change tax rates in order to influence variables such as inflation, unemployment and the balance of payments.

To redistribute income A government may judge that the distribution of resources is inequitable. To redistribute income, it may impose taxes which reduce the income and wealth of some groups in society and use the money collected to increase the income and wealth of other groups.

Types of taxes

Taxes can be classified in different ways. One way, explained in Unit 38, is to make the distinction between direct and indirect taxes. A direct tax, such as income tax or corporation tax, is a

Question 1

Each year in the Budget, the Chancellor of the Exchequer announces whether or not he will change the level of excise duties on tobacco. In most years, this is increased at least in line with inflation, although in some years, particularly election years, it is not increased at all. Why might the government change the level of excise duty on tobacco each year?

tax levied directly on individuals or companies. An indirect tax is a tax levied on goods or services such as value added tax (VAT), excise duties or council tax.

Another way, explained in Unit 73, is to make the distinction between progressive, proportional and regressive taxes. A progressive tax is one where as incomes increase, the proportion paid in tax increases. With a proportional tax, the proportion stays the same. With a regressive tax, it falls as income increases.

The canons of taxation

Taxation has been a source of much controversy since the first tax was introduced. Adam Smith wrote at length on the subject of taxation in his book *An Enquiry into the Nature and Causes of the Wealth of Nations*, published in 1776. He argued that a good tax was one which had four characteristics:

- the cost of collection should be low relative to the yield of the tax;
- the timing of collection and the amount to be paid should be clear and certain;
- the means of payment and the timing of the payment should be convenient to the taxpayer;
- taxes should be levied according to the ability to pay of the individual taxpayer.

These canons relate to efficiency and equity. For instance, the cost of collection is about productive efficiency. Ability to pay is about equity.

There have been examples in history where taxes did not possess these canons. For instance, at certain periods in Roman history tax collecting was privatised. The Roman government sold the right to collect taxes in a province to the highest bidder. This individual would buy the right, hoping to charge more in taxes than he paid to the Roman authorities. With luck he might make 100 per cent profit on the contract - in this case the cost of collection would hardly be low. He would terrorise the province, forcing anyone and everyone to pay as much tax as he could exact. No attempt was made to make means of payment or timing suitable to the taxpayer. It was not clear on what basis citizens were being taxed, and there was no attempt to link taxes to ability to pay, since it was the poor who were the most easily terrorised whilst better off citizens were left alone for fear that they might complain to Rome.

Economists today have argued that in addition to Adam Smith's canons, a 'good' tax should be one which:

- leads to the least loss of economic efficiency, or even increases economic efficiency;

- is compatible with foreign tax systems, and in the case of the UK, particularly with EU tax regimes;
- automatically adjusts to changes in the price level - this is particularly important in a high-inflation economy.
These three criteria relate to economic efficiency.

Sometimes it is argued that taxes should be linked to the benefits that taxpayers receive from the tax. For instance, road groups in the UK often point out that revenues from taxes on motorists far exceed government expenditure on roads. They then conclude that either taxes on motorists are too high or that spending on roads is too low. A tax whose revenue is specifically linked to an area of government spending is called a hypothecated tax. In the UK, National Insurance contributions could be argued to be a hypothecated tax because they are used solely to pay for spending on National Insurance benefits and make a small contribution towards the cost of the National Health Service. The benefit principle is one of equity. It is an argument which states that linking payment and benefit is 'fairer' than a tax which fails to do this.

Incentives to work and tax revenues

High marginal rates of tax (the rate of tax on the last £1 earned or spent) discourage economic activity. A tax on cigarettes leads to fewer cigarettes being bought. A tax on work (income tax) leads to people working less. A tax on profits (corporation tax) is a disincentive to firms to make profits. Lowering certain taxes will therefore raise the level of economic activity and increase aggregate supply.

Free market economists believe that the supply of labour is relatively elastic. A reduction in marginal tax rates on income will lead to a significant increase in 'work'. This could mean individuals working longer hours, being more willing to accept promotion, being more geographically mobile, or simply being prepared to join the workforce.

Work is, arguably, an inferior good, whilst leisure, its alternative, is a normal good. The higher an individual's income, the less willing he or she is to work. So a cut in marginal tax rates will have a negative income effect at the margin (i.e. the worker will be less willing to work). However, a cut in marginal tax rates will have a positive substitution effect because the relative price of work to leisure has changed in favour of work (i.e. the worker will be more willing to work).

Free market economists believe that the substitution effect of a tax cut is more important than the income effect and hence tax cuts increase incentives to work. If cutting marginal income tax rates encourages people to work harder and earn more, then in theory it could be that tax revenues will increase following a tax cut. For instance, if 10 workers, each earning £10 000 a year, pay an average 25 per cent tax, then total tax revenue is £25 000 (10 x £10 000 x 0.25). If a cut in the tax rate to 20 per cent were to make each worker work harder and increase earnings to, say, £15 000, tax revenues would increase to £30 000 (10 x £3 000).

This is an example of the **Laffer curve** effect, named after Professor Arthur Laffer who popularised the idea in the late 1970s. Figure 1 shows a Laffer curve, which plots tax revenues against tax rates. As tax rates increase, the rate of growth of tax revenue falls because of the disincentive effects of the tax. OA shows the maximum revenue position of the tax. At tax rates above OA, an increase in the tax rate so discourages economic activity that tax revenues fall. There is much debate about whether the Laffer curve reflects what happens in the real world. For example, if the top rate of income tax is 90 per cent and this is increased to 95 per cent, it is difficult to see why those already paying 90 per cent would suddenly stop working

Question 2

In 1990, the tax on houses, called local authority rates, was replaced by the community charge, more commonly known as the poll tax. Local authority rates were a tax on property based on notional rental values of the property. Broadly, the more valuable the property in a local area, the higher was the tax paid. The poll tax was a tax on every adult in a local area. The amount paid per person aged 18 and over was the same whatever their income, although students and the registered unemployed paid a reduced rate of 20 per cent. The cost of collection was much greater than under local authority rates. This was because there were nearly twice as many individual taxpayers to be sent bills and from whom to receive money. Large numbers of young adults disappeared from the population as they sought to evade paying the poll tax. Many others delayed payment in protest at the introduction of what was seen as an unfair tax. Individuals in rented housing on low incomes found it difficult to pay a tax they had never had to pay before. The poll tax was the most regressive form of tax that could be devised by a government because everyone, whatever their income, paid the same amount of tax.

Source: adapted from Alain Anderton, *Economics*, 5th Edition, Pearson.

Discuss whether the poll tax was a good tax.

Figure 1

The Laffer curve

As tax rates increase, economic activity is discouraged and hence the rate of growth of tax revenues falls. Above OA, an increase in tax rates so discourages economic activity that tax revenues fall.

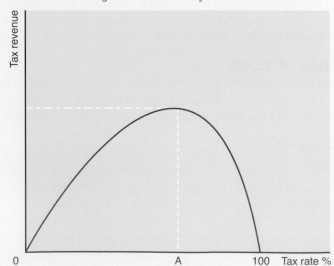

as hard or make extra efforts to avoid or evade tax. Equally, an increase in the top rate of tax from 40 per cent to 50 per cent is unlikely to have a major distinctive effect on those in work. In the United States, large tax cuts for those on high incomes under George Bush in the early 2000s saw a major cut in tax revenues paid by those individuals. Yet the tax cuts were justified on the grounds that cutting taxes on high-income earners would increase tax revenues.

Changes in tax and benefit rates also can have incentive effects for those in work and on low incomes or for those unemployed. These poverty and unemployment traps are discussed in more detail in Unit 39.

Income distribution

The impact of the tax system on income distribution was explained in detail in Unit 73. The impact of a change in tax revenues for the government on income distribution after tax will depend on why tax revenues have changed. Examples include the following.

- If the government increased the rate of Value Added Tax (VAT) or excise duties, the distribution of income is likely to become less equal. This is because VAT and excise duties are regressive taxes.
- If there is a rise in tax revenues because of a rise in the top rate of income tax, then the distribution of income is likely to become more equal. This is because the rise in tax revenues will be paid by top-income earners and not by lower-income earners.
- If the rate of corporation tax, the tax on company profits, rises, then the distribution of income is likely to become more equal. This is because a rise in corporation tax, the share of profits going to the government, is likely to lead to a fall in dividend payments to shareholders. Shares are disproportionally owned by those on high incomes. So the income of high earners is likely to fall.

Question 3

In 2014 David Cameron, Prime Minister and leader of the Conservative Party, said that if he won the next general election, in 2015, he would cut taxes. He pledged to increase the personal tax allowance, the amount of income on which no tax is paid, from £10 500 to £12 500. He also promised to raise the threshold at which people start paying the 40 per cent rate of income tax from its current rate of £41 865 to £50 000 by 2020. This, he said, would 'bring back some fairness to tax'. According to the Institute for Fiscal Studies (IFS), an independent think tank, the plans would mean that 40 per cent taxpayers would pay £430 less in tax per year in 2020 than they would if the thresholds had risen by inflation. Their savings would be nearly three times the £160 tax saving for a typical basic rate taxpayer. Stuart Adams of the IFS said the proposed tax cuts were skewed towards high earners. 'Most of the gains go to the top of the income spectrum - a lot of it to the top end of the top half.'

Source: adapted from © the *Financial Times* 2.10.2014, All Rights Reserved.

Explain whether the proposed tax cuts would make income tax more or less progressive.

Real output, the price level and employment

A change in tax rates is likely to have an effect on real output, the price level and employment. Some tax changes affect aggregate demand whilst others affect aggregate supply.

Aggregate demand Some taxes, such as income tax and Employees National Insurance contributions, affect aggregate demand. A rise in income tax rates, for example, will reduce household disposable income. Households will then spend less. This fall in consumption will reduce the output demanded at any given price. This is shown by a shift to the left in the aggregate demand curve in Figure 2. Equilibrium output falls from Y_1 to Y_2 in the short run and the price level falls from P_1 to P_2. So a rise in income tax rates leads to a fall in the short-run equilibrium price level.

What happens in the long run depends on the position of the vertical long-run aggregate supply curve. For example:
- Assume that the vertical LRAS curve is at Y_2. Aggregate demand of AD_1 had overheated the economy pushing it in the short run beyond its long run sustainable level of output. Then P_2 and Y_2 will represent the new long run equilibrium.
- If the LRAS curve were at Y_1, however, the economy at the new short-run equilibrium at Y_2 would be in long run disequilibrium. The economy would have experienced a recession in the move from Y_1 to Y_2. Unemployment would have risen. Eventually, aggregate demand is likely to rise again through a combination of increased consumption and investment, especially if the government pursues a looser monetary policy. The recovery in the economy, shown by the shift from AD_2 to AD_1, will restore the economy to its long-run equilibrium level of output of Y_1. Unemployment will have fallen whilst the price level will have risen.

Figure 2

An increase in tax leads to a fall in aggregate demand

An increase in income tax, for example, leads to a fall in disposable incomes. This leads to a fall in consumption and hence aggregate demand. This results in a fall in the price level and equilibrium output in the short run.

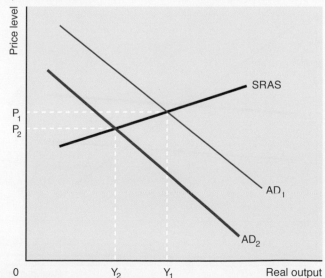

Aggregate supply Some taxes, such as VAT, excise duties and Employers' National Insurance contributions raise costs to firms. A rise in indirect taxes such as VAT and excise duties means that at any given level of output, firms have to charge a higher price for their products. They need to recoup the extra VAT or excise duties they will pass on to government. If the rise is an increase in Employers' National Insurance contributions, the cost of employing labour will increase. Higher costs will shift the short run aggregate supply curve up. This is shown in Figure 3. In the short run, a rise in these taxes will shift the short run aggregate supply curve from $SRAS_1$ to $SRAS_2$. Equilibrium output will fall from Y_1 to Y_2, whilst the price level will increase from P_1 to P_2. Unemployment will rise.

What happens in the long run depends on the position of the long-run aggregate supply curve. For example:

- If the vertical LRAS curve is at Y_2, then Y_2 will represent a new long-run equilibrium position.
- If the LRAS curve is at Y_1, then the move back to equilibrium depends on how the aggregate demand and aggregate supply change in the short run. At Y_2, the economy is below its full employment level if the LRAS curve is at Y_1. One possibility is that workers will respond to unemployment by accepting wage cuts. This will reduce costs of firms and the SRAS curve will shift back down to $SRAS_1$. Employment will rise. Another possibility is that workers will attempt to secure higher wages to cover the loss of real earnings they will have suffered from the rise in the price level. A wage-price spiral could then develop. Firms put up their prices to cover increased costs. Workers demand and receive higher wages to compensate them for the loss of their real earnings. Eventually, however, the economy will settle back to a long-run equilibrium where aggregate demand equals long-run aggregate supply.

Figure 3

An increase in tax leads to a fall in aggregate supply

An increase in VAT, for example, leads to an increase in costs for firms. This means that at any given level of output, firms will charge higher prices, shifting the SRAS curve upwards. This leads to a rise in the price level and a fall in equilibrium output in the short run.

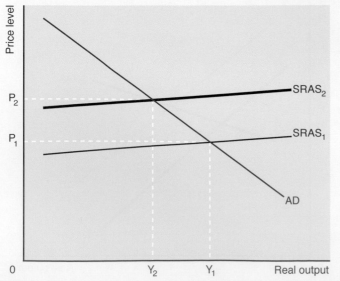

The trade balance

An increase in taxes on households will reduce their disposable income. This, in turn, will reduce their consumption including spending on imports. Hence the trade balance will improve. Equally, a cut in consumption will reduce aggregate demand. With aggregate demand falling from what it would otherwise have been, firms will need less capacity to meet demand and so they will need to invest less. This is what would be expected from the accelerator theory of investment. Some of the cut in investment will come from cuts in imports of capital equipment. Hence the trade balance in the short term will improve. In the long term, it could deteriorate if less investment makes domestic firms less internationally competitive over time.

Question 4

The 'Cut Tourism VAT' campaign wants to see VAT on hotels stays and tourist attractions cut from 20 per cent to 5 per cent, bringing the UK closer to the rates charged in other European countries. The campaign says the move would create 120 000 jobs and add £4bn to UK GDP, albeit at a cost to the exchequer in lost revenue. It is argued that because the UK's VAT rate on accommodation and attractions is one of the highest in the EU, it puts British tourism at a serious competitive disadvantage. Paul Maynard, MP for Blackpool North and Cleveleys, said his town was 'stifled by the uncompetitive VAT rate. 'Our long-term economic plan is working but our seaside resorts need to play a role in that recovery. I'm supporting the call for a tourism VAT cut, which will allow businesses in Blackpool to be more competitive, to invest in facilities and create more jobs.' Tourism is Britain's sixth largest export, according to a study by Oxford Economics, but many coastal towns have been hit hard by the rise of overseas package holidays since the 1980s.

Source: adapted from © the *Financial Times* 20.10.2014, All Rights Reserved.

Explain the possible impact of a cut in VAT on hotels and tourist attractions from 20 per cent to five per cent on (a) aggregate demand; (b) real output; (c) employment; (d) the current account on the balance of payments.

FDI flows

Foreign Direct Investment (FDI) is normally defined as investment by a foreign company where the foreign company acquires 10 per cent or more of the shares of the domestic company. For example, it could be Volkswagen (the foreign company) setting up a new vehicle manufacturing plant in Vietnam and owning 100 per cent of the company it sets up in Vietnam. It could be Volkswagen buying an existing vehicle manufacturing company in India. It could be Volkswagen buying a 20 per cent stake in a vehicle manufacturing company in China. Countries compete to attract FDI. For a country, it represents a way to increase investment in their own economies and to boost output and employment. For governments, it represents a way of increasing tax revenues because the ongoing operations will pay a variety of taxes from taxes on labour employed, to sales taxes like VAT, to taxes on profits.

Some countries have chosen to encourage FDI inflows by offering lower rates of tax on investment. In particular, some countries have deliberately lowered their rates of corporation tax, the tax on company profits. The justification is that any loss of tax revenues will be more than offset by increased economic growth and prosperity resulting from the investment. Also, in the long term, the government may collect more in tax despite the rate of tax being lower because if the investment had not been made, no tax would have been payable.

The problem with 'tax competition' is that it can become a 'race to the bottom'. If enough countries lower their taxes in an attempt to attract FDI, lower taxes will have little impact on a firm's decisions about where to make the investment. However, countries will see significantly lower tax revenues because all the existing firms in the country will now be paying lower tax. Using game theory, the strategy only works for a country lowering its tax rates if enough other countries keep their tax rates high. If every country lowers their tax rates, every government simply loses tax revenues.

Corporation tax rates have become a major international issue in the 2000s. Multinational companies have become increasingly aggressive about moving their assets around the world to avoid paying taxes. If a multinational can avoid billions of pounds in taxes by opening an office in the Cayman Islands, or routing all European sales through an office in Ireland, then there has been some foreign direct investment in the Cayman Islands and in Ireland. But it has come at a huge fiscal cost to many other countries.

Key Terms

Laffer curve - a curve which shows that at low levels of taxation, tax revenues will increase if tax rates are increased. However, if tax rates are high, then a further rise in rates will reduce total tax revenues because of the disincentive effects of the increase in tax.

Thinking like an economist

The main taxes in the UK

Over 90 per cent of government receipts come from taxes. Figure 4 gives a broad breakdown of estimated government receipts for 2015-16. The largest tax by revenue is income tax which raises approximately one quarter of all government receipts. The three largest taxes (income tax, National Insurance contributions and VAT) raise approximately 60 per cent. If corporation tax, local authority taxes (council tax and business rates) and excise duties (mainly on petrol, drink and tobacco)

are added to these, then these taxes contribute over 80 per cent of government revenues.

Income tax This is the single most important source of revenue for government. It is a tax on the income of individuals. Each person is allowed to earn a certain amount (called the personal tax allowance) income tax free. Then on any income over that amount, they have to pay tax at the basic rate (20 per cent in 2015). If incomes exceed the upper limit of the

Figure 4

Public sector receipts 2015-16

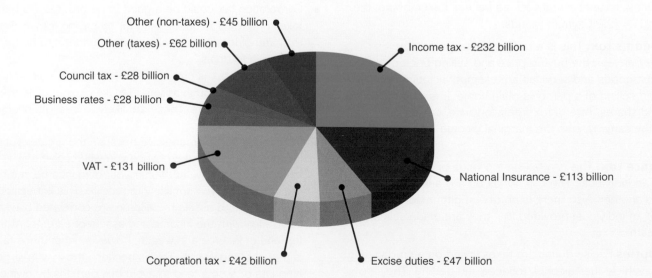

Source adapted from HM Treasury, Budget 2015.

519

basic rate, then any additional income over that is taxed at the higher rate of 40 per cent. In 2015, there was an additional rate of 45 per cent for income over £150 000. The majority of workers are in the 20 per cent tax bracket.

It is important to understand that the marginal rate of income tax differs from the average rate. Assume that workers can earn £10 000 tax free, then they pay 20 per cent tax on the next £40 000 and 40 per cent on earnings above this. Workers earning £100 000 would have a marginal rate of tax of 40 per cent. This is because the marginal rate of tax is the tax rate on the last £1 earned. But their average rate of tax would be the total tax paid divided by their income. Total tax paid is £28 000: this is £0 on the first £10 000, £8 000 on the next £40 000 (£40 000 x 20 per cent) and £20 000 on the next £50 000 (£50 000 x 40 per cent). With an income of £100 000, the average rate of tax is 28 per cent (100 per cent x £28 000 ÷ £100 000). If tax rates are rising with income, the average rate of tax is always below the marginal rate of tax.

National Insurance contributions (NICs) All taxes apart from National Insurance contributions (NICs) and local authority taxes are paid into one central fund (called the Consolidated Fund). However, there is a separate National Insurance Fund out of which is paid National Insurance benefits, such as state pensions. Strictly speaking, contributions are not taxes because they are a form of insurance premium. However, increasingly they have come to be seen and used, by government, as a form of tax. Employees and the self-employed pay NICs on their income. Employers too pay NICs based on the earnings of their workers.

Corporation tax Corporation tax is a tax on company profits. Companies pay a higher rate if their profits are larger. Companies can claim numerous allowances, including investment allowances which can be set against their profits. This reduces their taxable profits in any one year. A number of multinational companies operating in the UK and with substantial UK sales pay virtually no corporation tax by exploiting tax loopholes where costs, revenues and profits earned in the UK are redirected to tax havens such as Ireland, Luxembourg, the Netherlands or the Cayman Islands.

Capital gains tax This is a tax on capital gains - the difference between the buying price and selling price of an asset. Most goods and services are exempt, including the buying and selling of a person's main home. It is paid mainly on stocks and shares. After a tax free allowance, capital gains are taxed at the same rate as the marginal income tax rate of the tax payer.

Inheritance tax This is a tax on the value of assets left on death by an individual. There is no tax on any assets left by one spouse to another. Also there is no tax on gifts made during the lifetime of an individual provided that they are made seven years before death.

Excise duties Excise duties are taxes levied on a narrow range of goods: vehicle fuel, alcohol, tobacco and betting. They are mostly calculated not on value (as with VAT) but on the volume sold. For example, excise duty is paid per litre of petrol sold. If the price of petrol rises, the amount paid in VAT rises, but the excise duty remains the same. Excise duties should not be confused with customs duties which are taxes on imported goods. All revenues from customs duties collected by EU countries, including the UK, are paid directly to the EU to fund its budget.

Value Added Tax (VAT) This is a tax on expenditure. There are different rates of tax. Essential commodities - food, water, children's clothing, books, newspapers, magazines and public transport - are tax exempt (i.e. they are zero rated). Domestic fuel (gas electricity, heating oil and costs) is taxed at a reduced rate of five per cent. All other goods and services in 2015 were taxed at 20 per cent. VAT is collected by firms and is imposed on the valued added to a product by that firm.

Council tax Council tax is a tax imposed on domestic property by local authorities. Each dwelling has been assessed for sale value in April 1992. The property has been put into one of eight bands, from Band A for properties up to £240 000 to Band H for properties over £320 000. The local authority then fixes a charge each year for each band. The differences in charges between bands are fixed by law. For instance, properties in Band H, the highest band, pay three times the council tax of properties in Band A, the lowest band in a local area.

Business rates Business rates are a local authority tax on business property. Each business property has been given a rateable value based on an estimate of the yearly rent at which that property might reasonably have been let. Currently that is based on rents paid in April 2008. The amount paid by the business is the rateable value multiplied by a 'factor' called the 'Uniform Business Rate'. This is fixed by central government and not local government.

Progressive, proportional and regressive taxes

Some taxes in the UK are progressive, i.e. the higher the income, the higher the proportion of income paid in tax.

- Income tax is progressive because there are higher marginal rates of tax as income increases.
- Corporation tax could be argued to be progressive because taxes on profits might be paid for by paying less in dividends to shareholders. Individual shareholders tend to be higher income individuals.
- Capital gains tax is progressive because it is paid only by those with enough assets to make capital gains over the yearly allowance. These are likely to be high income individuals.
- Inheritance tax is progressive because the greater your income, the greater the chance you will receive an inheritance. Equally, the higher your own income, the higher the inheritance you are likely to receive. This is because the income and assets of children are correlated over a population with the income and assets of parents. At the top end of income and wealth, however, inheritance tax is probably regressive. This is because those with large amounts of assets tend to avoid tax, perhaps by giving their assets away before they die, putting them into trusts or moving the assets to a tax haven.

Table 1 Percentage of income paid in tax, 2012-13

	Quintile groups of all households ranked by equivalised disposable income					
	Bottom	2nd	3rd	4th	Top	All households
Original income	5 536	11 952	23 069	38 697	81 284	32 108
Gross income (original income plus benefits)	12 690	20 769	29 692	43 388	83 950	38 098
Direct taxes and employees, NIC	1 256	2 257	4 620	8 635	20 322	7 418
Indirect taxes	844	1 911	5 029	6 474	9 140	5 623
Direct taxes as a percentage of gross income	9.9	10.9	15.6	19.9	24.2	19.5
Indirect taxes as a percentage of gross income	27.5	19.2	16.9	14.9	10.9	14.8
Taxes as percentage of original income	85.7	52.2	41.8	39.0	36.2	40.6
Taxes as percentage of gross income	**37.4**	**30.1**	**32.5**	**34.8**	**35.1**	**34.2**

Source: adapted from *The Effects of Taxes and Benefits on Household Income*, 2012-13, www.ons.gov.uk.

Some taxes are regressive.

- VAT and excise duties are regressive. Higher-income households spend less of their income and save more than lower-income households. Hence they pay a lower proportion of their income in tax. Excise duties on alcohol, tobacco and betting are highly regressive.
- Council tax is highly regressive. The highest council taxpayer only pays a maximum three times that of the lowest council tax payer, but may earn considerably more.

National Insurance contributions paid by workers are mildly progressive up to mid ranges of income. This is because there is a tax free allowance for the first approximately £6 000 of earnings. However, there is also a limit on how much NICs can be made. Once that limit has been exceeded, high-income earners no longer pay NICs on the last pound earned. At high levels of income, NICs therefore become regressive.

Over time, there have been changes in the overall progressive or regressive nature of the UK tax system. Very large cuts in the top rate of income tax (from 83 per cent to 40 per cent) in the 1980s under Margaret Thatcher made the system considerably less progressive. The shift from local

authority taxation to the council tax in 1993, which also saw a rise in VAT from 15 per cent to 17.5 per cent, also made the system less progressive. The further rise in VAT in 2010 to 20 per cent equally reduced the progressive nature of the system.

Table 1 shows the proportion of tax paid by quintile groups of households ranked according to their disposable income (income after direct taxes and benefits have been taken into account). The tax system is progressive based upon the original income of households (income before taxes and benefits). However, once benefits are taken into account, the system is regressive between the two bottom quintiles of income earners and then very mildly progressive for the top three quintiles. The data in Table 1 shows clearly the progressive nature of direct taxes and the regressive nature of indirect taxes in the UK.

Comparisons of tax over time and between countries

Figure 5 shows how current receipts, almost all of which are tax receipts, as a percentage of GDP have changed since 1919. The large spike in 1939-45 represented the Second World War. In the post-war era, current receipts climbed to a peak of 44.3 per cent of GDP in 1981-82. However, large cuts particularly in income tax on high-income earners under Margaret Thatcher

Figure 5

Total public sector receipts as a percentage of GDP, UK

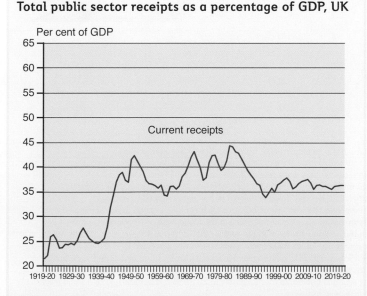

Source: adapted from Office for Budget Responsibility, *Economic and Fiscal Outlook*, March 2015.

Figure 6

Receipts from direct and indirect taxes, four quarter moving average, £ billion

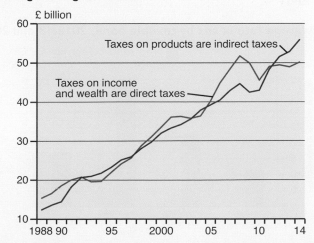

Source: adapted from ONS, *Longer-term trends - Public Sector Finance*, by A Jowett and M Hardie, 2014.

saw current receipts fall to 37.6 per cent when she left office in 1989-1990. Since then government receipts have averaged 36 per cent of GDP.

Figure 6 shows the balance between direct and indirect tax revenues over time. At the start of the period in 1988, indirect tax revenues were 25 per cent higher than direct tax revenues. By 2014, they were 13 per cent lower. It could be argued that this shift from direct to indirect taxation has been mainly due to the 2007-08 financial crisis and the consequent fall in incomes. However, between 2010 and 2015, the Coalition government has cut income tax and raised VAT. Overall, the tax changes between 1988 and 2015 have made the UK tax system less progressive.

Figure 7 gives an international comparison of taxes. In the 1970s and 1980s, it was strongly argued by some that Britain was highly taxed and that this had contributed to low economic growth rates. In fact, Britain has tended to tax less than the rest of the EU whilst taxing more highly than countries such as the US and Japan. Figure 7 shows that in 2014, the UK collected just 0.8 per cent more in revenue as a percentage of GDP than the average for the rich OECD countries but 8.1 per cent less of GDP than the euro area. The UK also tends to collect a lower proportion of taxes in direct taxes than in other EU countries. The result is that income inequality after tax on average is greater in the UK than in the rest of the EU.

Figure 7

Government total tax and non-tax receipts as a percentage of GDP, 2014

Per cent of nominal GDP

Country	%
Norway	55.9
Finland	55.6
France	52.9
Italy	48.1
Greece	46.5
Euro Area	46.5
Germany	44.3
United Kingdom	38.4
Spain	37.9
Canada	37.8
Total OECD	37.6
Japan	33.9
United States	33.4
Korea	31.7

Source: adapted from www.oecd.org.

Data Response Question

Flat tax

What is a flat tax?

A flat tax is any tax which has a single rate of tax. However, the flat tax debate centres round just one tax - income tax. A flat income tax would be one where there was just one rate of income tax for all income earners such as 25 per cent. Advocates of flat taxes tend to argue that there should also be a zero per cent band for the first £X of earnings such as £10 000. It would

Figure 8

Average rate of tax by taxable band, 2012-13 and 2014-15[1]

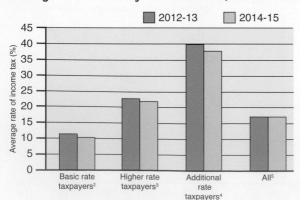

Source: adapted from HMRC, *Income tax liabilities statistics*, February 2015.

1. Data for 2012-13 are actual outturns, for 2014-15 are projections.
2. Basic rate taxpayers were individuals who earned enough to have some of their earnings taxed at the basic rate of 20 per cent.
3. Higher rate taxpayers were individuals who earned enough to pay some of their earnings at 20 per cent tax and the rest at the higher rate of 40 per cent.
4. Additional rate taxpayers were individuals who earned enough to pay some of their earnings at 20 per cent tax, some at the higher rate of 40 per cent and the rest at the additional rate of 50 per cent for 2012-13 and 45 per cent for 2014-15.
5. The average rate of tax for all income taxpayers was projected to stay the same in 2014-15 as in 2012-13 despite average rates of tax for basic, higher and additional rate taxpayers falling. This is because there are projected to be a larger number of higher rate and additional rate taxpayers in 2014-15 compared to 2012-13 and fewer basic rate only taxpayers.

be very difficult and administratively costly to collect small amounts tax from low-income earners. The cost of collection would be very high in proportion to the tax paid. It would also encourage some workers to disappear into the black economy. At the moment, when low-income individuals pay income tax, it tends to be automatically deducted from earnings through the PAYE system or by banks and building societies on interest earned. This is relatively cheap to collect for the tax authorities.

The argument for flat taxes

Some economists believe that flat taxes could help revitalise the British economy. There are four main arguments on favour of a flat tax on income.

- Flat taxes are much easier to understand than the present complex income tax system where there are many allowances and many different rates of tax. Simplifying the system would mean fewer loopholes for taxpayers to exploit in their drive to minimise the amount of tax they pay. Tax revenues would therefore go up because there would less tax avoidance.
- The top rate of tax would fall. This would act as a powerful incentive for higher-income earners to work harder and be more entrepreneurial. It would also act as a powerful incentive for lower-income earners because they would know that if they did increase their income, it would not be taxed at a higher rate.

- A flat tax would make the UK more attractive to foreign investors. Lower taxes would encourage foreign firms to set up in the UK and rich foreign individuals to take up residence in the UK.
- The combination of these three effects would boost the supply side of be economy and lead to higher economic growth. Tax revenues would increase as a result, allowing the government to cut tax rates even further.

The argument against flat taxes

Most economists believe that a flat tax has too many disadvantages to be viable. Assume that the same amount of income tax is to be collected under a flat tax as under the current system.

- The single rate of tax would have to be significantly higher than the current basic rate of tax. This is because in 2013-14, 66 per cent of the total amount of income tax collected was paid either by taxpayers who paid a top rate of tax of 40 per cent or 45 per cent. The proportion paid by these taxpayers was projected by HMRC to rise to 72 per cent in 2014-15.
- Most income taxpayers would pay considerably more tax. They would have to pay for the very large tax cuts that the highest-income earners would receive. There would be a few winners but a large number of losers.
- Income tax would be become significantly less progressive. It would mean that the UK tax system would move from being broadly proportional to being significantly regressive.

- There would be no positive supply-side effects. Cutting the top rate of tax from, say, 45 per cent to the flat rate of, say, 30 per cent, will not incentivise any significant number of workers to work harder or be more entrepreneurial. There would be no extra income tax paid because there would be no incentive effect to increase earnings. Moreover, if there are incentive effects in reducing tax rates, could there not be disincentive effects for the majority of earners who now pay a much higher average rate of income tax?
- Lowering tax rates for rich foreigners coming to live in the UK will lose the UK tax revenues. More rich foreigners might live in the UK and pay tax. But the tax lost from cutting the rate of income tax so much will more than offset any gains in tax.

Q

1. Explain the difference between current income tax system in the UK and a flat income tax system.

2. Discuss whether a flat tax would be more efficient, more equitable and lead to higher economic growth that the current income tax system.

Evaluation

There are three issues highlighted in the question. On each one, weigh up the advantages and disadvantages of the likely effects of a move to a flat tax.

Table 2 Income tax paid by taxable band, 2014-15[1]

	Number of taxpayers	Amount of tax paid	Proportion of total tax paid
Basic rate taxpayers	24.1m	54.9bn	33.10%
Higher rate taxpayers	4.5m	64.4bn	38.90%
Additional rate taxpayers	4.5m	46.4bn	28.00%

Source: adapted from HMRC, *Income tax liabilities statistics*, February 2015.

1. Projection.

Key points

1. Fiscal deficits and surpluses and the National Debt can be measured in money terms or as a percentage of GDP.
2. A distinction can be made between cyclical and structural fiscal deficits and surpluses, as well as current budgets deficits compared to primary budget deficits.
3. Factors affecting the fiscal budget balance include the spending and taxation decisions of government, the trade cycle and rates of interest on the National Debt.
4. The size of the National Debt in money terms is determined by the fiscal deficits or surpluses of government. Measured as a percentage of GDP, it is also determined by the level of national income.
5. The size of fiscal deficits and the National Debt can have an impact on interest rates, debt servicing, inter-generational equity, the rate of inflation, a country's credit rating and foreign direct investment.

Starter activity

Find out the current level of the fiscal deficit of the UK government and the value of the National Debt. Are these numbers a problem for the UK? If yes, what sort of problem do they pose and if no, why don't they pose a problem?

Fiscal surpluses and deficits and the National Debt

It was explained in Unit 38 that fiscal (or budget) deficits or surpluses had a direct impact on the size of the National Debt, the total of all unpaid government borrowing from previous years. If there is a fiscal deficit of, say, £20 billion in one year, then the National Debt will increase by £20 billion. If there is a fiscal surplus of, say, £30 billion, then the National Debt will decrease by £30 billion.

Fiscal balances and the National Debt can be measured in two main ways. One way is to measure them in money terms, like £10 billion. Another way is to measure them as a percentage of GDP, such as three per cent. The GDP measure is often more useful because it gives an indication of how easy it will be for the government to finance a deficit, or how easy it will be for the government to repay the National Debt. Compare this to an individual. If a worker borrows £1 000 and her income is £5 000 a year, the debt incurred is very significant. At 20 per cent of her income, it could show she is in serious financial difficulties. If a worker borrows £1 000 and her income is £100 000 a year, the debt is relatively trivial. At one per cent of her income, it is likely to be of little consequence.

It is important to understand that the National Debt of the UK is the debt owed by the UK government. Much of it is owed to UK citizens through the savings they have accumulated for their pensions and assurance policies. Also, in 2015, approximately one quarter of the National Debt was owned by the Bank of England, itself owned by the government.

Cyclical and structural deficits

A distinction can be made between **cyclical** and **structural deficits**. A **cyclical deficit** occurs because government spending and revenues fluctuate through the trade cycle. When the

economy is in boom, spending on welfare benefits such as unemployment benefit is likely to be relatively low and tax revenues are likely to be relatively high. When the economy is in

Question 1

Figure 1

UK National Debt, £ billions at current prices and as percentage of GDP

Source: adapted from House of Commons Library, Briefing Paper, Government borrowing, debt and debt interest: statistics by Matthew Keep, May 2015.

Figure 1 shows the UK National Debt expressed in £ billions at current prices and as a percentage of GDP.

(a) 'The UK National Debt increased 31 fold between 1974-74 and 2019/2020.' To what extent is this correct?

(b) 'The increase in the UK National Debt between 1974-75 and 2019-20 has imposed a crushing burden on every UK citizen. In 1974-75, the debt was just £927 per person but by 2019-20 this will have risen 26 fold to £24 247 per person.' To what extent is this correct given a rise in the population from 56.2 million in 1975 to an estimated 67.1 million in 2020?

Figure 2

Cyclical and structural deficits

There is a structural deficit in this economy of two per cent of GDP because the lowest level of the cyclical deficit is two per cent of GDP.

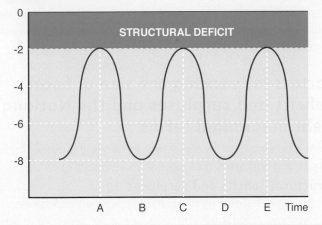

a recession, government spending will be relatively high and tax revenues relatively low. This pattern is shown in Figure 2. At time points A, C and E, the economy is in boom and the fiscal deficit is low at two per cent of GDP. When the economy is in a recession, as at time points B and D, the fiscal deficit is large at eight per cent of GDP. So the range of the cyclical deficit is six per cent (eight minus two per cent). At the peak of the boom, there is no cyclical deficit. At the bottom of the recession, the cyclical deficit has added six per cent to the actual deficit.

In Figure 2, at no point in the trade cycle is the budget in surplus. The best position it reaches is a deficit of two per cent. This two per cent then represents the structural deficit for the government. The structural deficit is the fiscal deficit which occurs when the cyclical deficit is lowest.

Figure 3

Cyclical and structural deficits and surpluses

There is a structural surplus in this economy of two per cent of GDP because the highest cyclical surplus is two per cent of GDP.

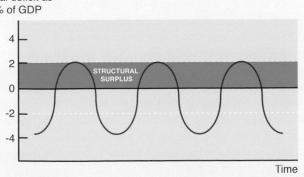

This means that the actual deficit is equal to the structural deficit plus the cyclical deficit.

Actual deficit = cyclical deficit + structural deficit

In Figure 2, at the point A, the structural deficit is two per cent and the cyclical deficit is 0 per cent. So the actual deficit is two per cent. At the point B, the structural deficit is two per cent and the cyclical deficit is six per cent. So the actual deficit is eight per cent.

Governments can also have structural balances or structural surpluses. A structural balance occurs when at the peak of a boom, the actual fiscal balance is zero. A structural surplus occurs when at the peak of a boom, there is an actual fiscal surplus. In Figure 3, the structural surplus is two per cent. This is because the cyclical surplus is two per cent at the top of the boom.

Question 2

Figure 4

Estimate of the structural balance, % of GDP

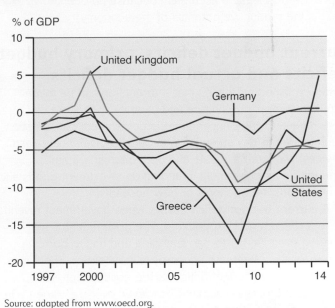

Source: adapted from www.oecd.org.

Figure 4 shows OECD estimates of the structural deficits or surpluses for four countries.

(a) Explain what is meant by a structural deficit.

(b) Which country over the whole period (i) had the highest average structural deficit (ii) saw the largest improvement in its structural deficit?

(c) Suggest why the structural deficits as a percentage of GDP of all four countries increased in 2009 compared to 2008.

(d) Greece cut its structural deficit from 2010 onwards by cutting public spending and raising taxes. These fiscal austerity measures cut Greek GDP by one quarter between 2009 and 2013. Explain (i) why fiscal austerity cut GDP and (ii) why the percentage cuts in the Greek fiscal deficit measured in money terms were larger than the percentage fall in the structural deficit when measured as a percentage of GDP.

If a government has a structural deficit, it is likely that the National Debt will grow over time. This is because, whether the economy is in boom or in recession, it will still have to borrow money to finance its spending. Therefore, economists argue that structural deficits need to be eliminated. Governments should either raise taxes, cut government spending or some combination of both to eliminate the structural deficit.

Some economists argue that in practice it is impossible to calculate the cyclical or structural deficit of an economy. This is because trade cycles are not regular occurrences. They also don't have the same amplitude each time. For example, the financial crisis of 2007-08 was the worst recession for many countries since the Great Depression of the 1930s. It was not predicted by the majority of economists and politicians. With hindsight, it is possible to see that many countries had structural deficits in the decade before 2007-08. However, at the time, economists and politicians were working on the assumption that many countries were running structural surpluses. The debate mirrors the one about output gaps. An output gap is a very helpful economic concept. But some economists argue that it is impossible to measure accurately because no one knows exactly what is the productive potential of the economy.

Current budget deficits, primary budget deficits and actual budget deficits

It was explained in Unit 79 that a distinction can be made between current expenditure and capital expenditure of government. Current expenditure is government consumption (such as day-to-day spending on education, defence, health services), welfare payments and debt interest. Capital expenditure is government spending on investment goods such as new roads, new schools or new hospitals.

A **current budget deficit** occurs when government revenues are less than current expenditure. The government is not covering even its day-to-day spending and has to borrow money for this. When the economy is in recession, there may well be a current budget deficit as the government attempts to increase aggregate demand. However, over the trade cycle, economists argue that the government needs to run a current budget surplus.

This is because governments must also invest for the future. The government faces the same choices as a household about how to finance investment. For example, a household might want to buy a new car. The car will be used over a number of years. Should it borrow the money and spread the payments over those years or should it buy in outright at the start? If it borrows money, it will pay interest. So the overall cost is likely to be higher. But if it spreads the payments, this more accurately reflects how the use of the car is spread over time.

So there are arguments for and against governments borrowing to finance their investment expenditure. With political pressure to keep taxes low, governments over the past 20 years have increasingly argued that at least a proportion of investment expenditure should be financed through borrowing. At the same time, over the trade cycle, there should be a current budget surplus. The surplus is then used to cover whatever investment spending will not be covered by borrowing.

A distinction can also be made between **primary budget deficits** or **surpluses** and actual budget deficits or surpluses. The primary deficit is the actual deficit but does not include interest payments on the National Debt. Therefore:

Primary deficit + debt interest payments = actual deficit

If a government is in financial difficulties, it might find it difficult to borrow more money on the world financial markets. In order not to increase the size of the National Debt, it then needs to run a primary surplus that is at least equal to debt interest payments.

Factors influencing the size of fiscal deficits and surpluses and the National Debt in nominal terms

There is a number of factors which influence the size of fiscal deficits and surpluses measured in money terms.

Structural deficits and surpluses Structural deficits and surpluses are caused by the planned spending and tax decisions of government. Most governments are under pressure to raise government spending and reduce taxes. In developing countries, government spending may be linked to economic development. When the economy is doing well, there is a temptation on the part of government decision makers to assume that it will continue to do well in the future. Borrowing a little more to finance a favourite spending project or provide a tax cut for core political voters can become irresistible.

Cyclical deficits and surpluses Cyclical deficits and surpluses are caused by changes in government spending and tax revenues which change as GDP changes. They are out of control of the government in the short term. For example, a downturn in the UK economy is likely to have a negative affect on house prices and the number of the houses being bought and sold. The result is that the government receives less in taxes on property transactions (called 'stamp duty'). The impact on government finances also varies with the severity of the recession or the size of the boom. The 2007-08 financial crisis hit government finances hard because, for many developed countries, it was the worst recession experienced since the 1930s.

Unforeseen events Occasionally, governments have to respond to major unforeseen events which are not covered in monies set aside for contingencies. Floods and other natural disasters are unlikely to have much impact on UK government finances but they might have a devastating impact on a small economy like Haiti or Jamaica. However, the financial crisis of 2007-08 showed that major economies can be at risk from unforeseen events. Between 2007-09, many developed countries were forced to nationalise (i.e. buy) banks and other financial institutions that were at risk of failing. These purchases are typically not seen on data relating to fiscal deficits in those years because they are excluded as 'one-off' items that would distort the underlying pattern of fiscal balances. However, a £60 billion purchase bail out of banks in one year is an extra £60 billion added to the fiscal deficit for that year.

Question 3

In 2008, the UK government was forced to bail out the UK banking system including buying part of Lloyds Bank and RBS (Royal Bank of Scotland). The cost was significant and added to the UK National Debt. The government has been selling off its stakes in banks since that time, reducing the National Debt.

(a) What, according to the data in Figure 5, was the cost to the UK government of the bank bail-outs of 2008?

(b) To what extent might the bank bail-outs increase or decrease the UK National Debt in the long term?

Figure 5

UK National Debt

% of normal GDP

[Bar and line chart showing UK National Debt from 2005 Q1 to 2014 Q1. Vertical axis labelled 0 to 160. Values start around 35-40 in 2005, rise sharply to about 140 in 2009 Q1, peak around 150 in 2010, and gradually decline to about 115 by 2014 Q1.]

— National Debt including cost of bank bail-outs
— National Debt excluding cost of bank bail-outs

Source: adapted from ONS, *Longer-term trends - Public Sector Finance* by A Jowett and M Hardie, 2014.

Debt interest Debt interest is part of a fiscal deficit or surplus. The larger the debt interest paid, the larger the deficit or the smaller the surplus. Debt interest is determined by two factors. One is the size of the National Debt, the total amount the government owes to its creditors. The other is the rate of interest it has to pay on its debt. The higher the average rate of interest on its borrowing, the higher will be debt repayments. New borrowing takes place at current market rates of interest. The rate of interest paid on new borrowing will depend on the two factors:

- the market rate of interest at the time;
- the credit rating of the government; if the government is seen as being able to repay in the future, its credit rating will be high and it will be able to borrow at relatively low rates of interest; if the government is seen as being at risk of not repaying, then it will have to offer a relatively high rate of interest to cover that risk.

Paradoxically, it can be the case that a government increases its borrowing substantially and yet the total amount of interest paid on its National Debt falls. This will happen if it is able to refinance part of its debt at much lower rates of interest. So an increase in the National Debt does not necessarily mean an increase in interest payments on the debt.

The size of the National Debt in money terms is entirely dependent on past fiscal surpluses or deficits and the current fiscal surplus or deficit. If the National Debt at the end of last year was £100 billion and the fiscal deficit this year was £15 billion, then the National Debt will be £115 billion at the end of this year.

Factors affecting fiscal deficits and surpluses and the National Debt as a percentage of GDP

The fiscal balance and the National Debt can be measured in nominal terms, such as £20 billion. However, they can also be measured as a percentage of GDP. This provides a much better indication of a government's ability to finance its debt. The fiscal balance, the National Debt and GDP are interlinked.

- If GDP is growing fast, the cyclical budget balance, whether deficit or surplus, is likely to improve. So the ratio of the budget balance to GDP is likely to fall. For example, assume there is a fiscal deficit of £2 billion and GDP is £100 billion. The fiscal deficit as a percentage of GDP is then 2.0 per cent (100% x 2 ÷ 100). If the next year, the fiscal deficit falls to £1 billion and GDP grows to £105 billion, the fiscal deficit as a percentage of GDP falls to 0.95 per cent (100% x 1 ÷ 105).
- If the economy falls into recession with GDP falling, the cyclical budget balance will deteriorate. So the ratio of the budget balance to GDP will rise. For example, assume there is a fiscal deficit of £2 billion and GDP is £100 billion. The fiscal deficit as a percentage of GDP is then 2.0 per cent (100% x 2/100). If the next year, the fiscal deficit rises to £5 billion and GDP falls to £90 billion, the fiscal deficit as a percentage of GDP is 5.6 per cent (100% x 5 ÷ 90).

The exact impact of rises or falls in GDP also depends on government policy about the structural balance. If the government in a recession decides to cut an existing structural deficit, it is likely to lead to a deterioration in the fiscal deficit as a percentage of GDP. This is because cuts in public spending or rises in taxes, combined with the consequent multiplier effects, are likely to lower aggregate demand and so lower GDP all other things being equal.

Implications for other variables of fiscal deficits and National Debts

The size of fiscal deficits or surpluses have implications for other economic variables.

Interest rates All other things being equal, a rise in government borrowing in a national economy should lead to a rise in market interest rates in that country. This is because the demand for borrowed funds rises relative to existing supply. The price of borrowed money is the rate of interest. So the rise in demand for borrowed funds leads to a rise in interest rates. This may then crowd out private sector spending. However, this rise in interest rates many not happen for a number of reasons.

- The increase in government borrowing may be relatively small and so have a barely noticeable impact on interest rates.
- If the central bank is operating a policy of quantitative easing,

explained in Unit 38, then the government is likely to be able to borrow more at virtually zero rates of interest.

- The government may borrow on international financial markets. This increases the potential supply of borrowed funds and so it may be able to borrow at no increase in interest rates.
- In a recession, government borrowing is likely to rise, but private sector borrowing will fall as investment and consumption fall. Less private sector borrowing reduce any impact on interest rates of higher government borrowing.

Debt servicing It has been explained above that a rise in government borrowing is likely to lead to a rise the amount of interest paid on the National Debt as it grows in size. However, the impact on debt servicing depends crucially on the rate of interest on current borrowing. If interest rates are rising, debt servicing will considerably add to the fiscal deficit and to the National Debt. If interest rates fall far enough, for example because of quantitative easing, then higher borrowing and a higher National Debt could even be associated with a fall in the total amount of interest paid on the National Debt.

Inter-generational equity Some economists and politicians have argued strongly that increasing fiscal deficits and National Debts benefit current citizens at the expense of future generations. If the National Debt doubles today, it will be left for people 50 years from now to pay it off. Equally, there are arguments to suggest that the 'baby boomer' generation has benefited from the financial crisis of 2007-08 at the expense of younger people. Both arguments have major flaws.

First, the National Debt is not something that most governments prioritise for repayment. What is important from year to year is the cost of financing the debt. If in 50 years' time, every adult is having, at today's prices, to pay £10 000 a year in extra taxes to finance interest payments on the debt, then it would be an inter-generational burden. But if the extra cost is £50, then it is irrelevant. The history of the past 100 years suggests that the National Debt declines in relative value over time because of the effects of inflation, which erodes the real value of the debt. Time also allows GDP to rise significantly making any interest payments more affordable to repay.

Second, the impact of a rise in the National Debt between today's generations is mixed. In the UK, the baby boomer generation who have retired have benefited from protection to their state pension from the government. They also have saved more than previous generations for private or occupational pensions and so are better off than pensioners 20 years ago. But quantitative easing has been reducing the interest on their savings to virtually zero. Also those having to buy private pensions are getting very low pensions for their money. Young people entering the job market between 2008 and 2014 have suffered, finding it difficult to get reasonably paid jobs. That has been a consequence of the financial crisis and not fiscal deficits or the National Debt. High house prices have also prevented many from buying a house. Those in their 30s and 40s with mortgages have made large gains because interest rates on those mortgages are so low due to quantitative easing. On the other hand, between 2008 and 2014, they saw a 10 per cent fall in their real take-home pay because inflation was much

Question 4

Figure 6

Net debt interest payments as percentage of GDP

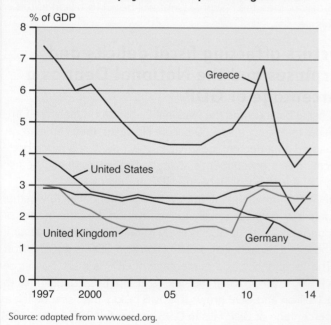

Source: adapted from www.oecd.org.

Consider Figure 6.

(a) (i) The government of which country had the highest debt interest payments as a percentage of GDP? (ii) Using the data in Question 2, Figure 4 of this unit, suggest why this was the case.

(b) The National Debt as a proportion of GDP of the UK doubled between 2008 and 2014. For the US, it increased by 50 per cent. (i) What happened to debt interest payments as a result? (ii) Suggest reasons why debt interest payments did not increase by as much.

higher than any pay increases they received.

What is absolutely certain is that nearly all groups in society, whether today or in the near future, have suffered significantly because of the 2007-08 financial crisis.

The rate of inflation The relationship between fiscal balances, the National Debt and inflation are complex. The traditional economic view has been that governments have a choice about how to finance a fiscal deficit. They can either borrow the money or they can print the money. If governments borrow the money they need, the government spends more and the private sector spends less because it has lent to the government. There is no increase in aggregate demand as a result (ignoring multiplier effects). Hence, there is no impact on inflation.

The outcome is different if governments print money. Down the ages, they have 'printed' money in a variety of ways. For example, in Roman or medieval times, governments controlled the mints which produced coins. These coins were made of valuable metals such as gold or silver. To print money, governments would accumulate old coins, melt them down and then reissue them with less of the valuable metal in them. This way they could produce more new coins compared to the old coins. When paper money became the main type of money, governments via their central banks, could literally just print more notes and spend them. In the modern age of electronic banking, central banks issue governments with bank credits which they then spend. The result is an increase in money in circulation. Monetarists argue that inflation is 'always and everywhere' the result of an increase in the money supply. More money chasing the same number of goods results in goods costing more, i.e. inflation. Put another way, governments have increased aggregate demand because they have increased their spending without reducing private sector spending. But aggregate supply has not increased. Hence there must be demand-pull inflation. Hyperinflation, such as experienced by Germany in 1923, or Zimbabwe in 2008-09, was caused by governments unable to borrow enough money to meet their spending needs. They resorted to the printing presses with disastrous results.

However, arguably, money was being printed in large amounts following the financial crisis of 2007-08. But it was given a different name: quantitative easing. The Bank of England, the Bank of Japan, the US Federal Reserve Bank and the European Central Bank have printed trillions of pounds between them. Their economists and those politicians who support quantitative easing would argue that quantitative easing is different from printing money. The reason is that, whilst these central banks are buying up the debt of their governments in return for money, at some point in the future the debt will be sold back to the private sector. Also, quantitative easing is designed directly to increase private sector spending. By buying assets (government bonds) from the private sector, the central bank is giving money to the private sector to spend. Hence it can't be 'printing money'. In practice, at this stage, it can be argued that whilst central banks are continuing to buy government debt, it has the same effect as government printing money. The Bank of England in 2015 owned approximately one

Figure 7

The impact of quantitative easing

Quantitative easing has shifted the aggregate demand curve to the right, raising short-run equilibrium output from Y_1 to Y_2. But it has not been enough to get the economy to its long-run equilibrium output of Y_3.

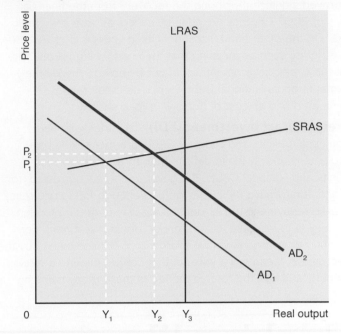

quarter of the UK National Debt. Put another way, half of the increase in the National Debt between 2008 and 2015 has ended up owned by the Bank of England, which in turn is owned by the UK government.

If governments have indeed printed trillions of pounds of money, why is there not rampant inflation in the USA, the UK, Japan or the eurozone? The answer is because of the relationship between aggregate demand and aggregate supply. In Figure 7, an economy is at output Y_1, a short-run equilibrium point. Quantitative easing, by raising spending in the economy, increases aggregate demand shifting the AD curve from AD_1 to AD_2. There is a mild inflationary impact as the price level rises, from P_1 to P_2. However, on this diagram, aggregate demand has not risen sufficiently to get the economy to its full employment level of Y_3.

Credit ratings In 2010, some economists and politicians were warning that the growing National Debt of the UK and its large fiscal deficit would reduce the credit rating of the government and consequently the rate of interest the UK government would have to pay on its borrowing would increase significantly. Credit ratings for large companies and governments are given by private sector companies such as Moody's and Standard & Poor's. They estimate the likelihood that a company or a government will default on its debt, i.e. not pay interest on it or not pay it back on time. The best credit rating is AAA and the worst is D. Credit ratings then influence the rate of interest at which companies and governments can borrow. The lower the credit rating, the higher the rate of interest savers demand to buy the bonds or debt issued. It could be argued that the more debt issued by a company or a government, the lower should be its credit ratings. More debt equals more risk. However, this is too simplistic. If a government or company has little debt in the first place, doubling its size is likely to have no impact on the risk of default. Equally, credit ratings are relative. Savers have to put their money somewhere. The US and UK governments have never defaulted on their debts. Despite the fact that they borrowed significantly during the recovery from the financial crisis of 2007-08, they are seen by savers as very low credit risks. On the other hand, fiscal deficits in Greece after 2010 were rightly seen as meaning that there was a high probability that the Greek government would not be able to make timely payments on its National Debt. Hence its credit ratings plummeted and its cost of borrowing rose sharply.

Foreign Direct Investment (FDI) Countries with very large fiscal deficits and National Debts are more likely have problems financing those deficits than those with low fiscal deficits and National Debts. If a government has borrowed from abroad, it may have difficulties getting enough foreign currency to make repayments on its debts. One way of getting foreign currency is to increase inward foreign direct investment. For example, a country may have a large copper mine owned by the government. It can sell a stake in that copper mine to a foreign company and use the foreign money to make repayments on

foreign currency denominated borrowing. Or the copper mine may be privately owned by a national owner. The owner sells the mine and the government forces the owner to sell it the foreign currency received in exchange for domestic currency.

However, far more commonly, countries which have severe fiscal problems are likely to see FDI decrease. This is because the economy may be going through a deep recession as the government cuts back on spending and increases taxes to deal with its fiscal problems. The recession is likely to make investing firms producing for the domestic market deeply unattractive.

Key Terms

Current budget deficit - occurs when government revenues are less than current expenditure. It does not include government capital expenditure.
Cyclical deficit - that part of the fiscal deficit which is caused by government spending and taxes changing through the trade cycle.
Primary deficit or surplus - the actual fiscal deficit or surplus not taking into account interest payments on the National Debt.
Structural deficit - that part of a fiscal deficit that exists even when the cyclical deficit is zero at the top of a boom.

Thinking like an economist

The UK fiscal balance and the National Debt

The financial crisis of 2007-08 led to large increases in fiscal deficits and National Debts throughout the developed world. In the UK, Public Sector Net Borrowing (PSNB), the UK measure of the fiscal deficit, increased from 2.7 per cent of GDP in the first quarter of 2008 to 10.2 per cent in the first quarter of 2010. With governments in countries like Greece, Portugal, Spain and Italy experiencing problems financing their debts and with the risk that some or all of these governments could default, some economists argued that cutting the fiscal deficit should be the main objective of UK government economic policy. Other economists agreed that the fiscal deficit certainly was a problem

and at 10.2 per cent of GDP would be unsustainable in the long run. However, the UK was in a very different position from Greece or Portugal. The key priority in 2010 was to sustain the recovery from the deep recession caused by the financial crisis. Higher economic growth would solve part of the problem and structural adjustments to government spending and taxation (i.e. the use of discretionary fiscal policy) to solve remaining problems could take place once the economy was in a strong economic position.

Figure 8 puts the UK fiscal deficit in a historical context. It shows that over the period 1956-2013, the fiscal deficit in 2010 was the highest over the whole period measured as a percentage of GDP. However, there were two other significant peaks in the mid-1970s and the early 1990s. The data also shows that it was relatively uncommon for the budget either to balance or to be in surplus. Until 2010, governments over the past 60 years have never made it a major fiscal objective to balance government spending and receipts. The data also shows the underlying cyclical nature of public finances.

At no point in the period from 1956 did the fiscal deficit ever get out of control. A mixture of cyclical improvements and discretionary fiscal policies brought fiscal deficit peaks down. The fall in the fiscal deficit as a percentage of GDP from 2010 was brought about partly by rises in GDP and partly by some tax rises and larger significant cuts in public spending.

One key issue with cutting the fiscal deficit quickly in 2010 was the size of the National Debt. Some economists argued that

Figure 8

Public sector net borrowing, % of GDP

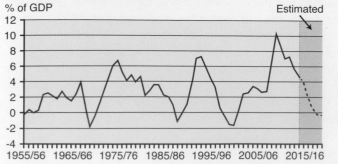

Source: adapted from House of Commons Library, Briefing Paper, Government borrowing, debt and debt interest: statistics by Matthew Keep, May 2015.

Figure 9

Ratio of National Debt to GDP

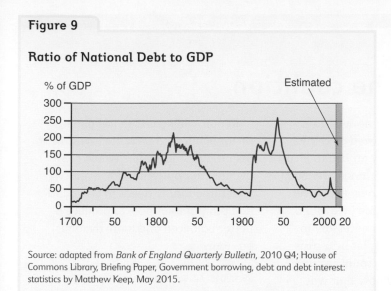

Source: adapted from *Bank of England Quarterly Bulletin*, 2010 Q4; House of Commons Library, Briefing Paper, Government borrowing, debt and debt interest: statistics by Matthew Keep, May 2015.

Figure 10

Debt interest payments, % of GDP

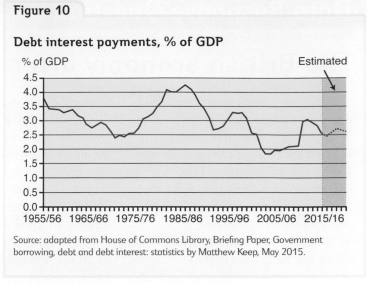

Source: adapted from House of Commons Library, Briefing Paper, Government borrowing, debt and debt interest: statistics by Matthew Keep, May 2015.

increases in the National Debt were so substantial that the UK, like Greece, would be in danger of defaulting on its debt. Figure 9 shows the National Debt as a percentage of GDP since 1830. By historical standards, the National Debt at around 80 per cent of GDP in 2014 is quite low. The main influence on the size of the National Debt has been war. The two World Wars in the 20th century saw the National Debt peak at over 250 per cent of GDP. National Debt levels of over 80 per cent were the norm in the 1950s and 1960s.

There are three main influences on the size of the National Debt over time. One is the fiscal deficit. During times of war, the fiscal deficit was very large. The second is inflation. Figure 8 shows, for example, that the UK had a large fiscal deficit in the mid-1970s but Figure 9 shows this had very little impact on the National Debt. This is because the mid-1970s were highly inflationary times. In 1975, inflation was 24 per cent. This substantially eroded the real value of the existing National Debt. The third factor is rises in real GDP. Between 1950 and 2008, the UK averaged 2.5 per cent growth each year. Between 1974 and 1988, the UK experienced fiscal deficits. But each year, because of economic growth, the fiscal deficit as a percentage of GDP fell.

Even at 80 per cent of GDP, the National Debt was arguably not much more of a burden on the economy than when it was 40 per cent in 2007. The key variable when discussing the burden of the National Debt is not its size but how much it costs to finance the debt. Figure 10 shows that the cost of financing the debt even at its peak in 2010 was lower than the average for 1955-2015. The main reason for this is the way in which the Bank of England has operated monetary policy. Following the financial crisis, it dropped interest rates to record lows. In 2009 it also began a policy of quantitative easing. This meant that new government borrowing or the National

Debt that was being rolled over (i.e. repaid at the end of its term and then reborrowed) was being financed at record low interest rates. There is also a less transparent reason why servicing the National Debt is relatively low. Quantitative easing between 2009 and 2015 meant that the Bank of England bought approximately one quarter of the UK National Debt. The government pays debt interest to the Bank of England on this. The Bank of England then repays the money in the form of dividends. So the headline cost of interest in 2015 shown in Figure 10 is in practice lower.

As for the risk of default, at no stage between 2008-15 was there any serious risk that the UK government would default on its debts. Nor did financial markets ever show they were unwilling to buy UK government debt. Some international credit rating agencies slightly down rated UK government debt but they did the same to US government debt too. International investors, on the other hand, saw UK government debt as a safe haven in comparison with many other countries round the world.

Economic historians will almost certainly still be arguing in 50 years' time whether the decision by the UK government to prioritise cutting the fiscal deficit over economic growth in 2010 was the right decision to make. Looking back to the 1930s, the consensus view is that the 1931 UK budget, which cut public sector spending significantly at the height of the Great Depression to defend the exchange rate value of the pound, was a mistake. It prolonged the recession in the UK at the time and caused considerable economic hardship amongst the poor and the unemployed. With further significant cuts in public spending due between 2015 and 2019, the question is two-fold: how much will this depress aggregate demand as did the spending cuts in the 1931 budget; and how much will it depress long-run aggregate supply as the government makes even more cuts to its capital expenditure programme?

Data Response Question

The British economy after the coalition

In 2010, the government talked as if the main challenge was the fiscal deficit, not the need to foster the recovery that had just begun. George Osborne, the Chancellor of the Exchequer, set himself the objective of eliminating the structural fiscal deficit by this financial year, 2015-16. In fact, the structural deficit will be 2.1 per cent in 2015-16, down from 3.9 per cent of GDP in 2010-11, the government's first year in office, according to the Office for Budget Responsibility. Similarly, cyclically-adjusted net borrowing is forecast to be 3.7 per cent of GDP this year, down from 6.5 per cent in 2010-11. The government's actual cuts in government spending and rises in taxes have proved less harsh than initial plans set out in 2010-11.

In 2010, there were two competing views about the speed with which

the fiscal deficit should be cut. The Conservative Party wanted quick cuts whilst the Labour Party argued that cuts should be made over a longer period of time to allow the economy to recover from the recession. Those in favour of quick cuts said this was necessary to stop the UK from being hit by a crisis similar to those hitting countries such as Greece. We know now that was wildly exaggerated for a country in the UK's position. Despite failing to hit its fiscal targets, interest rates on UK public debt have remained astonishingly low: 30-year and 50-year gilts (government borrowing) yield 2.4 per cent, whilst yields on comparable index-linked gilts are close to minus one per cent. Why should one be desperate to avoid a free loan? What is needed now is growth-promoting government borrowing. The fact is that supply-side constraints in the economy are now more important that demand-side constraints. We will never know whether

a greater willingness to use public sector finances to promote investment over the past five years would have avoided this outcome. However, government now needs to find policies and programmes able to produce a better-balanced and more dynamic economy.

Source: adapted from © the *Financial Times* 29.4.2015, All Rights Reserved.

Q

1. Explain the difference between a cyclical fiscal deficit and a structural fiscal deficit.

2. Analyse the links between a fiscal deficit, the National Debt and yields (rates of interest) on government borrowing.

3. Discuss the costs and benefits of cutting a fiscal deficit quickly when it is relatively high by historical standards at a time when the economy is just beginning to recover from a deep recession.

Figure 11

UK real GDP per head: index of actual GDP per head, index of long-term trend (1955-2007) and % deviation from the trend

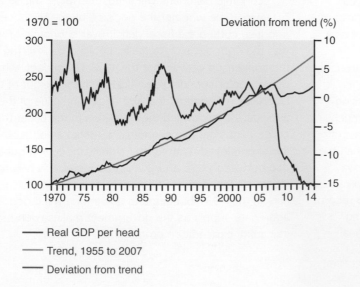

— Real GDP per head
— Trend, 1955 to 2007
— Deviation from trend

Source: adapted from Thomson Reuters Datastream; © the *Financial Times* 29.4.2015, All Rights Reserved.

Evaluation

In your answer, you need to weigh up the risks to the economy of maintaining a large fiscal deficit compared to the costs of bringing it down rapidly. Part of the evaluation must be commenting on what sort of economy this could be. Is it a Greek-type economy or a UK-type economy? Equally, you should say whether the answer would be different if the fiscal deficit was mainly structural or mainly cyclical.

Key points

1. Governments may use fiscal policy, monetary policy, exchange rate policy, supply-side policies and direct controls to influence variables such as fiscal deficits and national debts, interest rates and the money supply, poverty and inequality and international competitiveness.
2. Macroeconomic policies can be used to respond to external shocks.
3. Multinational companies have significant economic power and governments need to regulate their activities to prevent them abusing their power.
4. Policymakers face a number of problems when applying policies, including inaccurate information, risks and uncertainties and inability to control external shocks.

Starter activity

Between 2011 and 2014, the UK experienced almost no growth in labour productivity. Give five different measures the government could adopt to address this problem. One should be an example of fiscal policy, one of monetary policy, one of exchange rate policy, one of a supply-side policy and one of a direct control.

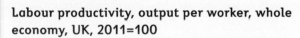

Figure 1

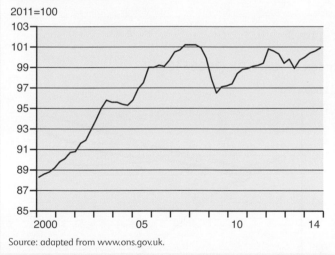

Labour productivity, output per worker, whole economy, UK, 2011=100

Source: adapted from www.ons.gov.uk.

Fiscal policy

Fiscal policy, explained in Unit 38, is the use of taxes, government spending and government borrowing to achieve its policy objectives. These objectives include:

- providing goods and services which private sector markets would either provide inefficiently, in too few quantities or not at all such as education or health care;
- achieving a desirable distribution of income and wealth for example through the use of taxes and welfare benefits (this is explained in detail in Unit 73);
- correcting market failure at a microeconomic level, for example by imposing environmental taxes;
- improving macroeconomic performance, such as increasing

economic growth or reducing unemployment through demand and supply-side policies;

- ensuring that the operation of fiscal policy is sustainable in the long term by controlling fiscal deficits and the size of the national debt.

Demand management

Fiscal policy can be used to manipulate the level of aggregate demand. This is known as **demand management**. A larger budget deficit or a smaller budget surplus will increase the government injection into the circular flow of money. There will be a multiplier impact, according to Keynesian economists, where every £1 of extra deficit or reduced surplus will lead to a more than £1 increase in final GDP. Because of this increase in GDP, policy which leads to larger budget deficits or smaller budget surpluses is known as **expansionary fiscal policy**.

In contrast, there is **deflationary fiscal policy** when the government decides to reduce a budget deficit or increase a budget surplus. This reduces the level of aggregate demand by reducing the government injection into the circular flow.

In the 1930s, large falls in export earnings and investment spending led to the Great Depression. Today, any reduction in

Question 1

In March 2006, the Chancellor of the Exchequer announced a number of changes to taxes and government spending at a time when the economy was growing very slightly below its trend rate of growth. Explain whether the following are likely to be examples of automatic stabilisers or active fiscal policy.

Source: adapted from Alain Anderton, *Economics*, 5th edition, Pearson.

(a) The introduction of a new higher band of Vehicle Excise Duty (the tax disk on cars) of £210 for cars which have a very high petrol consumption per mile travelled.

(b) A rise in tax revenues in 2005-06 of seven per cent, net of changes in tax rates in the 2005 Budget.

(c) A rise in average spending per pupil in state sector schools from £5 000 per annum to £8 000 over the period 2006 to 2012.

(d) Lower receipts from excise duties and VAT partly caused by moderation in household spending.

export earnings or investment would have less impact on the economy because **automatic** or **built-in stabilisers** are greater. Automatic stabilisers are expenditures which automatically increase when the economy is going into a recession. Conversely, they automatically fall when national income begins to rise.

Government spending and taxation are both automatic stabilisers. When the economy goes into recession and unemployment rises, the government automatically increases its social security spending, paying out more in unemployment benefits and other related benefits. The fall in aggregate demand is therefore less than it would otherwise have been. Tax revenues fall too at a faster rate than the fall in income. This is because tax rates tend to be higher on marginal income than on average income. For instance, a worker paid on commission may sell less in a recession. Her tax rate might then fall from the higher rate of 40 per cent to the basic rate of 20 per cent. If household spending has to be cut, then it is likely that consumption items such as consumer durables taxed at 20 per cent VAT will see falls rather than zero-rated food. With the government collecting less tax, disposable incomes are higher than they would otherwise be and therefore consumption can be at a higher level than would be the case without this automatic stabiliser.

When the economy goes into boom, government spending falls as the benefit budget falls automatically. Tax revenue increases at a faster rate than the increase in income. An unemployed person will pay very little tax. Once the unemployed get jobs, they start to pay substantial amounts of direct and indirect tax. So aggregate demand is lower than it would otherwise be with these automatic stabilisers.

Automatic stabilisers result from a set of rules which governments have made about how spending will change as income and unemployment changes. The opposite is discretionary (or active) policy. It is the deliberate manipulation of variables to influence the economy. **Active** or **discretionary fiscal policy** is deliberate decision making by government to change rates of tax, introduce new taxes, or change levels of government spending. Discretionary monetary policy is deliberate decision making by a central bank for example to change interest rates or introduce quantitative easing.

Measures to reduce fiscal deficits

Following the 2007-08 financial crisis, many developed countries were faced with increasing fiscal deficits and growing national debts. There is a consensus view that, for developed countries, fiscal deficits above three per cent of GDP are likely to lead to growing national debts as a percentage of GDP. Sooner or later, the national debt becomes so large that the costs of financing it (i.e. the interest on the debt) present a serious problem for governments trying also to spend money on education, roads or welfare benefits. In extreme circumstances,

Question 2

Figure 2

Fiscal balances[1] as a percentage of GDP

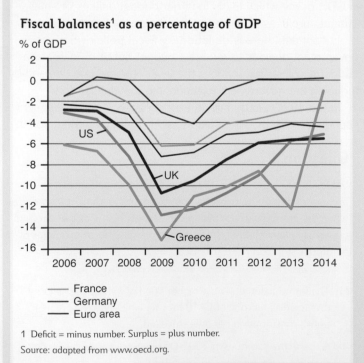

1 Deficit = minus number. Surplus = plus number.

Source: adapted from www.oecd.org.

Figure 3

Index of real GDP (2008=100)

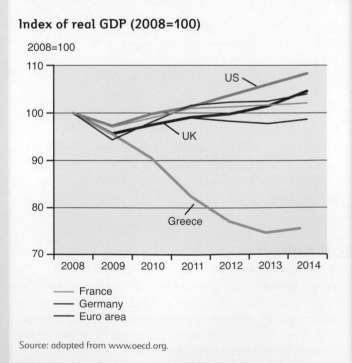

Source: adapted from www.oecd.org.

(a) Using the data, explain what is meant by an automatic fiscal stabiliser.

(b) Explain the link between fiscal austerity and GDP, using Greece as an example.

(c) Explain the possible link between Keynesian deflationary/reflationary policies and GDP growth, using the UK and the US as examples.

such as those experienced by Greece after 2012, the debt becomes impossible to finance on a long-term basis. At that point, either the government of the country defaults on its debts, as many countries have in the past, or it has to be bailed out by other governments or the IMF. Typically, some of the holders of the governments debts have to accept a write-down. This means they lose part of the value of their loan. There are two main ways in which governments can tackle fiscal deficits that are too large.

One is through **fiscal austerity**. The government cuts public spending or raises taxes or, more likely, does both. One problem with fiscal austerity is that it reduces the welfare of citizens both now and in the future. For example, higher taxes means that households have less to spend. Cutting welfare benefits hits those receiving benefits who are, on average, likely to be the poor and the disadvantaged. So this raises income inequalities. Cutting spending on roads or education is likely to reduce the future supply of physical and human capital leading to lower economic growth in the future. Some economists and politicians argue that cutting public spending can be achieved entirely through cutting 'waste'. Free market economists tend to argue that provision of government services is highly inefficient. It is possible to cut public spending by, say, 20 per cent and have no impact on services provided. However, even if some of the cuts can be financed through 'efficiency savings', it is highly unlikely that large cuts can be made in the short term without cutting services and benefits.

Another problem is that fiscal austerity causes, in the short term at least, a fall in GDP from what it would otherwise have been. The more severe the fiscal austerity measures, the greater the negative impact on GDP. If the economy is already in recession, it will make the recession even deeper. If the economy is recovering, it will knock back the recovery.

A third related problem with fiscal austerity is that, in the short term at least, for every £1 cut in public spending or rise in tax, there is a less than £1 cut in the budget deficit. Cuts in public spending or rises in taxes reduce aggregate demand. Unemployment will rise and economic activity will fall from what it would otherwise have been. The result is that welfare benefits associated with unemployment and low incomes will rise whilst tax revenues will fall.

The other way to reduce a fiscal deficit is for the government to do nothing and wait for the automatic stabilizers to do their work. This will only work if the fiscal deficit has arisen because the economy has gone into recession, i.e. the deficit is entirely cyclical and there is no structural deficit. If the government does nothing, the economy is likely to begin to grow again. This will increase tax revenues and reduce government spending. The fiscal deficit in (real) money terms will therefore fall. But it will also fall even faster as a percentage of GDP. As explained in Unit 81, with GDP growing and the fiscal deficit falling, the ratio of deficit to GDP will shrink.

Following the 2007-08 financial crisis, different countries had different policy choices about how to tackle their deficits. Countries such as Greece, Spain and Portugal went into the crisis arguably with significant structural deficits. Their economies were badly affected by the downturn in the world

economy and so they had high cyclical deficits. They had no choice but to adopt fiscal austerity measures because otherwise their deficits would have spiralled out of control. International lenders would also have not lent to them to finance their national debts. Countries such as the UK, the USA, France and Germany did have choices. France and the USA chose mainly to allow automatic stabilizers and the rise in GDP to correct their deficits. The US economy recovered relatively rapidly which led to a significant improvement in its fiscal position. France before the financial crisis was struggling with low growth. Its response to its fiscal deficit was less successful because it still struggled with low growth after the financial crisis. So it had problems reducing its deficit as a percentage of GDP. The UK government between 2008-10 did not adopt fiscal austerity measures as the economy recovered well from the financial crisis. A new government in 2010 reversed this and cut public spending and increased taxes. The result was much lower economic growth. This in turn meant that government spending was higher than it would otherwise have been with fast economic growth. It also led to lower tax revenues than were forecast. By 2015, the fiscal deficit as a percentage of GDP was about the same as that of the USA. However, it had come at a considerable cost in lower national income and the fiscal deficit in money terms was still two thirds of what it had been in 2010.

Measures to reduce the National Debt
Governments have a variety of ways of reducing the National Debt.
- Having a fiscal surplus will cut the debt in money terms.
- Balancing the government finances combined with economic growth will reduce the national debt as a percentage of GDP.
- Inflation will reduce the real value of the debt.
- If, as some economists argue, quantitative easing is a way of governments printing money to finance their deficits, then more quantitative easing will reduce the national debt held outside the central bank.
- Governments can default on their debts. The economic cost of this option to the economy is so large that governments only default as a last resort.

Monetary policy
The implementation of monetary policy, explained in Unit 38, is the responsibility of central banks. In many developed countries, as was explained in Unit 78, central banks are independent of government. In many developing countries, central banks are effectively part of government with politicians deciding on the monetary policy that central banks will pursue.

Central banks traditionally influence interest rates through the rate of interest that they are prepared to lend to commercial banks or other money market institutions. This 'bank rate' then influences other rates of interest through the economy.

Central banks may be able to set a bank rate that is influenced mainly by factors within its economy. For example, it may want to reduce inflationary pressures in the domestic economy and so it raises bank rate. It may want to stimulate domestic spending and so it reduces bank rate.

However, sometimes it may be forced to consider global events. For example, the exchange rate of its currency may be falling because other central banks are raising their bank rates. Higher interest rates in other countries will increase the demand for their currencies, pushing up their price. If the central bank doesn't want to see a fall in the exchange rate of its currency, it may be forced to raise its own bank rate. Or there may be a sharp rise in world commodity prices that sharply raises inflation rates in the country. To counteract the rise in inflation, the central bank may choose to raise interest rates in order to reduce aggregate demand.

A fall in bank rate is likely to increase the supply of money in the economy. This is because there will an increase in the demand for borrowed funds. Banks will respond by lending more money that is redeposited back in the banking system. These extra deposits constitute the increase in the money supply.

Whether the supply of money can be controlled by the central bank has been long-debated by economists. Monetarist economists in the 1970s and 1980s, for example, believed that central banks could control the money supply. By using a variety of measures, including interest rates and forcing banks to hold a fraction of their deposits in assets controlled by the central bank, central banks could choose their preferred level of the money supply. This was important because monetarists believe that inflation is caused by changes in the money supply. A famous monetarist economist of the second half of the 20th century, Milton Friedman, said that 'inflation is always and everywhere a monetary phenomenon'. So controlling the money supply allowed the central bank to fix the rate of inflation in the economy. Keynesian economists at the time argued that central banks could not control the money supply. Also, the link between changes in the money supply and inflation was not as simple as monetarists argued. Keynesian economists would agree that if the central bank allows the money supply to increase by 1 000 per cent in a year, then there will inevitably be hyperinflation. The German hyperinflation of 1923 was indeed caused by the German central bank printing ever-larger amounts of money. But if the money supply were to increase by 10 per cent this year, inflation might go up by two per cent or it might go up by 15 per cent. There is no simple relationship.

Today, the consensus view amongst central banks is that they cannot control the money supply; nor is there a simple link between changes in the money supply and inflation. The reason they cannot control the money supply is that they cannot control the ability of the financial system to create credit. If central banks rigidly control bank lending in their countries, then other financial institutions will begin to act like banks, arranging credit. As explained in Unit 77, central banks are currently worried that their attempts to regulate the banking system following the financial crisis of 2007-08 are being frustrated by the emergence of a shadow banking system. Moreover, the globalisation of financial markets makes it far more difficult to control the domestic money supply than 30 or 50 years ago.

Central bank control of inflation is today centred around interest rate policy. The consensus view is that central banks should allow inflation caused by supply-side factors such as rising commodity prices or a falling exchange rate to occur even if this put inflation above its target rate. However, central banks

should increase interest rates if there is a rise in demand-pull inflation.

Following the financial crisis of 2007-08, some central banks became more concerned about deflation than inflation. With interest rates as low they could be, they resorted to quantitative easing, buying up high-quality debt, much of it government debt, and issuing money in exchange. Quantitative easing remains a controversial policy. Some argue that it has done little to increase aggregate demand, which was its main purpose. Rather it has fuelled an increase in the price of assets such as shares and houses. Others argue that it has increased aggregate demand but the depth of the recession from the financial crisis has meant that it has been difficult to rebuild aggregate demand to its pre-2008 levels.

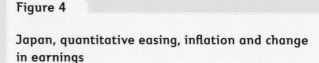

Question 3

Figure 4

Japan, quantitative easing, inflation and change in earnings

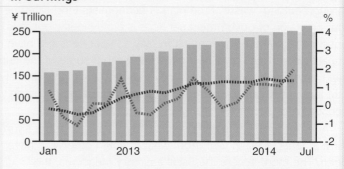

Bank of Japan balance sheet (¥tn) ▨
Inflation (annual % change) ▪▪▪▪▪
Average monthly earnings (annual % change) ▪▪▪▪▪

Source: adapted from Thomson Reuters Datastream; © the *Financial Times* 26.8.2014, All Right Reserved.

The Japanese government wants to encourage inflation. After two decades of slipping in and out of recession and deflation, it sees a positive inflation rate of around two per cent as essential to get its economy growing again. Part of its strategy is to encourage employers to increase the wages of their workers. Employers in a zero-inflation climate have become accustomed to not paying any annual wage increases. With zero inflation and no wage increases, consumers have been reluctant to increase their spending. Hence the zero-average growth.

The central bank of Japan, the Bank of Japan, has been engaged in quantitative easing since the early 2000s. Recently, it has been pumping large sums of money into the economy, shown by the growth in its balance sheet. It hopes that the extra money will encourage households to spend more and firms to pay more to their workers, raising inflation in accordance with government objectives.

Source: adapted from © the *Financial Times* 26.8.2014, All Rights Reserved.

(a) Explain why any government or central bank might want to encourage inflation.

(b) To what extent has quantitative easing resulted in higher inflation according to the data?

Exchange rate policies

Governments and central banks in developed countries mainly abandoned setting exchange rates in the 1970s, as explained in Unit 69. Since then, there have been a number of one-off interventions using currency reserves either to raise the value of a currency or to depreciate its value. However, for the most part, changes in exchange rates have resulted from changes in monetary policy.

If a central bank lowers interest rates to stimulate aggregate demand, one result will be a fall in its exchange rate. This is because a fall in interest rates makes the return on some investments in the country less attractive whilst returns on investments in other countries will be relatively more attractive. The demand for the currency will fall as a result whilst its supply will rise. This leads to a fall in the exchange rate which makes the economy more internationally price competitive. The fall in the exchange rate makes, on average, imports more expensive and exports cheaper. This leads to a rise in aggregate demand. The opposite occurs if the central bank raises interest rates.

Developing countries use a wide range of different exchange rate systems. As explained in Unit 70, countries may manipulate their exchange rates, for example, to improve their current account positions on the balance of payments, deal with problems caused by excessive fiscal deficits and national debts or encourage FDI flows. Some countries deliberately keep their exchange rate low in order to stimulate exports and drive economic growth.

Supply-side policies

Supply-side policies were explained in Unit 39. Their role in economic development was explained in Units 75 and 76. Supply-side policies are designed to increase the productive potential of the economy, shifting the long run aggregate supply curve to the right over time.

Governments in developed and developing countries implement a wide range of supply-side policies such as:
- improving education to increase the human capital of the population;
- improving health care, increasing the number of years that workers can use their acquired human capital for production;
- increasing levels of entrepreneurship, encouraging the growth of new businesses and the willingness to take calculated risks in the market place;
- reducing discrimination which is likely to lead to greater participation in the labour force and better use of scarce human capital.

As explained in Unit 71, successful supply-side policies can increase the international competitiveness of an economy. Improved relative competitiveness should increase exports and reduce imports, leading to higher economic growth and lower unemployment.

Direct controls

A **direct control** is a government measure that is imposed on the price or the quantity of a single product or factor of production. Examples of direct controls include:
- imposing a maximum price on a good such as bread, petrol or electricity;

- setting a minimum or maximum wage;
- fixing a quota on imports of beef;
- limiting the amount of foreign currency a citizen can buy during a year to £1 000;
- fixing a maximum interest rate that payday lenders can charge to their borrowers for small loans to 200 per cent per annum;

Question 4

Figure 5

Price of nickel ($ 000 per tonne)

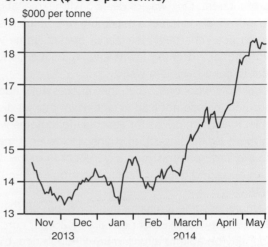

Source: adapted from Thomson Reuters Datastream; © the *Financial Times* 21.4.2014, All Rights Reserved.

In 2009, Indonesia passed a mining law which banned the export of nickel ore. Indonesia is a significant supplier of nickel ore onto world markets. In 2013, one quarter of all nickel was produced from Indonesian ore. The Indonesian government wanted to stop the export of ore to encourage nickel processors to build plants in Indonesia. This would add value to its mining industry creating both added exports and jobs.

The ban was not implemented at the time. Then, to the surprise of international markets, Indonesia imposed the ban in January 2014. At first, there was a muted reaction. World nickel stocks were high and traders believed that the ban would be circumvented. As time went on and the ban held, prices rose much higher.

A handful of Chinese companies have now started building processing plants in Indonesia but these are unlikely to start operating until mid-2105 at the earliest and will not come close to processing the amount of nickel ore that was exported in 2013.

Source: adapted from © the *Financial Times* 21.4.2014, 6.5.2014, All Rights Reserved.

(a) Explain what is meant by a direct control using nickel as an example.

(b) Using a demand and supply diagram, explain why the world price of nickel changed as shown in Figure 5.

(c) What might the advantages and disadvantages to (i) nickel ore mining companies in Indonesia and (ii) the Indonesian economy of banning the export of nickel ore?

- limiting the amount an individual can borrow for a mortgage to four times their income.

Governments or central banks impose direct controls because they are easy to understand and can be focussed on a specific problem such as poverty and inequality. In a developing country, for example, there may be malnutrition because poorer households cannot afford to buy enough of a staple like rice, maize or onions. To make these products more affordable, the government can set a maximum price below the current market price. In a developed country, there may be a problem with payday lenders. These are financial institutions which target low-income households providing them with small loans at very high rates of interest. One way of dealing with exploitation of vulnerable individuals is to set a maximum rate of interest that payday lenders can charge. In the labour market, some workers may be working for extremely low wages. A solution is for the government to set a minimum wage.

Direct controls work best when they successfully address a specific problem but do not lead to significant market distortions. For example, maximum prices for essential food items work well when there is little impact on supply. However, if market distortions are large enough, then any benefit from the direct controls can be wiped out and indeed the problem can be made worse.

For example, assume a maximum price is put on rice and as a result the quantity supplied of rice falls by 25 per cent. Poor households may be able to afford to buy enough rice, but the 25 per cent fall in supply may mean it is not available to buy in the shops. Black markets are likely to develop where much higher prices are charged and even less rice gets into shops charging the maximum price.

In the case of minimum wages, a minimum wage might be set so high that there is a significant negative effect on employment. Those who keep their minimum wage jobs are better off but a large number of other workers who become unemployed are worse off.

Macroeconomic policies and external shocks

Macroeconomic policies can be used to combat the effects of negative shocks to an economy. Two examples are given here.

Commodity price shocks Assume the world price of oil trebles in a year. This is going to provide a negative supply-side shock to any country that imports most or all of its oil requirements. In Figure 6, the economy is initially at the point E. Output is Y_1 and there is full employment. The oil price rise shifts the SRAS curve from $SRAS_1$ to $SRAS_2$ leading to lower real output and higher prices at the point F. In the long term, the oil price rise reduces the productive potential of the economy. This is because it makes some equipment, such as oil-fired power stations or fuel-inefficient cars, uneconomic to run. They are scrapped earlier than they would have been if oil prices had remained lower. This shifts the LRAS curve from $LRAS_1$ to $LRAS_2$. Whatever policies the government pursues, ignoring the fact that economies tend to grow over time anyway, the long run equilibrium output has now fallen to Y_3.

Governments may respond in a variety of ways. One approach is to accommodate the oil price increase. This means accepting the prices will rise, attempting to get the economy back to full employment quickly and protecting household incomes. Governments can do this by raising their spending, cutting taxes, whilst central banks can reduce interest rates and increase the money supply. This shifts the aggregate demand curve to the right. The danger is that a wage-price inflationary spiral will develop with workers fighting for pay rises to cover the increased inflation rate. The new long-run equilibrium level of output is Y_3. The result of expansionary fiscal and monetary policies might be eventually to shift the economy to the point G. The new price level is P_3 with the aggregate demand curve having risen to AD_3 and the SRAS curve to $SRAS_3$.

Another approach is for the government to attempt to squeeze the inflation caused by the oil price rise out of the economic system. It can do this by using deflationary fiscal and monetary policies and moving the economy to the point H. By shifting the aggregate demand curve back to AD_4 and accepting a slight rise in the SRAS curve, it can stabilise prices at the previous level of P_1. In the short term, this policy is likely to see a rise in unemployment and cuts in living standards of households. But, unlike the policy of accommodating the oil price crisis, inflation is kept to a minimum.

Alternatively, governments could pursue some mid course between these two policy alternatives. Whatever happens, the reality of a large oil price rise is that oil-importing countries will experience a cut in the GDP. That cut is the money that is transferred to oil exporting countries which raises their GDP. So equilibrium real output in oil-importing countries has to fall, all other things being equal.

Figure 6

A sharp oil price rise

Government can respond to a sharp oil price with expansionary fiscal and monetary policies but this raises the long-run price level from P_1 to P_3. Or it can use deflationary fiscal and monetary policies, keeping the price level at P_1 but creating short-term unemployment as a result.

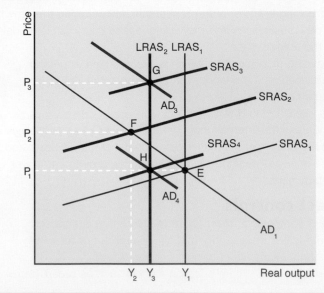

A major financial crisis The 2007-08 financial crisis severely tested governments. The monetary policy response was ultimately fairly similar. Governments supported the financial system and bailed out failing banks at a total cost of hundreds of billions of pounds. In the Great Depression of the 1930s, in contrast, the US government allowed hundreds of banks to fail. This cut credit to the economy and was a major cause of the fall in aggregate demand. Following 2007-08, governments and their central banks pursued expansionary monetary policies, cutting interest rates to almost zero. When this failed to stimulate spending sufficiently, they adopted policies of quantitative easing, buying up trillions of pounds between them of financial assets, most of which were government bonds. The US government pursued an expansionary fiscal policy too, prioritising economic growth over cutting its large fiscal deficit. From 2010 onwards, the UK chose to prioritise cutting its fiscal deficit over economic growth. Within the eurozone, Greece, Ireland, Spain and Portugal were forced to adopt deflationary fiscal policies because their fiscal deficits and national debts were too high. Countries such as France and Italy resisted fiscal austerity but high national debts and relatively high fiscal deficits meant they were unable to use the expansionary fiscal policies they would have liked to adopt.

Figure 7 shows the experience of a country like Ireland over the crisis using a Keynesian aggregate supply curve. In 2007, the economy was at output OY_{2007}. The financial crisis of 2007-08 and the subsequent fiscal austerity measures significantly lowered equilibrium output to OY_{2010}. By 2015, the Irish economy was beginning to recover with increased aggregate demand leading to equilibrium output of OY_{2015}. However, this output was still below its 2007 level.

Figure 7

The effects of fiscal austerity on an economy

The financial crisis of 2007-08 moves equilibrium output from OY_{2007} to OY_{2010}. The subsequent recovery increases output to OY_{2015} but this is still below its 2007 level.

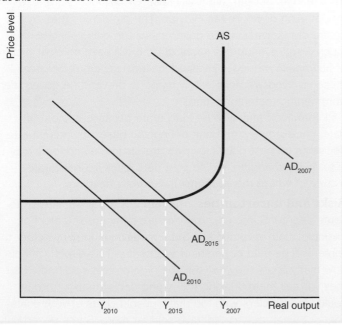

Measures to control global companies

The role of multinational (or transnational) companies in the global economy was explained in Unit 61. Multinational companies benefit the world economy through their ability to exploit economies of scale. Some also have knowledge, through research and development and practical experience, which smaller companies are never likely to have. This then creates new products or lowers prices. National economies often welcome the activities of multinational activities because they can create jobs, incomes, exports and tax revenues. Transfers of knowledge as well as foreign direct investment in building new manufacturing plants or opening new outlets can also benefit countries.

Multinational companies, however, can also have a negative economic and social impact. Some multinational companies such as oil and mining companies can have a negative impact on the local and global environment. Multinational companies in industries such as food and entertainment are accused of destroying local culture and loss of national identity. They can exploit countries with weak governments by taking out of a country far more in profits than they give back in terms of building blocks for economic development. Multinational companies have a long history of using legal and illegal means to influence politicians and state officials to take decisions that will favour their interests rather than the interests of the local people and the country. Many have also structured their business to pay the minimum amount of tax possible by shifting revenues and profits into low tax countries. One way they do this is through transfer pricing (explained in Unit 61).

Controlling multinational companies is difficult for individual governments. Many small developing countries have a lower GDP than the total revenues of a single large multinational company. Large multinational companies are run by highly educated, successful executives who can draw on considerable resources to find solutions which will benefit them. Individual countries may be run by far less gifted individuals who don't have the resources to understand the impact a multinational is having on their economy.

Large countries too find it difficult to control aspects of the behaviour of multinational companies. For example, in the EU, some multinationals use legal tax avoidance schemes called the 'double Irish' and the 'Dutch sandwich', routing costs, revenues and profits through Ireland, the Netherlands and Luxembourg before sending them to a tax haven such as the Bahamas or the Cayman Islands. Ireland, Luxembourg and the Bahamas are major beneficiaries of such tax schemes. The problem is that every other EU country is a major loser as is the United States where many multinational companies are based. The losses are very considerable. For every £1 gained in extra taxes by Luxembourg, for example, other countries are collectively losing possibly £1000 in tax revenues.

Some aspects of the unacceptable behaviour of multinational companies have been curtailed by countries. Examples include the following.

- In the EU and the USA, it is illegal for multinational companies operating in their countries to use bribery or corrupt practices anywhere in the world. A US-based multinational can be fined heavily by the United States government for using bribery to gain orders in, say, Nigeria.

- A number of developing countries don't allow multinational companies to set up in their countries without first setting up a joint company with a local partner. So at least some of the profits made are retained within the country. Also there is a transfer of knowledge and technology to local partners. This in future might create local competition to the multinational.

- Where a multinational wants to set up a manufacturing facility to make products for sale to individuals or firms in that country, governments can negotiate deals where a proportion of the production is exported. This helps the country earn foreign currency which can be used to pay for imports.

- Many contracts with governments involve clauses where the multinational has to manufacture at least some of the value of the order in the country. For example, a government may order 50 fighter aircraft from a multinational. The multinational then agrees that 40 per cent of the value of the contract is manufactured in the country. Or a government may order 50 high speed trains on condition that they are assembled in the country. This means that there is 'local content' in the order and offsets part of the cost to the economy.

Governments can be restricted in their treatment of multinational companies by the international they have signed. Some practices relating to local content requirements, for example, are illegal under World Trade Organization (WTO) agreements as examples of Trade-Related Investment Measures (TRIMs). However, developing countries are exempt from the WTO TRIMs rules.

In the case of widespread tax avoidance, a solution requires a worldwide agreement on taxing multinationals. Countries like Ireland, Luxembourg and the Bahamas would have much to lose if their tax arrangements were changed. Equally, there is disagreement within countries. In the United States, there is widespread agreement that the tax regime for company profits is losing the government large amounts of tax revenues. But government can't agree a solution because the two political parties, the Republicans and the Democrats, can't agree on a solution. Within this disagreement are multinationals who are spending millions of dollars each year lobbying US politicians to prevent any agreement which does not benefit them.

Problems facing policy makers

Policy makers such as governments face many problems when making decisions. These problems include the following.

Inaccurate information The information that policy makers hold can sometimes be inaccurate. Partly this is because the information may be very difficult to collect. For example, first estimates of GDP figures for the previous month can be inaccurate by several per cent. This is because it is not possible to collect accurate data within such a short time span. As more data comes in, GDP figures are revised and a more accurate picture emerges. Another example is tax evasion. Some governments today are making it a priority to collect taxes from individuals and companies who are illegally evading tax. In the UK, individuals may have money in the Cayman Islands that is not being declared to the UK tax authorities. A government may declare in its budget that it will raise £1 billion in extra taxes by clamping down on tax evasion. The problem is that, by the nature of tax evasion, the government can only estimate how much extra revenue this might raise. It will have no clear picture of how much money is invested in illegal schemes because those involved are deliberately trying to prevent the government from getting that information.

Information may also be inaccurate because it is out of date. For example, the Bank of England bases its interest rate decisions on past data. However, trends in the economy may actually be changing and so past data gives an inaccurate picture of where the economy is currently heading.

Risks and uncertainties The future is always uncertain to some degree. Some uncertainties are fairly predictable. For example, clothes retailers in September don't know whether the winter will be mild or harsh, or wet or dry. This directly affects how many coats they will sell, the type of coat sold and when they will sell them. Making the wrong decision about orders could lead retailers with too many unsold coats or with coats sold out when they could have sold far more. Some uncertainties

Question 5

European Commission investigators spelt out yesterday their preliminary conclusions to a probe into Amazon's tax-deal with Luxembourg. The tax-deal was negotiated in 2003. In the Commission's view, Luxembourg deviated from international standards to offer Amazon a ceiling on its tax exposure that did not reflect business risk assumed by its European headquarters in Luxembourg. The cap in income taxable in Luxembourg is less than one per cent - about €75 million in 2013 on Amazon operating company turnover of €13.6 billion. The European Commission claims the tax ruling at issue was not properly evidenced, used inappropriate methods and, crucially, permitted an intra-group royalty payment that - if proved to be exaggerated - 'would unduly reduce the tax paid by Amazon in Luxembourg by shifting profits to an untaxed entity from the perspective of corporate taxation'. The European Commission notes that the 2003 ruling was issued within 11 working days of the first Amazon request, 'a very short period of time had a transfer pricing report been submitted and assessed in this case'.

Amazon said it 'had received no special tax treatment from Luxembourg - we are subject to the same tax laws as other companies operating here'. Luxembourg-Amazon is one of four commission inquiries into tax rulings. Other deals include Ireland's arrangements with Apple, Luxembourg's clearance of structures used by Fiat and Holland's approval of Starbucks' tax base.

Source: adapted from © the *Financial Times* 17.1.2014, All Rights Reserved.

(a) Explain how multinationals can exploit different tax regimes in different countries to their advantage in ways that smaller national companies cannot.

(b) Discuss whether Amazon's tax agreement with Luxembourg in 2003 is likely to have benefited taxpayers in (i) Luxembourg and (ii) other EU countries.

are less predicable. In the UK, some are calling for the country to leave the EU. They make predictions about what would happen if it did so. However, those predictions are typically based on what they would like to happen. The reality is that it is difficult to predict the outcome. Some risks could have severe implications for the UK economy. For example, what would happen if foreign companies like car manufacturers Toyota and Nissan or banks like Deutsche Bank, moved out of the UK as a result? What would happen if the EU raised tariff and quota barriers against UK exports? Managing risk successfully is essential for good decision making.

External shocks External shocks cannot be controlled by national governments. In 1974-75, for example, the world experienced its first oil crisis as OPEC increased the price of oil from $2 a barrel to $11 a barrel. This created large inflationary pressures in oil-importing countries like the UK which contributed to the 25 per cent inflation experienced by the UK in 1975. In 2007-08, economies were thrown into the worst recession since the 1930s by the financial crisis originating in the US but spreading through the international financial markets into Europe and other parts of the world. The UK government

at the time saw the UK economy go from one of the fastest growing developed countries in the world to a deep recession. The risk of external shocks happening are increasing over time as globalisation deepens. It therefore makes it more difficult for policy makers to control events and pursue their policies successfully.

> ### Key Terms
>
> **Active or discretionary fiscal policy** - the deliberate manipulation of government expenditure and taxes to influence the economy.
> **Automatic or built-in stabilisers** - mechanisms that reduce the impact of changes in the economy on national income.
> **Demand management** - government use of fiscal or other policies to manipulate the level of aggregate demand in the economy.
> **Direct control** - a government measure that is imposed on the price or the quantity of a single product or factor of production.
> **Fiscal austerity** - tax rises or government spending cuts designed to reduce a government budget deficit.

Thinking like an economist

Economic growth in Greece

In the 1990s and the first half of the 2000s, Greece experienced strong economic growth as Figure 8 shows. However, part of the growth was being fuelled by excessive fiscal deficits. The financial crisis of 2007-08, which hit Greece just as much as other European countries, led to a recession. Tax revenues fell whilst government spending increased as economic theory would predict. An already bad fiscal deficit became even worse.

In 2009, Greece had the largest fiscal deficit in the EU with a rapidly rising national debt. At over 15 per cent of GDP, the fiscal deficit was more than five times the three per cent maximum permitted limit under eurozone rules. Its rapidly rising national debt at 128 per cent of GDP was more than twice the 60 per cent eurozone maximum limit. It became clear that the Greek government would be highly unlikely to repay its debts as they came due and pay interest on those debts. The financial markets responded by pushing up the interest rates on Greek government debt and virtually refusing to lend any more money.

In 2010, the Greek government was forced to make an agreement with a group of three lenders - the 'Trioka'. These were the International Monetary Fund (IMF), the European Central Bank and the European Commission. Emergency loans were provided and there was some element of debt forgiveness on the part of the EU. In return, the Greek government was forced to agree to a package of reform measures that cut government spending and raised taxes shown in Figure 9. Even in 2010, it was clear that in the long term the package of measures would not fully resolve the Greek government's financial problems. At some stage in the future, there would have to be more debt forgiveness, probably on the part of the EU.

By 2014, the Greek fiscal deficit was down to two per cent of GDP. It was also running a primary surplus (the fiscal balance excluding debt interest) of three per cent. However, it had come at a huge cost to the Greek economy. As Figure 10 shows, GDP was 25 per cent lower than at its peak in 2008. The unemployment rate, shown in Figure 11, was 27 per cent. The international financial crisis of 2007-08 was partly responsible for these statistics. But mostly, they were the result of fiscal austerity.

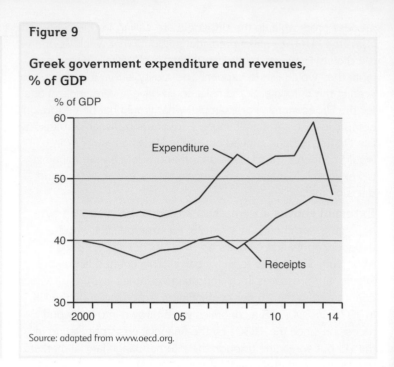

Figure 8

Greece, growth in GDP (%) and fiscal balance as % of GDP

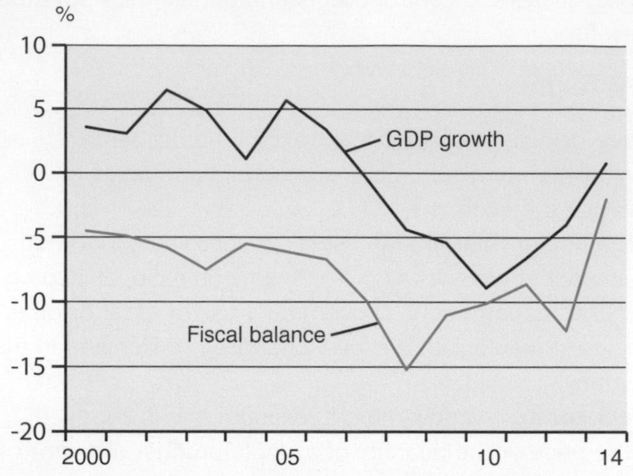

Source: adapted from www.oecd.org.

Figure 9

Greek government expenditure and revenues, % of GDP

Source: adapted from www.oecd.org.

In 2014, the Greek electorate voted in an anti-austerity coalition committed to reversing the austerity programme. Many Greeks blamed their problems on the Troika for pushing the Greek economy into such a deep recession. Most other countries in the EU had little sympathy for the Greeks. Portugal, Spain and Ireland had been through similar recessions and been forced to adopt austerity fiscal measures. They failed to see why, having experienced similar economic pain, the Greeks should not be forced to accept responsibility for the previous fiscal mistakes and continue to make sacrifices to put their economy on a stable footing. Some northern European countries, including Germany and Finland, failed to see why they should provide more loans to

Greece when it was not prepared to stabilise its economy. They were worried that there would be a continual flow of never-to-be-repaid loans from their countries to Greece.

In the long term, Greece can only make real economic progress through further supply-side reforms and control of government finances. The mathematics of its national debt says that at some point in the future, lenders to the Greek government will have to accept a write-off of some its debt. The Greek economy is likely to recover, but it could take decades to get back to the prosperity levels seen at the start of the 2007-08 financial crisis.

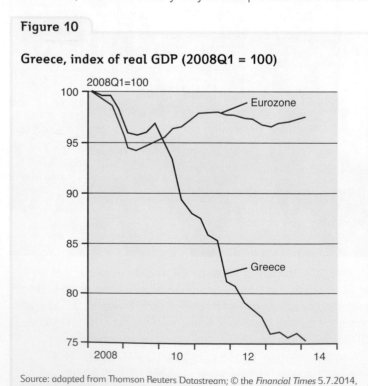

Figure 10

Greece, index of real GDP (2008Q1 = 100)

Source: adapted from Thomson Reuters Datastream; © the *Financial Times* 5.7.2014, All Rights Reserved.

Figure 11

Greece, unemployment rate (%)

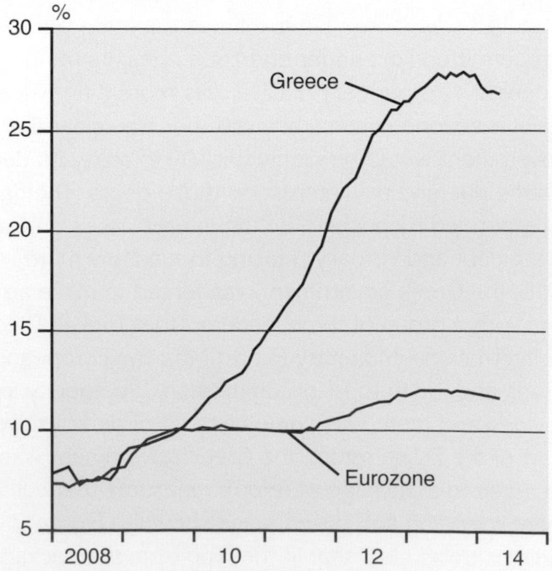

Source: adapted from Thomson Reuters Datastream; © the *Financial Times* 5.7.2014, All Rights Reserved.

Data Response Question

Argentina

In 1989 and 1990, Argentina was racked by hyperinflation. As part of a package of measures to get prices back under control, the Argentine government pegged its currency, the peso, against the US dollar. Having a fixed exchange rate against the US dollar was successful in controlling inflation. However, inflation in Argentina continued to be higher than in the USA. The result was that Argentina became less internationally price competitive as the 1990s progressed. The government found it ever-more difficult to borrow money long term on international markets. In 2001-02, there was an economic crisis and the fixed exchange rate between the peso and the US dollar was abandoned whilst the Argentinian government defaulted on its debts.

In the 2000s, the Argentine government pursued a mix of populist economic policies including nationalisation of key assets. However, these ultimately proved unsuccessful as the economy returned to high inflation and shrinking output.

In 2005 and 2010, it negotiated two debt-restructuring agreements. Most of the owners of the Argentine government debt agreed to reduce the amount they were owed to about 30 per cent of its 2002 value. However, seven per cent of the debt was still owned by bond holders who had refused to be party to the debt restructuring agreements. In 2014, they successfully challenged the right of the Argentine government to continue paying interest to the owners of the restructured bonds when they had not been paid in full. It meant that the Argentine government was once again unable to borrow in international financial markets.

In 2011, as the crisis developed, the Argentine government imposed currency controls on foreign currency movements. This meant that anyone wanting to buy foreign currency with Argentine pesos had to get permission to do so. A black market developed with pesos trading at a much lower price to US dollars than the official central bank price. By 2014, the Argentine government was limiting the amount of US dollars that

importers could buy. This meant that imports were cut. Since 80 per cent of imports are input for domestic industry, it meant that Argentine firms were severely restricted in their output. Economists expected about 350 000 people would lose their jobs as a result in 2014. Year-on-year production in the automobile industry, for example, was down 34.6 per cent because it was heavily reliant on imports for parts.

As part of its economic response, in 2014 the country's Congress passed a controversial 'supply' law that gives the government sweeping powers to control prices, profit margins and production levels.

Q

1. Explain what is meant by a 'direct control', using the data in the article to illustrate your answer.

2. Explain how the Argentine government in the 1990s used exchange rate policy to control domestic inflation.

3. Discuss whether the Argentine government should have adopted fiscal austerity measures to control its debt rather than using the mix of policies, including default and direct controls, that it chose to adopt.

Evaluation

How successful were the measures Argentina adopted? Did they produce a successful growing economy? What would have been the impact of an alternative strategy of fiscal austerity? Would the result have been worse or better in the short run and the long run compared to the mix of policies it did pursue?

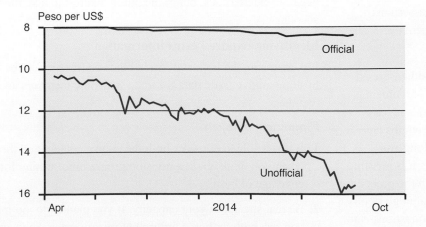

Figure 12

Argentine peso against the dollar

Peso per US$

Preparing for your AS and A level exams

Taking the UK driving test involves two parts: theory questions and a practical test. The contrast is obvious; the theory test is centred on knowledge and the practical test centres on skills. A first mistake to avoid is to think that economics exams, like the driving theory test, centre on knowledge. Edexcel economics exams use written papers to test four different skills. Across your course, the balance between these skills is roughly even.

The skills: knowledge and understanding

Knowledge and understanding of subject concepts, jargon and techniques is the first requirement. The most obvious test of this comes in the occasional definition question. However, a sharp grasp of concepts gives a foundation for the use of other skills so a fuzzy grasp will very seriously damage your prospects.

The skills: application

Most of the questions you are faced with start from a short 'stem' of information or a larger collection of data. The application skill is essentially the use of your concepts and techniques in the context (or situation) that you have been given. One example of application that you must expect is calculations; using a subject formula or standard technique to draw something out from data you are given.

The skills: analysis

Building an explanation is at the core of analysis. Three critical components are some economics, some steps in development and a logical chain of reasoning. Most often, analysis is concerned with either causes or consequences. If there is a chain there will be links: some experienced examiners see well-used link words such as 'so', 'because', 'unless' and 'therefore' as indicators of analysis. When weak answers fail to analyse they often use assertions – unsupported claims, with no explanation to back them up.

The skills: evaluation

More candidates struggle with this skill than any other. Sound evaluation has two key components: balance and judgement. Very little in economics is all good, even the best ideas have costs and risks. Balance centres on seeing both strengths and weaknesses, or winners and losers, or short- and long-run consequences, for example. Once there is balance, it is possible to move on to judgement. A simple parallel is with the procedure in law courts. Both sides of a case are put before a judge or jury comes to a decision. A bad mistake in evaluation questions is to rush to judgement. Evaluation questions carry the most marks and a judgement in the first sentence is generally an indicator of a very poor performance.

In longer answers, it is valuable to have more than one item of evaluation. The court comparison has a 'summative' judgement where the evidence is weighed to inform a conclusion. In extended writing, a concluding paragraph should normally contain evaluation. In addition, evaluative points can be made earlier. This entails commenting on points developed in an answer. Students from some centres seem to be trained to end their paragraphs with a 'however' sentence where they attempt to make an evaluative point. Some examples of possible evaluative points are listed below:

Commenting on significance

E.g. a 0.25 per cent rise in base rate has symbolic importance but only changes costs/returns slightly.

Identifying necessary conditions

E.g. a price cut only leads to increased revenue if demand is price elastic.

Judging the probability of a point

E.g. most covert cartels are (probably) successfully hidden but giving lenient treatment to the first culprit to confess is likely to encourage more 'whistleblowers'.

Separating short/long run outcomes

E.g. a VAT rise is likely to increase some prices in the short run but reduce real disposable income, consumption and prices in the medium/long term.

Distinguish private from public interest

E.g. it is in the private interest of a polluting firm to ignore negative externalities, but in the public interest to take them into account.

Identifying required extra information

E.g. assessing the impact of trade blocs on trade would be helped by comparative trade data for trade with bloc members and non-members.

Planning revision

1. It is sensible to consider both the course content and the skills when you think about a revision programme, aiming for sound coverage of both.

2. Be realistic about your capacity. If you plan to do too much you risk both feeling a failure before you reach the exam and suffering from diminishing returns. Make a timetable but be prepared to modify it after a few days if it proves unrealistic.

3. Sometimes 'the penny will drop' when you revisit a topic that you have struggled with, so it is foolish to neglect the areas you like least. Try to cover all of the course content.

4. For knowledge, first practise precise and concise definitions. Making your own glossary is good and so is talking through any differences over definitions with a friend.

5. One way to work on application is to look at news stories relevant to economics and ask yourself which concepts or theories are relevant. Exam questions are unlikely to be directly about current news as most were set almost a year ahead of the exam, but awareness of current issues can often be useful.

6. Try building chains of analysis and then checking how accurately you have used link words.

7. Think consciously about balance and judgement in your revision and beyond. Whenever you have decisions to make, choices tend to have both advantages and disadvantages.

In the exam

Some elements are found in all Economics AS and A level exams. The balance between the time for each exam and the marks available allows you 1 minute to earn each mark, plus a little extra thinking time. So, for example, when you tackle a four-mark short answer question in the theme 1 or theme 2 exam you should aim to take 4 minutes. Avoid the mistake of taking too long over questions with few marks. The opportunity cost of doing this would be having to rush the last part of the paper where questions have most marks. When a paper finishes with a 20-mark question, for example, that needs 20 minutes of your time.

Theme 1 and 2 AS exams: both these papers have 80 marks each and last for 90 minutes.

Paper 1: Introduction to markets and market failure.

Paper 2: The UK economy – performance and policies.

Section	Question type	Marks
A	Five short answer questions, each with two or three parts. Can include multiple choice, definition, annotation, calculation or brief explanation.	5 x 4 = 20
B	Data response question with six sections, including choice between two final 20-mark sections.	Sum of 60

A level Papers 1 and 2 have the same structure: both these papers have 100 marks and 120 minutes

Paper 1: Markets and business behaviour.

Paper 2: The national and global economy.

Section	Question type	Marks
A	Five short answer questions, structured as at AS but with 5 marks each at A level.	5 x 5 = 25
B	Data response question with five sections	Sum of 50
C	Choice from two extended open-response questions	Either for 25

Short answer questions carry an extra mark and the Section C extended writing questions have 25 marks. This last section carries us into the area of what were traditionally called essays.

A level Paper 3 again has 100 marks and 120 minutes

Paper 3: Microeconomics and macroeconomics

Section	Question type	Marks
A	Data response question with three compulsory sections (25 marks) plus choice of two final sections (25 marks).	50
B	Data response question with three compulsory sections (25 marks) plus choice of two final sections (25 marks).	50

This time there are no short answer questions but two data response questions, each with a final 25-mark question. These questions will be broadly similar to the final questions on Papers 1 and 2, but this time with the addition of data response stimulus material to provide context.

Section A questions

For a multiple choice question you are asked to choose the correct answer from four options, writing the letter corresponding to your answer in a box. The relevant subject idea is sometimes self-evident, making this a quick process. If unsure, you can mentally rule out obviously wrong answers and choose the best of what is left. A guess is better than leaving the answer box blank, as positive marking means there are no deductions for wrong answers so you can do no worse than score 0.

Where there is a 2-mark definition question, a clear and concise definition is fine. However, if your definition is slightly off-key this is likely to cost you a mark, so an example or brief extension can be worthwhile as it might tip the balance in your favour.

When the question has a diagram, you can be asked to shade a key area or to show the effect of some change. This 'annotation' should be straightforward for someone who understands the diagram and has some experience of identifying areas or changes. If this sounds daunting, build some confidence by adding practice to your revision programme.

Calculations in Section A should be straightforward and numbers are often rounded to keep things simple. If there are 2 or 3 marks available, identifying a correct relevant formula often earns a mark. It is important to write down the steps in your workings. If you use a calculator and just write down your answer, any slip would mean scoring no marks. If workings show that you were on the right lines but made a slip, this is likely to earn some credit.

Explanations (for 2 or 3 marks) need only be brief in this section, but they still require some economics and some logical development with a link or two. It would still be a mistake to leap straight to a conclusion with no explanation.

Section B questions

The best start to data response questions is to read the data or evidence carefully. Some people like to underline or star what they see as potential key points. Avoid the temptation to skip over diagrams or graphs, ask yourself what they are really showing you.

Questions carrying fewer marks (often 4-6) are likely to be calculations (= application) or analysis questions (most often with the command word 'explain'). Even a calculation depends on knowledge of what to do. Show your knowledge by writing the relevant formula where there is one. Your raw data will normally be found in the evidence, sometimes you will have to select the relevant figures from a table or graph.

As with calculation, explanation depends on underlying knowledge. You will be expected to make some use of the evidence too. This requires more than name dropping. Vague general statements such as 'the people want more income' would earn no credit, as this would be true of most people most of the time. However, if you can say why extra income would be important in the context of the question, this becomes useful application. Thus, an analysis question is actually testing the first three skills and the marks will normally be shared between them.

Once the mark allocation jumps up to 8 or more, evaluation is normally required. Now the marks will be shared between all four skills. In general, a greater the number of marks will also have a larger share of those marks tied to evaluation. Often, 8-mark questions include just two evaluation marks so basic balance and judgement can be enough (if accurate and relevant). A 15-mark question could have 6 evaluation marks so the emphasis on evaluation is greater and more is expected of you.

The longer final questions, either in Section B or labelled as Section C, want more time, thought and development. They continue the same approach as other evaluation questions. The marks will be shared between the four skills, though knowledge, application and analysis marks are sometimes grouped together. The biggest share of marks in these questions will be for evaluation.

The evaluation questions are not like arithmetical sums with just one right answer. Two people with contrasting views can both score full marks if their contrasting judgements are consistent with the evidence they explain and they demonstrate sound use of all four skills. There is no perfect judgement that is better than alternatives.

Sample question Section A, AS Paper I.

Centrica (formerly British Gas, the privatised supplier) retained a 40 per cent share of the domestic gas supply market 15 years after market liberalisation, despite charging prices seen as relatively high.

a) This information suggests that consumers are:

    A   rational
    B   better off
    C   maximising utility
    D   influenced by habit
Answer ☐   (1 mark)

b) Explain one reason why consumers might not behave rationally. (3 marks)

Sample answers:

a) D.

Comment: yes, 1 mark

b) Rational consumers seek to maximise the utility from their income so would choose the lowest price where products are homogeneous. If people are set in their ways and tend to repeat habitual behaviour, they might therefore stay with their existing supplier and not consider switching to an alternative. They might also have asymmetrical information, not being clear on price differences, on how to switch suppliers, or even on the homogeneous nature of gas supplied through the network.

Comment: 'so' in the first sentence is a first link word in explanation, 'therefore' is another. Last sentence might be a waste – only one reason wanted.

Sample question Section A, AS Paper 2

Figure 1

2014 UK OUTPUT GAP ESTIMATES

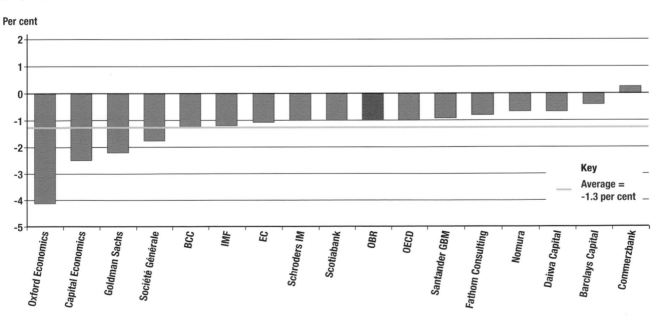

Source: adapted from HM Treasury, *OBR Economic and Fiscal Outlook*, March 2015.

a) Define the term 'output gap'.   (1 mark)

b) Briefly explain why there can be such variation in output gap estimates.   (2 marks)

c) The information given suggests that:

    A   the output gap can never be positive

    B   most estimates suggest the economy has around 1 per cent spare capacity

    C   economic growth is negative

    D   aggregate demand exceeds aggregate supply

    Answer ☐ (1 mark)

Sample answers:

a) The output gap is the difference between the actual output of an economy and its sustainable potential output.

Comment:

enough for the 1 mark

---

b) Estimates of actual output can be made using regularly collected data, though these are estimates and subject to errors. Potential output is much harder to identify so it is possible for one estimate to see possible evidence of four per cent unused capacity whilst another estimate sees evidence that output is above its sustainable potential.

Comment:

enough here again

---

c) B

Comment: 1 mark

Sample question Section B, AS Paper 2.

Productivity and growth

Extract A

Productivity problems

A February 2015 OECD economic report said: 'Weak export performance and productivity could be driven by infrastructure weaknesses and difficult access to bank finance, especially for small and medium-sized enterprises (SMEs), holding back the emergence of new firms and high-skilled jobs.'

Chancellor George Osborne told the CBI annual dinner in May 2015 that boosting productivity was vital to sustaining rises in living standards. He identified increased productivity as one of the government's central economic challenges over the next five years. Steps to upgrade transport links, reduce red tape, streamline planning and incentivise business ownership would be at the centre of a plan to rebalance the economy.

The BBC's economics editor, Robert Peston, said productivity in the UK was historically 30 per cent lower than in Germany and America - a gap that previous governments had wrestled with but failed to do much about.

The basic facts behind the productivity puzzle are that, since 2008, employment has risen substantially and working hours have increased but output per hour has fallen.

Source: adapted from OECD; © the *Financial Times*, All Rights Reserved; ONS.

Figure B

Some Index Numbers (January 2008 = 100)

Quarter	Output/hour	GDP	GDP per capita
2008 Q3	96	98.1	97.7
2010 Q3	98	96.5	94.7
2012 Q3	95	98.7	95.4
2014 Q3	96	102.9	98.2

Source: adapted from www.ons.gov.uk.

Figure C

What might have been?

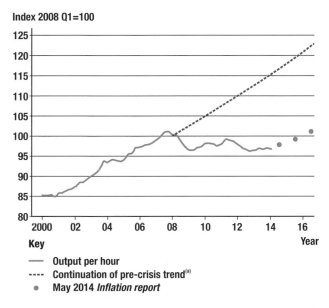

Index 2008 Q1=100

Key

— Output per hour
---- Continuation of pre-crisis trend[(a)]
• May 2014 *Inflation report*

Source: adapted from *The Productivity Puzzle*, Bank of England.

Questions

(a) Explain the link between productivity and economic growth.   (4 marks)

(b) Explain how Figure B can show GDP rising in 2014 despite productivity having fallen.   (5 marks)

(c) Explain **two** ways in which 'infrastructure weaknesses' (Extract A) could hold back productivity.   (6 marks)

(d) Assess the impact of the 2008-09 recession on the pre-crisis productivity trend (Figure C).   (10 marks)

(e) Discuss **two** ways in which a government could seek to increase productivity.   (15 marks)

EITHER

(f) Evaluate whether improvements to productivity and growth should be prioritised as a UK government objective.   (20 marks)

OR

(g) Evaluate the suggestion that increased labour market flexibility (e.g. by more use of zero-hours contracts) damages productivity.   (20 marks)

Sample answer

(a) Economic growth means increases in real GDP whereas productivity is about output per input of a factor of production. The output per hour column in Figure B gives a measure of labour productivity. If labour productivity grows workers will produce more per hour so total output will increase if the same hours are worked. Increased total output will increase GDP so labour productivity and GDP are linked. Of course, there are other variables that also influence GDP so there is not a perfect correlation between productivity and GDP.

Comment:

Knowledge, application and analysis all here and relevant. Last sentence goes beyond what is required.

(b) Figure B shows that productivity and growth don't always move in the same direction. Between 2008 and 2014 the GDP index has risen to 102.9, but productivity has fallen to 96. As productivity has fallen there is less output per hour worked, yet total output has gone up. This is probably because 'employment has risen substantially' (Extract A). 2008 was in a recession when unemployment was high. More hours are being worked. As the rise in employment is 'substantial' it can more than balance out the effect of lower productivity.

Comment: clear answer using the right skills.

(c) Infrastructure is the 'furniture' of the economy such as roads and utilities. If the transport system is in very bad repair or roads, railways and airports are excessively congested, this can reduce productivity for business, for example because it takes longer to deliver anything. It can also reduce geographical mobility of labour because workers might be reluctant to travel long distances to work. In some developing countries utilities such as power supplies are unreliable. This means that electrical machinery or heating equipment can go off for hours at a time in some cases. If all machinery is down, including computers, workers in many jobs will be unable to do much so their productivity will suffer.

Comment: 'furniture' is an odd choice of word, but the basic point is made in the first paragraph. The second paragraph makes a clear and separate point.

(d) What Figure C shows is a trend of about 2 per cent per annum increase in labour productivity per hour from 2000 to 2008, but then a drop and no sign of a return to the trend by 2014. Although there is no proof in the evidence that the recession caused this, it would be quite a coincidence otherwise.

One possibility is that lower demand in the recession decreased the amount firms could sell so they made less. If firms kept workers temporarily underemployed, rather than sack them and risk problems recruiting again after the recession, productivity would fall. This seems plausible, however, it should have made it possible to increase output by 2014 without the big increase in employment and the continuing low level of productivity.

Alternatively, investment generally falls in a recession. It could be that low investment left people working with ageing machinery and not able to get equipment using the latest technology. The infrastructure weaknesses are one example of the results of low investment. We have no evidence of firms' investment levels so it is hard to judge this point, but it is plausible.

There are also other possibilities that are not direct consequences of the recession. Since 2008 there has been an increase in casual employment, part-time and zero-hours contracts. Workers with insecure employment might be less motivated and so less productive. At the same time, firms using temporary or part-time labour might see less prospect of profit from training these casual workers to make them more productive, so not improve their skills. Average productivity might be reduced by these things.

There are commentators who suggest that austerity policies and prioritising reducing the level of public sector deficit have held back recovery in demand and output. Less output can mean firms working below capacity so less productively. Again, though, there must be some additional element to explain why productivity stayed low when output grew in 2014.

Certainty about the precise causes of the UK's move away from the previous productivity trend is elusive. If the causes were completely understood they could be addressed. Even if the recession was not itself directly responsible, it was involved in people's need to accept casual employment and in the growth of the public sector deficit so there is more than coincidence here.

Comment: the answer begins with two reasons why recession could damage productivity, followed with balance from possible causes other than directly the recession. The final paragraph contains a concluding judgement.

(e) Governments would welcome improvements in productivity as this could stimulate growth and competitiveness. Growth is a macroeconomic objective and competitiveness could help the balance of payments.

In Extract A the OECD report refers to infrastructure weaknesses and the Chancellor refers to 'steps to upgrade transport links' – one aspect of infrastructure. Governments often directly invest in infrastructure such as road improvements, high-speed rail lines and the London Crossrail project. They can also help the private sector with grants, tax allowances and planning permission (e.g. for runways to serve London). Such improvements could reduce transport costs, save time for business and improve journeys to work. Many businesses in rural areas say their productivity is held back by slow Internet speeds – waiting for things to download and upload. Making high-speed Internet available in more of the country would thus boost productivity.

All activities have their costs, financial or otherwise. Whilst the government prioritises reducing its deficit to slow the growth of the national debt, any spending proposals entail cutting across this priority. There are alternative such as the Private Finance initiative and Public/Private Partnerships whereby private sector funding is used, but such projects have frequently been criticised as very poor value for money. In the case of EDF (and Chinese finance) building a new nuclear power station it has been necessary to guarantee a high price for electricity generated. Thus the government avoids the issue of funding in the short term but perhaps at the cost of higher consumer prices in the long run. In the case of Heathrow expansion, delays are linked to real concerns over external costs such as noise and atmospheric pollution, so environmental objectives might be sacrificed if expansion went ahead.

The most direct way to approach productivity is to improve the quality of the labour force. Highly skilled workers in high value added jobs should be more productive. One of the UK's problems in recent years has been the high proportion of new jobs in unskilled work where less value is added. At the same time there have been skills shortages inhibiting growth in some areas. Better education and training can improve the quality of the labour force and its occupational mobility. General education for most children is in the public sector. Improvements here could develop more of the potential young people have. Support for apprenticeships and other incentives can improve the quality and quantity of training provided by businesses.

One problem here is the timescale involved. If, for example, primary education is improved, it is likely to be around seven years before any benefit feeds though to the working population and perhaps a generation for the full benefit. There have also been many graduates unable to find jobs to use their full abilities in recent years, so educating people is not sufficient, in itself. An issue with training is that we can identify present needs but technological change will alter future skills requirements in ways which might not be foreseen. There is a danger of training people in skills that will become obsolete.

Our understanding of the factors determining productivity is incomplete, making it difficult to be fully confident in measures to increase it. Improving both infrastructure and education and training can contribute as part of a rounded approach, but neither represents a quick and easy answer to increasing productivity.

Comment: the second paragraph shows good skills use to explain a first 'way', followed in the next paragraph with balance from the downside of spending on infrastructure. A second 'way' is explained, followed by balance again, with some judgement. The final paragraph contains a brief concluding judgement.

(f) The UK government has six macroeconomic objectives, one of which is economic growth. Policies which succeed in improving labour productivity, measured as output per hour worked, should increase output and GDP given ceteris paribus, and so improve economic growth. As GDP is now just 2-3 per cent higher than seven years ago, this would give a welcome boost to economic growth and the standard of living in the UK.

If UK workers become more productive, this should increase their earning power. This would be particularly important if it enabled unskilled workers to increase their ability to add value and their earnings. A feature of recent years has been increasing disparity in the UK income distribution. One of the macroeconomic objectives is greater income equality and increasing the relatively low incomes of unskilled workers would bring an improvement in this. However, many unskilled workers are in occupations such as retailing and catering, and there is limited potential to improve value added for a shop assistant or a waiter. Increasing value added has more often been found in already skilled occupations. Income distribution might not become more equal.

Another macroeconomic objective is to improve the balance of payments. In Extract A Robert Peston refers to UK productivity being 30 per cent behind levels in major developed rival countries. If improvements in UK productivity can narrow this gap and thereby reduce relative costs, this could make UK products more competitive. If home produced goods become more competitive with UK consumers, imports could fall. If UK goods become more competitive in overseas markets, exports could rise. More exports and fewer imports would improve the balance of payments situation. However, this depends on rivals not having similar improvements in productivity at the same time and it is hard to envisage closing the big cost disadvantage compared to China, for example. Improvement in the balance of payments cannot be guaranteed.

An increase in productivity can be expected to reduce unit costs as more is produced per hour worked, and so to be counter-inflationary. Control of inflation is another macroeconomic objective that could be helped by improved productivity. However, inflation is well below its 2 per cent target (in mid-2015) so measures to reduce costs and prices don't currently require high priority.

More significantly, more productive labour offering more output at lower unit costs should be more attractive to employers. If policies succeed in improving the potential productivity of currently unemployed workers, this would be of real benefit to the employment objective. The problem with this is that it is hard to see a policy that can rapidly improve the potential productivity of the unemployed.

The macroeconomic objective that is least likely to benefit from improvements in productivity is protection of the environment. If workers can and do produce more, then increases in pollution and other external costs are likely to follow. The environment could suffer additional damage. It is possible to argue that extra output would make the UK richer and so more able to afford to protect the environment, but there is no certainty that extra income would be spent in that way.

Improvements in productivity and growth could help a government to pursue five of its six macroeconomic objectives. It would also create extra resources which could be used for the sixth, environmental protection. Thus, potentially, there could be benefits for all six objectives. This suggests that policies to improve productivity and growth should have high priority. However, as Robert Peston suggests that previous governments have wrestled unsuccessfully with this problem, it is important to find policies that work and not just to prioritise this objective.

Comment: the six objectives and the three major policy types are often involved in macroeconomic evaluation questions. The second paragraph contains a sound link to another objective, ending with an evaluation point. Over the next three paragraphs, this approach is repeated three times. The sixth paragraph contains some balance from an objective that could be harmed. Finally, the conclusion rounds off a strong answer.

Sample question Section B, A level Paper I

Oligopolistic behaviour

Figure A

Collusion

In hypothetical models such as perfect competition, individual rival firms and individual consumers have tiny and anonymous market shares. There is little meaningful interaction, just impersonal exchange of products for payment. In oligopoly, the dominant large firms are interdependent; what each of them does will have an impact on the others. For example, if one large energy firm raises its prices significantly, that will have an impact on the others. The starting textbook assumption is that firms are intensely competitive and prioritise market share. UK Energy industry experience suggests that some form of collusion might be more likely than fierce competition. Why compete when firms can all have healthy profits at similar prices?

The most complex collusion is 'tacit'. This means that there is no agreement, either open or hidden. Firms independently find their way to a mutual realisation that strenuous competition could harm them all. They behave as if there was collusion, but without ever contacting each other. If we accept that the six leading UK Energy suppliers have not colluded overtly, they perhaps illustrate the potential of tacit collusion. They have each independently found the benefits of splitting operations into vertically integrated generation, trading and retail businesses. They all blend standing with charges variable in a different way, making clear price comparisons difficult. They all seem to change prices in the same direction (more often upwards) within a short time period. Despite this, their retail arms just make respectable profits whilst their trading businesses seem to make more money.

Source: adapted from 'Game Theory', *Economics Today*, March 2015.

Figure B

Competition & Markets Authority (CMA)

Amongst the possible issues that the CMA is investigating in its enquiry into UK energy supply are:

– that market power in electricity generation leads to higher prices

– that opaque prices in wholesale electricity markets distort competition in retail and generation

– that vertically integrated electricity companies act to harm the competitive position of non-integrated firms to the detriment of the consumer

– that suppliers face weak incentives to compete on price and non-price factors in retail markets, due in particular to inactive customers.

Source: adapted from CMA update, 15 March 2015, www.gov.uk.

Figure C

Shares of UK domestic households supplied with energy

Business	Share %
British Gas	29
SSE	15
EON	14
EDF	11
Scottish Power	11
RWE	10

Source: adapted from www.cornwallenergy.com.

Extract D

The role of Ofgem (Energy market regulator)

Over the next decade energy companies face an unprecedented challenge of securing significant investment to maintain a reliable and secure network, and dealing with the changes in demand and generation that will occur in a low carbon future.

As the regulator, we must ensure that this is delivered at a fair price for consumers.

Source: adapted from www.ofgem.gov.uk

Questions

(a) Explain the meaning and consequences of 'inactive customers' (Extract B).   (5 marks)

(b) Examine the benefits of vertical integration to the big six energy suppliers.   (8 marks)

(c) Assess potential gains from tacit collusion for major energy suppliers.   (10 marks)

(d) Discuss the contestability of the UK household energy market.   (12 marks)

(e) Evaluate difficulties facing Ofgem in regulating the energy market.   (15 marks)

Sample answer

(a) In this context, inactive customers are people who do not respond to market incentives. Consumers are theoretically expected to behave 'rationally' in order to maximise utility from their incomes. So, for example, if one energy supplier had a lower price than rivals consumers should buy from that company. Real consumers have inertia and often rely on habit. Many are still with British Gas from the time before privatisation. If they will not respond to an incentive by switching to a cheaper supplier, there is no point in reducing price. Even though this doesn't apply to all consumers, there is sufficient inertia to keep PED low and to discourage competing either by price or by non-price factors such as better service quality.

Comment: plenty here. Last sentence is an extension that is not necessary.

(b) One issue identified in Extract B is that vertically integrated companies can harm the competitive position of non-integrated firms. So, for example, generating and trading firms owned by the big six retailers might be reluctant to sell energy to new rivals or might charge them high prices to keep them uncompetitive. 'Opaque pricing' might help them to do this. This would protect the dominant position of the big six and allow them to use higher prices to make more profit.

Vertical integration can also make transfer pricing possible. Generators in the UK could sell cheaply to trading companies under the same ownership but based elsewhere – perhaps in a tax haven. Trading companies could then sell at high prices to their UK retail business. This means that neither the generator nor the retailer has high profits to declare to the regulator or the UK tax authorities. As Extract A says, 'their trading businesses seem to make more money'.

Extract B shows the big six supplying 90 per cent of households. Although this is still a dominant position, it does show that smaller firms have a foothold and some are increasing their market shares. Some of the smaller firms compete on non-price grounds, appealing to some consumers by being greener and relying as much as possible on wind and solar energy, for example. A second advantage here is that there are new generators of 'alternative' energies so reliance on the big integrated generators is reduced. Change is coming slowly to this market, but it is coming and vertical integration might slow change but cannot prevent it.

Comment: in the first two paragraphs, two benefits are successfully explained, in context. The examine command means some evaluation is wanted. There is enough in the final paragraph.

(c) The most obvious gain from collusion is that firms that dominate a market can collectively exploit monopoly power.

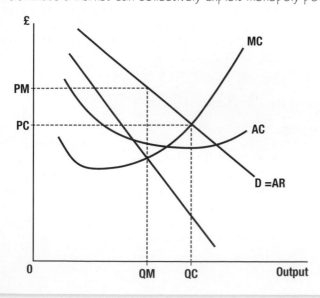

As the diagram shows, if in competition they produce where P = MC, output will be Q_C and price P_C. By colluding and creating a monopoly, they can raise price to PM, reduce output to QM and make supernormal profits. The more inelastic demand is, the greater are the potential profits. Household demand for energy is price inelastic so colluding energy companies can potentially make extensive profits. There is a deadweight loss of welfare from such behaviour and consumers pay higher prices, but there are large potential gains for the energy companies.

Overt and covert collusion are illegal, punishable by heavy fines. This means that either open or hidden agreements between firms are high risk and so unattractive. Tacit collusion has what Extract A calls 'a mutual realisation' rather than any form of agreement. Realising something, without collusion, is not against the law, so tacit collusion cannot be illegal and bring punishment. The dominant energy suppliers would not break the law by colluding tacitly, yet could still reap the benefits of collusion.

Comment: diagrams that support explanation are welcome. The final paragraph makes a classic error – this explains gains but lacks balance or judgement. The assess command means there are evaluation marks, which this answer cannot have.

(d) Contestability depends on the ease with which new entrants can join and leave a market. The advantage of contestability is that even when oligopolists (or a monopolist) dominate a market they are unable to fully exploit their market power if high profits would attract new entrants and so make the market more competitive.

Figure C shows that the big six serve 90 per cent of UK households, which immediately suggests that contestability is limited as other firms have evidently struggled to build market share. The large size of these six businesses suggests that they are able to exploit economies of scale. The expense of investing in generating capacity on a similar scale would be many millions of pounds, much of which would be a sunk cost unless the plants constructed could be transferred to alternative use – which seems unlikely. Funding such risky investment is a barrier to entry that would deter many potential entrants.

Extract B refers to inactive customers and this creates another barrier to entry. If consumers have inertia and stick with their established providers, new entrants would struggle to attract households to buy from them. The marketing expense per customer attracted could become prohibitive. Alternatively, setting exceptionally low prices as a way of attracting people would damage profitability. Knowing that consumers are inactive is thus another barrier to entry.

The alternative viewpoint is that several small firms do now have a foothold in this market, albeit with relatively small market shares. They have successfully established themselves and can now hope to gradually increase their market shares, so there is some contestability. The ability to focus on being greener and the fact that smaller firms tend to be seen as more customer friendly and more in touch with their consumers gives them strengths to exploit when growing. Whereas generation demands massive investment, retailing can have lower start-up costs for businesses which buy their energy wholesale and set up efficient online operations, making retail more contestable.

The combination of widespread discontent with the performance of the big 6 and the current CMA investigation suggests that change is likely in this market. If for example, the CMA decides that vertical integration is against the public interest, we could see a break-up that would open the market to more competition. Small non-integrated firms might well become able to compete on a more level basis. Even without such action, the swell of bad publicity for the big six seems likely to gradually increase the number of households willing to shop around and to find a better deal.

The UK household energy market has been characterised by low contestability since privatisation, dominated by the big six suppliers whose position has been helped by inactive consumers. However, it is not completely incontestable as there have been new entrants and their share of the market is slowly growing. There is also the possibility that action following the CMA investigation and growing consumer awareness could increase contestability in future.

Comment: the best start is often a relevant definition or some scene setting, as in the first paragraph. The next two paragraphs show good use of evidence in points suggesting contestability is low, followed by two balancing paragraphs indicating that there is some contestability. An evaluative conclusion rounds off the answer.

(e) Extract D identifies three areas in which OFGEM faces difficulties. These are securing investment to maintain a reliable and secure network, dealing with changes in demand and generation in a low carbon future and ensuring fair prices for consumers.

At first sight, securing investment should not be difficult in a profitable industry. The profit motive should attract entrepreneurs to invest and supply energy. Added incentives have been made available, for example for solar energy 'farms' and wind turbines, which have added to supply. However, these examples only add effectively to supply on sunny or windy days. The backbone of UK energy supply comes from coal- and oil-fired generation which should be run down in a low carbon future, plus ageing nuclear plants which the private sector seems reluctant to replace without heavy government support.

One of the problems here is that the low carbon vision is a response to external costs rather than to market forces. At present, renewable energy sources have relatively high construction costs and subsidisation has been necessary to stimulate investment in them. Where solar farms or wind turbines are proposed, there is often a NIMBY (not in my back yard) attitude from locals who fear a new type of external cost from noise and visual pollution. In addition, the economic case for the efficiency of most renewable systems is unproven. A 'reliable' network is also one which meets peak energy demand; we need energy consistently and with more capacity than is used most of the time. We cannot rely on wind and solar renewables on a still, foggy day, for example.

This mixture of considerations means that energy supply cannot simply be left to market forces. Complex planning is required, together with a mix of regulation (e.g. carbon trading) and incentives to attract private sector firms towards required actions. One of the issues here is that long-term vision is required to avoid stumbling into greater problems. Short termism could result in government failure as well as market failure, leading us away from desirable outcomes. Long-term planning is also dependent on assumptions about the state of technology and future market conditions. Is it reasonable, for example, to assume that there will be better future systems for the disposal of nuclear waste?

At present, energy suppliers are involved in schemes to improve insulation and promote energy saving developments such as smart meters. It seems slightly perverse to have suppliers taking actions that reduce future demand for their product. The regulator will need to keep a close eye on how this is done. One of the dangers of regulation is regulatory capture, the complexity of the situation and the desire to keep the suppliers investing will make it difficult for OFGEM to take actions which work against the interests of the suppliers.

Many of the incentives, such as those to go greener and to invest in nuclear energy, are ultimately funded by consumers via higher prices. This complicates the normative judgement on what is a 'fair' price for consumers. There are already some suspicions over pricing, for example that vertical integration allows the big six to obscure their true profitability. The argument that healthy profits are necessary both to attract investment and to help fund it is a powerful one which is likely to colour OFGEM's judgement. This adds to pressure to keep the market competitive and improve contestability.

Ultimately, these matters are out of OFGEM's hands, depending on the conclusions reached by the CMA investigation and subsequent political decisions and action. OFGEM faces complex difficulties that it cannot resolve alone. An effective balance between planning and competitive market forces will depend on concerted action from all those in authority.

Comment: after some initial scene setting there are good relevant points, but with more technical detail about electricity generation than an economics question can require.

A level Paper 3 Extended writing question

Development and external costs

Extract A

The Interoceanic Highway

The Interoceanic Highway is a 5 500 kilometres long route reaching right across South America. It cuts through the Amazonian rainforest, which is the largest area of its type in the world. This road significantly lowers costs for farmers and businesses, and can make a difference between life and death for people in remote areas far from hospitals. Land speculators, loggers, farmers, ranchers, gold miners and others can profit from exploiting opportunities along the route.

As the highway crosses the Peruvian Amazon region, a discreet sign urges travellers to protect the surrounding ecosystem. 'Let's care for the environment, let's conserve the forest', it reads. When the road was constructed, tall trees lined the route. The forest edge now lies about half a kilometre away, beyond a jumble of underbrush and freshly cut trees where a cattle pasture was recently carved out of the woods. As drivers head east into Brazil, the view is much the same for hundreds of kilometres. A study by South Dakota State University found that 95 per cent of deforestation in the region occurs within 7 kilometres of a road. Rapid deforestation early in this century was followed by a lull, but today the rainforests are being destroyed by 1.5 acres *every second*. Since 1978, over 750 000 square kilometres of Amazon rainforest have been destroyed. Once cleared, the soil is of such low quality that it can hardly be used to grow anything. After a year or two of farming, the land is totally stripped of nutrients – leaving a useless patch of ground.

Tropical rainforests only cover just 6 per cent of the Earth's surface, but are home to more than half the world's plant and animal species and bring extensive external benefits. Around 80 per cent of the foods we eat originally came from rainforests. Over a quarter of the medicines we use have their origins in the rainforests. With deforestation, 137 rainforest species (mainly plants) are exterminated completely every day. The drying brought about by roads influences local atmospheric circulation patterns and can also contribute to global warming by releasing carbon stored in the forest.

Source: adapted from *Markets, Consumers and Firms*, B. Ellis & N. Wall, Anforme

Figure B

GDP growth in the Amazonian region (%)

Country	2012	2013
Bolivia	5.2	6.8
Brazil	1.1	2.5
Colombia	4.0	4.7
Peru	6.0	5.8

Source: adapted from World Bank

Extract C

Smog in China

Question (e): With reference to the information provided and your own knowledge, evaluate the extent to which external costs are an inevitable consequence of economic development.   (25 marks)

Sample answer

Figure B shows that countries in the Amazonian region were growing in years when many developed economies were only slowly recovering from recession. Three of the four shown were growing at rates that most developed economies cannot match. Projects such as the Interoceanic Highway contribute to development by making transport quicker and easier whilst opening up new economic opportunities. For example, Extract A points out that loggers, farmers, ranchers, gold miners and others can exploit opportunities created by the road. This gives a stimulus to GDP growth and broader economic development.

The same extract also refers to deforestation, land stripped of nutrients, species extermination and a contribution to global warming. These are clear examples of external costs that will have an impact on future generations as well as in the short run. China has developed at an unprecedented rate for more than 25 years. Activity and incomes in the coastal Chinese regions have had sustained growth at around 10 per cent per year for decades. Extract C illustrates just one aspect of the external costs that have accumulated during this development process.

To focus on one aspect of development, a great deal of economic activity requires energy. Demand for electricity tends to increase rapidly during development, for example. The amount of coal burnt in electricity generation and for other industrial purposes helps to explain the prevalence of smog and also contributes to CO_2 emissions and so global warming. In the dash for growth in China it seems that such externalities were largely ignored for decades, so development was responsible for a surge in external costs.

We are moving away from a situation where around a quarter of the global population lived in relatively rich countries, with high-energy use, whilst others were too poor to consume and pollute on the same scale. As incomes rise in emerging countries it is only natural for people there to want electricity, cars and other consumer goods that entail pollution. It is not appropriate for developed countries to criticise others for doing as they do. Development was historically slower in the early countries to industrialise, yet they too have failed for long periods to deal effectively with issues such as global warming.

The word 'inevitable' in the question title is important. It is self-evident that development has created external costs in the past, but this does not make it inevitable that the same link must continue indefinitely. The EU emissions trading system has been used to get on target for a 20 per cent reduction in CO_2 emissions by 2020, compared with 1990. The next target will be 40 per cent reduction by 2030. Under the Kyoto Agreement, other developed countries have also agreed ambitious targets. This demonstrates that externalities can be reduced, once the will to do so is shared. To an extent, richer nations can more afford to be concerned and to target research at cutting externalities.

Just as countries which have developed more recently have grown faster and suffered problems from external costs faster, there must be the possibility that they can respond and take effective action faster. China has recognised extensive problems with air and water quality. Premier Li Keqiang said in 2014 that the government would 'resolutely declare war against pollution as we declared war against poverty'. Legislation has been introduced but there still appears to be a large gap between legislation and implementation.

The Amazonian basin is not yet suffering the consequences of externalities to the same extent as coastal China and this could help to explain why South American concern over the resulting issues seems less pronounced. Part of the problem here is that some of the costs are more global than localised. Perhaps global support for action will be necessary in this case. Although external costs have been associated with much economic development to date, we do now have examples of effective action to reduce external costs. It is not inevitable that future development will have inevitable consequences in external costs, but it will require concerted regulatory action around the world to break the link.

Comment: the answer starts well, with use of extracts and own knowledge tying development and external costs together. In the fifth paragraph, the close attention to the question wording is valuable and also brings balance. There is a sound evaluative conclusion.